Shooter's Bible

Shooter's Bible

102ND EDITION

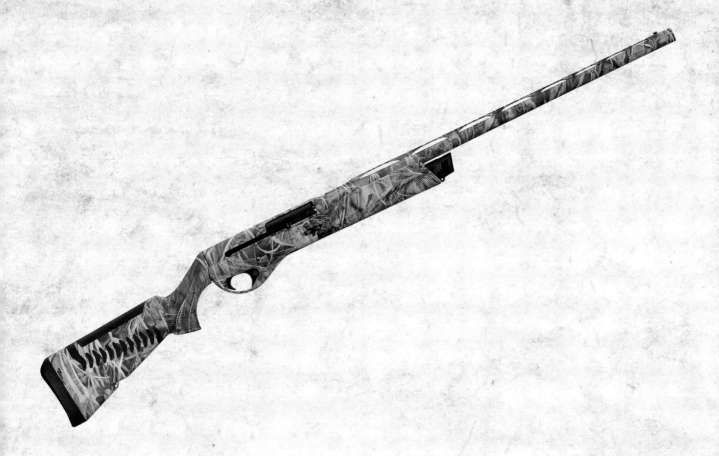

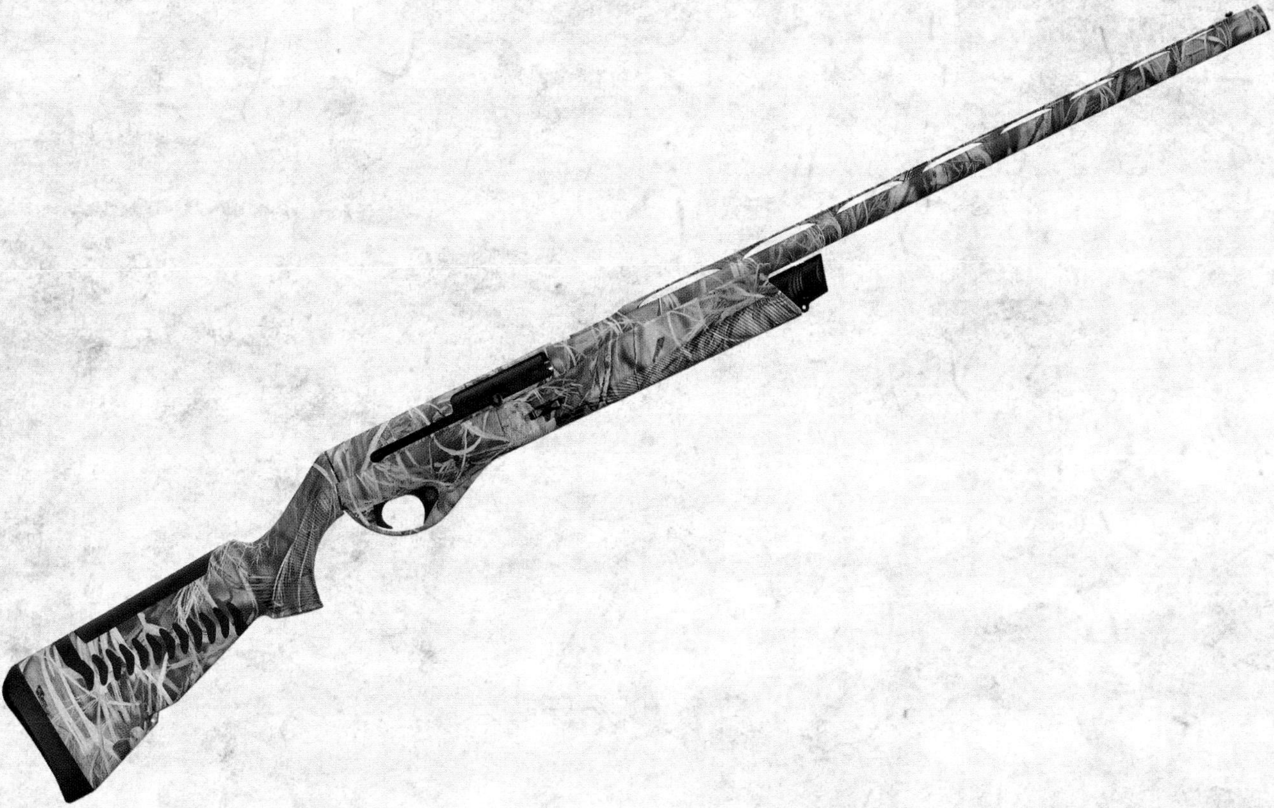

SKYHORSE PUBLISHING

Skyhorse Publishing books may be purchased in bulk at special discounts for sales promotion, corporate gifts, fund-raising, or educational purposes. Special editions can also be created to specifications. For details, contact the Special Sales Department, Skyhorse Publishing, 555 Eighth Avenue, Suite 903, New York, NY 10018 or info@skyhorsepublishing.com.

www.skyhorsepublishing.com

10 9 8 7 6 5 4 3 2 1

ISBN-13: 978-1-61608-087-7
ISSN: 0080-9365

Printed in the United States of America

Note: Every effort has been made to record specifications and descriptions of guns, ammunition, and accessories accurately, but the Publisher can take no responsibility for errors or omissions. The prices shown for guns, ammunition, and accessories are manufacturers' suggested retail prices (unless otherwise noted) and are furnished for information only. These were in effect at press time and are subject to change without notice. Purchasers of the book have complete freedom of choice in pricing for resale.

Special thanks to the National Rifle Association, for access to their image archives.

CONTENTS

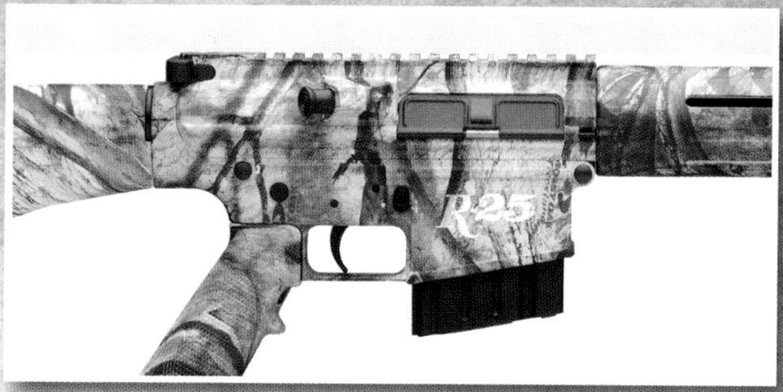

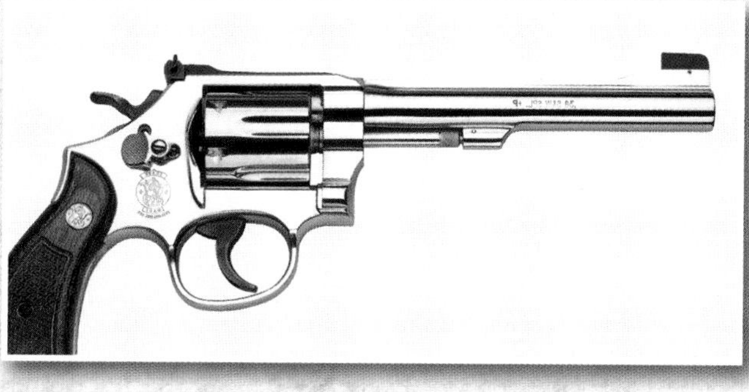

FOREWORD

Thank you for purchasing the 102nd edition of the *Shooter's Bible*. It is a book with a long history, dating all the way back to 1923, when it began as the mail-order catalog of the Stoeger Arms Corporation. The first numbered edition of the Shooter's Bible was published in 1925; it's been published annually, and in some cases bi-annually, ever since. More than 7 million copies have been sold in that time, and it continues to be the ultimate reference book for millions of people who want information on new guns, ammunition, optics, and other accessories, as well as up-to-date prices and specifications for thousands and thousands of firearms.

This year is the second year that the *Shooter's Bible* is being published by Skyhorse Publishing. Previous to that, it was produced by Stoeger books. In this edition, we have taken all of the new products from last year's *Shooter's Bible* and incorporated them into the main section of the book. Any guns, ammunition, or optics that have been discontinued have been removed. All prices have been updated, not only on the new products from 2008 and 2009, but on everything else as well. We have also listened to our readers in the past year and have added many guns that may have been omitted from the last edition. (Editor's Note: If you know of any new guns or guns currently in production that are missing, please let us know! It's tough keeping track of each and every gun or optic out there, and your input can help us put out as complete a book as humanly possibly. Send your emails to sb@skyhorsepublishing.com.)

This year we also, of course, have a 2010 New Products section, once again assembled by well-known firearms expert Wayne Van Zwoll. In this section, you'll find photos, specs, and descriptions of the very latest new rifles, shotguns, handguns, muzzleloaders, optics, ammunition, and more.

As a bonus, we have also included three feature-length stories: The first, by Wayne Van Zwoll, discusses the 10 best shotguns, rifles, and handguns produced since the turn of the century. Van Zwoll's choices will get you thinking. Did he miss anything? Why did he pick a Freedom Arms .500 Wyoming Express? How could he like the Beretta 391 Xtrema 2, but not include the new Caesar Guerini Ellipse (which I had the chance to drool over last week)? Food for thought, yes? Perhaps this will call for a follow-up article next year.

Van Zwoll's second article, on the .300 magnum, brings you back to 1913, when gunmaker Fred Adolph developed the .30 Adolph Express, a rimless round that sent 180-grain bullets downrange at an incredible (at the time) 2,880 fps. The history of the .300 is complex and fascinating, with most of the major and many of the smaller firearms and ammo manufacturers getting involved at some point. End result: If you currently don't own a .300 magnum, chances are you are going to think about getting one after reading this article.

You also won't want to miss Thomas McIntyre's piece on how to choose optics for big game hunting. In this thorough, well-researched piece, Tom explains how you should go about buying a new binocular (not "binoculars") or riflescope. Price, of course, comes into play. But there are many other factors to consider when buying optics, including glass quality, light transmission, IPD (interpupillary distance), eye relief, focus mechanism, power, housing, and more. Ultimately, Tom concludes that you should spend as much as you can, so long as it is not more than you can afford. Then he recommends that you should "plan on using those optics all that you can, and learning all that you can about them, in the years to come. Do not be a butterfly, flitting from new optics to newer optics, but pick something good and stick with it a while. The manufacturers will hate you (for not buying more of their products), but they shouldn't have made their riflescope or binocular so good to begin with." Good advice, but there's a lot more in there, including an extremely helpful glossary of optical terms.

The Skyhorse staff is very proud of this 102nd edition of the *Shooter's Bible*. We are honored to have the opportunity to publish it, and look forward to continuing a great tradition that began so many years ago.

—Jay Cassell
Consulting Editor

INTRODUCTION

As 2011 marks the 100th anniversary of John Browning's incomparable 1911 autoloading pistol, you'd anticipate a stampede of such handguns. Well, there are plenty, even from established long-gun specialists like Remington. And what's not a 1911 in the shooting press is likely an AR rifle. Both arms have spawned myriad variations in a market that can't get enough of either.

Truly, though, many other worthy guns have popped up this year—a record number, in fact. From the classy Fausti double shotguns (soon to have a home Stateside) to budget-friendly centerfire rifles courtesy Mossberg, Savage, and Thompson/Center, you'll find plenty to pique your interest. It's all here, too, in the pages of our most comprehensive *Shooter's Bible* yet!

Brand-conscious? Ruger fans won't be disappointed, as the firm trots out a new, lightweight LCR. Smith & Wesson has new Classic offerings, including the 48 in .22 WMR, and the iconic Model 10. Speaking of Icons, T/C's flagship rifle is now available in the mild but flat-shooting 6.5 Creedmoor —as are Ruger's 77 and No. 1. Winchester has announced a safari version of its Model 70 and, to no one's surprise, has brought back the Model 94. Marlin continues its run of compelling lever guns with a big-loop .45-70.

Hornady's Superformance ammunition brings magnum speed and power to ordinary chamberings. Federal and Norma expand their centerfire lines with cartridges as big as the .500 Nitro Express. Lead-free bullets get more attention at Winchester, where you'll also find exciting new defense loads for handguns and shotguns. A growing line of Nosler rifle ammunition includes popular wildcats.

In optics, too, shooters have more choices than ever. From range-compensating scopes with electronic brains (see the Burris Eliminator) to traditional favorites like the retro Weaver K4 and a user-friendly computer program from Nikon that makes tracking a load's performance almost as much fun as shooting it at the range—it's all here. In fact, there's so much, we can't afford more space for an introduction! We hope you enjoy this *Shooter's Bible!*

—Wayne van Zwoll

Shooter's Bible

BEST OF THE FIRST

—by Wayne van Zwoll

Ten years into the twenty-first century, we're inundated by new rifles, pistols, and shotguns. A few excel.

BERETTA 391 XTREMA2: PRETTY IS AS PRETTY DOES

Obesity has long been the curse of gas-driven autoloading shotguns. But Beretta shows how even beefy shotguns can be stripped of excess bulk. Its 391 Xtrema2 flaunts a supermodel profile and a refined mechanism. Its forend is as slim and shallow as the self-loading hardware permits. The wrist is longer and more slender. Length of pull is adjustable, with half-inch and 1-inch spacers.

The old 391Xtrema digested with monotonous predictability everything from dove loads to goose magnums with the payloads of siege cannons. While its great mass sapped the kick of bratwurst-size shells, shooters found it awkward to swing. The 12-bore Xtrema2 is gentle but relatively lithe. It handles 1-ounce, 2 ¾-inch loads interchangeably with magnums up to the heaviest 3½-inch. A signature grille just behind the magazine cap vents gas from high-octane loads. At the rear of the receiver, a bolt damper cushions the stop. The Gel-Tek pad and over-bored barrel help too, as does a spring inside the buttstock. Beretta offers, for $100, a "Kick-Off" hydraulic device that further trims recoil. Launching Federal turkey loads toward Texas toms *without* the device, I found the 391civil. Turkeys at 40 yards hit the ground dead.

This new shotgun's two-lug rotary bolt locks into a long barrel extension that adds rigidity to the barrel and enhances the accuracy of the slug version (with cantilever mount). The Xtrema2 trigger is

BERETTA HAS ADDED POWER AND VERSATILITY TO SELFLOADING SHOTGUN MECHANISMS. HERE IS THE 391 XTREMA2.

THE AUTHOR KILLED THIS TEXAS TURKEY WITH BERETTA'S FAST-HANDLING, SURE-CYCLING 391 XTREMA2.

better than its predecessor's—lighter, with less creep. I like the trigger pad, a slender steel arc well back in a racy guard, with tasteful sculpting around the forward crossbolt safety. A replacement trigger group offers a left-hand button. The Beretta 391 Xtrema2 sports a Tru-Glo bead. Its over-bored barrels accept Beretta Optima-Bore Field tubes (four provided). It is a reliable autoloader with the versatility and durability of less nimble guns, a profile your grandfather won't recognize.

BLASER'S R8: FASTEST BOLT RIFLE EVER!

Blaser (that's *blah*-zer, not *blay*-zer) came to life in 1957, but its products have steadily gained favor on both sides of the Atlantic. The finely-finished F3 over-under shotgun wears upscale walnut on a lean, taut frame so perfectly balanced that even mediocre bird shooters like me can shine. The R93 straight-pull rifle offers a selection of chamberings on a cleverly designed switch-barrel action. Now the R93 has been improved. The R8 is the first Blaser to make its debut in the States.

Norbert Hausman runs Blaser's North American operation from its headquarters in San Antonio, where I first fired the R8. He pointed out its R93 heritage: hammer-forged barrels; telescoping, radial-head bolt; target-quality trigger; screw-less scope mounting; straight-up, single-stack magazine tucked into a compact trigger group that trims more than 2 inches off over-all length. The bolt handle runs a telescoping, straight-pull mechanism you can cycle from the shoulder in a heartbeat. The thumb-piece that cocks the R8 is the only safety. Shove it up and forward; you're ready to fire. To de-cock, push ahead again, but down slightly, and let it slide rearward. The R93 and R8 are the only bolt rifles you can carry safely at the ready, because they're not cocked until you're ready to fire. R8s sold in Europe come standard with a trigger pull of 1.6 pounds. Stateside hunters get the same crisp break at 2.5 pounds. The R-8 has very fast lock time.

Like its predecessor, the R8 bolt head locks with a collett forced into a circumferential groove in the barrel shank. "But the R8 is stronger," said Norbert, a

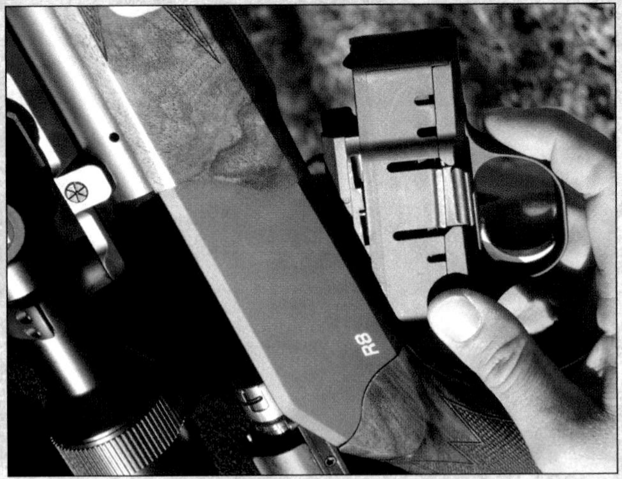

BLASER'S INGENIOUS R8 HAS A DETACHABLE MAGAZINE—AND TRIGGER GROUP. FEEDING IS SUPER-FAST, SILKY.

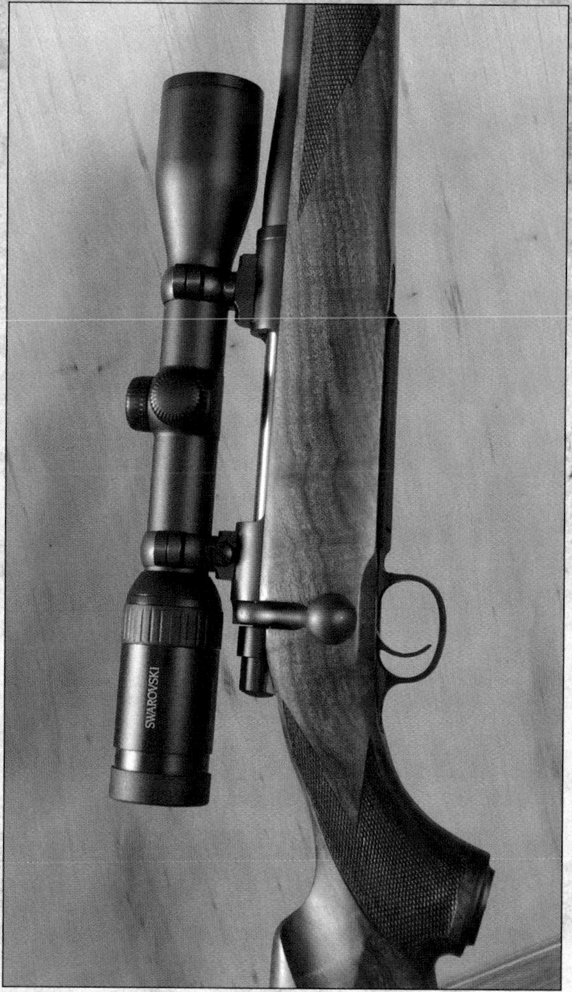

COOPER'S M52 IS EXCEEDINGLY ACCURATE, WITH FINE WOOD AND WORKMANSHIP, AND SMOOTH CYCLING.

master gunsmith. "Its locking angle is steeper. Also, a bushing slides into the collett's center during lock-up, for additional support. We've tested the R8 to pressures of 210,000 psi."

Plasma nitriding on the barrel's exterior boosts surface hardness. Saddle-style scope rings fit so precisely you can remove the scope and replace it without losing zero. I didn't believe that until Blaser's Tom Mack yanked the Zeiss scope from an R8 I was firing at a chalk-filled bucket 600 yards distant. After he replaced it, I fired again. A plume of white dust followed. "Bingo!" Tom cackled. I flicked the Blaser's bolt—an effortless event even prone, where a turn-bolt rifle requires enough arm movement to scuttle your position. Another squeeze. Another hit. Then a third. You can replace barrels with the same confidence.

Unlike the R93, the R8 has a detachable magazine. It's attached to the trigger group; the assembly falls into your hand when you squeeze a pair of latches. You can top-load the stack without removing the box or load it in your hand. The assembly can't drop accidentally, and when in place it does not rattle. One box accommodates all cartridges for which the R8 is chambered, from .223 to .416 Remington Magnum.

The R8's stock is also new—straight-combed and slightly longer than the R93's. It has cast-off at toe and heel, even in the grip. The Turkish walnut comes in several grades.

An engineering marvel, the lightning-quick Blaser R8 may also be the most effective hunting rifle of the decade!

COOPER MODEL 52: CLASSIC LINES, ASTOUNDING ACCURACY.

For a couple of years, 1980 and 1981, Dan Cooper and a friend hiked the spine of North America. He returned to Oregon and got a

A SILKY MECHANISM HOUSING BRUTE POWER: THE .500 WYOMING EXPRESS IN FREEDOM'S MODEL 83.

job mowing Jack Warne's lawn. The Australian entrepreneur had just started a gun company called Kimber. When the firm changed hands, Dan and three partners started building rifles. The first were single-shot rimfire target rifles, assembled in a garage at Bell Crossing, Montana. The Model 36 "cost $2000 to build and sold for $600." Models 38 and 22 centerfires followed. In 2001 the rimfire M57 appeared. I bought one in .17 HMR. The rifle averaged .9 inch for five 5-shot groups at 100 yards.

Short years later, Cooper had completed a big game rifle, the Model 52. Immediately I requested one for review. "We're shipping all we can make, filling back-orders," Dan said. Then: "Wait! We shipped a .270 today. We'll call it back!" I didn't believe he would. He did.

The M52 is ordinary in some ways. It has a bolt handle any numbskull can operate, three locking lugs, a Sako-style extractor, and fixed ejector. But a close look shows refinements. The two-position thumb safety rocks silently but solidly forward. The 52 is elegant, with a taut but graceful profile. Lines are clean and purposeful, from the sweep of the slender trigger and open, steel-capped grip to the vertical fall of the bolt handle. I like the deep-fluted comb. The magazine fits flush and snug; the latch is functional but unobtrusive. The matte-finished Classic I tested lacks the shadow-line cheek-piece and ebony forend tip, the steel bottom metal of highly polished Custom Classic and case-colored Western Classic M52s. Nominal weight for any M52 with a standard 24-inch barrel (.660 at the muzzle) is 7¾ pounds, save for the Jackson Hunter, a feathery 6¼. The trigger is Cooper's own mechanism, built in the Bitterroot. It's factory-set at 3½ pounds, adjusts to 1½.

To keep the magazine from influencing accuracy and reduce the size of the well, Dan latched a slender in-line, three-round box to the bottom metal. The 52 is glass bedded around a precision-ground, Remington-style recoil lug. The air-gauged, button-rifled barrel contacts the stock up front only, on "an isolated pillow of glass."

Cooper Arms uses mostly Claro in its stocks. They're CNC-machined to shape, checkered, and finished by hand.

Dan Cooper's accuracy guarantees seem almost unreasonable: ¼-inch five-shot groups at 50 yards for rimfire rifles, ½-inch five-shot groups at 100 yards for centerfires. That applies to the sporter-weight M52. Such hubris might put you off—until

IN THE BEGINNING . . .

In 1900 Colt manufactured John Browning's .38 self-loading pistol, the first of its kind in the United States—though Browning had a working model ready in 1895. Colt bought four pistols from the prolific inventor and based its subsequent self-loaders on those designs. Among the signature features of Browning pistols was an operating slide mated to the frame by rails. The slide comprised action housing, sighting rib, and bolt. It added mass to the recoil mechanism and permitted a range of chamberings—including Browning's own .25, .32, .380, and .45 ACP.

John refined the pistol in 1902, producing the .38 Military Model. But the Moro insurrection in the Philippines had soured soldiers on the .38 Colt, which had failed to stop frenzied attackers. Browning responded with two 45-caliber pistols, one with an exposed hammer, the other without. He marketed his exposed-hammer Model 1905 through Colt. To ensure his pistol was ready for Army trials in March, 1911, Browning (with protégé Fred Moore, of Colt's machine gun division) subjected a sample to a 6,000-round endurance run, in 100-shot stings. The gun functioned through an acid bath, dust and damaged ammo. The trials board approved John's .45 Automatic Pistol for service. It would see us through two world wars.

you shoot a 52. My .270 averaged .7 for five of six factory loads, first time out.

If the fetching lines of a Cooper 52 don't steal your heart, that level of accuracy certainly should!

FREEDOM ARMS .500 WYOMING EXPRESS: BELTED MAGNUM REVOLVER

In the Salt River Valley, not far from Olympic gold-medal wrestler Rulon Gardner's home, you'll find Freedom, Wyoming. No stop light. But here you can buy the best single-action revolver in the world.

Bob Baker, who steers the firm, is too modest to say that. But he believes it. When buyers balk at the price of a Freedom revolver, he tells them hunting is expensive; the best handgun is a good investment. If you compete in long-range silhouette matches, you may as well buy a Freedom revolver, "because you'll have to shoot against 'em."

Freedom revolvers are made *from scratch* on site. All major parts are of stainless steel machined to super-close tolerances, then hand-fitted. Freedom's flagship is its large-frame, five-shot Model 83, now twenty five years old. Once as he showed me the production line, Bob grabbed a proof target. Four shots had cut one hole, with the fifth ¾ inch away. "This gun is going back. It should do better at 50 yards."

FREEDOM ARMS MARRIED ITS EXQUISITE 83 SA TO A NEW ROUND: THE BELTED .500 WYOMING EXPRESS.

THE AUTHOR LIKES THE TRIM RECEIVERS OF THE KIMBER 84M AND 84L. THESE ARE LITHE, VERY HANDSOME RIFLES.

You can order a Model 83 in .454 Casull or .475 Linebaugh, in .44, .41, or .357 Magnum, even .22 LR. But the belted .500 Wyoming Express is the latest and most notable chambering. Bob explained: "The rim on a 50-caliber case would have been too small after sizing for a Model 83 cylinder. The belt adds beef and a headspacing shoulder. At 1.37 inches, .500 WE brass is loaded to an overall length of about 1.76. The head accepts large rifle primers. Freedom supplies dies, to size cases down to within .10 of the belt.

I used a Freedom Arms Premier revolver to fire factory-loaded .500 WE ammunition from Grizzly Cartridge Company (POB 1466, Rainier OR 97048). The beautiful 370-, 400-, and 440-grain hard-cast flat-noses proved civil—at 950 fps. But the .500 WE can drive 370-grain bullets at over 1,600 fps, 440s faster than 1,400! Such a potent single-action revolver should rotate in your hand during recoil. The 83 Premier's impregnated hardwood grips allow for slippage without compromising control. (Standard versions feature Pachmayr Presentation grips.) The trigger on the .500 broke crisply and consistently at just over 3 pounds. Nothing rattles on a Freedom 83. The cylinder rotates like the hand of a Rolex.

The Freedom Arms Model 83 offers more than fine fit and finish. Perfect balance, silky cycling, a glass-rod trigger break, and one-hole accuracy should seduce any shooter. Smith & Wesson, with its .500, has the most powerful handgun. But if you prefer the feel of a single-action, and a super-charged revolver that scales closer to 50 ounces than 70, you'll want an 83 in .500 Wyoming Express.

THE 1911: A CULT, NOT A PISTOL

Les Edelman didn't buy Kimber to produce pistols. But after Chapter 7 proceedings gave him a chance to resurrect the rifle company, he bought a factory in Yonkers, New York, and in 1995 introduced a nicely appointed 1911. Shooters bought the first 5,000 in a blink. Soon Kimber was shipping eight times that many pistols *annually*. By 2000 it had become the "world's largest manufacturer of 1911 pistols."

Kimber entered that market at just the right time. The public's demand for John Browning's iconic 1911 has since surged to the point of obsession. Other firms have offered their own upscale versions. Some are fetching indeed. But no firm has outmaneuvered Kimber, which hews to strict quality standards while churning out dozens of novel sub-models—some, for example, with Crimson Trace laser grips. The 2009 Kimber catalog carried seventy nine refined variations of the 1911!

The competition is heating up as more companies target the seemingly insatiable appetite of U.S. pistol buffs for 1911s. I've been most impressed by those from Rock River, Para USA, and Smith & Wesson. A "GI" version by Para is an outstanding value. So too the Legacy Sports Citadel series, expanded for 2010. Taurus offers refinements like a flared port, beveled magazine well, ambidextrous safety, checkered guard and grip, Heinie sights, all for "standard pistol" prices. Colt builds a high-quality 1911. So does SIG. Para's stable includes 1911s with double-stack magazines that hold as many as 14 rounds in .45 ACP, 18 in 9mm. The Hawg 9 packs 13 in a 24-ounce pistol! Custom shops like Les Baer's give shooters almost unlimited options. There's no way to pick one 1911 as the best—best pistol or best buy—without triggering myriad challenges. So I won't.

PARA USA BUILDS SEVERAL INNOVATIVE 1911-STYLE HANDGUNS, INCLUDING THIS DOUBLE-STACK WARTHOG.

PARA'S GI EXPERT IS A NEW, ECONOMICAL 1911 WITH FEATURES AND QUALITY OF HIGHER-PRICED GUNS.

If you can imagine an ideal 1911, it has probably been conceived, if not assembled. In fact, odds are you'll find it cataloged now, on the eve of the pistol's centennial celebration. While John Browning gave us the 1911, and Colt built the first military version, gunmakers have since made it an art-form.

KIMBER'S 84L: A PERFECT RIFLE—AGAIN

It looks right. Like the '65 Mustang, it has the right amount of straight, the right amount of curve. It feels nimble. But as with an automobile, there's more to a rifle than a sleek profile and simple obedience.

"We started with the best designs around," Kimber's designers told me in 1998, on the eve of the 84M (for "medium" or .308-length). Now there's an 84L, a long-action rifle for the .30-06 and kin.

MORE THAN ANY OTHER MAKER, KIMBER HAS CATERED TO THE CRAZE FOR REFINED 1911 PISTOLS.

It's actually the second long-action Kimber. The 8400, short and long versions, arrived three years ago. It has a bigger receiver ring than the 84M—which makes it quite ordinary. Kimber didn't make news building rifles of ordinary line. Kimbers, like Audrey Hepburn, Italian motorcycles and the F-16, are noted for their lithe profiles. They're lightweight without looking frail, elegant by way of trim, clean cosmetics.

The 84M is as good as lightweight rifles come. You get controlled feed, a crisp, consistent trigger pull, a three-detent safety, and nicely checkered walnut. The svelte receiver carries not an ounce of fat. Its traditional two-lug bolt features a Mauser claw that grabs case rims early and herds them smoothly forward. A fixed ejector kicks hulls away smartly. Trim steel bottom metal complements Kimber's own button-rifled barrel. The stock is neatly checkered 20 lpi in point patterns. Its straight comb puts your eye smack behind a low-mounted scope. Wood clings to metal like skin to a peach. Thank that slender profile for the feathery heft, smart engineering for balance that makes the 84M fly to your shoulder but swing as if on rails.

For several reasons, a long-action sequel didn't immediately follow the 84m. But now, a decade later, there *is* an 84L. Unlike the 8400, it boasts the slender receiver ring of its forebear. The .308 and .30-06 families share .473 heads—smaller than the .532 heads of belted rounds and the .535s on WSMs. So the 84L doesn't need extra metal up front. Insiders at Kimber confide that standard long-action rounds will soon leave the 8400. It will chamber only WSMs and traditional belted magnums.

Wrap your hand around the 84L's mid-section, slim as a maiden's wrist, and you won't guess the magazine holds five. To serve the fuel load of .30-06-length cases, Kimber installs a 24-inch barrel on the 84L. The forend is a trifle longer to match. But stock and barrel maintain a crisp, linear profile with perfect tapers and an economy of mass that makes the rifle look sculpted, not whippy. The 84L scales 6 pounds.

A rifle that carries easily but doesn't shoot well has limited utility. But a day's shooting with two 84Ls in .30-06 delivered several sub-minute clusters. A one-holer miked .3. Kimber's 84L comes in .25-06 and .270 as well. I stuck with that .30-06 for a couple of deer hunts. Two bucks died suddenly. More to the point, I enjoyed carrying that rifle. The steel and walnut in your hand can make any hunt memorable.

MARLIN XL7: SO MUCH FOR SO LITTLE!

The last decade has made many shooters price-sensitive. As rifles become better, they cost more. In a bid to offer an accurate, durable bolt rifle with good looks and handling qualities, Marlin dug out the blue-prints for a rifle it produced briefly some years ago—and married the best of those features with new

KIMBER'S 84L IS A BEAUTIFUL, LIGHTWEIGHT RIFLE THAT ALSO SHOOTS VERY WELL.

THE AUTHOR FIRES A MARLIN XL7, WHICH HE CONSIDERS ONE OF THE BEST BOLT-RIFLE BARGAINS IN DECADES.

ideas. Result: The XL7. Marlin had graciously asked my opinion during the rifle's design, and I managed to snare one of the first production-line XL7s for a range test.

I was immediately impressed with the Marlin's clean, conservative lines and fine balance. It has a look and feel that belies its low price—just $326 to start! Mike Jensen had assured me the rifle would not be expensive. Marling kept manufacturing costs down by using a tubular receiver, broached 22-inch barrel (also in .25-06 and .30-06), washer recoil lug, and Savage-style barrel nut for easy headspacing. The blind magazine isn't much of a cost savings; I like it because it keeps the rifle's profile clean and makes for an easy carry with your hand under the belly. Receiver ring and bridge match Winchester M70 contours. The XL7's right-hand locking lug has a slot that rides a rail to smooth bolt travel. It also houses the bolt-face extractor. Marlin adopted a plunger ejector and the M70 bolt release. A two-position thumb safety does not lock the bolt. The trigger resembles Savage's AccuTrigger, but operates differently. The blade is a *release* and does not engage the sear. If you bump the trigger shoe on a Savage rifle, you must re-cock to activate the blade. You cannot pull the Marlin shoe until you release it with the blade. The trigger on my .270 XL7 breaks crisply at 3¼ pounds. An injection-molded stock has a modest cheekpiece, open grip, 1-inch pad and18-lpi checkering. In my view, it has the most pleasing shape of any stock on an economy-class rifle.

The new Marlin XL7 shoots better than you'd expect, too. It is truly one of the best buys in bolt rifles in many years.

MARLIN 338MXLR: MOST POWERFUL LEVER EVER?

No, it is not. Among lever-action rifles, Browning's BLR Lightweight 81, with its rotating, front-locking bolt head and detachable box magazine, accommodates magnum cartridges as potent as the .300 Winchester Magnum and .325 WSM. But the BLR, like Winchester's Model 88 and the forgotten Sako Finnwolf, are not *traditional, exposed-hammer* lever-actions like Winchester's 94 and the classic Marlins.

Marlin's 336 and 1895 rifles (differing only in chamberings and ports, not receiver size) have been with us for decades. But the 338MLXR, an 1895 in stainless, with laminated stock, was engineered around a brand-new cartridge. Hornady's Dave Emary it up using new powders and the "Flex-Tip" bullet he had developed to extend the reach of grizzled lever-gun cartridges in LEVERevolution ammo. He drew on his recent work with the new .308 Marlin Express, based

THE MARLIN XL7 HAS PLEASING LINES AND BALANCE, FEATURES OF MORE COSTLY RIFLES. PRICE: UNDER $400!

THE AUTHOR TOOK THIS NEW MEXICO PRONGHORN WITH THE NEW .338 MARLIN EXPRESS, A POTENT ROUND IN A CLASSIC RIFLE.

on the .307 Winchester hull shortened from 2.015 to 1.920. The .308 ME outperforms not only the .300 Savage but the .307. Hornady's reconfigured powders make such efficiency possible, at pressures under 47,000 psi.

The even more potent sequel to the .308 ME derived from the .376 Steyr. Dave dubbed it the .338 Marlin Express. The 1.89-inch semi-rimmed case has a 25-degree shoulder, base diameter of .553. At 2,565 fps, the new .338's pointed 200-grain bullet matches the velocity and energy of the .348 Winchester's at the muzzle, then quickly leaves it behind. The .338 Marlin Express bullet can't quite deliver the energy of the much heavier (325-grain) .450 Marlin. But at the 100-yard mark, they have equal punch, and beyond that, the ballistically superior .338 takes over. It very nearly duplicates the arc and payload of a 210-grain Nosler Partition from the .338 Federal, but at significantly lower pressure. The 200-grain .338 ME all but mirrors the arc and energy figures of a 180-grain spitzer in a .30-06.

Marlin's new rifle has a magazine under a 24-inch barrel (blued-and-walnut rifles wear a 22-inch barrel). My first three-shot group measured a hair under one inch. The mechanism worked smoothly, cartridges feeding as if they were designed for the magazine and carrier. Hulls flew smartly from the port. Recoil was stiff but manageable, even in prone with my collarbone hard against the butt.

When in New Mexico I bellied through short grass to within iron-sight distance of a pronghorn, then squeezed the .338's trigger, I didn't feel the recoil at all. The buck collapsed on the spot. If like me you adore the feel of a traditional lever gun but the reach and power of bolt-rifle cartridges, Marlin's new 1895 XLR in .338 ME should be in your rack!

MONTANA: GREAT PLACE, GREAT RIFLE

A few years ago, I "custom-built" a rifle on a Montana 1999 action, with a Montana barrel and a stock by Serengeti. These two small firms both call Kalispell home, and they're both relatively new to the industry. Montana Rifles got its start in 1990, when founder Brian Sipe was repairing guns. Within three years he'd begun making barrels. By the end of the decade he and Rod Rogers had developed the Model

HORNADY ENGINEER DAVE EMARY TRIES OUT HIS BRAINCHILD, THE .338 MARLIN EXPRESS IN A MARLIN 1895.

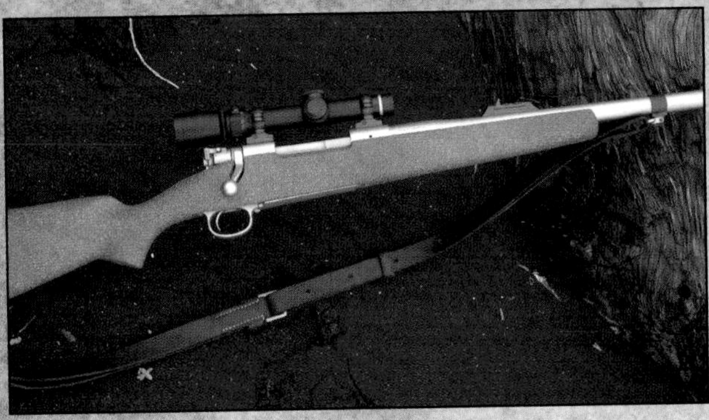

THIS STAINLESS MONTANA RIFLE IN .375 PROVED IDEAL FOR AN ALASKAN BEAR HUNT. NOTE M70 HERITAGE.

1999 bolt action, patterned after the early Model 70 Winchester. In 2003, Rod left to found Serengeti. It provided stocks for Montana Rifles, and offered a custom stocking service. The .257 Roberts in my rack is a delightful rifle, one of those that turned out just as I'd hoped.

The Model 1999 action is available in short and long versions, right-hand or left, in stainless or chrome-moly steel. Three magazine lengths for the long receiver accommodate cartridges from the short belted magnums to 2.85-inch cases. A Model 70-style bolt face (with coned breech) and a Mauser-style claw extractor secure the cartridge up front. But instead of requiring an extractor cut in the barrel, the 1999 features a collar inside the receiver ring to accept the extractor nose. A dovetail-shaped guide lug on the extractor clip reduces bolt bind. Ejector and three-position safety are vintage M70. The bolt release differs markedly, however. Instead of an unobtrusive tab operated from the rear, Montana's 1999 rifle employs a spring-loaded Sako-style latch. It's almost as big as a Mauser 98 gate, and to my eye less pleasing than the M70 release. The trigger mechanism is the Model 70's, arguably the best hunting trigger ever. The finger piece is smooth, polished steel, not grooved and blued as on Winchester rifles.

Receiver and bottom metal look to be dead ringers for the Winchester 70's; but the latter is of one-piece design. Another improvement: the 3.15-inch magazine box on the short action. It accommodates the 7x57 and its derivatives, the 6mm Remington and .257 Roberts.

I'd recommend a Serengeti stock to anyone. But I've found the synthetic handles on current 1999s eminently useful. The grip seems a bit small for my hands, but the .375 I took to Alaska, and then to Africa, handles like a wand. And it has never missed. It has killed game from impala to Cape buffalo with one shot. It nailed a leopard in tall grass quickly at twelve steps, and planted two bullets almost atop each other in a big eland's shoulder at 250. It cycles like the piston in a race engine, points as if possessed of its own eye. It shoots tighter groups than it should, and kills like a bolt from Zeus. I think it likes me.

THE AUTHOR KILLED THIS BUFFALO WITH A MONTANA 1999 RIFLE IN .375, WITH FEDERAL TROPHY BONDED AMMO.

NEW ULTRA LIGHT ARMS

If you really want to feel fresh at the end of a day's hunt, or climb faster, you'd best drop weight. From your middle. Paring rifle ounces helps about like rinsing the mud from your hubcaps boosts your gas mileage. Still, we who think more about tuning equipment than about physical conditioning are enamored of the lightweight rifle. So was Melvin Forbes when, in 1984, he designed his Ultra Light action.

From a distance, the Ultra Light mechanism looks like a Remington 700. But the bolt and receiver diameters are smaller. He configured the Model 20 for cartridges the size of a 7x57 Mauser. The magazine box is 3 inches long, not the 2.85 inches common in short-action rifles. Melvin didn't skeletonize anything, or use a carbine-length barrel. The key to his rifle's feathery heft is the stock, comprising carbon fiber and Kevlar. It weighs just 16 ounces but is "stiffer than the rifle's barrel," according to Melvin. There are no pillars; an alloy sleeve over the front guard screw prevents over-tightening. It's a straight-combed stock. It wears a roughened Dupont Imron finish. Paint remains a customer option.

The Ultra Light Model 20 was followed by the Model 24, lengthened to 3 inches for the .30-06. With 24-inch barrel, it weighs under 6 pounds. A Model 28 for magnum rounds is larger in diameter. The 3-inch M28 accommodates the WSMs. A 3-inch version handles the likes of the 7mm Remington and .338 Winchester. There's a longer M40 Ultra Light for cartridges as big as the .416 Rigby.

In March, 1999 Melvin Forbes sold Ultra Light Arms to Colt, which intended to build Model 28 actions while Melvin and his crew produced the stocks in Morgantown, West Virginia. But Colt got hit by cities suing the gun industry for criminals's use of firearms. Colt spent half a million dollars a month in court. It scrapped the rifle project. Melvin bought Ultra Light back and renamed it *New* Ultra Light Arms.

New Ultra Light rifles are built like before, with 4140 chrome-moly receiver, Douglas Premium barrel, Timney trigger, Sako-style extractor and a thumb safety that can be pushed to allow bolt cycling while on "safe." Melvin offers its own lightweight scope rings that mate directly to the receiver.

I used an Ultra Light rifle on a hunt in Alberta. The trim Model 20 carried like a wish. I killed a couple of black bears with 165-grain Trophy Bonded bullets in Federal loads. Soon thereafter I ordered a New Ultra Light rifle in 6.5/284. It weighs what I want it to—6½ pounds with 24-inch barrel—and shoots ¾-inch groups. Who needs more weight?

REMINGTON R-15: THE AR-15 GOES GREEN

It's hard to say if, over the last decade, the AR-15, or the 1911 pistol, has generated more coverage in the shooting press. Or which is manufactured by more companies. Certainly the AR-15 has sold

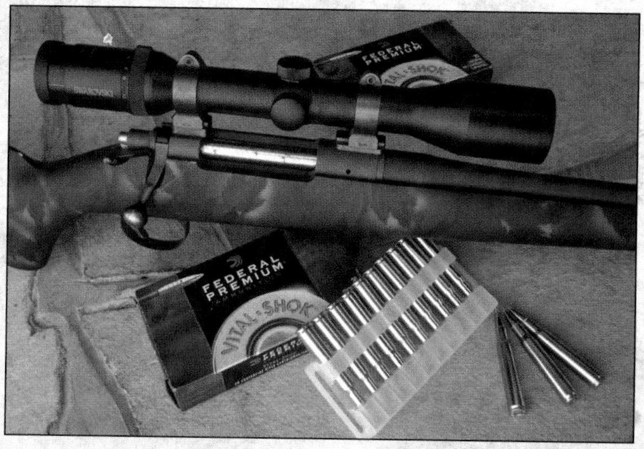

MELVIN FORBES BUILDS FINELY-FITTED 6-POUND RIFLES UNDER THE BANNER OF NEW ULTRA LIGHT ARMS.

THE R-15 FIRST APPEARED IN CARBINE AND RIFLE FORM. NEW CHAMBERINGS AND VARIATIONS HAVE FOLLOWED.

briskly since the election of 2008. Politics aside, its appeal derives from its semi-auto fire, saturation exposure on television, inexpensive ammunition, and myriad after-market accessories. Add the fact that a generation in uniform has now been trained on it.

Truly, this rifle has about as much in common with its military predecessors as a new mini-van has with a 1942 vegetable truck. It's unconventional, from the rear-mounted, T-shaped charging handle to the dorsal gas tube to the towering front sight and the cold black butt and forestock, from which the barrel protrudes like a serpent's tongue.

On the target range, AR-15s with stiff barrels and tuned triggers can shoot with the best bolt rifles—at least to 300 yards. Target rifles and AR-style varmint rifles, and the larger AR-10s chambered for big-game cartridges are not assault rifles. But repeating that truth hasn't done as much to soften—change—the AR's image as has Remington with its R-15.

"We call it the R-15 VTR Predator," said Remington's Al Russo at its unveiling. Varmint Target Rifle. The dipped

IN THE LAST DECADE, THE AR-15 HAS BECOME ALMOST UBIQUITOUS, SERVICE RIFLE TURNED JACK-OF-ALL-TRADES.

THIS RUGER HAWKEYE IN .300 RCM IS A WONDERFUL WOODS RIFLE.

camouflage on the first R-15 was a pleasing shade of green with white streaking. Pattern and hue distinguished the R-15 not only from its black siblings but the majority of camo-ed competitors. It sold briskly. "The R-15 is for hunters," added John Trull.

The rifle is actually assembled by Bushmaster, a sister company renowned for its myriad AR-type rifles and carbines. The R-15 Predator Rifle weighs just under 8 pounds, Carbines a pound less. Upper and lower are machined aluminum forgings. A machined aluminum forend tube floats free of the barrel; it is knurled and drilled and tapped for rails. The button-rifled barrel (22 inches on the rifle, 18 on the carbines) wears flutes forward of the gas block. A 1-in-9 twist for 5.56 barrels is designed to stabilize bullets up to 69 grains in weight. Or pick an R-15 in .204 Ruger, with 1-in-12 twist. Both have five-round magazines. The R-15 accepts standard AR-15 aftermarket accoutrements. Since its debut, the rifle has appeared in other configurations, and in new potent chamberings: 6.8 SPC (discontinued), .450 Bushmaster, and .30 Remington AR. The company has also come out with an AR-10 in more potent chambering. Camo patterns have changed.

Other makers have since built on Remington's success, fashioning AR *hunting* rifles. A favorite of high-volume prairie dog shooters, the AR is now showing up in big game fields. The Stag 7 and three Rock River ARs in my rack are accurate and dependable. So too the Smith & Wesson I've tested, and others I've fired. Olympic Arms catalogs an AR-15 in .300 Olympic, a ballistic match for the .30-06.

But Remington deserves special kudos for its R-15, the first AR to look like something other than a rifle built for people in helmets and dark glasses. Says John Trull: "Shooters with traditional taste should pick up a Predator, a brick of .223 ammo and a couple of extra magazines, then invade a prairie dog town."

If that doesn't wring a grin during magazine changes, you probably don't smile much at all.

RUGER HAWKEYE, 6.5 CREEDMOOR: BEST 77 IN THIRTY YEARS!

The Ruger Hawkeye arrived as a 77 upgrade. Like the Mark II makeover in 1989, it offers several substantive improvements. The Mark II gave us controlled-round feed (earlier rifles had that Mauser-like claw, but in practice it was a push-feed mechanism). It supplanted the tang safety with a three-position tab. Both those features are retained on the new Hawkeye. In addition, you get a one-piece stainless steel bolt, hammer-forged barrel, and, most noticeably, a trimmer walnut stock.

The Hawkeye's grip and forend are slimmer in cross-section—not so much as to cost you control, but just enough to make the rifle feel nimble. Checkering wraps entirely around the fore-stock, and the grip pattern is more generous than before. The ledges straddling the barrel channel have been reduced in

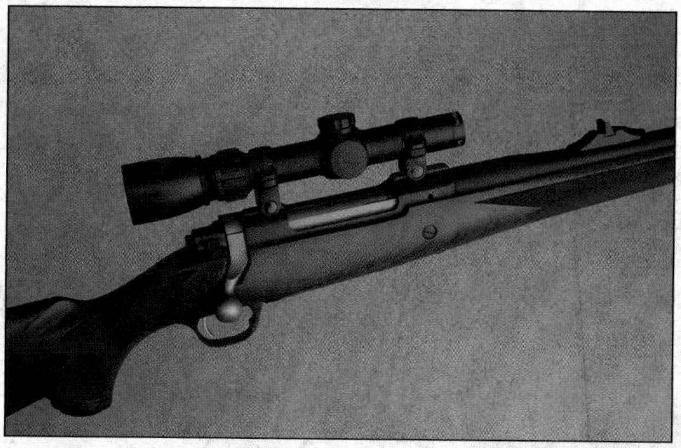

RUGER'S NEW HAWKEYE IS A TRIMMED, MORE ATTRACTIVE M77. ALL THE CHANGES ARE POSITIVE!

BUSHMASTER BUILDS THE R-15 FOR REMINGTON. THE .450 BUSHMASTER ROUND DELIVERS CLOSE-UP PUNCH.

width. The flat encompassing the bottom metal is less obtrusive now. Just as important is what *isn't* changed: the thin butt-pad, the straight comb with just the right drop and radius, and grip curve that seems to fit everyone.

The Hawkeye's metal has a matte finish that borders on satin but remains well off the high polish of early 77s. Stainless is an option on some versions (as are synthetic and laminated stocks and a left-side bolt handle). The guard, floorplate latch and floorplate have been tweaked. The trigger looks the same from the outside but differs in operation from the original. Called the LC6, it lacks an external adjustment screw.

You can select from 23 chamberings in a Hawkeye, not counting the Magnum Rifle in .375 H&H, .416 Rigby, and .458 Lott. The most recent cartridge on the list is the 6.5 Creedmoor, essentially the .30 TC necked down. Hornady ballistician Dave Emary got the idea from long-range rifle ace Dennis Demille at Camp Perry. Dennis noted that many shooters were turning to 6.5s but that none were short enough to use long match bullets in short actions. Dave went to work on the T/C round, applying new powders and the 140 A-Max bullet—which holds up better at distance than the heaviest match bullet practical in a .308.

Why wouldn't the 6.5 Creedmoor work as a hunting round? Dave and I had the same question. He beat me to the field, killing deer neatly at nearly a quarter mile. I made the longest shot I've yet taken at an elk. It died within seconds. Maybe there's no substitute for horsepower in a race engine. But in the hunting field, a svelte Ruger Hawkeye, chambered to the 6.5 Creedmoor offers instead flat trajectory, fine accuracy and mild recoil. And the package is most pleasing to the eye and hand.

SMITH & WESSON 500

The N-Frame revolver dates to before the .357 Magnum, circa 1935. Smith & Wesson used the husky double-action for its .44 Special, then in 1956, its .44 Magnum cartridges. Half a century later, after Dick Casull had upstaged the .44 Magnum with his .454 Casull in single-action guns, S&W committed to a DA

THE AUTHOR SHOT THIS WYOMING MULE DEER AT 95 YARDS WITH A SMITH & WESSON 500, COR-BON LOAD.

to trump all others. No revolver could accept the rifle cartridges chambered in single-shot pistols like JD Jone's T/C Contenders; so S&W product manager Herb Belin focused on a new revolver round. In early 2002, he and engineer Brett Curry, with Cor-Bon's Peter Pi and Terry Murback, came up with a 50-caliber round. The case was 1.625 inches long. Three Herculean loads stayed under the designated pressure lid of 48,000 psi (20 percent less than the Casull's). A 275-grain Barnes X clocked 1,675 fps, a 400-grain Hawk JSP 1,650, and a 440-grain hard cast bullet from Cast Performance 1,625. The .500 S&W delivered 700 ft-lbs more energy than a Casull and twice as much as a .44 Magnum!

Meanwhile, Belin and his crew developed an "X-frame" revolver. It had a five-shot cylinder 2¼ inches long, plus a sleeved barrel with a frame-to-yoke cylinder latch and a muzzle cap with top porting to reduce climb. Hogue-designed Sorbathane grips mitigated the slap of recoil, as did the pistol's weight. At 72 ounces, it was more than a pound heavier than a Model 629 .44 with a same-length (8 ⅜-inch) barrel. Listing at just under $1,000, the Smith & Wesson 500 (named after the round) was instantly back-ordered.

But Belin wasn't done. Even before the 500 went to dealers, an X-frame sequel was underway. It appeared in mid-2004. With a case even longer than the .500's, the .460 XVR pushed Hornady 200-grain SST at 2,211 fps. Cor-Bon fielded other loads, including a 395-grain Hard Cast at 1,511 fps. Pointed bullets extended the .460's reach. Zeroed to hit 3 inches high at 100 yards, the S&W revolver shot just 3.8 inches low at 200, where the Hornady SST bullet still clocked 1,373 fps and carried 837 ft-lbs of energy! Smith & Wesson's 460 DA revolver has gain-twist rifling, pitched 1-in-100 at the throat, 1-in-20 at the muzzle. The accelerating spin throttles pressures and minimizes bullet deformation without compromising accuracy.

I used one of the first S&W 500s on a deer and pronghorn hunt, killing both animals at just under 100 yards. Friend Bill Booth shot a deer at 200. The X-Frame redefines the hunting handgun.

STEYR: THE AUSTRIAN CLASSIC

"The gun room was disassembled, stick by stick, then trucked to a new factory and reassembled," says Franz Holzschuh, my host and co-owner of Steyr. Named for a thirteenth-century town established at the confluence of the Steyr and Enns Rivers, Steyr got its start in the 1860s when young Josef Werndl returned from a stint in the United States working for Colt. He applied his new knowledge in his father's gunshop. "In church one day Josef thought up a new rifle," said Franz. The mechanism would be called the "tabernacle breech." Not unlike our 1873 trap-door Springfield, it was first of many firearms bearing the Steyr stamp. Austria's army bought it, launching a company that at the end of the nineteenth century boasted more than ten thousand workers!

Steyr built rifles for other countries on their designs, notably the Norwegian Krag and the Mauser. It tacked other names onto its own sporting rifles too. Mannlicher-Schoenauer was not a manufacturer, but a series of rifles built by Steyr. Subsequent Steyr sporters have adopted the 98 Mauser in receiver design, with detachable box magazines instead of the Mannlicher's silky spools. Advantages of new Steyrs include a bridge to stiffen the receiver and facilitate scope mounting. The three-position tang safety also serves as a bolt release. Modern Steyr rifles boast a two-lug lock-up so strong it withstands test firing with a full-power load *fired behind a bullet deliberately lodged 30 cm up the barrel!* "We administer that test randomly," explained Franz. "Pressures are extremely high. Still, the hammer-forged barrels do not split. Usually we open the bolt by hand." Rifles doomed to this ordeal are, of course, scrapped.

The current Steyr Classic is more accurate than the old Mannlicher-Schoenauers, according to Dr.

STEYR HAS A LONG HISTORY OF BUILDING SMOOTH-SHUCKING RIFLES. ITS MAGAZINES ARE PEERLESS.

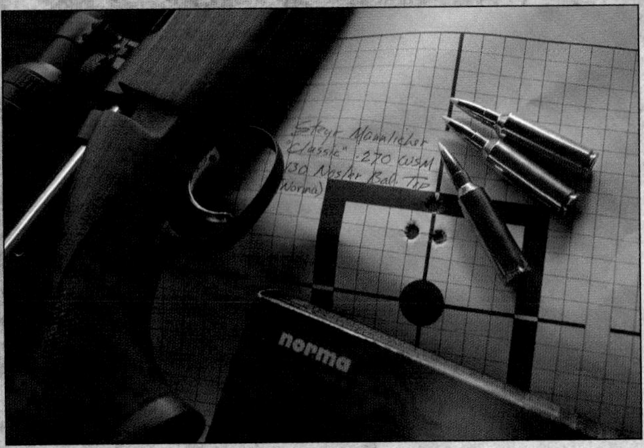

CURRENT STEYR RIFLES AND CARBINES DELIVER FINE ACCURACY. WAYNE FIRED THIS GROUP AT THE FACTORY.

Ernst Reichmayr, Franz's partner. At a range near the company plant, he handed me a carbine in 9.3x62. Handy and lightweight, it cycled RWS ammunition with buttery ease, hurling 258-grain H-Mantle bullets into sub-minute triangles. A Classic in .270 WSM I benched at the same time with Norma ammo kept its first three-shot groups to about .80. Both wore single-set triggers, standard now on Steyr rifles and much improved over earlier versions. A push forward, and you've readied the trigger to release at about a pound.

The handling qualities of Mannlicher-Schoenauer and now the Steyr full-stocked carbines endear them to hunters. The 19-inch barrel threads a slim, tapered fore-stock. Superb balance contributes to fast, natural pointing. In the Austrian woodlands I found the Classic carbine ideal for dashing boars. It downed five, and did not miss. The little 9.3 seemed not to need guidance.

A century and a half of gun-making can, at times, be downright obvious.

TIKKA BIG BOAR: SMOOTH, FROM SWEDEN

Since its debut at the turn of this century, the T3 has brought Tikka-seekers to gun counters like its more expensive Sako counterparts do not. The rifles, oddly enough, come from the same factory. The T3's reputation is deserved. So when, on a Finnish moose hunt, talk turned to a T3 *carbine*, I listened.

The short rifle entered Beretta's catalog soon thereafter (Beretta owns Sako and Tikka). It's called the Big Boar. Available in .308, .30-06, and .300 WSM, it features a 19-inch, hammer-forged, free-floated barrel. There are no sights; the receiver is prepped for scope mounts. The stock is of fiberglass-reinforced polymer. It has a pleasing profile, with a straight, fluted comb and a long grip. Raised bumps on the grip and forend panels secure your hands. This appears to be the same black stock as on the T3 Lite, with its 22- and 24-inch barrels. So it looks long on the Big Boar. Still, it is a comfortable handle.

SAM SHAW FIRES A TIKKA T3 BIG BOAR. ACCURATE AND SMOOTH-CYCLING, IT'S BUILT BY SAKO IN FINLAND.

FN BUILDS M70S (FIRST AS FNS) IN NORTH CAROLINA, FOLLOWING CLOSURE OF WINCHESTER'S NEW HAVEN PLANT.

I first saw the rifle at the plant in Riihimaki, Finland, after a humiliating shoot at a local range.

"You must shoot again," admonished the stern Finn at the controls of the running moose target.

The T3 in my hands that day, a .308, featured a two-lug bolt with a recessed face, a plunger ejector and Sako-style extractor. There's just one T3 receiver; bolt stops accommodate short and long cartridges. The detachable box magazines feed a single three-shot vertical stack. They're of lightweight polymer, more rigid than metal boxes. Deeper five- and six-round magazines are available. You can't load magazines through the receiver, partly because cartridges must be slipped in from the front, partly because the ejection port is small to keep the receiver stiff. Integral scope mount rails accept 17mm rings, but the rifle is also drilled and tapped for other bases. Except for the magazine and bolt shroud, and an alloy guard, the T3 action is all-steel. A pear-shaped bolt handle is one of four major bolt components, easy to take apart by hand. A two-position safety locks the bolt and trigger—which adjusts from 2 to 4 pounds pull with a hex key inserted through the magazine well. The recoil lug is a steel stock insert that engages a receiver slot.

Tikka imposes a minute-of-angle accuracy standard on its hunting rifles, including the Big Boar. I installed a Sightron 2-7x scope on my .308 test rifle, then gathered up ten boxes of ammo, all different, and hung a target. The rifle functioned without a hitch. Feeding was exceptionally smooth, I managed to punch groups as small as .70 inch. Average: 1.16. The top five came in at .86.

Overall, the Tikka T3 Big Boar is a delightful rifle, as pleasant to carry as to shoot. It points fast. It is better built, with a better trigger, than most rifles. And it is accurate enough to hit a peach at 200 yards.

Sako has some tough in-house competition indeed!

WINCHESTER MODEL 70: THE RIFLEMAN'S RIFLE—AGAIN.

When Winchester's New Haven factory shuttered its doors in March, 2006, shooters sprinted to local gunshops and quickly emptied racks of Model 70s. Not since 1964 has the firm's flagship rifle triggered such a response. That year, Winchester's accountants had their way with the 70, cutting production costs with changes that left customers cold. Almost overnight "pre-64" rifles rocketed in value, while new rifles with music-wire springs, stamped checkering, and bolt-face extractors drew ridicule.

Between 1964 and 2006 Winchester worked hard to improve the Model 70. Its long grind back up the hill reached a high bench in 1980 when a new, sleek Featherweight appeared and the Mauser extractor became a Custom Shop option. Months later Olin-Mattheson sold the Winchester Sporting Arms business. A short-action M70 came in 1984—and U.S. Repeating Arms filed for Chapter 11 bankruptcy. Six years later Winchester had a controlled-feed 70 "Classic." By then USRAC was a subsidiary of

WINCHESTER'S NEW MODEL 70 STABLE NOW INCLUDES A SAFARI-STYLE RIFLE IN .375 AND .458.

Fabrique Nationale (FN), a Belgian firm that already owned Browning. Under FN, the M70 kept evolving. But even as it claimed increasing market share, escalating labor costs were eroding profitability. Annual losses just before March, 2006 ran to seven figures. That year Winchester listed twenty one versions of the Model 70, starting at $525.

Before the Winchester assembly line shut down, a few Model 70 actions went to FNH USA, the U.S. subsidiary of FN Herstal. They came to market as FN rifles. The Columbia, South Carolina, facility building FN rifles now produces new Model 70s with most features of the last 2006 rifles. The "M.O.A." trigger replaces the excellent but less lawyer-friendly original. Factory set at just under 4 pounds, the new trigger has a finger-piece that pushes forward on an actuator that releases the sear that drops the striker. Pull weight is adjustable; sear engagement is not. The Mauser extractor and three-position safety are unchanged.

New Sporter Deluxe and Featherweight Deluxe M70s come in long- and short-action versions, in chamberings from .243 to .300 Winchester Magnum—including three WSMs. Their cut-checkered walnut stocks and hammer-forged barrels with high-polish blue appear also on the new Super Grade, with figured wood and black forend tip. An "Extreme Weather SS" features stainless steel receiver and barrel (fluted). New for 2010: a safari rifle in .375 and .458, with walnut stock, iron sights and barrel-mounted swivel stud.

The new M70s shoot well for me, albeit the original price of $61.25 is ancient history. I've owned more than fourty Model 70s. Most are now gone. I've regretted selling every one.

WEATHERBY D'ITALIA SHOTGUNS: QUICK AS A FERRARI

After a couple of false starts, Weatherby formed a partnership with an Italian gunmaker that could produce affordable shotguns that look and feel expensive. D'Italia over/under and side-by-side shotguns hail from the house of Fausti, a family whose smoothbores

exhibit the svelte lines and exquisite balance of the world's best double guns. Choose Orion or Athena versions, the latter with engraved sideplates. The O/U's four-lock action is exceptionally strong, and stubbornly refuses to shoot loose. Stocks are of nicely figured walnut, generously checkered twenty lines per inch. I like the round-knob Prince-of-Wales grip, but you can order a straight grip on the side-by-side D'Italia. It's appropriately paired with double triggers, while other D'Italias wear single selective inertia-activated triggers. Specify 12 or 20 gauge, or, in some models, 28. Frames are sized to the gauge and nicely fitted to the walnut. Chrome-lined barrels and ventilated ribs are standard. Weatherby's interchangeable chokes share thread patterns with Brileys.

Mostly, I like these new Weatherby shotguns for their handling. Lightweight and slender without feeling whispy, they leap to my cheek, swing smoothly. They're quick on target but balanced to pull you through the shot. On pheasants, chukars, and quail, I've shot as well with a Weatherby D'Italia 20-bore O/U as I've shot with any other scattergun. Almost as appealing is the Orion's price—not much more than that of a top-end autoloader.

If you're tired of feeling the machinery of pumps and autoloaders but can't stomach the divorce you'd trigger buying a British double, look at Weatherby D'Italias. You'll be hooked!

THREE HUN'ERD

—By Wayne van Zwoll

Once thought destructive, .300 magnums now fuel our most popular rifles. But are they versatile?

A .30 magnum is a fine elk round. I've been using various renditions for three decades. My first elk rifle, a Henriksen-built Mauser, was chambered in .300 Holland. In a darkening Oregon meadow long ago, I strained to see antlers on the lone elk at timber's edge. *Almost* sure, I decided not to shoot. I turned and found myself eyeball to brow tine with a six-point bull. Since then, I've clobbered elk with other .300 Hollands, as well as rifles in .300 Weatherby Magnum, .300 Winchester Magnum, .308 Norma Magnum, .300 Winchester Short Magnum, and .300 Remington Short Ultra Mag. My .30-.338 by Rick Freudenberg on a Model 70 action has not yet killed a bull. Nor has a Ruger Hawkeye in .300 Ruger Compact Magnum. One of my biggest elk succumbed to a .30-06 Improved—a magnum in performance if not name.

Short .30s have been around a long time, because "short" is relative. The .300 WSM measures just 2.76 inches *loaded*, compared to 3.31 inches for the .300 Winchester Magnum. The .300 WSM fits in rifle actions scaled for the .243 and .308 Winchester cartridges. But when I was growing up, short magnums were all those shorter than the 3.47-inch .300 H&H. Now as musty as news clippings of Sputnik, they still deliver a utility newer cartridges can only match.

THOMPSON/CENTER'S ICON IS ONE OF MYRIAD BOLT RIFLES SOLD IN .300 WINCHESTER MAGNUM SINCE 1963.

SHORT .300S; L–R: .300 REM. SHORT ACTION ULTRA MAG, .300 WSM, .300 RUGER COMPACT MAGNUM.

The first big .30 came from the drawing board of brilliant inventor Charles Newton. Called the .30 Adolph Express for gunmaker Fred Adolph, the rimless round booted 180-grain bullets downrange at 2,880 fps. In 1913, that was fast indeed. But few hunters were ready for such muscle. To riflemen of that day, the .30-06 seemed to pack the might of Zeus. Besides, Newton's .30, even when loaded by Western Cartridge, had no home except Newton rifles. Western dropped the loading in 1938.

Meanwhile, the .300 H&H appeared in Western's catalog. A long belted round designed for Cordite powder, the "Super .30" as it was called at its 1925 U.S. debut, duplicated .30 Newton performance. Custom rifles from Griffin & Howe and British shops kept it alive until Winchester chambered the Model 70 for it in 1937, two years after Ben Comfort won the 1,000-yard Wimbledon Match at Camp Perry with a .300 H&H. The Holland's 2.85-inch hull limits it to very long actions, like magnum Mausers and the Model 70 and Remington's later 721 and 700 (Comfort used a re-worked 1917 Enfield). Recent rifles from other makers have qualified too. The Super .30 got a tepid welcome compared to Winchester's fast-stepping .270, also announced in '25. Its fortunes rose, then gradually slid as newer, shorter .30s came along. But the .300 H&H has regained some traction of late, with factory loads from Hornady and Federal, as well as from Winchester and Remington. A pointed 180-grain bullet generates 3,315 foot-pounds at the muzzle and brings more than 1,700 to 400 yards. Given a 200-yard zero, that bullet strikes 7 inches low at 300 steps, and 21 inches low at 400. At one time, you could buy .300 H&H ammunition with 150-grain bullets at nearly 3,200 fps, and 220-grain bullets at 2,620. The 180-grain spitzers shoot 15 percent flatter than those from standard .30-06 loads, and deliver a 10 percent advantage in wind—but with 35 percent more recoil.

Despite its capacious hull and high-octane performance, the .300 H&H is quite pleasant to shoot, with significantly less felt recoil than the long magnum that came close on its heels.

Born in 1910 to a Kansas sharecropper, Roy Weatherby later moved to California, developed an insurance business and fashioned a line of magnum cartridges in his workshop. Roy's .300 was the .300 Holland blown out with minimum body taper. But his *first* magnums were necked to .257, .277, and .284 and shortened for .30-06-length magazines. In 1946, he pledged "everything I owned" to get a $5,000 loan and a start in the gun business.

In those halcyon days of surplused Mausers and Springfields, Weatherby's .300 made an anemic showing. Proprietary and expensive, the ammunition didn't suit lunch-bucket hunters who found the .30-06 and .270 deadly. Bankruptcy was looming when one day Gary Cooper walked in the door. Roy took full advantage of the moment and was soon tapping Hollywood to market rifles. He appeared in photographs with actors like Roy Rogers and John Wayne. He courted Elmer Keith and Jack O'Connor, Jimmy Doolittle and Joe Foss. High-profile associations implied that Weatherby owners belonged in elite company, that Weatherby rifles brought success. Sheldon Coleman became a customer, as did other industrialists like Texas oil man Herb Klein, who helped Roy financially. In 1957, having built rifles on Mauser actions, Roy and company engineer Fred Jennie came up with an action of their own: the magnum-length Mark V.

AFRICA WAS ROY WEATHERBY'S TESTING GROUND. HERE A HUNTRESS BEARS DOWN WITH HER MARK V IN .300.

High-performance cartridges got another boost from wildcatter Rocky Gibbs, who moved to Idaho from California during the March blizzard of 1955 and established a 500-yard range on 35 acres just out of Viola. Gibbs developed a stable of wildcats on the .30-06 case. The .30 Gibbs was perhaps most versatile. Unlike Parker Ackley's .30-06 Improved, the Gibbs cartridge had a shorter neck than the parent case. Case forming meant over-expanding the neck, then reducing it in a Gibbs sizing die to form a false shoulder. Or you could use the hydraulic case-forming tool marketed by the enterprising Gibbs.

Most early high-velocity rounds were .30-bore or smaller, no matter the case size. Then, just after the second world war, American wildcatters Charlie O'Neil, Elmer Keith and Don Hopkins designed the .333 OKH, the .30-06 necked for .333 bullets then available from Kynoch. Later OKH rounds were necked to .338 so they could employ American bullets. These became the .338-06 and .338 Winchester Magnum.

But the .338 Winchester didn't arrive until 1959. Remarkably, it predated every short commercial .300.

Winchester might have been thinking of a high-performance .30 earlier, but its first venture into short magnums gave us a far less versatile round. At its debut in 1956, the .458 Winchester Magnum was the first U.S. cartridge to compete with British Nitro Express rounds. With a 500-grain solid clocking 2,130 fps, the .458 developed 5,040 ft-lbs of muzzle energy, a tad shy of what you'd get from the .470 NE. But the case was much more compact: just 2.50 inches long, it fit in actions sized for the .30-06.

Winchester couldn't have expected to sell truckloads of .458s. At $310, a Model 70 so chambered cost nearly double what you'd pay for a .30-06. But the cartridge apparently pleased Olin's accountants, so another magnum followed. It was, astonish-

L–R: THE .300 H&H AND .300 WEATHERBY REQUIRE LONGER ACTIONS THAN DOES THE .308 NORMA.

ingly, not a .30. Like the .458 and Weatherby's short magnums of the early 1940s, the .264 Winchester employed the .300 H&H case (itself derived from the .375 Holland, circa 1912). It headspaced on a belt forward of the extractor groove. Designed into the slight-shouldered .375 case to ensure a definite "stop," the belt was useful on the rimless .458 but not necessary on the .264 with its ample 25-degree shoulder. First news of the .264 came in 1958; the 26-inch-barreled M70 dubbed the "Westerner" didn't appear until 1959. Alas, the .264 soon got a reputation as a barrel-burner, using big charges of slow powder to match the more efficient, hugely popular .270. When Winchester revised 140-grain velocities down to 3,030 fps, the .264 lost what little traction it had.

You'd think that Weatherby's success with its long .300 Magnum, and the unabashed affection many shooters had for the .30-06, 7x57 and .270 Winchester, would have influenced the folks at East Alton. But instead of a belted .300, 7mm or .270, they followed the .264 with the .338 Magnum. Even by today's standards, the .338 Winchester is on the brawny side of versatile. Recoil from the M70 "Alaskan" rifles that Winchester initially offered for the .338 discouraged even elk hunters. The name itself implied use on huge brown bears and moose taller than a carport.

Oddly enough, the first 30-caliber cartridge designed on a short magnum case hailed from Norma of Sweden. The case measures 2.56 inches, slightly longer than the .338, so it was not interchangeable with the .30-338—a logical wildcat engineered by shooters tired of waiting for Winchester to bring them a .300 magnum. Norma blunted its own entry into the U.S. market by first offering only *cases*. A year and a half later ammunition appeared, a "re" on the headstamp signifying reloadable Boxer-primed brass. Browning alone, among American gun companies, listed a rifle in .308 Norma: the lovely Mauser High Power. Had not Remington, then Winchester, come up with alternatives, the .308 Norma might have gained a foothold Stateside. From a design standpoint, many shooters consider it a superior medium-bore cartridge.

In 1962 Remington introduced its 7mm Magnum. A public that had shunned Winchester's .264 Magnum embraced Remington's 7, cleverly billed as a deer-elk round. The .264 had been offered up as a deer-varmint cartridge, a niche already filled by the less violent .243 and .25-06. The 7mm Remington Magnum also piggybacked on the same-year debut of the Model 700 rifle, sleek progeny of the 721. This rifle gave Remington an affordable platform for the cartridge, ensuring it would be better received

FLAT-SHOOTING, THE .300 MAGNUMS PERFORM AT DISTANCE AS THE .30-06 DOES 100 YARDS CLOSER.

than Weatherby's 7mm, then available only in the Mark V.

Winchester's response to Remington's belted 7mm appeared in 1963. Riflemen had expected a necked-down .338. Winchester instead delivered a belted case with the same head but an overall length of

HUNTERS BENEFIT MOST FROM .300 MAGNUMS IN OPEN, WINDY COUNTRY, LIKE THIS ALBERTA PLAIN.

L–R: .308 NORMA, .300 WINN MAG, .300 DAKOTA. THE DAKOTA IS RIMLESS, ON THE .404 JEFFERY CASE.

2.620 inches. With the neck shorter than bore diameter, it held more powder than Norma's hull, but actions for the .30-06 limited *useful* capacity by requiring that bullets be seated deep. Still, the .300 Winchester Magnum quickly ate market share away from the 7mm Remington Magnum. In my surveys of elk hunters during the 1990s, the .300 yielded in popularity to the .30-06 and Remington's 7mm Magnum but remains a strong contender. Recent surveys show it is closing the gap on the 7mm.

PUTTING UP WITH YOUR .300

The problem with any high-performance .30 is that it kicks. High bullet speed means high recoil velocity, according to this formula: V = bullet weight (grs.) / 7,000 x bullet velocity (fps) + powder weight (grs.) / 7,000 x powder gas velocity (fps). Powder and its gas figure in because like the bullet, they are "ejecta" and cause recoil. Gas velocity varies, but Art Alphin, in his A-Square loading manual, says 5,200 fps is a useful average. The "7,000" denominators simply convert grains to pounds so units make sense in the end. For a 180-grain bullet fired at 3,000 fps from my $8\frac{1}{2}$-pound .30-338 or .308 Norma rifles I'd calculate recoil this way: 180 / 7,000 x 3,000 + 70 / 7,000 x 5,200 = 8.5 x V. That simplifies to (77.143 + 52) 8.5 = V = 15.19 fps. Then I can calculate recoil using the first formula: KE = MV2 / GC. The result looks like this: 8.5 (15.19)2 / 64.32 = 30.49 foot-pounds of recoil, half again as much as from a .30-06. But the increase in felt recoil may be much less noticeable if your rifle has a straight, generous comb and a forgiving 1-inch recoil pad. Your hands help absorb recoil too, if grip and forend are properly shaped. Rifles approaching 8 pounds in weight, trailside, are much more comfortable to shoot than those under 7 pounds, which hit you quicker and harder because there's less inertia. Finally, install your scope well forward—recoil becomes much more noticeable if the ocular ring bangs your brow.

IN LITHE BOLT RIFLES, LIKE THIS HUNTER'S RUGER 77, THE .300 WINCHESTER HAS PERFORMED IN REMOTE PLACES.

For more than two decades, the .300 Winchester and 7mm Remington Magnums satisfied hunters looking for more power than available in a .270 or .30-06. Then Don Allen brought out the .300 Dakota, on a shortened .404 Jeffery hull. At 2.540 inches, the Dakota case is slightly shorter than the Winchester's, but it holds more powder and performs like the .300 Weatherby Magnum.

As if we didn't have enough .30 magnums, Weatherby announced, in 1996, a .300 to top all others. The .30-378 was based on the gigantic .378 Weatherby case, not only longer but bigger at the base than the .300 Winchester. By early 1997, the rifle plant in Maine was scrambling to fill orders—10 times as many as Weatherby had expected. More than a decade later, the .30-378 remains a strong seller. The only cartridge to challenge it is John Lazzeroni's 7.82 Warbird, a rimless round fashioned from scratch but similar to the .404 Jeffery. Both these .30s require a super-size action (McMillan receivers initially for the Warbird, then Sakos too). The .30-378 is factory loaded with 165-grain Nosler Ballistic Tips at an advertised 3,500 fps, 180-grain Barnes X bullets at 3,450. Given a 300-yard zero, these bullets strike less than 4 inches high at 200 yards, a mere 7 ½ inches low at 400. They carry well over a ton of energy to 500 yards.

Not to be left out of the .30-magnum game, Remington in 1998 brought out its .300 Ultra Mag on the .404 Jeffery hull. The Ultra Mag is about as big a round as the Model 700 action can stand. Its rim is slightly rebated to fit bolt faces engineered for the .532 H&H head common to most belted rounds. Though it has 13 percent more case capacity than the .300 Weatherby, you won't get 13 percent more velocity from the Ultra Mag. As case volume grows, cartridges lose efficiency. There's negligible difference between the .300 Ultra Mag as loaded by Remington and the .300 Weatherby as loaded by Norma. The Ultra Mag boots a 180-grain Nosler Partition at 3,250 fps; the Weatherby launches 180-grain Partitions at 3,240. Remington followed its first .30 magnum with other Ultra Mags, then trimmed the case for short actions to compete with Winchester's WSMs. I probably shot the first elk killed with the .300 Remington Short Action Ultra Mag. It remains a favorite cartridge, slightly smaller than the .300 WSM and suitable for Remington Model Seven actions.

Arguably even better is the .300 Ruger Compact Magnum, introduced by Hornady four years ago. It is more than a thinly veiled copy of the .300 WSM or .300 SAUM. It, and a companion .338 RCM, were developed to wring magnum velocities from 20-inch barrels. Mitch Mittelstaedt, who headed the project, explained to me that with new proprietary powders, his team was able to "tighten" pressure curves so the .300 RCM performs like ordinary .30 magnums in ordinary barrels but doesn't lose as much enthusiasm in carbines. Lab tests show velocity losses of 160 to 180 fps when .300 WSM barrels are chopped from 24 to 20 inches; with RCMs, the drop is about 100.

Inspired by the 2.58-inch .375 Ruger, the .300 and .338 RCM share its .532 head and base. WSM rounds are bigger, with rebated .535 heads. RCM shoulder angles are 30 degrees. Case capacities average 68 and 72 grains of water to the mouth. For comparison, Remington .30-06 hulls hold 67 grains of water, Winchester .300 WSM cases 79 grains. Ruger Compact Magnums cycle through WSM magazines, but you can sneak four RCMs into

THE AUTHOR USED A BROWNING A-BOLT IN .300 WSM TO KILL THIS NAMIBIAN ORYX, OR GEMSBOK.

most three-round WSM boxes. They're loaded to the same overall length (2.84 inches) as WSMs.

With chronograph guru Ken Oehler, I clocked .300 RCM loads from the 20-inch barrel of a Ruger carbine. The Oehler 35 gave me readings of around 2,840 fps with 180-grain bullets. Groups stayed around an inch. The accuracy was gratifying, though not surprising, as short barrels are stiff.

I can recall barrel stampings that read ".300 Magnum." Seventy years ago, no more identification was needed because the .300 Holland and Holland had no competition. Now, generations of high-octane cartridges later, .300 magnums come in a wide range of shapes, sizes and performance levels. And they're chambered in a multitude of bolt-action and single-shot rifles—even, now, lever-actions and autoloaders.

You may not need—or want—the heavy-handed muscle of the most powerful .30s. But the assortment of mid-size magnums that edge the .30-06 by a couple hundred feet per second add precious yards of lethal reach to your rifle. They may give you the confidence you need to turn the tide of a hunt in your favor.

ELAND CAN WEIGH A TON. BUT A SINGLE DEEP-DRIVING 180-GRAIN BULLET FROM A .300 DOWNED THIS BULL.

Dr. Wayne van Zwoll

A full-time journalist for the outdoors press, Wayne van Zwoll has published more than 2,000 articles and twice that many photos for more than two dozen magazine titles, including *Sports Afield*, *Outdoor Life*, and *Field & Stream*. Once the editor of *Kansas Wildlife*, he has also edited *Mule Deer* for the Mule Deer Foundation, and Stoeger's *Shooter's Bible*. His Rifles and Cartridges column in *Bugle* has run for twenty-one years—longer than any other in the Rocky Mountain Elk Foundation's flagship magazine. Wayne has authored thirteen books on hunting, shooting, and history. In 1996 he was named Shooting Sports Writer of the Year by the Outdoor Writers Association of America. In 2006 he received the Jack Slack Outdoor Writer of the Year award from Leupold and was recently presented with the John T. Amber award for excellence in gun writing. Now Special Projects Editor for *Intermedia Outdoors*, Wayne also contributes to Petersen's Hunting and Guns & Ammo television. He is a professional member of the Boone and Crockett Club and has served on the board of OWAA. Wayne lives in north-central Washington State with Alice, his wife of thirty-six years.

HOW TO PICK HUNTING OPTICS

—By Thomas McIntyre

A major part of the hunt for big game begins with finding good quality optics, whether a binocular or a riflescope. (And it is *binocular* and not *binoculars*, in the same way it's a *bicycle* and not *bicycles*, a bicycle a two-wheeled vehicle and a binocular a telescopic device with two eyepieces.)

It is difficult to imagine any big-game hunting situation in which a binocular would not come into play. You can't hunt game you can't see; and even a bowhunter will use a binocular to identify and judge an animal at close range—when it's in dark or heavy cover—before nocking an arrow.

Similarly, most serious big-game hunters have learned the value of the proper riflescope, even when hunting in dense timber where shots may be only a few yards away. Daniel Boone might have depended on "Kentucky windage" to bring down a distant deer; but if he'd had a good 3-9x42 with a duplex reticle, he'd have used it in a New York minute.

There are a number of ways of acquiring a binocular or riflescope. And whether it is purchased new or used, traded for, or passed along, there are several factors to be examined in order to determine an instrument's worth (not necessarily its monetary value) in the field.

When picking good hunting optics, here are some things to look at:

Price: Whether you can afford a little or a lot, be aware that there are usually four different prices for the same binocular or riflescope.

COMPARING TWO BINOCULARS

The first price is the *MSRP* ("manufacturer's suggested retail price"). This is the price that the maker publishes—often in product literature—and at which the maker believes, or says, the optical device should be sold. This price exists to allow retailers to show consumers how much of a bargain the retailers are offering with their own price, compared with the maker's. The writer Nelson Algren once wrote, "Never play cards with any man named 'Doc.' Never eat at any place called 'Mom's.' And never, never, no matter what else you do in your whole life, never sleep with anyone whose troubles are worse than your own." To which it should be added, never, under any circumstances, pay full MSRP.

MAP ("minimum advertised price") is second, and it is a figure approved by the manufacturer that retailers may show in their published or broadcast advertising. Obviously MAP will be less than MSRP, sometimes considerably. Its function is to enable smaller retailers to compete with the big-box stores, which could always undercut the little guy if permitted to blazon "low-low prices" set at a level so far beneath the floor established by the MAP that small-volume shop owners could never hope to receive a decent return from their far fewer number of sales.

Next comes the *real world price*. In case that term is not self-explanatory enough, this is the average price a consumer can expect to pay when purchasing a binocular or riflescope from a retailer, whether a local shop, big-box store, or a catalog. This price will sometimes appear in printed reviews of a binocular or riflescope, and it can fluctuate from retailer to retailer, depending on how much profit retailers hope to make. As a rule, though, it will not be too far from the MAP though can still be significantly different. To reiterate, a real world price below the MAP cannot be publicly advertised. A hunter has to walk into the store to find out what is actually written on the sticker.

The *Internet auction price* is a fourth possibility. It takes a certain degree of intestinal fortitude to bid on hunting optics at one of the auction sites, especially on used ones with more expensive names; but very substantial savings may be found. Fine-quality hunting optics have a lengthy shelf life, and ones made ten or even twenty years ago, although they may lack some of the more advanced antireflective coatings or newer glass—and as long as they have not been abused—

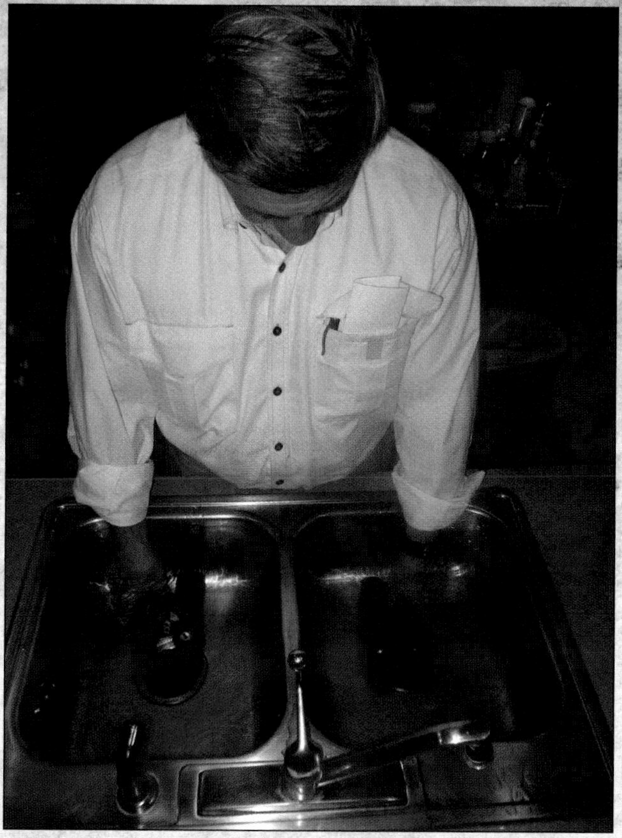

FIELD & STREAM'S DAVE PETZAL CHECKING WATERPROOFING ON BINOCULARS

can continue to function quite satisfactorily today. A hidden treasure to be on the lookout for is any really top-brand binocular or riflescope that has been refurbished and carries a factory warranty. Optics like this will be as good as new (and some think even better because if they had a manufacturing defect, that defect ought to have been remedied by the factory), and at a price that should to be well below what the binocular or riflescope originally sold for, in current dollars.

One last consideration with regard to the price of hunting optics is *where* that price should be paid. Leaving online auctions aside, the three choices are the small retailer, the big-box store, and a catalog. The first will almost always have the highest price, although there could be times when he is selling off, at an extremely attractive markdown, old stock that has long been gone from the other two outlets. The primary reason for purchasing from a small retailer, aside from an understandable desire to buy locally, is the hope that he will offer more insight into the quality of the optics than can some guy in a blue vest stacking boxes with a forklift in a mammoth warehouse operation or can the florid prose accompanying the grainy product photo in a catalog. The small retailer also holds out the promise of courteous, personal after-sale service—*promise*, remember, because the odds on finding this in any retailer's is about as likely as finding that home-cooked meal at "Mom's." Between the big box and the catalog, a hunter has to use time and gas to drive to the store; so even with shipping and handling, the catalog price may be less. One thing that hunters cannot do, though, when they buy a optics through a catalog is inspect them physically to see how well they "fit," an aspect of the buying experience that cannot be discounted.

When the question of price is understood, then the issue of a binocular's or riflescopes's cost—what a hunter is getting in exchange for the price he pays—can be balanced against the features that optical device offers:

DAVE PETZAL EXAMINES FROZEN BINOCULAR FOR FOGPROOFING IN SHERIDAN COLLEGE MEAT SCIENCE FREEZER

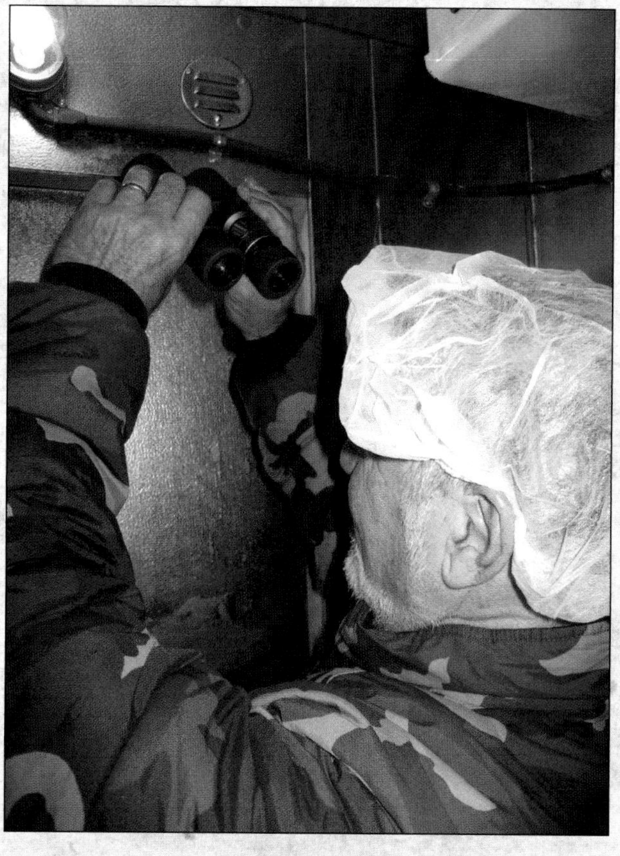

EARLY ZEISS PORRO-PRISM BINOCULAR, WITH THE PERMISSION OF CARL ZEISS, INC.

Glass: The alpha and omega of any binocular or riflescope. Optics can be thought of as nothing more than a convenient way of carrying around a lot of glass lenses and keeping them aligned and in focus. Considerations include low-dispersion and antireflective coatings, but at the bottom lies the quality of the optical glass—the better it is, the more it is likely to weigh, and the more, alas, it is likely to cost.

Light Transmission: *Exit pupil, twilight factor,* and *depth of field* [*please see glossary*], plus coatings, are involved in how much light actually passes through the optical system of a binocular or riflescope and reaches a hunter's eye. This is a figure that can make for delightfully entertaining bedtime reading in optics advertising brochures. Some manufacturers will underscore the fact that the layer of antireflective coating (reflected light being light that is lost to the hunter's eye) they apply will permit something like "99.8 percent" of the available light to pass through, which may be perfectly true. Yet, what they often fail to mention is how many layers of coating are applied to each surface, how many air-to-glass surfaces are contained in their binocular or riflescope (light loss being multiplied with each of those surfaces), and that a 0.2 percent loss of light is probably a reference to what is lost by the *best* (and most costly) layer of antireflective coating being used and not for all the other (cheaper) ones put on in order to call the lenses "multicoated" without being accused of false advertising, at least within the letter of the penal code. A relevant number is the percentage of the available light that travels through the *objective* and the entire optical system and exits from the *ocular*. If a binocular manufacturer can guarantee anywhere from 90 to 92 percent transmission of light through the binocular or riflescope, that is about as good as it gets, at least under the laws of physics as currently written.

IPD: *Interpupillary distance* is a term for describing how far apart someone's pupils are. For most adults this is between 58 and 72 millimeters; most binoculars can be adjusted within this range so that the eyepieces are the right distance apart in order for the centers of the eyes to coincide with the centers of the eyepieces, creating a single round sight picture rather than two overlapping ones. Some individuals can, though, have extremely narrow, or extremely wide-set, eyes. If a hunter believes he fits into one of those categories, then he does need to try a binocular before buying it to determine if it can be adjusted to the proper degree of spread. One of the several virtues of the *Porro-prism* binocular over the *roof prism* is that it can in general offer a more generous range of hinge adjustments.

Eye Relief: This is, lamentably, not another way of saying "Scarlett Johansson." It is the distance that the eyepiece may be held away from the eye and still provide the viewer with the complete field of view instead of a kind of tunnel vision. This distance can fall into a range that is sometimes called the "eye box." While

EXTENDED EYE RELIEF (EER) IS IMPORTANT WHEN SHOOTING PISTOLS.

GLASSING FOR BLACKTAIL ON KODIAK

riflescopes have eye relief measured in inches, and in extended-eye-relief (EER) scopes used on handguns in distances approaching feet, binoculars may have a very small eye box of 9 to 14 millimeters, which might be comfortable for most people who do not wear eyeglasses. For glasses wearers, though (and every shooter should always wear eye protection when using his firearm) it is estimated that an eye relief of at least 16 millimeters is required to see the whole picture. If that is something that cannot be ascertained by reading the technical data about a binocular, then a hunter needs, again, to get ahold of an actual sample in a store and put it to his eyes to find out if it will give him the relief he seeks. Eye relief on a scope, as exemplified in the EER example above, needs to be suited to the recoil of the firearm, to avoid that "ringing" sensation caused by the bell of the ocular bouncing off the hunter's eyebrow.

Eyecups: These are the soft rings around the eyepieces of a binocular that determine where a hunter places his eyes. These can be adjusted in several ways, depending on how they are manufactured. Some simply fold out or in to suit those with glasses and those without, or the eyecups can push in or pull out, or turn in or turn out. In the first instance, the synthetic rubber of the eyecup can fatigue and crack in time from the folding as well as from plain age. Better binoculars seem to use one of the latter two systems. Ideally a hunter would like to feel how the eyecups extend and retract to know that they are tight but smooth and will stay reliably locked in position and are not shaky to the touch.

Focus Mechanism: This can actually be more of an issue than might first be assumed. The three types are *fixed focus, individual eyepiece focusing* ("IF"), and *center focus*. A hunter needs to put the first one right out of his mind. A fixed-focus binocular assumes that a user has both perfect vision and vision that is perfectly matched in both eyes and that those eyes are young and flexible enough to do a great deal of accommodating (the focusing of the eye's lens itself) before a hammer of Thor eyestrain headache takes hold. "Fixed focus" fairly screams "shoddy!"

An IF binocular can adjust for the vision in each eye; but once that is accomplished, it is fundamentally the same as a fixed-focus. Images at varying distances will appear to be in focus, but this will be the result of unconscious accommodation and will bring on eventual visual weariness. A good center-focus binocular

MODERN IN-LINE MUZZLELOADERS REQUIRE GOOD SCOPES.

A HUNTER SHOOTING FROM THE CLASSIC SITTING POSITION

is always the best choice, assuming it has on one of the eyepieces an individual *dioptric adjustment* that will enable it to be properly focused for each of the viewer's eyes and can then be refocused as required for objects at different ranges through the use of the central-focus wheel.

One of the "small" touches that a hunter wants to look at in a hunting binocular is the location of that center-focus wheel. Most binoculars place it at the top of the hinge. This is fine, but for best use in the field, the wheel by all rights ought to be at the bottom. If at the top, the wheel will be under the brim of a hunter's cap, making it necessary for him to tip it back in order to adjust the focus on an animal or other object. Without fail, the wind will come up and blow the cap off his head every time he has to change focus while glassing. It also makes it nearly impossible to focus while squeezing down on the cap brim to help lock the binocular in place. A focus wheel at the bottom of the hinge will eliminate all these problems, if only more manufacturers understood enough about the needs of hunters to build their binoculars that way. Wherever the focus wheel is on the binocular, think about how you will use it in the field before making your purchase.

Riflescopes also need have their ocular focused. Usually, this may be done either with a ring at the end of the ocular, or by loosening a locking ring on the ocular and screwing it in and out until sharp focus is achieved. Then the locking ring is turned to hold the ocular in place. A non-locking ocular focus ring should be fairly stiff, to stay in focus.

Power: Less isn't always more, but what is enough? Personally, with a binocular, if I need magnification significantly over 10x, I will have a spotting scope. For me, for most hunting, I like a binocular around the 8x40 configuration, which gives me a good combination of magnification and exit pupil, such as light transmission, and which is about as big as I like to carry, comfortably, around my neck. For a scope, 3-9x seems to be the most popular choice these days, and it's hard to argue with it. A 4-16x seems like a great deal of scope to me, for big game, but would be all right for varmints. Again, personally, I used to use a lot of straight-power 4x32s or thereabouts; but as my eyes have gotten older, I tend toward the likes of 6x40s, still preferring the simplicity of fixed power. And for the same reason I like a duplex reticle—thick posts stepping down to thin wires—for visibility and being clean of additions such as *mil dots*. The main thing seems to be careful about getting much more scope than you are really going to need, or use, whether in terms of magnification, objective, or gizmos.

Housing: Some manufacturers are downright effusive about their binocular's "polymer" housing—as if

PORRO PRISM DIAGRAM

ROOF PRISM BINOCULAR, L., PORRO PRISM BINOCULAR, R.

they were Martha Stewart and this was a good thing. And perhaps it is. In time, no doubt, all binoculars and riflescopes will have housings ("tubes" in the case of riflescopes), not to mention lenses, of plastic, and hunters will probably wonder how they could have lived so long without them. For now, though, quality binocular and riflescope housings continue to be made of metal. When binoculars were known as "field glasses" that metal was brass; but now it may be magnesium or what is invariably described as "aircraft grade" aluminum or even titanium, of which most riflescope tubes are made because of weight considerations on the rifle. The goal is to use a metal that can be both strong and light. For optimum use by a hunter, a binocular housing should also be rubber armored to protect it and to reduce any alarm-inducing metallic clangs that might be produced by a branch or the like hitting the binocular as a hunter is closing those last few yards on a 7x7 bull elk.

As far as 1 inch versus 30mm riflescope tubes, the larger tube does not offer any more appreciable light transmission. The primary advantage of a 30mm comes in allowing room in the tube for a greater range of adjustment of windage and elevation, which might be of value to the long-range shooter.

Waterproof and Fogproof: Hunting can be a far-from-fair-weather pursuit, so hunting optics must be able to stand up to the elements by being both *waterproof* and *fogproof*. "Waterproof" ought to be clear, and the technical data for a binocular or riflescope will guarantee that it will remain free of any leakage when submerged to a particular depth, such as "down to 5 meters." The integrity of a guarantee of waterproofness can be tested by dunking the optics into a tub of water and holding them under while checking for streams of small bubbles emerging from the housing. (Stray air may be trapped around the housing when it is first submerged, and bubbles from this will be few, erratic, and larger, unlike the steady column of tiny champagne-like bubbles that represents a leak in the internal seals that is allowing the purging gas to escape.) "Fogproof" guarantees that the optics, if subjected to sharp changes in temperature, will not have condensation form within it; condensation is also capable of leading to corrosion. Fogproofing is obtained by replacing all the atmospheric air and any attendant moisture that may have entered a binocular or riflescope on dust during the assembly process with the pure, dry, nearly inert gas nitrogen or the even less reactive "noble gas" argon. Some manufacturers claim that argon is superior to nitrogen because even as a monatomic gas, as opposed to diatomic nitrogen, argon is much larger and so will escape (and all purging gases, over time, will escape) more slowly from the optics housing than will nitrogen, maintaining fogproofing better and longer; but this claim may be overblown, as it were.

What a Brochure Can't Tell a Hunter: Some individual qualities of a binocular or riflescope can be judged only when that it is in a hunter's hands or on his firearm, and that means picking one up and messing about with it. If a hunter enters a shop and asks to take a look at a particular binocular or riflescope, the person behind the counter will obligingly hand it to him and invite him to step outside to have a look

TWO TYPES OF CENTER-FOCUS CONTROL KNOBS

through it. This will tell a hunter almost exactly as much about that optical instrument as taking a test drive in "Park" would tell him about a new pickup. All but the worst possible optics will look good, or at least passing, when used in broad daylight. A hunter will be much better off to stay inside and focus the optics on something on the shop's far wall, something with small print on it, to gauge its *resolution*.

An optics brochure may or may not specify the type of glass that is used for the prism, but usually it will be either BK-7 borosilicate flint glass or BaK-4 barium crown glass. There is no reason for this to mean anything to a hunter, except that BaK-4 is considered superior to BK-7. The difference between the two, though, is noticeable when a binocular or riflescope is pointed toward the light (*no, not directly into the sun*), and the exit pupil is examined. On a binocular with a BK-7 prism the exit pupil will be squared off and gray edged, while one with a BaK-4 prism will produce a clean, well-lighted exit pupil, one that is round and evenly illuminated.

Stray light is reflections off the internal surfaces of the binocular or riflescope that can degrade the image the hunter sees through the eyepiece. The lens mounts, edges of the lenses themselves, or other places inside the housing can reflect stray light; a manufacturer of premium optics will take care to lessen or eliminate internal reflection by anodizing or painting bare metal and other shiny surfaces inside the housing, a process known as *baffling*. A hunter can check an optical instrument's baffling by looking for any loose gleams or reflections inside the housing while viewing a full, bright *field of view* (FOV)—everything around the image should be flat black. (The quality of the baffling can be even better judged by looking through the optics backward through the objective lens.)

One reason for carrying a binocular or riflescope out of the shop into the daylight is to check for *chromatic aberration*. A recommended method for doing this is to find a high-contrast image, such as a leafy tree, and place it in the center of the FOV against the sky. A hunter would then look for green or violet color fringing at the edges of the image. And as long as the hunter has the binocular or riflescope in his hands, he can work the hinges and eyecups, focus ring, the elevation and windage screws, power ring, parallax adjustment wheel, etc., so he can decide what he thinks about its overall construction while ruminating upon the weight, bulk, and shape of the optics—how it *feels* to him personally. (This kind of testing works better when comparing two optics simultaneously. Stack one on top of the over on a steady rest, and compare the images produced by each.)

About the only other thing that a hunter *may* be able to tell by a hands-on and eyes-on examination of a binocular is its *collimation*. This is frequently defined as the alignment between the two barrels of the binocular—do they point and focus on the same place—but it can also refer to the way the lenses are stacked up with one another inside the housing. Only rather severe collimation defects, such as double images, would be immediately detectable during a brief viewing through a binocular, with more minor, though finally no less annoying ones probably becoming apparent only after the purchase and some extended use in the field. Collimation problems can appear in any binocular, no matter how precisely made, after enough time in service, which is another reason for a hunter to make certain that any piece of optics he purchases comes with a lifetime warranty, and that he reads the fine print closely before paying his money.

A test of a riflescope that can't be done without mounting it on a rifle and carrying it to shooting range is called, for lack of a better term, "boxing the target" and tells a hunter how fine or precise the adjustment clicks are. Boxing is accomplished by zeroing in a scope at 100 yards then moving the elevation eight clicks (nominally equal to 2 MOA on a scope with ¼-inch clicks at 100 yards) up, and the windage eight clicks left, and seeing where the bullet goes. Ideally, it would be two inches left and two inches high from the X. Then move 16 clicks right, shoot, 16 clicks down, shoot, 16 clicks left, shoot. At this point, there should be a hole in each corner of the target, forming a four-inch square. Finally, move the elevation up eight clicks and the windage right eight clicks, and the shot should be right back in the bull's eye. I'm not really sure what this proves, but it's pretty cool when it works.

Conclusion: A hunter won't know how good or bad a binocular or riflescope is until he has used it for several seasons in the field. When first buying binoculars or riflescopes, the advice of other hunters can be useful to an inexperienced one, if those hunters actually know something about the subject upon which they are speaking. The good news is that most optics these days really aren't half bad. If you are looking for a perfectly arbitrary basic rule, almost anything that comes in a box that is kept behind the sales counter should be all right, while the optics found on the endcaps of the merchandise aisles, hanging in plastic clamshell packs, are probably the junk—but you never know.

In buying hunting optics, spend as much as you can, as long as it is not more than you can afford. And plan on using those optics all that you can, and learning all that you can about them, in the years to come. Do not be a butterfly, flitting from new optics to newer optics, but pick something good and stick with it a while. The manufacturers will hate you, but they shouldn't have made their riflescope or binocular so good to begin with.

TOM MCINTYRE

Tom McIntyre's a contributing editor at Sports Afield *and* Field & Stream *magazines. He also writes for the television production company Orion Multimedia. He's hunted on six continents and is the author of seven books, the latest* The Field & Stream Hunting Optics Handbook, *published by The Lyons Press, www.LyonsPress.com, from which this article is adapted, and* Wild and Fair: Tales of Hunting Big Game in North America, *from Safari Press, www.safaripress.com. He lives with his wife, son, dog, and cat in Wyoming and blogs at* www.mcintyrehunts.com.

GLOSSARY

Depth of field—the distance in front of and behind an object that is also in focus

dioptric adjustment—the adjustment independent of the center-focus wheel on a binocular, usually on the right eyepiece

exit pupil—the diameter of the light emitted from a binocular or riflescope's eyepiece, in millimeters, calculated by dividing the diameter of the objective lens by the power (e.g., 50mm divided by 10x equals an exit pupil of 5mm); the pupil of the human eye can expand in low light to a maximum of about 7mm, though this ability decreases with age

field of view—the wedge, or cone, of light entering the objective; thought of simply as width, this is how wide an area from which the objective is drawing light, such as "300 feet @ 1000 yards"

mil dots—a *mil* is a unit of measure for a circle, an abbreviation of *milliradian,* a *radian* being the angle that subtends an arc of a circle that is equal in length to the radius of that circle (e.g., a 10-inch-diameter circle would have a radius of 5 inches, and therefore the angle of a radian of that circle would subtend 5 inches of the circle's circumference); put another way, a mil is approximately 1/6283rd of a circle, or about .057 degree; effectively, the way this works out is that a mil dots subtends slightly less that 3.6 inches at 100 yards from center to center of the dots

minute of angle—minutes of angle or *minutes of arc* (both abbreviated as "MOA") refer to 1/60th divisions of one degree of arc, known as a *minute;* in most scopes one click of adjustment to the windage or elevation knobs equals approximately ¼ inch of movement of the crosshairs on the target at 100 yards

objective—the big end of the instrument that is pointed at, and nearest to, the object being viewed

ocular—the eyepiece

parallax—parallax is caused by the inability of the scope to remain focused at all distances, particularly farther ones; parallax can be seen in a riflescope by a hunter's holding the reticle on a target and then moving his eye around the ocular and noting whether or not the target moves in relation to the reticle; in the worst-case scenario, parallax can seriously affect the accuracy of the scope.

Porro prism—named for inventor Ignazio Porro, 19th century Italian artillery officer; his reflective prism resembles a toppled-over roof and changes the direction in which the light is traveling by 180 degrees, flipping the image so it reaches the hunter's eye right-side-up

resolution—ability to bring fine detail into sharp focus

reticle—the word *reticle* comes down from the Latin word for "net" and is related to "reticule" which is a woman's knitted handbag; but "reticle" is just a highfalutin word for "crosshairs," which may be "fine" to "dot" to "duplex" with thick-and-thin posts that can be further categorized from "fine" to "heavy duplex"

roof prism—essentially two Porro prisms cemented together so that the objective and ocular of the optical instrument can be in a straight line, the way most modern binoculars are made

twilight factor—a way of comparing the relative usefulness of different optics in low light, calculated by multiplying the objective diameter, in millimeters, by the power of magnification and finding the square root of this number

NEW PRODUCTS 2010–2011

ANSCHUTZ MODEL 1770

Action: bolt
Stock: walnut
Barrel: 22 in.
Sights: drilled and tapped for scope mounts
Weight: 7.5 lbs.
Caliber: .223 Rem.
Magazine: detachable, 3-shot, in-line
Features: six locking lug action for strength and reliability; adjustable, single-stage Match trigger; hand checkered stock with oval cheek piece and rubber butt pad; detachable sling swivel studs.
MSRP: $2499

ANSCHUTZ MODEL 1770

ARMALITE SPR MOD 1 LE CARBINE

Action: autoloader, short gas system
Stock: black tactical
Barrel: 16″ double lapped, chrome-lined
Sights: 3 detachable rails
Weight: 6.5 lbs.
Caliber: .223
Magazine: 30-shot detachable box
Features: muzzle flash suppressor, tactical 2-stage trigger; sling and case included.
MSRP: $1525

ARSENAL AK-74 JUBILEE SERIES

Action: gas-operated autoloader
Stock: U.S. made black polymer
Barrel: 16.3″ hammer forged, chrome lined
Sights: 1000 meter rear leaf sight and scope rail
Weight: 7.3 lbs.
Caliber: 5.45x39.5
Magazine: 10-shot Russian and 30-shot Bulgarian boxes included
Features: celebrating 35 years of AK-74 and 90th anniversary of M.T.Kalashnikov; limited edition of 500 rifles (100 gold inlay and 400 silver); Russian-made receiver; comes with matching rifle case, gloves and certificate.
MSRP: N/A

BARRETT MODEL 98 BRAVO

Action: bolt
Stock: tactical; adjustable butt
Barrel: 27″ fluted
Sights: none; 18-inch 1913 accessory rail
Weight: 13.5 lbs.
Caliber: .338 Lapua Magnum
Magazine: 10-shot detachable box
Features: adjustable rear monopod and front bipod stock with adjustable cheek piece; thumb operated safety, removable trigger module; two-port muzzle brake reduces recoil.
MSRP: $5040

BARRETT MODEL 98 BRAVO

BARRETT 82A1

BARRETT 82A1

Action: gas-operated autoloader
Stock: tactical-style, adjustable
Barrel: 29″ heavy fluted
Sights: flip-up iron sights
Weight: 29.7 to 30.9 lbs.
Caliber: .416 Barrett or .50 BMG
Magazine: 10-shot box (.416 non-detachable)
Features: M1913 steel optics rail, 27 MOA elevation; dual barrel springs, chrome chamber, non-detachable magazine; included Pelican case and cleaning kit.
MSRP: $9345

BENELLI MR1

BLASER R8

BENELLI MR1

Action: gas-operated autoloader
Stock: black synthetic tactical with pistol grip
Barrel: 16″
Sights: military-style aperture with Picatinny rail
Weight: 7.9 lbs.
Caliber: .223 Rem.
Magazine: 5-shot detachable box
Features: self-cleaning stainless piston system with gas port forward of chamber; accepts high-capacity M-16 magazines.
MSRP: $1299

BLASER R8

Action: straight-pull bolt
Stock: walnut or composite; straight comb
Barrel: 23″ to 25.75″
Sights: open
Weight: 6 lbs. 6 oz.
Caliber: .222 Rem. to .416 Rem. Mag.
Magazine: detachable flush-mounted box, 3- to 5-shot capacity
Features: detachable magazine, two trigger weights available; Blaser Saddle mount allows scope to be detached and reattached without the need to re-zero your optics; R8 Professional in dark green synthetic stock.
MSRP: . . . . . $3200 (R8 Professional with synthetic stock); from $3761 walnut

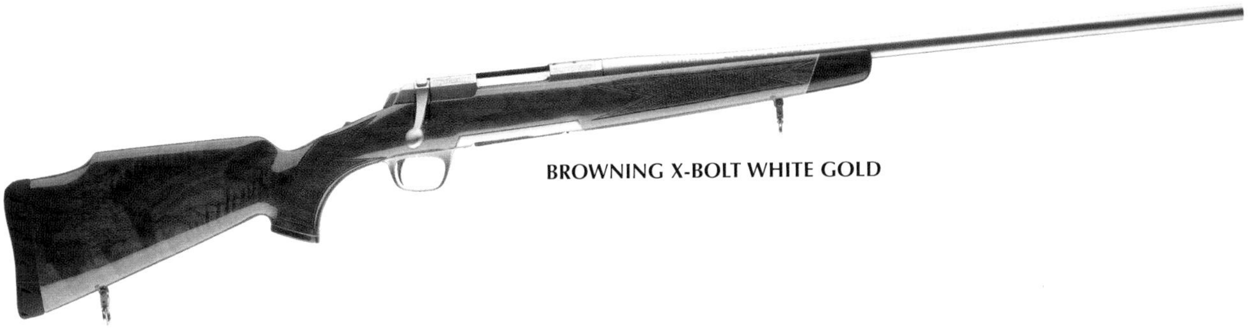

BROWNING X-BOLT WHITE GOLD

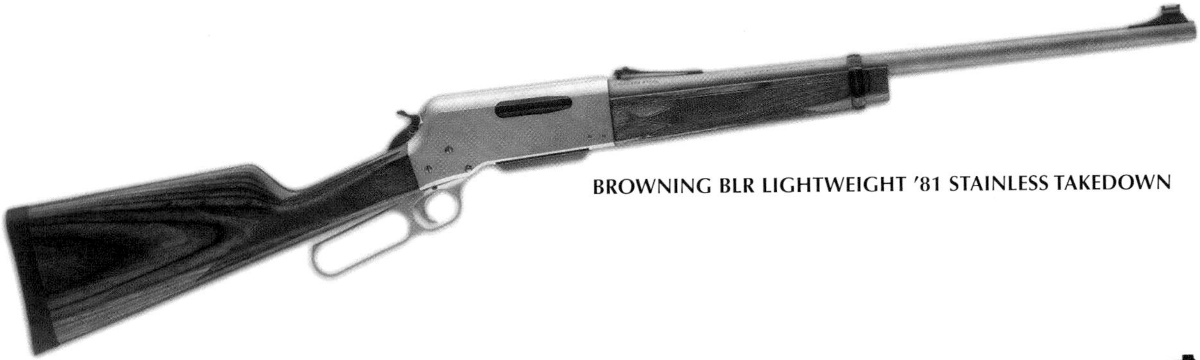

BROWNING BLR LIGHTWEIGHT '81 STAINLESS TAKEDOWN

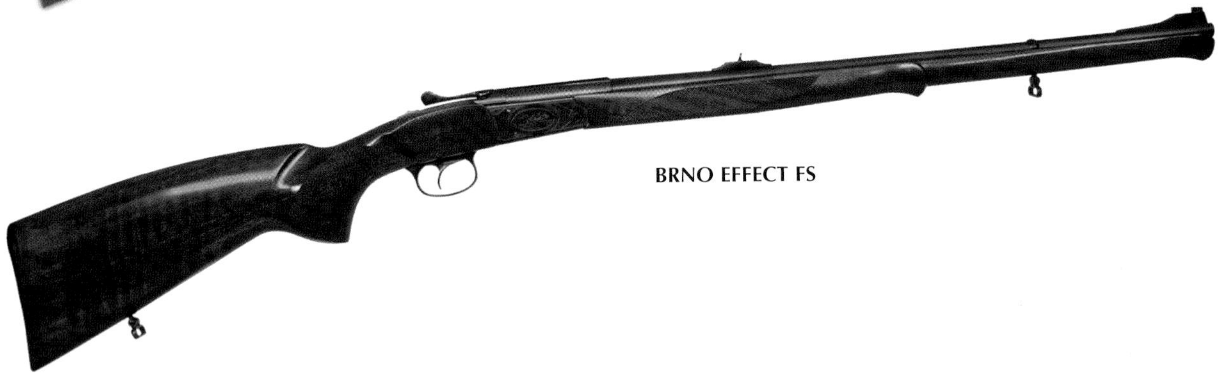

BRNO EFFECT FS

BROWNING X-BOLT WHITE GOLD

Action: bolt
Stock: gloss finish checkered walnut
Barrel: 22″ to 26″ stainless
Sights: none
Weight: 6 lbs. 8 oz to 7 lbs. (magnum)
Caliber: .243 Win. To .338 Win. Mag.
Magazine: detachable 4-shot (3 in magnums) rotary box
Features: scroll engraving on front and rear receiver; adjustable Feather Trigger, detachable rotary magazine, top-tang safety, rosewood fore-end grip and pistol grip cap.
MSRP: . . . . $1439–$1469

BROWNING BLR LIGHTWEIGHT '81 STAINLESS TAKEDOWN

Action: lever
Stock: gray laminate wood with straight grip
Barrel: 20″ to 24″ stainless
Sights: open
Weight: 6 lbs. 8 oz. to 7 lbs. 12 oz. (Magnum)
Caliber: .223 Rem. to .300 Win. Mag.
Magazine: detachable box 4-shot (3 in magnums)
Features: alloy receiver, satin nickel finish; drilled and tapped for scope mounts; detachable box magazine; checkered grip, recoil pad; separates for storage or transportation.
MSRP: . . . . $1149–$1199

BRNO EFFECT FS

Action: single-shot
Stock: walnut (full stock)
Barrel: 23.6″
Sights: open
Weight: 6 lbs.
Caliber: .30-06 or .308 Win.
Magazine: none
Features: select walnut stock (full in FS), big game engravings on receiver, single set trigger, automatic safety and iron sights.
MSRP: . . . . $1585; Full stock: $1699

BUSHMASTER ACR (ADAPTIVE COMBAT RIFLE)

Action: gas-piston semi-automatic
Stock: black or brown high-impact composite A-frame with rubber butt pad and sling mounts
Barrel: 16.5″
Sights: Magpul MBUS front/rear flip sights
Weight: 8.2 lbs.
Caliber: 5.56mm/.223 Rem. or 6.8mm Rem. SPC
Magazine: 30-shot detachable box
Features: carbine adaptable in minutes by switching bolt head, barrel and magazine without tools, from 5.56mm to 6.8mm to 6.5mm; enhanced features also available.
MSRP: . . . . $2685; Enhanced: $3061
Also*:* ACR Patrol and ACR Special Purpose

BUSHMASTER MOE M4 TYPE CARBINE

Action: gas-operated autoloader
Stock: composite Telestock
Barrel: 16″
Sights: Magpul MBUS rear flip sight
Weight: 6.22 lbs.
Caliber: 5.56 mm/.223 Rem.
Magazine: 30-round PMAG
Features: adjustable buttstock with A-frame design and rubber buttplate. Magpul MOE pistol grip accepts MIAD storage cores; available in black, foliage green and flat dark earth.
MSRP: $1295

BUSHMASTER ACR
(ADAPTIVE COMBAT RIFLE)

BUSHMASTER MOE M4
TYPE CARBINE

COOPER FIREARMS MODEL 54

Action: bolt
Stock: checkered walnut
Barrel: 22″ to 26″
Sights: none
Weight: 6.5 lbs.
Caliber: .22-250 Rem., .243 Win., .250 Savage, 7mm-08 Rem., .308 Win., .260 Rem.
Magazine: 3-round detachable box
Features: short action; three front locking lugs, air gauged lapped, match grade barrel.
MSRP: . . . . N/A

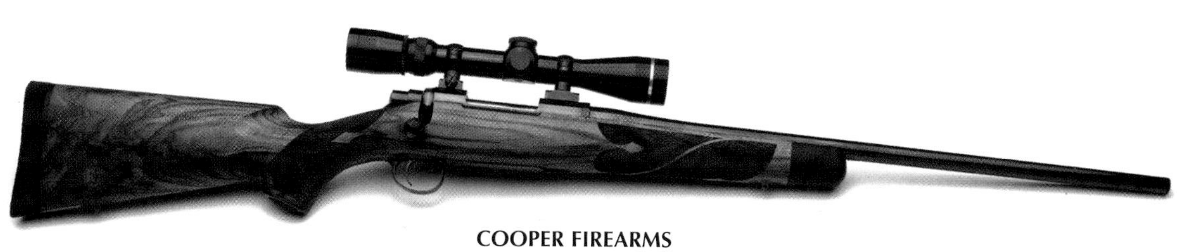

COOPER FIREARMS
MODEL 54

CVA SCOUT

Action: break-open single shot
Stock: black, ambidextrous
Barrel: 22″ fluted
Sights: open
Weight: 5.8 lbs.
Caliber: .243, 7mm-08, .270, .30-06, .35 Whelen
Magazine: none
Features: blued or stainless barrel, exposed hammer, CrushZone recoil pad, finger-operated breech release.
MSRP: . . . . . . $332 ($341 with rails)

CZ 550 URBAN COUNTER-SNIPER

Action: bolt
Stock: Kevlar-fiberglass composite
Barrel: 16″ with Surefire muzzle break
Sights: none
Weight: 8.3 lbs.
Caliber: .308 Win.
Magazine: 5 or 10 shot detachable box
Features: compact profile and reduced weight for maneuverability; short, stiff free-floated bull barrel with target crown, oversized bolt handle, polished action, Teflon coating and single-stage trigger.
MSRP: $2402

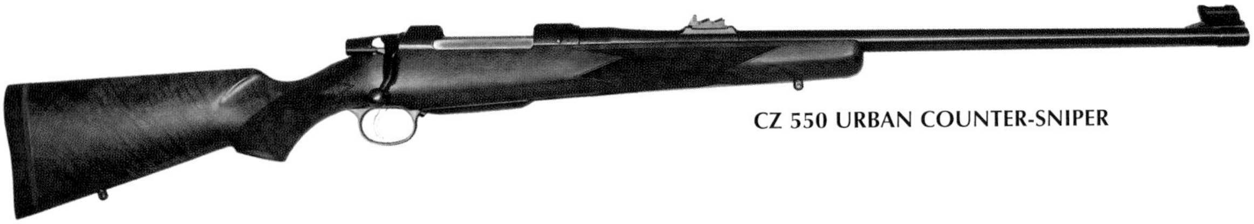

CZ 550 URBAN COUNTER-SNIPER

CZ 455 AMERICAN

CZ 512 SEMI AUTO

CZ 455 AMERICAN

Action: bolt
Stock: American walnut
Barrel: 22.5″
Sights: none
Weight: 5.4 lbs.
Caliber: .22 LR, .22 WMR, .17 HMR
Magazine: 5-shot detachable box
Features: CZ455 replaces the CZ452. Adjustable trigger, hammer-forged barrel and machined-billet receiver; as the 452 line changes to 455, barrels will be interchangeable.
MSRP: . . . . $463–$504

Also available*:* CZ 452 Thumbhole Varmint in .22 LR ($530) and .17 HMR ($555)

CZ 512 SEMI AUTO

Action: blow-back autoloader
Stock: beechwood
Barrel: 20.6″
Sights: adjustable
Weight: 5.9 lbs.
Caliber: .22 LR or .22 WMR
Magazine: 5-round
Features: aluminum alloy blued receiver, polymer frame and simple field stripping requiring no tools.
MSRP: . . . . N/A

CZ 550 SAFARI IN LEFT-HAND

Action: bolt
Stock: walnut with straight comb
Barrel: 25″ hammer forged
Sights: Express sights (1 standing, 2 folding)
Weight: 9.4 lbs.
Caliber: .375 H&H Mag.
Magazine: 5-shot internal box
Features: full-size magnum in left-hand; single set trigger, mauser claw extractor.
MSRP: $1799

DPMS PANTHER IN .308

Action: gas-operated autoloader
Stock: black synthetic with trap door assembly
Barrel: 24″ 416 stainless bull barrel, 6 grooves
Sights: none
Weight: 11.2 lbs.
Caliber: .308
Magazine: 19-round detachable box, two magazines provided
Features: gas operated rotating bolt; Teflon coated, raised Picatinny rail, no shell deflector; comes with web sling and cleaning kit.
MSRP: $1169

CZ 550 SAFARI IN LEFT-HAND

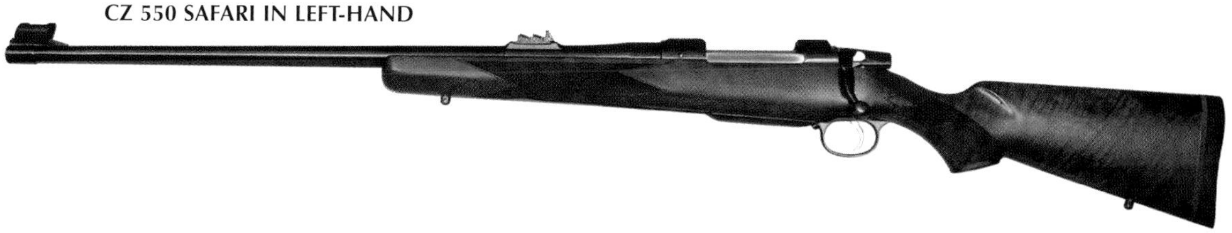

FNH FNAR STANDARD AND HEAVY

FNH SCAR 17S CARBINE

FNH FNAR STANDARD AND HEAVY

Action: gas-operated autoloader
Stock: matte black synthetic with pistol grip and adjustable comb
Barrel: 16″ or 20″ standard fluted or 20″ heavy fluted
Sights: receiver mounted rail
Weight: 8.8 to 10.0 lbs.
Caliber: .308 Win. (7.62x51mm NATO)
Magazine: 10 or 20-shot detachable box
Features: extended bolt handle, hammer-forged barrel with target crown; comes with one magazine, three recoil pads, three comb inserts and shims for adjusting for cast-on, cast-off and drop at comb.
MSRP: $1849

FNH SCAR 17S CARBINE

Action: gas-operated autoloader
Stock: tactical, telescoping, side-folding polymer
Barrel: 16.25″
Sights: adjustable, folding, removable
Weight: 8 lbs.
Caliber: .308 Win (7.62x51mm NATO)
Magazine: 10- or 20-round
Features: fully adjustable stock,
MIL-STD 1913 optical rail plus three accessory rails for attaching a variety of sights and lasers; free-floating, cold hammer-forged barrel. Available in black or Flat Dark Earth.
MSRP: .N/A

Also available: SCAR 16S in .223 (7.25 lbs, 10- or 30-round magazine)

HARRINGTON & RICHARDSON HANDI-GRIP HANDI RIFLE

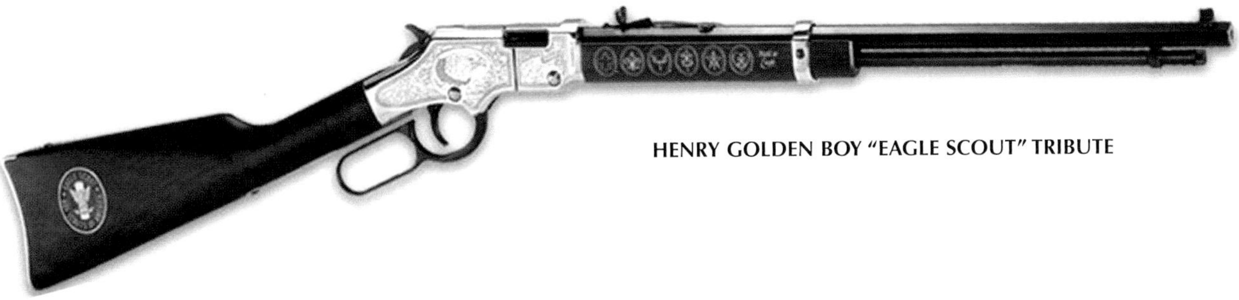

HENRY GOLDEN BOY "EAGLE SCOUT" TRIBUTE

HI-POINT 995TS

HARRINGTON & RICHARDSON HANDI-GRIP HANDI RIFLE

Action: hinged breech
Stock: ambidextrous thumbhole black polymer
Barrel: 22 to 26″
Sights: scope mount rail and hammer extension
Weight: 7 lbs.
Caliber: .204 Ruger, .223 Rem., .22-250, .308 Win., .45-70 Gov't., .243 Win., .25-06.
Magazine: none
Features: molded checkering at grip and fore-end for sure handling, Transfer Bar System.
MSRP: $298

HENRY GOLDEN BOY "EAGLE SCOUT" TRIBUTE

Action: lever
Stock: American walnut with Boy Scout medallion on side
Barrel: 20″
Sights: adjustable semi-buckhorn rear and brass bead front
Weight: 6.75 lbs.
Caliber: .22 LR and .22 short
Magazine: 16-round (LR) and 21-round (short)
Features: nickel-plated receiver with hand-engraved eagle and Boy Scout motto in 24-karat gold; brass buttplate, barrel band and receiver; blued barrel and lever.
MSRP: $1050

HI-POINT 995TS

Action: blow-back autoloader
Stock: black, skeleton-style, all weather molded polymer
Barrel: 16.5″
Sights: adjustable
Weight: 7 lbs.
Caliber: 9mm
Magazine: 10-shot detachable box
Features: sling, swivels and base mount included; last round lock-open latch, multiple Picatinny rails, internal recoil buffer.
MSRP: $274

HIGH STANDARD HSA-5 MIL-SPEC SERIES

Action: gas-operated autoloader
Stock: 6-position
Barrel: 20″ (16″ carbine)
Sights: adjustable
Weight: 8 lbs. (7.3 lbs. carbine)
Caliber: 5.56 Nato or 9mm Nato
Magazine: 30-shot detachable box
Features: matte black collapsible stock, G.I. style; hard chrome bore, A2 flash holder.
MSRP: . . . . $895–$945 (9mm $985 – $1025)

KIMBER MODEL 84L CLASSIC

Action: bolt
Stock: walnut (Select Grade features French walnut with ebony forend tip and hand-cut checkering)
Barrel: 24″ match grade
Sights: drilled and tapped for scope mounts
Weight: 6 lbs. 2 oz.
Caliber: .270, .30-06 (.25-06 Rem. also in 84L Classic Select Grade)
Magazine: 5 rounds + 1
Features: full-length Mauser claw exactor, 1″ Pachmayr recoil pad, full-length match-grade barrel with pillar and glass bedding; match-grade trigger and 3-position wing safety.
MSRP: . . . . $1172 ($1359 Select Grade)

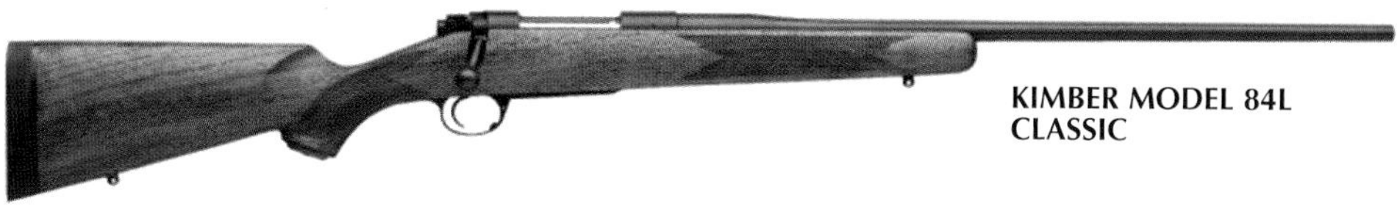

KIMBER MODEL 84L CLASSIC

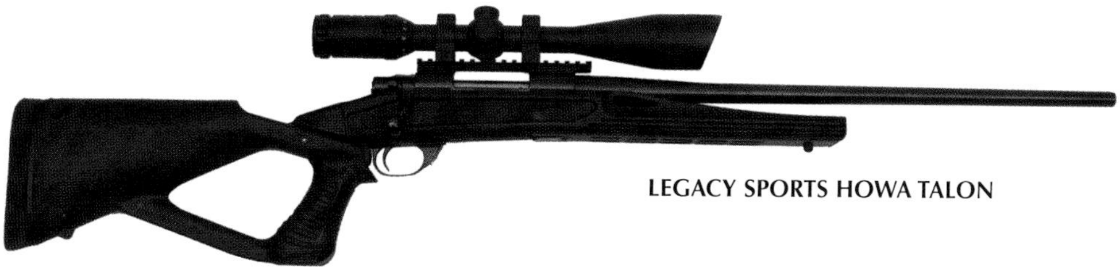

LEGACY SPORTS HOWA TALON

LEGACY SPORTS PUMA PPS .22 LR SEMI-AUTO

LEGACY SPORTS HOWA TALON

Action: bolt with two-stage dual Knoxx recoil system
Stock: thumbhole polymer and alloy
Barrel: 20″, 22″, 24″ standard or heavy
Sights: optional scope package available
Weight: 8.3 to 9.7 lbs.
Caliber: .223 Rem. to .375 Ruger
Magazine: internal box, 3- to 5-shot capacity
Features: combo includes 4-6x44 scope; ambidextrous stock that reduces felt recoil by 70%.
MSRP: . . . . $765–$850; scope package: $890–$975

LEGACY SPORTS PUMA PPS .22 LR SEMI-AUTO

Action: blow-back autoloader
Stock: wood, synthetic or tactical
Barrel: 20″ sporter
Sights: fixed front sight; tactical with Picatinny style accessory rail
Weight: 5.5 lbs.
Caliber: .22 LR
Magazine: 10- or 30-shot detachable box, or a 50-round drum
Features: available in 3 stock configurations with barrel shroud, rear pistol grip and tactical butt.
MSRP . . . . $$559–$609

LES BAER LBC TACTICAL RECON

Action: bolt
Stock: black composite Bell & Carlson adjustable comb and buttpad, pistol grip
Barrel: 24″ 416 barrel with 5 grooves
Sights: Picatinny 1–piece rail
Weight: 9 lbs.
Caliber: .308 Win., .260 Rem., .243 Win.
Magazine: 5-shot detachable box
Features: LBC precision match grade barrel; match trigger with 2.5 lb. pull, Harris bipod standard; guaranteed to shoot 10-shot groups under ½ MOA with match ammo.
MSRP: $3560

Also available: LBC Tactical Varmint Classic ($3410) with semi-pistol grip, butt hook and beavertail forend.

LES BAER LBC TACTICAL RECON

MARLIN M60 50TH ANNIVERSARY EDITION

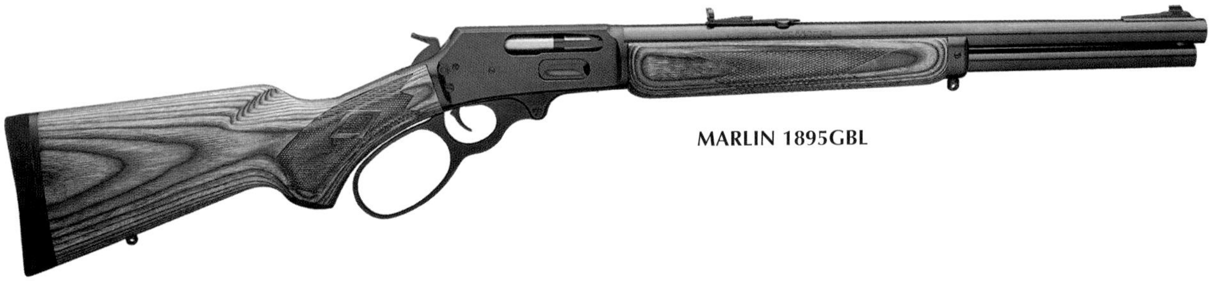

MARLIN 1895GBL

MARLIN M60 50TH ANNIVERSARY EDITION

Action: blow-back autoloader
Stock: walnut
Barrel: 19″
Sights: Semi-Buckhorn rear and ramp/hood front
Weight: 5.5 lbs.
Caliber: .22 LR
Magazine: 14-shot tube
Features: deluxe checkered stock, gold-plated trigger, rifle pad, customized roll stamp, special serial number.
MSRP: $252

MARLIN 1895GBL

Action: lever
Stock: brown laminate
Barrel: 18.5″
Sights: open
Weight: 7.5 lbs.
Caliber: .45/70 Govt.
Magazine: 6-shot tube
Features: full length magazine tube, pistol grip stock, big loop lever.
MSRP: $659

MARLIN 336BL

Action: lever
Stock: brown laminate
Barrel: 18.5″
Sights: open
Weight: 7 lbs.
Caliber: .30/30 Win.
Magazine: 6-shot tube
Features: pistol grip stock, big loop lever.
MSRP: $592

MCMILLAN TAC-50

Action: bolt
Stock: composite McMillan with butthook, adjustable saddle-type cheekpiece, LOP spacer; bipod
Barrel: 29″ Navy Contour, match-grade
Sights: drilled and tapped for scope
Weight: 26 lbs.
Caliber: .50 BMG
Magazine: detachable box
Features: finish available in black, olive, gray, tan and dark earth; NP3 bolt treatment, adjustable trigger.
MSRP: $7599

MARLIN 336BL

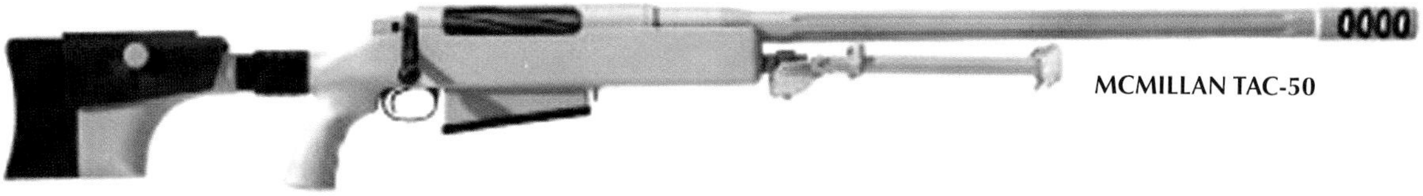

MCMILLAN TAC-50

MCMILLAN TAC-338

Action: bolt
Stock: composite A-5 with butthook, adjustable cheekpiece, sling loops
Barrel: heavy 27″ match-grade
Sights: none
Weight: 11 lbs.
Caliber: .338 Lapua Mag
Magazine: detachable box
Features: metal finish to match stock in black, olive, gray, tan and dark earth; muzzle brake.
MSRP: $5499

Also available*:* TAC-308 $4999 and TAC-300 $5299

MCMILLAN TAC-338

MERKEL KR1

Action: bolt
Stock: walnut with hogback comb and Bavarian cheek piece
Barrel: 22.24″ or 24.21″
Sights: scope mounts on barrel
Weight: 6.4 lbs.
Caliber: .223 Rem. to .270 WSM
Magazine: 3 (short magnum 2)
Features: short-stroke bolt action; modular design allows for quick disassembly for transport or change of caliber; disassembly has no effect on ***point of impact; left hand versions available.***
MSRP: . . . . . $1995 (Custom: $2995)

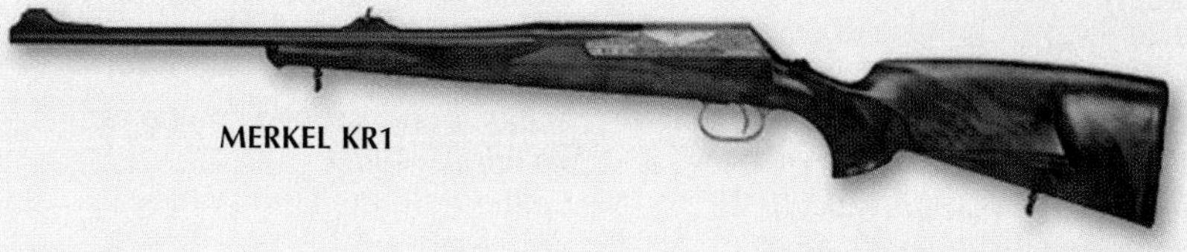

MERKEL KR1

MERKEL B3 'SUPER LIGHT'

Action: over/under, tilting breech-lock
Stock: checkered walnut
Barrel: 21.65″
Sights: "driven-hunt" sight with integrated light elements
Weight: 6.4 lbs.
Caliber: .30-06, .30R Blaser, 8x57IRS, 9.3x74R
Magazine: none
Features: short, light and responsive; manual cocking mechanism; tilting breech block can be removed without tools; adjustable single trigger; pistol grip, cheek piece and hogback comb, rubber buttpad.
MSRP: . . . . N/A

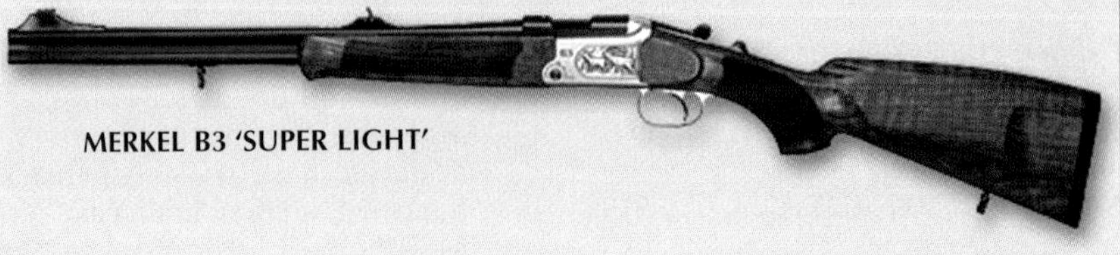

MERKEL B3 'SUPER LIGHT'

MOSSBERG MAVERICK BOLT-ACTION

MOSSBERG 4X4

NAVY LIGHTNING RIFLE

MOSSBERG MAVERICK BOLT-ACTION

Action: bolt
Stock: black synthetic
Barrel: 22″
Sights: Weaver-style bases attached
Weight: 7 lbs.
Caliber: .243, .308, .270, .30-06
Magazine: 4-shot internal box
Features: free-floating, button rifled barrel, recessed muzzle crown, top-load magazine. Maverick Super Bantam available with 20″ barrel in .243.
MSRP: $308

MOSSBERG 4X4

Action: bolt
Stock: polymer, gray laminate or American black walnut
Barrel: 22″
Sights: none; scoped combo available
Weight: 7.1 lbs.
Caliber: .30-06, .300 Win. Mag., .338 Win. Mag.
Magazine: 4- or 5-shot detachable box
Features: free-floating barrel, top-load magazine, matte blue finish, Monte Carlo style cheek-piece, slim grips, forend vents, and soft buttpád.
MSRP: $633

NAVY LIGHTNING RIFLE

Action: pump
Stock: straight grip checkered walnut
Barrel: 24″
Sights: gold front bead and semi-buckhorn rear
Weight: 6.8 lbs.
Caliber: .357 Mag., .45 Colt, .44-40
Magazine: 10-shot tube
Features: case-hardened receiver, octagonal barrel, tang drilled for peep sights
MSRP: $1399

NOSLER M48 TROPHY GRADE

Action: bolt
Stock: custom aluminum-bedded Bell and Carlson composite
Barrel: 24″
Sights: none
Weight: under 6.75 to 7.5 lbs.
Caliber: .270 Win to 325 WSM
Magazine: 3- or 4-shot, internal box
Features: NoslerCustom barreled action, match-grade chrome-moly barrel, Cerakote and MicroSlick finishes to prevent corrosion and weather damage, 3-pound trigger, guaranteed accuracy of sub-M.O.A. three-shot groups at 100 yards.
MSRP: $1746 (short action); $1895 (long action)

OLYMPIC ARMS GAMESTALKER

Action: gas-operated autoloader
Stock: ACE Skeleton stock in camo
Barrel: 22″ stainless fluted
Sights: Picatinny rail
Weight: 7.5 lbs.
Caliber: .243 WSSM, .25 WSSM, .300 OSSM
Magazine: 5-shot detachable box
Features: flat-top upper receiver, free-floating aluminum handguard, ERGO grip.
MSRP: $1359

OLYMPIC ARMS GAMESTALKER

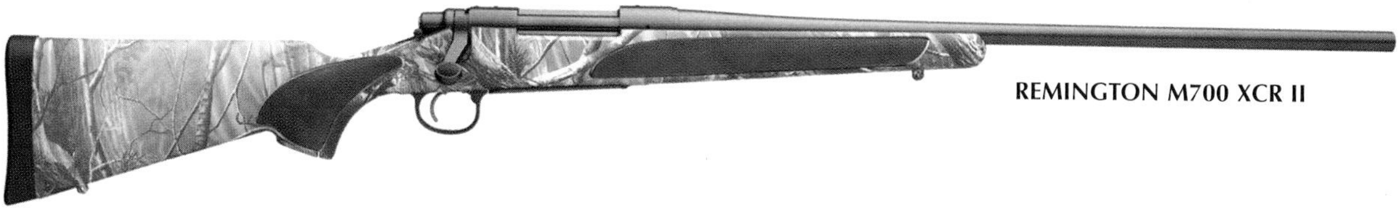

REMINGTON M700 XCR II

REMINGTON M700 VTR A-TACS

REMINGTON M700 XCR II

Action: bolt
Stock: camo or green composite with Hogue overmold
Barrel: 24″ or 26″ magnum
Sights: none
Weight: 7.5 lbs.
Caliber: .25-06, .270, .280 Rem., .30-06, 7mm Rem. Mag., .300 WSM, .300 Win. Mag., 7mm RUM, .300 RUM, .338 Win. Mag., .338 RUM, .375 H&H, .375 RUM
Magazine: 4 + 1 standard, 3 + 1 magnum
Features: all-weather rifle – 416 stainless steel barreled action, all exposed metal has satin TriNyte corrosion control, Physical Vapor Deposition finish.
MSRP:$930 standard, $956 Mag., $1005 WSM

REMINGTON M700 VTR A-TACS

Action: bolt
Stock: synthetic with vented beavertail forend in A-TACS camo
Barrel: 22″ triangular, target-grade
Sights: none
Weight: 7.5 lbs.
Caliber: .223 Rem., .308 Win.
Magazine: 5 + 1 (.223), 4 + 1 (.308)
Features: Hogue black overmolded grip, recoil pad; solid steel receiver in satin black oxide finish; integral muzzle brake, hinged floorplate.
MSRP: $872

REMINGTON R-15 IN .30 REM. AR OR 450 BUSHMASTER

Action: gas-operated autoloader
Stock: composite in Realtree AP HD Camo (Rem) or Mossy Oak New Break Up (Bushmaster)
Barrel: 18″ (.450 Bushmaster) or 22″ (.30 Rem. AR)
Sights: none
Weight: 7.5 lbs.
Caliber: .30 Rem. AR or .450 Bushmaster
Magazine: 4-shot detachable box
Features: pistol grip, free float tube, fluted barrel forward of gas block, single stage trigger
MSRP: $1255; Bushmaster $1567

REMINGTON M597 VTR

Action: blow-back autoloader
Stock: camo or black, fixed or collapsible
Barrel: 16″
Sights: Quad rail available
Weight: 5.5 lbs.
Caliber: .22 LR
Magazine: 10- or 30-shot detachable box
Features: available: A-2 stock, collapsible stock, A-2 grip; free float tubes.
MSRP: . . . . $445–$590

REMINGTON M597 VTR

RIFLES INC. PEAR FLAT

Action: bolt
Stock: checkered composite with Pear Flat paint scheme
Barrel: 24″
Sights: none
Weight: 6.25 lbs.
Caliber: 6.5x284
Magazine: 3-shot internal box
Features: engraved pear on floorplate with individual number (only 100 made); 1-8 twist, 3-groove Lilja barrel; ¾ M.O.A. accuracy.
MSRP: $3250 (plus customer-supplied Remington 700 short action)

ROSSI WIZARD

Action: hinged breech
Stock: wood or Hi-Def Green camo
Barrel: 23″
Sights: fiber optic front sight
Weight: 7 lbs.
Caliber: 18 chamberings, including shotguns, muzzleloaders, rimfire and centerfire
Magazine: none
Features: interchangeable barrel system allows barrels to be changed quickly without tools; blue finish, cushioned recoil pad, Monte Carlo stock.
MSRP: . . . . N/A
Also available: youth version, 6.25 lbs, 22″ barrel.

ROSSI CIRCUIT JUDGE

Action: DA revolver
Stock: wood
Barrel: 18.5″
Sights: fiber optic front sight
Weight: 4.75 lbs.
Caliber: .410 ga./.45LC
Magazine:6
Features: shotgun/rifle crossover allows you to fire .410 3-inch Magnum shotshells, .410 2 ½″ shotshells and .45 Colt ammunition in any order; available in smooth-bore shotgun or rifled barrel shotgun.
MSRP: . . . . N/A

ROSSI RIO GRANDE

Action: lever
Stock: wood or Hi-Def Green camo
Barrel: 20″
Sights: adjustable buckhorn
Weight: 7 lbs.
Caliber: .30-30 Win
Magazine: 6-shot tube
Features: side ejection, cushioned recoil pad, polished deep blue or stainless finish; hand assembled and tuned.
MSRP: $470

RUGER SR-556

Action: gas-operated autoloader
Stock: 6-position telescoping M4-style buttstock
Barrel: 16″
Sights: Troy Industries Folding Battlesights
Weight: 7.94 lbs.
Caliber: 5.56mm NATO/.223 Rem.
Magazine: 30-shot detachable box
Features: chrome-plated, two-stage piston driven operating system; 4-position gas regulator; quad rail handguard; includes 3 magazines and soft sided case.
MSRP: $1995

RUGER SR-22

Action: blow-back autoloader
Stock: Hogue Monogrip and six-position telescoping buttstock
Barrel: 16″
Sights: Picatinny rail
Weight: 6.5 lbs.
Caliber: .22 LR
Magazine: 10-shot rotary
Features: AR-style ergonomics; Mini-14 flash suppressor mounted on barrel.
MSRP: $625

RUGER SR-556

RUGER SR-22

SAKO 85 KODIAK

SAKO 85 KODIAK

Action: bolt
Stock: grey laminated hardwood
Barrel: 21.25″
Sights: open
Weight: 8 lbs.
Caliber: .338 Win. Mag., .375 H&H Mag
Magazine: 4-shot detachable box
Features: free-floating bull barrel, two crossbolts in stock, stainless barrel coated to resist weather; detachable magazine; integral rails for scope mounts.
MSRP: $1975

SAVAGE EDGE

Action: bolt
Stock: synthetic, black or Next Vista camo
Barrel: 22″
Sights: none
Weight: 6.5 lbs.
Caliber: .223, .22-250, .243, 7mm-08, .308 Win., .25-06, .270 Win., .30-06
Magazine: 4-shot detachable box
Features: dual pillar bedding, free-floating barrel, matte-black metal, two-position safety, swivel studs. 3-9x40 scope mounted and boresighted for $50 extra.
MSRP: . . . . $329 ($379 camo)

SAVAGE 110 BA LAW ENFORCEMENT

Action: bolt
Stock: Savage AccuStock with aluminum rail
Barrel: 26″
Sights: rail provided
Weight: 15.75 lbs.
Caliber: .300 Win. Mag and .338 Lapua
Magazine: 5-shot detachable box
Features: AccuTrigger, muzzlebrake, adjustable Magpul buttsotck.
MSRP: $2267

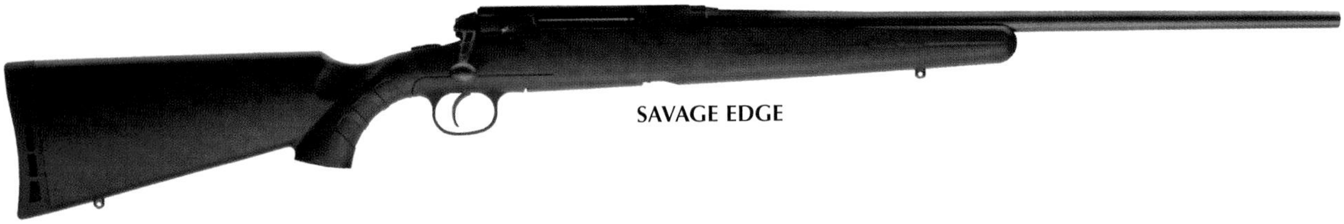

SAVAGE EDGE

SAVAGE 110 BA LAW ENFORCEMENT

SAVAGE M11/111 LONG RANGE HUNTER

SAVAGE M11/111 LONG RANGE HUNTER

Action: bolt
Stock: synthetic AccuStock with Karsten adjustable comb
Barrel: 26″ fluted
Sights: none
Weight: 8.4 lbs. (short action) 8.65 lbs. (long action)
Caliber: short Action*:* .308 Win., .300 WSM; long Action*:* .25-06, 6.5x284 Norma, 7mm Rem. Mag., .300 Win. Mag.
Magazine: internal box
Features: muzzlebrake, hinged floorplate, AccuTrigger.
MSRP: . . . . . .$934 ($972 .300 WSM)

E.R. SHAW MARK VII

Action: bolt
Stock: walnut, laminate wood, or synthetic
Barrel: from 16.25″ to 26″
Sights: drilled and tapped for scope mounts
Weight: depending upon specifications
Caliber: 75 calibers choices from .17 Rem. to .458 Lott
Magazine: internal box
Features: right- or left-hand actions, stainless receivers, contour barrels, polished or matte blue finish, recoil pads and swivel studs.
MSRP: $625

SIG SAUER M556 PATROL

Action: gas-operated autoloader
Stock: folding, length-adjustable
Barrel: 16″
Sights: Rotary Diopter
Weight: 7.7 lbs.
Caliber: 5.56 x 45mm NATO
Magazine: 30-shot detachable box
Features: short gas system; SWAT version has quad rail forend.
MSRP: . . .$2000; Patrol SWAT $2143

STAG ARMS MODEL 8

Action: gas-operated piston autoloader
Stock: 6 position collapsible
Barrel: chrome lined 20″
Sights: Midwest Industries front and rear flip-up
Weight: 6.8 lbs.
Caliber: 5.56 Nato
Magazine: 30-shot detachable box
Features: right and left-hand available
MSRP: $1145 ($1175 left-hand)

STEYR AUG/A3 SA

Action: gas-operated autoloader
Stock: black synthetic bullpup
Barrel: 16″ chrome-lined heavy
Sights: none
Weight: 8 lbs.
Caliber: 5.56x45 mm (.223 Rem)
Magazine: 30-shot detachable box (comes with two magazines)
Features: civilian version of the Steyr AUG.
MSRP: $2295

SIG SAUER M556 PATROL

STEYR AUG/A3 SA

STAG ARMS MODEL 8

STEYR SSG 08 IN .338 LAPUA

Action: bolt
Stock: aluminum folding stock with adjustable cheek piece and butt plate
Barrel: 23.6″ or 20″
Sights: Picatinny rail
Weight: 12.5 lbs.
Caliber: .338 Lapua (also available in .308 Win. and .300 Win. Mag.
Magazine: 10-shot detachable box
Features: folding stock so rifle can be transported in a small case; direct trigger, exchangeable pistol grip, Versa-Pod, muzzle brake; 3-position trigger safety.
MSRP: $5899

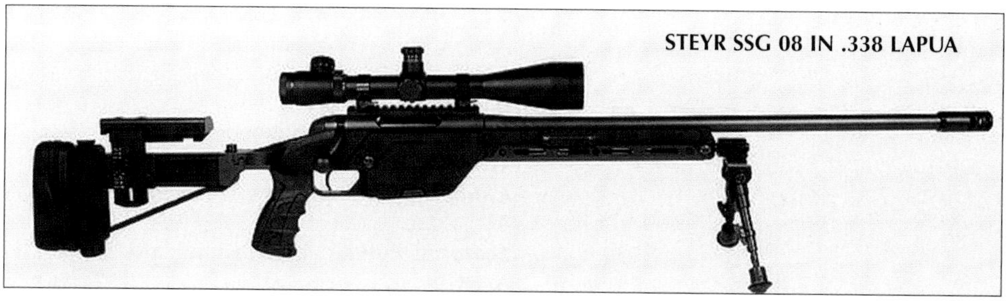

STEYR SSG 08 IN .338 LAPUA

THOMPSON/CENTER VENTURE PREDATOR

Action: bolt
Stock: Max I camo composite with Hogue panels
Barrel: 22″ fluted
Sights: Weaver-style scope bases factory installed
Weight: 6.75 lbs.
Caliber: .204 Ruger, .223 Rem., .22-250 Rem., .308 Win.
Magazine: 3-shot detachable box
Features: adjustable trigger, match grade barrel with 5R rifling, guaranteed MOA 1″ groups at 100 yards.
MSRP: . . . .$549–$599
Also new for 2010**:** Venture in 7 new calibers

THOMPSON/CENTER HOTSHOT .22LR

Action: hinged breech
Stock: composite black, Realtree AP camo or pink camo
Barrel: 19″
Sights: peep
Weight: 3 lbs.
Caliber: ,22 LR
Magazine: none
Features: a .22 for youngsters; exposed hammer for safety, precision rifled barrel and peep sight for easy training.
MSRP: $239

THOMPSON/CENTER VENTURE PREDATOR

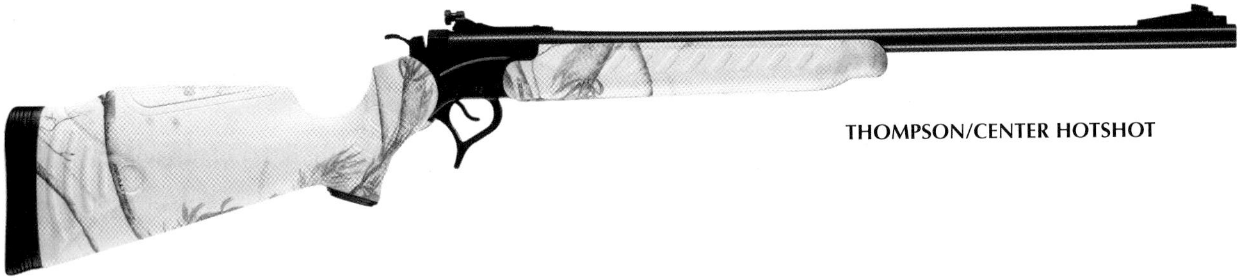

THOMPSON/CENTER HOTSHOT

THOMPSON/CENTER PROHUNTER PREDATOR

THOMPSON/CENTER PROHUNTER PREDATOR

Action: hinged breech
Stock: Max I camo with Flextech
Barrel: 28″
Sights: scope bases included
Weight: 7.75 lbs.
Caliber: .204 Ruger, .223 Rem., .22-250 Rem., .308 Win.
Magazine: none
Features: fluted barrel, Swing Hammer, FlexTech stock.
MSRP: $799

THOMPSON/CENTER ICON WARLORD

Action: bolt
Stock: Manner's carbon fiber in OD green, black or Desert Sand
Barrel: hand-lapped, heavy barrel with deep fluting
Sights: 20 MOA Picatinny Integra base
Weight: 12.75 lbs. (13.75 lbs. in .338 Lapua)
Caliber: .308 Win., .338 Lapua
Magazine: 5- or 10-shot detachable box
Features: sniper-style rifle with adjustable trigger, Interlok bedding system, tactical bolt handle, ½″ groups or less at 100 yards.
MSRP: $2995

TIKKA T3 SCOUT CTR (COMPACT TACTICAL RIFLE)

Action: bolt
Stock: black synthetic tactical
Barrel: 20″ match grade with target crown
Sights: Picatinny scope rail
Weight: 8 lbs.
Caliber: .223 Rem. and .308 Win.
Magazine: 5-shot
Features: free-floating cold hammer-forged barrel; 3-shot M.O.A. guaranteed; two-piece bolt with locking lugs; single-stage adjustable trigger.
MSRP: .N/A

THOMPSON/CENTER ICON WARLORD

UBERTI 1873 RIFLE & CARBINE

UBERTI 1883 BURGESS RIFLE & CARBINE

UBERTI 1873 RIFLE & CARBINE

Action: lever
Stock: A-grade walnut
Barrel: 16.25″ (Trapper), 18″ (half octagonal), or 19″ (carbine)
Sights: fixed
Weight: 7.4 to 8.2 lbs.
Caliber: .44 Magnum
Magazine: 9-, 10- or 13-shot tube
Features: blued or case-hardened barrel, straight grip; Old West styling.
MSRP: $1299

Also available: 1873 Trapper with 16.25″ barrel and 1873 Stallion with 10-shot magazine.

UBERTI 1883 BURGESS RIFLE & CARBINE

Action: lever
Stock: A-grade walnut
Barrel: 20″ carbine or 25.5″ rifle
Sights: fixed
Weight: 7.6 and 8.1 lbs.
Caliber: .45 Colt
Magazine: 10- or 13-shot tube
Features: case-hardened, round barrel; straight grip.
MSRP: $1499

UBERTI 1871 ROLLING BLOCK HUNTER CARBINE

Action: rolling block
Stock: A-grade walnut
Barrel: 22″ round
Sights: fixed
Weight: 4.5 lbs.
Caliber: .38/55, .30-30, .45/70
Magazine: none
Features: rubber butt pad, case-colored receiver.
MSRP: $799

VOLQUARTSEN TF-7

Action: blow-back autoloader
Stock: ambidextrous birch
Barrel: 18.5″ stainless
Sights: Picatinny mil spec rail
Weight: 8.5 lbs.
Caliber: .17 HMR
Magazine: 9-round rotary
Features: blowback design, TG2000 trigger unit with 2.25-lb. pull, black stainless barrel.
MSRP: $1041

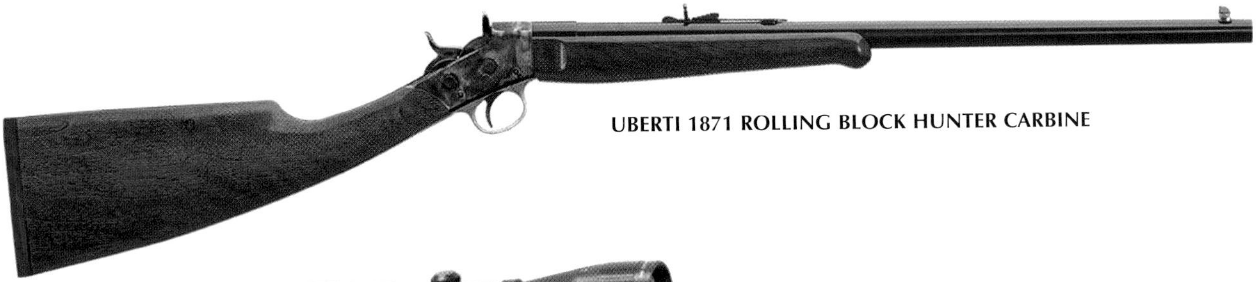

UBERTI 1871 ROLLING BLOCK HUNTER CARBINE

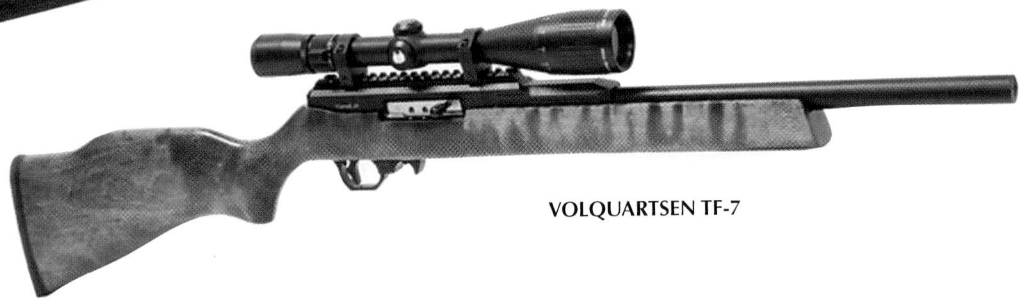

VOLQUARTSEN TF-7

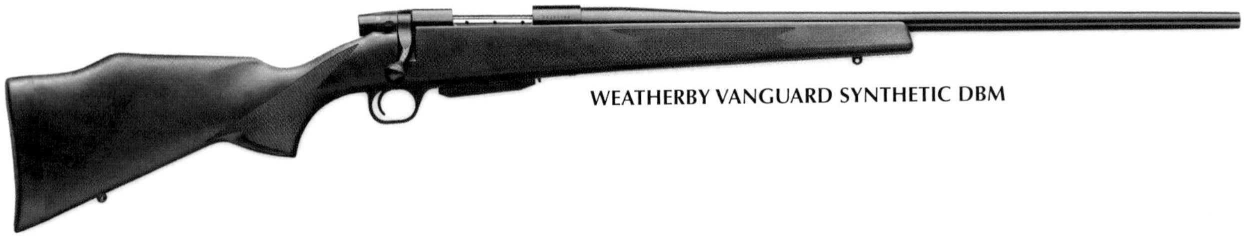

WEATHERBY VANGUARD SYNTHETIC DBM

WEATHERBY MARK V SUB-MOA TRR (THREAT RESPONSE RIFLE)

Action: bolt
Stock: hand-laminated with 3-position buttstock
Barrel: 26″ Krieger #3 contour barrel
Sights: none
Weight: 9 lbs.
Caliber: .300 Win. Mag., .300 Weatherby Mag., .30-378 Weatherby Mag., .338-378 Weatherby Mag.
Magazine: drop box "plus one" capacity
Features: guaranteed to shoot a 3-shot group of .99″ or less; hand-tuned, fully-adjustable trigger; stock has bi-pod attachment.
MSRP: $3999

WEATHERBY VANGUARD SYNTHETIC DBM

Action: bolt
Stock: injection-molded Monte Carlo
Barrel: 24″
Sights: none
Weight: 7 lbs.
Caliber: .25-06 Rem., .270 Win., .30-06 Springfield
Magazine: 3-shot detachable box
Features: matte black metalwork; low density recoil pad, adjustable trigger.
MSRP: $589

WEATHERBY VANGUARD SPORTER DBM

Action: bolt
Stock: walnut Monte Carlo
Barrel: 24″
Sights: none
Weight: 7 lbs.
Caliber: .25-06 Rem., .270 Win., .30-06 Springfield
Magazine: 3-shot detachable box
Features: rosewood forend, raised comb, satin urethane finish, matte black metalwork, adjustable trigger.
MSRP: $799

WEATHERBY VANGUARD YOUTH

Action: bolt
Stock: injection-molded Monte Carlo
Barrel: 20″
Sights: none
Weight: 6.5 lbs.
Caliber: .223 Rem., .22-250 Rem., .243 Win., 7mm-08 Rem. and .308 Win.
Magazine: 5-shot internal box
Features: removable spacer to allow stock to be lengthened as shooter grows; low-density recoil pad.
MSRP: $529

WEATHERBY VANGUARD YOUTH

WEATHERBY VANGUARD SPORTER DBM

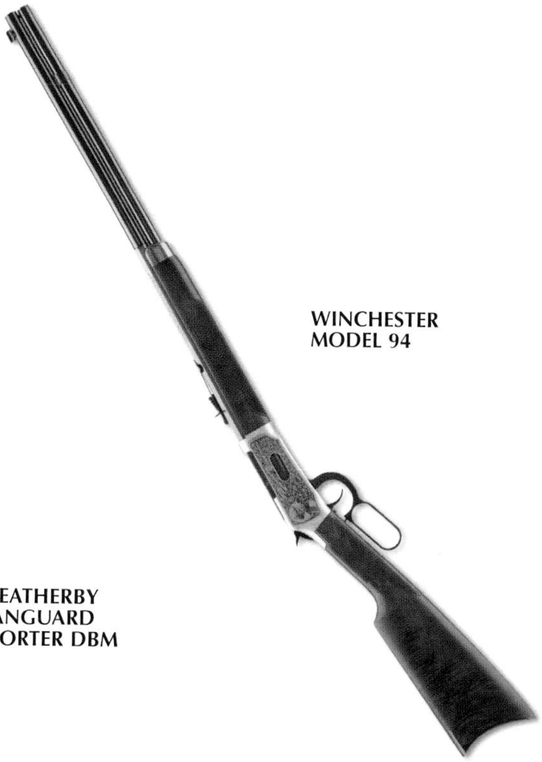

WINCHESTER MODEL 94

WILSON COMBAT M-4T TACTICAL CARBINE

Action: gas-operated autoloader
Stock: collapsible, 6-position tactical
Barrel: 16.25″ target-grade
Sights: optional quad-rail
Weight: 6.9 lbs.
Caliber: .223 Rem.
Magazine: 30-shot detachable box
Features: 2 MOA at 100 yards guaranteed; single stage trigger, pistol grip stock comes in tan, green, gray or black; CNC-machined receiver, muzzle brake.
MSRP: . . . . $2000 base model
Also available*:* UT-15Tac Carbine $2025

WINCHESTER MODEL 94

Action: lever
Stock: walnut
Barrel: 24″ half-round, half-octagon deeply blued
Sights: buckhorn rear sight with Marble's gold beat front
Weight: 8 lbs.
Caliber: .30-30 Win.
Magazine: 8-shot tube
Features: return of Winchester M94 commemorates the 200th anniversary of Oliver Winchester's birth; high-grade walnut and deep scroll engraving on receiver; Custom grade has gold inlays.
MSRP:$1469 High Grade; $1959 Custom Grade

NEW Products: Rifles

WINCHESTER M70 SAFARI EXPRESS

Action: bolt
Stock: satin-finished checkered walnut with deluxe cheekpiece
Barrel: 24″
Sights: hooded-blade front and express-style rear
Weight: 9 lbs.
Caliber: .375 H&H, .46 Rem. Mag., .458 Win. Mag.
Magazine: 3-shot internal box
Features: Pre-'64 type claw extractor, Pachmayr Decelerator recoil pad, barrel band front swivel base, dual recoil lugs and three-position safety. M.O.A. trigger system, matte blued finish; two steel crossbolts and one-piece steel trigger guard with hinged floorplate.
MSRP: $1279

WINCHESTER M70 SAFARI EXPRESS

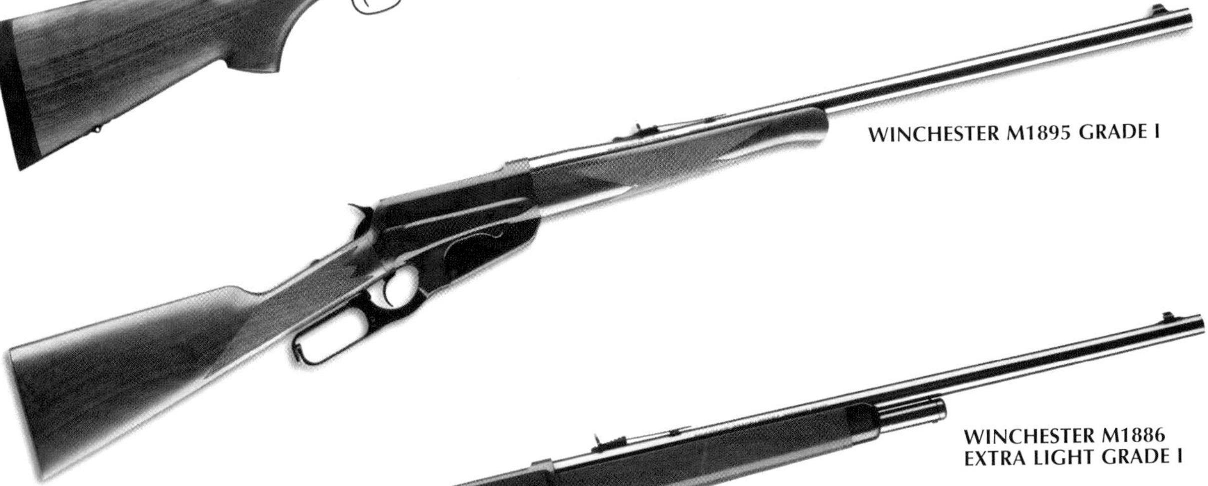

WINCHESTER M1895 GRADE I

WINCHESTER M1886 EXTRA LIGHT GRADE I

WINCHESTER M1886 EXTRA LIGHT GRADE I

Action: lever
Stock: walnut
Barrel: 22″
Sights: adjustable buckhorn rear and blade front
Weight: 7 lbs. 4 oz.
Caliber: .45-70
Magazine: 4-shot tube
Features: deeply blued receiver, lever and barrel, top-tang safety.
MSRP: $1269

WINCHESTER M1895 GRADE I

Action: lever
Stock: walnut with checkering and Schnabel fore-end
Barrel: 24″
Sights: adjustable buckhorn rear and blade front
Weight: 8 lbs.
Caliber: .405 Win., .30-06, .30-40 Krag
Magazine: 4-shot internal box
Features: limited production of the rifle designed by John Browning; Teddy Roosevelt favored the original 1895 for big game hunting.
MSRP: $1179

GAMO DYNAMAX

Action: PCP (Pre Charged Pneumatic)
Stock: synthetic tactical black
Barrel: 20.5″
Sights: 3-9x50 RGB Dot scope
Weight: 8.75 lbs. with scope
Caliber: .177 or .22
Magazine: 10-shot
Features: match-quality, full-floated barrel, 2-stage, adjustable trigger.
MSRP: $700

STOEGER X5

Power: break-barrel, spring-and-piston system
Stock: hardwood
Sights: open
Weight: 5.7 lbs.
Caliber: .177
Magazine: none
Features: automatic safety, fixed trigger.
MSRP: $109

NEW Products: Black Powder

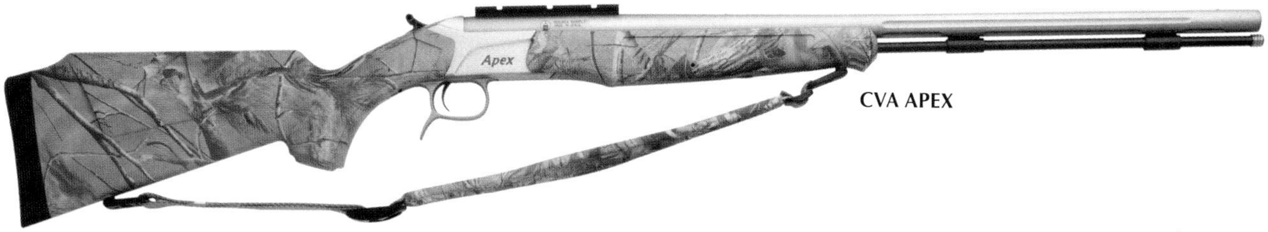

CVA APEX

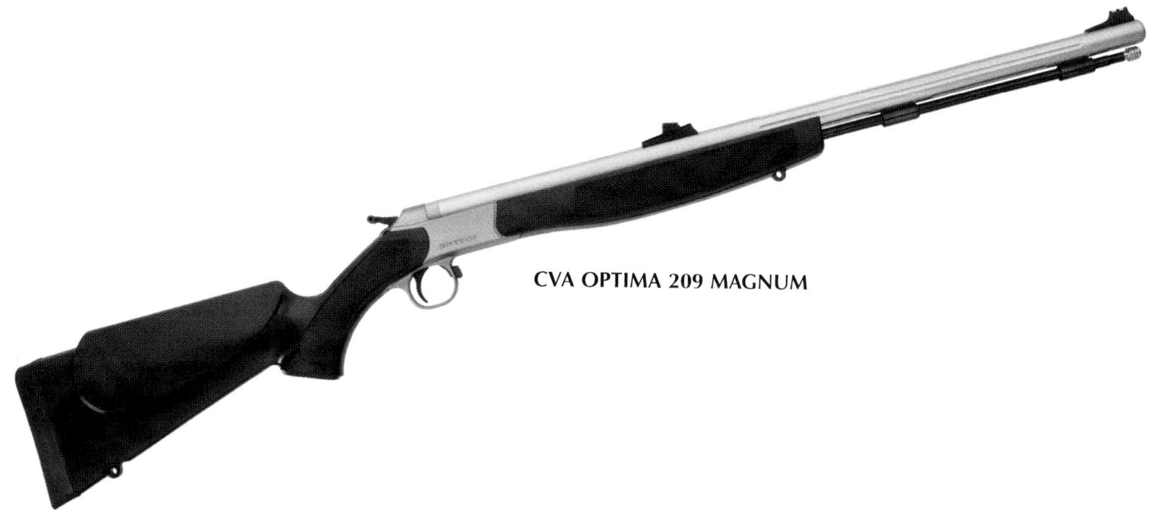

CVA OPTIMA 209 MAGNUM

CVA APEX

Lock: hinged breech muzzleloading
Stock: Realtree Hardwoods camo or black
Barrel: 27″ Bergara barrel
Sights: DuraSight rail mount
Weight: 7.5 lbs.
Bore/Gauge: .45 or .50 muzzleloading
Features: multi-barrel interchangeable rifle—13 styles, centerfire, rimfire, muzzleloading; E—Z open breech, includes Quake Claw sling.
MSRP: . . . . $615 to $695 (camo)

CVA OPTIMA 209 MAGNUM

Lock: hinged breech muzzleloading
Stock: standard and thumbhole, black or Realtree Hardwoods Green camo
Barrel: 26″ 416 stainless fluted
Sights: DuraSight fiber optic
Weight: 6.65 lbs.
Bore/Gauge: .50
Features: Optima has been re-designed. Quick release breech plug, Thumbhole stock has integral scope mounts; CrushZone recoil pad.
MSRP: . . . . $282 to $377

NEW Products: Black Powder

CVA ACCURA V2

Lock: hinged breech muzzleloading
Stock: composite stock in standard or Thumbhole with SoftTouch coating and rubber grip panels
Barrel: 27″ 416 stainless Bergara
Sights: DuraSight fiber optic sights
Weight: 7.3 lbs.
Bore/Gauge: .45, .50
Features: Quick-release breech plug, CrushZone reoil pad, drilled and tapped for scope mounts.
MSRP: . . . . $461 to $548

CVA ACCURA V2

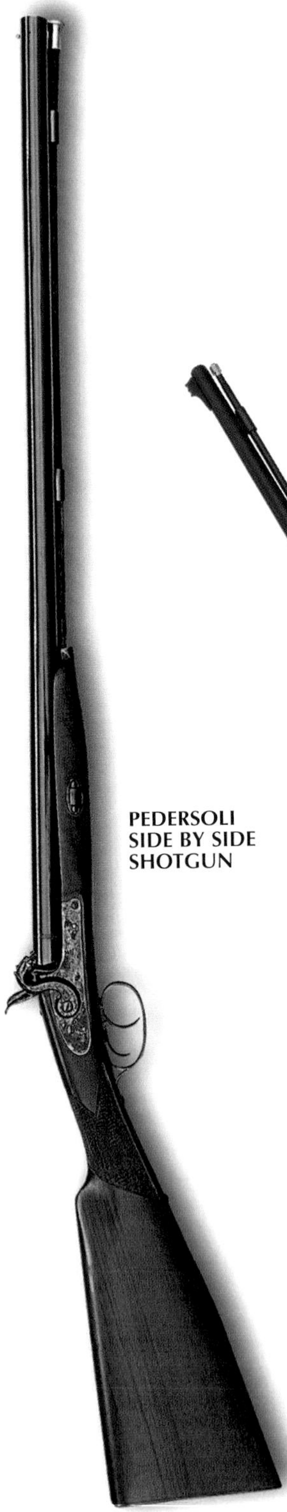

PEDERSOLI SIDE BY SIDE SHOTGUN

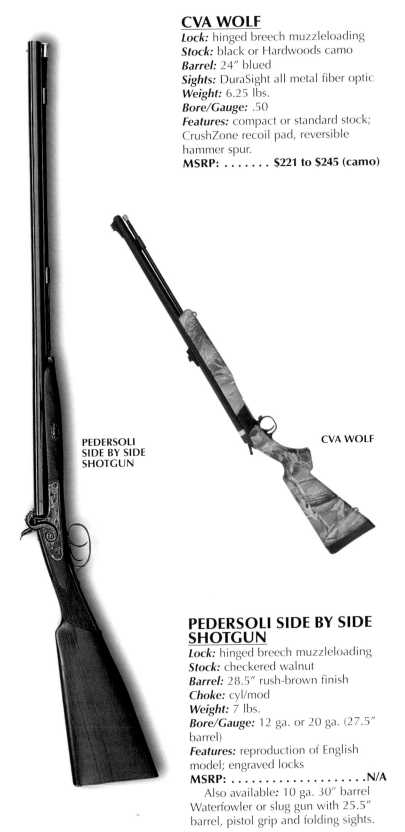

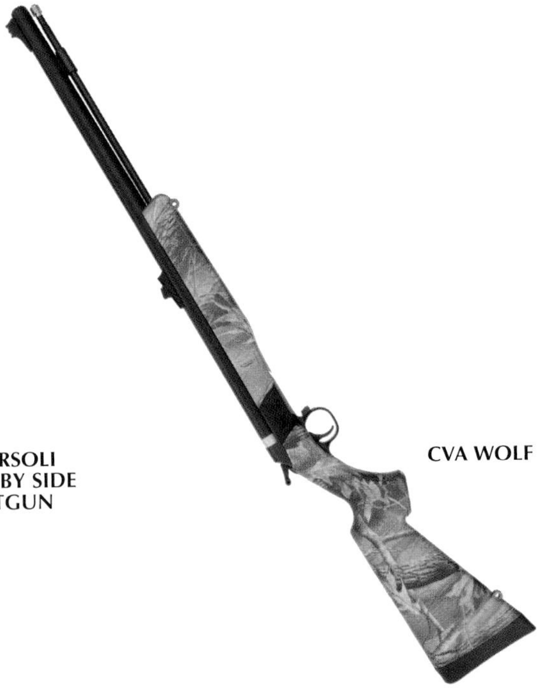

CVA WOLF

CVA WOLF

Lock: hinged breech muzzleloading
Stock: black or Hardwoods camo
Barrel: 24″ blued
Sights: DuraSight all metal fiber optic
Weight: 6.25 lbs.
Bore/Gauge: .50
Features: compact or standard stock; CrushZone recoil pad, reversible hammer spur.
MSRP: . . . . $221 to $245 (camo)

DIXIE FR4055 SPANISH MUSKET

Lock: flint lock muzzleloading
Stock: full, European walnut 56″
Barrel: smoothbore
Sights: steel stud front
Weight: 10 lbs.
Bore/Caliber: .68 round ball
Features: brass buttplate, triggerguard and barrel band; bright steel sideplates.
MSRP: $1400

PEDERSOLI SIDE BY SIDE SHOTGUN

Lock: hinged breech muzzleloading
Stock: checkered walnut
Barrel: 28.5″ rush-brown finish
Choke: cyl/mod
Weight: 7 lbs.
Bore/Gauge: 12 ga. or 20 ga. (27.5″ barrel)
Features: reproduction of English model; engraved locks
MSRP: .N/A

Also available: 10 ga. 30″ barrel Waterfowler or slug gun with 25.5″ barrel, pistol grip and folding sights.

TAYLOR'S & CO. 1873 TRAPPER

Lock: lever action
Stock: checkered walnut
Barrel: 18″ octagonal
Sights: front sight
Weight: 6.5 lbs.
Bore/Caliber: .44-40, .45 LC or .357 Mag.
Features: pistol or straight grip, case hardened finish, tapered barrel holds 10 rounds.
MSRP: . . . . $895 or $980 (checkered pistol grip)

THOMPSON/CENTER IMPACT!

Lock: hinged breech muzzleloading
Stock: black or LongLeaf camo
Barrel: blued 28″
Sights: fiber optic
Weight: 6.5 lbs.
Bore/Caliber: .50
Features: triple lead thread breech plug, 1″ adjustable buttstock.
MSRP: $249

TAYLOR'S & CO. 1873 TRAPPER

THOMPSON/CENTER IMPACT!

THOMPSON/CENTER ENCORE ENDEAVOR PROHUNTER XT

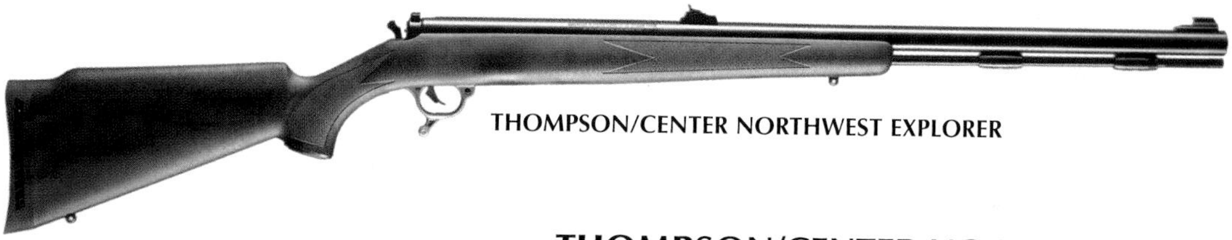

THOMPSON/CENTER NORTHWEST EXPLORER

THOMPSON/CENTER ENCORE ENDEAVOR PROHUNTER XT

Lock: hinged breech muzzleloading
Stock: camo or black FlexTech with SIMS recoil pad
Barrel: stainless, fluted 28″ Endeavor
Sights: fiber optic
Weight: 8.25 lbs.
Bore/Caliber: .50
Features: 209 ignition primer, Swing Hammer, power rod, QLA muzzle system; Speed Breech XT.
MSRP: $1005

THOMPSON/CENTER NORTHWEST EXPLORER

Lock: dropping-breech
Stock: black composite or Realtree Hardwoods camo
Barrel: 28″ blued
Sights: adjustable
Weight: 7 lbs.
Bore/Caliber: .50
Features: design meets legal regulations of western states: exposed breech system, #11 cap ignition and metal sights; QLA (Quick Load Accurizor). Weather Shield coating available.
MSRP: . . . . $329–$399

TRADITIONS VORTEK ULTRA LIGHT

Lock: hinged breech muzzleloading
Stock: synthetic black hogue overmold or Realtree AP camo
Barrel: 28″
Sights: fixed, open
Weight: 6.25 lbs.
Bore/Caliber: .50
Features: drop-out trigger assembly, recoil pad, 3-pound factory trigger, frame and barrel have CeraKote finish
MSRP: $439–499

Also available: Northwest edition featuring Tru-Glo fiber optic and black sights, exposed nipple and fires #11 percussion caps.

TRADITIONS VORTEK ULTRA LIGHT

TRADITIONS VORTEK PISTOL

Lock: hinged breech muzzleloading
Stock: select hardwood
Barrel: 13″
Sights: fixed open
Weight: 3.25 lbs.
Bore/Caliber: .50
Features: 209 primer ignition, Accelerator breech plug, Cerakote finish on frame and barrel.
MSRP: $369

TRADITIONS VORTEK PISTOL

TRADITIONS PURSUIT XLT

Lock: hinged breech muzzleloading
Stock: Realtree Tree Stand camo, monte carlo style comb
Barrel: 28″ fluted, nickel plated or camo
Sights: metal fiber optic
Weight: 7.5 lbs.
Bore/Gauge: .50
Features: alloy, lightweight frame, aluminum ramrod, QuickRelief recoil pad, SoftTouch rubberized coating on stock; 209 ignition primer, drilled and tapped for scope mounts; sling swivel studs included.
MSRP: . . . . $377 or $399 camo

TRADITIONS PURSUIT XLT

BENELLI LEGACY 28 GA.

Action: inertia autoloader
Stock: satin walnut with WeatherCoat
Barrel: 24″ or 26″
Chokes: screw-in tubes
Weight: 4.9 lbs.
Bore/Gauge***:*** 28 ga.
Magazine: 4 + 1
Features: red bar front sight and metal bead mid sight; game scene etchings, highly polished blued upper receiver.
MSRP: $1989

BERETTA A400 XPLOR UNICO

Action: gas-operated autoloader
Stock: walnut and polymer
Barrel: "Steelium" 26″, 28″ or 30″
Chokes***:*** Optima Choke HP
Weight: 6.6 lbs (26″ barrel)
Bore/Gauge***:*** 12 ga.
Magazine:
Features: Kick-off recoil system uses two hydraulic dampeners to decease recoil by 70%; green anodized receiver; Blink Operating System allows for fast, clean gas system; checkering features Beretta logo.
MSRP: $1725

BENELLI LEGACY 28 GA.

BERETTA TX4 STORM

BERETTA TX4 STORM

Action: gas-operated autoloader
Stock: black synthetic with rubber overlays
Barrel: 18″
Chokes: Optima Bore HP-Cylinder
Weight: 6.4 lbs.
Bore/Gauge***:*** 12 ga.
Magazine: 5 + 1
Features: adjustable length of pull with ½″ spacers; Picatinny rail mounted to receiver accepts your optics or the included ghost ring sight; plastic case included.
MSRP: $1450

BROWNING CYNERGY CLASS FIELD AND CLASSIC SPORTING

Action: Over/Under, reverse striker ignition system
Stock: gloss oil finish
Barrel: 26 to 30″
Chokes***:*** three Invector-Plus tubes
Weight: 6 lbs. 4 oz. to 7 lbs. 13 oz.
Bore/Gauge***:*** 12, 20, 28, .410
Magazine: none
Features: silver nitride finish receiver, low-profile, high-relief engraving, lightweight barrel has vented top and side ribs; ivory front and mid-bead sights; Classic Sporting has higher grade walnut
MSRP: .$2399 to $2429 Classic Field; $3469 to $3509 Classic Sporting

BROWNING CITORI LIGHTNING

Action: over/under
Stock: gloss walnut Lightning-style stock and forearm
Barrel: 26 to 32″ vent rib
Chokes***:*** Invector-Plus choke tubes (standard on 28 and .410)
Weight: 6 lbs.8 oz to 8 lbs. 10 oz.
Bore/Gauge***:*** 12, 20, 28, .410
Magazine: none
Features: blued engraved finish; vent rib barrel, recoil pad on 12 ga., ivory front bead sight, top-tang barrel selector/safety; single selective trigger.
MSRP: . . . . $1869–$1939

CONNECTICUT SHOTGUN MFG. CO. A-10 AMERICAN

Action: sidelock over/under
Stock: checkered American black walnut
Barrel: 26″ to 32″
Chokes: 5 TruLock tubes
Weight: 6.5 to 7.5 lbs.
Bore/Gauge: 12, 20, or 28 ga.
Magazine: none
Features: finely engraved, cut checkering, ventilated rib, pistol grip or straight grip, auto ejectors, single selective trigger, Galazan pad.
MSRP: . . . . standard starting $3995; deluxe starting $4995

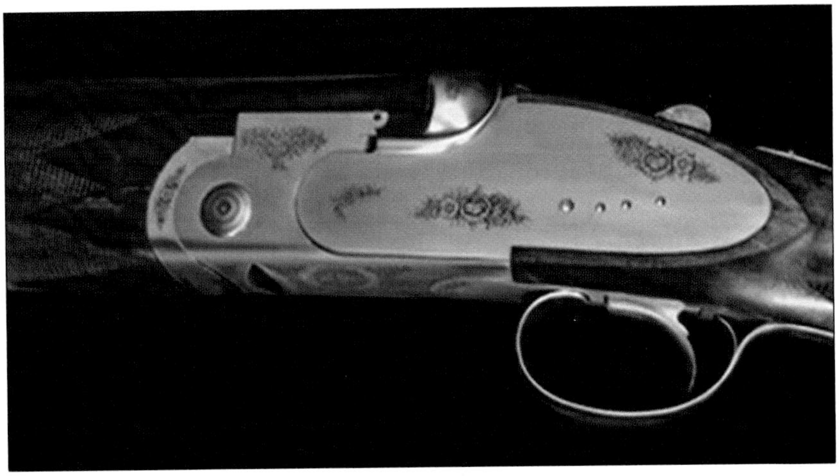

CZ UPLAND ULTRALIGHT

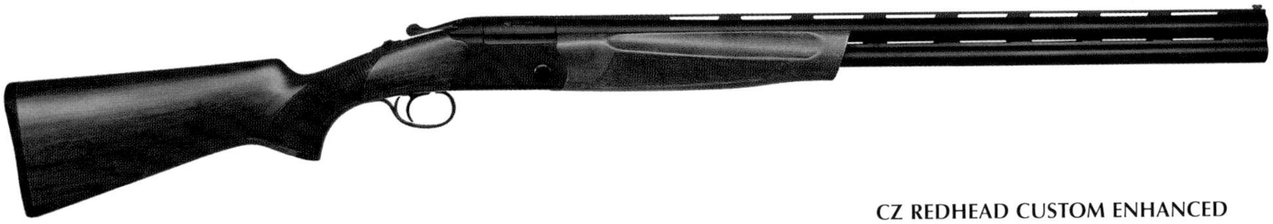

CZ REDHEAD CUSTOM ENHANCED

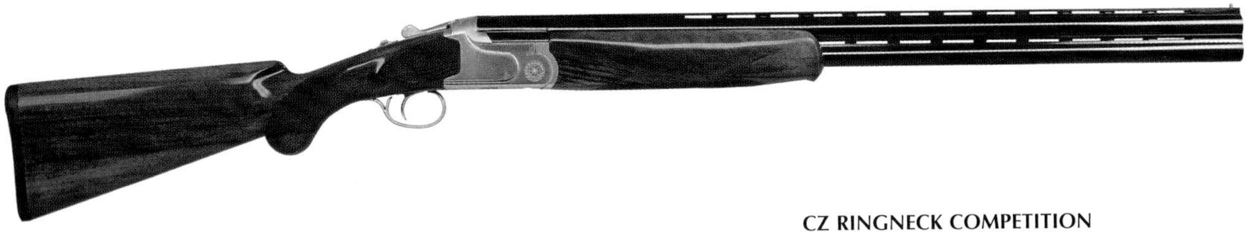

CZ RINGNECK COMPETITION

CZ UPLAND ULTRALIGHT

Action: over/under
Stock: Turkish walnut
Barrel: 26″ or 28″ black
Chokes: multi
Weight: 6 lbs.
Bore/Gauge: 12 ga.
Magazine: none
Features: lightweight, black alloy, vent rib.
MSRP: $749

CZ REDHEAD CUSTOM ENHANCED

Action: over/under
Stock: Circassian walnut, hand rubbed finish with Schnable fore-end
Barrel: 28″
Chokes: multi
Weight: 7.9 lbs.
Bore/Gauge: 12 ga.
Magazine: none
Features: hand cut checkering, silver receiver, 3.5 to 4-lb. trigger pull.
MSRP: $1899

CZ RINGNECK COMPETITION

Action: side-by-side
Stock: walnut, adjustable comb
Barrel: 28″
Chokes: multi
Weight: 7.3 lbs.
Bore/Gauge: 12 ga.
Magazine: none
Features: case-hardened receiver, ported barrels, center bead, fiber optic front sight, elongated forcing cones for reduced recoil.
MSRP: $2999

FAUSTI STEPHANO DEA ROUND BODY

Action: side-by-side
Stock: oil-finished select walnut
Barrel: 28″
Chokes*:* 5 choke tube options
Weight: 6 lbs. 3 oz.
Bore/Gauge*:* 20 ga.
Magazine: none
Features: English-style round-body action and stock, low-profile case-colored receiver, selective ejectors and extractors.
MSRP: $3895

Also available*:* DEA Duetto in 28-ga./.410 bore two-barrel set (4 lbs. 13 oz.); Caledon over/under available in 12 or 20 ga. in adult or youth versions

FRANCHI I-12 SPORTING

Action: inertia operated autoloader
Stock: A-Grade walnut with WeatherCoat
Barrel: 30″
Chokes: 5 extended choke tubes
Weight: 6.5 lbs.
Bore/Gauge*:* 12 ga.
Magazine: 4 + 1
Features: aluminum alloy receiver with steel inserts, tapered, target rib, ported; twin shock absorber reduces recoil; I-12 Limited has upland game bird etchings.
MSRP: $1329

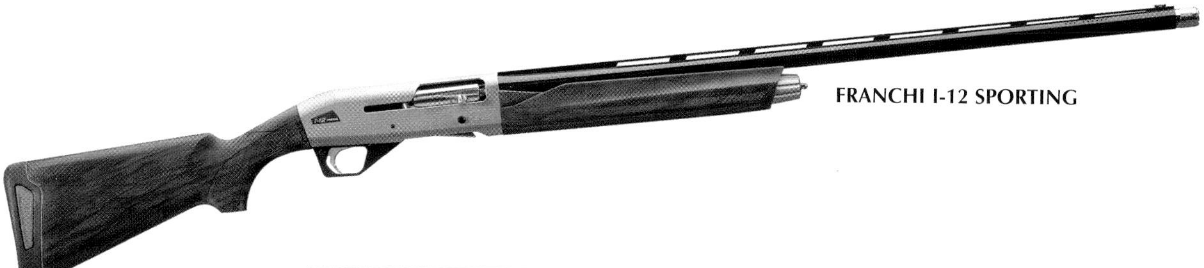

FRANCHI I-12 SPORTING

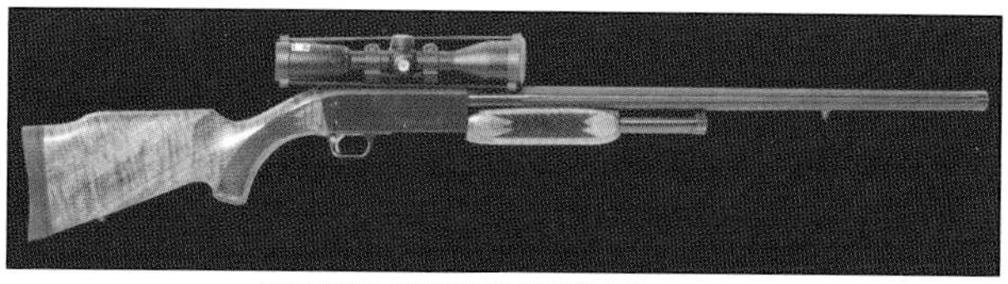

ITHACA DEERSLAYER III

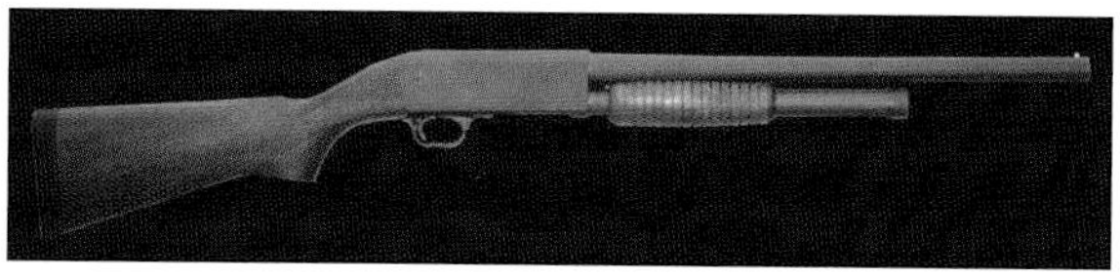

ITHACA MODEL 37 DEFENSE

CAESAR GUERINI MAXUM IMPACT

Action: over/under
Stock: checkered walnut with adjustable cheekpiece
Barrel: 30″ to 34″
Chokes*:* Maxis choke system
Weight: 7 lbs. 11 oz. to 8 lbs. 7 oz.
Bore/Gauge*:* 12 ga. or 20 ga.
Magazine: none
Features: engraved receiver, 17mm tall D.T.S. rib for more upright shooting, 5″ dual conical forcing cones, selective and non-selective triggers available, left hand available.
MSRP: . . . . N/A

ITHACA DEERSLAYER III

Action: pump
Stock: Grade-A black walnut, Monte Carlo
Barrel: 26″ heavy, fluted
Chokes: none
Weight: 8.1 lbs. (20 ga.), 9.5 lbs. (12 ga.)
Bore/Gauge*:* 20 ga. or 12 ga.
Magazine: 5-shot
Features: Model 37 action; Weaver #62 rail installed on receiver for mounting scope; deep blue finish, gold-plated trigger, deer head engraving on receiver.
MSRP: $1189

ITHACA MODEL 37 DEFENSE

Action: pump
Stock: walnut or black synthetic
Barrel: 18.5″ or 20″
Chokes: none
Weight: 6.5 to 7.1 lbs.
Bore/Gauge*:* 12 or 20 ga.
Magazine: 5-shot or 8-shot (20″ barrel)
Features: brass bead front sight; "Perma-Guard" finish, receiver machined from solid block of steel; Pachmayr Decelerator recoil pad.
MSRP: . . . . $499–$549

NEW Products: Shotguns

ITHACA MODEL 37 28 GAUGE FEATHERLIGHT

Action: pump
Stock: checkered black walnut
Barrel: 26″ or 28″ vent rib
Chokes: 3 Briley choke tubes
Weight: 6.1 lbs.
Bore/Gauge: 28 ga.
Magazine: 5-shot
Features: brass bead front sight or optional Turglo red fiber optic; black Pachmayr Decelerator recoil pad; engraved receiver with gold inlays.
MSRP: . . $999 ($1589 Fancy walnut)

ITHACA MODEL 37 28 GAUGE FEATHERLIGHT

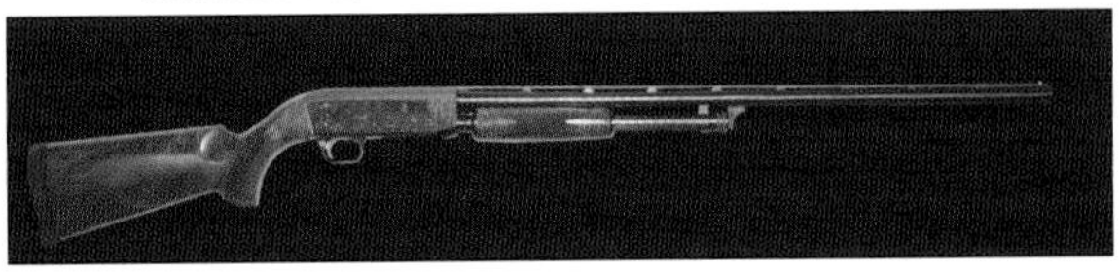

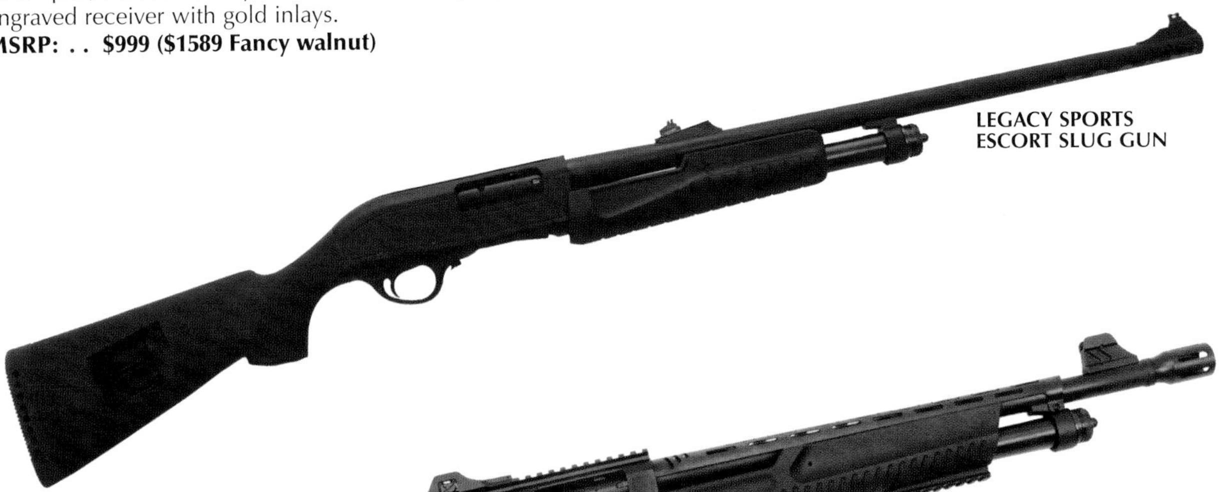

LEGACY SPORTS ESCORT SLUG GUN

LEGACY SPORTS ESCORT AIMGUARD HOME DEFENSE

LEGACY SPORTS ESCORT SLUG GUN

Action: autoloader or pump
Stock: black polymer
Barrel: 22″ Badger barrel
Chokes: rifled barrel
Weight: 6 lbs.
Bore/Gauge: 12 or 20 ga.
Magazine:
Features: fiber optic sights;
MSRP: . . . . $399 pump; $479 Semi-auto slug

LEGACY SPORTS ESCORT AIMGUARD HOME DEFENSE

Action: autoloader or pump
Stock: Pistol grip butt stock with rubber grip and 2-round built-in shell holder
Barrel: 18″ blued barrel
Chokes: cyl bore
Weight: 5.5 lbs.
Bore/Gauge: 12 ga.
Magazine: 5-round tubular
Features: drilled and tapped and installed upper Picatinny rail; ghost ring rear sight with windage and elevation adjustments and fiber optic front sight; large, easily accessible slide release, black matte finish.
MSRP: . . . . . $499; semi-auto: $280

LEGACY SPORTS CITADEL TACTICAL SHOTGUNS

Action: LE pump
Stock: Spec-Ops or Talon stock
Barrel: 18.75″
Chokes: none
Weight: 6 lbs.
Bore/Gauge: 12 ga.
Magazine: 5 or 10-shot detachable
Features: short combat; also available with traditional tube magazine, 7-round with 20″ barrel.
MSRP: $559

MOSSBERG 510 MINI SUPER BANTAM

Action: pump
Stock: adjustable synthetic
Barrel: 18.5″ VR
Chokes: Accu-set in 20 ga, Fixed-Modified in 410
Weight: 5 lbs.
Bore/Gauge: 20 ga. And .410
Magazine: 3 (.410) and 4 (20 ga.)
Features: good choice for petite or younger shooter; dual bead sights, blued finish, 1″ extension and recoil pad included.
MSRP: $364

LEGACY SPORTS CITADEL TACTICAL SHOTGUNS

MOSSBERG 510 MINI SUPER BANTAM

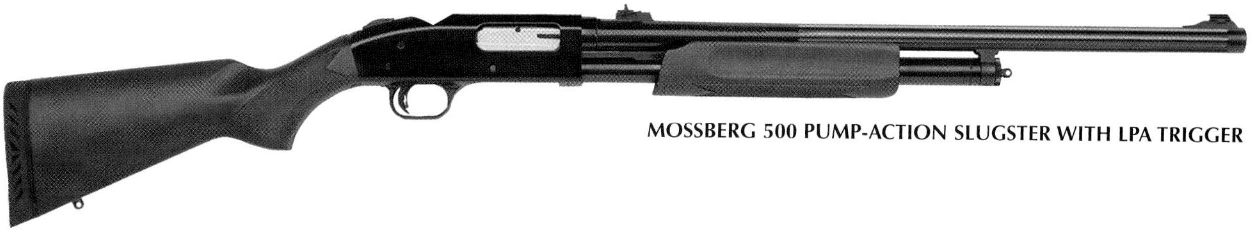

MOSSBERG 500 PUMP-ACTION SLUGSTER WITH LPA TRIGGER

MOSSBERG 500 PUMP-ACTION SLUGSTER WITH LPA TRIGGER

Action: pump
Stock: Realtree camo synthetic or wood
Barrel: 24″ fluted barrel
Chokes: fully rifled bore
Weight: 7 lbs.
Bore/Gauge: 12 ga.
Magazine: 3
Features: dual comb stock, integral scope base; new adjustable LPA (Lightning Pump Action) trigger system providing creep-free rifle-like trigger.
MSRP: $484

MOSSBERG MAVERICK HUNTER

Action: over/under
Stock: black synthetic
Barrel: 28″ matte blue
Chokes: interchangeable tubes
Weight: 7 lbs.
Bore/Gauge: 12 ga. 28 ga.
Magazine: none
Features: ventilated rib, dual locking lugs; two choke tubes included, bead sights.
MSRP: $394

REMINGTON 887 NITRO MAG CAMO COMBO

Action: pump
Stock: weather-impervious synthetic camo
Barrel: 22″ Turkey and 28″ Waterfowl
Chokes: Extended Waterfowl and Super Full Turkey
Weight: 7 and 7.25 lbs.
Bore/Gauge: 12 ga.
Magazine: 5-shot
Features: ArmorLokt seal on receiver and barrel; hammer forged barrel; built-in swivel studs. Comes with HiViz fiber-optic sights; both barrels included.
MSRP: $693

REMINGTON 887 NITRO MAG CAMO COMBO

REMINGTON 870 SPS SHURSHOT TURKEY PREDATOR

REMINGTON 870 SPS SHURSHOT TURKEY PREDATOR

Action: pump
Stock: pistol grip, overmolded panels in Mossy Oak Obsession camo
Barrel: 20″
Chokes: Wingmaster HD Turkey/Predator choke tube
Weight: 7 1/8 lbs.
Bore/Gauge: 12 ga.
Magazine: 5-shot
Features: bead front sight; Tru-Glo LUD optic sight; sling swivel studs, Super Cell recoil pad; finished in camo; sling included.
MSRP: $652

REMINGTON M11-87 SPORTSMAN FIELD

Action: gas-operated autoloader
Stock: walnut
Barrel: 26 or 28″ vent rib
Chokes: Rem-Choke tubes
Weight: 7.25 lbs. (20 ga.) 8.25 lbs. (12 ga.)
Bore/Gauge: 20 ga. or 12 ga.
Magazine: extended tube
Features: satin finish stock with Fleur-Di-Lis checkering, dual bead sights, nickel plated bolt and gold plated trigger, blued finish on barrel and receiver.
MSRP: $812

SAVAGE 220F SLUG GUN

Action: bolt
Stock: black synthetic
Barrel: 22″ rifled
Chokes: none
Weight: 7.5 lbs.
Bore/Gauge: 20 ga.
Magazine: 2-shot detachable box
Features: drilled and tapped for scope mounts; Accutrigger, matte blue.
MSRP: $519

REMINGTON M11-87 SPORTSMAN FIELD

SAVAGE 220F SLUG GUN

STEVENS TRAIL GUN

STEVENS TRAIL GUN

Action: side-by-side
Stock: checkered walnut
Barrel: 20″
Chokes: MC-5
Weight: 6 lbs.
Bore/Gauge: 20 ga., 12 ga.
Magazine: none
Features: compact and quick, 3″ chamber; front bead sight
MSRP: $799

STEVENS 350 PUMP SECURITY

Action: pump
Stock: black synthetic
Barrel: 18.25″
Chokes: none
Weight: 7.6 lbs.
Bore/Gauge: 12 ga.
Magazine: 5-shot
Features: bead sights.
MSRP: . . . . . $241 (with sights $282)
Also available: 350 Pump Field $267 and Field/Security Combo $307

STEVENS 350 PUMP SECURITY

STOEGER DOUBLE DEFENSE

STOEGER DOUBLE DEFENSE

Action: side-by-side
Stock: matte black hardwood
Barrel: 20″ tactical ported
Chokes: fixed: improved cylinder and cylinder
Weight: 6.5 lbs.
Bore/Gauge: 12 or 20 ga.
Magazine: none
Features: single-trigger design, tang-mounted auto safety; green fiber-optic sight. Comes with two Picatinny rails.
MSRP: $469

THOMPSON/CENTER PROHUNTER TURKEY

Action: hinged-breech single-shot
Stock: AP camo with Flextech
Barrel: 24 or 26″
Chokes: T/C Extra Full
Weight: 6.25 to 6.75 lbs.
Bore/Gauge*:* 12 or 20 ga.
Magazine: none
Features: fiber optic sights, 14″ length of pull.
MSRP: $799

WEATHERBY PA-459 HOME DEFENSE

Action: pump
Stock: pistol grip buttstock with rubber textured grip
Barrel: 9″ chrome-lined
Chokes: ported cylinder choke tube
Weight: 6.5 lbs.
Bore/Gauge*:* 12 ga.
Magazine: 5 (2 ¾″) or 4 (3″)
Features: low-density recoil pad, extended forend, Picatinny rail, LPA ghost ring rear sight and blade front sight with fiber optic pin; matte black finish on all metalwork.
MSRP: $469

THOMPSON/CENTER PROHUNTER TURKEY

WINCHESTER SUPER X3 20 GA.

WINCHESTER SUPER X3 20 GA.

Action: gas-operated autoloader
Stock: walnut, cut checkering
Barrel: 26″ or 28″
Chokes: F, M, IC
Weight: 6 ½ lbs.
Bore/Gauge*:* 20 ga.
Magazine: 4-shot
Features: machined rib with solid brass bead, self-adjusting gas system for reduced felt recoil, Pachmayr Decelerator recoil pad.
MSRP: $1199

WINCHESTER SUPERX PUMP DEFENDER

Action: pump
Stock: black composite
Barrel: 18″
Chokes: none
Weight: 6.8 lbs.
Bore/Gauge*:* 12 ga. buckshot or slugs
Magazine: 5-shot
Features: deeply grooved forearm.
MSRP: $349
Also available*:* SuperX Black Shadow Field with 26 or 28″ barrel $399

NEW Products: Handguns

BERETTA 92A1/96A1

Action: DA autoloader
Grips: Brunton/plastic
Barrel: 4.9″
Sights: white 3-dot sights, removable front sight
Weight: 34.4 oz.
Caliber: 9mm, 40 S&W (96)
Capacity: 17 (9mm), 12 (40 S&W)
Features: The new 92A1 and 96A1 include the best of Beretta's 92FS and 90two, with higher-capacity magazines (three magazines included), accessory rail, internal recoil buffer, and rounded trigger guard.
MSRP: $690

BERETTA PX4 STORM COMPACT

Action: DA autoloader
Grips: polymer
Barrel: 3.2″
Sights: 3-dot sight system
Weight: 27.3 oz.
Caliber: 9mm, .40 S&W
Capacity: 15 (9mm), 12 (.40 S&W)
Features: rotary barrel design of full-size Storm, but with a shorter slide and grip; ambidextrous slide stop lever; compact models accept the full size magazines, increasing capacity to 17 or 20 in 9mm and 17 in .40 S&W.
MSRP: $600

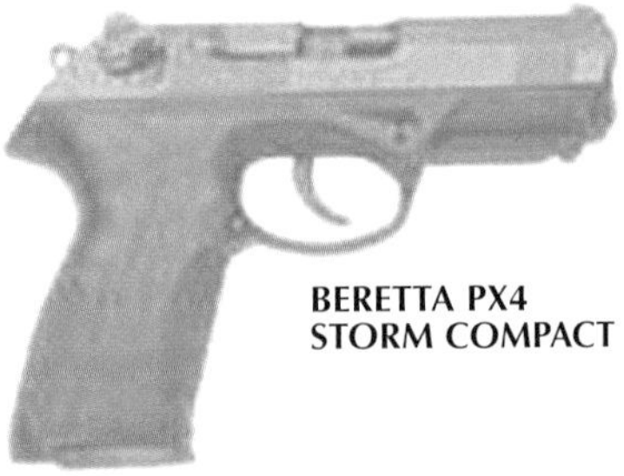

BERETTA PX4 STORM COMPACT

BERSA BP9CC/BP40CC

Action: DA autoloader
Grips: black polymer
Barrel: 3.2″
Sights: interchangeable front and rear sight
Weight: 21.5 oz.
Caliber: 9mm and .40 S&W
Capacity: 8 (9mm), 7 (.40 S&W)
Features: double action, alloy steel, slide, frame and trigger checkering, ambidextrous magazine catch button.
MSRP: $425

BROWNING BUCK MARK LITE GREEN/GRAY

Action: SA autoloader
Grips: Ultragrip RX ambidextrous
Barrel: 5.5″ and 7.25″
Sights: Pro-Target adjustable rear and fiber-optic front
Weight: 28 and 30 oz.
Caliber: .22 LR
Capacity: 10
Features: alloy CNC machined receiver and fluted barrel in matte green or gray finish.
MSRP: $519 (5.5″ barrel); $539 (7.25″ barrel)

BROWNING BUCK MARK PRACTICAL URX

Action: SA autoloader
Grips: Ultragrip RX ambidextrous
Barrel: tapered bull 5.5″, matte blued
Sights: Pro-Target adjustable rear with fiber-optic front
Weight: 34 oz.
Caliber: .22 LR
Capacity: 10
Features: alloy matte gray receiver.
MSRP: $399

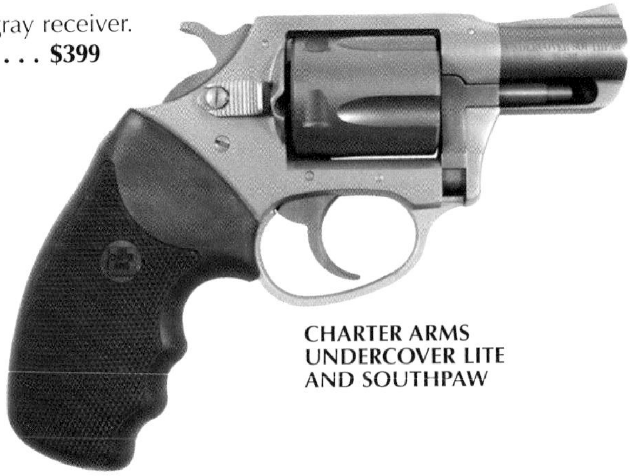

CHARTER ARMS UNDERCOVER LITE AND SOUTHPAW

CHARTER ARMS UNDERCOVER LITE AND SOUTHPAW

Action: DA revolver
Grips: rubber
Barrel: 2″
Sights: fixed
Weight: 12 oz.
Caliber: .38 Special + P
Capacity: 5
Features: aircraft-grade aluminum alloy one-piece frame and 3-point cylinder lock-up. American made.
MSRP: $477

Also available: Undercover Southpaw: a true left-handed revolver; completely reverse-configured with cylinder opening on right side allowing efficient reloading for left-handed shooters.

CHIAPPA RHINO REVOLVER

CHIAPPA RHINO REVOLVER

Action: DA revolver
Grips: wood or neoprene
Barrel: 2″, 4″, 6″, or 5″
Sights: fixed or adjustable
Weight: 25 oz. (4″ barrel)
Caliber: .357 Mag.
Capacity: 6
Features: barrel aligns with bottom chamber in the cylinder; aluminum frame, 3 grip sizes, hexagonal section on cylinder to lie flat against body.
MSRP: . . . .$775 (2″ barrel)

COLT CLASSIC SAA WITH GOLD ACCENTS

Action: SA revolver
Grips: walnut with gold medallions
Barrel: 5.5″
Sights: fixed, open
Weight: 46 oz.
Caliber: .45 LC
Capacity: 6
Features: full blue finish with gold barrel bands and cylinder bands
MSRP: $1620

COLT FRONTIER SIX SHOOTER

Action: SA revolver
Grips: black composite Eagle grips
Barrel: 4.75″ or 5.5″ or 7.5″
Sights: fixed
Weight: 46 oz.
Caliber: .44/40
Capacity: 6
Features: the revival of Colt Peacemaker classic
MSRP: $1547

Also available in nickel finish: SAA Sheriff's in .45 LC, 3″ barrel $1490 SAA Storekeeper's in .45 LC or .44/40, 4″ barrel $1490

COLT NEW AGENT DA

Action: DA autoloader
Grips: double-diamond slim-fit grips
Barrel: 3″
Sights: trench-style sight
Weight: 39 oz.
Caliber: .45
Capacity: 7 + 1
Features: double action only, black anodized frame with beveled magazine well, front strap serrations.
MSRP: $939

COLT RAIL GUN

Action: SA autoloader (1911)
Grips: double diamond rosewood
Barrel: 5″
Sights: white dot, Novak rear sight
Weight: 39 oz.
Caliber: .45 ACP
Capacity: 8 + 1
Features: mil standard rail will allow attachment of tactical lights and laser sights; skeletonized 3-hole trigger, enhanced hammer with elongated slot, upswept beavertail grip with palm swell, single slide tactical thumb safety, National Match barrel.
MSRP: $1055

CZ P-07 DUTY

Action: DA autoloader
Grips: polymer frame
Barrel: 3.8″
Sights: fixed
Weight: 27 oz.
Caliber: 9mm Luger or .40 S&W
Capacity: 16 (9mm), 12 (.40)
Features: Omega trigger system, improved trigger pull; shooter can choose the decocking lever (installed) or manual safety (included); accessory rail and two magazines included.
MSRP: . . . . . $579 (9mm); $599 (.40)

CZ P-07 DUTY

CZ 75 SP-01
SHADOW TARGET

CZ 75 SP-01 SHADOW TARGET

Action: SA/DA autoloader
Grips: cocobolo
Barrel: 4.72″
Sights: fiber optic
Weight: 39 oz.
Caliber: 9mm Luger
Capacity: 18
Features: manual safety, SA/DA, steel frame TRT rear sight, competition springs, CZ custom trigger and stainless guide rod.
MSRP: $1199

CZ 75 SA TARGET

Action: SA autoloader
Grips: aluminum
Barrel: 4.7″
Sights: fiber
Weight: 35 oz.
Caliber: 9mm Luger
Capacity: 16
Features: designed by Angus Hobdell, including custom trigger, Novak rear sight with fiber optic front, competition springs, Custom Aluminum grips, flat aluminum trigger and competition hammer.
MSRP: $1099

CZ 75 SA TARGET

DAN WESSON GUARDIAN

Action: SA autoloader
Grips: wood
Barrel: 4.25″
Sights: fixed tritium night sights
Weight: 29 oz.
Caliber: 9mm Luger
Capacity: 9
Features: bobtail frame, black receiver with "Duty" finish, ambidextrous thumb safety, Grip safety.
MSRP: $1530

DAN WESSON GUARDIAN

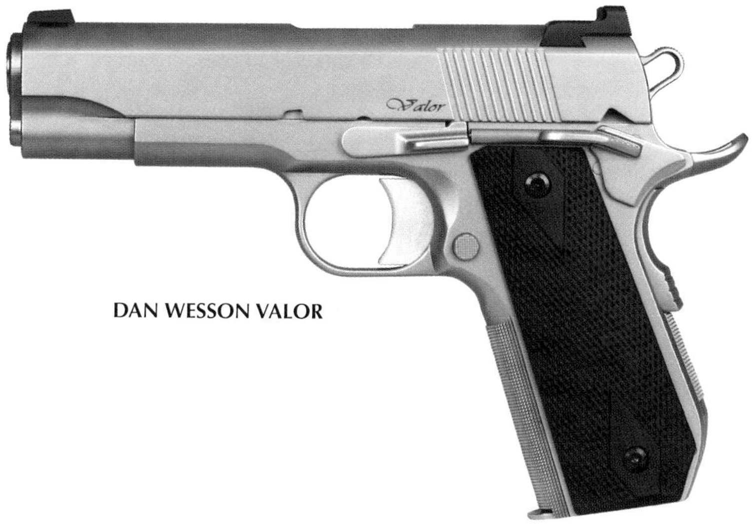

DAN WESSON VALOR

DAN WESSON VALOR

Action: SA autoloader
Grips: SlimLine V2
Barrel: 5″
Sights: adjustable
Weight: 39 oz.
Caliber: .45 Auto
Capacity: 8
Features: 1911 with manual thumb safety, grip safety.
MSRP: $1913

Also available: V-Bob (Valor series Bobtail Commander) 4.25″ barrel, fixed sights, various colored grips $1658 (stainless), $2040 (black)

FNH FNX-9/FNX-40

Action: SA/DA autoloader
Grips: interchangeable backstraps with lanyard eyelets
Barrel: 4″
Sights: 3-dot system
Weight: 22 oz. (9mm) and 24 oz. (.40)
Caliber: 9mm and .40 S&W
Capacity: 17 (9mm), 14 (.40)
Features: ergonomic polymer black frame with low bore axis; checkered and ribbed grip panels; stainless steel slide and hammer-forged stainless barrel. DA/SA ambidextrous operating controls.
MSRP: . . . . N/A

FNH FNX-9/FNX-40

FNH FNP-45 TACTICAL

FNH FNP-45 TACTICAL

Action: SA/DA autoloader
Grips: checkered polymer with interchangeable backstraps
Barrel: 5.3″
Sights: high-profile combat sights
Weight: 33.6 oz.
Caliber: .45 ACP
Capacity: 15
Features: DA/SA operation with decocker/manual safety; polymer frame in Flat Dark Earth with low bore axis for reduced felt recoil. Comes with three magazines and nylon soft case.
MSRP: . . . . N/A

FREEDOM ARMS M2008 SINGLE SHOT

Action: hinged breech with top slide latch
Grips: impregnated hardwood
Barrel: 10″ to 16″
Sights: none; drilled and tapped for scope mounts
Weight: 63 oz. (10″ barrel)
Caliber: .223 Rem. to .375 Win.
Capacity: one
Features: hammer block safety; stainless steel matte finish
MSRP: $495

HERITAGE MFG. GIRLY

Action: SA revolver
Grips: pink mother-of-pearl
Barrel: 3.5″
Sights: fixed
Weight: 30 oz.
Caliber: .22 LR and .22 Mag.
Capacity: 6
Features: alloy frame, blued finish, comes with both cylinders.
MSRP: $220

KAHR ARMS PM 9

Action: SA autoloader
Grips: polymer
Barrel: 3″
Sights: drift adjustable, white bar-dot combat
Weight: 15.9 oz.
Caliber: 9mm
Capacity: 6, 7 with extended magazine (included)
Features: polymer frame and stainless steel slide; external safety and LCI (Loaded Chamber Indicator).
MSRP: $924 ($1049 with night sights)
Also available*:* PM9/PM40 with Crimson Trace Laser Sight ($991)

KEL TEC PMR-30

Action: SA autoloader
Grips: nylon
Barrel: 4.3″ fluted
Sights: Picatinny accessory rail under barrel
Weight: 13.6 oz.
Caliber: .22 WMR
Capacity: 30
Features: blowback/locked breech system; lightweight but full size; urethane recoil buffer; disassembles for cleaning with removal of one pin.
MSRP: $415

KIMBER SUPER CARRY PRO

KIMBER SUPER CARRY PRO

Action: SA autoloader (1911)
Grips: checkered rosewood
Barrel: Custom (5″), Pro (4″), Ultra (3″)
Sights: fixed, low-profile, 3-dot
Weight: 25 to 31 oz.
Caliber: .45 ACP
Capacity: 7 or 8
Features: lightweight aluminum frame and machined stainless steel slide wear KimPro II, a high-tech finish that is self-lubricating and durable; rounded heel for concealed carry, night sights.
MSRP: $1530

KIMBER CENTENNIAL EDITION .45 ACP

Action: SA autoloader (1911)
Grips: ivory grips
Barrel: 5″
Sights: adjustable
Weight: 38 oz.
Caliber: .45 ACP
Capacity: 6 + 1
Features: To celebrate the 1911 centennial, Kimber has created an engraved .45 ACP in a wood-and-leather presentation case. Color case hardened finish by Turnbull Restoration. Only 250 made.
MSRP: $4352

KIMBER CENTENNIAL EDITION .45 ACP

KIMBER ULTRA CDP II

KIMBER ULTRA CDP II

Action: SA autoloader (1911)
Grips: Crimson Trace Lasergrips, rosewood, double diamond
Barrel: 3″ match-grade
Sights: Meprolight Tritium 3-dot night sights, fixed
Weight: 25 oz.
Caliber: .45 ACP
Capacity: 7
Features: aluminum frame, matte black, stainless slide, KimPro II frame finish, front strap checkering.
MSRP: $1603

KIMBER STAINLESS ULTRA TLE II

Action: SA autoloader (1911)
Grips: tactical gray, double diamond
Barrel: 3″ match-grade, ramped
Sights: Meprolight Tritium 3-dot night, fixed
Weight: 25 oz.
Caliber: .45 ACP
Capacity: 7
Features: aluminum frame, satin silver finish, front strap checkering.
MSRP: $1210

KIMBER STAINLESS ULTRA TLE II

LEGACY SPORTS PUMA M 1911-22

LEGACY SPORTS PUMA M 1911-22

Action: SA autoloader (1911)
Grips: walnut grip panels interchangeable with standard 1911 grips
Barrel: blued 4.75″
Sights: standard G.I.
Weight: 39 oz.
Caliber: .22 LR
Capacity: 10
Features: rimfire replica of Model 1911 designed by John Browning; polymer frame.
MSRP: $299

LEGACY SPORTS PUMA MODEL 1873

Action: SA revolver
Grips: hardwood
Barrel: 4.63″ blued
Sights: fixed front sight
Weight: 34 oz.
Caliber: .22 LR
Capacity: 6
Features: made by Chiappa Firearms to look and feel like Sam Colt's famous Single Action Army; traditional Peacemaker design; steel and alloy with matte black finish.
MSRP: $199

LEGACY SPORTS
PUMA MODEL 1873

MAGNUM RESEARCH
MICRO DESERT EAGLE

MAGNUM RESEARCH MICRO DESERT EAGLE

Action: DA autoloader
Grips: black polymer
Barrel: 2.22″
Sights: fixed, non-adjustable
Weight: 14 oz.
Caliber: .380 Auto (9mm Browning)
Capacity: 6
Features: gas-assisted blowback system, alloy frame, steel slide, oversized trigger guard.
MSRP: . . . .$535 nickel or nickel/blued, $500 blued

MAGNUM RESEARCH BABY DESERT EAGLE "FAST ACTION"

Action: DA autoloader
Grips: black polymer
Barrel: 4″ (9mm) 4.15″ (.40)
Sights: fixed
Weight: 24.8 oz. 9mm or 26.4 oz. .40 S&W
Caliber: 9mm or .40 S&W
Capacity: 10 or 15 (9mm), 10 or 12 (.40 S&W)
Features: 6-groove rifling
MSRP: . . . .$699, spare magazines: $31 each

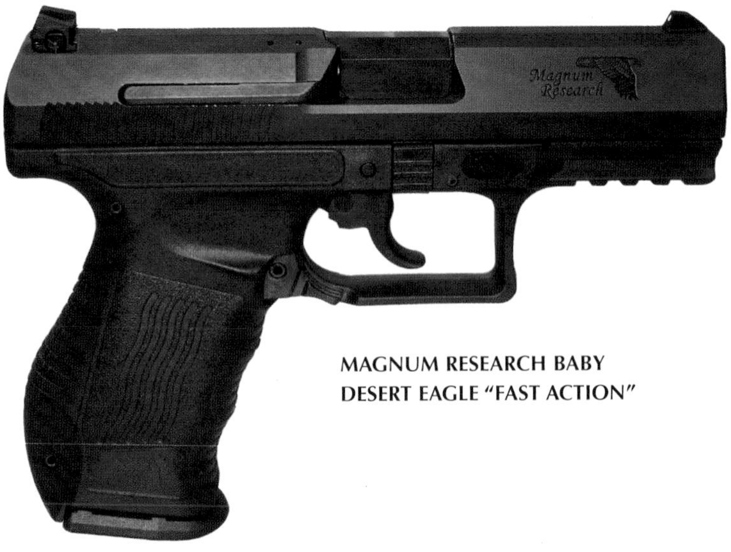

MAGNUM RESEARCH BABY
DESERT EAGLE "FAST ACTION"

MAGNUM RESEARCH DESERT EAGLE 1911

MAGNUM RESEARCH DESERT EAGLE 1911

Action: SA autoloader
Grips: checkered wood
Barrel: 5″ or 4.3″
Sights: fixed
Weight: 36 oz. (5″ barrel), 32 oz. (4.3″ barrel)
Caliber: .45 ACP
Capacity: 8
Features: grip safety, extended thumb safety, blued finish.
MSRP: $799

MOSSBERG 702 AND 802 PLINKSTER PISTOLS

MOSSBERG 702 AND 802 PLINKSTER PISTOLS

Action: SA auto (702) and bolt (802)
Grips: black synthetic or laminate
Barrel: 10″
Sights: grooved for scope mounts
Weight: 52 oz. or 64 oz.
Caliber: .22 LR
Capacity: 10
Features: detachable magazine, blued barrel, dovetail receiver, synthetic model features traditional pistol grip while the laminate features a grooved, ergonomic grip.
MSRP: . . . . $243–$274

NORTH AMERICAN ARMS "THE EARL"

Action: SA revolver
Grips: rosewood
Barrel: 4″ heavy octagonal
Sights: bead front
Weight: 8.6 oz.
Caliber: .22 Mag.
Capacity: 5
Features: 1860's style mini revolver – resembles 150-year-old percussion revolver.
MSRP: $289

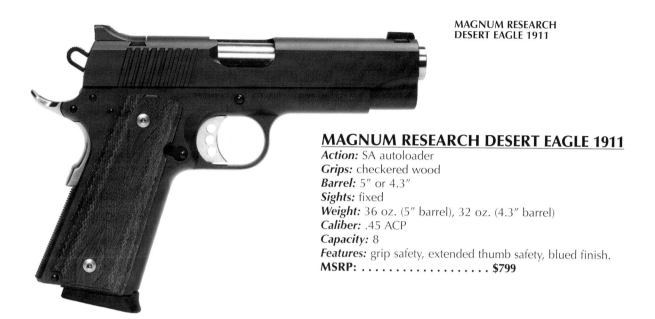

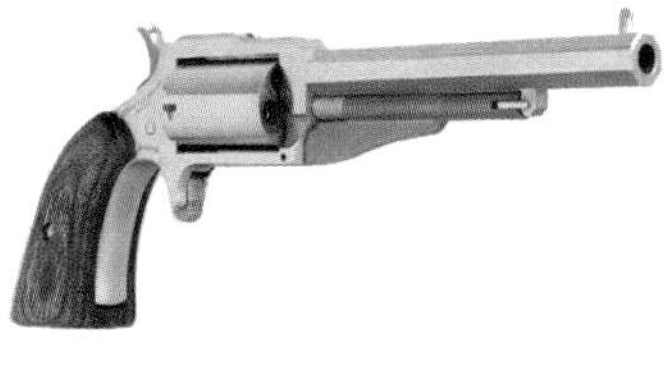

NORTH AMERICAN ARMS "THE EARL"

PARA G.I. EXPERT

Action: SA autoloader (1911)
Grips: checkered, polymer
Barrel: 5″ stainless
Sights: dovetail fixed, 3-white dot
Weight: 39 oz.
Caliber: .45 ACP
Capacity: 8
Features: covert black ParaKote finish; slide lock, internal firing block, lowered and flared ejection port, beveled magazine well.
MSRP: $599

PARA G.I. EXPERT

ROCK RIVER PPS PISTOL

Action: gas-operated autoloader with PPS (Performance Piston System) – AR style
Grips: Hogue rubber
Barrel: 8″ chrome moly
Sights: MS 1913 rail
Weight: 5 lbs.
Caliber: 5.56mm NATO chamber for 5.56mm & .223
Capacity: 30
Features: single-stage trigger.
MSRP: $1335

ROCK RIVER PPS PISTOL

RUGER LCR

RUGER LCR

Action: DA revolver
Grips: Hogue Tamer
Barrel: stainless steel 1.87″
Sights: replaceable, pinned ramp front and U-notch integral rear
Weight: 13.5 oz.
Caliber: .38 SPL + P
Capacity: 5
Features: Advanced Target Grey finish, polymer fire control housing, grip peg, stainless steel cylinder; soft case included.
MSRP: $525

Also available*:* LCR-LG with Crimson Trace Lasergrips $792

RUGER SR9C

Action: DA autoloader
Grips: black, glass-filled, nylon
Barrel: 3.5″
Sights: adjustable 3-dot sight
Weight: 23.4 oz.
Caliber: 9mm Luger
Capacity: 10 or 17
Features: compact version of SR9; black alloy or brushed stainless 6-groove rifling; high visibility sights, accessory mounting rail.
MSRP: $525

RUGER 22/45 RP

Action: SA autoloader
Grips: checkered cocobolo
Barrel: 5.5″ bull
Sights: adjustable rear
Weight: 33 oz.
Caliber: .22
Capacity: 10
Features: Replaceable Panels; Zytel polymer frame, blued; classic 1911-style pistol.
MSRP: $380

RUGER GP100 LE IN .327 FED. MAG.

Action: DA revolver
Grips: black with Hogue Monogrip
Barrel: 4.2″
Sights: adjustable rear
Weight: 40 oz.
Caliber: .327 Fed. Mag.
Capacity: 7
Features: Stainless medium frame; cushioned grips.
MSRP: $701

Also available in .327 Fed. Mag.: New Model Blackhawk, $681

SIG SAUER P238 SPECIAL EDITION NITRON

Action: SA autoloader
Grips: rosewood
Barrel: 2.7″
Sights: SIGLITE night sights
Weight: 15 oz. alloy frame, 20 oz. stainless frame
Caliber: .380 ACP
Capacity: 6
Features: for 2010, SigSauer has expanded its line of P238 concealed carry pistols; options include rainbow titanium finish, natural stainless or Nitron finish, two-tone with flat black anodized top, as well as new grip styles.
MSRP: . . . . $699 (Laser $749, SAS $735)

SIG SAUER P250 2SUM

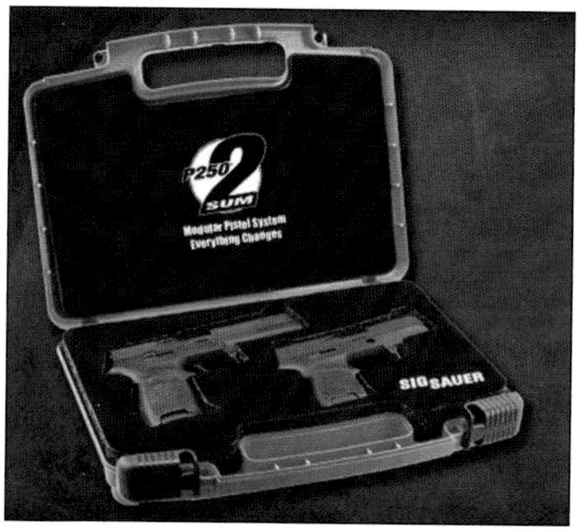

SIG SAUER P250 2SUM

Action: DA autoloader
Grips: black polymer
Barrel: 4.7″
Sights: SIGLITE night sights
Weight: 29.4 oz.
Caliber: 9mm, .40 S&W
Capacity: 17 (full-size 9mm), 14 (full-size .40 S&W)
Features: a full size P250 with all the components to rapidly convert it to the P250 subcompact with 3.6″ barrel (24.9 oz.)
MSRP: $945

SMITH & WESSON BODYGUARD 38

SMITH & WESSON BODYGUARD 38

Action: DA revolver
Grips: matte black synthetic
Barrel: 1.9″
Sights: integrated INSIGHT laser sighting system
Weight: 4.3 oz.
Caliber: .38 S&W Special + P
Capacity: 5
Features: stainless steel cylinder with PVD coating
MSRP: $625

NEW Products: Handguns

SMITH & WESSON BODYGUARD 380

Action: DA autoloader
Grips: polymer
Barrel: 2.75″
Sights: stainless steel drift-adjustable front and rear
Weight: 11.85 oz.
Caliber: .380 Auto
Capacity: 6 + 1
Features: manual thumb safety, external takedown lever, external slide stop, barrel and slide stainless with Melonite finish; integrated INSIGHT laser sighting system.
MSRP: $575

SMITH & WESSON BODYGUARD 380

SPRINGFIELD ARMORY USA XD (M)

Action: DA autoloader
Grips: polymer
Barrel: 3.8″ or 4.5″ match-grade
Sights: 3-dot
Weight: 28 oz (29-30 oz. in 4.5″)
Caliber: 9mm and .40 S&W
Capacity: 19 (9mm), 16 (.40 S&W)
Features: "M" features include carrying case, two magazines, paddle holster, mag loader, double mag pouch and 3 interchangeable backstraps and two magazines. "All-Terrain" texture and deep slide serrations are standard.
MSRP: $585

STI ECLIPSE

Action: SA autoloader (1911)
Grips: black polymer
Barrel: 3″ ramped, bull contour
Sights: 2-dot tritium night sights
Weight: 23.1 oz.
Caliber: .45 ACP, .40 S&W or 9x19
Capacity: 10
Features: 2011 double stack pistol; double-column magazine, steel frame, single sided blued thumb safety and bobbed, high-rise knuckle relief beavertail grip safety.
MSRP: $1825

TAURUS 24/7 G2

Action: DA/SA autoloader
Grips: checkered polymer with metallic inserts and 3 interchangeable backstraps
Barrel: 4.2″
Sights: low-profile, adjustable rear
Weight: 28 oz.
Caliber: 9mm, .40, .45 ACP
Capacity: 15 (9mm), 13 (.40), 10 (.45 ACP)
Features: blued or stainless steel; DA/SA trigger system, SA or DA only; contoured thumb rests, "Strike Two" trigger, Picatinny accessory rail.
MSRP: . . . . $498–$545

Also available*:* 24/7 G2 Compact (3.5″ barrel) and G2 Long Slide (5″ barrel)

TAURUS 24/7 G2

TAURUS 800 SERIES COMPACT

TAURUS 800 SERIES COMPACT

Action: DA/SA autoloader
Grips: polymer grips with metallic inserts
Barrel: 3.5″
Sights: 3-dot fixed
Weight: 24.7 oz.
Caliber: 9mm, .40, .357 Sig
Capacity: 10 (12 in 9mm)
Features: blued or stainless in 9mm; DA/SA; shorter grip for easy carry, ambidextrous magazine release, "Strike Two" trigger.
MSRP: . . . . $539–$555

TAURUS SLIM 740/SLIM 708

Action: DA/SA autoloader
Grips: polymer with metallic inserts
Barrel: 3.2″
Sights: adjustable rear sights
Weight: 19 oz.
Caliber: .380 ACP or .40
Capacity: 7 (.380), 6 (.40)
Features: sub-compact pistol in blued or stainless steel. Loaded chamber indicator, low-profile sights; short, crisp DA/SA trigger pull.
MSRP: . . . . $399–$499

TAURUS SLIM 740/SLIM 708

TAURUS 822 PISTOL

TAURUS 822 PISTOL

Action: DA autoloader
Grips: polymer with metallic inserts
Barrel: 4.5″ or 6″
Sights: adjustable rear
Weight: 21.3 oz. or 22.7 oz. with 6″ barrel
Caliber: .22 LR
Capacity: 10
Features: stainless or blue; loaded chamber indicator; Picatinny accessory rail; "Strike Two" trigger; extended grip for additional hold.
MSRP: . . . . $586–$602

TAURUS PUBLIC DEFENDER ULTRA-LITE

Action: DA revolver
Grips: Ribber
Barrel: 2.5″
Sights: fixed
Weight: 20.7 oz.
Caliber: .410 ga./.45 LC
Capacity: 5
Features: blue or stainless; generous profile hammer; fiber optic front sight.
MSRP: . . . . $648–$680

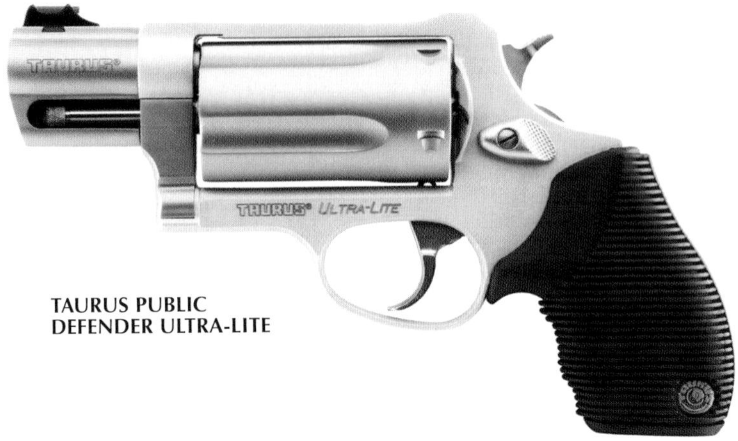

TAURUS PUBLIC DEFENDER ULTRA-LITE

TAURUS PUBLIC DEFENDER POLYMER

TAURUS PUBLIC DEFENDER POLYMER

Action: DA revolver
Grips: Ribber
Barrel: 2.5″
Sights: red fiber optic fixed front
Weight: 27 oz.
Caliber: .45/.410
Capacity: 5
Features: newest version of the Judge; polymer frame, blued or stainless finish, target hammer and trigger; fires both .410 shotshells and .45 Colt ammunition.
MSRP: . . . . $570–$67

TAURUS PROTECTOR POLYMER

Action: DA revolver
Grips: Rubber-Wooden style
Barrel: 2.5″
Sights: fixed
Weight: 18.2 oz.
Caliber: .38 Special + P
Capacity: 5
Features: blued finish, fully shrouded zero-profile hammer; ambidextrous thumb rest; wood-colored polymer grips.
MSRP: $445

TAURUS PROTECTOR POLYMER

TAURUS RAGING JUDGE MAGNUM

Action: DA revolver
Grips: soft cushion insert
Barrel: 3″ (or 6″)
Sights: fixed
Weight: 60.6 oz. (72.7 oz. with 6″ barrel)
Caliber: .410 ga./ .45 LC/.454 Casull
Capacity: 6
Features: stainless steel finish; "Raging Bull" backstrap for added cushioning.
MSRP: $936

Also available: Raging Judge Ultra-Lite in .410 ga./.45 LC with blue ultra-lite finish (41.4 oz. or 47.2 oz.)

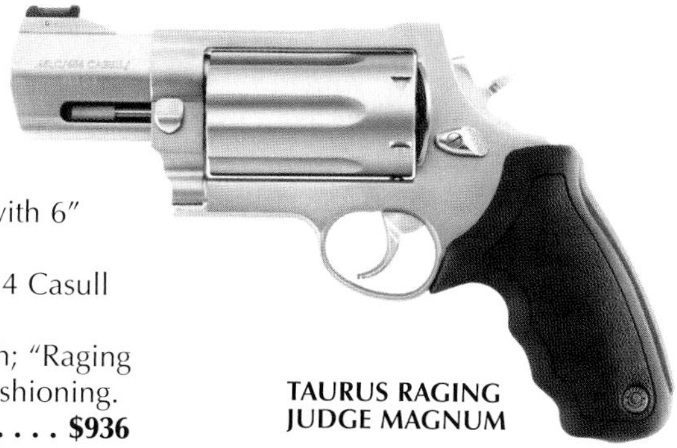
TAURUS RAGING JUDGE MAGNUM

TAYLOR'S & CO. RUNNIN' IRON

Action: SA revolver
Grips: checkered walnut
Barrel: 3.5″ to 5.5″
Sights: wider fixed, open
Weight: 39 oz.
Caliber: .45 LC or .357 Mag.
Capacity: 6
Features: designed for the sport of Mounted Shooting; offered in stainless or blue finish with low, wide hammer spur, checkered, one-piece gunfighter-style grips in walnut or black polymer. Wide trigger and extra clearance at font and rear of cylinder.
MSRP: . . . . . . $530 (stainless: $630)

UBERTI 1873 CATTLEMAN CALLAHAN NM

UBERTI 1873 CATTLEMAN CALLAHAN NM

Action: SA revolver
Grips: walnut, black or mother-of-pearl synthetic
Barrel: 4.75 or 6″ (target version 6 or 7.5″)
Sights: fixed
Weight: 42 oz.
Caliber: .44 Mag.
Capacity: 6
Features: blue, stainless, case-hardened or Old West finish; target model has angled front target sight and adjustable notched rear blade sight.
MSRP: . . . $569 Target version: $639

WALTHER P99AS

Action: DA autoloader
Grips: black polymer frame and grips
Barrel: 4″ stainless steel with Tenifer finish
Sights: front and rear tritium night sight
Weight: 21 to 23 oz.
Caliber: 9mm or .40 S&W
Capacity: 15 (9mm), 12 (.40 S&W)
Features: the first pistol with a firing pin block combines advantages of a traditional DA pull with SA trigger and a decocking button safety integrated into slide, allowing users the ability to decock the striker, preventing inadvertent firing in both DA and SA mode.
MSRP: $825

Also available with Night Sight Defense Kit: Walther PPS with 3.2″ barrel.

WALTHER P99AS

NEW Products: Handloading Equipment

FORSTER

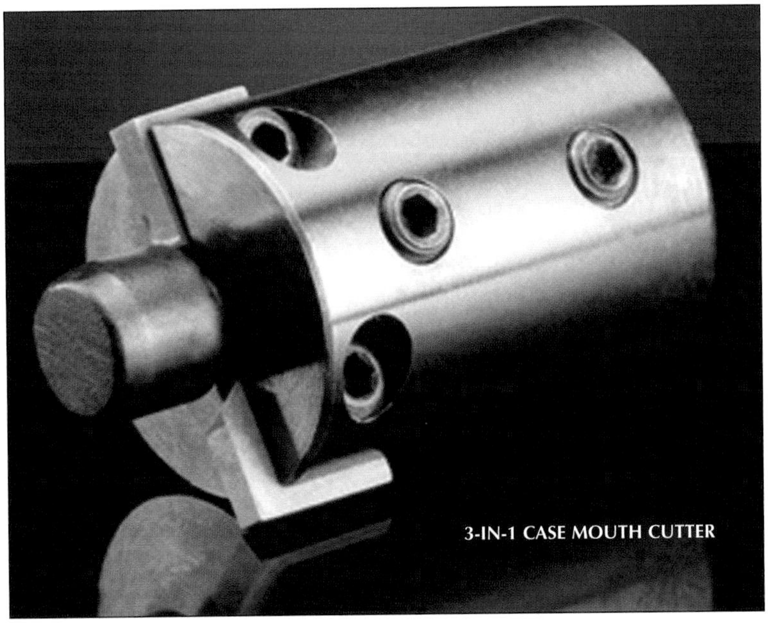
3-IN-1 CASE MOUTH CUTTER

3-in-1 Case Mouth Cutter

This carbide case trimmer accessory performs three functions simultaneously: It trims the case to length, chamfers the inside of the case mouth to an angle of 14 degrees and the outside of the mouth at 30 degrees. Blades never need sharpening if used on brass only. The 3-in-1 Cutter is currently available for three bullet diameters: .224, .243, .308.

Co-Ax Press

Since its introduction several years ago, the Co-Ax press has become known for its perfect die-ram alignment and quick-change die slot. The unique top priming device ensures that primers are seated "square" with the case head and to factory specifications. The shell holder floats, so the case naturally finds the die center. Shell holder jaws open and close on the case automatically, for positive extraction and easy case removal. Now there's a short-throw handle for the Co-Ax – handier if you don't need lots of leverage. An optional shell holder adapter plate allows use of standard shell holders. Tight tolerances make the Co-Ax one of the best choices for loading match ammo.

Co-Ax Case and Cartridge Inspector

Measure neck wall thickness, case neck concentricity and bullet run-out in thousandths. Ensure that bullet and case share the same axis for top accuracy on the range. I wide range of pilots,.204 to .458, adapt the Inspector to almost all popular cartridges, to loaded lengths of 3 ½ inches. The dial indicator is easy to read. Forster offers a full complement of handloading and gunsmithing tools for shooters demanding the best performance from their rifles.

LYMAN

Revolution Rotating Gun Vise

This versatile gun vise is engineered with a full range of adjustments. It tilts, revolves, clamps and has inserts to securely hold any firearm. Padded contact points protect gun surfaces during cleaning and gunsmithing, bore- sighting. 9 lbs. $89.95.

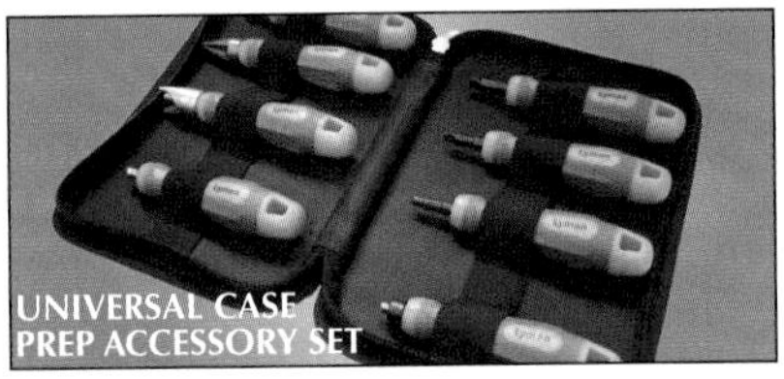
UNIVERSAL CASE PREP ACCESSORY SET

Universal Case Prep Accessory Set

This new accessory features all the items necessary for case preparation in one set. It includes large and small primer pocket reamers, primer pocket cleaners, outside deburring tool, inside (VLD) chamfer tool and large and small primer pocket uniformer tools. All individual items have their own molded handles with rubber inserts for sure grip. There's a zippered case for storage and transport to the range; 12.6 lbs. $69.95.

Magnum Inertia Bullet Puller

This inertia puller safely strips loaded rounds in seconds without damage to bullet or case. Its newly engineered head allows use on a full range of cartridges, from the tiny 5.7 X 28FN to the largest magnums. A new full-size ergonomic molded handle features a rubber insert for comfort and sure grip. This too traps components for easy retrieval; 9 oz. $21.50. Lymanproducts.com

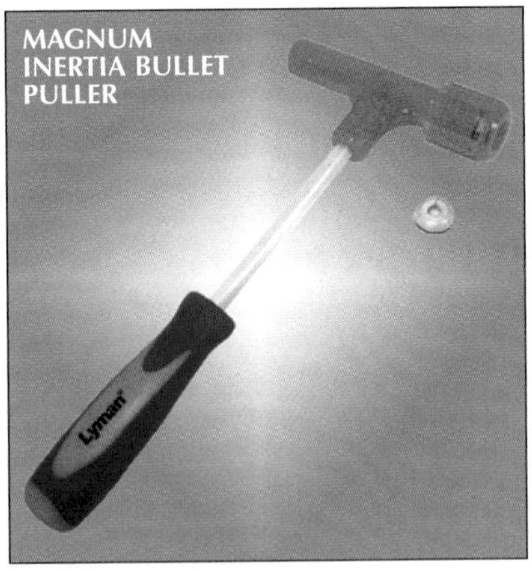

MAGNUM INERTIA BULLET PULLER

REVOLUTION ROTATING GUN VISE

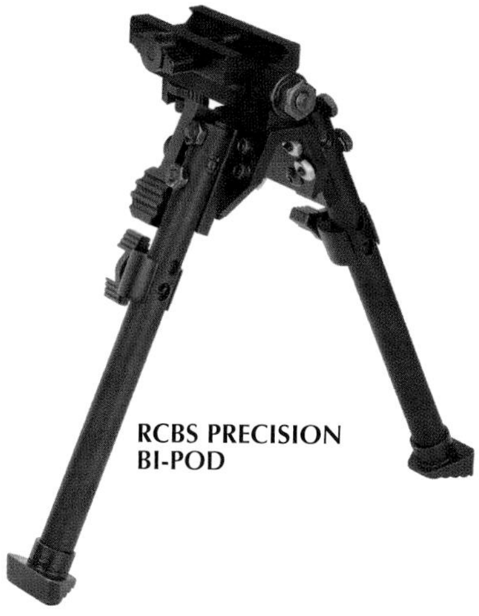

RCBS PRECISION BI-POD

RCBS

Precision Bi-Pod

Quick-adjust telescoping legs of 6061 T6 alloy secure your rifle for accurate shooting on uneven ground. Range of movement: 7 to 10 inches, with 25 degrees of cant. Skid-resistant polyurethane feet grip slick surfaces. Tool-free mounting adapts this bi-pod to any Picatinny rail. Paddle locks make for quick, easy deployment. Hard-coat anodizing endures tough use. $219.95.

Bullet Feeder—Rifle Kit (Progressive Press)

Designed to fit most progressive presses with 7/8-14" platform holes, this automatic unit features a rotating collator that orients the bullets to drop into the feed mechanism/seat die. Choose .22 or .30. The hopper holds 250 .22 caliber bullets over .30s. Powered by 110-240 VAC, the unit comes with plug adapters for foreign outlets. $595.95.
Also available: Pistol Kit with fittings for 9mm/.38 Spl./.357 Magnum, 10mm/.40 and .45 ACP. The hopper holds up to 200 bullets. As with the rifle version, this bullet feeder can boost production rates by 50 percent! $510.95

Other Products

RCBS offers the most complete line of handloading hardware in the industry. Besides new accessories like cleaning and lube kits for dies and presses, and a Pow'r Pull bullet extraction kit, it offers a variety of presses, from the famous Rock Chucker to a single-stage press for 50-caliber BMG cartridges and progressive turret and auto-indexing machines. A variety of measuring tools deliver accuracy to .0001. Manual and electronic powder measures and new scope mounting and gunsmithing tool sets complement trigger pull gauges, portable benches, even a quick-setup chronograph. The die selection defies count. RCBS.com.

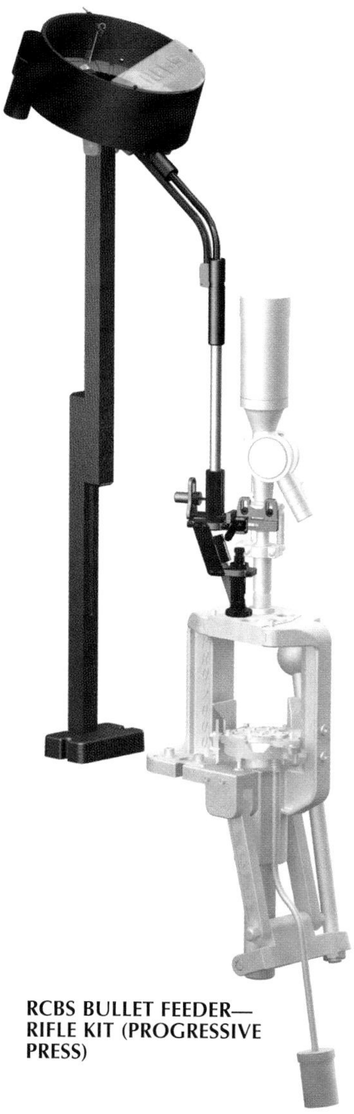

RCBS BULLET FEEDER—RIFLE KIT (PROGRESSIVE PRESS)

REDDING

Versa Pak Reloading Kit

Versa Pak was developed to give the handloader all he or she needs after purchasing a press and dies -- at a substantial savings over the cost of the individual items. Versa Pak includes all items listed in the Pro Pak (less press and dies) plus a Model 3 Master Powder Measure, a 1400 XT Case Trimmer, Imperial Dry Neck Lube in Application Media, a starter size of Imperial Sizing Die Wax and the DVD, "Advanced Handloading, Beyond the Basics." A bargain at $549!

Instant Indicator Headspace and Bullet Comparator

This instrument helps you quickly compare bullets and cases, plus trim lengths, seating depths and loaded ammunition for uniformity. You'll be able to easily sort hulls fired in different chambers, set your sizing dies to individual rifles, find variations in case and chamber dimensions and check headspace. The comparator comes supplied with one bore-diameter bushing, surface contactor, shoulder contactor, headspace gauge. $168.30.

G-RX Push Thru Base Sizing Die

The new G-RX Push Thru Base Sizing Die is designed to restore fired cases from .40 S&W autoloading pistols. Passing the case through the new G-RX Die, you remove the bulge that commonly appears upon firing. Presto! The case is back in service. A must-have if you shoot a .40 in autoloaders that induce case bulge. $49.80.

National Match Die Set

This specialized die set for military match shooters is available in .223, .308 and 30-06. The set includes a Full-Length Sizing Die, a Competition Bullet Seating Die and a Taper Crimp Die. $208.80. Redding offers an enormous selection of Competition and bushing-style dies for handgun and rifle cartridges, even wildcats, British Nitro Express rounds and 19th-century straight-wall rounds. Presses and other bench tools, including

NEW Products: Handloading Equipment

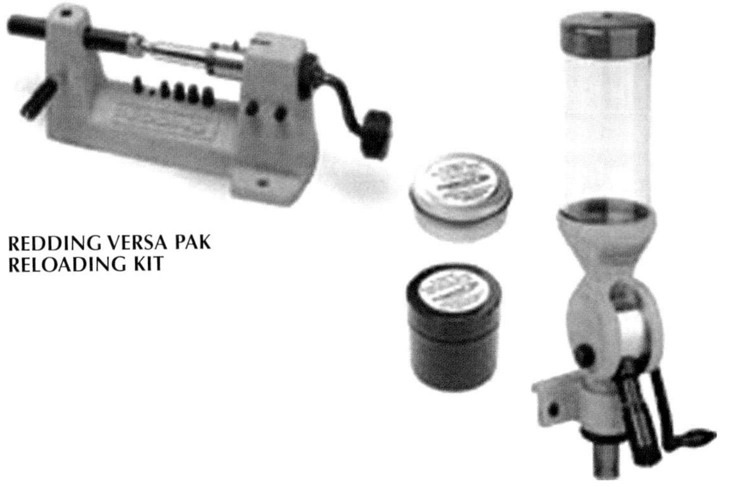

REDDING VERSA PAK RELOADING KIT

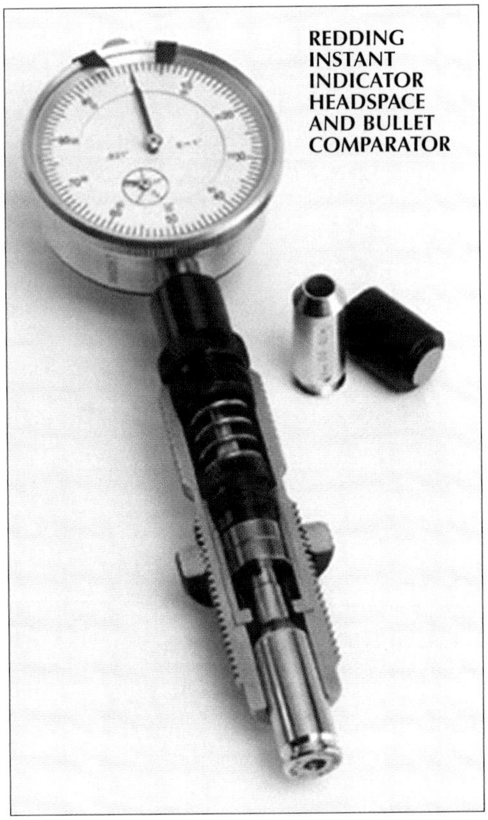

REDDING INSTANT INDICATOR HEADSPACE AND BULLET COMPARATOR

high-precision measuring instruments and bullet-casting equipment, round out the extensive Redding line. Redding-reloading.com.

NEW Products: OPTICS

AIMPOINT

Gunnar Sandberg's first "single-point sight" had no optical tunnel. You couldn't look through this sight; you looked into the tube with one eye while your other registered a dot superimposed on the target. That was in 1974. Sandberg refined the device and founded Aimpoint to produce it. The front lens of a modern Aimpoint is a compound glass that corrects for parallax by bringing the floating illuminated dot to your eye in a line parallel with the sight's optical axis. You hit where you see the dot, even when your eye is off-axis. A 1x Aimpoint gives you unlimited eye relief. Circuitry on the newest models reduces power demand. Batteries last up to 50,000 hours at mid-level brightness settings. A new Hunter series comprises four models with long and short tubes, 34mm and 30mm in

AIMPOINT

diameter and waterproof. They all feature 1x images, 2-minute dots and half-minute windage and elevation clicks. A 12-stop dial controls dot intensity. One CR-2032 battery lasts 5 years of continuous use! Fully multi-coated lenses (43mm objective on the 30mm sight, 47mm on the 34mm) deliver sharp images. Durable enough for military use, Aimpoints have been adopted by the armed forces in the U.S. and France. Sportsmen in 40 countries favor them. One of every 10 Swedish moose hunters with optical sights carries an Aimpoint. Aimpoint.com.

ALPEN

While 2010 adds just a few new products to the Alpen catalog, they're all worth a look. The Rainier 20-60x80 spotting scope has a fine-focus dial now, and accommodates a camera adapter for extended-range photography. AR rifle-scopes for air guns stand up to their double-shuffle recoil. Rainier 8x32 and 10x32 binoculars are 20 percent lighter than the 42mm originals but still feature BAK4 lenses, phase-corrected coatings, twist-out eyecups, a locking diopter dial. The AlpenPro Porro series includes an 8x30 ideal for woods-hunting. Alpen's Vickie Gardner is filling back-orders because some 2009 introductions were pre-mature. Wings binoculars, for example, weren't available until mid-year. ED glass is an option in both 8x42 and 10x42 models. Four new Apex scopes include three with turret-mounted parallax dial and new bullet-drop-compensating reticle. Alpenoutdoors.com.

BSA

The new BSA PMRGSLL multi-reticle illuminated sight attaches with Weaver-style components. Choose from seven brightness settings and four reticles. An integrated light and laser help you hit close targets. BSA's traditional scopes are getting a cosmetic overhaul, to match the value-loaded internals. A 3-12x44 Catseye recently announced has push/pull zero reset windage and elevation dials, plus parallax correction on the turret. Fully multi-coated optics, a fast-focus eyepiece and 4 inches of eye relief make this scope a must-see if you're seeking an all-around big game sight with the features of optics costing much more! Bsaoptics.com.

BURRIS

Like its Euro Diamond and Black Diamond lines, Burris' Six Series sights have 30mm tubes and 4 inches of eye relief. They also feature six-times magnification (the 2-12x covers nearly every hunting situation). Illuminated reticles define the Fullfield II LRS scopes; Fullfield 30s (3-9x40 and 3.5-10x50) boast 30mm tubes at affordable prices. The headliner at Burris in 2010 is the Eliminator, a programmable laser range-finding scope. You enter the ballistic path of your cartridge (drop figures at 500 yards, with a 100- or 200-yard zero) to get reads for a correct hold. The sight – a 4-12x42 LaserScope – tells you the exact distance to 800 yards on reflective objects, 550 on deer and elk. A dot on the reticle stem lights up instantly as the Eliminator determines bullet drop. Aim center with that lighted dot and fire. Given still conditions, your bullet should strike point of aim. The Eliminator weighs a hefty 26 ounces. It functions as

BURRIS ELIMINATOR LASERSCOPE

BURRIS SIXX SERIES RIFLESCOPE

BURRIS XTR 4-16X50

advertised and is most at home on long-range rifles. For deer in thickets, try the FastFire II, a 1.6-ounce reflex red dot sight, now waterproof. Battery-saver mode extends the life of the lithium CR2032 battery to five years. FastFire II mounts fit popular lever rifles; a plate slipped between receiver and buttstock on a repeating shotgun makes it what Burris calls the SpeedBead. For 2010, Fullfield II Tactical scopes and Fullfield TAC30 variables (3-9x40, 3.5-10x50 and 4.5-14x42) have been joined by a 3x AR-332 prism sight, and an AR-Tripler, which mounts behind any red dot sight for extra magnification. Burrisoptics.com.

BUSHNELL TROPHY XLT

BUSHNELL

Elite 6500-series rifle-scopes (2.5-16x42, 2.5-16x50 and 4.5-30x50) appeared in 2009 with nearly seven-times magnification, the broadest range practical. Now the scopes feature the DOA (Dead On Accurate) range-finding reticle, which can also be ordered on Elite 3200 and Trophy sights. The new Elite 4200 FFP 30mm scope has 1-mil adjustment gradations and a green illuminated reticle. Choose the 3-12x44 or a 6-24x50. For hunters on budgets, Bushnell has up-graded the Trophy series. Trophy XLT scopes feature fully multi-coated lenses and fast-focus eyepiece in magnification ranges to 6-18x50. RainGuard HD lens coatings and ED Prime glass have been added to Bushnell's top-end Elite 8x42 and 10x42 binoculars. A step down in price are new 21-ounce Legend 8x36 and 10x36 binoculars. They have many Elite features, including ED glass and RainGuard. The Excursion spotting scope, with a folded light path, comes in 15-45x60 and 20-60x80 versions. The new 15-45x Legend HD spotting scope is compact enough to stow in a backpack. Dual-speed focus gives you coarse and fine focusing. Bushnell's Scout 1000 laser range-finder with ARC technology reads shot angle so you get corrected range from tree stands and on steep pitches. Single-button control makes this 6 ½-ounce unit easy to use one-handed. Bushnell.com.

CABELA'S

No optics company, Cabela's nonetheless offers its own lines of imported scopes to augment its catalog selection of brand-name optics. High-volume marketing keeps prices modest for the excellent Alaska Guide series of fixed-power and variable rifle-scopes, including 4-12x AO and 6.5-20x AO models with 40mm objectives and 1-inch tubes. They list for less than $400. There's also a series of Cabela's tactical scopes with interchangeable turrets and left-side parallax knobs – starting at under $100. They have fully multi-coated lenses, fast-focus eyepieces and adjustable objectives. A new Lever-Action scope features a reticle that helps you adjust your hold for long distances. Five inches of eye relief give you fast aim. Cost: $100. Cartridge-specific EXT reticles in some Cabela's scopes compensate for bullet drop. Cabelas.com.

DOCTER

In 1991 the Carl Zeiss Jena factory in Thuringia, Germany began manufacturing Docter optics. In 2006 Merkel USA became the U.S. importer.

Docter Optic has since courted the U.S. market with 1-inch rifle-scopes featuring rear-plane reticles. The 3-9x40, 3-10x40, 4.5-14x40 AO and 8-25x50 AO Docter Sport scopes and 1-inch 6x42 and 8x56 fixed-power Classics complement 30mm Classic variables: 1-4x24, 1.5-6x42, 2.5-8x48 and 3-12x5 with helical eyepieces, resettable windage/elevation dials and lighted reticles. In the Unipoint series, an electronic rear-plane dot stays a constant size, while the first-plane main reticle maintains a relationship with the target as you change power. Doctor's magnesium-frame binoculars (8x42, 10x42 and 8x58) feature a central diopter dial with a vernier scale that helps you achieve precise focus to just 3 feet! Merkel-usa.com and docter-germany.com

GREYBULL PRECISION

John Burns is a Wyoming gun-builder who, with Coloradans Scott Downs and Don Ward, runs GreyBull Precision. The product: mid-weight hunting rifles for hunters who want to shoot far. The firm contracts with Leupold to install its own reticle in Leupold's 4.5-14x VX III sight. The GreyBull reticle is a Duplex with fine horizontal lines for range estimation, and one-minute tics to help you shade for wind. Each sight is set up for a specific load and marked so you can quickly dial the distance and hold center. Adjusting windage dials, most hunters agree, is unwise. Wind changes speed and direction, and you can quickly get lost correcting off-zero. Numbers on the dials of GreyBull scopes show minutes of adjustment needed in a 10-mph crosswind. GreyBull can tailor dials to nearly any cartridge. "But ballistic coefficients in catalogs and loading manuals aren't always right," John warns. "If the C number is off a little, you won't notice it out to about 400 yards. But the farther the bullet travels, the steeper its arc, and the more important the accuracy of the data." Third-minute clicks replace standard quarter-minute elevation detents on GreyBull scopes so you can get more distance per dial revolution. Greybullprecision.com.

LEICA

This storied German firm has up-graded its Geovid range-finding binoculars with the HD fluorite glass of its own Ultravid HD binoculars. These fluorite lenses enhance brightness and resolution, and can reduce overall weight. All four Geovids (8x42, 10x42, 8x56 and 12x56) have alloy frames and deliver accurate reads to 1,200 yards. Duovid dual-power binoculars come in 8+12x42 and 10+15x50 versions. Switch from 8x to 12x (or 10x to 15x) for a close-up view. At 37 and 44 ounces, Duovids aren't light. But they're relatively compact and certainly more portable than spotting scopes. Big news at Leica this year is two rifle-scopes, the company's first under its own logo. The 2.5-10x42 and 3.5-14x42 have 30mm tubes, rear-plane reticles and AquaDura hydrophobic lens coating to shed water. They weigh 15 and 17 ounces, and give you plenty of free tube for rings. Four inches of eye relief make these attractive scopes practical for rifles of heavy recoil. Leica-sportoptics.com.

LEUPOLD

Two years ago Leupold introduced its top-end VX-7 scopes. The low-profile VX-7L, with a concave belly up front, followed. These sights feature European-style eyepieces and "lift and lock" SpeedDial turret knobs. Xtended Twilight glass features scratch-resistant DiamondCoat 2 lens coating. The power ring is matched to a "Ballistic Aiming System" so you can tailor magnification and reticle to the target and the range. Nitrogen was replaced by Argon/Krypton gas to prevent fogging. The VX-7 was joined last year by the VX-3, which replaced the Vari-X III. Nearly 40 models have stainless adjustments that move 1/4, 1/8 and 1/10 m.o.a. per click in standard, competition and target/varmint versions. An improved spring system ensures precise erector movement. The fast-focus eyepiece has a rubber ring. These features also appear on new fixed-power FX-3 6x42, 6x42 AO, 12x40 AO and on 25x40 AO and 30x40 AO metallic silhouette scopes. Leupold gives you 18 reticle options for the VX-3 and FX-3 series, For the popular AR-10 and AR-15 rifles, there's a new Mark AR series: 1.5-4x20, 3-9x40, 4-12x40 and 6-18x40. The Mark 4 tactical line includes an ER/T M1 4.5-14x50 sight with front-plane reticle. Leupold's new pocket range-finders, the RX-1000 and RX-1000 TBS, boast higher light transmission. Leupold.com.

MEOPTA

After 77 years building high-quality optics, Meopta has just introduced a series of 1-inch rifle-scopes for the American market. The MeoPro 3-9x42,

LEUPOLD MARK 6-18X40

4-12x50 and 6-18x50 have handsome profiles and plenty of free tube. Compact eyepieces permit forward mounting. The 6-18x50 wears a parallax dial on the turret. "MB550 Ion Assisted" lens coatings boost light transmission. These Czech scopes complement three new binoculars: 6.5x32, 8x42 and 10x42. That 6.5x, with its wide field and great depth of focus, is just what hunters need in cover – and has plenty of power for most open-country hunting. Meopta lines include 30mm MeoStar variable rifle-scopes. The newest R1 series comprises seven models, from 1-4x22 to 4-16x44. Meostar S1 spotting scopes (75mm objective) come with standard or APO glass, straight or angled eyepiece, and 30x, 30x wide-angle or 20-60x zoom eyepiece. Meopta.com.

NIGHTFORCE

Since 1993, more world records in long-range Benchrest events have been set with Nightforce scopes than with any other. The 8-32x56 and 12-42x56 Precision Benchrest models have resettable dials with 1/8-minute clicks, plus glass-etched illuminated reticles. Their four-times magnification range is shared by the NXS series, from 3.5-15x50 to 12-42x56. Compact scopes for hunting are new at Nightforce. The 1-4x24, 2.5-10x2 and, now, a 2.5-10x32 weigh just over a pound with turret-mounted focus/parallax dials and 30mm bronze alloy tubes. A new 3.5-15x50 F1 with first-plane reticle serve hunters who want the reticle to stay in constant relationship to the target. Nightforce lists 11 illuminated reticles, distinctive and appealing because they cover little of the field. Long-range shooters can specify a turret with 1-minute elevation and half-minute windage graduations, for big changes in yardage with short dial movement. A "zero-stop" turret has an elevation dial that can be set to return to any of 400 detents in its range. All Nightforce rifle-scopes endure rigorous tests. Each must remain leak- and fog-proof after submersion in 100 feet of water for 24 hours, freezing in a box at a minus 80 degrees F, then heating to 250 degrees F. Every scope gets pounded in a device that delivers 1,250 Gs, backward and forward. Lens coatings must pass mil-spec abrasion tests. The Idaho firm also has scope mounts and rings in five heights. Unimount, machined from 7075-T6 alloy, boasts titanium crossbolts and a 20-minute taper for long shots. Nightforce has produced a Ballistic Program for Windows and pocket PCs. Nightforceoptics.com.

NIGHTFORCE COMPACT 2.5-10X32

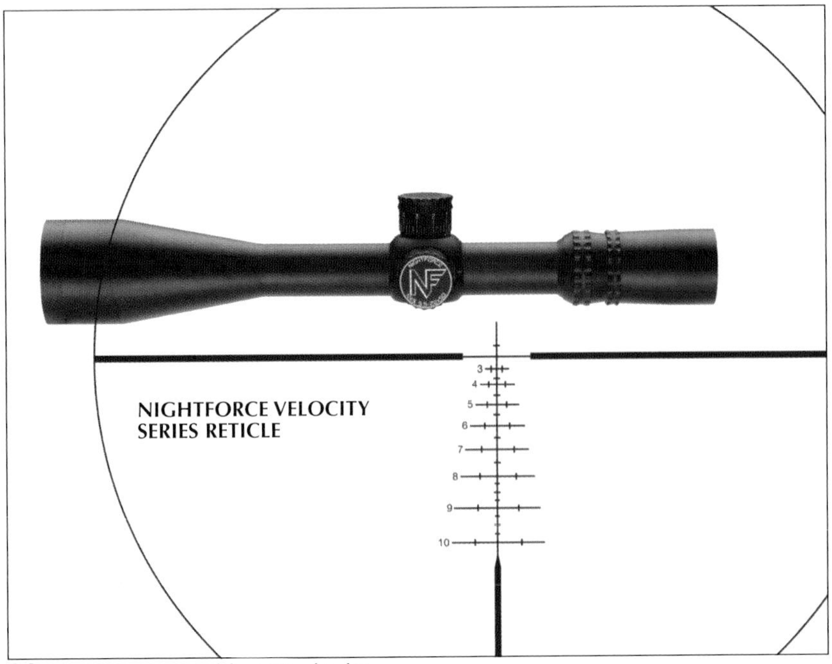

NIGHTFORCE VELOCITY SERIES RETICLE

NIKON

Biggest news for this optics giant may be its rifle ballistics program, which you can access without charge from Nikon's website. Specify a cartridge, bullet type and velocity to get down-range speed and energy data. Plug in a zero range, and you see the bullet's arc. Or work backward to find the sight-in range that gives you longest point-blank distance. The program has a database with dozens of popular centerfire rounds. Nikon rifle-scopes now include an M-223 series for AR shooters. BDC reticles for the 2-8x and 3-12x are tailored for popular AR-15 loads. The Monarch line remains Nikon's flagship, with "African" and "Long Range" subsets. The 1-4x20 has a 1-inch tube, the 1.1-4x24 a 30mm. Both provide 4 inches of eye relief. The African scopes round out a series tilted to high-power optics by the recent debut of an 8-32x50ED SF with 1/8-minute clicks. Omega and Slughunter 1.65-5x36 scopes have 5 inches of eye relief, and BDC reticles. Omega's parallax setting is 100 yards, that of the SlugHunter 75. For 2010 the value-oriented ProStaff stable

NIKON M223

NIKON PROSTAFF 4-12X40

includes a 4-12x40. Nikon also lists two new range-finders. Carriage-class EDG binoculars (7x42, 8x42, 10x42, 8x32, 10x32) have an open-bridge design and a locking diopter – plus the ED lenses also used in the EDG Fieldscope, 85mm or 65mm. Nikonhunting.com.

PENTAX

A new series of value-priced rifle-scopes called the GameSeeker II head the list of new Pentax optics for 2010. Six models, from the 3-9x40 to a light-grabbing 2.5-10x56, feature one-piece, 1-inch alloy tubes, fully multi-coated optics and finger-adjustable windage and elevation dials. Reticle options: a standard plex or the Precision Plex BDC. Last year Pentax has introduced a 3-15x50 GameSeeker with five-times magnification. Now you can choose from eight 1-inch variable GameSeekers, plus 4x32 and 6x42 fixed-power sights. Variables in the 30mm Lightseeker 30 series include a 3-10x40, 4-16x50, 6-24x50 and 8.5-32x50. Pentax's PF-63 Zoom spotting scope with integral 20-50x eyepiece complements the PF-80ED and PF-100ED with interchangeable eyepieces. Pentaxsportoptics.com.

REDFIELD

It has an unlikely new home. Last year the Redfield brand was bought by Leupold, which promptly began manufacturing a fresh line of Redfield rifle-scopes in its Beaverton, Oregon plant. Starting at just $160, the 2-7x33, 3-9x40, 3-9x50 and 4-12x40 "Revolution" scopes have fully multi-coated optics and finger-adjustable dials. A classic profile, satin finish and generous eye relief add curb appeal. Three knurled rings on the eyepiece are signature Redfield. Subdued red logos grace the turret and objective bell. Pick a 4-Plex reticle or a range-finding "Accu-Range" with a circle at the center. At 4x the circle subtends one foot at 100 yards. There's a dot on the wire, for aim to 400 yards with many cartridges. Redfield.com.

SCHMIDT & BENDER

A small company by most standards, S&B still caters to people who want the very best in optical

REDFIELD REVOLUTION 2-7X33

sights. Last year S&B announced its first 1-inch rifle-scope for the American market. The 16-ounce 2.5-10x40 Summit has a rear-plane reticle and precise finger-adjust dials. The company has brought innovation to the tactical table with a 3-12x recently adopted by the U.S. Marine Corps for its 30- and 50-caliber sniper rifles. S&B's 34mm Police/Marksman scopes rank among the most sophisticated in the industry. Lighted mil dot reticles, as on the 4-16x42 P/M II, feature 11-setting turret-mounted rheostats. The automatic shutoff saves battery while the previous setting automatically engages when you hit the illumination switch again. A side-mounted parallax knob hides the battery cage. Windows on "Posicon" windage and elevation adjustments show where the reticle is in its adjustment range. Flash-Dot reticles incorporate a beam-splitter to illuminate a center dot, which vanishes at a touch if you want only a black reticle. The Police/Marksman line now comprises 17 scopes with 30mm and 34mm tubes. The latest is a 5-25x56 PM II with locking turrets. Schmidt-bender.de or (U.S. importer) scopes@cyberportal.net

SCHMIDT & BENDER 5-25X56PMII

SCHMIDT & BENDER 1-8X24 SHORT DOT

SHEPHERD

A front-plane reticle grows in apparent size as you dial up the power but stays the same size in relation to the target. As a range-finding device, it gives you the same picture no matter the magnification. But at long range, where targets appear small and you need precise aim, the reticle can obscure the target. Up close, when you power down for shots in thickets, the reticle becomes too fine to see quickly. A second-plane reticle stays the same apparent size throughout the power range, so it won't hide distant targets at high magnification, and it won't vanish when you turn down the power to see close targets fast. But in practice, a second-plane reticle limits range-finding to one power setting. Shepherd scopes offer both reticles, including range-finding rings that you can read at any power setting. Superimposed, the reticles appear as one. To determine yardage, match a deer-size (18-inch) target with one of the rings. Correct holdover is factored in because the circles are stacked to compensate for bullet drop. The 6-18x M556 Shepherd is designed for AR-style rifles. Shepherdscopes.com.

SIGHTRON

Several rifle-scopes joined the Sightron family in 2010. The SIII Tactical Fixed Power stable comprises 10x, 16x, and 20x scopes with 42mm objectives, 30mm tubes. An SII 1.25-5x20 Dangerous Game sight with over 6 inches of clear tube has replaced the 2.5x20. Dot reticles come in scopes like the 5-20x42. Sightron's Hunter Holdover reticle incorporates a couple of simple hash marks on the lower wire. Specify it on 3-9x42, 3-12x42 and 45.5-14x42 SIIs, and on the 3-9x40 SI. Sightron lists more than 50 scopes in its SI, SII and SIII series. Long Range models feature 30mm tubes, target knobs and turret-mounted parallax dials. Reticles include a mil dot and an illuminated German #4A. From the 3.5-10x44 to the 8-32x56, these scopes feature fully multi-coated optics in one-piece tubes, with resettable ExacTrack windage and elevation adjustments and a fast-focus eyepiece. External lenses wear "Zact-7," a seven-layer coating to reduce light loss. A hydrophobic wash disperses rain. New SIIIMS magnesium-frame binoculars (8x32, 10x32, 8x42 and 10x42) weigh 20 to 25 ounces. Sightron.com.

SWAROVSKI

The Z6 rifle-scope line at Swarovski has grown to include 2.5-15x56 and 2.5-15x44 sights. All 30mm Z6 scopes also come in illuminated versions. The switch atop the eyepiece has an automatic shutoff and two memory locations, one for daytime, one for night use. The 1-6x24 Z6 has the broadest power range of any "dangerous game" sight. At 4¾ inches, its eye relief is most generous. Swarovski's new Z5 rifle-scopes offer five-times magnification in 1-inch tubes. A 3-15x42 may be the perfect scope for shooters who want the greatest versatility in a relatively lightweight scope. Swarovski borrowed from subsidiary Kahles to install a Ballistic Turret that can store several zero settings. If you change loads or zero after sighting in, you can return to the original setting instantly. Ballistic Turret is offered on selected Swarovski scopes. Another long-range option: the BR reticle with ladder-type reticle. BR is available in three AV models, plus 1.7-10x42 and 2-12x50 Z6 rifle-scopes. Swarovskioptik.com.

TRIJICON

The AccuPoint is Trijicon's main hunting optic, a scope with two sources of reticle illumination. The fiber optic window in the ocular bell complements tritium in the reticle itself. A rotating cover lets you control light from the fiber optic coil. Last year, after selling more than half a million ACOGs (Advanced Combat Optical Gunsights) to military units, Trijicon ramped up its marketing efforts to civilian shooters. Now it offers plex and crosswire-and-dot reticles as alternatives to its original super-fast delta, available in red, green and amber. Trijicon's fully multi-coated glass gives you brilliant, razor-edged images. Besides the versatile 3-9x40 AccuPoint, you can choose a 1.25-4x24 or a 2.5-10x56 with 1-inch tube. A 1-4x24 and a powerful 5-20x50 have 30mm tubes. For quick shots in thickets, Trijicon builds reflex sights with lighted dots of various sizes. The RMR (Ruggedized Miniature Reflex)

SWAROVSKI Z5 3.5-18X44

SWAROVSKI BALLISTIC TURRET

can be ordered with a light-emitting diode that automatically adjusts to incident light. The battery-free RMR uses tritium and fiber optics only; an electronic version is powered by a 17,000-hour lithium battery. Trijicon.com.

TRUGLO

On the heels of its shotgun beads and rifle-sight inserts with tritium and fiber-optic elements, TruGlo is making red dot sights and rifle-scopes. Waterproof and compatible with any Weaver-style mount, the red dot sights come in 1-inch and 30mm and 40mm tubes – also in lightweight reflex form. All versions of the tube sight have unlimited eye relief, multi-coated lenses, click-stop windage/elevation dials, an 11-level rheostat to control reticle brightness. Some offer instant selection of reticle color. Reflex sights weigh as little as 2 ounces, carry a 4-minute dot with manual and light-sensitive automatic brightness modes. TruGlo markets several series of rifle-scopes, topped by the Maxus XLE in 1.5-6x44, 3-9x44 and 3.5-10x50. Tru-Brite Xtreme Illuminated rifle-scopes feature dual-color plex and range-finding reticles. There are scopes for muzzleloaders, even crossbows. TruGlo 's line of illuminated iron sights includes a green fiber optic AR-15 gas-block front sight. Truglo.com.

VORTEX

The boom in tactical rifles prompted Vortex to introduce New Razor scopes for AR enthusiasts. The 1.4-4x24 has a 30mm tube, the 5-20x50 a 35mm tube. Both feature extra-low-dispersion lenses. Illuminated, etched-glass reticles lie in the first focal plane. A zero-stop mechanism prevents the elevation dial from passing the sight-in setting, for fast return to zero. Pick mil-dot graduations or minutes of angle. Vortex Vipers (also available in tactical form) come in six versions, five power ranges. Reticle options include dot, BDC and mil-dot, in 30mm and 1-inch tubes. More affordable Vortex Diamondbacks have 1-inch tubes only. So do entry-level Crossfire scopes. That line features 2-7x32 and 4x32 sights for rimfires, a 2x20 handgun scope and a 3x32 for crossbows. Specify a mil dot or illuminated mil dot reticle on the 6-24x50 AO scope for varmint rifles. Vortex also lists a red dot sight, the Strikefire, with fully multi-coated lenses. Choose red or green dot to suit conditions. In spotting scopes, the20-60x80 and budget-priced 20-60x60 accept adapters for pocket-size digital cameras. The top-end Razor HD boasts apochromatic lenses, coarse and fine focusing, an 85mm objective. It weighs 66 ounces with a 20-60x eyepiece. Vortex.com.

WEAVER

The 330 scope Bill Weaver designed 80 years ago started a popular trend away from iron sights For 2010 Weaver is re-introducing the iconic steel-tube K4 that followed the 330 and for decades defined the big game hunting scope. The new version has fully multi-coated glass and modern innards with permanently centered Dual-X reticle. Weaver also just announced a 1-5x24 Dangerous Game Super Slam scope with thick Dual-X. Besides Grand Slam, Classic V, Classic K and T series, there's now a Buck Commander line, with 2.5-10x42, 3-12x50 and 4-16x42 models. Prices start at just $280. For close shooting, Weaver offers a red/green dot sight with five brightness settings. It has a 30mm tube, an integral Weaver-style base. The firm's 4-20x50 Tactical scope, fresh in 2009, features a 30mm tube, front-plane mil dot reticle and side-focus parallax dial. But you can still buy K-series fixed-power scopes (still great bargains too!). Classic binoculars have been added to Weaver's line this year: 8x32, 8x36, 8x42 and 10x42. Incidentally, ATK, parent to several brands, has folded its

TRUGLO MAXUS XLE

TRUGLO TRU-BRITE XTREME RIFLE SCOPE

WEAVER 1-5X24 DANGEROUS GAME

Nitrex optics into the Weaver family, albeit the lines remain separate. Nitrex TR One scopes (similar to the Weaver Grand Slams) are joined by TR Two (Super Slam) scopes with additional reticles: glass-etched EBX (ballistic), dot and illuminated. These sights boast five-times magnification – 2.5-10x42 to 4-20x50 – and turret parallax dials. Pull-up, resettable w/e knobs need no caps. Weaveroptics.com, Nitrexoptics.com.

ZEISS

The three newest Zeiss rifle-scopes all fatten the top-end Victory line, with magnification to help you hit ill-defined targets far off. The husky 6-24x72, a 34mm scope, debuted in 2005 but now features quarter-minute clicks and FL glass. It and the new 6-24x56 and 4-16x50 deliver brilliant, tack-sharp images – like the proven and less specialized Victory 2.5-10x42. The good news in Recession Bleakdom is that Zeiss's economical 1-inch Conquest sights offer almost everything you get in a Victory. And, Zeiss has just cut the list price on its 3-9x40 Conquest from $499 to $399! A new Compact Point red dot sight has a 3.5-minute dot with five brightness levels. Weight: less than 3 ounces with two 3V lithium batteries. Zeiss still tops the field of laser-ranging scopes, with its 3-12x56 Diarange. Varipoint models combine a rear-plane illuminated dot with a front-plane black reticle. The 8x45 and 10x45 T* RF binoculars introduced last year lure shooters with a laser ranging unit that requires no "third eye" emitter but delivers 1,300-yard range on reflective targets. This unit is fast – you get a read in about a second. Its LED self-compensates for brightness. The binocular itself has peerless optics, with rain-repellent LotuTec coating on ocular and objective lenses. (Program the RF with computer data to get holdover for six standard bullet trajectories.) The Zeiss PhotoScope is a 20-60x80 Diascope with 7-megapixel digital camera built in. Its 15-45x power range matches a 600-1800mm zoom in a 35mm camera. The field sweeps 68 degrees at 15x! Zeiss.com.

ZEISS COMPACT POINT RED DOT SIGHT

ZEISS VICTORY FL DIAVARI 4-16X50

NEW Products: AMMUNITION AND COMPONENTS

BARNES TRIPLE SHOCK (TSX) BULLETS

BARNES BULLETS

The Triple-Shock X-Bullet powers on in 2010, with and without the recently introduced polymer tip. The new offerings range in weight from a 50-grain .224 (flat-base) to a 350-grain .375 (flat-base). There's a 200-grain .308 tipped boat-tail and a 285 .338 boat-tail, even a 300-grain tipped boat-tail for the .458 SOCOM, plus sleek new TSX offerings in .264, .277, .284 and .323. Barnes has also expanded its stable of jacketed hard-cast handgun bullets. New Barnes Busters include: 300-grain .429, 325-grain .454, 400-grain .458 (for .45-70s) and .400-grain .500. Barnes also catalogs Varmint Grenade and Multi-Purpose Green rifle bullets, Expander MZ and Spit-Fire MZ, TMZ and T-EZ muzzleloader bullets, plus its Banded Solids and the lead-core Barnes Original. Five TAC bullets – four for rifles, one for handguns – serve the military and law enforcement contingents. Barnesbullets.com.

BLACK HILLS

High product quality and fast service with a personal touch have catapulted Black Hills Ammunition from a backroom handloading enterprise using once-fired brass to a manufacturing firm with a new (renovated) facility that turns out – in huge quantities – first-cabin rifle and pistol ammo for hunters, target shooters, the Cowboy Action clan, law enforcement agencies and military units. This year, Jeff and Kristi Hoffman have added to the14 loads cataloged for the .223. A new 62-grain Barnes TSX offering at 3,100 fps will get the attention of both hunters and people who need a rifle for LE work or home defense. It works well in barrels cut with 1-in-7 to 1-in-9 twist. In flesh, it typically opens to double its original diameter. Other Black Hills .223 loads feature bullets from 36 to 77 grains. The impressive line of Cowboy Action loads includes traditional rounds like the .38-40, .38 Long Colt, .44 Russian and the .38-55 rifle cartridge. New for 2010 in the centerfire stable is a 300-grain MatchKing at 2,725 fps in .338 Lapua. Black-Hills.com.

COR-BON

Known for specialty bullets, such as the shot-filled Glaser Safety Slug for Sky Marshal handgun ammo, Cor-Bon has deep roots in the development of hunting handgun bullets and cartridges (the .500 S&W, for example). Now it has an extensive line of loaded ammo, for defensive pistol (jacketed hollowpoints in .32 Auto to 10mm Auto), hunting handgun (.357 Magnum to .454 Casull), hunting rifle (.223 to .375) and match purposes. Cor-Bon loads its Pow'RBall bullet (a polymer ball capping a hollowpoint nose) in auto pistol cartridges for smooth feeding, deeper penetration. The Safety Slug appears in rounds from .25 Auto to .30-06. The DPX line of handgun ammo features solid-copper hollowpoints. So does the DPX rifle line (Barnes TSX). Cor-Bon includes Glaser and Dakota Ammunition in its Sturgis SD facility. Corbon.com.

ENVIRON-METAL

Makers of Hevi-Shot, this company now loads No. 7 pellets in its Hevi-13 line. The 20-gauge 3-inch has 1¼ ounces, the 12 3-inch and 3½-inch hold 2 and 2¼ ounces. No. 7 is also an option in the Classic Doubles series. Magnum Blend 12-bore 3- and 3½-inch loads contain No. 5, 6, and 7 shot, proportioned to improve pattern density. Environ-Metal has extended its market reach with Dead Coyote loads that hurl heavy charges of 00 Buckshot from 3 ½-inch 12- and 10-gauge shells. Hevishot.com.

FEDERAL

News from Federal typically captures not just headlines but the whole front page. In brief, the Minnesota firm, now an arm of ATK, has these notable entries for 2010: Prairie Storm shotshells with FliteControl wads and mixed shot charges comprising 70 percent copper-plated lead and 30 percent nickel-plated lead, come in 12 and 20 gauge, shot sizes 4, 5 and 6. Black Cloud Snow Goose FS Steel loads (3-inch 12-bore) launch 1⅛ ounces of 2s or BBs at 1,635 fps. Personal Defense

FEDERAL PERSONAL DEFENSE SHOTSHELLS

FEDERAL PRAIRIE STORM SHOTSHELLS

FEDERAL PREMIUM SAFARI CAPE SHOK CENTERFIRE CARTRIDGES

shells in 12 and 20 feature 34 and 24 No. 4 buckshot, respectively, and two new 3-inch .410 loads serve the Taurus Judge revolver. Varmint hunters get 30- and 32-grain Speer TNT Green bullets in .22 Hornet and .204 Ruger, plus a new .220 Swift load with a 50-grain Sierra BlitzKing. The Vital-Shok big game line is now includes a 140 Trophy Bonded Tip bullet in 7mm Remington Magnum and 7mm WSM. The .30-06 comes with a 110-grain Barnes TTSX. The TSX bullet has joined the Premium Safari stable in 9.3x62, 9.3x74, .470 N.E. and .500 N.E. All big-bore rounds except the .370 Sako are available with Swift A-Frame bullets and Barnes Banded Solids. Handgunners will find six new potent revolver loads with Swift A-Frames. Shotgunners who favor slugs for deer can now load a harder, high-antimony TruBall 12-gauge copper-plated slug. Also new : Federal components, from Trophy Bonded bullets to rifle and handgun brass. Federalpremium.com.

FIOCCHI

Dating to 1877, the Fiocchi enterprise served the European ammunition market. A partnership with S&W during the 1950's put Fiocchi manufacturing on U.S. soil, in Illinois. Subsequently the firm withdrew to the Old Country, returning Stateside in 1984. Known best for its shotshells and rimfire ammo, Fiocchi put more resources into the North American market, expanding its line into pistol and centerfire rifle rounds. In the last five years, Fiocchi of America (FOA) sales have increased 500 percent. New for 2010 are loads for the .222, .223, .204 Ruger, .22-250, .30-30, .308 and .30-06. Handgunners get the 9x19 (9mm Luger) and 7mm Penna, a novel IPSC cartridge with a .277 bullet for use in STI guns. Shot loads include Tundra composition shot in three densities, 12-gauge only in 2¾- and 3-inch shells. Tundra will also debut in 20 and 28 gauge ammunition. Target shooters will have new 12-bore paper loads with 1- and 1⅛ ounces of shot, and Light White Rino competition shells. Fiocchi rifle ammo includes lead-free and match bullet options. The pistol category comprises five types of ammo, notably a Classic line for old rounds like the .455 Webley. Fiocchi also offers cartridge components to handloaders. Fiocciusa.com.

FUSION

This ATK product was developed in by Federal's research and development team, but it's now marketed separately. For 2010 Fusion plated bullets are new in.22-250 (50-grain), 7mm-08 (120-grain), 7.62x39 (123-grain) and .35 Whelen (180-grain). There's a 325-grain load for the .500 S&W as well, and Fusion slugs in 12- and 20-bore shells, 2 ¾ and 3 inches. The Fusion line came about as a hunter's alternative to more costly bullet types. Fusion bullets have proven deadly on deer! Fusionammo.com.

HODGDON (AND

FUSION RIFLE AMMUNITION

FUSION SLUG

FUSION PISTOL AMMUNITION

IMR AND WINCHESTER) POWDERS

The Hodgdon firm has grown. "We market about 120 types of powder," says J.B. Hodgdon. That includes IMR and Winchester powders now, and accounts for about 70 percent of the market. Bruce Hodgdon's business began 60 years ago with just one powder: war-surplus H4895. To sell it, he advertised a special package with primers, then hard to find. Bruce offered a 150-pound keg and 15,000 primers for $49.95!

H4831 came next. Developed for 20mm cannons, it was available in huge quantities after WW II. Newly manufactured powders have since become the focus at Hodgdon. For 2010 there's IMR 8208 XBR, a fuel especially useful in the .204 Ruger and the .223 and .22-250 Remington. It's also ideal for the short 6mms and the .308. IMR 8208 XBR meters well and performs across a wide temperature range. Lab tests show no appreciable change in bullet velocity from minus 40 F to 165 F! IMRpowder.com.

HORNADY

The LeverEvolution series of ammunition that gave a huge boost to the performance – and popularity – of traditional lever-action rifles keeps getting longer. For 2010 FlexTip technology is combined with the lead-free GMX design in a 150-grain .30-30 load and a 250-grain .45-70 load. The Dangerous Game line has a new 286-grain InterLock load for the 9.3x62, a cartridge Europeans have favored for decades on heavy African game. At the other end of the weight spectrum, Hornady has announced .17 Mach 2 and .17 HMR loads with 15.5-grain NTX bullets, a .22WMR offering with a 25-grain NTX. In between, you can find the hard-to-find – such as lads for the 5.45x39, the 6.5 Grendel and, of course, the Hornady's own 6.5 Creedmoor, Critical Defense handgun cartridges now include 125-, 165- and 185-grain loads in .357 Magnum, .40 S&W and .45 ACP, respectively. Handloaders will get new component bullets, in the configurations Hornady favors in loaded ammo. The biggest news this year, though, is Superformance ammunition, the culmination of extensive work at Hornady with more efficient non-canister powders. A handful of cartridges have made the jump; others will follow. Unlike the earlier Light Magnum rounds (and Heavy Magnums), the new Superformance cartridges will cost very little more than standard ammo. But the ballistic advantages are significant: more power, flatter flight, less temperature sensitivity. Look for Hornady to make Superformance the flagship of its centerfire rifle ammunition lines. Hornady.com.

LAPUA

Renowned for its super-accurate rimfire ammo and the .338 Lapua cartridge, this Finnish firm offers a wide selection of hunting and match loads for centerfire rifles, with six bullet types. New in its stable of high-quality brass is the .22-250 and a .308 Palma case with small-rifle primer pocket. Lapua's North American distributors, Kaltrone-Pettibone (IL) and Graf & Sons (MO) also handle an expanding line of Vihta Vuori powders, including 17 for rifles, nine for handguns. Lapua.com.

NORMA

LAPUA .22-250 BRASS

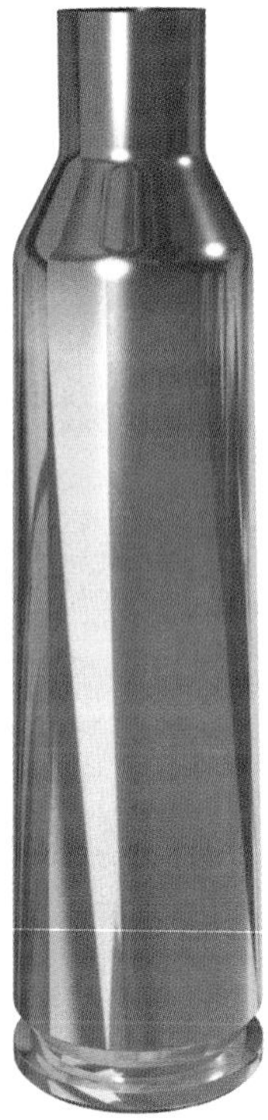

The African PH line of ammunition now includes soft-point and solid loads for eight heavy hitters, from .375 H&H to .505 Gibbs. Fetchingly boxed, this ammo is as effective as it is attractive. The belted .308 and .358 Norma Magnums introduced in the early 1960s are due for some companions. Norma is now producing brass for the brand-new .300 and .338 Norma Magnum on a shortened .338 Lapua (or .416 Rigby) case. A .375 Norma Magnum is in the wings. The firm is definitely courting American shooters, with loads that feature bullets from Swift, Nosler, Barnes and Woodleigh. Norma's own Oryx has earned a following too. For 2010 there are 19 new centerfire rifle loads, from .222 Remington to .500 Jeffery – plus brass offerings that include old but dear .300 H&H, .35 Whelen and .375 Weatherby. Norma rocks! Norma.cc.

MAGTECH

Now comprising the box names of CBC, MEN and Sellier & Bellot, the Magtech enterprise has grown to catalog pistol ammunition from .25 Auto to .500 S&W. Bullet options include "green" frangibles (in front of lead-free primers), solid-copper and jacketed hollowpoints, softpoints, wadcutters and lead missiles for Cowboy Action events. Rifle ammo, from .22 Hornet to .50 BMG, features FMJs and hollow-points, soft-points and polymer-tipped bullets, plus Barnes TSX and Sierra GameKing spitzers. The shotshell stable has loads for waterfowl, upland birds, clay targets, with slug and buckshot options for deer. Magtech also sells primers, bullets and cases. Magtechammunition.com.

NOSLER

Now manufacturing ammunition as well as bullets, Nosler has many new offerings for 2010. Companion to the popular Ballistic Tip, the lead-free, frangible Ballistic Tip Varmint comes in .204 (32-grain), .223 (35- and 40-grain) and .243 (55-grain). The Ballistic Silvertip loaded by Winchester is sold by Nosler as a component bullet. The selection now includes a 32-grain .204 and a 180-grain .323.

There's also a round-nose 300 in .458. Nosler's AccuBond stable has a new entry: a 100-grain .277. E-Tip component bullets include new weights in .257, .277, .284, .308 and .323. Handgunners get a 135-grain 10mm JHP. You can now find Trophy Grade ammunition featuring 40-grain .223 and 50-grain .22-250 Ballistic Tip loads, also 6.5x55 and 7mm Remington Magnum with 140 AccuBonds and the .300 Remington Ultra Mag with 180 Partition. A 168-grain .308 load joins the Custom Competition clan. Nosler.com.

PMC

Three years ago, PMC entered into an agreement with Poonsan to increase its market share in the U.S. ammo market. For 2010 PMC has announced five new ammunition lines! Its shotshells include 12, 16, 20, 28 and .410 loads. The Frangible centerfires encompass both pistol and rifle rounds typically used by law enforcement and military units. Precision rifle ammo in .223 and .308 is mainly for target shooting and varmint hunting. It complements the existing hunting rifle offerings and new X-Tac tactical 5.56. Cowboy Action loads in six traditional rifle and revolver chambering have, naturally, distinctive boxes reminiscent of the Old West. PMCammo.com.

REMINGTON

The Premier Copper Solid line of big game centerfire ammo now includes 150-grain .30-30 loads, plus 165s in .30-06, .300 Winchester and .300 Ultra Mag. There's a 250-grain softpoint load for the .338 Marlin Express, a 260 AccuTip for the .450 Bushmaster. The .30 Remington AR gives you four bullet choices now. Remington.com.

WEATHERBY

Just when shooters need help to keep their sport affordable, Weatherby announces new lower-priced ammunition in .257 and .300 Weatherby Magnum. Loaded by Norma of Sweden (which has furnished Weatherby's ammo for decades, the new cartridges feature top-quality components – for just $39 a box, retail. Word is that standard chamberings will soon be available at even lower cost. Weatherby.com.

WINCHESTER

This year marks the 200th anniversary of Oliver F. Winchester's birthday. So the company is marketing a commemorative line of ammunition in .22 Long Rifle, .45 Colt and .30-30. New offerings include Bonded PDX1 cartridges for law enforcement and personal defense. Available in popular handgun rounds, it's an option for shotgun owners too. The 12-gauge load marries a slug with three 00 buckshot pellets; a .410 PDX1 cartridge holds three wafer-like Defense Disks with BB shot. Varmint hunters can tap Winchester's Explosive Technology with fragmenting copper bullets in .223 and .22-250 ammo. Big game enthusiasts will find Power Max Bonded cartridges an economical but accurate, deadly alternative to the Supreme stable. Like the Power-Point, the Power Max Bonded is really a lead-core bullet, but it has its own packaging as loaded ammunition under the Super-X umbrella. Speaking of Supreme, Winchester has announced a new Supreme Elite Dual Bond sabot round that employs a "bullet within a bullet" for deer hunters in shotgun country. Winchester.com.

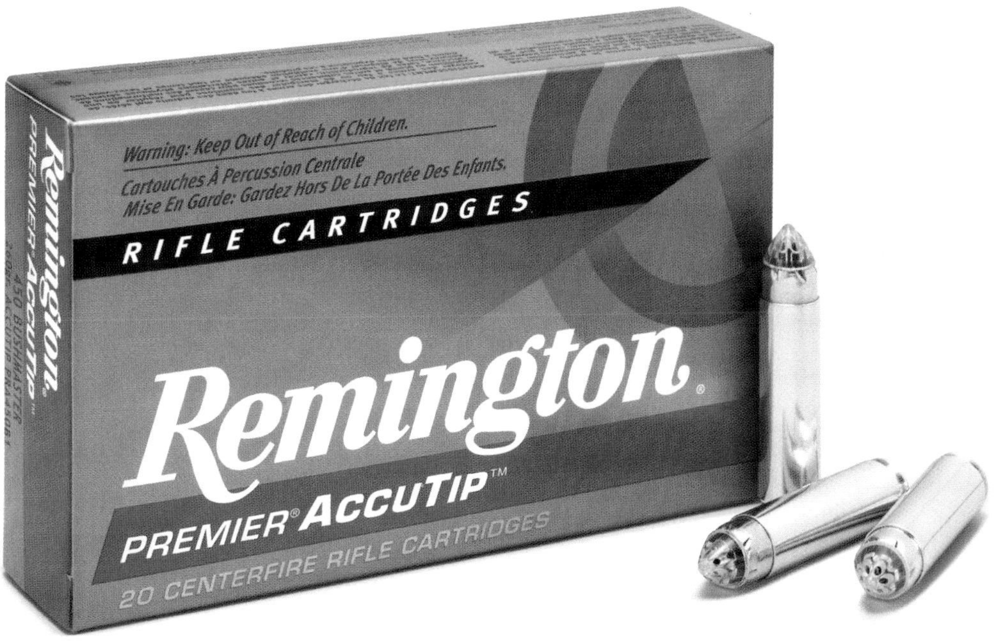

REMINGTON PREMIER .450 BUSHMASTER AMMUNITION WITH ACCUTIP BULLETS

Anschütz Rifles

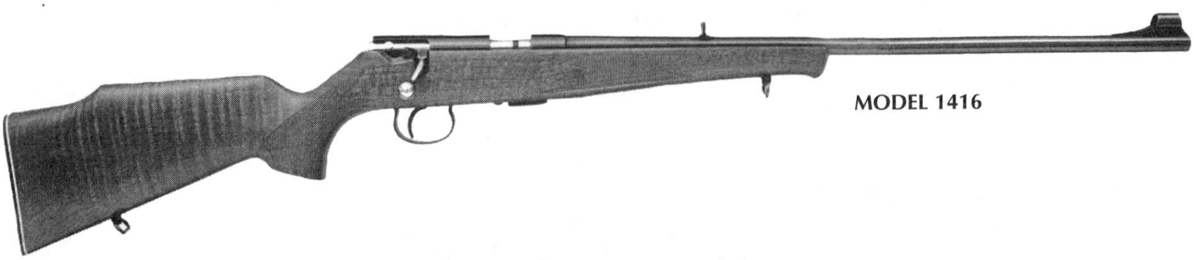

MODEL 1416

1416 D HB

MODEL 1451

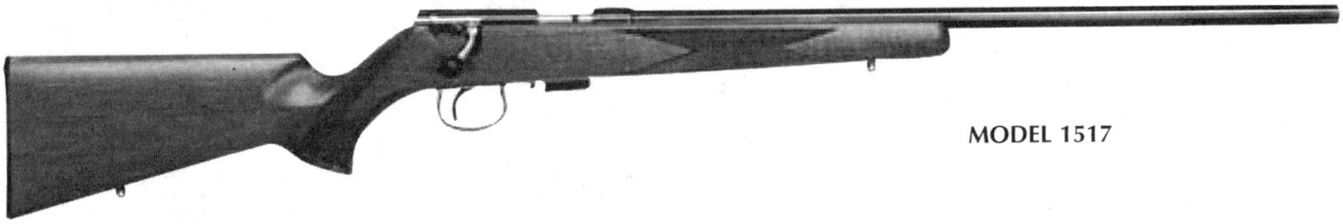

MODEL 1517

MODEL 1416

Action: bolt
Stock: walnut
Barrel: 22 in.
Sights: open
Weight: 5.5 lbs.
Caliber: .22LR, .22 WMR
Magazine: detachable box, 5 rounds .22 LR, 4-round .22 WMR
Features: M64 action; 2-stage match trigger; checkered stock available in classic or Monte Carlo
Classic: $630–795
Monte Carlo: $630–795

1416 D HB, 1502 D HB, 1517 D HB

Action: bolt
Stock: walnut
Barrel: 23 in.
Sights: none
Weight: 6.2 lbs.
Caliber: .22 LR, .17 Mach 2 and .17 HMR, respectively
Magazine: detachable box, 5 rounds
1416 D HB, 1507 D HB,
1517 D HB: $799–1000

MODEL 1451

Action: bolt
Stock: Sporter Target, hardwood
Barrel: heavy 22 in.
Sights: open
Weight: 6.3 lbs.
Caliber: .22 LR
Magazine: detachable box, 10 rounds
Features: M64 action
1451: $397–480

MODEL 1517

Action: bolt
Stock: walnut
Barrel: target-grade sporter, 22 in.
Sights: none
Weight: 6.0 lbs.
Caliber: .17 HMR
Magazine: 4 rounds
Features: M64 action, heavy and sporter barrels; Monte Carlo and Classic stocks available; target-grade barrel; adjustable trigger (2.5 lbs.)
Classic: $899–1079
Monte Carlo: $1139

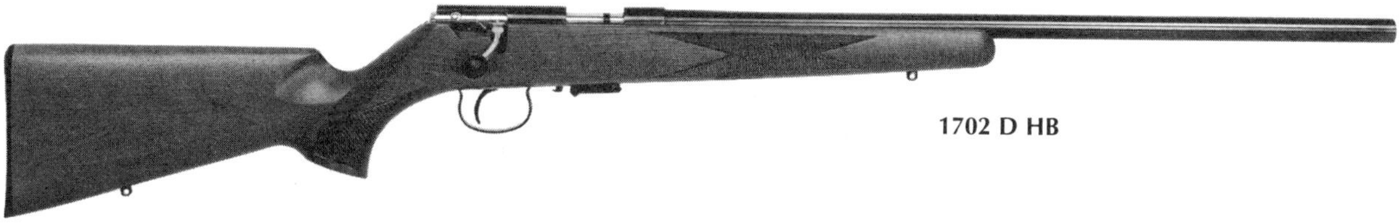

1702 D HB

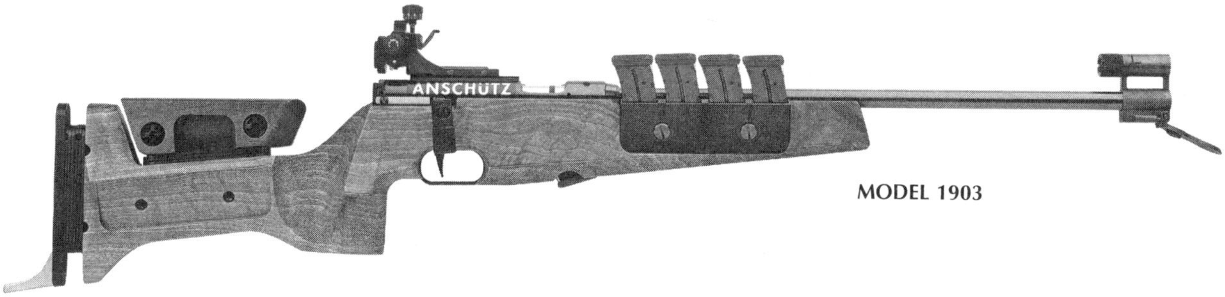

MODEL 1903

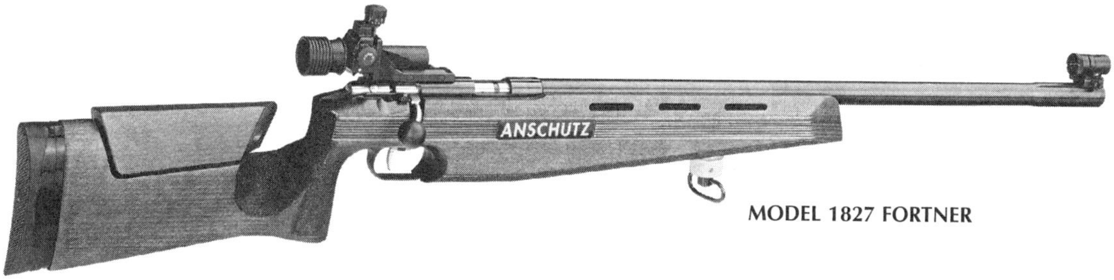

MODEL 1827 FORTNER

MODEL 1710

Action: bolt
Stock: walnut
Barrel: target-grade sporter, 22 in.
Sights: none
Weight: 6.7 lbs
Caliber: .22 LR
Magazine: 5 rounds
Features: M54 action; two-stage trigger; Monte Carlo stock; silhouette stock available

Model 1710: $1095–1595
With fancy wood: $1095–1595
Silhouette Model 1712: $1850

MODEL 1730 AND 1740 CLASSIC SPORTER

Action: bolt
Stock: sporter, walnut
Barrel: 23 in.
Sights: none
Weight: 7.3 lbs.
Caliber: .22 Hornet and .222
Magazine: detachable box, 5 rounds
Features: M54 action; Meister grade about $250 additional

1730 .22 Hornet, Monte Carlo: $1895–2199
1730 .22 Hornet with heavy barrel: $1649–1745

MODEL 1827 FORTNER

Action: bolt
Stock: Biathlon, walnut
Barrel: medium 22 in.
Sights: none
Weight: 8.8 lbs.
Caliber: .22 LR
Magazine: detachable box, 5 rounds
Features: M54 action

1827: $3010–3597
With thumbhole stock: . $3189–3698

MODEL 1903

Action: bolt
Stock: Standard Rifle, hardwood
Barrel: heavy 26 in.
Sights: none
Weight: 10.5 lbs
Caliber: .22 LR
Magazine: none
Features: M64 action; adjustable cheekpiece; forend rail

1903: $1150
Left-hand: $1150

Anschütz Rifles

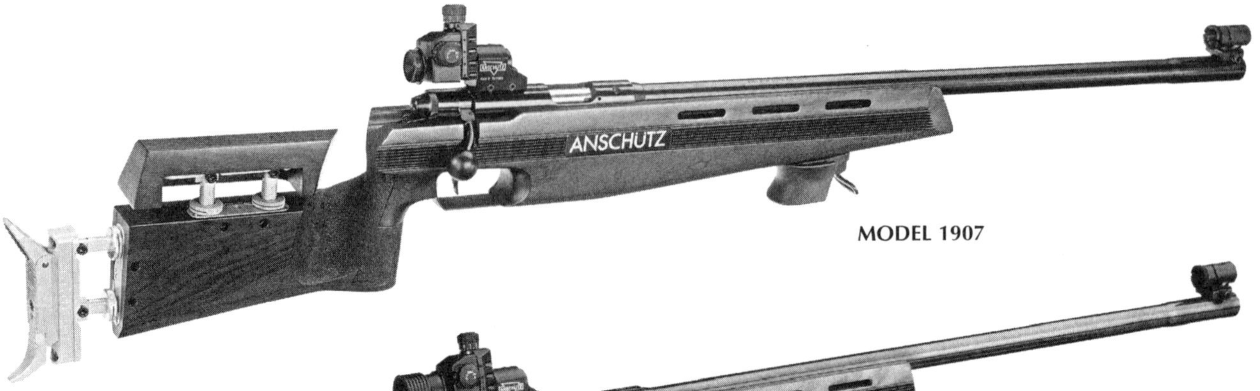

MODEL 1907

MODEL 1912 SPORT

MODEL 1907

Action: bolt
Stock: standard rifle, walnut
Barrel: heavy 26 in.
Sights: none
Weight: 10.5 lbs.
Caliber: .22 LR
Magazine: none
Features: M54 action; adjustable cheekpiece and butt; forend rail
1907: $2365–2975
Left-hand: $2100–2975

MODEL 1912 SPORT

Action: bolt
Stock: International, laminated
Barrel: heavy 26 in.
Sights: none
Weight: 11.4 lbs.
Caliber: .22 LR
Magazine: none
Features: M54 action; adjustable cheekpiece and butt; forend rail
1912: $2400–2600
Left-hand: $2500–2700

Armalite Rifles

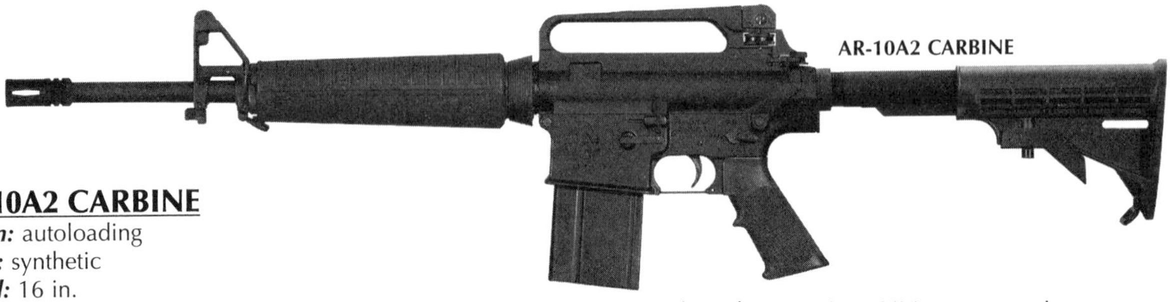

AR-10A2 CARBINE

AR-10A2 CARBINE

Action: autoloading
Stock: synthetic
Barrel: 16 in.
Sights: open
Weight: 9.0 lbs.
Caliber: .308
Magazine: detachable box, 10 rounds
Features: forged A2 receiver; NM two stage trigger; chrome-lined barrel; recoil check muzzle device; green or black synthetic stock
MSRP: $1561

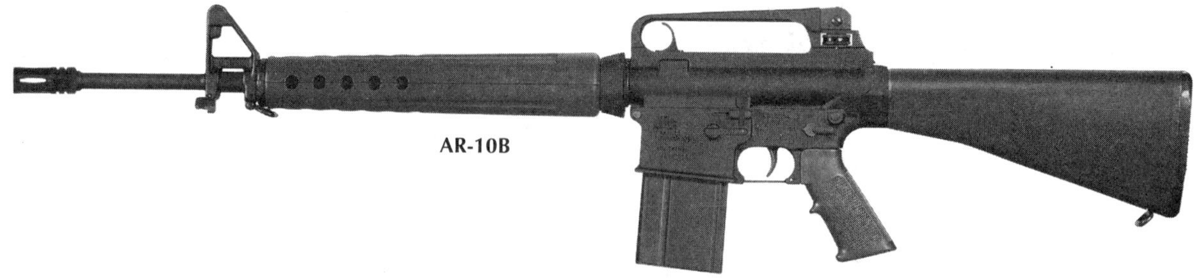

AR-10B

AR-10T

AR-10A4 SPR (SPECIAL PURPOSE RIFLE)

Action: autoloading
Stock: synthetic
Barrel: 20 in.
Sights: none
Weight: 9.6 lbs.
Caliber: .308, .243 WIN
Magazine: detachable box, 10 rounds
Features: forged flattop receiver; chrome-lined heavy barrel; optional recoil-check muzzle device; green or black synthetic stock; Picatinny rail sight base
MSRP: $1300–1500

AR-10B

Action: autoloading
Stock: synthetic
Barrel: 20 in.
Sights: open
Weight: 9.5 lbs.
Caliber: .308
Magazine: detachable box, 20 rounds
Features: multi-slot recoil-check muzzle device; M-16 style front sight base, single stage trigger (two stage NM optional); chrome-lined barrel; forged aluminum upper receiver; M-16 style tapered handguards; AR-10 SOF with M4 type fixed stock
MSRP: $1600

AR-10T AND AR-10A4 CARBINE

Action: autoloading
Stock: synthetic
Barrel: 24 in.; (Carbine: 16 in.)
Sights: open; (Carbine: none)
Weight: 10.4 lbs.; (Carbine: 9 lbs.)
Caliber: .308
Magazine: detachable box, 10 rounds
Features: forged flattop receiver; stainless T heavy barrel; carbine with chrome-lined barrel and recoil check muzzle device; two stage NM trigger
AR-10T: $1892
AR-10A4 Carbine: $1557

AR-10 SUPERSASS

Action: semiautomatic
Stock: composite
Barrel: 24 in. SST T Heavy
Sights: Leupold 3.5 X 10 tactical telescopic sight
Weight: 11.97 lbs.
Caliber: .308 and 7.62mm
Magazine: 10-round box
Features: selectable gas valve; sound suppressor; full-length rail mounting system; adjustable buttstock; main accessories: flip up rear and front sights, high power throw lever rings, Harris bipod and ARMS throw lever adapter; complete rifle system: flip up front and rear sights, Leupold Vari X III 3.5-10X40 scope, high power throw lever rings, Harris bipod and ARMS throw lever adapter, Starlight case, Sniper Cleaning Kit; dummy sound suppressor available for display
MSRP: $3078

Armalite Rifles

AR-30M

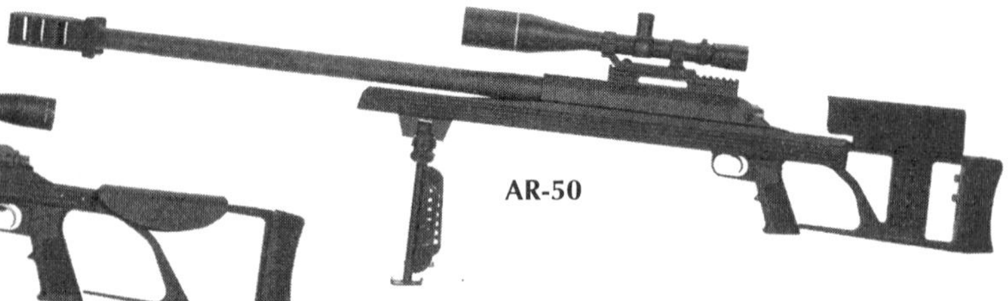

AR-50

M-15 A2 CARBINE

M-15 A4 SPRII

AR-30M RIFLE

Action: bolt
Stock: synthetic
Barrel: 26 in.
Sights: none *Weight:* 12.0 lbs.
Caliber: .300 Win Mag, .308 Win, .338 Lapua
Magazine: detachable box
Features: triple-lapped match grade barrel; manganese phosphated steel and hard anodized aluminum finish; forged and machined removable buttstock; available with bipod adapter, scope rail and muzzle brake; receiver drilled and slotted for scope rail

.308 Win & .300 Win Mag: . . . $1742
.338 Lapua: $1882

AR-50

Action: bolt
Stock: synthetic *Barrel:* 31 in.
Sights: none *Weight:* 35.0 lbs.
Caliber: .50BMG *Magazine:* none
Features: receiver drilled and slotted for scope rail; Schillen standard single stage trigger; vertically adjustable buttplate; vertical pistol grip; manganese phosphated steel and hard anodized aluminum finish; available in right- or left-handed version

MSRP: $3359

M-15 A2, M-15 A2 CARBINE AND M-15 A2 NATIONAL MATCH RIFLE

Action: autoloading
Stock: synthetic
Barrel: 16 in., (M-15A2), 20 in.
Sights: open
Weight: 7.0 lbs. (Carbine); 8.27 lbs.
Caliber: .223 REM
Magazine: detachable box, 10 rounds; 7 rounds (Carbine)
Features: forged A2 receiver; heavy, stainless, chrome-lined floating match barrel; recoil check muzzle device; green or black synthetic stock; Carbine with M-16 style front sight base; National Match Rifle with NM two stage trigger and NM sleeved floating barrel; M-15 A4 (T) with flattop receiver and tubular handguard

M-15A2: $1150
Carbine: $1150
National Match Rifle: $1388

M-15 A4 SPR II (SPECIAL PURPOSE RIFLE)

Action: autoloading
Stock: synthetic
Barrel: 20 in.
Sights: none
Weight: 9.0 lbs.
Caliber: .308, .243 WIN
Magazine: detachable box, 10 rounds
Features: forged flattop receiver; NM sleeved floating stainless barrel; Picatinny rail; two stage trigger; green or black synthetic stock; Picatinny gas block front sight base

M-15 A4 SPR 11: $1413

Auto-Ordnance Rifles

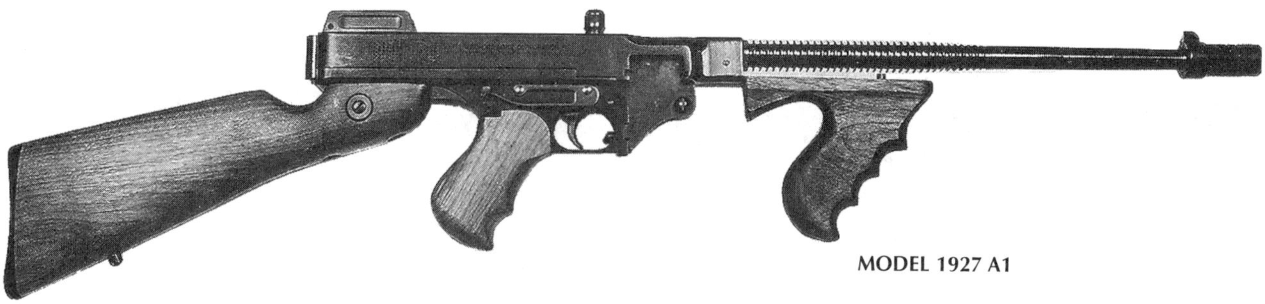

MODEL 1927 A1

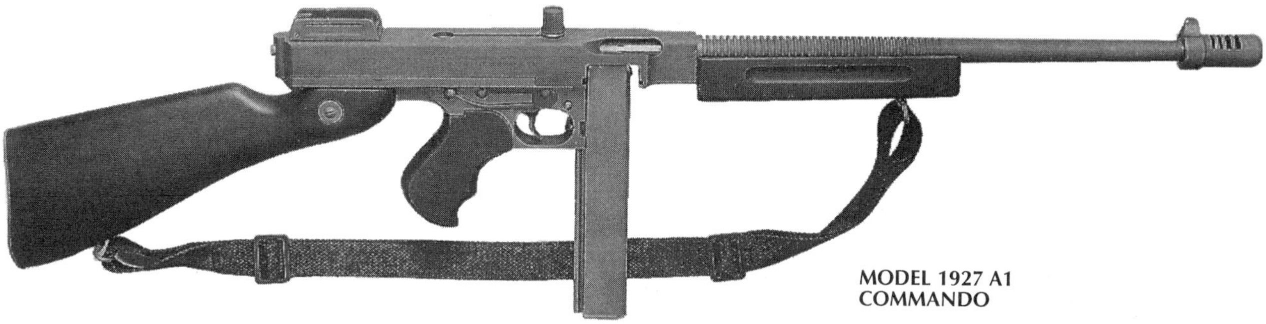

MODEL 1927 A1
COMMANDO

RIFLES

MODEL 1927 A1

Action: autoloading
Stock: walnut, vertical foregrip
Barrel: 16 in.
Sights: open
Weight: 13.0 lbs.
Caliber: .45 ACP
Magazine: detachable box, 20-rounds
Features: top-cocking, autoloading blowback; lightweight version 9.5 lbs.
Standard:............ $1420–2000
Lightweight:.......... $1286–1699

MODEL 1927 A1 COMMANDO

Action: autoloading
Stock: walnut, horizontal fore-grip
Barrel: 16 in.
Sights: open
Weight: 13.0 lbs.
Caliber: .45 ACP
Magazine: detachable box, 20-rounds
Features: top-cocking, autoloading blowback; carbine version with side-cocking lever, 11.5 lbs.
1927: $1393
Carbine: $1393

It is not as essential for your rifle to shoot quarter-inch, half-inch or even one-inch groups as it is to really know what you and your rifle are capable of under ideal conditions. This builds confidence and lets you know what you can and cannot attempt in the field. Spend as much time shooting across a solid bench rest with good ammo as you can and really get to know your rifle.

Barrett Rifles

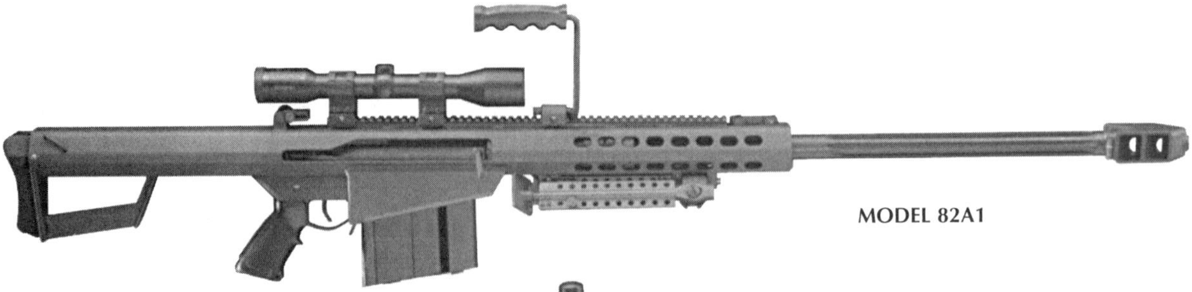

MODEL 82A1

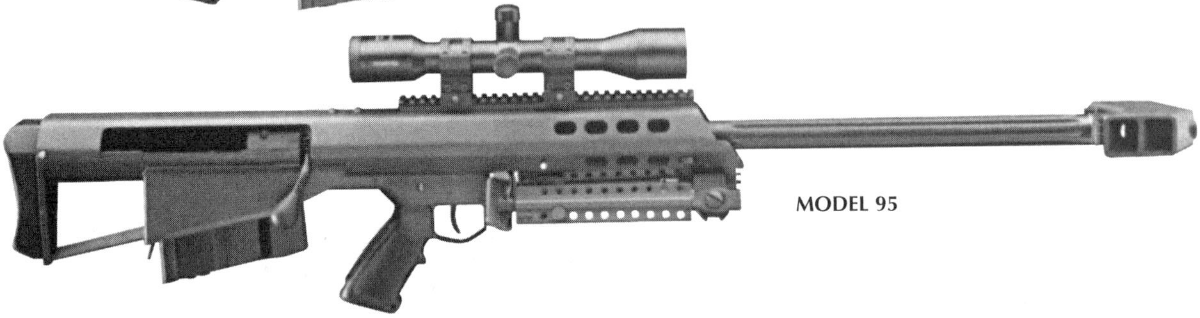

MODEL 95

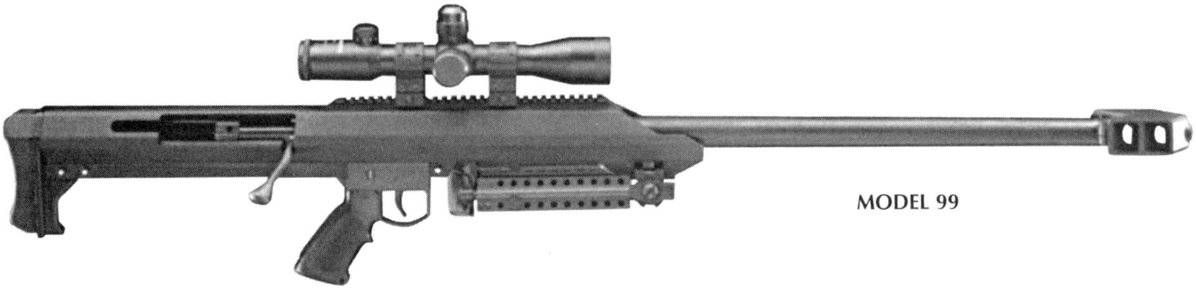

MODEL 99

MODEL 82A1

Action: autoloading
Stock: synthetic
Barrel: 29 in.
Sights: target
Weight: 28.5 lbs.
Caliber: .50 BMG
Magazine: 10 rounds
Features: Picatinny rail and scope mount; fluted barrel, detachable bipod and carrying case
MSRP: $9345

MODEL 95, MODEL 99

Action: bolt
Stock: synthetic
Barrel: 29 in. or 33 in. (M99)
Sights: none
Weight: 25.0 lbs.
Caliber: .50 BMG
Magazine: 5 (M95) or none (M99)
Features: Picatinny rail; detachable bipod; M95 has fluted barrel and weighs 22 lbs.
M95: $6825
M99: $4410–4725

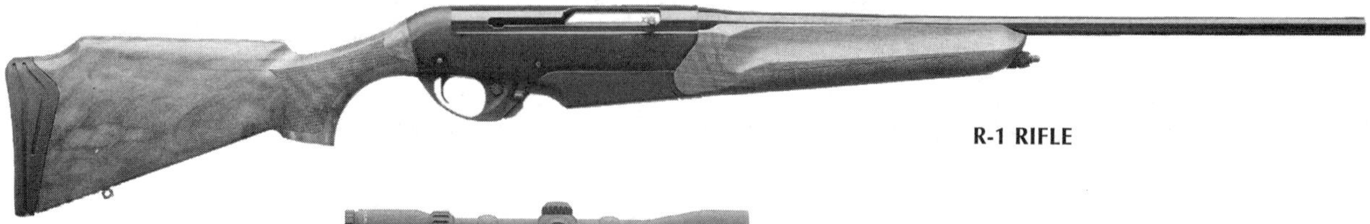

R-1 RIFLE

R-1 RIFLE COMFORTECH

R1 REALTREE APG HD

R1 SYNTHETIC

R-1 RIFLE

Action: autoloading
Stock: walnut
Barrel: 22 in. (Standard Rifle); 20 in. (Standard Carbine); 24 in. (Magnum Rifle)
Sights: none (option for riflesights available)
Weight: 7.1 lbs. (Standard Rifle); 7.0 lbs. (Standard Carbine); 7.2 lbs. (Magnum Rifle); 7.0 lbs. (Magnum Carbine)
Caliber: .30-06; .300 Win. Mag., .308 Win., .270 WSM, .300 WSM
Magazine: detachable box, 3-4 rounds (optional 10 rounds in 30-06)
Features: auto-regulating gas-operated system; three lugged rotary bolt; select satin walnut stock; receiver drilled and tapped for scope mount; base included
Standard Rifle:. $1429

R1 RIFLE-COMFORTECH

Action: autoloader
Stock: synthetic
Barrel: 24 in. (.270 WSM, 300 WSM & .300 Win.); 22, 22 in. (.30-06) .308
Sights: None
Weight: 7.3 lbs.
Caliber: .270 WSM, .30-06 Springfield, .300 WSM, .300 WM
Magazine: 3 rounds
Features: ComforTech recoil absorbing stock system; optional interchangeable barrels; GripTight stock and fore-end; receiver is drilled and tapped for scope mount; Picatinny rail scope base included; open sights available
MSRP: $1599

R-1 RIFLE COMORTECH, .30-06 SPRINGFIELD, REALTREE APG HD

Action: autoloading
Stock: synthetic (Realtree APG HD)
Barrel: 22 in.
Sights: none
Weight: 7.2 lbs.
Caliber: .30-06 Springfield
Magazine: detachable box, 4 + 1 rounds
Features: Comfortech recoil dampening stock; auto-regulating gas-operated system; three lugged rotary bolt; receiver drilled and tapped for scope; optional extra-high gel comb
MSRP: $1759

Beretta Rifles

1873 RENEGADE SHORT-STROKE LEVER ACTION RIFLE

C X 4 STORM

1873 RENEGADE SHORT-STROKE LEVER ACTION RIFLE

Action: lever
Stock: walnut
Barrel: 20 in.
Sights: open, adjustable
Weight: 7.1 lbs.
Caliber: .357 Mag., .45 Colt
Magazine: under-barrel tube, 10 rounds
Features: tapered, octagon barrel; color case-hardened frame with blued hammer, lever and barrel; gold bead front sight; straight, walnut stock with checkered fore-end; rubber butplate
MSRP: $1350

CX4 STORM

Action: autoloader
Stock: synthetic
Barrel: 16.6 in.
Weight: 5.75 lbs.
Caliber: 9mm, .40 S&W, .45 ACP
Magazine: removable box, 10-17 rounds
Features: cold hammer-forged chrome-lined barrel; blued finish; optional 30-round magazine; accepts full-size Beretta magazines from the 92/96 and Cougar series pistols
MSRP: $915

Blaser Rifles

K95 BARONESSE STUTZEN

BLASER K95 BARONESSE STUTZEN

Action: tilting-block single-shot
Stock: checkered Turkish walnut
Barrel: 19 3/4″
Sights: open rear, bead front on ramp
Weight: 5 lbs. 12 oz.
Caliber: .222 Rem, 5.6x50 RM, 5.6x52 R, .243 Win., 6.5x57 R, 7x57 R, .308 Win., .30-06, 8x57 IRS
Magazine: none
Features: Full-length stock, engraved receiver with side-plates, strong action that's safe to carry with a chambered cartridge before thumb-cocking.
MSRP: $15,500

Blaser Rifles

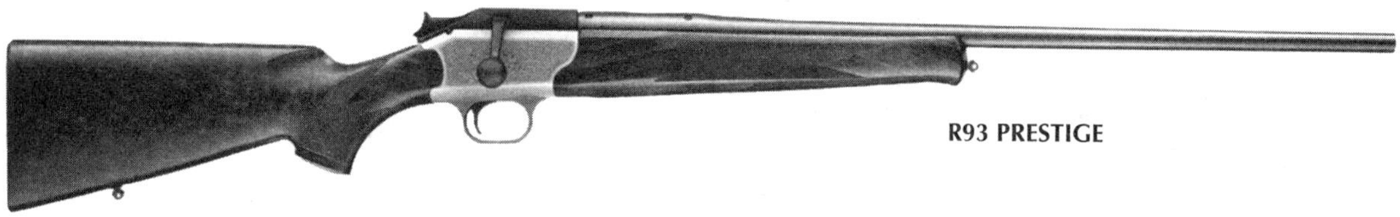

R93 PRESTIGE

R93

Action: bolt
Stock: walnut or synthetic
Barrel: 22 in.
Sights: none
Weight: 6.5 lbs., 7.0 lbs. (Magnum)
Caliber: .22-250, .243, .25-06, 6.5x55, .270, 7x57, 7mm/08, .308, .30-06; Magnums: .257 Wby. Mag., 7mm Rem. Mag., .300 Win. Mag., .300 Wby. Mag., .300 Rem. UM, .338 Win. Mag., .375 H&H, .416 Rem. Mag.
Magazine: in-line box, 5 rounds
Features: straight-pull bolt with expanding collar lockup
Left-hand versions: . . . . . . add $163
Prestige: $3373
Luxus: $4594
Attache: $6360

BLASER R93 PRESTIGE

Action: straight-pull, collet-locking bolt
Stock: Grade 3 walnut
Barrel: 22 ¾″ or 25 ½″
Sights: none (open sights standard on some models)
Weight: 6 lbs. 13 oz.
Caliber: choice of many popular chamberings
Magazine: single-stack, top-loading
Features: sideplates with English scroll on an action with smooth-feeding straight-up magazine, optional recoil reducer in stock. R93 action allows quick change of barrels/chamberings within cartridge groups.
MSRP: $3,275

R93 LONG RANGE SPORTER 2

Action: bolt
Stock: tactical composite
Barrel: heavy, fluted 26 in.
Sights: none
Weight: 8.0 lbs.
Caliber: .223 Rem., .243, .22-250, 6mm Norma, 6.5x55, .308, .300 Win. Mag., .338 Lapua Mag.
Magazine: in-line box, 5 rounds
Features: straight-pull bolt; fully adjustable trigger; optional folding bipod, muzzle brake and hand rest
Long Range Sporter: $3963

S2 SAFARI

Action: tilting block, double-barrel
Stock: select Turkish walnut, checkered
Barrels: 24 in., gas-nitrated, sand-blasted, independent
Sights: open rear, blade front on solid rib
Weight: 10.1-11.2 lbs., depending on caliber
Caliber: .375 H&H, .500/.416 NE, .470 NE, .500 NE
Magazine: none
Features: selective ejectors; Pachmayr Decelerator pad; snap caps; leather sling; Americase wheeled travel case; scope mount of choice
MSRP (standard grade): $10,032
(extra barrel set): $6070
Also available: S2 double rifle in standard chamberings, from .222 to 9.3x74R, 7.7 lbs

RIFLES

BPI Rifles

BPI APEX

Action: hinged-breech single-shot
Stock: synthetic, black or camo, ambidextrous design, configured for scope use, Crush-Zone recoil pad
Barrel: 25″ (centerfire) and 27″ (muzzleloader)
Sights: none
Weight: 7 ½ lbs.
Caliber: 10 popular centerfire chamberings, .222 to .300 Win. Mag and .45-70; barrels interchangeable with black powder, .22 rimfire barrels.
Magazine: none
Features: Bergara barrel and adjustable (3-5 pounds) trigger on this exposed-hammer, switch-barrel rifle enhance accuracy
Black, stainless: $615–652
Realtree camo, stainless: . . $695–732

Brown Precision Rifles

CUSTOM HIGH COUNTRY

HIGH COUNTRY YOUTH

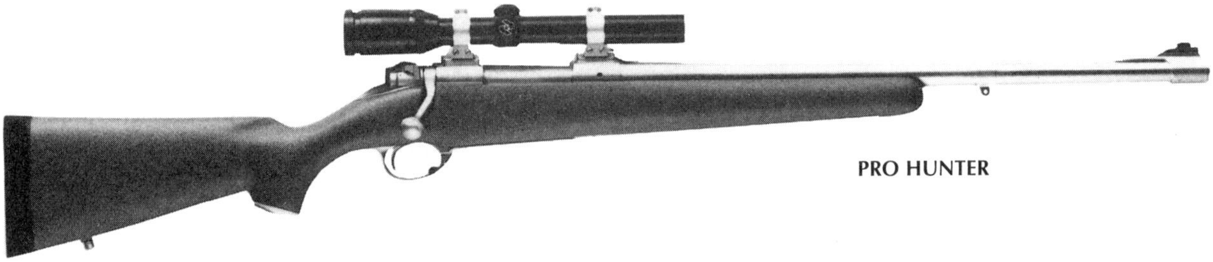

PRO HUNTER

RIFLES

CUSTOM HIGH COUNTRY

Action: bolt
Stock: composite classic stock
Barrel: choice of contours, lengths
Sights: none
Weight: 6.0 lbs.
Caliber: any popular standard caliber
Magazine: box, 5 rounds
Features: Remington 700 barreled action; tuned trigger; choice of stock colors and dimensions
MSRP: $5199

CUSTOM HIGH COUNTRY YOUTH

Action: bolt
Stock: composite sporter, scaled for youth
Barrel: length and contour to order
Sights: none
Weight: 5.0 lbs.
Caliber: any popular standard short action
Magazine: box, 5 rounds
Features: Remington Model 700 or Model 7 barreled action; optional muzzle brake, scopes, stock colors and dimensions; included: package of shooting, reloading and hunting accessories
MSRP: $1895

PRO HUNTER

Action: bolt
Stock: composite sporter
Barrel: Shilen match grade stainless
Sights: none
Weight: 8.0 lbs.
Caliber: any standard and belted
Magnum caliber up to: .375 H&H
Magazine: box, 3-5 rounds
Features: Model 70 action with Mauser extractor; tuned trigger; optional Talley peep sight and banded ramp front sight or Talley mounts with 8-40 screws; optional muzzle brake, Mag-Na-Porting; Americase aluminum hard case
Pro Hunter: $2899
Left-hand: $2999

Brown Precision Rifles

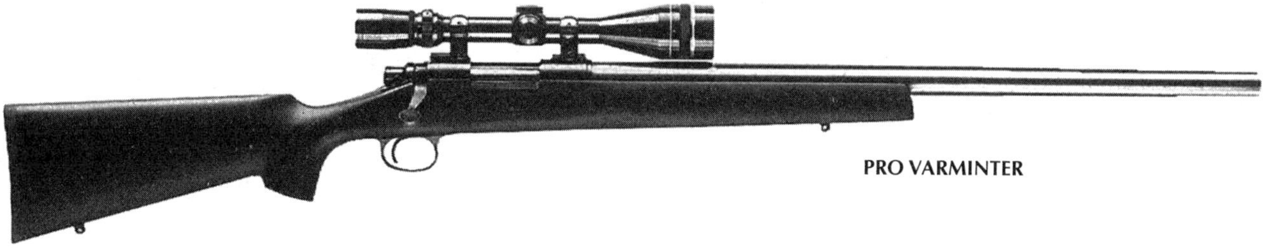

PRO VARMINTER

TACTICAL ELITE

PRO VARMINTER

Action: bolt
Stock: composite, varmint or bench rest
Barrel: heavy stainless match
Grade: 26 in.
Sights: none
Weight: 9.0 lbs.
Caliber: all popular calibers
Magazine: box (or single shot)
Features: Remington 40X or 700 action (right or left-hand); bright or bead-blasted finish; optional muzzle brake; after-market trigger; scope and mounts optional
Model 700, right-hand: $3295
Model 700, left-hand: $3595
Rem. 40X (with target trigger): $3895

TACTICAL ELITE

Action: bolt
Stock: composite tactical
Barrel: Shilen match-grade, heavy stainless
Sights: none
Weight: 9.0 lbs.
Caliber: .223, .308, .300 Win. Mag., (others on special order)
Magazine: box, 3 or 5 rounds
Features: Remington 700 action; Teflon metal finish; adjustable buttplate; tuned trigger; optional muzzle brakes, scopes
MSRP: $3295–3995

Browning Rifles

BROWNING X-BOLT MICRO HUNTER

Action: three-lug bolt
Stock: satin finish walnut, sized for smaller shooters
Barrel: 20 or 22″, low-luster blued finish
Sights: none
Weight: 6 to 6 ½ lbs.
Caliber: .223, .22-250, .243, 7mm-08, .308 Win, .270 WSM, 7mm WSM, .300 WSM, .325 WSM
Magazine: detachable rotary box
Features: adjustable "Feather" trigger, top-tang safety, bolt-unlock button, sling swivel studs. Also*:* new .223 and .22-250 chamberings in other X-Bolt versions, some in stainless/synthetic form.
MSRP: .... $899-$919

BROWNING A-BOLT TARGET

Action: three-lug bolt
Stock: checkered gray laminate with adjustable comb
Barrel: heavy contour, 28″
Sights: none
Weight: 13 lbs.
Caliber: .223, .308, .300 WSM
Magazine: detachable box
Features: the latest of an extensive line of long- and short-action A-Bolt rifles. Target-style beavertail forend, floating barrel, glass-bedded receiver, single-set trigger, top-tang safety. Stainless and carbon-steel versions are available.
.223,.308 carbon steel:...... $1359
.300 WSM stainless:........ $1589–1629

Browning Rifles

.22 SEMI-AUTOMATIC

Action: autoloading
Stock: walnut
Barrel: 19 in.
Sights: open
Weight: 5.2 lbs.
Caliber: .22 LR
Magazine: tube in stock, 11 rounds
Features: Grade VI has high grade walnut, finer checkering, engraved receiver
Grade I: $659
Grade VI: $1419

A-BOLT HUNTER

Action: bolt
Stock: walnut
Barrel: 20-26 in.
Sights: none
Weight: 7.0 lbs.
Caliber: all popular cartridges from .22 Hornet to .30-06, including WSMs and WSSMs.
Magazine: detachable box, 4-6 rounds
Features: BOSS (Ballistic Optimizing Shooting System) available; Micro Hunters weigh 6.3 lbs. with 20 in. barrel and shorter stock; left-hand Medallion available; Eclipse thumbhole stock available with light or heavy barrel (9.8 lbs.) and BOSS
Micro Hunter: $739–819
Eclipse Hunter: $1349–1379
Hunter: $719
Medallion: $869–979
Medallion BOSS: $1059–1079
Medallion, white gold: $1229–1259

A-BOLT HUNTER MAGNUM

Action: bolt
Stock: walnut
Barrel: 23 in. and 26 in.
Sights: none ***Weight:*** 7.5 lbs.
Caliber: popular magnums from 7mm Rem. to .375 H&H, including .270, 7mm and .300 WSM plus .25, .223 and .243 WSSMs
Magazine: detachable box, 3 rounds
Features: rifles in WSM calibers have 23 in. barrels and weigh 6.5 lbs.; WSSM have 22 in. barrels; BOSS (Ballistic Optimizing Shooting System) available; left-hand available
Medallion Magnum BOSS: . . $1079
Eclipse BOSS: $1349–1379

.22 SEMI-AUTOMATIC

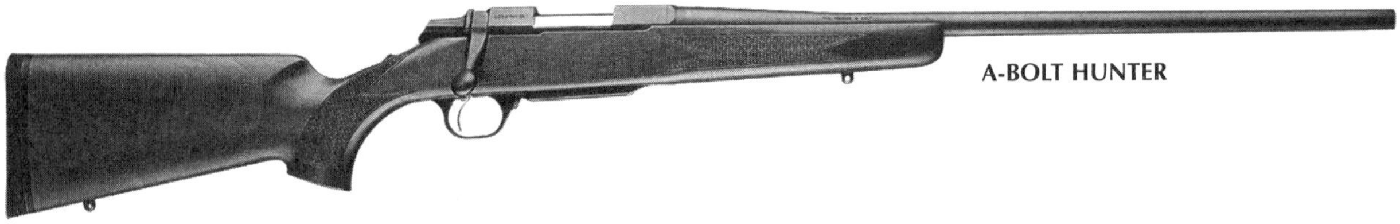

A-BOLT HUNTER

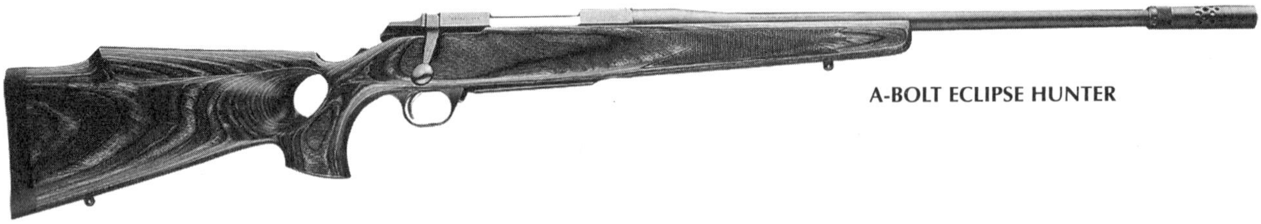

A-BOLT ECLIPSE HUNTER

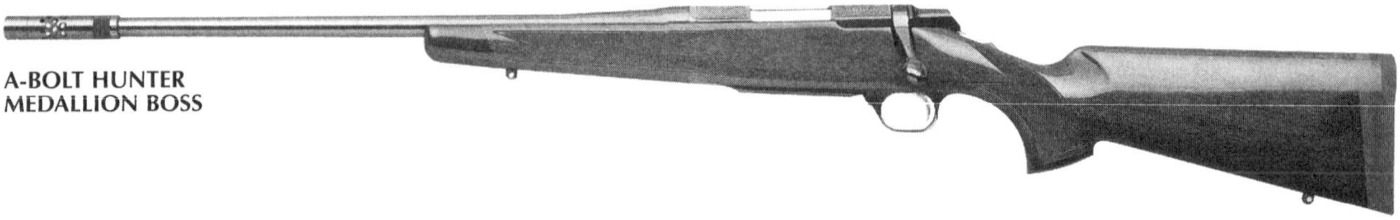

A-BOLT HUNTER MEDALLION BOSS

Browning Rifles

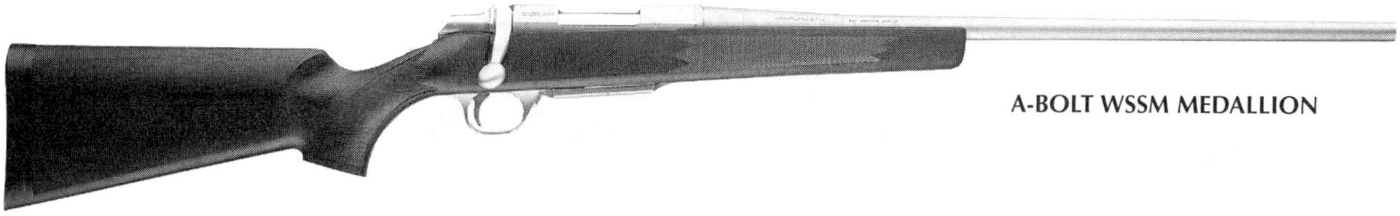

A-BOLT WSSM MEDALLION

A-BOLT STALKER

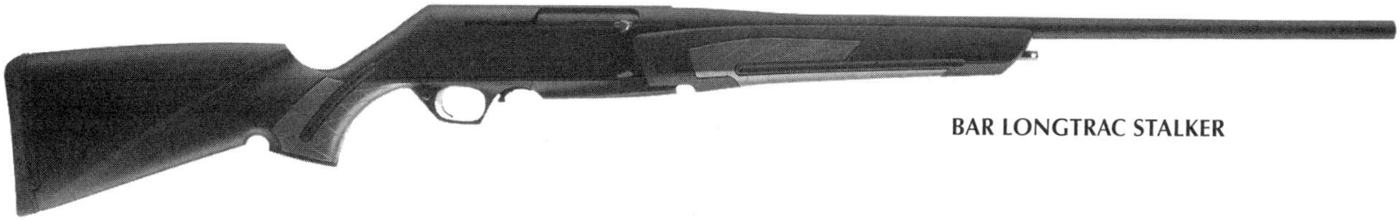

BAR LONGTRAC STALKER

A-BOLT STALKER

Action: bolt
Stock: synthetic
Barrel: 22, 23 and 26 in.
Sights: none
Weight: 7.5 lbs.
Caliber: most popular calibers and magnums, including .270, 7mm and .300 WSMs; .25, .223 and .243 WSSMs
Magazine: detachable box, 3-6 rounds
Features: BOSS (Ballistic Optimizing Shooting System) available; stainless option; rifles in WSM calibers have 23 in. barrels and weigh 6.5 lbs.

Stalker: $719–749
Stainless: $915–1079
Stainless, left-hand: $1099–1139
BOSS: $939–959
Stainless, BOSS: $1159–1189
Stainless, left-hand, Boss: $1189–1229
Varmint Stalker: $915
TCT Varmint: $1299

BAR

Action: autoloading
Stock: walnut or synthetic
Barrel: 20, 23, and 24 in.
Sights: open ***Weight:*** 7.5 lbs.
Caliber: .243, .25-06, .270, .308, .30-06, 7mm Rem. Mag., .300 Win. Mag., .270 WSM, 7mm WSM, .300 WSM, .338 Win. Mag.
Magazine: detachable box, 3-5 rounds
Features: gas operated; lightweight model with alloy receiver and 20 in. barrel weighs 7.2 lbs.; magnum with 24 in. barrel weighs 8.6 lbs.; BOSS (Ballistic Optimizing Shooting System) available; higher grades also available

Lightweight Stalker: $1119–1229
Safari (no sights): $1139–1229
WSMs: $1149–1239
Safari, BOSS: $1259–1359
WSM & Mag: $1179

BAR LONGTRAC STALKER

Action: autoloader
Stock: composite
Barrel: 22 and 24 in.
Weight: 6.9 lbs. and 7.5 lbs.
Caliber: .270 Win, .30-06, 7mm Rem Mag, .300 Win Mag
Magazine: detachable box, 3-4-rounds
Features: matte black finish; recoil pad

MSRP: $1149–1239

Browning Rifles

BAR LIGHTWEIGHT STALKER

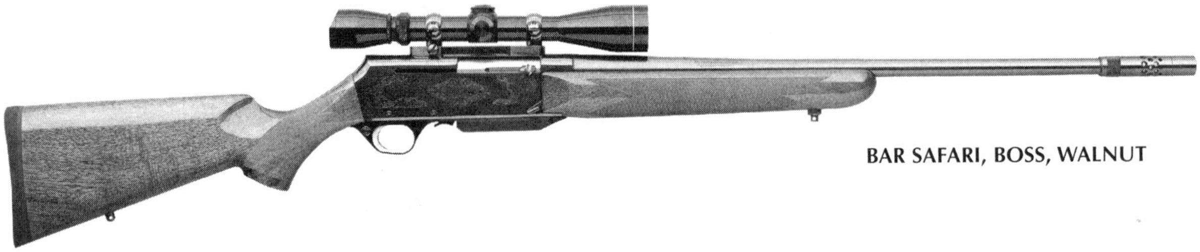

BAR SAFARI, BOSS, WALNUT

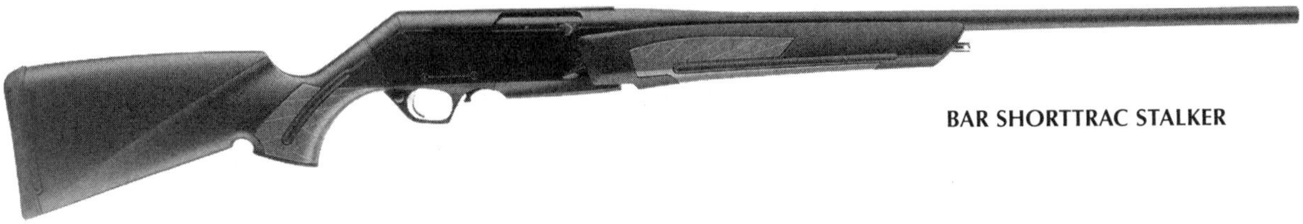

BAR SHORTTRAC STALKER

BL 22

BAR SHORTTRAC STALKER

Action: autoloader
Stock: composite
Barrel: 22 and 23 in.
Weight: 6.9 lbs. and 7.5 lbs.
Caliber: .243 Win, .308 Win, .270 WSM, 7mm WSM, .300 WSM
Magazine: detachable box, 3-4-round
Features: matte blued finish; recoil pad
MSRP: $1149–1239

BL 22

Action: lever
Stock: walnut
Barrel: 20 or 24 in.
Sights: open
Weight: 5.0 lbs.
Caliber: .22 LR or .17 MACH2
Magazine: under-barrel tube, 15 rounds
Features: short stroke, exposed hammer, lever-action; straight grip; also available in Grade II with fine checkered walnut
Grade I: $559
Grade II: $639
With 24″ octagon bbl.: $899
FLD Series
(nickel receiver): $599–679

BLR LIGHTWEIGHT

Action: lever
Stock: checkered walnut
Barrel: 18 or 20 in.
Sights: open
Weight: 6.5-7.75 lbs.
Caliber: .22-250, .243, 7mm-08, .308, .358, .450, .270 WSM, 7mm WSM, .300 WSM, .325 WSM, .270, .30-06, 7mm Rem. Mag., .300 Win. Mag.
Magazine: detachable box, 3-5 rounds
Features: Long- and short-actions; rotating bolt heads; sporter barrel; stock with pistol grip and Schnabel forend
MSRP: $919

BLR LIGHTWEIGHT '81

Action: lever
Stock: straight-grip walnut
Barrel: 20, 22 or 24 in.
Sights: open
Weight: 6.5 or 7.3 lbs.
Caliber: .22-250, .243, 7mm-08,.308, .358, .450 Marlin, .270,.30-06 (22 in.), 7mm Rem. Mag.,.300 Win. Mag. (24 in.)
Magazine: 5 and 4 rounds (magnums)
Features: long- and short-action; alloy receiver; front-locking bolt; rack-and-pinion action
MSRP: $879

BLR TAKEDOWN RIFLE

Action: lever
Stock: gloss finish walnut
Barrel: 20, 22 and 24 in.
Sights: adjustable
Weight: 6.5-7.7 lbs.
Caliber: .22-250 Rem., .243 Win., 7mm-08 Rem., .308 Win., .358 Win., .270 Win., .30-06 Splfd., 7mm Rem. Mag., .300 Win. Mag., .300 WSM, .270 WSM, 7mm WSM, .450 Marlin, .325 WSM
Magazine: detachable box
Features: separates for storage or transportation; aircraft-grade alloy receiver; blued finish; drilled and tapped for scope mounts; scout-style scope mount available as accessory; sling swivel studs installed; recoil pad
MSRP: . . . . starting at $999

RIFLES

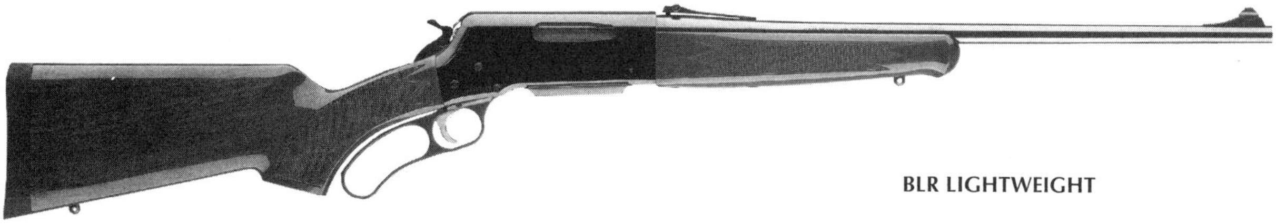

BLR LIGHTWEIGHT

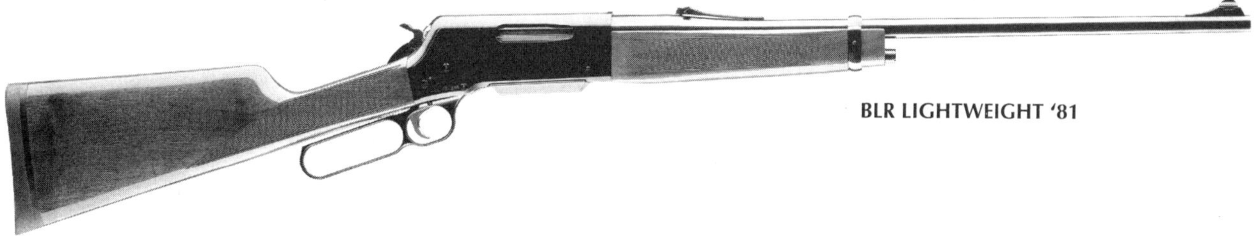

BLR LIGHTWEIGHT '81

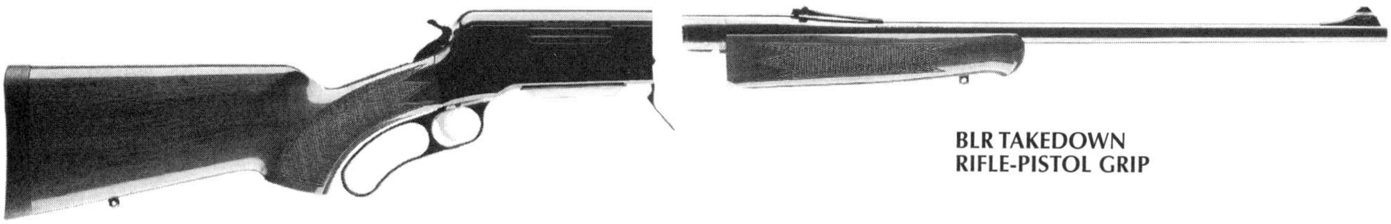

BLR TAKEDOWN
RIFLE-PISTOL GRIP

Browning Rifles

BUCKMARK

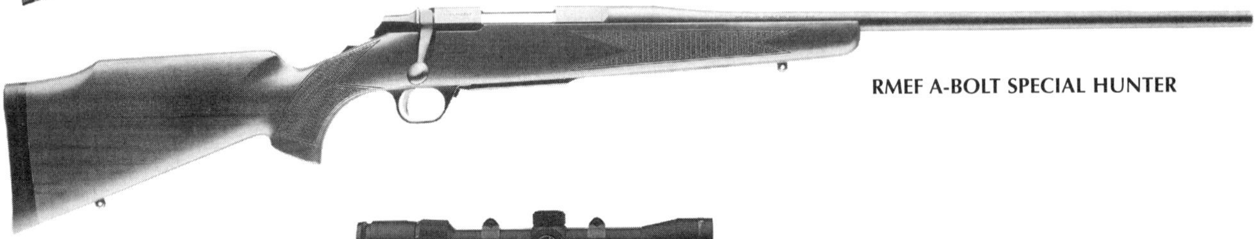

RMEF A-BOLT SPECIAL HUNTER

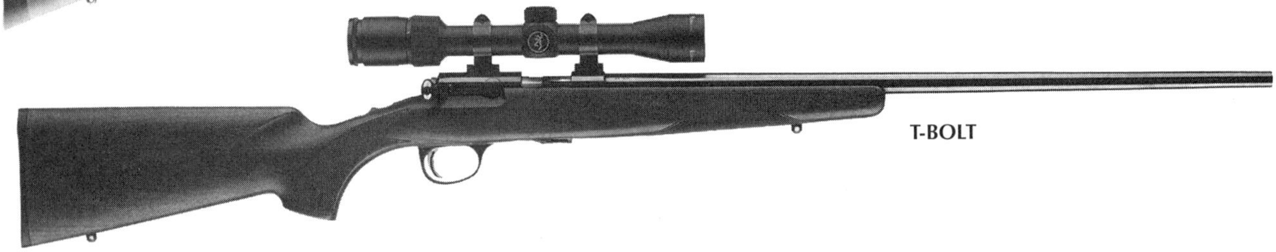

T-BOLT

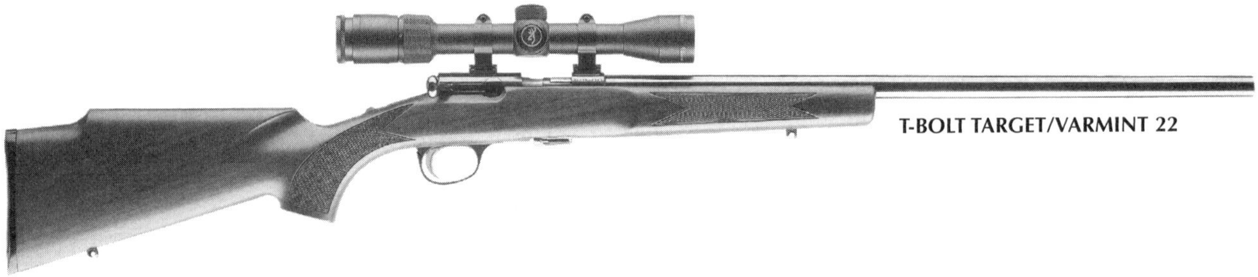

T-BOLT TARGET/VARMINT 22

BUCKMARK

Action: autoloading
Stock: laminate
Sights: open
Weight: 5.2 lbs.
Caliber: .22 LR
Magazine: detachable box, 10 rounds
Features: also in target model with heavy barrel
Buckmark: $619

ROCKY MOUNTAIN ELK FOUNDATION A-BOLT SPECIAL HUNTER

Action: bolt
Stock: satin finish walnut; inset with RMEF logo
Barrel: 23 in.
Sights: none; drilled and tapped for scope mounts
Weight: 7.7 lbs.
Caliber: 325 WSM
Magazine: detachable box
Features: sling swivels; recoil pad; hinged floorplate
MSRP: $979

T-BOLT

Action: bolt
Stock: checkered walnut
Barrel: 22 in.
Sights: none
Weight: 4.25 lbs. (average)
Caliber: .22 LR
Magazine: rotary box, 10-round
Features: straight-pull T-Bolt; receiver drilled and tapped for scope mounts; Double HelixT rotary box magazine; overall length 401/8 in.
MSRP: $702

T-BOLT TARGET/VARMINT 22

Action: bolt
Stock: satin finish walnut
Barrel: 22 in.
Sights: none; drilled and tapped for scope mounts
Weight: 5.7 lbs.
Caliber: .22 L.R.
Magazine: Double Helix magazine
Features: blued steel receiver and barrel; free-floating, heavy target barrel with semi-match chamber; straight pull bolt; gold-colored trigger; sling swivel studs installed
MSRP: $749

X-BOLT

Action: bolt
Stock: composite, gloss finish walnut or satin finish walnut
Barrel: 22, 23, 24, 26 in.
Weight: 6.3-7 lbs.
Caliber: variety of calibers from 243 Win. to 375 H & H Mag
Magazine: detachable rotary
Features: available in several models: Stainless Stalker and Composite Stalker with composite stocks; Medallion and Hunter with wood stocks; all with adjustable three-lever Feather Trigger, bolt unlock button allows bolt to be unlocked and opened with safety on, X-Lock scope mounting system. Blued, stainless steel, low luster blued or matte blued barrels.

Composite Stalker: $899–939
Hunter: $899–939
Medallion: $1019–1039
Stainless Stalker: $1119–1149

Bushmaster Rifles

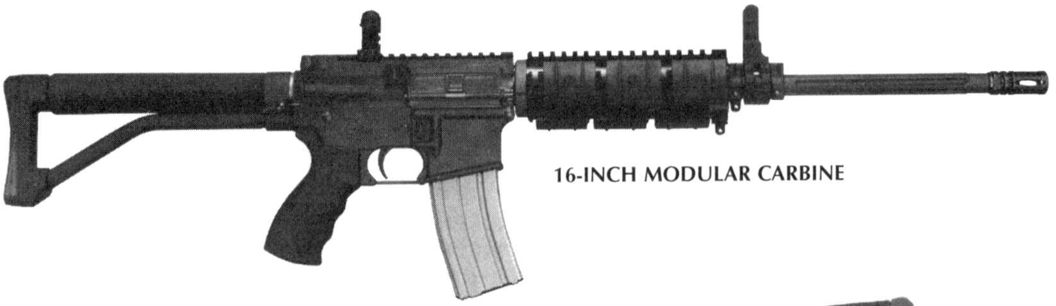

16-INCH MODULAR CARBINE

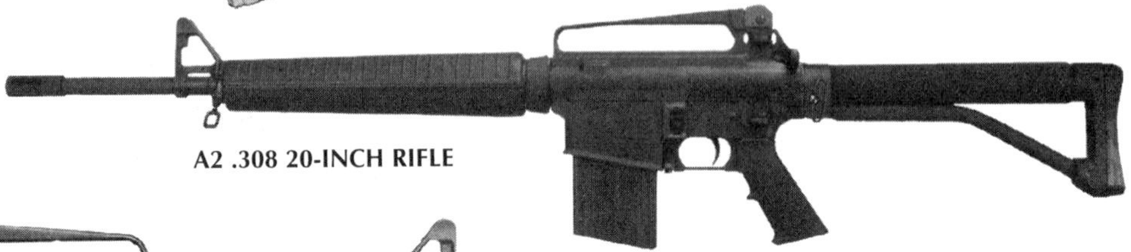

A2 .308 20-INCH RIFLE

A2 CARBINE

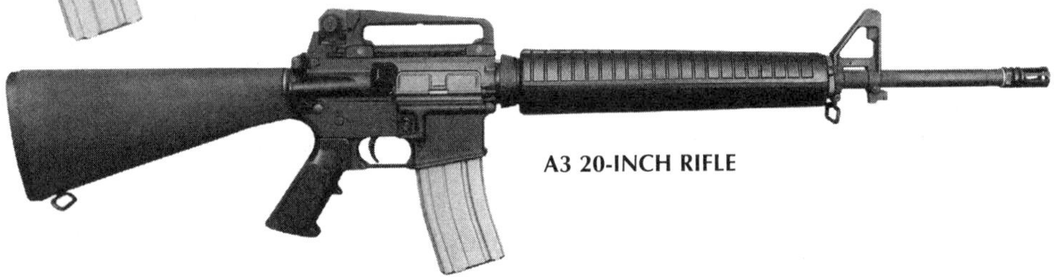

A3 20-INCH RIFLE

16-INCH MODULAR CARBINE

Action: autoloader
Stock: synthetic
Barrel: 16 in.
Sights: open adjustable
Weight: 7.3 lbs.
Caliber: .223 Rem. (5.56mm)
Magazine: detachable box, 10 rounds (accepts all M16 types)
Features: forged aluminum A3 type flat-top upper receiver; chrome-lined moly steel fluted barrel with milled gas block; A. B.M.A.S. four rail free-floater tubular forend with Picatinny rails; skeleton stock; ambidextrous pistol grip; overall length 34.5 in.
MSRP: $1780

A2 .308 20-INCH RIFLE

Action: autoloader
Stock: polymer
Barrel: 20 in.
Sights: open
Weight: 9.57 lbs.
Caliber: .308 Winchester
Magazine: detachable box, 20 rounds (accepts all FN-FAL types)
Features: heavy alloy steel barrel with Bushmaster's Izzy muzzle brake; forged aluminum receiver; integral solid carrying handle with M16 A2 rear sight; overall length 42.75 in.
A2 .308 20-inch Rifle: . . . $1725–1755

A2 CARBINE

Action: auto loader
Stock: polymer
Barrel: 16 in.
Sights: open, adjustable
Weight: 7.22 lbs.
Caliber: 223 Rem. (5.56mm)
Magazine: detachable box, 10 rounds
Features: lightweight forged aluminum receiver with M16 A2 design improvements; heavy profile barrel with chrome-lined bore and chamber; M16 A2 sight system; overall length 34.74 inches; manganese phosphate finish
MSRP: $985

A2 AND A3 20-INCH RIFLES

Action: autoloader
Stock: polymer
Barrel: 20 in.
Sights: open, adjustable
Weight: 8.27 lbs.
Caliber: 223 Rem. (5.56mm)
Magazine: detachable box, 10 rounds
Features: forged aluminum receivers; A3 upper receiver with slotted rail; optional removable carry handle; military spec. heavy barrel with chrome-lined bore and chamber; ribbed front handguard; M16 A2 rear sight system; overall length 38.25 in.; manganese phosphate finish
A2 20 inch Rifle:. $1095
A3 20 inch Rifle:. $1195

Bushmaster Rifles

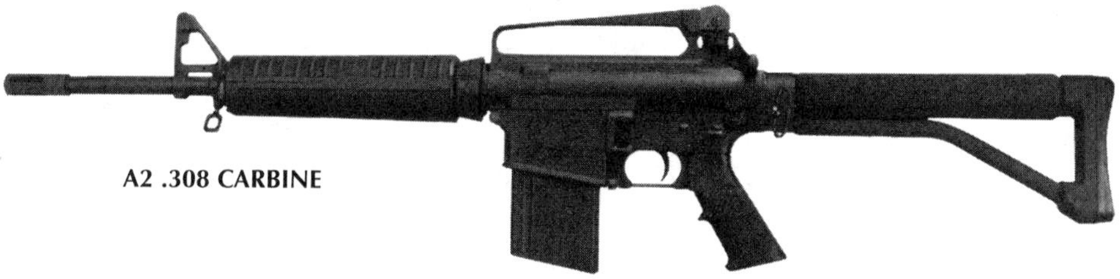

A2 .308 CARBINE

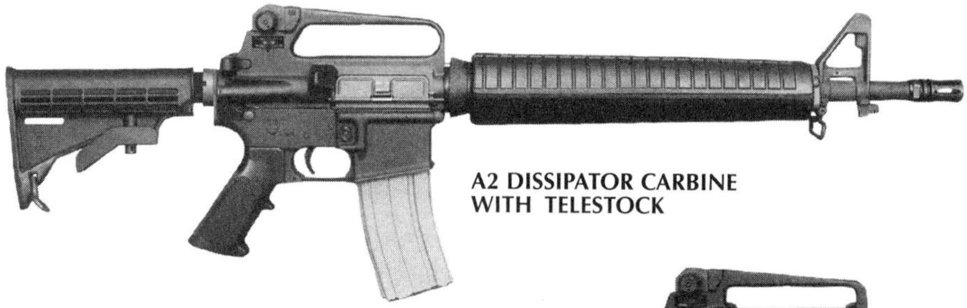

A2 DISSIPATOR CARBINE
WITH TELESTOCK

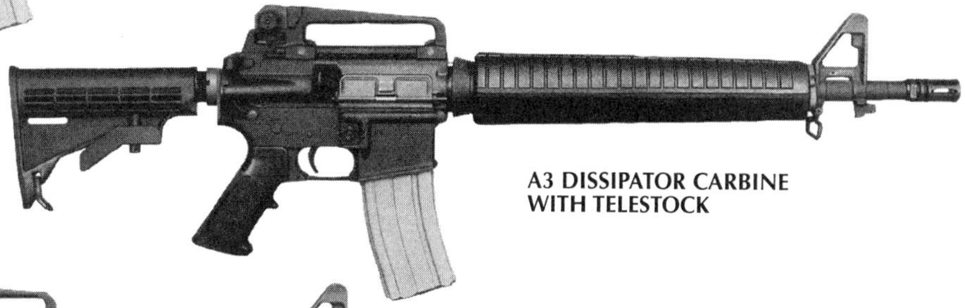

A3 DISSIPATOR CARBINE
WITH TELESTOCK

AK A3 CARBINE

A2 AND A3 DISSIPATOR CARBINES

Action: autoloader
Stock: polymer
Barrel: 16 in.
Sights: adjustable
Weight: 7.68 lbs.
Caliber: .223 Rem. (5.56mm)
Magazine: detachable box, 10 rounds
Features: lightweight forged aluminum receivers; manganese phosphate finished heavy profile barrel with chrome lined bore and chamber; ribbed full length Dissipator handguards; M16 A2 sight system; removable carry handle; overall length 34.74 inches

A2 Dissipator: $1140
With Telestock: $1170
A3 Dissipator: $1240
With Telestock: $1270

A3 CARBINE, AK A3 CARBINE AND AK A2 RIFLE

Action: autoloader ***Stock:*** polymer
Barrel: 16 in., 14.5 in, (AK A3 Carbine and Rifle)
Sights: open, adjustable
Weight: 6.7 lbs., 7.33 lbs. (AK A3 Carbine and Rifle)
Caliber: .223 Rem. (5.56mm)
Magazine: detachable box, 10 rounds
Features: forged upper and lower receivers with M16 A2 design improvements; heavy-profile barrel with chrome-lined bore and chamber; M16 A2 sight system; overall length 34.75 inches; manganese phosphate finish; AK muzzle brake permanently attached

AK A2 Rifle: $1115
AK A3 Carbine: $1215

Bushmaster Rifles

CARBON 15 TYPE 21

M4 A2 CARBINE

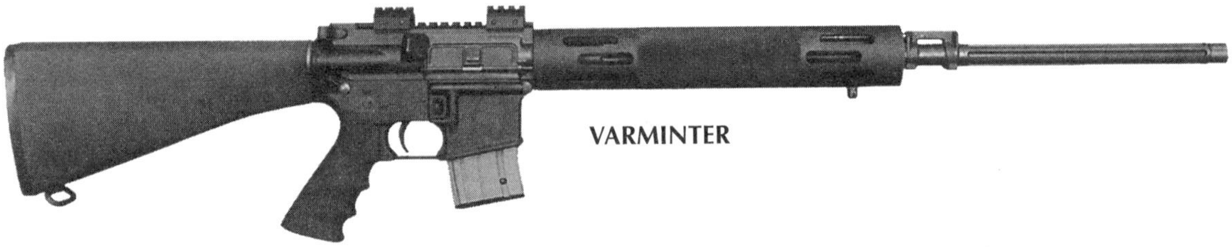

VARMINTER

CARBON 15 TYPE 21 RIFLE

Action: autoloader
Stock: synthetic
Barrel: 16 in.
Sights: none
Weight: 4.0 lbs.
Caliber: .223 Rem. (5.56mm)
Magazine: detachable box, 10 rounds (accepts all M16 types)
Features: carbon fiber upper and lower receivers; anodized aluminum Picatinny rail; stainless match grade barrel; quick-detach compensator; overall length 35 inches
MSRP: **$1100**

M4 TYPE CARBINE

Action: autoloader
Stock: polymer
Barrel: 16 in.
Sights: open adjustable
Weight: 6.59 lbs.
Caliber: .223 Rem. (5.56 mm)
Magazine: detachable box, 10 rounds
Features: forged aluminum receivers with M16 A2 design improvements; M4 profile chrome-lined barrel with permanently attached Mini Y Comp muzzle brake; M16 A2 rear sight system; BATF approved, fixed position tele-style buttstock; manganese phosphate finish
MSRP: **$1395**

VARMINTER RIFLE

Action: autoloader
Stock: synthetic
Barrel: 24 in.
Sights: none
Weight: 8.75 lbs.
Caliber: .223 Remington (5.56 mm)
Magazine: detachable box, 5 rounds (accepts all M16 types)
Features: free-floating fluted heavy DCM competition barrel; V Match tubular forend with special cooling vents and bipod stud; Bushmaster competition trigger; overall length 42.25 in.
MSRP: **$1360**

Bushmaster Rifles

VARMINT SPECIAL

V MATCH RIFLE

XM15 E2S A2 20-INCH STAINLESS STEEL

RIFLES

VARMINT SPECIAL RIFLE

Action: autoloader
Stock: synthetic
Barrel: 24 in.
Sights: none
Weight: 8.75 lbs.
Caliber: .223 Rem. (5.56 mm)
Magazine: detachable box, 5 rounds
Features: flat-top upper receiver with B.M.A.S. scope risers; lower receiver includes two stage competition trigger and tactical pistol grip; polished stainless steel barrel
MSRP: $1365

V MATCH RIFLE AND CARBINE

Action: autoloader
Stock: synthetic
Barrel: 16 in. (Carbine), 20 in. or 24 in. (Rifle)
Sights: none
Weight: 6.9 lbs. (Carbine), 8.05 lbs. (Rifle)
Caliber: .223 Rem. (5.56mm)
Magazine: detachable box, 10 rounds
Features: forged aluminum V Match flat-top upper receiver with M16 A2 design improvements and Picatinny rail; heavy, chrome-lined free-floating barrel; front sight bases available in full sight or no sight versions; overall length 34.75 in.
Carbine: $1140
Rifle: $1150

XM15 E2S A2 20-INCH STAINLESS STEEL RIFLE

Action: autoloader
Stock: synthetic
Barrel: 20 in.
Sights: open
Weight: 8.27 lbs.
Caliber: .223 Rem. (5.56 mm)
Magazine: detachable box, 5 rounds (accepts all M16 types)
Features: heavy configuration, match grade stainless barrel; available in either A2 or A3 (with removable carry handle) configurations
MSRP: $1150

Chey-Tac Rifles

M-200

M-200

Action: bolt
Stock: synthetic; retractable
Barrel: 30 in.
Sights: none
Weight: 27 lbs., 24 lbs. (carbon fiber barrel)
Caliber: .408 CheyTac
Magazine: detachable box, 7 rounds
Features: heavy, free floated detachable fluted barrel; rear of barrel enclosed by shroud mount for bipod and handle; muzzle brake; receiver fitted with fixed MilStd Picatinny rail; fully collapsible, retractable buttstock containing integral hinged monopod.
MSRP: $11495

RIFLES

Cimarron Rifles

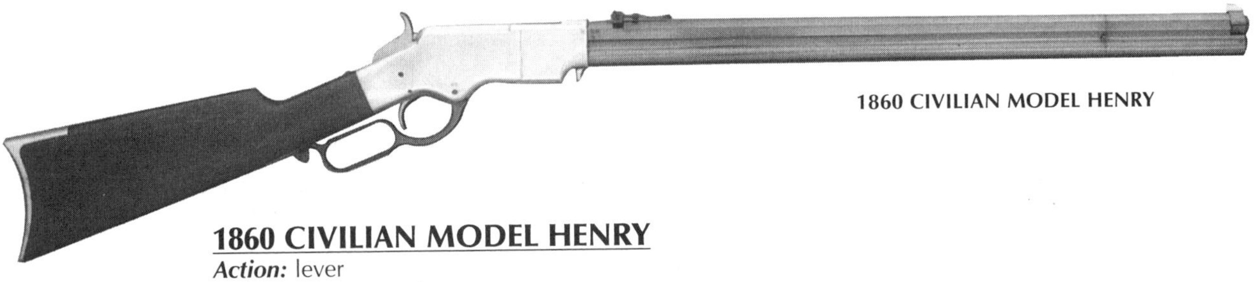

1860 CIVILIAN MODEL HENRY

1860 CIVILIAN MODEL HENRY

Action: lever
Stock: walnut, straight grip
Barrel: 24 in.
Sights: open
Weight: 7.5 lbs.
Caliber: .44 WCF, .45 LC
Magazine: under-barrel tube, 11 rounds
Features: replica of the most famous American rifle of the Old West
MSRP: . . . . starting at $1484

Cimarron Rifles

1873 WINCHESTER

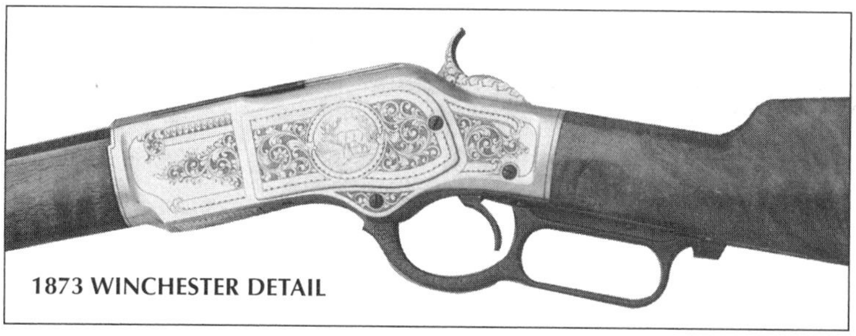

1873 WINCHESTER DETAIL

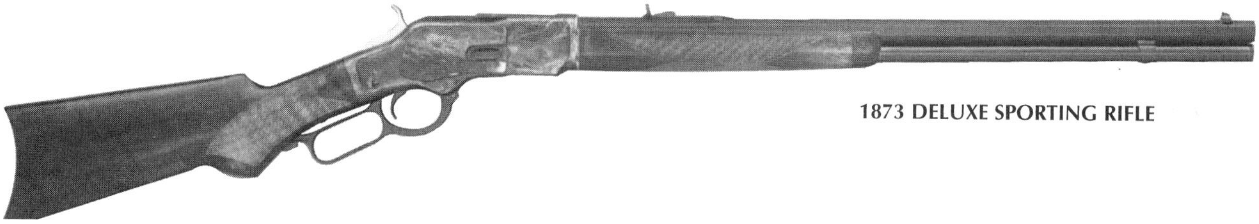

1873 DELUXE SPORTING RIFLE

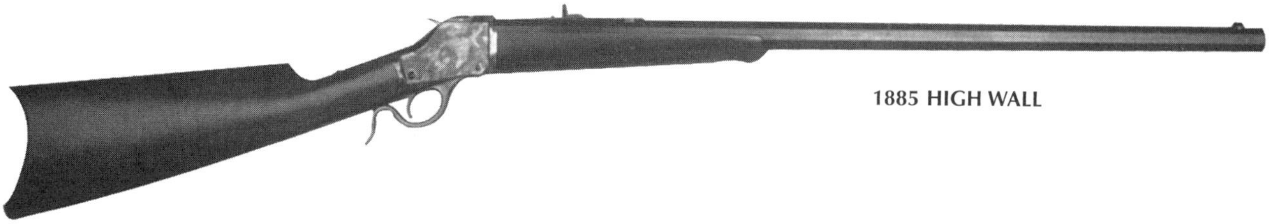

1885 HIGH WALL

1873 WINCHESTER

Action: lever
Stock: walnut, straight grip
Barrel: 24 in.
Sights: open
Weight: 7.5 lbs.
Caliber: .45 Colt, .44 WCF, .357, .32 WCF, .38 WCF, .44 Special
Magazine: under-barrel tube, 11 rounds
Features: Available: "Sporting" model, "Deluxe" model, "Long Range" model (30 in. barrel), and carbine (19 in. barrel); Deluxe model has pistol grip
Sporting: $1357.86
Deluxe: $1513.48
Long Range: $1424.36
Long Range Deluxe: $1558.04
Carbine: $1364.95

1885 HIGH WALL

Action: dropping block
Stock: walnut, straight grip
Barrel: octagon 30 in.
Sights: open
Weight: 9.5 lbs.
Caliber: .45-70, .45-90, .45/120, .40-65, .38-55, .348 Win., .30-40 Krag
Magazine: none
Features: reproduction of the Winchester single-shot hunting rifle popular in the 1880s
1885: $1112.46–1320.40

Cimarron Rifles

BILLY DIXON 1874
SHARPS SPORTING

QUIGLEY
MODEL 1874 SHARPS

BILLY DIXON 1874 SHARPS SPORTING

Action: dropping block
Stock: walnut, straight grip
Barrel: octagon 32 in.
Sights: open
Weight: 10.5 lbs.
Caliber: .45-70, .45-90, .45-110, .50-90
Magazine: none
Features: single-shot reproduction
MSRP: 1370.60

QUIGLEY MODEL 1874 SHARPS

Action: dropping block
Stock: walnut, straight grip
Barrel: octagon 34 in.
Sights: open
Weight: 10.5 lbs.
Caliber: .45-70, .45-90, .45-120
Magazine: none
Features: single-shot reproduction
MSRP: $1524.60

Colt Rifles

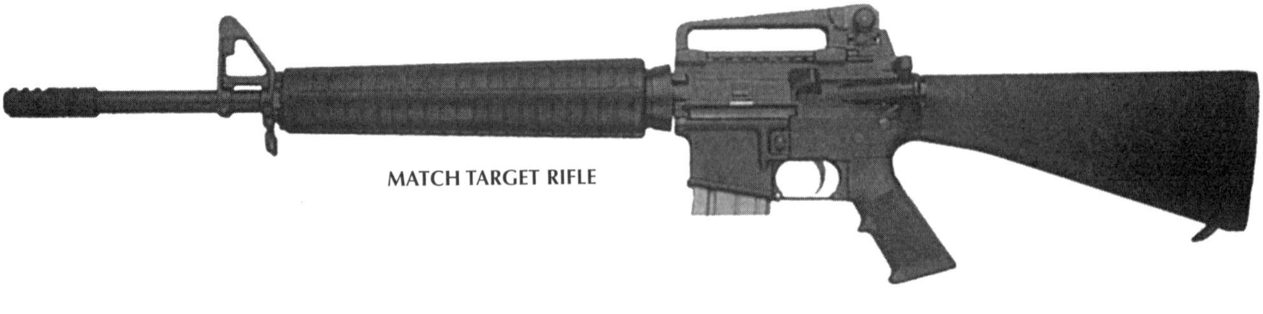

MATCH TARGET RIFLE

MATCH TARGET RIFLE

Action: autoloading
Stock: combat-style, synthetic
Barrel: 16 or 20 in.
Sights: open
Weight: 8.0 lbs.
Caliber: .223
Magazine: detachable box, 9 rounds
Features: suppressed recoil; accepts optics; 2-position safety; available with heavy barrel, compensator
Match Target: $1218–1328

Cooper Rifles

COOPER 52

Action: three-lug bolt
Stock: checkered walnut
Barrel: 24″
Sights: none
Weight: 7 ¾ lbs.
Caliber: .25-06, .270, .280, .280 Imp., .30-06, .338-06, .35 Whelen
Magazine: detachable box, single stack
Features: semi-controlled feed, match-dimension chamber in air-gauged barrel, glass-bedded action, Remington-style recoil lug,
Price: from $1450
MSRP: $1790

Cooper Arms Rifles

CLASSIC

JACKSON SQUIRREL RIFLE

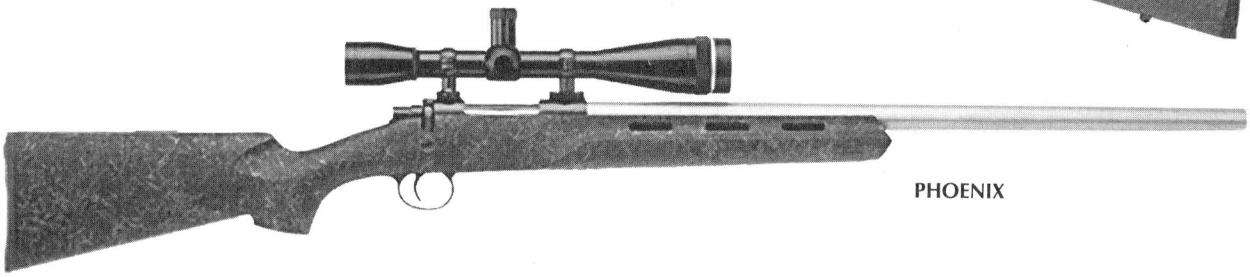

PHOENIX

CLASSIC SERIES

Action: bolt
Stock: checkered, Claro walnut
Barrel: match grade 22 in.
Sights: none
Weight: 6.5 lbs.
Caliber: .22 LR, .22 WMR, .17 HMR, .38 Hornet, .223, .308
Magazine: none
Features: single-shot; 3-lug bolt; also available in Custom Classic and Western Classic with upgraded wood
Classic: $1595–1695
Custom Classic: $2495–3195
Western Classic: $3295–3895

JACKSON SQUIRREL RIFLE

Action: bolt
Stock: walnut
Barrel: 22 in.
Sights: none (fitted with scope bases)
Weight: 6.5 lbs.
Caliber: .22LR, .22WMR, .17HMR, .17 Mach 2
Magazine: detachable box, 4 or 5 rounds
Features: Stainless match grade barrel; Pachmayr butt pad; matte finished
MSRP: $1755

PHOENIX

Action: bolt
Stock: synthetic (Kevlar)
Barrel: 24 in.
Sights: none (fitted with scope bases)
Weight: 7.5 lbs.
Caliber: .17 Rem, .17 Mach IV, .223 Tactical, .204 Ruger, . 221 Fireball, .222 Rem, .222 Rem Mag, .223 Rem, .223 Rem AI, .22 PPC, 6mm PPC, 6x45, 6x47, 6.8 SPC
Magazine: single shot
Features: matte stainless barrel; aircraft-grade aluminum bedding block; stock: hand-laid synthetics with Kevlar reinforcing surround; Model 21 and 22, right-hand option only
MSRP: $1495–1775

Cooper Arms Rifles

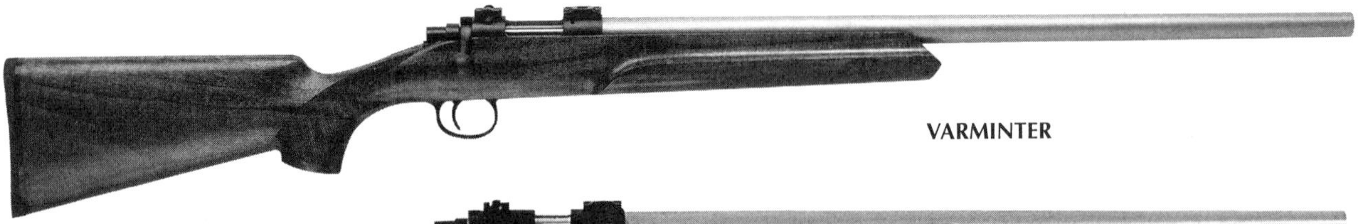

VARMINTER

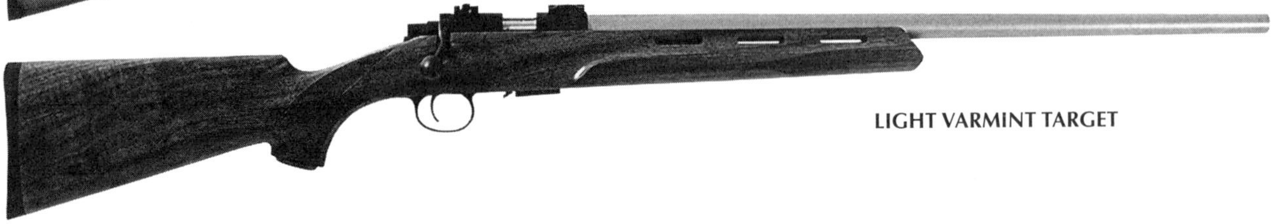

LIGHT VARMINT TARGET

RIFLES

VARMINT SERIES
Action: bolt
Stock: checkered, Claro walnut
Barrel: stainless steel match, 24 in.
Sights: none
Weight: 7.5 lbs.
Caliber: .223, .38 Hornet, .308
Magazine: none
Features: 3-lug action in 4 sizes;
Also available: Montana Varminter, Varminter Extreme and Lightweight LVT

Varminter: $1495–1855
Montana Varminter:. . . . $1695–1995
Varminter Extreme: $2095–2395
Light Varmint Target: $1755

CZ (Ceska Zbrojovka Uhersky Brod) Rifles

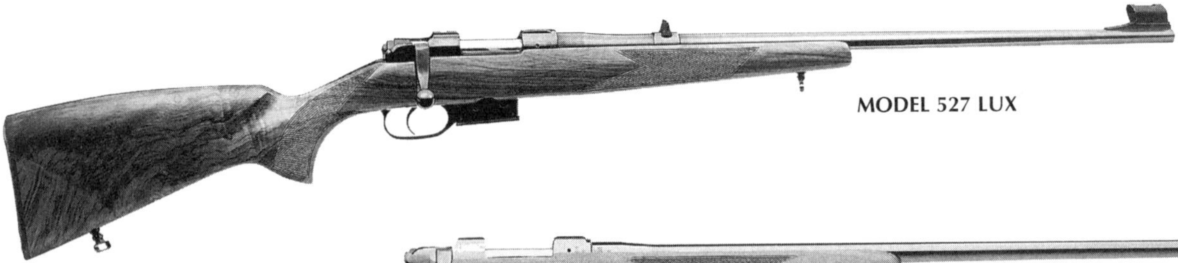

MODEL 527 LUX

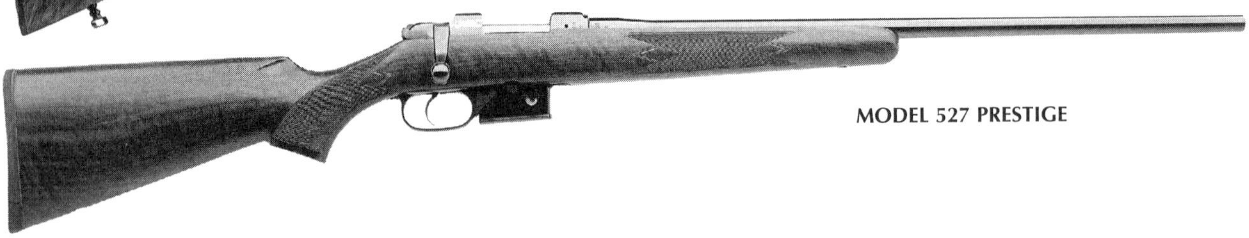

MODEL 527 PRESTIGE

MODEL 527
Action: bolt
Stock: checkered, walnut sporter
Barrel: 24 in.
Sights: open
Weight: 6.2 lbs.
Caliber: .22 Hornet, .222, .223
Magazine: detachable box, 5 rounds
Features: CZ 527 Carbine in .223, 7.62x39, CZ 527 full stock (FS) in .22 Hornet, .222 and .223 with 20 in. barrel and 527 Prestige in .22 Hornet and .223 with 22 in. barrel

Varmint:. $718
Lux: $718
American: $751
Carbine: $727
FS: $827
Varmint Kevlar: $955

CZ (Ceska Zbrojovka Uhersky Brod) Rifles

MODEL 550

MODEL 550

Action: bolt
Stock: checkered walnut sporter
Barrel: 24 in.
Sights: open
Weight: 7.3 lbs.
Caliber: .243, 6.5x55, .270, 7x57, 7x64, .308, .30-06, 9.3x62
Magazine: box, 5 rounds
Features: adjustable single set trigger; detachable magazine optional; full-stocked model (FS) available; CZ 550 Safari Magnum has magnum length action, express sights in calibers .375 H&H, .416 Rigby, .458 Win.
American: $827
Medium Magnum:. $950
FS: $894
Safari Magnum: $1179

MODEL 550 ULTIMATE HUNTING RIFLE

Action: bolt
Stock: walnut
Barrel: 23.6 in.
Sights: iron, adjustable
Weight: 7.7 lbs.
Caliber: .300 Win Mag
Magazine: box, 3 rounds
Features: broke-in hammer forged blued barrel; boresighted 5.5-22 x 50 Nightforce scope w/ R2 reticle mounted on 1 piece rings; aluminum hard case; minute of angle accuracy guarantee to 1000 yards
MSRP: $4242

MODEL 550 VARMINT

Action: bolt ***Stock:*** walnut
Barrel: heavy varmint 24 in.
Sights: open ***Weight:*** 8.5 lbs.
Caliber: .308 Win., 22-250
Magazine: box, 5 rounds
Features: adjustable single set trigger; laminated stock optional; detachable magazine optional; also available: CZ 550 medium magnum in .7mm Rem. Mag. and .300 Win. Mag.
Varmint: $841
Varmint Laminate: $966

Dakota Arms Rifles

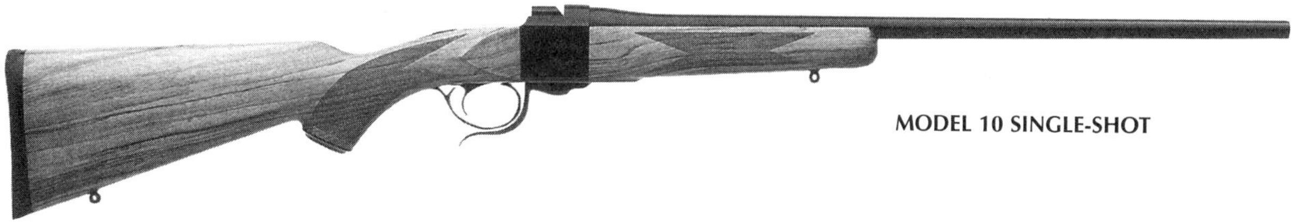

MODEL 10 SINGLE-SHOT

MODEL 10 SINGLE-SHOT

Action: dropping block
Stock: select walnut
Barrel: 23 in.
Sights: none
Weight: 5.5 lbs.
Caliber: from .22 LR to .375 H&H; magnum: .338 Win. to .416 Dakota
Magazine: none
Features: receiver and rear of breech block are solid steel; removable
trigger plate
Action only: $1875
Standard or Magnum: $4695

Dakota Arms Rifles

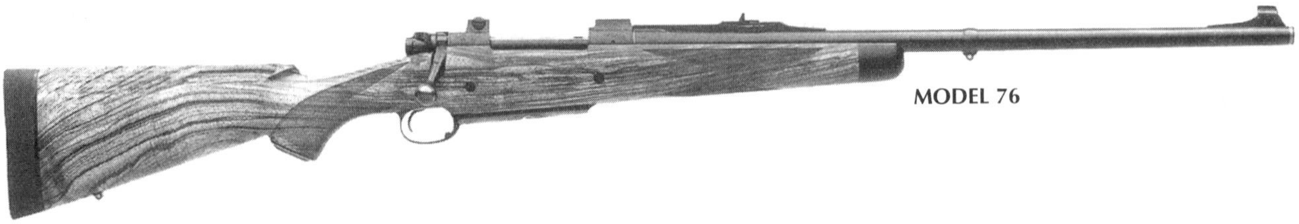

MODEL 76

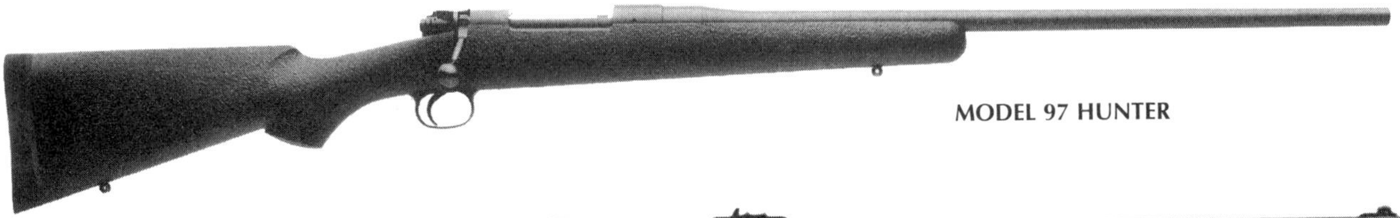

MODEL 97 HUNTER

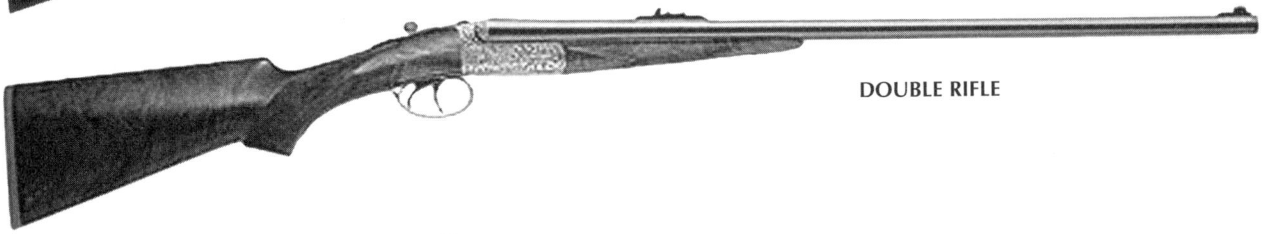

DOUBLE RIFLE

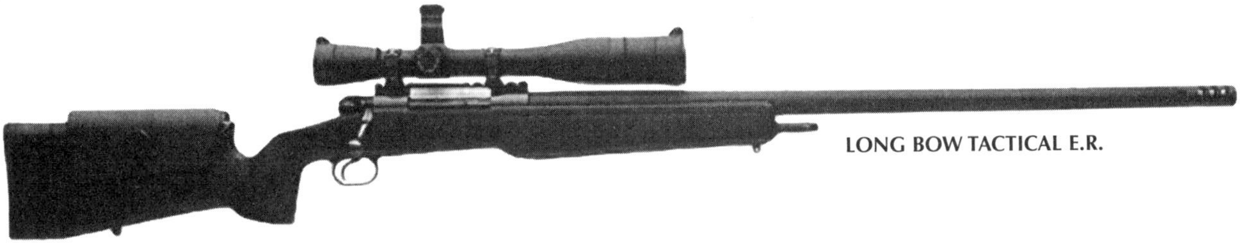

LONG BOW TACTICAL E.R.

MODEL 76

Action: bolt
Stock: select walnut
Barrel: 23-24 in.
Sights: none
Weight: 6.5 lbs.
Caliber: Safari: from .257 Roberts to .458 Win. Mag.; Classic: from .22-250 through .458 Win. Mag.(inc. WSM); African: .404 Jeffery, .416 Dakota, .416 Rigby, .450 Dakota
Magazine: box, 3-5 rounds
Features: three-position striker-blocking safety allows bolt operation with safety on; stock in oil-finished English, Bastogne or Claro walnut; African model weighs 9.5 lbs. and the Safari is 8.5 lbs.
Classic: $4995
Safari: $6795
African: $7595

MODEL 97 HUNTER SERIES

Action: bolt
Stock: walnut or composite
Barrel: 24 in.
Sights: open
Weight: 7.0 lbs.
Caliber: .25-06 through .375 Dakota
Magazine: blind box, 3-5 rounds
Features: 1 in. black recoil pad, 2 sling swivel studs
Long Range Hunter.............. $3395

DOUBLE RIFLE

Action: hinged breech
Stock: exhibition walnut, pistol grip
Barrel: 25 in.
Sights: open
Weight: 9.5 lbs.
Caliber: most common calibers
Magazine: none
Features: round action; elective ejectors; recoil pad; Americase
MSRP: . . . . .Price on request

LONG BOW TACTICAL E.R.

Action: bolt
Stock: McMillan fiberglass, matte finish
Barrel: stainless, 28 in.
Sights: open
Weight: 13.7 lbs.
Caliber: .338 Lapua, .300 Dakota and .330 Dakota
Magazine: blind, 3 rounds
Features: adjustable cheekpiece; 3 sling swivel studs; bipod spike in forend; controlled round feeding; one-piece optical rail; 3-position firing pin block safety; deployment kit; muzzle brake
MSRP: $4795

Dakota Arms Rifles

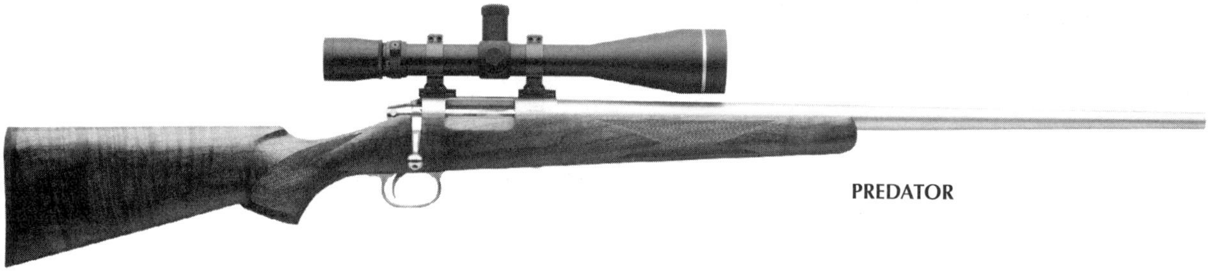

PREDATOR

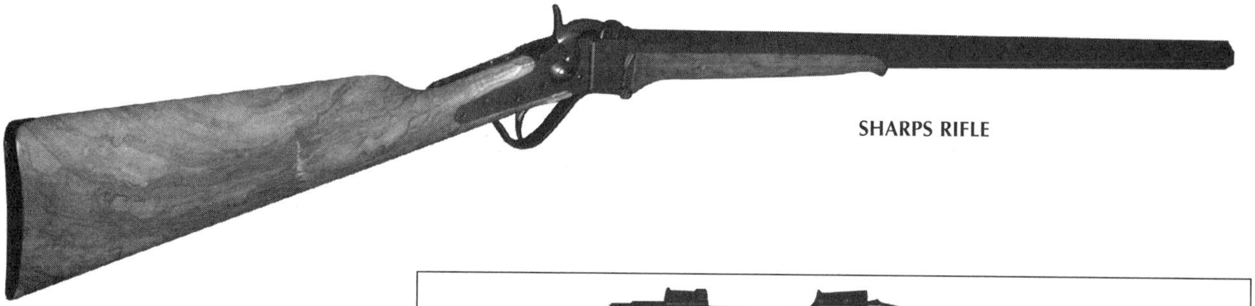

SHARPS RIFLE

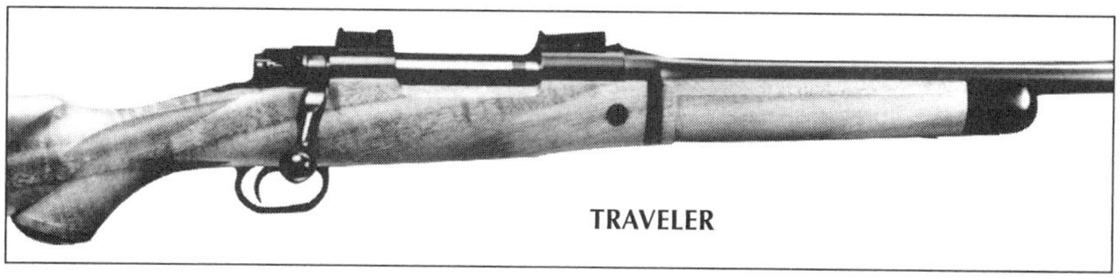

TRAVELER

PREDATOR

Action: bolt
Stock: checkered walnut
Barrel: match-grade stainless
Sights: none ***Weight:*** 9.0 lbs.
Caliber: .17 VarTarg, .17 Rem., .17 Tactical, .20 VarTarg, .20 Tactical, .20 PPC, .204 Ruger, .221 Fireball, .222 Rem., .222 Rem. Mag., .223 Rem., .22 BR, 6 PPC, 6 BR
Magazine: none
Features: many options, including fancy walnut
MSRP: $1995–4295

SHARPS RIFLE

Action: dropping block
Stock: walnut, straight grip
Barrel: octagon 26 in.
Sights: open ***Weight:*** 8.0 lbs.
Caliber: .17 HRM to .30-40 Krag
Magazine: none
Features: small frame version of 1874 Sharps
MSRP: $4295

TRAVELER

Action: bolt
Stock: take-down, checkered walnut
Barrel: choice of contours, lengths
Sights: none
Weight: 8.5 lbs.
Caliber: all popular cartridges
Magazine: box, 3-5 rounds
Features: the Dakota Traveler is based on the Dakota 76 design. It features threadless disassembly. Weight and barrel length depend on caliber and version.
Classic: $6095
Safari: $7895
African: $9495

Dixie Rifles

1873 SPRINGFIELD "TRAPDOOR"

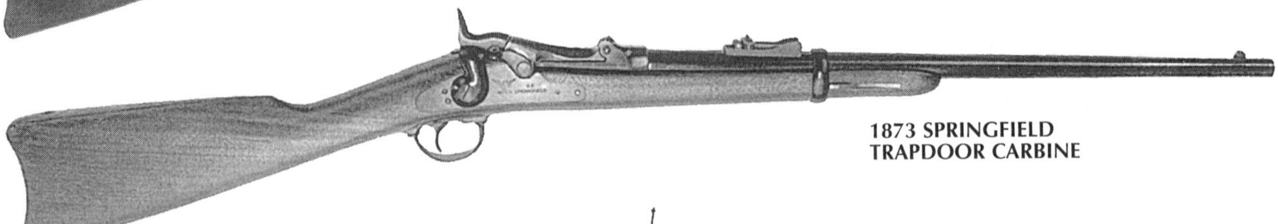

1873 SPRINGFIELD
TRAPDOOR CARBINE

1874 SHARPS LIGHTWEIGHT
HUNTER SILHOUETTE

1874 SHARPS HUNTER

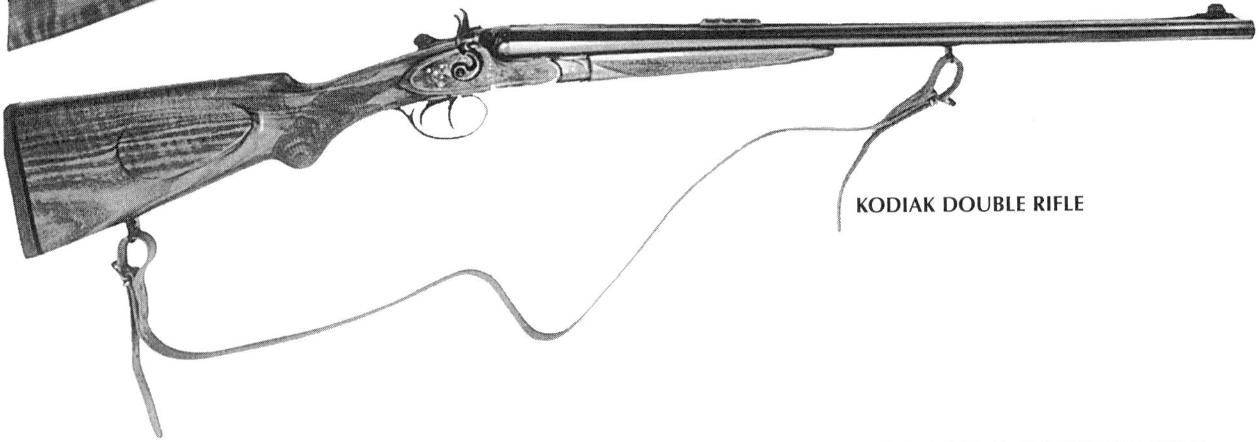

KODIAK DOUBLE RIFLE

1873 SPRINGFIELD "TRAPDOOR"

Action: hinged breech
Stock: walnut
Barrel: 26 or 32 in. (22 in carbine)
Sights: adjustable
Weight: 8.0 lbs.
Caliber: .45-70
Magazine: none
Features: single-shot rifle; first cartridge rifle of U.S. Army; Officer's Model (26 in.) has checkered stock; weight with 32 in. Barrel: 8.5 lbs. and 7.5 lbs. for carbine
1873 Springfield "Trapdoor": . $1225
Officer's Model: $1600
Carbine: $1200

1874 SHARPS LIGHTWEIGHT HUNTER

Action: dropping block
Stock: walnut
Barrel: 30 in.
Sights: adjustable
Weight: 10.0 lbs.
Caliber: .45-70
Magazine: none
Features: case-colored receiver, drilled for tang sights; also 1874 Sharps Silhouette Hunter in .40-65 or .45-70
Hunter: $1050
Silhouette:. $1200

KODIAK DOUBLE RIFLE BY PEDERSOLI

Action: hinged breech
Stock: walnut
Barrel: 24 in.
Sights: open, folding leaf
Weight: 10.0 lbs.
Caliber: .45-70
Magazine: none
Features: double-barrel rifle with exposed hammers
MSRP: $4500

DPMS Panther Rifles

16-INCH AP4

A2 TACTICAL 16-INCH

AP4 CARBINE

16-INCH AP4 POST BAN W/MICULEK COMP.

Action: autoloader
Stock: synthetic
Barrel: 16 in.
Sights: open
Weight: 7.25 lbs.
Caliber: 5.56 x 45mm
Magazine: detachable box, 30 rounds
Features: forged aluminum alloy A3 flattop upper receiver with detachable carry handle; forged aluminum alloy lower receiver with semi-auto trigger group; AP4 contour chrome-moly steel barrel with fixed Miculek compensator; length*:* 34 in.
MSRP: $989

A2 TACTICAL 16-INCH

Action: autoloader
Stock: synthetic
Barrel: 16 in.
Sights: open
Weight: 9.75 lbs.
Caliber: 5.56 x 45mm
Magazine: detachable box, 30 rounds
Features: forged aluminum alloy upper receiver with A2 fixed carry handle; forged aluminum alloy lower receiver with semi-auto trigger group; heavy chrome-moly steel barrel with A2 flash hider; length*:* 34.75 inches
MSRP: $829

AP4 CARBINE

Action: autoloader
Stock: synthetic
Barrel: 16 in.
Sights: none
Weight: 6.7 lbs.
Caliber: 5.56 x 45mm
Magazine: detachable box, 30 rounds
Features: forged aluminum alloy A3 flattop upper receiver with detachable carry handle and adjustable rear sight; forged aluminum alloy lower receiver with semi-auto trigger group; chrome-moly steel barrel; telescoping stock*:* 36.24 in. extended, 32.5 collapsed
MSRP: $894

DPMS Panther Rifles

ARCTIC

SUPER BULL 24

BULL TWENTY

ARCTIC

Action: autoloader
Stock: synthetic
Barrel: 20 in.
Sights: none
Weight: 9.0 lbs.
Caliber: .223 Rem.
Magazine: detachable box, 30 rounds
Features: forged aluminum alloy A3 flattop upper receiver; forged aluminum alloy lower receiver with semi-auto trigger group; stainless steel fluted bull barrel; white coated, vented aluminum free float handguards
MSRP: $1099

BULL 24 SPECIAL & SUPER BULL 24

Action: autoloader
Stock: synthetic
Barrel: 24 in.
Sights: none
Weight: 10.25 lbs. (Bull 24 Special), 11.75 lbs.
Caliber: .223 Rem.
Magazine: detachable box, 30 rounds
Features: forged aircraft aluminum alloy A3 flattop upper receiver; forged aluminum alloy lower receiver with semi-auto trigger group; stainless steel fluted bull barrel; length: 43 inches (Bull 24 Special)
Bull 24 Special: $1189

BULL SWEET SIXTEEN, TWENTY AND TWENTY-FOUR

Action: autoloader
Stock: synthetic
Barrel: 16, 20, or 24 in.
Sights: none
Weight: 7.75 lbs. (16 in.), 9.5 lbs. (20 in.), 9.8 lbs. (24 in.)
Caliber: .223 Rem.
Magazine: detachable box, 30 rounds
Features: forged aircraft aluminum alloy A3 flattop upper receiver; forged aluminum alloy lower receiver with semi-auto trigger group; stainless steel bull barrel
Bull Sweet Sixteen: $909
Bull Twenty:. $939
Bull Twenty-Four:. $969

DPMS Panther Rifles

16-INCH CARBINE

CLASSIC

DCM

LITE 16

CARBINE

Action: autoloader
Stock: synthetic
Barrel: 11.5 in. and 16 in.
Sights: none
Weight: 6.9 lbs. (11.5 in.), 7.06 lbs. (16 in.)
Caliber: 5.56 x 45mm
Magazine: detachable box, 30 rounds
Features: forged aluminum alloy upper receiver with A2 fixed carry handle and adjustable rear sight; forged aluminum alloy lower receiver with semi-auto trigger group; chrome-moly steel barrel flash hider; telescoping AP4 (6 position) stock*:* 35.5 in. extended, 31.75 collapsed (11.5 in.), 36.26 in. extended, 32.75 collapsed (16 in.)
11.5-inch Carbine: $894
16-Inch Carbine: $894

CLASSIC

Action: autoloader
Stock: synthetic
Barrel: 16 in., 20 in. (Classic)
Sights: open
Weight: 7.06 lbs. (Classic Sixteen), 9 lbs. (Classic)
Caliber: 5.56 x 45mm
Magazine: detachable box, 30 rounds
Features: forged aircraft aluminum alloy upper receiver with A2 fixed carry handle; forged aluminum alloy lower receiver with semi-auto trigger group; heavy chrome-moly steel barrel with A2 flash hider; chrome-plated steel bolt carrier with phosphated steel bolt
Classic Sixteen: $829
Classic: $849

DCM

Action: autoloader
Stock: synthetic
Barrel: 20 in.
Sights: none
Weight: 9.0 lbs.
Caliber: .223 Rem.
Magazine: detachable box, 30 rounds
Features: forged aluminum alloy upper receiver with A2 fixed carry handle and adjustable NM rear sight; forged aluminum alloy lower receiver with two stage semi-auto trigger group; stainless steel heavy barrel; length*:* 38.5 inches
MSRP: $1099

LITE 16

Action: autoloader
Stock: synthetic
Barrel: 16 in.
Sights: open
Weight: 5.7 lbs.
Caliber: 5.56 x 45mm
Magazine: detachable box, 30 rounds
Features: forged aluminum alloy upper receiver with A1 fixed carry handle; forged aluminum alloy lower receiver with semi-auto trigger group; chrome-moly steel lite-contour barrel with A2 flash hider; chrome plated steel bolt carrier with phosphated steel bolt; A1 rear and front sights
MSRP: $759

DPMS Panther Rifles

LONG RANGE .308

LO-PRO CLASSIC

RIFLES

LONG RANGE .308

Action: autoloader
Stock: synthetic
Barrel: 24 in.
Sights: none
Weight: 11.28 lbs.
Caliber: .308 Winchester
Magazine: detachable box, 9 rounds
Features: extruded aluminum upper receiver; milled aluminum lower receiver; Picatinny rail; stainless steel bull barrel; A-15 trigger group; length 43.6 in.
MSRP: $1099

LO-PRO CLASSIC

Action: autoloader
Stock: synthetic
Barrel: 16 in.
Sights: none
Weight: 7.75 lbs.
Caliber: .223 Rem.
Magazine: detachable box, 30 rounds
Features: extruded aluminum alloy flattop Lo-Pro upper receiver; forged aluminum alloy lower receiver with semi-auto trigger group; chrome-moly steel bull barrel; length: 34.75 in.
MSRP: $759

Ed Brown Rifles

DAMARA

DAMARA

Action: bolt
Stock: McMillan composite
Barrel: #1.5, 22 in.
Sights: none ***Weight:*** 6.1 lbs.
Caliber: .22-250, .243, 6mm, .260, 7mm/08, .308, .270 WSM, 7mm WSM, .300 WSM
Magazine: box, 5 rounds (WSM: 3)
Features: lapped barrel, 3 position safety, steel bottom metal; Talley scope mounts with 8-40 screws; also available in long-action: .25/06, .270, .280, 7mm Rem. Mag., 7mm Wby., .300 Win. Mag., .300 Wby. Mag.
MSRP: $3995–4095

Ed Brown Rifles

SAVANNAH

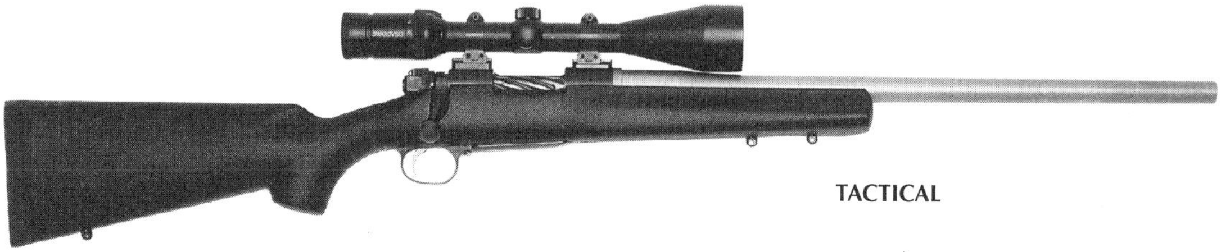

TACTICAL

VARMINT

RIFLES

SAVANNAH

Action: bolt
Stock: McMillan composite
Barrel: #3 lightweight, 24 in.
Sights: open ***Weight:*** 7.5 lbs.
Caliber: .270 WSM, 7mm WSM, .308, .300 WSM
Magazine: box, 3 or 5 rounds
Features: short-action; lapped barrel, 3 position safety, steel bottom metal; long-action model in .270, .280, 7mm Rem. Mag., .30-06, 7mm Wby. Mag., .340 Wby., .300 Win. Mag., .300 Wby. Mag., .338 Win. Mag. with 26 in.; #4 barrel in magnums: 8.0 lbs.
MSRP: $3895–3995

TACTICAL A5

Action: bolt
Stock: McMillan composite tactical
Barrel: heavy 26 in.
Sights: none ***Weight:*** 11.3 lbs.
Caliber: .308, .300 Win. Mag.
Magazine: box, 3 or 5 rounds
Features: Jewell trigger; Talley scope mounts with 8-40 screws
MSRP: $4495

VARMINT

Action: bolt
Stock: McMillan composite varmint
Barrel: medium 24 in. or heavy 24 in.
Sights: none ***Weight:*** 9.0 lbs.
Caliber: .22-250
Magazine: none
Features: lapped barrel, 3 position safety, steel bottom metal; optional 2 oz. trigger
Varmint: $3895

EMF Replica Rifles

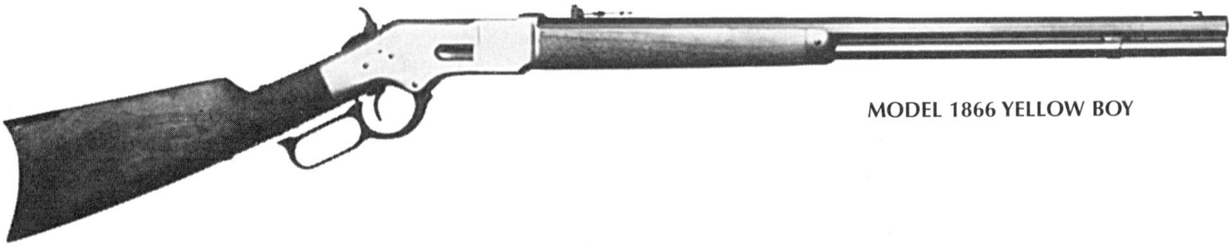

MODEL 1866 YELLOW BOY

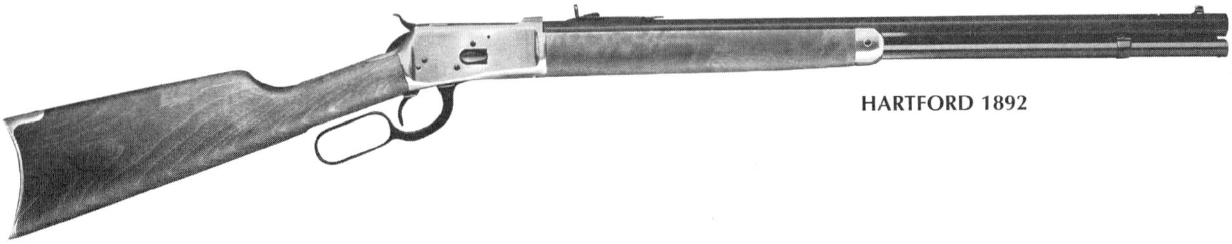

HARTFORD 1892

RIFLES

MODEL 1866 YELLOW BOY

Action: lever
Stock: walnut
Barrel: 24 in.
Sights: open
Weight: 8.0 lbs.
Caliber: .45 LC, .38 Special and .44-40
Magazine: under-barrel tube, 11 rounds
Features: blued barrel; brass frame
MSRP $1075

HARTFORD 1892

Action: lever
Stock: walnut
Barrel: octagon or round 24 in.
Sights: open
Weight: 7.5 lbs.
Caliber: .357 and .45 LC
Magazine: under-barrel tube, 11 rounds
Features: blued, casehardened or stainless steel; carbine has 20 in. barrel
Case-hardened: $610
Blued: $610
Stainless: $610
Carbine, blued, round barrel: $540
Carbine, case-hardened, round barrel: $550
Carbine, stainless, round barrel: $580

Excel Industries Rifles

ACCELERATOR

Action: autoloading
Stock: synthetic
Barrel: 18 in.
Sights: none
Weight: 8.0 lbs.
Caliber: .17 HMR, .22 WMR
Magazine: detachable box, 9 rounds
Features: fluted stainless steel bull barrel; pistol grip stock; aluminum shroud with integral Weaver scope and sight rail; manual safety and firing pin block; last round bolt hold-open feature
MSRP: $488

Harrington & Richardson Rifles

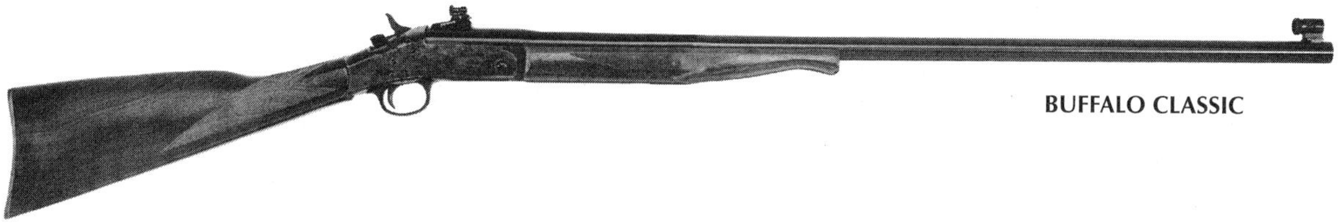

RIFLES

BUFFALO CLASSIC

Action: hinged breech
Stock: checkered walnut
Barrel: 32 in.
Sights: target
Weight: 8.0 lbs.
Caliber: .45-70
Magazine: none
Features: single-shot, break-open action; steel buttplate; Williams receiver sight; Lyman target front sight; antique color case-hardened frame
MSRP: $469.59

CR CARBINE

Action: hinged breech
Stock: checkered American black walnut
Barrel: 20 in.
Sights: carbine-style open sights
Weight: 6.2 lbs.
Caliber: .45 Long colt
Magazine: none
Features: case-colored receiver; case-colored crescent steel buttplate
MSRP: $469.59

ULTRA HUNTER

Action: hinged breech
Stock: hand-checkered, laminate
Barrel: 22, 24, and 26 in.
Sights: none
Weight: 7.0 lbs.
Caliber: .22 WMR, .223 Rem. and .243 (Varmint), .25-06, .30-06, .270, .308 Win
Magazine: none
Features: single-shot with break-open action and side lever release; Monte Carlo stock with sling swivels on stock and forend; scope mount included; weight varies to 8 lbs. with bull barrel
Ultra: $373.73
Ultra in .22 WMR: $5060

Heckler & Koch Rifles

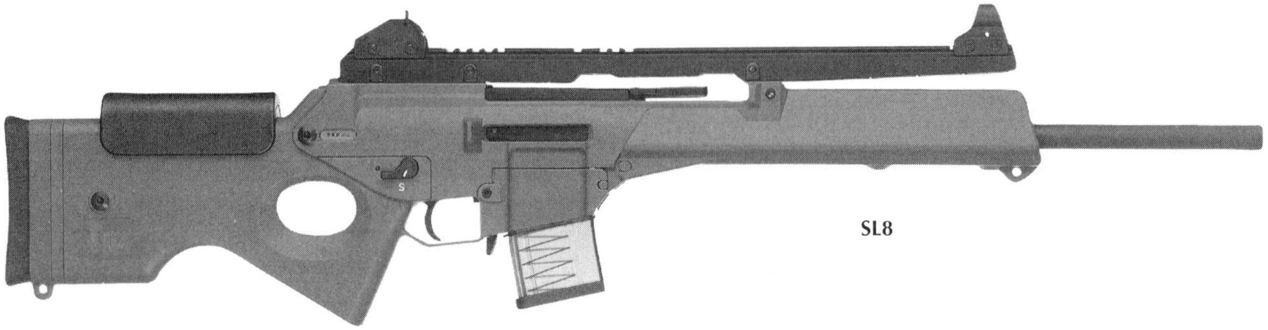

SL8

SL8
Action: autoloading
Stock: synthetic
Barrel: 20.80 in.
Sights: open
Weight: 8.60 lbs.
Caliber: 5.56x45mm
Magazine: detachable box, 10 rounds
Features: delayed roller-locked bolt system; match grade barrel with external fluting; available with Weaver type scope/sight rail or 13-inch Picitinny rail
MSRP: $2053.88

RIFLES

Henry Repeating Arms Rifles

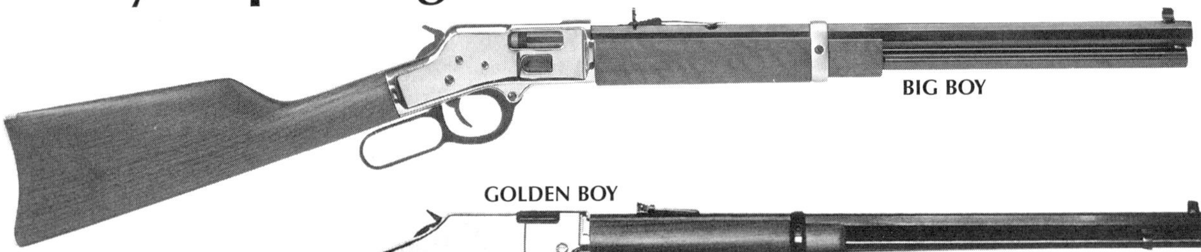

BIG BOY

GOLDEN BOY

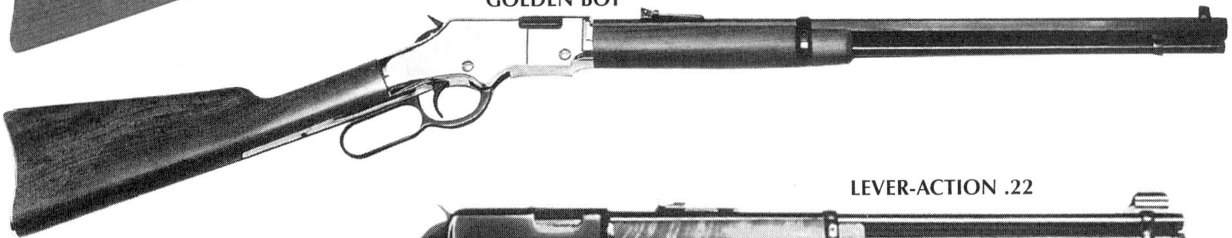

LEVER-ACTION .22

BIG BOY
Action: lever
Stock: walnut
Barrel: 20 in. octagon
Sights: open
Weight: 8.7 lbs.
Caliber: .44 Mag., .45 LC
Magazine: 10 rounds
Features: brass receiver, barrel band, buttplate
MSRP: $900

GOLDEN BOY
Action: lever
Stock: walnut, straight-grip
Barrel: octagon 20 in.
Sights: open *Weight:* 6.8 lbs.
Caliber: .22 LR, .22 WMR, .17 HMR
Magazine: under-barrel tube, 16-22 rounds
Features: brass receiver and buttplate per Winchester 66
Golden Boy (.22 LR): $515
.22 Mag: $595
.17 HMR: $615

LEVER-ACTION .22
Action: lever
Stock: American walnut
Barrel: 18 in.
Sights: open
Weight: 5.5 lbs.
Caliber: .22 S, .22 L, .22 LR
Magazine: under-barrel tube, 15-21 rounds
Features: also available: carbine and youth model; .22 WMR with checkered stock, 19 in. barrel
Rifle, carbine or youth: $325–340
Magnum: $475

Henry Repeating Arms Rifles

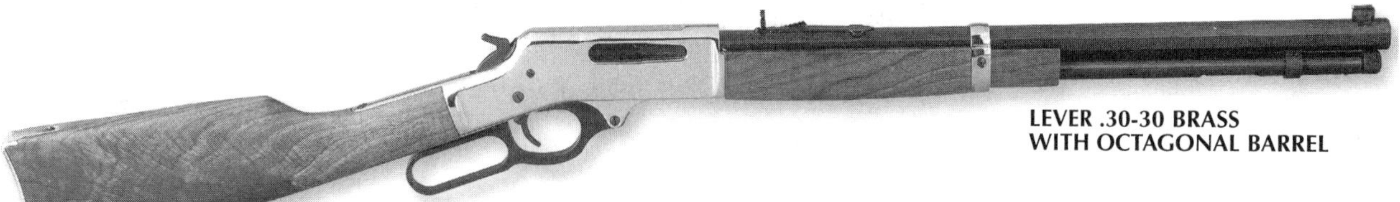

LEVER .30-30 BRASS WITH OCTAGONAL BARREL

MINI BOLT .22

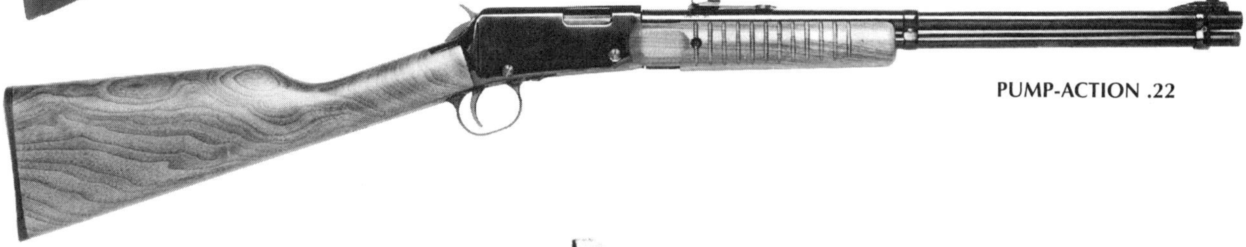

PUMP-ACTION .22

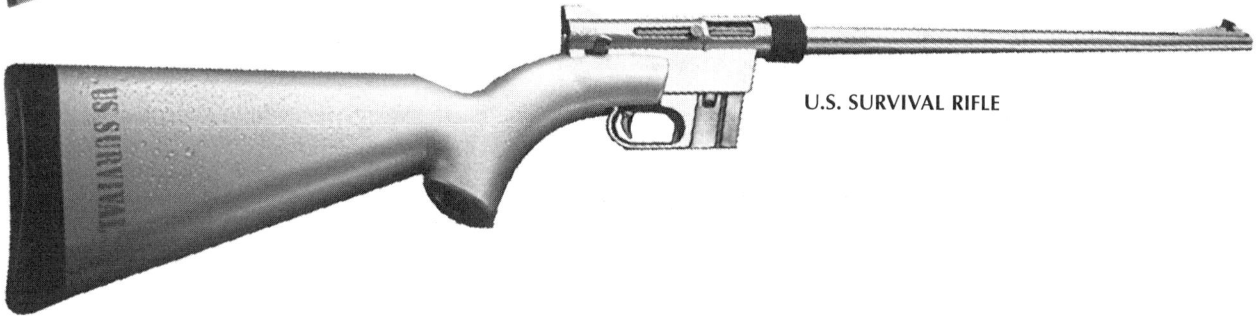

U.S. SURVIVAL RIFLE

LEVER .30-30

Action: lever
Stock: Straight grip American Walnut with buttplate
Barrel: 20-in. round bull (steel version), 20-in. octagonal (brass version)
Sights: Marbles adjustable Semi-Buckhorn rear and brass beaded front
Weight: 8.3 lbs.
Caliber: .30-30
Magazine: 6 rounds
Features: drilled and tapped for scope; tubular feed design
Steel:. $749
Brass:. $970

MINI BOLT .22

Action: bolt
Stock: synthetic
Barrel: stainless 16 in.
Sights: illuminated
Weight: 3.3 lbs.
Caliber: .22 S, .22 L, .22 LR
Magazine: none
Features: single-shot; designed for beginners
Mini Bolt:. $250
Acu-Bolt (20 in. bbl. & 4x scope included): $400

PUMP-ACTION .22

Action: pump
Stock: walnut
Barrel: 18 in.
Sights: open
Weight: 5.5 lbs.
Caliber: .22 LR
Magazine: under-barrel tube, 15 rounds
Features: alloy receiver
MSRP: $515

U.S. SURVIVAL RIFLE

Action: Autoloading
Stock: synthetic butt stock
Barrel: 16 in.
Sights: open
Weight: 4.5 lbs.
Caliber: .22 LR
Magazine: detachable box, 8 rounds
Features: barrel and action stow in water-proof, floating stock
Survival Rifle (black or silver):. $275
Camo: $340

Henry Repeating Arms Rifles

VARMINT EXPRESS

VARMINT EXPRESS

Action: lever
Stock: walnut
Barrel: 20 in.
Sights: none
Weight: 5.8 lbs.
Caliber: .17 HMR
Magazine: 11 rounds
Features: Monte Carlo stock; scope mount included
MSRP: $550

RIFLES

HOWA Rifles

HOWA M-1500 RANCHLAND CAMO

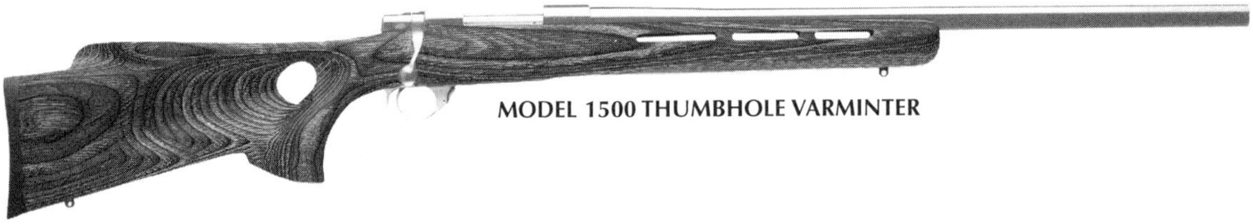

MODEL 1500 THUMBHOLE VARMINTER

HOWA M-1500 RANCHLAND CAMO

Action: two-lug bolt
Stock: composite King's Desert Shadow pattern
Barrel: 20″
Sights: scope included
Weight: 8 ¼ lbs.
Caliber: .204, .223, .22-250, .243, 7mm-08, .308
Magazine: internal box
Features: Full camo combo packages includes Nikko Stirling 3-10x42 camo scope mounted to a one-piece base.
MSRP: $625

MODEL 1500 THUMBHOLE VARMINTER

Action: bolt
Stock: laminated
Barrel: heavy 22 in.
Sights: none ***Weight:*** 9.9 lbs.
Caliber: .223, .22-250, .243 Win., .308
Magazine: 5 rounds
Features: nutmeg, pepper or black stock color, blued or stainless; also*:* Sporter thumbhole version (7.6 lbs.) in 19 calibers including WSMs
Blued sporter: $565
Magnum: $585
Blue: $595
Stainless: $695
Stainless Sporter: $665
Magnum: $685

H-S Precision Rifles

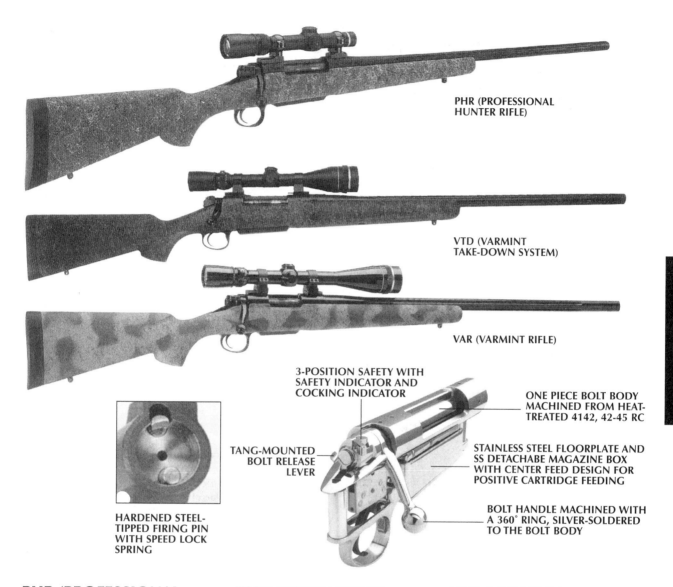

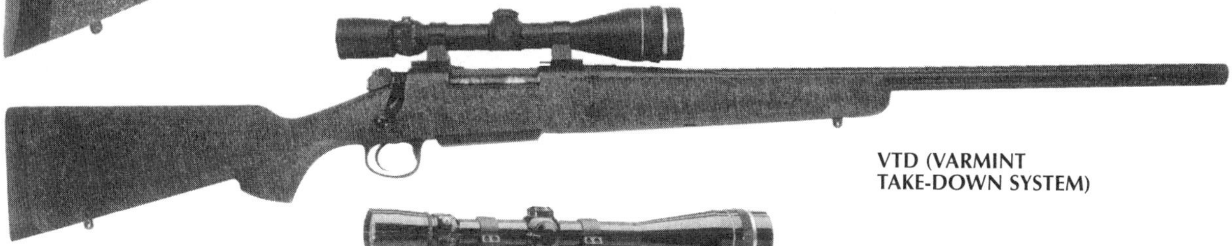

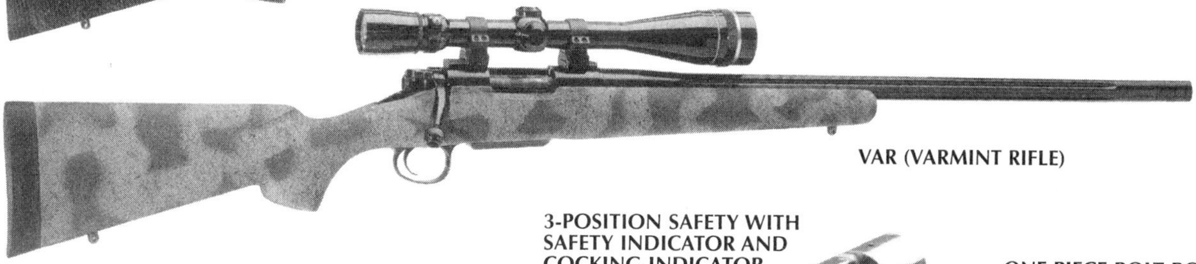

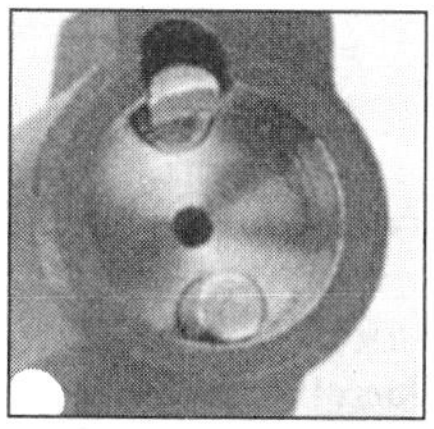

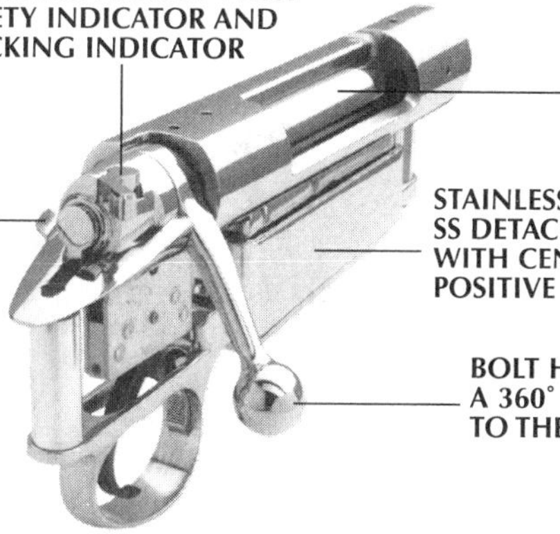

PHR (PROFESSIONAL HUNTER RIFLE)

Action: bolt
Stock: composite
Barrel: 24-26 in.
Sights: none
Weight: 8.0 lbs.
Caliber: all popular magnum calibers up to .375 H&H and .338 Lapua
Magazine: detachable box, 3 rounds
Features: Pro series 2000 action: full-length bedding block, optional 10x Model with match-grade stainless, fluted barrel, muzzle brake, built-in recoil reducer; Lightweight SPR rifle is chambered in standard calibers
MSRP: $3045

TAKE-DOWN RIFLES

Action: bolt
Stock: 2-piece composite
Barrel: any contour and weight 22-26 in.
Sights: none
Weight: 8.0 lbs.
Caliber: any popular standard or magnum chambering
Magazine: detachable box, 3 or 4 rounds
Features: rifle disassembles in front of action and reassembles to deliver identical point of impact; price includes carrying case, TD versions with sporter or tactical stocks; customer's choice of barrels and chambering
Left-hand model: $4700–5200
MSRP: $4500–5000

VAR (VARMINT)

Action: bolt
Stock: composite
Barrel: heavy 24 in.
Sights: none
Weight: 11.0 lbs.
Caliber: all popular varmint calibers
Magazine: detachable box, 4 rounds
Features: Pro-series 2000 action; full-length bedding block; also 10x version with fluted, stainless barrel, optional muzzle
MSRP: $2910

Jarrett Custom Rifles

ORIGINAL BEANFIELD

PROFESSIONAL HUNTER

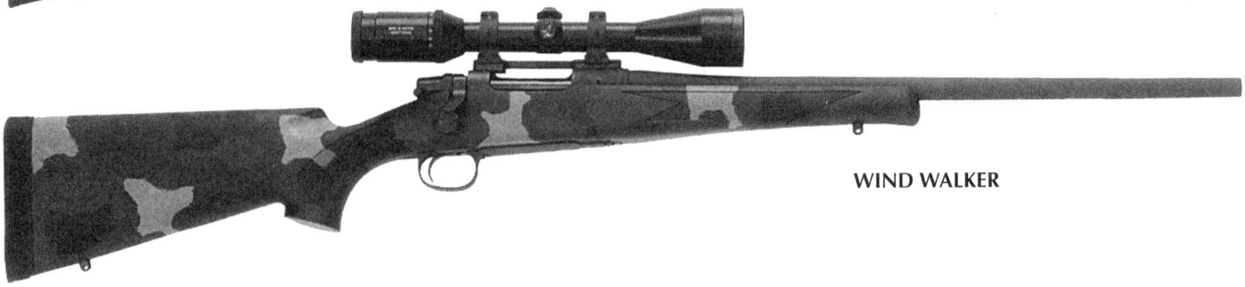

WIND WALKER

ORIGINAL BEANFIELD

Action: bolt
Stock: McMillan synthetic
Barrel: #4 match grade, 24 in.
Sights: none
Weight: 8.5 lbs.
Caliber: any popular standard or magnum
Magazine: box, 3 or 5 rounds
Features: Shilen trigger; Remington 700 or Winchester 70 action; Talley scope mounts, case, sling, load data and 20 rounds of ammunition; Wind Walker has skeletonized 700 action (7.3 lbs.); muzzle brake
MSRP: . . . . starting at $5380

PROFESSIONAL HUNTER

Action: bolt
Stock: synthetic
Barrel: 24 in.
Sights: open
Weight: 9.0 lbs.
Caliber: any popular standard or wildcat chambering
Magazine: 3 or 5 rounds
Features: muzzle brake; also two Leupold 1.5-5x scopes zeroed in Talley QD rings
MSRP: . . . . starting at $10400

WIND WALKER

Action: bolt
Stock: synthetic
Barrel: 20 in.
Sights: none
Weight: 7.5 lbs.
Caliber: any popular short-action
Magazine: box, 3 or 5 rounds
Features: Remington Model 700 short-action; includes Talley scope mounts, choice of scope plus case, sling, load data and 20 rounds of ammunition
MSRP: . . . . starting at $7380

Do you jerk the trigger when shooting a rifle? Adjust the grip of your shooting hand so your thumb doesn't wrap around the wrist of the stock. Sometimes eliminating your ability to "grip" the stock will solve the problem.

Kimber Rifles

MODEL 84M CLASSIC

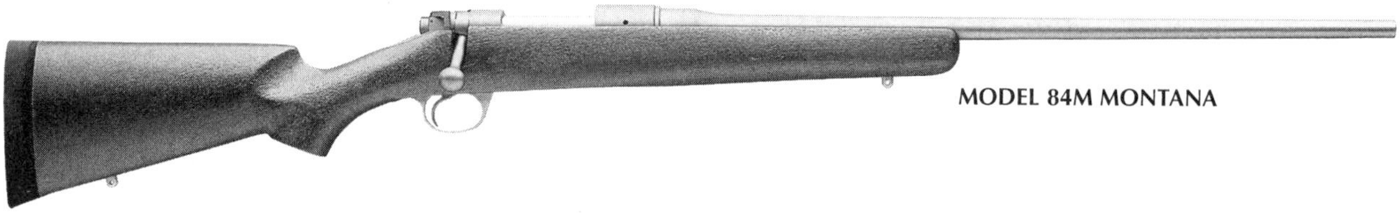

MODEL 84M MONTANA

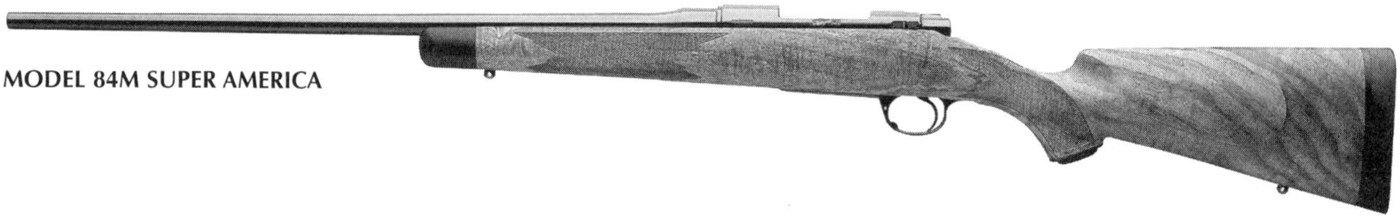

MODEL 84M SUPER AMERICA

KIMBER M 8400 POLICE TACTICAL

KIMBER M 8400 POLICE TACTICAL

Action: two-lug bolt, extended handle
Stock: black, laminated with beavertail forend and three swivel studs (extra for bipod)
Barrel: match grade, 26″ fluted
Sights: none, 20 MOA rail installed
Weight: 8 lbs. 11 oz.
Caliber: .300 Win Mag
Magazine: internal box
Features: fourth in a series of tactical rifles from Kimber, the new Police Tactical is a more powerful version of the Light Police Tactical in .308.
MSRP: $1476

MODEL 84M

Action: bolt
Stock: checkered, Claro walnut
Barrel: light sporter, 22 in.
Sights: none
Weight: 5.6 lbs.
Caliber: .243, .22-250, .260, 7mm-08, .308
Magazine: box, 5 rounds
Features: Varmint model (7.4 lbs.) in .22-250 & .204 Ruger with 26 in. stainless, fluted barrel; Long Master Classic (7.4 lbs) in .223, .243 and .308 with 24 in. stainless, fluted barrel; Long Master VT (10 lbs.) in .22-250 with stainless, bull barrel, laminated target stock; Pro Varmint with 22 in. barrel in .204 Ruger and .223 Rem., 24 in. barrel in .22-250; Short Varmint/ Target (SVT) with 18.25 in. barrel in .223 Rem.
Classic: $1114
Varmint: $1255
Long Master Classic: $1255
Long Master VT: $1391
ProVarmint: $1391
SVT: $1391

MODEL 84M MONTANA

Action: bolt
Stock: synthetic
Barrel: 22 in.
Sights: none
Weight: 5.3 lbs.
Caliber: .308, .243, .260, 7mm-08
Magazine: 5 rounds
Features: stainless steel 84M Montana, standard
MSRP: $1312

MODEL 84M SUPER AMERICA

Action: bolt
Stock: AAA walnut
Barrel: 22 in.
Sights: none
Weight: 5.3 lbs.
Caliber: .308, .243, .260, 7mm-08, .223 Rem.
Magazine: 5 rounds
Features: 24 LPI wrap checkering on select wood
MSRP: $2124

Kimber Rifles

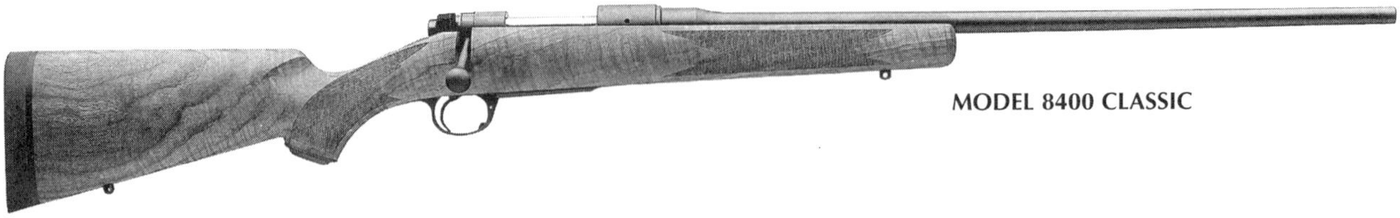

MODEL 8400 CLASSIC

MODEL 8400 CLASSIC
Action: bolt
Stock: walnut
Barrel: 24 in.
Sights: none
Weight: 6.6 lbs.
Caliber: .270, 7mm, .325 WSM and .300 WSM
Magazine: 3 rounds
Features: 3-position safety
8400 Classic: $1172
8400 Montana, WSMs: $1312
8400 Super America: $2240

RIFLES

Krieghoff Rifles

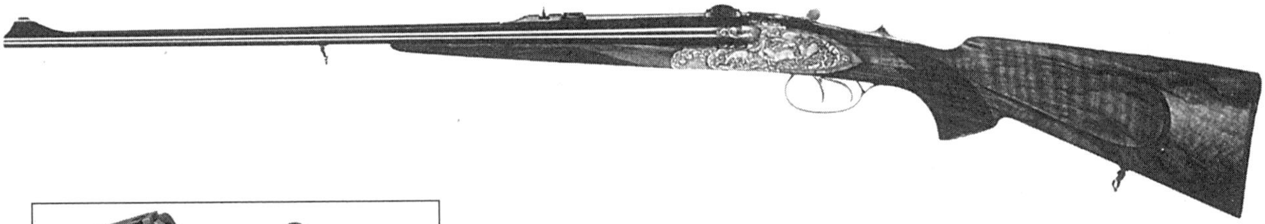

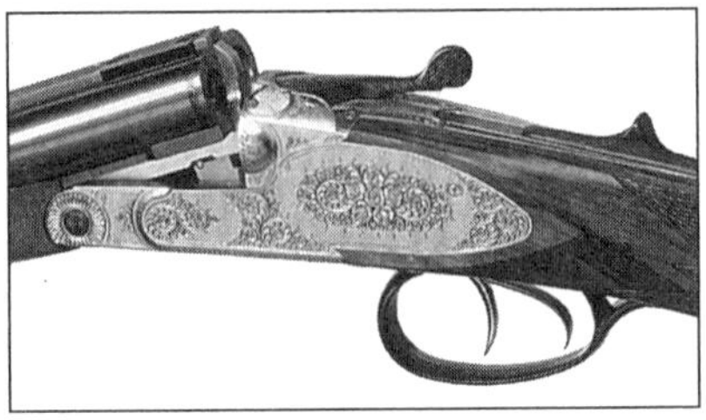

CLASSIC SIDE-BY-SIDE
Action: hinged breech
Stock: select walnut
Barrel: 23.5 in.
Sights: open
Weight: 8.0 lbs.
Caliber: 7x65R, .308, .30-06, .30R Blaser, 8x57, 9.3x74, .375 H&H, .416 Rigby, .458 Win., .470 N.E., .500 N.E.
Magazine: none
Features: thumb-cocking, break-action; double triggers; optional 21.5 in. barrel; engraved side plates; weight depends on chambering and barrel contour
Standard calibers: $9850
Magnum calibers: $12795
Extra barrels
with forearm (fitted): . $4200–8950
Magnum barrels: $8950

L.A.R. Rifles

GRIZZLY BIG BOAR
Action: bolt
Stock: all steel sleeve with rubber butt pad
Barrel: 36 in.
Sights: none
Weight: 30.4 lbs.
Caliber: .50 BMG
Magazine: none
Features: Bull Pup single-shot; descending pistol grip; bi-pod; finish options
Grizzly: $2350
Parkerized: $2450
Nickel-frame: $2600
Full nickel: $2700
Stainless $2600

Lazzeroni Rifles

MODEL 2005 GLOBAL HUNTER
Action: bolt
Stock: synthetic
Barrel: 22 or 26 in.
Sights: none
Weight: 6.1 lbs. (short-action) or 7.4 lbs. (long-action)
Caliber: nine Lazzeroni chamberings, from 6.53 Scramjet to 10.57 Meteor
Magazine: internal box, 3 rounds
Features: fluted stainless sporter barrel; long- or short-action; lightweight graphite composite stock and alloy bottom metal
MSRP: $5499–7999

Legacy Sports International Rifles

PUMA M-92 RIFLES AND CARBINE
Action: lever
Stock: walnut
Barrel: 16, 18 and 20 in.
Sights: open
Weight: 6.0-7.5 lbs.
Caliber: .38/.357, .44 Mag., .45 Colt, .454 Casull, .480 Ruger
Magazine: full-length tube; capacity varies with barrel length
Features: 18-inch barrel ported; available with 24-inch octagon barrel; HiViz sights; .45 carbine with large-loop lever; stainless and blued finishes available
MSRP: . . . . from $899–990

Legacy Sports International Rifles

PUMA SCOUT

Action: lever
Stock: wood
Barrel: 20 in. blued
Sights: 2.5-32 Nikko Stirling riflescope
Weight: unavailable
Caliber: .17 Rem., .38 Spl./.357 Mag., .44 Mag., .45 Colt, .454 Casull
Magazine: 10+1
Features: .454 model fitted with shotgun-style recoil pad; crescent steel buttplates on other models.
MSRP: . . . . $739–$849

PUMA SCOUT

Les Baer Rifles

AR .223 SUPER VARMINT MODEL

Action: autoloader
Stock: synthetic
Barrel: 18 in. and 24 in.
Sights: none
Weight: 13.0 lbs.
Caliber: .204 Ruger
Magazine: detachable box, 5-rounds
Features: Les Baer 416-R stainless barrel; chromed National Match carrier and extractor; titanium firing pin; aluminum gas block with Picatinny top; match-grade stainless; two-stage, 24-inch Jewell trigger; Picatinny rail; optional Leupold Long Range 8.5-25x50mm Vari-X III package; Versa Pod bipod; all-weather Baer Coat finish; camo finish and special rifling twist available as options
MSRP: . . . . starting at $2690

Do most of your live-fire rifle practice with a quality rimfire. It will save money and help overcome flinching.

Lone Star Rifles

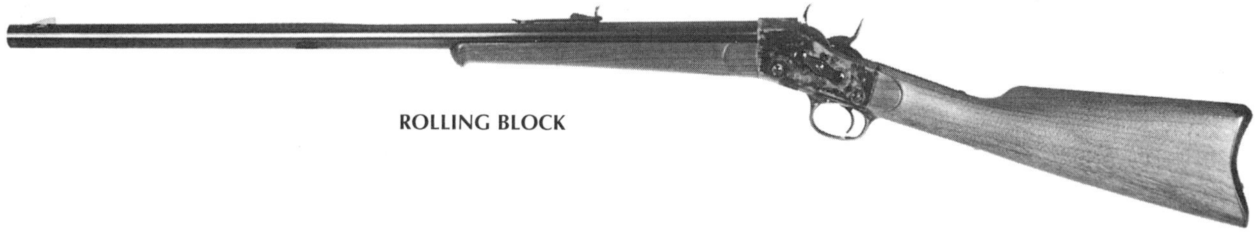

ROLLING BLOCK

ROLLING BLOCK

Action: single shot
Stock: walnut ***Barrel:*** 28-34 in.
Sights: many options
Weight: 6.0-16.0 lbs.
Caliber: .25, .20 WCF, .25-35, .30-30, .30-40, .32-20, .32-40, .38-50, .38-55, .40-50SS, .40-50SBN, .40-70SMB, .40-70SS, .40-82, .40-90SS, .45-70, .45-90, .45-100, .45-110, .45-120, .44-60, .44-77SBN, .44-90SBN, .44-100 Rem. Sp., .50-70, .50-90, .50-140
Magazine: none
Features: true-to-form replicas of post-Civil War Remington rolling blocks; single set or double set triggers; case-colored actions on Silhouette, Creedmoor, Sporting, Deluxe Sporting, Buffalo, Custer Commemorative, #5, #7
Sporting: $2195
Buffalo Rifle: $3200

Magnum Research Rifles

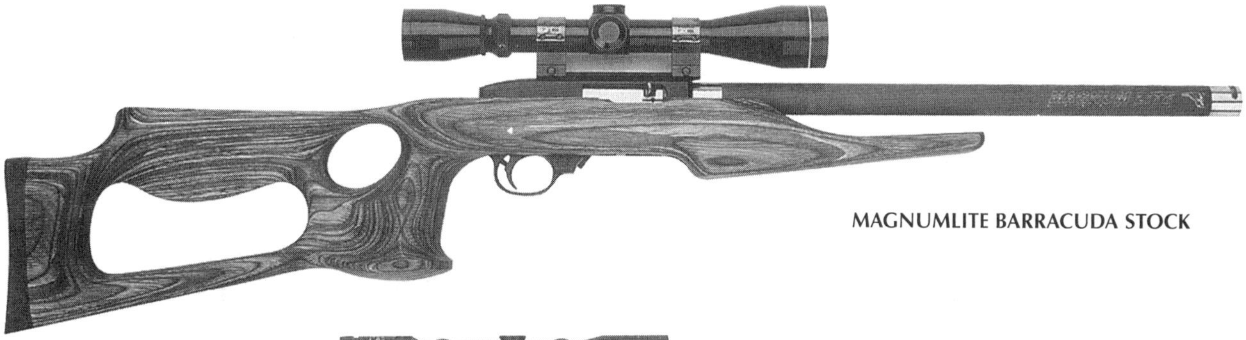

MAGNUMLITE BARRACUDA STOCK

MOUNTAIN EAGLE
MAGNUMLITE GRAPHITE CENTERFIRE

MAGNUMLITE RIMFIRE

Action: autoloading
Stock: composite or laminated
Barrel: graphite sleeved, 16.75 in.
Sights: none
Weight: 5.2 lbs.
Caliber: .22LR, .22 WMR, .17 HMR and .17M2
Magazine: rotary, 9 rounds
Features: Ruger 10/22 action; carbon-fiber barrel with steel liner
With composite stock: $665
.17 M2: $665
.17 HMR: $665
With laminated stock: $665
Magnum with composite: $665
Magnum with laminated: $791

MOUNTAIN EAGLE MAGNUMLITE GRAPHITE CENTERFIRE

Action: bolt
Stock: composite
Barrel: graphite sleeved, 24 or 26 in.
Sights: none
Weight: 7.8 lbs.
Caliber: .280, .30-06, 7mm Rem. Mag., .300 Win. Mag., 7 WSM, .300 WSM
Magazine: box, 3 or 4 rounds
Features: adjustable trigger, free-floating match-grade barrel; platform bedding; left-hand available
MSRP: $2173

Marlin Rifles

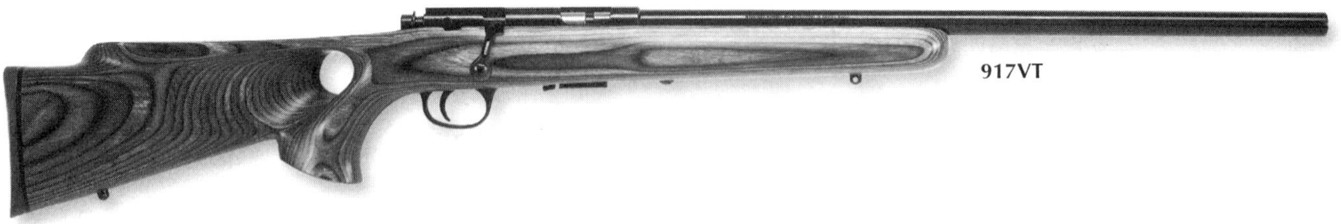

917VST

Action: bolt
Stock: gray and black laminate, thumbhole pistol grip
Barrel: heavy 22 in. with microgroove rifling, stainless steel
Sights: none
Weight: 7 lbs.
Caliber: .17 HMR
Magazine: 4-shot and 7-shot clips
Features: nickel receiver; sling swivel studs; rubber butt pad; grooved, drilled and tapped for scope bases (2 included); thumb safety; red cocking indicator
MSRP: $450

RIFLES

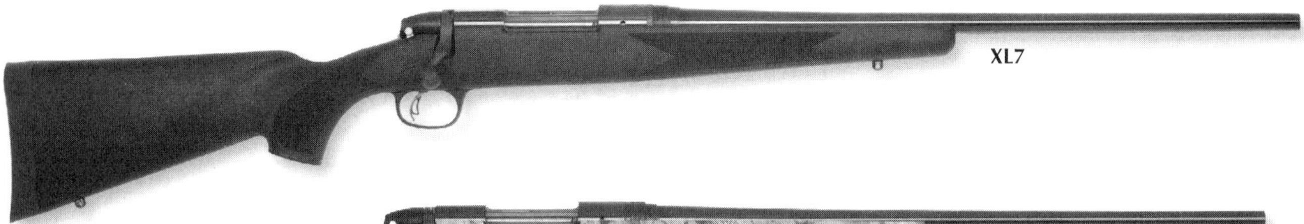

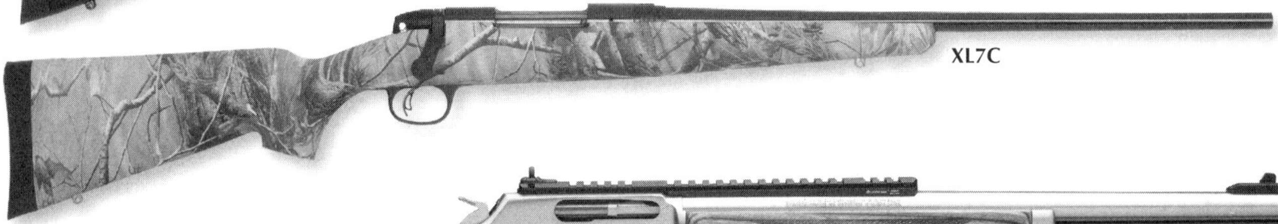

XL7

Action: centerfire bolt
Stock: black synthetic or RealTree APG-HD camo
Barrel: 22 in.
Sights: none; 1-piece Weaver-style scope base included
Weight: 6.5 lbs.
Caliber: .30-06 Spg., .270 Win., .25-06 Rem.
Magazine: 4+1
Features: Fluted bolt; Pro-Fire trigger; Soft-Tech recoil pad; steel swivel studs; Weaver-style 1-piece scope base
MSRP: $397

MARLIN 1895 SBL

Action: lever
Stock: black/gray laminated, pistol grip with fluted comb, cut checkering, deluxe recoil pad
Barrel: stainless steel, 18 ½″
Sights: XS Ghost ring sights, attached Weaver-style rail
Weight: 8 lbs.
Caliber: .45-70 Govt.
Magazine: full-length tube
Features: big loop lever, length*:* 37 inches
MSRP: $1014

MARLIN XL7W

Action: two-lug fluted bolt
Stock: checkered walnut (synthetic and brown laminate stocks also available)
Barrel: 22″
Sights: none, one-piece scope mount included
Weight: 6 ½ lbs.
Caliber: .270 or .30-06 (also new this year*:* short-action XS7 in .243, 7mm-08 and .308)
Magazine: internal box
Features: Pro-Fire Trigger System, Soft-Touch recoil pad, button rifling.
MSRP: $89

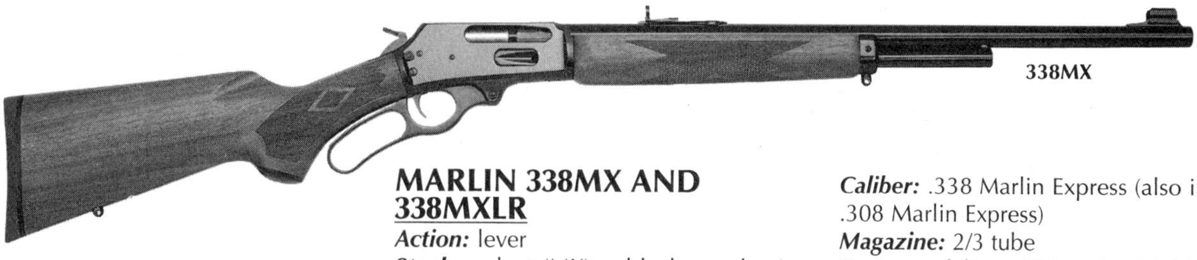

338MX

MARLIN 338MX AND 338MXLR

Action: lever
Stock: walnut (MX) or black-gray laminate (MXLR)
Barrel: 22 or 24 inch blue or stainless
Sights: adjustable semi-buckhorn folding rear, ramp front with brass bead
Weight: 7 ¼ and 7 ½ lbs.
Caliber: .338 Marlin Express (also in .308 Marlin Express)
Magazine: 2/3 tube
Features: delivers 180-grain .30-06 ballistics with a 200-grain bullet at 2,565 fps., 1-in-12 twist
Laminated:. $860
Walnut: $652

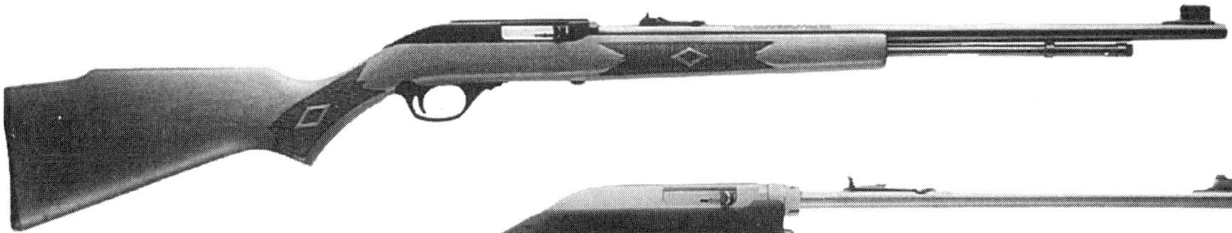

MODEL 60

MODEL 70PSS

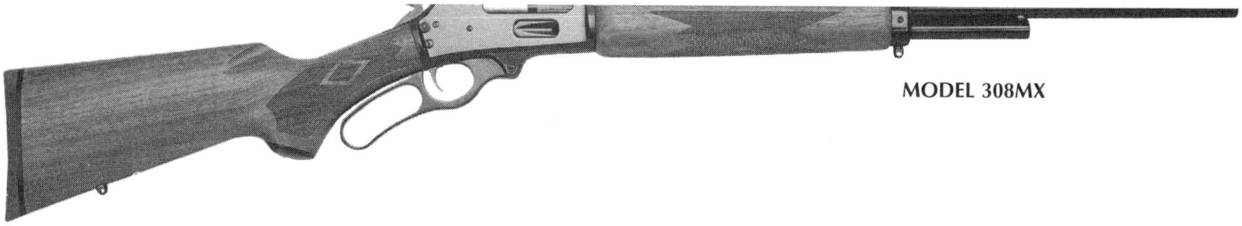

MODEL 308MX

MODEL 60

Action: autoloading
Stock: hardwood
Barrel: 19 in.
Sights: open
Weight: 5.5 lbs.
Caliber: .22 LR
Magazine: under-barrel tube, 14 rounds
Features: last shot hold-open device; stainless, synthetic and laminated stocked versions available; also available with camo-finished stock
Standard:. $190.31
Camo: $224.36
Stainless: $241.31
Stainless, synthetic:. $197.75
Stainless,
laminated two-tone: . . . $165–204

MODEL 70PSS

Action: autoloading
Stock: synthetic
Barrel: 16 in.
Sights: open
Weight: 3.3 lbs.
Caliber: .22 LR
Magazine: detachable box, 7 rounds
Features: take-down rifle; nickel-plated swivel studs; floatable, padded carrying case included
MSRP: $291.59

MODEL 308MX

Action: lever
Stock: American black walnut
Barrel: 22 in.
Sights: adjustable semi-buckhorn folding rear; ramp front sight with brass bead and Wide-Scan hood
Weight: 7 lbs.
Caliber: .308 Marlin Express
Magazine: 5-shot tubular
Features: traditional blued barrel and receiver; full pistol grip; solid-top receiver tapped for scope mount; offset hammer spur (right or left hand) for scope use; deluxe recoil pad; swivel studs; tough Mar-Shield finish
MSRP: $519

Marlin Rifles

MODEL 308MXLR

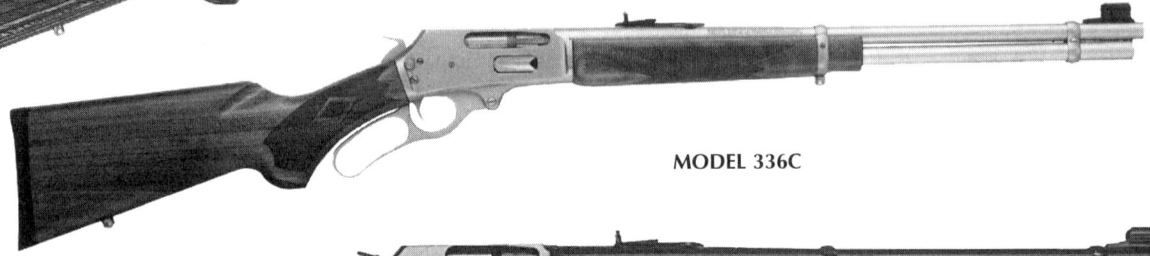

MODEL 336C

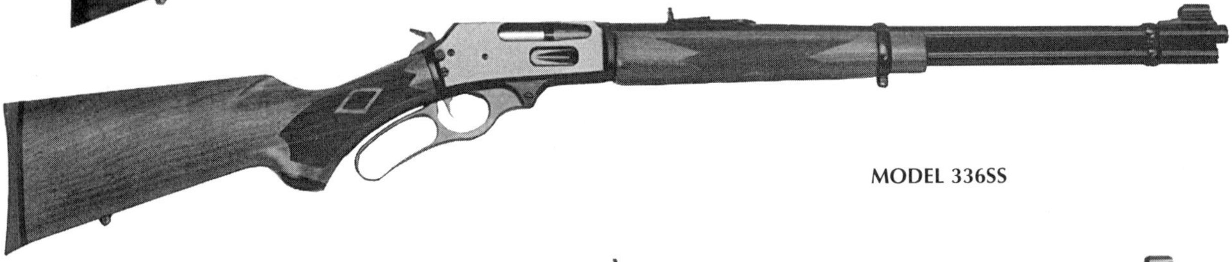

MODEL 336SS

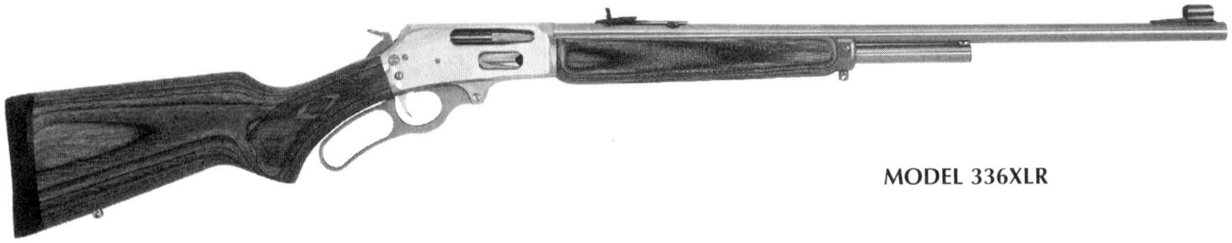

MODEL 336XLR

MODEL 308MXLR

Action: lever
Stock: black/gray laminated hardwood
Barrel: 24 in.
Sights: adjustable semi-buckhorn folding rear; ramp front sight with brass bead and Wide-Scan hood
Weight: 7.0 lbs.
Caliber: .308 Marlin Express
Magazine: 5-shot tubular
Features: stainless-steel barrel and receiver; full pistol grip; Marlin signature solid-top receiver with side-ejection; deluxe recoil pad; nickel plated swivel studs
MSRP: $684

MODEL 336C

Action: lever
Stock: checkered walnut, pistol grip
Barrel: 20 in.
Sights: open
Weight: 7.0 lbs.
Caliber: .30-30 Win., and .35 Rem.
Magazine: tube, 6 rounds
Features: blued; hammer-block safety; offset hammer spur for scope use
Model 336C: $5582
Model 336W, .30-30 only, gold-plated: $424.28

MODEL 336SS

Action: lever
Stock: checkered walnut, pistol grip
Barrel: 20 in.
Sights: open
Weight: 7.0 lbs.
Caliber: .30-30
Magazine: under-barrel tube, 6 rounds
Features: stainless steel; Micro-Groove rifling
MSRP: $545.26

MODEL 336XLR

Action: lever
Stock: laminated
Barrel: 24 in.
Sights: adjustable
Weight: 7.0 lbs.
Caliber: .30/30
Magazine: tube, 5 rounds
Features: 24 in. stainless barrel w/ broached Ballard rifling; stainless solid-top receiver with side-ejection —tapped for scope mount; semi-buckhorn folding rear sight, ramp front sight with Wide-Scan hood; black/gray laminated hardwood pistol grip stock, cut checkering; nickel plated swivel studs; decelerator recoil pad
MSRP: $640.71

MODEL 444

Action: lever
Stock: walnut, pistol grip, fluted comb, checkering
Barrel: 22 in.
Sights: open
Weight: 7.5 lbs.
Caliber: .444 Marlin
Magazine: tube, 5 rounds
Features: blued; hammer-block safety; offset hammer spur for scope use
MSRP: $439.52

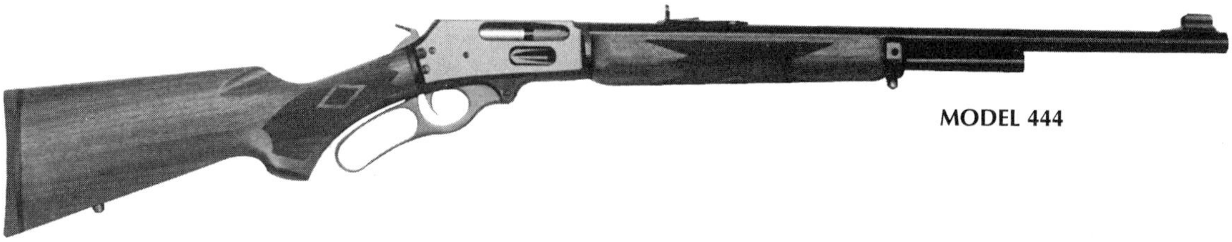

MODEL 444

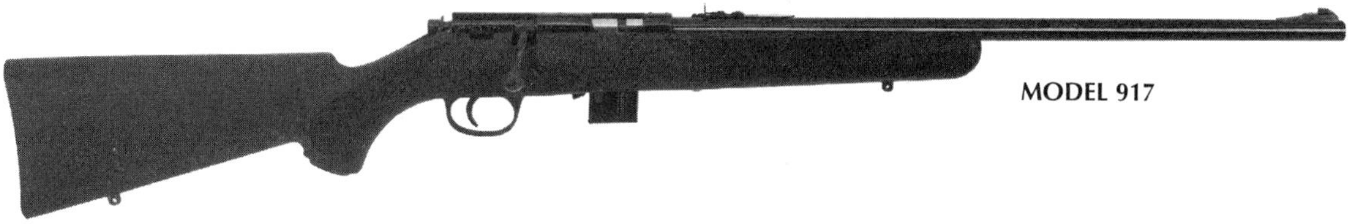

MODEL 917

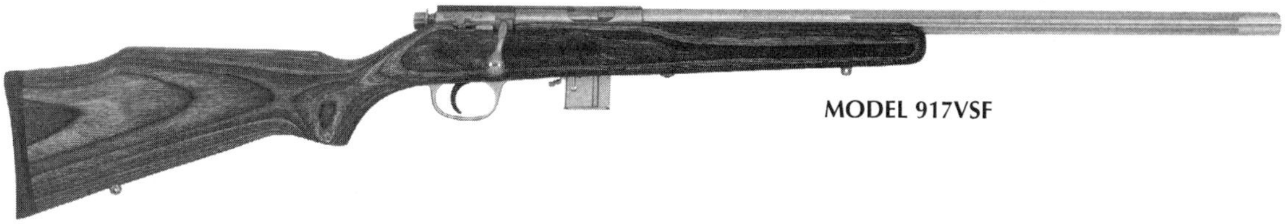

MODEL 917VSF

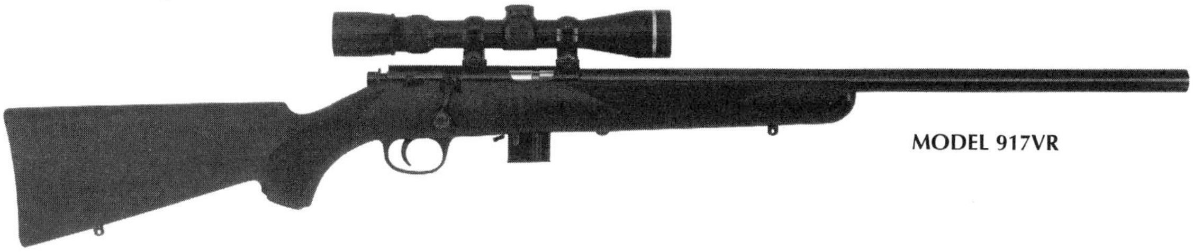

MODEL 917VR

MODEL 444XLR

Action: lever
Stock: laminated
Barrel: 24 in.
Sights: adjustable
Weight: 7.5 lbs.
Caliber: .444 Marlin
Magazine: tube, 5 rounds
Features: 24 in. stainless barrel w/ broached Ballard rifling; stainless solid-top receiver with side-ejection —tapped for scope mount; semi-buckhorn folding rear sight, ramp front sight with Wide-Scan hood; black/gray laminated hardwood pistol grip stock; cut checkering; nickel plated swivel studs; decelerator recoil pad
MSRP: $640.71

MODEL 917

Action: bolt
Stock: synthetic
Barrel: 22 in.
Sights: adjustable
Weight: 6.0 lbs.
Caliber: .17 HMR
Magazine: clip, 7 rounds
Features: Sporter barrel; adjustable T-900 trigger system; fiberglass-filled synthetic stock with full pistol grip, swivel studs and molded-in checkering; adjustable open rear, ramp front sights
MSRP: $273.99

MODEL 917V

Action: bolt
Stock: hardwood
Barrel: heavy 22 in.
Sights: none
Weight: 6.0 lbs.
Caliber: .17 HMR
Magazine: detachable box, 7 rounds
Features: T-900 Fire Control System; 1-in. scope mounts provided; also available: 917VS stainless steel with laminated hardwood stock (7 lbs.)
917V: $220.07
917VS: $312.11
917 VSF (fluted barrel): $330.83

MODEL 917VR

Action: bolt
Stock: synthetic
Barrel: 22 in.
Sights: none
Weight: 6.0 lbs.
Caliber: .17 HMR
Magazine: clip, 7 rounds
Features: Varmint barrel; thumb safety; red cocking indicator; receiver is grooved for scope mount; drilled and tapped for scope bases (scope bases included); fiberglass-filled synthetic stock with full pistol grip, swivel studs and molded-in checkering
MSRP: $235.39

Marlin Rifles

MODEL 925

Action: bolt
Stock: hardwood
Barrel: 22 in.
Sights: open
Weight: 5.5 lbs.
Caliber: .22 LR
Magazine: detachable box, 7 rounds
Features: T-900 Fire Control System; Micro-Groove rifling; can be ordered with scope; also available with Mossy Oak camo stock finish
925: $174.48
925 with scope: $196.07
925C (camo): $200.61

MODEL 925R

Action: bolt
Stock: synthetic
Barrel: 22 in.
Sights: adjustable
Weight: 5.5 lbs.
Caliber: .22 LR
Magazine: clip, 7 rounds
Features: Micro-Groove sporter barrel; patented T-900 Fire Control System; black synthetic stock with molded-in checkering and swivel studs; adjustable open rear, ramp front sights
MSRP: $172.99

MODEL 981T

Action: bolt
Stock: synthetic
Barrel: 22 in.
Sights: open
Weight: 6.0 lbs.
Caliber: .22 L, S or LR
Magazine: under-barrel tube, 17 rounds
Features: Micro-Groove rifling; T-900 Fire Control System
918T: $174

MODEL 983T

Action: bolt
Stock: synthetic
Barrel: 22 in.
Sights: open
Weight: 6.0 lbs.
Caliber: .22 WMR
Magazine: under-barrel tube, 12 rounds
Features: T-900 Fire Control System; Micro-Groove rifling; available as Model 983 with walnut stock or laminated stock and stainless barrel
983T: $201.99
Model 983:. $243.69
Model 983S:. $279.98

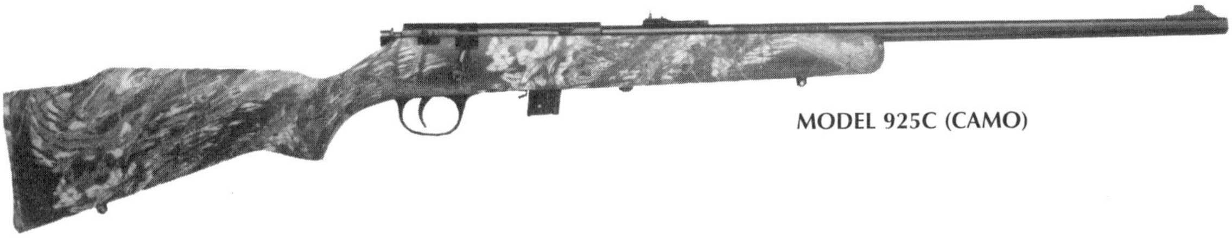
MODEL 925C (CAMO)

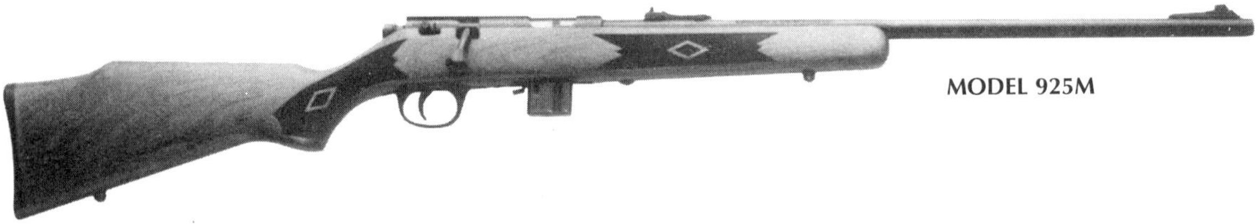
MODEL 925M

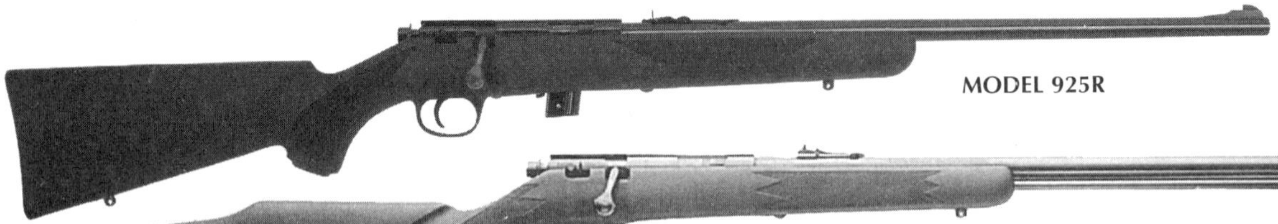
MODEL 925R

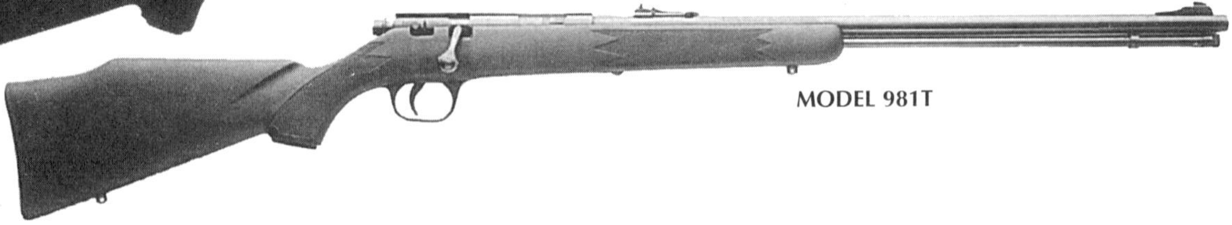
MODEL 981T

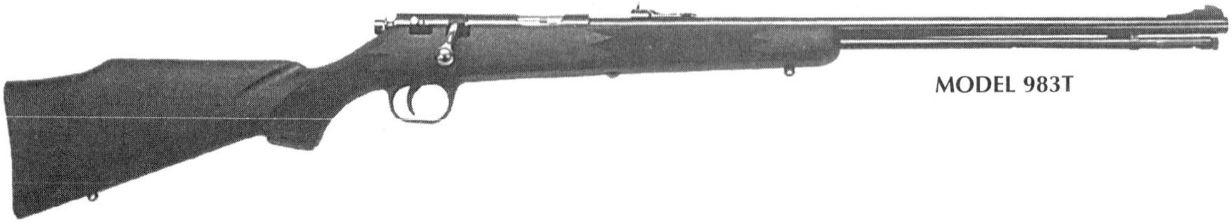
MODEL 983T

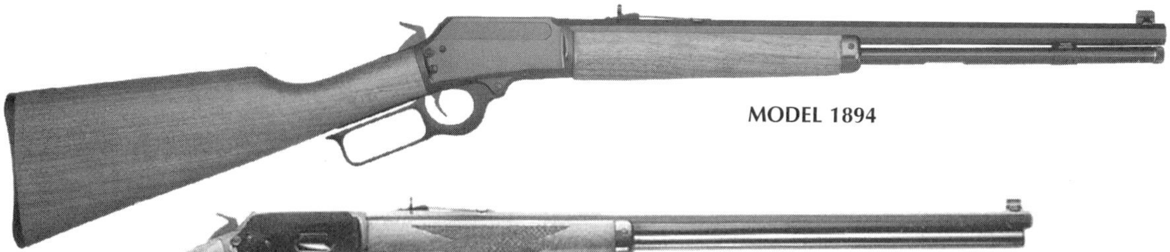
MODEL 1894

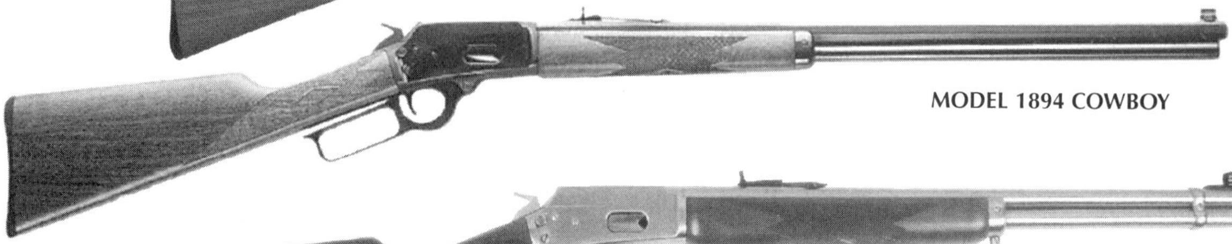
MODEL 1894 COWBOY

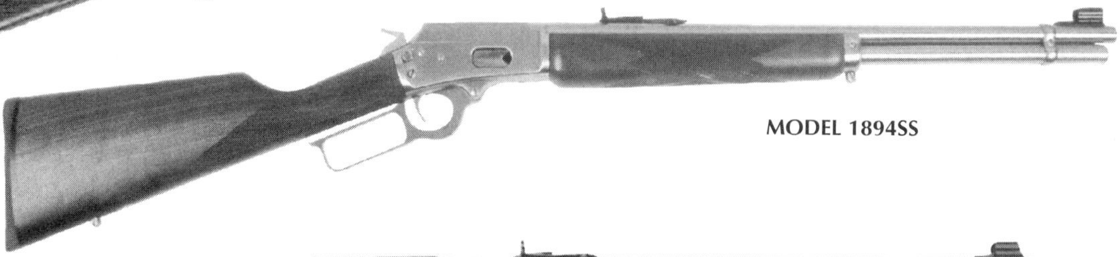
MODEL 1894SS

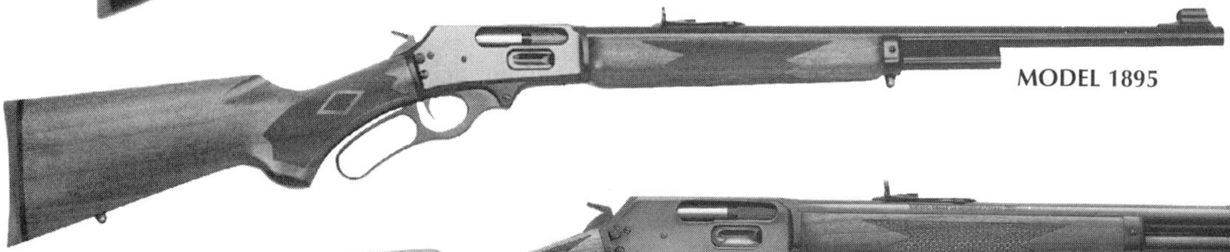
MODEL 1895

MODEL 1895M

MODEL 1894

Action: lever
Stock: checkered American walnut
Barrel: 20 in.
Sights: open
Weight: 6.0 lbs.
Caliber: .44 Rem. Mag./.44 Special
Magazine: tube, 10 rounds
Features: straight grip stock with Mar-Shield finish
MSRP: $555.93

MODEL 1894 COWBOY

Action: lever
Stock: walnut, straight grip, checkered
Barrel: tapered octagon, 24 in.
Sights: open
Weight: 6.5 lbs.
Caliber: .357 Mag./.38 Special, .44 Mag./.44 Special and .45 Colt
Magazine: tube, 10 rounds
Features: blued finish; hammer-block safety; hard rubber buttplate; Competition model available in .38 Special or .45 Colt with 20 in. barrel
1894 Cowboy: $788.24

MODEL 1894SS

Action: lever
Stock: checkered walnut, straight grip
Barrel: 20 in. ***Sights:*** open
Weight: 6.0 lbs.
Caliber: .44 Rem. Mag.
Magazine: under-barrel tube, 10 rounds
Features: Micro-groove rifling
1894C (blued): $591
1894 SS: $722

MODEL 1895

Action: lever
Stock: checkered walnut, pistol grip
Barrel: 22 in. ***Sights:*** open
Weight: 7.5 lbs.
Caliber: .45-70 Govt.
Magazine: tube, 4 rounds
Features: blued; hammer-block safety, offset hammer spur for scope use; Model 1895G has 18.5 in. barrel and straight grip
1895: $611
1895G: $621
1895GS in stainless steel: $742
1895 Cowboy (26″ octagonbarrel): $775

MODEL 1895M

Action: lever
Stock: checkered walnut, straight grip
Barrel: Ballard rifled, 18.5 in.
Sights: open
Weight: 7.0 lbs.
Caliber: .450
Magazine: tube, 4 rounds
Features: blued finish; hammer-block safety; offset hammer spur for scope use
MSRP: $559

Marlin Rifles

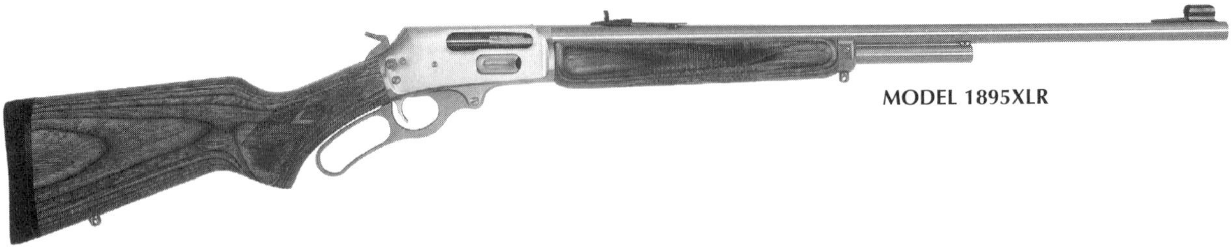

MODEL 1895XLR

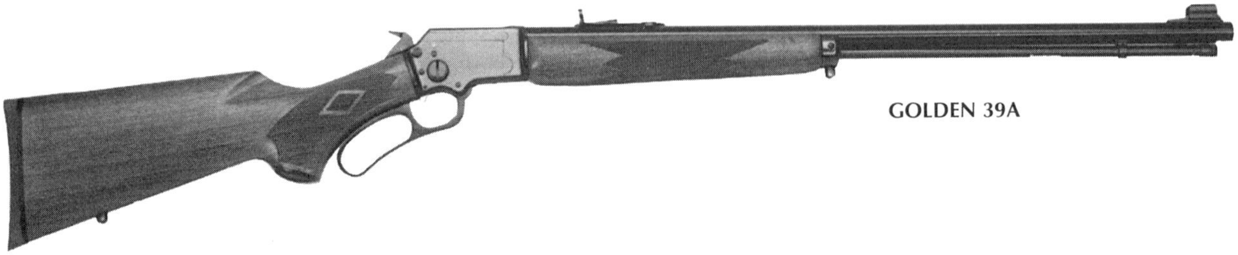

GOLDEN 39A

MODEL 1895MXLR

Action: lever
Stock: laminated
Barrel: 24 in.
Sights: adjustable
Weight: 7.0 lbs.
Caliber: .450 Marlin
Magazine: tube, 4 rounds
Features: 24 in. stainless steel barrel w/ Ballard rifling; stainless solid-top receiver with side-ejection—tapped for scope mount; semi-buckhorn folding rear sight, ramp front sight with brass bead and Wide-Scan hood; black/gray laminated hardwood pistol grip stock, cut checkering; nickel-plated swivel studs; decelerator recoil pad
MSRP: $655

MODEL 1895XLR

Action: lever
Stock: laminated
Barrel: 24 in.
Sights: adjustable
Weight: 7.5 lbs.
Caliber: .45/70
Magazine: tube, 4 rounds
Features: 24 in. stainless steel barrel w/ Ballard rifling; stainless solid-top receiver with side-ejection—tapped for scope mount; semi-buckhorn folding rear sight, ramp front sight with brass bead and Wide-Scan hood; black/gray laminated hardwood pistol grip stock with fluted comb, cut checkering; nickel-plated swivel studs; decelerator recoil pad
MSRP: $697

MODEL 7000

Action: autoloading
Stock: synthetic
Barrel: target weight, 28 in.
Sights: none
Weight: 5.3 lbs.
Caliber: .22 LR
Magazine: detachable box, 10 rounds
Features: also available as Model 795 and 795 SS, with sights and lighter barrel (weight: 4.5 lbs.)
795: $126.22
795 SS: $180.47

GOLDEN 39A

Action: lever
Stock: checkered walnut, pistol grip
Barrel: 24 in.
Sights: open
Weight: 6.5 lbs.
Caliber: .22 LR
Magazine: under-barrel tube, 19 rounds
Features: Micro-Groove rifling, single-screw take-down; swivel studs
MSRP: $496

McMillan Rifles

MCMILLAN PRODIGY

Action: Two-lug bolt
Stock: McMillan hand-laid synthetic; slim open grip with straight comb; Pachmayr recoil pad
Barrel: 24″ Shilen stainless
Sights: none; drilled & tapped, Talley bases supplied
Weight: 7 lbs.
Caliber: popular standard and magnum chamberings
Magazine: internal box
Features: Glass bedding and alloy pillars, Jewell trigger, stainless receivers, washer-type recoil lug and MP-3 nickel two-lug bolts (spiral fluted). Bolt-face extractor and plunger ejector.
MSRP: $4770

Merkel Rifles

MODEL K1 LIGHTWEIGHT STALKING RIFLE

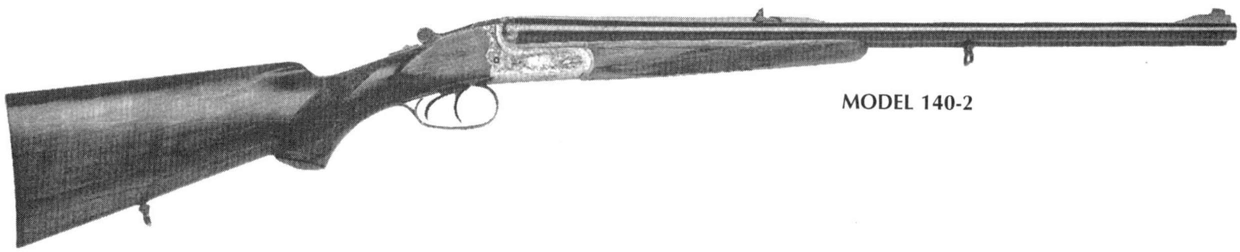

MODEL 140-2

MODEL K1 LIGHTWEIGHT STALKING RIFLE

Action: hinged breech
Stock: select walnut
Barrel: 24 in.
Sights: open
Weight: 5.6 lbs.
Caliber: .243, .270, 7x57R, 7mm Rem. Mag., .308, .30-06, .300 Win. Mag., 9.3x74R
Magazine: none
Features: single-shot; Franz Jager action; also available: Premium and Hunter grades
MSRP: $3795

SAFARI SERIES MODEL 140-2

Action: hinged breech
Stock: select walnut
Barrel: length and contour to order
Sights: open
Weight: 9.0 lbs.
Caliber: .375 H&H, .416 Rigby, .470 N.E.
Magazine: none
Features: Anson & Deely box-lock; double triggers; includes oak and leather luggage case; higher grade available; also Model 141.1, lightweight double in .308, .30-06, 9.3x74R
MSRP: . . . . from $11995

Mossberg Rifles

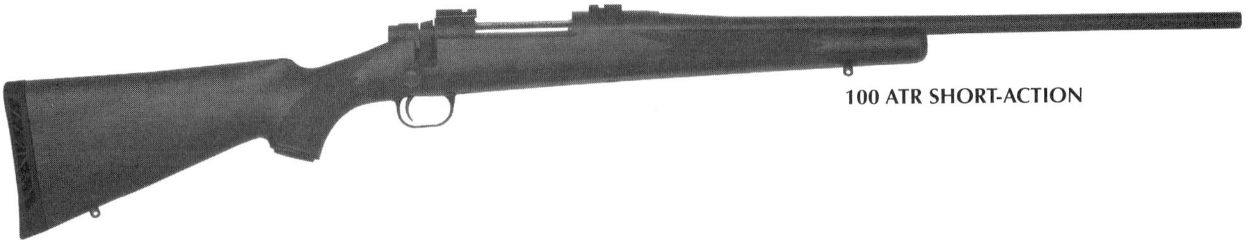

100 ATR SHORT-ACTION

464 22LR

464 30-30

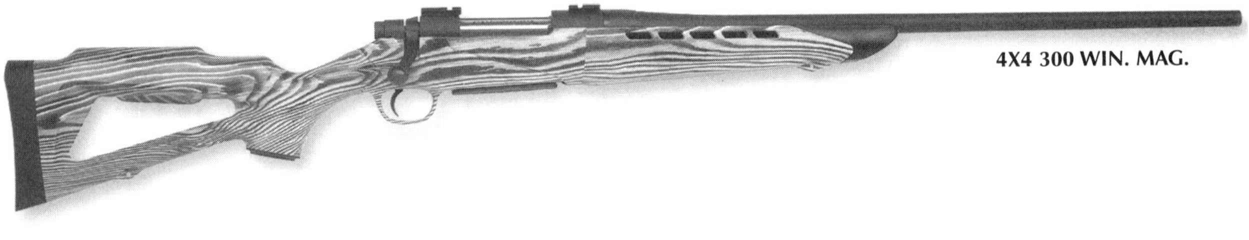

4X4 300 WIN. MAG.

RIFLES

100 ATR SHORT-ACTION

Action: bolt
Stock: hardwood
Barrel: 22 in.
Sights: none
Weight: 7 lbs.
Caliber: .243 Win, .308 Win.
Magazine: internal box, 4 + 1 rounds
Features: free floating matte blued barrel; side-lever safety; factory installed Weaver style scope bases; walnut finished hardwood stock; rubber recoil pad
MSRP: $424–471

464 LEVER-ACTION

Action: lever
Stock: wood
Barrel: 20 in.
Weight: 6.7 lb. (.30-30), 5.6 lb. (.22 LR)
Caliber: .30-30 Win., .22 LR
Magazine: 6+1 (.30-30), 13+1 (.22LR) rounds
Features: button-rifled barrel, recessed muzzle crown, top-tang safety, recoil softening rubber buttpad
MSRP: $468–535

4x4 .300 WIN. MAG. LAMINATE

Action: bolt
Stock: synthetic with laminate finish
Barrel: 24 in., matte blue
Weight: 6.7 lb.
Caliber: .300 Win. Mag.
Magazine: 3+1 rounds, drop box
Features: free-floating, button-rifled barrel, recessed muzzle crown, two-piece factory installed Weaver scope bases
MSRP: $633

Mossberg Rifles

802 BLACK SYNTHETIC CHROME

802 PINK MARBLE SYNTHETIC

802 SCOPED COMBO

802 THUMBHOLE TIPDOWN

702 & 802 PLINKSTER BOLT-ACTIONS

Action: bolt
Stock: synthetic (black, pink, pink marble) or wood
Barrel: 18, 21 in., blue or brushed chrome
Sights: Adjustable rifle
Weight: 4.1-5.2 lb.
Caliber: .22 LR
Magazine: 10 rounds, detachable
Features: 702 Plinkster Bantam models feature a shortened 12-¼-in. LOP and 18-in. barrel for young shooters or smaller stature adults; offered in factory-mounted 4X scoped combo sets.
MSRP: . . . . from $162

Mossberg Rifles

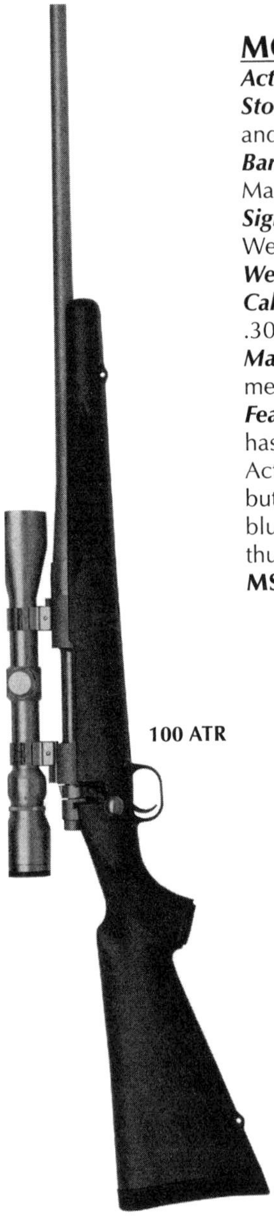

100 ATR

MOSSBERG 100 ATR

Action: two-lug bolt
Stock: black synthetic, camo and synthetic walnut
Barrel: 22″, matte blue or Marinecote
Sights: none, installed Weaver-style scope bases
Weight: 6 ½ to 7 lbs.
Caliber: .270, .30-06, .243, .308
Magazine: detachable polymer box
Features: All Terrain Rifle now has LBA (Lightning Bolt Action) trigger, free-floating, button-rifled barrel, matte blue or Marinecote finish, thumb safety.
MSRP: . . . . $424-$518

MOSSBERG 4X4 CLASSIC

Action: Bolt
Stock: polymer, gray laminate or American black walnut with forend barrel vents
Barrel: 24″
Sights: none, installed Weaver-style scope bases
Weight: 6 ¾ to 7 ¾ lbs.
Caliber: from .25-06 to .338 Win. Mag.
Magazine: detachable polymer box
Features: new LBA (Lightning Bolt Action) trigger adjustable to 2 lbs., thumb safety, classic stock.
MSRP: $633

MOSSBERG 464 LEVER-ACTION

Action: lever
Stock: hardwood, new pistol grip buttstock
Barrel: 20″, blued finish
Sights: open rear, bead front
Weight: 6 ¾ lbs.
Caliber: .30-30
Magazine: full-length tube
Features: button-rifled barrel, top-tang safety, rubber buttpad
MSRP: . . . . $468-$535

4X4 CLASSIC

Navy Arms Rifles

MODEL 1866 YELLOW BOY

MODEL 1866 YELLOW BOY

Action: lever
Stock: walnut, straight grip
Barrel: octagon, 20 in.
Sights: open
Weight: 7.5 lbs.
Caliber: .38 Special, .44-40, .45 Colt
Magazine: under-barrel tube, 10 rounds
Features: also available: Yellow Boy with 24 in. barrel (8.3 lbs.)
MSRP: $1015

RIFLES

Navy Arms Rifles

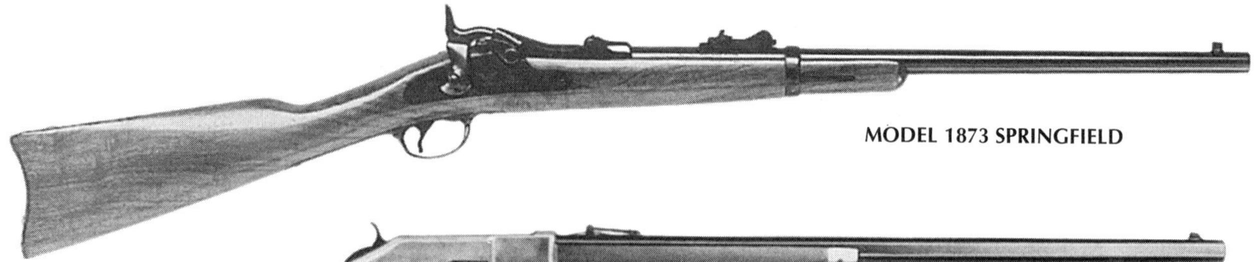

MODEL 1873 SPRINGFIELD

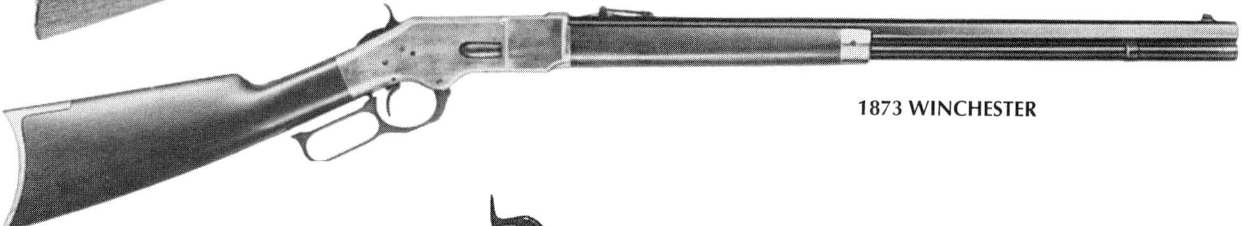

1873 WINCHESTER

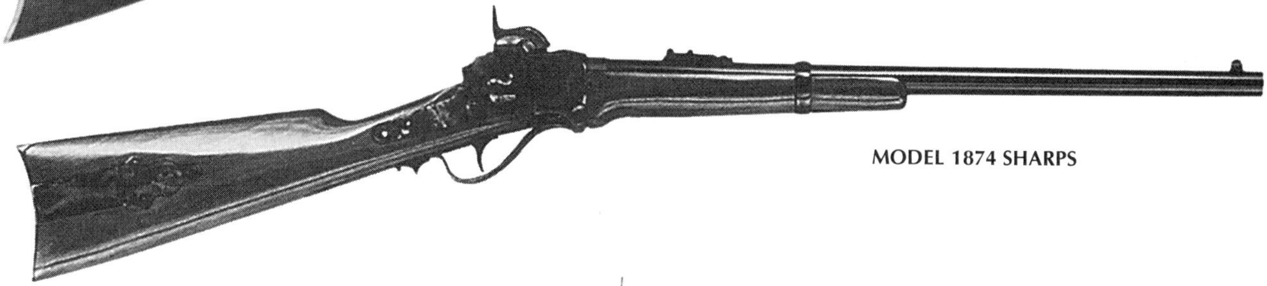

MODEL 1874 SHARPS

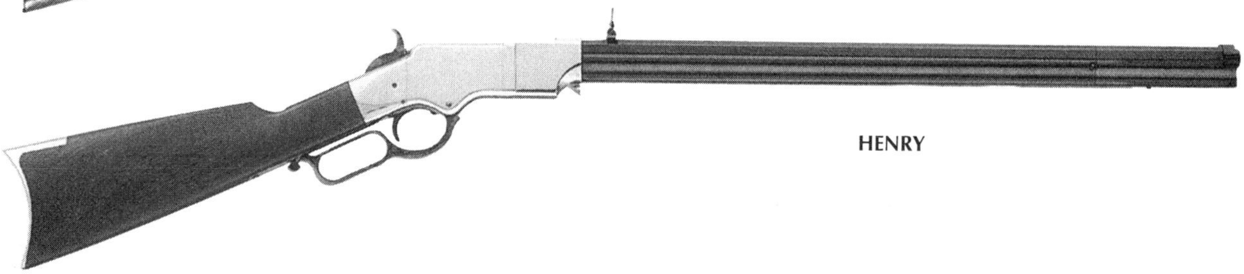

HENRY

MODEL 1873 SPRINGFIELD

Action: dropping block
Stock: walnut
Barrel: 22 in.
Sights: open
Weight: 7.0 lbs.
Caliber: .45-70
Magazine: none
Features: "Trapdoor" replica; saddle bar with ring
MSRP: $1475

MODEL 1873 WINCHESTER

Action: lever
Stock: walnut, straight grip
Barrel: 24 in.
Sights: open
Weight: 8.3 lbs.
Caliber: .357 Mag., .44-40, .45 Colt
Magazine: under-barrel tube, 13 rounds
Features: case-colored receiver; also: Carbine, Border, Deluxe (checkered) Border and Sporting models
1873 Winchester: $1132
Deluxe Border Model: $1241

MODEL 1874 SHARPS

Action: dropping block
Stock: walnut
Barrel: 22 in.
Sights: open
Weight: 7.8 lbs.
Caliber: .45-70
Magazine: none
Features: also: No. 3 Long Range Sharps with double set triggers, 34 in. barrel (10.9 lbs.) and Buffalo Rifle with double set triggers, 28 in. octagon barrel (10.6 lbs.)
Carbine: $1210
No. 3: $2379

HENRY

Action: lever
Stock: walnut, straight grip
Barrel: 24 in.
Sights: open
Weight: 9.0 lbs.
Caliber: .44-40, .45 Colt
Magazine: under-barrel tube, 13 rounds
Features: blued or case-colored receiver
Military Henry: $1212
Henry: $1281

Navy Arms Rifles

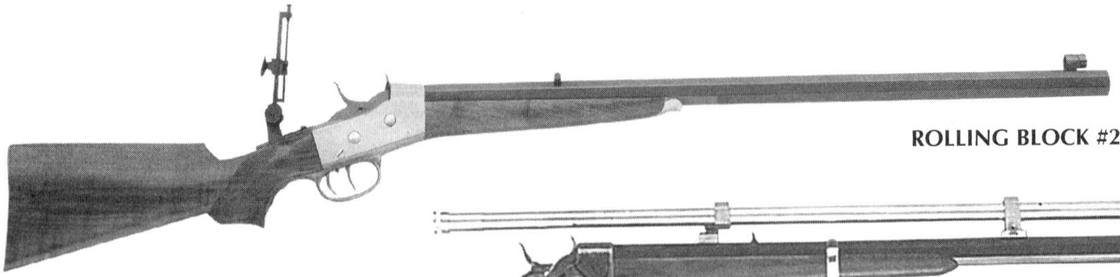
ROLLING BLOCK #2 JOHN BODINE

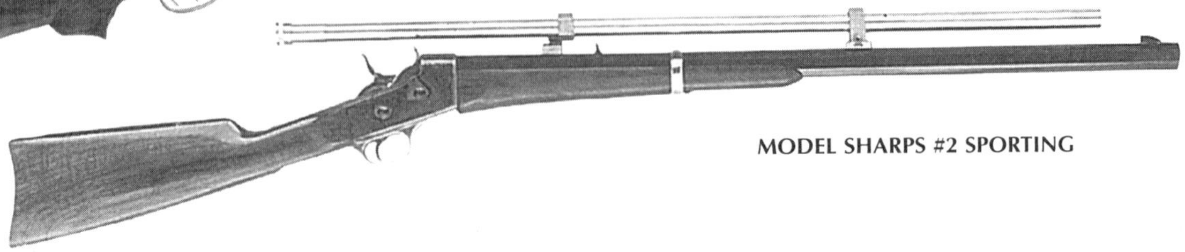
MODEL SHARPS #2 SPORTING

ROLLING BLOCK #2 JOHN BODINE

Action: dropping block
Stock: walnut ***Barrel:*** 30 in.
Sights: adjustable tang
Weight: 12.0 lbs.
Caliber: .45-70 ***Magazine:*** none
Features: double set triggers; nickel-finish breech
MSRP: $1940

MODEL SHARPS #2 SPORTING

Action: dropping block
Stock: walnut
Barrel: 30 in.
Sights: target ***Weight:*** 10.0 lbs.
Caliber: .45-70 ***Magazine:*** none
Features: also #2 Silhouette Creedmoor and Quigley
(with 34 in. barrel)
Quigley $1981
Creedmoor: $1844

New England Firearms Rifles

HANDI-RIFLE HARDWOOD

HANDI-RIFLE

Action: hinged breech
Stock: Monte Carlo synthetic or hardwood
Barrel: 22 in. or 26 in.
Sights: none
Weight: 7.0 lbs.
Caliber: .223, .22-250, .243, .270, .30-06
Magazine: none
Features: offset hammer; open-sight version of Handi-Rifle in .22 Hornet, .30-30, .357 Mag., .44 Mag., .45-70 Govt.; Youth models in .223, .243 and 7mm-08
Handi-Rifle: $307.42
With hardwood stock: $246
Synthetic Stainless: $316.39

New England Firearms Rifles

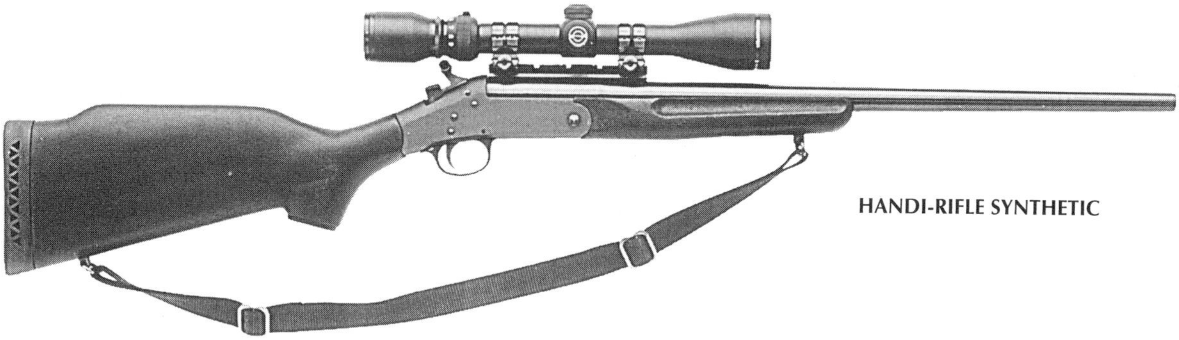

HANDI-RIFLE SYNTHETIC

SPORTSTER 17 HMR

RIFLES

SURVIVOR

SPORTSTER 17 HMR & 17 MACH2

Action: hinged breech
Stock: synthetic
Barrel: heavy varmint, 22 in.
Sights: none
Weight: 6.0 lbs.
Caliber: .17 Hornady Magnum Rimfire, .17 MACH 2
Magazine: none
Features: Monte Carlo stock; sling swivel studs; recoil pad; Sportster Youth available with 20 in. barrel (5.5 lbs.), in .22 LR or .22 WMR
Youth: $161.38
Sportster:. $165.99

SURVIVOR

Action: hinged breech
Stock: synthetic
Barrel: 22 in. bull
Sights: open
Weight: 6.0 lbs.
Caliber: .223 & .308
Magazine: none
Features: single-shot; recoil pad; hollow synthetic stock with storage compartment; thumbscrew take down
MSRP: $320.02

New Ultra Light Arms Rifles

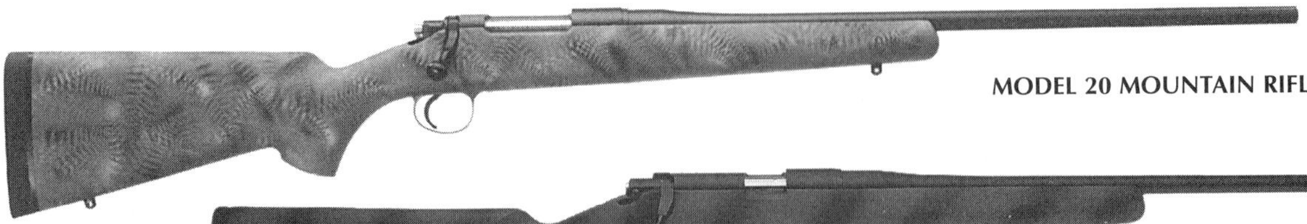

MODEL 20 MOUNTAIN RIFLE

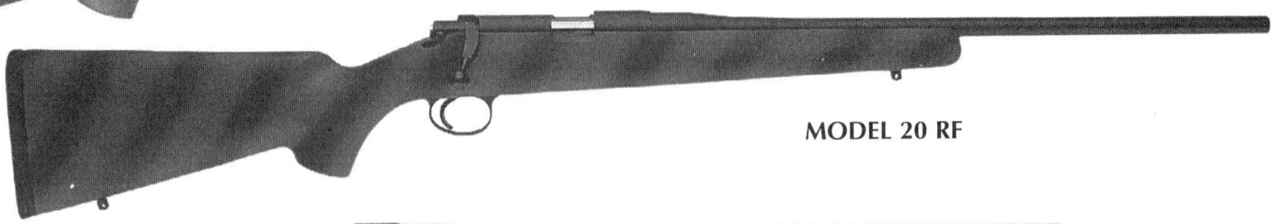

MODEL 20 RF

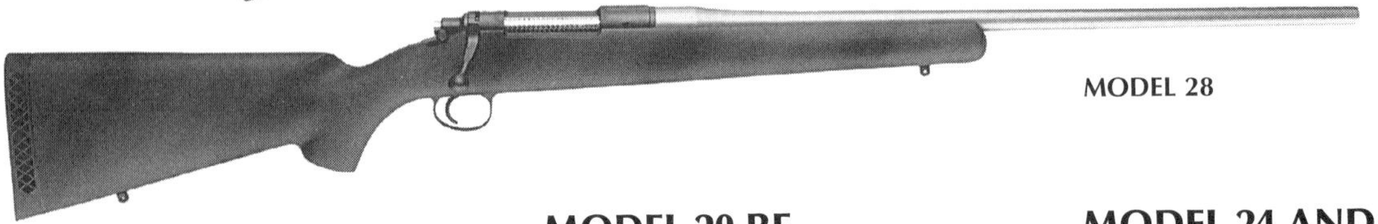

MODEL 28

MODEL 20 MOUNTAIN RIFLE

Action: bolt
Stock: Kevlar/graphite composite
Barrel: 22 in.
Sights: none
Weight: 4.75 lbs.
Caliber: short action: 6mm, .17, .22 Hornet, .222, .222 Rem. Mag., .22-250, .223, .243, .250-3000 Savage, .257, .257 Ackley, 7x57, 7x57 Ackley, 7mm-08, .284, .300 Savage, .308, .358
Magazine: box, 4, 5 or 6 rounds
Features: two-position safety; choice of 7 or more stock colors; available in left-hand
Mountain Rifle: $3000
Left-hand: $3100

MODEL 20 RF

Action: bolt
Stock: composite
Barrel: Douglas Premium #1 Contour, 22 in.
Sights: none
Weight: 5.25 lbs.
Caliber: .22 LR
Magazine: none (or detachable box, 5 rounds)
Features: single-shot or repeater; drilled and tapped for scope; recoil pad, sling swivels; fully adjustable Timney trigger; 3-position safety; color options
Single-shot: $1300
Repeater: $1350

MODEL 24 AND 28

Action: bolt
Stock: Kevlar composite
Barrel: 22 in.
Sights: none
Weight: 5.25 lbs.
Caliber: long action: .270, .30-06, .25-06, .280, .280 Ackley, .338-06, .35 Whelen; Model 28: .264, 7mm, .300, .338, .300 WSM, .270 WSM, 7mm WSM; Model 40: .300 Wby. and .416 Rigby
Magazine: box, 4 rounds
Features: Model 28 has 24 in. bbl. and weighs 5.5 lbs.; Model 40 has 24 in. bbl. (6.5 lbs.); all available in left-hand versions
Model 24: $3100
Model 24, left-hand: $3200
Model 28 or Model 40: $3400
Model 28 or Model 40, left-hand: $3500

Nosler Rifles

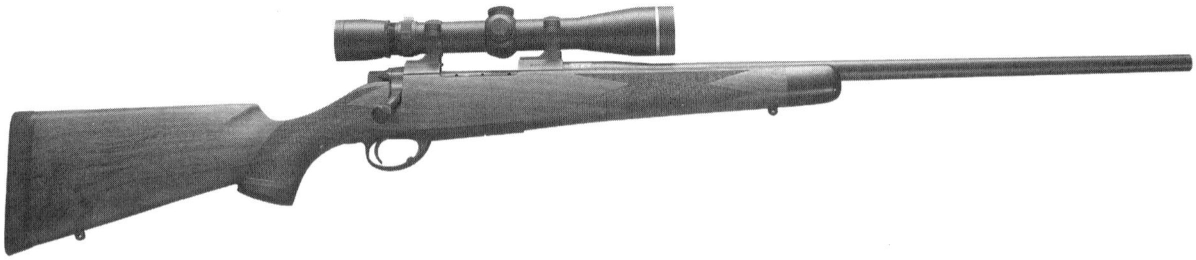

NOSLER BOLT-ACTION

Action: bolt
Stock: Turkish walnut
Barrel: 24 in.
Sights: optical
Weight: 7.75 lbs.
Caliber: .300 WSM
Magazine: internal box, 3 rounds
Features: hand-lapped, match-grade Wiseman barrel; three-position safety; Timney trigger; Leupold VX-III 2.5-8x36 scope serial-numbered to the rifle; production limited to 500 units
MSRP: $4195

Pedersoli Replica Rifles

.45-70 OFFICER'S MODEL TRAPDOOR SPRINGFIELD

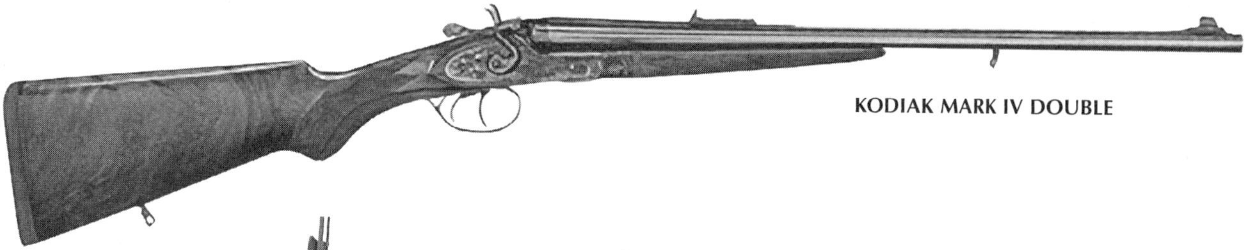

KODIAK MARK IV DOUBLE

ROLLING BLOCK TARGET

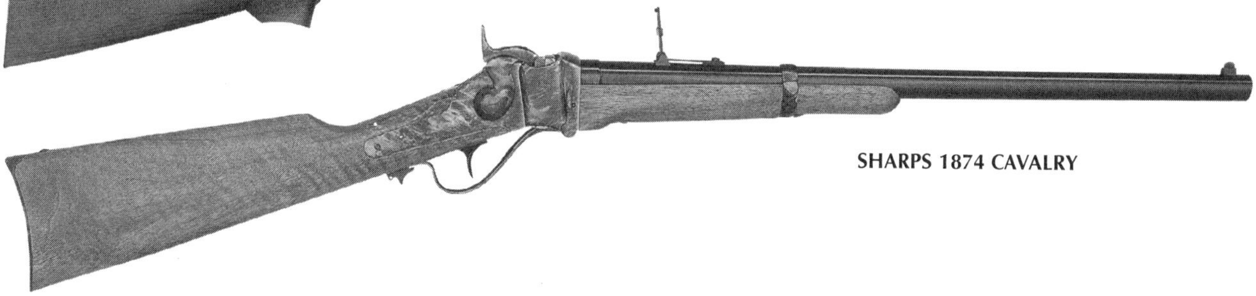

SHARPS 1874 CAVALRY

.45-70 OFFICER'S MODEL TRAPDOOR SPRINGFIELD

Action: single-shot hinged breech
Stock: walnut
Barrel: 26 in.
Sights: Creedmoor style tang
Weight: 7.72 lbs.
Caliber: .45-70
Magazine: none
Features: blued, 26 in. tapered round barrel, precision broach rifled with 6 lands and grooves with a one turn-in-18 inches rifling twist; color case-hardened receiver, breechblock, trigger guard, barrel band, buttplate and lock plate; satin-finished American black walnut stock
MSRP: $1500

KODIAK MARK IV DOUBLE

Action: hinged breech
Stock: walnut
Barrel: 22 in. and 24 in.
Sights: open
Weight: 8.2 lbs.
Caliber: .45-70, 9.3x74R, 8x57JSR
Magazine: none
Features: .45-70 weighs 8.2 lbs.; also available: Kodiak Mark IV with interchangeable 20-gauge barrel
45-70: . . . . special order only
8x57, 9.3x74: . . . special order only
Kodiak Mark IV: . special order only

ROLLING BLOCK TARGET

Action: dropping block
Stock: walnut
Barrel: octagon, 30 in.
Sights: target
Weight: 9.5 lbs.
Caliber: .45-70 and .357 (10 lbs.)
Magazine: none
Features: Creedmoor sights; also available: Buffalo, Big Game, Sporting, Baby Carbine, Custer, Long Range Creedmoor
MSRP: $1540

SHARPS 1874 CAVALRY & INFANTRY MODEL

Action: dropping block
Stock: walnut
Barrel: 22 in.
Sights: open
Weight: 8.4 lbs.
Caliber: .45-70
Magazine: none
Features: also available: 1874 Infantry (set trigger, 30 in. bbl.), 1874 Sporting (.40-65 or .45-70, set trigger, 32 in. oct. bbl.), 1874 Long Range (.45-70 and .45-90, .45-120, 34 in. half oct. bbl., target sights)
Cavalry: $1281
Infantry (one trigger): $1561
Infantry (two triggers): $1624
Sporting: $1350
Long Range: $1761
Long Range Big Bore: $1916

PGW Defense Technology Rifles

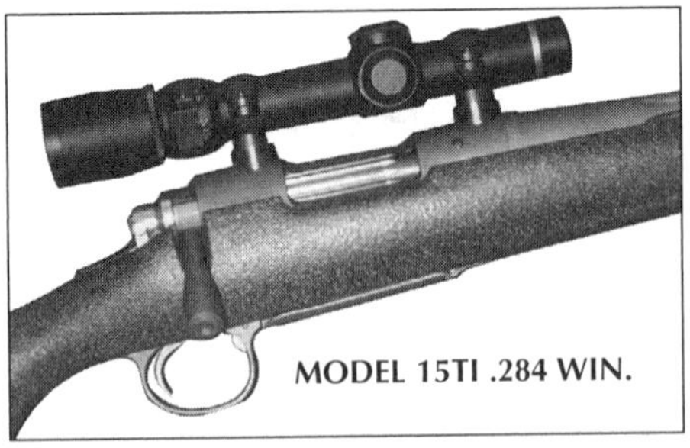

MODEL 15TI ULTRA LIGHT

Action: bolt
Stock: composite *Barrel:* 22 in.
Sights: none *Weight:* 5.0 lbs.
Caliber: most short-action calibers
Magazine: box, 5 rounds
Features: Rem. 700 short-action, custom alloy scope mounts; new firing pin and bolt shroud tuned; also: Model 18Ti with long 700 action

TIMBERWOLF

Action: bolt
Stock: McMillan fiberglass
Barrel: fluted, match grade
Sights: none
Caliber: .338 Lapua
Magazine: 5 rounds
Features: stainless receiver; adjustable trigger; 3-position safety, titanium rail with guide rib

Timberwolf:. $7000
Coyote in 7.62
(5 or 10-shot magazine): . . $5500

RIFLES

Puma Rifles

PUMA CHUCK CONNORS COMMEMORATIVE

Action: lever
Stock: walnut
Barrel: 20″
Sights: open
Weight: 6 ½ lbs.
Caliber: .44-40
Magazine: full-length tube
Features: limited edition of 1000 made in Italy by Chiappa Firearms, imported by Legacy Sports. This rifle commemorates the popular 1950's TV show, "The Rifleman." Large loop with set screw in trigger guard, Chuck Connors' signature etched on receiver and laser engraved on stock.
MSRP: $1299

Purdey Rifles

DOUBLE BARREL RIFLE .577 NITRO

Purdey's double-barrel Express rifles are built to customer specifications on actions sized to each particular cartridge. Standard chamberings include .375 H&H Magnum and .470, .577 and .600 Nitro Express. The Purdey side-by-side action patented in 1880, designed by Frederick Beesley, retains a portion of the energy in the mainsprings to facilitate the opening of the gun.

The over-under is derived from the Woodward, patented in 1913. The action blocks for all guns are cut from certified forgings, for consistency of grain throughout, and are fitted to the barrels to make an absolute joint. The actioner then fits the fore-part, the locks, the strikers and the safety work before finally detonating the action.

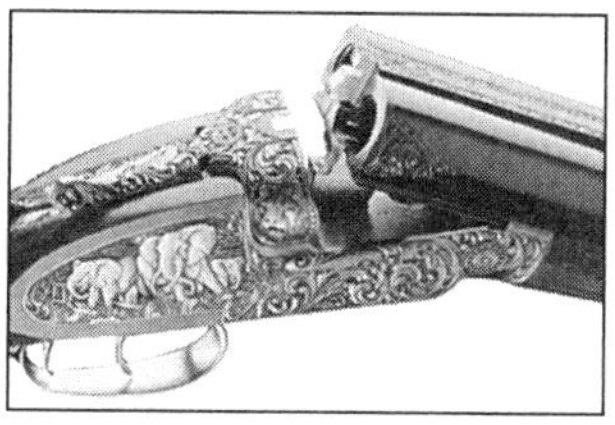

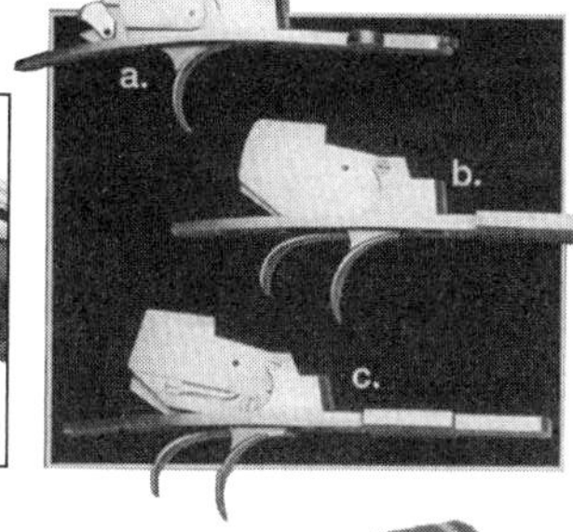

SINGLE TRIGGER

DOUBLE TRIGGER

SPRING BLADED FRONT TRIGGER

"RAIL MOUNT" SYSTEM WITH INTEGRAL RECOIL BAR

A – SINGLE TRIGGER

The Purdey single trigger works both by inertia and mechanically. It is simple, effective and fast. The firing sequence is fixed, therefore no barrel selection is possible.

B & C – DOUBLE TRIGGERS

The standard double triggers (B) can be augmented with an articulated front trigger (C). This device alleviates damage to the back of the trigger finger on discharge.

Purdey makes its own dedicated actions for bolt rifles in the following calibers: .375 H&H, .416/450 Rigby or other, .500 and .505 Gibbs. The action length is suited to cartridge length in each caliber. Mauser Square Bridge and Mauser '98 actions are available.

RAIL MOUNT SYSTEM

This is Purdey's own system for big bolt rifles. It is very secure and facilitates fast on/off. Rings and mounts are all made with an integral recoil bar from a single piece of steel. This system is recommended for Purdey actions and Mauser Square Bridge actions.

Remington Arms Rifles

MODEL 40-XBBR KS

MODEL 40-XBBR KS

Action: bolt
Stock: fiberglass
Barrel: 24 in.
Sights: none
Weight: 9.75 lbs.
Caliber: .22 LR
Magazine: single shot
Features: benchrest with stainless barrel; Aramid-fiber reinforced Remington green stock
Custom order

Remington Arms Rifles

MODEL R-15 VTR

Action: semi-auto
Stock: synthetic; Advantage MAX-1 HD finish
Barrel: 22 in. (Predator); 18 in. (Carbine and Carbine CS)
Weight: 7.75 lbs. (Predator); 6.75 lbs. (Carbine and Carbine CS)
Caliber: .223 Rem., .204 Ruger
Magazine: 5 rounds
Features: free-floating button-rifled chrome-moly fluted barrels with recessed hunting crown; single-stage hunting trigger; receiver-length Picatinny rail; ergonomic pistol grip; fore-end tube drilled and tapped for accessory rails; compatible with aftermarket AR-15 magazines; lockable hard case included.
MSRP: $1225

R-15VTR PREDATOR CARBINE

R-15VTR PREDATOR CARBINE CS

MODEL 40-XB TACTICAL

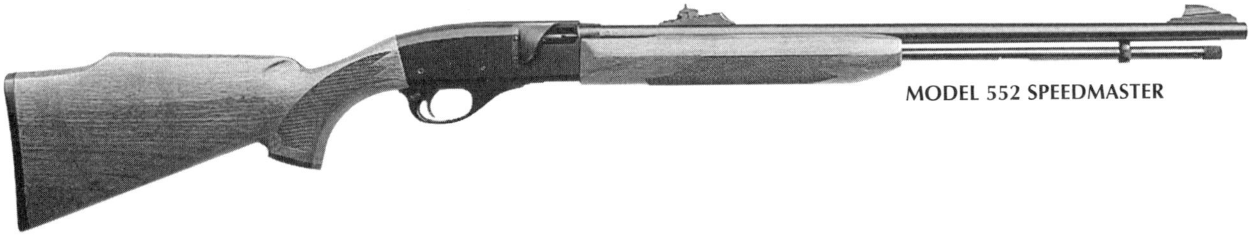

MODEL 552 SPEEDMASTER

MODEL 40-XB TACTICAL

Action: bolt
Stock: black with green fiberglass
Barrel: 27.25 in.
Sights: none
Weight: 10.25 lbs.
Caliber: .308 Win.
Magazine: hinged floorplate, 5 rounds
Features: built to order
Custom order

MODEL 40-X TARGET

Action: bolt
Stock: target, benchrest or tactical
Barrel: 24 in. or 27 in.
Sights: none
Weight: 10.25-11.25 lbs.
Caliber: 18 popular standard and magnum calibers
Magazine: box, 3 or 5 rounds
Features: rimfire and single-shot versions available; walnut, laminated and composite stocks; forend rail, match trigger
40-X: $2561–3014
Left-hand: $1884–2555
Custom 40-XR Sporter: $4523

MODEL 552 BDL DELUXE SPEEDMASTER

Action: autoloading
Stock: walnut
Barrel: 21 in.
Sights: Big Game
Weight: 5.75 lbs.
Caliber: .22 S, .22 L, .22 LR
Magazine: under-barrel tube, 15-20 rounds
Features: classic autoloader made 1966 to date
MSRP: $617

Remington Arms Rifles

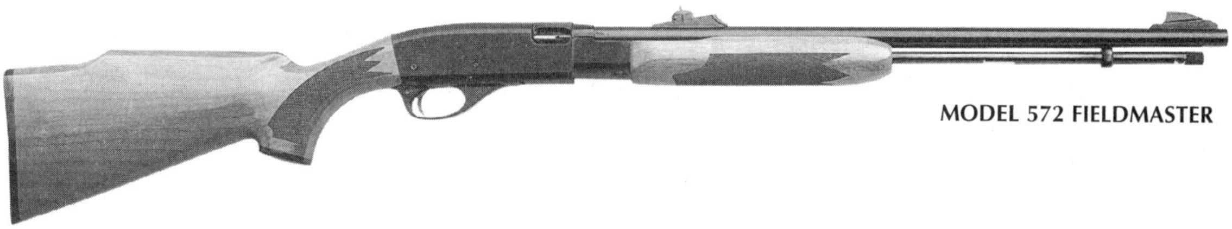

MODEL 572 FIELDMASTER

MODEL 597

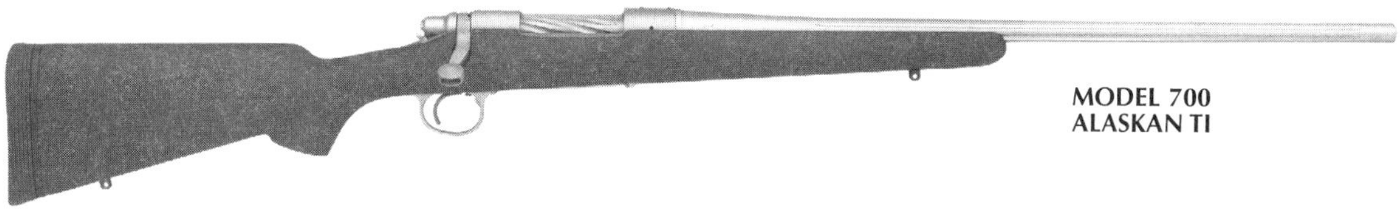

MODEL 700
ALASKAN TI

MODEL 572 BDL DELUXE FIELDMASTER

Action: pump
Stock: walnut
Barrel: 21 in.
Sights: Big Game
Weight: 5.5 lbs.
Caliber: .22 S, .22 L, .22 LR
Magazine: under-barrel tube, 15-20 rounds
Features: grooved receiver for scope mounts
MSRP: $607

MODEL 597

Action: autoloading
Stock: synthetic or laminated
Barrel: 20 in.
Sights: Big Game
Weight: 5.5-6.5 lbs.
Caliber: .22 LR, .22 WMR, .17 HMR
Magazine: detachable box, 10 rounds (8 in magnums)
Features: magnum version in .22 WMR and .17 HMR (both 6 lbs.); also: heavy-barrel model
Model 597: $193
22 WMR: $492

MODEL 700 AFRICAN BIG GAME

Action: bolt
Stock: laminated
Barrel: 26 in.
Sights: open
Weight: 9.5 lbs.
Caliber: .375 H&H, .375 RUM, .458 Win, .416 Rem.
Magazine: box, 3 rounds
Features: barrel-mounted front swivel
MSRP: $3241

MODEL 700 ALASKAN TI

Action: bolt; short, long and magnum
Stock: Bell & Carlson carbon fiber synthetic, matte finish, Maxx Guard protective coating
Barrel: 24 in.
Sights: none; drilled and tapped for scope mounts
Weight: 6-6.3 lbs.
Caliber: .270 Win, 7mm-08 Rem, .25-06 Rem, .280 Rem, .30-06 Sprg, 7mm Rem Mag, .270 WSM, .300 WSM, .300 Win Mag
Magazine: hinged floorplate, 4 rounds (short, long action calibers), 3 rounds (magnum)
Features: titanium receiver; spiral flutes on bolt body and handle; 416 stainless steel barrel with Light Varmint style fluting; Remington X-Mark Pro trigger; R3 recoil pad; sling swivel studs
MSRP: . . . . Custom made

Remington Arms Rifles

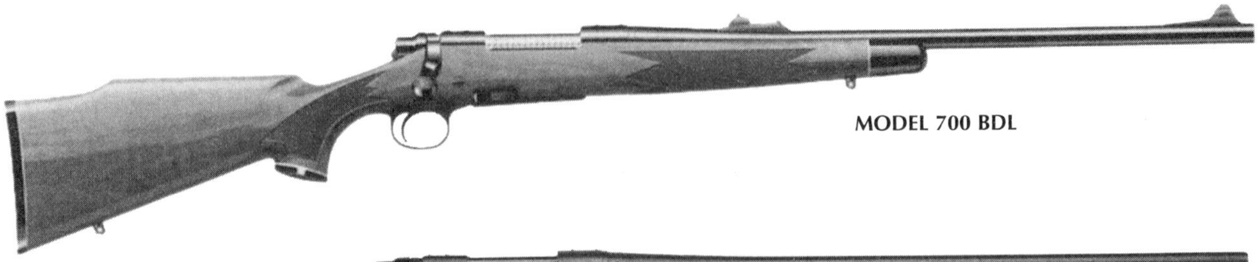

MODEL 700 BDL

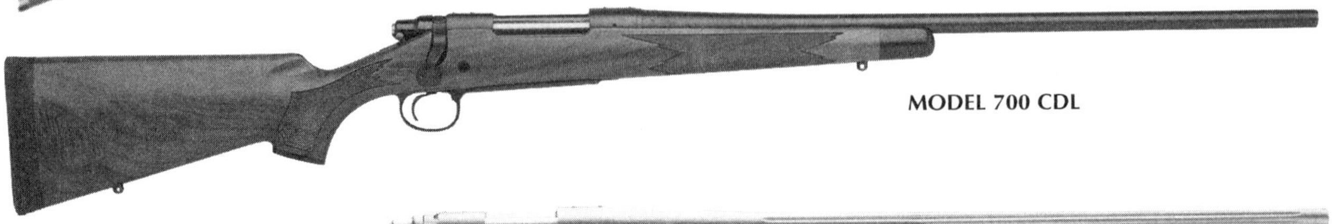

MODEL 700 CDL

MODEL 700 CDL SF

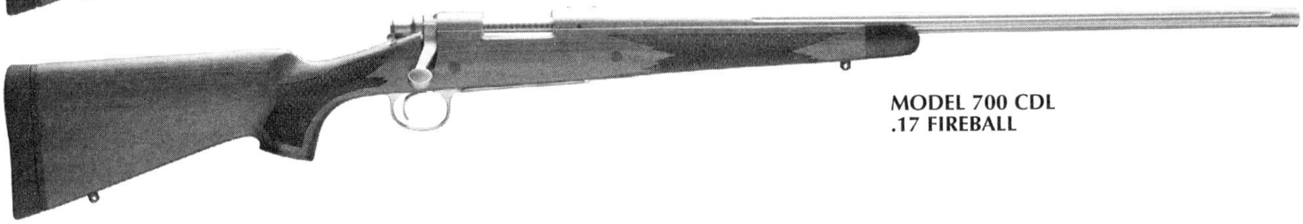

MODEL 700 CDL
.17 FIREBALL

MODEL 700 BDL CUSTOM DELUXE

Action: bolt
Stock: walnut
Barrel: 22-26 in.
Sights: open ***Weight:*** 7.25-7.5 lbs.
Caliber: popular standard calibers from .17 Rem. to .300 RUM
Magazine: box, 3 or 5 rounds
Features: hinged floorplate; sling swivel studs; hooded ramp front & adjustable rear sights
BDL:.................... $927
BDL Magnum: $955
BDL Ultra-Mags: $955

MODEL 700 CDL

Action: bolt
Stock: walnut
Barrel: 24 in. (standard) and 26 in. (magnum, Ultra Mag)
Sights: none (drilled and tapped for scope mounts)
Weight: 7.5 lbs.
Caliber: .243, .25-06 Rem., .35 Whelen, .270, 7mm-08, 7mm Rem. Mag., 7mm Ultra Mag, .30-06, .300 Win. Mag., .300 Ultra Mag
Magazine: box, 4 rounds (3 in magnums, Ultra Mags)
Features: fully adjustable trigger
Standard:................. $959
Ultra Mag: $987
Mag & Ultra Mag, left-hand (6 calibers): $987–1013

MODEL 700 CDL SF

Action: bolt; short, long and magnum
Stock: American walnut, satin finish
Barrel: 24 in. (short, long, short magnum), 26 in. (magnum)
Sights: none; drilled and tapped for scope mounts
Weight: 7.4-7.6 lbs.
Caliber: .270 Win, 7mm-08 Rem, .30-06 Sprg, 7mm Rem Mag, .270 WSM, .300 WSM
Features: 416 stainless steel fluted barrel; solid steel cylindrical receiver; hammer-forged barrel; Remington X-Mark Pro trigger; jeweled bolt; R3 recoil pad; sling swivel studs
MSRP: $1100

MODEL 700 CDL SF LIMITED, .17 REMINGTON FIREBALL

Action: bolt, short
Stock: American walnut, satin finish
Barrel: 24 in.
Sights: none; drilled and tapped for scope mounts
Weight: 7.6 lbs.
Caliber: .17 Remington Fireball
Magazine: 4 rounds
Features: commemorative engraving on the hinged floorplate denoting the introduction of the .17 Remington Fireball cartridge and "Model 700 Limited" rollmark on the receiver; limited production quantities; right-handed cheek piece; 416 stainless fluted barreled action; hammer-forged barrel; Remington X-Mark Pro trigger; jeweled bolt; R3 recoil pad; sling swivel studs
MSRP: $1132

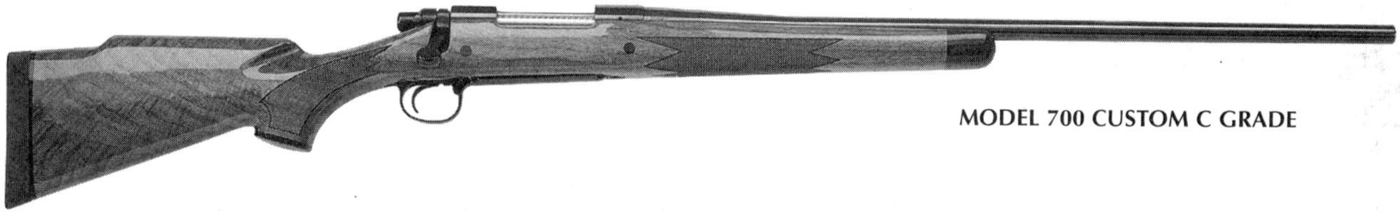

MODEL 700 CUSTOM C GRADE

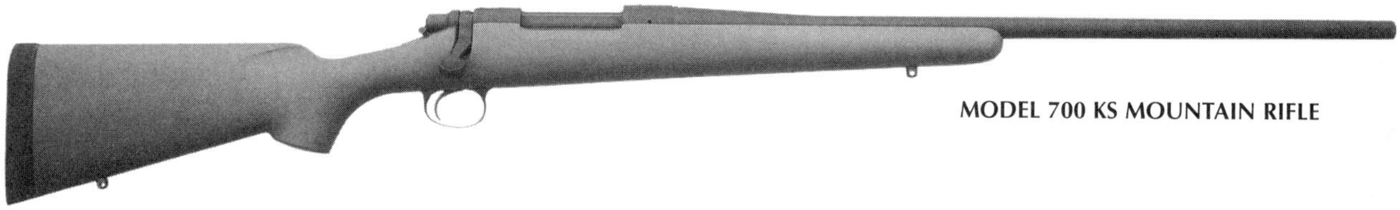

MODEL 700 KS MOUNTAIN RIFLE

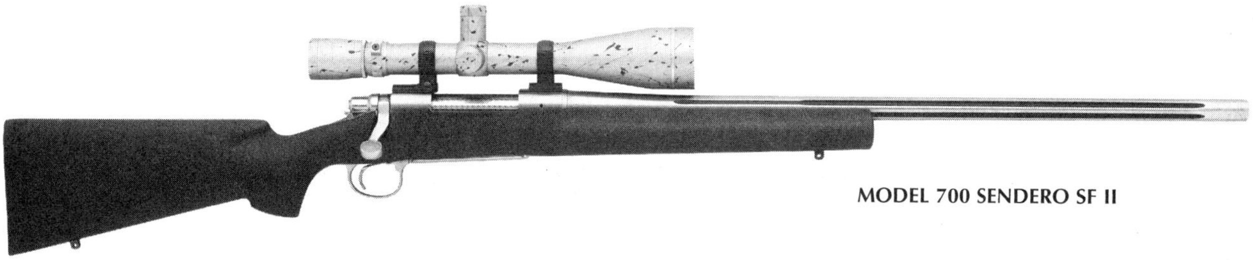

MODEL 700 SENDERO SF II

MODEL 700 CUSTOM C GRADE

Action: bolt
Stock: fancy American walnut
Barrel: 24 in. (Ultra Mag 26 in.)
Sights: none
Weight: 7.5 lbs.
Caliber: any popular standard or magnum chambering
Magazine: 3-5 rounds
Features: some custom-shop options available
MSRP: **$3236**

MODEL 700 SENDERO SF II

Action: bolt
Stock: composite
Barrel: 26 in.
Weight: 8.5 lbs.
Caliber: .264 Win. Mag., 7mm Rem. Mag., 7mm Rem. Ultra Mag., .300 Win. Mag., .300 Win. Ultra Mag.
Features: heavy-contour (0.820″ Muzzle O.D.) polished stainless fluted barrel; full-length aluminum bedding blocks; black with gray webbing H.S. Precision aramid fiber reinforced composite stock with contoured beavertail forend with ambidextrous finger grooves and palm swell; twin front swivel studs for sling and a bipod
MSRP: **$1359**

MODEL 700 SPS

Action: bolt
Stock: synthetic
Barrel: 24 in. or 26 in.
Sights: none
Weight: 7.25-7.5 lbs.
Caliber: .204 Ruger to .300 Ultra Mag
Magazine: detachable box, 3-5 rounds
Features: also available in youth models with 20- and 22-inch barrels; chrome-moly or stainless, sporter
MSRP: **$639–673**

Remington Arms Rifles

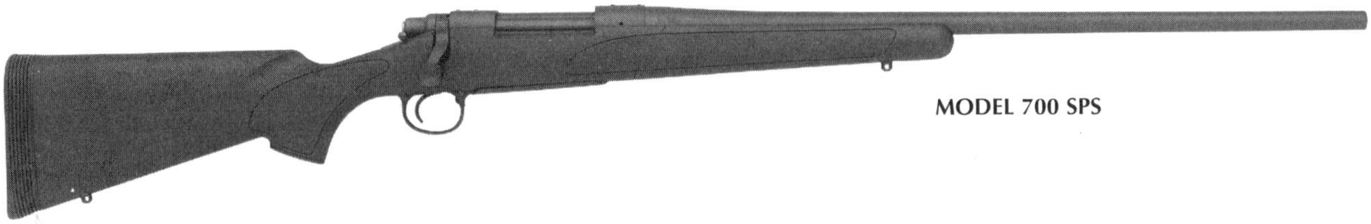

MODEL 700 SPS

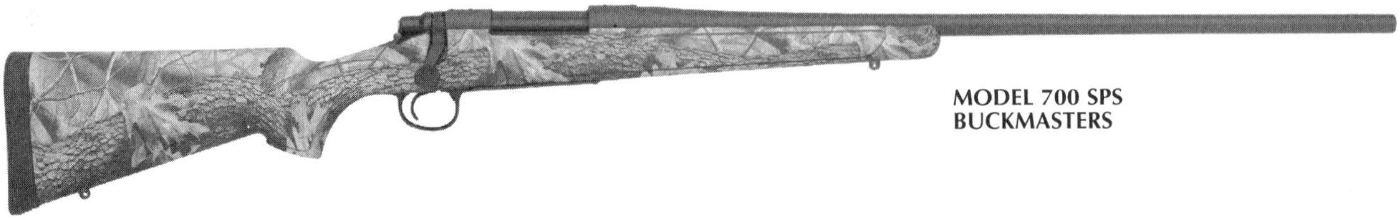

MODEL 700 SPS BUCKMASTERS

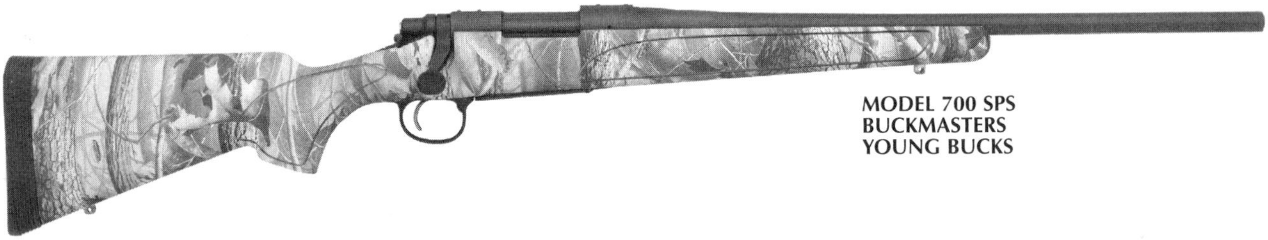

MODEL 700 SPS BUCKMASTERS YOUNG BUCKS

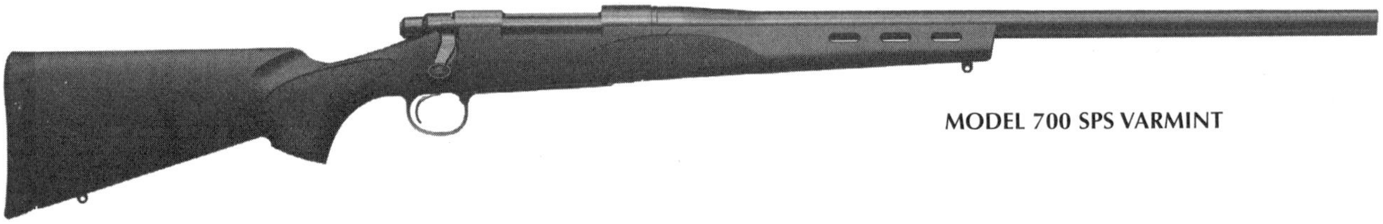

MODEL 700 SPS VARMINT

MODEL 700 SPS BUCKMASTERS

Action: bolt; short, long and magnum
Stock: camo-covered synthetic, Realtree Hardwoods HD
Barrel: 24 in. (short and long), 26 in. (magnum)
Sights: none; drilled and tapped for scope mounts
Weight: 7.3-7.6 lbs.
Caliber: .243 Win, 7mm-08, .270 Win, .30-06 Sprg, 7mm Rem Mag, .300 Win Mag
Magazine: hinged floorplate
Features: specially engraved floorplate with Buckmasters logo; fully camouflaged stock; carbon steel barrel with matte blued finish; sling swivel studs, R3 recoil pad
MSRP: $707

MODEL 700 SPS BUCKMASTERS YOUNG BUCKS YOUTH EDITION

Action: bolt; short
Stock: camo-covered synthetic, Realtree Hardwoods HD
Barrel: 20 in.
Sights: none; drilled and tapped for scope mounts
Weight: 6.8 lbs.
Caliber: .243 Win
Magazine: hinged floorplate
Features: specially engraved floorplate with Buckmasters logo; fully camouflaged stock; carbon steel barrel with matte blued finish; sling swivel studs, R3 recoil pad
MSRP: $707

MODEL 700 SPS VARMINT

Action: bolt; short
Stock: synthetic, matte black
Barrel: 26 in.
Sights: none; drilled and tapped for scope mounts
Weight: 7.4 lbs.
Caliber: .204 Ruger, .22-250 Rem, .223 Rem, .243 Win, .308 Win, .17 Rem Fireball
Magazine: 4 or 5 rounds, hinged floorplate
Features: carbon steel, heavy varmint-contour barrel with matte blued finish; Remington X-Mark Pro trigger; sling swivel studs
MSRP: $665

Remington Arms Rifles

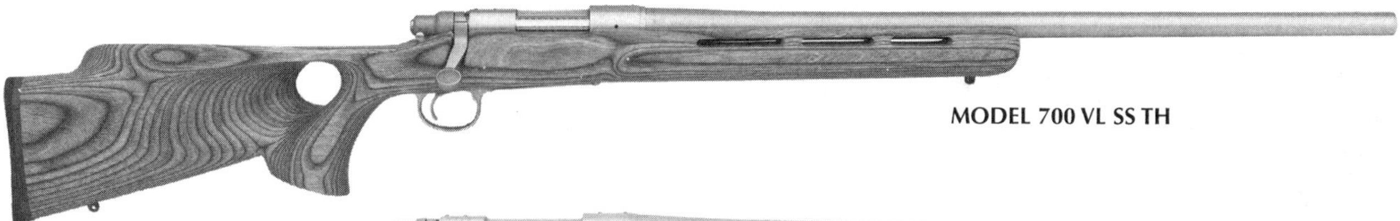

MODEL 700 VL SS TH

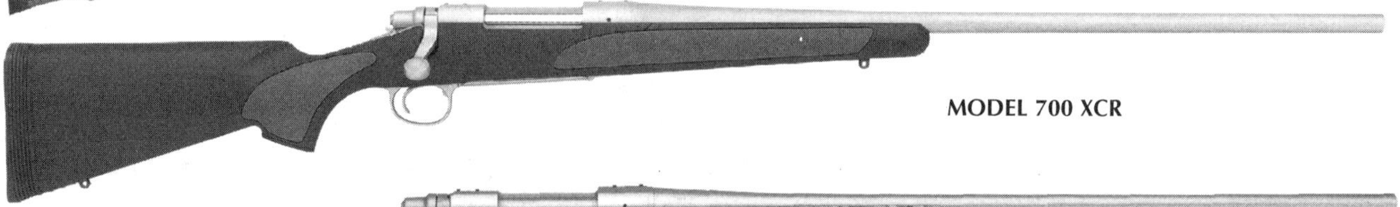

MODEL 700 XCR

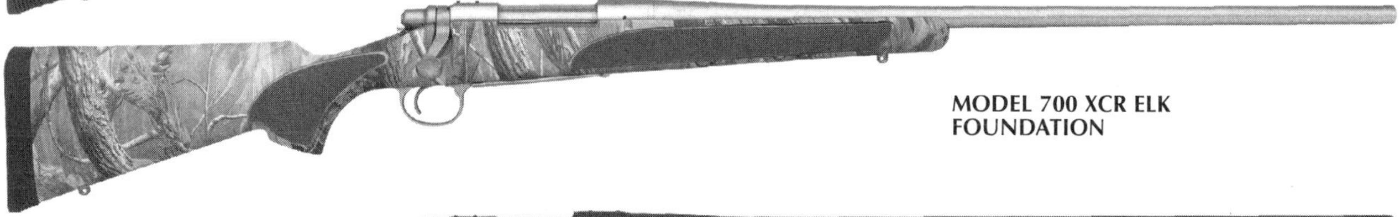

MODEL 700 XCR ELK FOUNDATION

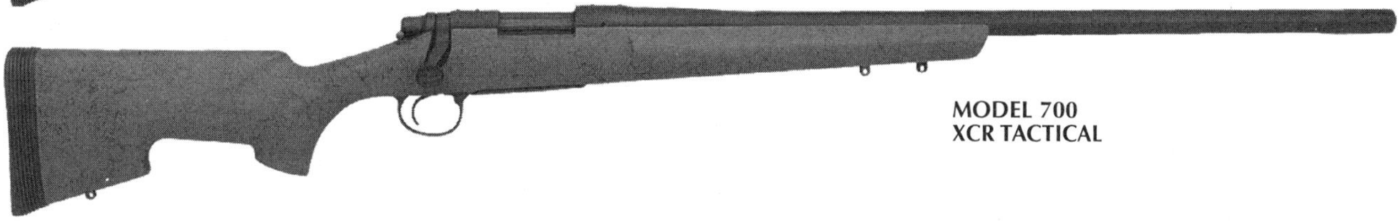

MODEL 700 XCR TACTICAL

MODEL 700 VL SS TH

Action: bolt; short
Stock: satin finish brown laminate; thumbhole style
Barrel: 26 in.
Sights: none; drilled and tapped for scope mounts
Weight: 9.2 lbs.
Caliber: .204 Ruger, .22-250 Rem, .223 Rem
Magazine: 4 rounds, hinged floorplate
Features: cylindrical solid steel receiver; hammer-forged, heavy-contour barrel with satin finish; Remington X-Mark Pro trigger; sling swivel studs
MSRP: $1085

MODEL 700 VSF TARGET

Action: bolt
Stock: composite
Barrel: heavy, 26 in.
Sights: none
Weight: 9.5 lbs.
Caliber: .223, .22-250, .243, .308
Magazine: box, 5 rounds
Features: fluted barrel, stock with beavertail forend, tactical style dual front swivel studs for bi-pod; VSSF II also available in .204 Ruger and .220 Swift
VSSF II: $1332
VLS (laminate): $979

MODEL 700 XCR

Action: bolt
Stock: synthetic
Barrel: 24 in. or 26 in.
Sights: none
Weight: 7.5 lbs.
Caliber: 11 chamberings, from .270 to .375 Ultra Mag
Magazine: internal box, 3-5 rounds
Features: stainless barreled action; TriNyte corrosion control coating; Hogue grip panels; stock finish is Realtree Hardwoods Gray HD; R3 recoil pad
MSRP: $1068–1141

MODEL 700 XCR ELK FOUNDATION RIFLE, .300 REM. ULTRA MAG

Action: bolt
Stock: camo-covered synthetic, overmolded, Realtree All-Purpose HD
Barrel: 26 in.
Sights: none; drilled and tapped for scope mounts
Weight: 7.6 lbs.
Caliber: .300 Rem. Ultra Mag
Magazine: hinged floorplate
Features: Rocky Mtn. Elk Foundation logo engraved on the hinged floorplate and stock; stainless-steel barrel with TriNyte Satin finish; sling swivel studs; R3 recoil pad; Remington X-Mark Pro trigger
MSRP: $1199

MODEL 700 XCR TACTICAL LONG RANGE RIFLE

Action: bolt, short and magnum
Stock: Tactical Bell and Carlson; synthetic composite, OD Green/Black Webbed
Barrel: 26 in.
Sights: none; drilled and tapped for scope mounts
Weight: 8.5 lbs.
Caliber: .300 Rem. Ultra Mag
Magazine: 3, 4 or 5 rounds
Features: 416 stainless-steel, varmint-contour, fluted barrel with black TriNyte finish; sling swivel studs; Remington X-Mark Pro trigger; recessed thumb hook behind the pistol grip
MSRP: $1407

Remington Arms Rifles

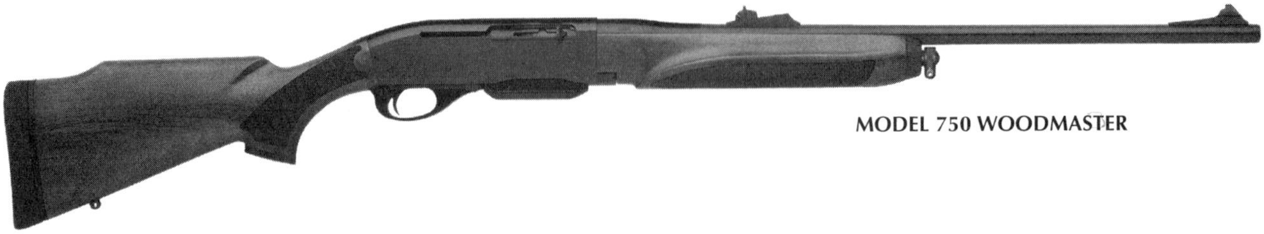

MODEL 750 WOODMASTER

MODEL 770

MODEL 770 YOUTH

MODEL 750 WOODMASTER

Action: autoloader
Stock: walnut
Barrel: 18.5 (carbines) and 22 in.
Sights: open, adjustable
Weight: 7.25 lbs. and 7.5 lbs.
Caliber: .243 Win., .308 Win., .270 Win., .30-06 Sprng., .35 Whelen, .308 Win. (carbine), .30-06 (carbine), .35 Whelen (carbine)
Features: improved gas system; low-profile design; R3 recoil pad; receiver drilled and tapped for Model 7400 scope mounts; satin finish American walnut forend and stock with machine-cut checkering
MSRP: $879

MODEL 770

Action: bolt; short, long and magnum
Stock: synthetic, matte black
Barrel: 22 or 24 in.
Sights: none; drilled and tapped for scope mounts
Weight: 8.5-8.6 lbs.
Caliber: .243 Win, .270 Win, .30-06 Sprg, 7mm Rem Mag, .300 Win Mag, 7mm-08 Rem, .308 Win
Magazine: 3 or 4 rounds, center-feed steel box
Features: complete with factory-mounted and bore-sighted Bushnell Sharpshooter 3-9x40mm scope; all steel receiver; ordnance-grade steel barrel with six-groove, button-rifling; all steel bolt cams; ergonomically contoured stock; sling swivel studs
MSRP: $460

MODEL 770 YOUTH

Action: bolt; short
Stock: synthetic, matte black
Barrel: 20 in.
Sights: none; drilled and tapped for scope mounts
Weight: 8.5-8.6 lbs.
Caliber: .243 Win
Magazine: 4 rounds, center-feed steel box
Features: 12 3/8 in length of pull (1 in. shorter than standard model); complete with factory-mounted and bore-sighted Bushnell Sharpshooter 3-9x40mm scope; all steel receiver; ordnance-grade steel barrel with six-groove, button-rifling; all steel bolt cams; ergonomically contoured stock; sling swivel studs
MSRP: $460

MODEL 7600

MODEL 7600

Action: pump
Stock: walnut or synthetic
Barrel: 22 in.
Sights: open
Weight: 7.5 lbs.
Caliber: .243, .270, .308, .30-06
Magazine: detachable box, 4 rounds
Features: also 7600 carbine with 18 in. barrel (7.25 lbs.)
Synthetic: $665
Walnut: $792

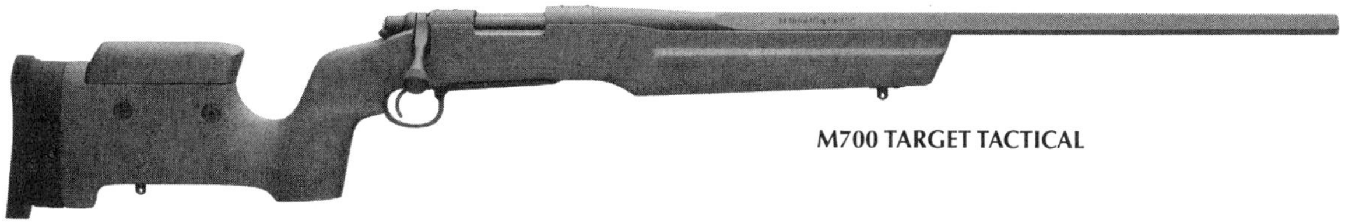

M700 TARGET TACTICAL

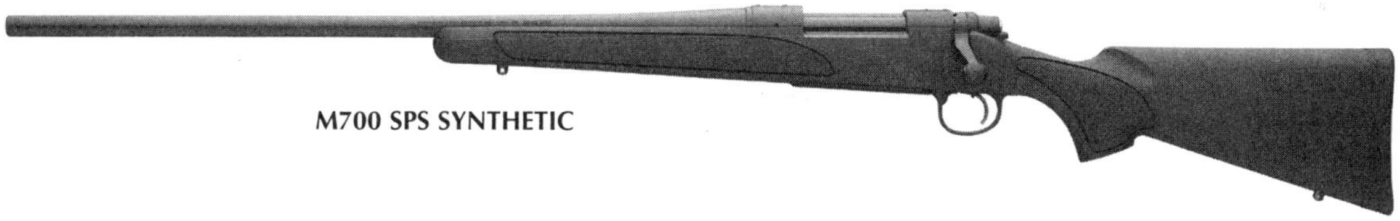

M700 SPS SYNTHETIC

REMINGTON M700 TARGET TACTICAL

Action: two-lug bolt
Stock: Bell & Carlson Medalist Varmint/Tactical stock with adjustable comb and length of pull
Barrel: 26″ triangular VTR Barrel Profile with muzzle counter-bore
Sights: none
Weight: 9 lbs.
Caliber: .308 Win.
Magazine: internal box
Features: tactical extended bolt knob, all-steel hinged floorplate, 5-R hammer-forged target rifling, X-Mark-Pro externally adjustable trigger, thumb safety.
MSRP: $1972

REMINGTON M700 SPS SYNTHETIC, LEFT-HAND (ALSO VARMINT VERSION)

Action: two-lug bolt
Stock: black synthetic
Barrel: 24″ or 26″
Sights: none
Weight: 7 ½ to 7 ¾ lbs (9 lbs in Varmint)
Caliber: .270 Win., .30-06, 7mm-08 Rem., .300 Win. Mag. (.17 Rem. to .308 in Varmint)
Magazine: internal box
Features: affordable left-hand version of most popular American bolt rifle.
MSRP: $639

Remington Arms Rifles

REMINGTON M700 XHR XTREME HUNTING RIFLE

Action: two-lug bolt
Stock: synthetic in camo with Hogue overmolded accents on grip and fore-end
Barrel: 24″ or 26″ triangular contoured barrel, hammer forged, matte finish
Sights: none
Weight: 7 1/4 to 7 3/4
Caliber: .243 Win to .300 Rem Ultra Mag
Magazine: internal box
Features: X-Mark-Pro adjustable trigger, hinged floorplate, SuperCell recoil pad, polished jewel bolt.
MSRP: $915

REMINGTON M597 FLX

Action: autoloading, recoil operated
Stock: Next Digital FLX camo
Barrel: 20″ carbon steel matte
Sights: TruGlo fiber optic
Weight: 5 1/2 lbs.
Caliber: .22 LR
Magazine: detachable 10-round box
Features: bolt-guidance system with twin tool-steel guide rails, last-shot, hold-open bolt for added safety.
MSRP: $260

R-25

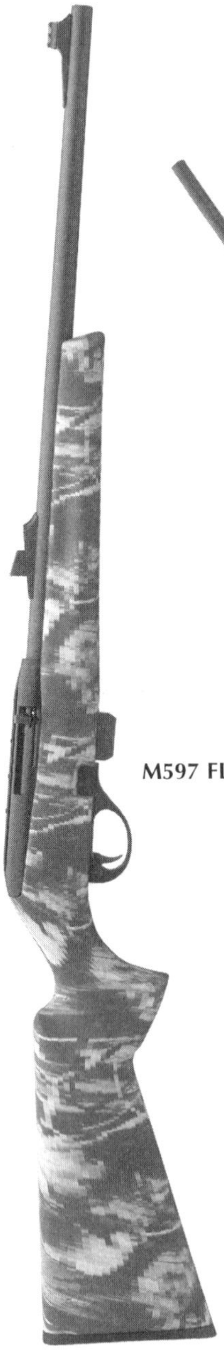

M597 FLX

R-15

REMINGTON R-25 MODULAR REPEATING RIFLE

Action: autoloading, gas operated
Stock: synthetic camo (Mossy Oak Treestand)
Barrel: 20″ carbon steel, matte blue
Sights: none, receiver-length Picatinny rail and gas block rail furnished
Weight: 7 3/4 lbs.
Caliber: .243 Win., 7mm-08 Rem., .308 Win.
Magazine: detachable 4-round box
Features: AR-style hunting rifle, single-stage hunting trigger, free-floated ChroMoly barrel.
MSRP: $1567

REMINGTON R-15 HUNTER

Action: autoloading, gas operated
Stock: synthetic camo
Barrel: 22″
Sights: receiver-length Pitcatinny rail for adding optics
Weight: 7 3/4 lbs.
Caliber: .30 Rem (also .223)
Magazine: detachable 4-round box
Features: New for 2009: .30 Remington addition to R-15 line that includes carbine and predator versions and new Thumbhole and Stainless Steel Varmint versions in .223.
MSRP: $1225

Rifles Inc. Rifles

CLASSIC

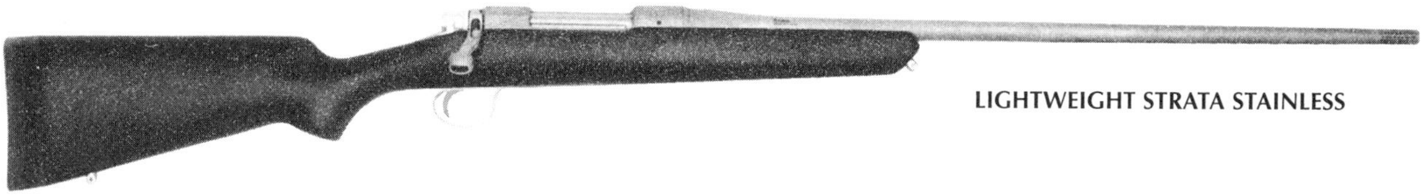

LIGHTWEIGHT STRATA STAINLESS

MASTER SERIES

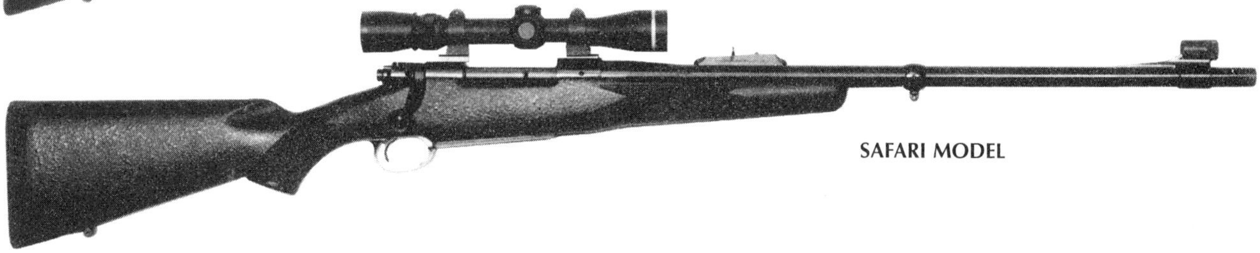

SAFARI MODEL

CLASSIC

Action: bolt
Stock: laminated fiberglass
Barrel: stainless steel, match grade 24-26 in.
Sights: none
Weight: 6.5 lbs.
Caliber: all popular chamberings up to .375 H&H
Magazine: box, 3 or 5 rounds
Features: Winchester 70 or Rem. 700 action; lapped bolt; pillar glass bedded stock; adjustable trigger; hinged floor-plate; also 27 in. fluted barrel, synthetic stock in .300 Rem. UM
MSRP: $2300

LIGHTWEIGHT STRATA STAINLESS

Action: bolt
Stock: laminated with textured epoxy
Barrel: stainless match grade 22-25 in.
Sights: none
Weight: 5.0 lbs.
Caliber: all popular chamberings up to .375 H&H
Magazine: box, 3 or 5 rounds
Features: stainless Rem. action, fluted bolt and hollowed-handle; pillar glass bedded stock; stainless metal finish; blind or hinged floorplate; custom Protektor pad; also Lightweight 70 (5.75 lbs.); Lightweight Titanium Strata
Lightweight Strata:. $2600
Lightweight 70: $2500
Titanium Strata:. $2600

MASTER SERIES

Action: bolt
Stock: laminated fiberglass
Barrel: match grade, 24-27 in.
Sights: none
Weight: 7.75 lbs.
Caliber: all popular chamberings up to .300 Rem. Ultra Mag.
Magazine: box, 3 rounds
Features: Remington 700 action
MSRP: $2750

SAFARI MODEL

Action: bolt
Stock: laminated fiberglass
Barrel: stainless match grade 23-25 in.
Sights: optional Express
Weight: 8.5 lbs.
Caliber: all popular chamberings
Magazine: box, 3 or 5 rounds, optional drop box
Features: Win. Model 70 action; drilled and tapped for 8-40 screws; stainless Quiet Slimbrake; stainless or black Teflon finish; adjustable trigger; hinged floor-plate; barrel band optional
MSRP: $2950

Rock River Rifles

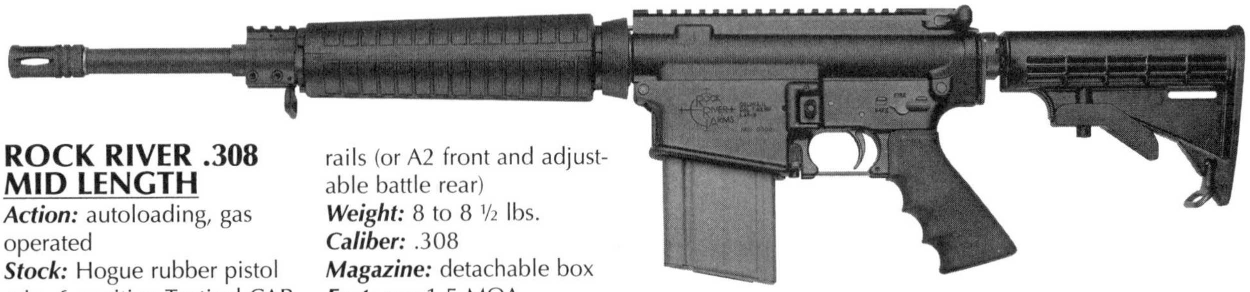

ROCK RIVER .308 MID LENGTH

Action: autoloading, gas operated
Stock: Hogue rubber pistol grip, 6-position Tactical CAR Stock
Barrel: 16″
Sights: none on flattop verison, with front and rear rails (or A2 front and adjustable battle rear)
Weight: 8 to 8 ½ lbs.
Caliber: .308
Magazine: detachable box
Features: 1.5 MOA accuracy standard at 100 yards, RRA two-stage trigger
MSRP: $1265

RIFLES

Rogue Rifle Company

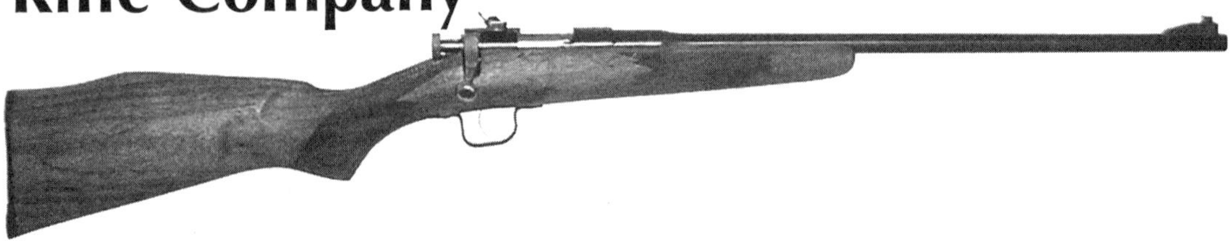

CHIPMUNK

Action: bolt
Stock: walnut, laminated black, brown or camo
Barrel: 16 in.
Sights: target
Weight: 2.5 lbs.
Caliber: Sporting rifle in .17 HMR and .17 MACH 2; Target model in .22, .22 LR, .22 WMR
Magazine: none
Features: single-shot; manual-cocking action; receiver-mounted rear sights; Target model weighs 5 lbs. and comes with competition-style receiver sight and globe front and adjustable trigger, extendable buttplate and front rail
Standard:. $140-200
Stainless: $160-220
Bull barrel:. $175-220
Bull barrel/stainless: $263–277

Rossi Rifles

ROSSI TRIFECTAMATCHED SET IN LAMINATED STOCK

Action: hinged-breech single-shot
Stock: synthetic laminate available in 3 colors
Barrel: set of 3; 22″ 20 gauge, 18 ½″ .22LR; 22″ .243 Win. Youth
Sights: shotgun barrel has brass bead front, .243 and .22 LR have fiber-optic open sights
Weight: 6 ½ to 7 lbs.
Caliber: 20 ga. Shotgun, .22 LR, .243 Win.
Magazine: none
Features: Three guns in one! Carrying case included, removable cheekpiece.
MSRP: $334–363

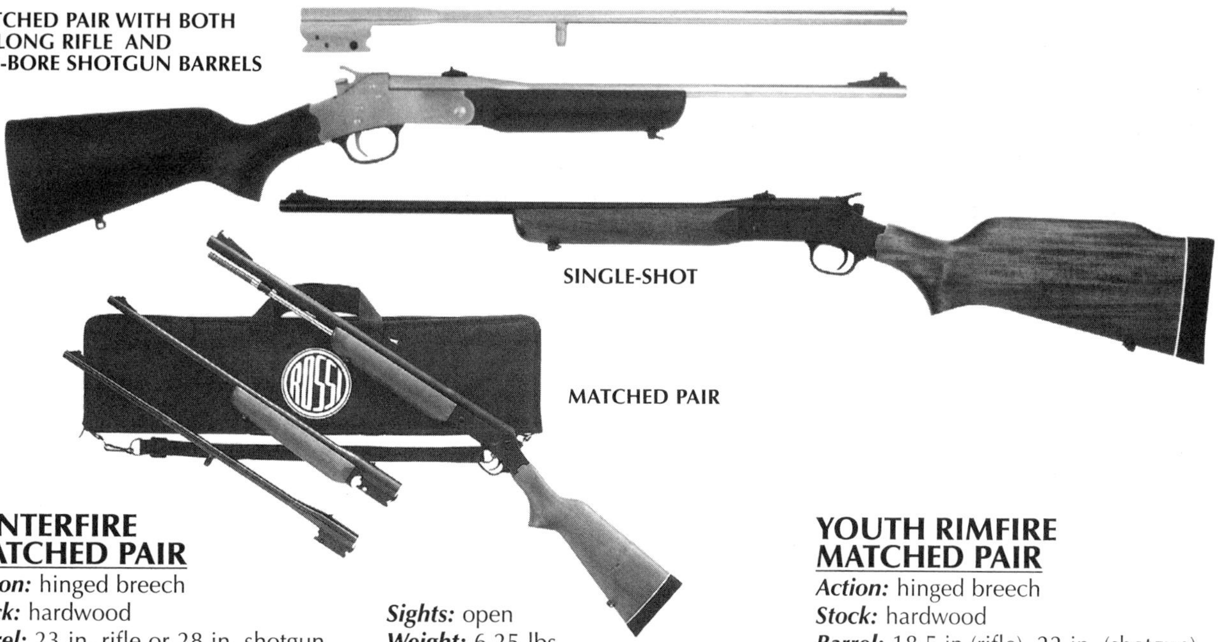

CENTERFIRE MATCHED PAIR

Action: hinged breech
Stock: hardwood
Barrel: 23 in. rifle or 28 in. shotgun
Sights: open
Weight: 5.0-6.0 lbs.
Caliber: 12 or 20 ga. with .223 Rem., .243 Rem., .243 Win., .308, .30-06, .270 and .22-250 (Youth only)
Magazine: none
Features: carry case and sling included; adjustable sights
MSRP: $327

SINGLE-SHOT

Action: hinged breech
Stock: hardwood
Barrel: 23 in.
Sights: open
Weight: 6.25 lbs.
Caliber: .17 HMR, .223, 243, .308, .30-06, .270, .22-250 , 7.62x39
Magazine: none
Features: single shot; recoil pad; sling swivels; extra-wide positive-action extractor; good rifle for first time shooters; all calibers except .17 HMR have Monte Carlo stock
.17 HMR blue: $175
.17 HMR stainless: $221
Single Shot with heavy barrel (.223, .243, .22-250): $272
Youth model: $263

YOUTH RIMFIRE MATCHED PAIR

Action: hinged breech
Stock: hardwood
Barrel: 18.5 in (rifle), 22 in. (shotgun)
Sights: open
Weight: 4.0-6.0 lbs.
Caliber: 20 ga/.22 LR, .410/.22 LR, .410/.17 HMR
Magazine: none
Features: single shot; blue or stainless steel; single-stage trigger, adjustable sights; full size 12 or 20 gauge with .22 LR, .22 Mag or .17 HMR
Blued: $197
Stainless: $213
.410 and .17 HMR, blue: $223
Stainless: $252
Full-size: $252

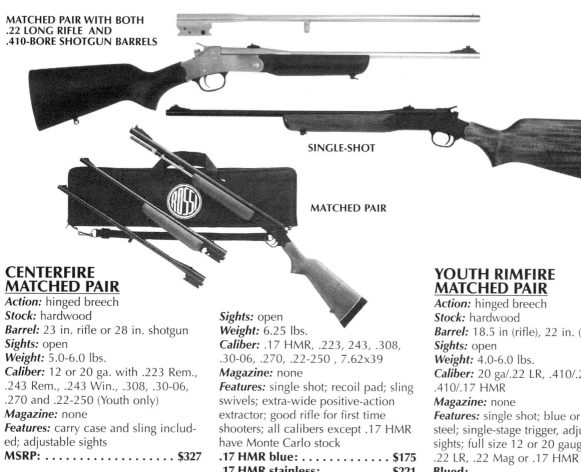

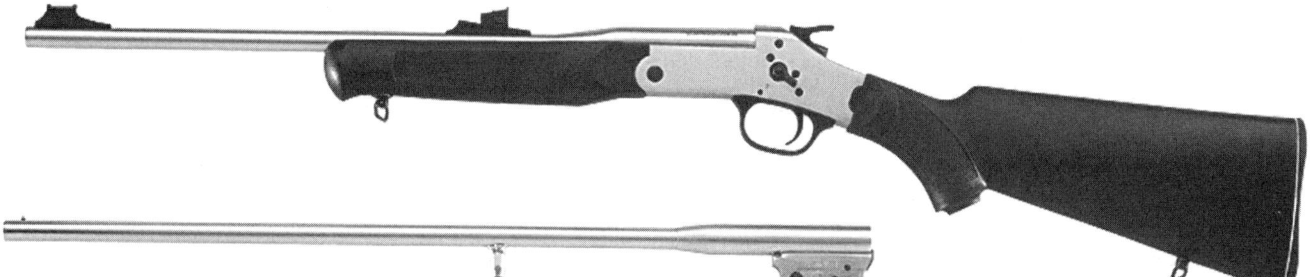

YOUTH MATCHED PAIR

Action: break-open single shot
Stock: black synthetic
Barrel: 22 in./18.5 in.
Sights: adjustable fiber optic front (rifle barrels), brass bead front (shotgun)
Weight: 3.75 lbs./5.6 lbs.
Caliber: .17 HMR or .22 LR rifle barrel and .410 gauge shotgun barrel
Features: quick-interchange rifle and shotgun barrels; matte nickel finish; rifle barrel drilled and tapped to hold included scope mount base and hammer extension; Taurus Security System lock; carrying case and dual purpose strap included
.410/.17 HMR: $221
.410/.22 LR: $188

Ruger Rifles

MODEL 10/22 RBM

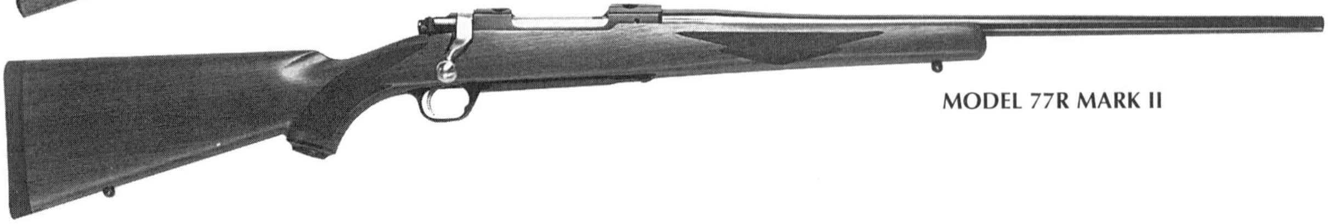

MODEL 77R MARK II

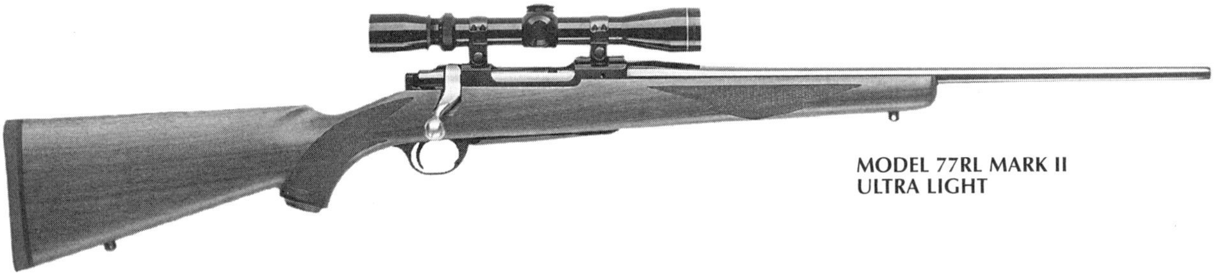

MODEL 77RL MARK II
ULTRA LIGHT

MODEL 10/22

Action: autoloading
Stock: walnut, birch, synthetic or laminated
Barrel: 18 in.
Sights: open
Weight: 5.0 lbs.
Caliber: .22 LR
Magazine: rotary, 10 rounds
Features: blowback action; also International with full-stock, heavy-barreled Target and stainless steel versions; Magnum with 9-shot magazine
Model 10/22: $269
Stainless: $318
Walnut: $355
Target: $485
Target stainless, laminated: . . . $533

MODEL 77R MARK II

Action: bolt
Stock: walnut
Barrel: 22 in.
Sights: none
Weight: 7.25-8.25 lbs.
Caliber: most popular standard and magnum calibers
Magazine: box, 3-5 rounds
Features: scope rings included; RBZ has stainless steel, laminated stock; RSBZ with sights
MSRP: $935.63

MODEL 77 RFP MARK II

Action: bolt
Stock: synthetic
Barrel: 22 in.
Sights: none
Weight: 7.0-8.0 lbs.
Caliber: most popular standard and magnum calibers
Magazine: box, 3-5 rounds
Features: stainless steel barrel and action, (magnums with 24 in. barrel); scope rings included
MSRP: $935.63

MODEL 77RL MARK II ULTRA LIGHT

Action: bolt
Stock: walnut
Barrel: 20 in.
Sights: none
Weight: 6.25-6.75 lbs.
Caliber: .223, .243, .257, .270, .308
Magazine: box, 4 or 5 rounds
77RL Ultra Light: $612.02
International Model
(18 in. bbl.): $612.02

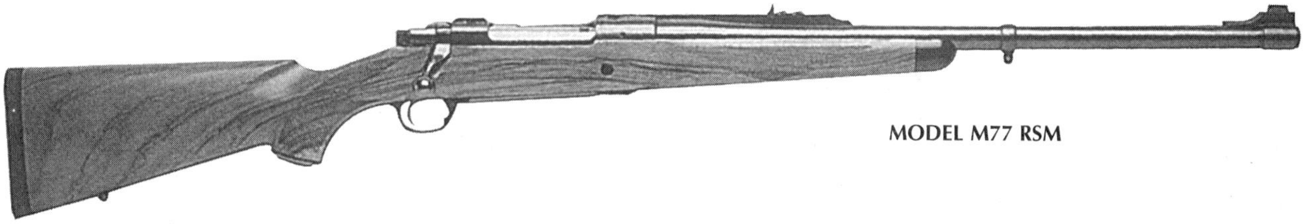

MODEL M77 RSM

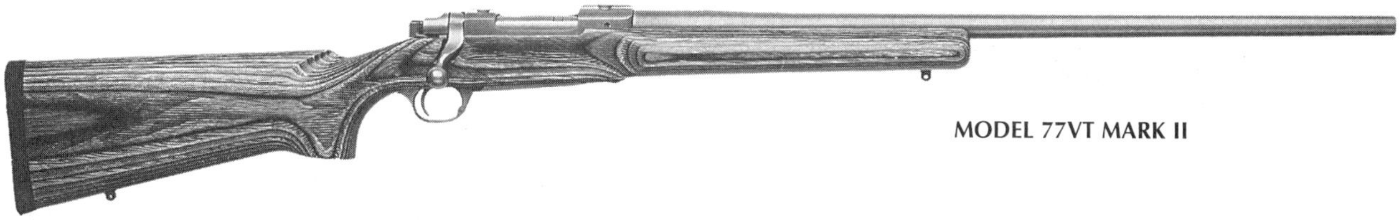

MODEL 77VT MARK II

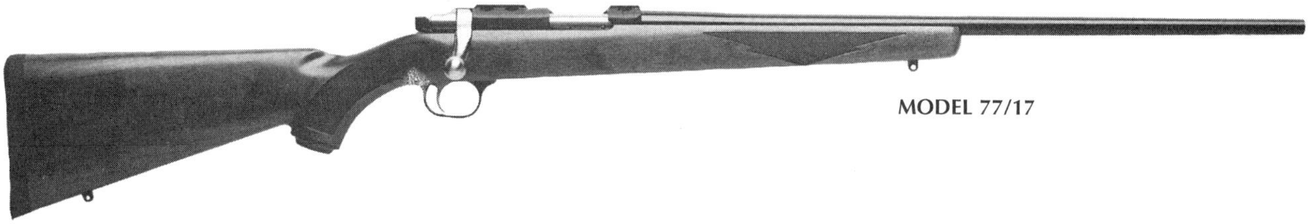

MODEL 77/17

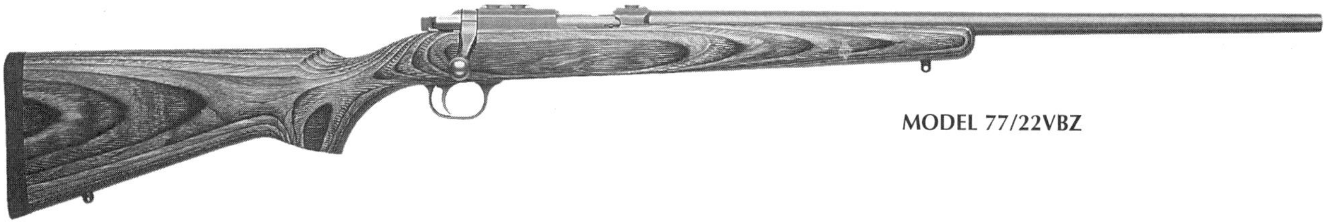

MODEL 77/22VBZ

MODEL 77 RSM MAGNUM

Action: bolt
Stock: Circassian walnut
Barrel: 23 in. with quarter rib
Sights: open
Weight: 9.5-10.0 lbs.
Caliber: .375 H&H, .416 Rigby (10.3 lbs.), .458 Lott
Magazine: box, 3 or 4 rounds
Features: barrel-mounted front swivel; also Express rifle in popular standard and magnum long-action calibers
MSRP: $1766.82

MODEL 77 VT MARK II

Action: bolt
Stock: brown laminate
Barrel: heavy stainless 26 in., target gray finish
Sights: none
Weight: 9.8 lbs.
Caliber: .223, .204, .22-250, .220 Swift, .243, .25-06, .308
Magazine: box, 4 or 5 rounds
MSRP: $935

MODEL 77/17

Action: bolt
Stock: walnut, synthetic or laminated
Barrel: 22 in.
Sights: none
Weight: 6.5 lbs.
Caliber: .17 HMR
Magazine: 9 rounds
Features: also stainless (P) and stainless varmint with laminated stock (VMBBZ), 24 in. barrel (6.9 lbs.)
77/17 RM: $612.99
K77/17 VMBBZ: $630.96

MODEL 77/22 RIMFIRE RIFLE

Action: bolt
Stock: walnut
Barrel: 20 in.
Sights: none
Weight: 6.0 lbs.
Caliber: .22 LR, .22 Mag., .22 Hornet
Magazine: rotary, 6-10 rounds
Features: also Magnum (M) and stainless synthetic (P) versions; scope rings included for all; sights on S versions; VBZ has 24 in. medium stainless barrel (6.9 lbs.)
77/22R: $612
77/22RM: $612
K77/22RP: $612.99
K77/22 RMP: $612
77/22RH (.22 Hornet): $612
K77/22VBZ: $612
K77/22VMBZ: $665.15

Ruger Rifles

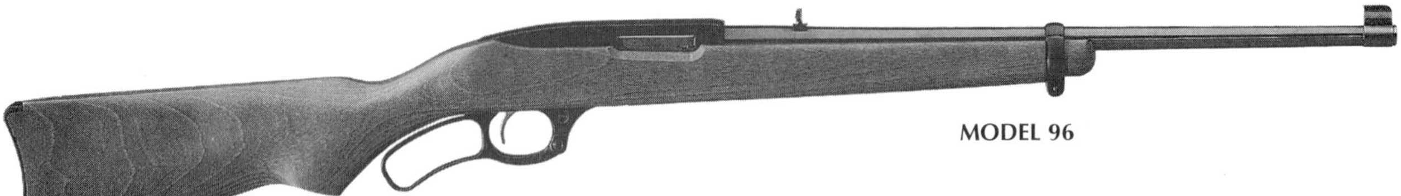

MODEL 96

M77 HAWKEYE

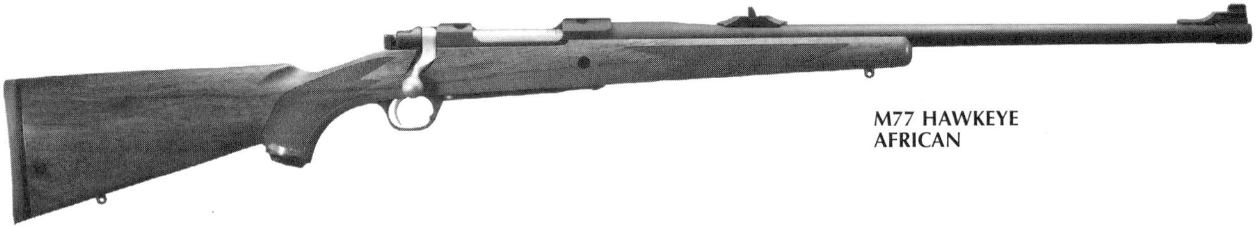

M77 HAWKEYE AFRICAN

M77 HAWKEYE ALASKAN

MODEL 96 LEVER-ACTION RIFLE

Action: lever
Stock: hardwood
Barrel: 18½ in., blued
Sights: adjustable rear sight
Weight: 5.25 lbs.
Caliber: .17 HMR, .22 WMR, .44 Mag.
Magazine: rotary magazine, 9 rounds
Features: enclosed short-throw lever action; cross bolt safety; standard tip-off scope-mount base
Model 96: $390
.44 Mag. (4-round): $546

M77 HAWKEYE

Action: bolt
Stock: American walnut (Standard models) or black synthetic (All-Weather models)
Barrel: 22 or 24 in.
Sights: none
Weight: 8 lbs.
Caliber: .204 Ruger, .22-250 Rem, .223 Rem, .243 Win, .25-06 Rem, .270 Win, .280 Rem, .30-06 Sprgfld., .300 Win Mag, .308 Win, .338 Federal, .338 Win Mag, .358 Win, 7mm Rem Mag, 7mm-08 Rem
Magazine: 4 rounds
Features: Matte blued or matte stainless finish; Ruger LC6 trigger; non-rotating, Mauser-type controlled-feed extractor; fixed-blade type ejector; hinged steel floor plate with Ruger logo; scope rings included; three-position safety
MSRP: $643.39

M77 HAWKEYE AFRICAN

Action: bolt
Stock: American walnut
Barrel: 23 in.
Sights: front: white bead; rear: shallow V, windage adjustable
Weight: 7.8 lbs.
Caliber: .375 Ruger
Magazine: 3 rounds
Features: Matte blue finish; Ruger LC6 trigger; non-rotating, Mauser-type controlled-feed extractor; fixed-blade type ejector; hinged steel floor plate with Ruger logo; scope rings included; three-position safety
MSRP: $782.38

M77 HAWKEYE ALASKAN

Action: bolt
Stock: Black Hogue rubber overmolded
Barrel: 20 in.
Sights: front: white bead; rear: shallow V, windage adjustable
Weight: 8 lbs.
Caliber: .375 Ruger
Magazine: 3 rounds
Features: Alaskan Black finish; Ruger LC6 trigger; non-rotating, Mauser-type controlled-feed extractor; fixed-blade type ejector; hinged steel floor plate with Ruger logo; scope rings included; three-position safety
MSRP: $793

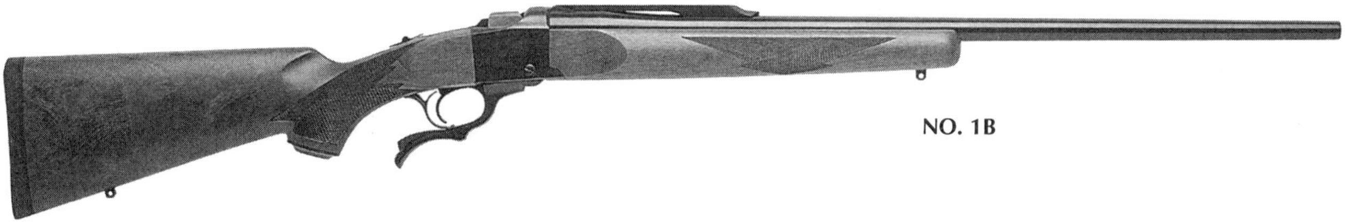

NO. 1B

NO. 1 STAINLESS VARMINTER (.204)

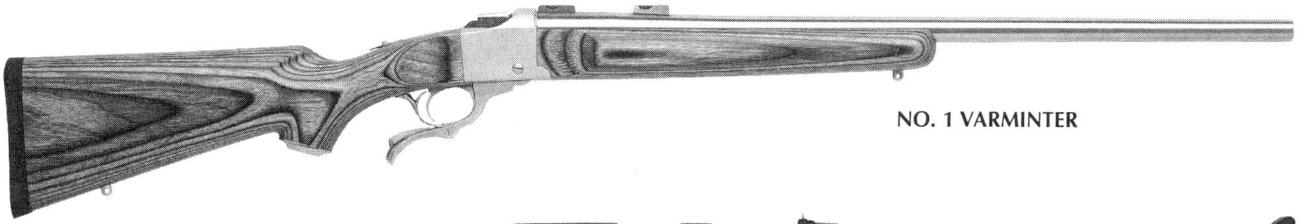

NO. 1 VARMINTER

MODEL PC4

MODEL PC4 CARBINE

Action: autoloading
Stock: synthetic
Barrel: 16.25 in.
Sights: open
Weight: 6.3 lbs.
Caliber: 9mm, .40 S&W
Magazine: detachable, 10-15 rounds
Features: delayed blowback action; optional ghost ring sight
Carbine: $623
With ghost ring sights: $647

NO. 1 SINGLE-SHOT

Action: dropping block
Stock: select checkered walnut
Barrel: 22, 24 or 26 in. (RSI: 20 in.)
Sights: open
Weight: 7.25-8.25 lbs.
Caliber: all popular chamberings in Light Sporter, Medium Sporter, Standard Rifle
Magazine: none
Features: pistol grip; all rifles come with Ruger 1″ scope rings; 45-70 is available in stainless; No. 1 Stainless comes in .243, .25-06, 7mm Rem. Mag., .204, .30-06, .270, .300 Win. Mag., .308
No. 1:.................. $868.72

NO. 1 VARMINTER

Action: dropping block
Stock: select checkered walnut
Barrel: heavy 24 or 26 in. (.220 Swift)
Sights: open
Weight: 8.75 lbs.
Caliber: .22-250, .220 Swift, .223, .25-06
Magazine: box, 5 rounds
Features: Ruger target scope block; stainless available in .22-250; also No. 1H Tropical (heavy 24 in. bbl.) in .375 H&H, .416 Rigby, .458 Lott, .458 Win. Mag., .405; No.1 RSI International (20 in. light bbl. and full-length stock) in .243, .270, .30-06, 7x57
MSRP: $904.90

Ruger Rifles

RANCH RIFLE

TARGET MODEL
MINI-14 RANCH

RANCH RIFLE

Action: autoloading
Stock: hardwood
Barrel: 18 in.
Sights: target
Weight: 6.5-7.0 lbs.
Caliber: .223
Magazine: detachable box, 5 rounds
Features: also stainless, stainless synthetic versions of Mini-14/5; Ranch Rifle (with scope mounts) and Mini-thirty (in 7.62x39)
Deerfield Carbine .44 Mag.: . . $702
Ranch Rifle: $872
Ranch rifle, stainless: $938
Ranch rifle, stainless synthetic: $938
Mini-Thirty, stainless synthetic: $949–966

TARGET MODEL MINI-14 RANCH RIFLE

Action: autoloading
Stock: gray laminated target stock
Barrel: 22 in.
Sights: none; factory set-up for scope use
Weight: 9 lbs.
Caliber: .223 Rem
Magazine: 5 rounds
Features: satin-finished stainless steel receiver; hammer-forged matte stainless-steel target barrel with recessed target crown and adjustable barrel weight; Garand-style breech bolt locking system, with a fixed-pistol gas system and self-cleaning, moving gas cylinder; ventilated handguard; stainless-steel Ruger scope rings; non-slip grooved rubber buttpad; Garand-type safety
MSRP: $1098

RUGER M77 HAWKEYE PREDATOR

Action: two-lug bolt
Stock: Green Mountain Laminate
Barrel: stainless 22″ or 24″
Sights: none
Weight: 7 3/4 to 8 lbs.
Caliber: .223 Rem, .22-250 Rem. or .204 Ruger
Magazine: internal box (.223 Rem and .204 Ruger)
Features: lightweight varminter, trim version of M77, two-stage trigger, 3-position safety.
MSRP: $963

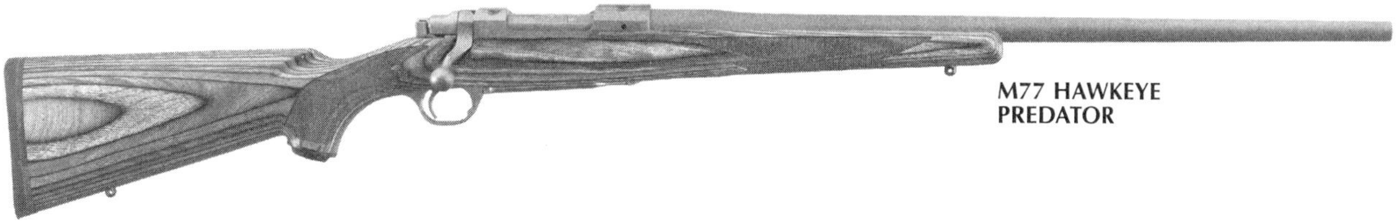

M77 HAWKEYE PREDATOR

NO. 1 IN .300 RCM

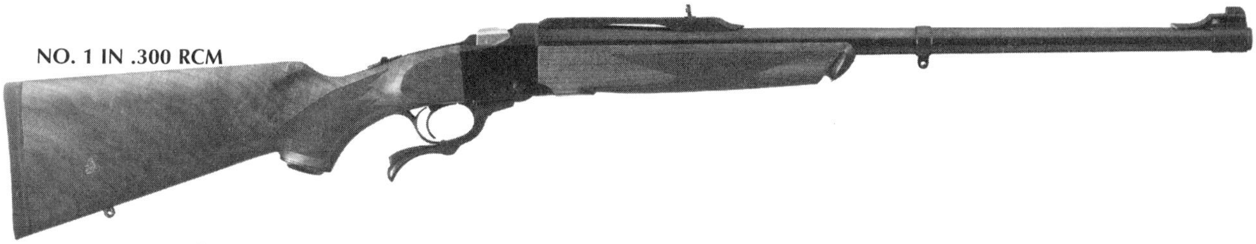

RUGER NO. 1 IN .300 RCM

Action: dropping-block single-shot
Stock: American walnut
Barrel: 22″
Sights: adjustable open rear sight on quarter-rib, blade front sight
Weight: 7 1/4 lbs.
Caliber: .300 RCM
Magazine: none
Features: lightweight hunting rifle with Alexander Henry-style forend
MSRP: $1182

RUGER SR-556

Action: autoloading, gas-operated
Stock: 6-position telescoping M4-style buttstock
Barrel: 16″ chrome-lined, cold hammer-forged
Sights: Troy Industries folding battle sights (provided standard)
Weight: 8 lbs.
Caliber: 5.56 Nato/.223 Rem.
Magazine: detachable 30-round box (3 included)
Features: chrome-plated, two-stage piston driven operating system, 4-position gas regulator, Hogue Monogrip pistol grip, Troy Industries quad rail, handguard and rail covers.
MSRP: $1995

SR-556

Sako Rifles

A7

Action: bolt
Stock: synthetic
Barrel: 22.4-24.4 in.
Sights: none
Weight: 6.3-6.6 lbs.
Caliber: .243 Win., .22-250 Rem., 7mm-08 Rem., .308 Win., .338 Federal, .270 WSM, .300 WSM,
.25-06 Rem., .270 Win., .30-06 Sprg., 7mm Rem. Mag., .300 Win. Mag.
Magazine: 3-round detachable
Features: match-grade hammer-forgedbarrel in blued or no-glare stainless steel finish; forged steel bolt; adjustable single-stage trigger; "Total Control" magazine latch; comes with Weaver-style scope mounting blocks
MSRP: $1000

MODEL 85 GRAY WOLF

Action: bolt
Stock: laminated
Barrel: 22.25 or 22.75 in.
Sights: none
Weight: 7.75 lbs.
Caliber: .223, .22-05, .260, .270 Win., .270 WSM,
Magazine: detachable box, 4-6 rounds
Features: stainless, cold hammer-forged barrel; four action sizes; gray laminated stock
MSRP: $1626

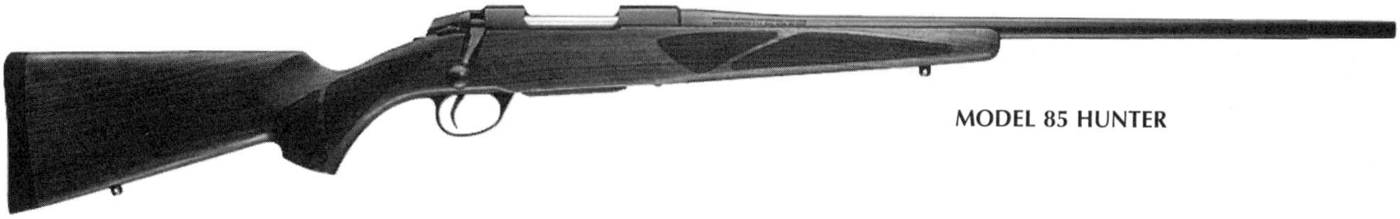

MODEL 85 HUNTER

MODEL TRG-22

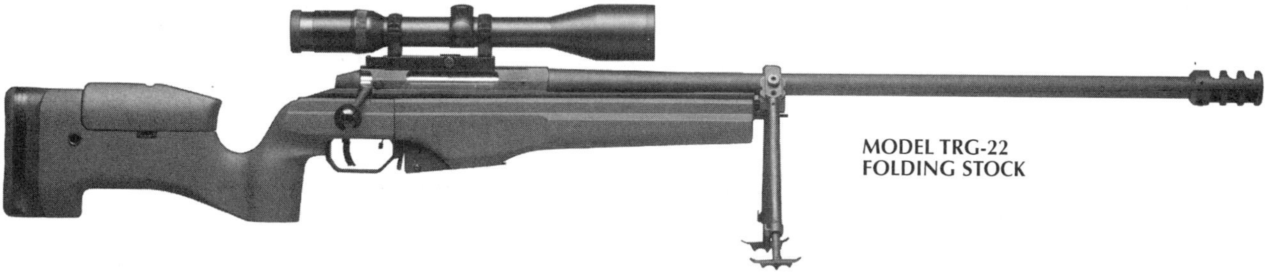

MODEL TRG-22
FOLDING STOCK

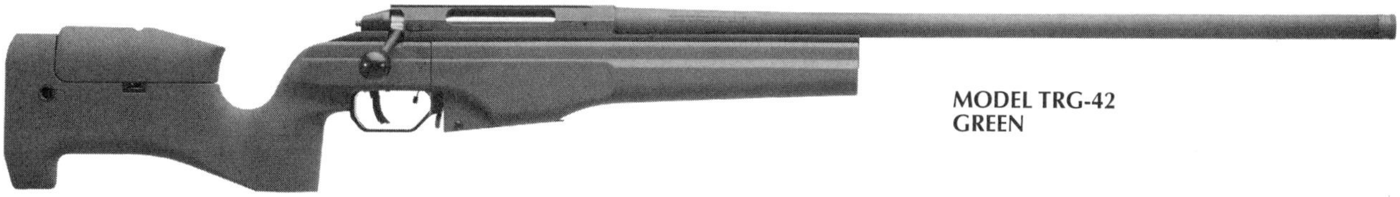

MODEL TRG-42
GREEN

MODEL 85 HUNTER

Action: bolt
Stock: walnut or synthetic
Barrel: hammer-forged 22.5 or 24.25 in.
Sights: none
Weight: 7.75 lbs.
Caliber: most popular standard and magnum calibers from .222 Rem. to .270 and 300 WSM and .375 H&H
Magazine: detachable box, 4-5 rounds
Features: barrel length depends on caliber; 4 action lengths; also stainless synthetic and short-barreled Finnlight versions; Deluxe Grade with fancy walnut stock
Hunter: $1626
.270 WSM & .300 WSM: $1626

MODEL TRG-22

Action: bolt
Stock: synthetic
Barrel: 26 in.
Sights: none
Weight: 10.3 lbs.
Caliber: .308
Magazine: detachable box, 10 rounds
Features: 3-lug bolt; fully adjustable trigger; optional bipod, brake; also TRG 42 in .300 Win. Mag. and .338 Lapua (5-round magazine, 27 in. barrel, 11.3 lbs.)
TRG-22: $2698
TRG-22, folding stock: $4560
TRG-42: $3250
TRG-42, green: $3250

Sako Rifles

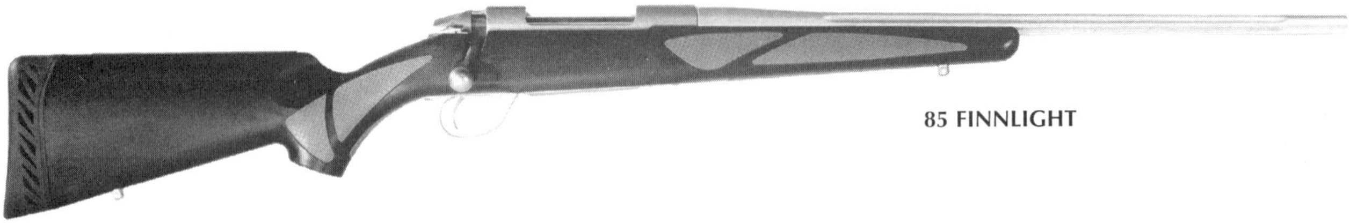

85 FINNLIGHT

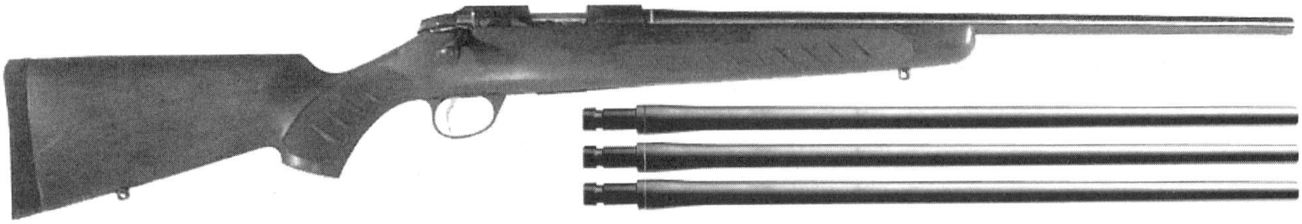

QUAD HUNTER COMBO

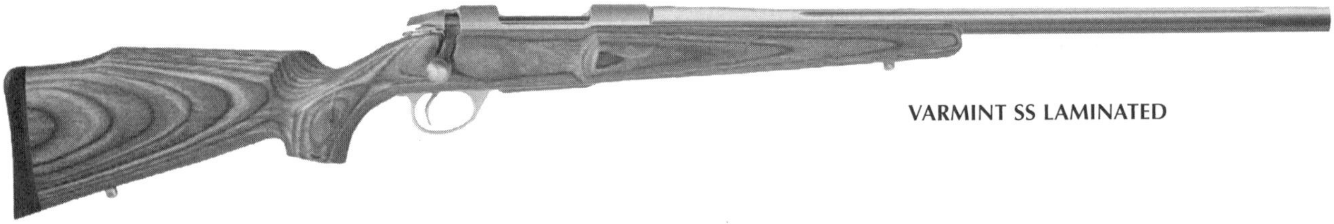

VARMINT SS LAMINATED

85 FINNLIGHT

Action: bolt
Stock: synthetic
Barrel: 20 or 24 in.
Sights: none
Caliber: .243 Win, 25-06 Rem, .260 Rem, .270 Win, .270 WSM, .30-06 Sprg, .300 Win Mag, .300 WSM, .308 Win, .338 Federal, 6.5x5.5 Swedish Mauser, 7mm Rem Mag, 7mm WSM, 7mm-08 Rem
Magazine: detachable box
Features: stainless-steel barreled action; available in 4 action lengths; stainless inner parts
MSRP: $1545–1590

QUAD HUNTER

Action: bolt
Stock: hardwood
Barrel: 22 in.
Sights: none
Caliber: .17 HMR, .17 Mach 2, .22 LR, .22 WMR,
Magazine: box, 5 rounds
Features: Quad barrel system—four interchangeable barrels; stainless-steel barreled action; stainless inner parts; adjustable trigger
Quad Hunter
Two-Barrel Combo. $1209
(2 barrels; .22 LR & .22 WMR)
Quad Hunter
Four-Barrel Combo:. $2189
(4 barrels; .17 HMR, .17 Mach 2, .22 LR & .22 WMR)

VARMINT SS LAMINATED

Action: bolt
Stock: laminated
Barrel: 23.5 in.
Sights: none
Weight: 7.7 lbs.
Caliber:.204 Ruger, .222 Rem, .223 Rem, .223 Rem, .22-250 Rem, .243 Win. .260 Rem, .7mm-08 Rem, .308 Win, .338 Federal
Features: cold hammer-forged stainless steel, free-floating, heavy fluted barrel (available with short barrel threaded for muzzle brake or suppressor); short & extra short actions available; adjustable trigger; safety allows loading and unloading rifle with safety engaged; extended recoil lug; integral scope mount rail
Laminated SS Varmint:. $2069

Sauer Rifles

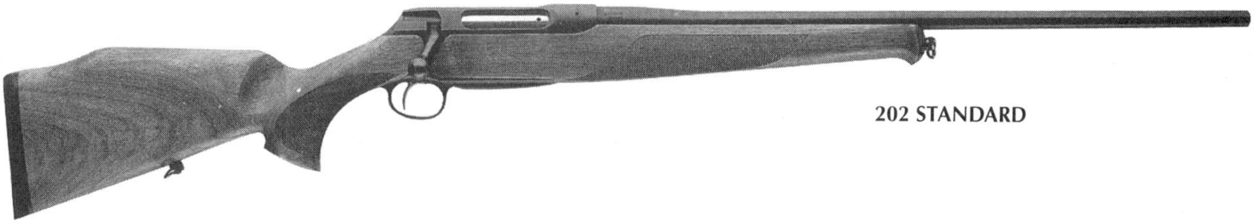

202 STANDARD

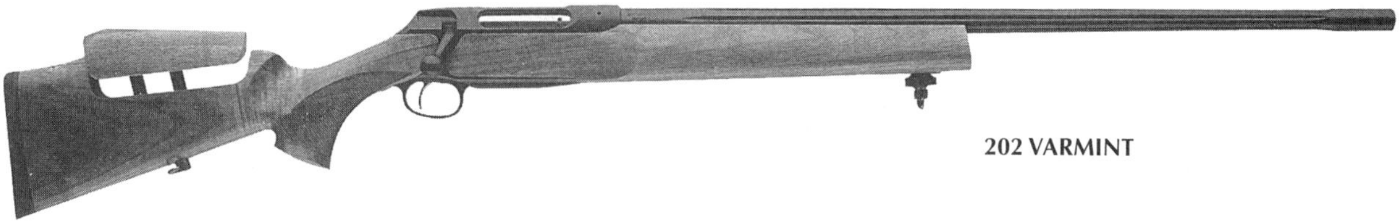

202 VARMINT

MODEL 202

Action: bolt
Stock: Claro walnut
Barrel: 24 in. ***Sights:*** none
Weight: 7.7 lbs.
Caliber: .243, .25-06, 6.5x55, .270, .308, .30-06
Magazine: detachable box, 5 rounds
Features: adjustable trigger; quick-change barrel; also Supreme Magnum with 26 in. barrel in 7mm Rem., .300 Win., .300 Wby., .375 H&H; Varmint and Tactical versions too
Model 202: $4250
Magnum: $4250
Synthetic: $2875
Varmint: $3400
Left-hand (.30-06, walnut): . . . $3700
SSG 3000 Tactical: $2900–5000

RIFLES

Savage Rifles

64 BTV

Action: semi-auto rimfire
Stock: synthetic thumbhole laminate
Barrel: 20.5 in.
Sights: Adjustable notched rear, bead post front
Weight: 5 lbs.
Caliber: .22 LR
Magazine: detachable 10 round
Features: side ejecting
MSRP: $359

CUB T PINK

Action: single shot bolt
Stock: pink thumbhole laminate
Barrel: 16.1 in.
Sights: post bead front, rear peep
Weight: 3.5 lbs.
Caliber: .22 S, L, LR
Magazine: single shot
Features: Accutrigger; recoil pad
MSRP: $288

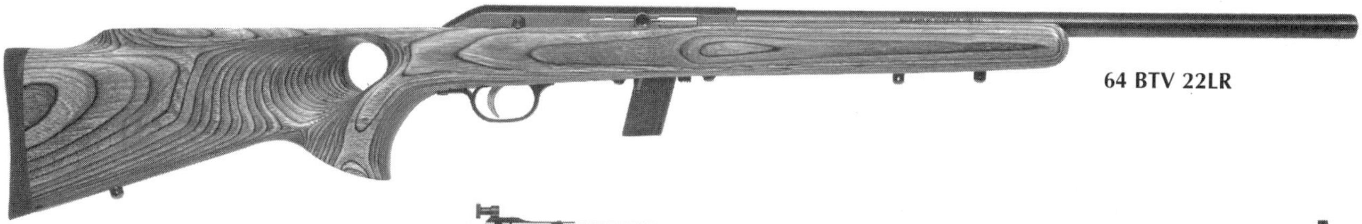

64 BTV 22LR

CUB T PINK

Savage Rifles

MODEL 25

Action: centerfire bolt
Stock: laminated
Barrel: 22 or 24 in. satin blue
Sights: none, Weaver-style scope bases installed
Weight: 8.35 lbs.
Caliber: .223 Rem., .204 Ruger
Magazine: 4-round detachable box
Features: available in Classic, Lightweight Varminter and Lightweight Varminter Thumbhole models; brown laminated or brown laminated thumbhole stocks
Lightweight Varminter: $667
Thumbhole: $712
Classic: $692

MODEL 11F

Action: bolt
Stock: synthetic
Barrel: 22.0 in.
Sights: none
Weight: 6.8 lbs.
Caliber: .223, .22-250, .243, 7mm-08, .308, .270 WSM, 7mm WSM, .300 WSM,
Magazine: box, 5 rounds
Features: open sights available; also 11G with walnut stock, 10 GY Youth with short stock in .223, .243 and .308
11F: $489.63
11G: $526.32

MODEL 11/111

Action: bolt
Stock: hardwood or synthetic
Barrel: 24.0 in.
Sights: none
Weight: 7.0 lbs.
Caliber: .270 WSM, 7mm WSM, .300 WSM, 7mm SUM, .300 SUM
Magazine: 3 rounds
Features: top tang safety; adjustable sights available
MSRP: $591

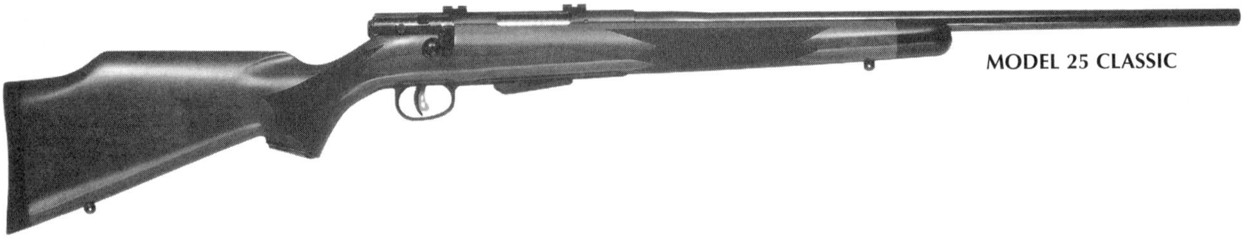

MODEL 25 CLASSIC

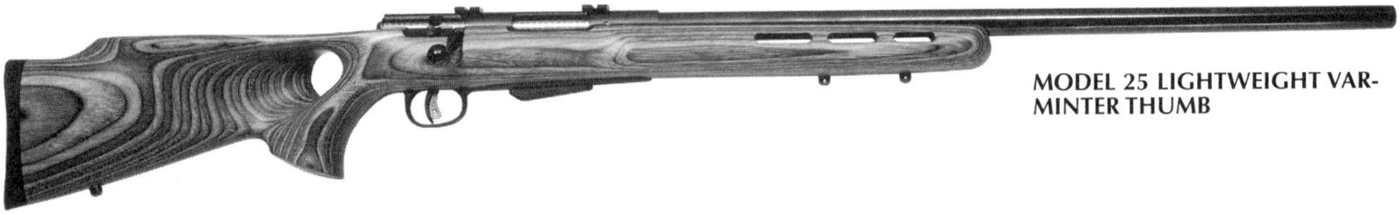

MODEL 25 LIGHTWEIGHT VARMINTER THUMB

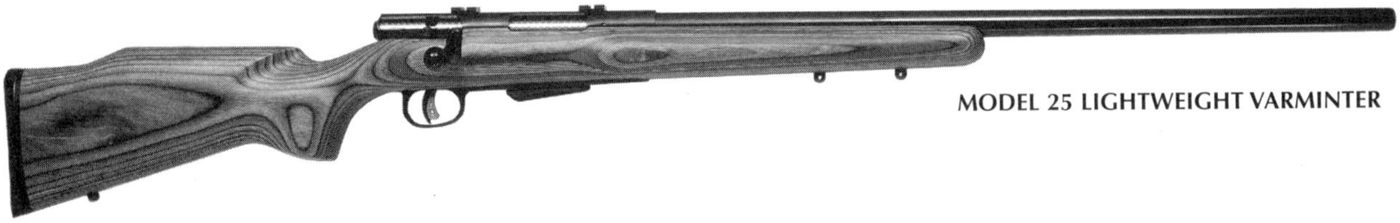

MODEL 25 LIGHTWEIGHT VARMINTER

MODEL 11G

MODEL 12FV

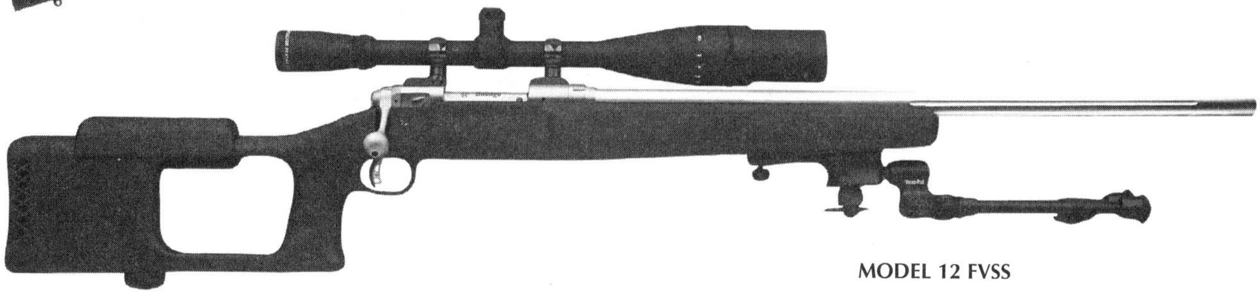

MODEL 12 FVSS

MODEL 114

MODEL 16FSS

MODEL 12, 112 10FP SERIES

Action: bolt
Stock: synthetic or laminated
Barrel: 20.0 in. or 26.0 in.
Sights: none
Weight: 8.3 lbs.
Caliber: .223, .22-250, .243, .25-06, 7mm Rem. Mag., .308, .30-06, .300 WSM, .300 Win. Mag.
Magazine: 3 or 4 rounds
Features: single-shot or box magazine; Savage AccuTrigger
MSRP: **$719**

MODEL 12FV (SHORT-ACTION)

Action: bolt
Stock: synthetic
Barrel: varmint, 26.0 in.
Sights: none
Weight: 9.0 lbs.
Caliber: .223, .22-250, .243, .308, .300 WSM, .204 Ruger
Magazine: box, 5 rounds
Features: also 12 VSS with fluted stainless barrel, Choate adjustable stock (11.3 lbs.) and V2 BVSS with stainless fluted barrel, laminated or synthetic stock (9.5 lbs.)
FV: **$676**
FVSS: **$840**
BVSS laminated: **$925**

MODEL 14/114

Action: bolt
Stock: checkered walnut
Barrel: 22.0 in. and 24.0 in.
Sights: none
Weight: 7.25 lbs.
Caliber: .223 to .300 Win. Mag.
Magazine: detachable box, 3-5 rounds
Features: AccuTrigger
MSRP: **$860–894**

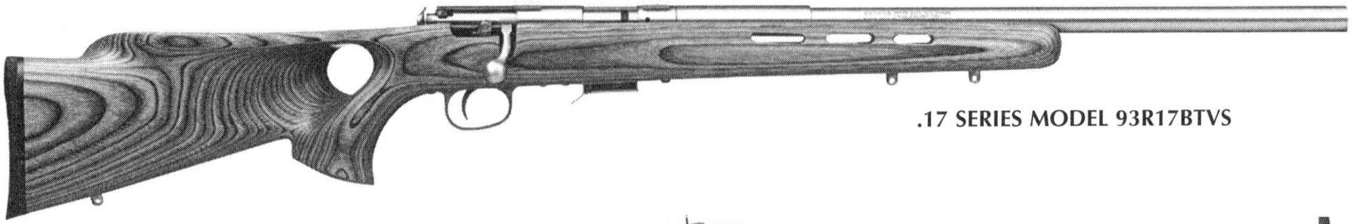

.17 SERIES MODEL 93R17BTVS

MODEL 30G

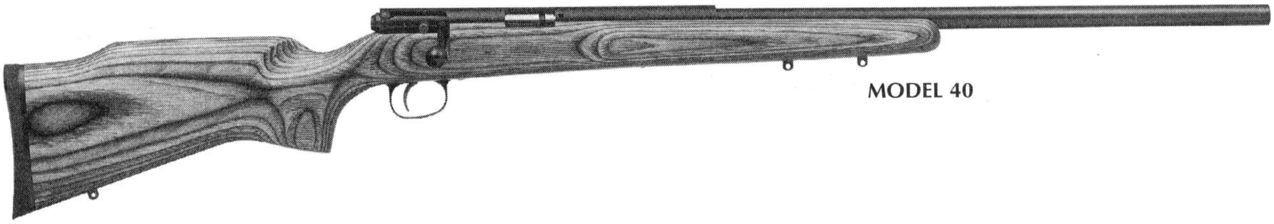

MODEL 40

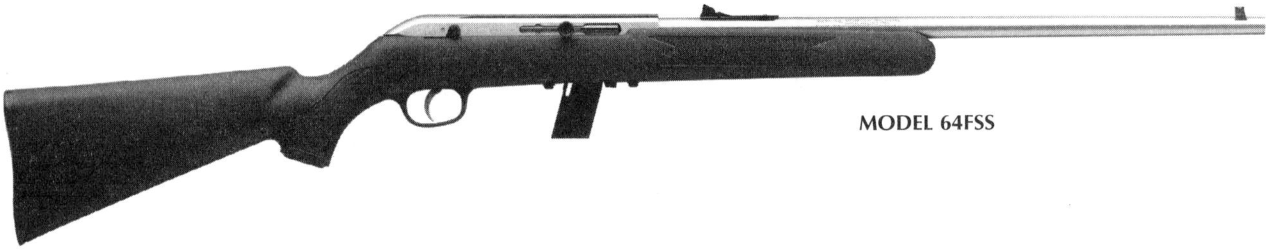

MODEL 64FSS

MODEL 16FSS (SHORT-ACTION)

Action: bolt
Stock: synthetic
Barrel: stainless, 22 or 24 in.
Sights: none
Weight: 6.0 lbs.
Caliber: .223, .243, .204 Ruger, 7mm WSM, .22-250 REM, 7mm-08, .308, .270 WSM, .300 WSM
Magazine: box, 3 or 4 rounds
Features: also 16BSS with checkered laminated stock in .300 WSM only
MSRP: $699

.17 SERIES MODEL 93R17BTVS

Action: bolt
Stock: laminated
Barrel: 21 in.
Sights: none
Weight: 6.0 lb.
Caliber: .17 HMR
Magazine: detachable box, 5 rounds
Features: AccuTrigger; stainless steel bolt-action; button-rifled heavy varmint barrel; swivel studs; brown laminated vented thumbhole stock
MSRP: $462

MODEL 30

Action: dropping block
Stock: walnut
Barrel: octagon, 21 in.
Sights: open
Weight: 4.3 lbs.
Caliber: .22 LR, .22 WMR, .17 HMR
Magazine: none
Features: re-creation of Steven's Favorite
30G: $358
Take-down .22: $374

MODEL 93

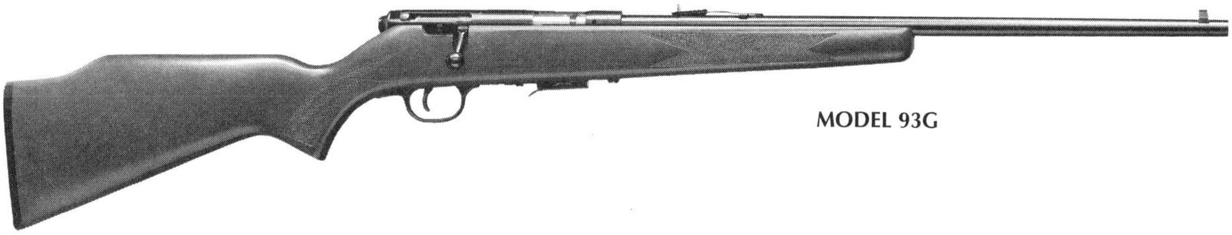

MODEL 93G

MODEL 64F

Action: autoloading
Stock: synthetic
Barrel: 21 in.
Sights: open
Weight: 5.5 lbs.
Caliber: .22 LR
Magazine: detachable box, 10 rounds
Features: also 64 FSS stainless, 64FV and FVSS heavy barrel, 64G hardwood stock
64F: $156
64G: $193

MODEL 93

Action: bolt
Stock: synthetic, hardwood or laminated
Barrel: 21 in.
Sights: none
Weight: 5.0 lbs.
Caliber: .17 HMR ***Magazine:*** 5 rounds
Features: scope bases included; eight versions with stainless or C-M steel, different stocks; varmint models weigh 6.0 lbs.
Synthetic F: $248
Laminated stainless FVSS: $359

MODEL 93G

Action: bolt
Stock: synthetic
Barrel: 21 in.
Sights: open ***Weight:*** 5.8 lbs.
Caliber: .22 WMR, .17 HMR
Magazine: detachable box, 5 rounds
Features: 93G with hardwood stock; 93 FSS stainless; 93FVSS with heavy barrel; 93G with hardwood stock
MSRP: $268

MODEL 116FSS (LONG-ACTION)

Action: bolt
Stock: synthetic
Barrel: stainless 22, 24 or 26 in.
Sights: none ***Weight:*** 6.5 lbs.
Caliber: .270, .30-06 (22 in.), 7mm Rem. Mag., .300 Win. Mag., .338 Win. Mag., .300 RUM (26 in.)
Magazine: box, 3 or 4 rounds
Features: also 116BSS with checkered laminated stock
MSRP: $699

MARK I

Action: bolt
Stock: hardwood
Barrel: 19 in. or 21 in.
Sights: open
Weight: 5.5 lbs.
Caliber: .22 S, .22 L, .22 LR
Magazine: none
Features: also MkIG Youth (19 in. barrel), MkILY Youth laminated stock, MIY Youth camo stock
Mark I FVT (with peep sights):. $406
Mark I G: $233
G Youth: $233

Savage Rifles

MARK II FSS

MARK II FV HEAVY-BARREL

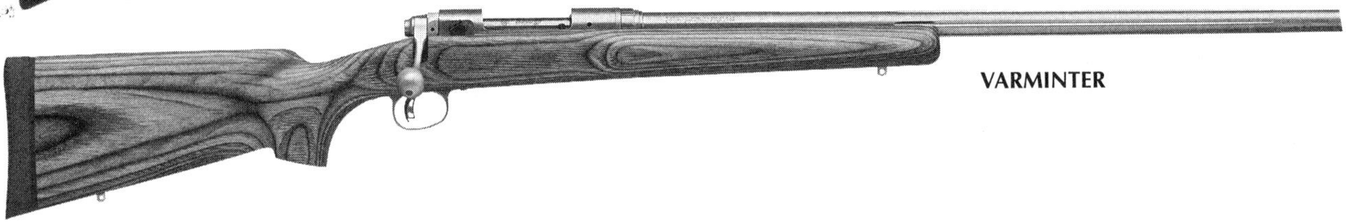

VARMINTER

MARK II F

Action: bolt
Stock: synthetic
Barrel: 21 in.
Sights: open
Weight: 5.0 lbs.
Caliber: .22 LR
Magazine: detachable box, 5 rounds
Features: also MkIIG with hardwood stock, MkIIFSS stainless, MkIIGY with short stock and 19 in. barrel

F: **$207–268**
G: **$233**
FSS: **$281**
GY: **$233**
Camo: **$253**

MARK II FV HEAVY-BARREL

Action: bolt
Stock: synthetic
Barrel: heavy 21 in.
Sights: none
Weight: 6.0 lbs.
Caliber: .22 LR
Magazine: detachable box, 5 or 10 rounds
Features: Weaver scope bases included; also MkII LV with laminated stock (6.5 lbs.)

FV: **$280–299**
BV: **$352**

VARMINTER

Action: bolt
Stock: laminated
Barrel: heavy fluted stainless, button-rifled
Sights: none (drilled and tapped for scope mounts)
Weight: 9.0 lbs.
Caliber: .223 and .22-250, .204 Ruger
Magazine: 4-round box or single-shot
Features: fully adjustable AccuTrigger

MSRP: **$838.95**

SAVAGE 10XP PREDATOR HUNTER IN SNOW

Action: two-lug bolt
Stock: composite in Snow camo
Barrel: 22″
Sights: none
Weight: 7 ¼ lbs.
Caliber: .204 Ruger, .223 Rem., .22-250 Rem., .243 Win.
Magazine: detachable box
Features: AccuTrigger, also available as a "package" rifle with scope.

MSRP: **$864**

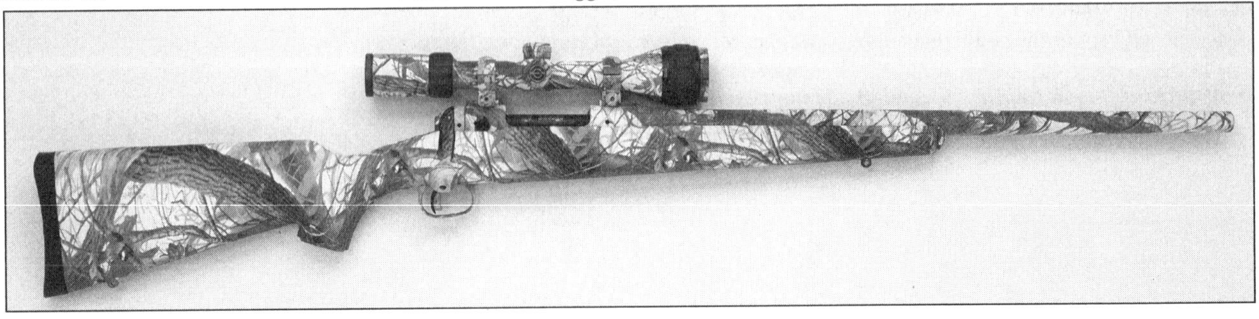

Sig Sauer Rifles

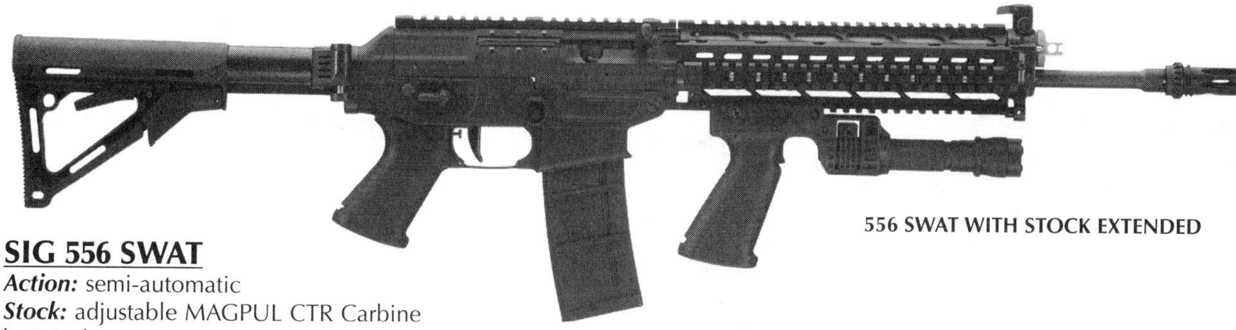
556 SWAT WITH STOCK EXTENDED

SIG 556 SWAT

Action: semi-automatic
Stock: adjustable MAGPUL CTR Carbine buttstock
Barrel: 16 in.
Sights: flip up combat front and rear
Weight: 8.7 lbs.
Caliber: 5.56mm NATO
Magazine: 30 rounds
Features: alloy Quad Rail forearm; Nitron X durable, corrosion resistant finish; two position adjustable gas piston operating rod system; flash suppressor
MSRP: $2000

Smith & Wesson Rifles

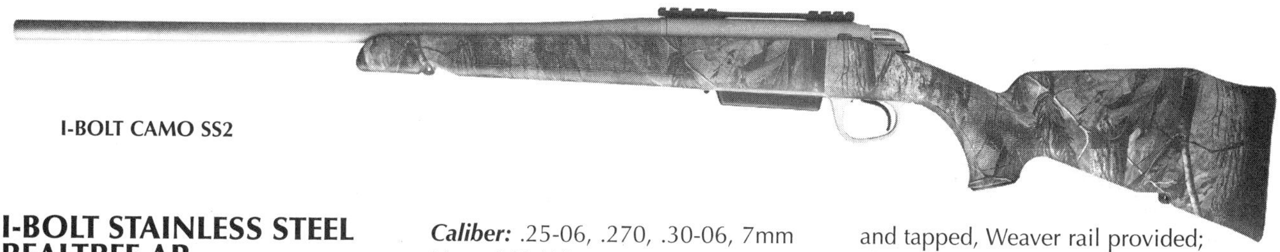
I-BOLT CAMO SS2

I-BOLT STAINLESS STEEL REALTREE AP

Action: bolt
Stock: composite
Barrel: 23, 25-in.
Sights: none
Weight: 6.8 lbs.
Caliber: .25-06, .270, .30-06, 7mm Mag, .300 Win.
Magazine: 3+1 or 4+1
Features: free-floated Thompson/Center stainless steel, match grade barrel; adjustable trigger; three-position, semi-lineal safety; receiver drilled and tapped, Weaver rail provided; checkered Monte Carlo stock in RealTree AP; flush sling swivel mounts
MSRP: $637

M&P15

M&P15 & M&P15A

Action: autoloader
Stock: synthetic
Barrel: 16 in.
Sights: adjustable
Weight: 6.74 lbs.
Caliber: 5.56/.223 NATO
Magazine: detachable box, 30 rounds
Features: gas-operated semi automatic; 4140 steel barrel; black anodized finish; adjustable post front sight; adjustable dual aperture rear sight; 6-position telescopic black synthetic stock—rifle measures 35 in. long when fully extended and 32 in. with the stock collapsed; M&P15A available with folding rear combat sight in place of the flat-top handle
M&P15: $1730
M&P15A: $1704

Smith & Wesson Rifles

M&P15A

M&P15T

SMITH & WESSON M&P 15-22

M&P15T

Action: autoloader
Stock: synthetic
Barrel: 16 in.
Sights: adjustable post front sight; adjustable dual aperture rear sight
Weight: 6.85 lbs.
Caliber: 5.56 mm NATO / .223
Magazine: detachable box, 30 rounds (5.56 mm or .223)
Features: gas-operated semi automatic; free floating chrome-lined 4140 steel barrel; black anodized finish; folding front and rear combat sights with four-sided Picatinny fore-end; 6-position telescopic hard coat black anodized synthetic stock—rifle measures 35 in. long when fully extended and 32 in. with stock collapsed; front rail system with Smith & Wesson handrails
MSRP: $1600

SMITH & WESSON M&P 15-22

Action: autoloading, recoil activated
Stock: polymer, collapsible 6-position
Barrel: 16″
Sights: AR-style adjustable
Weight: 6 lbs.
Caliber: .22 LR
Magazine: 25 round detachable box
Features: Upper and lower of high-strength polymer, front quad rail, accessories interchangeable with standard AR-15 5.56mm rifles.
MSRP: $568

Springfield Rifles

M1A STANDARD

M1A

Action: autoloading
Stock: walnut
Barrel: 22 in.
Sights: target
Weight: 9.2 lbs.
Caliber: .308
Magazine: detachable box, 5 or 10 rounds
Features: also with fiberglass stock and M1A/Scout with 18 in. barrel and scope mount (9.0 lbs.)
M1A: $1448

Steyr Rifles

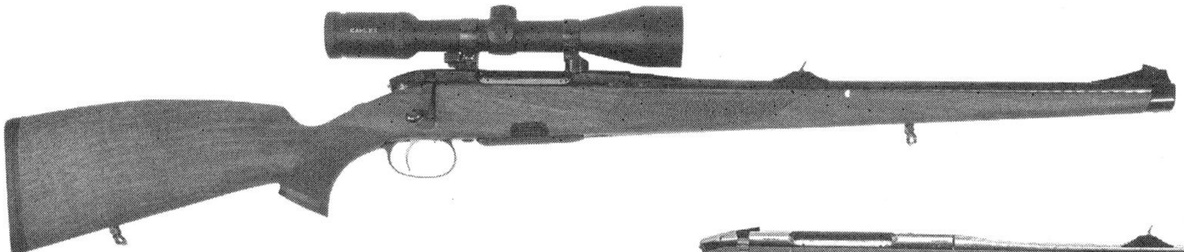

MANNLICHER CLASSIC

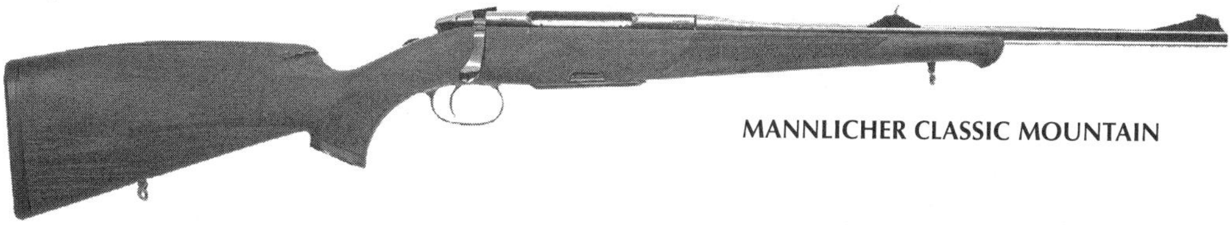

MANNLICHER CLASSIC MOUNTAIN

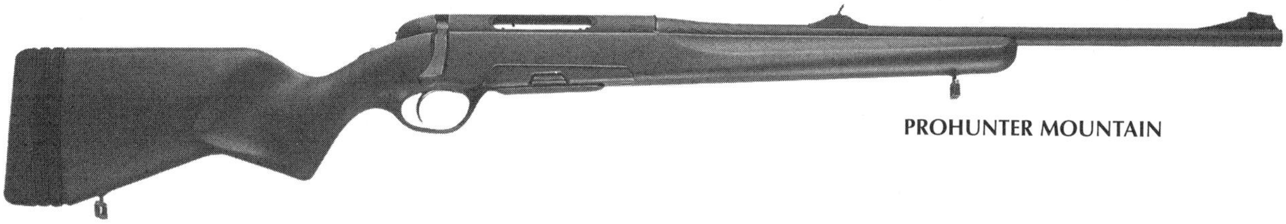

PROHUNTER MOUNTAIN

MANNLICHER CLASSIC

Action: bolt
Stock: European walnut
Barrel: 20 in., 23.6 in. and 25.6 in.
Sights: open
Weight: 7.4 lbs., 7.7 lbs. (magnum)
Caliber: .222, .223, .243, 6.5x55 SE, 6.5x57, 25-06, .270, 7x64, 7mm-08, 308, 30-06, 8x57 JS, 9, 3x62, 7 mm Rem. Mag., .300 Win. Mag., 7 mm WSM, .270 WSM, .300 WSM
Magazine: box, 4 rounds
Features: three-position roller tang safety with front locking lugs and ice/residue groove; full stock or half stock models; total length 41.7 in.; set or direct trigger; sights as optional extras on half-stock models
Half-stock: $3799
Mountain: $3269
Classic: $4199

PROHUNTER

Action: bolt
Stock: synthetic
Barrel: 20 in. (Mtn.), 23.6 in. and 25.6 in.
Sights: open
Weight: 7.8 lbs. (std.), 8.2 lbs. (mag.), 7.4 lbs. (Mtn.)
Caliber: .222, .223, .243, 6.5x55 SE, 6.5x57, .25-06, .270, 7x64, 7mm-08, .308, .30-06, 8x57 JS, 9.3x62, 7mm Rem. Mag., .300 Win. Mag., 7mm WSM, .270 WSM, .300 WSM
Magazine: detachable box, 5 rounds
Features: high-strength aluminum receiver; SBS safety system; three position roller tang safety; set or direct trigger; charcoal-gray, charcoal-black or Realtree Hardwoods HD stocks; heavy barrel available in .308 or .300 Win. Mag.
ProHunter: $1150
ProHunter Stainless: $1250
ProHunter Mountain: $1150
ProHunter Mountain Stainless: $1250

Steyr Rifles

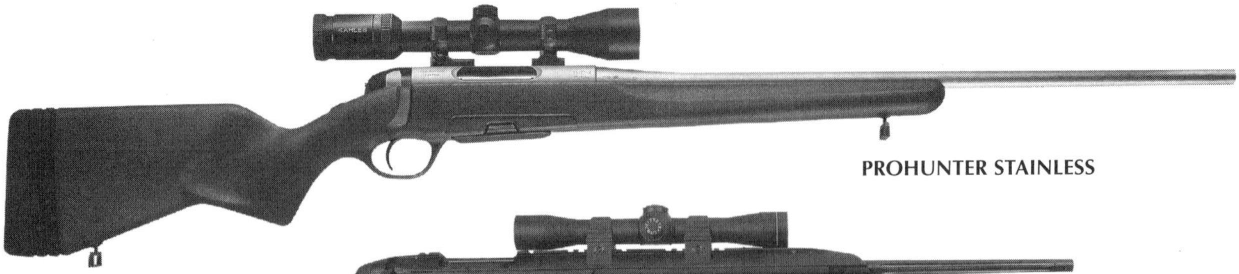

PROHUNTER STAINLESS

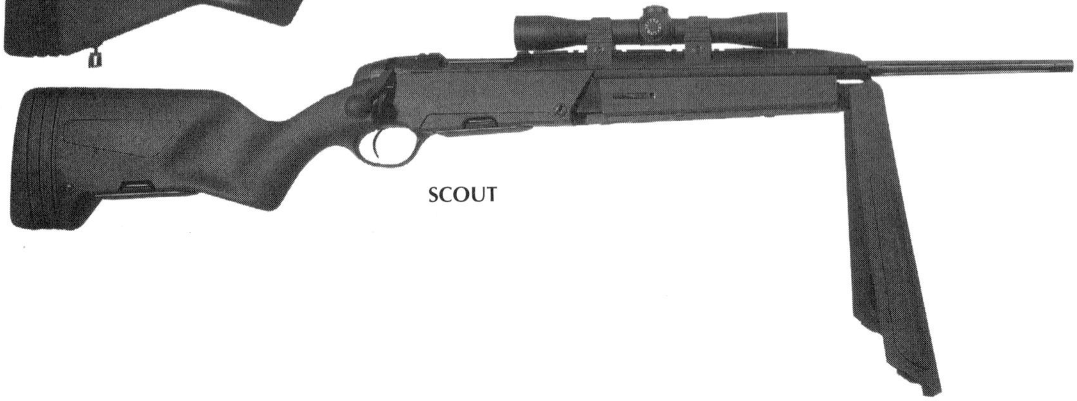

SCOUT

ULTRA LIGHT

SCOUT

Action: bolt
Stock: synthetic
Barrel: 19 in.
Sights: open ***Weight:*** 7.0 lbs.
Caliber: .223, .243, 7mm-08, .308, .376 Steyr
Magazine: detachable box, 5 rounds
Features: high-strength aluminum receiver; SBS (Safe Bolt System) safety; system; three position roller tang safety full, set or direct trigger; Weaver-type rail; spare magazine in the butt stock; integral folding bipod; matte black finish; total length 38.5 in.
Scout: $2099–2199

ULTRA LIGHT

Action: bolt
Stock: European walnut
Barrel: 19 in.
Sights: none
Weight: 5.9 lbs.
Caliber: .222, .223, .243 Win., 7mm-08 Rem., .308
Magazine: detachable box, 4 rounds
Features: high-strength aluminum receiver; bolt lugs lock into steel safety bushing; SBS (Safe Bolt System) safety system; three position roller tang safety with front locking lugs and ice/residue groove; set trigger or direct trigger; integral Weaver-type scope mounting rail; total length 38.5 in.
MSRP: 2799

Szecsei & Fuchs Rifles

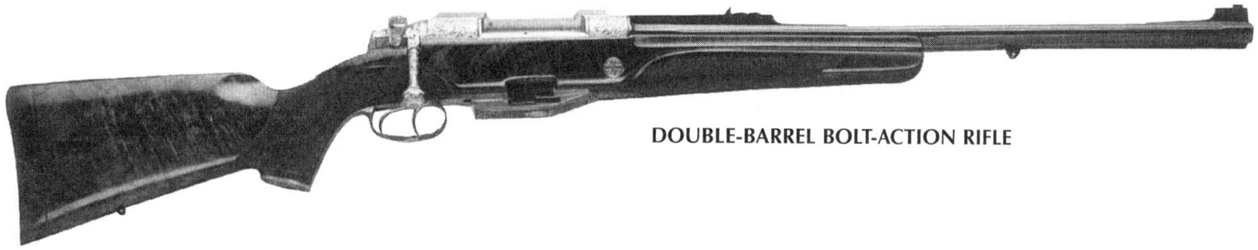

DOUBLE-BARREL BOLT-ACTION RIFLE

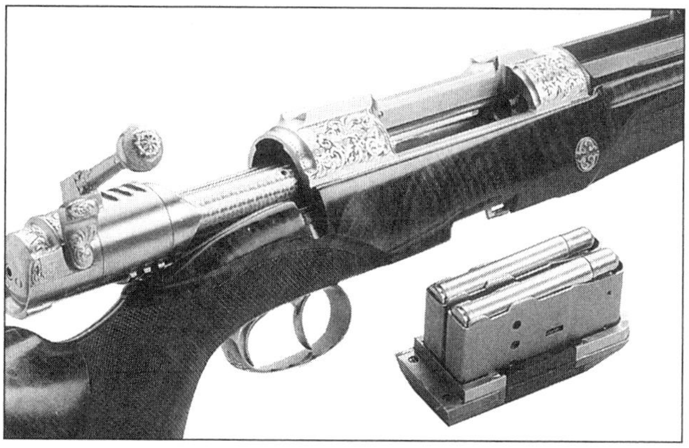

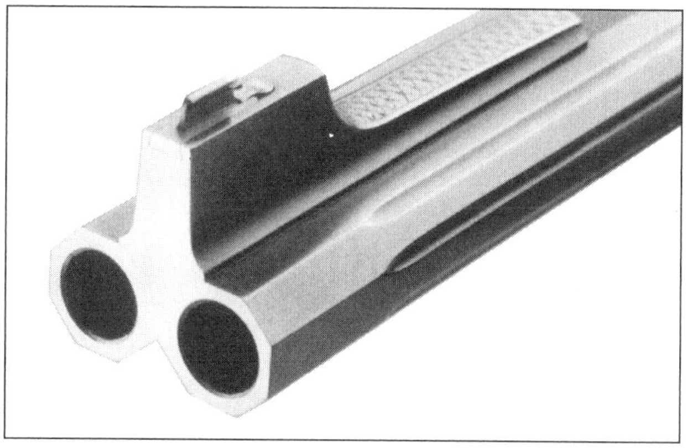

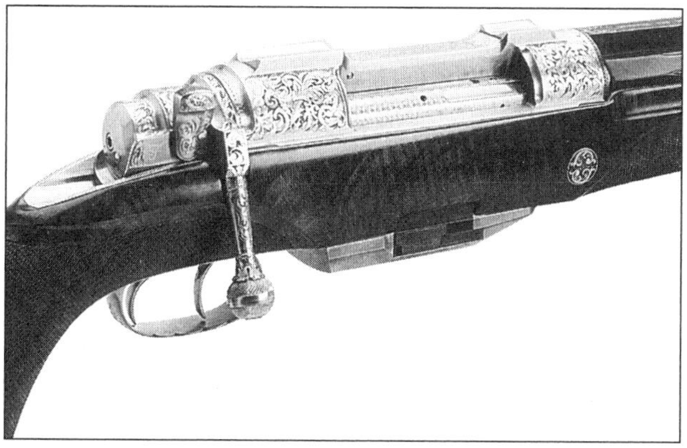

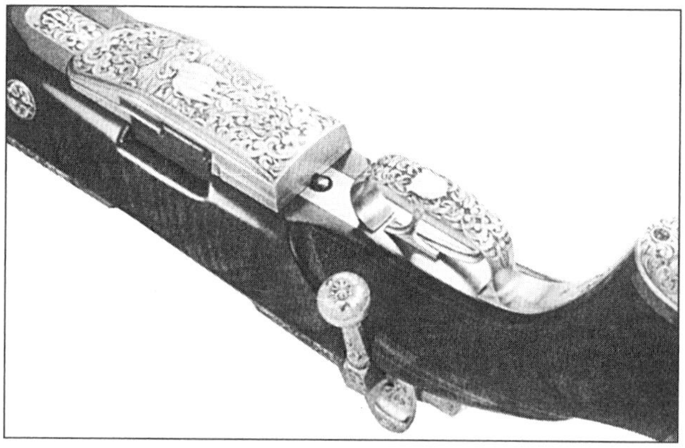

The Szecsei & Fuchs double-barrel bolt-action rifle may be the only one of its kind. Built with great care and much handwork from the finest materials, it follows a design remarkable for its cleverness. While the rifle is not light-weight, it can be aimed quickly and offers more large-caliber firepower than any competitor. The six-shot magazine feeds two rounds simultaneously, both of which can then be fired by two quick pulls of the trigger.

Chamberings: .300 Win, 9.3 x 64, .358 Norma, .375 H&H, .404 Jeff, .416 Rem., .458 Win., .416 Rigby, .450 Rigby, .460 Short A-Square, .470 Capstick, .495 A-Square, .500 Jeffery

Weight: 14 lbs. with round barrels, 16 with octagon barrels.

Price:. $499

To help steady a rifle, raise your shooting elbow so it is parallel to the ground or at a 90-degree angle to your body. This pinches the rifle between your shoulder and cheek, providing a rigid shooting platform.

Tactical Rifles

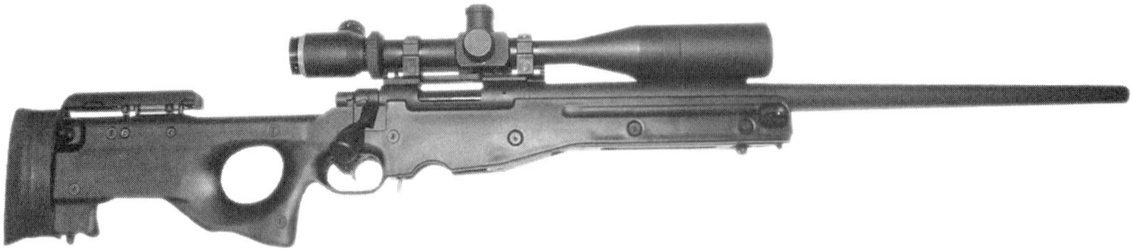

TACTICAL L.R.

Action: bolt, M700 Remington
Stock: thumbhole aluminum, with resin panels, optional adjustable cheekpiece
Barrel: heavy, match-grade, 26 in.
Sights: none (drilled and tapped for scope, supplied with Picatinny rail)
Weight: 13.4 lbs.
Caliber: 7.62 NATO (Magnum version available, in .300 WSM)
Magazine: detachable box, 5 rounds (10-round boxes available)
Features: adjustable trigger; soft rubber recoil pad, swivel studs; options include stainless fluted barrel
MSRP: $2450

RIFLES

Taylor's Rifles

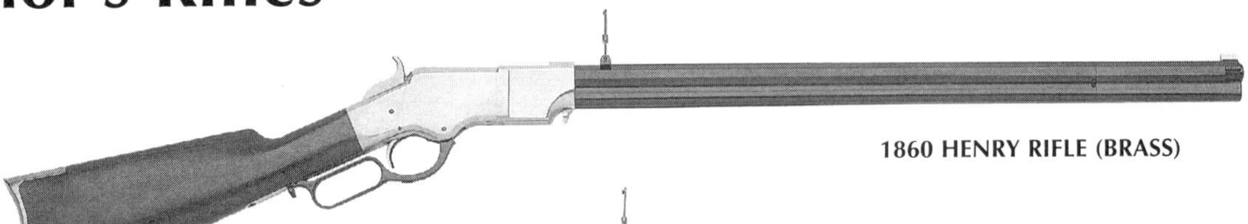

1860 HENRY RIFLE (BRASS)

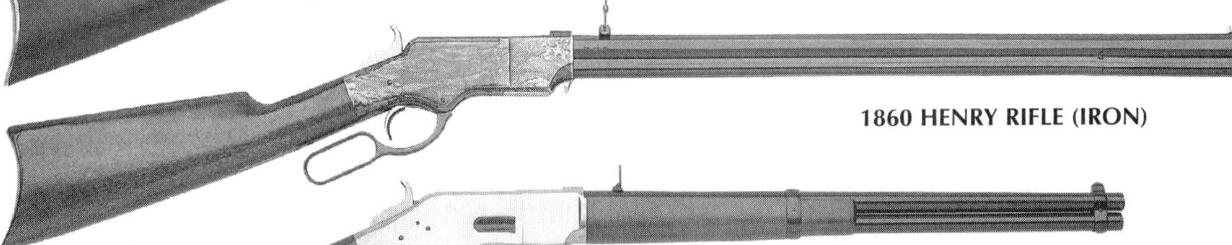

1860 HENRY RIFLE (IRON)

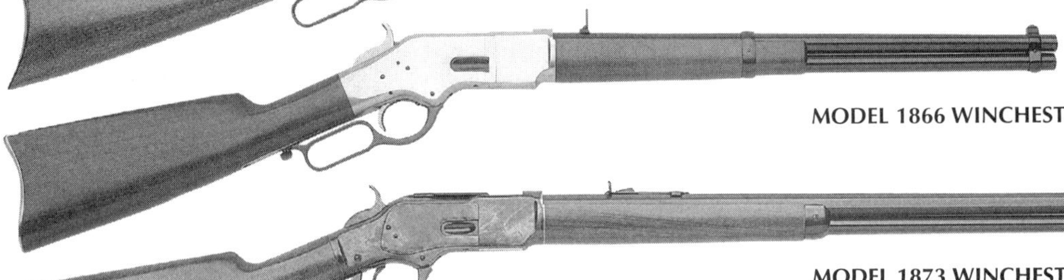

MODEL 1866 WINCHESTER

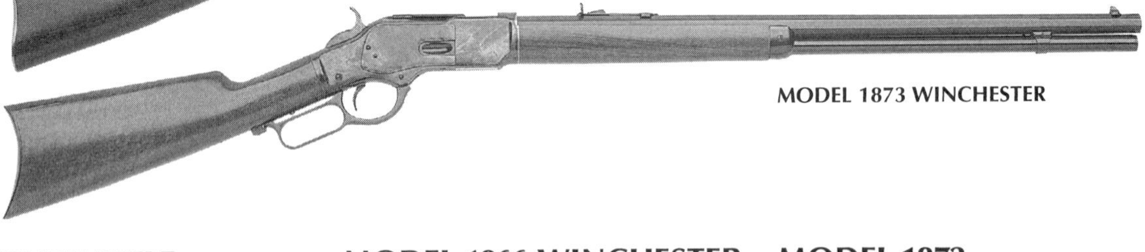

MODEL 1873 WINCHESTER

1860 HENRY RIFLE

Action: lever
Stock: walnut
Barrel: 24 in.
Sights: open
Weight: 7.5 lbs.
Caliber: .44-40, .45 Long Colt
Magazine: under-barrel tube, 13 rounds
Features: brass frame; also original-type steel-frame in .44-40 only
MSRP: $1290–1525

MODEL 1866 WINCHESTER

Action: lever
Stock: walnut
Barrel: 20 in.
Sights: open
Weight: 6.5 lbs.
Caliber: .38 Spl., .45 Long Colt
Magazine: under-barrel tube, 9 rounds
Features: brass frame, octagon barrel
1866: $925–1045

MODEL 1873 WINCHESTER RIFLE

Action: lever
Stock: walnut
Barrel: 24 in.
Sights: open
Weight: 7.5 lbs.
Caliber: .44-40, .45 Long Colt
Magazine: under-barrel tube, 13 rounds
Features: optional front globe and rear tang sights
1873: $1150–1351

Thompson/Center Rifles

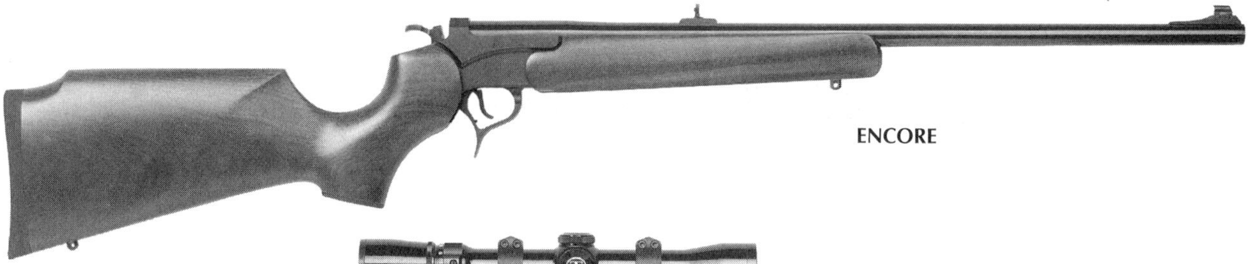

ENCORE

G2 CONTENDER

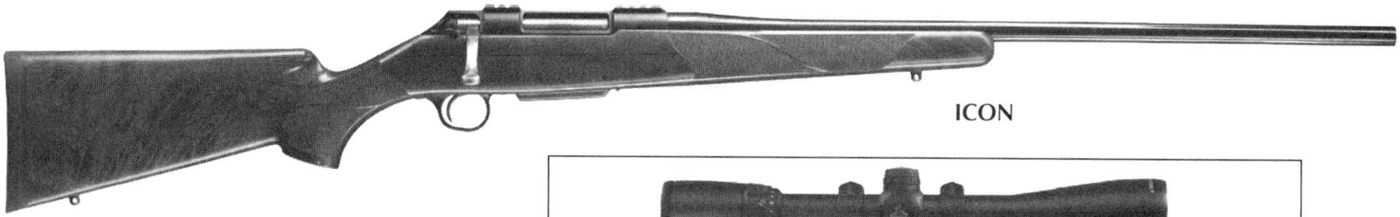

ICON

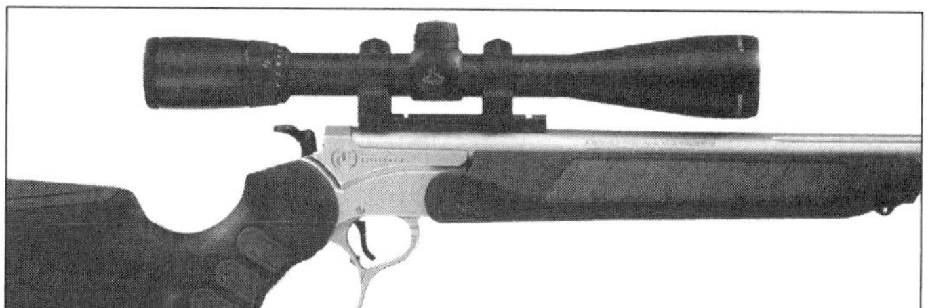

PRO HUNTER RIFLE

ENCORE
Action: hinged breech
Stock: walnut
Barrel: 24 and 26 in.
Sights: open
Weight: 6.8 lbs.
Caliber: most popular calibers, from .22 Hornet to .300 Win. Mag. and .45-70
Magazine: none
Features: also synthetic and stainless versions; Hunter package with .308 or .300 includes 3-9x40 T/C scope and hard case
Synthetic: **$798**
Walnut: **$700**
Stainless: **$734**

G2 CONTENDER
Action: hinged breech
Stock: walnut
Barrel: 23 in.
Sights: none
Weight: 5.4 lbs.
Caliber: .17 HMR, .17 MACH 2, .22 LR, .223, 6.8 Rem., .30-30, .204 Ruger, .45/70, .375 JDJ
Magazine: none
Features: recocks without opening rifle
G2 Rifle: **$727**

ICON
Action: bolt
Stock: high-grade walnut
Barrel: 23.5 in.
Sights: none
Weight: 7.25 to 7.75 lbs.
Caliber: .243, .308, .22-250, .30 TC
Magazine: 3-round removable box
Features: receiver machined from solid steel; button rifled match grade barrel; 3-lug bolt with T-slot extractor; Interlock Bedding Block System; cocking indicator integrated into the bolst sleeve; fully adjustable trigger; two-position safety
MSRP: **$942–1038**

PRO HUNTER RIFLE
Action: hinged breech
Stock: synthetic
Barrel: 28 in.
Sights: none
Caliber: .204 Ruger, .22-250 Rem, .223 Rem, .243 Win, .25-06, .270 Win, .30-06, .300 Win, .308 Win, .338 Win, .7mm Mag, 7mm-08
Magazine: none
Features: stainless steel fluted barrel; machined target crown and chamber; Swing Hammer rotating hammer; all-steel one-piece extractor; FlexTech stock system
Pro Hunter: **$804–867**

Thompson/Center Rifles

T/C R55

THOMPSON/CENTER TRIUMPH BONE COLLECTOR MUZZLELOADER

RIFLES

T/C R55

Action: blowback autoloader
Stock: synthetic/stainless or lam./ blued
Barrel: 20.0 in.
Sights: adjustable, with fiber optic inserts
Weight: 5.5 lbs.
Caliber: .17 Mach 2
Magazine: detachable box, 5-rounds
Features: available in blued or stainless steel
Laminated/blued:. $467–546
Synthetic/stainless: $604

THOMPSON/CENTER TRIUMPH BONE COLLECTOR MUZZLELOADER

Action: muzzleloading with Toggle Lock breech
Stock: composite camo and black
Barrel: 28″ fluted, Weather Shield finish
Sights: open, fiber-optic
Weight: 8 lbs.
Caliber: .50 caliber
Magazine: none
Features: short Flex Tech stock. Reversible hammer extension, QLA muzzle system, Toggle Lock Action, Power Rod for easy field loading.
Price: $550-$650

Tikka Rifles

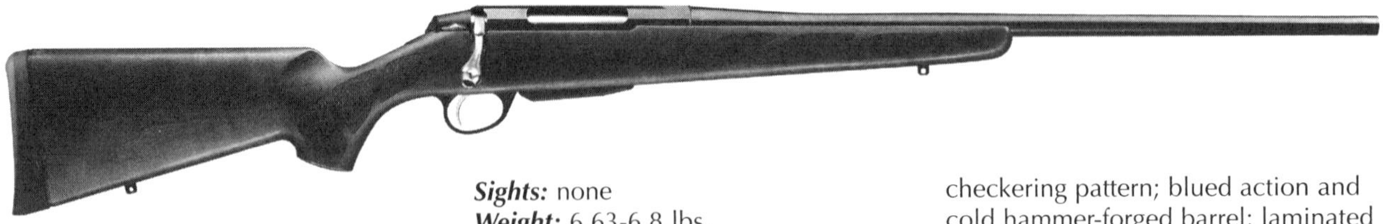

T3 HUNTER

Action: bolt
Stock: walnut, (T3 Lite, synthetic)
Barrel: 22.44, 24.38 in.
Sights: none
Weight: 6.63-6.8 lbs.
Caliber: .22-250 Rem, .223 Rem, .243 Win, .25-06 Rem, .270 Win, .270 WSM, .30-06, .308 Win, 6.5 x 55
Magazine: detachable box, 3 rounds
Features: walnut stock with distinctive checkering pattern; blued action and cold hammer-forged barrel; laminated stock with stainless action and barrel, 2- to 4-lb. adjustable trigger; integral scope rail, required rings are supplied with each gun
MSRP: $577

Tikka Rifles

T3 LITE

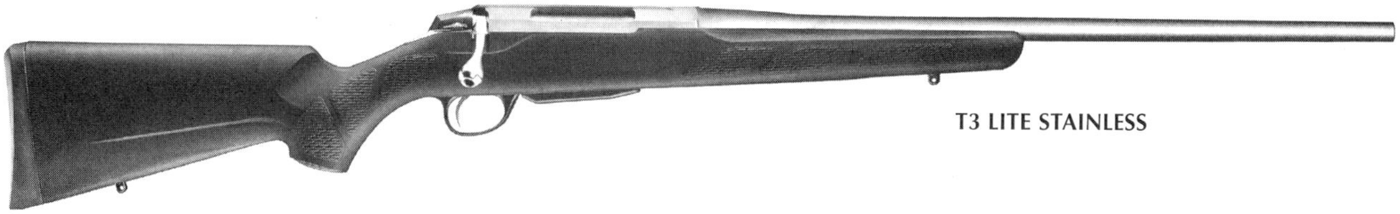

T3 LITE STAINLESS

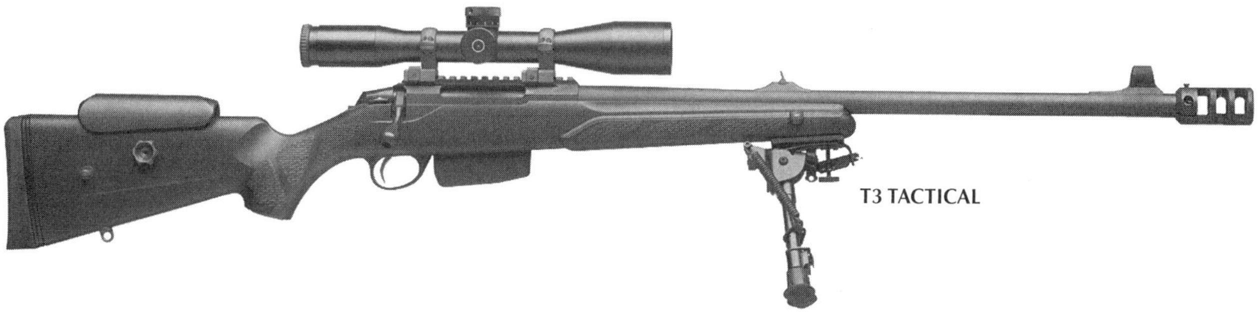

T3 TACTICAL

T3 VARMINT

T3 LITE

Action: bolt
Stock: synthetic
Barrel: 23.0, 24.0 in.
Sights: none
Weight: 6.19-6.38 lbs.
Caliber: 22-250 Rem, .223 Rem, .243 Win, .25-06 Rem, .270 Win, .270 WSM, .30-06 Sprg, .300 Win Mag, .300 WSM, .308 Win, .338 Win Mag, 7mm Rem Mag, 7mm-08 Rem
Magazine: 3 or 4 rounds
Features: blue or stainless; 3-shot 1 in. group at 100 yds. in factory testing
T3 Lite:.................... $477
Stainless:.................. $505

T3 TACTICAL

Action: two-lug bolt
Stock: synthetic
Barrel: 20 in.
Sights: none
Weight: 7.25 to 7.75 lbs.
Caliber: .223, .308
Magazine: detachable box, 5 rounds
Features: free-floating, hammer-forged barrel, fully adjustable trigger; Picatinny rail; black phosphate finish, a synthetic varmint-style stock with adjustable cheek piece
Tactical:.................. $1482

T3 VARMINT

Action: bolt
Stock: synthetic
Barrel: 23.27 in.
Sights: none
Weight: 6.63 lbs.
Caliber: .22-250 Rem, .223 Rem, .308 Win
Magazine: detachable box, 5 rounds
Features: heavy contour, free-floating, varmint type barrel, fully adjustable trigger; blued finish; drilled and tapped for scope mounts
T3 Varmint: $804

Traditions Rifles

TRADITIONS VORTEK MUZZLELOADER

Action: hinged-breech muzzleloader
Stock: synthetic black or Soft Touch camo (thumbhole option)
Barrel: 28″ blued or stainless
Sights: Williams fiber-optic
Weight: 12 ½ lbs.
Caliber: .50
Magazine: none
Features: aluminum ramrod, Accelerator Breech Plug, quick-release drop-out trigger, 209 shotgun primer ignition, over-molded stock and forend, recoil pad
MSRP: . . . . $449–$499
Thumbhole: . . . . $419–$519

TRADITIONS OUTFITTER

Action: hinged-breech centerfire
Stock: synthetic black or Soft Touch camo (thumbhole option)
Barrel: 24″ blued fluted Wilson
Sights: Williams fiber optic
Weight: 7 ¼ lbs.
Caliber: .243, .270, .308, .30-06, .444
Magazine: none
Features: This model uses a true drop-in design that requires no factory fitting for replacement barrels and can be quickly converted from centerfire rifle to muzzleloader to shotgun. Rifle barrel drilled and tapped for scope mounting.
MSRP: $543
Thumbhole: $565

VORTEK MUZZLELOADER

OUTFITTER

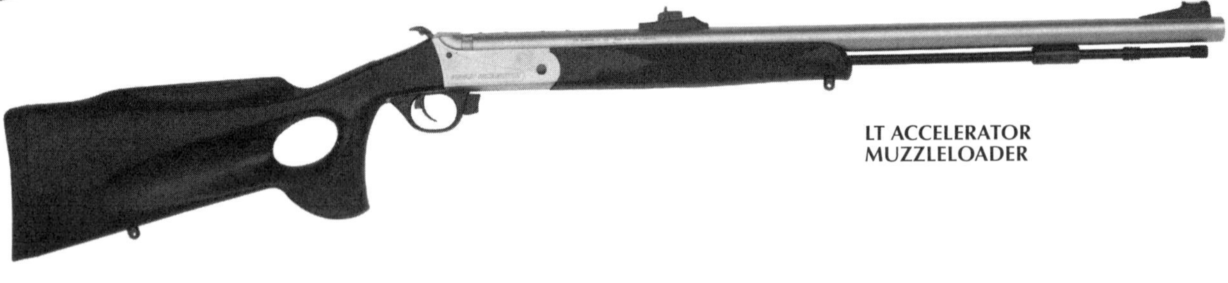

LT ACCELERATOR MUZZLELOADER

TRADITIONS LT ACCELERATOR MUZZLELOADER

Action: hinged-breech muzzleloader
Stock: synthetic black or Soft Touch camo (thumbhole option)
Barrel: 26″ blued or nickel
Sights: TruGlo fiber-optic
Weight: 6 ¾ lbs.
Caliber: .50
Magazine: none
Features: aluminum ramrod, accelerator breech plug, light-weight, 1:28 twist rifling, 209 shotgun primer ignition, Fast Action release button, drilled and tapped for scope
MSRP: $229–399
Thumbhole: $329–390

Uberti Rifles

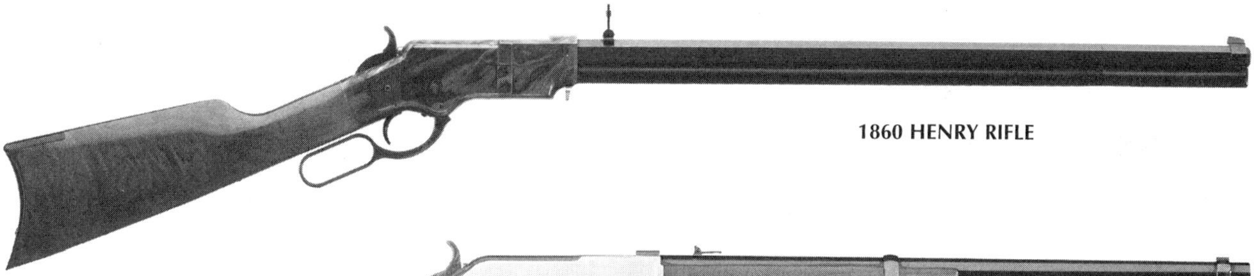

1860 HENRY RIFLE

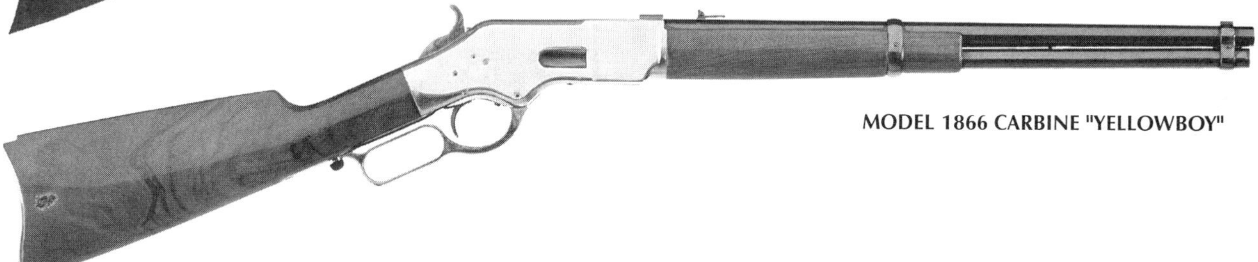

MODEL 1866 CARBINE "YELLOWBOY"

MODEL 1873 SPORTING RIFLE

1874 CALVARY CARBINE
SHARPS

1860 HENRY RIFLE

Action: lever
Stock: walnut
Barrel: 18.5 in. and 24.25 in.
Sights: adjustable
Weight: 9 lbs
Caliber: .44-40, .45 Colt
Magazine: tube, 10 or 13 rounds
Features: octagon barrel; brass or steel frame; lever lock; front loading, under-barrel tube magazine; A-grade straight walnut stock
MSRP: $1329

MODEL 1866 WINCHESTER "YELLOWBOY"

Action: lever
Stock: walnut
Barrel: 19 (Carbine), 20, or 24.25 in.
Sights: adjustable
Weight: 7.4 lbs.
Caliber: .38 Spl., .44-40, .45 Colt
Magazine: tube, 10 or 13 rounds
Features: brass frame; under-barrel tube magazine with loading gate on frame; lever lock; A-grade straight walnut stock
1866 Yellowboy Carbine: $1079
1866 Yellowboy Rifle: $1129

MODEL 1873 WINCHESTER RIFLE

Action: lever
Stock: walnut
Barrel: 19 (Carbine), 20 or 24.25 in.,
Sights: adjustable
Weight: 7.5 lbs.
Caliber: .357 Mag., .44-40, .45 Colt
Magazine: tube, 10 or 13 rounds
Features: Rifle & Special Sporting Rifle with 20 or 24-in. octagonal barrel and color case-hardened frame; Carbine with 19-in. round barrel and blued frame; under-barrel tube magazine with loading gate; lever lock; straight or pistol grip A-grade walnut stock
Carbine: $1199
Rifle: $1249
Special Sporting Rifle: $1379

1874 CALVARY CARBINE SHARPS

Action: falling block
Stock: walnut
Barrel: 22 in.
Weight: 8 lbs.
Caliber: .45-70
Magazine: 1 round
Features: round barrel; color-case-hardened receiver; A-grade walnut stock
MSRP: $1569

Uberti Rifles

1874 SHARPS

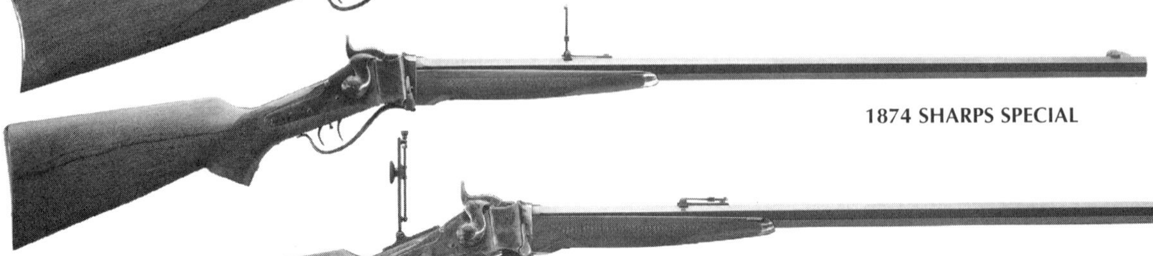

1874 SHARPS SPECIAL

1874 BUFFALO HUNTER SHARPS

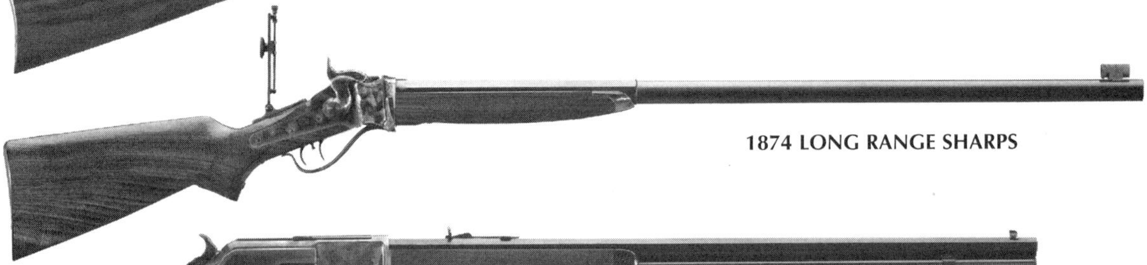

1874 LONG RANGE SHARPS

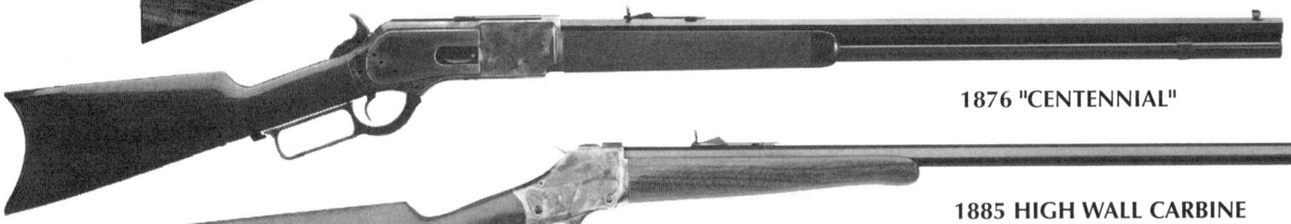

1876 "CENTENNIAL"

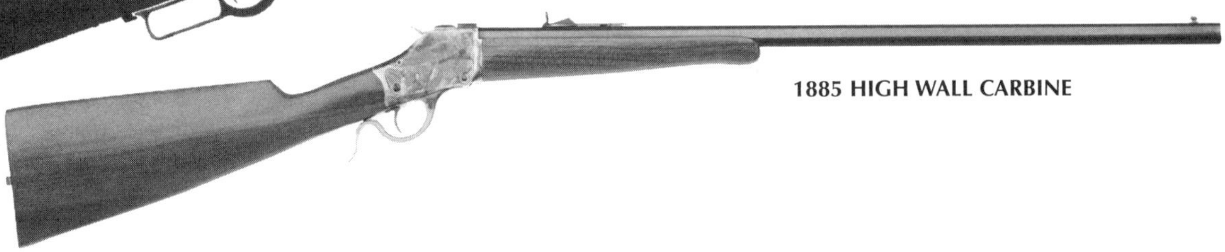

1885 HIGH WALL CARBINE

1874 SHARPS RIFLE

Action: falling block
Stock: walnut
Barrel: 30, 32 or 34 in.
Sights: adjustable ***Weight:*** 10.5 lbs.
Caliber: .45-70 ***Magazine:*** none (capacity 1 round)
Features: color case-hardened frame, buttplate and lever; blued barrel; Standard*:* 30-in. round barrel; Special*:* 32-in. octagonal barrel; Deluxe*:* 34-in. octagonal barrel; Down Under*:* 34 in. octagonal barrel; Buffalo Hunter*:* 32-in. octagonal barrel; Long Range*:* 34-in. half octagonal barrel; adjustable ladder or Creedmore rear sights

Standard:. $1459
Special: $1729
Buffalo Hunter: $2219
Down Under:. $2249
Long Range: $2279
Deluxe: $2749

1876 "CENTENNIAL"

Action: lever
Stock: walnut
Barrel: 28 in.
Sights: adjustable buckhorn
Weight: 10 lbs.
Caliber: .40-60, .45-60, .45-75, .50-95
Magazine: 11 + 1 rounds
Features: octagonal, blued barrel; color case-hardened receiver; A-grade, oil finished straight walnut stock

MSRP: $1569

1885 HIGH-WALL SINGLE-SHOT

Action: falling block
Stock: walnut
Barrel: 28 in. (carbine), 30 or 32 in.
Sights: adjustable
Weight: 9.5
Caliber: .45-70 (carbine) .45-70, .45-90, .45-120
Magazine: none (capacity 1 round)
Features: single shot, Special Sporting rifle with walnut checkered pistol grip stock; Sporting Rifles with straight stock; optional Creedmore sights; color case-hardened frame with blued barrel

1885 Carbine:. $969
1885 Sporting: $1029
1885 Special Sporting: $1179

LIGHTNING

Action: pump
Stock: walnut
Barrel: 20 in. and 24.25 in.
Sights: adjustable
Weight: 7.5 lbs
Caliber: .357 mag, .45 Colt
Magazine: 10 + 1 rounds
Features: blued or color case-hardened finish; straight walnut stock with checkered forend

MSRP: $1179

LIGHTNING

SHARPS HUNTER

SPRINGFIELD TRAPDOOR CARBINE

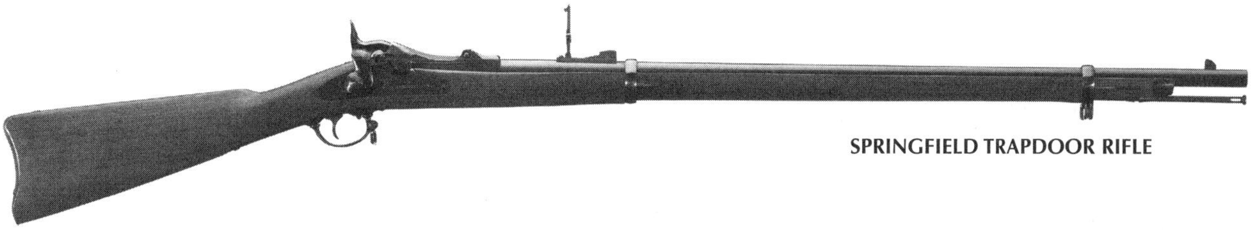

SPRINGFIELD TRAPDOOR RIFLE

SHARPS HUNTER

Action: falling block
Stock: walnut
Barrel: 28 in.
Sights: adjustable
Weight: 9.5 lbs.
Caliber: .45-70
Magazine: none (capacity 1 round)
Features: round, matte blued barrel; color-case-hardened receiver and buttplate; adjustable fiber optic sights; A-grade straight walnut stock
MSRP: $1459

SPRINGFIELD TRAPDOOR CARBINE

Action: hinged breech
Stock: walnut
Barrel: 22 in.
Sights: adjustable ladder
Weight: 7.2 lbs.
Caliber: .45-70
Magazine: none (capacity 1 round)
Features: ladder 1000-yd rear sight; carbine ring; blued barrel and action; case-hardened trapdoor and buttplate
MSRP: $1429

SPRINGFIELD TRAPDOOR RIFLE

Action: hinged breech
Stock: walnut
Barrel: 32.5 in.
Sights: adjustable ladder
Weight: 8.8 lbs.
Caliber: .45-70
Magazine: none (capacity 1 round)
Features: rear ladder sight adjustable up to 1000 yds.; blued barrel and action; case-hardened trapdoor and buttplate; cleaning rod
MSRP: $1669

Walther Rifles

G22 CARBINE

Action: blowback autoloading
Stock: synthetic
Barrel: 20 in.
Sights: adjustable on handle and front strut
Weight: 6 lbs.
Caliber: .22 LR
Magazine: detachable box
Features: Weaver-style accessory rail; black or green synthetic stock
MSRP: $509–615

Weatherby Rifles

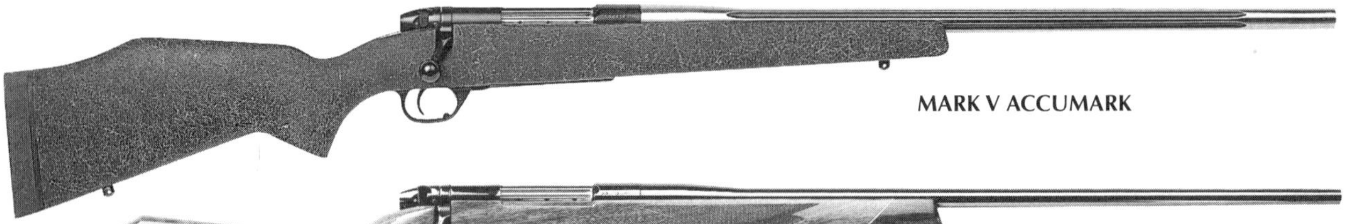

MARK V ACCUMARK

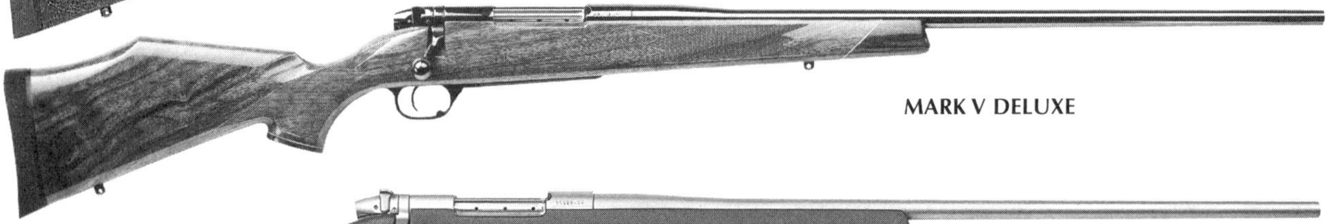

MARK V DELUXE

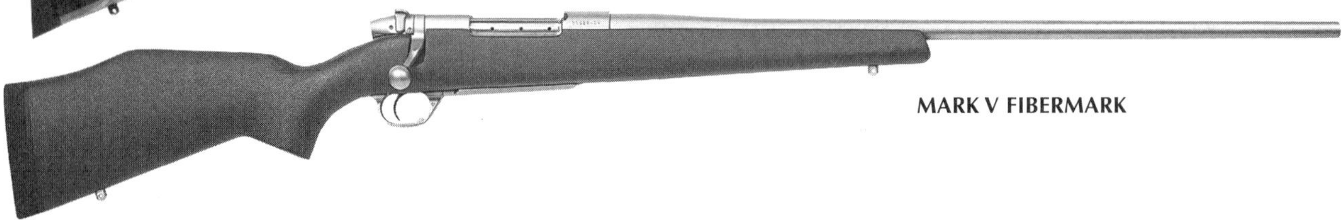

MARK V FIBERMARK

MARK V ACCUMARK

Action: bolt ***Stock:*** composite
Barrel: 26 in. and 28 in.
Sights: none
Weight: 7.0 lbs.
Caliber: Wby. Magnums: .257, .270, 7mm, .300, .340, .30-378, .338-378 and .300 Win. Mag., 7mm Rem. Mag.
Magazine: box, 3 or 5 rounds
Features: weight depends on caliber; hand-laminated; raised comb, Pachmayr recoil pad
Magnums: $1879
With Accubrake: $1939

MARK V DELUXE

Action: bolt
Stock: Claro walnut
Barrel: 26 in. and 28 in.
Sights: none
Weight: 8.5 lbs.
Caliber: .257 Wby. Mag to .460 Wby. Mag.
Magazine: box, 3 or 5 rounds
Features: 26 in. barrels for most magnum calibers; 28 in. barrel for .378, .416, .460
With Accubrake: $2279
.378, .416 with Accubrake: . . . $2679
.460: $3149

MARK V FIBERMARK

Action: bolt ***Stock:*** synthetic
Barrel: 24 in. and 26 in.
Sights: none ***Weight:*** 8.0 lbs.
Caliber: popular magnum chamberings from .257 Wby. Mag. to .375 H&H Mag.
Magazine: box, 3-5 rounds
Features: Krieger Criterion barrel; one-piece forged fluted bolt with three gas ports; hand-laminated, raised comb, pillar-bedded Monte Carlo composite stock; adjustable trigger; Pachmayr Decelerator recoil pad
Magnum: $1449
With Accubrake: $1739

Weatherby Rifles

MARK V LAZERMARK

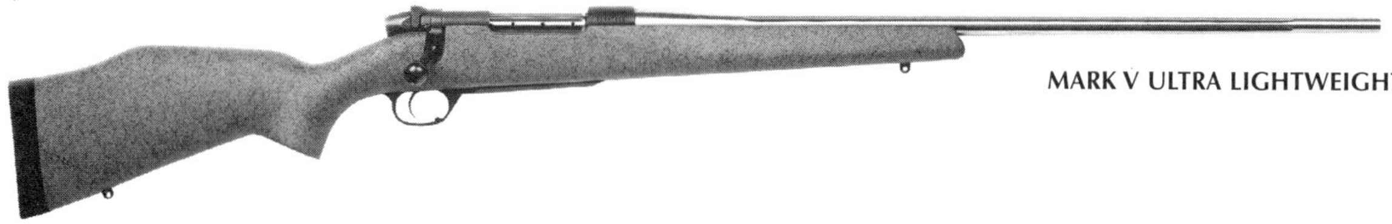

MARK V ULTRA LIGHTWEIGHT

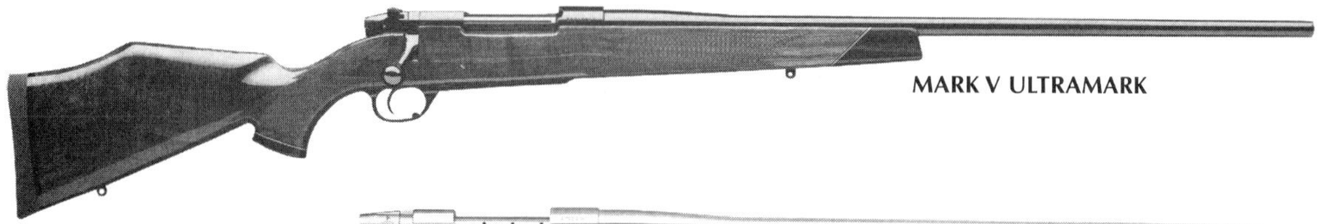

MARK V ULTRAMARK

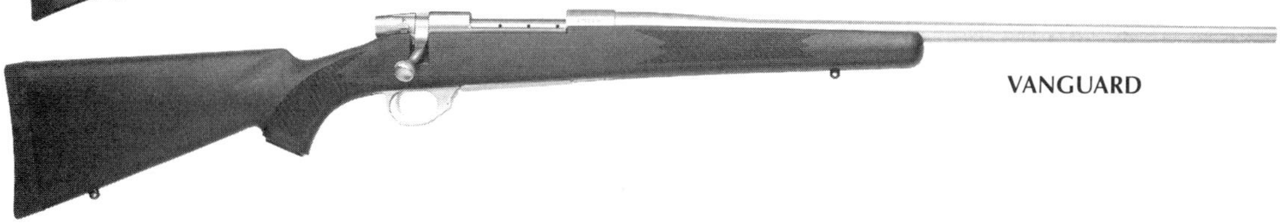

VANGUARD

MARK V LAZERMARK

Action: bolt
Stock: walnut *Barrel:* 26 in.
Sights: none *Weight:* 8.5 lbs.
Caliber: Wby. Magnums from .257 to .340
Magazine: box, 3 rounds
Features: laser-carved stock; button rifled Krieger barrel
MSRP: $2519

MARK V SPORTER

Action: bolt
Stock: walnut
Barrel: 24 and 26 in.
Sights: none *Weight:* 8.0 lbs.
Caliber: popular magnum chamberings from .257 Wby. Mag. to .340 Wby. Mag.
Magazine: box, 3 or 5 rounds
Features: checkered grip and forend
MSRP: $1529

MARK V SYNTHETIC

Action: bolt
Stock: synthetic
Barrel: 24, 26 and 28 in.
Sights: none
Weight: 8.5 lbs.
Caliber: popular standard and magnum calibers from .22-250 to .257 Wby. Mag.
Magazine: box, 3 or 5 rounds
Features: also stainless version
Mark V Synthetic: $1229
Magnum: $1299
With Accubrake: $1529

MARK V ULTRA LIGHTWEIGHT

Action: bolt
Stock: composite
Barrel: 24 in. and 26 in.
Sights: none
Weight: 6.0 lbs.
Caliber: .243, .240 Wby., .25-06, .270, 7mm-08, .280, 7mm Rem. Mag., .308, .30-06, .300 Win. Mag., Wby. Magnums: .257, .270, 7mm, .300
Magazine: box, 3 or 5 rounds
Features: lightweight action; 6-lug bolt
Ultra Lightweight: $1909
Magnums: $1999

MARK V ULTRAMARK

Action: bolt *Stock:* walnut
Barrel: 26 in. *Weight:* 8.5 lbs.
Caliber: .257 Weatherby Magnum, .300 Weatherby Magnum
Magazine: box, 3 + 1 rounds
Features: six locking lugs for a 54-degree bolt lift; high gloss, raised comb Monte Carlo stock from hand-selected highly figured, exhibition grade walnut
MSRP: $3029

VANGUARD

Action: bolt
Stock: composite *Barrel:* 24 in.
Sights: none *Weight:* 7.8 lbs.
Caliber: .223, .22-250, .243, .270, .308, .30-06, .257 Wby. Mag., 7mm Rem. Mag., .300 Win. Mag., .300 WSM, .270 WSM, .300 Wby. Mag., .338 Win. Mag.
Magazine: internal box, 3-5 rounds
Features: 2-lug action; made in Japan; 1½-inch guarantee for 3-shot group
Synthetic: $439

Weatherby Rifles

VANGUARD SPORTER

VANGUARD SPORTER

Action: bolt
Stock: checkered walnut
Barrel: 24 in.
Sights: none
Weight: 7.75 lbs.
Caliber: 13 chamberings, from .223 to .338 Win. Mag.
Magazine: internal box, 3-5 rounds
Features: Chrome-moly or stainless steel barrel; pillar-bedded composite stock with Aramid, fiberglass and graphite components.
Blue: $719

WEATHERBY VANGUARD AXIOM

Action: two-lug bolt
Stock: synthetic Knoxx adjustable, with pistol grip and recoil-absorbing mechanism
Barrel: 22″ or 24″
Sights: none
Weight: 8 ½ to 8 ¾ lbs.
Caliber: .25-06, .270, .30-06, .257 Wby. Mag., 7mm Rem. Mag., .330 Win. Mag., .300 Wby. Mag. (Varmint version: .223 Rem., .22-250 Rem., .308 Win.)
Magazine: internal box
Features: new Vanguard from Weatherby's Custom Shop. 4″ of buttstock adjustment to fit any shooter, vertical pistol grip. Also: new Vanguard Thumbhole Laminate with varmint-style forend, 22″ mid-weight barrel in .204, .223, .22-250, .308.
Varmint:. . . . . starting from $879
Big Game: . . . . starting from $965

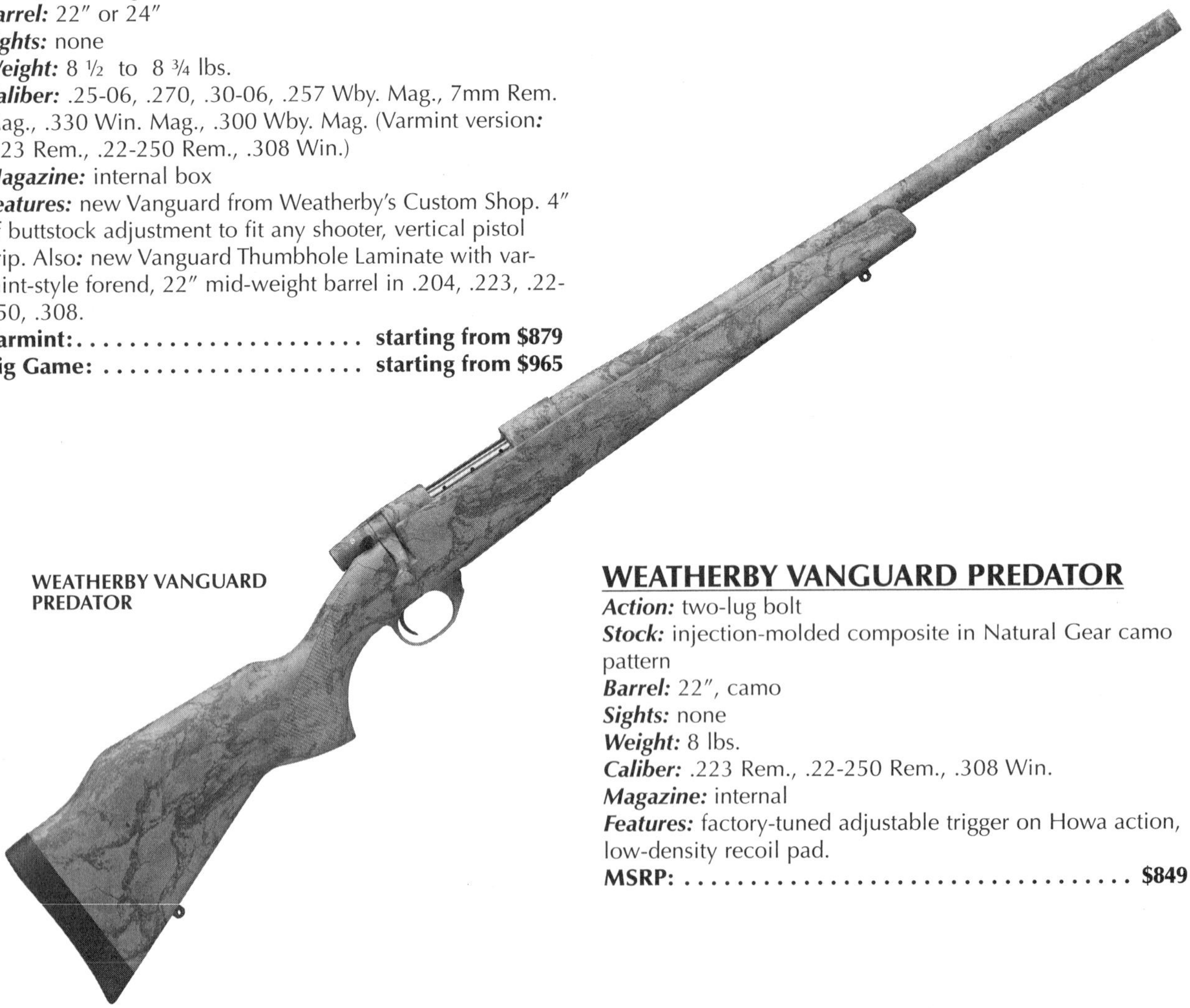

WEATHERBY VANGUARD PREDATOR

WEATHERBY VANGUARD PREDATOR

Action: two-lug bolt
Stock: injection-molded composite in Natural Gear camo pattern
Barrel: 22″, camo
Sights: none
Weight: 8 lbs.
Caliber: .223 Rem., .22-250 Rem., .308 Win.
Magazine: internal
Features: factory-tuned adjustable trigger on Howa action, low-density recoil pad.
MSRP: $849

Wild West Guns

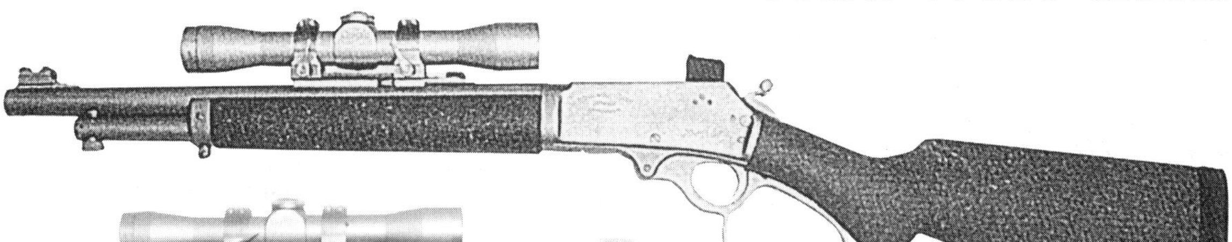

CO-PILOT

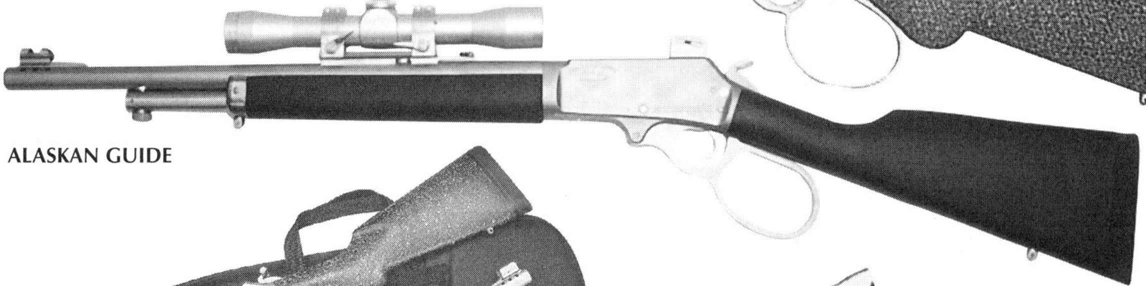

ALASKAN GUIDE

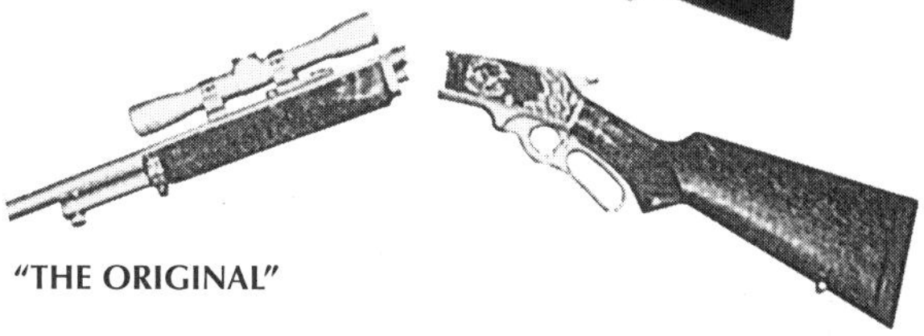

"THE ORIGINAL"

CO-PILOT

Action: lever
Stock: walnut
Barrel: 16, 18 or 20 in.
Sights: illuminated
Weight: 7.0 lbs.
Caliber: .45-70, .457 Magnum, .50 Alaskan
Magazine: under-barrel tube
Features: 1895 Marlin action; ported barrels; take-down feature; Alaskan Guide similar, not take-down

.50 Alaskan conversion:...... $250
Alaskan on supplied 1895:
Marlin:................. $935
Alaskan Guide:......... $1320
Take-Down on supplied:
1895G:................ $1595
Master Guide Take-Down:. $1865
Co-Pilot:.............. $1980

Winchester Rifles

MODEL 70 SUPER GRADE

MODEL 70
FEATHERWEIGHT DELUXE

MODEL 70

Action: bolt
Stock: walnut or composite
Barrel: cold hammer-forged steel
Sights: none
Weight: not available
Caliber: available in popular calibers
Magazine: 3+1 to 5+1
Features: M.O.A. Trigger System; Pre-64 Controlled Round Feeding, 3-position safety; blade-type ejector

Super Grade:......... $1159–1189
Featherweight Deluxe:... $999–1049
Sporter Deluxe:.........$799–859
Extreme Weather SS:... $1069–1119

Winchester Rifles

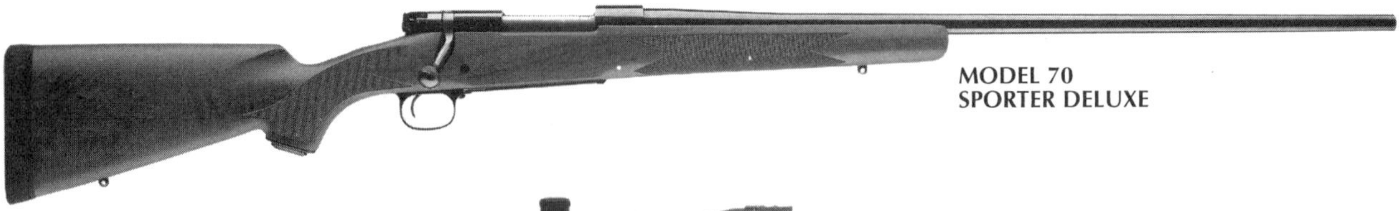

MODEL 70
SPORTER DELUXE

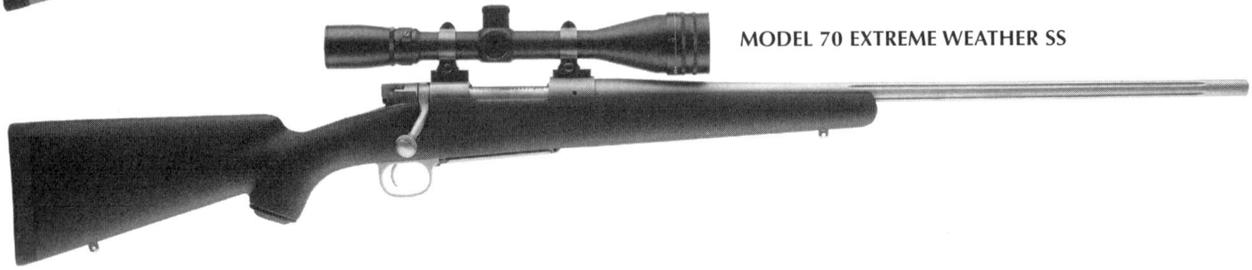

MODEL 70 EXTREME WEATHER SS

SUPER X RIFLE-SXR

WILDCAT
BOLT-ACTION .22

WILDCAT
TARGET/VARMINT .22

SUPER X RIFLE-SXR

Action: autoloader
Stock: walnut
Barrel: 22-24 in.
Sights: none
Weight: 7.0-7.25 lbs.
Caliber: .30-06, .300 Win Mag, .300 WSM, .270 WSM
Magazine: 4 rounds (.30-06); 3 rounds (other calibers), detachable box
Features: Rotary bolt semi-auto, center-fire system; crossbolt safety; single-stage trigger w/ enlarged trigger guard; Pachmayr Decelerator recoil pad; sling swivel studs
.30-06: $864
.300 WSM, .270 WSM,
.300 Win Mag: $892

WILDCAT BOLT-ACTION .22

Action: bolt
Stock: checkered hardwood
Barrel: 21 in.
Sights: none
Weight: 6.5 lbs.
Caliber: .22
Magazine: one 5-round and three 10-round magazines
Features: checkered black synthetic Winchester buttplate; Schnabel fore-end; steel sling swivel studs
MSRP: $259
DISCONTINUED

WILDCAT TARGET/ VARMINT .22

Action: bolt
Stock: checkered hardwood
Barrel: 21 in.
Sights: none
Weight: 6.5 lbs.
Caliber: .22
Magazine: one 5-round and three 10-round magazines
Features: heavy .866 in. diameter bull barrel; adjustable trigger; receiver drilled and tapped for bases, as well as grooved for mounting a scope; dual front steel swivel studs; scope not included
MSRP: $309
DISCONTINUED

WINCHESTER M70 COYOTE LIGHT

Action: two-lug bolt
Stock: black composite
Barrel: 22 or 24″ stainless
Sights: none
Weight: 7 ½ lbs.
Caliber: .22-250, .243 Win, .308 Win, .270 WSM, .300 WSM, .325 WSM
Magazine: internal box
Features: Bell & Carlson carbon fiber stock with Pachmayr Decelerator recoil pad, flow-through vents on forend to reduce weight and help cool barrel. Skeletonized aluminum bedding block.
MSRP: . . . . $1069-$1119

WINCHESTER M70 ULTIMATE SHADOW

Action: two-lug bolt
Stock: black synthetic
Barrel: 22″, 24″, or 26″
Sights: none
Weight: 6 ½ to 7 lbs.
Caliber: .243, .308, .270, .30-06; 7mm Mag and .300 Win. Mag.; .270 .300 and .325 WSM.
Magazine: internal box
Features: WinSorb recoil pad, MOA trigger system, controlled round feed with external claw extractor.
MSRP: . . . . $749-$789

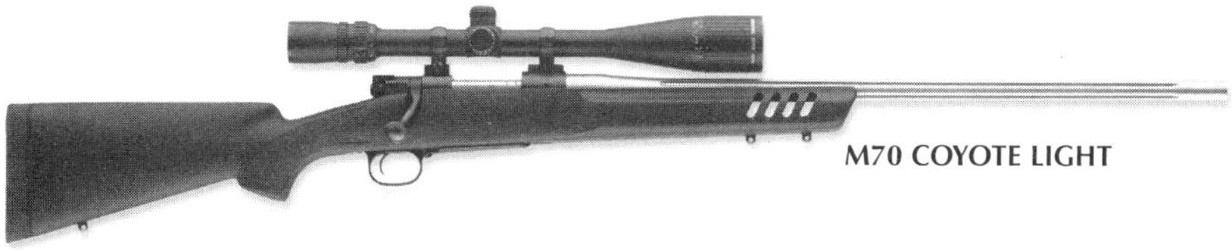
M70 COYOTE LIGHT

SUPER X RIFLE

WINCHESTER 1895 SAFARI CENTENNIAL 1909-2009

Action: Model 1895 lever
Stock: High Grade and Custom Grade, both finely checkered fancy walnut
Barrel: 24″
Sights: buckhorn rear sight, Marble's gold bead front sight
Weight: 8 lbs.
Caliber: .405 Win.
Magazine: detachable 4-round box
Features: receiver engraved with African big game animals, commemorating the 100th anniversary of Theodore Roosevelt's safari. Only 1,000 Custom Grade rifles to be built, and sold in sets with 1,000 High Grade rifles. An additional 500 High Grade rifles will be sold separately.
High Grade:. $1749
Custom Grade: $3649

WINCHESTER SUPER X RIFLE

Action: autoloading, gas operated
Stock: checkered walnut
Barrel: 22 or 24″ barrel
Sights: none
Weight: 7 ½ lbs.
Caliber: 270 WSM, 300 WSM, .30-06, .300 Win Mag.
Magazine: detachable box
Features: bolt-action accuracy from a combination of multi-lug rotating bolt and hammer-forged free-floating barrel. Hinged floorplate. Easily removable trigger assembly. Crossbolt safety. Low felt recoil.
MSRP: $1199

AIR RIFLES

Anschütz Air Rifles

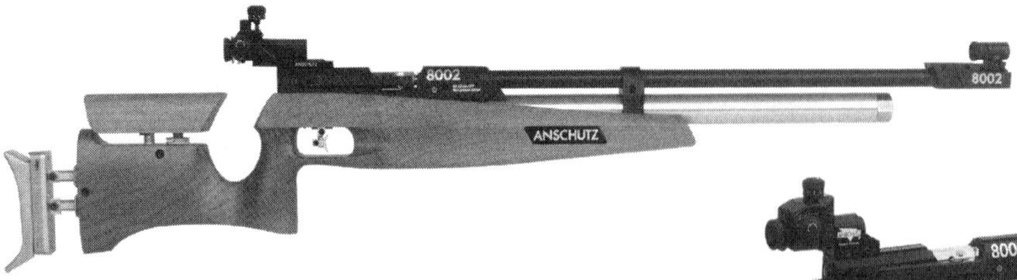

8002 COMPRESSED

8002 CA ALU

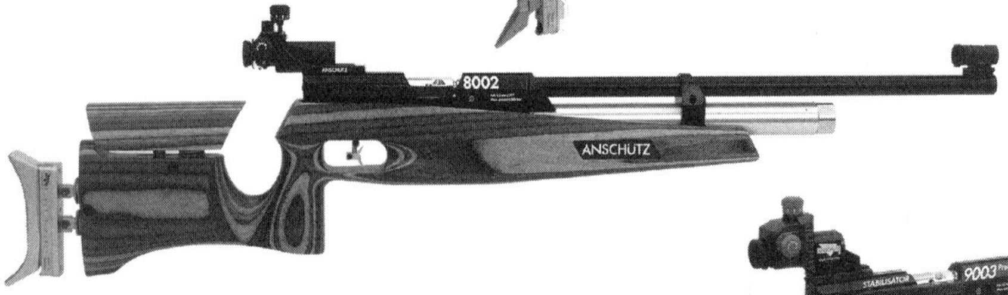

8002 COMPRESSED JUNIOR

MODEL 9003 PREMIUM

8002 COMPRESSED AIR RIFLE

Power: compressed air
Stock: walnut
Barrel: 26.2 in.
Sights: none
Weight: 10.36 lbs
Caliber: .177
Features: single loader; vibration free shot release; carrier with special aluminum regulation valve; capacity for compressed air cylinder appr. 300 shots; adjustable cheek piece and buttplate
MSRP: $2178–2224

8002 CA ALU METAL STOCK

Power: compressed air
Stock: aluminum
Barrel: 25.2 in.
Sights: none
Weight: 10.8 lbs.
Caliber: .177
Features: single loader; recoil & vibration free barreled action; compressed air cylinder with monometer (max 200 bar filling pressure); capacity for filled compressed air cylinder appr. 350 shots; special aluminum regulation valve; barrel weights & weight rings
MSRP: $2740–2832

8002 COMPRESSED AIR RIFLE JUNIOR

Power: compressed air
Stock: laminated
Barrel: 23.2
Sights: none
Weight: 9.9 lbs.
Caliber: .177 cal
Features: single loader; vibration free shot release; carrier with special aluminum regulation valve; capacity for compressed air cylinder appr. 280 shots; adjustable cheek piece and buttplate; stock can be lengthened by spacers; right & left hand cheek piece
MSRP: $1965

MODEL 9003 PREMIUM

Power: compressed air
Stock: aluminum
Sights: none
Weight: 9.92 lbs
Length: 42.52 in.
Caliber: .177
Features: single shot; vibration damping barrel/stock connection; adjustable match trigger and trigger blade; cocking lever mountable left and right; soft link shock absorber; adjustable pistol grip; fully adjustable fore-end; exchangeable compressed air cylinder; air filter with manometer; filling adapter with air release screw
MSRP: $2125–3420

Airforce Air Rifles

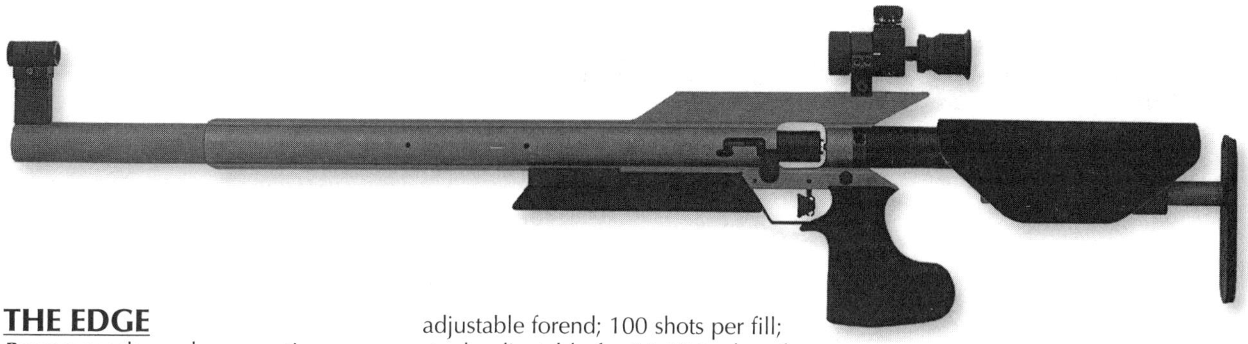

THE EDGE

Power: precharged pneumatic
Stock: composite
Sights: precision peep sight
Weight: 6.75 lb.
Caliber: .177
Features: ambidextrous cocking knob; adjustable forend; 100 shots per fill; stock adjustable for 35-42 in. length of pull; approved by the Civilian Marksmanship Program for Sporter Class competition
MSRP: $466–600

Beeman Air Rifles

MODEL 1024 COMBO

MODEL 1082 SS1000-H

MODEL 1024 COMBO

Power: break barrel/spring piston
Stock: hardwood
Sights: tapped for scope
Weight: 10.0 lbs
Caliber: .177
Length: 45.5 in.
Features: velocity 550 fps; removable barrel; all-steel receiver; raised cheek piece; comes with 4x20 wide-angle scope
MSRP: $60

MODEL 1082 SS1000-H

Power: break barrel/spring piston
Stock: hardwood
Sights: adjustable
Weight: 7.9 lbs.
Caliber: .177, .22
Length: 46.5 in
Features: velocity: 1000fps, 850 (.22); rifled steel barrel; ported muzzlebrake; blued finish; automatic safety; two-stage adjustable trigger; Monte Carlo cheek piece; rubber pad buttplate; 3-9x32 AO scope
MSRP: $170

Beeman Air Rifles

MODEL R1

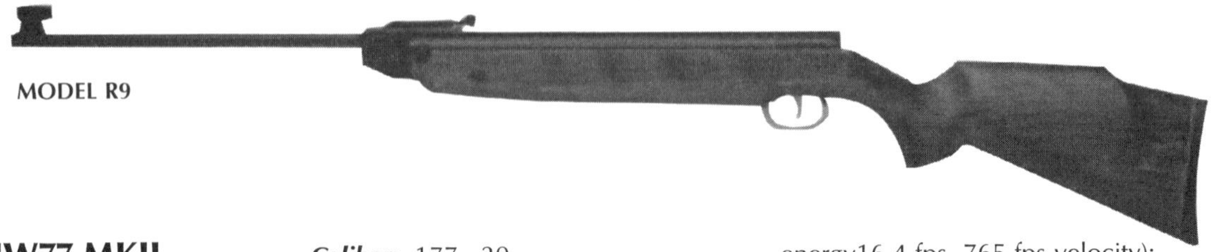

MODEL R9

MODEL HW77 MKII

Power: under lever/spring piston
Stock: hardwood
Sights: none
Weight: 8.7 lbs.
Caliber: .177
Length: 39.7 in.
Features: velocity 930 fps; two-stage adjustable trigger; automatic safety; receiver grooved to except 11mm ring or one-piece mounts; beech sporter stock, with tapered forend, hand-cut checkering on the pistol grip, high comb with raised cheek piece
MSRP: $710

MODEL HW97 MK III

Power: under lever/spring piston
Stock: hardwood
Sights: none
Weight: 9.2 lbs.
Caliber: .177, .20
Length: 44.1 in.
Features: velocity 930 fps; two-stage adjustable trigger; automatic safety; receiver grooved to except 11mm ring or one-piece mounts; beech sporter stock, with tapered forend, hand-cut checkering on the pistol grip, high comb with raised cheek piece
MSRP: $695–720

MODEL R1, R1 CARBINE

Power: break barrel/spring piston
Stock: hardwood
Sights: adjustable
Weight: 8.8 lbs.
Caliber: .177, .20
Length: 45.2 in., 42.0 in. (Carbine)
Features: 14.23 fp muzzle energy; 950 fps velocity; (.22 cal. — muzzle energy16.4 fps, 765 fps velocity); automatic safety; two-stage adjustable trigger; beech stained hardwood stock
MSRP: $800

MODEL R9

Power: break barrel/spring piston
Stock: hardwood
Sights: adjustable
Weight: 7.3 to 7.5 lbs.
Caliber: .177, .20
Length: 43 in.
Features: Velocity 930 fps (.177), 800 fps. (.20);
R9: $500–525

AIR RIFLES

Crosman Air Rifles

BENJAMIN DISCOVERY

BENJAMIN DISCOVERY

Power: compressed air or CO2
Stock: walnut
Barrel: 39 in. rifled steel
Sights: open
Weight: 5 lb. 2 oz.
Caliber: .177 or .22
Features: built-in pressure gauge; quick-disconnect fittings; receiver grooved to accept 11mm scope mounts; comes with three-stage hand pump; optional CO2 adapter; Williams Firesight fiber optic front and rear sights
MSRP: $270

BENJAMIN SUPER STREAK

BENJAMIN SUPER STREAK

Power: break barrel/spring piston
Stock: hardwood
Barrel: rifled steel, silver or black
Sights: micro-adjustable rear sight, hooded front sight
Weight: 8.5 lb.
Caliber: .177 or .22
Features: two-stage adjustable trigger; factory mounted CenterPoint Precision Optics 4-16x40mm scope with red/green illuminated Mil Dot reticle; ambidextrous thumbhole stock
Black:.................... $315
Silver: $315

MODEL 760XLS

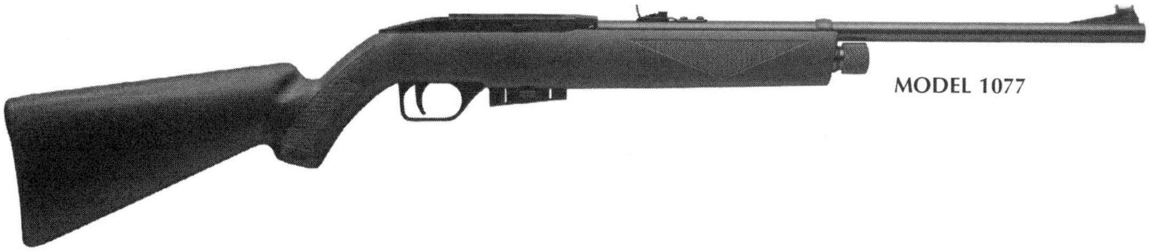

MODEL 1077

MODEL 760 PUMPMASTER

Power: pneumatic pump
Stock: synthetic
Sights: adjustable
Weight: 3.69 lbs
Caliber: .177
Length: 33.5 in.
Features: velocity: BB*:* up to 625 fps (190.5 m/s) Pellet*:* up to 600 fps (182.8 m/s); smooth bore steel barrel; reservoir*:* 200 BBs, magazine*:* 18 BBs; Model 760 XLS with hardwood stock, variable power short-stroke pump action, optional BB repetition or single-shot pellet fire
Model 760:.................. $49
Model 760XLS:.............. $75

MODEL 764SB

Power: pneumatic pump
Stock: synthetic
Sights: adjustable
Weight: 2.69 lbs.
Caliber: .177
Length: 33.5 in.
Features: velocity: BB*:* up to 625 fps (190.5 m/s) Pellet*:* up to 600 fps (182.9m/s); smooth bore steel barrel; reservoir*:* 200 BBs, magazine*:* 18 BBs; available with 4-power precision scope
MSRP: $64

MODEL 1077

Power: CO2
Stock: synthetic
Sights: adjustable
Weight: 3 lbs. 11 oz.
Caliber: .177
Length: 36.88 in.
Features: velocity: 625 fps; rifled steel barrel; 12-shot rotary clip; Model 1077W with hardwood stock
Model 1077:................ $138

Crosman Air Rifles

MODEL 2100

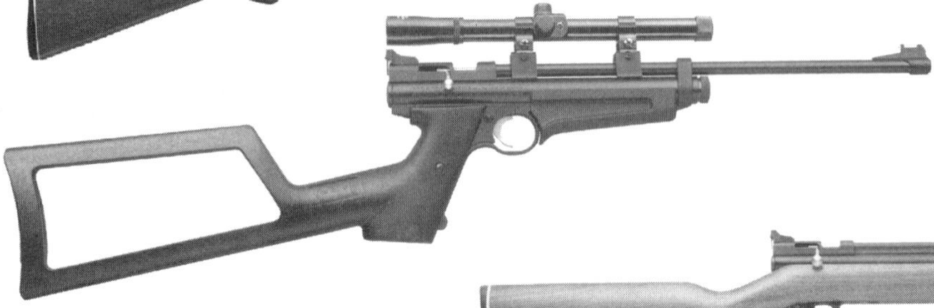

MODEL 2250B

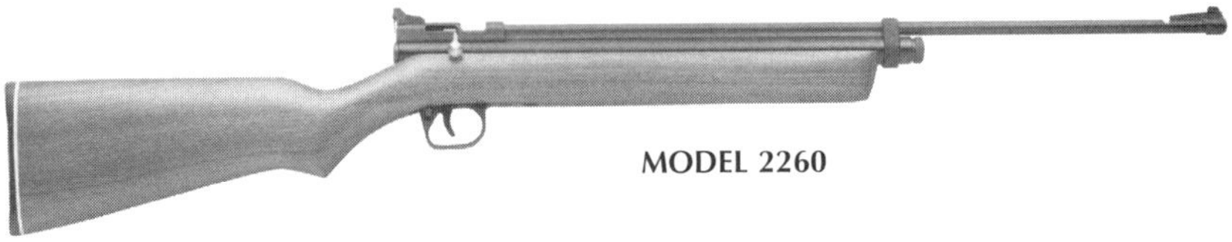

MODEL 2260

CHALLENGER CH 2000

MODEL 2100

Power: pneumatic pump
Stock: synthetic
Sights: adjustable
Weight: 4 lbs. 13 oz.
Caliber: .177
Length: 39.75 in.
Features: velocity: BB*:* up to 755 fps(230.2 m/s) Pellet*:* up to 725 fps(221.1 m/s); rifled steel barrel; reservoir*:* 200 BBs, magazine*:* 17 BBs
MSRP: $82

MODEL 2250B

Power: CO^2
Stock: synthetic
Sights: adjustable
Weight: 3 lbs. 6 oz.
Caliber: .22
Length: 30.25 in.
Features: velocity: 550 fps; rifled steel barrel; single shot; 4-power scope
MSRP: $78

MODEL 2260

Power: CO^2
Stock: hardwood
Sights: adjustable
Weight: 4 lbs. 12 oz.
Caliber: .22
Length: 39.75 in.
Features: velocity: 600 fps; rifled steel barrel; single shot
MSRP: $90

CHALLENGER CH 2000

Power: CO^2
Stock: synthetic
Sights: adjustable
Weight: 6 lbs. 15.2 oz.
Caliber: .177
Length: 36.25 in.
Features: velocity: 485 fps; single shot; rifled steel barrel; ambidextrous steel straight pull bolt; trigger overtravel screw; adjustable stock, buttplate and cheek piece; molded pistol-style grip, available with hooded front aperture sight and fully adjustable rear sight
MSRP: $403.82

PHANTOM 1000

Power: break barrel/spring piston
Stock: synthetic
Sights: adjustable
Weight: 6.02 lbs.
Caliber: .177
Length: 44.5 in.
Features: velocity: 1,000 fps; rifled steel barrel; two-stage, adjustable trigger; fiber optic front sight, micro-adjustable fiber optic rear sight; checkered grip and forearm
MSRP: $107

Crosman Air Rifles

TAC 1 EXTREME

Power: break barrel/spring piston
Stock: synthetic
Sights: optical or red dot
Weight: 6.02 lbs.
Length: 44.5 in.
Caliber: .22
Features: velocity: 800 fps; single shot; rifled steel barrel; two-stage adjustable trigger; totally ambidextrous; all-weather synthetic stock with pistol grip; contoured forearm; TAC 1 comes with a 3-9X32mm scope, flashlight, bipod and red dot sight.
MSRP: $330

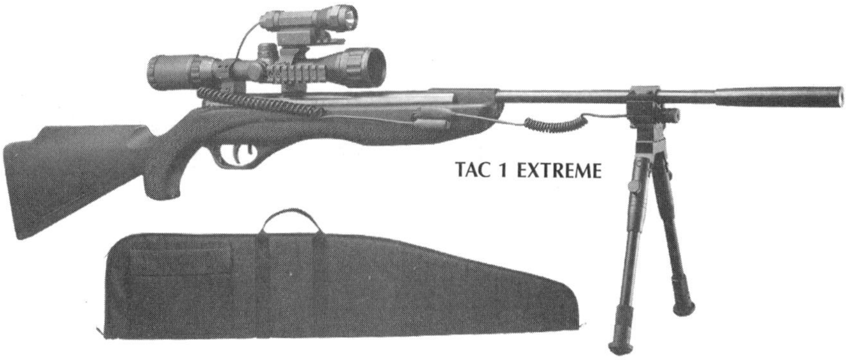

TAC 1 EXTREME

Daisy Air Rifles

MODEL 880

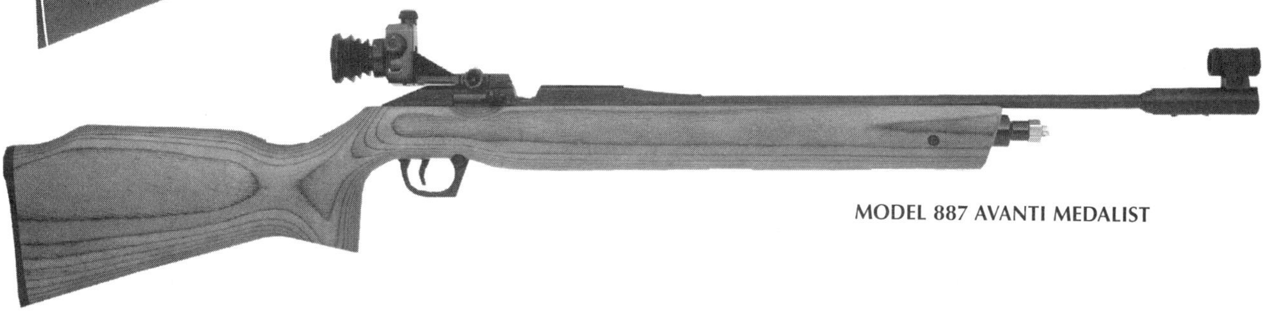

MODEL 887 AVANTI MEDALIST

MODEL 853 LEGEND

Power: pneumatic pump
Stock: hardwood
Sights: adjustable
Weight: 5.50 lbs.
Length: 38.5 in.
Caliber: .177
Features: velocity: 510 fps., 490 fps. (853C Legend EX); single-shot, straight pull-bolt; diecast receiver; Lothar Walther rifled steel barrel; manual crossbolt trigger block safety; hooded front sight, micrometer adjustable rear sight; sporter-style hardwood stock
Model 853 Legend: $280
Model 853C Legend EX: $280

MODEL 880

Power: pneumatic pump
Stock: synthetic
Sights: adjustable
Weight: 3.70 lbs.
Length: 37.6 in.
Caliber: .177
Features: velocity:750 fps/BB; 665 fps/ pellet; capacity:50 shot/BB; single shot/pellet; resin receiver with dovetail mount for scope; crossbolt trigger block safety; Truglo fiber optic front, adjustable rear sights; woodgrain Monte Carlo stock and forearm
MSRP: $72

MODEL 887 AVANTI MEDALIST

Power: CO^2
Stock: laminated
Sights: target
Weight: 6.90 lbs.
Length: 38.5 in.
Caliber: .177
Features: velocity: 500 fps; single-shot bolt action; Lothar Walther rifled steel crowned, barrel; manual, crossbolt trigger block safety; refillable 2.5 oz. CO2 cylinder; hooded front sight, micrometer adjustable rear peep sight; rail adapter; sporter-style multicolored laminated hardwood stock
MSRP: $462

Daisy Air Rifles

MODEL 1000

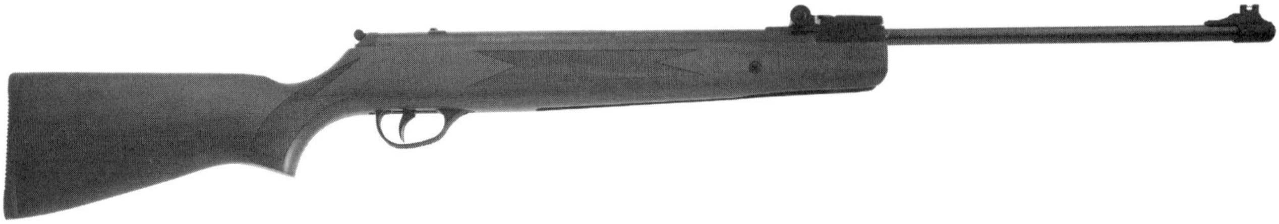

POWERLINE 500

AIR RIFLES

MODEL 1000

Power: break barrel/spring piston
Stock: synthetic or walnut (1000X)
Sights: adjustable
Weight: 6.60 lbs.
Length: 44.5 in.
Caliber: .177
Features: velocity: 1000 fps; rifle steel barrel; rear button safety; fiber optic hooded front and micro adjustable rear sight; available with Winchester 3-9X 32 scope; sporter-style black composite stock; 1000X with solid steel barrel shroud, auto rear button safety and sporter-style select walnut stock
Model 1000: $232

POWERLINE 800

Power: break barrel/spring piston
Stock: synthetic
Sights: adjustable
Weight: 5.70 lbs.
Length: 45.7 in.
Caliber: .177
Features: velocity: 800 fps; rifled steel barrel, grooved to accept optics; rear button safety; micro-adjustable rear sight; sporter style black composite stock; Model 800X with sporter-style select walnut stock
MSRP: $111

POWERLINE 500 BREAK BARREL

Power: break barrel/spring air
Stock: hardwood
Barrel: rifled steel
Sights: adjustable open
Weight: 6.6 lb.
Caliber: .177
Features: single shot; hooded front and micro-adjustable rear sights; variable 4x32 air rifle scope included
MSRP: $150

POWERLINE 800 BREAK BARREL

Power: break barrel/spring air
Stock: black composite
Barrel: rifled steel
Sights: adjustable open
Weight: 6.6 lb.
Caliber: .177
Features: single shot; hooded front and micro-adjustable rear sights; variable 4x32 air rifle scope included
MSRP: $121

POWERLINE 1000 BREAK BARREL

Power: break barrel/spring air
Stock: sporter-style black composite
Barrel: rifled steel
Sights: adjustable open
Weight: 6.6 lb.
Caliber: .177
Features: single shot; hooded front and micro-adjustable rear sights; variable 3-9x32 air rifle scope included
MSRP: $135

Daisy Air Rifles

POWERLINE 800

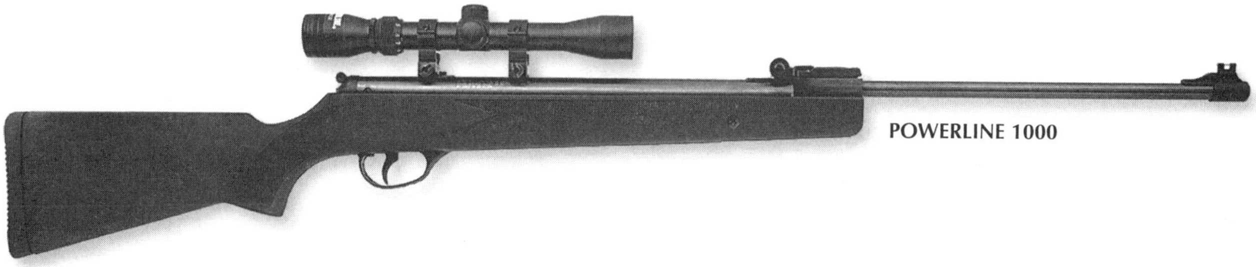

POWERLINE 1000

POWERLINE 901

Power: pneumatic pump
Stock: synthetic
Sights: adjustable, open
Weight: 3.70 lbs.
Length: 37.5 in.
Caliber: .177
Features: velocity: 750 fps. (BB); shoots either BBs or pellets - 50 shot BB, single shot pellet; composite receiver with dovetail mounts for optics; rifled steel barrel; crossbolt trigger block safety; TruGlo fiber optic front sight; black composite stock and forearm
MSRP: **$63**

Gamo Air Rifles

BIG CAT 1200

WHISPER

BIG CAT 1200

Power: break barrel/spring piston
Stock: synthetic
Sights: 4x32 Air Rifle Scope with rings
Weight: 6.1 lb.
Caliber: .177
Features: 1200 fps with PBA ammunition; all-weather molded synthetic stock
MSRP: **$170**

WHISPER

Power: break barrel/spring piston
Stock: synthetic
Sights:open adjustable
Weight: 5.3 lb.
Caliber: .177
Features: single shot; integrated noise dampener; second stage adjustable trigger; 1200 fps with PBA or 1000fps with standard lead; all-weather molded synthetic stock; fiber optic front sight with sight guard; fiber optic adjustable rear sight
MSRP: **$300**

RWS Air Rifles

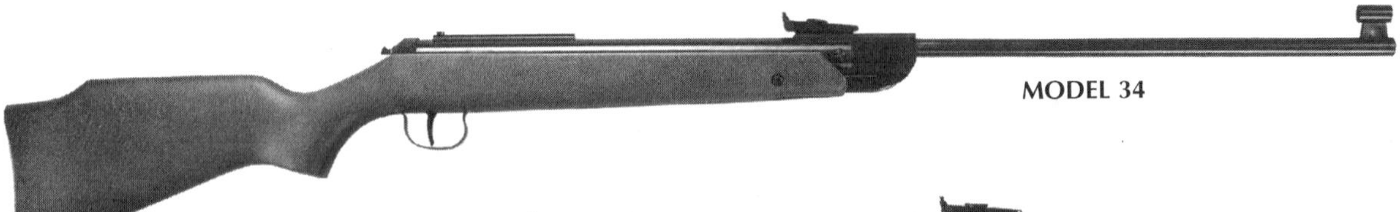

MODEL 34

MODEL 48

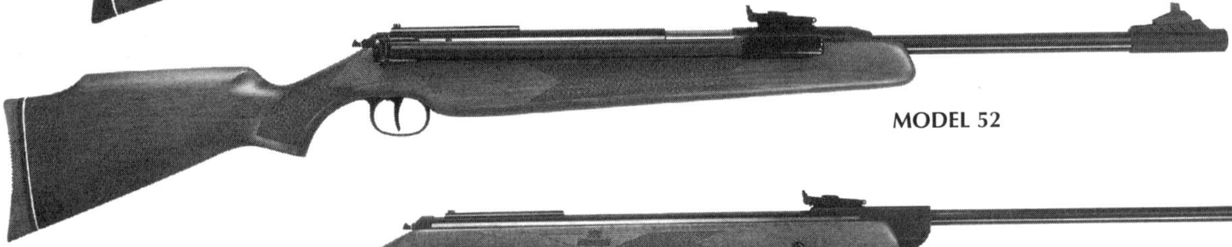

MODEL 52

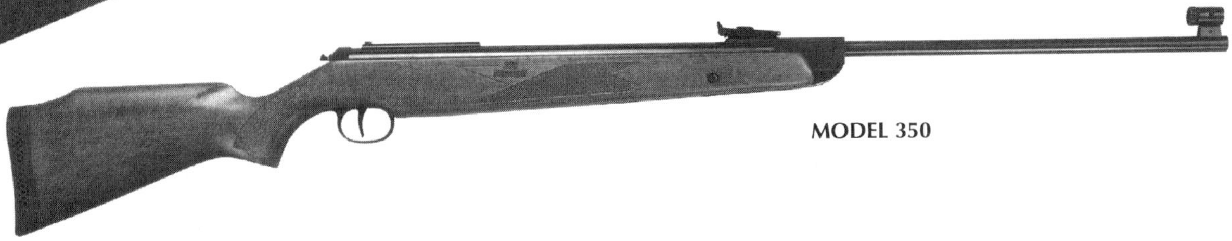

MODEL 350

MODEL 24 RIFLE AND CARBINE

Power: break barrel/spring piston
Stock: hardwood
Barrel: 17 in. (13.5 in. carbine)
Sights: adjustable
Weight: 6 lbs. (5 lbs. Carbine)
Caliber: .177, .22
Features: velocity: .177/700 fps, .22/400 fps, Carbine: .177/700 fps; rifled barrel; automatic safety; scope rail
Model 24 Rifle: $196–220
Model 24 Carbine: $196–220

MODEL 34 RIFLE AND CARBINE

Power: break barrel/spring piston
Stock: synthetic
Barrel: 19 in. (15.5 in. Carbine)
Sights: adjustable
Weight: 7.5 lbs. (7 lbs. Carbine)
Caliber: .177, .22
Features: velocity: .177/1000 fps; .22/800 fps; rifled barrel, adjustable trigger; automatic safety; blued finish
Model 34: $295–299
Model 34BC (matte black): $305–515
Carbine: $203–290
Model 36 Rifle: $435–450
Model 36 Carbine: $435–451

MODEL 45

Power: side lever/spring piston
Stock: hardwood
Barrel: 19 in.
Sights: adjustable
Weight: 8 lbs.
Caliber: .177
Features: velocity: .177 1000 fps; automatic safety; two stage adjustable trigger; scope rail
MSRP: $470

MODEL 48

Power: side lever/spring piston
Stock: hardwood
Barrel: 17 in.
Sights: adjustable
Weight: 8.5 lbs.
Caliber: .177, .22, .25
Features: velocity: .177 1100 fps/.22 900 fps; fixed rifled barrel with sliding breech opening; automatic safety; adjustable trigger
Model 48, .177: $479–600
Model 48, .22: $470–516

MODEL 52

Power: side lever/spring piston
Stock: walnut or rosewood
Barrel: 17 in.
Sights: adjustable
Weight: 8.5 lbs.
Caliber: .177, .22, .25
Features: velocity: .177 1100 fps; .22 900 fps; Monte Carlo stock, sculpted cheek piece with checkering on wrist and forearm; Deluxe version with select walnut stock, rosewood forearm cap, pistol grip caps, palm swell, and hand cut checkering
Model 52, .177: $525
Model 52, .22: $550

MODEL 350

Power: break barrel/spring piston
Stock: hardwood
Barrel: 18 in.
Sights: adjustable
Weight: 8.2 lbs.
Caliber: .177, .22
Features: velocity: .177 1250 fps; .22 1050 fps.; Monte Carlo stock w/ cheek piece and checkering
MSRP: $519–550

SHOTGUNS

AYA Shotguns

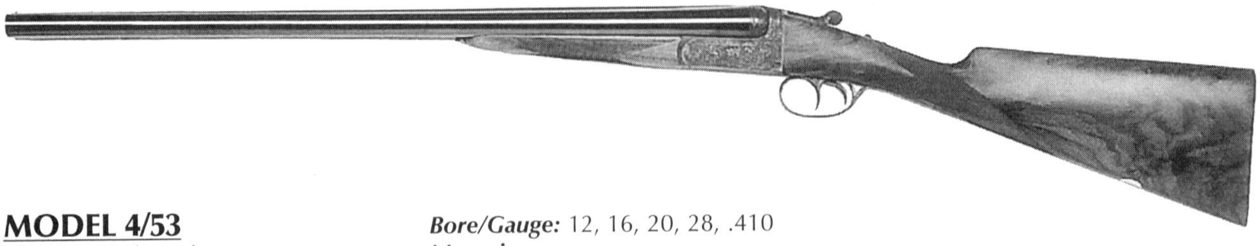

MODEL 4/53

Action: side-by-side
Stock: walnut, straight grip
Barrel: 26, 27 or 28 in.
Chokes: improved cylinder, modified, full
Weight: 7.0 lbs.
Bore/Gauge: 12, 16, 20, 28, .410
Magazine: none
Features: boxlock; chopper lump barrels; bushed firing pins, automatic safety and ejectors
MSRP: $3900

Benelli Shotguns

BENELLI VINCI MAX4

Action: autoloading, inertia operated
Stock: black synthetic or camo (including new Max-4 HD)
Barrel: 26″ or 28″
Chokes: set of 5 included
Weight: 6.8 to 6.9 lbs.
Bore/Gauge: 12 ga., 3″
Magazine: 3 + 1
Features: in-line inertial driven system, oversize lugs, Red Bar front sight, recoil reduction system
Camo: . . . . $1379-$1479

CORDOBA 12 GA.

CORDOBA

Action: inertia operated semi-auto
Stock: synthetic with Grip-Tight surface coating
Barrel: 28 or 30 in.
Chokes: 5 extended Crio screw-in tubes
Weight: 7.85 lbs. (12)
Bore/Gauge: 12
Magazine: 4 + 1 rounds
Features: Comfortech recoil reduction system; ported Crio barrel; inertia operated; 3 in. chamber
MSRP: $2659–2769

CORDOBA,
COMFORTECH 12 GA.
ADVANTAGE MAX-4 HD

CORDOBA,
COMFORTECH 20 GA.

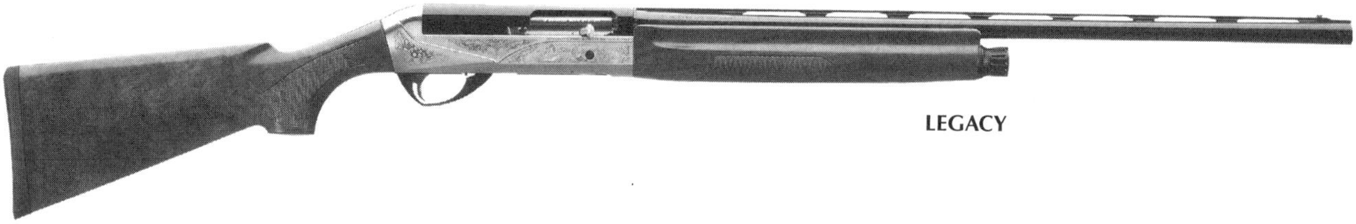

LEGACY

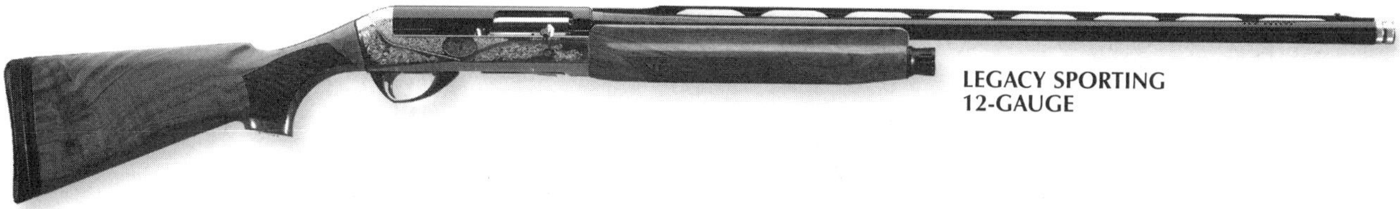

LEGACY SPORTING
12-GAUGE

CORDOBA COMFORTECH 12-GA. ADVANTAGE MAX-4 HD

Action: inertia operated semi-auto
Stock: synthetic (Advantage Max-4 HD)
Barrel: 28 in.
Chokes: 5 extended Crio screw-in tubes
Weight: 7.9 lbs. (12)
Bore/Gauge: 12
Magazine: 4 + 1 rounds
Features: Comfortech recoil reduction system; ported Crio barrel; 3 in. chamber; optional gel-combs
MSRP: **$1949–2119**

CORDOBA COMFORTECH 20-GA.

Action: inertia operated semi-auto
Stock: black synthetic with GripTight surface coating.
Barrel: 28 in.
Chokes: 5 extended Crio screw-in tubes
Weight: 6.3 lbs.
Bore/Gauge: 20
Magazine: 4 + 1 rounds
Features: Comfortech recoil reduction; ported Crio barrel; inertia operated; 3 in. chamber; shell view magazine
MSRP: **$1949**

LEGACY

Action: inertia operated semi-auto
Stock: select AA grade walnut
Barrel: 24, 26 or 28 in.
Chokes: screw-in crio tubes
Weight: 7.5 lbs. (12); 5.8lbs (20)
Bore/Gauge: 12, 20
Magazine: 4 + 1 rounds
Features: 3 in. chambers; inertia operated; rotating bolt with dual lugs; two-toned receiver with engraved game scenes.
MSRP: **$1759**

LEGACY SPORTING

Action: inertia operated semi-auto
Stock: walnut
Barrel: 28 in., 30 in.
Chokes: screw-in tubes
Weight: 7.5 lbs.
Bore/Gauge: 12
Magazine: 4+1 rounds
Features: vent target rib; Crio polished blue barrel; chambered for 2-3/4 and 3-in. shells, Extended Chrome Crio Choke tubes (C, IC, IM, M, F); AA grade walnut stock; contoured gel recoil pad; black titanium insert with game scene on receiver.
MSRP: **$1689–2269**

Benelli Shotguns

M2 FIELD 12 GA., WALNUT STOCK

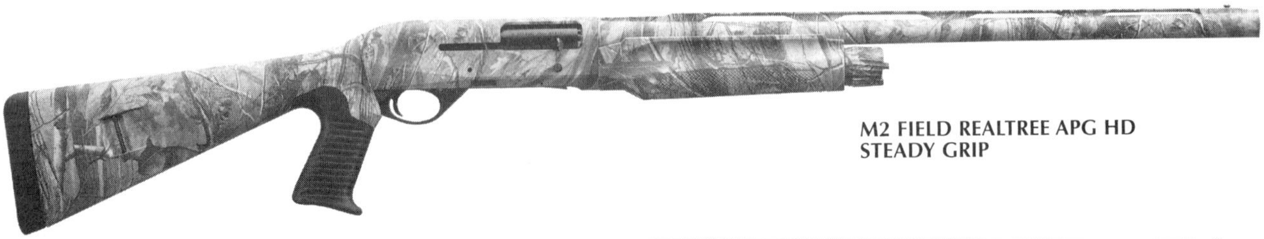

M2 FIELD REALTREE APG HD
STEADY GRIP

M-2 FIELD, 20 GA.
COMFORTECH

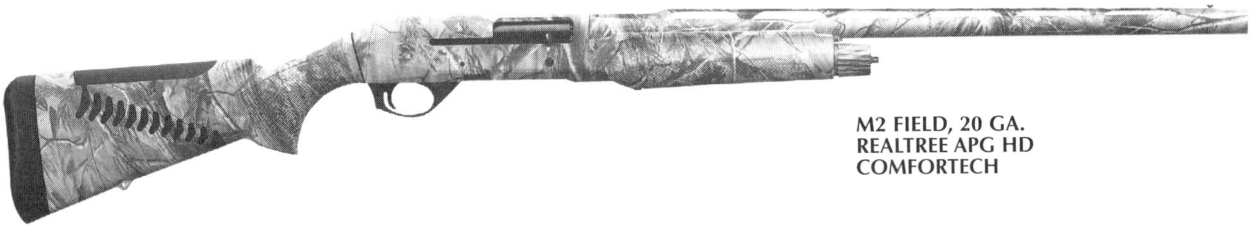

M2 FIELD, 20 GA.
REALTREE APG HD
COMFORTECH

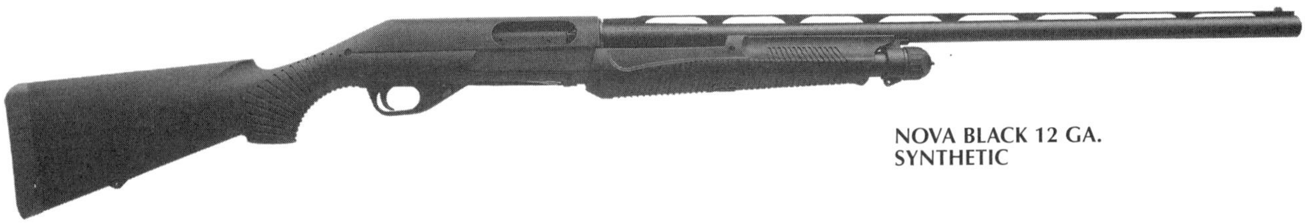

NOVA BLACK 12 GA.
SYNTHETIC

M2 FIELD - 12 GA.

Action: inertia operated semi-auto
Stock: synthetic, satin walnut, APG or Max 4
Barrel: 21, 24, 26 or 28 in.
Chokes: screw-in crio tube
Weight: 6.9-7.1 lbs.
Bore/Gauge: 12
Magazine: 3 + 1 rounds
Features: Comfortech recoil reduction; inertia operated; 3 in. chamber; dual lug rotating bolt

Walnut: $1269
Synthetic: $1319
Camo: $1429
Steady Grip $1489

M2 FIELD - 20 GA.

Action: inertia operated semi-auto
Stock: synthetic or Realtree APG HD
Barrel: 24 and 26 in.
Chokes: screw-in crio tube
Weight: 5.7-5.5 lbs.
Bore/Gauge: 20
Magazine: 3 + 1 rounds
Features: Comfortech recoil reduction system; Inertia operated; 3 in. chamber; optional Comfortech gel recoil pads to adjust LOP

Black synthetic: $1379
APG: $1489

NOVA - 12 GA.

Action: pump
Stock: synthetic or camo
Barrel: 24, 26 or 28 in.
Chokes: screw-in tubes
Weight: 8.1 lbs
Bore/Gauge: 12
Magazine: 4 rounds
Features: 3.5-inch magnum chamber; molded polymer (steel reinforced) one- piece stock and receiver; rotating bolt locks into steel barrel extension; screw-in choke tubes (IC, M, F); available in Max-4 HD or APG HD camo

Synthetic: $449
Camo: $529

SHOTGUNS

Benelli Shotguns

NOVA PUMP
REALTREE APG HD

NOVA PUMP YOUTH, 20 GA.
SHORT STOCK, SYNTHETIC

NOVA H_2O PUMP

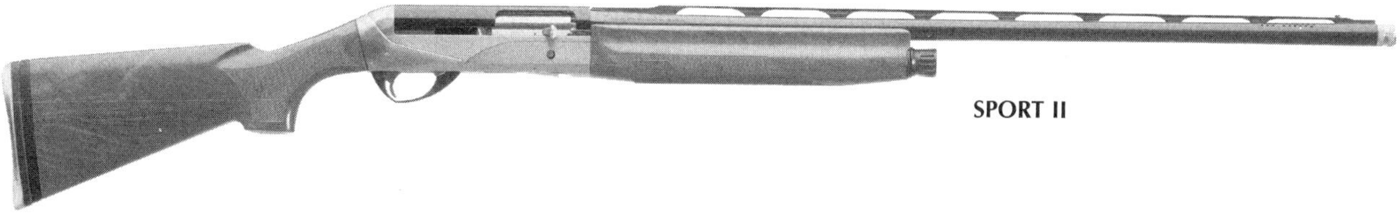

SPORT II

NOVA - 20 GA.

Action: pump
Stock: synthetic or APG Realtree
Barrel: 24 or 26 in.
Chokes: screw-in tubes
Weight: 6.6 lbs
Bore/Gauge: 20
Magazine: 4 rounds
Features: 3-inch magnum chamber; molded polymer (steel reinforced) one-piece stock and receiver; rotating steel bolt locks into steel barrel extension; screw-in choke tubes (IC, M, F)
Synthetic: $459
Realtree APG HD: $559
Youth: $459

NOVA H_2O PUMP

Action: pump
Stock: synthetic
Barrel: 18.5 in.
Chokes: cylinder, fixed
Weight: 7.2 lbs.
Bore/Gauge: 12
Magazine: 4 + 1 rounds
Features: matte nickel finish; open rifle sights
MSRP: $629

SPORT II

Action: inertia operated semi-auto
Stock: select walnut, with spacers to adjust drop, cast
Barrel: 28 or 30 in.
Sights: red bar on tapered stepped rib
Chokes: screw-in extended crio tubes
Weight: 7.5 lbs. (12 ga.) 6.3 (20 ga.)
Bore/Gauge: 12, 20
Magazine: 4+1 rounds
Features: ultra-reliable operating system; hammer-forged, ported, cryo barrel; light and heavy loads interchangeably without adjustment; extended screw-in crio tubes (C, IC, M, IM, F); select walnut stock with spacers to adjust drop & cast; red bar sight
MSRP: $1759

Benelli Shotguns

SUPER BLACK EAGLE II WITH SCOPE
STEADYGRIP, APG

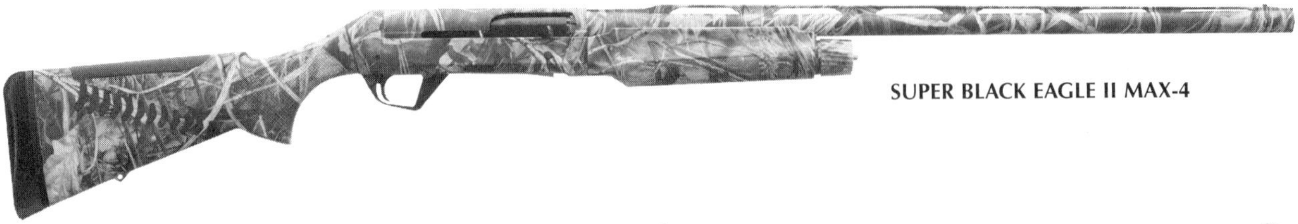

SUPER BLACK EAGLE II MAX-4

SUPER BLACK EAGLE II, 12 GA.
COMFORTECH, APG, SLUG

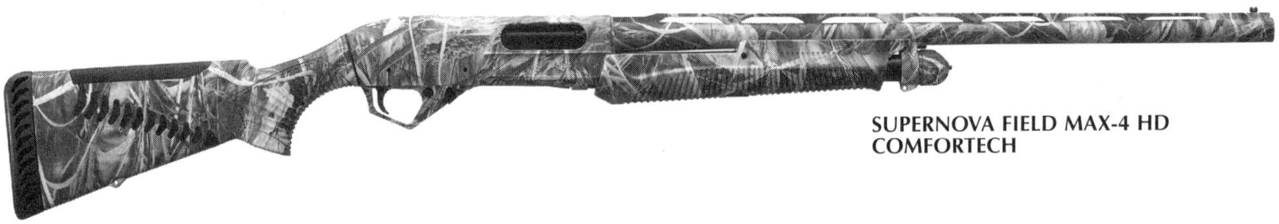

SUPERNOVA FIELD MAX-4 HD
COMFORTECH

SUPER BLACK EAGLE II

Action: inertia operated semi-auto
Stock: synthetic, walnut, APG or Max-4
Barrel: 24, 26 or 28 in.
Chokes: screw-in Crio tubes
Weight: 7.2 lbs.
Bore/Gauge: 12
Magazine: 3+1 rounds
Features: Comfortech recoil reduction system; Crio barrel; 3½ in. chamber; drilled & tapped receiver; SteadyGrip stock option for one-hand control
Walnut: $1609
Synthetic Comfortech: $1649
APG, MAX-4: $1759
Steady Grip:. $1839

SUPER BLACK EAGLE II, COMFORTECH SLUG GUN

Action: inertia operated semi-auto
Stock: synthetic or APG
Barrel: 24 in.
Chokes: none
Weight: 7.4 lbs. (slug);
Bore/Gauge: 12
Magazine: 3+1 rounds
Features: available with fully rifled slug barrel with 3in. chamber; drilled and tapped receiver; Comfortech recoil reduction system; inertia-operated; adjustable sights; optional high comb; stock in Realtree APG HD camo
Rifled: $1879

SUPERNOVA FIELD

Action: pump
Stock: synthetic
Barrel: 24, 26 or 28 in.
Chokes: screw-in tubes
Weight: 7.8-8.0 lbs.
Bore/Gauge: 12
Magazine: 4+1rounds
Features: two-lug rotary bolt; lightweight steel skeleton frame over-molded with high-tech polymer; dual-action bars; 2 ¾, 3 and 3 ½-in. chambers; Comfortech recoil reduction system; optional SteadyGrip stock; stock available in Realtree APG HD, Advantage Max-4 HD camo. screw-in choke tubes (IC, M, F)
SuperNova ComforTech: $529
SuperNova ComforTech Camo (APG or Max-4): $639
SuperNova SteadyGrip: $659
SuperNova SteadyGrip, APG HD: $659

Benelli Shotguns

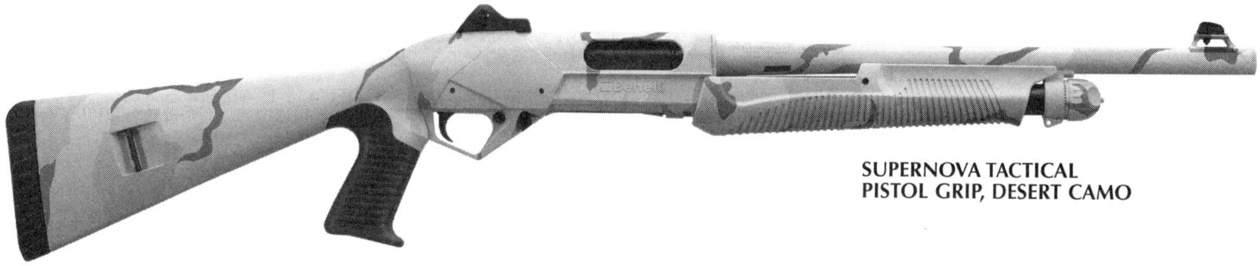

SUPERNOVA TACTICAL
PISTOL GRIP, DESERT CAMO

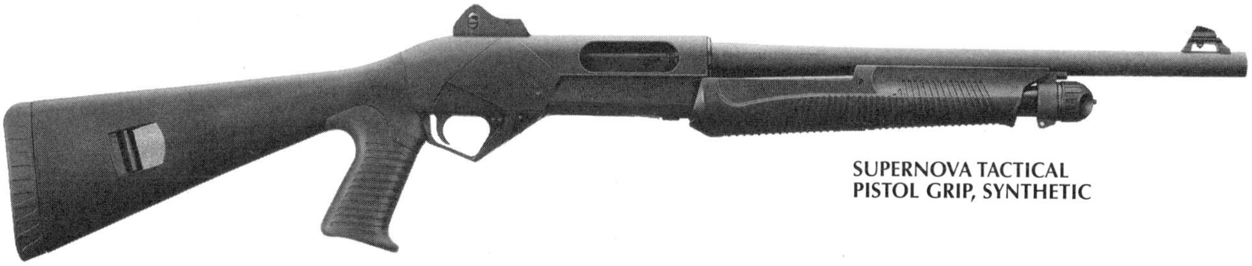

SUPERNOVA TACTICAL
PISTOL GRIP, SYNTHETIC

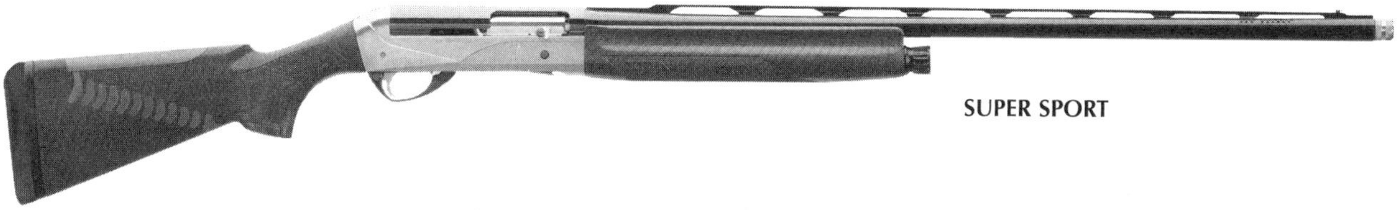

SUPER SPORT

ULTRA LIGHT 20-GAUGE

SUPERNOVA TACTICAL

Action: pump
Stock: synthetic
Barrel: 18 in.
Chokes: fixed cyl.
Weight: 7.8 lbs.
Bore/Gauge: 12
Magazine: 4+1rounds
Features: rotary bolt; $2^{3}/_{4}$, 3 and $3^{1}/_{2}$-in. chambers; open rifle sights or ghost ring rear sight with optional 3-dot tritium inserts; receiver drilled and tapped for scope mounting; stock available with ComforTech and pistol grip in black synthetic or Desert Camo.
SuperNova Tactical, Comfortech: $489
SuperNova Tactical, Pistol Grip: $499
SuperNova Tactical, Desert Camo: $619

SUPER SPORT

Action: inertia operated semi-auto
Stock: synthetic
Barrel: 28 or 30 in.
Chokes: screw-in extended crio tubes
Weight: 7.2 lbs. (12) 6.4 (20)
Bore/Gauge: 12, 20
Magazine: 4 rounds
Features: Comfortech recoil reduction system; ported Crio barrel; inertia operated; 3 in. chamber; rotating bolt with dual lugs; Carbon Fiber synthetic stock application; Shellview in 20 ga.
MSRP: $2069

ULTRA LIGHT 20-GAUGE

Action: inertia operated semi-auto
Stock: walnut
Barrel: 24 in.
Chokes: screw-in tube
Weight: 5.2 lbs.
Bore/Gauge: 20
Magazine: 2+1 rounds
Features: carbon-fiber vent rib; Crio barrel; chambered for 2-$^{3}/_{4}$ and 3-in. shells; Crio tube chokes - IC, M, F; WeatherCoat finished stock; lightest 20-gauge auto made!
MSRP: $1539

SHOTGUNS

Beretta Shotguns

MODEL 471 EL SILVER HAWK

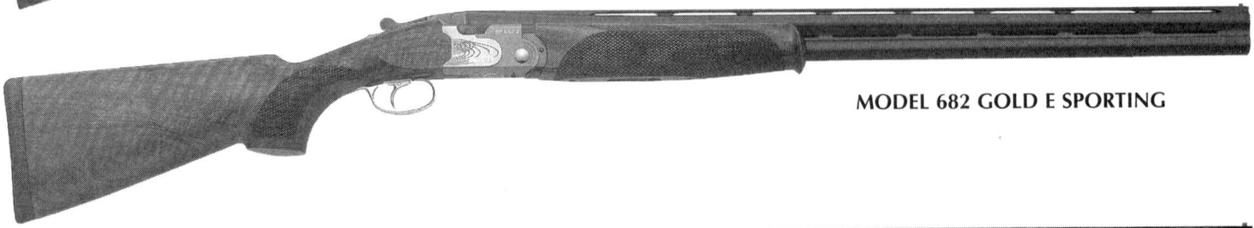

MODEL 682 GOLD E SPORTING

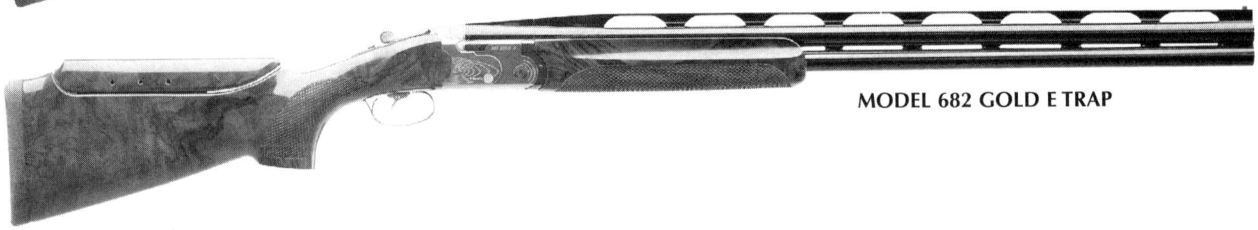

MODEL 682 GOLD E TRAP

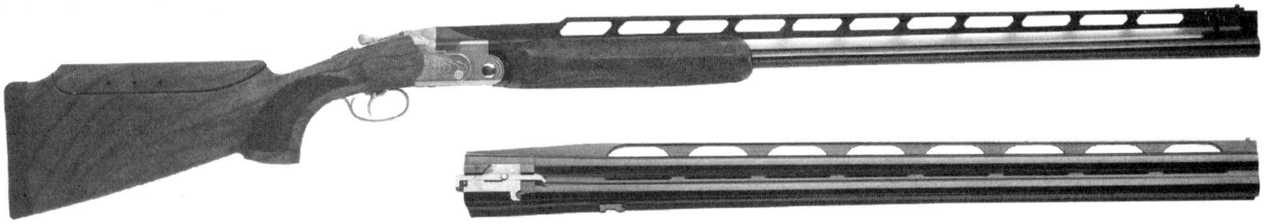

MODEL 682 GOLD E TRAP
BOTTOM SINGLE

MODELS 471 & 471 EL SILVER HAWK

Action: side-by-side
Stock: walnut
Barrel: 26 or 28 in.
Chokes: 12 Gauge Optima Chokes, 20 Gauge Mobilechokes or fixed chokes
Weight: 6.5 lbs. (5.9 lbs. 20 ga.)
Bore/Gauge: 12, 20
Magazine: none
Features: boxlock; satin chromed or case-colored receiver; single selective trigger or double triggers; automatic ejectors; EL has case-colored receiver; gold inlay; straight or pistol grips
Model 471:. $3850

MODEL 682 GOLD E

Action: over/under
Stock: walnut
Barrel: 28, 30 or 32 in.
Chokes: screw-in tubes
Weight: 7.5-8.8 lbs.
Bore/Gauge: 12
Magazine: none
Features: boxlock; single selective adjustable trigger; automatic ejectors; adjustable combs on Skeet and Trap models
Sporting: $4250
Skeet: $4450
Trap: $5150

MODEL 682 GOLD E TRAP BOTTOM SINGLE

Action: over/under
Stock: walnut
Barrel: 30, 34 or 32 in.
Chokes: screw-in tubes
Weight: 6.5 lbs.
Bore/Gauge: 12
Magazine: none
Features: boxlock; single selective adjustable trigger; automatic ejectors; fully adjustable unsingle rib; combo versions available with 34 in. unsingle w/ 30 in. O/U and 34 in. unsingle w/ 32 in. O/U barrels; adjustable comb
Bottom Single:. $4350
Bottom Single Combo 30/34: $5150
Bottom Single Combo 32/34: $5150

MODEL 686 ONYX SERIES

Action: over/under
Stock: walnut
Barrel: 26, 28 or 30 in.
Chokes: screw-in tubes
Weight: 6.8-7.7lbs. (12 ga.)
Bore/Gauge: 12, 20, 28, .410
Magazine: none
Features: boxlock; 3 in. chambers; single selective trigger; automatic ejectors; 3.5 has 3½ in. chambers
White Onyx Sporting: $2275

Beretta Shotguns

MODEL 686 WHITE ONYX SPORTING

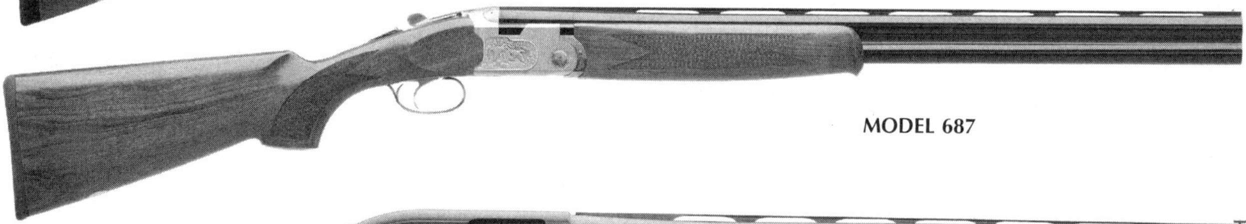

MODEL 687

3901 AMERICAN STATESMAN

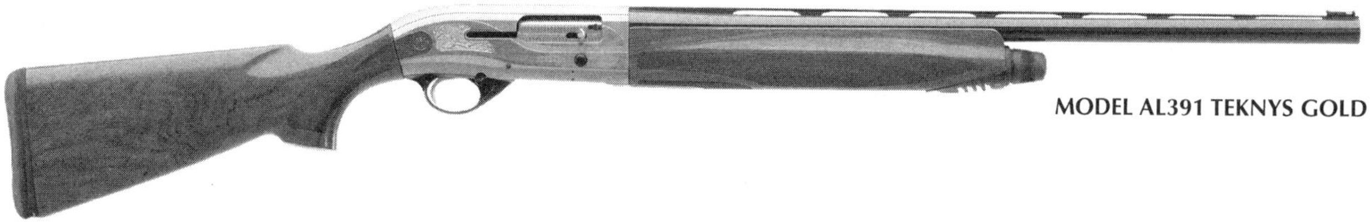

MODEL AL391 TEKNYS GOLD

MODEL 687 PIGEON SERIES

Action: over/under
Stock: walnut
Barrel: 26, 28, 30 in.
Chokes: screw-in tubes
Weight: 6.8 lbs. (12 ga.)
Bore/Gauge: 12, 20, 20/28 & 28/.410 Combo
Magazine: none
Features: boxlock; 3-inch chambers; single selective trigger; automatic ejectors;
Silver Pigeon II: $3050
Silver Pigeon III: $3175
EELL Diamond Pigeon: $7650

3901 AMERICAN SERIES

Action: autoloader
Stock: walnut or synthetic
Barrel: 24 (rifled),26 or 28 in.
Chokes: screw-in tubes
Weight: 6.6 (20 ga.); 7.4 - 7.6 lbs.
Bore/Gauge: 12, 20
Magazine: 3 rounds
Features: steel alloy, hammer forged barrel; self-compensating gas operation; 3-in. chamber; Gel-Tek & Tru-Glo sights (Ambassador); adjustable comb (Target RL only); Mobil-choke (F, M. IC); stock shim
Citizen: $743
Rifled Slug: $787
Statesman: $905
Target RL: $972

MODEL AL391 TEKNYS

Action: autoloader
Stock: walnut
Barrel: 26, 28, 30 or 32 in.
Chokes: screw-in tubes
Weight: 7.3 lbs. (12 ga.), 5.9 lbs. (20 ga.)
Bore/Gauge: 12, 20
Magazine: 3 rounds
Features: self-compensating gas system; reversible cross-bolt safety; Optima-Bore overbored barrels (12 ga.); Optima Choke flush tubes; Gold target model with additional stepped rib
AL391 Teknys Gold: $2075

Beretta Shotguns

AL 391 URIKA 2
X-TRA GRAIN

AL 391 URIKA 2
GOLD

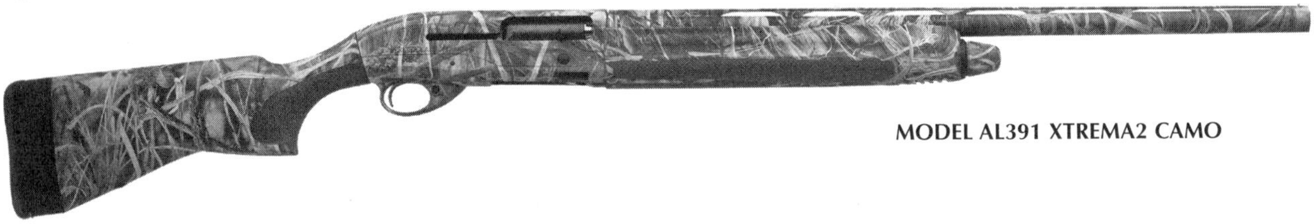

MODEL AL391 XTREMA2 CAMO

MODEL DT 10 TRIDENT

AL 391 URIKA 2

Action: autoloader
Stock: X-tra Grain wood finish
Barrel: 22, 24, 26, 28 or 30 in.
Chokes: Mobilchoke, Optimachoke and/or Cylinder choke
Weight: 5.7-6.6 lbs.
Bore/Gauge: 12 or 20
Magazine: 3 rounds
Features: gas operation system with self-cleaning and self-compensating valve; 3 in. chamber; receivers of Urika 2 Gold models engraved with "gold" game scenes; Classic and Gold models available with slug barrel, short rib with ramp, V-shape rear sight and anti-glare front sight
Urika 2 Classic: $1125–1500
Urika 2 Gold: $1400

MODEL A391 XTREMA2

Action: autoloader
Stock: synthetic
Barrel: 26, 28 in.
Chokes: screw-in tubes
Weight: 7.8 lbs.
Bore/Gauge: 12
Magazine: 3 + 1 rounds
Features: 3½ in. chambers; self-cleaning gas system; Kick-Off recoil reduction; spring/mass recoil reducer; Gel-Tek; Aqua Technology; stock adjustment shims; quick-detach sling swivel
Synthetic: $1257
Camo: $1257

MODEL DT 10 TRIDENT

Action: over/under
Stock: walnut
Barrel: 28, 30, 32 or 34 in.
Chokes: screw-in tubes
Weight: 8 - 8.8 lbs.
Bore/Gauge: 12
Magazine: none
Features: boxlock; single selective trigger; automatic ejectors; Skeet, Trap and Sporting models are Beretta's best competition guns; combo with top single or bottom single; Trap versions available
Sporting: $7650
Trap, Bottom Single: $8650

KING RANCH SERIES

Action: over/under
Stock: walnut, oil finish
Barrel: 26, 28 in.
Chokes: Mobilchoke
Weight: various
Bore/Gauge: 12, 20, 28
Magazine: 2 rounds
Features: engraving motifs derived from King Ranch executed on popular Beretta models; Limited Editions
686 Silver Pigeon S: $2800
687 Silver Pigeon IV: $3780
687 Diamond Pigeon EELL: . . $7650

Beretta Shotguns

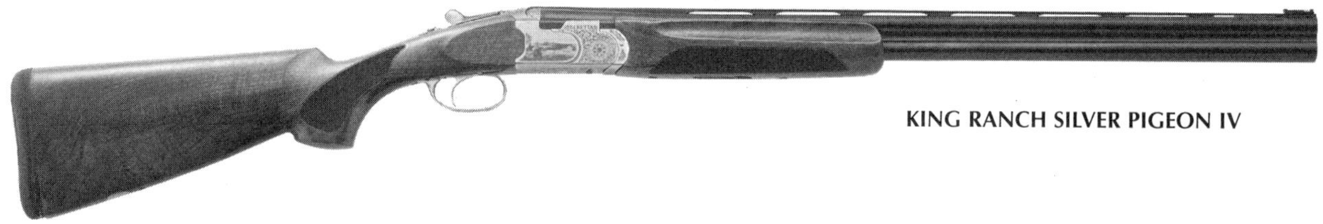

KING RANCH SILVER PIGEON IV

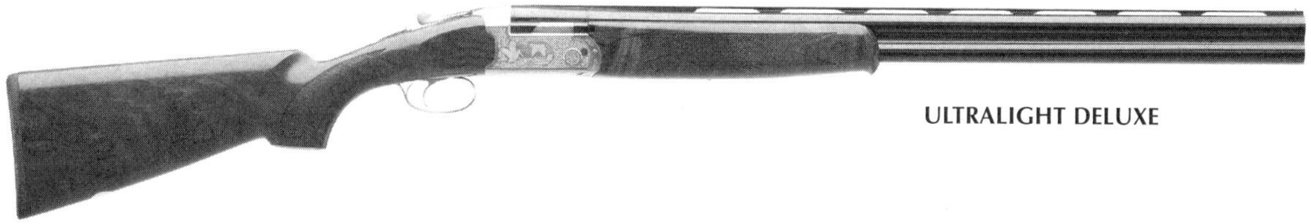

ULTRALIGHT DELUXE

SV10 PERENNIA

UGB25 XCEL

SV10 PERENNIA

Action: over/under
Stock: walnut
Barrel: 26 or 28 in.
Chokes: screw-in tubes
Weight: 7.3 lbs.
Bore/Gauge: 12
Magazine: none
Features: Optima-Bore high-performance cold, hammer-forged barrels; long guided extractors; chrome-lined bore and chamber; manual or auto matic shell extraction; single selective trigger group; automatic safety; Optimachoke choke tubes; available with or without Kick-Off technology; semi-beavertail fore-end with constant fit fore-end iron; 3rd generation Beretta Over/Under to be launched
MSRP (with Kick-Off): $3650
(without Kick-Off): $3250

UGB25 XCEL

Action: break-open semi-auto
Stock: walnut
Barrel: 30 in.
Chokes: screw-in tubes
Weight: 8.1-9 lbs.
Bore/Gauge: 12
Magazine: 1 (in side carrier)
Features: short barrel recoil system; light alloy receiver; Optima-Bore barrel with lengthened forcing cone; locking system with break-open action for safe operation — second round is visible in side cartridge carrier; 2¾ in. chambers; select walnut stock with water-resistant finish; adjustable drop, cast-on and cast-off; fore-end with extended checkered configuration; comes in case with accesories
MSRP: $3500–3650

ULTRALIGHT SERIES

Action: O/U, improved box lock
Stock: select walnut
Barrel: 28 in.
Chokes: screw-in tubes (Mobilchoke)
Weight: 5.75 lbs.
Bore/Gauge: 12
Magazine: none
Features: aluminum, titanium-reinforced frame; single selective trigger; automatic safety; 2¾ in. chamber; Schnabel fore-end; checkered stock; gold inlay
Ultralight: $2075
Ultralight Deluxe: $2450

Bernardelli Shotguns

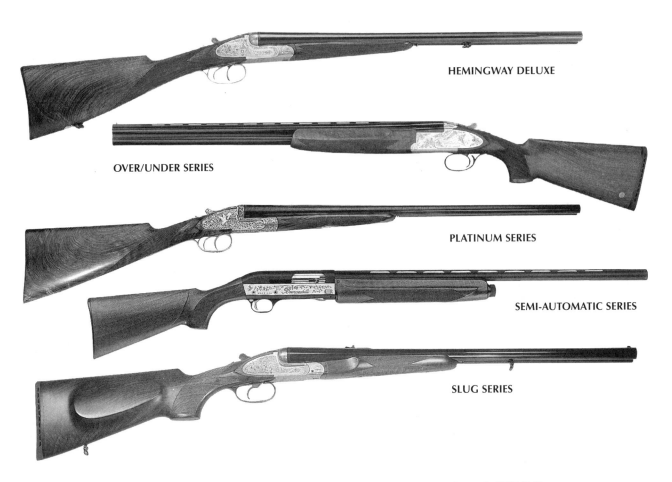

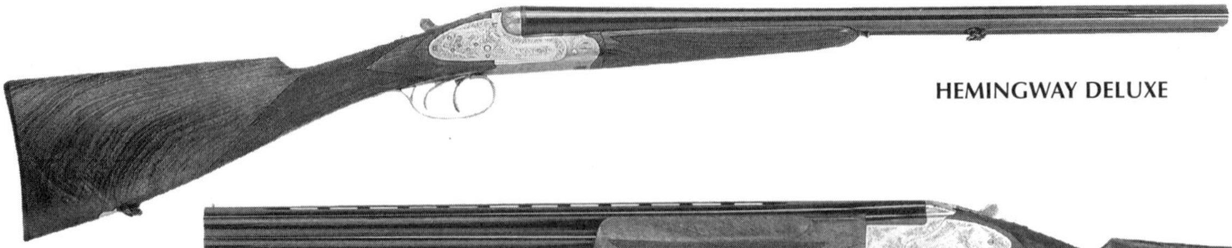

HEMINGWAY DELUXE

OVER/UNDER SERIES

PLATINUM SERIES

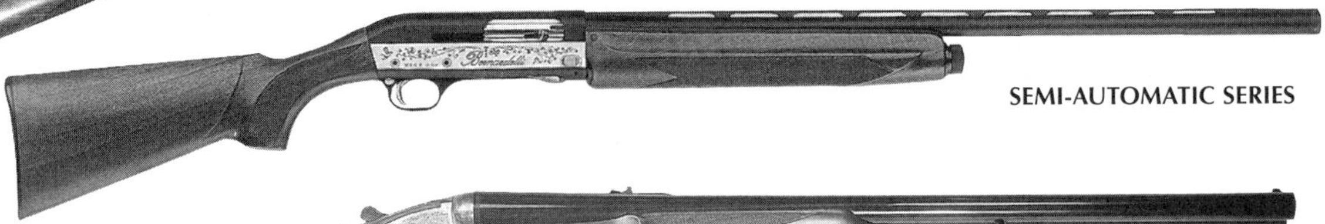

SEMI-AUTOMATIC SERIES

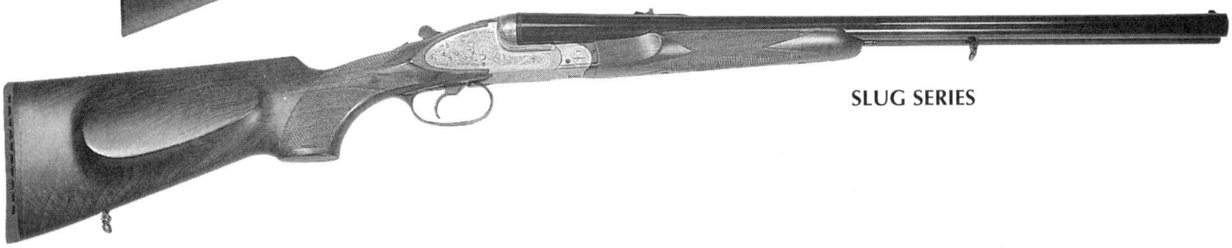

SLUG SERIES

HEMINGWAY DELUXE

Action: side-by-side
Stock: walnut, straight grip
Barrel: 26 in.
Chokes: modified, improved modified, full
Weight: 6.25 lbs.
Bore/Gauge: 16, 20, 28
Magazine: none
Features: boxlock double; single or double trigger; automatic ejectors
MSRP: . . . . price on request

OVER/UNDER SERIES

Action: over/under
Stock: walnut, pistol grip
Barrel: 26 or 28 in.
Chokes: modified, improved modified, full, screw-in tubes
Weight: 7.2 lbs.
Bore/Gauge: 12, 20
Magazine: none
Features: boxlock over/under; single or double triggers; vent rib, various grades
MSRP: . . . . price on request

PLATINUM SERIES

Action: side-by-side
Stock: walnut, straight or pistol grip
Barrel: 26 or 28 in.
Chokes: modified, improved modified, full
Weight: 6.5 lbs.
Bore/Gauge: 12
Magazine: none
Features: sidelock double; articulated single selective or double trigger; triple-lug Purdey breeching automatic ejectors; various grades
MSRP: . . . . price on request

SEMI-AUTOMATIC SERIES

Action: autoloader
Stock: walnut, synthetic or camo
Barrel: 24, 26 or 28 in.
Chokes: screw-in tubes
Weight: 6.7 lbs.
Bore/Gauge: 12
Magazine: 5 rounds
Features: gas-operated; concave top rib; ABS case included
MSRP: . . . . price on request

SLUG SERIES

Action: side-by-side
Stock: walnut, pistol grip
Barrel: 24 in.
Chokes: modified, improved modified, full
Weight: 7.0 lbs.
Bore/Gauge: 12
Magazine: none
Features: boxlock double; single or double trigger; automatic ejectors; rifle sights
MSRP: . . . . price on request

Blaser Shotguns

BLASER F3 28-GAUGE

Action: over/under, hinged breech
Stock: European walnut
Barrel: 28″, 30″ or 32″
Chokes: Briley Spectrum
Weight: 7 lbs.
Bore/Gauge: 28 gauge
Magazine: none
Features: Blaser introduces a 28-gauge to their F3 over/under shotgun line, including 12-bores (shown above) offered in Competition and Game models.
MSRP: . . . . from $6197

Browning Shotguns

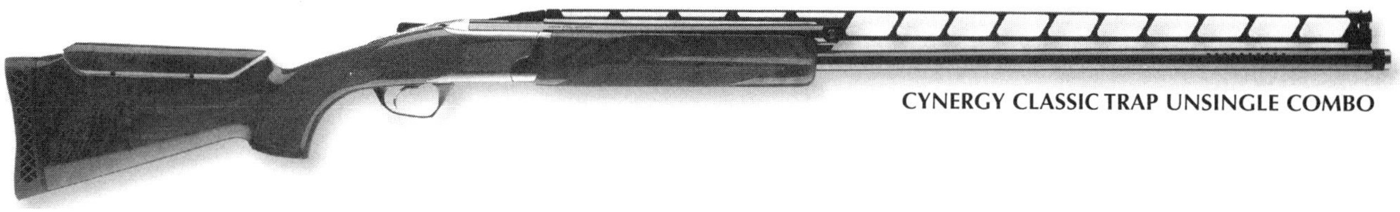

CYNERGY CLASSIC TRAP UNSINGLE COMBO

BROWNING MAXUS STALKER AND MAXUS DUCK BLIND

Action: autoloading, gas operated
Stock: matte black composite (Duck blind camo composite)
Barrel: 26″ or 28″
Chokes: interchangeable
Weight: 6 lbs. 14 oz.
Bore/Gauge: 12 gauge
Magazine: tube
Features: Flat, ventilated rib. 3″ and 3 ½″ chamber models.
Maxus Stalker: . . . . $1199-$1379
Duck Blind: . . . . $1339-$1509

CYNERGY CLASSIC TRAP UNSINGLE COMBO

Action: single-shot and over/under
Stock: walnut
Barrel: 32/34, 32/32, 30/34 and 30/3-in. combinations
Chokes: interchangable tubes
Weight: 8 lbs. 13 ozs., 8 lbs. 15 ozs.
Bore/Gauge: 12
Magazine: none
Features: barrel set: single barrel with adjustable Unsingle Rib and over/under barrel; Monolock hinge low-profile receiver; Reverse Striker ignition system; 4 Invector Plus Midas Grade choke tubes; HiViz Pro-Comp fiber optic sights; gloss-finish Monte Carlo grade III/IV walnut stocks; aluminum case
MSRP: $3999

Browning Shotguns

L.C. SMITH .410, 28-GAUGE

Action: side-by-side, hinged breech
Stock: checkered walnut, pistol grip, semi-beavertail
Barrels: 26″, solid rib
Chokes: 3 tubes supplied
Weight: 6 ½ lbs.
Bore/Gauge: .410, 3″ or 28 ga.
Magazine: none
Features: box-lock action with engraved, case-colored side-plates, European manufacture, single selective trigger, automatic ejectors. Also: 12- and 20-gauge 3″ models, and 12- and 20-gauge 3″ over/under models.
MSRP: . . . . available on request

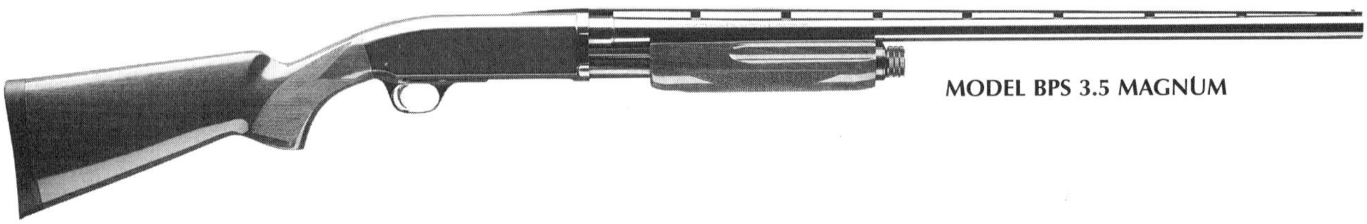

MODEL BPS 3.5 MAGNUM

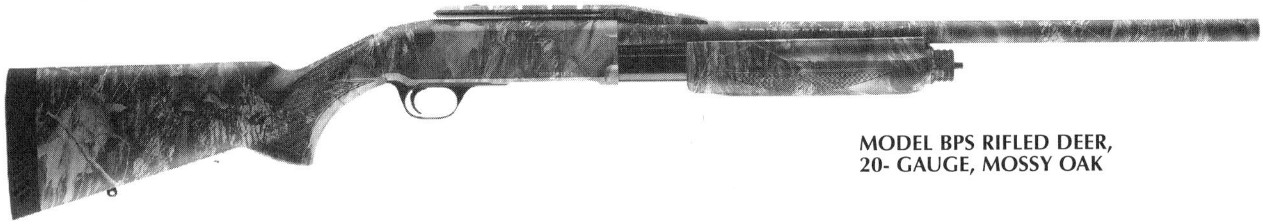

MODEL BPS RIFLED DEER, 20- GAUGE, MOSSY OAK

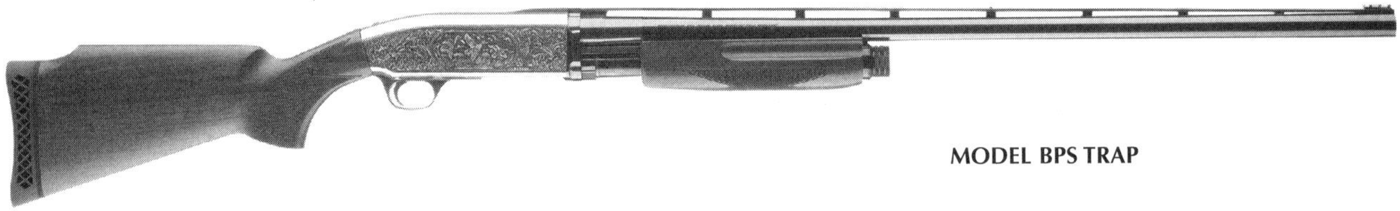

MODEL BPS TRAP

MODEL BPS

Action: pump
Stock: walnut or synthetic
Barrel: 20, 22, 24, 26, 28 or 30 in.
Chokes: screw-in tubes
Weight: 8.0 lbs.
Bore/Gauge: 10, 12, 20, 28, .410
Magazine: 4 rounds
Features: Both 10 and 12 ga. available with 3 in. chambers; Upland Special has short barrel, straight grip; Deer Special has rifled barrel; Micro BPS has short barrel, stock
Stalker (synthetic):. $579–709
Hunter (walnut): $599–639
Upland Special: $569–609
Micro (20): $599
Rifled Deer (12): $739

MODEL BPS RIFLED DEER, 20-GA.

Action: bottom-ejection pump
Stock: satin finish walnut or composite
Barrel: 22 in.; rifled
Chokes: none
Weight: 7.3 lbs.
Bore/Gauge: 20
Magazine: 2¾ in: 4+1;
3 and 3½ in.: 3+1
Features: Satin wood or Mossy Oak New Break-Up camo finish with Dura-Touch armor coating. Included is a cantilever scope base for consistent accuracy, even if the barrel is removed and reinstalled.
Mossy Oak: $749

MODEL BPS TRAP

Action: bottom-ejection pump
Stock: satin finish walnut
Barrel: 30 in.
Chokes: 3 Invector-Plus choke tubes
Weight: 8.1 lbs.
Bore/Gauge: 12
Magazine: 2¾in: 4+1;
3 and 3½ in.: 3+1
Features: bottom feed, bottom eject system; magazine cut-off; HiViz TriComp fiber optic sight; top tang safety; available in standard and youth models.
MSRP: $759

Browning Shotguns

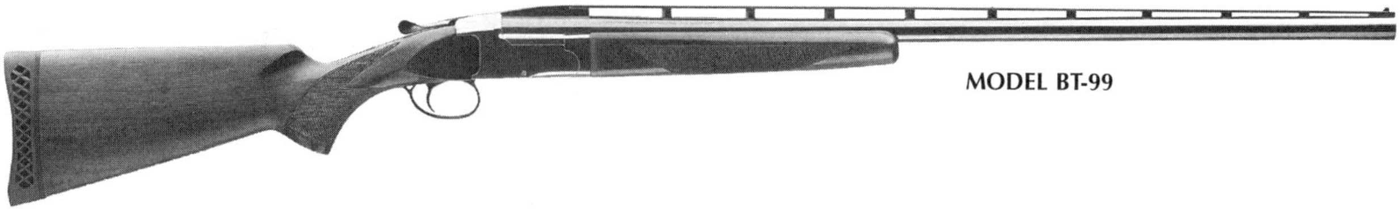

MODEL BT-99

CITORI COMPETITION

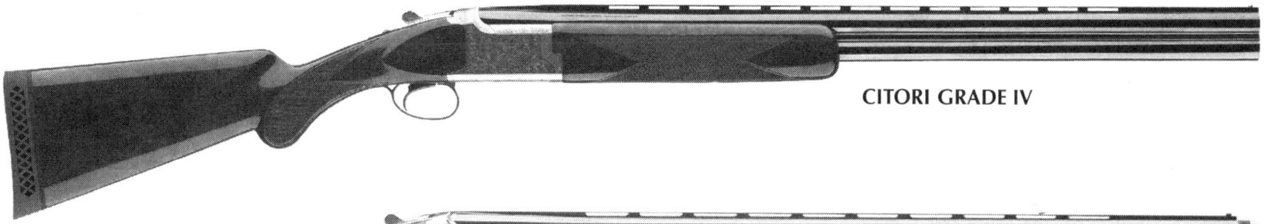

CITORI GRADE IV

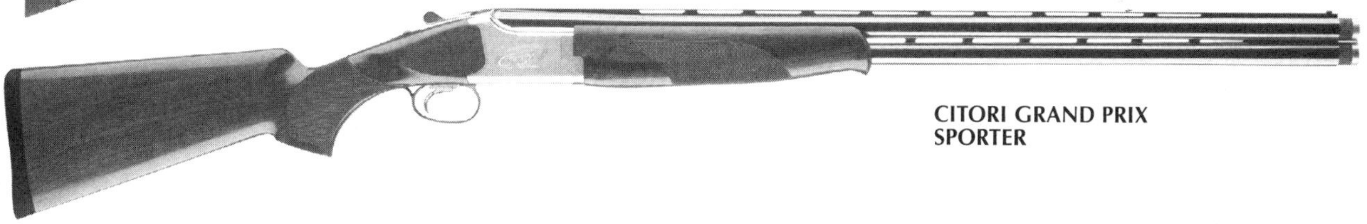

CITORI GRAND PRIX SPORTER

MODEL BT-99

Action: hinged single-shot
Stock: walnut, trap-style
Barrel: 30, 32 or 34 in.
Chokes: screw-in tubes
Weight: 8.0 lbs.
Bore/Gauge: 12 ***Magazine:*** none
Features: boxlock single-shot competition gun with high-post rib
BT-99: $1399
With adjustable comb: $7599
Micro: $1339
Golden Clays with adjustable comb: $3999

CITORI COMPETITION

Action: over/under
Stock: walnut
Barrel: 26, 28 or 30 in.
Chokes: screw-in tubes
Weight: 8.0 lbs.
Bore/Gauge: 12
Magazine: none
Features: boxlock; XS Pro-Comp has ported barrels, adjustable stock comb, GraCoil recoil reducer; Trap and Skeet Models are stocked and barreled accordingly
XT Trap: $2789
XT Trap with adjustable comb: $3399
XT Trap Gold with adjustable comb: $5179
XS Skeet: $2989
XS Skeet with adjustable comb: $3319

CITORI GRADE IV AND VII LIGHTNING

Action: over/under
Stock: select walnut
Barrel: 26 and 28 in., back-bored, 3 in. chambers in 12, 20 and .410
Chokes: screw-in tubes
Weight: 6.5-8.0 lbs.
Bore/Gauge: 12, 20, 28 and .410
Magazine: none
Features: Boxlock action with automatic ejectors; engraved receivers
12, 20 Grade IV: $3179
28, .410 Grade IV:.......... $3229
12, 20 Grade VII: $5039
28, .410 Grade VII:......... $5109

CITORI GRAND PRIX SPORTER

Action: over/under
Stock: oil finish walnut
Barrel: 28, 30 or 32 in.
Chokes: 5 Invector-Plus Midas Grade choke tubes
Weight: 8.1-8.5 lbs.
Bore/Gauge: 12
Magazine: none
Features: steel receiver with silver nitride finish; Browning's exclusive Selection Ejection System; lightweight, back-bored barrels; gold enhancements
MSRP: $3519

Browning Shotguns

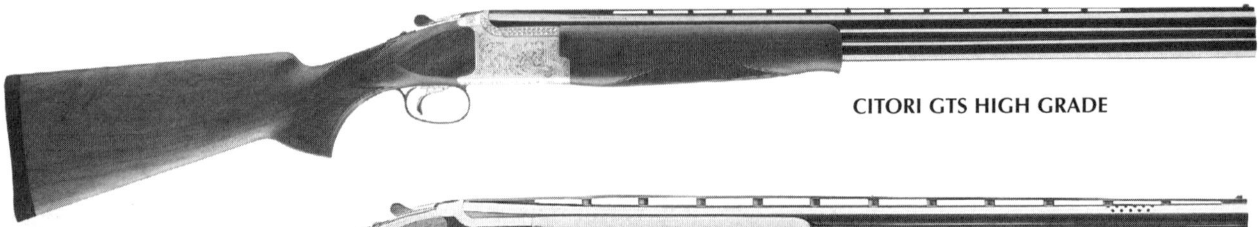
CITORI GTS HIGH GRADE

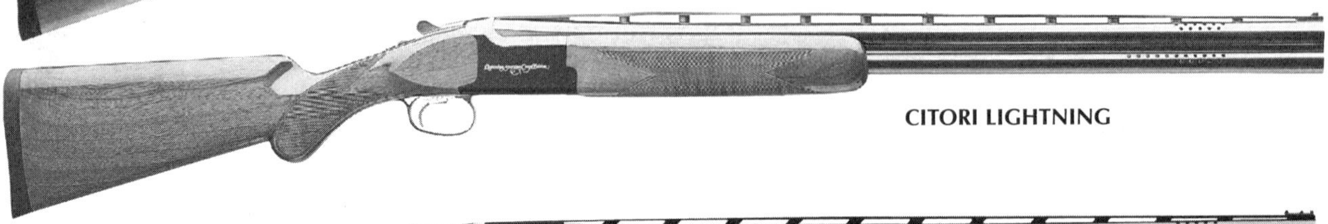
CITORI LIGHTNING

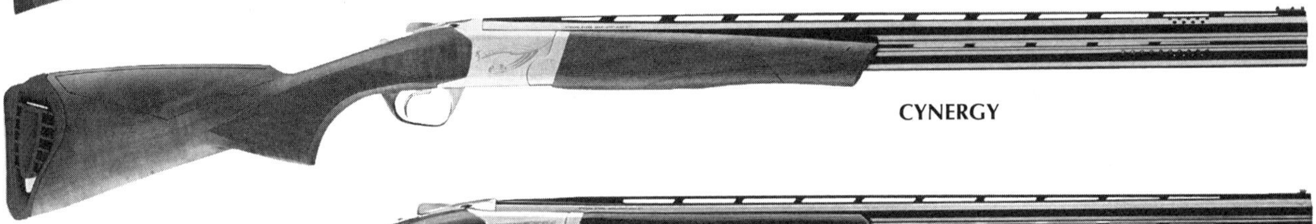
CYNERGY

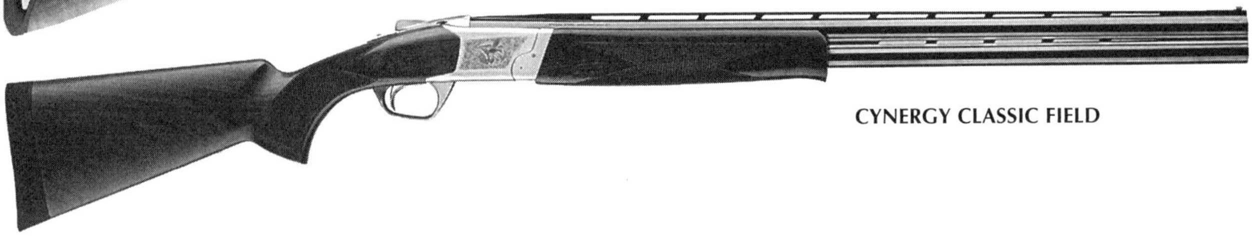
CYNERGY CLASSIC FIELD

CITORI GTS GRADE I

Action: over/under
Stock: oil finish grade II/III walnut
Barrel: 28 or 30 in.
Chokes: 5 Invector-Plus choke tubes
Weight: 8.1-8.3 lbs.
Bore/Gauge: 12
Magazine: none
Features: 3 in. chambers; steel receiver with silver nitride finish; engraving of a game bird transforming into a clay target; Triple Trigger System; HiViz Pro-Comp fiber-optic sight; ABS case included
MSRP: $2349

CITORI GTS HIGH GRADE

Action: over/under
Stock: oil finish grade III/IV walnut
Barrel: 28 or 30 in.
Chokes: 5 Invector-Plus choke tubes
Weight: 8.1-8.3 lbs.
Bore/Gauge: 12
Magazine: none
Features: 3 in. chambers; steel receiver with silver nitride finish; gold engraving of a game bird transforming into a clay target; Triple Trigger System; HiViz Pro-Comp fiber-optic sight; ABS case included
MSRP: $4309

CITORI LIGHTNING

Action: over/under
Stock: walnut
Barrel: 26 or 28 in.
Chokes: screw-in tubes
Weight: 6.3-8.0 lbs.
Bore/Gauge: 12, 20, 28, .410
Magazine: none
Features: boxlock; single selective trigger, automatic ejectors; higher grades available; ported barrels optional
Citori Lightning: $1869
Citori White Lightning: $1939
Citori Lightning Feather: $3699
Citori Superlight Feather: . . . $2359

CYNERGY

Action: box-lock over/under, with reverse striker firing mechanism
Stock: walnut, oil-finished and checkered, or composite, both with black recoil pad
Barrel: 26, 28, 30 or 32 in., fitted with removable choke tubes
Sights: double beads on tapered rib
Chokes: screw-in tubes (three provided)
Weight: 7.7 lbs.
Bore/Gauge: 12
Magazine: none
Features: single selective trigger; manual safety; selective ejectors
Cynergy: $2832
Also available:
20 & 28 ga.: $2923

CYNERGY CLASSIC FIELD

Action: over/under
Stock: walnut
Barrel: 26 or 28 in.
Chokes: screw-in tubes
Weight: 7.69-7.8 lbs
Bore/Gauge: 12
Magazine: none
Features: back-bored barrels; silver nitride receiver; impact ejectors; low profile Monolock hinge; mechanical triggers; Inflex recoil pad; conventional butt stock configuration; satin finish walnut stock; three Invector-Plus choke tubes
MSRP: $2399

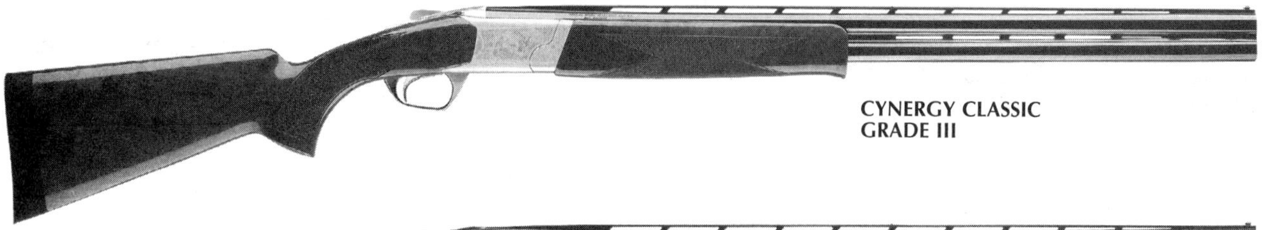

CYNERGY CLASSIC
GRADE III

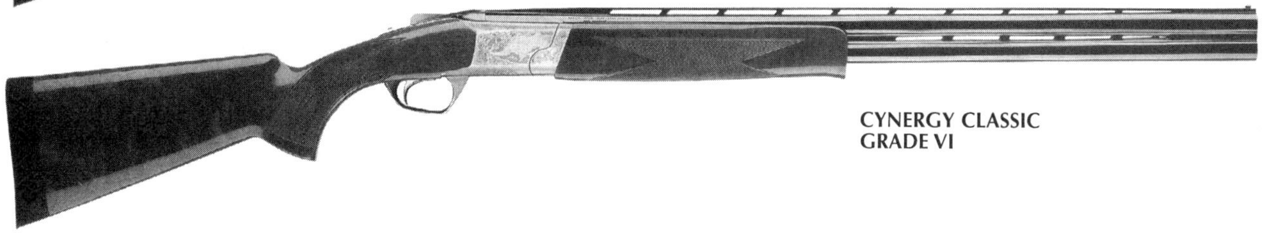

CYNERGY CLASSIC
GRADE VI

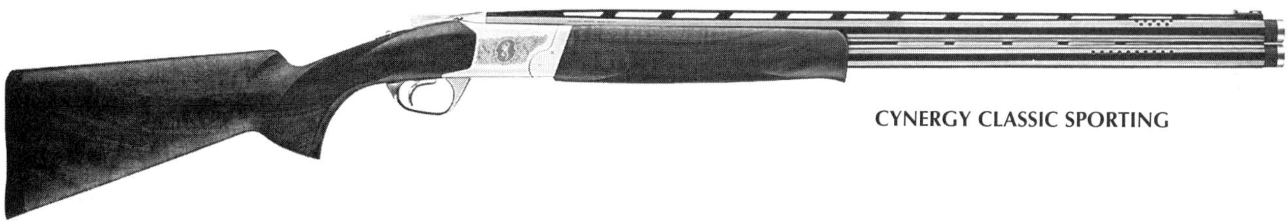

CYNERGY CLASSIC SPORTING

CYNERGY CLASSIC GRADE III

Action: over/under
Stock: gloss finish grade III/IV walnut
Barrel: 26 or 28 in.
Chokes: 3 Invector-Plus choke tubes
Weight: 6.5-8.1 lbs.
Bore/Gauge: 20 and 12
Magazine: none
Features: steel receiver with silver nitride finish; Reverse Striker ignition system; impact ejectors. Full receiver coverage with high-relief engraving. The 12 gauge depicts pheasants on the left side and mallards on the right, while the 20 gauge highlights teal on the left and partridge on the right side of the receiver. Recoil pad on the 12 ga. model.
Grade III, 12 ga.: $3099
Grade III, 20 ga.: $3739

CYNERGY CLASSIC GRADE VI

Action: over/under
Stock: gloss finish grade V/VI walnut
Barrel: 26 or 28 in.
Chokes: 3 Invector-Plus choke tubes
Weight: 6.5-8.1 lbs.
Bore/Gauge: 20 and 12
Magazine: none
Features: steel receiver with silver nitride finish; Reverse Striker ignition system; impact ejectors; ultra-low profile. Full coverage high-relief engraving is gold enhanced and includes the trigger guard, tang and lever. 12 ga. models illustrate pheasants on the right, mallards on the left. 20 ga. models feature quail and grouse. Recoil pad on the 12 ga. model.
Grade VI, 12 ga.: $5519
Grade VI, 20 ga.: $5549

CYNERGY CLASSIC SPORTING

Action: over/under
Stock: walnut
Barrel: 28, 30 or 32 in.
Chokes: screw-in tubes
Weight: 7.69-7.94 lbs.
Bore/Gauge: 12
Magazine: none
Features: steel, silver nitride receiver; ultra-low profile; MonoLock Hinge; grade III/IV walnut stock; 3 Invector-Plus Midas Grade choke tubes
MSRP: $3469

CYNERGY CLASSIC TRAP

Action: over/under
Stock: gloss finish Monte Carlo walnut
Barrel: 30 or 32 in.
Chokes: 3 Invector-Plus Midas Grade choke tubes
Weight: 8.7 lbs.
Bore/Gauge: 12
Magazine: none
Features: steel receiver with silver nitride finish; monolock hinge; mechanical triggers; chrome chambers; Reverse Striker ignition system; impact ejectors; ultra-low profile; modified semi-beavertail forearm with finger grooves; Inflex Recoil Pad System; HiViz Pro-Comp fiber-optic sight. Available in Monte Carlo or adjustable comb configurations.
Monte Carlo: $3739
Adjustable: $4069

Browning Shotguns

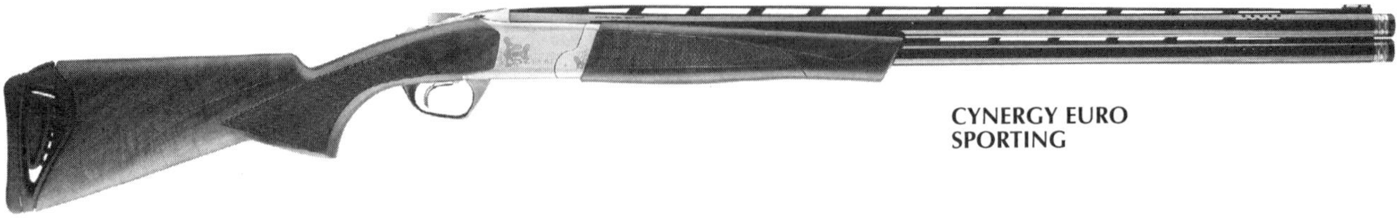

CYNERGY EURO SPORTING

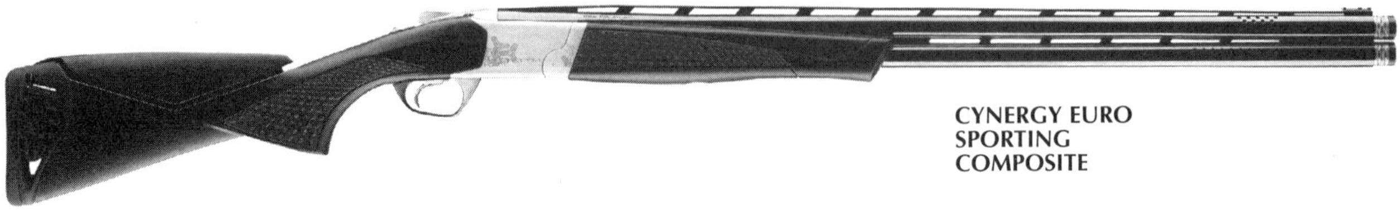

CYNERGY EURO SPORTING COMPOSITE

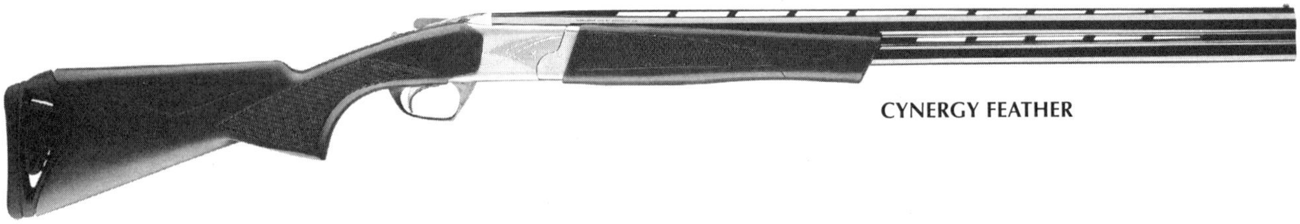

CYNERGY FEATHER

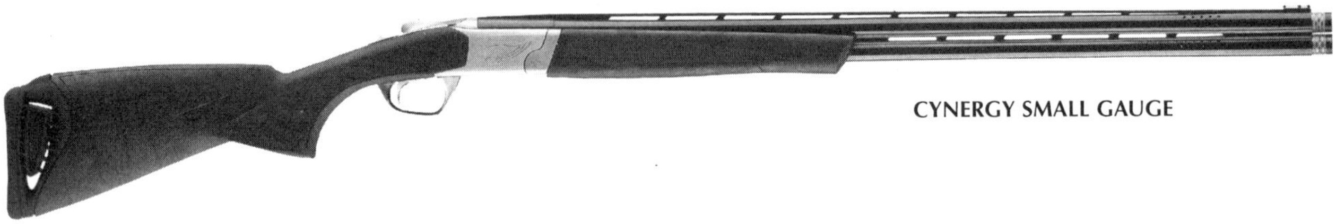

CYNERGY SMALL GAUGE

CYNERGY EURO SPORTING

Action: over/under
Stock: oil finish walnut or black composite
Barrel: 28, 30 or 32 in.
Chokes: 3 Invector-Plus Diana Grade choke tubes
Weight: 7.5-8.0 lbs.
Bore/Gauge: 12
Magazine: none
Features: steel receiver with silver nitride finish; gold enhanced engraving; Reverse Striker ignition system; impact ejectors; ultra-low profile; Inflex Recoil Pad System; HiViz Pro-Comp fiber-optic sight. Adjustable model has comb adjustment for cast and drop. Available in three models.
Sporting: $3249
Sporting Adjustable: $3291
Sporting Composite: $3080

CYNERGY FEATHER

Action: over/under
Stock: satin finish walnut or black composite
Barrel: 26 or 28 in.
Chokes: 3 Invector-Plus choke tubes
Weight: 6.5-6.7 lbs.
Bore/Gauge: 12
Magazine: none
Features: lightweight alloy receiver with steel breech face; gold enhanced grayed finish; ultra-low profile; MonoLock Hinge; Inflex Recoil Pad System
Feather: $2719
Feather Composite: $2659

CYNERGY SMALL GAUGE

Action: over/under
Stock: walnut
Barrel: 26 or 28 in. (Field), 30 or 32 in. (Sporting)
Chokes: screw-in tubes
Weight: 6.25-6.5 lbs
Bore/Gauge: 20 and 28
Magazine: none
Features: Boxlock action; 20 ga. comes with ported barrels; mechanical single trigger
Field: $2870
Sporting: $2953

GOLD

Action: autoloader
Stock: walnut (Hunter) or syn. (Stalker)
Barrel: 24, 26, 28 or 30 in.
Chokes: screw-in tubes
Weight: 8.0 lbs.
Bore/Gauge: 10, 12, 20
Magazine: 3 rounds
Features: gas-operated, 3½ in. chambers on 10 and one 12 ga. version; Youth and Ladies' versions available
Gold Light (10 ga.): $1619

Browning Shotguns

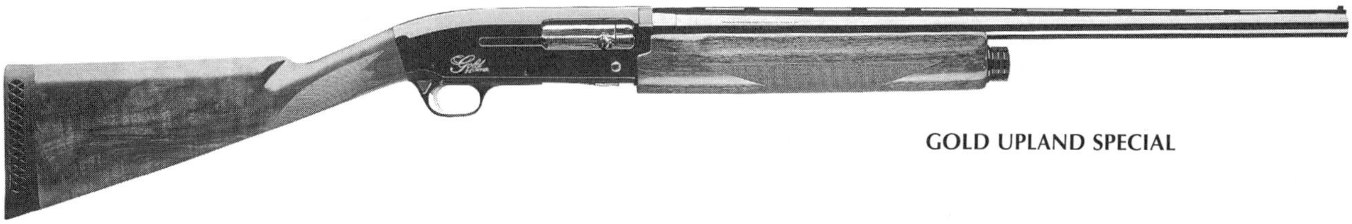

GOLD UPLAND SPECIAL

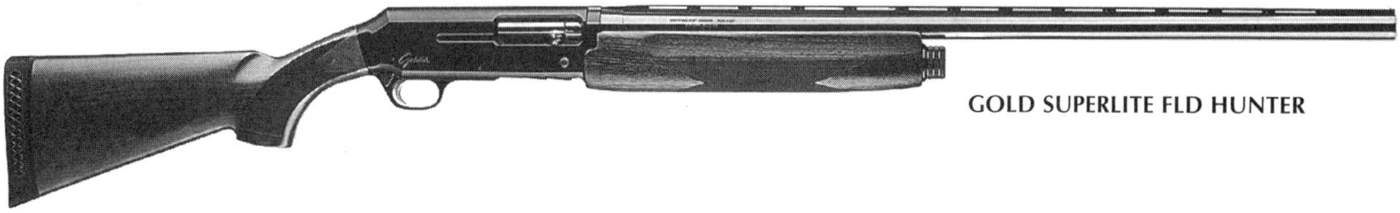

GOLD SUPERLITE FLD HUNTER

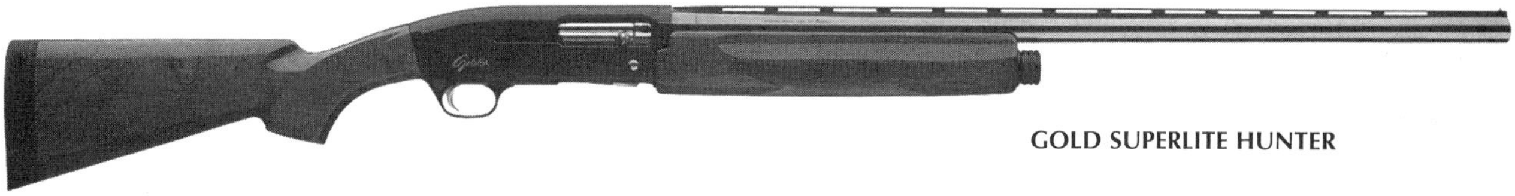

GOLD SUPERLITE HUNTER

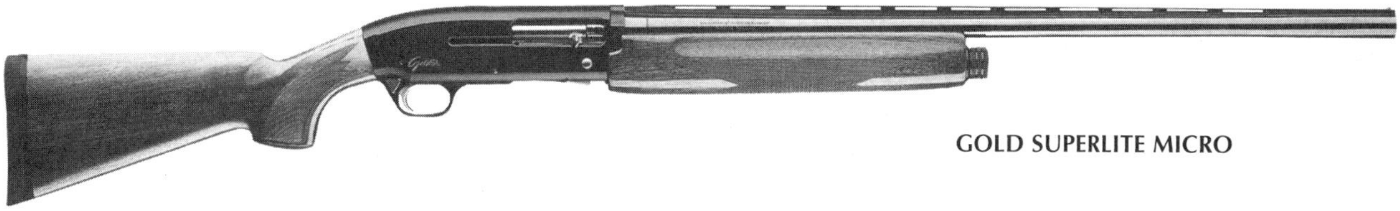

GOLD SUPERLITE MICRO

NRA GOLD SPORTING

GOLD SUPERLITE

Features: gas-operated, 3½ in. chambers on 10 and one 12 ga. version; Youth and Ladies' versions available
Hunter: $1002
Gold Light (10 ga.): $1619

GOLD SUPERLITE MICRO

Action: autoloader
Stock: walnut
Barrel: 26 in.
Chokes: screw-in tube
Weight: 9.6 lbs.
Bore/Gauge: 20, 12
Magazine: 3 rounds
Features: aluminum alloy receiver; 3 in. chamber lightweight alloy magazine tube; magazine cut-off; compact, gloss finish walnut stock; three Invector-Plus choke tubes.
MSRP: $1002

Browning Shotguns

SILVER CAMO

SILVER HUNTER

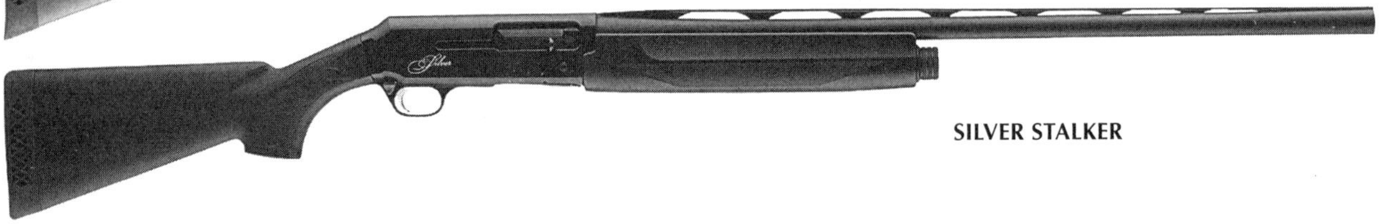

SILVER STALKER

SILVER CAMO

Action: autoloader
Stock: composite
Barrel: 26 or 28 in.
Chokes: screw-in tube
Weight: 7.5-7.88 lbs.
Bore/Gauge: 12 ***Magazine:*** 3 rounds
Features: 3 or 3½ in. chamber; Mossy Oak New Break-Up and Mossy Oak New Shadow Grass finish, Dura-Touch armor coating; F, M and IC Invector-PlusT choke tubes
Silver Camo 3 in.: $1035
Silver Camo 3½ in.: $1229

SILVER HUNTER

Action: autoloader
Stock: checkered satin finish walnut
Barrel: 26, 28 and 30 in.
Chokes: screw-in tubes
Weight: 7.25-7.56 lbs.
Bore/Gauge: 12
Magazine: 3 rounds
Features: silver finish aluminum alloy receiver; hump back configuration; available with 3 or 3½ in. chambers; interchangeable F, M and IC Invector-PlusT tubes
Silver Hunter 3 in.: $1069
Silver Hunter 3½ in.: $1259

SILVER STALKER

Action: autoloader
Stock: composite
Barrel: 26 or 28 in.
Chokes: screw-in tube
Weight: 7.5-7.56 lbs.
Bore/Gauge: 12
Magazine: 3 rounds
Features: black matte finish, 3 or 3½ in. chamber; Dura-Touch armor coating; interchangeable F, M and IC Invector-PlusT tubes
Silver Stalker 3½ in.: $1199

Charles Daly Shotguns

EMPIRE II EDL HUNTER

FIELD II

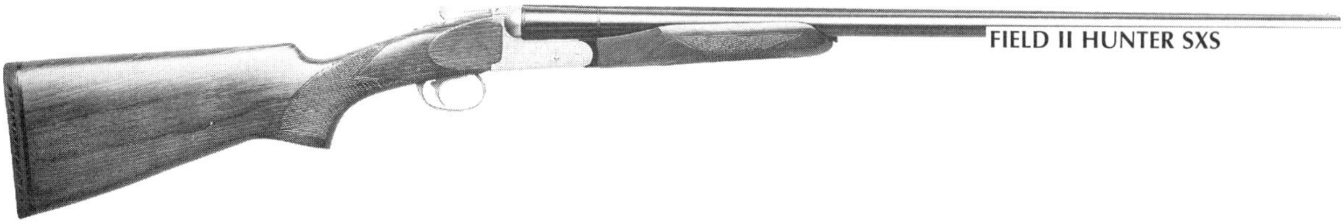

FIELD II HUNTER SXS

FIELD HUNTER CAMO

EMPIRE II EDL HUNTER

Action: over/under
Stock: walnut
Barrel: 26 or 28 in.
Chokes: screw-in tubes
Weight: 7.2 lbs.
Bore/Gauge: 12, 20, 28, .410
Magazine: none
Features: boxlock; single selective trigger; automatic safety; automatic ejectors
28 ga.: $2100
.410: $2100
12 or 20 ga.: $2100

FIELD II

Action: over/under
Stock: walnut
Barrel: 26 or 28 in.
Chokes: mod/full (28 in.), imp.cyl/mod (26 in.), full/full (.410)
Weight: 7.2 lbs.
Bore/Gauge: 12, 16, 20, 28, .410
Magazine: none
Features: boxlock; single selective trigger; automatic safety
Field II: $959–1219

FIELD II HUNTER SXS

Action: side-by-side
Stock: walnut
Barrel: 26, 28 or 30 in.
Chokes: imp.cyl/mod (26 in.), mod/full (28, 30 in.), full/full (.410)
Weight: 10.0 lbs.
Bore/Gauge: 12, 16, 20, 28, .410
Magazine: none
Features: boxlock; single selective trigger; automatic safety
12 or 20 ga.: $1100
16, 28 ga. or .410: $1100

Charles Daly Shotguns

FIELD II ULTRA-LIGHT

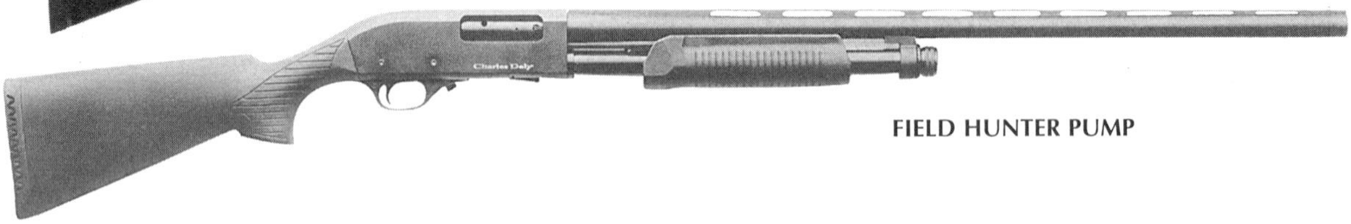

FIELD HUNTER PUMP

FIELD HUNTER AUTOLOADER

Action: autoloader
Stock: synthetic
Barrel: 22, 24, 26, 28 or 30 in.
Chokes: screw-in tubes
Weight: 7.5 lbs.
Bore/Gauge: 12, 20, 28
Magazine: 4 rounds
Features: ventilated rib; Superior II Grade has walnut stock, ported barrel

12 or 20 ga.: $429
28 ga.: $429
Camo: $429
3.5-in. magnum synthetic: $499
3.5-in. magnum camo: $574
Superior Hunter: $499
Superior Trap: $499

FIELD HUNTER PUMP

Action: pump
Stock: synthetic
Barrel: 26 or 28 in.
Chokes: screw-in tubes
Weight: 7.0 lbs.
Bore/Gauge: 12, 20
Magazine: 4 rounds
Features: ventilated rib

Field Hunter: $219
Camo: $219
3.5-in. magnum synthetic: $329
3.5-in. magnum camo: $320

CZ Shotguns

RINGNECK

BOBWHITE AND RINGNECK

Action: side-by-side
Stock: Turkish walnut ***Barrel:*** 26 in.
Chokes: Screw-in chokes (12 & 20); fixed chokes in .410. (IC & Mod)
Weight: 5.2 lbs.
Bore/Gauge: 20, 28, 12, .410
Magazine: none
Features: Color case-hardened finish and hand engraving; 20 and 28 ga. built on appropriate size frame; straight English-style grip and double triggers (Bobwhite); American pistol grip with a single trigger (Ringneck); hand checkered; overall length 43 in.; 14½ in. LOP

Bobwhite: $789–987
Ringneck: $1036–1244

HAMMER COACH SHOTGUN

Action: side-by-side
Stock: walnut
Barrel: 20 in.
Chokes: IC and Mod
Weight: 6.7 lbs.
Bore/Gauge: 12
Magazine: none
Features: chambered for shells up to 3 in.; external hammers; double triggers

MSRP: $905

Escort Shotguns

AS YOUTH SELECT

Action: semi-auto
Stock: walnut
Barrel: 22 in.
Chokes: M, IC, F
Weight: 6.7 lbs.
Bore/Gauge: 20
Magazine: 4
Features: 3-in. chamber; blued finish; magazine cut-off for single shot loading; extra O rings in box; Trio recoil pad with shims
MSRP: $479

Flodman Shotguns

FLODMAN SHOTGUN

Action: over/under
Stock: walnut, fitted to customer
Barrel: any standard length
Chokes: improved cylinder, modified, full
Weight: 7.0 lbs.
Bore/Gauge: 12, 20
Magazine: none
Features: boxlock offered in any standard ga. or rifle/shotgun combination; true hammerless firing mechanism; single selective trigger; automatic ejector
Flodman shotgun: $9500–15000

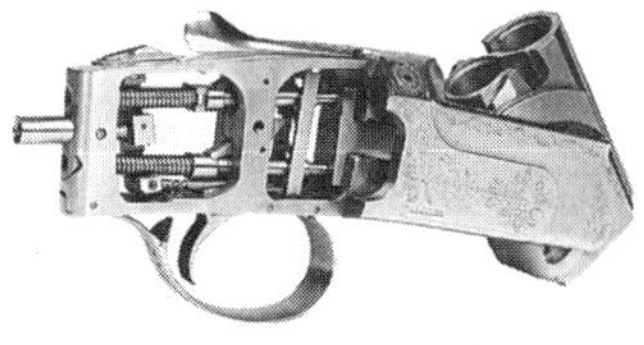

STRAIGHT-LINE RECOIL

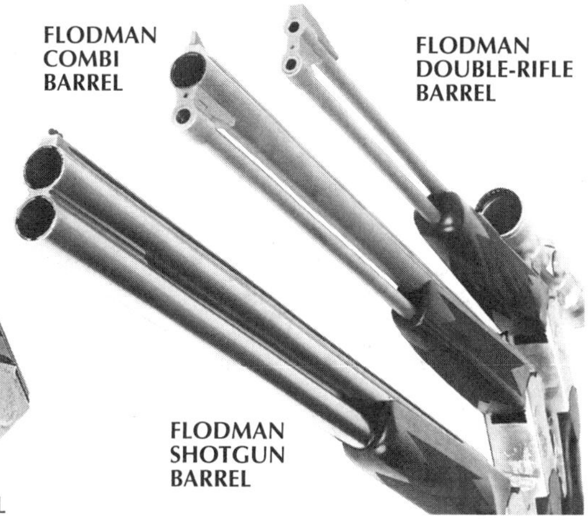

Franchi Shotguns

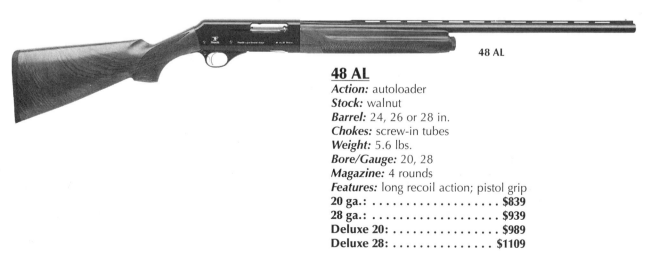

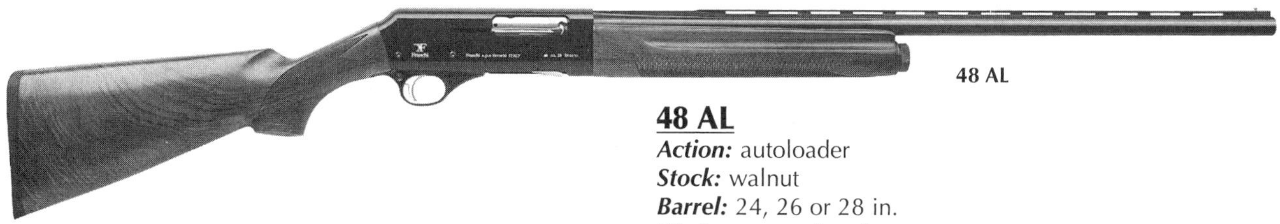

48 AL

48 AL

Action: autoloader
Stock: walnut
Barrel: 24, 26 or 28 in.
Chokes: screw-in tubes
Weight: 5.6 lbs.
Bore/Gauge: 20, 28
Magazine: 4 rounds
Features: long recoil action; pistol grip
20 ga.: $839
28 ga.: $939
Deluxe 20: $989
Deluxe 28: $1109

Franchi Shotguns

720 COMPETITION

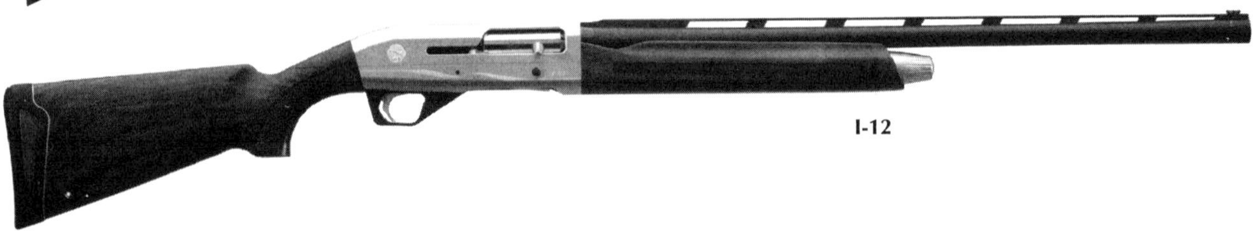

I-12

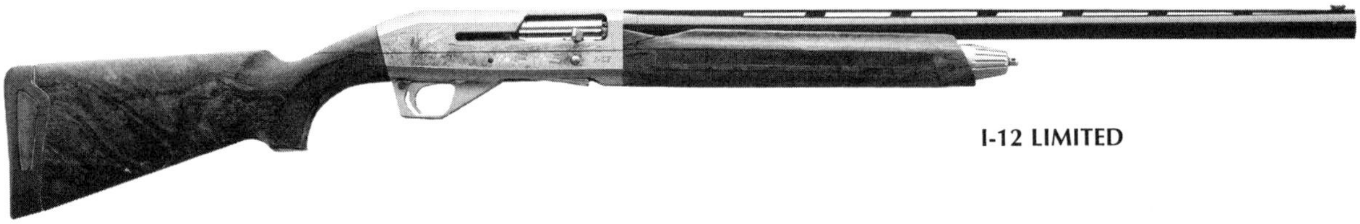

I-12 LIMITED

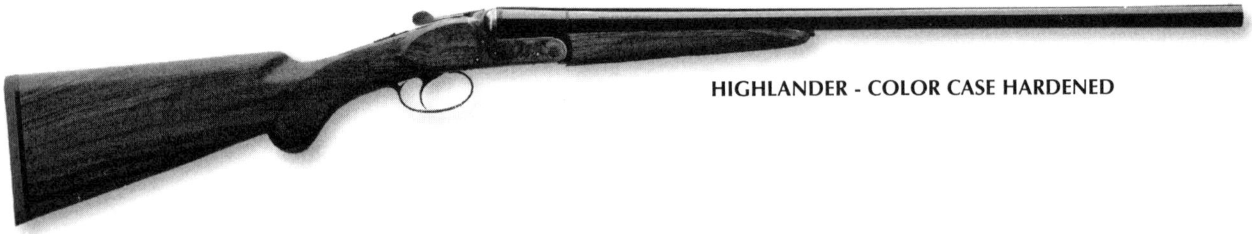

HIGHLANDER - COLOR CASE HARDENED

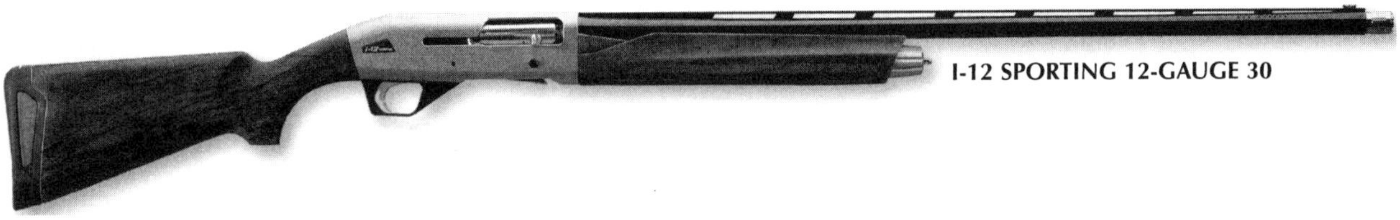

I-12 SPORTING 12-GAUGE 30

720 COMPETITION

Action: autoloader
Stock: walnut
Barrel: 28 in.
Chokes: screw-in tubes
Weight: 6.25 lbs.
Bore/Gauge: 20
Magazine: *4 rounds*
Features: ported barrel; rotary bolt; satin nickel receiver finish; accepts 2½ and 3 in. shells; screw-in extended chokes (C, IC, M); walnut stock with with WeatherCoat protection
MSRP: $1109

HIGHLANDER - COLOR CASE HARDENED

Action: side-by-side
Stock: walnut
Barrel: 26 in.
Chokes: IC, M
Weight: 6 lbs.
Bore/Gauge: 20
Features: box-lock action; automatic safety and ejectors; single trigger; fine scroll engraving; A-grade walnut stock
MSRP: $2799

I-12

Action: inertia operated semi-auto
Stock: walnut or synthetic
Barrel: 24, 26, or 28 in.
Chokes: screw-in tubes
Weight: 7.5 lbs.
Bore/Gauge: 12
Magazine: 4 + 1 rounds
Features: inertia-recoil; lightweight aluminum alloy receiver with steel inserts; rotary bolt; TSA recoil reduction; available with walnut Weathercoat or black or camo synthetic stocks; screw-in extended choke tubes (C, IC, M, IM, F)
MSRP: $939

Franchi Shotguns

I-12 UPLAND HUNTER
12-GAUGE 26

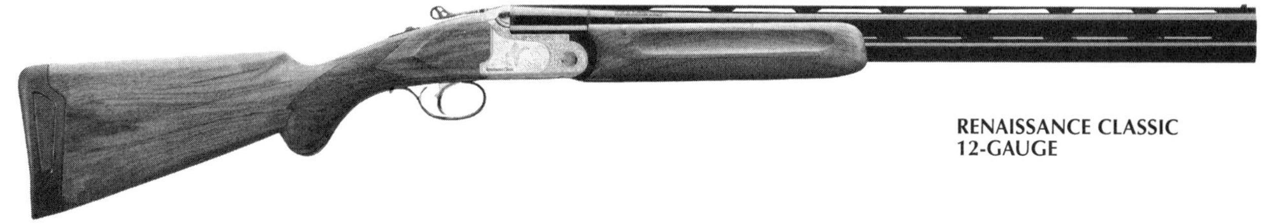

RENAISSANCE CLASSIC
12-GAUGE

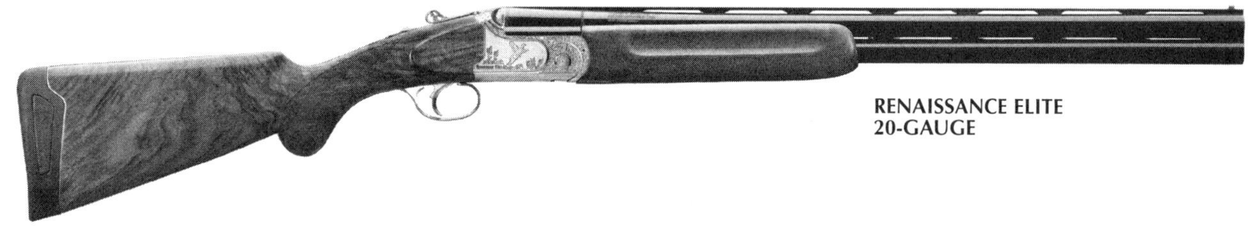

RENAISSANCE ELITE
20-GAUGE

I-12 LIMITED

Action: inertia operated semi-auto
Stock: walnut
Barrel: 28 in.
Chokes: screw-in tubes
Weight: 7.7 lbs.
Bore/Gauge: 12
Magazine: 4 + 1 rounds
Features: chambered for 3 in.; nickel receiver accented with white gold game birds; Inertia Driven operating system; Twin Shock Absorber recoil pad with gel insert; oil finished AA-grade figured walnut stock w/ cut checkering; screw-in chokes (C, IC, M, IM, F); shim kit to adjust drop
MSRP: $1699

I-12 SPORTING

Action:inertia operated semi-auto
Stock: walnut
Barrel: 30 in.
Chokes: screw-in tubes
Weight: 6.5 lbs.
Bore/Gauge: 12
Magazine: 4+1 rounds
Features: ported, polished blue barrel; lengthened forcing cone; chambered for 2¾- and 3-in. shells; screw-in extended choke tubes (C, IC, IM, M, F); 10-mm target rib; Twin Shock Absorber recoil reducing system; WeatherCoat walnut stock
MSRP: $1379

I-12 UPLAND HUNTER

Action: inertia operated semi-auto
Stock: walnut
Barrel: 26 in.
Chokes: 5 tubes - C, IC, IM, M, F
Weight: 6.3 lbs.
Bore/Gauge: 12
Magazine: 4+1 rounds
Features: vent rib; polished blue barrel; chambered for 2¾- and 3-in. shells; Twin Shock Absorber recoil reducing system.
MSRP: $1169

Franchi Shotguns

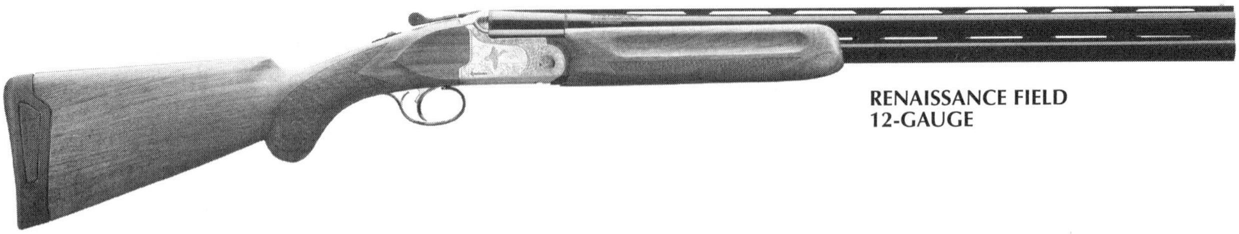

RENAISSANCE FIELD
12-GAUGE

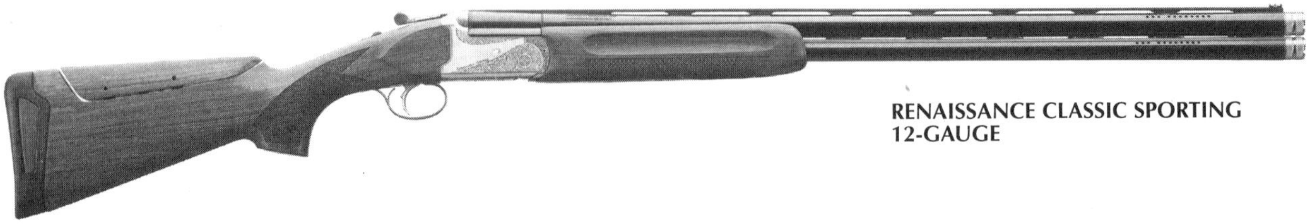

RENAISSANCE CLASSIC SPORTING
12-GAUGE

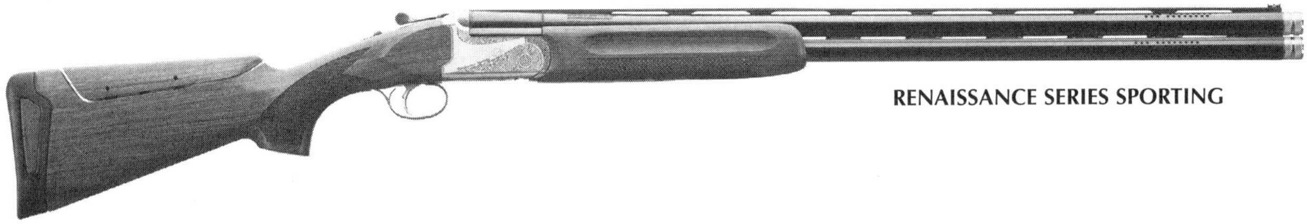

RENAISSANCE SERIES SPORTING

RENAISSANCE SERIES FIELD, CLASSIC, CLASSIC SPORTING AND ELITE MODELS

Action: over/under
Stock: walnut
Barrel: 26 and 28 in. (20, 12 ga.); 26 in. (28 ga.)
Chokes: screw-in tubes
Weight: 6.0 lbs.
Bore/Gauge: 20, 28 and 12
Magazine: none
Features: lightweight aluminum alloy receiver; Twin Shock Absorber recoil pad with gel insert; oil finish select walnut stock with Prince of Wales pistol grips, cut checkering; screw-in choke tubes (C, IC, M, IM, F)
MSRP: $1659–2729

RENAISSANCE SERIES SPORTING

Action: over/under
Stock: walnut
Barrel: 30 in.
Chokes: screw-in tubes
Weight: 8 lbs.
Bore/Gauge: 12
Magazine: none
Features: ported barrel; stainless, box-lock action; lengthened forcing cones; engraving and gold embellishments on receiver; oil finished, select A grade walnut stock w/ adjustable comb & cut checkering; Twin Shock Absorber system; screw-in extended choke tubes
MSRP: $2219

Harrington & Richardson Shotguns

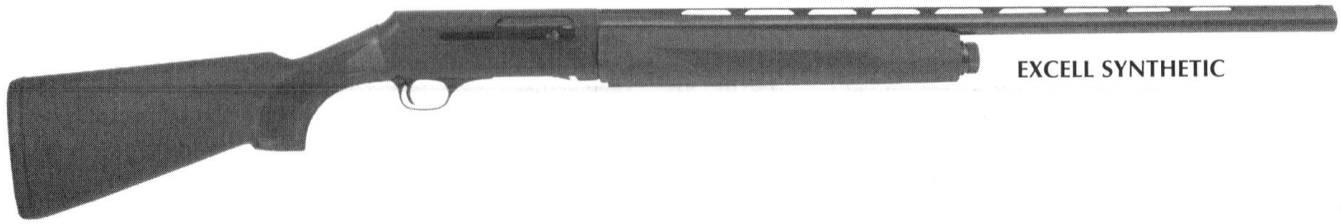

EXCELL SYNTHETIC

EXCELL AUTO

Action: autoloader
Stock: synthetic
Barrel: 28 in. (Synthetic, Walnut, Waterfowl); 22 in. (Turkey); 28 in. w/ ventilated rib, 24 in. rifled barrel (Combo)
Chokes: screw-in tubes
Weight: 7.0 lbs.
Bore/Gauge: 12
Magazine: 5 rounds
Features: vent rib barrels (except slug barrel); 3 in. magnum capability; magazine cut-off; ventilated recoil pads; stock available in black, American walnut, Real Tree Advantage Wetlands or Real Tree Advantage Hardwoods; 4 screw-in tube chokes IC,M,IM,F
Synthetic: $420.93
Walnut: $454.75
Waterfowl: $513.46
Turkey: $513.46
Combo: $472

SHOTGUNS

Harrington & Richardson Shotguns

EXCELL TURKEY

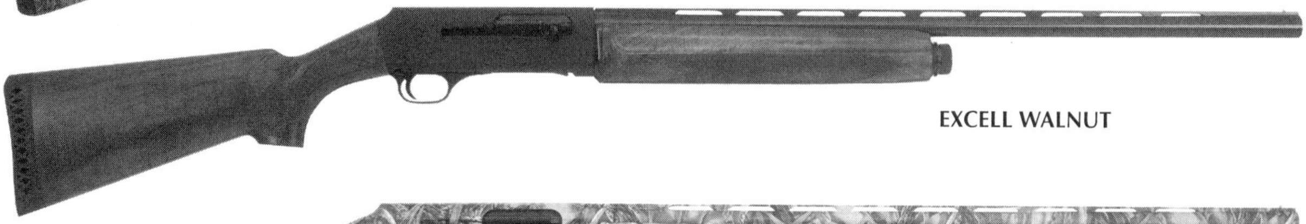

EXCELL WALNUT

EXCELL WATERFOWL

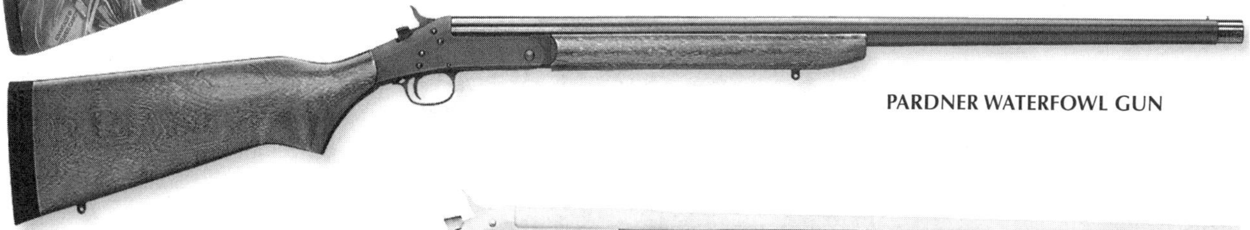

PARDNER WATERFOWL GUN

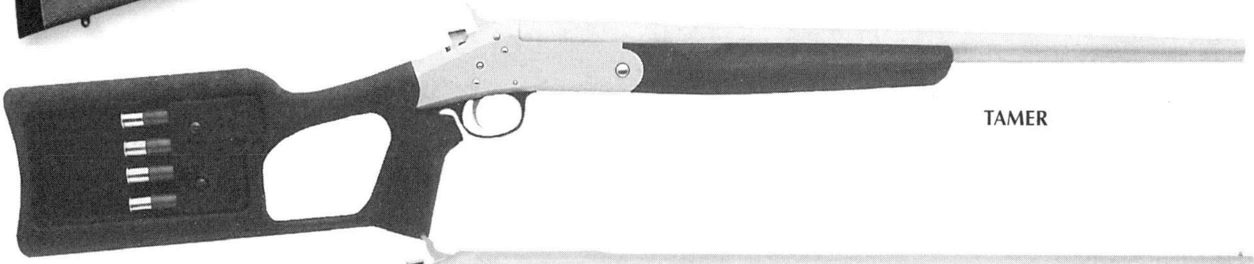

TAMER

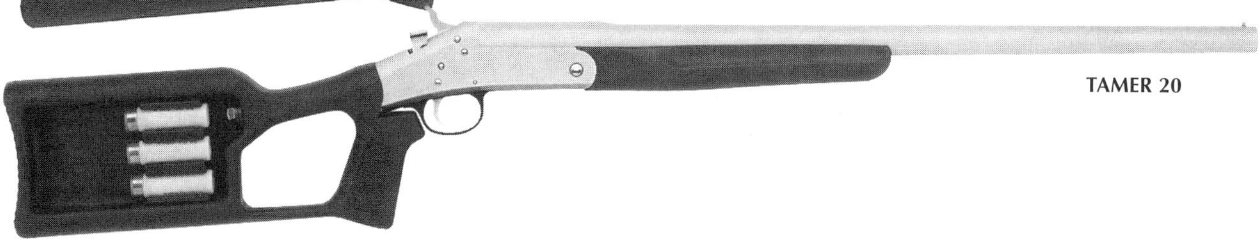

TAMER 20

PARDNER WATERFOWL GUN

Action: break-open single shot
Stock: walnut
Barrel: 30 in.
Chokes: screw-in tubes
Weight: 9 lbs.
Bore/Gauge: 10
Magazine: none
Features: blued carbon steel action and barrel; transfer bar safety; modified WinChoke tubes; bead front sight; ventilated recoil pad; pistol grip stock; sling swivel studs.
MSRP: $228

TAMER

Action: hinged single-shot
Stock: synthetic
Barrel: 19 in.
Chokes: full
Weight: 6 lbs.
Bore/Gauge: .410
Magazine: none
Features: thumbhole stock with recessed cavity for ammo storage
MSRP: $182.13

TAMER 20

Action: hinged single-shot
Stock: high-density polymer
Barrel: 20 in.
Chokes: full
Weight: 6 lbs.
Bore/Gauge: 20
Magazine: none
Features: weather-resistant nickel-plated receiver and barrel; black matte finish pistol grip stock; thumbhole design with storage compartment; automatic shell ejection; Transfer Bar System to prevent accidental firing; locking system for safe storage
MSRP: $182.13

Harrington & Richardson Shotguns

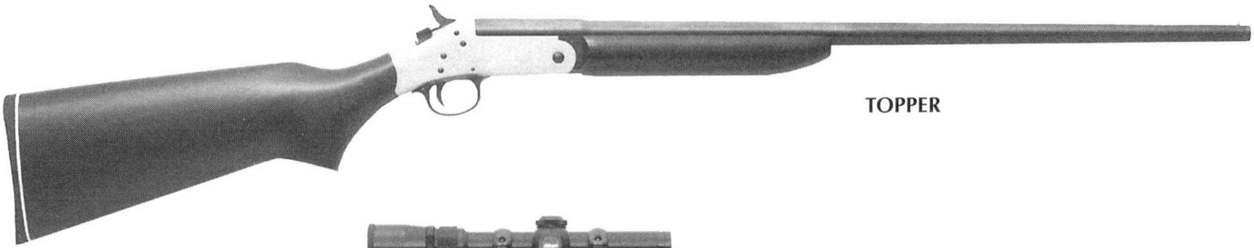

TOPPER

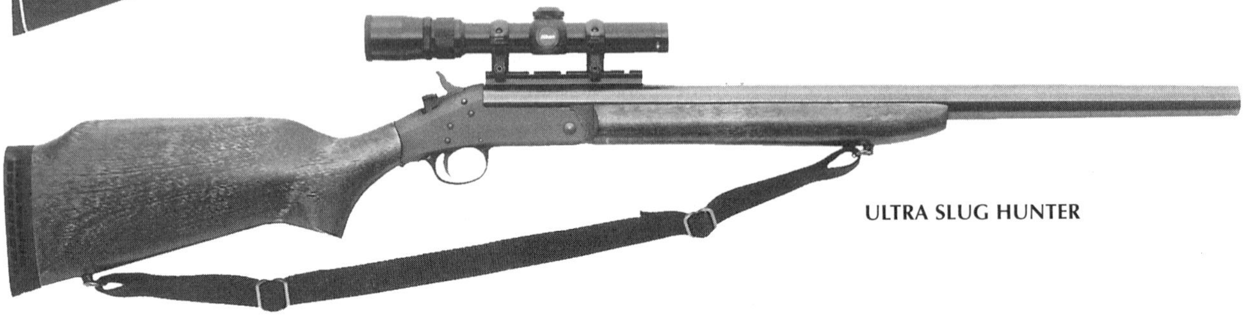

ULTRA SLUG HUNTER

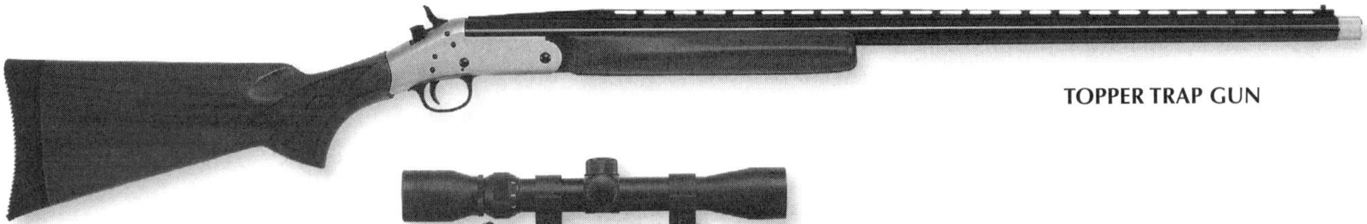

TOPPER TRAP GUN

ULTRA LIGHT SLUG HUNTER

TOPPER TRAP GUN

Action: break-open single shot
Stock: walnut
Barrel: 30 in.
Chokes: screw-in tube
Weight: 7 lbs.
Bore/Gauge: 12 ga.
Magazine: none
Features: blued carbon steel barrel with ventilated rib; electroless nickel coated carbon steel receiver; stainless steel IM extended choke tube; double white bead sighting system; select walnut checkered Monte Carlo stock Pachmayr trap recoil pad
MSRP: $362

ULTRA LIGHT SLUG HUNTER

Action: break-open single shot
Stock: hardwood
Barrel: 24-in.
Chokes: none
Weight: 5.25 lbs.
Bore/Gauge: 12, 20
Magazine: none
Features: blued, polished carbon steel action and barrel; 24-in. Ultragon rifling; transfer bar safety; hammer extension; barrel with installed scope base; ventilated recoil pad; walnut-stained, Monte Carlo pistol-grip stock
MSRP: $194

TOPPER

Action: hinged single-shot
Stock: hardwood
Barrel: 26 or 28 in.
Chokes: screw-in tubes
Weight: 6.0 lbs.
Bore/Gauge: 12, 20, 28, .410
Magazine: none
Features: hinged-breech with side lever release; automatic ejection
Topper: $161.18
12 ga. 3.5-inch: $182
Junior with walnut stock: . . . $169.03
Deluxe Classic: $237.68

ULTRA SLUG HUNTER

Action: hinged single-shot
Stock: hardwood
Barrel: 24 in., rifled
Chokes: none
Weight: 7.5 lbs.
Bore/Gauge: 12, 20
Magazine: none
Features: factory-mounted Weaver scope base, swivels and sling
Ultra Slug Hunter: $285.05
With camo laminated wood: . . $387

Ithaca Shotguns

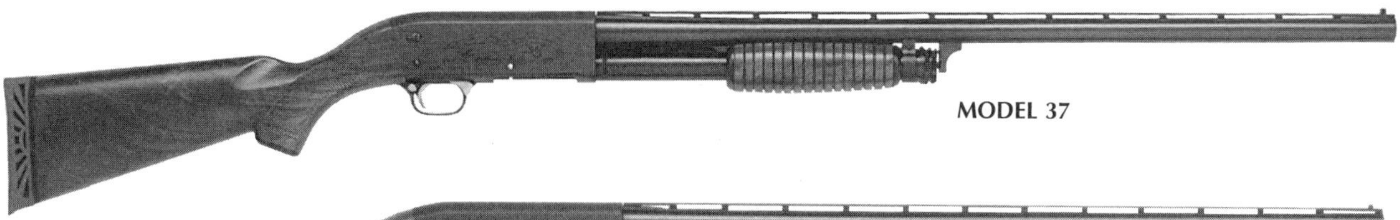

MODEL 37

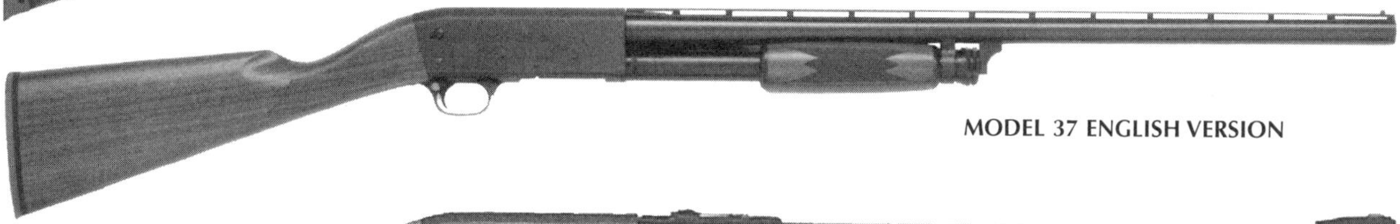

MODEL 37 ENGLISH VERSION

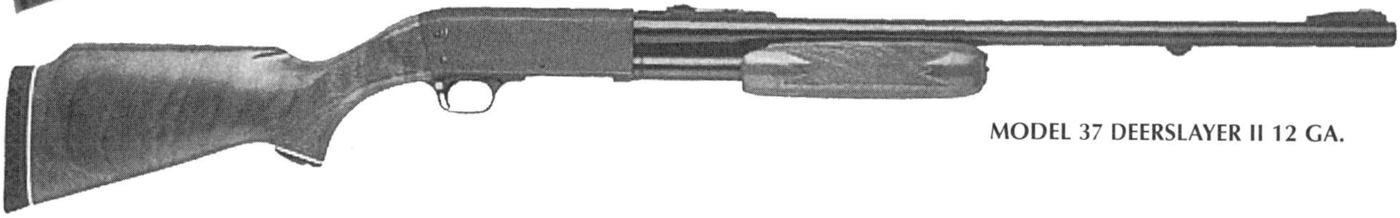

MODEL 37 DEERSLAYER II 12 GA.

MODEL 37

Action: pump
Stock: walnut or synthetic
Barrel: 20, 22, 24, 26 or 28 in.
Chokes: screw-in tubes
Weight: 7.0 lbs.
Bore/Gauge: 12, 16, 20
Magazine: 4 rounds
Features: bottom ejection
12 or 20: $499–499
Turkey Slayer Guide: $627
Deluxe vent rib: $651
Classic: $859
Ultralight 20 ga.: $959
English straight-grip: $713
Trap or Sporting Clays with Briley tubes, starting: $1845

MODEL 37 DEERSLAYER II

Action: pump
Stock: walnut
Barrel: 20 or 25 in., rifled or smoothbore
Weight: 7.0 lbs.
Bore/Gauge: 12, 16, 20 *Magazine:* 4
Features: open sights; receiver fitted with Weaver-style scope base; also available: Deerslayer III with 26-in. heavy rifled barrel and Turkeyslayer (12 or 20) with 22 in. barrel, extra-full tube
Deerslayer II: $899

Krieghoff Shotguns

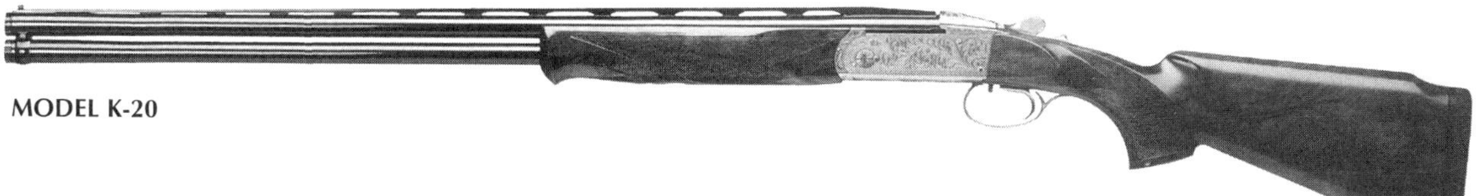

MODEL K-20

MODEL K-20

Action: over/under
Stock: walnut
Barrel: 28 or 30 in.
Chokes: screw-in tubes
Weight: 7.2 lbs.
Bore/Gauge: 20, 28, .410
Magazine: none
Features: boxlock; single selective trigger, automatic ejectors; tapered rib; choice of receiver finish; fitted aluminum case
MSRP: $10695

Krieghoff Shotguns

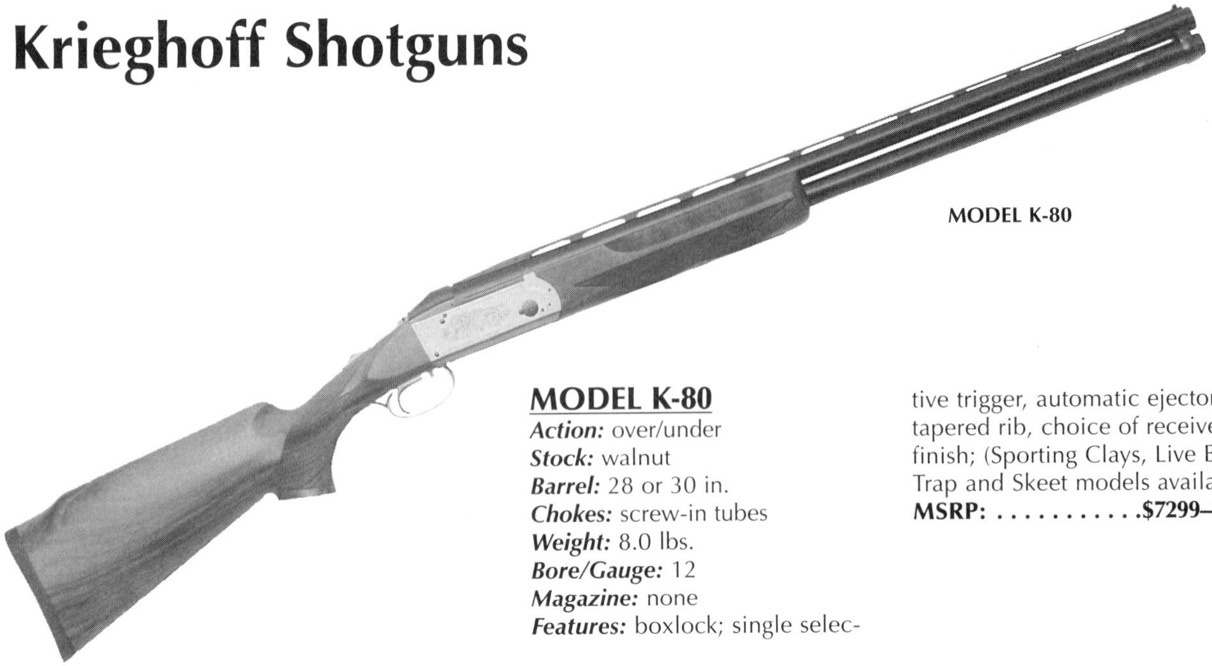

MODEL K-80

MODEL K-80

Action: over/under
Stock: walnut
Barrel: 28 or 30 in.
Chokes: screw-in tubes
Weight: 8.0 lbs.
Bore/Gauge: 12
Magazine: none
Features: boxlock; single selective trigger, automatic ejectors; tapered rib, choice of receiver finish; (Sporting Clays, Live Bird, Trap and Skeet models available)
MSRP: $7299–8999

L.C. Smith Shotguns

MODEL LC28-DB

MODEL LC410-DB

SHOTGUNS

MODEL LC28-DB

Action: side-by-side
Stock: checkered walnut
Barrel: 26 in. with solid rib
Chokes: 3 tubes (IC, M, F)
Weight: 6.5 lbs.
Bore/Gauge: 28
Magazine: none
Features: 2¾ in. chamber; color case hardened receiver with gold game bird decorations on sides and bottom; single selective trigger; selective automatic ejectors; chrome-lined barrels with solid rib; bead front sight
MSRP: $1464

MODEL LC410-DB

Action: side-by-side
Stock: checkered walnut
Barrel: 26 in. with solid rib
Chokes: 3 tubes (IC, M, F)
Weight: 6.5 lbs.
Bore/Gauge: .410
Magazine: none
Features: 3 in. chamber; color case hardened receiver with gold game bird decorations on sides and bottom; single selective trigger; selective automatic ejectors; chrome-lined barrels with solid rib; bead front sight
MSRP: $1464

Legacy Sports Shotguns

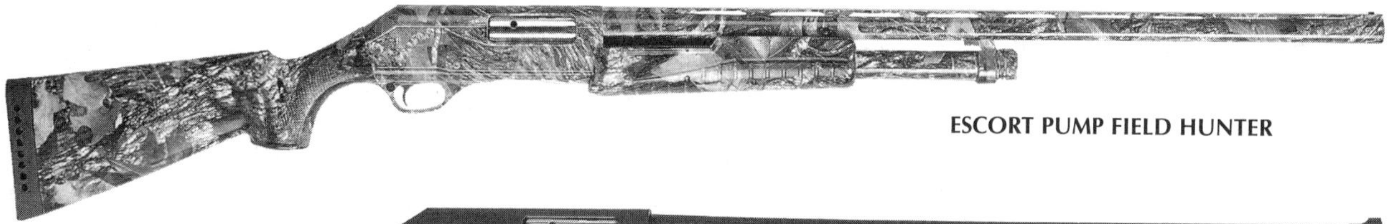

ESCORT PUMP FIELD HUNTER

ESCORT SEMI-AUTO PS AIM GUARD

ESCORT PUMP-ACTION SHOTGUN

Action: pump
Stock: black or chrome polymer
Barrel: 18, 22, 26 or 28 in.
Sights: Hi Viz
Chokes: IC, M, F
Weight: 6.4-7.0 lbs.
Bore/Gauge: 12, 20
Magazine: 5-shot with cut-off button
Features: alloy receiver with 3/8 in. milled dovetail for sight mounting; black chrome or camp finish; black chrome bolt; trigger guard safety; 5-shot magazine with cut-off button; two stock adjustment shims; three choke tubes: IC, M, F (except AimGuard); 24 in. Bbl comes with extra turkey choke tube and HI Viz TriViz sight combo.

Aim Guard, 18 in. bbl.: $280
Field Hunter, black: $359
Field Hunter Camo: $359
Field Hunter slug, black: $399

ESCORT SEMI-AUTOMATIC SHOTGUN

Action: autoloader
Stock: polymer or walnut
Barrel: 18, 22, 26 & 28 in.
Sights: HiViz
Weight: 6.4-7.8 lbs.
Bore/Gauge: 12, 20
Magazine: 5 rounds
Features: gas operated and chambered for 2¾ or 3in. shells; barrels are nickel-chromium-molybdenum steel with additional chrome plating internally and a ventilated anti-glare checkered rib; bolts are chrome plated; extras include three chokes, a migratory plug and two spacers to adjust the slope of the stock; camo waterfowl and turkey combo available with Hi Viz sights, 28 in. barrel; hard case.

AS walnut: $469
AS Youth walnut: $469
PS polymer: $399
PS Slug, black: $479
PS blue, 3.5 mag.: $489
PS Waterfowl & Turkey: $659
Combo, Waterfowler/Turkey 24-28 in. bbl., TriViz Sights, Turkey choke: $659

Ljutic Shotguns

MONO GUN

Action: single barrel
Stock: AAA English walnut
Barrel: 32-34 in.
Chokes: Fixed, Ljutic SIC, Briley SIC
Weight: 10 lbs.
Bore/Gauge: 740 bore, 12 gauge
MSRP: $7495

SHOTGUNS

Ljutic Shotguns

LJUTIC MONO GUN
ADJUSTABLE RIB

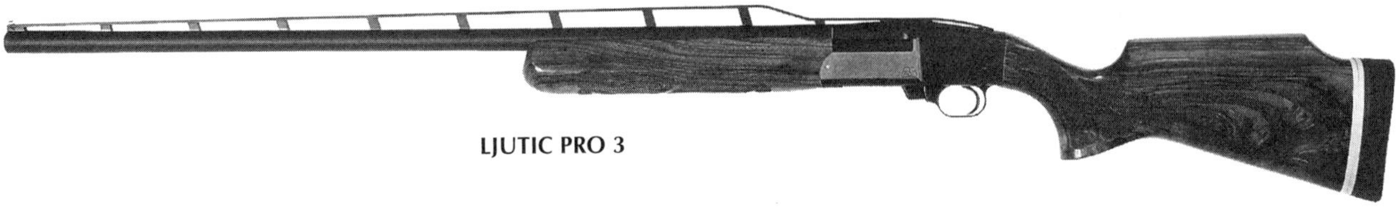

LJUTIC PRO 3

MONO GUN, ADJUSTABLE RIB
Action: single barrel
Stock: AAA English walnut
Barrel: 34 in.
Chokes: Fixed or Ljutic SIC
Weight: 10 lbs.
Bore/Gauge: 740 bore, 12 gauge
Features: adjustable "One Touch" impact from 60 to 100%, adjustable comb, adjustable base plate
MSRP: **$7995**

MONO GUN, ADJUSTABLE RIB, STAINLESS STEEL
Action: single barrel
Stock: AAA English walnut
Barrel: 34 in.
Chokes: Fixed or Ljutic SIC
Weight: 10 lbs.
Bore/Gauge: 740 bore, 12 gauge
Features: adjustable "One Touch" impact from 60 to 100%, adjustable comb, adjustable base plate
MSRP: **$8995**

MONO GUN, STAINLESS STEEL
Action: single barrel
Stock: AAA English walnut
Barrel: 32-34 in.
Chokes: Fixed, Ljutic SIC, Briley SIC
Weight: 10 lbs.
Bore/Gauge: 740 bore, 12 gauge
MSRP: **$8495**

PRO 3
Action: single barrel
Stock: high quality English walnut and checkering
Barrel: 34 in.
Chokes: Fixed, Ljutic Extended Chokes or Ljutic Internal Flush Mount
Weight: 9 lbs.
Bore/Gauge: Special bore, 12 gauge
Features: adjustable Comb, adjustable Aluminum Base Plate with 2 pad system
MSRP: **$8995**

PRO 3, ADJUSTABLE RIB
Action: single barrel
Stock: high quality English walnut and checkering
Barrel: 34 in.
Chokes: Fixed or Ljutic SIC
Weight: 9 lbs.
Bore/Gauge: 740 bore, 12 gauge
Features: adjustable "One Touch" impact from 60 to 100%, adjustable comb, adjustable base plate with 2 pad system
MSRP: **$9520**

PRO 3 STAINLESS STEEL
Action: single barrel
Stock: high quality English walnut and checkering
Barrel: 34 in.
Chokes: Fixed, Ljutic Extended Chokes or Ljutic Internal Flush Mount
Weight: 9 lbs.
Bore/Gauge: Special bore, 12 gauge
Features: adjustable comb, adjustable aluminum base plate with 2 pad system
MSRP: **$9995**

PRO 3 STAINLESS STEEL, ADJUSTABLE RIB
Action: single barrel
Stock: high quality English walnut and checkering
Barrel: 34 in.
Chokes: Fixed or Ljutic SIC
Weight: 9 lbs.
Bore/Gauge: 740 bore, 12 gauge
Features: adjustable "One Touch" impact from 60 to 100%, adjustable comb, adjustable base plate with 2 pad system
MSRP: **$10520**

SLE PRO
Action: single barrel
Stock: AAA English walnut
Barrel: 32-34 in.
Chokes: Fixed, Ljutic SIC, Briley SIC
Weight: 10 lbs.
Bore/Gauge: Special bore, 12 gauge
Features: adjustable comb, adjustable aluminum base plate, SLE forearm
MSRP: **$8495**

SLE PRO STAINLESS STEEL
Action: single barrel
Stock: AAA English walnut
Barrel: 32-34 in.
Chokes: Fixed, Ljutic SIC, Briley SIC
Weight: 10 lbs.
Bore/Gauge: Special bore, 12 gauge
Features: adjustable comb, adjustable aluminum base plate, SLE forearm
MSRP: **$8995**

SHOTGUNS

Marocchi Shotguns

MODEL 99

Action: over/under ***Stock:*** walnut
Barrel: back-bored 28, 29, 30 or 32 in.
Chokes: screw-in tubes
Weight: 8.0 lbs. ***Bore/Gauge:*** 12
Magazine: none
Features: boxlock; single adjustable trigger, BOSS locking system
Model 99: $2750

"Shotgun technique is directly opposite that of a rifle. With a rifle, you place your single bullet with perfect aiming and slow precision trigger squeezing. With a shotgun, you 'throw' a cloud of shot with lightning reaction." —John Cartier

Merkel Shotguns

MODEL 147EL BOXLOCK

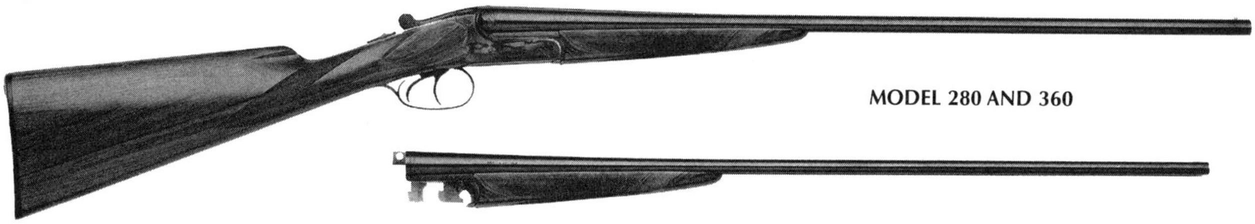

MODEL 280 AND 360

MODEL 147E

Action: side-by-side
Stock: walnut, straight or pistol grip
Barrel: 27 or 28 in.
Chokes: imp.cyl/mod or mod/full
Weight: 7.2 lbs.
Bore/Gauge: 12, 20
Magazine: none
Features: boxlock; single selective or double triggers; automatic ejectors; fitted luggage case
47E: $4595–5795
147E (deluxe): $5795
147EL (super deluxe): $7195

MODEL 280 AND 360

Action: side-by-side
Stock: walnut, straight grip
Barrel: 28 in.
Chokes: imp.cyl/mod (28 ga.), mod/full (.410)
Weight: 6.0 lbs.
Bore/Gauge: 28, .410
Magazine: none
Features: boxlock; double triggers, automatic ejectors; fitted luggage case (Model 280*:* 28 ga. and Model 360*:* .410)
Model 280 or Model 360: $4995
two-barrel sets: $7695
S models
with sidelocks: . . . $10995–11595

Merkel Shotguns

MODEL 303 EL

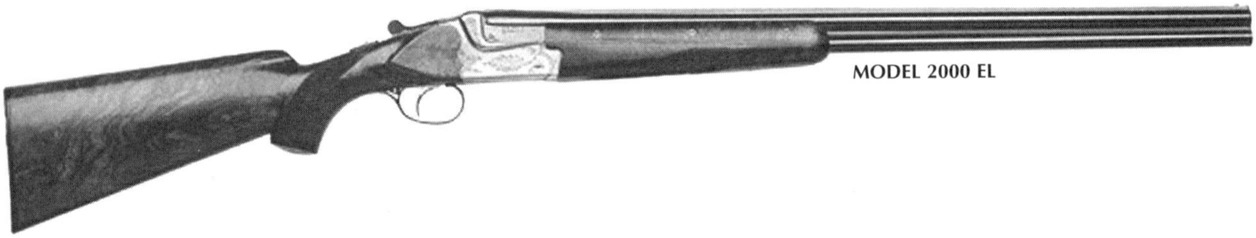

MODEL 2000 EL

MODEL 303 EL

Action: over/under
Stock: walnut, straight or pistol grip
Barrel: 27 or 28 in.
Chokes: improved cylinder, modified, full
Weight: 7.3 lbs.
Bore/Gauge: 16, 20, 28
Magazine: none
Features: sidelock; automatic ejectors; special-order features
MSRP: **$24995**

MODEL 2000 CL

Action: over/under
Stock: walnut, straight or pistol grip
Barrel: 27 or 28 in.
Chokes: improved cylinder, modified, full
Weight: 7.3 lbs.
Bore/Gauge: 12, 20, 28
Magazine: none
Features: boxlock; single selective or double trigger; three-piece forend, automatic ejectors
MSRP: **$8495**

Mossberg Shotguns

500 J.I.C. (JUST IN CASE) MARINER

Action: pump
Stock: black synthetic
Barrel: 18.5 in.
Chokes: cylinder bore
Weight: 5.5 lb.
Bore/Gauge: 12 ga.
Magazine: 4+1 capacity
Features: Marinecoat finish barrel; 3-inch chamber; pistol grip; impact-resistant tube with strap, multi-tool and knife; 28.75-in. overall length
MSRP: **$547**

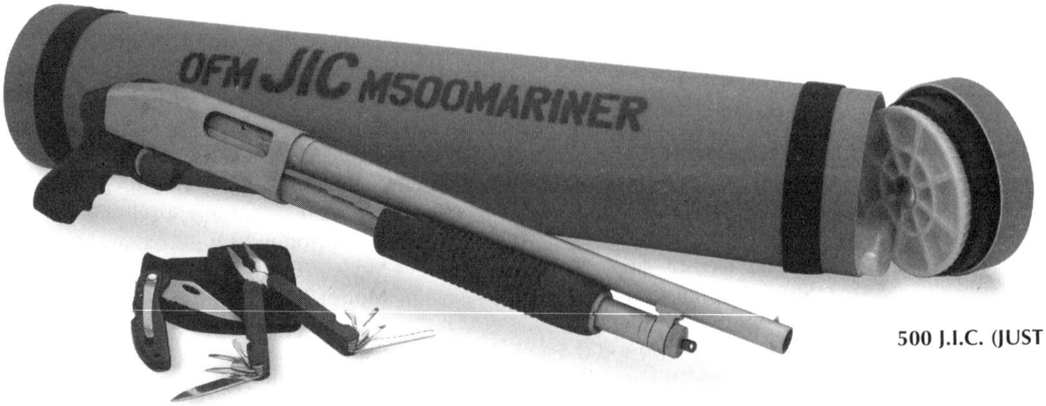

500 J.I.C. (JUST IN CASE) MARINER

SHOTGUNS

Mossberg Shotguns

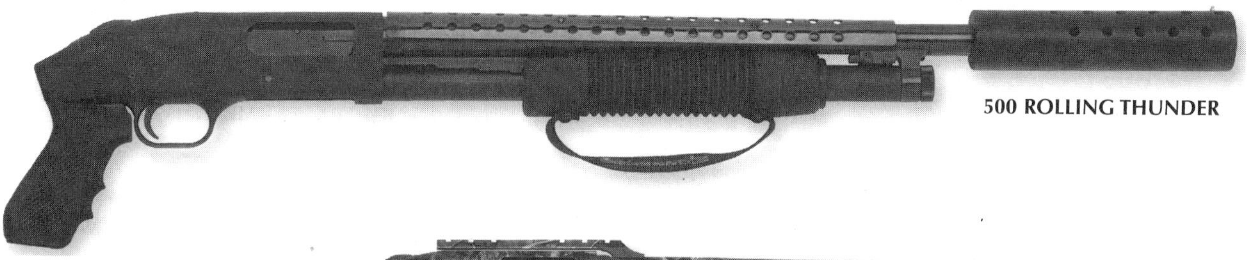

500 ROLLING THUNDER

500 SUPER BANTAM SLUGSTER

500 SUPER BANTAM TURKEY

MODEL 500 SPORTING

500 ROLLING THUNDER 6-SHOT

Action: pump
Stock: black synthetic
Barrel: 23 in.
Chokes: cylinder bore
Weight: 5.75 lb.
Bore/Gauge: 12 ga.
Magazine: 4+1 capacity
Features: barrel with heat shield and barrel stabilizer; 3-inch chamber; pistol grip; 33.5-in. overall length
MSRP: $471

500 SUPER BANTAM SLUGSTER

Action: pump
Stock: synthetic
Barrel: 24 in.
Chokes: none
Weight: 5.25 lb.
Bore/Gauge: 20 ga.
Magazine: 4+1 capacity
Features: fully rifled bore; 3-in. chamber; ISB sights; blue or RealTree AP finish; stock with 12-13-in. adjustable LOP; gun lock
MSRP: . . . . from $354

500 SUPER BANTAM TURKEY

Action: pump
Stock: synthetic
Barrel: 22 in.
Chokes: X-Full
Weight: 5.25 lb.
Bore/Gauge: 20 ga.
Magazine: 4+1 capacity
Features: 3-inch chamber; adjustable FO sights; adjustable synthetic stock with 12-13-in. adjustable LOP, available in Mossy Oak Obsession or RealTree Hardwoods HD green finish; gun lock
MSRP: $410

MODEL 500

Action: pump
Stock: wood or synthetic
Barrel: 18, 22, 24, 26 or 28 in.
Chokes: screw-in tubes
Weight: 7.5 lbs.
Bore/Gauge: 12, 20, .410
Magazine: 5 rounds
Features: barrels mostly vent rib, some ported; top tang safety; camouflage stock finish options; 10-year warranty
Model 500:. $364–543
Camo: $422

SHOTGUNS

Mossberg Shotguns

MODEL 835 PUMP ULTI-MAG CAMO

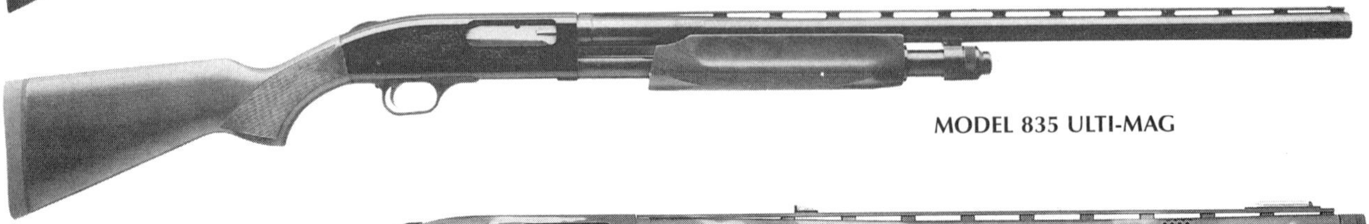

MODEL 835 ULTI-MAG

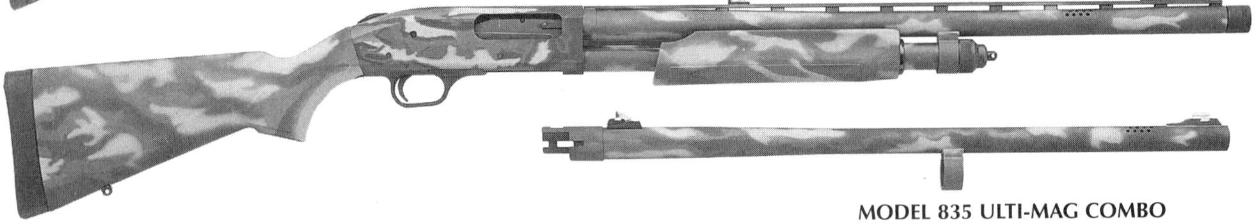

MODEL 835 ULTI-MAG COMBO

MOSSBERG 535 ATS THUMBHOLE TURKEY

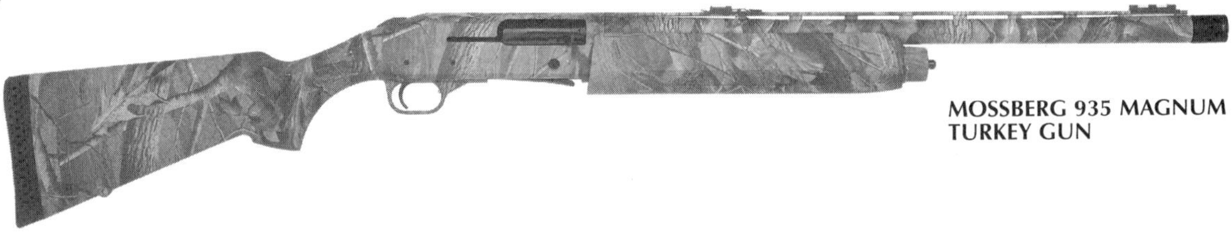

MOSSBERG 935 MAGNUM TURKEY GUN

MODEL 835 ULTI-MAG

Action: pump
Stock: synthetic or camo
Barrel: 24 or 28 in.
Chokes: full
Weight: 7.0 lbs.
Bore/Gauge: 12
Magazine: 4 rounds
Features: barrel ported, back-bored with vent rib; 3½ in. chamber; top tang safety; rifled slug barrel and combination sets available; 10-year warranty
Model 835:. $450–655
Model 835, camo: $450–525
Combo: $575–612

MOSSBERG 535 ATS THUMBHOLE TURKEY

Action: pump
Stock: synthetic black or camo
Barrel: 28″ matte blue or camo
Chokes: interchangeable
Weight: 7 lbs.
Bore/Gauge: 12 ga.
Magazine: tube
Features: 3½″, length: 40.5″, X-Factor Ported Tube.
MSRP: . . . . $433–$507

MOSSBERG 935 MAGNUM TURKEY GUN

Action: autoloading, gas operated
Stock: synthetic camo
Barrel: 22″ overbored
Chokes: interchangeable
Weight: 7.5 lbs.
Bore/Gauge: 12 ga. 3″ or 3½″
Magazine: tube
Features: magnum autoloading shotgun with X-Factor Ported Tube, drilled and tapped for bases and optics. Front and rear fiber optic sights. Overall length: 41.5″
MSRP: . . . . $754–$855

Mossberg Shotguns

ONYX RESERVE 20-GAUGE 26

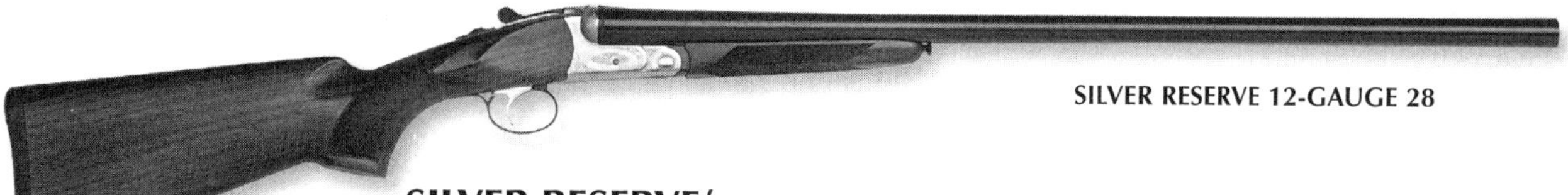

SILVER RESERVE 12-GAUGE 28

SILVER RESERVE/ ONYX RESERVE SIDE-BY-SIDES

Action: side-by-side
Stock: Turkish walnut
Barrel: 26, 28 in.
Chokes: Sport Set (5 total)
Weight: 6.4-7.2 lb.
Bore/Gauge: 12, 20, 28 ga.
Magazine: none
Features: chrome-plated chambers and bores; ambidextrous thumb-operated safety and integrated barrel selector, located on the top tang; checkered Turkish black walnut stock; gun lock
MSRP: $672

"You will never attain maximum shotgunning potential if you hold your shotgun as if you're choking it. Relax your grip. Caress the pistol grip and forearm with gentle but confident hands. Holding them too firmly will tighten up the muscles in your arms and, shoulders, making a smooth, flowing swing virtually impossible. Golfers grip the club as if it were a tiny bird, tightly enough to prevent escape, but not enough to cause harm. Try the same with your shotgun."
—Grits Gresham

New England Arms/FAIR Shotguns

PARDNER PUMP

PARDNER PUMP SHOTGUN

Action: hammerless pump
Stock: walnut, synthetic or camo
Barrel: 28 in., with vent rib, screw-in choke tube; 22-in. Turkey model; combo comes with 22-in. rifled slug barrel
Sights: gold bead front, TruGlo front & rear on Turkey model
Chokes: screw-in Browning/ Winchester/ Mossberg tubes (one provided), turkey choke
Weight: 7.5 lbs. ***Bore/Gauge:*** 12
Magazine: 5-shot tube, with 2-shot plug provided
Features: twin action bars; easy takedown
MSRP: $205-305

New England Arms/FAIR Shotguns

PARDNER YOUTH

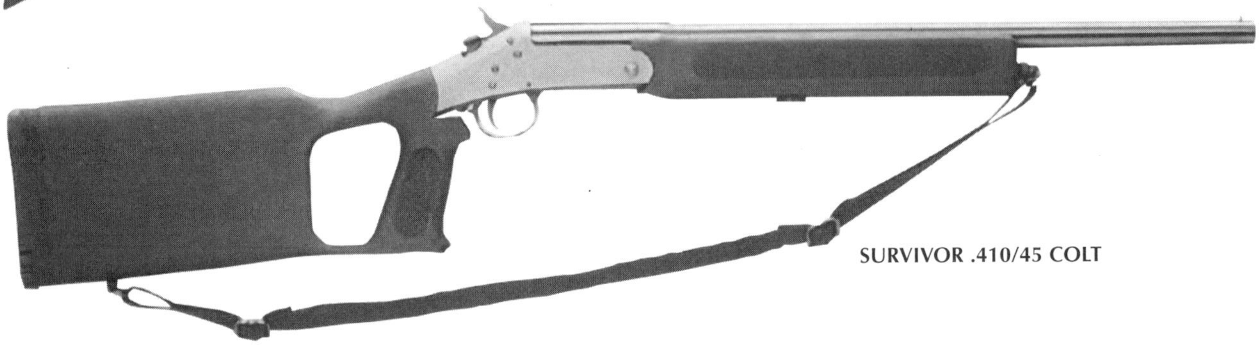

SURVIVOR .410/45 COLT

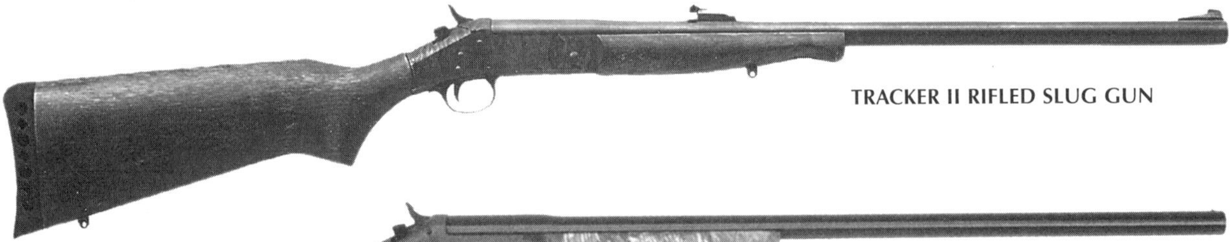

TRACKER II RIFLED SLUG GUN

TURKEY & SPECIAL PURPOSE

SURVIVOR AND PARDNER

Action: hinged single-shot
Stock: synthetic
Barrel: 22, 26, 28 or 32 in.
Chokes: modified, full ***Weight:*** 6.0 lbs.
Bore/Gauge: 12, 16, 20, 28, .410
Magazine: none
Features: Youth and camo-finish Turkey models available; Survivor has hollow pistol-grip buttstock for storage; chambers .410/.45 Colt
Pardner:. $129–137
Pardner Youth: $180–195
Pardner
Turkey Camo Youth: . . . $180–195
Survivor blue or silver: . . . $286–288

TRACKER II RIFLED SLUG GUN

Action: hinged single-shot
Stock: hardwood
Barrel: rifled 24 in.
Chokes: none
Weight: 6.0 lbs.
Bore/Gauge: 12, 20
Magazine: none
Features: adjustable rifle sights; swivel studs standard
MSRP: $193

TURKEY & SPECIAL PURPOSE

Action: hinged single-shot
Stock: hardwood
Barrel: 24 in. (Turkey) or 28 in. (Waterfowl)
Chokes: full, screw-in tubes
Weight: 9.5 lbs.
Bore/Gauge: 10, 12
Magazine: none
Features: Turkey and Waterfowl models available with camo finish; swivel studs standard (Turkey Gun)
Turkey Gun
(black, tubes): $175
(camo, full choke): $185
Special Purpose Waterfowl
10 ga.: $227
With 28 in. barrel, walnut: $206

SHOTGUNS

Perazzi Shotguns

MX8 SPORTING

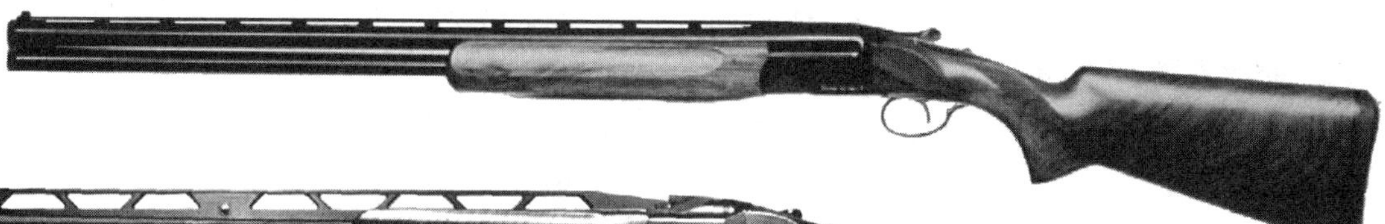

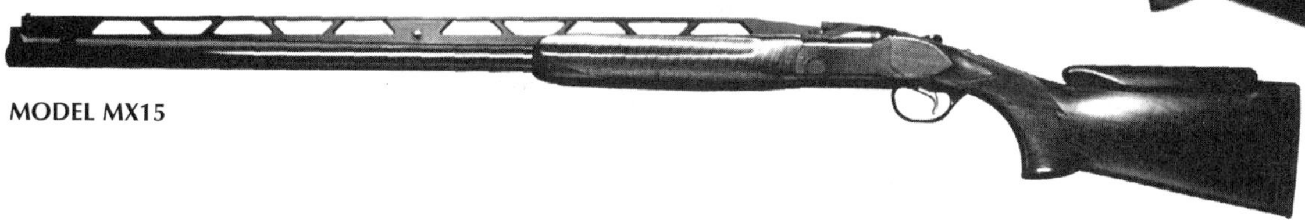

MODEL MX15

MODEL MX8

Action: over/under
Stock: walnut
Barrel: 28 or 34 in.
Chokes: screw-in tubes
Weight: 7.3 lbs.
Bore/Gauge: 12, 20
Magazine: none
Features: hinged-breech action; double triggers or single selective or non-selective trigger; Sporting, Skeet and Trap models and 28 ga. and .410 also available
MX8: . . . . from $7990–12,322

MODEL MX15

Action: hinged single-shot
Stock: walnut, adjustable comb
Barrel: 32 or 35 in. *Chokes:* full
Weight: 8.4 lbs. *Bore/Gauge:* 12
Magazine: none
Features: high trap rib
MX15: . . . . from $7333

Purdey Shotguns

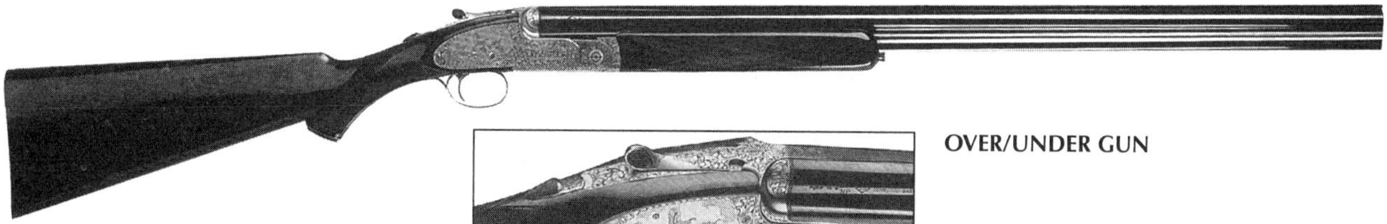

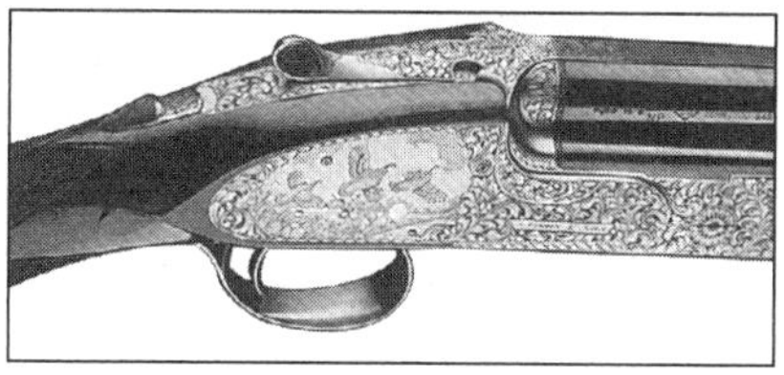

OVER/UNDER GUN

OVER/UNDER GUN

The over/under gun is available in 12, 16, 20, 28 and .410, with each bore made on a dedicated action size. As with side-by-side, the shape of the action has an effect on the weight of the gun. Conventionally, the Purdey over-under will shoot the lower barrel first, but can be made to shoot the top barrel first if required. The standard for regulating and patterning the shooting of a gun is the percentage of the shot charge, which is evenly concentrated in a circle of 30 in. diameter at a range of 40 yards.
MSRP: . . . . from $105,000

Purdey Shotguns

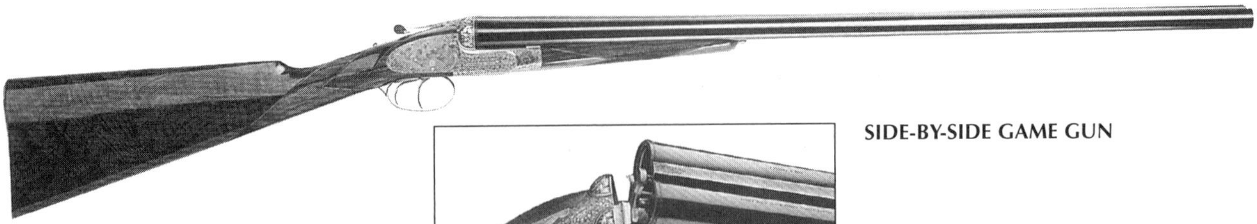

SIDE-BY-SIDE GAME GUN

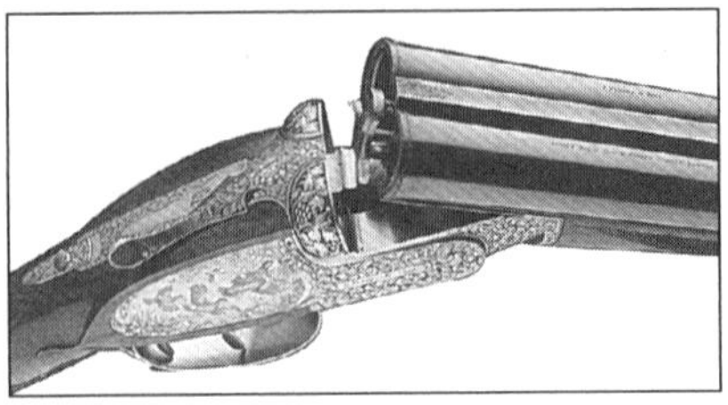

SIDE-BY-SIDE GAME GUN

Purdey easy opening action: All side-by-side guns are built on the easy opening system invented by Frederick Beesley. This system is incorporated in guns built from 1880 onwards.

Purdey offers dedicated action sizes for each of the bores 10, 12, 20, 28 & .410 cores. An extra pair of barrels can be ordered, even if you want a barrel set one ga. smaller. For example, you can have fitted 28 ga. barrels on a 20 ga., and .410 on a 28 ga. These guns are made with a single forend for both bores.
All Purdey barrels, both SxS and O/U, are of chopper lump construction. Each individual tube is hand filled and then "struck up" using striking files. This gives the tube the correct Purdey profile.

Once polished, the individual tubes are joined at the breech using silver solder. The loop iron is similarly fixed. Once together, the rough chokes can be cut and the internal bores finished using a traditional lead lapping technique.

Ribs are hand-filed to suit the barrel contour exactly, and then soft-soldered in place, using pine resin as the fluxing agent. Pine resin provides extra water resistance to the surfaces enclosed by the ribs.

MSRP: . . . . .from $89,000

NEED TO CALL FOR PRICES +44 (0) 20 7499 1801

The world's largest annual shooting tournament is the Grand American World Trapshooting Championships conducted by the Amateur Trapshooting Association. At this competition, 100 trap fields set side by side stretch for 1.75 miles. Several thousand competitors (ages 8 to 80) shoot as many as 5 million clay targets during the 10-day event. Since the first Grand American in 1900, many famous shooters have participated, including Annie Oakley, John Philip Sousa and Roy Rogers.

Remington Shotguns

SHOTGUNS

MODEL 870 EXPRESS

Action: pump
Stock: synthetic, hardwood or camo
Barrel: 18-28 in.
Chokes: screw-in tubes
Weight: 6.0-7.5 lbs.
Bore/Gauge: 12, 16, 20, 28, .410
Magazine: 5 rounds
Features: Super Magnum chambered for 3½ in. shells; deer gun has rifled barrel, open sights

Express: $383
Express Deer w/RS: $398
Express Turkey: $445
Express Deer FR: $425
Express Super Magnum: $431
Express LH: $426
Turkey camo: $471
Express Deer w/cantilever: $554
Combo with Rem choke barrel and slug barrel: $581
Express Super Mag. Turkey, camo: $564
Express Super Mag. Combo with deer barrel: $601

Remington Shotguns

MODEL 870 EXPRESS

MODEL 870 MARINE MAGNUM

MODEL 870 SPS

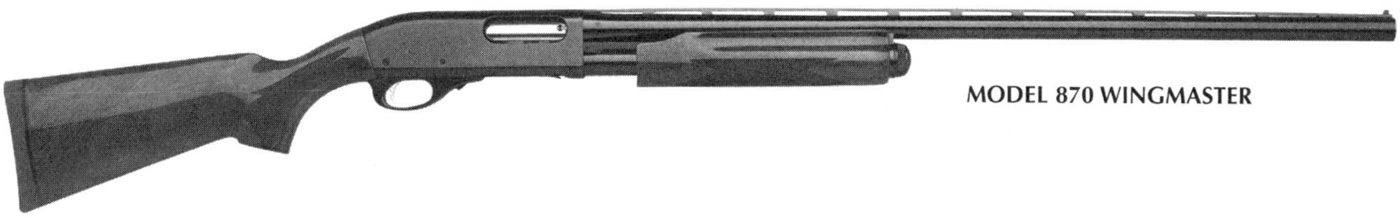

MODEL 870 WINGMASTER

MODEL 870 MARINE MAGNUM

Action: pump
Stock: synthetic
Barrel: 18 in.
Chokes: none, cylinder bore
Weight: 7.5 lbs.
Bore/Gauge: 12
Magazine: 7 rounds
Features: nickel-plated exterior metal; R3 recoil pad
MSRP: $772

MODEL 870 SPS

Action: pump
Stock: camo ***Barrel:*** 20-28 in.
Chokes: screw-in tubes
Weight: 6.25-7.5 lbs.
Bore/Gauge: 12 & 20
Magazine: 4 (3: 3½ in.) rounds
Features: turkey models available; R3 recoil pad
Turkey:. $625

MODEL 870 WINGMASTER

Action: pump
Stock: walnut
Barrel: 25-30 in.
Chokes: screw-in tubes
Weight: 6.5-7.5 lbs.
Bore/Gauge: 12, 16, 20, 28 & .410
Magazine: 3-4 rounds
Features: machine-cut checkering; blued receiver
3 in.: $785
Classic Trap:. $1039
LW-20 (3 in.): $818
LW-Small Bore: $873–928

SHOTGUNS

Remington Shotguns

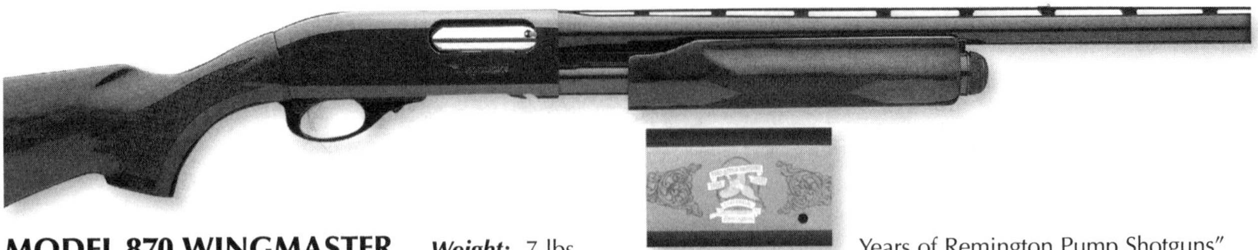

MODEL 870 WINGMASTER 100TH ANNIVERSARY COMMEMORATIVE EDITION

Action: pump
Stock: American walnut
Barrel: 28 in.
Chokes: screw-in tubes
Weight: 7 lbs.
Bore/Gauge: 12
Magazine: 3+1
Features: hammer-forged, carbon steel barrel with vent rib; limited edition, one-year issue with fine-line embellishments on receiver, left side with gold-inlayed centennial logo banner — "100 Years of Remington Pump Shotguns" flushing pheasant with anniversary years 1908–2008; high polish blued finish; gold-plated trigger; 3 RemChoke tubes: IC, M, F; high-gloss, B-grade American walnut stock
MSRP: **$1035**

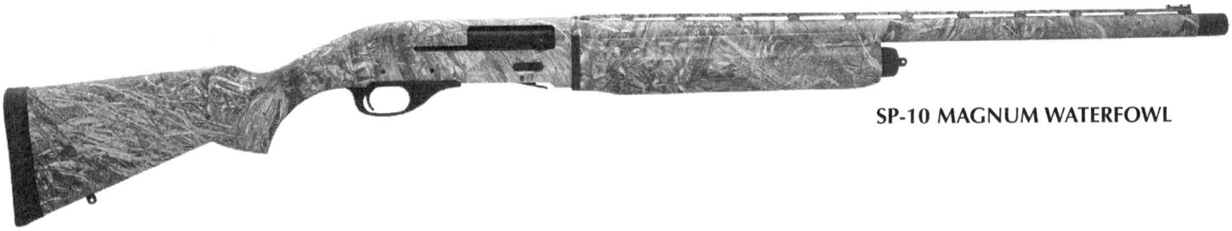

SP-10 MAGNUM WATERFOWL

SP-10 MAGNUM THUMBHOLE CAMO

MODEL SP-10

Action: autoloader
Stock: walnut, synthetic or camo
Barrel: 26 or 30 in.
Chokes: screw-in tubes
Weight: 10.75-11.0 lbs.
Bore/Gauge: 10
Magazine: 2 rounds
Features: the only gas-operated 10 ga. made; stainless piston and sleeve; R3 recoil pad on synthetic
SP-10: **$1772**
Camo: **$1932**

SP-10 MAGNUM WATERFOWL

Action: autoloader
Stock: camo-covered synthetic, Mossy Oak Duck Blind
Barrel: 26 in.
Chokes: 3 Briley Waterfowl tubes
Weight: 10.8 lbs.
Bore/Gauge: 10
Magazine: 2 rounds 3½ in. mag.
Features: soft-recoiling, gas-operating system; fully camouflaged with Mossy Oak Duck Blind pattern; HiViz Fiber Optic front sight; vent rib Rem Choke barrel; rear swivel studs; black padded sling; R3 recoil pad.
MSRP: **$1945**

SP-10 MAGNUM THUMBHOLE CAMO

Action: autoloader
Stock: camo-covered synthetic/laminate, Mossy Oak Obsession
Barrel: 23 in.
Chokes: Briley straight-rifled ported turkey choke tube
Weight: 10.8 lbs.
Bore/Gauge: 10
Magazine: 2 rounds 3½ in. mag.
Features: laminated thumbhole stock; soft-recoiling, gas-operating system; Limbsaver recoil reducing technology; fully camouflaged with Mossy Oak Obsession pattern; fiber optic sights; Rem Choke rifle-sighted barrel; R3 recoil pad
MSRP: **$2052**

SHOTGUNS

Remington Shotguns

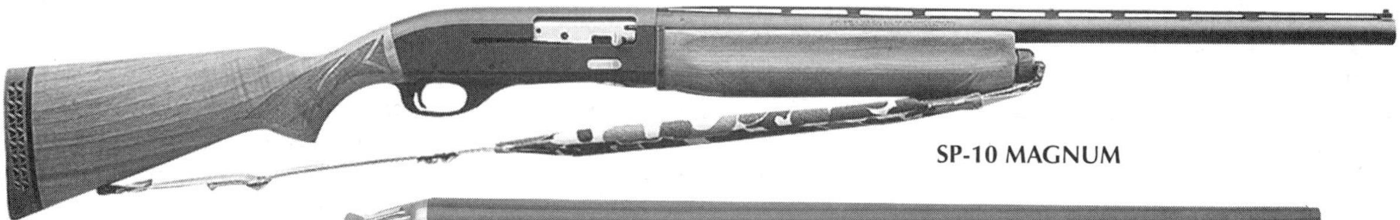

SP-10 MAGNUM

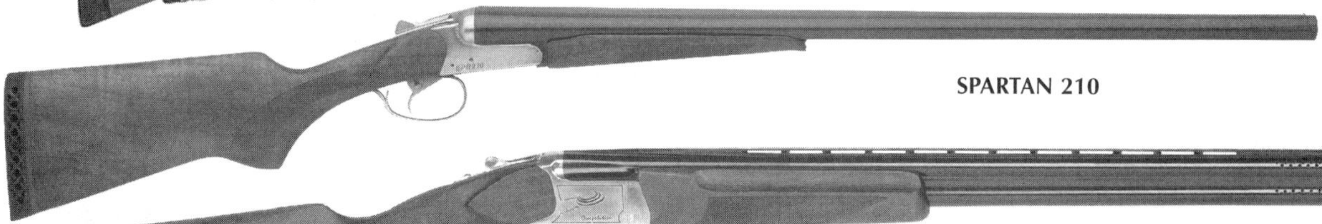

SPARTAN 210

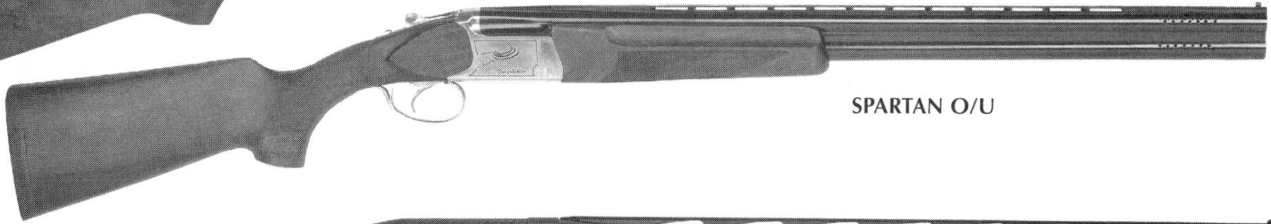

SPARTAN O/U

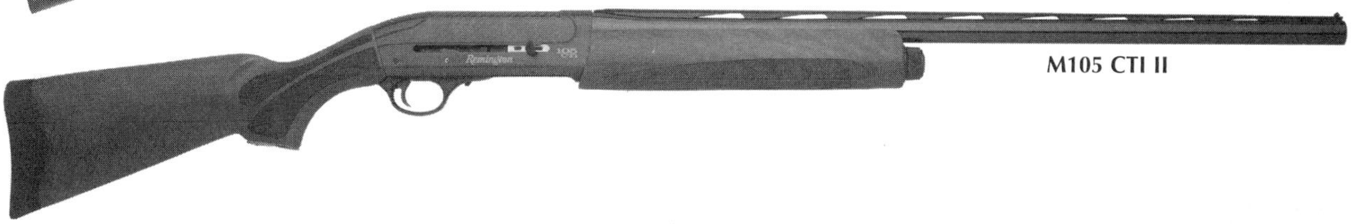

M105 CTI II

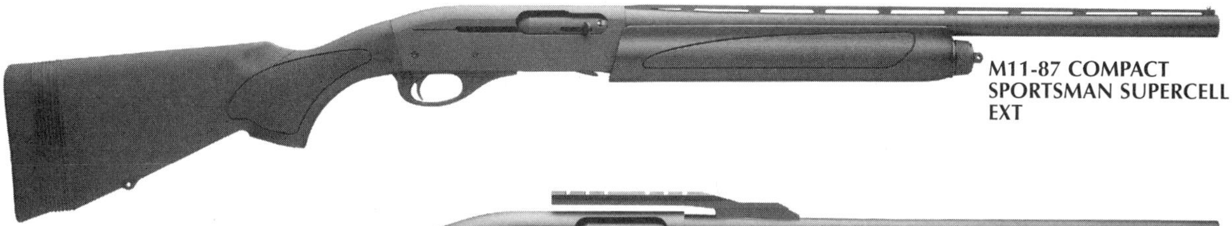

M11-87 COMPACT SPORTSMAN SUPERCELL EXT

M870 EXPRESS TACTICAL

REMINGTON M105 CTI II

Action: autoloading, gas operated
Stock: American walnut
Barrel: 26″ or 28″, vent rib
Chokes: interchangeable Rem Chokes
Weight: 7 lbs.
Bore/Gauge: 12 ga. 3″
Magazine: tube
Features: Remington's lightest, softest-recoiling shotgun with 48% reduction in recoil. Autoloading 12 gauge with 3″ chamber. Made from aircraft-grade titanium with carbon-fiber shell. "Double-down" bottom feed and ejection mechanism. CTi II improvements ensure performance with light 2 ¾-inch loads.
MSRP: $810

REMINGTON M 11-87 COMPACT SPORTSMAN SUPERCELL EXT

Action: autoloading, gas operated
Stock: synthetic, black or camo
Barrel: 21″ with vent rib
Chokes: modified
Weight: 6.5 lbs.
Bore/Gauge: 20 ga. 3″
Magazine: tube
Features: adjustable length of pull (LOP) system to fit young shooters as they grow. Supercell recoil pad.
MSRP: . . . . $772–$878

REMINGTON M870 EXPRESS TACTICAL

Action: pump
Stock: synthetic, gray powder coat finish
Barrel: 18.5″
Chokes: Extended Tactical Rem choke tube
Weight: 7.5 lbs.
Bore/Gauge: 12 ga. 3″
Magazine: extended tube
Features: XS Ghost Ring Sights, ribbed forend. Overall length: 38 ½″.
MSRP: . . . . from $505

Remington Shotguns

REMINGTON M870 SPS SURESHOT SUPERSLUG

Action: pump
Stock: synthetic, Mossy Oak Treestand camo
Barrel: extra-heavy, fluted, fully rifled, 25 ½″
Chokes: none
Weight: 7 7/8 lbs.
Bore/Gauge: 12 ga. 3″
Magazine: tube
Features: sights*:* drilled and tapped receiver with Weaver 429M rail. Finish*:* matte black, 47″ long.
MSRP: . . . . from $772

REMINGTON M887 NITRO MAG

Action: pump
Stock: synthetic, black or Waterfowl camo, built-in swivel studs
Barrel: 28″, solid rib, H-Viz bead
Chokes: interchangeable Rem Chokes
Weight: 7 1/ 2 lbs.
Bore/Gauge: 12 ga. 3 ½″
Magazine: tube
Features: steel receiver, hammer-forged barrel, ArmorLokt polymer coating on all exposed steel, twin action bars, 48″ long.
MSRP: $399

M870 SPS SURESHOT SUPERSLUG

M887 NITRO MAG

Renato Gamba Shotguns

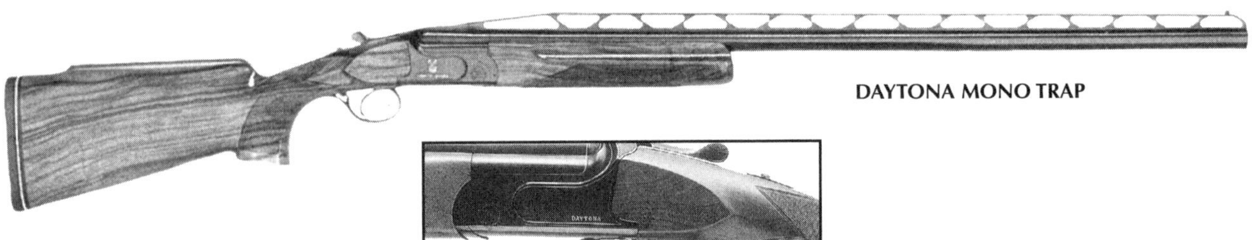

DAYTONA MONO TRAP

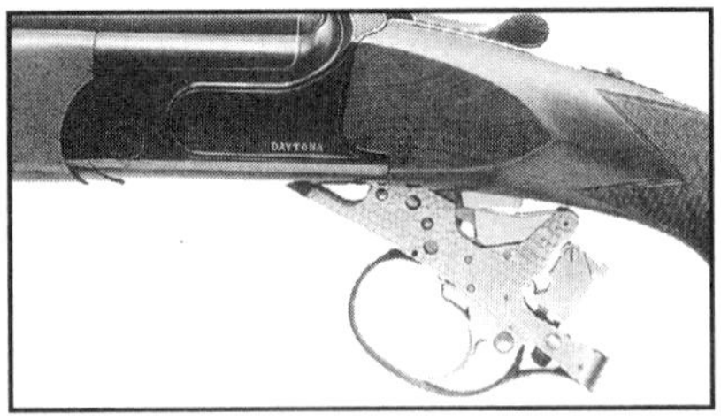

DETACHABLE TRIGGER GROUP WITH GUIDE-PROTECTED COIL SPRINGS

THE DAYTONA SHOTGUN

The Daytona shotgun is available in several styles oriented specifically to American Trap, International Trap, American Skeet, International Skeet and Sporting Clays. The Daytona SL, (the side plate model), and the Daytona SLHH, (the side lock model), are the top of the Daytona line.
All employ the Boss locking system in a breech milled from one massive block of steel.

The trigger group*:* The trigger group is detachable and is removable without the use of tools. The frame that contains the hammers, sears and springs is milled from a single block of special steel and jeweled for oil retention. On special order, an adjustable trigger may be produced with one inch of movement that can accommodate shooters with exceptionally large or small hands. Internally, the hammer springs are constructed from coils that are contained in steel sleeves placed directly behind the hammers. With the fail safe capsule surrounding the springs, the shotgun will fire even if breakage occurs.

Concorde o/u: $3,999–5999
Daytona 2K o/u: $5,999–6999

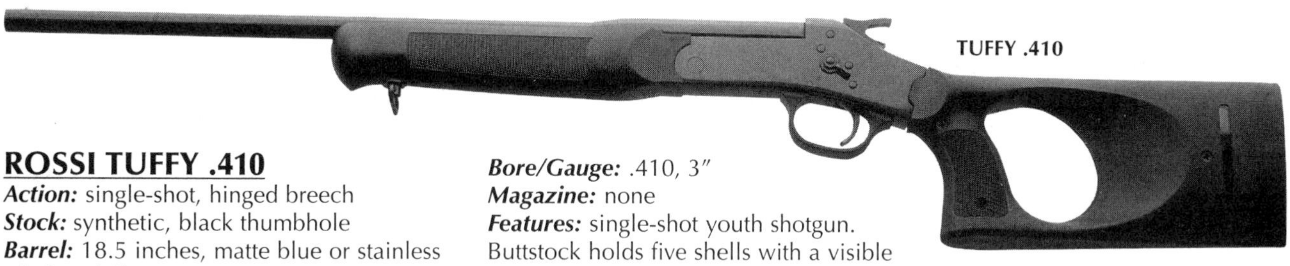

TUFFY .410

ROSSI TUFFY .410

Action: single-shot, hinged breech
Stock: synthetic, black thumbhole
Barrel: 18.5 inches, matte blue or stainless
Chokes: full
Weight: 3 lbs.
Bore/Gauge: .410, 3″
Magazine: none
Features: single-shot youth shotgun. Buttstock holds five shells with a visible shell capacity window.
MSRP: $164–172

TURKEY GUN

Action: break-open single shot
Stock: hardwood
Barrel: 24 in.
Chokes: screw-in tube
Weight: 6.25 lbs.
Bore/Gauge: 12 ga.
Magazine: none
Features: 3.5-in. chamber; button rifled; matte blue finish; fiber optic sights; drilled and tapped barrel with included scope mount base; ambidextrous operation; removable Briley Extended Turkey Choke; installed sling swivels; satin oil-finished exotic wood, pistol grip stock; Taurus Security System
MSRP: $187

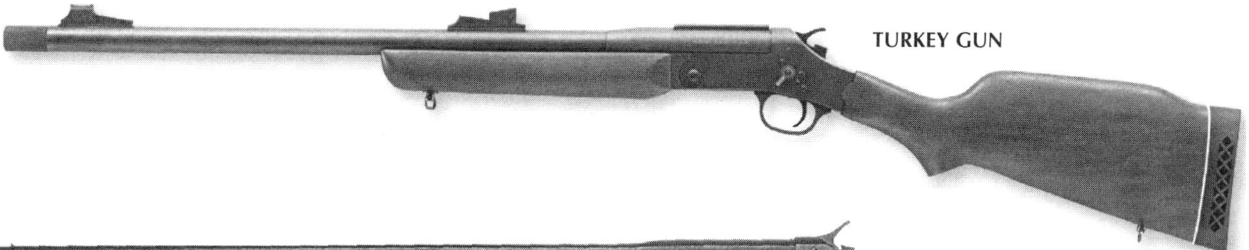

TURKEY GUN

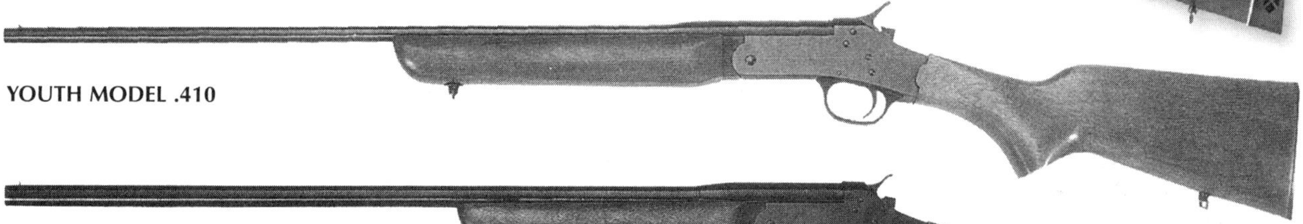

YOUTH MODEL .410

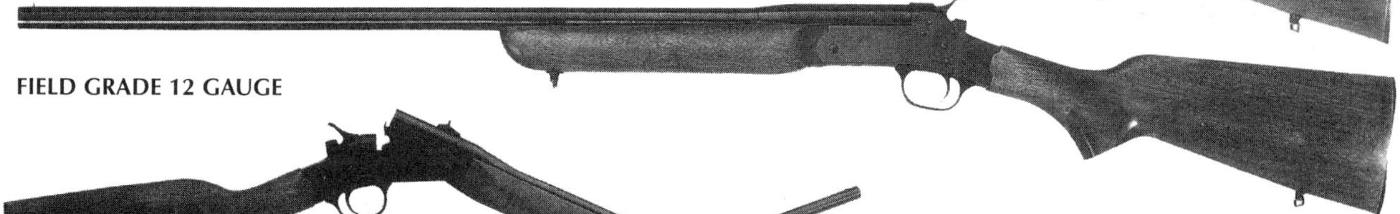

FIELD GRADE 12 GAUGE

MATCHED PAIR

THE DAYTONA SHOTGUN

The Daytona shotgun is available in several styles oriented specifically to American Trap, International Trap, American Skeet, International Skeet and Sporting Clays. The Daytona SL, (the side plate model), and the Daytona SLHH, (the side lock model), are the top of the Daytona line.
All employ the Boss locking system in a breech milled from one massive block of steel.

The trigger group*:* The trigger group is detachable and is removable without the use of tools. The frame that contains the hammers, sears and springs is milled from a single block
of special steel and jeweled for oil retention. On special order, an adjustable trigger may be produced with one inch of movement that can accommodate shooters with exceptionally large or small hands. Internally, the hammer springs are constructed from coils that are contained in steel sleeves placed directly behind the hammers. With the fail safe capsule surrounding the springs, the shotgun will fire even if breakage occurs.

Concorde o/u: $3,999–5999
Daytona 2K o/u: $5,999–6999

Rossi Shotguns

TURKEY GUN

SINGLE BARREL SHOTGUNS

Action: hinged single-shot
Stock: hardwood
Barrel: 28 in.
Chokes: modified, full
Weight: 5.3 lbs.
Bore/Gauge: 12, 20, .410
Magazine: none
Features: exposed-hammer, transfer-bar action; Youth model available; rifle barrels have open sights
Single-Shot: $138
Youth, 22 in. barrel: $138
Rifled barrel slug gun
(23 in. bbl., 12 or 20 ga.): . . . $234
Matched Pair
(.50 cal/12 ga. rifled slug): . . $334

TURKEY GUN

Action: hinged single-shot
Stock: satin, oil-finished exotic hardwood
Barrel: 24 in.
Chokes: removable Briley Extended Turkey Choke
Bore/Gauge: 12
Magazine: none
Features: 3½ in. chamber; fiber optic sights; drilled and tapped barrel; spur hammer with an integral linkage system that prevents the action from opening or closing when the hammer is cocked; pistol grip; ambidextrous operation; installed sling swivels;
Taurus Security System utilizes a key to lock the firearm
MSRP: $187

Ruger Shotguns

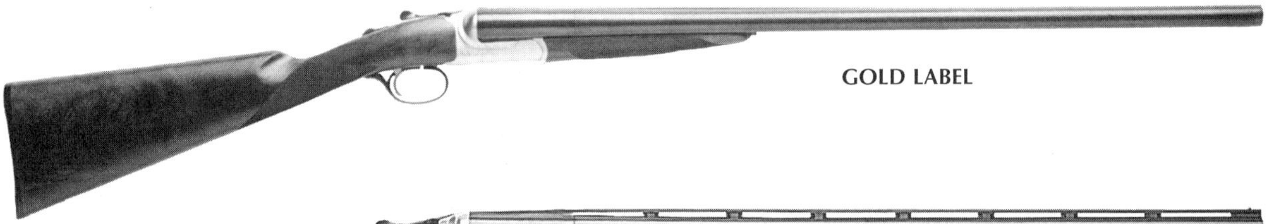

GOLD LABEL

RED LABEL

RED LABEL SHOTGUNS

Action: over/under
Stock: walnut or synthetic, straight or pistol grip
Barrel: 26, 28, 30 in.
Chokes: screw-in tubes
Weight: 6.0-8.0 lbs.
Bore/Gauge: 12, 20, 28
Magazine: none
Features: boxlock; All-Weather version has stainless steel, synthetic stock; 28 ga. only available in 26 or 28 in. barrel
Standard or All-Weather: . . $1249.95
Engraved: $1438.62

SHOTGUNS

Savage Shotguns

MODEL 210F SLUG WARRIOR

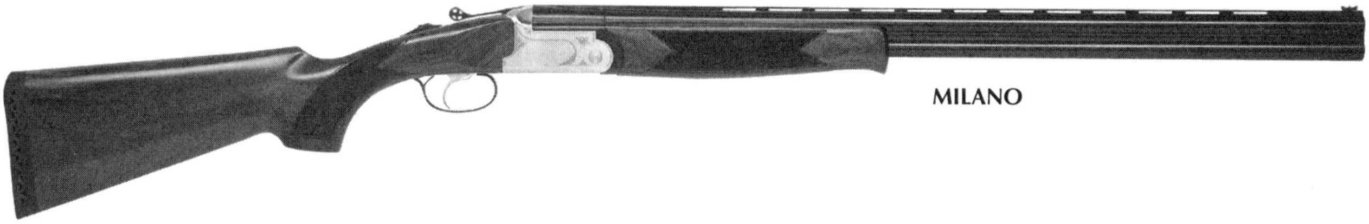

MILANO

MODEL 210F SLUG WARRIOR

Action: bolt
Stock: synthetic
Barrel: rifled, 24 in.
Chokes: none
Weight: 7.5 lbs.
Bore/Gauge: 12
Magazine: 2 rounds
Features: top tang safety; no sights; new camo version available
210F: $529
Camo: $560

MILANO

Action: over/under
Stock: walnut
Barrel: 28 in.
Chokes: screw-in tubes
Weight: 6.25-7.5 lbs.
Bore/Gauge: .410, 20, 28, 12
Magazine: none
Features: chrome-lined barrel w/ elongated forcing cone; automatic ejectors; single selective trigger; fiber optic front sight with brass mid-rib bead; satin finish Turkish walnut stock; F, M, IC included; .410 chokes: M, IC
MSRP: $1417.27

High-visibility, fiber-optic front sights are an accessory every shotgun shooter should consider using. Usually seen in orange or yellow-green, these little beauties collect and concentrate ambient light (diffused light that's already there). They can help your shooting by catching the shooting eye so you are instantly aware of the gun and its muzzle orientation and can immediately start focusing on and tracking the target as you should.

SKB Shotguns

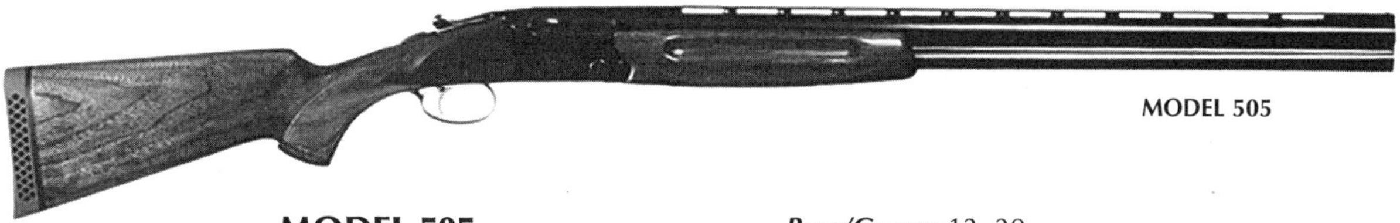

MODEL 505

MODEL 505

Action: over/under
Stock: walnut
Barrel: 26 or 28 in.
Chokes: screw-in tubes
Weight: 8.4 lbs.
Bore/Gauge: 12, 20
Magazine: none
Features: boxlock; ventilated rib, automatic ejectors
MSRP: $1429

Smith & Wesson Shotguns

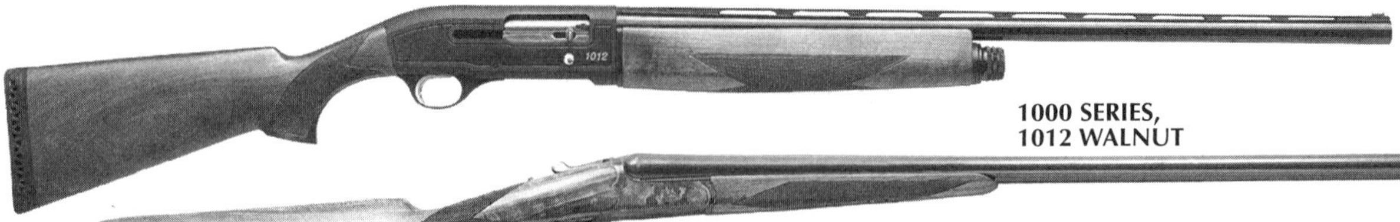

1000 SERIES,
1012 WALNUT

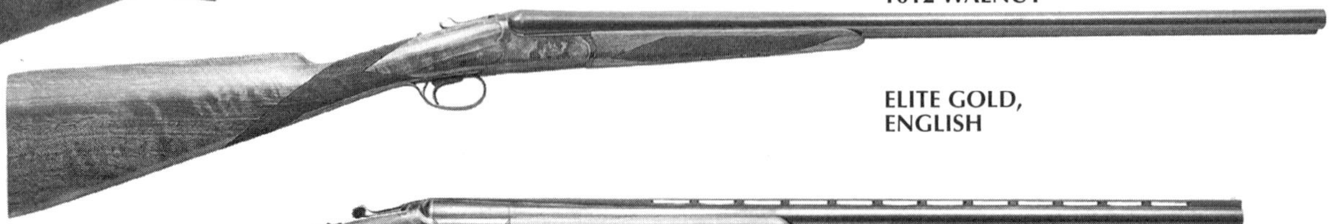

ELITE GOLD,
ENGLISH

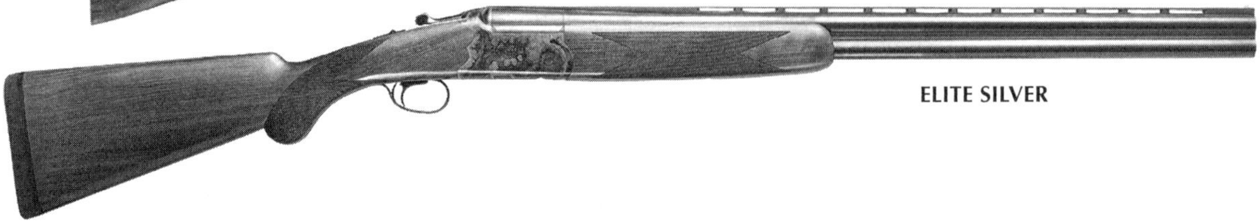

ELITE SILVER

1000 SERIES

Action: autoloader
Stock: walnut or synthetic (satin, black, Realtree MAX-4 and Realtree APG)
Barrel: 24 to 30 in.
Chokes: 5 choke tubes
Weight: 6.5 lbs.
Bore/Gauge: 20 or 12
Magazine: 3+1 or 4+1
Features: offered in 29 configurations; chrome-lined barrel; 4-piece shim kit for stock adjustments; TRUGLO fiber-optic sights; dual-piston feature allows shooting heavy or standard loads
MSRP: $623–882

ELITE GOLD SERIES, GRADE 1

Action: side-by-side
Stock: grade III Turkish walnut
Barrel: 26 or 28 in.
Chokes: 5 English-Teague choke tubes
Weight: 6.5 lbs.
Bore/Gauge: 20
Magazine: none
Features: hand-engraved receiver with bone-charcoal case hardening and triggerplate round body action; rust-blued, chopper-lump barrels; Prince of Wales pistol grip or straight English style grips; white front bead sight; brass mid-bead sight
MSRP: $2380

ELITE SILVER SERIES, GRADE 1

Action: over/under
Stock: grade III Turkish walnut with proprietary catalytic finish
Barrel: 26, 28 or 30 in.
Chokes: 5 English-Teague style choke tubes
Weight: 7.7-7.9 lbs.
Bore/Gauge: 12
Magazine: none
Features: receiver with bone-charcoal case hardening and triggerplate round body action; rust-blued, chopper-lump barrels; Prince of Wales pistol grip; white front bead sight; brass mid-bead sight; solid rubber recoil pad
MSRP: $2380

Stoeger Shotguns

MODEL 2000 REALTREE APG HD

Action: inertia operated semi-auto
Stock: synthetic
Barrel: 24, 26 and 28 in.
Chokes: screw-in tubes
Weight: 6.7-6.8 lbs.
Bore/Gauge: 12
Magazine: 4+1 rounds
Features: inertia operating system; bolt assembly with inertia spring and rotating locking head; cavity in buttstock accommodates 13 oz. mercury-filled recoil reducer (synthetic stock; wood stock 11 oz.); fires 2¾ and 3 in. ammunition; screw-in choke tubes (C, IC, M, F, XF); Red Bar front sight; synthetic, pistol grip stock in Realtree APG HD camo
MSRP: $549

SHOTGUNS

Stoeger Shotguns

MODEL 2000

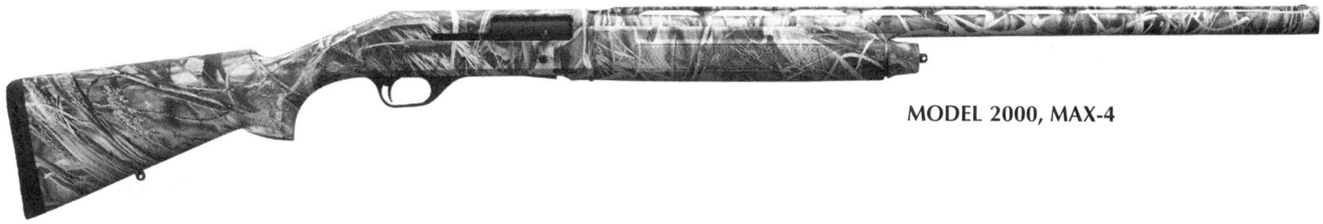

MODEL 2000, MAX-4

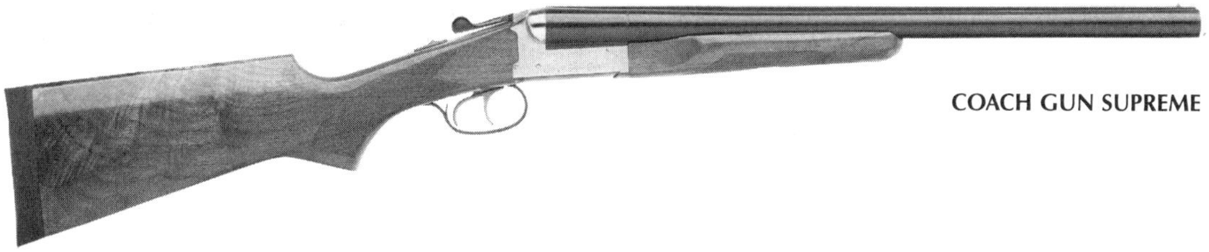

COACH GUN SUPREME

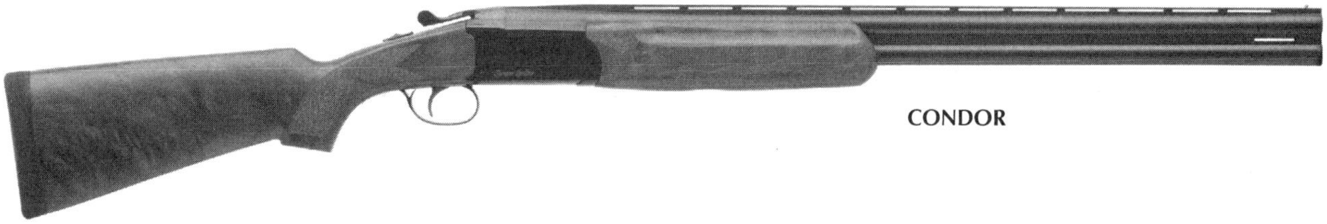

CONDOR

MODEL 2000 WALNUT, SYNTHETIC, APG, MAX-4

Action: inertia operated semi-auto
Stock: synthetic or walnut
Barrel: 18.5(Defense), 24, 26 or 28 in.
Chokes: screw-in tubes
Weight: 6.5-7.2 lbs.
Bore/Gauge: 12
Magazine: 4+1 rounds
Features: inertia-recoil system; ventilated rib; recoil reducers; 2¾ and 3 in. shells; barrels: Max-4 (26 or 28 in.), walnut (26, 28 or 30 in.); chokes (C, IC, M, F, XF); Defense: fixed cylinder

Max 4 Camo: $549
Walnut: $499
Black synthetic: $499
Defense: $499
APG $549

COACH GUN

Action: side-by-side
Stock: walnut
Barrel: 20 in.
Chokes: screw-in or fixed (.410)
Weight: 6.4-6.5 lbs.
Bore/Gauge: 12, 20, .410
Magazine: none
Features: boxlock, double triggers; automatic safety; flush & extended screw-in and fixed chokes (IC & M); available w/ stainless receiver and blued or polished nickel finish; walnut or black hardwood stocks

Coach Gun: $399
Nickel Coach Gun: $469
Silverado Coach Gun: $469
Silverado Coach Gun w/English stock: $469

CONDOR

Action: over/under
Stock: American Walnut
Barrel: 26, 28 in.
Chokes: screw-in or fixed
Weight: 6.7 to 7.4 lbs., 5.5 lbs. (Youth)
Bore/Gauge: 12, 20, 16 & .410
Magazine: none
Features: single trigger; 2¾ and 3 in. shells; 16-gauge w/ 2¾ in.; Standard and Supreme grades; Supreme available with 24 in. barrel; screw-in (IC & M) and fixed chokes (M & F), .410 (F & F); American walnut stock

Condor: $399
Condor Supreme: $599
Condor Youth: $399

Stoeger Shotguns

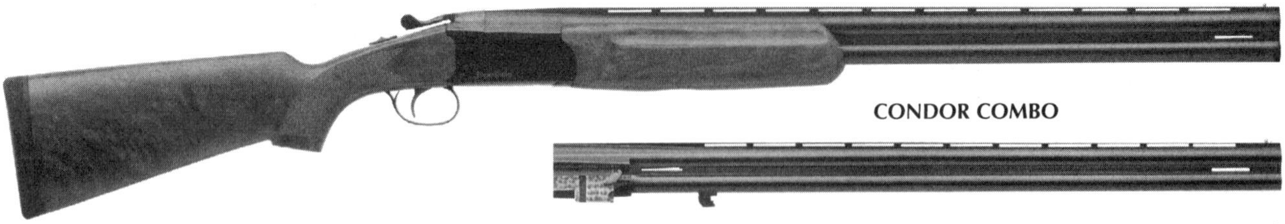

CONDOR COMBO

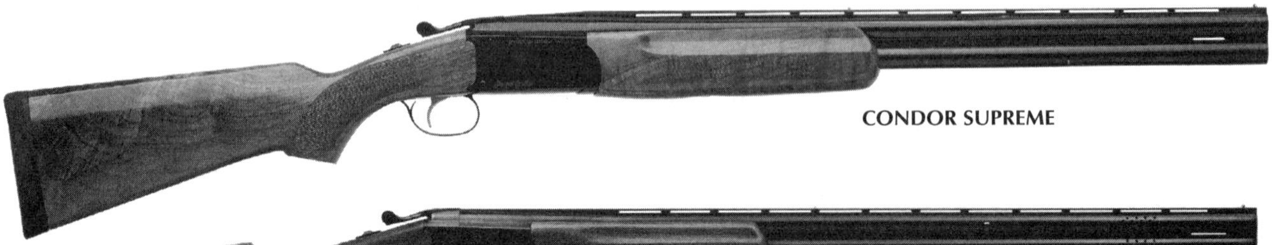

CONDOR SUPREME

CONDOR COMPETITION COMBO

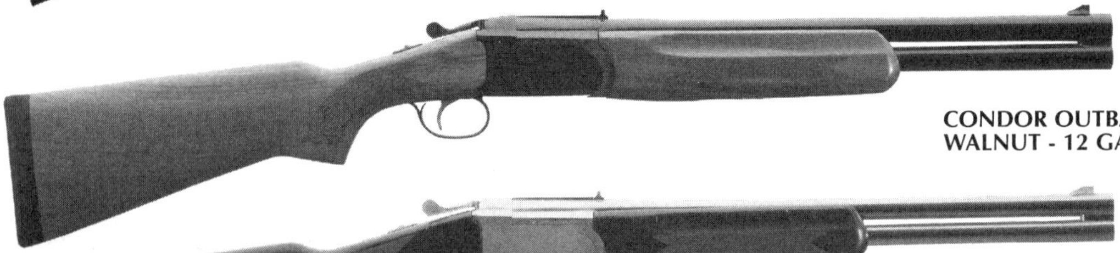

CONDOR OUTBACK
WALNUT - 12 GAUGE

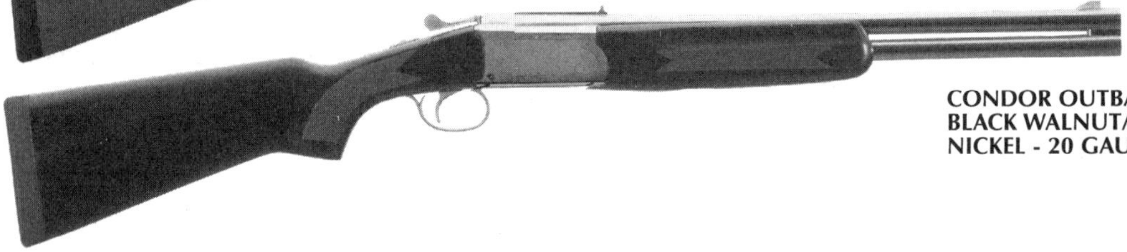

CONDOR OUTBACK
BLACK WALNUT/
NICKEL - 20 GAUGE

CONDOR COMBO

Action: over/under
Stock: walnut ***Barrel:*** 28/26 in.
Chokes: screw-in
Weight: 7.4 /6.8-lbs.
Bore/Gauge: 12, 20 ***Magazine:*** none
Features: boxlock; single trigger; screw-in chokes (I & M); 2 barrel sets (12 and 20 ga.); A-grade (Condor) or AA-grade (Supreme) American walnut stocks; ejectors (Supreme only)
Condor:. $549
Condor Supreme: $739

CONDOR COMPETITION

Action: over/under
Stock: walnut ***Barrel:*** 30 in.
Chokes: screw in
Weight: 7.8 (12 ga.), 7.3 (20 ga.)
Bore/Gauge: 12, 20 ***Magazine:*** none
Features: single trigger; ported barrels; barrel selector and ejectors; screw-in chokes (IC, M, F; brass bead front & silver bead mid sights; right- and left-hand models w/ palm swell; adjustable comb; AA-grade American walnut stocks
MSRP: $629

CONDOR COMPETITION COMBO 12 GA./20 GA.

Action: over/under
Stock: walnut ***Barrel:*** 30/30 in.
Chokes: screw in
Weight: 7.8/7.3
Bore/Gauge: 12/20 ***Magazine:*** none
Features: single trigger; ported barrels; barrel selector and ejectors; screw-in chokes (IC, M, F); brass bead front & silver bead mid sights; right- and left-hand models w/ palm swell; adjustable comb; AA-grade walnut stocks
MSRP: $839

CONDOR OUTBACK

Action: over/under
Stock: walnut; black hardwood
Barrel: 20 in.
Chokes: screw-in tubes
Weight: 6.5 to 7.0 lbs.
Bore/Gauge: 12, 20
Magazine: none
Features: box-lock action; single trigger; extractors; 3 in. chambers; notched rear and fixed blade front sights; screw-in tube chokes (IC & M) optional flush & extended screw-in tubes (C, IC, M, F); A-grade walnut or black finished hardwood stocks
Walnut/high polish blue: $399
Black hardwood/polished nickel: $449

Stoeger Shotguns

P350 APG, 12-GA.

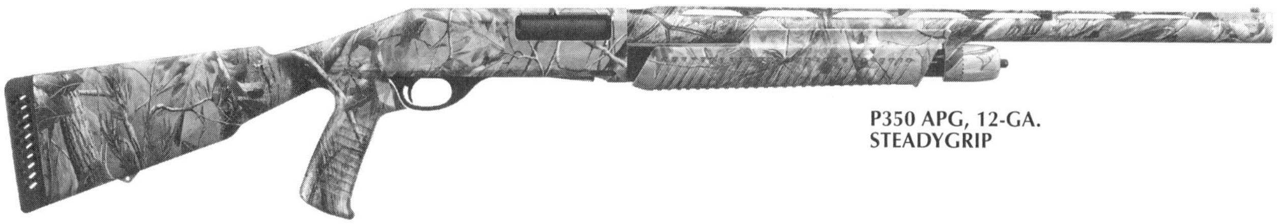

P350 APG, 12-GA.
STEADYGRIP

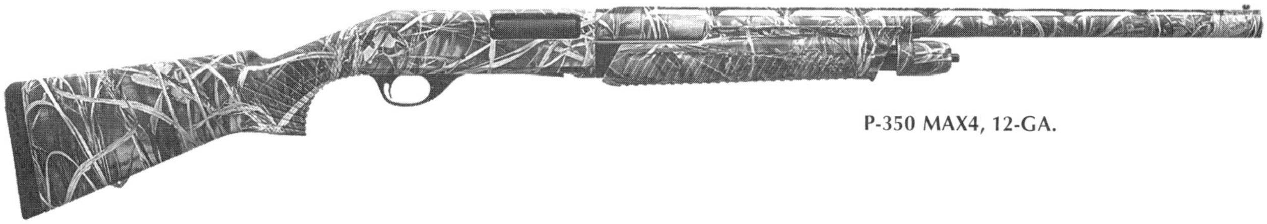

P-350 MAX4, 12-GA.

P-350 SYNTHETIC, 12-GA.

P-350 SYNTHETIC DEFENSE

P350 PUMP

Action: pump
Stock: synthetic
Barrel: 24, 26 and 28 in. 18.5 in. (Defense)
Chokes: screw-in
Weight: 6.4 to 6.9 lbs
Bore/Gauge: 12
Magazine: 4 + 1 rounds
Features: bolt with rotating lugs; raised rib; fires all types of 12-gauge ammunition — accepts 2¾ in., 3 in., 3½ in. Magnum (target loads, steel shot, lead shot and slugs); available with optional 13-oz. mercury filled recoil reducer; screw-in choke tubes (C, IC, M, F, XF turkey); stocks available in black synthetic, Advantage Max-4 HD or synthetic available in pistol grip, Max-4 HD & APG HD available in Steady Grip configuration; red bar front and metal bead mid sights; Defense model with black synthetic pistol-grip stocks, 3½-in. chamber, blade front sight, fixed cylinder choke

Synthetic: **$329**
Synthetic Pistol Grip: **$329**
APG HD Camo: **$429**
Max 4 Camo: **$429**
APG HD Steady Grip: **$429**
Timber HD Steady Grip: **$429**
Defense: **$329**

Stoeger Shotguns

UPLANDER

Action: side-by-side
Stock: walnut
Barrel: 22 (youth), 24, 26 and 28 in.
Chokes: screw-in and fixed
Weight: 7 to 7.5 lbs, 6.5 to 6.8 (Youth)
Bore/Gauge: 12, 20, 16, 28 and .410
Magazine: none
Features: single selective trigger; tang-mounted automatic safety; extractors; brass bead front sight; 2¾ and 3-in. chambers (16- and 28-ga. in 2¾ in. chambers only); screw-in chokes 12 & 20 ga. (IC & M), fixed chokes 16, 28 ga. and .410 bore (F&F); optional flush and extended screw-in choke tubes available for 12 & 20 ga. (C, IC, M, IM, F); A-grade satin walnut stocks; Youth model 20 ga. or .410 with 13-in. length-of-pull and 22-in. barrel; Combo sets available in 12/20 or 20/28-ga. configurations

Uplander: $399
Uplander Combo: $659
Uplander Supreme: $499
Uplander Youth: $399

Tristar Sporting Arms Shotguns

COBRA TACTICAL PUMP

COBRA TACTICAL PUMP

Action: pump
Stock: black synthetic
Barrel: 20 in.
Chokes: screw-in tubes
Weight: 6.9 lbs.
Bore/Gauge: 12 ga.
Magazine: 5+1 rounds
Features: return spring in forearm, allows user to pull back on the forearm to eject the shell, spring returns the forearm back to position and shucks another shell into the chamber; 3 Beretta-style tubes (IC, M, F); matte black, separate pistol grip folding stock
MSRP: $349

Verona Shotguns

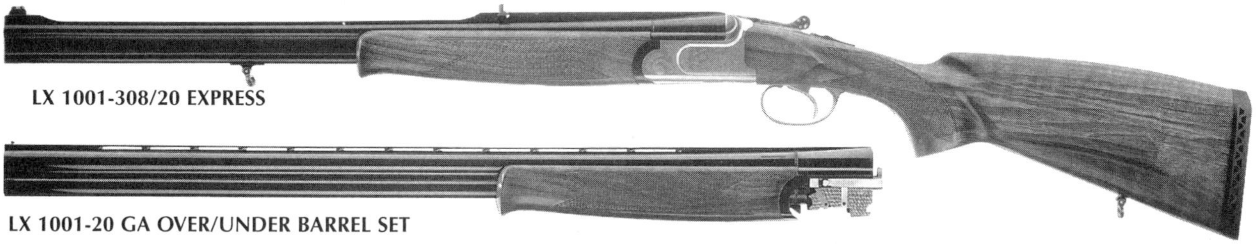

LX 1001-308/20 EXPRESS

LX 1001-20 GA OVER/UNDER BARREL SET

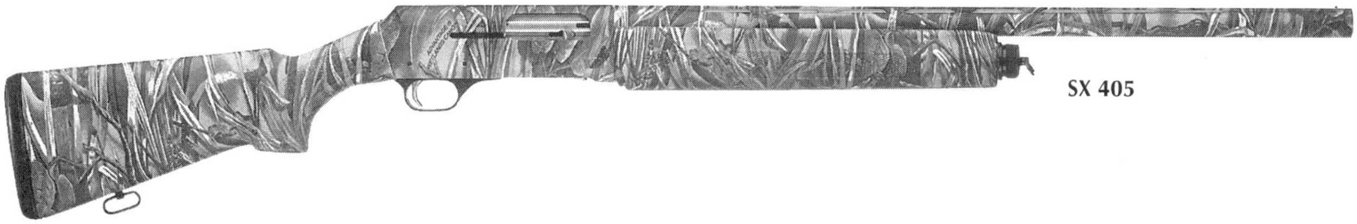

SX 405

MODEL LX EXPRESS

Action: over/under
Stock: Turkish walnut
Barrel: 28 in.
Chokes: screw-in tubes
Weight: 8.0 lbs.
Bore/Gauge: .223, .243, .270, .308 or .30-06 over 20 ga.
Magazine: none
Features: single selective trigger; automatic ejectors
Express Combo with Express and 20 ga. over/under set: $2599

VERONA 401, 405, 406 SHOTGUN

Action: autoloading, inertia operated
Stock: oil-finished walnut with forend checkering
Barrel: 26″
Chokes: interchangeable
Weight: 7 lbs.
Bore/Gauge: 12 ga, 3″ or 3 ½", or 20 ga., 3″
Magazine: tube
Features: Legacy Sports offers the Semi-automatic Verona shotgun (made by Pietta in Italy). Brass sight on standard model; fiber optic on deluxe. Pivoting bolt with integral double-charging lever and sleeve. Black nylon recoil pad. Silver, blue or pewter finish. 401 and 405 with 3″ chambering and the 406 series in 3 ½″.
401: $1199-1250
405: $1099
406: $1199

VERONA 501 SHOTGUN OVER/UNDER

Action: hinged breech
Stock: oil-finished walnut with round pistol grip and rounded forend
Barrel: 28 inches
Chokes: interchangeable
Weight: 7 lbs
Bore/Gauge: 20 and 28 ga.
Magazine: none
Features: Made by Fausti in Italy and imported by Legacy Sports. Two barrel sets in 20 and 28 gauge. 3″ magnum in 20 ga. Receiver has gold inlay of quail. Action features automatic safety and single, selective gold trigger. Black recoil pad.
MSRP: $1299

Weatherby Shotguns

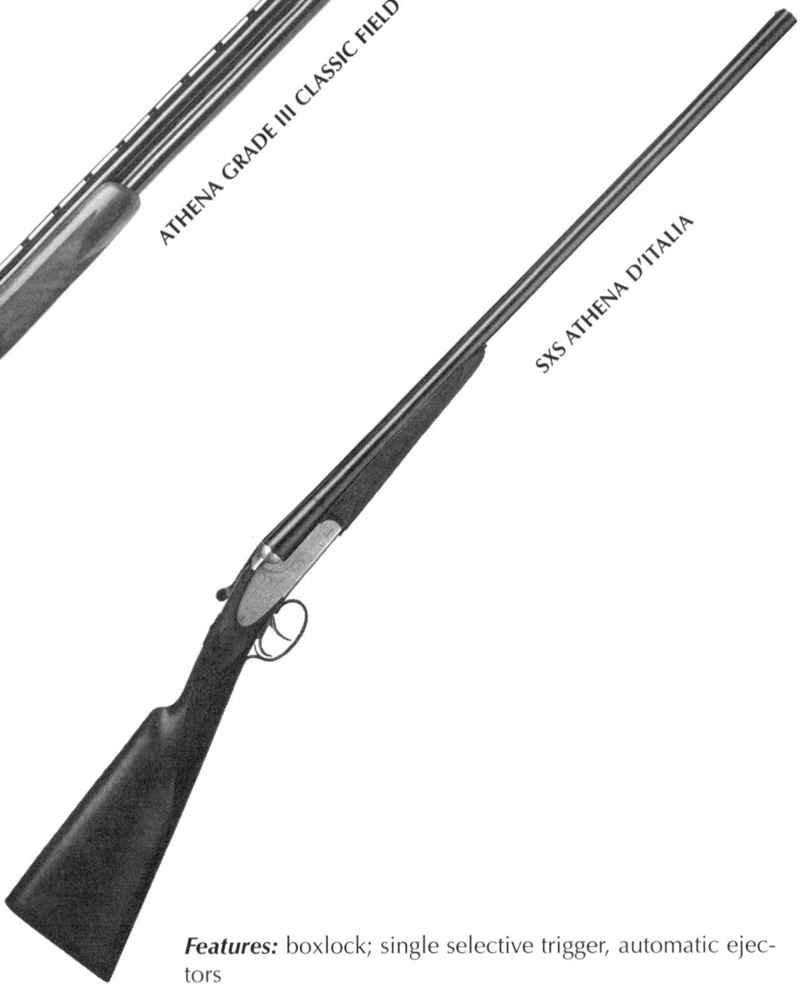

ATHENA

Action: over/under
Stock: walnut
Barrel: 26 or 28 in.
Chokes: screw-in tubes
Weight: 8.0 lbs.
Bore/Gauge: 12, 20, 28
Magazine: none
Features: boxlock; single selective mechanical trigger, automatic ejectors
Grade III Classic Field:. $2599
Grade V Classic Field: $3999

ORION

Action: over/under
Stock: walnut, straight or pistol grip
Barrel: 26, 28, 30 or 32 in.
Chokes: screw-in tubes
Weight: 8.0 lbs.
Bore/Gauge: 12, 20 or 28
Magazine: none
Features: boxlock; single selective trigger, automatic ejectors
Grade II: $1899
Grade III:. $2199

SXS ATHENA DÍITALIA

Action: side-by-side
Stock: Turkish walnut
Barrel: 26 or 28 in.
Chokes: screw-in tubes
(fixed chokes in 28 ga.)
Weight: 6.75-7.25 lbs.
Bore/Gauge: 12, 20, 28
Magazine: none
Features: chrome-lined and back-bored barrels; Anson and Deeley
boxlock mechanism; automatic
ejectors; engraved sideplates; double triggers and a straight grip, IC and
M chokes in 28 ga.
MSRP: $3125

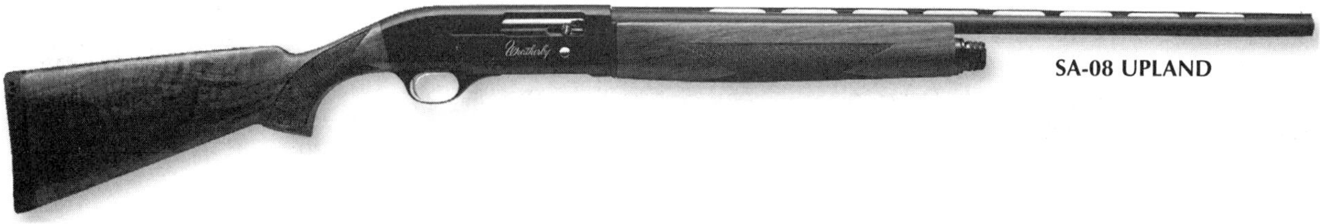

SA-08 UPLAND

SA-08 YOUTH

UPLAND PA-08

SA-08 UPLAND

Action: autoloader
Stock: walnut
Barrel: 26 or 28 in.
Chokes: adjustable integral
Weight: 6 or 6.75 lbs.
Bore/Gauge: 20, 12 ga.
Magazine: 4+1 rounds
Features: adjustable gas system; screw on valve caps; chambers 7/8 oz. to 3-in. loads; integral Multi-choke System (IC, M, F); oil-finish walnut stock
MSRP: **$669**

SA-08 YOUTH

Action: autoloader
Stock: walnut
Barrel: 26 in.
Chokes: adjustable integral
Weight: 5.75 lbs.
Bore/Gauge: 20 ga.
Magazine: 4+1 rounds
Features: vented top rib; dual valve system; matte black metal finish; integral Multi-choke System (IC, M, F); oil-finish walnut stock with 12 ½-in. length of pull to fit women and younger shooters
MSRP: **$669**

WEATHERBY UPLAND PA-08

Action: pump
Stock: checkered walnut
Barrel: 26 or 28″ with vent rib
Chokes: 3 screw-in choke tubes
Weight: 6½ to 7 lbs.
Bore/Gauge: 12 ga. 3″
Magazine: tube
Features: Ventilated top rib and brass bead front sight. 3″ chamber.
MSRP: **$409**

Winchester Shotguns

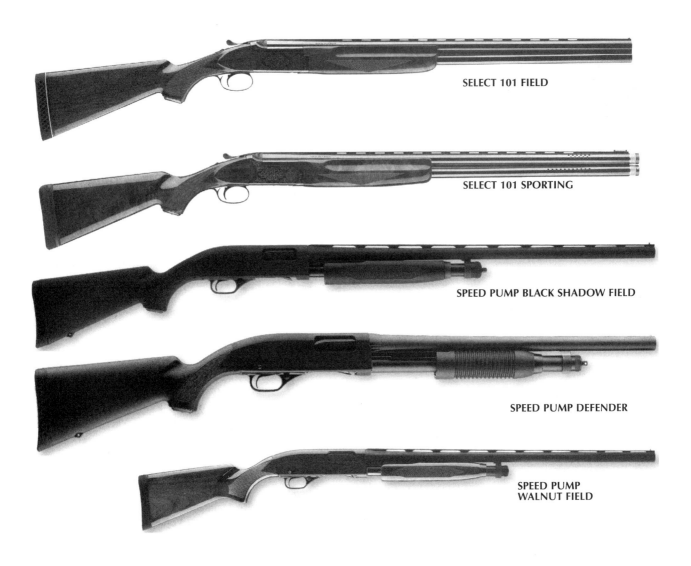

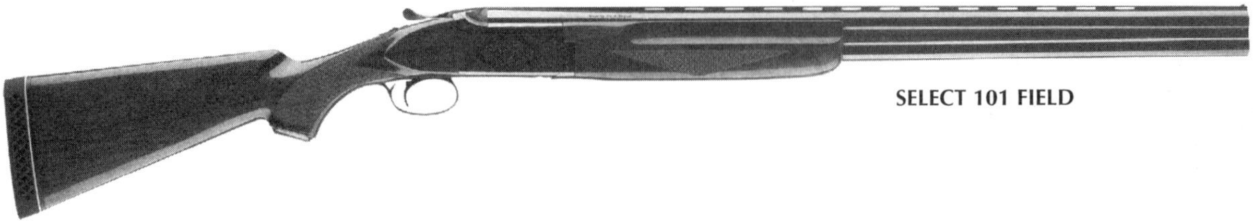

SELECT 101 FIELD

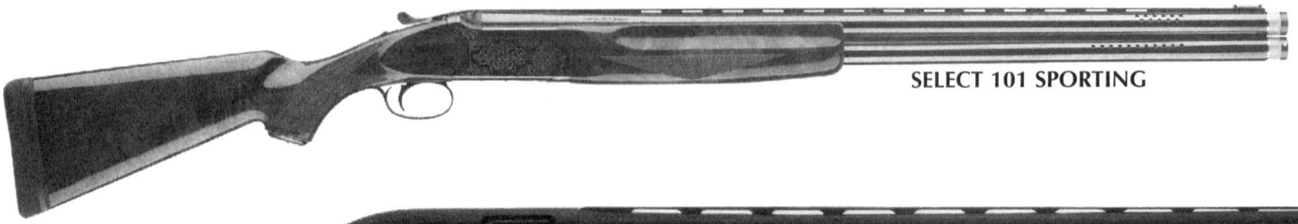

SELECT 101 SPORTING

SPEED PUMP BLACK SHADOW FIELD

SPEED PUMP DEFENDER

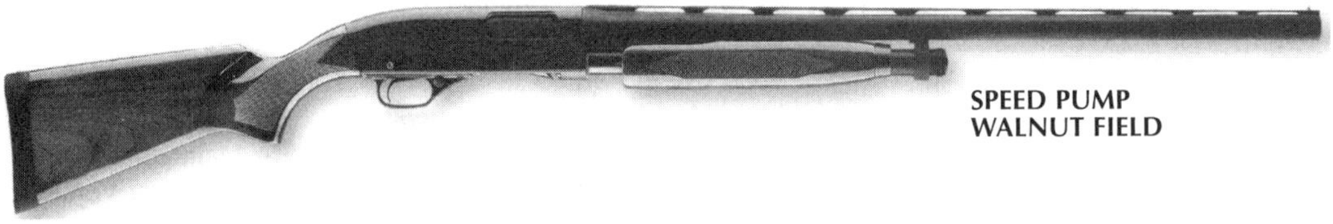

SPEED PUMP
WALNUT FIELD

SELECT 101

Action: over/under
Stock: high gloss grade II/III walnut
Barrel: 26 or 28 (Field model); 28, 30 or 32 in. (Sporting)
Chokes: Invector-Plus with three tubes (Field model) or five Signature extended tubes (Sporting model)
Weight: 7.0-7.7 lbs.
Bore/Gauge: 12
Magazine: none
Features: blued receiver with deep-relief engraving; lightweight ported barrels; Pachmayr Decelerator sporting pad control recoil; 10mm runway rib and white mid-bead; TRUGLO front sight round
101 Field: **$1759**
101 Sporting: **$2179**

SPEED PUMP BLACK SHADOW FIELD

Action: pump
Stock: composite
Barrel: 26, 28 in.
Chokes: screw-in tubes
Weight: 7 lbs., 7.25 lbs.
Bore/Gauge: 12
Magazine: 5+1
Features: 4-lug rotary bolt design; chrome plated barrels; fires all factory 2¾ in. and 3 in. steel, tungsten, bismuth and lead loads; Invector-Plus choke system
MSRP: **$399**

SPEED PUMP DEFENDER

Action: pump
Stock: composite
Barrel: 18 in.
Chokes: open
Weight: 6.5 lbs.
Bore/Gauge: 12
Magazine: 5+1
Features: 4-lug rotary bolt design; chrome plated barrels; handles buckshot or rifled slugs; non-glare metal surfaces; deeply grooved forearm
MSRP: **$349**

Winchester Shotguns

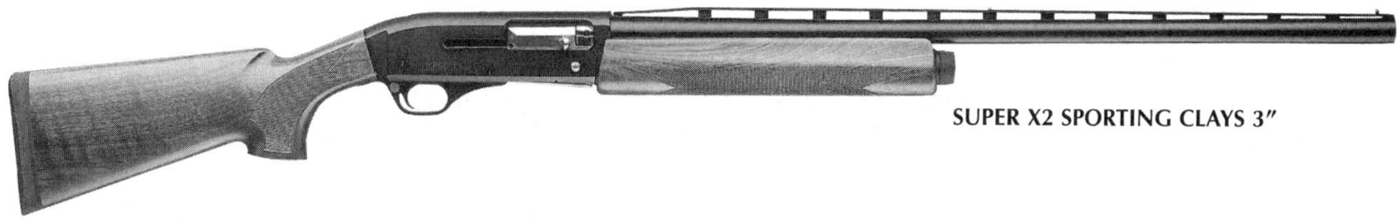

SUPER X2 SPORTING CLAYS 3″

SUPER X2 MAGNUM
STANDARD COMPOSITE

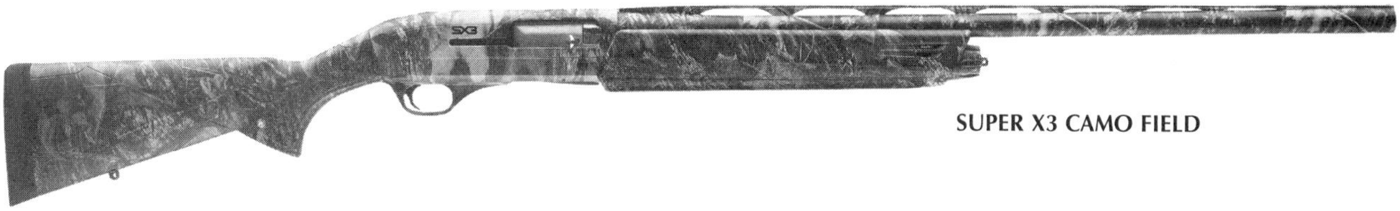

SUPER X3 CAMO FIELD

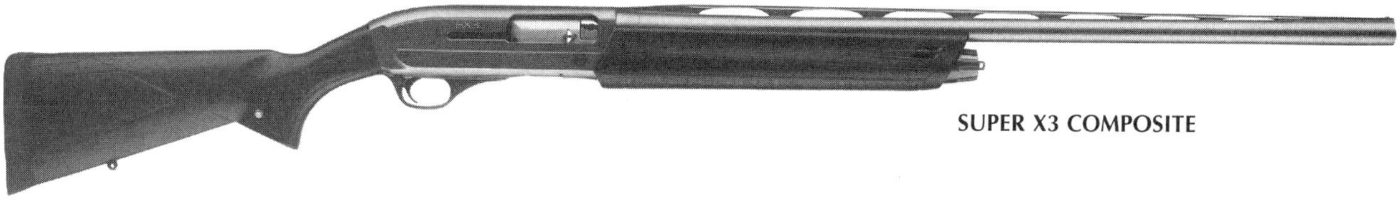

SUPER X3 COMPOSITE

SUPER X2

Action: autoloader
Stock: walnut or synthetic
Barrel: 22, 24, 26, 28 or 30 in.
Chokes: screw-in tubes
Weight: 8.0 lbs.
Bore/Gauge: 12
Magazine: 4 rounds
Features: gas-operated mechanism, back-bored barrels; all with Dura-Touch finish, some with Tru-Glo sights
Sporting Clays: $1459

SUPER X3 CAMO FIELD

Action: autoloader
Stock: composite
Barrel: 26 or 28 in.
Chokes: screw-in tubes
Weight: 7.5 lbs.
Bore/Gauge: 12
Magazine: 4 rounds
Features: Mossy Oak New Break-Up finish; composite stock w/ shims and Dura-Touch Armor Coating finish; Invector-Plus choke tube system
MSRP: $1469

SUPER X3 COMPOSITE

Action: autoloader
Stock: composite
Barrel: 26 or 28 in.
Chokes: screw-in tubes
Weight: 7.5 lbs.
Bore/Gauge: 12
Magazine: 4 rounds
Features: slim barrel with machined rib; lightweight alloy receiver; light-weight alloy magazine tube and recoil spring system; self-adjusting Active Valve gas system; Pachmayr Decelerator recoil pad; composite stock w/ Dura-Touch Armor Coating finish; Invector-Plus choke tube system
Super X3 Composite 3 in.: . . . $1139
Super X3 Composite 3¾ in.:. . . $1269

Winchester Shotguns

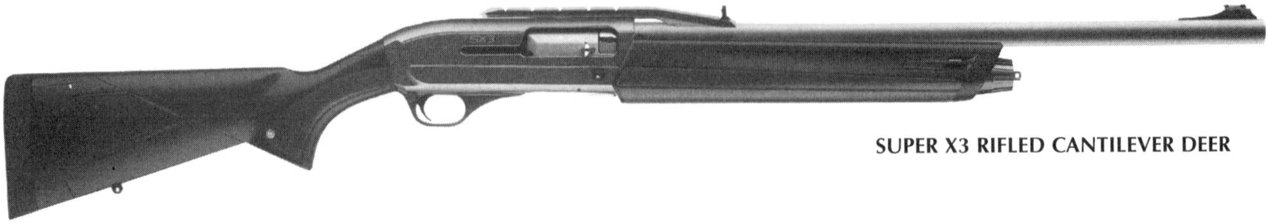

SUPER X3 RIFLED CANTILEVER DEER

SUPER X3 WATERFOWL

SUPER X3 RIFLED CANTILEVER DEER

Action: autoloader
Stock: composite
Barrel: 22 in.
Chokes: none
Weight: 7.0 lb.
Bore/Gauge: 12
Magazine: 4 rounds
Features: fully rifled barrel; cantilever scope base mount and rifle style sights; lengthwise groove in the cantilever; TruGlo fiber-optic front sight; Weaver-style rail on the cantilever; composite stock w/ Dura-Touch armor coating
MSRP: $1269

SUPER X3 SELECT SUPER X3 WATERFOWL

Action: autoloader ***Stock:*** composite
Barrel: 26 or 28 in.
Chokes: screw-in tubes
Weight: 7.5 lb. ***Bore/Gauge:*** 12
Magazine: 4 rounds
Features: barrel with improved ventilated rib design; Active Valve system; weather-resistant composite stock and forearm with Dura-Touch Armor Coating finish; available in Mossy Oak New Shadow Grass finish; stock shims for cast and comb height adjustability; sling swivel studs are included; Invector-Plus choke tube system
MSRP: $1469

SHOTGUNS

HANDGUNS

Accu-Tek Handguns

AT-380 II

Action: autoloader
Grips: composite
Barrel: 2.8 in.
Sights: target
Weight: 23.5 oz
Caliber: 380 ACP
Capacity: 6 + 1 rounds
Features: exposed hammer; one-hand manual safety; European type magazine release on bottom of grip; adjustable rear sight; stainless steel magazine
MSRP: $262

American Derringer Handguns

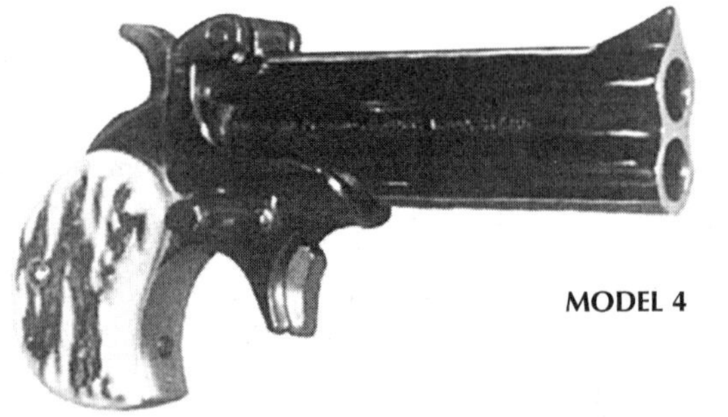

MODEL 4

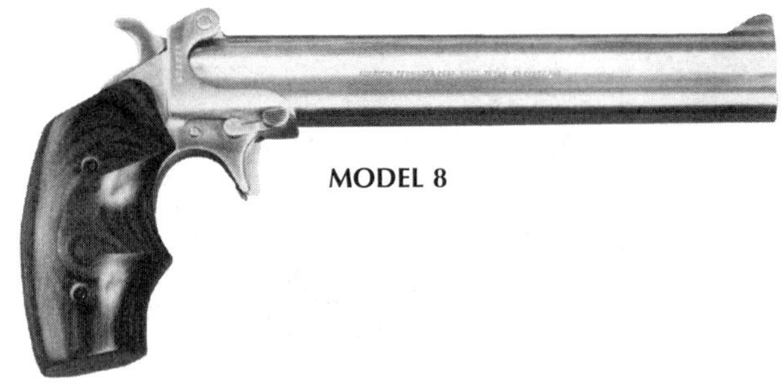

MODEL 8

MODEL 1

Action: hinged breech
Grips: rosewood or stag
Barrel: 3 in. ***Sights:*** fixed open
Weight: 15.0 oz.
Caliber: .45 Colt/.410
Capacity: 2 rounds
Features: single-action; automatic barrel selection; manually operated hammer-block type safety
MSRP: $705

MODEL 4

Action: hinged breech
Grips: rosewood or stag
Barrel: 4.1 in., 6 in. (Alaskan Survival)
Sights: fixed open ***Weight:*** 16.5 oz.
Caliber: .32 H&R, .357 Mag., .357 Max., .44 Mag., .45 Colt/.410, .45-70
Capacity: 2 rounds
Features: satin or high polish stainless steel finish; single-action; automatic barrel selection; manually operated hammer-block type safety
.357 Mag.: $760
.357 Max.: $760
.44 Mag.: $815
Alaskan Survival (.45 Colt/.410): $815

MODEL 6

Action: hinged breech
Grips: rosewood, walnut, black
Barrel: 6 in.
Sights: fixed open
Weight: 21.0 oz.
Caliber: .357 Mag; .45 Auto; .45 Colt/.410
Capacity: 2 rounds
Features: satin or high polish stainless steel finish; single-action; automatic barrel selection; manually operated hammer-block type safety
MSRP: $860

MODEL 7 LIGHTWEIGHT & ULTRA LIGHTWEIGHT

Action: hinged breech
Grips: blackwood
Barrel: 3 in.
Sights: fixed open
Weight: 7.5 oz.
Caliber: .22LR; .22 Mag;.32 Mag/.32 S&W Long; .380 Auto;.38 Special; .44 Special
Capacity: 2 rounds
Features: gray matte finish; single-action; automatic barrel selection; manually operated hammer-block type safety
MSRP: $705

MODEL 8

Action: hinged breech
Grips: rosewood, walnut, black
Barrel: 8 in.
Sights: red-dot scope
Weight: 24.0 oz.
Caliber: .357 Mag; .45 Auto; .45 Colt/.410
Capacity: 2 rounds
Features: satin or high polish stainless steel finish; single-action; automatic barrel selection; manually operated hammer-block type safety—automatically disengages when the hammer is cocked
.357 Mag.: $910
.45 Auto: $910
.45 Colt/.410: $910

Auto-Ordnance Handguns

MODEL 1911A1

Action: autoloader
Grips: plastic
Barrel: 5 in.
Sights: fixed open
Weight: 39.0 oz.
Caliber: .45 ACP
Capacity: 7 + 1 rounds
Features: single-action 1911 Colt design; Deluxe version has rubber wrap-around grips, 3-dot sights; Thompson 1911C stainless; 1911 SE in blued finish
WWII Parkerized: $813

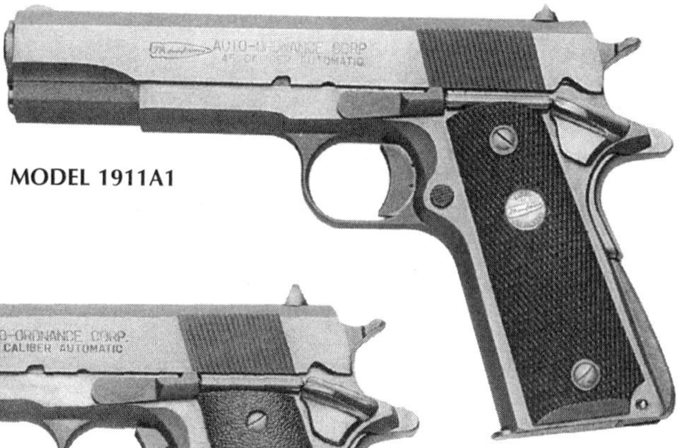

MODEL 1911A1

1911WGSE
DELUXE

Beretta Handguns

MODEL 21 BOBCAT

MODEL 84
CHEETAH

MODEL 21 BOBCAT

Action: autoloader
Grips: plastic or walnut
Barrel: 2.4 in.
Sights: fixed open
Weight: 11.5 oz.
Caliber: .22 LR, .25 Auto
Capacity: 7 (.22) or 8 (.25) rounds
Features: double-action; tip-up barrel; alloy frame; walnut grips extra
Matte: $271.95
Stainless: $355.60

MODEL 84 CHEETAH

Action: autoloader
Grips: plastic or wood
Barrel: 3.8 in.
Sights: fixed open
Weight: 23.3 oz.
Caliber: .380 Auto
Capacity: 13 + 1 rounds (10+1 restricted capacity)
Features: double-action; ambidextrous safety
Cheetah 84: $770
Cheetah 84 nickel: $830

Beretta Handguns

MODEL 85 CHEETAH

MODEL 87 TARGET

90-TWO

MODEL 92

92FS INOX

MODEL 3032 TOMCAT

MODEL 85 CHEETAH

Action: autoloader
Grips: plastic or wood
Barrel: 3.8 in.
Sights: fixed open
Weight: 23.3 oz.
Caliber: .380 Auto
Capacity: 8 + 1 rounds
Features: double-action; ambidextrous safety; single stacked magazine
Cheetah 85: $770
Cheetah 85 nickel: $830

MODEL 87 CHEETAH

Action: autoloader
Grips: wood
Barrel: 3.8 in. ***Sights:*** fixed open
Weight: 23.3 oz.
Caliber: .22LR
Capacity: 7 + 1 rounds
Features: double-action; ambidextrous safety
MSRP: $845

MODEL 87 TARGET

Action: autoloader
Grips: plastic or wood
Barrel: 5.9 in. ***Sights:*** fixed open
Weight: 20.1 oz.
Caliber: .22 LR
Capacity: 10 + 1 rounds
Features: blowback design; Target weighs 40.9 oz. with target sights
MSRP: $880

90-TWO

Action: autoloader
Grips: technopolymer single-piece wraparound, standard or slim size
Barrel: 4.9 in.
Sights: Super-LumiNova
Weight: 32.5 oz.
Caliber: 9mm, .40 S&W
Capacity: 10, 12 or 17 rounds
Features: aluminum frame with Beretta's exclusive Bruniton non-reflective matte black finish; short recoil, delayed blowback system; front accessory rail with removable cover; internal recoil buffer
MSRP: $795

MODEL 92/96 SERIES

Action: autoloader
Grips: plastic
Barrel: 4.7 to 4.9 in. ***Sights:*** 3-dot
Weight: 34.4-41.0 oz.
Caliber: 9mm
Capacity: 15+ 1 rounds (10 + 1 restricted capacity)
Features: chrome-lined bore; double-action tritium sights available; reversible magazine catch; manual safety doubles as de-cocking lever; visible/touch sensitive loaded chamber indicator
Model 92FS: $650
Model 92FS Inox: $795

MODEL 3032 TOMCAT

Action: autoloader
Grips: plastic
Barrel: 2.5 in.
Sights: fixed open
Weight: 14.5 oz.
Caliber: .32 Auto
Capacity: 7 + 1 rounds
Features: double-action; tip-up barrel
Matte: $435
Stainless: $555
Tritium with laser grip: $555

Beretta Handguns

MODEL M9

MODEL PX4

PX4 STORM .45

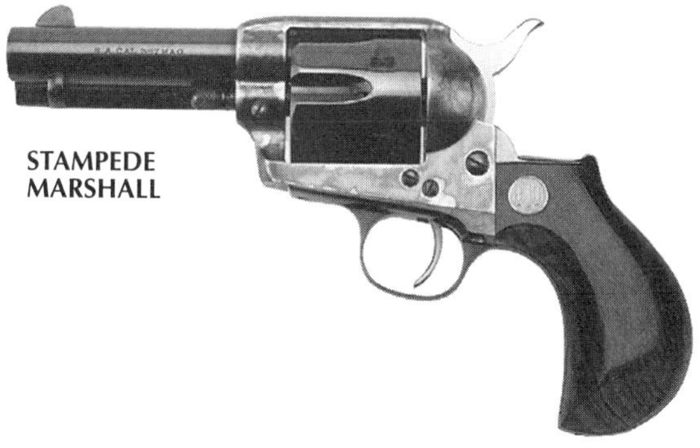

STAMPEDE MARSHALL

MODEL M9

Action: autoloader
Grips: plastic
Barrel: 4.9 in.
Sights: dot and post, low profile, windage adjustable rear
Weight: 34.4 oz.
Caliber: 9mm
Capacity: 15 + 1 rounds (10 + 1 restricted capacity)
Features: chrome-lined bore; double-action; reversible magazine release; short recoil, delayed locking block system; lightweight forged aluminum alloy frame w/ combat-style trigger guard, manual safety doubles as decocking lever; visible/touch sensitive loaded chamber indicator; open slide design; automatic firing pin block; ambidextrous manual safety; disassembly latch
MSRP: $650

MODEL M9A1

Action: autoloader
Grips: plastic
Barrel: 4.9 in.
Sights: post and dot, low profile, windage adjustable rear
Weight: 34.4 oz.
Caliber: 9mm
Capacity: 15+ 1 rounds (10 + 1 restricted capacity)
Features: chrome-lined bore; double-action; reversible magazine release button; sand resistant magazine; short recoil; delayed locking block system; lightweight forged aluminum alloy frame w/ combat-style trigger guard and integral MIL-STD-1913 "Picatinny" rail; checkered front and back strap; manual safety doubles as decocking lever; visible/touch sensitive loaded chamber indicator; open slide design, automatic firing pin block; ambidextrous manual safety; disassembly latch
MSRP: $700

MODEL PX4

Action: autoloader
Grips: 3 sizes, interchangeable polymer
Barrel: 4 in.
Sights: Super-LumiNova
Weight: 27.7 oz
Caliber: 9mm and .40 S&W
Capacity: 9mm*:* 17 + 1 rounds (10 + 1 restricted capacity) 40 S&W*:* 14 + 1 rounds (10 + 1 restricted capacity)
Features: double-action; cold hammer forged barrel; chrome-lined bore and chamber; MIL-STD -1913 "Picatinny" accessory rail for laser sight; flashlight; interchangeable/ambidextrous magazine release buttons; interchangeable back-straps; Night sights available as option
MSRP: $550

PX4 STORM .45

Action: autoloader
Grips: synthetic
Barrel: 4 in.
Sights: 3-dot dovetail
Weight: 27.7 oz.
Caliber: .45 ACP
Capacity: 10 rounds
Features: locked breech rotating barrel system; ambidextrous manual safety; reversible magazine release button; interchangeable slide catch; Picatinny rail; interchangeable backstraps
MSRP: $650

STAMPEDE

Action: single-action revolver
Grips: polymer, plastic or Walnut
Barrel: 4.75-7.5 in.
Sights: fixed, open
Weight: 36.8-38.4 oz.
Caliber: .45 Colt, .357 Mag.
Capacity: 6 rounds
Features: single-action; color case-hardened frame; blue, charcoal blue, Inox, or Old West finish
Blued: $575
Deluxe: $695
Old West: $650
Marshall: $650
Old West Marshall: $650

Beretta Handguns

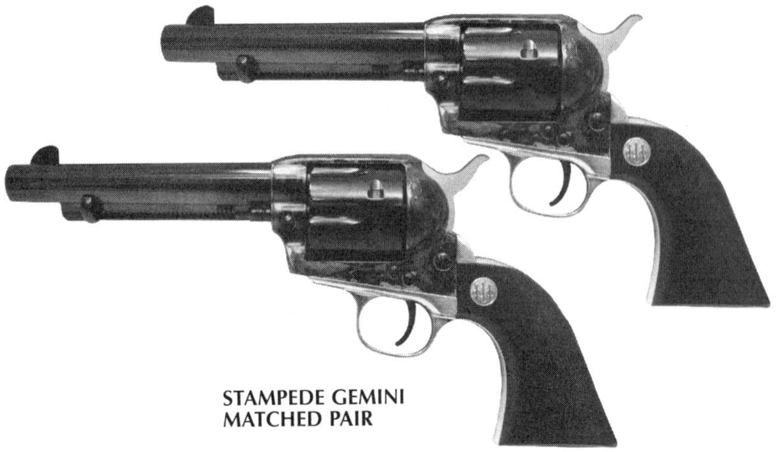

STAMPEDE GEMINI
MATCHED PAIR

STAMPEDE PHILADELPHIA
MATCHED PAIR, CUSTOM
ENGRAVED

MODEL U22 NEOS

STAMPEDE GEMINI, MATCHED PAIR

Action: single-action revolver
Grips: oil finished, hand rubbed walnut fitted with a gold Beretta medallion
Barrel: 5.5 in.
Sights: open, fixed
Caliber: .45 LC
Capacity: 6 rounds
Features: German silver trigger guards and backstraps; matching paired serial numbers; "UGB" inspector cartouche stamped on outside panel of each grip; optional custom fitted deluxe wood case
Stampede Gemini:. . . . . $1288 pair, $644 each

STAMPEDE PHILADELPHIA, MATCHED PAIR, CUSTOM ENGRAVED

Action: single-action revolver
Grips: walnut with checkering and inlaid gold Beretta medallions
Barrel: 5.5 in.
Sights: open, fixed
Caliber: .45 LC
Capacity: 6 rounds
Features: inspired by the limited edition Philadelphia Centennial engraving (1876); laser engraved then hand finished on the receiver cylinder and barrel; gold-filled "1" and "2" on top of backstrap; paired serial numbers
Stampede Philadelphia:. .$2100 pair, $1050 each

MODEL U22 NEOS

Action: autoloader
Grips: plastic
Barrel: 4.5 in. or 6 in.
Sights: target
Weight: 31.7 oz.
Caliber: .22 LR
Capacity: 10 + 1 rounds
Features: single-action; removable colored grip inserts; model with 6 in. barrel weighs 36.2 oz.; Deluxe model features adjustable trigger, replaceable sights; optional 7.5 in. barrel
U22 Neos: $275
Inox: $375

Bersa Handguns

THUNDER 9
ULTRA COMPACT

THUNDER 40

THUNDER 45
ULTRA COMPACT

THUNDER 380

THUNDER 9 ULTRA COMPACT

Action: autoloader
Grips: black polymer
Barrel: 3.5 in.
Sights: target
Weight: 24.5 oz.
Caliber: .9mm
Capacity: 10 + 1 rounds
Features: double-action; manual and firing pin safeties; anatomically designed grips
Matte: $377.23
Satin Nickel: $359

THUNDER 40

Action: autoloader
Grips: black polymer
Barrel: 4.2 in.
Sights: target
Weight: 28 oz.
Caliber: .40 ACP
Capacity: 16 + 1 rounds
Features: double-action; manual and firing pin safeties; anatomically designed grips
Matte: $338.53
Satin Nickel: $359

THUNDER 45 ULTRA COMPACT

Action: autoloader
Grips: black polymer
Barrel: 3.6 in.
Sights: target
Weight: 27 oz.
Caliber: .45 ACP
Capacity: 7 + 1 rounds
Features: double-action; manual and firing pin safeties; anatomically designed grips
Matte: $389.23
Stainless: $480
Duotone: $374.91

THUNDER 380

Action: autoloader
Grips: black polymer
Barrel: 3 in.
Sights: fixed open
Weight: 19.75 oz.
Caliber: .380 ACP
Capacity: 7 + 1 rounds
Features: double-action; safeties: integral locking system, manual, firing pin
Deluxe Blue: $325.34
Matte: $282.45
Matte CC: $336
Satin nickel: $299.99

Bond Arms Handguns

TEXAS DEFENDER

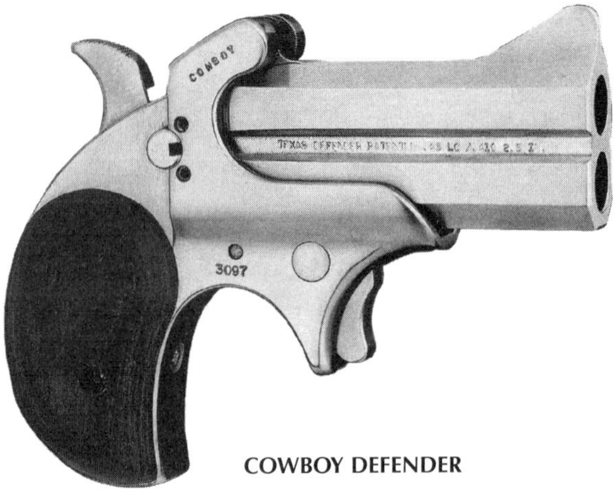

COWBOY DEFENDER

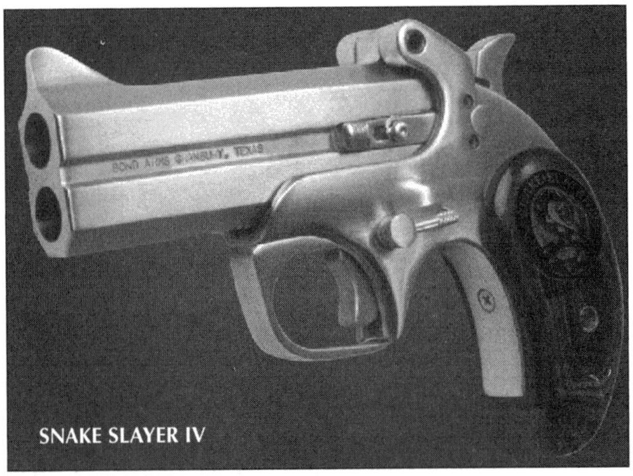

SNAKE SLAYER IV

CENTURY 2000

Action: single-action
Grips: laminated
Barrel: 3.5 in.
Sights: fixed, open
Weight: 21 oz.
Caliber: .410/45LC
Capacity: 2 rounds
Features: interchangeable barrels; automatic extractor; rebounding hammer; crossbolt safety; stainless steel with satin polish finish; black ash or rosewood laminated grips
MSRP: $432.99

DEFENDER

Action: single-action
Grips: laminated
Barrel: 3 or 5 in.
Sights: fixed, open
Weight: 19 oz., 20 oz.
Caliber: .22 LR, 9 mm, 32 H & R Mag, .357 Mag/.38 Spl., .357 Max., 10 mm, .40 S&W, .45 LC; .45 ACP, .45 Glock; .44 Sp., .44-40 Win., .45 Colt/.410 Shot Shell (rifled)
Capacity: 2 rounds
Features: interchangeable barrels; automatic extractor; rebounding hammer; crossbolt safety; stainless steel with satin polish finish; black ash or rosewood laminated grips
Texas Defender:. . . . $342.70–352.99
Cowboy Defender: . $352.99–359.77

SNAKE SLAYER

Action: single-action
Grips: rosewood
Barrel: 3.5 in.
Sights: fixed, open
Weight: 22 oz.
Caliber: .410/45LC
Capacity: 2 rounds
Features: interchangeable barrels; automatic extractor; rebounding hammer; crossbolt safety; stainless steel with satin polish finish; extended grips
MSRP: $407.99

SNAKE SLAYER IV

Action: hinged breech
Grips: rosewood
Barrel: 4.25 in.
Sights: blade front, fixed rear
Weight: 23.5 oz.
Caliber: .410/45LC with 3 in. chambers
Capacity: 2 rounds
Features: stainless steel double barrel; automatic extractor; rebounding hammer; retracting firing pins; crossbolt safety; extended custom rosewood grips
MSRP: $466.99

Browning Handguns

BUCK MARK STANDARD
(5.5" BARREL)

BUCK MARK
5.5 TARGET

BUCK MARK HUNTER

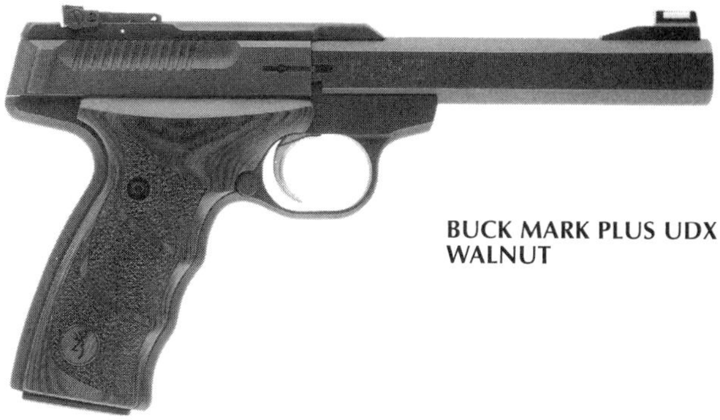

BUCK MARK PLUS UDX
WALNUT

BUCK MARK PLUS UDX
ROSEWOOD

BUCK MARK PLUS UDX
BLACK LAMINTED, STAINLESS

BUCK MARK

Action: autoloader
Grips: composite, laminated or wood
Barrel: 4, 5.5 or 7.5 in.
Sights: target
Weight: 34 oz.
Caliber: .22 LR
Capacity: 10 + 1 rounds
Features: standard, camper, target, bullseye models available with various grips, barrel contours; Plus with adjustable rear and Truglo/Marble fiber-optic front sights; FLD Plus with rosewood grips and adjustable rear and Truglo/Marble fiber-optic front sights
Buck Mark: $619
Camper: $349
Stainless: $389
Field: $619
Hunter (7.5 in. bbl): $459
Micro (4 in. bl.): $429
Stainless: $469
Plus: $499
FLD: $571
Target: $579

BUCK MARK PLUS UDX

Action: autoloader
Grips: walnut, black laminated or rosewood Ultragrip DX ambidextrous
Barrel: 5.5 in.
Sights: adjustable Pro-Target rear sight; Truglo/Marble's fiber-optic front sight
Weight: 34 oz.
Caliber: .22 L.R.
Capacity: 15 rounds (9mm), 10 rounds (.40 S&W)
Features: alloy receiver; stainless slab-side barrel; single-action trigger
Walnut: $499
Rosewood: $499
Black laminated, stainless: $539

Browning Handguns

HI-POWER

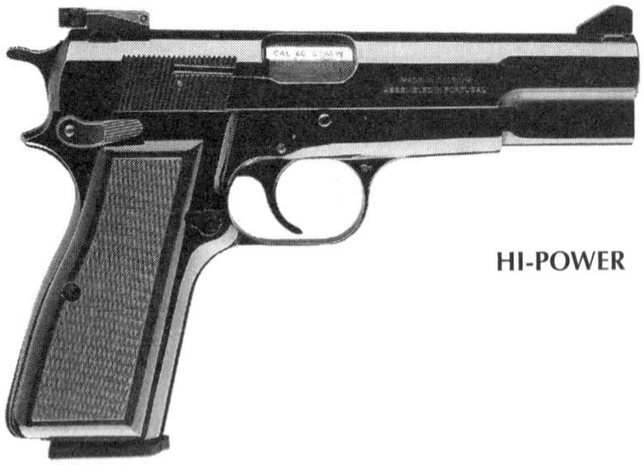

PRO-9

HI-POWER

Action: autoloader
Grips: walnut, rubber or composite
Barrel: 4.74 in.
Sights: fixed or adjustable
Weight: 33 oz.; 35 oz. (.40 S&W)
Caliber: 9mm, .40 S&W
Capacity: 10+1 rounds
Features: single-action; locked breech action; ambidextrous thumb safety; polished blued finish on slide
MSRP: $933

PRO-9 & PRO-40

Action: autoloader
Grips: polymer
Barrel: 4 in.
Sights: fixed
Weight: 30-35 oz.
Caliber: 9mm, .40 S& W
Capacity: 10 rounds
Features: Pro-9 (9mm only) polymer receiver; has stainless steel slide and replaceable backstrap inserts; double-action; polymer receiver; stainless steel slide; under-barrel accessory rail; ambidextrous safety/decocker; interchangeable backstrap inserts
Pro-9: $639.99
Pro-40: $617.04

Charles Daly Handguns

MODEL 1911 A-1

Action: autoloader
Grips: walnut
Barrel: 3.5, 4 or 5 in.
Sights: target
Weight: 34, 38 or 39.5 oz.
Caliber: .45 ACP
Capacity: 6+1 (ECS), 8 + 1 rounds
Features: extended hi-rise beavertail grip safety; combat trigger; combat hammer; beveled magazine well; flared and lowered ejection port; dovetailed front and low profile rear sights; ECS series with contoured left hand safety
G-4 Series: $838

M-5 COMMANDER

MODEL M-5

Action: autoloader
Grips: walnut, rubber or composite
Barrel: 3.1, 4.4 in., 5 in.
Sights: fixed or adjustable
Weight: 28 oz., 30.5 oz., 33.5 oz.
Caliber: 9mm (Compact), .40 S&W, .45 ACP
Capacity: 10+1 rounds
Features: single-action; polymer frame; tapered bull barrel and full-length guide rod; stainless steel beaver-tail grip safeties; grip with raised contact pad with serrations
M-5: $776
M-5 Commander: $776
M-5 Ultra X Compact: $776

Charter Arms Handguns

Known for concealable, affordable revolvers, Charter Arms chambers them for the .22 Long Rifle as well as for the centerfire .38 Special, .327 Federal, .357 Magnum, and .44 Special. The iconic Bulldog in .44 Special became available in a limited-edition model in 2010. A 40-year-old company headquartered in New England's "Gun Valley," Charter Arms employs chrome-moly and stainless steel in its handguns—also 7075 aluminum to trim ounces. The Undercover On Duty in .38 Special (a five-shot revolver with 2-inch barrel) weighs just 12 ounces. You can also get factory-installed Crimson Trace Laser Grips (on the .327 Patriot, for example, and the .32 H&R Pink Lady). Specify colored finishes on alloy frames, and tiger striping, dark olive and black, on steel frames. Charter Arms makes Derringer-style handguns as well—five-shot rimfires that scale a feathery 6 ounces. Prices across the Charter line range from about $240 to $740. *Shooter's Bible 103rd Edition* will include the full line of Charter Arms handguns.

Cimarron Handguns

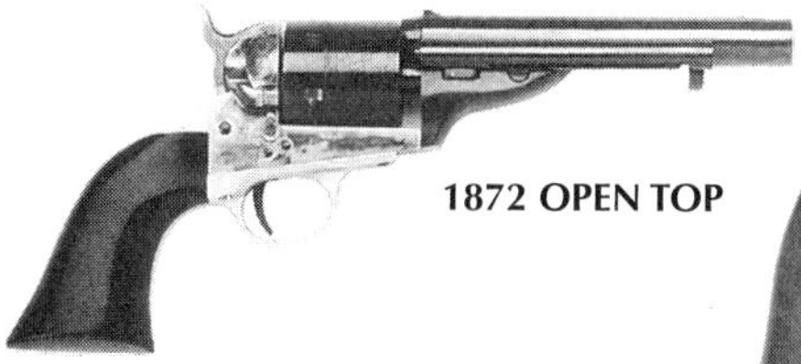
1872 OPEN TOP

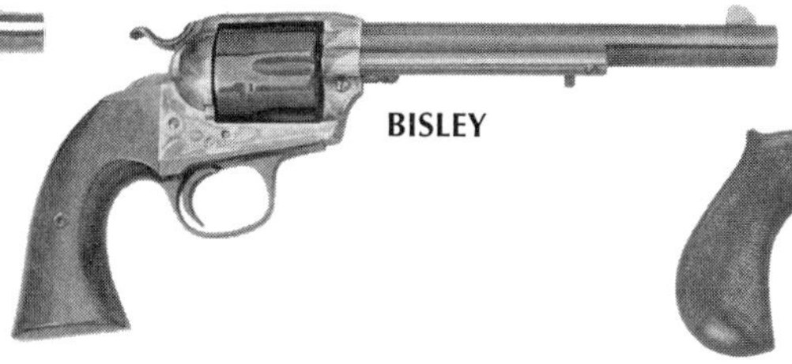
BISLEY

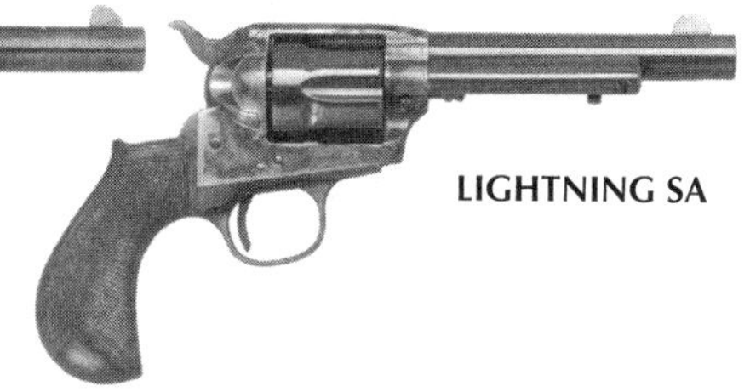
LIGHTNING SA

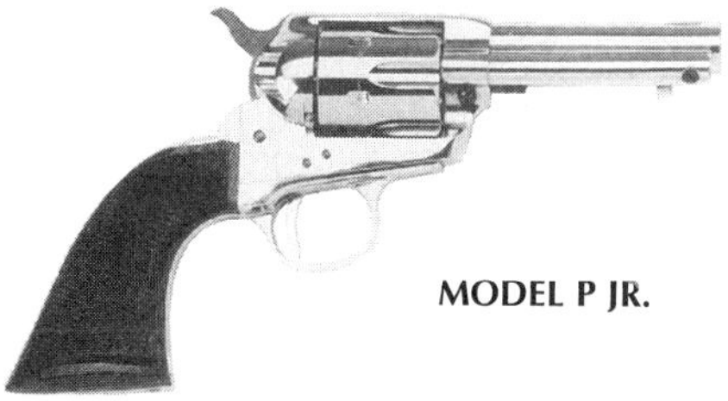
MODEL P JR.

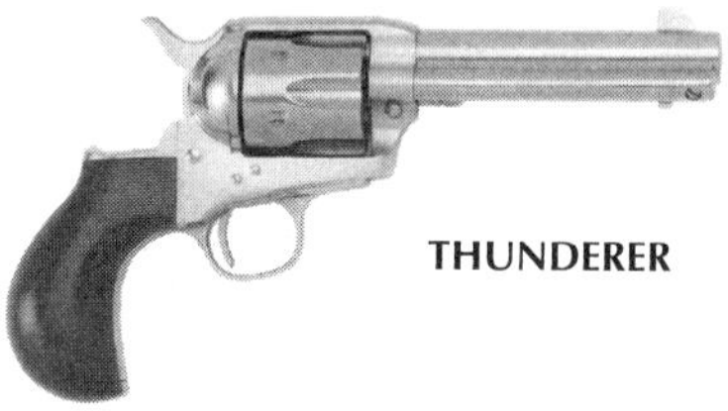
THUNDERER

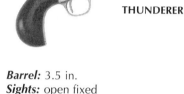

MODEL 1872 OPEN TOP

Action: single-action revolver
Grips: walnut
Barrel: 5.5 and 7.5 in.
Sights: fixed open
Weight: 40.0 oz.
Caliber: .38 Spec, .44 Colt and .45 S&W
Capacity: 6 rounds
Features: forged, color case-hardened frame; blue, charcoal blue or nickel finish; weight varies up to 46 oz.
1872: $562.91
1872 Navy grip: $518.36

BISLEY

Action: single-action revolver
Grips: walnut
Barrel: 4.75, 5.5 & 7.5 in.
Sights: open, fixed
Weight: 40.3, 40.6, 44.0 (.357 Mag.) oz.
Caliber: .357, .45LC, .44 Sp., .44 WCF
Capacity: 6 rounds
Features: reproduction of the original Colt Bisley; forged, color case-hardened frame; blue, charcoal blue, nickel finish
MSRP: $637.18

GEORGE ARMSTRONG CUSTER 7TH U.S. CAVALRY MODEL

Action: single-action revolver
Grips: walnut
Barrel: 7.5 in.
Sights: open, fixed
Weight: 40.4 oz.
Caliber: .45 LC.
Capacity: 6 rounds
Features: forged, color case-hardened frame; blue, charcoal blue or US Armory finish
MSRP: $607.47

LIGHTNING SA

Action: single-action revolver
Grips: walnut
Barrel: 3.5, 4.75 or 5.5 in.
Sights: open, fixed
Weight: 28.5, 29.5, 30.75 (.38 Colt) oz.
Caliber: .38 Colt and .38 Special
Capacity: 6 rounds
Features: forged, color case-hardened frame; blue, charcoal blue or nickel finish
MSRP: $533.21

MODEL P 1873

Action: single-action revolver
Grips: walnut, hard rubber, ivory
Barrel: 4.75, 5.5 and 7.5 in.
Sights: none
Weight: 44.0 oz.
Caliber: .32 WCP, .357, .38 WCF, 45 ACP, .45 LC, .45 Schofield, .38 WCF, .32 WCF, .44 WCF.
Capacity: 6 rounds
Features: fashioned after the 1873 Colt SAA but 20% smaller
MSRP: $548.06

MODEL P JR.

Action: single-action revolver
Grips: walnut
Barrel: 3.5, 4.75 and 5.5 in.
Sights: open
Weight: 35.2 oz.
Caliber: .38 Special
Capacity: 6 rounds
Features: fashioned on the 1873 Colt SAA but 20% smaller; color case-hardened frame; blue, charcoal blue or nickel finish
MSRP: $507.48

NEW SHERIFF'S MODEL

Action: single-action revolver
Grips: walnut, black hard rubber
Barrel: 3.5 in.
Sights: open fixed
Weight: 33.5 oz.
Caliber: .45 Colt, 44 WCF
Capacity: 6 rounds
Features: forged, color case-hardened frame; blue, charcoal blue, nickel finish
MSRP: $546.08

THUNDERER

Action: single-action revolver
Grips: walnut, ivory, mother of pearl or black hard rubber
Barrel: 3.5 w/ejector, 4 .75, 5.5 or 7.5 in.
Sights: open, fixed
Weight: 38, 40, 40.75, 43.60 (.357 Mag.) oz.
Caliber: .357 Mag., .44 SP, .44 WCF, .45 ACP, .45 Colt
Capacity: 6 rounds
Features: forged, color case-hardened frame; blue, charcoal blue or nickel finish
MSRP: $592.62

U.S.V. ARTILLERY MODEL

Action: single-action revolver
Grips: walnut
Barrel: 5.5 in.
Sights: open, fixed
Weight: 40 oz.
Caliber: .45 LC.
Capacity: 6 rounds
Features: forged, color case-hardened frame; blue, charcoal blue or US Armory finish
MSRP: $607.47

Citadel Handguns

CITADEL 1911 PISTOLS
Action: SA autoloading, recoil operated
Grips: checkered walnut
Barrel: 5″ or 3 ½″ (small frame)
Sights: Novak combat
Weight: 38 (5″) or 30 ounces
Caliber: .45 ACP
Capacity: 8 or 6
Features: forged all-steel 1911 made for Legacy Sports Int'l, with skeleton loop hammer, lowered ejection port, full-length guide rod. Full-size model has extended ambidextrous thumb safety, front slide serrations.
MSRP: $649–899

Colt Handguns

.38 SUPER

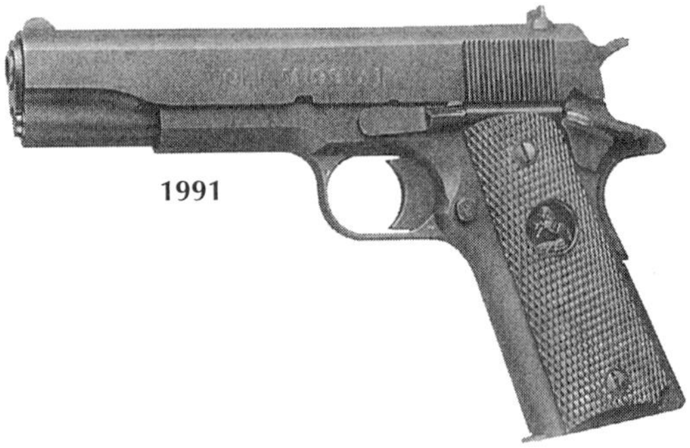
1991

DEFENDER

GOLD CUP

.38 SUPER
Action: autoloader
Grips: rosewood or composite
Barrel: 5 in.
Sights: fixed open
Weight: 39.0 oz.
Caliber: .38 Super
Capacity: 9 + 1 rounds
Features: M1911 stainless models available; aluminum trigger
Blue: $837
Stainless: $866
Bright stainless: $1090

1991 SERIES
Action: autoloader
Grips: rosewood or composite
Barrel: 5 in.
Sights: fixed open
Weight: 39.0 oz.
Caliber: .45 ACP
Capacity: 7 + 1 rounds
Features: M1911 Commander with 4.3 in. barrel available; both versions in stainless or chrome moly
1991: $786
Stainless: $839

DEFENDER
Action: autoloader
Grips: rubber finger-grooved
Barrel: 3 in.
Sights: 3-dot
Weight: 30.0 oz.
Caliber: .45 ACP
Capacity: 7 + 1 rounds
Features: stainless M1911; extended safety; upswept beavertail; beveled magazine well
MSRP: $885

GOLD CUP
Action: autoloader
Grips: black composite
Barrel: 5 in.
Sights: target
Weight: 39.0 oz.
Caliber: .45 ACP
Capacity: 8 + 1 rounds
Features: stainless or chrome-moly; Bo-Mar or Eliason sights
Gold Cup, blue: $1022
Stainless: $1071

Colt Handguns

SERIES 70

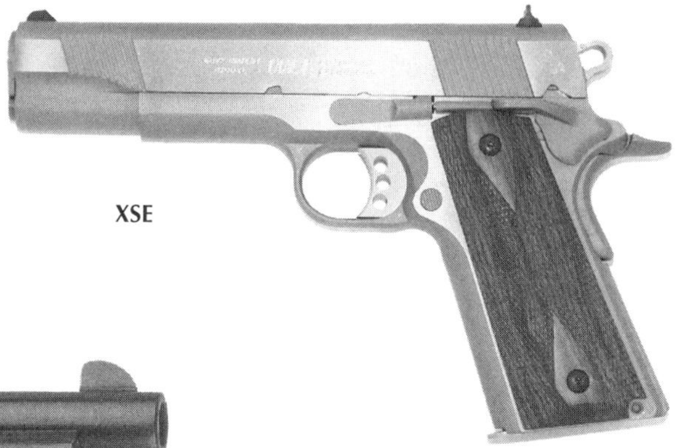

XSE

SINGLE-ACTION ARMY

XSE COMMANDER

SERIES 70

Action: autoloader
Grips: walnut
Barrel: 5 in.
Sights: fixed open
Weight: 39.0 oz.
Caliber: .45 ACP
Capacity: 7 + 1 rounds
Features: single-action M1911 design
Series 70: $919–990

SINGLE-ACTION ARMY

Action: single-action revolver
Grips: composite
Barrel: 4.3, 5.5 or 7.5 in.
Sights: fixed open
Weight: 46.0 oz.
Caliber: .32/20, .357 Mag., .38 Spl., .44-40, .45 Colt, .38/40
Capacity: 6 rounds
Features: case-colored frame; transfer bar; weight for .44-40, 48 oz. and 50 oz. for .45 Colt
Single-Action Army:. $1290
Nickel: $1350

MODEL XSE

Action: autoloader
Grips: rosewood
Barrel: 5 in.
Sights: 3-dot
Weight: 39.0 oz.
Caliber: .45 ACP
Capacity: 8 + 1 rounds
Features: stainless; M1911 with extended ambidextrous safety; upswept beavertail; slotted hammer and trigger; also available as 4.3 in. barrel Commander
MSRP: $900–1050

When shooting a handgun, accuracy walks hand-in-hand with consistency. Be as consistent as possible with things such as how you raise the gun to the target, how you establish your sight picture, and how long it takes to settle and discharge the shot. Also try to keep physical conditions constant, such as barrel temperature (this is controlled to some extent by the time between shots) and ammunition type.

CZ Handguns

MODEL 75

MODEL 75 CHAMPION

MODEL 75 COMPACT
.40 S&W

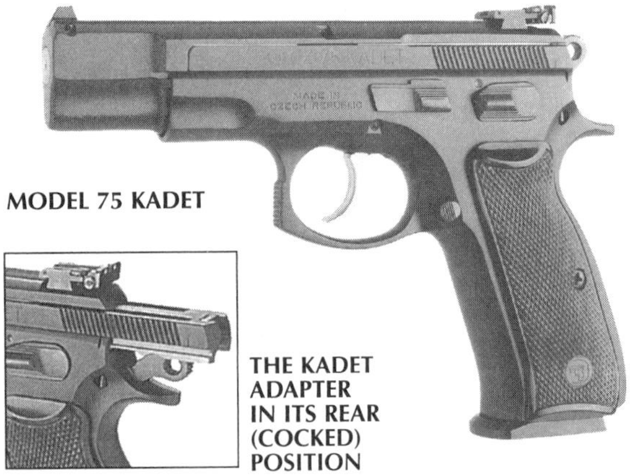

MODEL 75 KADET

THE KADET ADAPTER IN ITS REAR (COCKED) POSITION

MODEL 83

MODEL 75

Action: autoloader
Grips: composite
Barrel: 4.7 in.
Sights: 3-dot
Weight: 35.0 oz.
Caliber: 9mm or .40 S&W
Capacity: 10 + 1 rounds
Features: single- or double-action
9mm: $597–756
.40 S&W: $615–669

MODEL 75 CHAMPION

Action: autoloader
Grips: composite
Barrel: 4.5 in.
Sights: target
Weight: 35.0 oz.
Caliber: 9mm or .40 S&W
Capacity: 10 + 1 rounds
Features: also available*:* IPSC version with 5.4 in. barrel
Champion: $1739

MODEL 75 COMPACT

Action: autoloader
Grips: composite
Barrel: 3.9 in.
Sights: fixed open
Weight: 32.0, 37.8 (40 S&W) oz.
Caliber: 9mm or .40 S&W
Capacity: 10 rounds
Features: single- or double-action; ambidextrous safety
Compact:. $631–651
Compact .40 S&W:. $672

MODEL 75 KADET

Action: autoloader ***Grips:*** composite
Barrel: 4.9 in.
Sights: target
Weight: 38.0 oz.
Caliber: .22 LR
Capacity: 10 + 1 rounds
Features: single- or double-action
Kadet: $689

MODEL 83

Action: autoloader
Grips: composite
Barrel: 3.8 in. ***Sights:*** fixed open
Weight: 26.0 oz.
Caliber: 9mm
Capacity: 10 + 1 rounds
Features: single- or double-action
MSRP: $495–522

CZ Handguns

MODEL 85 COMBAT

MODEL 97

2075 RAMI

MODEL 85 COMBAT
Action: autoloader
Grips: composite
Barrel: 4.7 in.
Sights: target
Weight: 35.0 oz.
Caliber: 9mm
Capacity: 10 + 1 rounds
Features: single- or double-action
MSRP: $702–732

MODEL 97
Action: autoloader
Grips: composite
Barrel: 4.8 in.
Sights: fixed open
Weight: 41.0 oz.
Caliber: .45 ACP
Capacity: 10 + 1 rounds
Features: single- or double-action
MSRP: $779–799

2075 RAMI
Action: single- and double-action autoloader
Grips: lack composite
Barrel: 3 in.
Sights: blade front, shrouded rear
Weight: 25.0 oz.
Caliber: 9mm Luger, .40 S&W
Capacity: 10 rounds (9mm), 8 rounds (.40 S&W)
Features: firing pin block; manual safety; double-stack magazine
MSRP: $671

MODEL P-01
Action: autoloader
Grips: rubber
Barrel: 3.8 in.
Sights: 3-dot
Weight: 27.3 oz.
Caliber: 9mm
Capacity: 13 + 1 rounds
Features: single- or double-action; decocking lever; safety stop on hammer; firing pin safety
MSRP: $672

Downsizer Handguns

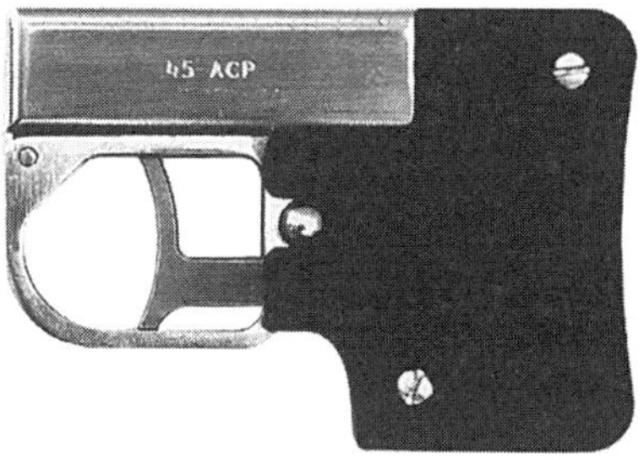

WSP (WORLD'S SMALLEST PISTOL)
Action: tip-up hinged breech
Grips: composite
Barrel: 2.1 in.
Sights: none
Weight: 11.0 oz.
Caliber: .357 Mag., .38 SP, .45 ACP
Capacity: 1 round
Features: double-action; stainless steel frame & barrel; internal firing pin block
MSRP: $499

Ed Brown Handguns

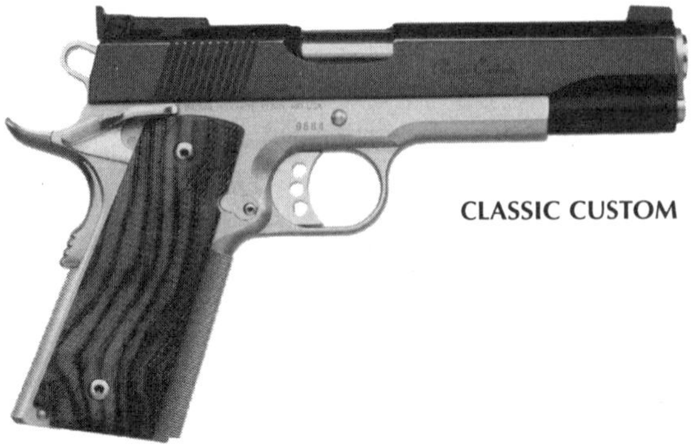

CLASSIC CUSTOM

EXECUTIVE CARRY

EXECUTIVE ELITE

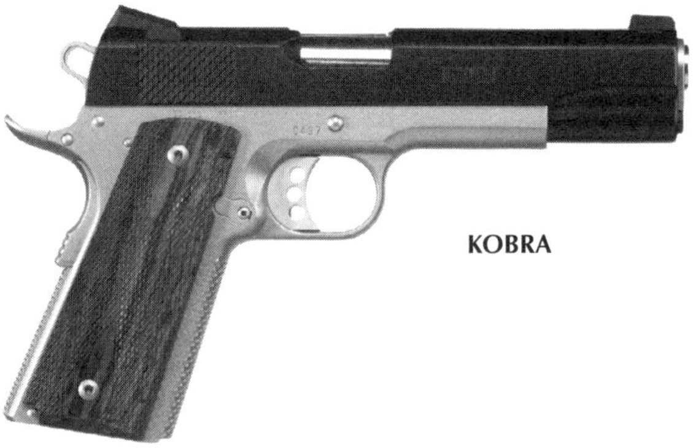

KOBRA

CLASSIC CUSTOM

Action: autoloader
Grips: cocobolo wood
Barrel: 5 in. ***Sights:*** target
Weight: 37.0 oz.
Caliber: .45 ACP
Capacity: 7 + 1 rounds
Features: single-action, M1911 Colt design; Bo-Mar sights; checkered forestrap; ambidextrous safety; stainless

Classic Custom: **$3155**
Stainless/blue: **$3155**
Stainless: **$3155**

EXECUTIVE CARRY

Action: autoloader
Grips: checkered cocobolo wood
Barrel: 4.25 in.
Sights: low-profile combat
Weight: 33.0 oz.
Caliber: .45 ACP
Capacity: 7 + 1 rounds
Features: Bob-tail butt; checkered forestrap; stainless optional

Executive Carry: **$2645**
Stainless/blue: **$2645**
Stainless: **$2645**

EXECUTIVE ELITE

Action: autoloader
Grips: checkered cocobolo wood
Barrel: 5 in. ***Sights:*** to order
Weight: 36.0 oz.
Caliber: .45 ACP
Capacity: 7 + 1 rounds
Features: custom-grade M1911 Colt

Elite: **$2395**
Stainless/blue: **$2395**
Stainless: **$2395**

KOBRA

Action: autoloader
Grips: cocobolo wood
Barrel: 4.3 (Kobra Carry) or .5 in.
Sights: low-profile combat
Weight: 36.0 oz.
Caliber: .45 ACP
Capacity: 7 + 1 rounds
Features: single-action M1911 Colt design; matte finish with Snakeskin treatment on forestrap; mainspring housing and rear of slide; stainless models

Kobra: **$2195**
Stainless/blue: **$2195**
Stainless: **$2195**
Kobra Carry: **$2445**
Stainless/blue: **$2445**
Stainless: **$2445**

EMF Handguns

1873 DAKOTA

1875 REMINGTON

MODEL 1890
REMINGTON POLICE

1873 HARTFORD

Action: single-action revolver
Grips: walnut
Barrel: 4, 4.75, 5.5, 7.5 in.
Sights: fixed open
Weight: 46.0 oz.
Caliber: 32/20, 38/40, 44/40, 44SP, 45LC, .357.
Capacity: 6 rounds
Features: Birdshead grip; steel backstrap and trigger guard; Great Western II features various combinations of deluxe nickel, satin nickel, casehardened or blue finish with bone, ultra stag or ultra ivory grips
Great Western II: $520
Great Western II Californian (walnut grips): $520

1875 REMINGTON

Action: single-action revolver
Grips: walnut
Barrel: 5.5 or 7.5 in.
Sights: fixed open
Weight: 48.0 oz.
Caliber: .357 Mag., .44/40, .45 LC
Capacity: 6 rounds
Features: case-hardened colored steel frame
Model 1875: $424
Engraved: $659
Nickel: $599

1890 REMINGTON POLICE

Action: single-action revolver
Grips: walnut
Barrel: 5.8 in.
Sights: fixed open
Weight: 48.0 oz.
Caliber: .357 Mag., .44-40, .45 Colt
Capacity: 6 rounds
Features: lanyard loop; case-colored frame
Model 1890: $450
Nickel: $675

"Handgun shooting is widely considered to be the most difficult of the shooting arts. Pistols are relatively light, hard to hold steady and, unlike rifles and shotguns, not supported against the shooter's body when fired. Concentration and self-discipline are required to reliably hit the target with a handgun. Even after a satisfactory level of skill is acquired, regular practice is necessary to maintain that skill. Continuing practice is far more important with a handgun than it is with a rifle." —Chuck Hawks

Entréprise Arms Handguns

ELITE

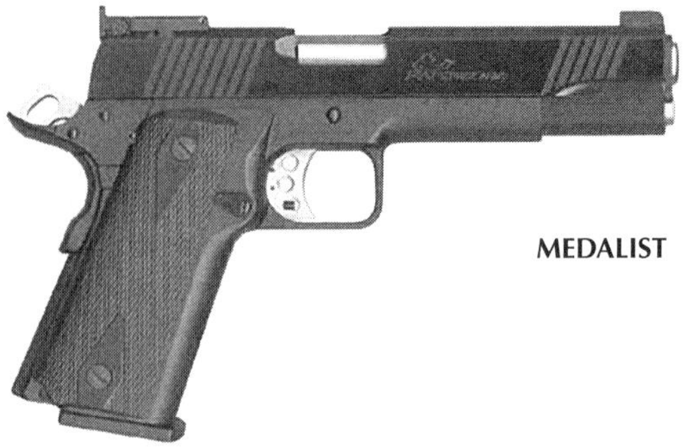

MEDALIST

ELITE

Action: autoloader
Grips: composite
Barrel: 3.25, 4.25 or 5 in.
Sights: adjustable
Weight: 38, 40.0 oz.
Caliber: .45 ACP
Capacity: 10 + 1 rounds
Features: lowered and flared ejection port; reinforced dust-cover; bolstered front strap; high grip cut; high-ride beaver-tail grip safety; steel flat mainspring housing; extended thumb lock; adjustable rear sights
MSRP: $999

MEDALIST

Action: autoloader
Grips: composite
Barrel: 5 in. ***Sights:*** target
Weight: 44.0 oz.
Caliber: .40 S&W, .45 ACP
Capacity: 10 + 1 rounds
Features: up-turned beavertail, stainless hammer and sear; flared ejection port; match trigger, lapped slide
.45: $979
.40 S&W: $1099

European American Armory Handguns

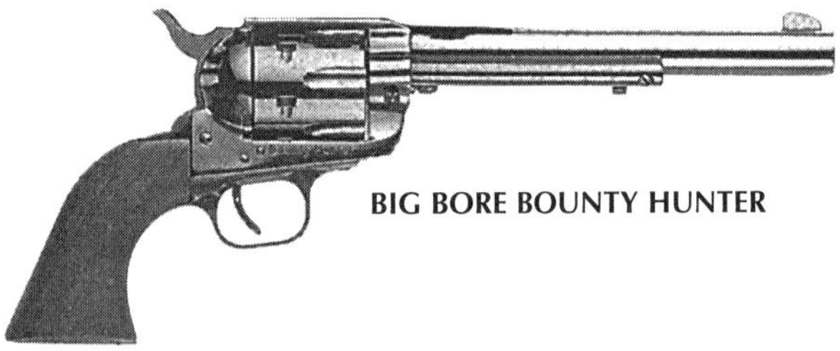

BIG BORE BOUNTY HUNTER

SMALL BORE BOUNTY HUNTER

BOUNTY HUNTER

Action: single-action revolver
Grips: walnut
Barrel: 4.5 or 7.5 in.
Sights: fixed open
Weight: 39.0-41.0 oz.
Caliber: .357 Mag., .44 Mag., .45 Colt
Capacity: 6 rounds
Features: case-colored or blued or nickel frame; version with 7.5 in. barrel weighs 42 oz.
Bounty Hunter: $340
Nickel: $464.20
Case color: $433.15
Also available:
Small Bore Bounty Hunter
(.22 LR or .22 WMR): $281.99
Nickel: $275

WITNESS

Action: autoloader
Grips: rubber
Barrel: 4.5 in.
Sights: 3-dot
Weight: 33.0 oz.
Caliber: 9mm, .38 Super, .40 S&W, 10 mm, .45 ACP
Capacity: 10 + 1 rounds
Features: double-action; polymer frame available
Steel: $541.82
Polymer: $432.99
"Wonder" finish: $541.82
Gold Team: $2001.17

European American Armory Handguns

WITNESS

WITNESS P COMPACT

WITNESS COMPACT

Action: autoloader
Grips: rubber
Barrel: 3.6 in.
Sights: 3-dot
Weight: 29.0 oz.
Caliber: 9mm, .40 S&W, .45 ACP
Capacity: 10 + 1 rounds
Features: double-action; polymer frame and ported barrels available
Steel: $555.99
Polymer: $539.95
Witness P Carry: $634.97

WITNESS S/A HUNTER

Action: autoloader
Grips: rubber
Barrel: 6 in.
Sights: adjustable
Weight: 41.0 oz.
Caliber: 10mm, .45 ACP
Capacity: 10+1 rounds
Features: single-action; auto firing pin block; drilled & tapped for scope mount
Hunter Pro 10: $989
Hunter Pro 45: $989

Firestorm Handguns

MODEL 45

Action: autoloader
Grips: rubber
Barrel: 4.3 or 5.2 in. ***Sights:*** 3-dot
Weight: 34.0 oz.
Caliber: .45 ACP
Capacity: 7 + 1 rounds
Features: single-action; 1911 Colt design; from cocking grooves
Model 45: $415
Duotone: $410

MODEL 45

Firestorm Handguns

MODEL 380

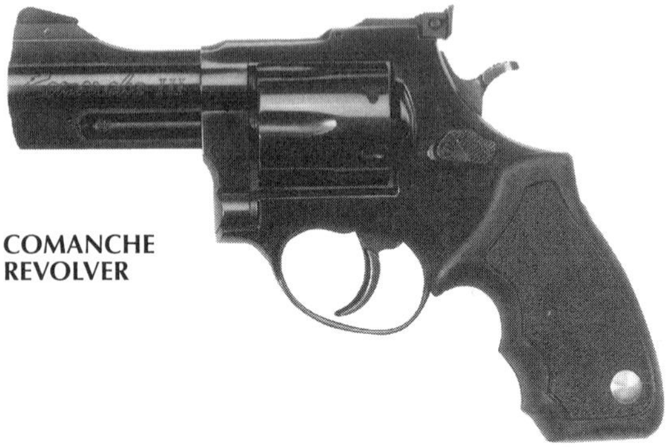

COMANCHE
REVOLVER

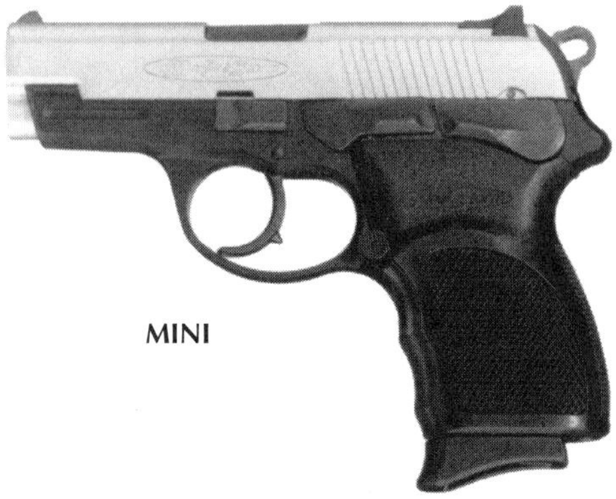

MINI

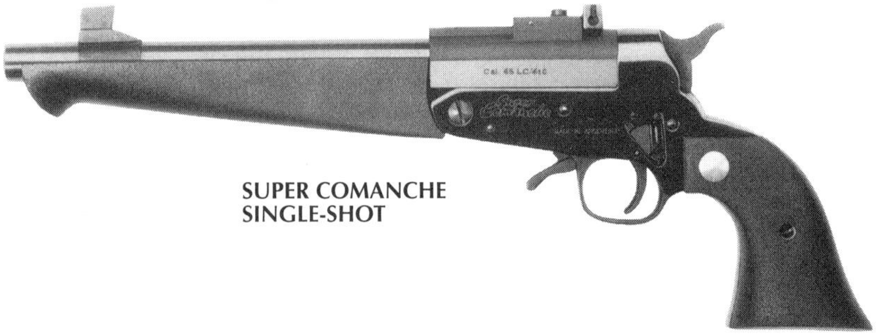

SUPER COMANCHE
SINGLE-SHOT

MODEL 380

Action: autoloader
Grips: rubber *Barrel:* 3.5 in.
Sights: 3-dot *Weight:* 23.0 oz.
Caliber: .380
Capacity: 7 + 1 rounds
Features: double-action; also available in .22 LR; 10-shot magazine
Model 380:. $270
Duotone:. $300
22 LR:. $260

COMANCHE REVOLVER

Action: double-action revolver
Grips: rubber
Barrel: 3 or 6 in. *Sights:* target
Weight: 22.0 oz.
Caliber: .38 Spl. (also in .22, .357)
Capacity: 6 rounds
Features: adjustable sights; stainless or blue finish
Comanche I (.22, 6 in.) blue:. . $207
Comanche I (.22, 6 in.) SS: . . . $230
Comanche II (.38 Spl., 3or 4 in.) blue: $207
Comanche II (.38 Spl., 3or 4 in.) SS:. $230
Comanche III(.357, 3, 4 or 6 in.) blue: $230
Comanche III (.357, 3, 4 or 6 in.) SS:. $235.69

MINI

Action: autoloader
Grips: polymer
Barrel: 3.5 in. *Sights:* target
Weight: 24.5 oz.
Caliber: 9mm, .40 S&W, .45 ACP
Capacity: 10 + 1 rounds (7 + 1 in .45)
Features: double-action
Mini: $344.45
Duotone:. $350.69
Duotone .45: $350.69
Nickel:. $350.69
.45 nickel: $369.99

SUPER COMANCHE

Action: hinged breech
Grips: composite
Barrel: 10 in. *Sights:* target
Weight: 47.0 oz.
Caliber: .45 LC/.410
Capacity: 1 round
Features: adjustable sight; accepts 2.5 or 3 in. shells; rifled slugs or buckshot(.410); blue or satin nickel finish
Nickel:. $172.44
Blue: $158.70

FNH USA Handguns

FIVE-SEVEN USG

FNP 40

FIVE-SEVEN USG

Action: autoloader ***Grips:*** plastic
Barrel: 4.75 in. ***Sights:*** fixed, open
Weight: 19.2 oz.
Caliber: 5.7 x 28mm
Capacity: 10 +1 rounds
Features: single-action; forged barrel with hard chrome finish; polymer frame and slide cover; reversible magazine release
MSRP: $1082

FNP 9

Action: autoloader ***Grips:*** plastic
Barrel: 4.75in. ***Sights:*** fixed, open
Weight: 25.2 oz. (24.8 Compact)
Caliber: 9mm ***Capacity:*** 10 +1 rounds
Features: double/single-action; polymer frame w/tactical accessory rail; ambidextrous de-cocking levers and reversible magazine release
MSRP: $530–570

FNP 40

Action: autoloader ***Grips:*** plastic
Barrel: 4 in. ***Sights:*** fixed, open
Weight: 26.7 oz. ***Caliber:*** .40 S&W
Capacity: 10 + 1 rounds
Features: double/single-action operation; molded polymer frame w/ tactical accessory rail; ambidextrous de-cocking levers and reversible magazine release; numerous sight configurations available
MSRP: $530–630

Freedom Arms Handguns

MODEL 83
PREMIER GRADE

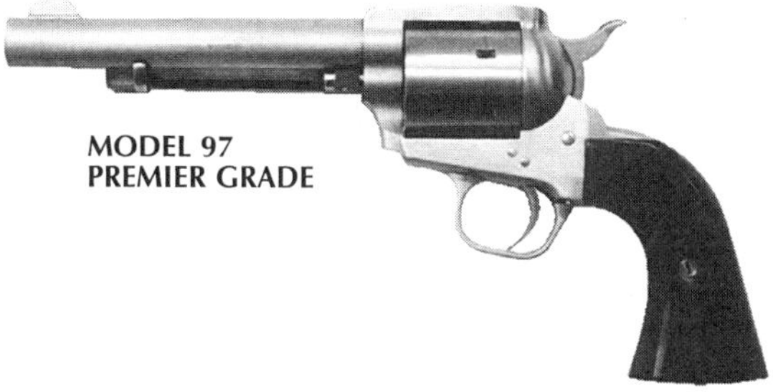

MODEL 97
PREMIER GRADE

MODEL 83 PREMIER GRADE

Action: single-action revolver with manual safety bar
Grips: hardwood or optional Micarta
Barrel: 4.75, 6, 7.5, 9 or 10 in.
Sights: fixed or adjustable
Weight: 52.5 oz.
Caliber: .357 Mag., .41 Mag., .44 Mag., .454 Casull, .475 Linebaugh
Capacity: 5 rounds
Features: sights, scope mounts and extra cylinders optional
MSRP: $2230–2320

MODEL 83 RIMFIRE FIELD GRADE

Action: single-action revolver
Grips: Pachmyr or optional hardwood or Micarta
Barrel: 4.75, 6, 7.5, 9 or 10 in.
Sights: adjustable
Weight: 55.5 oz.
Caliber: .22 LR, .357 Mag., .41 mag., .44 Mag., .454 Casull, .475 Linebaugh
Capacity: 5 rounds
Features: sights, scope mounts and extra cylinders optional
MSRP: $1970

MODEL 97 PREMIER GRADE

Action: single-action revolver with automatic transfer bar safety
Grips: hardwood or optional Micarta
Barrel: 4.5, 5.5, 7.5 or 10 in.
Sights: fixed or adjustable
Weight: 39.0 oz.
Caliber: .17 HMR, .22 LR, .32 H&R Mag., .357 Mag., .41 Mag., .44 Spl., .45 Colt
Capacity: 5 rounds for .41 and bigger, 6 rounds for smaller calibers
Features: sights; scope mounts and extra cylinders optional
MSRP: $1891–1907

Glock Handguns

MODEL G19

MODEL G23

MODEL G17

MODEL G20

MODEL G22

MODEL G26

MODEL G27

MODEL G29

MODEL G30

MODEL G33

GLOCK HANDGUNS COMPACT PISTOLS G-19, G-23, G-25, G-38, G-32

Action: autoloader
Grips: composite
Barrel: 4.0 and 6.0 in.
Sights: fixed open
Weight: 20.19 to 24.16 oz.
Caliber: 9mm, .40 S&W, .357 Mag., 10mm, .45 ACP
Capacity: 9, 10, 13, 15 rounds
Features: trigger safety; double-action
MSRP: $595

STANDARD PISTOLS G-17, G-20, G-21, G-22, G-37

Action: autoloader
Grips: composite
Barrel: 4.5 in.
Sights: fixed open
Weight: 22.4 to 27.68 oz.
Caliber: 9mm, .40 S&W, .357 Mag., 10mm, .45 ACP
Capacity: 10, 13, 15, 17 rounds
Features: trigger safety; double-action
MSRP: $640

SUBCOMPACT PISTOLS G-26, G-27, G-29, G-39, G-30, G-28, G-33

Action: autoloader
Grips: composite
Barrel: 5.67 in.
Sights: fixed open
Weight: 18.66 to 24.69 oz.
Caliber: 9mm, .40 S&W, .357, .45
Capacity: 9, 10, 6 rounds
Features: trigger safety; double-action
MSRP: $580–595

Glock Handguns

MODEL G34

MODEL G35

G-36 SLIMLINE

COMPETITION G-34, G-35

Action: autoloader
Grips: synthetic
Barrel: 5.32 in.
Sights: fixed open
Weight: 22.9 oz.
Caliber: 9x19
Capacity: 17 + 1 rounds
Features: extended barrel; 7.56-in. line of sight; right hand, hexagonal barrel rifling, 9.84-in. length-of-twist; Glock safe action system
MSRP: $670

G-36 SLIMLINE

Action: autoloader
Grips: synthetic
Barrel: 3.8 in.
Sights: fixed open
Weight: 21.0 oz.
Caliber: .45 ACP
Capacity: 6 + 1 rounds
Features: single-stack magazine for thinner grip
MSRP: $646

Hämmerli Handguns

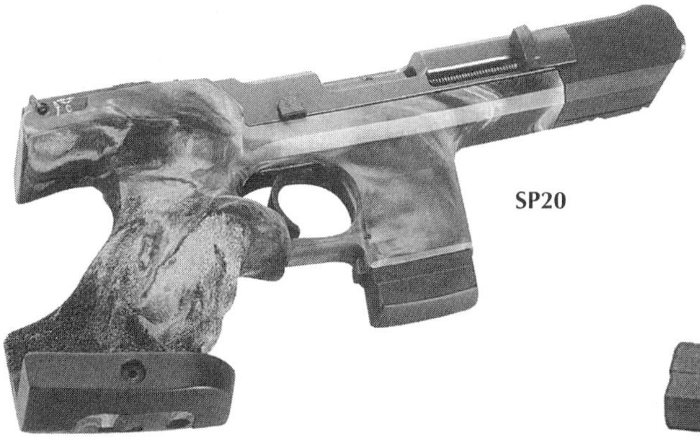
SP20

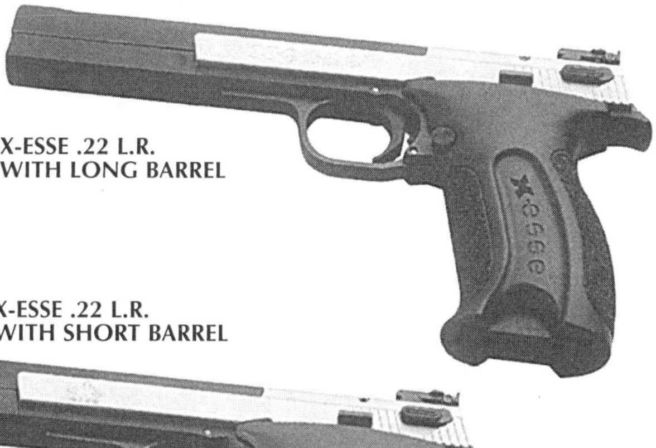
X-ESSE .22 L.R.
WITH LONG BARREL

X-ESSE .22 L.R.
WITH SHORT BARREL

MODEL SP20

Action: autoloader
Grips: synthetic
Barrel: 4.6 in.
Sights: target
Weight: 40.0 oz.
Caliber: .22 LR, .32 S&W
Capacity: 5 rounds
Features: front-end magazine
.22: $1348
.32: $1498

MODEL X-ESSE SPORT

Action: autoloader
Grips: composite
Barrel: 4.5 or 5.5 in.
Sights: target
Weight: 36.0 oz.
Caliber: .22 LR
Capacity: 10 rounds
Features: single-action
MSRP: $1099

Heckler & Koch Handguns

COLOR FRAME PISTOLS

MARK 23
SPECIAL OP

P2000

USP 9

COLOR FRAME PISTOLS

Heckler & Koch is offering a limited edition run of color frame versions of its most popular pistol models. These guns are functionally identical to their black-framed counterparts but are unique alternatives with molded-in colors especially suited for desert, jungle or urban environments.

Offered in select models of HK's USP, USP Compact, USP Tactical and Mark 23 pistols, Desert Tan, Green and Gray frame variations feature a tough, matte black corrosion resistant finish on all metal parts. Each color frame model comes with two magazines, a cleaning kit and nylon carry case.

Heckler & Koch color frames are available in: Gray (USP 45 & USP 40 Compact); Green (USP 45, USP 40, USP 40 Compact & USP 45 Tactical); Desert Tan (USP 45, USP 40, USP 40 Compact, USP 45 Tactical and Mark 23).

Suggested retail prices for the color frame models are the same as for the black frame variation.

MARK 23 SPECIAL OP

Action: autoloader
Grips: polymer
Barrel: 5.9 in.
Sights: 3-dot
Weight: 42.0 oz.
Caliber: .45 ACP
Capacity: 10 + 1 rounds
Features: military version of USP
MSRP: $2000

P2000 AND P2000 SK

Action: autoloader
Grips: polymer
Barrel: 3.6 in. (2000) and 2.5 in. (2000 SK)
Sights: 3-dot
Weight: 24 oz. (2000) and 22 oz. (2000 SK)
Caliber: 9mm, .357 SIG, .40 S&W
Capacity: 9-13 rounds
Features: double-action; pre-cock hammer; ambidextrous magazine releases and interchangeable grip straps; mounting rail for lights and lasers
P2000: $856
P2000 SK: $890

USP 9 & 40

Action: autoloader
Grips: polymer
Barrel: 4.25 in. Sights: 3-dot
Weight: 27.0 oz.
Caliber: 9mm, .40 S&W
Capacity: 13 rounds
Features: short-recoil action; also in kit form
MSRP: $850

Heckler & Koch Handguns

USP 40
COMPACT LEM

USP 45

USP 40 COMPACT LEM

Action: autoloader
Grips: composite
Barrel: 3.6 in.
Sights: fixed open
Weight: 24.0 oz.
Caliber: .40 S&W
Capacity: 12 rounds
Features: double-action only with improved trigger pull; also in 9mm
MSRP: $900–1350

USP 45

Action: autoloader
Grips: polymer
Barrel: 4.4 in.
Sights: 3-dot
Weight: 30.0 oz.
Caliber: .45 ACP
Capacity: 12 rounds
Features: short-recoil action
MSRP: $1060

Heritage Handguns

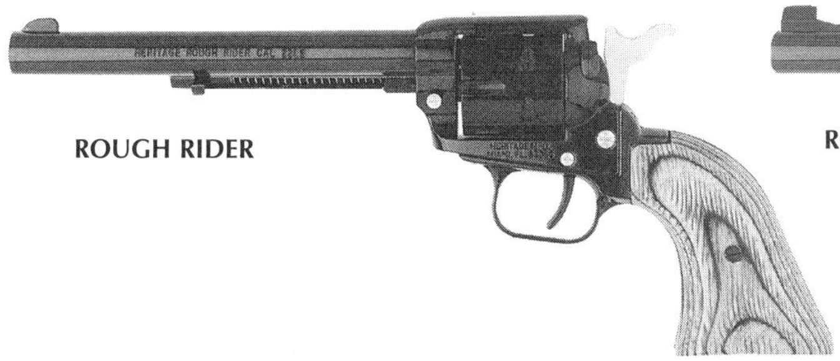

ROUGH RIDER

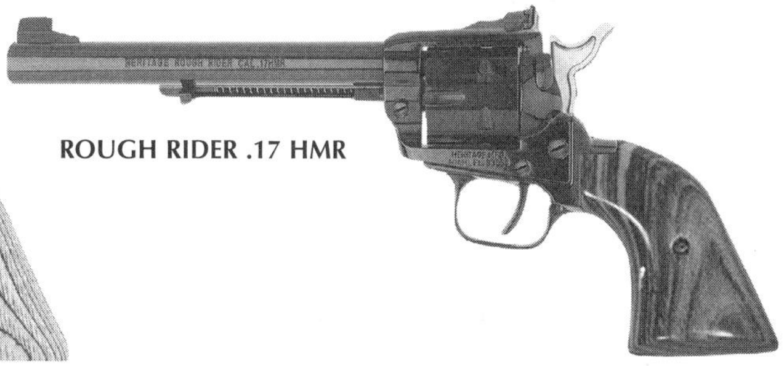

ROUGH RIDER .17 HMR

ROUGH RIDER

Action: single-action revolver
Grips: hardwood, regular or birdshead
Barrel: 3.5, 4.75, 6.5, 9 in.
Sights: fixed open
Weight: 31.0 oz.
Caliber: .22, .22 LR (.22 WMR cylinder available)
Capacity: 6 rounds
Features: action on Colt 1873 pattern; transfer bar; satin or blued finish; weight to 38 oz. dependent on barrel length

Rough Rider: $160–400
With WMR cylinder: $260
Satin, with WMR cylinder:. . . . $246
Satin, adjustable sights, WMR cylinder: $204
Bird's head grip: $185

ROUGH RIDER IN .17 HMR

Action: single-action revolver
Grips: laminated camo
Barrel: 6.5 or 9 in.
Sights: adjustable
Weight: 38.0 oz.
Caliber: .17 HMR
Capacity: 6 rounds
Features: Williams Fire Red ramp front sight and Millet rear
MSRP: $236

High Standard Handguns

OLYMPIC

SUPERMATIC CITATION MS

SUPERMATIC TROPHY

M1911 TARGET PISTOLS

Action: autoloader
Grips: walnut
Barrel: 5 in. (6 in. Supermatic)
Sights: fixed or target
Weight: 40 oz.
Caliber: .45 ACP
Capacity: 7 + 1 rounds
Features: Mil spec. slide; mil. spec. barrel and bushing; flared ejection port; beveled magazine well; match trigger with overtravel stop; 4-pound trigger pull; stippled front grip; available in stainless steel, blued or Parkerized finish
Camp Perry Model
Fixed sights: $1095
Adjustable sights:................. $1095
Supermatic Tournament: $1195

CRUSADER COMBAT

Action: autoloader
Grips: cocobolo wood
Barrel: 4.5 in. ***Sights:*** fixed open
Weight: 38 oz.
Caliber: .45 ACP
Capacity: 7+1 rounds
Features: precision fitted frame and slide; flared ejection port; lightweight long trigger with over-travel stop; trigger pull tuned at 5-6 lbs.; extended slide stop and safety; wide beavertail grip safety; available in stainless steel, blued or Parkerized finish
MSRP: $625

CRUSADER M1911 A-1

Action: autoloader
Grips: cocobolo wood
Barrel: 5 in.
Sights: fixed open
Weight: 40 oz.
Caliber: .38 Super, .45 ACP
Capacity: 7+1 (.38 Super), 9 + 1 rounds
Features: precision fitted frame and slide; flared ejection port; lightweight long trigger with over-travel stop; trigger pull tuned at 5-6 lbs.; extended slide stop and safety; wide beavertail grip safety; available in stainless steel, blued or Parkerized finish
MSRP: $615

G-MAN MODEL

Action: autoloader
Grips: cocobolo wood
Barrel: 5 in.
Sights: fixed open
Weight: 39 oz.
Caliber: .45 ACP
Capacity: 8+1 rounds
Features: custom-fit match grade stainless barrel and National Match bushing; polished feed ramp; throated barrel; lightweight trigger with over-travel stop; flared ejection port; wide, beavertail grip and ambidextrous thumb safeties; black Teflon finish
MSRP: $1395

OLYMPIC

Action: autoloader
Grips: walnut
Barrel: 5.5 in.
Sights: target
Weight: 44.0 oz.
Caliber: .22 Short
Capacity: 10 + 1 rounds
Features: single-action, blowback mechanism
MSRP: $875

SUPERMATIC CITATION

Action: autoloader
Grips: walnut
Barrel: 10 in.
Sights: target
Weight: 54.0 oz.
Caliber: .22 LR
Capacity: 10 + 1 rounds
Features: optional scope mount; slide conversion kit for .22 short
MSRP: $895

SUPERMATIC TROPHY

Action: autoloader
Grips: walnut
Barrel: 5.5 (bull) or 7.3 (fluted) in.
Sights: target
Weight: 44.0 oz.
Caliber: .22 LR
Capacity: 10 + 1 rounds
Features: left-hand grip optional
5.5 in. barrel: $845
7.3 in barrel (46 oz.): $895

High Standard Handguns

VICTOR

Action: autoloader
Grips: walnut ***Barrel:*** 4.5 or 5.5 in.
Sights: target ***Weight:*** 45.0 oz.
Caliber: .22 LR
Capacity: 10 + 1 rounds
Features: optional slide conversion kit for .22 Short
4.5 in. barrel: $845
5.5 in. barrel (46 oz.):. $845
4.5 in. barrel with universal scope base: $785
5.5 in. barrel with universal scope base: $785

VICTOR

Hi-Point Handguns

C-9

C-9 COMP

CF-380

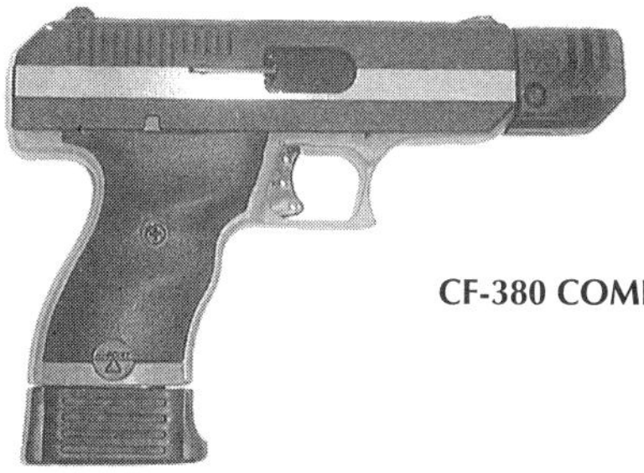

CF-380 COMP

MODEL 40S&W/POLY & .45 ACP

Action: autoloader
Grips: polymer
Barrel: 4.5 in.
Sights: 3-dot adjustable
Weight: 32 oz.
Caliber: .40 S&W, .45 ACP
Capacity: 9 + 1 rounds (10 round magazine available for COMP)
Features: high-impact polymer frame; last-round lock-open; quick on-and-off thumb safety; magazine disconnect safety; powder coat black finish
MSRP: $199.95

MODEL C-9 AND C-9 COMP

Action: autoloader
Grips: polymer
Barrel: 3.5 in.
Sights: 3-dot
Weight: 25.0, 30.0 (COMP) oz.
Caliber: 9mm
Capacity: 8 + 1 rounds (10 round magazine available for COMP)
Features: high-impact polymer frame; COMP models feature a compensator, last-round lock-open
MSRP: $165

MODEL CF-380 AND 380 COMP

Action: autoloader
Grips: polymer
Barrel: 3.5 or 4 in. (COMP)
Sights: 3-dot adjustable
Weight: 25.0, 30.0 (COMP) oz.
Caliber: .380 ACP
Capacity: 8 + 1 rounds (10 round magazine available for COMP)
Features: high-impact polymer frame; last-round lock-open; COMP models feature a compensator; powder coat black finish with chrome rail
CF-380:. $140
380 COMP: $140

Kahr Handguns

CW .45 ACP

PM .45 ACP

CW .45 ACP

Action: autoloader
Grips: textured polymer
Barrel: 3.64 in.
Sights: adjustable
Weight: 19.7 oz.
Caliber: .45 ACP
Capacity: 6+1 rounds
Features: DAO; lock breech; Browning -type recoil lug; passive striker block; no magazine disconnect; drift adjustable white bar-dot combat rear sight, pinned-in polymer front sight
MSRP: $606

PM .45 ACP

Action: autoloader
Grips: polymer
Barrel: 3.14 in.
Sights: adjustable
Weight: 17.3 oz.
Caliber: .45 ACP
Capacity: 5+1 rounds
Features: DAO; lock breech; Browning-type recoil lug; passive striker block; no magazine disconnect; drift adjustable, white bar-dot combat sights (tritium night sights optional)
MSRP: $855–974

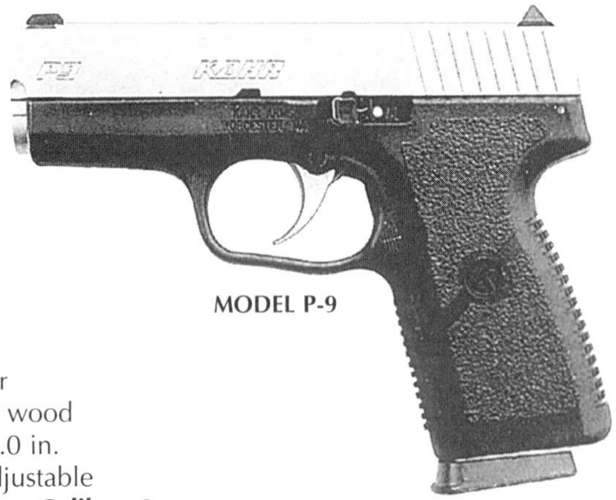

MODEL P-9

P-9 SERIES

Action: autoloader
Grips: polymer or wood
Barrel: 3.5, and 4.0 in.
Sights: fixed or adjustable
Weight: 15-26 oz. ***Caliber:*** 9mm
Capacity: 6 + 1 to 8 + 1 rounds
Features: trigger cocking DAO; lock breech; "Browning-type" recoil lug; passive striker block; no magazine disconnect; black polymer frame

CW9093, polymer, matte stainless slide (3.5 in. bl, 15.8 oz.): . . $549
KT9093, Hogue grips, matte stainless (4.0 in. bl, 26.0 oz.): $831
KT9093-Novak, Hogue grips, Novak sights, matte stainless: $968
KP9093, polymer frame, matte stainless slide (3.5 in. bl, 15.8 oz.): $739
KP9094, polymer frame, blackened stainless slide w/Tungsten DLC: $786
PM9093, polymer frame, matte stainless slide (3 in. bl, 14.0 oz.): $786
PM9094 polymer frame, blackened stainless steel slide w/Tungsten DLC: $837
K9093, matte stainless steel (3.5 in. bl, 23.1 oz.): $855
K9094, matte blackened stainless w/Tungsten DLC: . . $891
K9098 K9 Elite 2003, stainless: $932
M9093 matte stainless (4 in. bl, 22.1 oz.): $855
M9093-BOX, matte stainless frame, matte black slide (3 in. bl, 22.1 oz.): $475
M9098 Elite 2003, stainless steel: $932

Kahr Handguns

MODEL P-45

KP4544

MODEL P-40

P-40 SERIES

Action: autoloader
Grips: polymer or wood
Barrel: 3.5-4 in.
Sights: target or adjustable
Weight: 15.0-22.1 oz.
Caliber: .40 S&W
Capacity: 5+1 (Covert) to 7+1 rounds
Features: trigger cocking DAO; lock breech; "Browning-type" recoil lug; passive striker block; no magazine disconnect; black polymer frame

KT4043 4-in. barrel, Hogue grips, matte stainless (4-in. bl): . . . $831
KT4043-Novak, Hogue grips, Novak sights, matte stainless (4-in. bl): $838
KP4043 polymer frame, matte stainless slide (3.08-in. bl): . $739
KP4044 polymer frame, blackened stainless slide w/Tungsten DLC (3.5-in. bl): $786
KPS4043 Covert, polymer frame w/shortened grip, matte stainless slide (3.5-in.): $697
PM4043 polymer frame, matte stainless slide (3.08-in. bl): . $786
PM4044 polymer frame, blackened stainless slide w/Tungsten DLC (3.08-in.): $837
K4043 matte stainless steel (3.5-in.): $855
K4044 matte blackened stainless w/ Tungsten DLC (3.5-in. bl.): $891
K4048 Elite, stainless steel (3.5-in.): $932
M4043 matte stainless steel (3-in.): $855
M4048 Elite, stainless steel (3-in.): $932

P-45 SERIES KP4543

Action: autoloader
Grips: polymer *Barrel:* 3.54 in.
Sights: target or adjustable
Weight: 18.5 oz. *Caliber:* .45 ACP
Capacity: 6 + 1 rounds
Features: trigger cocking DAO; lock breech; "Browning-type" recoil lug; passive striker block; no magazine disconnect; polymer frame; matte stainless slide

P45: $805
Matte stainless slide with night sights: $921

KP4544

Action: autoloader *Grips:* polymer
Barrel: 3.54 in. *Sights:* bar-dot
Weight: 18.5 oz.
Caliber: .45 ACP *Capacity:* 6 rounds
Features: black textured polymer frame; matte blackened stainless steel slide; drift-adjustable, white bar-dot combat sights (tritium night sights optional); textured polymer grips

MSRP: $855

Kel-Tec Handguns

P-3AT

Action: autoloader
Grips: polymer
Barrel: 2.8 in.
Sights: fixed open
Weight: 7.3 oz.
Caliber: .380
Capacity: 6 + 1 rounds
Features: locked-breech mechanism

P-3AT: $318
Parkerized: $361
Chrome: $377

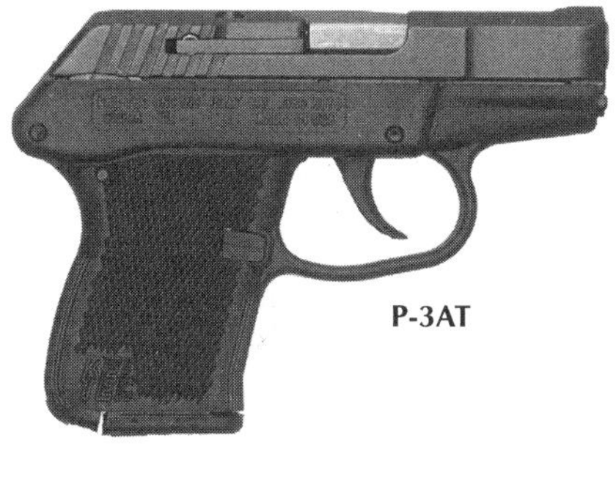

P-3AT

Kel-Tec Handguns

P-11

P-32

PF-9

SUB RIFLE 2000

SUB RIFLE 2000 (READY TO FIRE)

P-11

Action: autoloader
Grips: polymer
Barrel: 3.1 in.
Sights: fixed open
Weight: 14.4 oz.
Caliber: 9mm
Capacity: 10 + 1 rounds
Features: locked-breech mechanism
P-11: $333
Parkerized: $377
Chrome: $390

P-32

Action: autoloader
Grips: polymer
Barrel: 2.7 in.
Sights: fixed open
Weight: 6.6 oz.
Caliber: .32 Auto
Capacity: 7 + 1 rounds
Features: locked-breech mechanism
P-32: $318
Parkerized: $361
Chrome: $377

PF-9

Action: autoloader
Grips: plastic
Barrel: 3.1 in.
Sights: open, adjustable
Weight: 12.7 oz.
Caliber: 9mm Luger
Capacity: 7+1 rounds
Features: firing mechanism, double-action only with automatic hammer-block safety; available in blued, Parkerized, and hard chrome finishes; single stack magazine; black, gray or olive drab grips
Blued: $333
Parkerized: $377
Hard chrome: $390

SUB RIFLE 2000

Action: autoloader
Grips: polymer
Barrel: 16 in.
Sights: target
Weight: 64.0 oz.
Caliber: 9mm and .40 S&W
Capacity: 10 + 1 rounds
Features: take-down, uses pistol magazines
Sub Rifle:................. $409
SU-16 in .223:...........$374–665

Kimber Handguns

KIMBER STAINLESS PRO RAPTOR II

Action: SA autoloading, recoil operated
Grips: rosewood, scaled surface
Barrel: 4″
Sights: Tactical Wedge three dot (green) fixed night
Weight: 35 oz.
Caliber: .45 ACP
Capacity: 8
Features: Full size 1911 chambered in .45 ACP. Stainless steel slide and frame with hand-polished flat surfaces, satin finish over curves. Flat top slides with back-cut row of scales in gripping area and beavertail grip safety, ambidextrous thumb safety.
MSRP: $1359

STAINLESS PRO RAPTOR II

KIMBER TACTICAL ENTRY II

Action: SA autoloading, recoil operated
Grips: checkerd gray laminate
Barrel: 5″ match grade
Sights: Kimber Tactical Rail for mounting; night sights
Weight: 40 oz.
Caliber: .45 ACP
Capacity: 7
Features: Stainless steel frame with front-strap checkering, extended magazine well. Also new: Tactical Custom HD
MSRP: $1428

KIMBER ULTRA CRIMSON CARRY II

Action: SA autoloading, recoil operated
Grips: Crimson Trace laser grips, checkered rosewood
Barrel: 3″ bushingless match grade
Sights: combat iron sights
Weight: 25 oz.
Caliber: .45 ACP
Capacity: 7
Features: satin silver alloy frame, matte black steel slide, one of three new Crimson Carry pistols with laser grips.
MSRP: $1156

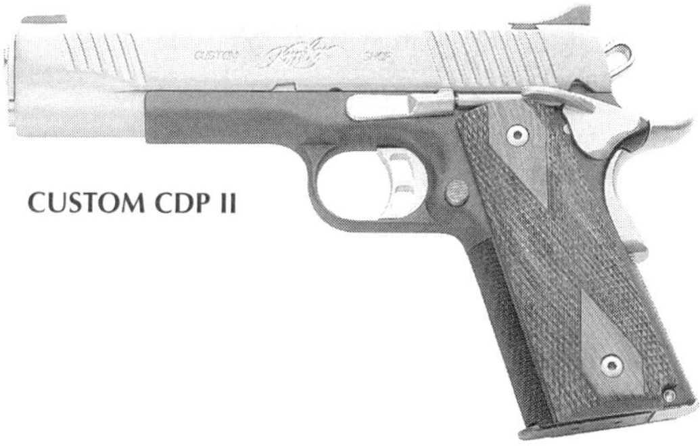

CUSTOM CDP II

COMPACT II

CDP II SERIES

Action: autoloader
Grips: rosewood
Barrel: 3, 4, or 5 in.
Sights: low-profile night
Weight: 25.0-31.0 oz.
Caliber: .45 ACP
Capacity: 7 + 1 rounds
Features: alloy frame, stainless slide; also in 4 in. (Pro Carry and Compact) and 3 in. (Ultra) configurations
MSRP: $1318

COMPACT II

Action: autoloader
Grips: synthetic ***Barrel:*** 4 in.
Sights: low-profile combat
Weight: 34.0 oz.
Caliber: .45 ACP, .40 S&W
Capacity: 7 + 1 rounds
Features: shortened single-action 1911; also Pro Carry with alloy frame at 28 oz.; match-grade bushingless bull barrel
Compact II stainless: $1009
Pro Carry II: $888
Pro Carry II stainless: $979
Pro Carry HD II: $1008

Kimber Handguns

CUSTOM TARGET II

DESERT WARRIOR

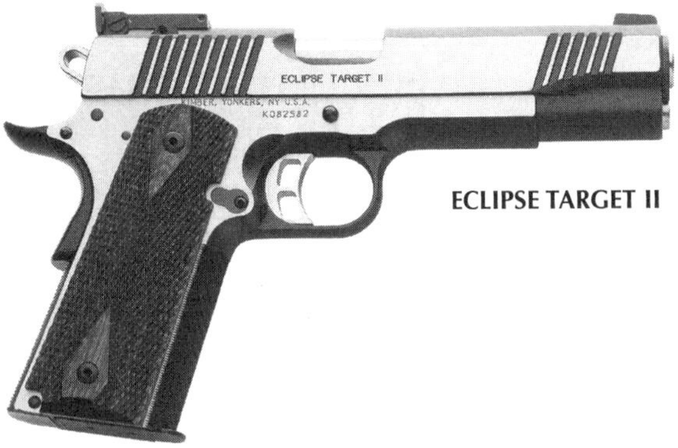

ECLIPSE TARGET II

GOLD MATCH II

CUSTOM II

Action: autoloader
Grips: synthetic or rosewood
Barrel: 5 in.
Sights: target or fixed
Weight: 38.0 oz.
Caliber: .38 Super, .40 S&W, .45 ACP, 10mm, 9mm
Capacity: 7 + 1 rounds
Features: single-action; 1911 Colt design; front cocking serrations; skeleton trigger and hammer
Custom II: **$828**
Stainless II: **$964**
Stainless Target II: **$1068**

DESERT WARRIOR .45ACP

Action: autoloader ***Grips:*** synthetic
Barrel: 5 in.
Sights: Tactical wedge
Weight: 39 oz.
Caliber: .45 ACP
Capacity: 7 + 1 rounds
Features: match grade solid steel barrel; ambidextrous thumb safety; bumped and grooved beavertail grip safety and bumper pad on the magazine; integral Tactical Rail; G-10 Tactical Grips; Tactical Wedge Tritium low profile night sights; KimPro II Dark Earth finish; lanyard loop
MSRP: **$1458**

ECLIPSE II

Action: autoloader
Grips: laminated
Barrel: 5 in. ***Sights:*** 3-dot night
Weight: 38.0 oz.
Caliber: .45 ACP, 10mm
Capacity: 7 + 1 rounds
Features: matte-black oxide finish over stainless, polished bright on flats; also 3-in. Ultra and 4 in. Pro Carry versions; sights also available in low profile combat or target
Ultra Target II: **$1345**
Ultra II: **$1236**
Pro II: **$1236**
Pro Target II: **$1345**

GOLD MATCH II

Action: autoloader
Grips: rosewood
Barrel: 5 in.
Sights: adjustable target
Weight: 38.0 oz.
Caliber: .45 ACP
Capacity: 7 + 1 rounds
Features: single-action 1911 Colt design; match components; ambidextrous safety
Gold Match II: **$1345**
Stainless: **$1519**
Team Match II: **$1535**

Kimber Handguns

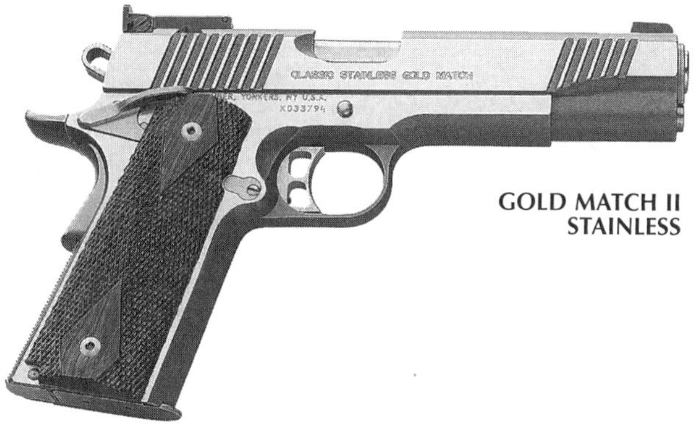

GOLD MATCH II
STAINLESS

PRO TLE II (LG)

ULTRA CARRY II
STAINLESS

PRO TLE II (LG) .45 ACP

Action: autoloader
Barrel: 4 in.
Sights: 3 dot
Weight: 36 oz.
Caliber: .45 ACP
Capacity: 7 + 1 rounds
Features: bushingless match grade bull barrel; steel frame; Crimson Trace Lasergrips (normal grip pressure activates a laser mounted in a grip panel); Meprolight Tritium 3 dot night sights
MSRP: **$1102**

ULTRA CARRY II

Action: autoloader
Grips: synthetic
Barrel: 3 in.
Sights: low-profile combat
Weight: 25.0 oz.
Caliber: .40 S&W, .45 ACP
Capacity: 7 + 1 rounds
Features: smallest commercial 1911-style pistol
Ultra Carry II: **$888**
Stainless II: **$980**

Magnum Research Handguns

BABY EAGLE

BABY EAGLE

Action: autoloader
Grips: plastic composite
Barrel: 3.5, 4, 4.5 in.
Sights: 3-dot combat
Weight: 26.8-39.8 oz.
Caliber: 9mm, .40 S&W, .45 ACP
Capacity: 10 rounds (15 for 9mm)
Features: squared, serrated trigger guard
MSRP: **$699**

Magnum Research Handguns

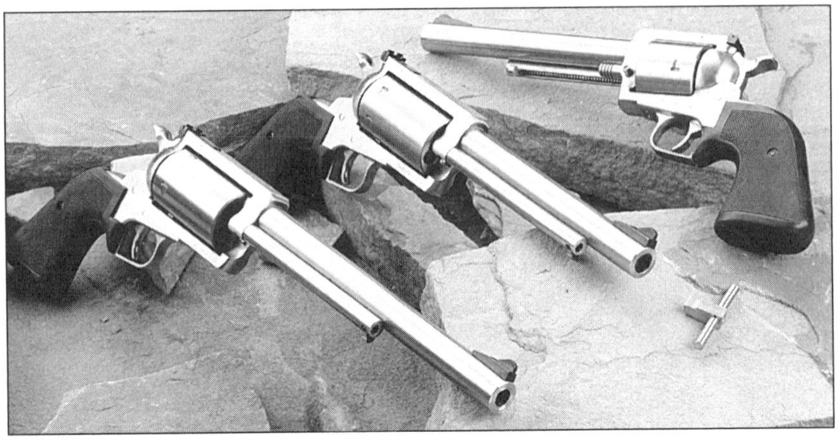

BFR

BFR (BIGGEST FINEST REVOLVER)

Action: single-action revolver
Grips: rubber
Barrel: 6.5, 7.5 or 10 in.
Sights: open adjustable
Weight: 50.0-67.3 oz.
Caliber: .45/70, .444, .450, .500 S&W, .30-30 Win. (long cylinder), .480 Ruger, .475 Linbaugh, .22 Hornet, .45 Colt/.410, .50 AE (short cylinder)
Capacity: 5 rounds
Features: both short and long-cylinder models entirely of stainless steel
MSRP: $1050

MARK XIX DESERT EAGLE
.50 MAGNUM TITANIUM FINISH

MARK XIX DESERT EAGLE

Action: autoloader
Grips: plastic composite
Barrel: 6 or 10 in.
Sights: fixed combat
Weight: 70.2 oz.
Caliber: .357 Mag., .44 Mag., .50 AE
Capacity: 9 + 1 rounds, 8 + 1 rounds, 7 + 1 rounds
Features: gas operated; all with polygonal rifling, integral scope bases
Desert Eagle, 6 in. barrel: . . . $1563
10 in. barrel (79 oz.): $1650
6 in. chrome or nickel: $1838
6 in. Titanium Gold:. $2055

MOA Handguns

MAXIMUM

Action: hinged breech
Grips: walnut
Barrel: 8.5, 10.5 or 14 in.
Sights: target *Weight:* 56.0 oz.
Caliber: most rifle chamberings from .22 Hornet to .375 H&H
Features: stainless breech; Douglas barrel; extra barrels; muzzle brake available
Maximum: $865
With stainless barrel: $966

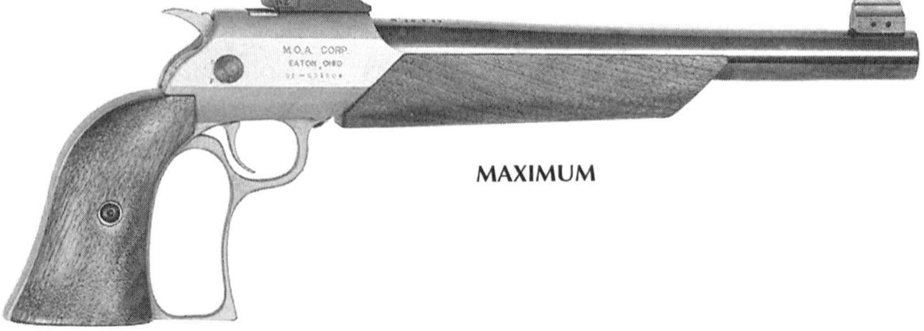

MAXIMUM

Navy Arms Handguns

1875 SCHOFIELD
CAVALRY MODEL

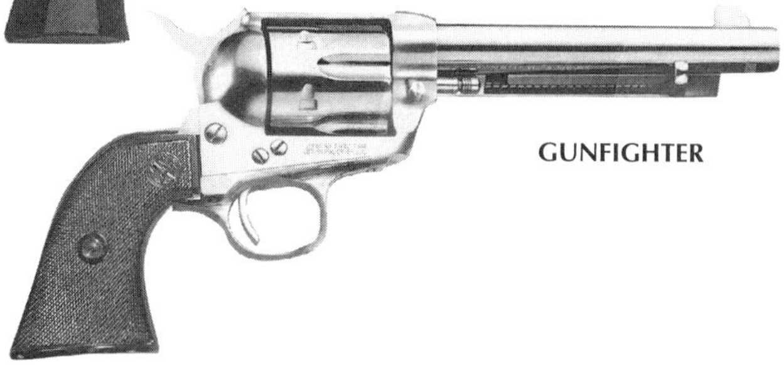

GUNFIGHTER

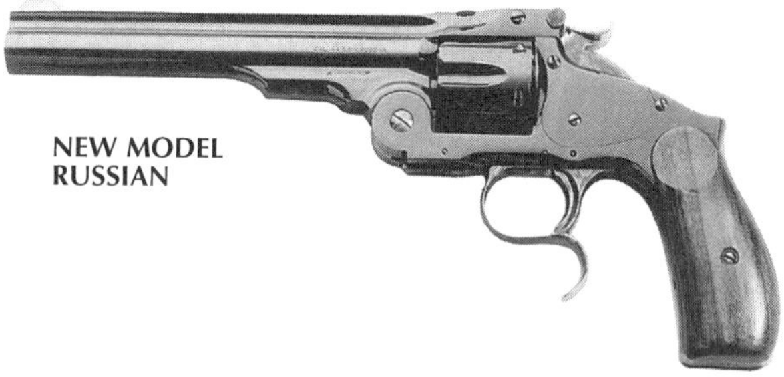

NEW MODEL
RUSSIAN

MODEL 1875 SCHOFIELD CAVALRY MODEL

Action: single-action revolver
Grips: walnut
Barrel: 3.5, 5.0 or 7.0 in.
Sights: fixed open
Weight: 35.0 oz.
Caliber: .38 Spl.,. 44-40, .45 Colt,
Capacity: 6 rounds
Features: top-break action, automatic ejectors; 5 in. barrel (37 oz.) and 7 in. barrel (39 oz.)
.38 Spl.: $899
44-40: $899
.45 Colt: $899

BISLEY

Action: single-action revolver
Grips: walnut
Barrel: 4.8, 5.5 or 7.5 in.
Sights: fixed open ***Weight:*** 45.0 oz.
Caliber: .44-40, .45 Colt
Capacity: 6 rounds
Features: Bisley grip case-colored frame; weight to 48 oz.
MSRP: $532

GUNFIGHTER SERIES

Action: single-action revolver
Grips: walnut
Barrel: 4.8, 5.5, 7.5 in.
Sights: fixed open
Weight: 47.0 oz.
Caliber: .357, .44-40, .45 Colt
Capacity: 6 rounds
Features: case-colored frames, after 1873 Colt design
Gunfighter: $585
Stainless: $591

Nighthawk Custom Handguns

10-8 GUN

Action: autoloader
Grips: VZ Diamondback, green or black linen micarta accented with the 10-8 logo
Barrel: 5 in.
Sights: 10-8 Performance rear sight, serrated front sights with a tritium insert
Caliber: .45 ACP
Features: long, solid trigger with a hidden fixed overtravel stop designed by Hilton Yam; front and rear cocking serrations on the slide; strong-side-only safety; 25-lpi checkered front strap; lanyard loop mainspring housing; black Perma Kote finish; low-profile Dawson Light Speed rail for easy attachment of Surefire X200 Series lights for use at night
MSRP: $2595

North American Arms Handguns

PUG MINI-REVOLVER

Action: revolver
Grips: rubber
Barrel: 1 in.
Sights: Tritium or white dot
Weight: 6.4 oz.
Caliber: .22 Mag
Capacity: 5 rounds
Features: XS sighting system
MSRP: $299–319

GUARDIAN .32

GUARDIAN .380

GUARDIAN .32

Action: autoloader
Grips: polymer
Barrel: 2.5 in.
Sights: fixed open
Weight: 12.0 oz.
Caliber: .32 ACP or .25 NAA
Capacity: 6 + 1 rounds
Features: stainless, double-action
MSRP: $402

GUARDIAN .380

Action: autoloader
Grips: composite
Barrel: 2.5 in.
Sights: fixed open
Weight: 18.8 oz.
Caliber: .380 ACP or .32 NAA
Capacity: 6 rounds
Features: stainless, double-action
MSRP: $449

North American Arms Handguns

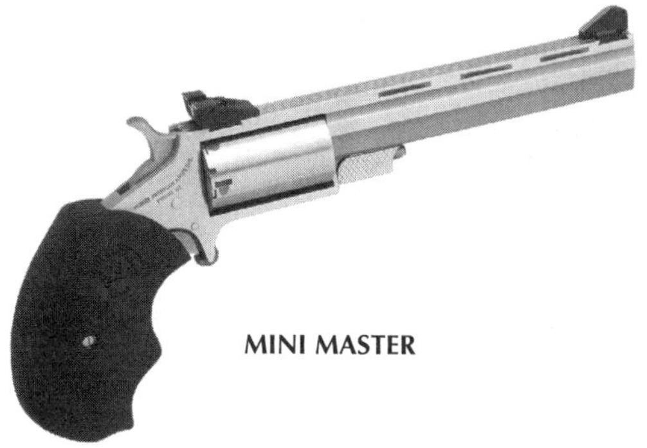

MINI MASTER

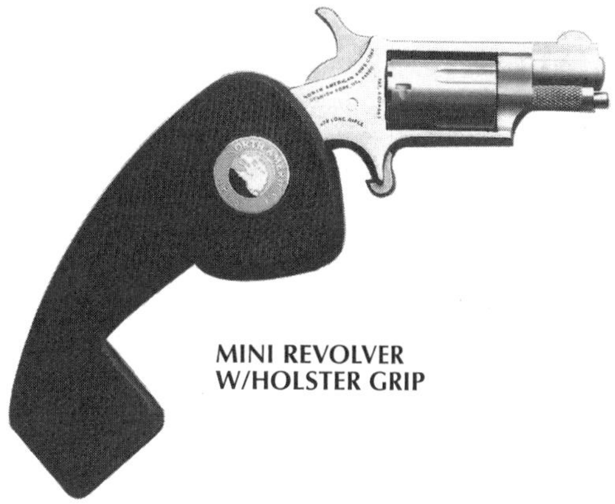

MINI REVOLVER W/HOLSTER GRIP

MINI MASTER SERIES REVOLVER

Action: single-action revolver
Grips: rubber
Barrel: 2 or 4 in.
Sights: fixed or adjustable
Weight: 8.8 oz. (2 in.) or 10.7 oz. (4 in.)
Caliber: .22LR or .22 Mag., .17 MACH 2, .17 HMR
Capacity: 5 rounds
Features: conversion cylinder or adjustable sights available

.22 Mag, LR (2 in.), .17 MACH2 or .17 HMR: $269
.22 Mag w/conversion .22 LR (2 in.): $334
.22 Mag or LR (4 in.): $284
.22 Mag w/conversion .22 LR (4 in.) or .17 HMR with .17 MACH2 conversion: $349

MINI REVOLVER

Action: single-action revolver
Grips: laminated rosewood
Barrel: 1.2 in.
Sights: fixed open
Weight: 5.0 oz.
Caliber: .22 Short, .22 LR, .22 WMR, .17 MACH 2, .17 HMR
Capacity: 5 rounds
Features: holster grip

.22 Short, .22 LR, .17 MACH2: . $215
With holster grip: $244
.22 Magnum, .17 HMR: $244
.22 Magnum with holster grip: . . $319

Olympic Arms Handguns

COHORT

Action: autoloader
Grips: walnut
Barrel: 4 in. bull ***Sights:*** target
Weight: 38.0 oz.
Caliber: .45 ACP
Capacity: 7 + 1 rounds
Features: single-action on 1911 Colt design; extended beavertail; stainless or parkerized
MSRP: $879

ENFORCER

Action: autoloader
Grips: walnut
Barrel: 4 in. bull
Sights: low-profile combat
Weight: 36.0 oz.
Caliber: .45 ACP
Capacity: 6 + 1 rounds
Features: single-action on 1911 Colt design; extended beavertail; stainless or parkerized
MSRP: $969

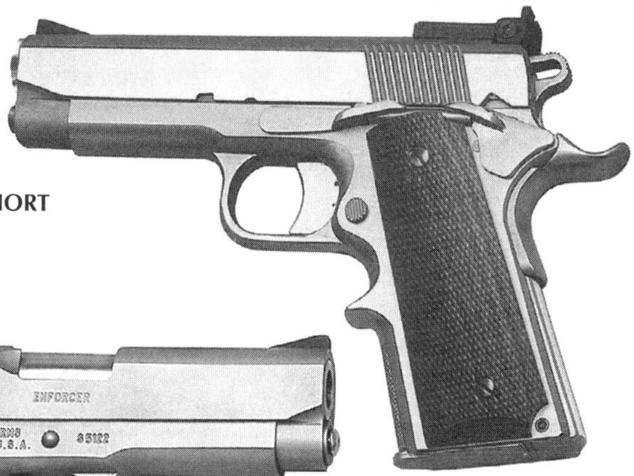

COHORT

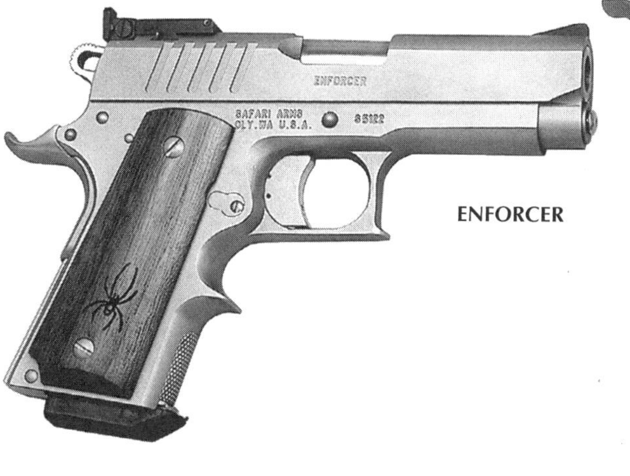

ENFORCER

Olympic Arms Handguns

HANDGUNS

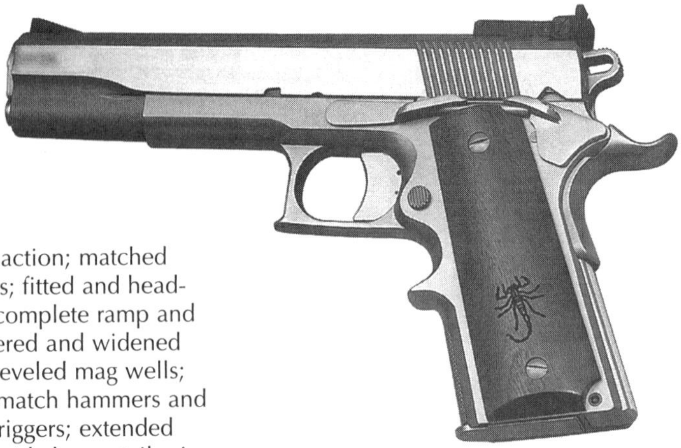

MATCHMASTER

MATCHMASTER
Action: autoloader
Grips: walnut
Barrel: 5 or 6 in. *Sights:* target
Weight: 40.0-44.0 oz.
Caliber: .45 ACP
Capacity: 7 + 1 rounds
Features: single-action on 1911 Colt design; extended beavertail; stainless or parkerized
Matchmaster 5 in.:. $903
6 in. barrel (44 oz.): $975
RS (40 oz.): $739

WESTERNER
Action: autoloader
Grips: walnut
Barrel: 4, 5, or 6 in. *Sights:* target
Weight: 35-43 oz. *Caliber:* .45 ACP
Capacity: 7 + 1 rounds
Features: single-action; matched frames and slides; fitted and head-spaced barrels; complete ramp and throat jobs; lowered and widened ejection ports; beveled mag wells; hand-stoned-to-match hammers and sears; adjusted triggers; extended thumb safeties; wide beavertail grip safeties; adjustable rear sights; dovetail front sights
Westerner:. $1039
Trail Boss (6 in. bbl): $1099
Constable (4 in. bbl):. $1164

Para Ordnance Handguns

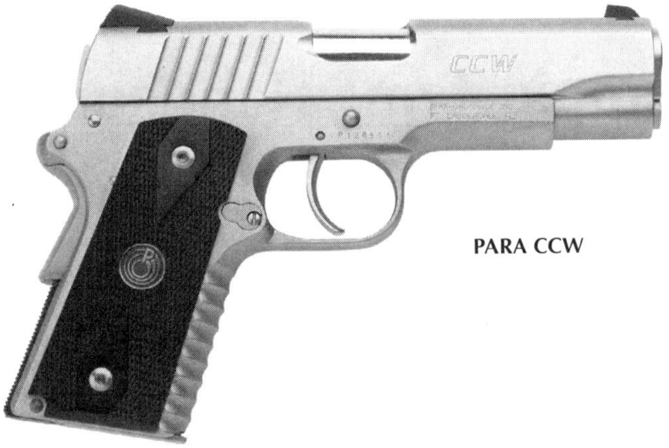

PARA CCW

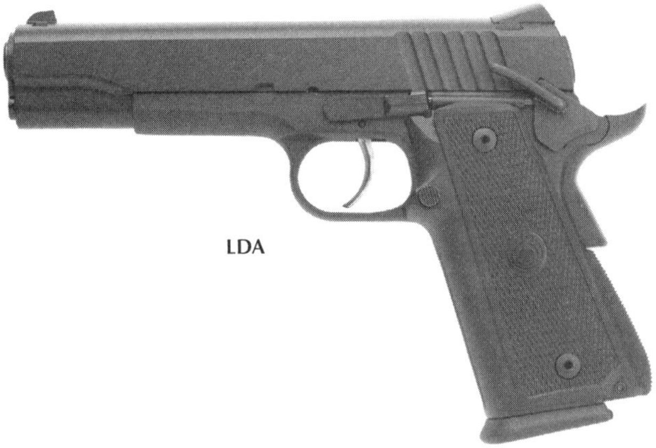

LDA

CCW AND COMPANION CARRY
Action: double-action autoloader
Grips: cocobolo
Barrel: 2.5, 3.5 or 4.1 in.
Sights: low-profile combat
Weight: 32.0-34.0 oz.
Caliber: .45 ACP
Capacity: 7 + 1 rounds
Features: double-action; stainless; Tritium night sights available
4.25 in. CCW:. $1129
3.5 in. Companion Carry: . . . $1129

LDA HIGH CAPACITY
Action: double-action autoloader
Grips: composite
Barrel: 4.25 or 5.0 in. ramped
Sights: target
Weight: 37.0-40.0 oz.
Caliber: 9mm, .40 S&W or .45 ACP
Capacity: 14 + 1 rounds, 16 + 1 rounds, 18 + 1 rounds
Features: double-action, double-stack magazine; stainless
LDA:. $999–1269
Carry option, 3.5 in. barrel:. . $1199

LDA SINGLE STACK
Action: double-action autoloader
Grips: composite
Barrel: 3.5, 4.25 or 5 in.
Sights: target
Weight: 32.0-40.0 oz.
Caliber: .45 ACP
Capacity: 7 + 1 rounds
Features: ramped, stainless barrel
MSRP: $999–1269

Para Ordnance Handguns

MODEL P12 .45 ACP
(3.5" BARREL, STAINLESS)

PXT 1911

PXT 14 .45 HIGH
CAPACITY LIMITED

PXT WARTHOG

TAC-FOUR

P-SERIES

Action: single-action autoloader
Grips: composite
Barrel: 3.0, 3.5, 4.25 or 5.0 in.
Sights: fixed open
Weight: 24.0-40.0 oz.
Caliber: 9mm, .45 ACP
Capacity: 10 + 1 to 18 + 1 rounds
Features: customized 1911 Colt design; beveled magazine well; polymer magazine; also available with 3-dot or low-profile combat sights; stainless
MSRP: $855–995

PXT 1911 PISTOLS

Action: single-action autoloading
Grips: cocobolo wood with gold medallion and beavertail extension
Barrel: 3.5, 4.25 and 5 in.
Sights: blade front, white 3 dot rear
Weight: 32.0-39.0 oz.
Caliber: .45 ACP
Capacity: 7+1 rounds
Features: single-action match trigger; extended slide lock; Para Kote Regal finish; stainless competition hammer; ramped stainless barrel
MSRP: $959–1149

PXT 14 .45 HIGH CAPACITY LIMITED

Action: single-action autoloader
Grips: polymer
Barrel: 5 in.
Sights: adjustable
Weight: 40.0 oz.
Caliber: .45 ACP
Capacity: 14 + 1 rounds
Features: stainless receiver: sterling finish
MSRP: $1259

PXT WARTHOG

Action: autoloader
Grips: black plastic
Barrel: 3 in.
Sights: 3 dot
Weight: 24 oz.
Caliber: .45 ACP
Capacity: 10 + 1 rounds
Features: single-action; ramped barrel; alloy receiver; spurred hammer
Warthog: $959
Nite Hawg:. $1099

TAC-FOUR

Action: double-action autoloader
Grips: black polymer
Barrel: 4.25 in.
Sights: low-profile combat
Weight: 36.0 oz.
Caliber: .45 ACP
Capacity: 13 + 1 rounds
Features: double-action; stainless; flush hammer; bobbed beavertail
MSRP: $1099

Para USA Handguns

1911 LIMITED

P14-45

P14-45
GUN RIGHTS

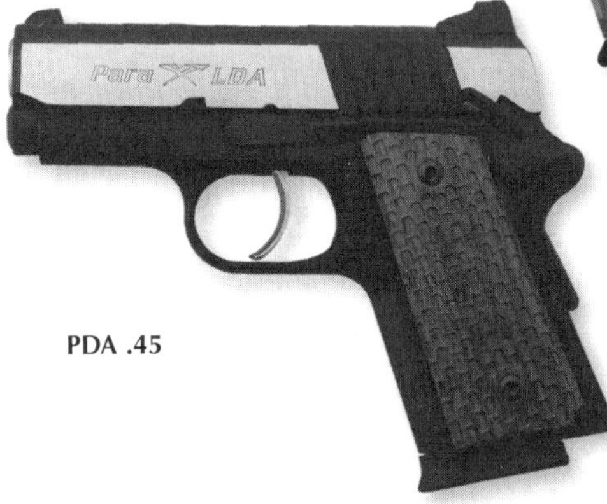

PDA .45

PDA 9MM

1911 LIMITED

Action: single-action autoloader
Barrel: 5 in. ramped, match, stainless
Sights: fiber optic front, adjustable rear
Weight: 40 oz.
Caliber: .45 ACP
Capacity: 8+1 rounds
Features: SA; stainless steel receiver; ambidextrous slide-lock safety; sterling stainless finish; two 8-round magazines included
MSRP: $1249

P14-45

Action: single-action autoloader
Grips: Ultra Slim polymer
Barrel: 5 in. ramped, match, stainless
Sights: 3-white dot fixed
Weight: 40 oz.
Caliber: .45 ACP
Capacity: 14+1 rounds
Features: SA; carbon steel receiver; Para Triple Safety System (slide lock, firing pin and grip); Covert Black Para Kote finish; two 14-round magazines included (10-round magazines available in those states with restricted capacity)
MSRP: $919

P14-45 GUN RIGHTS

Action: single-action autoloader
Grips: polymer
Barrel: 5 in.
Sights: fixed rear, fiber optic front
Weight: 40 oz.
Caliber: .45 ACP
Capacity: 14+1 rounds (10-round magazine available)
Features: SA; ramped, match, stainless barrel; stainless Classic Satin finish; specially made to support the N.R.A.'s Institute for Legislative Action
MSRP: $1149

PDA (PERSONAL DEFENSE ASSISTANT)

Action: double-action autoloader
Grips: cocobolo wood
Barrel: 3 in. ramped, match, stainless
Sights: 3-dot tritium night sights
Weight: 24 oz.
Caliber: .45, 9mm
Capacity: 6+1 rounds
Features: DA; stainless slide; Covert Black frame; Para Triple Safety System (slide lock, firing pin and grip); two 6-round (.45) or 8-round (9mm) magazines; PDA logo on grips
PDA 9MM: $1219–1269

Para USA Handguns

PXT SSP

SUPER HAWG
HIGH CAPACITY

SUPER HAWG
SINGLE STACK

PXT SSP

Action: autoloader
Grips: rubber
Barrel: 5 in.
Sights: 3-dot white fixed
Weight: 39 oz.
Caliber: .45 ACP
Capacity: 8+1 rounds
Features: SA; ramped, match, stainless barrrel; Para Triple Safety System (slide lock, firing pin and grip); Covert Black Para Kote finish; two 8-round magazines
MSRP: **$1149**

SUPER HAWG HIGH CAPACITY

Action: autoloader
Grips: polymer
Barrel: 6 in.
Sights: fiber optic front, adjustable rear
Weight: 41 oz.
Caliber: .45 ACP
Capacity: 14+1 rounds
Features: SA; ramped, match, stainless barrel; Classic Stainless finish; ambidextrous Para Triple Safety System (slide lock, firing pin and grip); two 14-round magazines included (10-round magazines available in those states with restricted capacity)
MSRP: **$1369**

SUPER HAWG SINGLE STACK

Action: autoloader
Grips: Double Diamond Checkered Cocobolo
Barrel: 6 in.
Sights: adjustable
Weight: 40 oz.
Caliber: .45 ACP
Capacity: 8+1 rounds
Features: SA; ramped, match, stainless barrel; Classic Stainless finish; ambidextrous Para Triple Safety System (slide lock, firing pin and grip); fiber optic front, adjustable rear sights; two 8-round magazines
MSRP: **$1369**

PARAUSA GI EXPERT

Action: SA autoloading, recoil operated
Grips: checkered composite
Barrel: 5″
Sights: fixed white-dot combat
Weight: 39 oz.
Caliber: .45 ACP
Capacity: 8
Features: a plain-jane military-style 1911 with some refinements—skeleton loop hammer, stainless barrel, white dot sights and grooved, drilled trigger.
MSRP: **$599–699**

Puma Handguns

STAINLESS STEEL MODEL
WITH WHITE GRIPS

PUMA WESTERNER SA REVOLVERS

Action: SA revolver
Grips: white or walnut
Barrel: 4.75, 5.5 or 7.5 inch
Sights: strap groove and fixed blade
Weight: 36-40 oz.
Caliber: .45 LC, .357 Mag., .44-40
Capacity: 6
Features: Made in Italy by Pietta, imported by Legacy Sports Int'l. Stainless steel or color case hardened or nickeled carbon steel frame
MSRP: $589–829

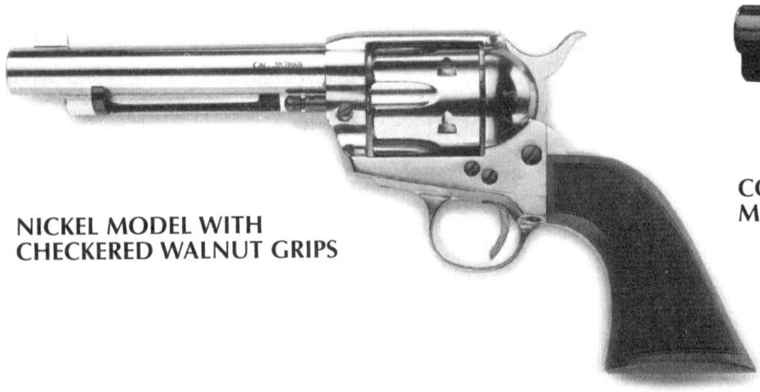

NICKEL MODEL WITH
CHECKERED WALNUT GRIPS

COLOR CASE HARDENED
MODEL

Rossi Handguns

MODEL R351 AND R352

Action: double-action revolver
Grips: rubber
Barrel: 2 in.
Sights: fixed open
Weight: 24.0 oz.
Caliber: .38 Spl.
Capacity: 6 rounds
Features: stainless; R351 chrome-moly also available
R35202 stainless: $452
R35102 blue: $389

MODEL R352

Rossi Handguns

MODEL R461

MODEL R972 .357
MAGNUM 6-SHOT

MODEL R462 & R461

Action: double-action revolver
Grips: rubber
Barrel: 2 in.
Sights: fixed open
Weight: 26.0 oz.
Caliber: .357 Mag.
Capacity: 6 rounds
Features: stainless; R461 chrome-moly also available
R462 stainless: $452
R461 blue: $389

MODEL R851

Action: double-action revolver
Grips: rubber
Barrel: 4 in.
Sights: adjustable
Weight: 32.0 oz.
Caliber: .38 Spl.
Capacity: 6 rounds
Features: adjustable rear sight; blue finish
R85104: $389

MODEL R972

Action: double-action revolver
Grips: rubber
Barrel: 6 in.
Sights: target
Weight: 34.0 oz.
Caliber: .357 Mag.
Capacity: 6 rounds
Features: stainless after S&W M19 pattern; also R971 chrome-moly with 4 in. barrel
R972 stainless: $508
R971 blue: $452

Ruger Handguns

RUGER MARK III HUNTER

Action: SA autoloading, recoil operated
Grips: checkered cocobolo
Barrel: 4.5″ target-crowned, fluted bull
Sights: HiViz front sight with 6 interchangeable LitePipes
Weight: 38 oz.
Caliber: .22
Capacity: 10
Features: Stainless steel frame. V-notch rear sight blade. Length*:* 8 ¾″. Visible loaded chamber indicator.
MSRP: $638–811

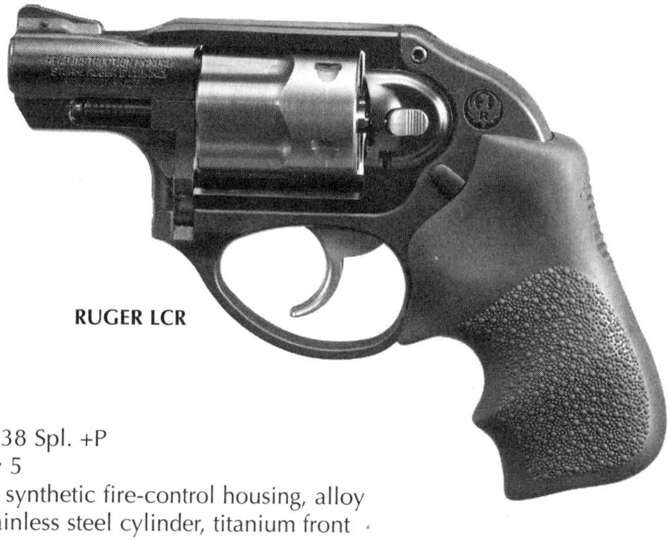

RUGER LCR

RUGER LCR (LIGHTWEIGHT COMPACT REVOLVER)

Action: DA revolver
Grips: Hogue
Barrel: 2″
Sights: fixed U-notch and ramp
Weight: 13 ½ oz.
Caliber: .38 Spl. +P
Capacity: 5
Features: synthetic fire-control housing, alloy frame, stainless steel cylinder, titanium front latch
MSRP: $525–792

Ruger Handguns

.22 CHARGER

LCP

.22 CHARGER
Action: autoloader
Grips: black laminate
Barrel: 10 in.
Sights: N/A
Weight: 56 oz.
Caliber: .22 LR
Capacity: 10 rounds
Features: cross bolt safety; extended magazine release; combination Weaver-style and "tip-off" sight mount; bipod and gun rug with Ruger logo included
MSRP: $380

LCP (LIGHTWEIGHT COMPACT PISTOL)
Action: double-action autoloader
Grips: integral
Barrel: 2.75 in.
Sights: none
Weight: 9.4 oz.
Caliber: .380
Capacity: 6+1 rounds
Features: through-hardened blued steel slide; glass-filled nylon frame height
3.6 in., width .82 in.; includes soft case
MSRP: $364

BISLEY
Action: single-action revolver
Grips: walnut
Barrel: 6.5 (.22 LR) or 7.5 in.
Sights: target
Weight: 43.0-50.0 oz.
Caliber: .22 LR, .357 Mag., .44 Mag., .45 Colt
Capacity: 6 rounds
Features: rimfire and centerfire
(48 oz.); low-profile hammer
.357, .44, .45: $591.64

BISLEY SINGLE-ACTION TARGET

BISLEY VAQUERO
Action: single-action revolver
Grips: rosewood
Barrel: 4.6, 5.5 in.
Sights: fixed open
Weight: 43.5-44.0 oz.
Caliber: .45 Colt or .44 Rem. Mag
Capacity: 6 rounds
Features: stainless or color case blued; transfer bar operating mechanism/loading gate interlock
Stainless: $566.73

A semi-auto pistol is designed to operate as the slide moves against the abutment of a firmly held frame. A low grasp allows the muzzle to whipsaw upward from recoil as the mechanism is automatically cycling, diverting momentum from the slide through the frame. Now the slide can run out of momentum before it has completed its work. This is why holding a pistol too low can cause it to jam.

GP-100 .357 MAGNUM
6" HEAVY BARREL

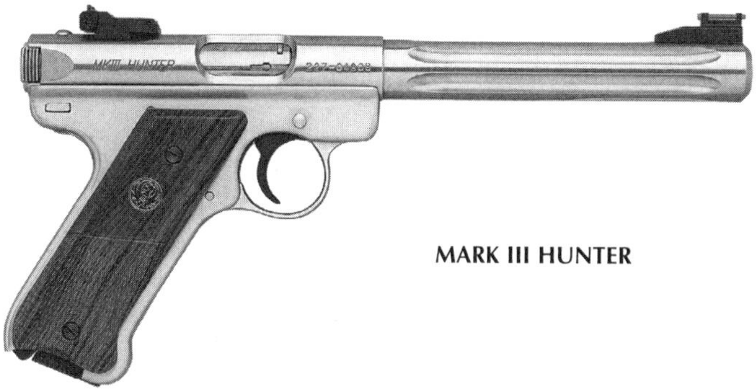

MARK III HUNTER

NEW BEARCAT

MODEL GP100

Action: double-action revolver
Grips: rubber with rosewood insert
Barrel: 4.3 or 6 in.
Sights: fixed open
Weight: 38.0-46.0 oz.
Caliber: .38 Spl. or .357
Capacity: 6 rounds
Features: chrome-moly or stainless; weight to 46 oz. depending on barrel length
Blued: $452.95
Stainless: $497.95–565.99

MARK II

Action: autoloader
Grips: synthetic or rosewood
Barrel: 4 in., 4 in. Bull, 6.7 in. Bull
Sights: open, fixed or adjustable
Caliber: .22 LR
Capacity: 10 rounds
Features: slab bull barrel; manual safety; loaded chamber indicator; magazine disconnect; adjustable rear sight; blued finish
4 in. Bull (Limited Edition rosewood grips): . . . . .price on request
6.7 in. Bull: $637
6.7 in slab Bull: $637

MARK III

Action: autoloader
Grips: black synthetic or wood
Barrel: 5.5 in. Bull or 6.7 in. Bull
Sights: open, adjustable
Weight: 41 oz.
Caliber: .22 LR
Capacity: 10 rounds
Features: Bull barrel; contoured ejection port and tapered bolt ears; manual safety; loaded chamber indicator; magazine disconnect; adjustable rear sight; stainless finish; drilled and tapped for a Weaver-type scope base adapter
Stainless, 5.5 in. Bull bl.: $627
Stainless, 6.7 in. bl.: $644
Stainless, 6.7 in. slab Bull bl.: $646
Blue, 4.75 in. bl.: $439
Blue, 6 in. bl.: $439
22/45 Mark III (4-in slab bull bl.): $435

NEW BEARCAT

Action: single-action revolver
Grips: rosewood
Barrel: 4 in.
Sights: fixed open
Weight: 24.0 oz.
Caliber: .22 LR
Capacity: 6 rounds
Features: transfer bar
New Bearcat: $423.25
Stainless: $479.99

Ruger Handguns

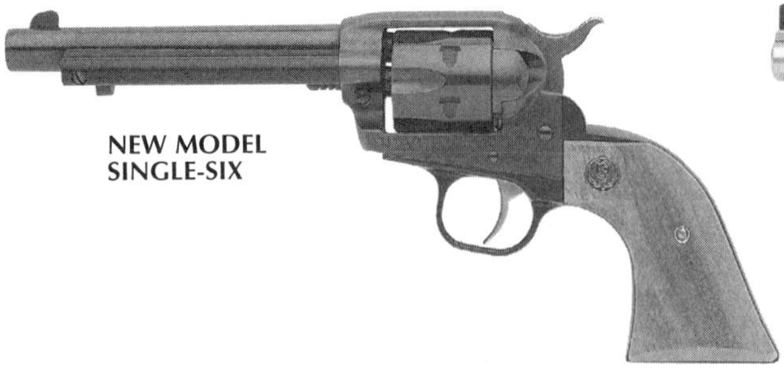

NEW MODEL SINGLE-SIX

NEW MODEL SUPER BLACKHAWK

NEW VAQUERO

MODEL P94

P345

NEW MODEL SINGLE SIX

Action: single-action revolver
Grips: rosewood or Micarta
Barrel: 4.6, 5.5, 6.5 or 9.5 in.
Sights: fixed open
Weight: 33.0-45.0 oz.
Caliber: .22 LR, .22 WMR, .17 HMR, .17 MACH 2
Capacity: 6 rounds
Features: adjustable sights available; weight to 38 oz. depending on barrel length

Single Six: $549.99
Stainless: $482–598
17 HMR: $402.98

NEW MODEL SUPER BLACKHAWK

Action: single-action revolver
Grips: walnut
Barrel: 4.6, 5.5, 7.5 or 10.5 in.
Sights: target
Weight: 45.0-55.0 oz.
Caliber: .41 Rem Mag, .44 Rem Mag .45 Colt
Capacity: 6 rounds
Features: weight to 51 oz. depending on barrel length; also available: Super Black-hawk Hunter, stainless with 7.5 in. barrel, black laminated grips, rib, scope rings

Blue: $529.99
Stainless: $701.86

NEW VAQUERO

Action: single-action revolver
Grips: black, checkered
Barrel: 4.6, 5.5 or 7.5 in.
Sights: fixed open
Weight: 37.0-41.0 oz.
Caliber: .45 Colt or .357
Capacity: 6 rounds
Features: gloss stainless or color case, reverse indexing pawl

Vaquero: $525.77

P-SERIES

Action: autoloader
Grips: polymer
Barrel: 3.9 or 4.5 in.
Sights: fixed open
Weight: 30.0 oz.
Caliber: 9mm, .40 S&W, .45 Auto
Capacity: 10 + 1 rounds (8 + 1 in .45, 15 + 1 in 9mm)
Features: double-action; ambidextrous grip safety; decocker on some models; manual safety on others (9mm)

KP95PR Stainless 3.9 in. bl.: $340
P95PR Blued 3.9 in. bl.: . . $316.56
KP89 Stainless 4.5 in. bl.:. . . $525
KP94 Stainless 4.1 in. bl.:. . . $628
KP95 Stainless 3.9 in. bl.:. $329.95
P89 Blued 4.5 in. bl.: $475
P95 Blued 3.9 in. bl.: $349.99

(.40 S&W)

P94 .40 S&W
Blued 4.1 in. bl.: $479.95

(.45 ACP)

KP345 Stainless 4.5 in. bl.: $427.95
KP345PR 4.25 in. bl.: $453.47
P345PR Blued 4.25 in. bl.: $424.07
KP90 Stainless 4.5 in. bl.:. $467.43
P90 Blued 4.5 in. bl.: $469.95

Ruger Handguns

REDHAWK STAINLESS

REDHAWK

MODEL SP101

SUPER REDHAWK

SUPER REDHAWK ALASKAN

REDHAWK

Action: double-action revolver
Grips: rosewood
Barrel: 5.5 or 7.5 in.
Sights: target
Weight: 49.0 oz.
Caliber: .44 Rem Mag.
Capacity: 6 rounds
Features: stainless model available; 7.5 in. version weighs 54 oz.; scope rings available
Stainless: $757.55
Stainless with rings: $813.70

MODEL SP101

Action: double-action revolver
Grips: rubber with synthetic insert
Barrel: 2.3, 3.0 or 4.0 in.
Sights: fixed open (adjustable on .32 H&R)
Weight: 25.0-30.0 oz.
Caliber: .22 LR, .32 H&R, 9mm, .38 Spl., .357
Capacity: 5 or 6 rounds
Features: chrome-moly or stainless; weight to 30 oz. depending on barrel length
Stainless 2.25 in. bl.: $439–708
Stainless 3.1 in. bl.: $439

SUPER REDHAWK

Action: double-action revolver
Grips: rubber/black laminate
Barrel: 7.5 or 9.5 in. (2.25 Alaskan)
Sights: target
Weight: 53.0 oz.
Caliber: .44 Mag., .454 Casull, .480 Ruger
Capacity: 6 rounds
Features: stainless or low glare stainless finish; 9.5 in. version weighs 58 oz.
.44 Magnum: $746.00
.454, .480 Ruger: $813.70
Alaskan: $849–869

Sig Sauer Handguns

SIG SAUER P238 NITRON

Action: SA autoloading, recoil operated
Grips: aluminum
Barrel: 2 ½″
Sights: SIGLITE night sights
Weight: 15 oz.
Caliber: .380
Capacity: 6
Features: Small frame. Overall length: 5.5″, 3.96″ high. Anodized alloy beavertail style frame with fluted aluminum grips. Stainless serrated slide. Available in black or two-tone with corrosion resistant Nitron slide.
MSRP: $629

P250

Action: locked breech DAO semiauto
Grips: polymer
Barrel: variable length
Sights: SIGLITE® Three Dot Night Sights
Weight: 24.6-30.8 oz.
Caliber: .45ACP, .40 S&W, .357 SIG, 9mm
Capacity: variable
Features: steel receiver with Nitron or two-tone finish; reversible magazine release; ambidextrous slide release; interchangable mechanism allows immediate change in caliber and size (subcompact, compact and full); integral accessory rail; interchangeable grips
MSRP: $570–870

MODEL P226

MODEL P220

Action: autoloader
Grips: polymer or laminated
Barrel: 4.4 in., 3.9 in. (Carry)
Sights: adjustable
Weight: 27.8 oz., 30.84 oz. (Carry), 31.2 (Compact)
Caliber: .45 ACP
Capacity: 8 rounds, 6 rounds (Compact)
Features: DA/SA; de-cocking lever; automatic firing pin safety block; Nitron or two-tone finish; Picatinny rail; available with SIGLITE Night Sights
Nitron:. $976
Two-tone: $1110
Elite: $1200
Carry Nitron:. $975
Carry Two-tone:. $1100
Carry Elite:. $1200
Carry Elite Two-tone: $1107
Compact Nitron: $1050
Compact Two-tone: $1110

Sig Sauer Handguns

MODEL P226

Action: autoloader
Grips: polymer or laminated hardwood
Barrel: 4.4 in.
Sights: adjustable
Weight: 34 to 34.2 oz w/ mag.
Caliber: 9mm; 357 SIG, 40 S&W
Capacity: 10 or 5 rounds (9mm), 10 or 12 + 1 rounds (357 SIG, 40 S&W)
Features: DA/SA; de-cocking lever; automatic firing pin safety block; reversible magazine release; Picatinny rail; available with SIGLITE Night Sights
Nitron:. $976
Two-tone: $1110
Elite: $1200
Elite two-tone:. $1200
Elite stainless: $1350

MODEL P229

SIG CLASSIC COMPACT P229 ST

MODEL P229

Action: autoloader
Grips: polymer or laminated wood
Barrel: 3.9 in.
Sights: fixed open
Weight: 32 to 32.4 oz. w/ mag.
Caliber: 9mm, .357 SIG, .40 S&W
Capacity: 10 + 1 rounds
Features: DA/SA; de-cocking lever; automatic firing pin safety block; available with SIGLITE Night Sights
MSRP: $976

MODEL SP2022

MODEL SP2022

Action: autoloader *Grips:* polymer
Barrel: 3.6 in. *Sights:* fixed open
Weight: 30.2 oz.
Caliber: 9mm, .357 SIG, .40 S&W
Capacity: 7 + 1 rounds
Features: DA/SA; Nitron coated stainless slide, polymer frame; can be converted from DA to SA.
MSRP: $613

MODEL P232

MODEL P232

Action: autoloader *Grips:* polymer
Barrel: 3.6 in.
Sights: fixed open
Weight: 16.2 oz.
Caliber: .380
Capacity: 7 + 1 rounds
Features: double-action; Picatinny rail; available with SIGLITE Night Sights
Blued: $720
Two-tone: $826
Stainless:. $900

Sig Sauer Handguns

MODEL P239

MOSQUITO

MODEL P239

Action: autoloader
Grips: polymer
Barrel: 3.6 in.
Sights: fixed open
Weight: 27.0 oz.
Caliber: 9mm, .357 Sig, .40 S&W
Capacity: 7 + 1 rounds
Features: DA/SA; lightweight alloy frame
Nitron:. $840
Two-tone: $1006

MOSQUITO

Action: autoloader
Grips: polymer, composite
Barrel: 4 in. ***Sights:*** adjustable
Weight: 24.6 oz. w/ mag.
Caliber: .22 LR
Capacity: 10 rounds
Features: DA/SA; polymer frame; Picatinny rail; slide mounted ambidextrous safety; internal locking device
Blued: $390
Two-tone: $405

REVOLUTION 1911

Action: autoloader
Grips: custom hardwood
Barrel: 5 in.
Sights: foxed open or target
Weight: 30.3 to 40.3 oz.
Caliber: .45 ACP
Capacity: 8+1 rounds
Features: 1911 series pistol; SA; hand-fitted stainless steel frame and slide available in black Nitron finish; match grade barrel; available with 4¼ in. barrel (Compact); hammer/sear set and trigger; beavertail grip safety; firing pin safety and hammer intercept notch; available with Novak night sights
Nitron:. $1200
Stainless:. $1170
Stainless Carry: $1170
Compact Nitron: $1200
Compact Stainless: $1170

Smith & Wesson Handguns

SMITH & WESSON CLASSIC M57 AND M58

Action: DA N-frame revolver
Grips: checkered square-butt walnut (target style on M57, standard on M58)
Barrel: 4″ or 6″
Sights: Pinned red ramp front, micro-adjustable white outline rear (M57) or strap-groove rear (M58)
Weight: 45 or 48 oz.
Caliber: .41 Magnum
Capacity: 6
Features: This Classic Series six-shot revolver is available in bright blue or nickel. M57 has target hammer and trigger, M58 has lanyard fixture.
M57: $1098–1153
M58: $1090–1146

CLASSIC M57

Smith & Wesson Handguns

SMITH & WESSON M14 NICKEL

Action: DA K-frame revolver
Grips: checkered square-butt walnut
Barrel: 6″
Sights: partridge-style front sight and micro-adjustable rear
Weight: 40 oz.
Caliber: .38 Special
Capacity: 6
Features: This Classic Series six-shot revolver is available in bright blue or nickel.
MSRP: $1027–1106

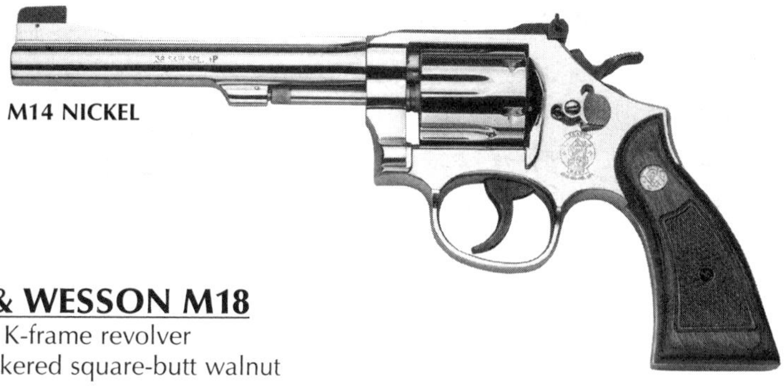
M14 NICKEL

SMITH & WESSON M18

Action: DA K-frame revolver
Grips: checkered square-butt walnut
Barrel: 4″
Sights: ramp front sight and micro-adjustable rear
Weight: 33 oz.
Caliber: .22 Long Rifle
Capacity: 6
Features: This Classic Series six-shot revolver is finished in bright blue.
MSRP: $1043

M&P9L

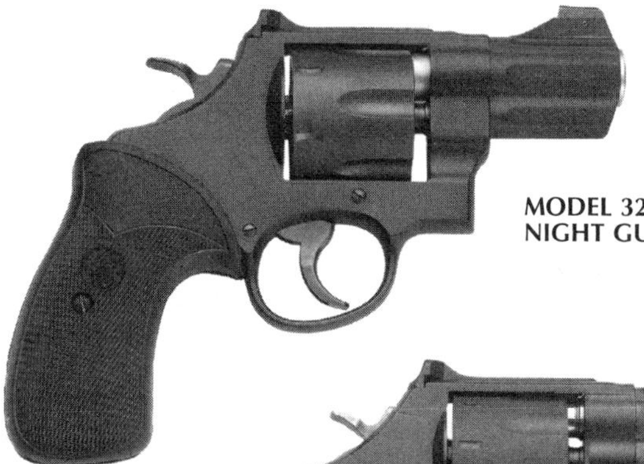
MODEL 325 NIGHT GUARD

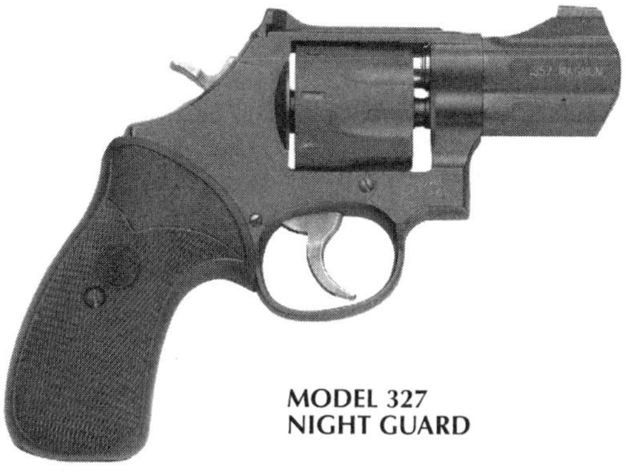
MODEL 327 NIGHT GUARD

M&P9L

Action: striker fire action
Grips: synthetic
Barrel: 5 in.
Sights: open
Weight: 25.2 oz.
Caliber: 9mm
Capacity: 17 rounds
Features: through-hardened black Melonite stainless steel barrel; Zytel polymer frame reinforced with steel chassis; loaded chamber indicator on top of slide; ambidextrous slide stop; reversible magazine release; steel white-dot dovetail front, steel Novak Lo-Mount carry rear sights, (tritium sights available); enlarged trigger guard; 3 interchangeable grip sizes
MSRP: $758

MODEL 325 NIGHT GUARD

Action: single/double action revolver
Grips: synthetic
Barrel: 2.5 in.
Sights: open
Weight: 28 oz.
Caliber: .45 ACP
Capacity: 6 rounds
Features: scandium alloy frame; stainless PVD cylinder; matte black finish; XS Sight 24/7 Standard Dot Tritium front, Cylinder & Slide Extreme Duty Fixed back sights; Pachmayr Compac Custom grips
MSRP: $1185

MODEL 327 NIGHT GUARD

Action: single/double action revolver
Grips: synthetic
Barrel: 2.5 in.
Sights: open
Weight: 27.6 oz.
Caliber: .357 Magnum, .38 S&W Special
Capacity: 8 rounds
Features: scandium alloy frame; stainless PVD cylinder; matte black finish; XS Sight 24/7 Standard Dot Tritium front, Cylinder & Slide Extreme Duty Fixed back sights; Pachmayr Compac Custom grips
MSRP: $1185

Smith & Wesson Handguns

MODEL 329 NIGHT GUARD

MODEL 386 NIGHT GUARD

MODEL 396 NIGHT GUARD

MODEL 27 CLASSIC

MODEL 327PD

MODEL 627 PRO SERIES

MODEL 329 NIGHT GUARD

Action: single/double action revolver
Grips: synthetic
Barrel: 2.5 in.
Sights: XS Sight 24/7 Standard Dot Tritium front, Cylinder & Slide Extreme Duty Fixed back
Weight: 29.3 oz.
Caliber: .44 Magnum, .44 Special
Capacity: 6 rounds
Features: scandium alloy frame; stainless PVD cylinder; matte black finish
MSRP: $1185

MODEL 386 NIGHT GUARD

Action: single/double action revolver
Grips: Pachmayr Compac Custom
Barrel: 2.5 in.
Sights: XS Sight 24/7 Standard Dot Tritium front, Cylinder & Slide Extreme Duty Fixed back
Weight: 24.5 oz.
Caliber: .357 Magnum, .38 Special +P
Capacity: 7 rounds
Features: scandium alloy frame; stainless PVD cylinder; matte black finish
MSRP: $1106

MODEL 396 NIGHT GUARD

Action: single/double action revolver
Grips: Pachmayr Compac Custom
Barrel: 2.5 in.
Sights: XS Sight 24/7 Standard Dot Tritium front, Cylinder & Slide Extreme Duty Fixed back
Weight: 24.5 oz.
Caliber: .44 Special
Capacity: 5 rounds
Features: scandium alloy frame; stainless PVD cylinder; matte black finish
MSRP: $820

MODEL 27 CLASSIC

Action: single/double action revolver
Grips: checkered square butt walnut
Barrel: 6.5 in.
Sights: pinned partridge front, micro adjustable rear with cross serrations
Caliber: .357 Magnum, .38 S&W Special
Capacity: 6 rounds
Features: carbon steel; classic style thumbpiece; color case wide spur hammer; color case serrated target trigger; High Bright Blue or Bright Nickel finish
MSRP: $1122

MODEL 327PD

Action: single/double action revolver
Grips: slip-resistant synthetic rubber
Barrel: 4 in.
Sights: red Hi-Viz pinned front, fully adjustable V-notch rear
Weight: 24.3 oz.
Caliber: 357 Magnum, .38 S&W Special + P
Capacity: 8 rounds
Features: lightweight scandium alloy frame; titanium cylinder; black matte finish
MSRP: $974

MODEL 627 PRO SERIES

Action: single/double action revolver
Grips: synthetic
Barrel: 4 in.
Sights: interchangeable front, adjustable rear
Weight: 41.2 oz.
Caliber: .357 Magnum, .38 S&W Special
Capacity: 8 rounds
Features: stainless precision crowned muzzle, chamfered charge holes, bossed mainspring, internal lock, cable lock
MSRP: $1090

Smith & Wesson Handguns

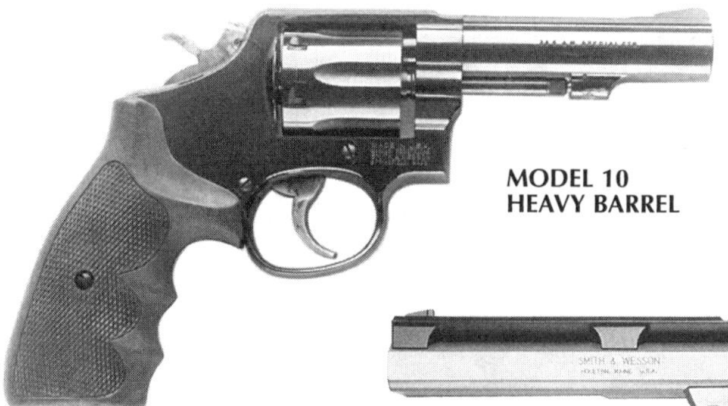

MODEL 10
HEAVY BARREL

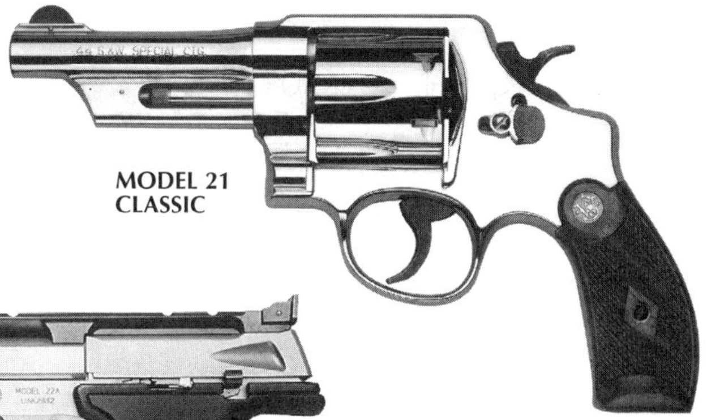

MODEL 21
CLASSIC

MODEL 22A
SPORT

MODEL 22 CLASSIC

MODEL 22 OF
1917 CLASSIC

MODEL 10

Action: double-action revolver
Grips: Uncle Mike's Combat
Barrel: 4.0 in. heavy
Sights: fixed open
Weight: 33.5 oz.
Caliber: .38 Spl.
Capacity: 6 rounds
Features: "military and police" model; also in stainless, K-frame
Model 10: $814

MODEL 21 CLASSIC

Action: revolver
Grips: Altamont walnut
Barrel: 4 in.
Sights: front: pinned half moon service; rear: service
Weight: 37 oz.
Caliber: .44 SP
Capacity: 6 rounds
Features: carbon steel frame and cylinder; blue, color case or nickel finish; square butt; serrated trigger
MSRP: $924

MODEL 22A SPORT

Action: autoloader
Grips: polymer
Barrel: 4, 5.5 or 7 in.
Sights: target
Weight: 28.0 oz.
Caliber: .22 LR
Capacity: 10 + 1 rounds
Features: scope mounting rib; 5½ in. bull barrel available
4 in.:. $324
5.5 in. (31 oz.):. $356
5.5 in. bull: $356
5.5 in. bull, Hi-Viz sights:. $356
7 in. (33 oz.): $324
5.5 in. stainless:. $356

MODEL 22 CLASSIC

Action: revolver
Grips: Altamont walnut
Barrel: 4 in.
Sights: front: pinned half moon service; rear: service
Weight: 36.8 oz.
Caliber: .45 ACP
Capacity: 6 rounds
Features: carbon steel frame and cylinder; blue, color case or nickel finish; comes with two six-shot full-moon clips
MSRP: $1090

MODEL 22 OF 1917 CLASSIC

Action: revolver
Grips: Altamont walnut
Barrel: 5.5 in.
Sights: front: pinned half moon service; rear: service
Weight: 37.2 oz.
Caliber: .45 ACP
Capacity: 6 rounds
Features: carbon steel frame and cylinder; blue, color case or nickel finish; comes with two six-shot full-moon clips
MSRP: $1098

Smith & Wesson Handguns

MODEL 29 .44 MAGNUM

MODEL 29 CLASSIC, ENGRAVED

MODEL 36 CHIEFS SPECIAL CLASSIC

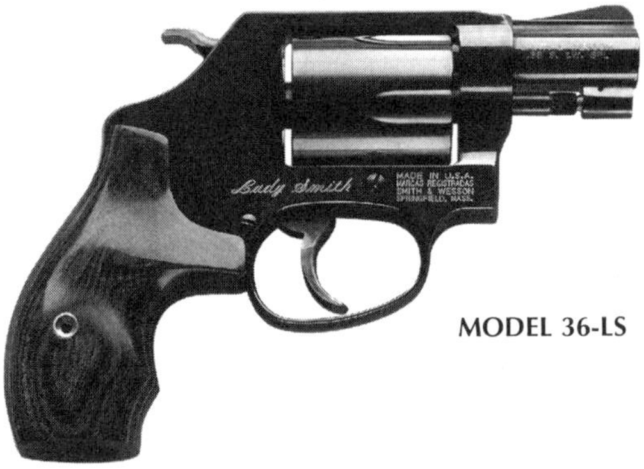

MODEL 36-LS

MODEL 29 .44 MAGNUM 50TH ANNIVERSARY EDITION

Action: double-action revolver
Grips: African cocobolo wood
Barrel: 6.5 in.
Sights: target
Weight: 48.5 oz.
Caliber: .44 MAG
Capacity: 6 rounds
Features: 24kt gold-plated anniversary logo on the frame; red ramp front sight, adjustable white outline rear sight; shipped with a mahogany presentation case and a Smith & Wesson cleaning kit with screwdriver
MSRP: $1280

MODEL 29 CLASSIC, ENGRAVED

Action: revolver
Grips: African cocobolo wood
Barrel: 6.5 in.
Sights: front: red ramp; rear: adjustable white outline
Weight: 48.5 oz.
Caliber: .44 Magnum
Capacity: 6 rounds
Features: carbon steel frame and cylinder; blue or nickel finish; square butt frame; serrated trigger; Smith & Wesson logo engraved on the four-screw side plate and decorative scrolling down the length of the barrel; shipped in a glass-top wooden presentation case, with a traditional cleaning rod, brush and replica screwdriver
MSRP: . . . . Custom

MODEL 36 CHIEFS SPECIAL CLASSIC

Action: revolver
Grips: Altamont walnut
Barrel: 1-1/8 in.
Sights: front: integral; rear: fixed
Weight: 20.4 oz.
Caliber: .38 Spl.+P
Capacity: 5 rounds
Features: carbon steel J frame; blue, color case or nickel finish
MSRP: $822

MODEL 36-LS

Action: double-action revolver
Grips: laminated rosewood, round butt
Barrel: 1.8, 2.2, 3 in.
Sights: fixed open
Weight: 20.0 oz.
Caliber: .38 Spl.
Capacity: 5 rounds
Features: weight to 24 oz. depending on barrel length; stainless version in .357 Mag. available (60 LS)
60 LS: $845

Smith & Wesson Handguns

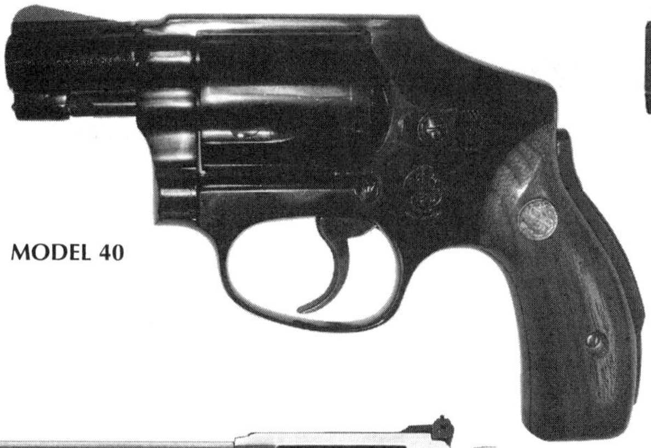

MODEL 40

MODEL 41

MODEL 60

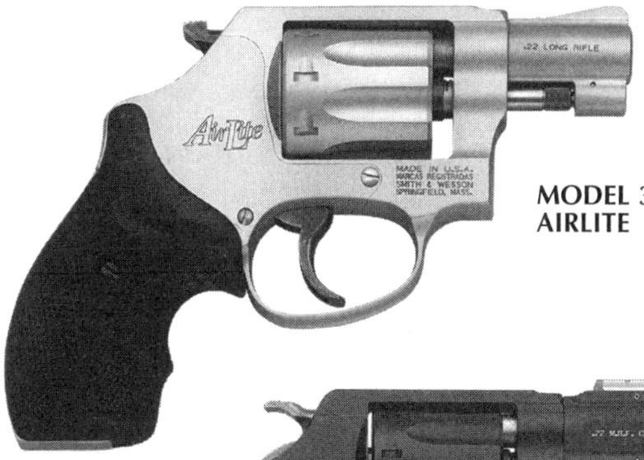

MODEL 317 AIRLITE

MODEL 325 PD

MODEL 351 PD

MODEL 40

Action: hammerless revolver
Grips: Altamont walnut
Barrel: 1-7/8 in.
Sights: front***:*** integral; rear***:*** fixed
Weight: 20.4 oz.
Caliber: .38 Spl.+P
Capacity: 5 rounds
Features: carbon steel construction; safety hammerless design; grip safety; blue, color case or nickel finish
MSRP: $877

MODEL 41

Action: autoloader
Grips: walnut
Barrel: 5.5 or 7 in.
Sights: target
Weight: 41.0 oz.
Caliber: .22 LR
Capacity: 12 + 1 rounds
Features: adjustable trigger; 7 in. barrel***:*** 44 oz.
MSRP: $1288

MODEL 60

Action: double-action revolver
Grips: wood
Barrel: 5 in.
Sights: adjustable open
Weight: 30.5 oz.
Caliber: .357
Capacity: 5 rounds
Features: stainless frame
MSRP: $853

MODEL 317

Action: double-action revolver
Grips: rubber
Barrel: 1.8 or 3 in.
Sights: fixed open
Weight: 10.5 oz.
Caliber: .22 LR
Capacity: 8 rounds
Features: alloy frame
1.8 in.: $822
3 in.: $853

MODELS 325 PD AND 351 PD REVOLVER

Action: double-action revolver
Grips: wood (.45), rubber (.22)
Barrel: $2\frac{3}{4}$ in. (.45), $1\frac{7}{8}$ in. (.22)
Sights: adjustable rear, HiViz front (.45), fixed rear, red ramp front (.22)
Weight: 21.5 oz. (.45), 10.6 oz. (.22)
Caliber: .45 ACP (Model 325), .22 WMR (Model 351)
Capacity: 6 (.45), 7 (.22) rounds
.22: $1258
.45: $1258

Smith & Wesson Handguns

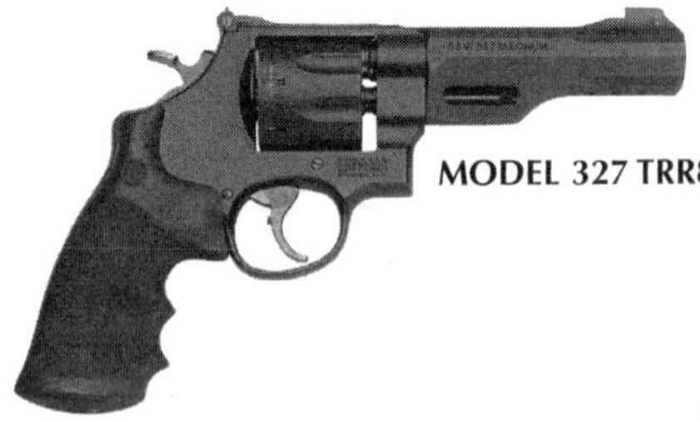

MODEL 327 TRR8

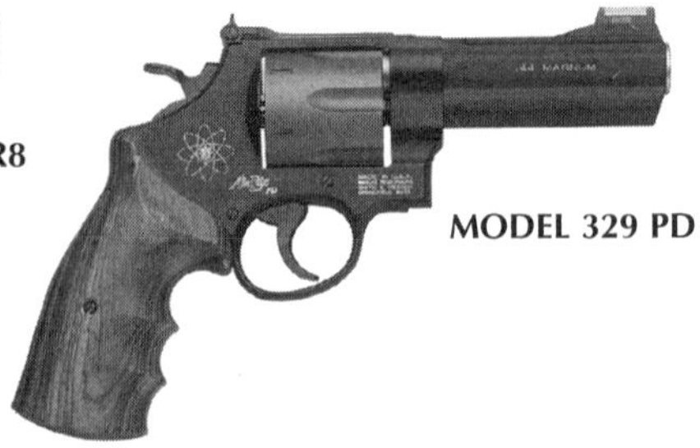

MODEL 329 PD

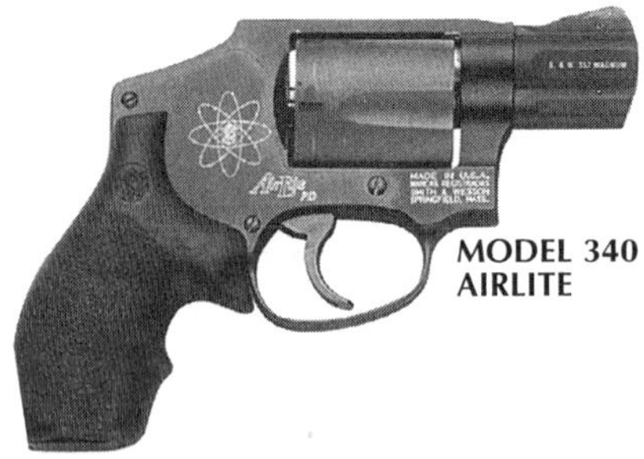

MODEL 340 AIRLITE

MODEL 386 MOUNTAIN LITE

MODEL 442

MODEL 442, "WOMEN OF THE NRA" LIMITED EDITION

MODEL 327 TRR8

Action: double-action revolver
Grips: rubber
Barrel: 5 in., two-piece shrouded steel
Sights: interchangeable front sight, adjustable rear sight
Weight: 35.3 oz.
Caliber: .357 Magnum, .38 S&W Special
Capacity: 8 rounds
Features: precision barrel forcing cone, optimum barrel and cylinder gap; ball and detent cylinder lockup and chamfered charge holes; wide range of options for mounting optics, lights, laser aiming devices and other tactical equipment
MSRP: $1438

MODEL 329 PD

Action: double-action revolver
Grips: wood
Barrel: 4 in.
Sights: adjustable fiber optic
Weight: 27.0 oz.
Caliber: .44 Mag.
Capacity: 6 rounds
Features: scandium frame, titanium cylinder
MSRP: $1280

MODEL 340

Action: double-action revolver
Grips: rubber
Barrel: 1.8 in.
Sights: fixed open
Weight: 12.0 oz.
Caliber: .357 Mag.
Capacity: 5 rounds
Features: Scandium alloy frame, titanium cylinder
MSRP: $1153

MODEL 386

Action: double-action revolver
Grips: rubber
Barrel: 3.2 in.
Sights: low-profile combat
Weight: 18.5 oz.
Caliber: .357 Mag.
Capacity: 7 rounds
Features: scandium alloy frame; titanium cylinder
Model 386: $1019

MODEL 442

Action: double-action revolver
Grips: rubber
Barrel: 1.8 in.
Sights: fixed open
Weight: 15.0 oz.
Caliber: .38 Spl.
Capacity: 5 rounds
Features: concealed-hammer, double-action only
Model 442: $600

MODEL 442, "WOMEN OF THE NRA" LIMITED EDITION

Action: hammerless revolver
Grips: synthetic ivory
Barrel: 1-7/8 in.
Sights: front: black blade; rear: fixed
Weight: 15 oz.
Caliber: .38 Spl.
Capacity: 5 rounds
Features: limited edition; aluminum alloy frame with blue finish; machined-engraved NRA logo; inscription on the carbon steel cylinder reads "Original Defender of Freedom 2nd Amendment" and an inscription on the backstrap reads "Women of the NRA"; decorative engraving along the barrel; special serial numbers starting with NRA0001; glass-top, wooden presentation case
MSRP: $697

MODEL 460XVR

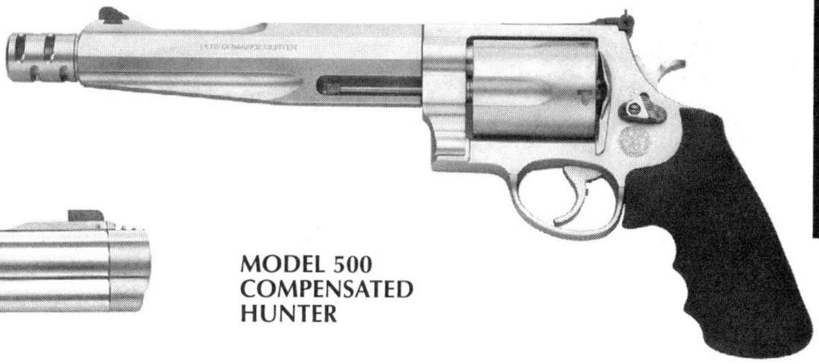

MODEL 500 COMPENSATED HUNTER

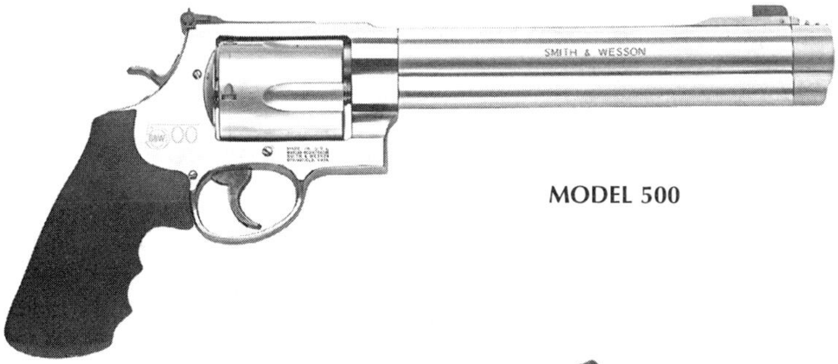

MODEL 500

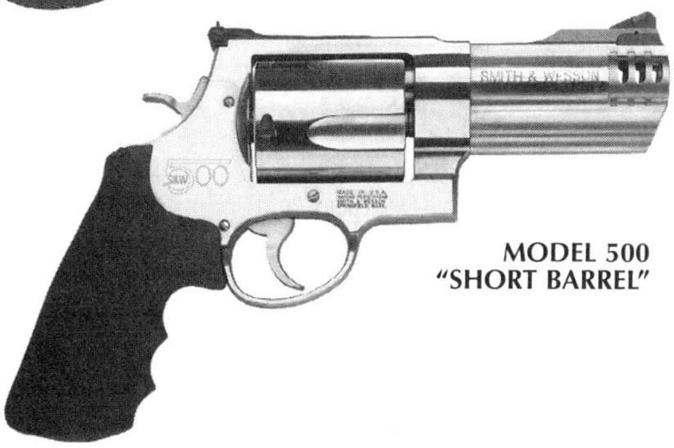

MODEL 500 "SHORT BARREL"

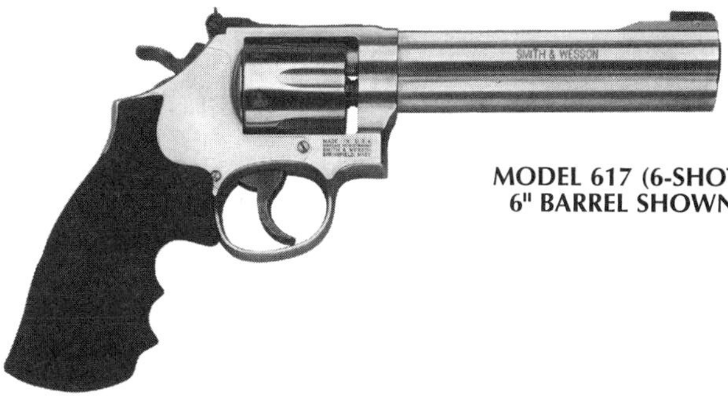

MODEL 617 (6-SHOT, 6" BARREL SHOWN)

MODEL 460XVR

Action: double-action revolver
Grips: stippled rubber
Barrel: 8.375 in., stainless
Sights: adjustable open
Weight: 72 oz.
Caliber: .460 S&W
Capacity: 5 rounds
Features: ported barrel also fires .454 Casull and .45 Colt
MSRP: $1714

MODEL 500

Action: double-action revolver
Grips: Hogue Sorbathane
Barrel: ported 8.4 in.
Sights: target
Weight: 72.5 oz.
Caliber: .500 S&W
Capacity: 5 rounds
Features: X-Frame, double-action stainless revolver
Model 500:. $300

MODEL 500 COMPENSATED HUNTER

Action: revolver
Grips: synthetic Hogue Dual Density Monogrips
Barrel: 7.5 in.
Sights: front: orange ramp dovetail; rear: adjustable black blade
Weight: 71 oz.
Caliber: .500 S&W
Capacity: 5 rounds
Features: stainless-steel frame and cylinder; 360-degree muzzle compensator; two-piece barrel with button rifling and removable scope mount; precision-crowned muzzle; flashed-chromed forged hammer and trigger; ball and detent cylinder lock up; solid ejector rod
MSRP: $1390

MODEL 500 "SHORT BARREL"

Action: double-action revolver
Grips: rubber
Barrel: 4 in., sleeved, with brake
Sights: adjustable rear, red ramp front
Weight: 56 oz.
Caliber: .500 S&W
Capacity: 5
Features: double-action; Hogue grip; comes with 2 mukkle compensators
MSRP: $1485

MODEL 617

Action: double-action revolver
Grips: Hogue rubber
Barrel: 4.0, 6.0, 8.4 in.
Sights: target
Weight: 42.0 oz.
Caliber: .22 LR
Capacity: 6 rounds
Features: stainless; target hammer and trigger; K-frame; weight to 54 oz. depending on barrel length
4 in.: $940
6 in.: $940
6 in., 10-shot:. $940

Smith & Wesson Handguns

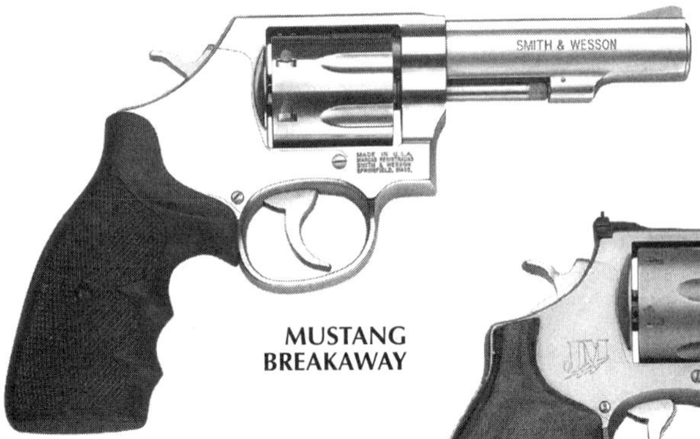

MUSTANG BREAKAWAY

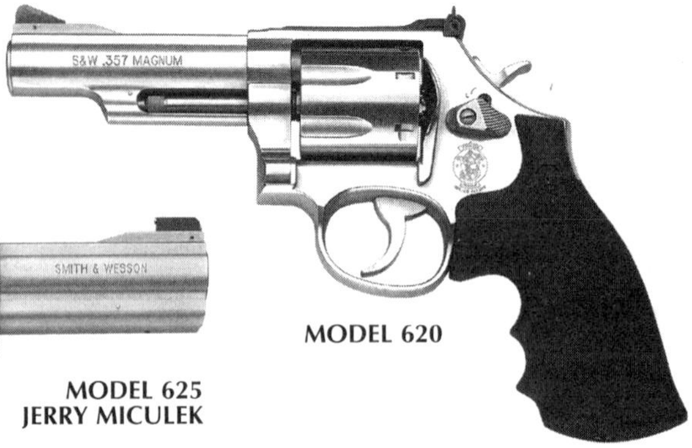

MODEL 620

MODEL 625 JERRY MICULEK

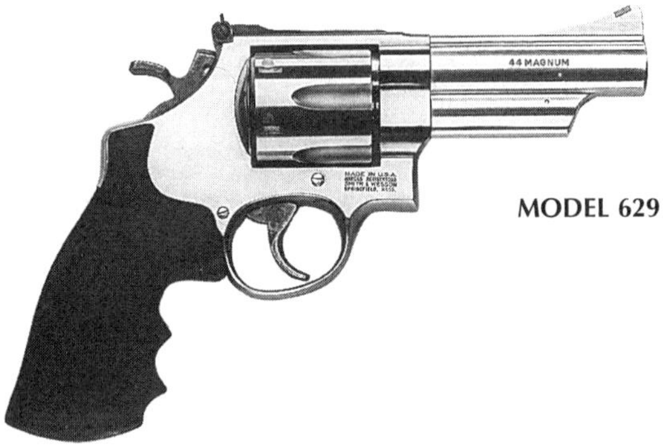

MODEL 629

MODEL 629 CLASSIC

MODELS 619 AND 620

Action: double-action revolver
Grips: checkered rubber
Barrel: 4 in.
Sights: adjustable open (M620) and fixed (M619)
Weight: 38 oz.
Caliber: .357 Mag.
Capacity: 7 rounds
Features: stainless; semi-lug barrel
Model 619:. $711
Model 620:. $893

MODEL 625

Action: double-action revolver
Grips: Hogue rubber, round butt
Barrel: 4 or 5 in.
Sights: target
Weight: 49.0 oz.
Caliber: .45 ACP
Capacity: 6 rounds
Features: N-frame, stainless; also in Model 610 10mm with 4 in. barrel; 5 in. barrel 51 oz.
Model 625:. $1106

MODEL 625 JERRY MICULEK PROFESSIONAL SERIES REVOLVER

Action: double-action revolver
Grips: wood
Barrel: 4 in.
Sights: adjustable open, removable front bead
Weight: 43 oz.
Caliber: .45 ACP
Capacity: 6 rounds
Features: wide trigger; smooth wood grip; gold bead front sight on a removable blade; comes with five full-moon clips for fast loading
MSRP: $1185

MODEL 629

Action: double-action revolver
Grips: Hogue rubber
Barrel: 4 or 6 in.
Sights: target
Weight: 44.0 oz.
Caliber: .44 Mag.
Capacity: 6 rounds
Features: N-frame, stainless; 6 in. weighs 47 oz.
4 in.: $1114
6 in.: $1114

MODEL 629 CLASSIC

Action: double-action revolver
Grips: Hogue rubber
Barrel: 5, 6.5 or 8.4 in.
Sights: target
Weight: 51.0 oz.
Caliber: .44 Mag.
Capacity: 6 rounds
Features: N-frame, stainless, full lug; weight to 54 oz. depending on barrel length
MSRP: $1185

Smith & Wesson Handguns

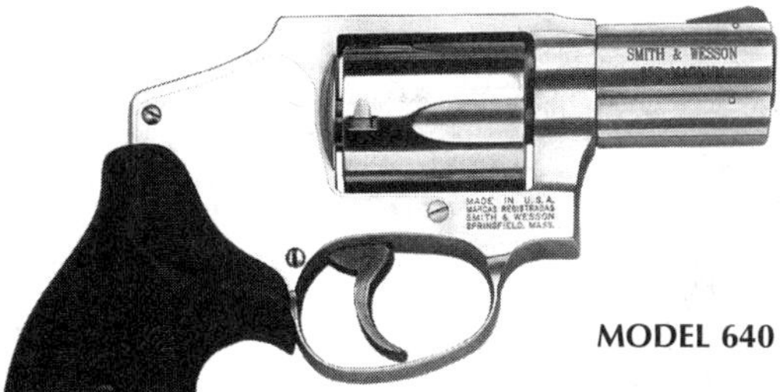

MODEL 640

MODEL 686

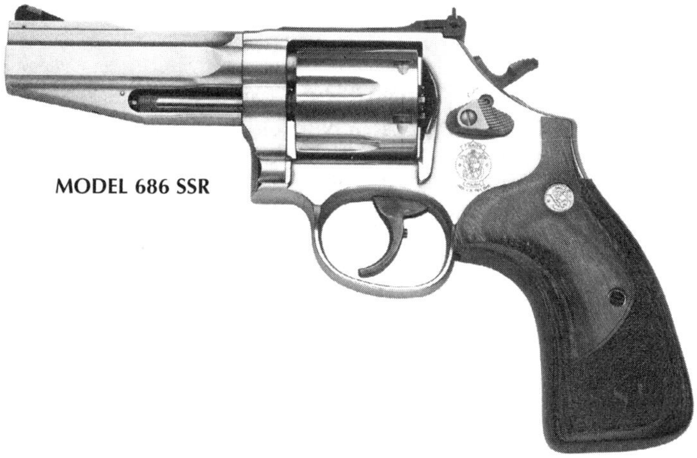
MODEL 686 SSR

MODEL 945

MODEL 640 CENTENNIAL

Action: double-action revolver
Grips: rubber
Barrel: 2.2 in.
Sights: fixed open
Weight: 23.0 oz.
Caliber: .357
Capacity: 5 rounds
Features: stainless; concealed-hammer; double-action-only; also M649 Bodyguard single- or double-action
MSRP: $822

MODEL 686

Action: double-action revolver
Grips: combat or target
Barrel: 2.5, 4, 6 in.
Sights: target
Weight: 34.5 oz.
Caliber: .357 Mag.
Capacity: 6 rounds
Features: stainless; K-frame 686 Plus holds 7 rounds; to 48 oz. depending on barrel length
MSRP.: $938

MODEL 686 SSR

Action: double-action revolver
Grips: wood laminate
Barrel: 4 in.
Sights: front: interchangeable; rear: micro adjustable
Weight: 38.3 oz.
Caliber: 357 MAG, .38+P
Capacity: 6 rounds
Features: stainless-steel frame and cylinder; satin stainless finish; forged hammer and trigger; chamfered charge holes; bossed mainsprings; "SSR" inscription on butt
MSRP: $1090

MODEL 945

Action: autoloader
Grips: Hogue black/silver checkered laminate
Barrel: 5 in.
Sights: front: dovetail black blade; rear: adjustable Wilson Combat
Weight: 40.5 oz.
Caliber: .45 ACP
Capacity: 8 + 1 rounds
Features: stainless-steel frame and slide; hand-polished and fitted spherical barrel bushing and feed ramp; competition-grade serrated hammer and match trigger with overtravel stop; 3.5 to 4-pound trigger pull; ambidextrous frame-mounted thumb safety; beveled magazine; aluminum carry case
MSRP: $2410

Smith & Wesson Handguns

MODEL 3913 LADYSMITH

MODEL 3913TSW

CS 9

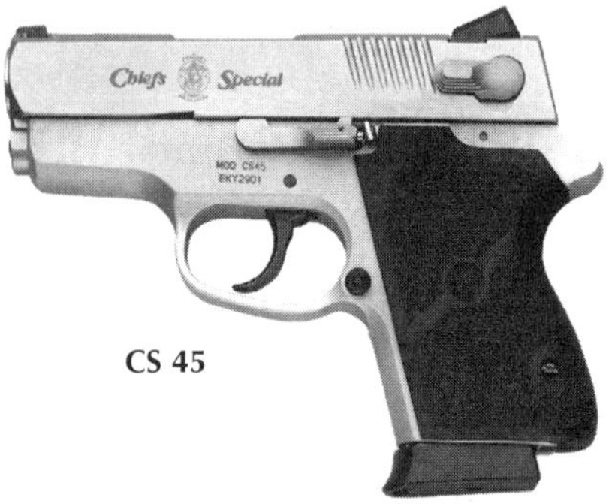

CS 45

M&P 9MM

M&P9 COMPACT

MODEL 3913 LADYSMITH

Action: autoloader
Grips: Hogue rubber
Barrel: 3.5 in.
Sights: low-profile combat
Weight: 24.8 oz.
Caliber: 9mm
Capacity: 8 + 1 rounds
Features: double-action; stainless
MSRP: $682

MODEL 3913TSW (TACTICAL SERIES)

Action: autoloader
Grips: rubber
Barrel: 3.5 in.
Sights: 3 dot
Weight: 24.8 oz.
Caliber: 9mm
Capacity: 8 + 1 rounds
Features: alloy frame, stainless slide; also: 3953TSW double-action-only
MSRP: $755

MODEL CS9 AND CS45 (CHIEF'S SPECIAL)

Action: autoloader
Grips: rubber
Barrel: 3 or 3.25 in.
Sights: 3 dot
Weight: 20.8-24.0 oz.
Caliber: 9mm, .45 ACP
Capacity: 7 + 1 rounds (9mm) and 6 + 1 (.40 S&W)
Features: lightweight; compact
CS 9: $618
CS 45: $728

MODELS M&P 9MM, M&P .40 AND M&P .357 SIG

Action: autoloader
Barrel: 4.25 in.
Sights: fixed open
Weight: 24 oz. (empty)
Caliber: 9mm, .40, .357 SIG
Capacity: 17 + 1 rounds (9mm),15 + 1 rounds (.40 and.357 SIG)
Features: part of the Smith & Wesson Military & Police Pistol Series; Zytel polymer frame reinforced with a ridged steel chassis; thru-hardened black melonite stainless steel barrel and slide; dovetail-mount steel ramp front sight; steel Novak Lo-mount carry rear sight; optional Tritium sights
MSRP: $719

M&P9 COMPACT

Action: autoloader
Grips: 3 interchangeable grip sizes
Barrel: 3.5 in.
Sights: front: steel dovetail mount; rear: steel Novak Lo-Mount carry (Tritium sights available)
Weight: 21.7 oz.
Caliber: 9mm
Capacity: 10+1 or 12+1 rounds
Features: Zytel polymer frame reinforced with a rigid stainless steel chassis and through-hardened black Melonite finished stainless steel barrel and slide; passive trigger safety; sear lever release; loaded chamber indicator on top of the slide; internal lock system; ambidextrous slide stop; reversible magazine release; enlarged trigger guard
MSRP: $719

Smith & Wesson Handguns

M&P45 FULL SIZE

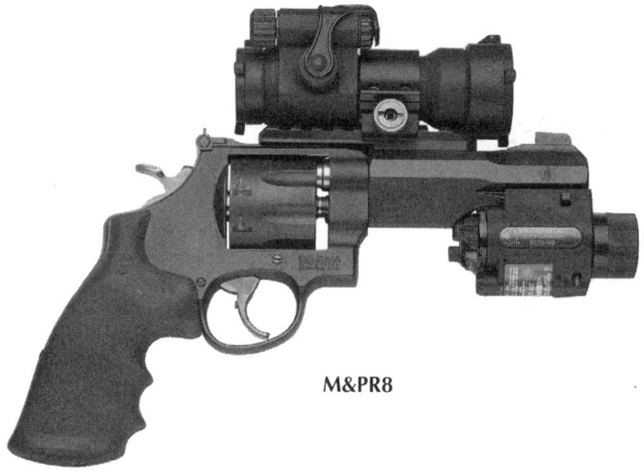

M&PR8

MODEL SW9 VE

MODEL 99OL .40

M&P45 FULL SIZE

Action: autoloader
Grips: 3 interchangeable grip sizes
Barrel: 4.5 in.
Sights: front: steel dovetail mount; rear: steel Novak Lo-Mount carry (Tritium sights available)
Weight: 29.6 oz.
Caliber: .45ACP
Capacity: 10+1 or optional 14+1 rounds
Features: Zytel polymer frame reinforced with a rigid stainless steel chassis and through-hardened black Melonite finished stainless steel barrel and slide; offered with a traditional black frame or bi-tone, dark earth brown frame; frame-mounted thumb safety on the bi-tone model; universal Picatinny-style equipment rail for tactical lights and lasers; passive trigger safety; sear lever release; loaded chamber indicator on top of the slide; internallock system; ambidextrous slide stop; reversible magazine release; enlarged trigger guard
MSRP: $758

M&PR8

Action: revolver
Grips: rubber
Barrel: 5 in. 2-piece
Sights: front: Interchangeable Partridge White Dot; rear: adjustable V-notch
Weight: 36.3 oz.
Caliber: 357MAG, .38+P
Capacity: 8 rounds
Features: integral accessory Picatinny style rail for lights or lasers; removable Picatinny-style mount for optics; crisp single action; smooth double action with wolff mainspring and traditional sear; polished button polygonal rifling; precision barrel forcing cone; optimum barrel cylinder gap; 2 full moon clips; chamfered charge holes; ball detent lock-up; aluminum gun case
MSRP: $1454

MODEL SW9 VE

Action: autoloader
Grips: polymer
Barrel: 4 in.
Sights: 3 dot
Weight: 24.7 oz.
Caliber: 9mm
Capacity: 10 + 1 rounds
Features: double-action; stainless slide; polymer frame; finish options
SW9 VE: $363

MODEL SW990L

Action: autoloader
Grips: polymer
Barrel: 3.5, 4 or 5 in.
Sights: low-profile combat
Weight: 22.5-25.0 oz.
Caliber: .40 S&W, 9mm
Capacity: 8-16 rounds
Features: double-action pistol made in collaboration with Walther
MSRP: $615

Smith & Wesson Handguns

MODEL SW1911

SW 1911 TACTICAL RAIL

MODEL SW1911

Action: autoloader
Grips: checkered composite, checkered wood
Barrel: 5 in. (4 in. for Model 945)
Sights: adjustable open
Weight: 28-41 oz.
Caliber: .45 ACP (.38 Super in SW1911DK)
Capacity: 8+1 rounds (10 in SW1911DK)
Features: single-action; extended beavertail; match trigger
MSRP: $1225–2700

MODELS SW1911PD AND SW1911 TACTICAL RAIL SERIES

Action: autoloader
Barrel: 5 in.
Sights: fixed open
Weight: 32 oz. (1911PD), 39 oz. (1911)
Caliber: .45 ACP
Capacity: 8 + 1 rounds
Features: Model SW1911 stainless steel slide w/ melonite finish; black anodized Scandium Alloy frame; non-reflective matte gray finish; white dot front sight and Novak Lo Mount Carry rear sight; Picatinny-style rail with standard 1911 configuration
1911PD: $1057–1120

Springfield Handguns

9MM ENHANCED MICRO PISTOL (EMP)

Action: autoloader
Grips: thinline cocobolo hardwood
Barrel: 3-in. stainless steel match grade, fully supported ramp
Sights: fixed low profile combat rear; dovetail front, tritium 3-dot
Weight: 33 oz.
Caliber: .40
Capacity: two 9-round, stainless steel magazines
Features: dual-spring recoil system with full-length guide rod; long aluminum match-grade trigger; forged steel slide with satin finish
MSRP: $1060–1400

SPRINGFIELD ARMORY EMP

Action: SA autoloading, recoil operated
Grips: checkered cocobolo or composite
Barrel: 3″
Sights: fixed combat tritium
Weight: 26 or 30 oz.
Caliber: 9mm or .40 S&W
Capacity: 9 or 8
Features: true short-action 1911 with 15 re-engineered parts. Stainless slide; matte black frame, extended grip safety, ambidextrous thumb safety.
MSRP: $1345

Springfield Armory Handguns

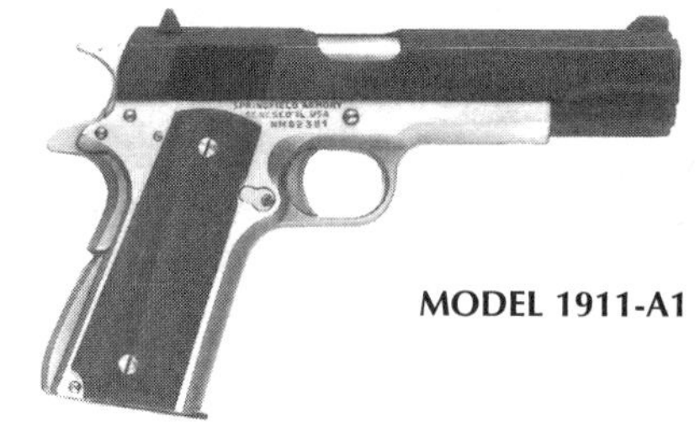
MODEL 1911-A1

1911-A1 ULTRA-COMPACT

1911-A1 MICRO COMPACT

MODEL 1911-A1 TROPHY MATCH

MODEL XD SERVICE

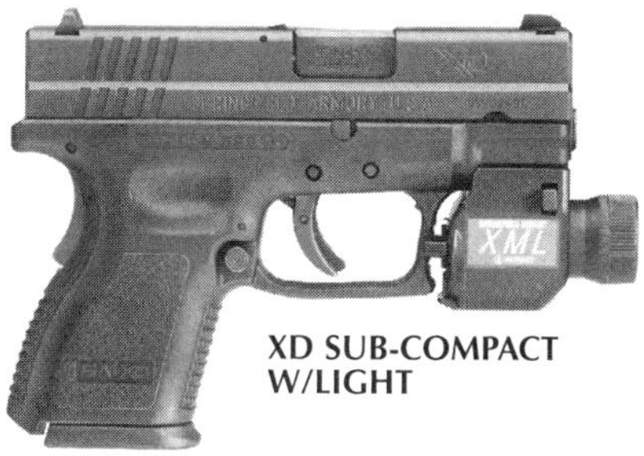
XD SUB-COMPACT W/LIGHT

1911-A1

Action: autoloader
Grips: cocobolo
Barrel: 5 in.
Sights: fixed or adjustable
Weight: 38.0 oz.
Caliber: 9mm, .45 ACP
Capacity: 7 + 1 rounds
Features: steel or lightweight aluminum frames; stainless, blued and parkerized finishes; V-12 barrel porting; fixed combat or fully adjustable rear sights
Black stainless: $1219
Stainless: $979

1911-A1 COMPACT MODELS

Action: autoloader
Grips: plastic or cocobolo
Barrel: 3 (Micro-Compact) or 3.5 in.
Sights: Fixed, open
Weight: 32.0 oz.
Caliber: .45 ACP
Capacity: 6+1 rounds
Features: forged aluminum anodized alloy frame; forged steel slide; ambidextrous thumb safety
Ultra-Compact: $1099
Micro-Compact: $1437

1911-A1 MIL-SPEC

Action: autoloader
Grips: plastic *Barrel:* 5 in.
Sights: fixed open
Weight: 35.6-39.0 oz.
Caliber: .38 Super, .45 ACP
Capacity: 7 + 1 rounds
Features: traditional M1911 A-1
Parkerized: $610
Stainless Steel: $661
.38 Super: $580

MODEL 1911 A-1 TROPHY MATCH

Action: autoloader
Grips: cocobolo
Barrel: 5 in. *Sights:* target
Weight: 38.0 oz.
Caliber: .45 ACP
Capacity: 7 + 1 rounds
Features: match barrel and bushing; Videcki speed trigger; serrated front strap; stainless
MSRP: $1437

MODEL XD SERVICE

Action: autoloader *Grips:* walnut
Barrel: 4 or 5 in. *Sights:* fixed open
Weight: 22.8-27.0 oz.
Caliber: 9mm, .357 Sig, .40 S&W, .45 GAP
Capacity: 10 + 1 rounds
Features: single-action; short recoil; black or OD green
XD: $540
W/ Tritium sights: $558
V-10 Ported: $550
XD Tactical (5 in. bl.): $515
Bi-Tone (.45 GAP only): $575
Trijicon Sights: $587

MODEL XD SUB COMPACTS

Action: autoloader
Grips: black composite
Barrel: 3.1 in. *Sights:* fixed, open
Weight: 20.5 oz.
Caliber: 9mm, .357 SIG, .40, .45 GAP
Capacity: 10+1 rounds
Features: cold hammer forged barrel; polymer frame with heat-treated steel slide and rails; short-recoil, locked-breech action; dual recoil springs; three safeties; cocking indicator; light rail (Mini Light optional); 3-dot sights; black or OD green finish
MSRP: $510–590

STI International Inc. Handguns

EAGLE

EDGE

EXECUTIVE

LSA LAWMAN

LS

EAGLE

Action: autoloader
Grips: polymer ***Barrel:*** 5 or 6 in.
Sights: target (5 in.), open fixed (6 in.)
Weight: 34.5oz. (5 in.), 40 oz. (6 in.)
Caliber: 9mm, 9X21, .38 Super, .40 S&W, .45 ACP
Capacity: 10+1 rounds
Features: modular steel frame; classic slide; long curved trigger; fully supported, ramped bull barrel; stainless STI grip and ambidextrous thumb safeties; blue finish
Eagle (5 in.):. $1994
Eagle (6 in.):. $2050

EDGE

Action: autoloader
Grips: polymer ***Sights:*** target
Weight: 39 oz.
Caliber: 9mm, .40 S&W, 10mm, .45 ACP
Capacity: 6+1 rounds
Features: modular steel; long wide frame; overall length $8\frac{5}{8}$ in.; fully supported, ramped bull barrel; long curved trigger; stainless STI grip and ambidextrous thumb safeties; blue finish
MSRP: $1994

EXECUTIVE

Action: autoloader
Grips: polymer
Barrel: 5 in.
Sights: target
Weight: 39 oz.
Caliber: .40 S&W
Capacity: 10+1 rounds
Features: modular steel; long wide frame; overall length $8\frac{5}{8}$ in.; fully supported, ramped bull barrel; long curved trigger; stainless STI grip and ambidextrous thumb safeties
MSRP: $2464

LAWMAN

Action: autoloader
Grips: rosewood
Barrel: 5 in.
Sights: fixed open
Weight: 40 oz.
Caliber: .45 ACP
Capacity: 6+1 rounds
Features: forged steel government-length frame; overall length $8\frac{1}{2}$ in.; 1911 style slide; fully supported, ramped barrel with match bushing; STI aluminum trigger; STI grip and single sided thumb STI high rise beavertail safeties; two tone polymer finish (light brown over olive drab)
MSRP: $1420

LS

Action: autoloader
Grips: rosewood
Barrel: 3.4 in.
Sights: fixed open
Weight: 28 oz.
Caliber: 9mm, .40 S&W
Capacity: 7+1 rounds (9mm), 6+1 rounds (.40 S&W)
Features: government-size steel frame with full size grip; fully supported, ramped bull barrel; undercut trigger guard and front strap; long curved trigger; STI grip and single-sided thumb safeties; integral front sight with Heinie low-mount rear sight; flat blue finish; slide does not lock back after last round is fired
MSRP: $992

STI International Inc. Handguns

RANGEMASTER

RANGER II

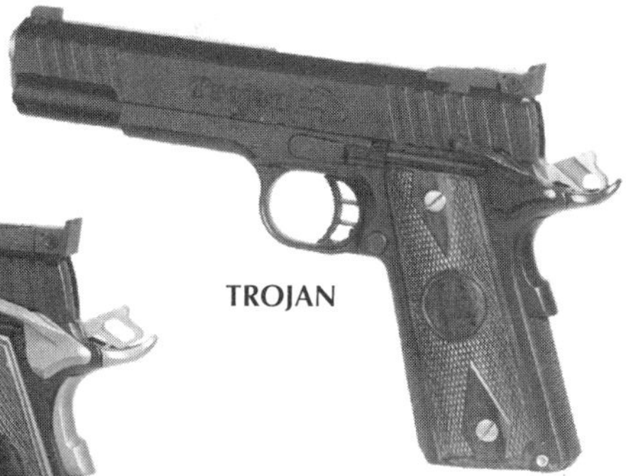
TROJAN

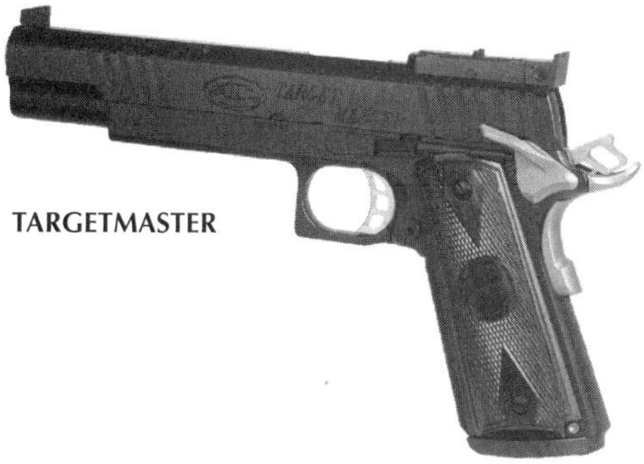
TARGETMASTER

VIP

RANGEMASTER

Action: autoloader
Grips: rosewood
Barrel: 5 in. ***Sights:*** target
Weight: 38 oz.
Caliber: 9mm, .45 ACP
Features: single stack government length steel frame; flat top slide; full length dust cover; fully supported, ramped bull barrel; aluminum long curved trigger; polished stainless grip and ambidextrous thumb safeties; overall length 8.5 in.; polished blue finish
MSRP: $1521

RANGER II

Action: autoloader
Grips: rosewood
Barrel: 4.15 in. ***Sights:*** fixed open
Weight: 30 oz.
Caliber: .45 ACP
Capacity: 7+1 rounds
Features: commander size with full length 1911-style frame and fully supported barrel; hi-rise trigger guard; 1911-style flat topped slide; long curved trigger with stainless bow; hi-rise grip and single sided thumb safeties; blue finish
MSRP: $1110

TARGETMASTER

Action: autoloader
Grips: rosewood
Barrel: 6 in.
Sights: target
Weight: 40 oz.
Caliber: 9mm, .45 ACP
Features: single stack government length frame; classic flat top slide; fully supported ramped match bull barrel; overall length 9½ in.; tri-level adjustable sights; aluminum long curved trigger; STI stainless grip and ambidextrous thumb safeties; polished blue finish
MSRP: $1695

TROJAN

Action: autoloader
Grips: rosewood
Barrel: 5 or 6 in.
Sights: target
Weight: 36 oz. (5 in.); 38 oz. (6 in.)
Caliber: 9mm, .38 Super, .40 S&W, .45 ACP
Features: single stack government size frame; 5 in. or 6 in. classic flat top slide; fully supported match barrel; high rise grip safety, STI long curved polymer trigger and undercut trigger guard; flat blue finish
Trojan (5 in.): $1110
Trojan (6 in.): $1420

VIP

Action: Autoloader (SA)
Grips: polymer
Barrel: 3.9 in.
Sights: fixed open
Weight: 25 oz.
Caliber: 9mm, .38 Super, 9X21, .40 S&W,.45 ACP
Capacity: 10 + 1 rounds
Features: modular aluminum frame; overall length 7½ in.; classic flat top slide; fully supported, ramped bull barrel; STI long curved trigger; STI stainless grip and single-sided thumb safeties
MSRP: $1646

Stoeger Handguns

COUGAR 8000

COUGAR 8000

Action: double/single
Grips: black plastic
Barrel: 3.6 in.
Sights: fixed
Weight: 32.6 oz.
Caliber: 9mm Parabellum, .40 S&W
Capacity: 15 rounds (9mm), 11 rounds (.40 S&W)
Features: cold hammer-forged barrel; rotary lock action; chrome-lined bore; ambidextrous safety; combat-style trigger guard; fixed 3-Dot dovetail rear and removable blade front sights; matte black finish
MSRP: $469

Swiss Arms Handguns

P210 SPORT

MODEL P210 SPORT

Action: autoloader
Grips: wood
Barrel: 4.8 in.
Sights: target
Weight: 24.0 oz.
Caliber: 9mm
Capacity: 8 + 1 rounds
Features: chrome-moly, single-action
P210 . . . . $1500

One of the most fantastic firearms ever created is a working, scaled-up copy of a Remington 1859 revolver built by Ryszard Tobys of Czempin, Poland. Listed by the Guinness Book of World Records as the world's largest revolver, this 99.2-pound, 4-foot-long gun holds six bullets, each weighing more than a quarter of a pound. In 2002, the gigantic revolver was used in a shooting competition between NATO Reserve Forces from Great Britain, Denmark, the Czech Republic, Germany and Poland. The Czechs won.

TAURUS 22 PLY/25PLY

Action: DAO autoloading, recoil operated
Grips: polymer
Barrel: 2⅓″
Sights: fixed
Weight: 11 oz.
Caliber: .22 LR or .25 ACP
Capacity: 8 or 9
Features: ultra-light, polymer frame with tip-up barrel for safety and convenience during loading. Extended magazine for added grip.
MSRP: . . . . price on request

TAURUS M709 SLIM

Action: SA/DA autoloading, recoil operated
Grips: polymer
Barrel: 3¼″
Sights: low-profile for easy concealment
Weight: 19 oz
Caliber: 9mm
Capacity: 7 (9 with extended magazine)
Features: blued, stainless or titanium versions.
MSRP: $498

TAURUS M738 TCP

Action: SA/DA autoloading, recoil operated
Grips: polymer
Barrel: blued or stainless
Sights: low-profile fixed
Weight: 8½ oz. titanium, 10 oz. blue or stainless
Caliber: .380 ACP
Capacity: 6, 8 with extended magazine
Features: the lightest Taurus available, but with a lethal chambering for self defense.
MSRP: $336–453

TAURUS JUDGE PUBLIC DEFENDER

Action: DA revolver
Grips: Ribber
Barrel: 3″ or 6½″ stainless or blue
Sights: fixed rear and fiber optic front
Weight: 22 oz. (3″ UltraLight), 29 oz. (3″ std), 32 oz. (6½″ std), 37 oz. (3″ magnum for 3″ .410 shells)
Caliber: .45 Colt and .410 shotgun, interchangeably
Capacity: 5 shot
Features: The new compact frame of alloy trims weight by half a pound. Available in stainless, blue steel or blue steel frame with titanium cylinder.
MSRP: $429–505

M709 SLIM

M738 TCP

22PLY

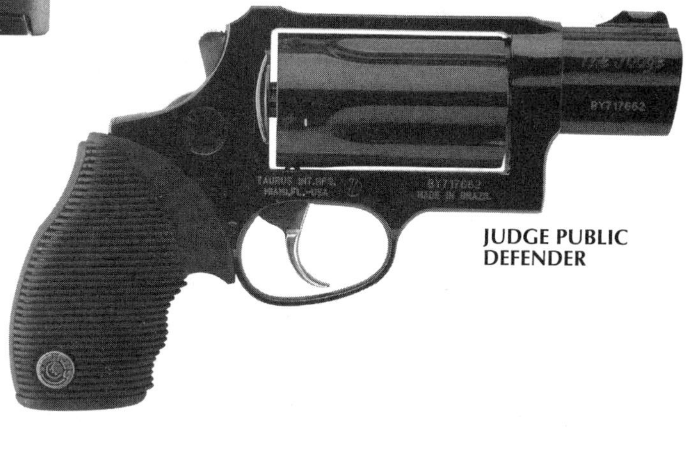

JUDGE PUBLIC DEFENDER

Taurus Handguns

24/7 OSS
STAINLESS STEEL

MODEL 709B

MODEL 709SS

MODEL
856B2

MODEL
856HL2MG

MODEL
856SS2

24/7 OSS STAINLESS STEEL

Action: single/double action autoloader
Grips: checkered polymer with Ambidextrous Indexed Memory Pads
Barrel: 5.25 in. Match Grade steel
Sights: Novak rear night sight option
Weight: 29.1 oz.
Caliber: .45 ACP, .40 S&W., 9mm
Capacity: 10+1, 12+1, 15+1 or 17+1 rounds
Features: integral Picatinny rail system accommodates slide-on lights or laser sights; SA/DA indicator on the rear of the slide that shows whether the pistol is in "cocked" or "decocked" mode, front slide serrations and reversible magazine release combine for increased versatility; Taurus Security System allows users to securely lock the gun
MSRP: $514

MODEL 709

Action: double action autoloader
Grips: checkered polymer
Barrel: 6 in., stainless steel or black matte finish
Sights: fixed
Weight: 19 oz.
Caliber: 9mm
Capacity: 8+1 rounds
Features: 6 in. long and less than 1 in. thick; visual loaded chamber indicator; Taurus Security System allows users to securely lock the gun
MSRP: $283–498

MODEL 856

Action: revolver
Grips: soft rubber
Barrel: 2 in.
Sights: fixed
Weight: 13.2 oz. (Hy-Lite magnesium frame)
Caliber: .38 Special, .38 Special +P
Capacity: 6 rounds
Features: offered in several configurations, including a Hy-Lite magnesium model in .38 Special and standard version (.38 Special +P) in blue or matte stainless; Taurus Security System allows users to securely lock the gun
MSRP: $441–492

Taurus Handguns

MODEL 24/7

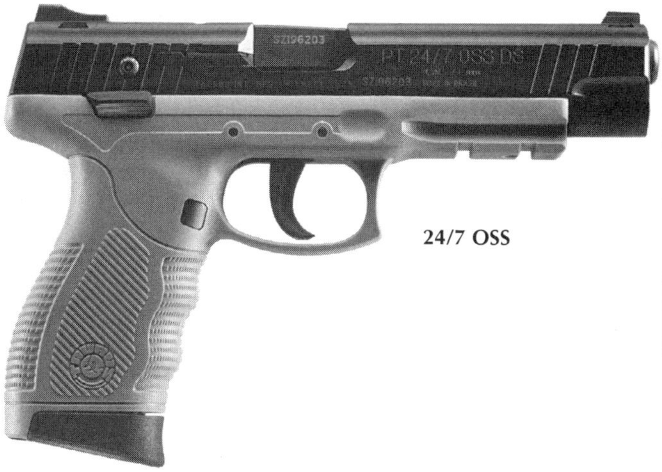

24/7 OSS

MODEL 44

MODEL 82

MODEL 24/7

Action: autoloader
Grips: polymer with rubber overlay
Barrel: 6 in.
Sights: 3 dot
Weight: 32.0 oz.
Caliber: .40 S&W
Capacity: 15 rounds
Features: double-action; reversible magazine release; Picatinny rail
MSRP: $475

24/7 OSS

Action: autoloader
Grips: checkered polymer
Barrel: 5.25 in.
Sights: Heinie 1-dot (front), Heinie Straight Eight (rear)
Weight: 31.4-32.5 oz.
Caliber: .45ACP, .40 S&W, 9mm
Capacity: 12 + 1, 15 + 1 or 17 +1 rounds
Features: Single Action/Double Action trigger system; checkered grip; combat-necessary ambidextrous decock/safety levers that allow for "cocked and locked" and/or double-action carry; an SA/DA indicator on the rear of the slide that shows whether the pistol is in cocked or decocked mode; reversible magazine release; 18.5-lb. recoil spring that cycles the slide faster; stainless-steel guide rod adds just the right amount of front-end weight for improved recoil control and rapid fire accuracy
MSRP: $623

MODEL 44

Action: double-action revolver
Grips: rubber
Barrel: 4, 6.5 or 8.4 in.
Sights: target
Weight: 44.0 oz.
Caliber: .44 Mag.
Capacity: 6 rounds
Features: vent rib, porting; weight to 57 oz. depending on barrel length
Stainless, 4 in.: $711
Stainless, 6.5 in.: $711
Stainless, 8.4 in.: $711

MODEL 82

Action: double-action revolver
Grips: rubber
Barrel: 4 in.
Sights: fixed open
Weight: 36.5 oz.
Caliber: .38 Spl. +P
Capacity: 6 rounds
Features: also, 21-ounce model 85 in .38 Spl, with 2 in. barrel, grip options
Model 82, blue: $424
Model 82, stainless: $472
Model 85, blue: $433
Model 85, stainless: $480

Taurus Handguns

HANDGUNS

1911

Action: autoloader
Grips: checkered black
Barrel: 5 in.
Sights: Heinie "Straight Eight" 2-dot
Weight: 32-38 oz.
Caliber: .45 ACP
Capacity: 8 + 1 rounds
Features: forged frame, slide and barrel; ambidextrous safety; skeletonized trigger; target hammer; serrated slide; checkered trigger guard; mainspring housing and front strap; polished feed ramp; lowered and flared ejection port; custom internal extractor; beavertail grip safety with memory pad; extended magazine release; two 8-round magazines with bumper pads; finishes and variations include matte blue steel, matte blue steel with integral accessory rail, two-tone matte/high polished blue steel, stainless steel, stainless steel with rail and an Ultra-Lite model with forged alloy frame
MSRP: $757–905

1911

JUDGE .45/.410

Action: double-action revolver
Grips: ergonomic Ribber Grips
Barrel: 3.0 or 6.5 in.
Sights: fixed rear, fiber optic front
Caliber: 410 bore, 2.5-in., .45 Colt,
Capacity: 5 rounds
Features: capable of chambering both .410 bore shotgun shells and .45 Colt ammunition; Taurus Security System allows users to securely lock the gun using an inconspicuous key-lock system; several models and variations, including blue, blue steel, stainless steel and titanium
MSRP: $556–652

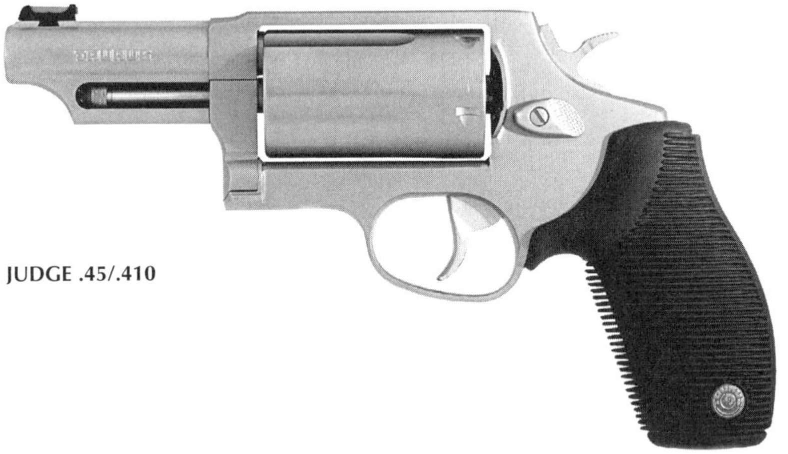

JUDGE .45/.410

PROTECTOR

Action: double-action revolver
Grips: rubber
Barrel: 2 in.
Sights: fixed open
Weight: 24.5 oz.
Caliber: .357 Mag. or .38 Spl.
Capacity: 5 rounds
Features: shrouded but accessible hammer; also Titanium and UltraLight versions to 17 oz.
Blue: $433
Stainless: $480
Shadow Gray Titanium: $650

Ed McGivern of Montana was one of the most incredible handgun shooters who ever lived. At South Dakota's Lead Club Range on August 20, 1932, he shot a .45-caliber revolver five times from 15 feet into an area with a diameter of 1.1875 inches. He accomplished this in 45/100s of a second and did it twice that same day.

Taurus Handguns

MODEL 92

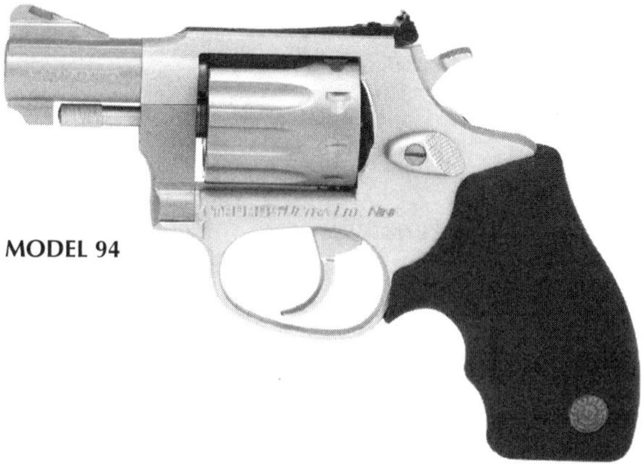

MODEL 94

MODEL 444
ULTRALITE

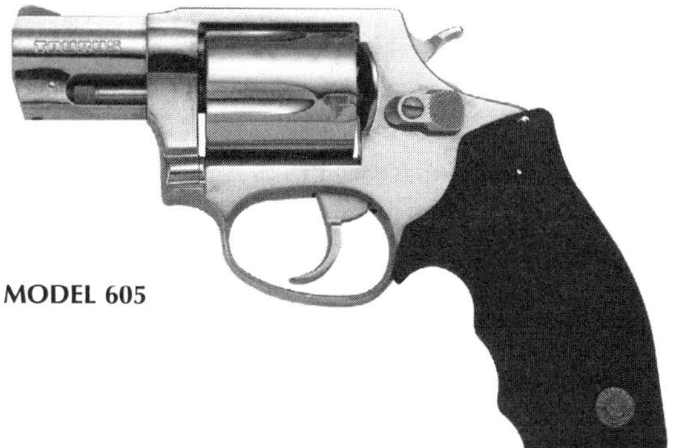

MODEL 605

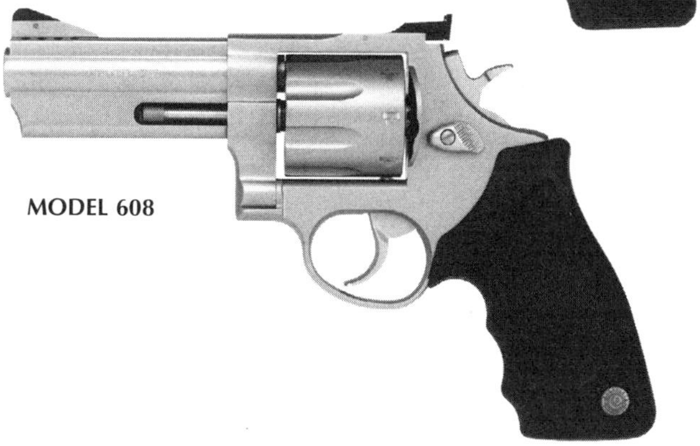

MODEL 608

MODEL 92

Action: autoloader
Grips: rosewood or rubber
Barrel: 5 in.
Sights: fixed open ***Weight:*** 34.0 oz.
Caliber: 9mm
Capacity: 10 + 1 rounds or 17 + 1
Features: double-action; also PT99 with adjustable sights
Blue: $435
Stainless: $439
Stainless gold, Mother of Pearl: $663

MODEL 94/941

Action: double-action revolver
Grips: hardwood
Barrel: 2, 4 or 5 in.
Sights: target
Weight: 18.5-27.5 oz.
Caliber: .22 LR, .22 Mag.
Capacity: 8-9 rounds
Features: small frame, solid rib
Blue: $430
Magnum, blue: $461
Stainless: $477
Magnum, stainless: $452
.22 LR, Ultralite: $452
.22 Mag., Ultralite: $477

MODEL 605

Action: double-action revolver
Grips: rubber
Barrel: 2 in.
Sights: fixed open
Weight: 24.5 oz.
Caliber: .357 Mag.
Capacity: 5 rounds
Features: small frame, transfer bar; porting optional
Model 605: $424
Titanium (16 oz.): $472
Stainless: $472

MODEL 608

Action: double-action revolver
Grips: rubber
Barrel: 4, 6.5 or 8.4 in., ported
Sights: target ***Weight:*** 49.0 oz.
Caliber: .357 Mag.
Capacity: 8 rounds
Features: large frame; transfer bar; weight to 53 oz. depending on barrel length
Stainless, 4 in.: $615
Stainless, 6.5 or 8.4 in.: $641

Taurus Handguns

MODEL 905

MODEL 22B

MODEL PT945

MILLENNIUM PRO

MODEL 905

Action: double-action revolver
Grips: rubber
Barrel: 2 in. ***Sights:*** fixed open
Weight: 21.0 oz.
Caliber: 9mm, .40 S&W, .45 ACP 9 with 2, 4 or 6.5 in. barrel
Capacity: 5 rounds
Features: stellar clips furnished; UltraLite weighs 17 oz.

Blue: $433
Stainless: $480
.32 Mag.: $433

MODEL 22B

Action: autoloader
Grips: rosewood
Barrel: 2.8 in. ***Sights:*** fixed open
Weight: 12.3 oz.
Caliber: .22 LR
Capacity: 8 + 1 rounds
Features: double-action only; blue, nickel or DuoTone finish; also in .25 ACP (PT25)

Blued: $262
With checkered wood: $262
With gold trim: $280
With Mother of Pearl grips: . . . $280

MODEL 911B

Action: autoloader
Grips: checkered rubber
Barrel: 4 in.
Sights: 3 dot
Weight: 28.2 oz.
Caliber: 9mm
Capacity: 10 + 1 rounds or 15 + 1
Features: double-action only; ambidextrous decocker

Blued: $677
Stainless: $789

MODEL 945

Action: autoloader
Grips: checkered rubber, rosewood or Mother of Pearl
Barrel: 4.3 in.
Sights: 3 dot
Weight: 29.5 oz.
Caliber: .45 ACP, .38 Super
Capacity: 8 + 1 rounds (.38: 10 + 1)
Features: double-action; also PT38 in .38 Super

Blued: $658
Stainless: $674
Stainless, gold, Mother of Pearl: $743

Stainless rosewood: $727
Model 940 blue: $615
Model 940 stainless: $633

MILLENNIUM PRO

Action: autoloader
Grips: polymer
Barrel: 3.25 in. ***Sights:*** 3 dot
Weight: 18.7 oz.
Caliber: 9mm, .40 S&W, .45 ACP, .32 ACP, .380 ACP
Capacity: 10 + 1 rounds
Features: double-action; polymer frame; also comes with night sights (BL or SS), add $78

.40 blue: $441
.40 stainless: $459
.45 blue/composite: $441
.45 stainless/composite: $459
9mm, .32 or .380 BL: $441
9mm, .32 or .380 SS: $459
9mm Titanium: $623

Taurus Handguns

NINE BY SEVENTEEN
Action: autoloader
Grips: hard rubber
Barrel: 4 in.
Sights: 3 dot
Weight: 26 oz.
Caliber: 9mm
Capacity: 17 rounds
Features: double-action with de-cocker
Blued: $571
Stainless: $589

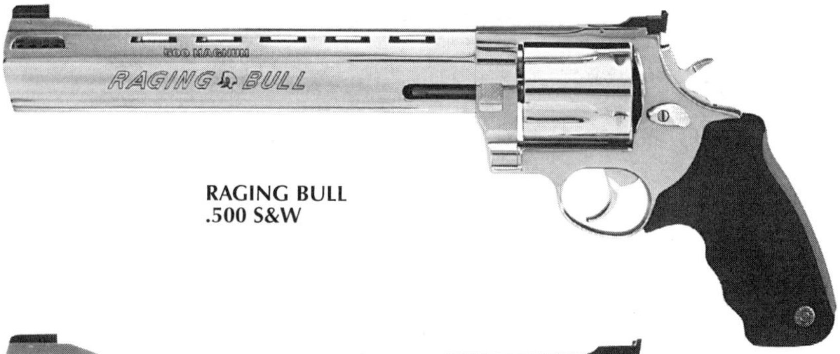

RAGING BULL
.500 S&W

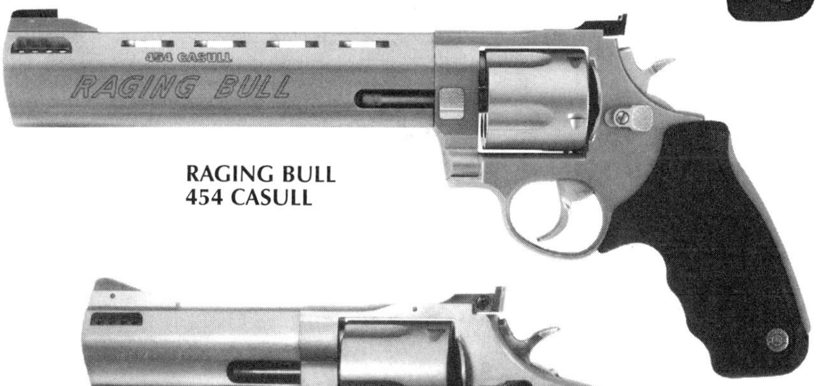

RAGING BULL
454 CASULL

TRACKER
TITANIUM

RAGING BULL
Action: double-action revolver
Grips: rubber
Barrel: 5, 6.5 or 8.3 in.
Sights: target
Weight: 53.0-63.0 oz.
Caliber: .41 Mag., .44 Mag., .480 Ruger, .454 Casull
Capacity: 6 rounds
Features: stainless vent rib, ported; also 72 oz. 5 round Raging Bull in .500 Mag with 10 in. barrel
.41: $780
.44 Mag, blue: $711
stainless .44 & .480 Ruger: . $674–722
454 Casull, blue: $923–992
454 Casull, stainless: $992

TRACKER
Action: double-action revolver
Grips: rubber with ribs
Barrel: 4 or 6.5 in. *Sights:* target
Weight: 24.0-45.0 oz.
Caliber: .22 LR, .41 Mag., .357 Mag., .44 Mag., .17 HMR, .500 S&W
Capacity: 5-7 rounds (full-moon clips)
Features: ported barrel on .44 Mag., .357 and .41 Mag.; available in Titanium
.17 HMR: $477
.22 LR: $489
.357 Mag.: $600
.357 Mag. (Shadow Gray): $688
.41 Mag., stainless: $597
.44 Mag., blue: $581
.44 Mag., stainless: $632
.500 S&W: $899

Taylor's & Company Handguns

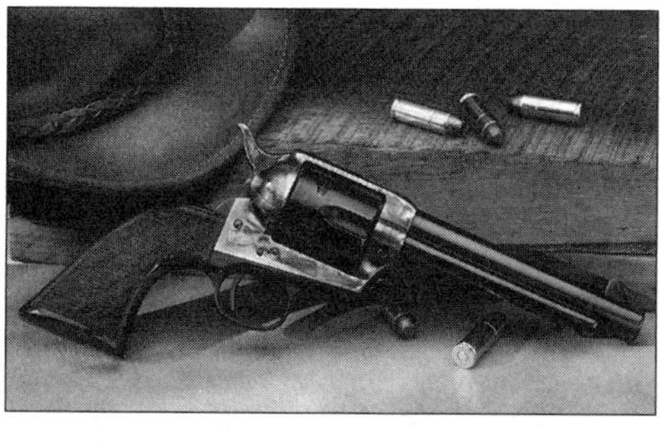

SMOKE WAGON
Action: single-action revolver
Grips: checkered wood
Barrel: 4.75 or 5.5 in.
Sights: open rear sight groove, wide angle front sight blade
Weight: unavailable
Caliber: .38 Special, .357 Mag., .45 LC, .44-40
Capacity: 6 rounds
Features: low profile hammer; deluxe edition model includes custom tuning, custom hammer and base pin springs, trigger-spring at 3 pounds, jig-cut positive angles on trigger and sears, wire bolt and trigger springs
MSRP: . . . . (standard) $485
. . . .(deluxe) $620

Thompson/Center Handguns

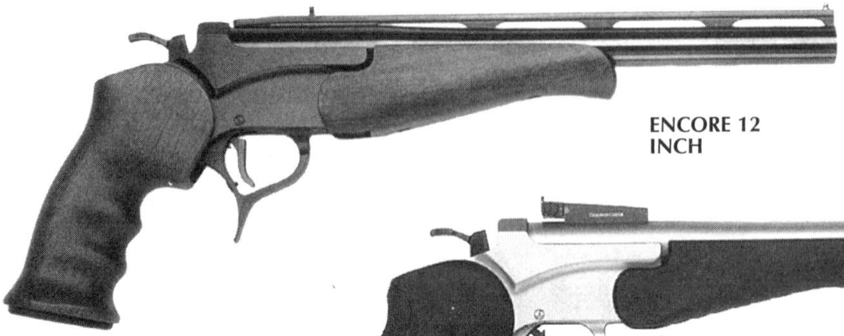

ENCORE 12 INCH

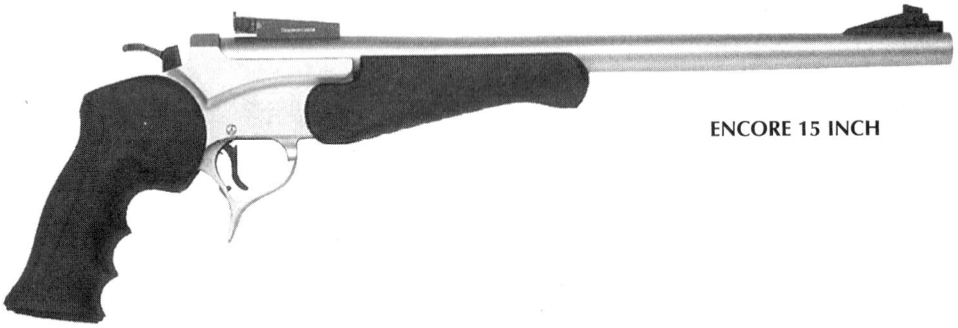

ENCORE 15 INCH

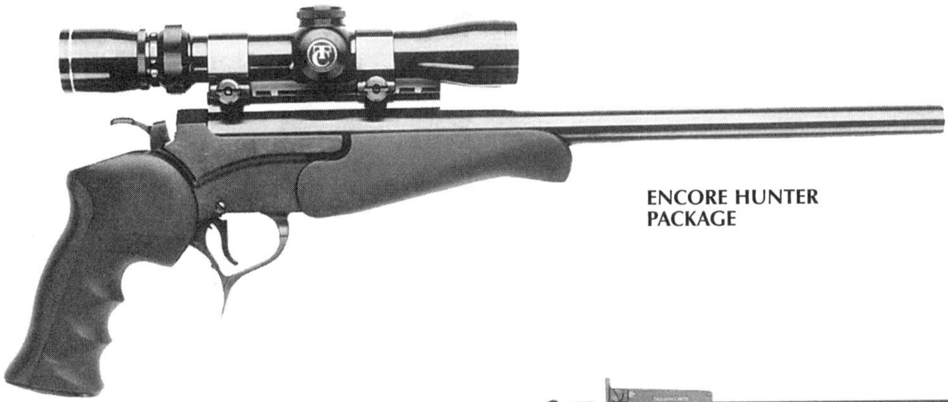

ENCORE HUNTER PACKAGE

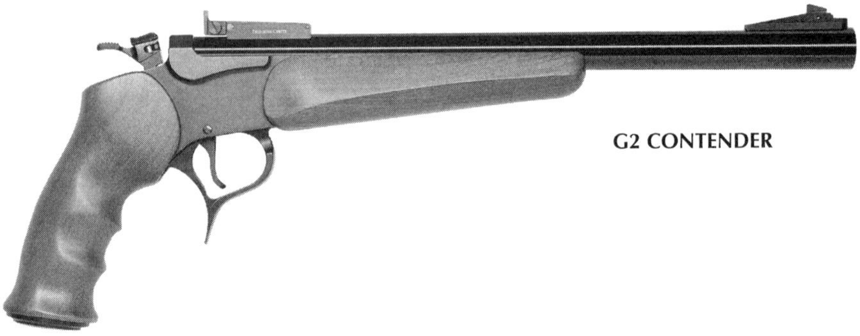

G2 CONTENDER

ENCORE

Action: hinged breech
Grips: walnut or rubber
Barrel: 12 or 15 in.
Sights: target
Weight: 68.0 oz.
Caliber: many popular rifle and big-bore pistol rounds, from the .22 Hornet to the .30-06 and .45-70, the .454 Casull and .480 Ruger
Capacity: 1 round
Features: also in package with 2-7x scope, carry case; prices vary with caliber, options

12 in.: $753
15 in. (72 oz.): $730
.45/.410 with rib: $730
Stainless with rubber grips: . . . $753

G2 CONTENDER

Action: hinged breech
Grips: walnut
Barrel: 12 or 14 in.
Sights: target
Weight: 60.0 oz.
Caliber: .22 LR, .22 Hornet, .357 Mag., .17 MACH 2, 6.8 Rem SPC, .44 Mag., .45/.410 (12 in.), .17 HMR, .22 LR, .22 Hornet, .223, 7-30, .30-30, .44 Mag., .45/.410, .45-70 (15 in.), .204 Ruger, .375 JDJ
Capacity: 1 round
Features: improved, stronger version of Contender

12 in.: $555–600
14 in. (64 oz.): $555–600

1851 NAVY CONVERSION

Action: single-action revolver
Grips: walnut
Barrel: 4.75, 5.5 and 7.5 in.
Sights: fixed, open
Weight: 41.6 oz.
Caliber: .38 Special
Capacity: 6 rounds
Features: engraved cylinder; frame retro-fitted with loading gate to accommodate cartridges, just like original; fitted with ejector rod for removing casings from cylinder; brass backstrap and trigger guard
MSRP: $519

1851 NAVY CONVERSION

1860 ARMY CONVERSION

Action: single-action revolver
Grips: walnut
Barrel: 4.75, 5.5 and 8 in. (.38 Special); 5.5 and 8 in. (.45 Colt)
Sights: fixed, open
Weight: 41.6 oz.
Caliber: .38 Special, .45 Colt
Capacity: 6 rounds
Features: cylinder adapted for center-fire metalic cartridges; frame retro-fitted with loading gate; engraved cylinder; ejector rod; blued steel backstrap and trigger guard
MSRP: $549

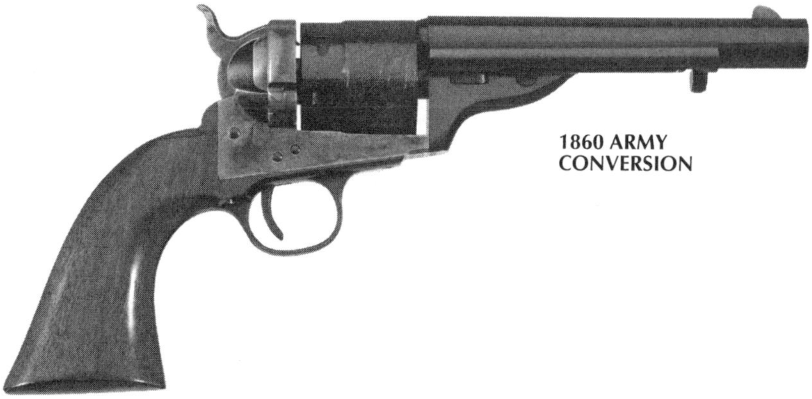

1860 ARMY CONVERSION

1871-1872 OPEN-TOP

Action: single-action revolver
Grips: walnut
Barrel: 4.75, 5.5 and 7.5 in. (1871 Open-Top); 7.5 in. (1872 Open-Top)
Sights: fixed, open
Weight: 41.6 oz.
Caliber: .38, .45 Colt
Capacity: 6 rounds
Features: cylinder adapted for center-fire metalic cartridges; engraved cylinder; 1871 Model with frame and cylinder designed for cartridges, brass backstrap and trigger guard; 1872 Model with blued steel backstrap and trigger guard; both models fitted with ejector rods
1871 Open-Top: $499
1872 Open-Top: $519

1871 OPEN-TOP (EARLY MODEL)

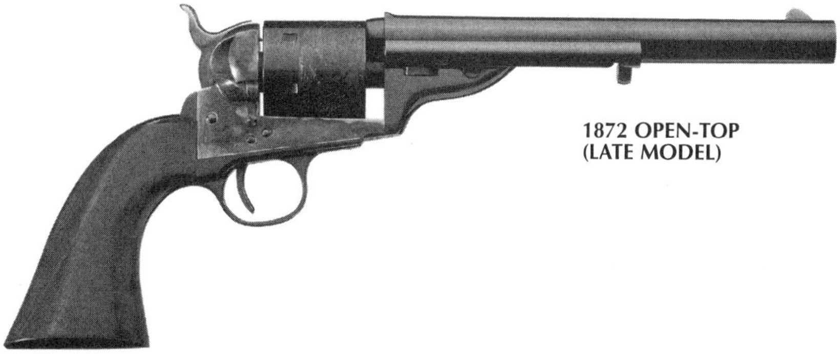

1872 OPEN-TOP (LATE MODEL)

Uberti Handguns

1873 CATTLEMAN BIRD'S HEAD

1873 CATTLEMAN CHISHOLM

1873 CATTLEMAN DESPERADO

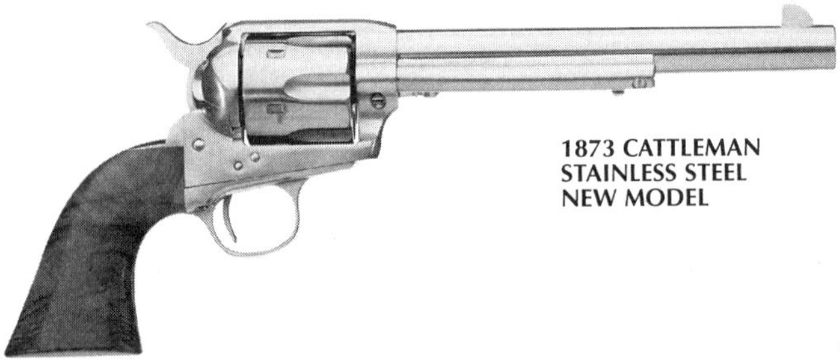

1873 CATTLEMAN STAINLESS STEEL NEW MODEL

1873 STALLION

1873 CATTLEMAN BIRD'S HEAD

Action: single-action revolver
Grips: walnut
Barrel: 3.5, 4, 4.5 or 5.5 in.
Sights: fixed, open ***Weight:*** 36.8 oz.
Caliber: .357 Mag., .45 LC
Capacity: 6 rounds
Features: fluted cylinder; round barrel; forged steel; color case-hardened frame; curved grip frame and grip
MSRP: $539

1873 CATTLEMAN CHISHOLM

Action: single-action revolver
Grips: walnut
Barrel: 4.75, 5.75 or 7.5 in.
Sights: fixed, open
Weight: 35 oz.
Caliber: .45 Colt ***Capacity:*** 6 rounds
Features: 6-shot fluted cylinder; checkered walnut grip; matte blue finish
MSRP: $539

1873 CATTLEMAN DESPERADO

Action: single-action revolver
Grips: black horn
Barrel: 4.75, 5.5 or 7.5 in.
Sights: fixed, open
Weight: 35 oz.
Caliber: .45 Colt ***Capacity:*** 6 rounds
Features: 6-shot fluted cylinder; nickel finish; black bison horn style grips
MSRP: $789

1873 SINGLE-ACTION CATTLEMAN

Action: single-action revolver
Grips: walnut
Barrel: 4.75, 5.5, 7.5 or 18 in.
Sights: fixed, open
Weight: 37 oz.
Caliber: .357 Mag., .44-40, .45 Colt
Capacity: 6 rounds
Features: 6-shot fluted cylinder; color case-hardened frame; more than 100 configurations available
1873: $489
Nickel finish: $609
Old West antique finish: $629
Matte black Hombre: $429
Charcoal blue: $579
Stainless New Model: $649
Buntline: $639

1873 STALLION

Action: single-action revolver
Grips: walnut
Barrel: 5.5 in.
Sights: fixed, open or target
Weight: 22.3 oz.
Caliber: .22 LR, .38 SP
Capacity: 6 rounds
Features: color case-hardened frame; fluted cylinder, brass or steel backstrap & trigger guard; optional target sights
MSRP: $429–539

Uberti Handguns

1875 OUTLAW

1875 FRONTIER

1890 POLICE

BISLEY

TOP BREAK
NO. 3 2ND MODEL

TOP BREAK
NO. 3 NEW MODEL
RUSSIAN

1875 OUTLAW & FRONTIER

Action: single-action revolver
Grips: walnut
Barrel: 7.5 in. (5.5 Frontier)
Sights: fixed, open
Weight: 44.8 oz. (40 oz. Frontier)
Caliber: .45 Colt
Capacity: 6 rounds
Features: color case-hardened frame with blued barrel; fluted cylinder
Outlaw: $539
Outlaw, Nickel: $629
Frontier: $539

1890 POLICE REVOLVER

Action: single-action revolver
Grips: walnut
Barrel: 5.5 in.
Sights: fixed, open
Weight: 41.6 oz.
Caliber: .357 Mag., .45 Colt,
Capacity: 6 rounds
Features: fluted cylinder; blued finish; lanyard loop
MSRP: $549

BISLEY

Action: single-action revolver
Grips: walnut
Barrel: 4.75, 5.5, 7.5 in.
Sights: fixed, open
Weight: 40.2 oz.
Caliber: .357 Mag., .45 LC
Capacity: 6 rounds
Features: Bisley style grip; color case-hardened frame; fluted cylinder
MSRP: $569

TOP BREAK REVOLVERS

Action: single-action revolver
Grips: walnut
Barrel: 3.5, 5, 7 in.
Sights: fixed open
Weight: 36 oz.
Caliber: .38 sp., .44/40, .45 Colt,
Capacity: 6 rounds
Features: top break action; blue finish; fluted cylinder
No. 3 2nd Model: $999
No. 3 2nd Model, Nickel, mother of pearl grips: $1369

NEW MODEL RUSSIAN REVOLVER

Action: single-action revolver
Grips: walnut
Barrel: 6.5 in.
Sights: fixed, open
Weight: 40 oz.
Caliber: 44 Russian, .45 Colt
Capacity: 6 rounds
Features: improved top latch, 6-shot fluted cylinder; blued frame, barrel and backstrap; color case-hardened trigger guard with spur; lanyard loop
New Model Russian: $1049
New Model Russian Nickel, mother of pearl grips: $1399

Walther Handguns

PPS (POLICE PISTOL SLIM)

P99 COMPACT

PPK/S

PPS (POLICE PISTOL SLIM)

Action: Striker Fire Action autoloader,
Grips: black polymer
Barrel: 3.2 in.
Sights: 3-dot low profile contoured
Weight: 19.4 oz. (9mm), 20.8 oz (.40)
Caliber: 9mm, .40 S&W
Capacity: 6 and 7 round magazines (9mm), 5 and 6 round magazines (.40)
Features: Striker Fire Action pre-cocked; flat slide stop lever; Picatinny-style accessory; adjustable grip length and size; Walther QuickSafe technology; loaded chamber indicator on top of slide; cocking indicator on rear of slide; optional 8-round magazine available for 9mm and 7-round magazine for .40 S&W; Pachmayr Compac Custom grips
MSRP: $735

P22

Action: autoloader
Grips: polymer
Barrel: 3.4 or 5 in. ***Sights:*** 3 dot
Weight: 19.6 oz.
Caliber: .22 LR
Capacity: 10 + 1 rounds
Features: double-action; 20.3 oz. 5 in. barrel
MSRP: $375–472

P99 COMPACT

Action: autoloader ***Grips:*** polymer
Barrel: 4 in. ***Sights:*** low-profile combat
Weight: 25.0 oz.
Caliber: 9mm, .40 S&W
Capacity: 10 + 1 rounds
Features: double-action; ambidextrous magazine release; high-capacity magazines available
P99 Compact: $825

PPK AND PPK/S

Action: autoloader
Grips: polymer
Barrel: 3.4 in. ***Sights:*** fixed open
Weight: 22.0 oz.
Caliber: .380 and .32 ACP
Capacity: 7 + 1 rounds
Features: double-action; blue or stainless; decocker
MSRP: $626

Weatherby Handguns

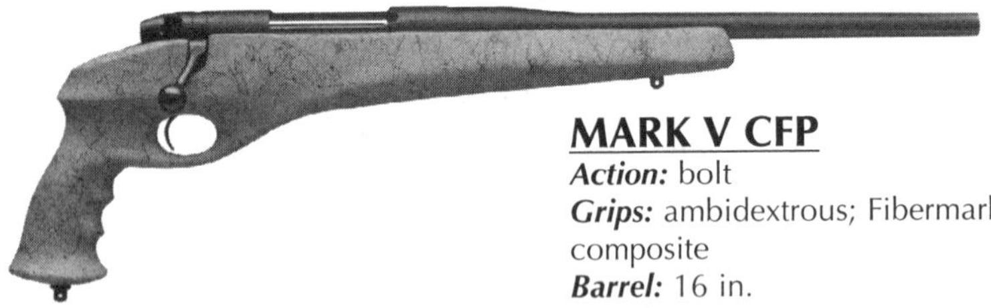

MARK V CFP

Action: bolt
Grips: ambidextrous; Fibermark composite
Barrel: 16 in.
Weight: 84 oz.
Caliber: .223 Rem., .22-250 Rem., .243 Win., 7mm-08 Rem.
Capacity: 5 + 1 rounds
Features: Button-rifled, #2 contour, chrome moly (4140 steel) barrel; one-piece forged and fluted bolt; cocking indicator; adjustable trigger
MSRP: $1499

Wildey Handguns

WILDEY AUTOMATIC PISTOL

Action: autoloader
Grips: composite
Barrel: 5, 6, 7, 8, 10, 12 or 14 in.
Sights: target ***Weight:*** 64.0 oz.
Caliber: .45 Win. Mag., .44 Auto Mag., .45 and .475 Wildey
Capacity: 7 + 1 rounds
Features: gas operated; ribbed barrel
MSRP: $1571–2149

BLACK POWDER

BLACK POWDER

Cabela's Black Powder

BLUE RIDGE FLINTLOCK RIFLE

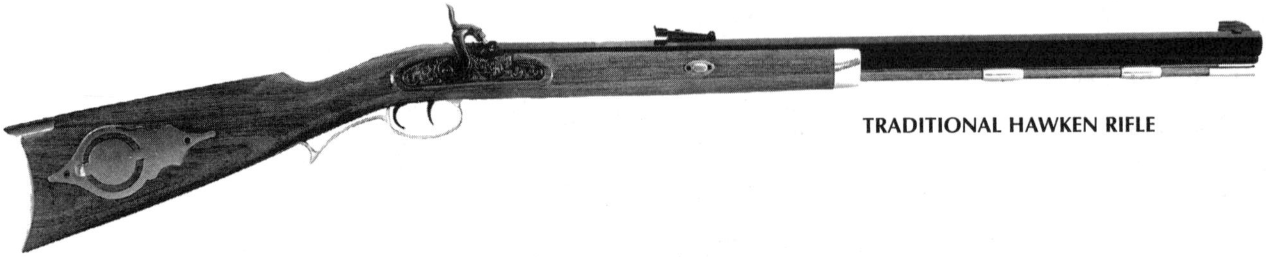

TRADITIONAL HAWKEN RIFLE

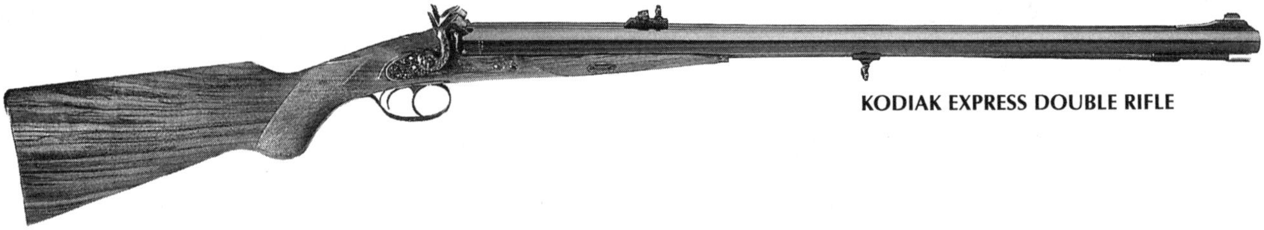

KODIAK EXPRESS DOUBLE RIFLE

BLUE RIDGE FLINTLOCK RIFLE

Lock: side-hammer caplock
Stock: walnut
Barrel: 39 in., 1:48 twist
Sights: none
Weight: 7.75 lbs. (7.25 lbs., .45, .50, .54 cal.)
Bore/Caliber: .32, .36, .45, .50 and .54
Features: double set triggers; case-colored locks
MSRP: $749

DOUBLE SHOTGUN

Lock: traditional caplock
Stock: walnut
Barrel: 27, 28 or 30 in.
Sights: none
Weight: 7.0 lbs. (6.5 20 ga.)
Bore/Caliber: 20, 12 or 10 ga.
Features: screw-in choke tubes: X-Full, Mod, IC; double triggers; weight to 10 lbs. depending on ga.
MSRP: $939–999

HAWKEN

Lock: traditional cap or flint
Stock: walnut
Barrel: 29 in., 1:48 twist
Sights: adjustable open
Weight: 9.0 lbs.
Bore/Caliber: .50 or .54
Features: brass furniture; double-set trigger
Traditional percussion (right or left-hand): $399
Sporterized percussion (28-in. bl.):. $499

KODIAK EXPRESS DOUBLE RIFLE

Lock: traditional caplock
Stock: walnut, pistol grip
Barrel: 28 in., 1:48 twist
Sights: folding leaf
Weight: 9.3 lbs.
Bore/Caliber: .50, .54, .58 and .72
Features: double triggers
MSRP: $1199–1299

Use only powders specific to each particular muzzleloader and recommended by that firearms manufacturer. To do otherwise can cause damage to the firearm and may cause serious injury, and even death, to the shooter and/or spectators.

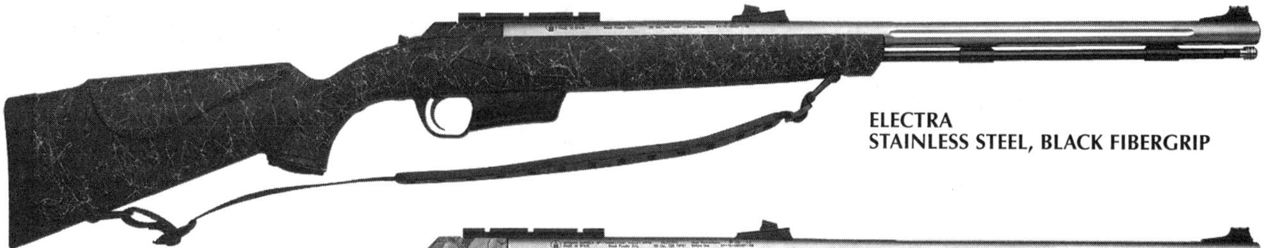

ELECTRA
STAINLESS STEEL, BLACK FIBERGRIP

ELECTRA
STAINLESS STEEL, REALTREE

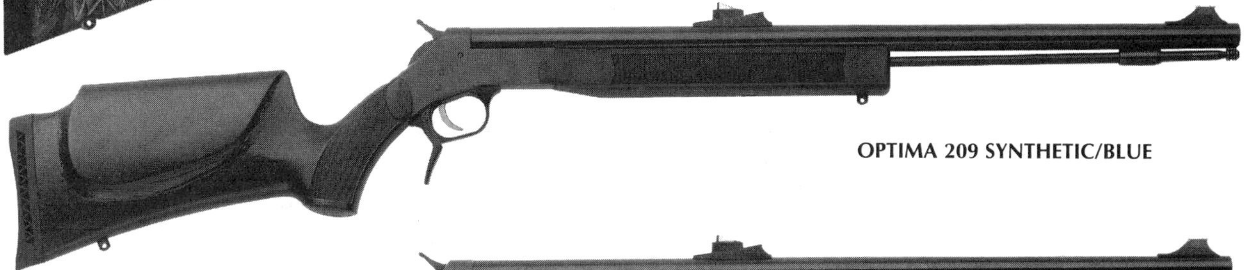

OPTIMA 209 SYNTHETIC/BLUE

OPTIMA 209 CAMO/BLUE

OPTIMA 209 CAMO/NICKEL

ELECTRA

Lock: in-line
Stock: composite; RealTree HD camo or Black FiberGrip; ambidextrous
Barrel: 26-in. Bergara Barrel, stainless steel or blued steel; 1:28 twist
Sights: DuraSight Fiber Optic
Weight: 7.5 lbs.
Bore/Caliber: .50
Features: world's first electronic ignition muzzleloader; Electronic ARC Ignition (completely sealed from the elements) eliminates the need for 209 primers; when the trigger is pulled, ignition is instantaneous; powered by a 9-volt lithium battery, which will reliably fire the gun up to 500 times; when the system is activated, the gun is ready to fire in approximately 20 seconds; Quake Claw Sling; Crush-Zone recoil pad; DuraSight rail scope mount
Stainless Steel/Realtree HD: . . $350
Stainless Steel/Black FiberGrip: $300
Blued/Black FiberGrip: $250

OPTIMA 209 AND OPTIMA PRO 209

Lock: in-line
Stock: synthetic or camo
Barrel: 26 in. (Pro: 29 in.), 1:28 twist
Sights: adjustable fiber optic
Weight: 8.2 lbs. (Pro: 8.8 lbs.)
Bore/Caliber: .45 or .50
Features: stainless steel 209 breech plug, ambidextrous stock
Optima, synthetic/blue: $256
Camo/nickel: $286

CVA Black Powder

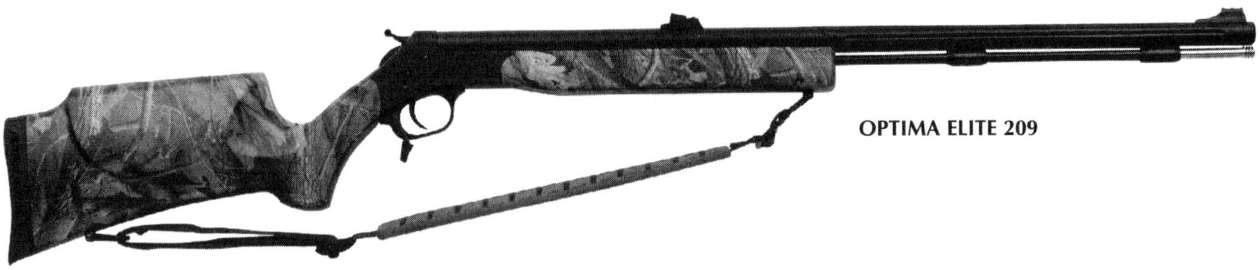

OPTIMA ELITE 209

OPTIMA ELITE 209 FIBER GRIP

OPTIMA ELITE 209 REALTREE HD

OPTIMA ELITE 209 MAGNUM BREAK-ACTION

Lock: in-line
Stock: composite
Barrel: 29 in. blued or stainless fluted
Sights: DuraBright adjustable fiber optic
Weight: 8.8 lb.
Bore/Caliber: .45 and .50
Features: Bergara button rifled barrel with bullet guiding muzzle (Optima Pro and Optima barrels cannot be installed on the Optima Elite frame); stainless 209 breech plug; reversible cocking spur available; extendable loading rod; ambidextrous solid composite stock in standard or thumbhole design in Realtree HD or Black FiberGrip; CrushZone recoil pad; Quake Claw sling
MSRP: $338

OPTIMA ELITE COMPACT 209 MAGNUM

Lock: in-line, break-action
Stock: synthetic or camo
Barrel: 24 in., 1:28 twist
Sights: adjustable fiber optic
Weight: 6.0 lbs.
Bore/Caliber: .45 or .50
Features: in-line break-action; available with Bergara muzzleloading barrel; ambidextrous solid composite stock; adjustable fiber optic sights; drilled and tapped for scope mounts
MSRP: $250

Dixie Black Powder

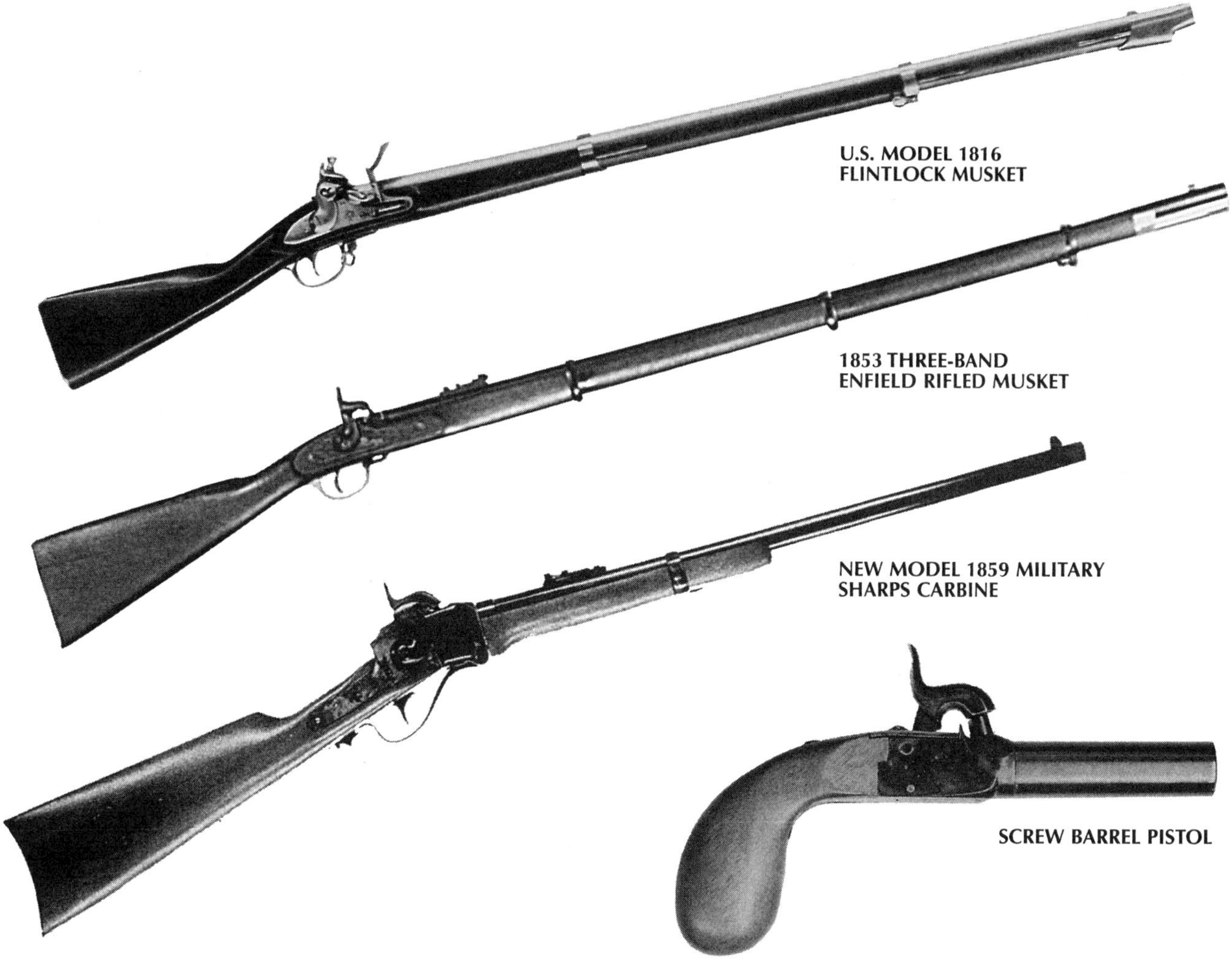

U.S. MODEL 1816
FLINTLOCK MUSKET

1853 THREE-BAND
ENFIELD RIFLED MUSKET

NEW MODEL 1859 MILITARY
SHARPS CARBINE

SCREW BARREL PISTOL

MODEL U.S. 1816 FLINTLOCK MUSKET

Lock: traditional flintlock
Stock: walnut
Barrel: 42 in. smoothbore
Sights: fixed
Weight: 9.8 lbs.
Bore/Caliber: .69
Features: most common military flintlock from U.S. armories, complete with bayonet lug and swivels
MSRP: $1395

1853 THREE-BAND ENFIELD

Lock: traditional caplock
Stock: walnut ***Barrel:*** 39 in.
Sights: fixed
Weight: 10.5 lbs.
Bore/Caliber: .58
Features: case-colored lock, brass furniture; also 1858 two-band Enfield with 33 in. barrel
Three-band: $650
Two-band: $725

NEW MODEL 1859 MILITARY SHARPS CARBINE

Lock: dropping block
Stock: walnut ***Barrel:*** 22 in.
Sights: adjustable open
Weight: 7.8 lbs.
Bore/Caliber: .54
Features: case-colored furniture, including saddle ring; also 1859 military rifle with 30 in. barrel (9 lbs.); both by Pedersoli
MSRP: $1200

SCREW BARREL PISTOL

Lock: traditional caplock
Grips: hardwood
Barrel: 3 in.
Sights: none
Weight: 0.75 lbs.
Bore/Caliber: .445
Features: barrel detaches for loading; folding trigger
MSRP: $185

EMF Hartford Black Powder

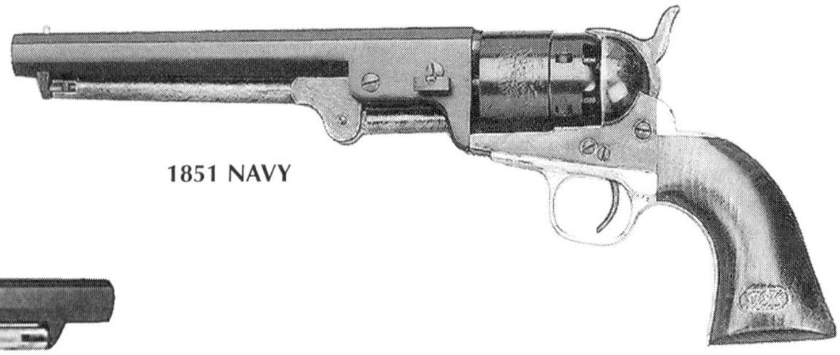

1851 NAVY

1851 NAVY SHERIFF'S

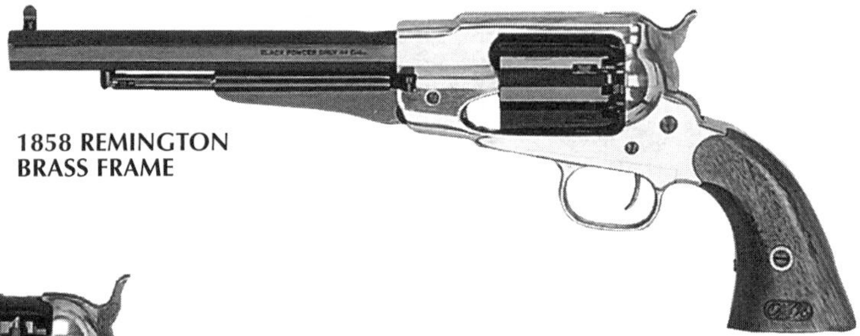

1858 REMINGTON
BRASS FRAME

1860 ARMY REVOLVER

1851 NAVY

Lock: caplock revolver
Grips: walnut
Barrel: 7.5 in.
Sights: fixed
Weight: 2.5 lbs.
Bore/Caliber: .36 or .44
Features: octagonal barrel; brass or steel frame
Brass frame:. $200
Case-hardened steel frame:. . . $215

1851 NAVY SHERIFF'S

Lock: caplock revolver
Grips: walnut
Barrel: 5.5 in.
Sights: none
Weight: 2 lbs.
Bore/Caliber: .44
Features: brass guard; strap
MSRP: $215

1858 REMINGTON ARMY REVOLVER

Lock: caplock revolver
Grips: walnut
Barrel: 8 in.
Sights: fixed
Weight: 2.5 lbs.
Bore/Caliber: .44
Features: brass or stainless steel frame
Brass frame:. $210
Blued steel frame: $260
Stainless frame:. $390

1860 ARMY REVOLVER

Lock: caplock revolver
Stock: walnut
Barrel: 8 in.
Sights: fixed
Weight: 2.6 lbs.
Bore/Caliber: .44
Features: case-colored frame; brass guard; strap
MSRP: $215

Euroarms of America Black Powder

1803 HARPER'S FERRY FLINTLOCK RIFLE

1841 MISSISSIPPI RIFLE

COOK & BROTHER CONFEDERATE CARBINE

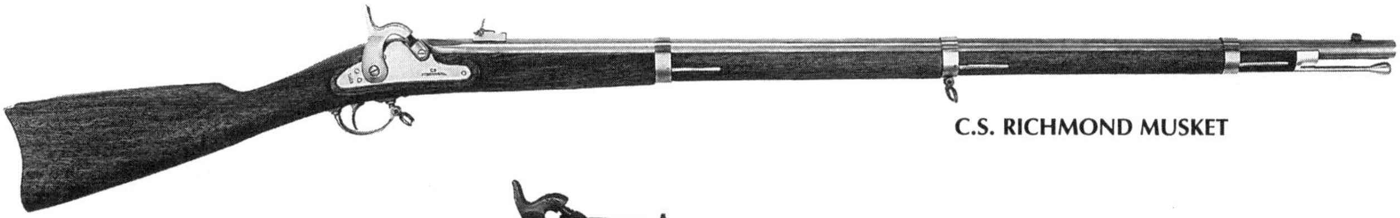

C.S. RICHMOND MUSKET

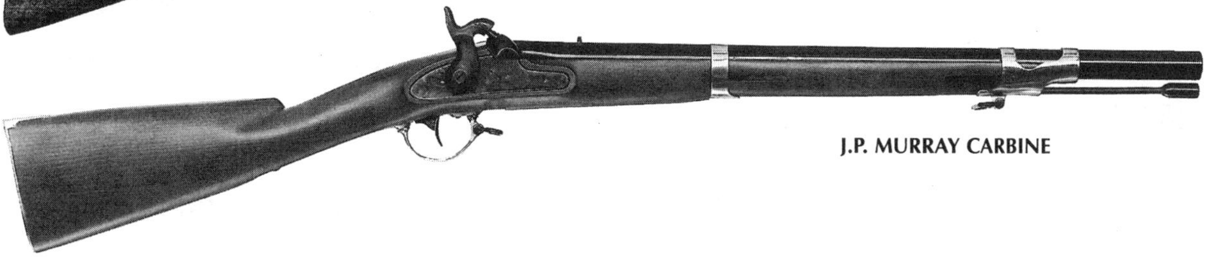

J.P. MURRAY CARBINE

1803 HARPER'S FERRY FLINTLOCK

Lock: traditional flintlock
Stock: walnut
Barrel: 35 in.
Sights: fixed
Weight: 10.0 lbs.
Bore/Caliber: .54
Features: half-stock, browned steel
MSRP: $809

1841 MISSISSIPPI RIFLE

Lock: traditional caplock
Stock: walnut
Barrel: 33 in.
Sights: fixed
Weight: 9.5 lbs.
Bore/Caliber: .54 or .58
Features: brass furniture
MSRP: $631

COOK & BROTHER CONFEDERATE CARBINE

Lock: traditional caplock
Stock: walnut
Barrel: 24 in.
Sights: fixed
Weight: 7.9 lbs.
Bore/Caliber: .577
Features: carbine; also rifle with 33 in. barrel
Rifle: $563

C.S. RICHMOND MUSKET

Lock: traditional caplock
Stock: walnut ***Barrel:*** 40 in.
Sights: fixed
Weight: 9.0 lbs.
Bore/Caliber: .58
Features: 3-band furniture; swivels
MSRP: $730

J.P. MURRAY CARBINE

Lock: traditional caplock
Stock: walnut
Barrel: 23 in.
Sights: fixed
Weight: 7.5 lbs.
Bore/Caliber: .58
Features: brass furniture; replica of rare Confederate Cavalry Carbine
MSRP: $573

Euroarms of America Black Powder

LONDON ARMORY P-1858 ENFIELD

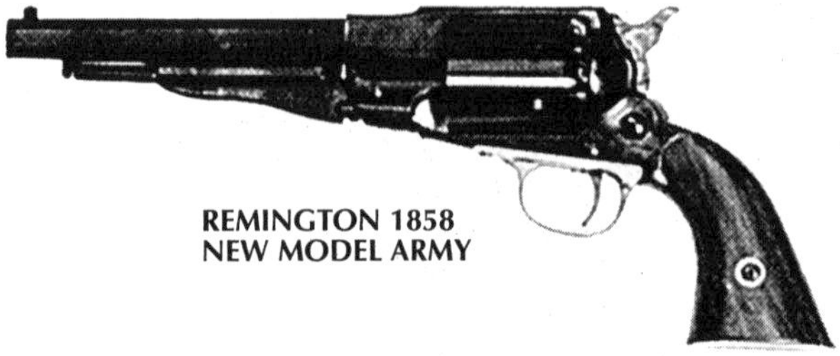

REMINGTON 1858
NEW MODEL ARMY

ROGERS AND
SPENCER TARGET

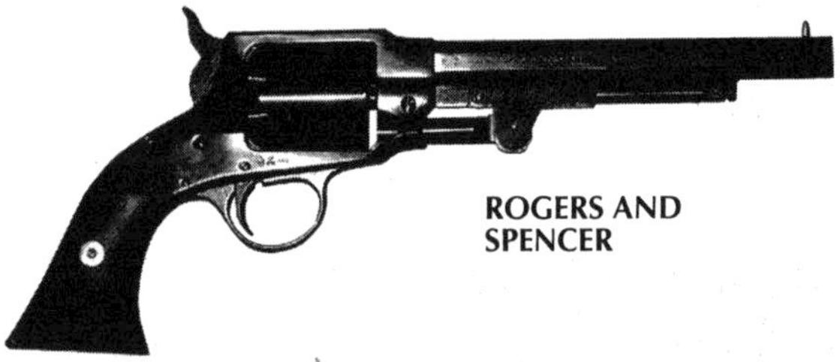

ROGERS AND
SPENCER

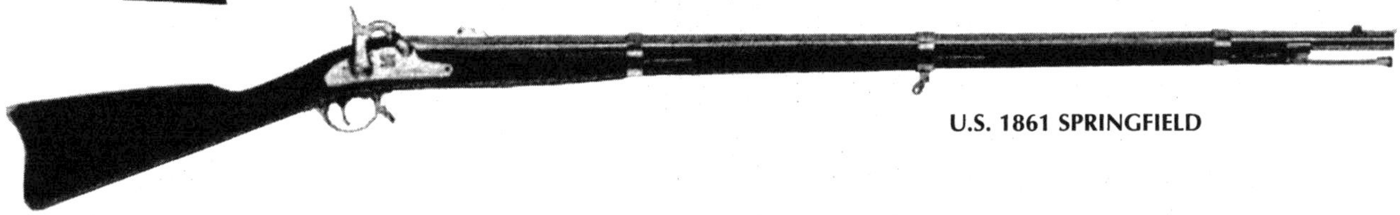

U.S. 1861 SPRINGFIELD

LONDON ARMORY P-1858 ENFIELD

Lock: traditional caplock
Stock: walnut
Barrel: 33 in.
Sights: adjustable open
Weight: 8.8 lbs.
Bore/Caliber: .58
Features: steel ramrod; 2-band
1861 London Enfield: $495
P-1858 Enfield: $495
1853 rifled musket: $575

REMINGTON 1858 NEW MODEL ARMY

Lock: caplock revolver
Grips: walnut
Barrel: 8 in.
Sights: fixed
Weight: 2.5 lbs.
Bore/Caliber: .44
Features: brass guard; engraved version
New Model Army: $242
Engraved:. $332

ROGERS AND SPENCER

Lock: caplock revolver
Grips: walnut
Barrel: 7.5 in.
Sights: fixed
Weight: 2.9 lbs.
Bore/Caliber: .44
Features: recommended ball diameter .451; also target model with adjustable sight
Rogers and Spencer: $340
London gray finish: $370
Target: $360

U.S. 1841 MISSISSIPPI RIFLE

Lock: traditional caplock
Stock: walnut
Barrel: 33 in.
Sights: fixed
Weight: 9.5 lbs.
Bore/Caliber: .54 or .58
Features: brass furniture
Mississippi: $545

U.S. 1861 SPRINGFIELD

Lock: traditional caplock
Stock: walnut
Barrel: 40 in.
Sights: fixed
Weight: 10.0 lbs.
Bore/Caliber: .58
Features: sling swivels; also London P-1852 rifled musket; London Enfield P-1861 (7.5 lbs.)
MSRP: $610

Green Mountain Black Powder

LIMITED EDITION .32-CALIBER SMALL GAME RIFLE

Lock: in-line
Stock: brown laminated
Barrel: 22.5 in., Green Mountain octagonal, blue-black finish
Sights: none; Redfield scope bases and rings provided
Weight: 5.8 lbs.
Bore/Caliber: .32
Features: Knight DISC Extreme action; limited edition with a production of 250 rifles, with its own exclusive serial number range; one-piece receiver; custom jeweled bolt, raised cheek-piece on stock
MSRP: $500

BLACK POWDER

Lenartz Black Powder

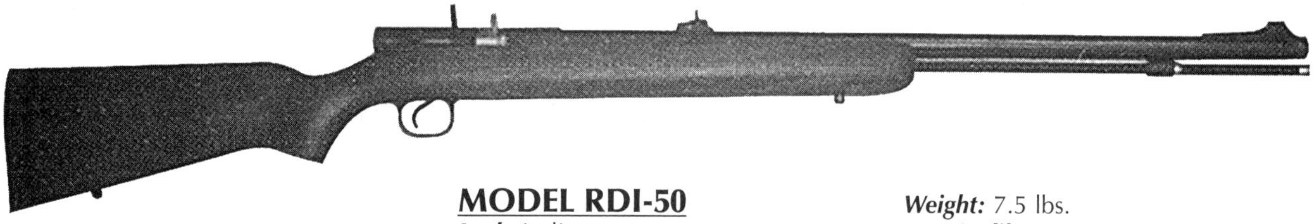

MODEL RDI-50

Lock: in-line
Stock: walnut
Barrel: 26 in., 1:28 twist
Sights: adjustable open
Weight: 7.5 lbs.
Bore/Caliber: .50
Features: adjustable trigger; uses 209 primers, converts to #11
MSRP: . . . . price on request

A short-started (unseated) load in your black-powder gun can cause big problems. This happens when the bullet is not firmly seated on the powder. Though the phenomenon is not well understood, it appears that the air space created by an unseated load causes the powder to detonate rather than burn. That is not good. For safety's sake, make certain every powder/projectile combination is seated correctly.

Lyman Black Powder

MUSTANG BREAKAWAY

Lock: in-line
Stock: hardwood
Barrel: 26 in.
Sights: fiber optic front and rear
Weight: 7.5 lbs.
Bore/Caliber: .50
Features: 1/28-in. twist rifling; tang mounted shotgun-style safety; magnetized primer retention system; drilled and tapped for scope; Pachmayr "decelerator" recoil pad
MSRP: $525

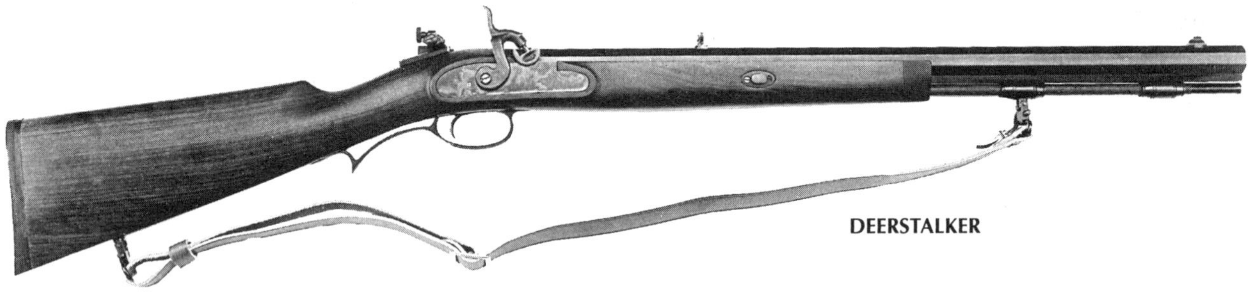

DEERSTALKER

GREAT PLAINS RIFLE

DEERSTALKER

Lock: traditional cap or flint
Stock: walnut
Barrel: 24 in.
Sights: aperture
Weight: 7.5 lbs.
Bore/Caliber: .50 or .54
Features: left-hand models available
Caplock: $500
Left-hand: $525
Flintlock: $545
Left-hand: $580
Stainless caplock: $625

GREAT PLAINS RIFLE

Lock: traditional cap or flint
Stock: walnut
Barrel: 32 in., 1:66 twist
Sights: adjustable open
Weight: 8.0 lbs.
Bore/Caliber: .50 or .54
Features: double set triggers, left-hand models available; also Great Plains Hunter with 1:32 twist
Caplock: $675
Flintlock: $725

Lyman Black Powder

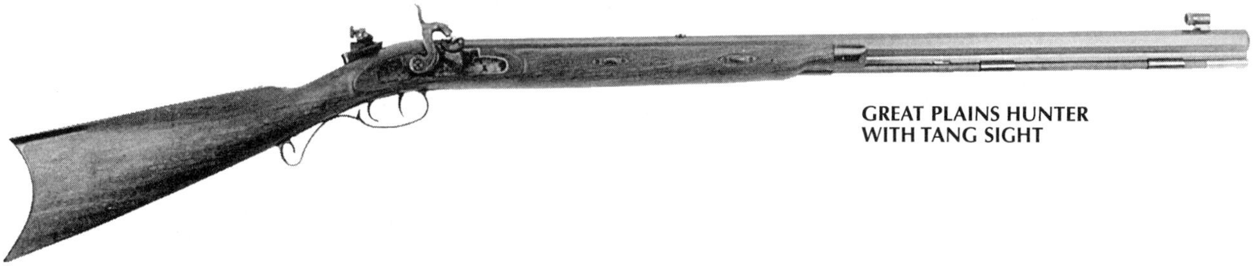

GREAT PLAINS HUNTER
WITH TANG SIGHT

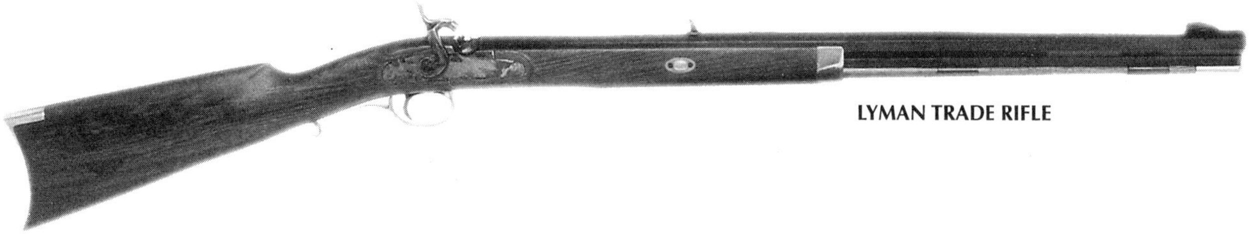

LYMAN TRADE RIFLE

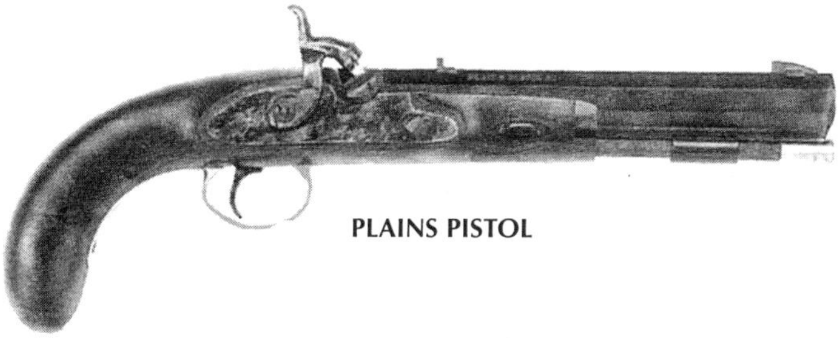

PLAINS PISTOL

BLACK POWDER

LYMAN TRADE RIFLE

Lock: traditional cap or flint
Stock: walnut
Barrel: 28 in., 1:48 twist
Sights: adjustable open
Weight: 8.0 lbs.
Bore/Caliber: .50 or .54
Features: brass furniture
Caplock: $500
Flint: $525

PLAINS PISTOL

Lock: traditional caplock
Stock: walnut
Barrel: 6 in.
Sights: fixed
Weight: 2.2 lbs.
Bore/Caliber: .50 or .54
Features: iron furniture
Plains Pistol: $360
Kit:. $300

Markesbery Black Powder

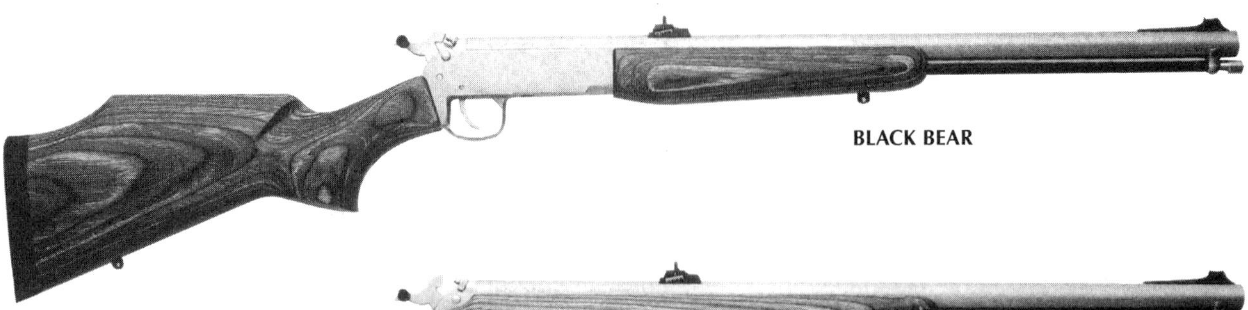

BLACK BEAR

BROWN BEAR

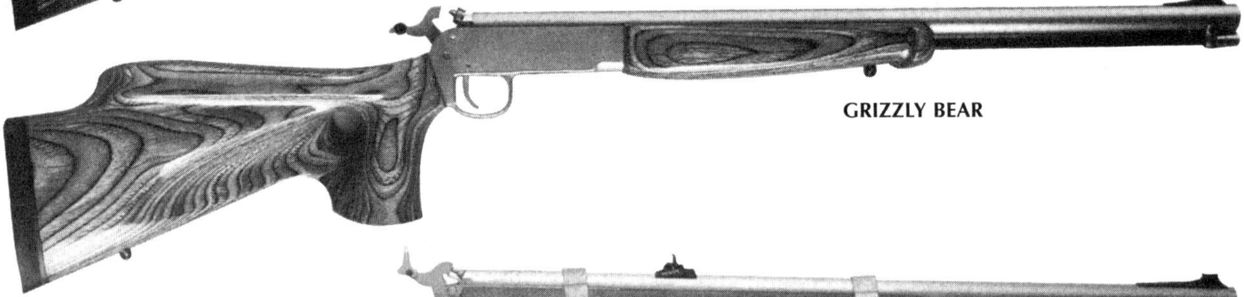

GRIZZLY BEAR

COLORADO ROCKY MOUNTAIN RIFLE

POLAR BEAR

BLACK BEAR

Lock: in-line
Stock: two-piece walnut, synthetic or laminated
Barrel: 24 in., 1:26 twist
Sights: adjustable open
Weight: 6.5 lbs.
Bore/Caliber: .36, .45, .50, .54
Features: also Grizzly Bear with thumbhole stock, Brown Bear with one-piece thumbhole stock, both checkered, aluminum ramrod
Black Bear: $532–556
Brown Bear: $658–680
Grizzly Bear: $642–664

POLAR BEAR

Lock: in-line
Stock: laminated
Barrel: 24 in., 1:26 twist
Sights: adjustable open
Weight: 7.8 lbs.
Bore/Caliber: .36, .45, .50, .54
Features: one-piece stock
MSRP: $536–570

Navy Arms Black Powder

1805 HARPER'S FERRY PISTOL

1805 HARPER'S FERRY PISTOL

Lock: traditional flintlock
Stock: walnut
Barrel: 10 in.
Sights: fixed
Weight: 2.75 lbs.
Bore/Caliber: .58
Features: browned rifled barrel; case-hardened lock
MSRP: $495

Pedersoli Black Powder

GIBBS SHOTGUN

GIBBS SHOTGUN

Lock: standard percussion
Stock: walnut
Barrel: 30.7 in.
Weight: 8.38 lbs.
Bore/Caliber: 12 ga.
Features: octagonal to round barrel; case hardened color-finished lock; grip and forend caps with ebony inserts; pistol grip stock
MSRP: $1214

SWISS MATCH STANDARD FLINTLOCK

Lock: flint
Stock: walnut
Barrel: 29.5 in.
Sights: adjustable
Weight: 16.9 lbs.
Bore/Caliber: .4
Features: octagonal; rust-brown finished 1:47 twist barrel; case-hardened color lock; double set trigger; steel ramrod; hook-shaped steel buttplate; moveable rear sight with windage and elevation adjustments
MSRP: $2700

SWISS MATCH FLINTLOCK

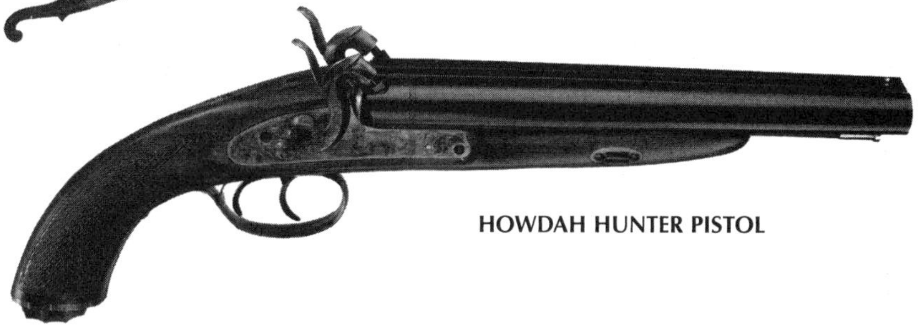

HOWDAH HUNTER PISTOL

HOWDAH HUNTER PISTOL

Lock: standard percussion
Stock: walnut
Barrel: 11.25 in. double
Weight: 4.41-5.07 lbs.
Bore/Caliber: 20 ga. or .50 cal.
Features: engraved locks with wild animals scenes; case-hardened color finish; checkered walnut pistol grip with steel butt cap
MSRP: $649

Pedersoli Black Powder

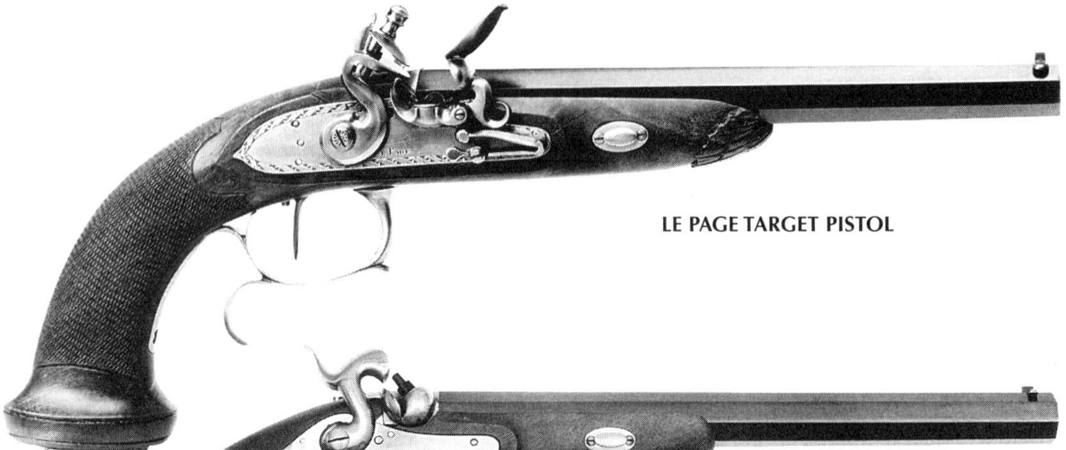

LE PAGE TARGET PISTOL

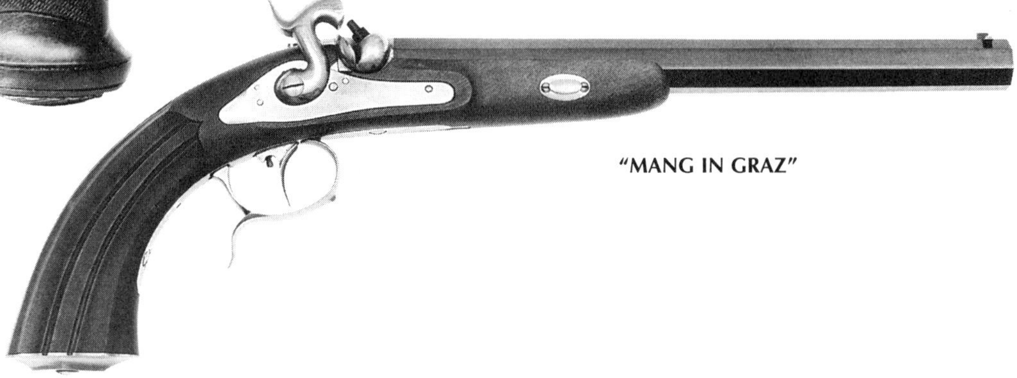

"MANG IN GRAZ"

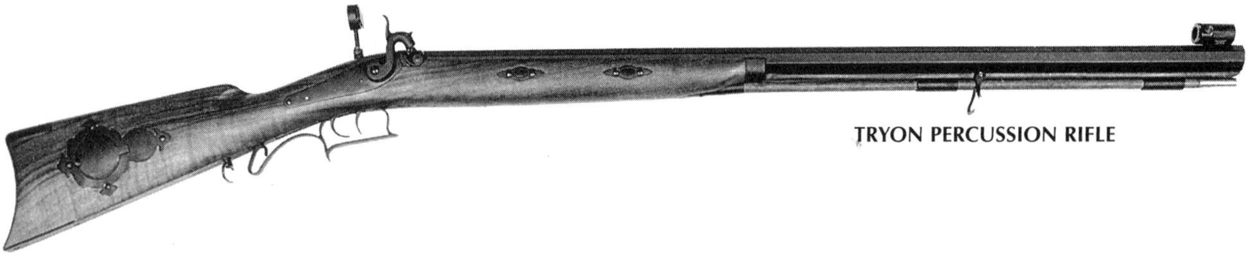

TRYON PERCUSSION RIFLE

LEPAGE TARGET PISTOL

Lock: traditional flintlock
Grips: walnut
Barrel: 10.5 in., 1:18 twist
Sights: fixed
Weight: 2.5 lbs.
Bore/Caliber: .44 or .45
Features: smoothbore .45 available
LePage flintlock: $880–1110
Percussion in .36, .38, .44: . $750–825

"MANG IN GRAZ"

Lock: traditional caplock
Grips: walnut
Barrel: 11 in., 1:15 or 1:18 (.44) twist
Sights: fixed
Weight: 2.5 lbs.
Bore/Caliber: .38 or .44
Features: grooved butt
MSRP: $1515

MORTIMER TARGET RIFLE

Lock: flintlock
Stock: English-style European walnut
Barrel: octagon to round 36 in.
Sights: target
Weight: 8.8 lbs.
Bore/Caliber: .54
Features: case-colored lock; stock has cheek piece and hand checkering; 7-groove barrel
MSRP: $975–1040

TRYON PERCUSSION RIFLE

Lock: traditional caplock
Stock: walnut
Barrel: 32 in., 1:48 or 1:66 (.54) twist
Sights: adjustable open
Weight: 9.5 lbs.
Bore/Caliber: .45, .50, .54
Features: Creedmoor version with aperture sight available
Tryon Percussion: $869
Creedmoor: $1200

Savage Black Powder

MODEL 10ML-11

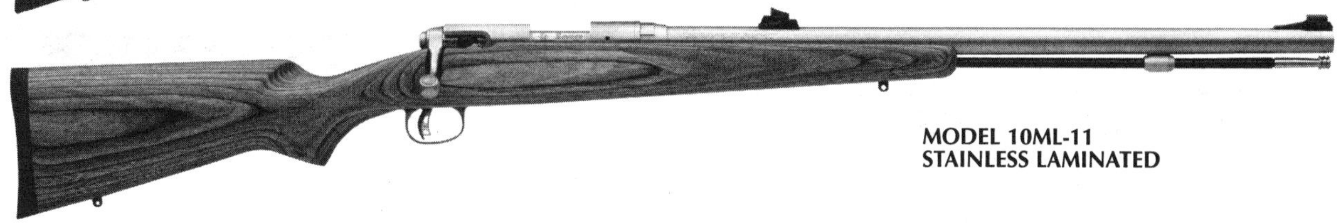

MODEL 10ML-11
STAINLESS LAMINATED

MODEL 10ML-11 MUZZLELOADER

Lock: in-line
Stock: synthetic, camo or laminated
Barrel: 24 in.
Sights: adjustable fiber optic
Weight: 8.0 lbs.
Bore/Caliber: .50
Features: bolt-action mechanism; 209 priming

Blue synthetic:............. $680
Stainless:.................. $758
Blue camo: $731
Stainless camo: $797
Stainless laminated:......... $908

Shiloh Black Powder

1863 SHARPS

1874 CREEDMOOR TARGET RIFLE
(WITHOUT SIGHTS)

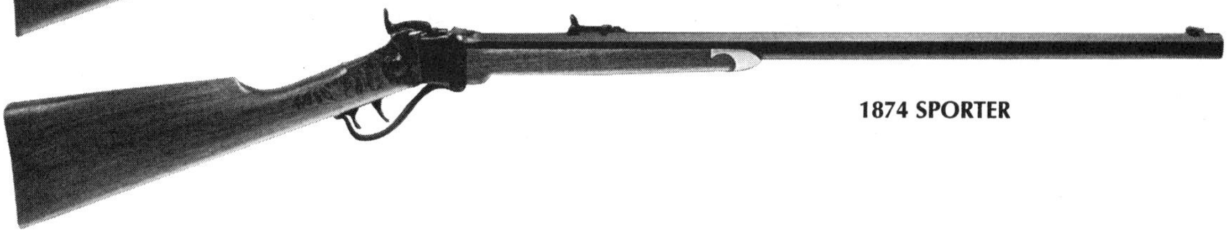

1874 SPORTER

MODEL 1863 SHARPS

Lock: traditional caplock
Stock: walnut ***Barrel:*** 30 in.
Sights: adjustable open
Weight: 9.5 lbs.
Bore/Caliber: .50 or .54
Features: sporting model with half-stock; double set trigger military model with 3-band full stock; also carbine with 22 in. barrel (7.5 lbs.)
Sporting rifle and carbine: .. $1800
Military rifle: $2092

MODEL 1874 CREEDMOOR TARGET

Lock: black powder cartridge
Stock: walnut
Barrel: 32 in. half octagon
Sights: none
Weight: 9.0 lbs.
Bore/Caliber: all popular black powder cartridges from .38-55 to .50-90
Features: shotgun buttstock, pistol grip; single trigger; fancy walnut, pewter tip
MSRP: $2743
#2 Creedmoor Silhouette (30 in. round, tapered barrel): ... $2743

Thompson/Center Black Powder

BLACK DIAMOND XR
MUZZLELOADING RIFLE

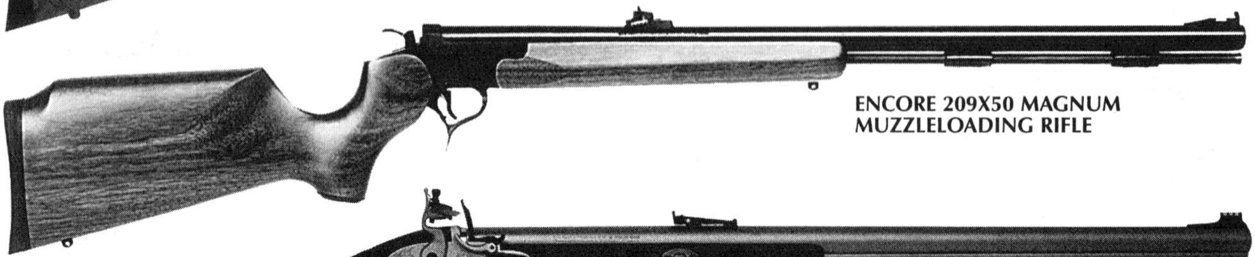

ENCORE 209X50 MAGNUM
MUZZLELOADING RIFLE

FIRE STORM

ENCORE 209X50 RIFLE

Lock: in-line
Stock: walnut or synthetic
Barrel: 26 in., 1:28 twist
Sights: adjustable fiber optic
Weight: 7.0 lbs.
Bore/Caliber: .50
Features: automatic safety; interchangeable barrel with Encore centerfire barrels; also available 209x45 9.45
Blue walnut: $722
Blue camo: $792
Stainless synthetic: $771
Stainless Camo: $832

FIRE STORM

Lock: traditional cap or flint
Stock: synthetic
Barrel: 26 in., 1:48 twist
Sights: adjustable fiber optic
Weight: 7.0 lbs.
Bore/Caliber: .50
Features: aluminum ramrod
Blue: $507
Stainless: $567

Always use the right muzzleloading projectile. A heavy, round-nosed bullet might drop 2 feet at 200 yards, while a lighter, sleeker, saboted bullet will only drop a foot. Guess which one is easier to connect with when that buck steps clear at 200 yards?

PRO HUNTER 209 X 50 MUZZLELOADER

TRIUMPH BLUED COMPOSITE

TRIUMPH CAMO COMPOSITE

TRIUMPH WEATHERSHIELD COMPOSITE

PRO HUNTER 209 X 50 MUZZLELOADER

Lock: in-line
Stock: FlexTech composite
Barrel: 28 in., stainless, fluted; interchangeable with shotgun and rifle barrels
Sights: fiber-optic
Weight: N/A
Bore/Caliber: .50
Features: stainless, fluted precision barrel—interchangeable with shotgun and rifle barrels; Swing Hammer design; engraved receiver; FlexTech (recoil system) composite stock in black or Realtree Hardwoods camo with or without thumbhole
Black:. $832–928
Realtree Hardwoods camo stainless: $991

TRIUMPH

Lock: in-line
Stock: composite, black or Realtree AP HD camo
Barrel: Weather Shield metal coating with QLA
Sights: none; Redfield scope bases and rings provided
Bore/Caliber: .50
Features: only four moving parts so there's no need to remove the trigger group, disassemble or use tools to clean the rifle; alloy receiver; tip-up barrel with Toggle Lock action; solid aluminum ramrod; SIMS Limbsaver recoil pad; sling swivel studs; breech plug (Speed Breech XT) can be removed by hand; Set trigger with automatic hammer block safety
MSRP: $428–559

Traditions Black Powder

1851 NAVY

1858 NEW ARMY

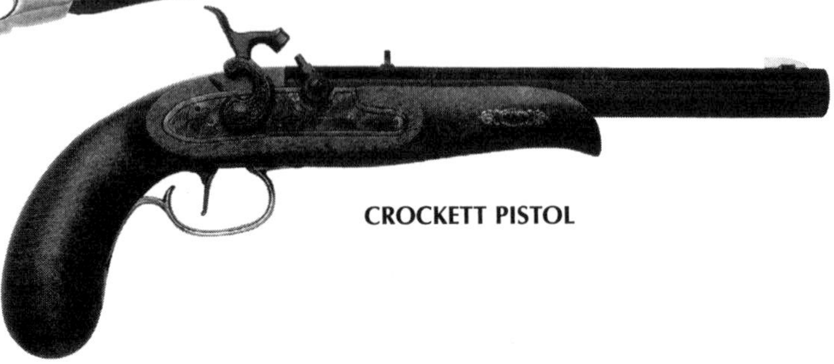

CROCKETT PISTOL

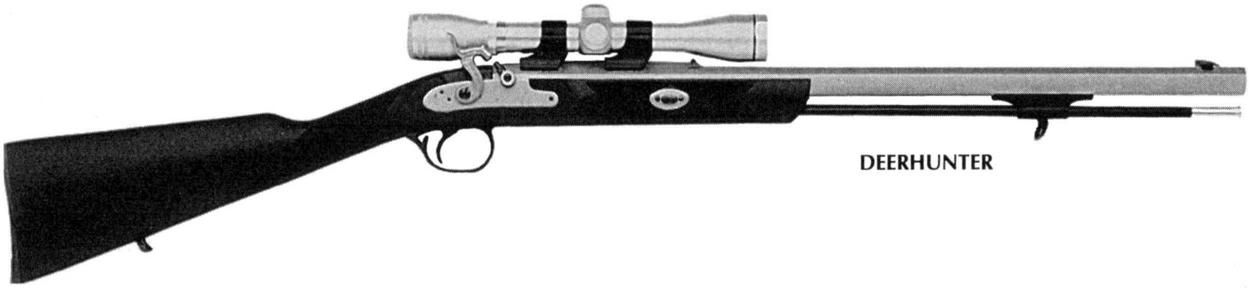

DEERHUNTER

1851 NAVY REVOLVER

Lock: caplock
Grips: walnut
Barrel: 7.5 in.
Sights: fixed
Weight: 2.7 lbs.
Bore/Caliber: .36
Features: blued, octagon barrel; steel or brass frame
Brass frame:. $239
Steel frame: $269
1851 Navy U.S. Marshall (old silver, 5 in. bbl.): $399
1851 Navy Old Silver (7.5 in. bbl.): $339

1858 NEW ARMY REVOLVER

Lock: caplock
Grips: walnut
Barrel: 8 in.
Sights: fixed
Weight: 2.6 lbs.
Bore/Caliber: .44
Features: octagon barrel; steel frame
1858 New Army (brass): $279
1858 New Army (steel): $329
1858 New Army (stainless): . . . $549

1860 ARMY REVOLVER

Lock: caplock
Grips: walnut
Barrel: 8 in.
Sights: fixed
Weight: 2.8 lbs.
Bore/Caliber: .44
Features: blued; round barrel; steel or brass frame
Brass frame:. $260
Steel frame: $299
Nickel:. $349

CROCKETT PISTOL

Lock: traditional caplock
Grips: hardwood
Barrel: 10 in.
Sights: fixed
Weight: 2.0 lbs.
Bore/Caliber: .32 caplock
Features: blued, octagon barrel
MSRP: $229

DEERHUNTER RIFLE

Lock: traditional cap or flint
Stock: hardwood, synthetic or camo
Barrel: 24 in., 1:48 twist
Sights: fixed
Weight: 6.0 lbs.
Bore/Caliber: .32, .50, .54
Features: blackened furniture; also economy-model Panther, 24 in .50 or .54
Cap, nickel, synthetic:. $239
Flint, blue, synthetic:. $279
Flint, nickel, synthetic: $299
Cap, blue, hardwood: $279
Flint, blue, hardwood:. $339

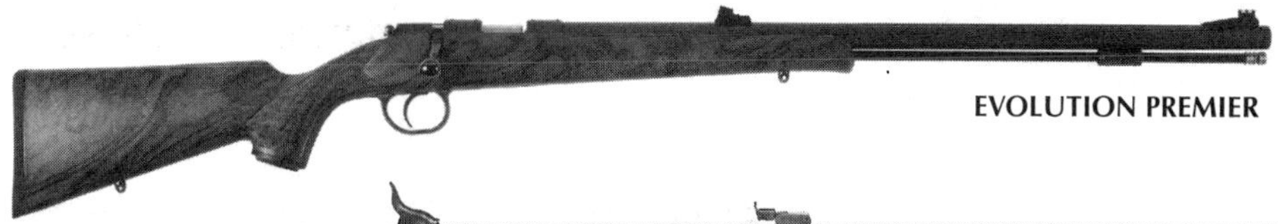
EVOLUTION PREMIER

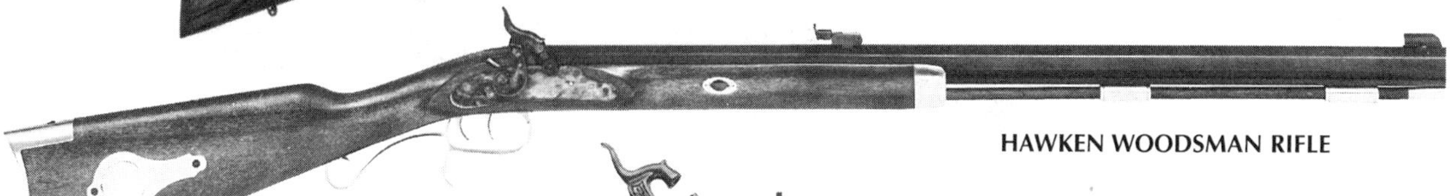
HAWKEN WOODSMAN RIFLE

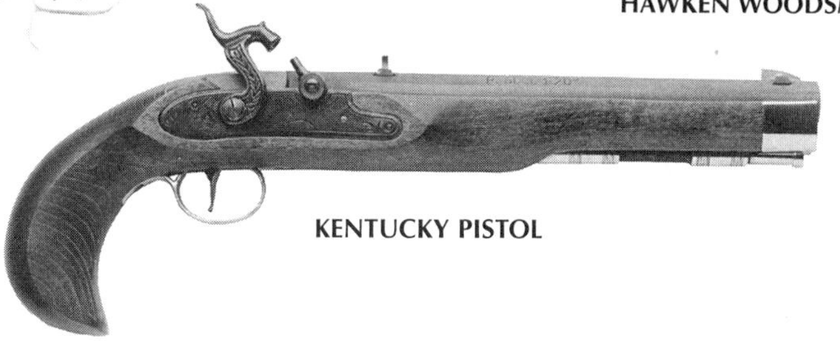
KENTUCKY PISTOL

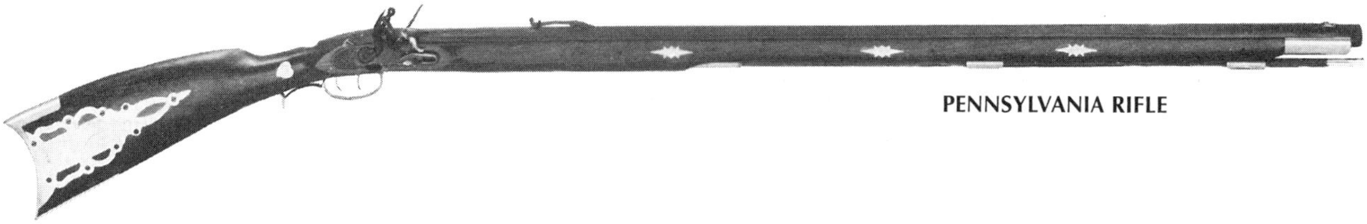
PENNSYLVANIA RIFLE

EVOLUTION

Lock: bolt
Stock: synthetic, laminated or camo
Barrel: 26 in.
Sights: fiber optics
Weight: 7.0 lbs.
Bore/Caliber: .50
Features: fluted, tapered barrel, drilled & tapped for scope; 209 ignition; swivel studs, rubber butt pad; LD model in .45 or .50 has Tru-Glo sights.
LD nickel synthetic: $230
LD nickel camo: $240

EXPRESS DOUBLE OVER & UNDER MUZZLELOADER

Lock: 209 primer top break
Stock: synthetic ***Barrel:*** 24 in.
Sights: adjustable ***Weight:*** 12.5 lbs.
Bore/Caliber: .50
Features: double barrel over/under; 209-ignition system; blued barrels; double trigger, top tang safety; fiber optic sights; drilled & tapped for a scope
MSRP: $1599–1766
Close-out $799

HAWKEN WOODSMAN RIFLE

Lock: traditional cap or flint
Stock: beech
Barrel: 28 in., 1:48 twist
Sights: adjustable open
Weight: 7.7 lbs.
Bore/Caliber: .50 or .54
Features: brass furniture
Caplock: $429
Left-hand caplock: $439
Flintlock: $469

KENTUCKY PISTOL

Lock: traditional caplock
Grips: beech ***Barrel:*** 10 in.
Sights: fixed ***Weight:*** 2.5 lbs.
Bore/Caliber: .50
Features: brass furniture
MSRP: $219

PENNSYLVANIA RIFLE

Lock: traditional cap or flint
Stock: walnut
Barrel: 20 in., 1:66 twist
Sights: adjustable open
Weight: 8.5 lbs.
Bore/Caliber: .50
Features: brass furniture
MSRP: $719–789

Traditions Black Powder

SHENANDOAH RIFLE

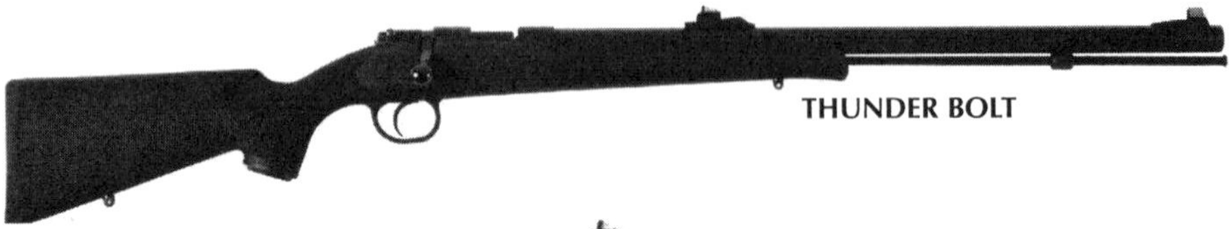
THUNDER BOLT

TRACKER 209

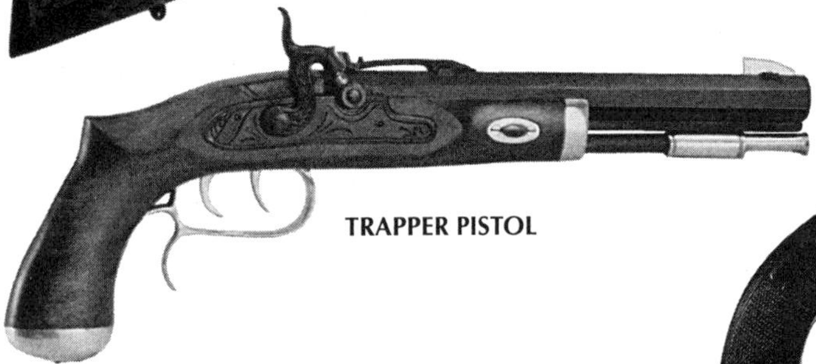
TRAPPER PISTOL

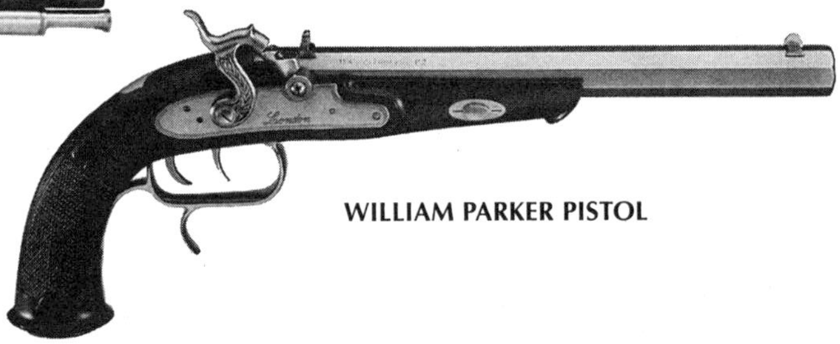
WILLIAM PARKER PISTOL

PURSUIT LT BREAK OPEN

Lock: break-open, 209 ignition system
Grips: synthetic
Barrel: 28 in. ***Sights:*** adjustable
Weight: 8.25 lbs.
Bore/Caliber: .45
Features: 209-ignition; fluted barrel; cross block trigger safety; fiber optic sights
Nickel/black: $289
Realtree Hardwoods/blue: $329

SHENANDOAH RIFLE

Lock: traditional cap or flint
Stock: beech
Barrel: 33 in., 1:66 twist
Sights: fixed
Weight: 7.2 lbs.
Bore/Caliber: .50
Features: brass furniture; squirrel rifle in .36
Caplock: $599
Flintlock: $629
Caplock .36: $599
Flintlock .36: $659
Kentucky,
flint or caplock: $455

THUNDER BOLT

Lock: bolt
Stock: synthetic
Barrel: 24 in. (21 in. youth)
Sights: adjustable
Weight: 7.0 lbs.
Bore/Caliber: .45 or. 50
Features: 209-ignition; checkered stock; sling swivels; rubber butt pad; drilled & tapped for scope
Blue synthetic: $163
Blue camo: $163
Nickel camo: $322

TRACKER 209

Lock: in-line
Stock: synthetic or camo
Barrel: 22 in., 1:28 twist (1:24 .45)
Sights: fiber optic
Weight: 6.5 lbs.
Bore/Caliber: .45 or .50
Features: 209 primer ignition
Blue synthetic: $169
Nickel synthetic: $189

TRAPPER PISTOL

Lock: traditional cap or flint
Grips: beech
Barrel: 9.8 in.
Sights: adjustable open
Weight: 2.9 lbs.
Bore/Caliber: .50
Features: brass furniture
Trapper: $299
Flintlock: $329

WILLIAM PARKER PISTOL

Lock: traditional caplock
Grips: walnut
Barrel: 10.4 in.
Sights: fixed
Weight: 2.3 lbs.
Bore/Caliber: .50
Features: checkered with brass furniture
MSRP: $399

Uberti Black Powder

1847 WALKER

1848 DRAGOON

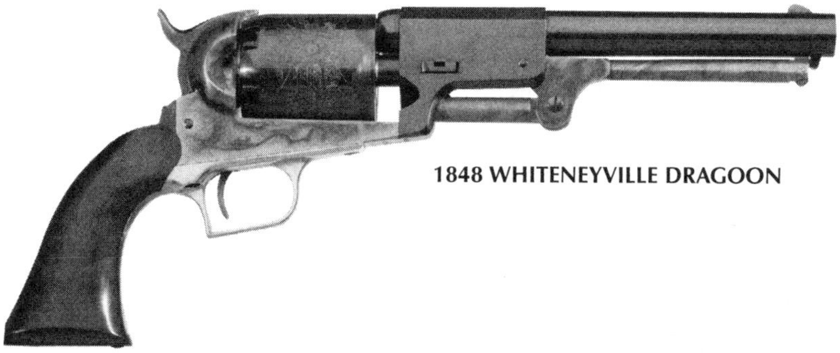

1848 WHITENEYVILLE DRAGOON

1851 NAVY REVOLVER

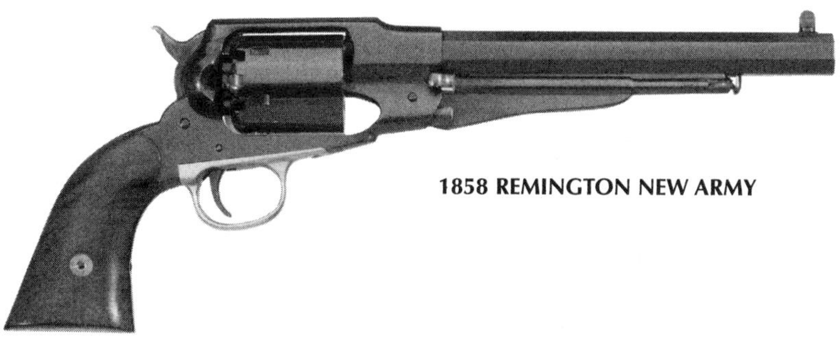

1858 REMINGTON NEW ARMY

WALKER

Lock: caplock revolver
Grips: walnut grips
Barrel: 9 in.
Sights: fixed, open
Weight: 71.2 oz.
Bore/Caliber: .44
Features: color case-hardened frame; brass trigger guard
MSRP: $429

1848 DRAGOON

Lock: caplock revolver
Grips: walnut
Barrel: 7.5 in.
Sights: fixed, open
Weight: 64.9 oz.
Bore/Caliber: .44
Features: comes in 1st, 2nd and 3rd models; color case-hardened frame; brass trigger guard
1848 Dragoon: $409
1848 Whiteneyville Dragoon: . . $429

1851 NAVY REVOLVER

Lock: caplock revolver
Grips: walnut
Barrel: 7.5 in.
Sights: fixed, open
Weight: 44.8 oz.
Bore/Caliber: .36
Features: color case-hardened frame; brass round or square trigger-guard
MSRP: $329

1858 REMINGTON NEW ARMY

Lock: caplock revolver
Grips: walnut
Barrel: 8 in.
Sights: fixed, open
Weight: 44.8 oz.
Bore/Caliber: .44
Features: octagonal barrel; brass trigger guard, blue finish
New Army: $349
Stainless: $429
18 in. barrel, carbine: $549

Uberti Black Powder

1860 ARMY REVOLVER

Lock: caplock revolver
Grips: walnut
Barrel: 8 in.
Sights: fixed, open
Weight: 41.6 oz.
Bore/Caliber: .44
Features: color case-hardened frame
1860 Army:. $339
Fluted cylinder: $349

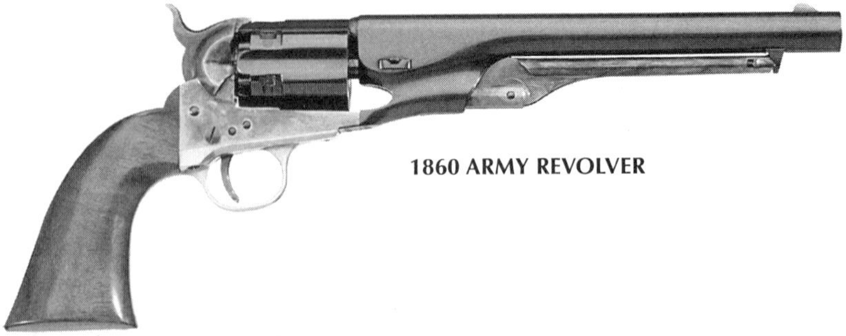

1860 ARMY REVOLVER

1861 NAVY REVOLVER

Lock: caplock revolver
Grips: walnut
Barrel: 7.5 in. ***Sights:*** fixed, open
Weight: 44.8 oz.
Bore/Caliber: .36
Features: color case-hardened frame; brass or steel trigger-guard
MSRP: $349

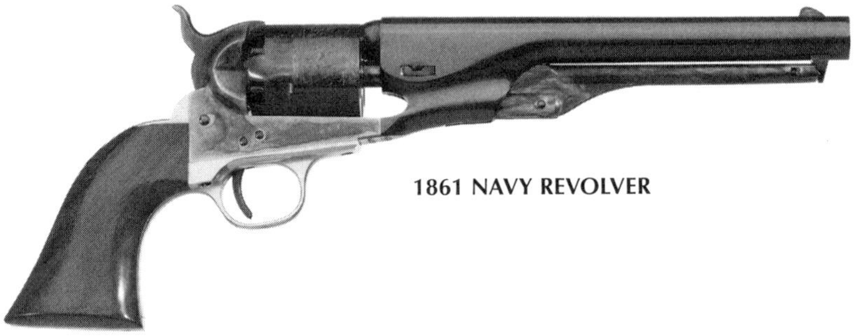

1861 NAVY REVOLVER

1862 POCKET NAVY

Lock: caplock revolver
Grips: walnut
Barrel: 5.5 or 6.5 in.
Sights: fixed, open
Weight: 26.9 oz.
Bore/Caliber: .36
Features: color case-hardened frame; 6-shot cylinder; forged steel barrel, brass backstrap and trigger guard.
MSRP: $349

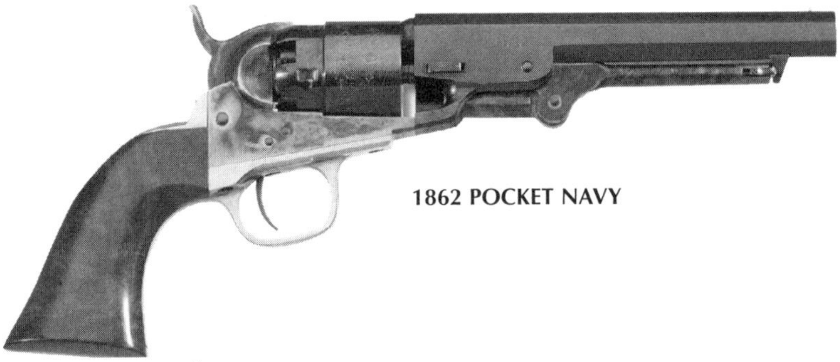

1862 POCKET NAVY

1862 POLICE

Lock: caplock revolver
Grips: walnut
Barrel: 5.5 or 6.5 in.
Sights: fixed, open
Weight: 26.9 oz.
Bore/Caliber: .36
Features: color case-hardened frame; 6-shot cylinder; forged steel barrel; brass backstrap and trigger guard.
MSRP: $349

1862 POLICE

1848-1849 POCKET REVOLVERS

Lock: caplock revolver
Grips: walnut
Barrel: 4 in.
Sights: fixed, open
Weight: 23.8 - 24.9 oz.
Bore/Caliber: .31
Features: color case-hardened frame; 5-shot cylinders; forged steel barrel, brass backstrap and trigger guard.
1849 Wells Fargo:. $339
1849 Pocket:. $339

1849 POCKET

White Rifles Black Powder

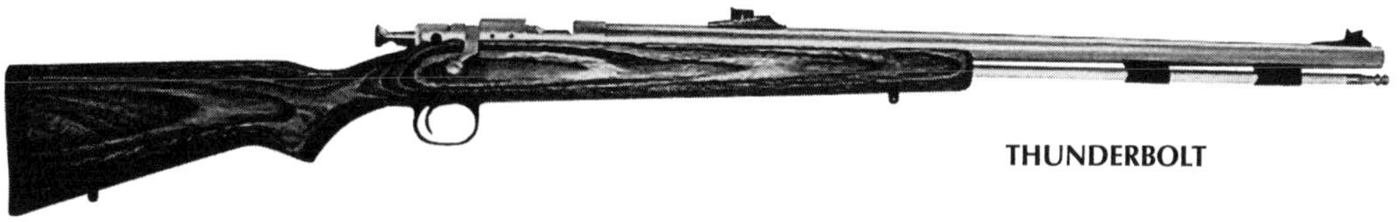

THUNDERBOLT

HUNTER SERIES

Lock: in-line
Stock: synthetic or laminated
Barrel: stainless, 22 in. (24 in. Elite)
Sights: fiber-optic
Weight: 7.7 lbs.
Bore/Caliber: .45 or .50
Features: elite weighs 8.6 lbs.; aluminum ramrod with bullet extractor; also: Thunderbolt bolt action with 209-ignition, 26 in. barrel

Whitetail:.................. $399
Blacktail and Elite: $499
Thunderbolt:............... $699
Odyssey (ss/laminated thumbhole stock):....... $1299

BLACK POWDER

Alpen Optics Scopes

APEX 3.5-10x50

KODIAK 4-12

APEX AND KODIAK SCOPES

Alpen Optics offers two lines of riflescopes, comprising 11 models. Apex variables feature fully multi-coated lens systems, plus resettable finger-adjustable windage and elevation adjustments with 1/4-min. clicks. Kodiak scopes are fully waterproof and fogproof.

APEX SCOPES				
Magnification (x obj. dia.)	Field of View (ft., 100 yds)	Dia./Length (in.)	Weight (oz.)	MSRP
3-9x42	40/14	1/12.5	17	$319
3.5-10x50	28-10	1/12.8	17	$363
4-16x50	23.6/-62	1/14.8	23	$269
6-24x50	15-4	1/16	16	$418

KODIAK SCOPES				
Magnification (x obj. dia.)	Field of View (ft., 100 yds)	Dia./Length (in.)	Weight (oz.)	MSRP
4x32	34	1/12.3	12	$75
1.5-4.5x32	50-21	1/11.7	14	$86
3-9x32	37-14	1/12	12	$77
3-9x40	42-14	1/13	13	$136
2.5-10x44	42-12	1/13	20	$129
3.5-10x50	35-12	1/13.2	21	$189
4-12x40	32-11	1/13.4	16	$165
6-24x50	18-6	1/16.2	26	$218

BSA Scopes

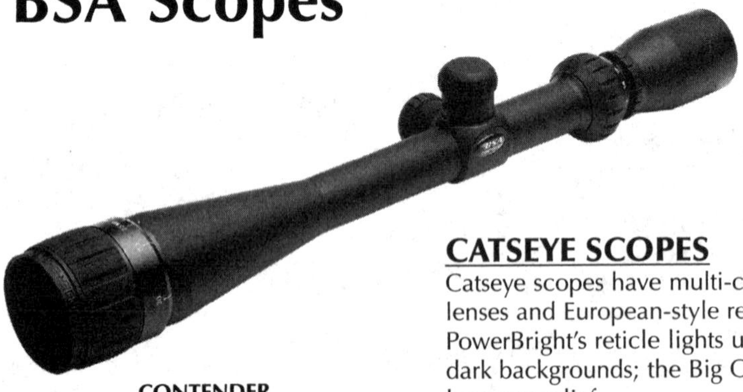

CONTENDER

CATSEYE SCOPES

Catseye scopes have multi-coated lenses and European-style reticles; the PowerBright's reticle lights up against dark backgrounds; the Big Cat has long eye relief

3-12x44: $229.95
3.5-10x50: $219.95
3.5-10x50 Illum. Reticle: $239.95
4-16x50 AO: $229.95
6-24x50: $239.95

CONTENDER SCOPES

Feature multicoated lenses; eyepiece focusing from -4 to +4 diopter for duplex reticle; focusing for 10 yds. & 300 yds.; power ring & turret caps; finger adjustable windage & elevation

3-12x40 A/O TT: $219.95
4-16x40 A/O TT: $199.95
6-24x40mm A/O TT:.............$219.95

BSA Scopes

HUNTSMAN 3-9x40

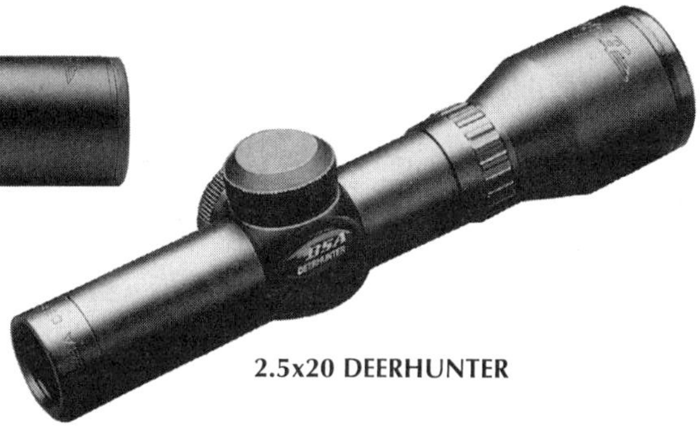

2.5x20 DEERHUNTER

DEERHUNTER SCOPES

Deerhunter Scopes are nitrogen gas filled and feature a one piece, 1 in. tube; camera quality lenses; black textured finish; easy focus eyepiece

1.5-4.5x32mm: $80
2.5-10x44mm: $110
2.5x20mm (Shotgun): $49.95
3-9x40mm: .... : $69.95
3-9x40mm Illuminated Reticle: $130
3-9x40mm: $124.95
3-9x50mm: $89.95

HUNTSMAN SCOPES

The Huntsman series features multi-coated lenses, finger-adjustable windage and elevation and generous eye relief; warranted waterproof, fogproof and shockproof

3-12x50mm: $119.95
3-9x40mm: $109.95
4-16x40mm: $114.95
18x40mmAO: $129.95

MIL-DOT SCOPES

Mil-Dot scopes have multicoated objective & ocular lenses; eyepiece focusing from -4 to +4 diopter for dupleX reticle; finger adjustable windage & elevation knobs

4-16x40: $99.95
6-24x40: $149.95
6-24x40 Illum.: $179.95
4-16x40 Illum.: $159.95

PANTHER ALL-WEATHER SCOPES

Feature BSA Standard Reticles; fully multicoated camera quality glass lenses; ocular speed focus; European style eyeball; finger adjustable windage and elevation with "push/pull" locking system

2.5-10x44: $99.95

PLATINUM TARGET SCOPES

Platinum target scopes are fitted with finger-adjustable windage and elevation dials; these scopes have a three-piece objective lens systems

PT 6-24x44 AO: $149.95–159.95
PT 8-32x44 AO: $149.95–179.95
PT 6-24x44 AO
Mildot Reticle: $169.95–179.95
PT 8-32x44 AO
Mildot Reticle: $169.95–179.95

SWEET 17 SCOPES

Designed for the .17 HMR, these scopes feature a 1-in. mounting tube; fully-coated optics; finger-adjustable windage and elevation

2-7x32 A/O: $89.95
3-12x40: $129.95
6-18x40: $169.95

SCOPES

Brunton Scopes

BRUNTON LITE-TECH 1.5-6X40

Features: Fully Broadband Multi-Coated lenses, waterproof/fogproof/shockproof. Available in 1.5-6x40 to 6-24x50 with Mil Dot or duplex reticle.

MSRP: $104–194

BRUNTON ECHO 6-24X50

Features: Fully Broadband Multi-Coated lenses, waterproof/fogproof/shockproof. Available in 1.5-5x20 to 6-24x50 with glass-etched Mil Dot, Duplex or Ballistic reticle.

MSRP: $148–448

Burris Scopes

BURRIS AR-332 PRISM SIGHT

Features: 3x tactical prism sight, waterproof to 5m, compact with Ballistic/CQ (close quarters) reticle, 1/3 MOA clicks, multicoated lenses and Picatinny rail mounting bracket, length: 5 inches, weight: 14 oz., matte black.

MSRP: $319

BURRIS AR TRIPLER

Features: 3x magnification with dot sight (or flip it away when you don't need it). Mounts with AR-Pivot Ring or other 30mm fixed mount. Wire tethers prevent loss of caps. Waterproof to 5 meters.

MSRP: $199

BURRIS SIXX 2-12X50

Features: 6x magnification range, 4.5 inches eye relief, fixed position eye piece, 30mm tube, tactile rubber coated power ring, rapid-adjust diopter setting, HiLume StormCoat lens finish, waterproof/shockproof/fogproof, matte finish, 2-12x50 or 2-12x40.

MSRP: $1051–1201

BURRIS XTR 3-12X50 (ALSO 1.5-6X40, 6-24X50)

Features: Fully multi-coated, Ballistic Mil-Dot reticle calibrated for 7.62-175MK and 5.56-77MK loads, turret parallax dial, tactical adjustment knobs, coyote brown finish on 30mm tube with walls 25% thicker for greater strength.

MSRP: $1080

AR-322 PRISM SIGHT

AR TRIPLER

SIXX 2-12X50

XTR 3-12X50

Burris Scopes

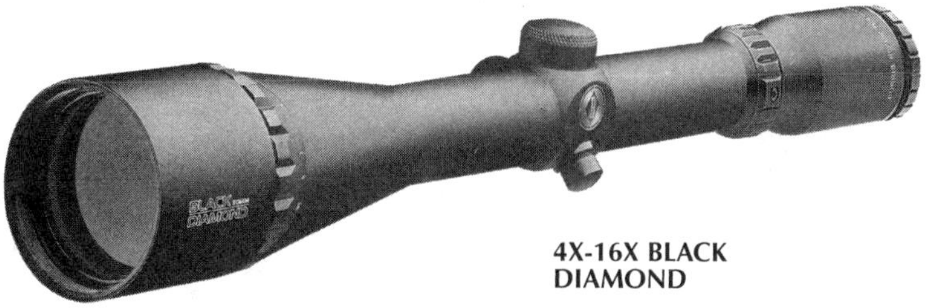

4X-16X BLACK DIAMOND

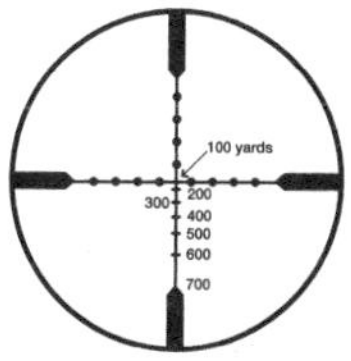

BALLISTIC MIL-DOT

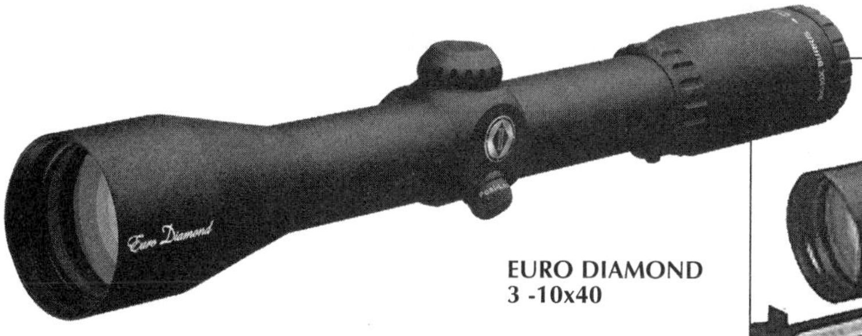

EURO DIAMOND 3 -10x40

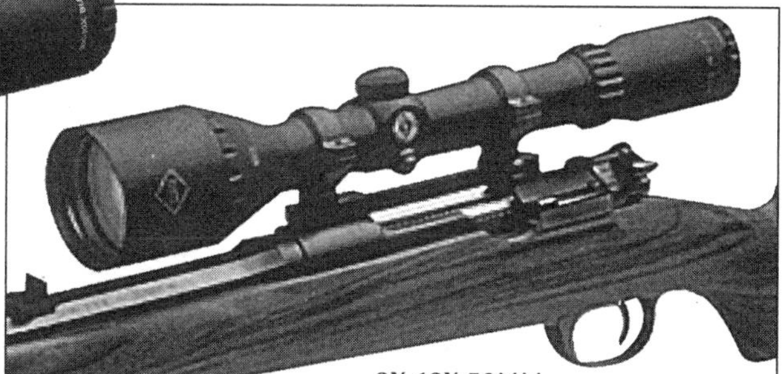

3X-12X-50MM

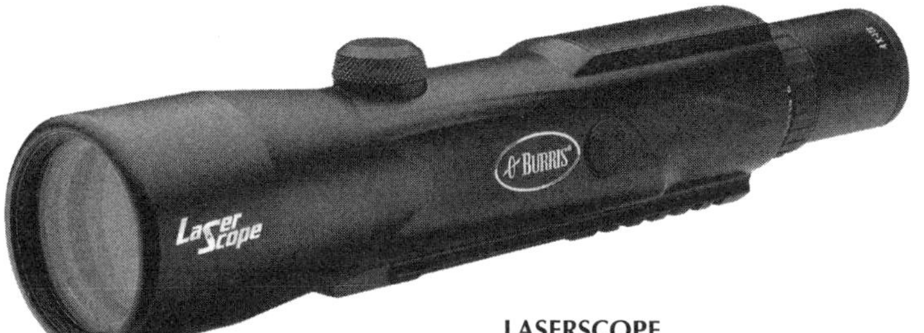

LASERSCOPE

BLACK DIAMOND RIFLESCOPES

Features a 50mm objective and heavy 30mm matte finish tube. The Black Diamond line includes three models of a 30mm main tube with various finishes, reticles and adjustment knobs. These scopes have rubber-armored parallax-adjust rings, an adjustable and resettable adjustment dial and an internal focusing eyepiece. Available with BallPlex, Ballistic Mildot, BallM-Dot/PosiLock reticles. Black Diamond Titanium scopes are made of solid titanium, coated with molecularly bonded aluminum titanium nitride. Black Diamond Titanium scope lenses have a scratch-proof T-Plate coating applied to the objective and eyepiece lenses.

EURO DIAMOND SCOPES

All Euro Diamond scopes come in matte black finish, with fully multi-coated lenses and ¼-min. clicks on resettable dials. Eye relief is 3½ to 4 in. The eyepiece and power ring are integrated and the scopes have a helical rear ocular ring. Options include: ballistic Plex or German 3P#4 reticle and PosiLock or illuminated.

FULLFIELD II VARIABLE SCOPES

Feature one piece main tubes; multi-coated lenses; one-piece power ring/eyepiece; soft rubber eyeguard; double integral springs; available with Ballistic Plex, Ballistic Mildot, Fine Plex reticles; finished in matte, silver or black; nitrogen filled with special quad seals.

LASERSCOPE

Burris' LaserScope is the successful integration of a laser rangefinder and a quality riflescope into an affordable package that stands up under severe recoil and with a moderate size and weight. The Burris Ballistic Plex reticle incorporated in the LaserScope lets you quickly range the target, hold dead on and squeeze off your shot without losing sight of your target. Although fully functional as a self-contained single unit, the LaserScope also comes with a remote activation switch that straps to the forearm of a rifle to allow more convenient and steady operation of the laser.

LIGHTED RETICLE SCOPES

The Burris Electro-Dot adds a bright pinpoint aiming spot to the center of the crosshair. Available with Ballistic Plex or Fast Plex reticles. Battery Life: Medium Power—50-60 hrs; High Power—40-50 hrs.

Burris Scopes

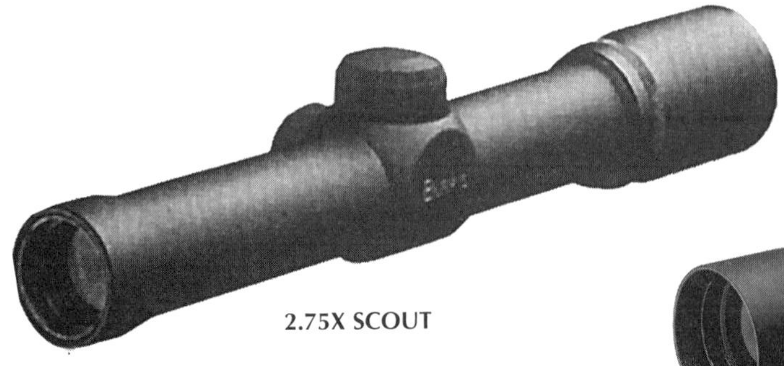

2.75X SCOUT

3-9X SHORT MAG SCOPE

4.5-14X SHORT MAG SCOPE

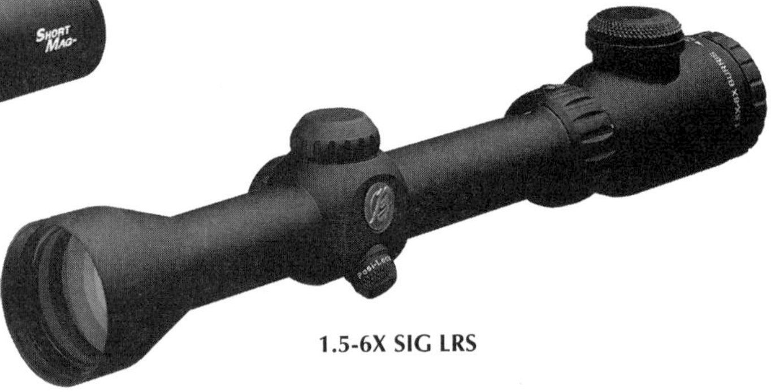

1.5-6X SIG LRS

3x10 SIG LRS

SCOUT SCOPES

For hunters who need a 7- to 14-in. eye relief for mounting in front of the ejection port; this scope allows you to shoot with both eyes open. The 15-ft. field of view and 2.75X magnification are ideal for brush guns and shotgunners.

SHORT MAG SCOPES

Short Mag riflescopes feature top grade optical glass and index-matched HiLume lens multicoatings; generous 3½-5 in. eye relief; re-settable windage and elevation dials. Lens system formulation combines edge-to-edge clarity with 3½-5 in. of light rifle magnum eye relief. Each variable power Short Mag features a Ballistic Plex reticle.

SIGNATURE SCOPES

Features include premium quality lenses with Hi-Lume multi-coat; large internal lenses; deep relief grooves on the power ring and parallax adjust ring and centrally located adjustment turret; shooter-viewable, easy-to-grip power ring integrated with the eyepiece; non-slip ring of rubber on the internally focusable eyepiece ring. Available with Ball Plex, Ball Plex/PosiLock, Ballistic MilDot and 3P#4/PossiLock reticles.

Burris Scopes

Item	Model	Reticle	Finish	Features	List
BLACK DIAMOND T-PLATES SCOPES (30MM)					
200929	4X-16X-50-mm	Ballistic MDot	mat	PA	$1212
BLACK DIAMOND SCOPES (30MM)					
200955	4X-16X-50-mm	Ballistic MDot	mat	Side PA	$1212
200926	4X-16X-50-mm	Ballistic Plex	mat	—	$1130
200933	6X-24X-50-mm	Fine Plex	mat	Tar-Side /PA	$1224
200934	6X-24X-50-mm	Ballistic MDot	mat	Tar-Side /PA	$1339
200942	8X-32X-50-mm	Fine Plex	mat	Tar-Side /PA	$1226
200943	8X-32X-50-mm	Ballistic MDot	mat	Tar-Side /PA	$1416
EURO DIAMOND SCOPES					
200960	1.5X-6X-40-mm	German 3P#4	mat	Posi-Lock	$835
200966	3X-10X-40-mm	Ballistic Plex	mat	—	$862
200918	2.5X-10X-44mm	Ballistic Plex	mat	—	$888
200915	3X-12X-50-mm	German 3P#4	mat	Illuminated	$1108
200916	3X-12X-50-mm	Ballistic Plex	mat	—	$955
Fullfield II Scopes					
200052	6X-40mm	Plex	mat		$397
200154	3X-9X-50-mm	Ballistic Plex	mat	—	$524

Item	Model	Reticle	Finish	Features	List
200160	3X-9X-40-mm	Plex	blk	—	$331
200161	3X-9X-40-mm	Plex	mat	—	$331
200162	3X-9X-40-mm	Ballistic Plex	mat	—	$349
200163	3X-9X-40-mm	Plex	nic	—	$384
200169	3X-9X-40-mm	Ballistic Plex	nic	—	$384
200172	3.5X-10X-50mm	Ballistic Plex	mat	—	$608
200180	4.5X-14X	Plex	blk	PA	$611
200181	4.5X-14X	Plex	mat	PA	$611
200191	6.5X-20X-50mm	Fine Plex	mat	PA	$731
200193	6.5X-20X-50mm	Ballistic MDot	mat	PA	$856
LASERSCOPES					
200111	4-12x42mm	XTR Ballistic Mil-Dot	mat	Remote activation	$1176
LRS LIGHTED RETICLE SCOPES					
200719	1.5X-6X-40 Sig Select	Electro-Dot	mat	—	$667
200772	4X-16X-44 Sig Select	Ballistic Plex	mat	PA	$1078

Item	Model	Reticle	Finish	Features	List
SCOUT SCOPES					
200269	2.75X	Heavy Plex	mat	—	$391
SIGNATURE SERIES SCOPES					
200717	1.5X-6X-40-mm	Taper Plex	mat	—	$667
200560	3X-10X-40-mm	Ballistic Plex	mat	—	$738
200616	3X-12X-44-mm	Ballistic Plex	mat	—	$778
200617	3X-12X-44-mm	Ballistic Plex	mat	Posi-Lock	$831

Item	Model	Reticle	Finish	Features	List
200768	4X-16X-44-mm	Ballistic Plex	mat	PA	$844
200769	4X-16X-44-mm	Ballistic Mdot	mat	PA	$937
200770	4X-16X-44-mm	Ballistic Plex	mat	Posi-Lock/PA	$1078
200823	6X-24X-44mm	Fine Plex	mat	Target/PA	$912
200824	6X-24X-44-mm	Ballistic MDot	mat	Target/PA	$1031
200867	8X-32X	Fine Plex	mat	Target/PA	$922
200868	8X-32X	Ballistic MDot	mat	Target/PA	$1039

Bushnell Riflescopes

ELITE 2.5-10X50

ELITE 2.5-16

ELITE 4.5-30

ELITE 6500 SERIES

a 6.5x magnification range (1:6.5 ratio from low to high power); push/pull turrets with resettable zero for easy sighting-in.; extended range of windage and elevation travel (60 inches on the 2.5-16x models), with .25 MOA quick adjust clicks, suitable for a broad range of game and distances; all models have a one-piece, 30mm tube to deliver plenty of light, and up to 4 inches of eye relief and a finer Multi-X reticle (Mil Dot versions of each model are also available); each model has side parallax adjustment; the 2.5x models can be adjusted from 10 yards to infinity and the 4.5 x models adjusts from 25 yards to infinity

Model	Field of View @100 yds.	Eye Relief (in.)	Click Value @ 100 yds.	Length (in.)	Weight (oz.)	Reticle	MSRP
2.5-16x42	41 ft @ 2.5 x 6.55 ft. @ 16x	3.9	0.25 in.	13.5	17.3	Multi-X or Mil-Dot	$749
2.5-16x50	42 ft @ 2.5 x 7 ft. @ 16x	3.9	0.25 in.	13.5	21.0	Multi-X or Mil-Dot	$779
4.5-30x50	21.6 ft @ 4.5 x 3.4 ft. @ 30x	4.0	0.25 in.	13.5	21.0	Multi-X or Mil-Dot	$899

BUSHNELL ELITE 3200 WITH DOA 600

Features: Fully multi-coated lenses with Rainguard coating for a clear image in wet weather. One-piece, 1-inch aluminum tube, waterproof/fogproof/shockproof, ¼ MOA. Available with DOA 600 (Dead On Accuracy) reticle in 3-9x40 and 4-12x40 in matte finish. Extended-yardage aiming points reach to 600 yards with most rounds.
MSRP: **. $300–400**

Bushnell Riflescopes

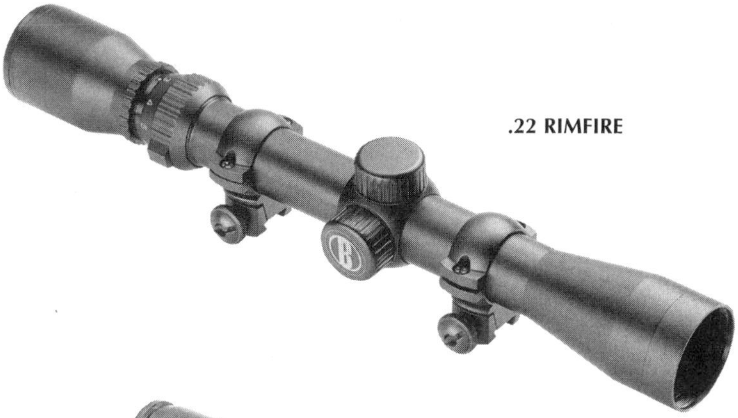

.22 RIMFIRE

BANNER

.22 RIMFIRE RIFLESCOPES

Bushnell .22 Rimfire scopes are designed with a 50-yd parallax setting and fully coated optics. The one-piece 1 in. tube is waterproof and fogproof; 1/4 MOA windage and elevation adjustments are fingertip-easy to turn. Scopes come with rings for grooved receivers.

BANNER RIFLESCOPES

Banner Dusk & Dawn riflescopes feature DDB multi-coated lenses to maximize dusk and dawn brightness for clarity in low and full light. A fast-focus eyepiece and wide-angle field of view complement a one-piece tube and 1/4 in. MOA resettable windage and elevation adjustments. An easy-trip power change ring allows fast power changes. This scope is waterproof, fogproof and shockproof.

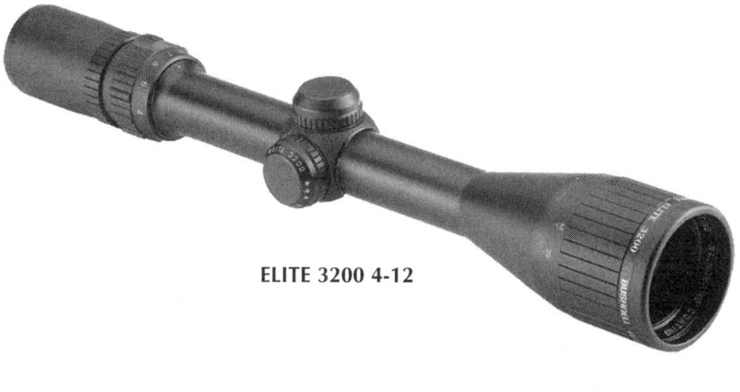

ELITE 3200 4-12

ELITE 3200 RIFLESCOPES

Riflescopes are made with multi-coated optics and a patented Rainguard lens coating that reduces large water drops to near-microscopic specks. Bushnell's FireFly reticle is available on several 3200 models, illuminating the crosshairs. The FireFly reticle glows green after a 10-second flashlight charge. Elite 3200 riflescopes are dry-nitrogen filled and feature a one-piece hammer-forged aluminum tube, 1/4 MOA fingertip, audible/ resettable windage and elevation adjustment and are waterproof, fogproof, and shockproof.

Bushnell Riflescopes

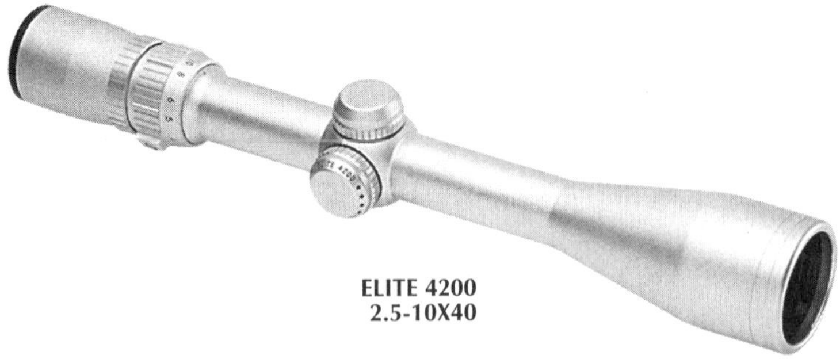

ELITE 4200
2.5-10X40

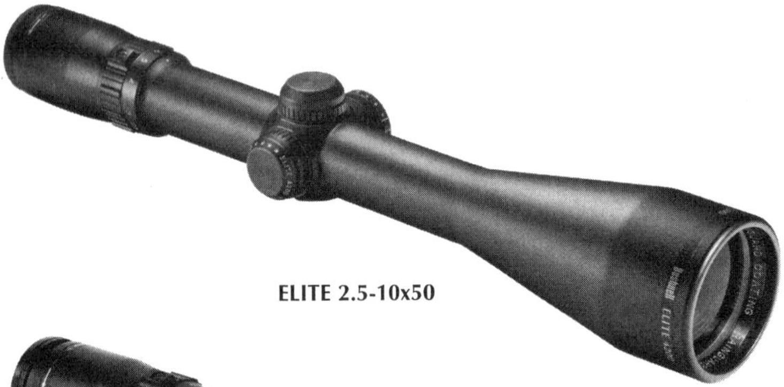

ELITE 2.5-10x50

ELITE 3-9x40

ELITE 4200
1.5-4X24

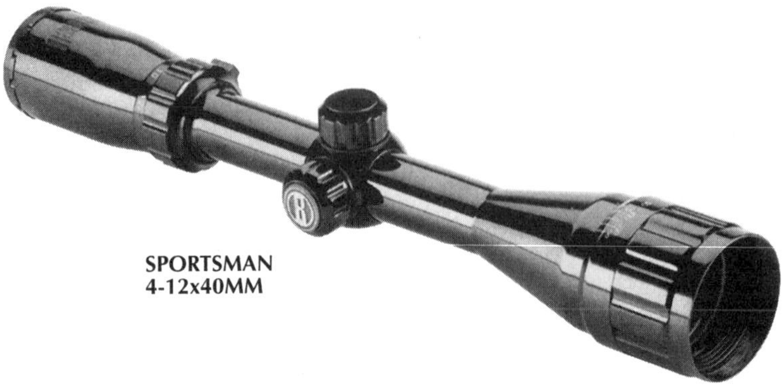

SPORTSMAN
4-12x40MM

ELITE 4200 RIFLESCOPES

Riflescopes feature 95% light transmission at 550mm. 4200s have multi-coated optics with hydrophobic Rainguard lens coating. These scopes feature hammer-forged one-piece aluminum/titanium alloy dry-nitrogen filled tubes, 1/4 MOA fingertip, audible/resettable windage and elevation adjustment; and are waterproof, fog-proof and shock-proof. 4200 scopes are available with Bushnell's FireFly reticle.

ELITE 4200 1.25-4X24

To better address the needs of the tactical and law enforcement market, Bushnell has added a 1.25-4x24mm model to its Elite 4200 line of precision riflescopes. It is equipped with a European reticle with an illuminated 1 MOA mil dot for quicker target acquisition and precise aiming. It has fingertip adjustments for windage and elevation with audible clicks, plus a Fast Focus eyepiece and fully multi-coated optics. It is nitrogen-purged and O-ring sealed, making it waterproof and fog proof inside and out. RainGuard, a permanent water repellent coating, is applied to the objective and ocular lenses to prevent fogging from rain, snow or sudden temperature changes. All Elite 4200 series riflescopes are constructed with titanium-reinforced tubes and recoil tested to 10,000 rounds of a .375 H&H.

SPORTSMAN RIFLESCOPES

Featuring multi-coated optics and a fast-focus eyepiece, easy-grip power change ring and 1/4 MOA fingertip windage and elevation adjustments. The rigid one-piece 1 in. tube is waterproof, fogproof and shockproof.

TROPHY RIFLESCOPES

Riflescopes feature multi-coated optics, Amber-Bright high contrast lens coating, one-piece dry-nitrogen filled tube construction, 1/4 MOA fingertip, audible/resettable windage and elevation adjustment, a fast-focus eyepiece and are waterproof, fogproof and shockproof.

3-9x40MM TROPHY WIDE ANGLE RIFLESCOPE

TROPHY 1X28MM RED DOT WITH AUTO ON/OFF

Bushnell's Trophy 1x28mm Red Dot scope features an automatic On/Off switch that conserves battery life by automatically turning the batteries on when the gun is raised to a shooting position and then off when the gun is on its side. It also has a manual override so that the sight can be switched to ALWAYS ON and ALWAYS OFF by hand. Shooters can choose any of four reticle options — 3 MOA dot, 10 MOA dot crosshair, and circle with dot in center— with just a simple twist of the reticle selector knob. The scope is constructed with a one-piece body tube that is dry nitrogen purged and then sealed with an "O" ring to protect the optics against moisture and fog.

MSRP. $116.49

TROPHY MP RED DOT RIFLESCOPE

TROPHY 1X32MM MP RED DOT RIFLESCOPE

This scope, used on tactical firearms, has integrated Weaver style mounts, and its bright optics, low magnification and T-Dot reticle make for fast target acquisition. The Trophy MP Red Dot offers a choice between a green T-Dot for low-light conditions and a red T-Dot reticle under brighter conditions. It features unlimited eye relief and is dry nitrogen purged and sealed with an o-ring to protect the optics against moisture and fog. Windage and elevation adjustments are 1/4 MOA It comes in a matte black finish.

MSRP: $223.49

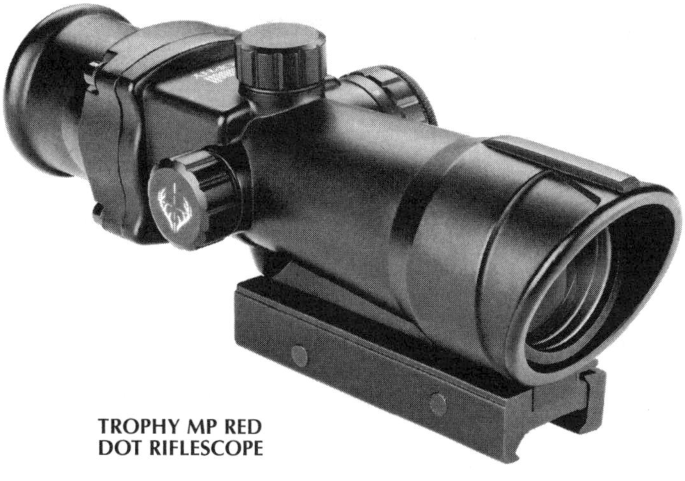

TROPHY MP RED DOT RIFLESCOPE

SCOPES

Bushnell Riflescopes

YARDAGE PRO LASER RANGEFINDER RIFLESCOPE

This new riflescope combines premium, fully multi-coated optics with a laser rangefinder that accurately ranges targets from 30 to 800 yds. with Bullet Drop Compensator turrets that quickly and easily adjust elevation to the displayed range. The scope comes with five Bullet Drop Compensator (BDC) turrets calibrated to match the most popular calibers and bullet weights. In the field or at the range, the shooter uses a wireless trigger pad to activate the laser rangefinder. Once the distance is displayed in the scope, the BDC turret is adjusted to match the range, eliminating the need for hold-over. Once the shooter knows the range, the Mil Dot reticle can be used to compensate for windage and elevation. Other features include fully multi-coated optics, and waterproof/fog proof construction. Eye relief is set at 3½ in. It is compact in design and weighs just 25.3 oz.

MSRP: $989.99

.22 RIMFIRE

Model	Finish	Power / Obj. Lens (mm)	Reticle	Field-of-View (ft@100yds)	Weight (oz)	Length (in)	Eye Relief (in)	Exit Pupil (mm)	Click Value (in@100yds)	Adj. Range (in@100yds)	Suggested Retail
76-2239	Matte	3–9x32	Multi-X®	40–13	11.2	11.75	3.0	10.6–3.6	.25	40	$53.99
76-2239S	Silver	3–9x32	Multi-X®	40–13	11.2	11.75	3.0	10.6–3.6	.25	40	$53.99
76-2243	Matte	4x32	Multi-X®	30 / 10@4x	10	11.5	3.0	8	.25	40	$46.99

BANNER DUSK & DAWN

Model	Finish	Power / Obj. Lens (mm)	Reticle	Field-of-View (ft@100yds)	Weight (oz)	Length (in)	Eye Relief (in)	Exit Pupil (mm)	Click Value (in@100yds)	Adj. Range (in@100yds)	Suggested Retail
71-0432	Matte	4x32	Circle-X®	31.5–10.5@4x	11.1	11.3	3.3	8@4x	.25	50	$96.95
71-1432	Matte	1–4x32	Circle-X®	78.5–24.9	12.2	10.5	4.3	16.9@1x / 8@4x	.25	50	$115.95
71-1436	Matte	1.75–4x32	Circle-X®	35–16	12.1	10.8	6	18.3@1.75x –6.4@4x	.25	100	$109.95
71-1545	Matte	1.5–4.5x32	Multi-X®	67v23	10.5	10.5	4.0	17@1.5x / 7@4.5x	.25	60	$109.95
71-3510	Matte	3.5-10x36	Multi-X®	30-10.415.0	12.5	3.4		10.3@ 3.5/3.6 @10	.25	85	$143.95
71-3944	Matte	3–9x40	Circle-X®	36–13	12.5	11.5	4.0	13@3x / 4.4@9x	.25	60	$117.95
71-3947	Matte	3–9x40	Multi-X®	40–13.6	13	12	3.3	13@3x / 4.4@9x	.25	60	$119.95
71-3948	Matte	3–9x40	Multi-X®	40–14	13	12	3.3	13.3@3x / 4.4@9x	.25	60	$112.95
71-3949I	Matte	3–9x40	R/G illuminated	40/13.6@3x–14/4.7@9x	13	12	3.3	13.3@3x / 4.4@9x	.25	60	$143.95
71-3950	Matte	3–9x50	Multi-X®	26–12	19	16	3.8	16@3x / 5.6@9x	.25	50	$175.95
71-3959I	Matte	3–9x50	R/G illuminated	36/12@3x–12/4@9x	20	16	3.8	16@3x / 5.6@9x	.25	50	$186.95
71-4124	Matte	4–12x40	Multi-X®	29–11	15	12	3.3	10@4x / 3.3@12x	.25	60	$148.95
71-4164I	Matte	4–16x40	illuminated	22/7@4x–6/2@16x	16	14	3.3	10@4x / 2.5@16x	.25	70	$186.95
71-6185	Matte	6–18x50	Multi-X®	17–6	18	16	3.5	8.3@6x / 2.8@18x	.25	40	$197.95
71-6244	Matte	6–24x40	Mil Dot	17–5	19.6	16.1	3.4	6.7@6x / 1.7@24x	.25	36	$197.95

ELITE 3200

Model	Finish	Power / Obj. Lens (mm)	Reticle	Field-of-View (ft@100yds)	Weight (oz)	Length (in)	Eye Relief (in)	Exit Pupil (mm)	Click Value (in@100yds)	Adj. Range (in@100yds)	Suggested Retail
32-1040M	Matte	10x40	Mil Dot	11	15.5	11.7	3.5	4.0	.25	100	$219.99
32-2632S	Silver	2–6x32	Multi-X®	10/3@2x	10	9	20	16–5.3	.25	50	$299.99
*32-2636M	Matte	2–6x32	FireFly™	10/3@2x	10	9	20	16–5.3	.25	50	$299.99
32-2732M	Matte	2–7x32	Multi-X®	44.6/15@2x	12	11.6	3.0	12.2–4.6	.25	50	$200.99
32-3104M	Matte	3-10 x40	Multi-X®	35.5/11.803x	14.5	11	3.7	13.1-4	.25	85	$229.99
32-3940G	Gloss	3–9x40	Multi-X®	33.8/11@3x	13	12.6	3.3	13.3–4.4	.25	50	$199.00
32-3940S	Silver	3–9x40	Multi-X®	33.8/11@3x	13	12.6	3.3	13.3–4.4	.25	50	$199.00
32-3944B	Matte	3-9x40	Ballistic	9.8@3x	13	12.6	3.3	13.3-4.4	.25	50	$299.95
32-3944M	Matte	3–9x40	Multi-X®	33.8/11@3x	13	12.6	3.3	13.3–4.4	.25	50	$199.00
32-3946M	Matte	3–9x40	FireFly™	33.8/11@3x	13	12.6	3.3	13.3–4.4	.25	50	$249.00
32-3954M	Matte	3–9x50	Multi-X®	31.5/10@3x	19	15.7	3.3	16–5.6	.25	50	$299.99
32-3956M	Matte	3–9x50	FireFly™	31.5/1.50@3x	19	15.7	3.3	16.7–5.6	.25	50	$364.49
32-4124A	Matte	4–12x40	Multi-X®	26.9/9@4x	15	13.2	3.3	10–3.33	.25	50	$319.99
32-4124B	Matte	4-12x40	Ballistic	26.9/9@4x	15	13.2	3.3	10-3.33	.25	50	$399.99
32-5154M	Matte	5–15x40	Multi-X®	21/7@5x	19	14.5	4.3	9–2.7	.25	50	$339.95
32-5155M	Matte	5–15x50	Multi-X®	21/7@5x	24	15.9	3.4	10–3.3	.25	40	$359.99
32-7214M	Matte	7-21x40	MilDot	13.5/4.5@7x	15	12.8	3.3	14.6-6	.25	40	$419.95

Bushnell Riflescopes

ELITE 4200											
Model	Finish	Power / Obj. Lens (mm)	Reticle	Field-of-view (ft@100yds)	Weight (oz)	Length (in)	Eye Relief (in)	Exit Pupil (mm)	Click Value (in@100yds)	Adj. Range (in@100yds)	Suggested Retail
42-2104M	Matte	2.5–10x40	Multi-X®	41.5/13.8@2.5x	16	13.5	3.3	15.6–4	.25	50	$429.99
42-2105M	Matte	2.5–10x50	Multi-X®	40.3/13.4@2.5x	18	14.3	3.3	15–5	.25	50	$539.99
42-2152M	Matte	2.5–10x50	4A w/1 MOA illumated Dot	12@2.5x	22	14.5	3.3	15–5	.25	60	$579.99
42-6242M	Matte	6–24x40	Mil Dot	18/6@6x	20.2	16.9	3.3	6.7–1.7	.125	26	$549.99
42-6243A	Matte	6–24x40	¼ MOA Dot	18/6@6x	20.2	16.9	3.3	6.7–1.7	.125	26	$519.99
42-6244M	Matte	6–24x40	Multi-X®	18/4.5@6x	20.2	16.9	3.3	6.7–1.7	.125	26	$519.99
42-8324M	Matte	8–32x40	Multi-X®	14/4.7@8x	22	18	3.3	5–1.25	.125	20	$559.99

SPORTSMAN® RIFLESCOPES											
Model	Finish	Power / Obj. Lens (mm)	Reticle	Field-of-view (ft@100yds)	Weight (oz)	Length (in)	Eye Relief (in)	Exit Pupil (mm)	Click Value (in@100yds)	Adj. Range (in@100yds)	Suggested Retail
**72-0039	Gloss	3–9x32	Multi-X®	40 13.1	163	12.2	430	3.6–11	.25	100	$100.99
72-1393S	Silver	3–9x32	Multi-X®	37–14	13.5	12	3.5	10–3.6	.25	100	$59.49
72-1398	Matte	3–9x32	Multi-X®	37–14	13.5	12	3.5	10–3.6	.25	100	$59.49
72-1403	Matte	4x32	Multi-X®	29	11	11.7	3.4	8	.25	110	$50.49
*Airgun scope **Target Airgun scope											

TROPHY® RIFLESCOPES											
Model	Finish	Power / Obj. Lens (mm)	Reticle	Field-of-view (ft@100yds)	Weight (oz)	Length (in)	Eye Relief (in)	Exit Pupil (mm)	Click Value (in@100yds)	Adj. Range (in@100yds)	Suggested Retail
73-0131	Matte	1x28	6 MOA Red Dot	68–22.6	6	5.5	Unlimited	28	.5	50	$96.95
73-0132A	Matte	1x28	5 MOA Red Dot	68–22.6	7.0	5.5	Unlimited	28	3.3	50	$170.95
73-0132P	Matte	1x32	Red/Green T- dot	44	15.6	13.7	3.3	32	.25	70	
73-0134	Matte	1x28	4 Dial-In Electronic	68–22.6	6	5.5	Unlimited	28	.5	50	$128.95
73-0135	Matte	1x30	4 Dial-Fn	68–22.6	6	5.5	Unlimited	28	.5	50	$141.95
73-1422AP	Camo	1.75–4x32	Circle-X®	73–30	10.9	10.8	4.1	18@1.75x / 8@4x	.25	120	$158.49
73-2632	Matte	2–6x32	Multi-X®	11–4	10.9	9.1	9–26	16@2x / 5.3@6x	.25	50	$213.99
73-2632S	Silver	2–6x32	Multi-X®	11–4	10.9	9.1	9–26	16@2x / 5.3@6x	.25	50	$243.99
73-3940	Gloss	3–9x40	Multi-X®	42–14	13.2	11.7	3.4	13.3@3x / 4.4@9x	.25	60	$130.49
73-3940S	Silver	3–9x40	Multi-X®	42–14	13.2	11.7	3.4	13.3@3x / 4.4@9x	.25	60	$130.49
73-3946	Matte	3–9x40	Mil Dot	42–14	13.2	11.7	3.4	13.3@3x / 4.4@9x	.25	60	$144.99
73-3948	Matte	3–9x40	Multi-X®	42–14	13.2	11.7	3.4	13.3@3x / 4.4@9x	.25	60	$129.99
73-3949	Matte	3–9x40	Circle-X®	42–14	13.2	11.7	3.4	13.3@3x / 4.4@9x	.25	60	$144.99
73-4124M	Matte	4–12x40	Multi-X®	32–11	16.1	12.6	3.4	10@4x / 3.3@12x	.25	60	$215.49
73-6184	Matte	6–18 x 40	Multi-X®	17.3–6	17.9	14.8	3.0	6.6@6x / 2.2@18x	.125	40	$321.49

Cabela's Scopes

PINE RIDGE								
Power	Finish	Reticle	Objective Diameter (mm)	Eye Relief (in.)	Length (in.)	Weight (oz.)	FOV 100 yards (ft)	Price
2-7	Matte	MX(5-4)	32	4.1	12.2	16	47-15	$69–189
3-9	Matte	MX(5-7)	40	4.3	13.3	17.6	39-13	$69–189
3-12SF	Matte	MX(5-7)	40	3.3	13.1	17.1	36-9	$69–189
6-18SF	Matte	MX(5-7)	40	3.4	15.7	18.6	17-6	$69–189

PINE RIDGE .17 TACTICAL RIFLESCOPES

Cabela's scopes are specially engineered for rifles in the .17 HMR caliber. The Pine Ridge .17 Tactical Riflescopes are incrementally calibrated to adjust for bullet drop out to 300 yds. Waterproof, fogproof and shockproof, these scopes have fully coated optics. Mounting tube is 1 in., and eye relief is 3 in. The scopes also have finger-adjustable windage and elevation with trajectory compensation turret and parallax adjustment. The 3-12x40 and 6-18x40 feature side-focus parallax adjustment. These scopes have all the quality features and high-performance optics of the regular .17 Tactical Scopes above, but by repositioning the parallax setting knob location on the scope, Cabela's has enabled the user to keep the target in sight while making adjustments from 50 to 300 yds. and beyond. Side-focus models also have a larger field of view for quicker target acquisition.

CenterPoint Precision Optics Scopes

ADVENTURE 2-7x32

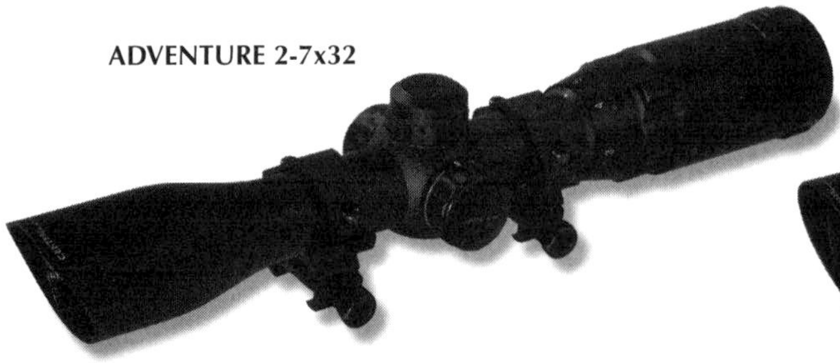

POWER CLASS 1TL 3-9x42 MM

ADVENTURE CLASS 2-7x32MM

Adventure Class 2-7x32mm combination scope for shotgun and muzzleloader hunting. 2x to 7x magnification allows the shooter to dial in the target at closer distances; the 5.2 inches of eye relief allows for a comfortable shooting position for heavy recoil rifles. The 2-7x32mm is designed for all light conditions.
Features: Mil-Dot reticle illuminates red or green at various brightness settings; angled front objective for built-in sun or rain protection; true hunter windage and elevation dials; flip open lens covers; medium-profile Weaver-style rings; CenterPoint limited lifetime warranty
MSRP: $90

POWER CLASS 1TL SERIES

Power Class 1TL Series scopes include 3-9x42mm and 1.5-6x44mm scopes.
Features: dual illuminated reticles; One Touch Lightning (1TL) technology with +/- brightness control; low profile design; completely sealed base; nitrogen filled, European-style sealed 30mm, one-piece waterproof, shockproof and fog-proof tube; multi-coated lens surfaces; angled objective and integral windage and elevation housing with dual-sealed o-rings; target adjustable windage and elevation dials with zero locking and resetting capability; side focus parallax adjustment; etched glass floating duplex reticle; flip open lens covers; sunshade
MSRP: $253

Columbia Sportswear Co. Scopes

TIMBERLINE PHG 3-12x40

TIMBERLINE PHG 3-12x50

TIMBERLINE PHG

Performance Hunting Gear (PHG) riflescopes (manufactured by Kruger Optics).
Features: one-piece aircraft grade aluminum dry nitrogen filled body construction; fully-coated optics; water tested for reliable, fog-free performance; re-settable windage and elevation adjustments in accurate ¼–minute clicks; armored power selector rings with ribbed surfaces
3-12x40: $120
4-16x40SF: $200

Docter Sports Optics Scopes

3-10x40MM

Description	Magnification	Objective Lens Dia.	Color	Reticle	Price
ONE-INCH TUBE SCOPES					
3-9x40 Variable	3x to 9x	40mm	Matte Black	Plex	$599–999
3-9x40 Variable	3x to 9x	40mm	Matte Black	German #4	$599–999
3-10x40 Variable	3x to 10x	40mm	Matte Black	Plex	$599–999
3-10x40 Variable	3x to 10x	40mm	Matte Black	German #4	$599–999
4.5-14x40 Variable	4.5x to 14x	40mm	Matte Black	Plex	$599–999
4.5-14x40 Variable	4.5x to 14x	40mm	Matte Black	Dot	$599–999
8-25x50 Variable	8x to 25x	50mm	Matte Black	Dot	$599–999
8-25x50 Variable	8x to 25x	50mm	Matte Black	Plex	$599–999
30mm TUBE SCOPES					
1.5-6x42 Variable	1.5x to 6x	42mm	Matte Black	Plex	$899
2.5-10x48 Variable	2.5x to 10x	48mm	Matte Black	Plex	$899
2.5-10x48 Variable	2.5x to 10x	48mm	Matte Black	German #4	$899
2.5-10x48 Var., Aspherical Lens	2.5x to 10x	48mm	Matte Black	Plex	discontinued
3-12x56 Variable	3x to 12x	56mm	Matte Black	Plex	$989
3-12x56 Var., Aspherical Lens	3x to 12x	56mm	Matte Black	Plex	$989
3-12x56 Var., Aspherical Lens	3x to 12x	56mm	Matte Black	German #4	$989

RIFLE SCOPES

Features: High strength, one-piece tube; high grade multi-coating; joints sealed with statically and dynamically loaded ring gaskets; diopter focus; precise click-stop adjustments of 1/4 in. at 100 yds. for windage and elevation; more than 3 in. of eye relief; wide rubber ring on the eye-piece; wide range of adjustment (50 in.) for easier mounting error compensation.

Insight Scopes

INSIGHT MINI RED DOT SIGHT

Features: 1 MOA click adjustable for elevation and windage, manual control with 4 settings, impact-resistant polymer lens, waterproof up to 66 feet for 2 hours, weight: .85 oz.
MSRP: $575

Kahles Riflescopes

HELIA CL 1-IN.
3-9x42

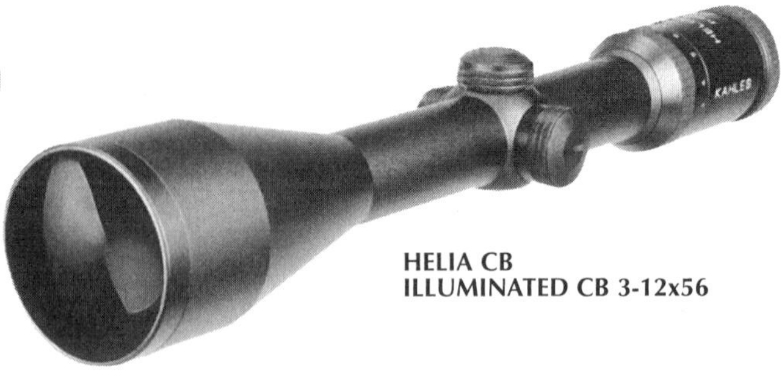

HELIA CB
ILLUMINATED CB 3-12x56

HELIA COMPACT C 1,1-4x24

HELIA CSX 1.5-6x42

HELIA CL 1-INCH RIFLESCOPES

Features of Helia CL 1-in. scopes include the Kahles multizero system, a revolutionary "micro-mechanic" ballistic system that will allow users to pre-set up to five different sight settings on the scope; third turret parallax; enhanced AMV Lens Coating technology on all air-to-glass surfaces which now maximizes low light performance by transmitting a higher percentage of the visible light spectrum; waterproof submersible turrets even when protective caps are removed; expanded point-of-impact total range of adjustment; and an 18% larger ocular diameter which has expanded the eye relief, expanded the field-of-view, fast focus ocular dial and enhanced the edge-to-edge resolution.

All Kahles CL riflescopes have the reticle located in the (non-magnifying) second image focal plane that maintains its size throughout the magnification range, come standard with a technologically advanced, scratch-resistant matte finish.

HELIA COMPACT

Kahles AMV-multi-coatings transmit up to 99.5% per air-to-glass surface. This ensures optimum use of incident light, especially in low light level conditions or at twilight. These 30mm Kahles rifle scopes are shockproof, waterproof and fogproof, nitrogen purged several times to assure the elimination of any moisture.

HELIA CB ILLUMINATED

Adjustable for illumination, and minimizes stray light. Battery life: 110 hrs.

HELIA CL RIFLESCOPES

Model	Power/Obj. Lens (mm)	Field of View (ft/100yds)	Eye Relief (in.)	Click Value (in.@100yds)	Length (in.)	Weight (oz.)	Price
CL 2-7x36	2-7x36	48-17	3.6	.36	11	13.6	$999
CL 3-9x42	3-9x42	39-13.5	3.6	.36	12.1	14.1	$769
CL 3-10x50	3-10x50	34-12	3.6	.36	12.1	14.1	$799
4-12x52	4-12x52	29-10	3.6	.25	13.9	18.0	$899

HELIA COMPACT RIFLESCOPES

Model	Power/Obj. Lens (mm)	Field of View (ft/100yds)	Eye Relief (in.)	Click Value (in.@100yds)	Length (in.)	Weight (oz.)	Price
C 1.1-4x24	1.1-4x24	118.8-32	3.6	.54	10.8	14.6-21.5	$2100
C 1.5-6x42	1.5-6x42	75.5-21.5	3.6	.36	12.0	16.4-24.2	$2850
C 2.5-10x50	2.5-10x50	45.3-13	3.6	.36	12.8	17.3-25.4	$2460
C 3-12x56	3-12x56	37.8-10.9	3.6	.36	14.0	19.4-28.5	$2820

HELIA CB ILLUMINATED

Model	Power/Obj. Lens (mm)	Field of View (ft/100yds)	Eye Relief (in.)	Click Value (in.@100yds)	Length (in.)	Weight (oz.)	Price
CBX 2.5-10X50	2.5-10X50	45.3-13	3.5	.36	12.8	18.3-19.4	$2926
CBX 3-12x56	3-12x56	37.8-10.9	3.5	.36	14.0	20.5-21.5	$2868
CSX 1.5-6x42	1.5-6x42	81.5-21.5	3.6	.36	12.0	17.3-18.3	$2250
CSX 2.5-10x50	2.5-10x50	43.8-12.7	3.6	.36	12.8	18.3-19.4	$2550

Kaps Optics Scopes

Kap scopes feature high-quality glass and state-of-the-art coatings, illuminated reticles, 30mm alloy tubes, satin finish.

KAPS				
Magnification x Obj. Dia.	Field of View (Ft., 100 yds.)	Dia./Length (in.)	Weight (oz.)	MSRP
4x36	32.8	1.18/12.8	14.1	$699
6x42	20.3	1.18/12.8	15.9	$799
8x56	18	1.18/14.2	20.8	$899
10x50	13.8	1.18/14.1	20.6	$999
1-4x22	98-33	1.18/14.2	20.6	$899
1.5-6x42	62-23	1.18/12.4	17.3	$999
2-8x42	57-17	1.18/13.2	17.3	$1099
2.5-10x50	40.7-13.8	1.18/14.1	20.6	$1199
2.5-10x56	40.7-13.8	1.18/14.6	20.6	$1199

Konus USA Scopes

KONUSPRO M-30 SERIES

Features: black matte finish 30mm nitrogen-purged, fogproof and waterproof tubes; lockable tactical turrets, 1/8 minute audible tactical adjustments; lockable fast-focus eyeball; greater windage/elevation and resolution; illuminated Blue Mil. Dot. Reticle; laser-etched glass reticle system; flip-up eye covers and detachable sunshade

4.5-16x40mm:. $470–550
6.5-25x44mm:. $530–580
8.5-32x52mm:. $600–640

SCOPES

PRO SHOTGUN/BLACKPOWDER SCOPE

Two new KonusPro scopes in a fixed 2.5X32mm and a variable 1.5X-5X32mm configuration, both with etched reticles, are available for shotgun and blackpowder applications. Other features include long-eye relief, Aim-Pro reticle design (circle/diamond pattern), multi-coated optical glass for increased light transmission and a nitrogen purged tube assembly for 100% waterproof and fogproof integrity.

2.5X32mm: $69.99
1.5X-5X32mm: $79.99

PRO SHOTGUN/BLACKPOWDER

KONUS USA PRO SHOTGUN/BLACKPOWDER SCOPE							
Model	Power/Obj. Lens (mm)	Field of View (ft/100yds)	Eye Relief (in.)	Reticle Type	Length (in.)	Weight (oz.)	Price
7248	2.5x32	37	5	Grabada Aim-Pro	10.9	11.6	$83.99

Leatherwood/Hi-Lux Scopes

SHORT MALCOLM SCOPE

SHORT MALCOLM SCOPE

Leatherwood/Hi-Lux Optics' shorter 17-in. version of the original Wm. Malcolm scopes can be used on a wide range of vintage-style breech-loading rifle models dating from the 1880s into the first half of the 20th Century. The 3/4 in. diameter, blued-steel scope comes standard with Unertl-style mounting blocks, requiring gunsmith installation (two holes drilled and tapped for each block) on many rifles. Optional "no gunsmithing" mounts now also make it easy for the Winchester Model 1873 and Model 1876 rifle owner to off-set mount this scope, utilizing the rear sight dovetail and raised dust-cover rail of the receiver. The mounts move the scope just enough to the left to permit top-ejected cases to clear. Leatherwood/Hi-Lux Optics also offers specialty mounts to fit a variety of other current production rifles, such as the Henry Repeating Arms lever-actions, the Marlin Model 1895 Cowboy, Sharps 1874 side-hammer rifles and the break-open H&R Buffalo Classic and Model .38-55 Target rifles.

The company chose to produce this scope in 3x, making it an ideal hunting scope. The caged rear mount is easily adjusted for windage and elevation, making sighting in a snap. Like the originals, this scope does not offer micrometer click adjustment. Instead, the shooter unlocks a collar under the adjustment screw (with either windage or elevation). Then, once an adjustment has been made, the lock collar is turned to lock that adjustment in place. When the scope is fully adjusted, the lock collars for both adjustments can be snugged tight and the scope will hold that setting. The scope has super bright, sharp and crisp multi-coated lenses.

MSRP: $278.99

"WM. MALCOLM" SCOPE AND MOUNTS

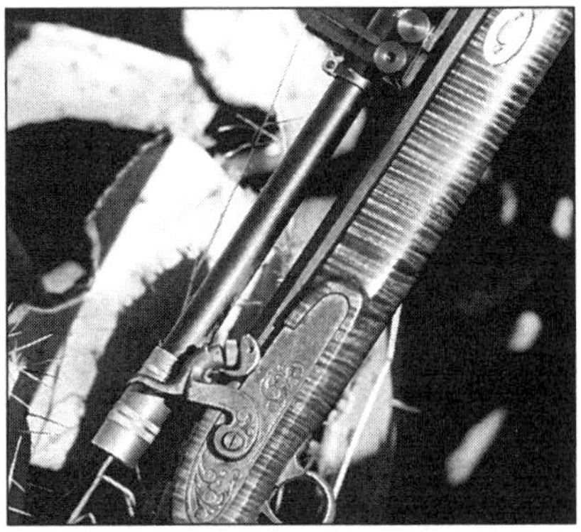

"WM. MALCOLM" SCOPE AND MOUNTS

The Wm. Malcolm scope offers authentic 1870s looks and styling, but has been built with the benefits of modern scope-making technology. Unlike the originals used on Sharps, Winchester High Wall and Remington Rolling Block black powder cartridge rifles, this 6X long tube-type scope is built with light gathering full multi-coated lenses. This scope is built with a nitrogen-filled 3/4 in. tube for fog-free service. The scope can be mounted on old-style rifles with barrel lengths from 28 to 34 in. using the factory cut front and rear sight dovetails. Comes with fully adjustable external mounts.

MSRP: $399.99

SCOPES

Leupold Scopes

LEUPOLD ULTIMATESLAM

Features: Leupold's new 1-inch scope for black powder or slug guns. New SABR reticle, waterproof/fogproof, available in 2-7x33 and 3-9x40 in silver or black matte.

MSRP: . . . . $259-$269

LEUPOLD VX-3 5-10X50

Features: New Xtended Twilight Lens System giving brighter, sharper images in low-light, high-strength aluminum adjustment dials, dual spring erector. The VX-3L offers Leupold's Light Optimization Profile – the cut crescent shape delivering maximum light with a lower mount. Waterproof/fogproof/shockproof, Argon/Krypton gas blend. Blackened lens edges maximizes clarity. Available in power ranges from 1.5-5x20 to 8.5-25x50 with 1-inch tube (30mm on Long Range versions) and 1/4 MOA adjustments.

MSRP: $580-$660 (5-10x50); VX-3 line from $430 to $1049

VX-3 . . . . $430–1049

5-10x50 . . . . $580–660

VX-3 5-10X50

ILLUMINATED VX-L 3.5-10x50 MM

PRISMATIC 1x14 MM

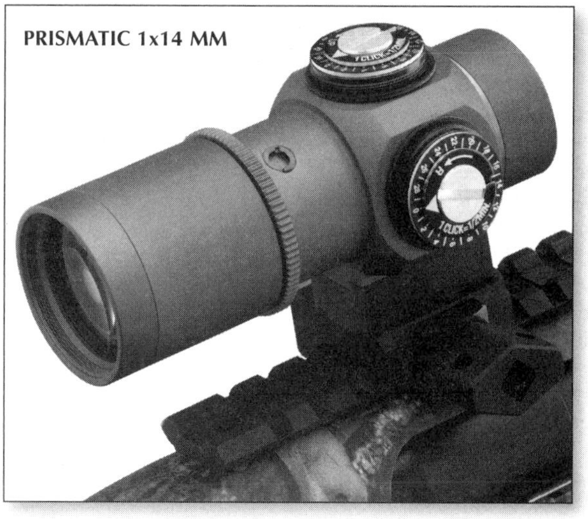

ILLUMINATED VX-L SERIES

The Illuminated VX-Ls feature Leupold 11-setting illumination system with variable intensity rheostat. The illuminated reticle and Light Optimization Profile provide low-light performance with reduced weight. Available with German#4 Dot and Boone & Crockett illuminated reticle options.

Features: Leupold Index Matched Lens System; DiamondCoat lens coatings; Leupold Second Generation waterproofing; dual-spring titanium nitride coated stainless steel adjustment system.

3.5-10x50mm:. $900
4.5-14x50mm:. $1185
3.5-10x56mm:. $1080
4.5-14x56mm LR: $1080

PRISMATIC 1x14 MM HUNTING

The Prismatic 1x14mm Hunting scope has an etched glass reticle that remains functional even if the batteries die. Available in Illuminated Circle Plex or Illuminated Duplex.

Features: removable illumination module; 1x true power magnification; waterproof, shockproof and fog proof; Leupold Dark Earth finish easily adjusted focusing eyepiece; ½-MOA click windage and elevation adjustment dials; compact 4.5-inch length

MSRP: $500

QD MANAGER SERIES

Developed by Leupold in association with the Quality Deer Management Association (QDMA). Based on Leupold's VX-L riflescope models.

Features: Light Optimization Profile (a concave crescent in the bottom of the objective lens and bell that allows large objective riflescopes to be mounted low); 11 brightness setting illumination system with variable intensity rheostat; matte black finish; QDMA identity on the Leupold Golden Ring and QDMA logo medallion

3.5-10x50mm:. $900
4.5-14x50mm:. $1185
3.5-10x56mm:. $1080
4.5-14x56mm LR: $1080

Leupold Scopes

VX-7 LONG RANGE MODELS

Features: Leupold's Xtended Twilight Lens System and Light Optimization Profile (a concave crescent in the bottom of the objective lens and bell that allows large objective riflescopes to be mounted low); 34mm main tube; SpeeDial adjustment system; Leupold Ballistics Aiming System reticles; dual erector springs; 34mm PRW rings; the VX-7L 3.5-14x56mm Long Range is available with XT Duplex, Boone & Crockett Big Game and Varmint Hunter's reticles; VX-7L 4.5-18x56mm Long Range reticle options include Fine Duplex, Boone & Crockett Big Game and Varmint Hunter

VX-7L 3.5-14x56mm LR: $1599
VX-7L 4.5-18x56mm LR: $1699

VX-7L 4.5-18x56 MM LONG RANGE

COMPETITION SERIES 45X45MM

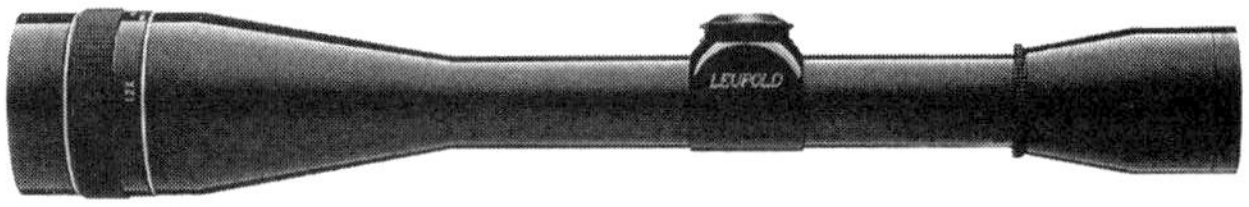

FX-II 12x40MM STANDARD

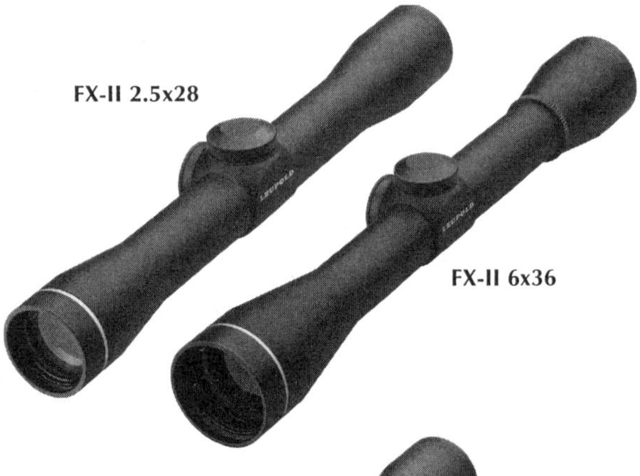

FX-II 2.5x28

FX-II 6x36

FX-II 4X33

FX-II 2.2x20MM COMPACT

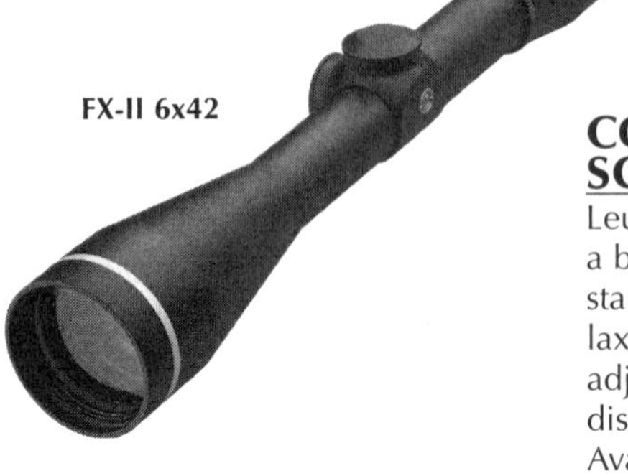

FX-II 6x42

COMPETITION SERIES SCOPES

Leupold's new Competition series offer a bright, crisp sight picture with outstanding contrast. The side-focus parallax adjustment knob allows you to adjust your scope to be parallax-free at distances from 40 yds. to infinity. Available in matte finish with target dot or target crosshair reticle.

FX-II (FIXED POWER) SCOPES

Features: Multicoat 4 lens system; _ MOA click windage and elevation dials; special 9 in. eye relief; available in matte or gloss finish; duplex or wide duplex reticles; Leupold full lifetime guarantee.

Leupold Scopes

HANDGUN SCOPES

Features: Compact scope for handguns; multicoat 4 lens system; 1/4 MOA click windage and elevation dials; special 9 in. eye relief; available in matte or gloss finish; duplex or wide duplex reticles; Leupold full lifetime guarantee.

LPS PREMIERE SCOPES

Leupold's Premiere Scope (LPS) line features 30mm tubes, fast-focus eyepieces, armored power selector dials that can be read from the shooting position, 4 in. constant eye relief, Diamondcoat lenses for increased light transmission, scratch resistance, and finger-adjustable, low-profile elevation and windage adjustments.

MARK 2 TACTICAL RIFLESCOPES

Leupold's new Mark 2 tactical riflescopes include the 1.5-4x20mm, 3-9x40mm Hunter, 3-9x40mm T2, 4-12x40mm Adjustable Objective T2 and 6-18x40mm Adjustable Objective T1. Each riflescope in the series is completely waterproof and features Leupold's Multicoat 4 lens coating for superior clarity and brightness, edge-to-edge sharpness across the visual field and optimal contrast for easy target identification in virtually any light or atmospheric condition. Additionally, the riflescopes also feature lockable, fast-focus eyepieces and tactile power indicators.

MARK 4 TACTICAL SCOPES

Fixed and variable power. 1/4 MOA audible click windage and elevation adjustments (Except M-3s). Duplex or MilDot reticle. Waterproof. Leupold Long Range/Tactical optics feature: 30mm (1.18 in.) main tubes–increased windage and elevation adjustment; index matched lens system; finger-adjustable dials. Fully illuminated Mil Dot, Duplex or TMR reticles available in select models. Front Focal model with the reticle in the front focal plane of the scope increases in magnification along with the image.

LPS 3.5-14x50MM SIDE FOCUS (SATIN FINISH)

MARK 2 TACTICAL

MARK 4 3.5-10x40 LRT M1

MARK 4 2.5-8x36

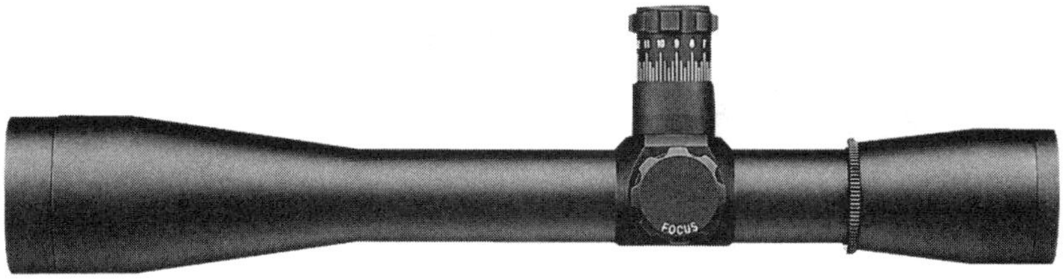

MARK 4 16x40MM

Leupold Scopes

MARK 4 8.5-25x50MM ER/T M1

VX-1 2-7x28
RIMFIRE

3-9x40MM DUPLEX

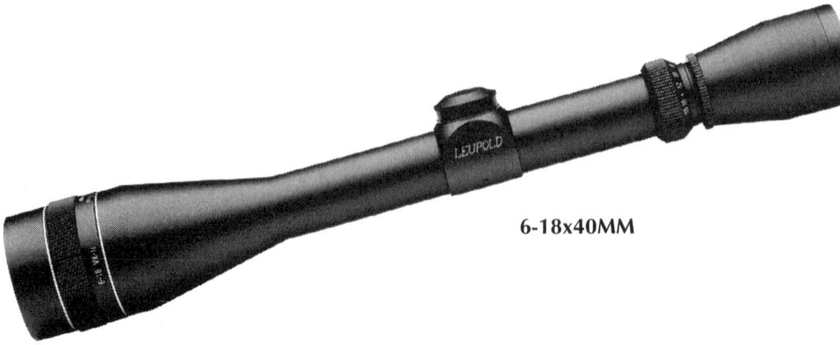

6-18x40MM

MARK 4 8.5-25X50MM ER/T M1 RIFLESCOPE

Engineered with its reticles in the front focal plane, Leupold's 8.5-25x50mm Mark 4 Extended Range/Tactical ER/T M1 riflescope allows tactical shooters to range targets at all magnifications. The front focal design allows a shooter to increase the riflescope's magnification, as well as the magnification of the reticle. By doing so, shooters maintain the versatility of a variable magnification optic as well as the ability to use the Mil Dot or TMR reticle to engage a target at any magnification setting. Designed for the U.S. Marine Corps, the Mil Dot reticle features a series of dots in one milliradian increments on the crosshair. Bracketing the target between dots allows the shooter to estimate range. The TMR expands on the Mil Dot principle incorporating a series of various sized and spaced hash marks for increased ranging precision and more accurate shot placement. The ER/T M1 also features Leupold's Index Matched Lens System for maximum light transmission and clarity, as well as reduced glare. Additionally, the lockable, fast-focus eyepiece delivers long eye relief to provide the shooter with nearly instant target acquisition and protection from the hardest recoiling extreme range firearms such as the .50 BMG and .338 Lapua.

RIMFIRE SCOPES

Adapted to the unique requirements of rimfire shooting. Features: Standard multicoat lens system; micro-friction windage and elevation dials; 60 yds. parallax correction distance; Leupold full lifetime guarantee.

SHOTGUN & MUZZLELOADERS SCOPES

Leupold shotgun scopes are parallax-adjusted to deliver precise focusing at 75 yds. Each scope features a special Heavy Duplex reticle that is more effective against heavy, brushy backgrounds. All scopes have matte finish and Multicoat 4 lens coating.

SCOPES

TACTICAL PRISMATIC 1X14MM RIFLESCOPE

With an etched-glass reticle that is always crisp, and provides military and law enforcement professionals with unmatched reliability, the Leupold 1x14mm Tactical Prismatic separates itself from red dot sights by remaining functional if the batteries die.

The Leupold Tactical Prismatic features a unique, removable Illuminated Module which illuminates the circle dot reticle in red. The riflescope also allows instant target acquisition by virtue of its wide field of view and one true power magnification that allows sighting with both eyes open. In addition, shooters experience no need to change focus from the target to the sight. The sight features a focusing eyepiece, allowing the Tactical Prismatic to be easily adjusted, and is compatible with A.R.M.S. #22-34mm throw-lever rings base and spacer system as well as the conventional 30mm ring. Different height mounting spacers are included, and DiamondCoat 2 lens coatings exceed the military's durability standard with 500 rub performance.

ULTRALIGHT SCOPES

Ultralight riflescopes have about 17% less weight than their full-size counterparts, but retain all of the features of the larger scopes. Ultralight scopes have a Multicoat 4 lens system, are waterproof and are covered by the Leupold Full Lifetime Guarantee. They are available in matte finish with Duplex or Heavy Duplex reticles.

VX-I SCOPES

A tough, gloss black finish and Duplex reticle.

TACTICAL PRISMATIC 1x14MM

ULTRALIGHT VX-II 3-9x33

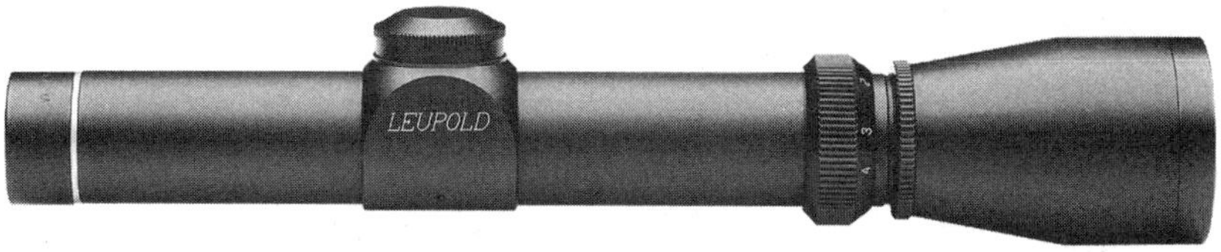

VX-I 1-4x20MM SHOTGUN/ MUZZLELOADER

VX-I 3-9x40MM

If a scope is mounted too far to the rear, the eyepiece can injure the shooter's brow. Shooting at an uphill angle also increases this hazard because it shortens the distance between the brow and the rear of the scope. Therefore, when mounting your scope, position it as far forward in the mounts as possible to take full advantage of the scope's eye relief.

SCOPES

Leupold Scopes

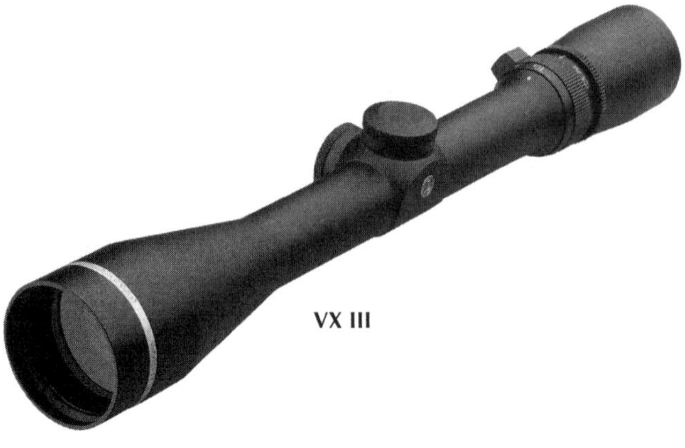

VX III

VX-III 4.5-14x40

VX-II SCOPES

The VX-II line offers Multi-Coated 4 lens coatings for improved light transmission; ¼ MOA click adjustments; a locking eyepiece for reliable ocular adjustment; a sealed, nitrogen-filled interior for fog-free sighting.

VX-III SCOPES

The VX-III scopes, which replace the Vari-X III line, feature new lens coatings and the Index Matched Lens System (IMLS). The IMLS matches coatings to the different types of glass used in a scope's lens system. Other refinements include finger-adjustable dials with resettable pointers to indicate zero, a fast-focus, lockable eyepiece and a 30mm main tube for scopes with side-mounted focus (parallax correction) dials.

ULTRALIGHT SCOPES				
Magnification (x obj. dia.)	Field of View (ft., 100 yds)	Dia./Length (in.)	Weight (oz.)	MSRP
VX-II 2-7x28mm	41.7(2x) 16.5(7x)	1/9.9	8.2	$415
VX-II 3-9x33mm	34.0(3x) 13.5(9)	1/10.96	8.8	$439
VX-II 3-9x33mm EFR	34.0(3x) 13.50(9x)	1/11.32	11.0	$475
COMPETITION SERIES SCOPES				
Magnification (x obj. dia.)	Field of View (ft., 100 yds)	Dia./Length (in.)	Weight (oz.)	MSRP
35x45mm	3.3	1/15.9	20.3	$1249
40x45mm	2.7	1/15.9	20.3	$1249
45x45mm	2.5	1/15.9	20.3	$1249
FX-II (FIXED POWER)				
Magnification (x obj. dia.)	Field of View (ft., 100 yds)	Dia./Length (in.)	Weight (oz.)	MSRP
2.5x28mm Scout	22.0	1/10.10	7.5	$375
4x33mm	24.0	1/10.47	9.3	$375
6x36mm	17.7	1/11.35	10.0	$375
HANDGUN SCOPES				
Magnification (x obj. dia.)	Field of View (ft., 100 yds)	Dia./Length (in.)	Weight (oz.)	MSRP
FX-II 2x20mm	21.20	1/8.0	6.0	$440
FX-II 4x28mm	9.0	1/8.43	7.0	$440
RIMFIRE SCOPES				
Magnification (x obj. dia.)	Field of View (ft., 100 yds)	Dia./Length (in.)	Weight (oz.)	MSRP
FX-I 4x28mm	25.5	1/9.2	7.5	$275
VX-I 2-7x28mm	41.7(2x) 16.5(7x)	1/9.9	8.2	$275
X-II 3-9x33mm EFR	34.0(3x) 13.50(9x)	1/11.32	11.0	$499
MUZZLELOADER				
Magnification (x obj. dia.)	Field of View (ft., 100 yds)	Dia./Length (in.)	Weight (oz.)	MSRP
VX-I 1-4x20mm	75.0(1x) 28.5(4x)	1/9.2	9.0	$250
VX-I 2-7x33mm	42.5(2x) 17.8(7x)	1/11.0	10.5	$265
VX-I 3-9x40mm	32.9(3x) 13.1(9x)	1/12.2	12.0	$289
MARK 4 TACTICAL SCOPES				
Magnification (x obj. dia.)	Field of View (ft., 100 yds)	Dia./Length (in.)	Weight (oz.)	MSRP
10x40mm LR/T M1	11.1	1.18/13.10	21.0	$1749
10x40mm LR/T M3	3.7	1.18/13.10	21.0	$1874
16x40mm LR/T M1	6.8	1.18/12.90	22.5	$1999
4 3.5-10x40mm LR/T M3	29.9(3.5x) 11.0(10x)	1.18/13.50	19.5	$1324
4.5-14x50mm LR/T M1	14.3(6.5x) 5.5(20x)	1.18/14.5	22.0	$1344
8.5-25x50mm	4.4-11.2	1.2/14.5	22.5	$1749
TACTICAL PRISMATIC SCOPES				
Magnification (x obj. dia.)	Field of View (ft., 100 yds)	Dia./Length (in.)	Weight (oz.)	MSRP
1x14mm	83.0	1.2/4.5	12.0	$624
VX-I SCOPES				
Magnification (x obj. dia.)	Field of View (ft., 100 yds)	Dia./Length (in.)	Weight (oz.)	MSRP
3-9x40mm	32.9(3x) 13.1(9x)	1/12.2	12	$289
3-9x50mm	33.0(3x) 13.1(9x)	1/12.4	14.1	$375
4-12x40mm	19.9(4x) 9.4(12x)	1/12.2	13	$375
VX-II SCOPES				
Magnification (x obj. dia.)	Field of View (ft., 100 yds)	Dia./Length (in.)	Weight (oz.)	MSRP
2-7x33mm	42.5(2x) 17.8(7x)	1/11.0	10.5	$374
3-9x40mm	32.3(3x) 14.0(9x)	1/12.4	12	$374
3-9x50mm	32.3(3x) 14.0(9x)	1/12.1	13.7	$474
4-12x40mm Adj. Obj.	22.8(4x) 11.0(12x)	1/12.4	14	$564
4-12x50mm	33.0(4x) 13.1(12x)	1/12.2	14.5	$599
6-18x40mm Adj. Obj.	14.5(6x) 6.6(18x)	1/13.5	15.8	$624
VX-III SCOPES				
Magnification (x obj. dia.)	Field of View (ft., 100 yds)	Dia./Length (in.)	Weight (oz.)	MSRP
1.5-5x20mm	65.7(1.5x) 23.7(5x)	1/9.4	9.7 oz.	$499
1.75-6x32mm	17.0(1.75x) 6.4(6x)	1/11.23	11.2	$499
2.5-8x36mm	37.3(2.5x) 13.7(8x)	1/11.4	11.2	$499
3.5-10x40mm	29.7(3.5x) 11.0(10x)	1/12.6	13.0	$599
3.5-10x50mm	29.8(3.5x) 11.0(10x)	1/12.2	15.1	$689
4.5-14x40mm	19.9(4.5x) 7.4(14x)	1/12.6	13.2	$664
4.5-14x40mm Adj. Obj.	20.8-7.4	1/12.5	15	$750
6.5-20x40mm EFR Target	14.3(6.5x) 5.6(20x)	1/14.4	19.0	$939

Meopta Scopes

MEOPTA MEOSTAR R1 4-16X44 TACTIC

Features: Adjustable objective setting zero from 3m to infinity, low-profile target knobs, ¼ MOA, Mil Dot reticle, waterproof/fogproof.

MSRP: **$880–980**

MEOPTA ARTEMIS 3000 3-9X42

Features: Solid steel tube, shock resistant, Nitrogen purged for fog and waterproof performance, ¼ MOA.

MSRP: **$500–550**

ARTEMIS 3000
3-9X42

R1 4-16X44

Nightforce Scopes

SCOPES

NIGHTFORCE 2.5-10X32 NXS

Features: Slim design with larger exit pupil allows fast target acquisition and improved light. Length: 12 inches. Weight: 19 ounces, with ¼ MOA adjustments in fully-enclosed hunting-style dials or exposed target knobs. ZeroStop technology with windage limiter. Three ballistic reticles offered in 2.5-10x32 and 2.5-10x24 compact versions.

MSRP: . . . . **$1345-$1613**

NIGHTFORCE F1 3.5-15X50

Features: Tactical scope with 30mm tube, turret parallax dial, reticle in the first focal plane. Offered in choice of three windage/elevation adjustments: ¼ MOA, .1 Mil Radian, or 1.0 MOA elevation/.5 MOA windage (optional turret caps available). Several long-range reticles,

MSRP: **$2410**

NIGHTFORCE TOP OF RING BUBBLE LEVEL

Features: Nightforce's new built-in bubble level replaces the top half of a ring mount, helping the shooter eliminate cant – critical at long range.

MSRP: **$160**

Nikon Scopes

NIKON COYOTE SPECIAL 3-9X40

Features: Nikon's new BDC Predator Hunting Reticle with circle design, Anti reflective, multicoated lenses, ¼ MOA click adjustments, generous eye relief and quick-focus eyepiece, 1-inch tube, waterproof/fogproof, two camo finishes available, 3-9x40 or 4.5-14x40.

MSRP: $260–280

COYOTE SPECIAL 3-9X40

NIKON AFRICAN 1-4X20

Features: Monarch African series offers Ultra ClearCoat lens systems, German #4 reticle, one-piece main body tubes, ½ MOA click adjustments (¼ MOA in 1.1-4x24), quick-focus eyepiece, waterproof/fogproof/shockproof, matte finish. Offered in 1-4x20 with 1-inch tube and 1.1-4x24 with 30mm tube (two versions).

MSRP: 1-4x20: $290
1-4x24: $780–870

AFRICAN 1-4X20

NIKON EDG 65 AND 85 FIELDSCOPE SPOTTING SCOPES

Features: ED (Extra-low Dispersion) fully multi-coated lenses, 65mm or 85mm objective lenses, zoom eyepiece, sliding sunshade, straight and angled body versions, waterproof/fogproof.

MSRP: 65MM: $2700
85MM: $3300

NIKON OMEGA MUZZLELOADER 1.65-5X36

Features: Nikon's BDC 250 reticle with easy-to-see "ballistic circles," 1-inch alloy tube, 5 inches eye relief, ¼ MOA click adjustments, 100-yard parallax setting, multicoated lenses, waterproof/fogproof/shockproof, matte or camo finish.

MSRP: $200–230

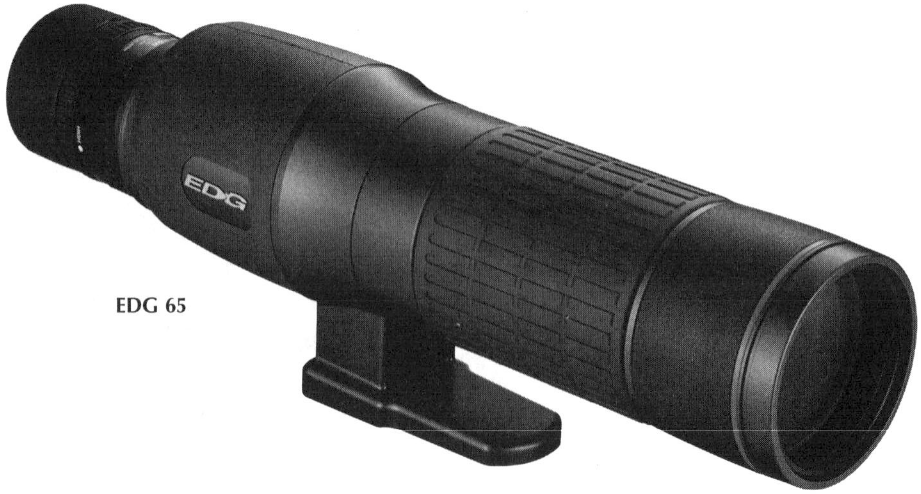

EDG 65

ENCORE HANDGUN 2.5-8x28 EER

MONARCH 2-8x32

MONARCH 4-16x50

MONARCH 8-32x50

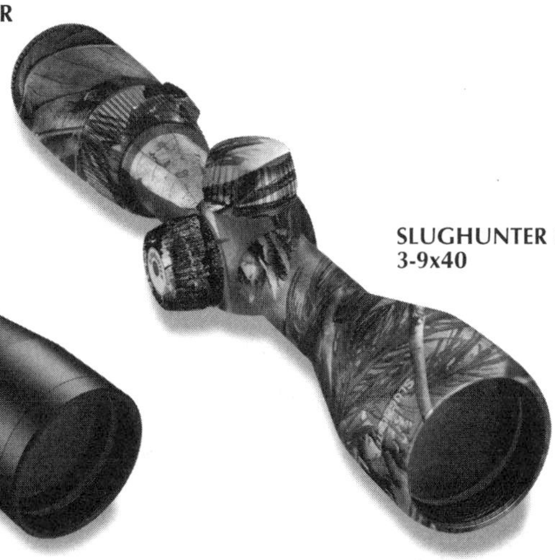

SLUGHUNTER REALTREE 3-9x40

ENCORE HANDGUN 2.5-8x28 EER

The Encore 2.5-8x28 is designed to work with single shot handguns or revolvers and integrates the Nikon BDC reticle.

Features: waterproof, fogproof and shockproof; 2.5-8 variable zoom 1-inch tube; 28-inch objective; hand-turn adjustments and positive clicks; available in a matte or silver finish

Matte: **$455**
Silver: **$465**

MONARCH 2-8x32, 4-16x50SF, 8-32x50ED SF

The Monarch 2-8x32 features a large objective and superior low light performance.

Features: Nikon ED glass; Nikon BDC reticle; lead-and-arsenic-free Eco-Glass lenses; Ultra ClearCoat anti-reflective multicoatings; locking side-focus parallax adjustment; hand-turn reticle adjustment, Monarch Eye Box design with 4-time zoom range; constant 4 inches of eye relief; rear-facing magnification indicators on zoom control; quick-focus eyepiece

2-8X32: **$290–300**
4-16X50SF: **$490–500**
8-32X50ED SF: **$690–700**

SLUGHUNTER REALTREE APG HD

The Nikon 3-9x40 SlugHunter BDC 200 riflescope in RealTree APG HD (All-Purpose Green) camo.

Features: Nikon BDC (Bullet Drop Compensating) 200 reticle system (a trajectory compensating reticle with aiming points for various shot distances; calibrated to be sighted-in on the crosshair at 50 yards with two ballistic circles that represent 100-yard and 150-yard aiming points — lower reticle post becomes a 200-yard aiming point); 5 inches of eye relief; Nikon multicoated optics; ¼-MOA click adjustments; 100-yard parallax setting; waterproof, fogproof and shock proof; 11.3 inches long, weighs 13.7 oz

MSRP: **$260–270**

Nikon Scopes

LASER IRT RIFLESCOPE

The Laser IRT riflescope system combines Nikon's BDC (Bullet Drop Compensating) reticle with an integral Laser Rangefinder. The rangefinder and reticle work together to provide hunters precise distance measurement, proper aiming point and speed for immediate shot placement. The riflescope is also available with Nikon's Nikoplex reticle.

The patent-pending IRT technology returns precise and continuous distance readings for 12 seconds, allowing the hunter time to range the animal and select the appropriate aiming circle. When the animal is spotted, simply hit the button and settle in for the shot. The IRT keeps the hunter current on the range as the animal moves. The one-touch rangefinding capabilities also can be operated using the included remote control switch, which can be attached to the rifle with a Velcro strap. O-ring sealed and nitrogen-filled for true waterproof, fogproof and shockproof performance.

The scope operates on a 3-volt CR-2 battery, ranges up to 766 yds. and has a bright, 3-digit electroluminescent display that measures in yds. or meters.

LASER IRT

MONARCH RIFLE SCOPES

Monarch Rifle Scopes feature multi-coated Ultra ClearCoat optical system; ¼ min. positive click windage and elevation; one-piece aluminum tube construction. All Monarch scopes are shockproof, waterproof and fogproof. The Monarch series includes scopes specifically designed for use with blackpowder rifles shooting sabots or shotguns shooting sabot-style slugs. Available in matte or lustre finish.

MONARCH GOLD 2.5-10x56

OMEGA BLACK

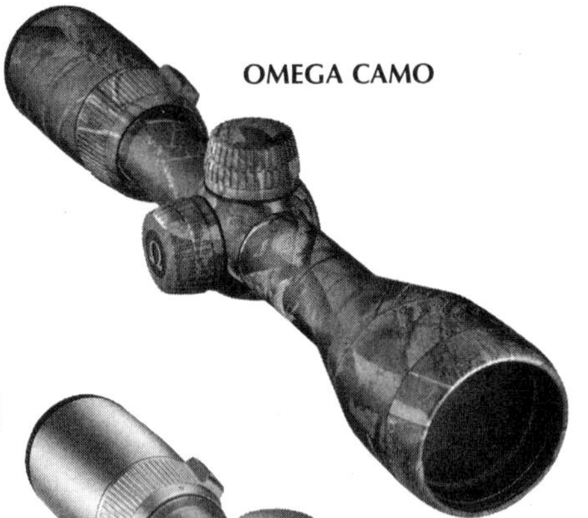
OMEGA CAMO

MONARCH GOLD

1.5-6x42: $858.95
2.5-10x50: $1062.95
2.5-10x56: $1184.95

OMEGA MUZZLELOADING RIFLESCOPE

The Nikon Omega 3-9x40 with BDC-250 reticle was created to help shooters take advantage of the full accuracy potential of their muzzleloaders. The Omega offers a bullet drop compensating reticle designed specifically for muzzleloading loads and ranges and was designed to utilize .50 caliber muzzleloading loads –150 grains of Pyrodex (pellets or powder), 250-grain bullets and ranges (out to 250-yds).

The BDC-250 is a trajectory-compensating reticle designed and calibrated to provide fast, simple aiming points for various shot distances. This unique system integrates a series of small "ballistic circles"—each subtending 2 in. @ 100 yds.—allowing an unimpeded view of the target. (At 200 yds., the circles are 4 in.; at 250 yds., they are 5 in.) The reticle is designed to be sighted-in at 100 yds., with aiming-point circles at 150, 200, 225 and 250 yds. A generous 25.2 8.4-foot field-of-view also makes getting on a trophy animal a breeze. The Omega Riflescope is equipped with precise, ¼-MOA click reticle adjustments. Available in Matte, Silver and Realtree Hardwoods Green HD finishes.

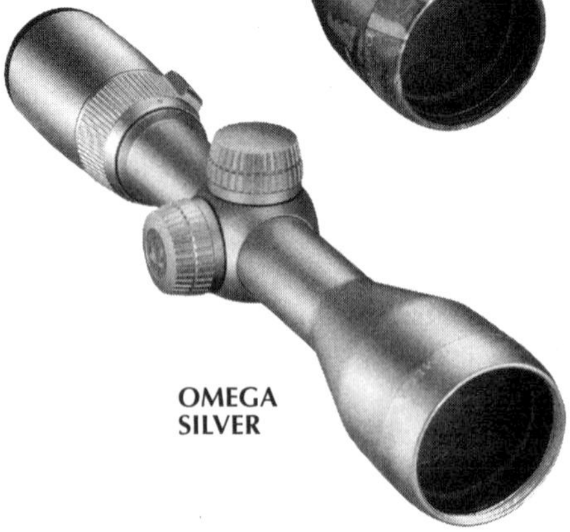
OMEGA SILVER

PROSTAFF RIFLESCOPES

Nikon's Prostaff line includes the 4x32, 2-7x32 and 3-9x40 scopes. The 4x is parallax-corrected at 50 yds.. It measures 11.2 in. long and weighs just 11.6 ounces, in silver, matte black or Realtree camo finish. The 2-7x, parallax-free at 75 yds., is a 12-ounce scope available in matte black or camo. The 13-ounce 3-9x is available in all three finishes. The Prostaff scopes have multicoated lenses and 1/4-min. adjustments and are waterproof, and fogproof.

4x32 Rimfire Classic: $152.95
2-7x32: $194.95
3-9x40: $224.95
3-9x40 Realtree Nikoplex: . . $254.95

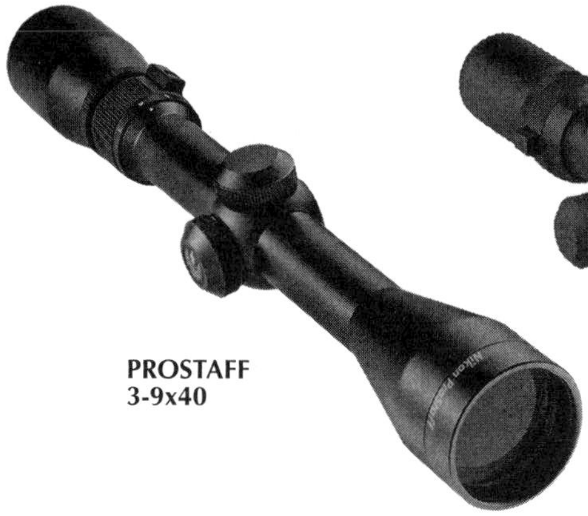

PROSTAFF 3-9x40

TACTICAL 2.5-10x44

SLUGHUNTER

SLUGHUNTER

Nikon's 3-9x40 SlugHunter is the first scope dedicated to the slug gun. It's designed around Nikon's BDC 200, a trajectory compensating reticle that provides fast, simple aiming points for various shot distances. Calibrated to be sighted in on the crosshair at 50 yds., the BDC 200 has two ballistic circles that represent 100-yard and 150-yard aiming points. For exceptionally accurate gun and load combinations, the lower reticle post becomes a 200-yard aiming point as well. Multicoated optics produce crisp, clear images, while 92 percent light transmission keeps the hunter in the field when the game is moving. Waterproof, fogproof and shockproof.

TACTICAL RIFLESCOPES

Nikon's Tactical Riflescopes are available in 2.5-10x44 and 4-16x50. The 2.5-10x44 features a choice of reticles: Nikoplex, Mildot, and Dual Illuminated Mildot. The 4-16 is offered with Nikoplex or Mildot. Both are equipped with turret mounted parallax adjustment knobs, have a tough, black-anodized matte finish and have easy-to-grip windage and elevation knobs for accurate field adjustments.

Tactical 2.5-10x44
(Nikoplex): $1388.95
Tactical 4-16x50
(Nikoplex): $1490.95

1.5-4x20 TURKEYPRO

2.5-8X28 EER HANDGUN SCOPE

Nikon's 2.5-8x28 EER (Extended Eye Relief) has a wide field of view at low power, but a twist of the power ring instantly supplies 8x magnification for long shots.

MSRP: $434.95

MONARCH UCC RIFLESCOPE

Model	4x40	1.5-4.5x20	2-7x32	3-9x40	3.5-10x50	4-12x40AO	5.5-16.5x44AO	6.5-20x44AO	2x20EER
Lustre	6500	N/A	6510	6520	6530	6540	6580	6550/6556	6560
Matte	6505	6595	6515	6525	6535	6545	6585	6555/6558	6562
Silver	N/A	N/A	N/A	6528	N/A	N/A	N/A	N/A	6565

Nikon Scopes

MONARCH UCC RIFLESCOPE									
Actual Magnification	4x	1.5x-4.5x	2x-7x	3x-9x	3.5x-10x	4x-12x	5.5x-16.5x	6.5x-19.46x	1.75x
Objective Diameter (mm)	40	20	32	40	50	40	44	44	20
Exit Pupil (mm)	10	13.3-4.4	16-4.6	13.3-4.4	14.3-5	10-3.3	8-2.7	6.7-2.2	11.4
Eye Relief (in)	3.5	3.7-3.5	3.9-3.6	3.6-3.5	3.9-3.8	3.6-3.4	3.2-3.0	3.5-3.1	26.4-10.5
FOV @ 100 yds (ft)	26.9	50.3-16.7*	44.5-12.7	33.8-11.3	25.5-8.9	25.6-8.5	19.1-6.4	16.1-5.4	22
Tube Diameter (in.)	1	1	1	1	1	1	1	1	1
Objective Tube(mm/in)	47.3-1.86	25.4/1	39.3-1.5	47.3-1.86	57.3-2.2	53.1-2.09	54-2.13	54-2.13	25, 4/1
Eyepiece O.D. (mm)	38	38	38	38	38	38	38	38	38
Length (in)	11.7	10	11.1	12.3	13.7	13.7	13.4	14.6	8.1
Weight (oz)	11.2	9.3	11.2	12.6	15.5	16.9	18.4	20.1	6.6
Adjustment Gradation	¼ MOA	¼ MOA	¼ MOA	¼ MOA	¼ MOA	¼ MOA	¼ MOA	1/8 MOA	¼ MOA
Max Internal Adjustment	120 MOA	120 MOA	70 MOA	55 MOA	45 MOA	45 MOA	40 MOA	38 MOA	120 MOA
Parallax Setting (yds)	100	75	100	100	100	50 to ∞	50 to ∞	50 to ∞	100

BUCKMASTER SCOPES					
MODEL	1x20	4x40	3-9x40	3-9x50	4.5-14x40AO
Matte	6465	6405	6425	6435	6450
Silver	N/A	N/A	6415	N/A	6455
Actual Magnification	1x	4x	3.3-8.5x	3.3-8.5x	4.5-13.5x
Objective Diameter (mm)	20	40	40	50	40
Exit Pupil (mm)	20	10	12.1-4.7	15.1-5.9	8.9-2.9
Eye Relief (in)	4.3-13.0	3.5	3.5-3.4	3.5-3.4	3.6-3.4
FOV @ 100 yds (ft)	52.5	30.6	33.9-12.9	33.9-12.9	22.5-7.5
Tube Diameter (in.)	1	1	1	1	1
Objective Tube (mm/in)	27/1.06	47.3/1.86	47.3/1.86	58.7/2.3	53/2.1
Eyepiece O.D. (mm)	37	42.5	42.5	42.5	38
Length (in)	8.8	12.7	12.7	12.9	14.8
Weight (oz)	9.2	11.8	13.4	18.2	18.7
Adjustment Gradation	¼: 1 click	¼: 1 click	¼: 1 click	¼: 1 click	—
Max Internal Adjustment	50	80	80	70	40
Parallax Setting (yds)	75	100	100	100	50 to ∞

OMEGA 3-9X40 MUZZLELOADING RIFLESCOPE						
POWER/OBJ. LENS (MM)	FIELD OF VIEW (FT/100YDS)	EYE RELIEF (IN.)	TUBE DIAMETER (IN.)	LENGTH (IN.)	WEIGHT (OZ.)	PRICE
3-9x40	25.2-8.4	5	1	11.3	13.7	$368.95

LASER IRT SCOPES						
POWER/OBJ. LENS (MM)	FIELD OF VIEW (FT/100YDS)	EYE RELIEF (IN.)	TUBE DIAMETER (IN.)	LENGTH (IN.)	WEIGHT (OZ.)	PRICE
4-12X42	24.9-8.3	3		13.1	26	$1320.95

SLUGHUNTER SCOPES						
POWER/OBJ. LENS (MM)	FIELD OF VIEW (FT/100YDS)	EYE RELIEF (IN.)	TUBE DIAMETER (IN.)	LENGTH (IN.)	WEIGHT (OZ.)	PRICE
3-9X40	25.2-9.4	5.0		11.3	13.7	$368.95

Nitrex Scopes

NITREX TR TWO SERIES RIFLE-SCOPES

NITREX TR TWO SERIES RIFLE-SCOPES

Features: Available in EBX (Enhanced Ballistic-X), Fine-X with dot, and illuminated reticles. 2-10x42, 3-15x42, 3-15x50 and 4-20x50mm versions. TruCoat multi-coated lenses, pull-up resettable turrets, power selector ring and argon-filled 1-inch tubes, matte or silver, shockproof/fogproof/waterproof.
MSRP: $465–727

Pentax Scopes

PENTAX PIONEER II 4.5-14X42

Features: Available in 3-9x40 and 4.5-14x42. One-piece, 1-inch tube, waterproof, nitrogen-filled with fully multi-coated PentaBright lenses, ¼ MOA adjustments, quick-focus eyepiece, PentaPlex reticle.
MSRP: $190–280

PIONEER II 4.5-14X42

PENTAX GAMESEEKER 5X

Features: 3-15x magnification and 50mm objective for maximum light transmission. Waterproof, nitrogen-filled 1-inch tube, fully multi-coated lenses. ¼ MOA finger-adjustable dials.
MSRP: $109–149

GAMESEEKER 5X

Pentax Scopes

4X-16XAO LIGHTSEEKER 30

8.5X-32XAO LIGHTSEEKER 30

6X-24XAO LIGHTSEEKER 30

LIGHTSEEKER 2.5xSG PLUS
MOSSY OAK BREAK-UP

LIGHTSEEKER-XL 3-9x50

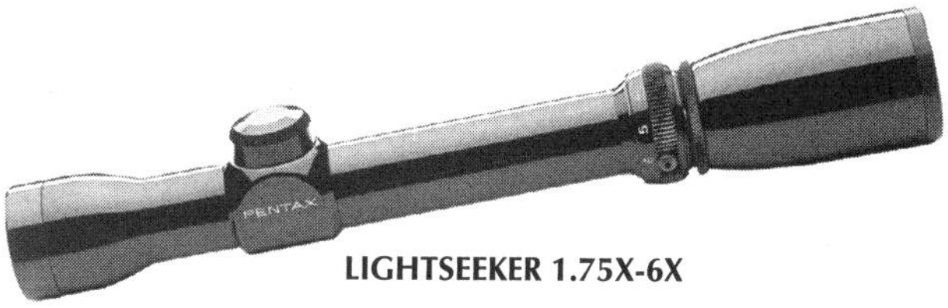

LIGHTSEEKER 1.75X-6X

GAMESEEKER

WHITETAILS UNLIMITED

GAMESEEKER

Featuring one in., one-piece tube construction, Pentax Gameseeker riflescopes are extremely durable and fully waterproof for the most extreme hunting situations. Each scope is nitrogen filled to prevent internal fogging of optical elements, and the fully-multi-coated optics with PentaBright technology help increase light transmission to deliver sharp, clear images. Every Gameseeker includes the new bullet drop compensating Precision Plex reticle.

LIGHTSEEKER

The Lightseeker features a scratch-resistant outer tube. High Quality cam zoom tube made of a bearing-type brass with precision machined cam slots. The zoom control screws are precision-ground to ½ of one thousandth tolerance. Power rings are sealed on a separate precision-machined seal tube. The scopes are filled with nitrogen and double-sealed with heavy-duty "O" rings, making them leakproof and fogproof.

Lightseeker optics are multi-coated. The Lightseeker-30 has the same features as the Lightseeker II, but with a 30mm tube. Ballistic Plex reticles are available on the 3X-9X and 6.5X-20X Whitetails Unlimited Scopes.

Pentax Scopes

Model	Tube Diameter (in)	Objective Diameter (mm)	Eyepiece Diameter (mm)	Exit Pupil (mm)	Eye Relief (in)	Field of View (ft@ 100 yd)	Adj. Grad. (in@ 100 yd)	Max. Adjust. (in@ 100 yd)	Length (in)	Weight (oz)	Reticle	Price
RIFLE SCOPES												
Lightseeker 3X - 9X	1	40	39	12.0-5.0	3.5-4.0	36-14	1/4	50	12.7	15	P, MD	$439
Lightseeker 3X - 9X	1	50	39	16.1-5.6	3.5-4.0	35-12	1/4	50	13.0	19	TW, BP	$459
Lightseeker 2.5X - 10X	1	50	39	16.3-4.6	4.2-4.7	35-10	1/4	100	14.1	23	TW	$569
Lightseeker 4X - 16X	1	44	36	10.4-2.8	3.5-4.0	33-9	1/4	35	15.4	23.7	BP	$589
LIGHTSEEKER-30												
3X-10X AO	30mm	40	35	13.3-4.4	3.5-4.0	34-14	1/4	90	13.1	20.0	BP	$519
4X-16X AO	30mm	50	42	12-3.1	3.3-3.8	27-7.5	1/4	74	15.2	23	TW, MD	$619
6X-24X AO	30mm	50	42	7.6-2.1	3.2-3.7	18-5	1/8	52	16.9	27	MD, FP	$832
8.5X-32X AO	30mm	50	42	6.2-1.7	3.0-3.5	14-4	1/8	39	18.0	27	MD, FP	$729
WHITETAILS UNLIMITED												
2X-5X WTU	1	20	39	11.1-4.2	3.1-3.8	65-23	1/2	70	10.7	10	TW	$279
3X-9X WTU	1	40	39	12.9-4.7	3.1-3.8	31-13	1/4	50	12.4	13	TW	$299
3X-9X WTU	1	50	39	16.0-5.3	3.1-3.8	32-13	1/4	50	13.2	17	BP	$299

Scopes are available in high gloss black, matte black, or camouflage, depending on model.
P=Penta-Plex, FP=Fine-Plex, DW=Deepwoods Plex, MD=Mil-Dot, CP=Comp-Plex, TW=Twilight Plex, BP=Ballistic Plex, LBP=Laser Ballistic Plex

GAMESEEKER						
Power/Obj. Lens (mm)	Field of View (ft/100yds)	Eye Relief (in.)	Adj. Gradation (in.@100yds)	Length (in.)	Weight (oz.)	Price
3-9x40	38-13.1	3	.25	12.3	14.2	$109
3-9x50	33-12.1	3	.25	13.1	18.2	$129
1.5-6x40	56-15.7	3-3.6	.25	11.9	13.5	$129
4-12x40	27.3-10-5	3	.25	13.0	14.8	$139
2.5-10x56	34.6-8.9	3-3.4	.25	13.7	22.1	$159
4-16x50	24.0-6.2	3-3.4	.25	13.9	18.8	$136
3.5-10x50	28.6-9.4	3	.25	13.0	18.8	$129

Schmidt & Bender Scopes

ZENITH 1.1-4X24

SCHMIDT & BENDER 2.5-10X40 SUMMIT

Features: S&B's first 1-inch scope for the American market, with A7 or A8 reticle in second focal plane. 3½ inches eye relief, fully multi-coated, first-quality S&B optics, ¼-minute clicks, quick-focus eyepiece

MSRP: $1400

SCHMIDT & BENDER ZENITH 1.1-4X24

Features: A great choice for dangerous or fast-moving game at close quarters. Reticle is located in the second focal plane, so size remains constant throughout the magnification range. At lower magnification a wide field of view (36 yds/100 yds).

MSRP: $1730–2289

Schmidt & Bender Scopes

2.5-10x56 VARIABLE HUNTING SCOPE

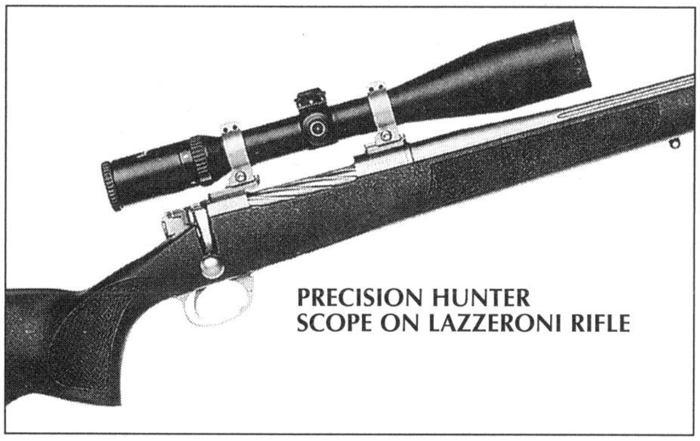

PRECISION HUNTER SCOPE ON LAZZERONI RIFLE

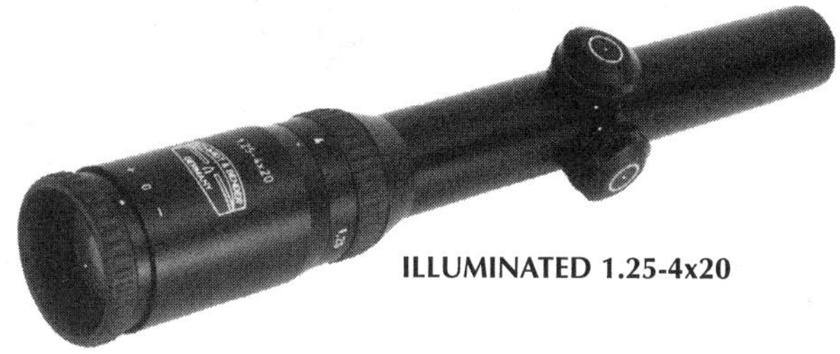

ILLUMINATED 1.25-4x20

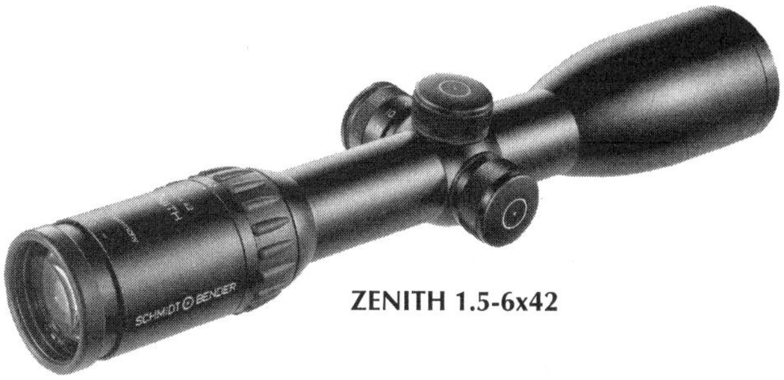

ZENITH 1.5-6x42

RIFLESCOPES

Redfield's scopes feature ED glass objective lenses; one-piece aluminum tubes; water resistant lens coating; TrueZero windage and elevation dials; 3-cam 5X zoom system; side focus adjustments (on select models); black matte finish.

This German firm manufactures carriage-class optics for discriminating sportsmen and tactical shooters. Variable scopes have 30mm and 34mm tubes. Note: All variable power scopes have glass reticles and aluminum tubes.

FIXED POWER SCOPES

4x36: $1069
6x42: $1189
8x56: $1490

ILLUMINATED SCOPES

Designed for use on magnum rifles and for quick shots at dangerous game. Long eye relief, and a wide field of view (31.5 yds. at 200 yds.) speed your aim. The Flash Dot reticle shows up bright against the target at the center of the crosswire. Illuminated scopes feature illuminated reticles; hard multi-coating on lenses; 30mm tubes

2.5-10x56:................ $2299
3-12x50: $2279
3-12x42: $2249

PRECISION HUNTER

Precision Hunter scopes combine the optical quality of S&B hunting scopes, with a sophisticated mil-dot reticle (developed by the U.S. Marine Corps) with a bullet drop compensator to give shooters the ability and confidence to place an accurate shot at up to 500 yds.

2.5-10x56 with #9 Reticle:.... $2549
3-12x42 with P3 Reticle:..... $2399
3-12x50 with P3 Reticle:..... $2399
4-16x50 with P3 Reticle:..... $2749

PRECISION HUNTER WITH PARALLAX ADJUSTMENT

4-16x50 Parallax:........... $2749

VARIABLE HUNTING SCOPES

2.5-10x56:................ $1839
3-12x42: $1799
3-12x50: $1829
4-16x50: $2179

ZENITH SERIES SCOPES

1.1-4x24: $1699–2079
1.1-4x24: $1699–2079
1.5-6x42: $1699–2349
1.5-6x42: $1699–2349
2.5-10x56:............. $1699–2479
2.5-10x56:............. $1699–2479
3-12x50 h:............. $1699–2549

Sightmark Scopes

TACTICAL 8.5-25x50

TACTICAL 3-9x40

TACTICAL 3-9X

Features: multicoated lenses; oversized windage, elevation and focusing adjustment knobs; 30mm nitrogen filled and purged tube; waterproof and fog-proof

MSRP: $180

TACTICAL 8.25-25x50

Features: multicoated lenses; oversize windage, elevation and focusing adjustment knobs; internally-illuminated mil-dot reticle; 1/8-in. locking MOA; front diopter adjustment; nitrogen filled and purged tube; waterproof and fog-proof; comes with two 30mm mounting rings

MSRP: $240

Sightron Scopes

SII 6.5-20x42 TARGET

SII BIG SKY 6-24x42

SII 6.5-20x42 TARGET

The Sightron SII variable-power target scope is available with dot, mil-dot or duplex reticles.

Features: low-profile target knobs; 720-degree adjustable objective; 3-in. detachable sun shade; one piece, aircraft quality aluminum tube; Sightron Exactrack no-drift windage and elevation adjustment system; fully coated precision ground lenses with Sightron ZACT-7 Revcoat seven layer multicoating; nitrogen filled tube

Duplex: $510

Dot: $570

Mil Dot: $600

SII BIG SKY 6-24x42

Designed for small bore and high power silhouette competitive shooters.

Features: ¼ MOA click target knobs with 20 MOA per revolution, 60 MOA of windage and elevation adjustment; ½ inch MOA Target Dot reticle; one piece, aircraft quality nitrogen filled aluminum tube; waterproof and fog proof with climate control coating on exterior lens surfaces; Sightron no-drift windage and elevation adjustment Exactrack system; fully coated precision ground lenses with ZACT-7 Revcoat seven layer multicoating; 3-inch sun shade

MSRP: $735–765

SIGHTRON HIGH-POWER SII SCOPES

Features: variable 3-12x42, 4.5-14x50, 6-24x42 and fixed 6x42 and 36x42 scopes with fully multi-coated optics, 1/8 and ¼ minutes per click, depending on magnification, AO and target knobs on target versions.

MSRP: . . . $320–650, approximately

Sightron Scopes

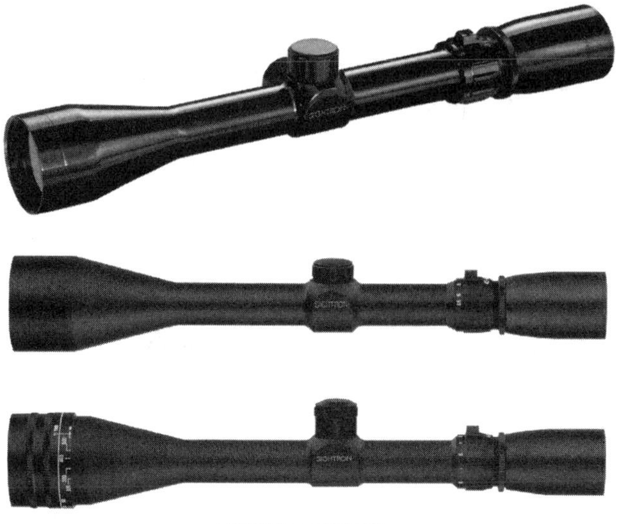

SERIES I SCOPES

SERIES II COMPETITION SCOPES

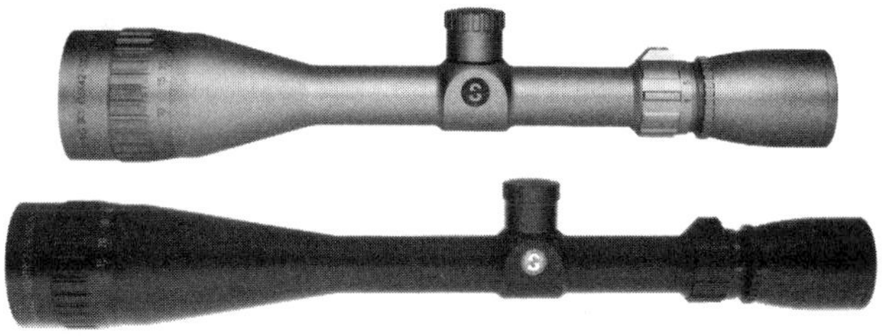

SII BIG SKY 4-16x42MM AND 6-24x42

SII BIG SKY 1.25-5x20MM BIG GAME SCOPE

SERIES I SCOPES

Series I scopes include multi-coated objective and ocular lenses; finger adjustable windage and elevation; scopes are shockproof, waterproof.

1x20: $168.99
2.5-10x44: $175.99
2.5x32: $118.37
3-9x32RF: $162.99
3-9x40ST: $146.25
3-9x40GL: $146.25
3-9x40MD: $154.38
3.5-10x50: $250

SERIES II SCOPES

Series II riflescopes feature the ExacTrack windage and elevation system; one piece body tube; multi-coated optics. SII Series scopes are waterproof, shockproof, fogproof and nitrogen filled. Available in stainless with a wide choice of reticles from plex and double diamond to mildot.

SII BIG SKY 4-16X42MM AND 6-24X42

Three new rifle scopes in Sightron's SII Big Sky line have been designed and built to meet the demanding needs of competitive shooters and hunters who shoot long range.

The three scopes include two 4-16x42mm models, one with a satin black finish and the other stainless, plus one 6-24x42 satin black model. All three scopes incorporate a mil-dot reticle that makes adjustments for wind and elevation simple. This reticle has proven itself in both military and civilian applications.

Each Sightron SII Big Sky scope starts with a one-piece mono-tube design, crafted from a bar of aluminum that is 400 times stronger than jointed scopes that may have several pieces in the tube.

Features on all three models include a one-piece tube, ExacTrack adjustment system and Zact-7 Climate Control Coatings. Each scope has target knobs and an adjustable objective lens. Eye relief is between 3.7 and 4 in.

The scopes come with a Lifetime Replacement Warranty. Should a Sightron product ever fail, consumers can return the product to Sightron or a participating dealer for replacement.

MSRP: $767.84

SII BIG SKY 1.25-5X20MM BIG GAME SCOPE

With big dangerous game in mind, Sightron has added a compact 1.25-5x20mm scope to their SII Big Sky line. This scope is built with a one-piece, mono-tube design to give it maximum strength. Lenses are precision ground and multi-coated with Sightron's Zact-7 multi-layer coating with Climate Control Coatings. These coatings will disperse moisture on the outside lens in rainy and foggy hunting conditions. Mounting surface is a consideration when scopes of these designs have to be mounted on magnum rifle actions. The SII Big Sky 1.25x5 scope has a 6.18 inch maximum mounting length between rings, one of the longest in the industry.

MSRP: $505.69

Sightron Scopes

SII BIG SKY 36x42MM TARGET RIFLE SCOPE

SERIES II COMPACT RIFLE SCOPE

SERIES III SCOPES

SII BIG SKY 36X42MM TARGET RIFLE SCOPE

Sightron's new 36-power rifle scope is sure to catch the eye of avid benchrest target shooters. This addition to the SII Big Sky line of scopes has several features that serious benchrest shooters look for in a quality scope. It's built around a one-piece mono-tube, the perfect platform for a large scope, giving it strength and durability. The glass lenses are precision ground and hand-fitted. Outside lens surfaces are multi-coated with Zact-7, Revcoat with Climate Control Coating. These lenses will enable the shooters to see clearly in all types of weather, including rain.

The SII Big Sky 36x42mm scope uses Sightron's enhanced ExacTrack adjustment system with ⅛ MOA target knobs. By loosening three set screws on the turret, the scope can be reset to zero. The scope also incorporates a 1/8 MOA dot reticle. Focus goes all the way down to 10 yds.. Each scope comes with a sunshade and lens covers.

MSRP: $806.28

SII COMPACT SCOPES

2.5-10x32:. $306.49
4x32: $241.69
6x42: $364.54

SII SIDE FOCUS RIFLE SCOPES

3.5-10x44:. $567.69
4.5-14x44:. $607.29
6.5-20x50:. $623.99

SII VARIABLE POWER RIFLE SCOPES

3.5-10x42:. $381.29
3-9x36: $340.64
3-9x42ST: $414.79

COMPETITION SCOPES

3-6x42: $612.89
4-16x42: $583.69
6-24x42: $601.29
6-24x42: $586

SERIES III SCOPES

Series III scopes feature one-piece aluminum main tubes; multi-coated objective and ocular lenses; windage and elevation adjustment; side focus; fast-focus eyepiece. SIII scopes are waterproof, shockproof, fogproof and nitrogen charged.

624x50 . . . . $1030.55
624x50MD $935.99
3.510x44MD $936.38
1.56x50. . . . . $788.69

Sightron Scopes

RETICLE DIMENSION REFERENCES

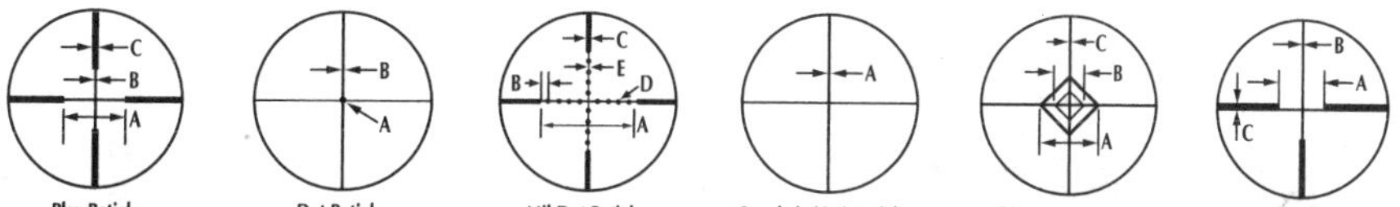

Plex Reticle — Dot Reticle — Mil Dot Reticle — Crosshair (CH) Reticle — Double Diamond Reticle — German 4A Reticle

Magnification	Objective Diameter (mm)	Field of View (ft@ 100 yd)	Eye Relief (in)	Recticle Type	Reticle Subtension Min. Power A/B/C/D/E (in.@100 yds)	Reticle Subtension Max. Power A/B/C/D/E (in.@100 yds)	Click Value	Windage Elevation Travel (in)	Tube (Dia.)	Weight (oz)	Finish
SERIES II BIG SKY RIFLESCOPES											
4-16X	42	26-7	3.6	Plex			1/8 MOA	56		16	Satin Black
6-24X	42	15.7-4.4	4.0-3.7	Mil-Dot			1/8 MOA	55		17.6	Satin Black
1.5-5X	20	79.0-19.2	4.0-3.8	Duplex			½ MOA	100		10.1	Satin Black
36X	42	4.4	3.7	Dot			1/8 MOA	40		17.3	Satin Black
SERIES II RIFLESCOPES – Side Focus											
3.5-10X	44	25.4-8.9	4.7-3.7	Plex	102.6/10.26/3.25/2.2/.69	36/3.6/1.15/.8/.23	¼ MOA	80	1.0 in.	19.0	Satin Black
4.5-14X	44	20.5-6.8	4.7-3.7	Plex	79.0/1.33/5.32	19.8/.33/1.32	¼ MOA	70	1.0 in.	19.80	Satin Black
6.5-20X	50	14.9-4.0	4.3-3.4	Plex	79.0/1.33/5.32	19.8/.33/1.32	¼ MOA	45	1.0 in.	20.50	Satin Black
SERIES II RIFLESCOPES – Variable Power											
1.5-6X	42	50-15	4.0-3.8	Plex	79.0/1.33/5.32	19.8/.33/1.32	¼ MOA	70	1.0 in.	14.00	Satin Black
2.5-8X	42	36-12	3.6-4.2	Plex	48.0/.80/3.20	15.0/.25/1.0	¼ MOA	90	1.0 in.	12.82	Satin Black
3-9X	42	34-12	3.6-4.2	Plex	39.9/.66/2.66	13.2/.22/.88	¼ MOA	95	1.0 in.	13.22	Satin Black
3-9X	42	34-12	3.6-4.2	Plex	39.9/.66/2.66	13.2/.22/.88	¼ MOA	95	1.0 in.	13.22	Stainless
3-9X	42	34-12	3.6-4.2	Dot	4/.66	1.3/.22	¼ MOA	95	1.0 in.	13.22	Satin Black
3-12X	42	32-9	3.6-4.2	Plex	39.9/.66/2.66	9.9/.16/.66	¼ MOA	80	1.0 in.	12.99	Satin Black
3.5-10X	42	32-11	3.6	Plex	34.2/.57/2.28	12.0/.20/.80	¼ MOA	60	1.0 in.	13.80	Satin Black
4.5-14X	42	22-7.9	3.6	Plex	26.4/.44/1.76	8.5/.14/.56	¼ MOA	50	1.0 in.	16.07	Satin Black
3-9X	50	34-12	4.2-3.6	Plex	39.9/.66/2.66	13.2/.22/.88	¼ MOA	*	1.0 in.	15.40	Satin Black
3-12X	50	34-8.5	4.5-3.7	Plex	39.9/.66/2.66	9.9/.16/.66	¼ MOA	*	1.0 in.	16.30	Satin Black
3.5-10X	50	30-10	4.0-3.4	Plex	34.2/.57/2.28	12.0/.20/.80	¼ MOA	50	1.0 in.	15.10	Satin Black
4.5-14X	50	23-8	3.9-3.25	Plex	26.4/.44/1.76	8.4/.14/.56	¼ MOA	60	1.0 in.	15.20	Satin Black
SERIES II RIFLESCOPES –Variable Power Target Scopes											
4-16X	42	26-7	3.6	Plex	30/.50/2.0	7.5/.125/.50	1/8 MOA	56	1.0 in.	16.00	Satin Black
4-16X	42	26-7	3.6	Plex	30/.50/2.0	7.5/.125/.50	1/8 MOA	56	1.0 in.	16.00	Stainless
4-16X	42	26-7	3.6	Dot	1.7/.10	.425/.025	1/8 MOA	56	1.0 in.	16.00	Satin Black
4-16X	42	26-7	3.6	Dot	1.7/.10	.425/.025	1/8 MOA	56	1.0 in.	16.00	Stainless
6-24X	42	15.7-4.4	3.6	Plex	19.8/.33/1.32	4.8/.08/.32	1/8 MOA	40	1.0 in.	18.70	Satin Black
6-24X	42	15.7-4.4	3.6	Plex	19.8/.33/1.32	4.8/.08/.32	1/8 MOA	40	1.0 in.	18.70	Stainless
6-24X	42	15.7-4.4	3.6	Dot	1.12/.066	.27/.016	1/8 MOA	40	1.0 in.	18.70	Satin Black
6-24X	42	15.7-4.4	3.6	Dot	1.12/.066	.27/.016	1/8 MOA	40	1.0 in.	18.70	Stainless
3-12X	42	32-9	3.6-4.2	Mil-Dot	144/14/4.7/3.1/.7	36/3.6/1.2/.79/.1	¼ MOA	80	1.0 in.	12.99	Satin Black
4-16X	42	26-7	3.6	Mil-Dot	144/14/4.7/3.1/.6	36/3.6/1.2/.79/.1	1/8 MOA	56	1.0 in.	16.00	Satin Black
4-16X	42	26-7	3.6	Mil-Dot	144/14/4.7/3.1/.6	36/3.6/1.2/.79/.1	1/8 MOA	56	1.0 in.	16.00	Stainless
6-24X	42	15.7-4.4	3.6	Mil-Dot	144/14/4.7/3.1/.4	36/3.6/1.2/.79/.1	1/8 MOA	40	1.0 in.	18.70	Satin Black
6-24X	42	15.7-4.4	3.6	Mil-Dot	144/14/4.7/3.1/.4	36/3.6/1.2/.79/.1	1/8 MOA	40	1.0 in.	18.70	Stainless
24X	44	4.4	4.33	Dot	.27/.016	.27/.016	1/8 MOA	60	1.0 in.	15.87	Satin Black
6X	42	20	4.00	Dot	.375/.070	.375/.070	1/8 MOA	100	1.0 in.	16.00	Satin Black
SERIES II RIFLESCOPES-Compact Scopes											
4X	32	25	4.52	Plex	30/.50/2.0	30/.50/2.0	¼ MOA	120	1.0 in.	9.80	Satin Black
2.5-7X	32	41-11.8	3.8-3.2	Plex	48/.80/3.20	17.2/.29/1.2	¼ MOA	120	1.0 in.	11.60	Satin Black
2.5-10X	32	41-10.5	3.8-3.5	Plex	48/.80/3.20	12/.20/.80	¼ MOA	120	1.0 in.	10.93	Satin Black
6X	42	20	3.60	Plex	19.8/.33/1.32	19.8/.33/1.32	¼ MOA	100	1.0 in.	12.69	Satin Black
SERIES II SHOTGUN SCOPES											
2.5X	20	41	4.33	Plex	48.0/.80/3.20 ¼ MOA	48.0/.80/3.20	¼ MOA	160.	1.0 in.	9.00	Satin Black
2.5-7X	32	41-11.8	3.8-3.2	DD	48/24/.60	17/8.5/.26	¼ MOA	120	1.0 in.	11.60	Satin Black

**Specifications not available at press time*

Simmons Scopes

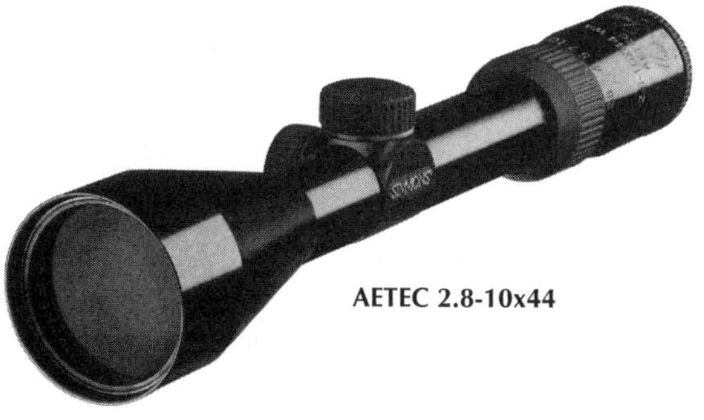

AETEC 2.8-10x44

AETEC RIFLESCOPES

Features TrueZero flex erector system; Quick Target Acquisition eyepiece, with constant minimum 3½ in. of eye relief; one-piece tube construction; aspherical lens technology and fully multi-coated optics; HydroShield lens coating; SureGrip rubber surfaces on all eyepieces and side-focus parallax adjustments.

Simmons Scopes

BLAZER 3-9x50

PROHUNTER

MODEL 807732 (2X)

PROSPORT

BLAZER RIFLESCOPES

The Blazer line of riflescopes feature the TrueZero adjustment system; QTA eyepiece; high-quality optical glass and fully coated optics; HydroShield lens coating SureGrip rubber surfaces.

PRODIAMOND SHOTGUN SCOPES

Master Series ProDiamond shotgun scopes feature TrueZero adjustment system QTA eyepiece; up to 5½ in. of eye relief; ProDiamond reticle; one-piece tube construction; high–quality optical glass and multi-coated optics; HydroShield lens coating; SureGrip rubber surfaces on power change rings and eyepieces.

PROHUNTER HANDGUN SCOPES

ProHunter handgun scopes feature long eye relief, ½ and ¼ MOA adjustments, and are waterproof, fogproof and shockproof. Available in black and silver matte finishes.

PROHUNTER RIFLESCOPES

Master Series ProHunter rifle and shotgun scopes feature the TrueZero adjustment system; QTA eyepiece; one-piece tube construction; high-quality optical glass and multi-coated optics; HydroShield lens coating; SureGrip rubber surfaces and side-focus parallax adjustments.

PROSPORT SCOPES

Master Series ProSport scopes feature TrueZero adjustment system and QTA eyepiece with up to 5½ in. of eye relief; one-piece tube construction; high-quality optical glass and fully coated optics; HydroShield lens coating; SureGrip rubber surfaces.

RIMFIRE RIFLESCOPES

The Rimfire collection is scaled down in size with ¾ in. tubes for smaller rifles. All are calibrated parallax free at 50 yds. for shorter rimfire ranges. They come complete with a set of rings ready to be mounted on your favorite rimfire rifle.

22 MAG RIMFIRE SCOPES

Featuring TrueZero adjustment system; QTA quick target acquisition eyepiece; high-quality optical glass and fully coated optics; HydroShield lens coating; SureGrip rubber surfaces; scopes come with a set of rimfire rings. Scopes come in gloss or matte finish.

RED DOT SCOPES

Simmons Red Dot scopes work great on handguns, crossbows, shotguns and paintball guns with rapid target acquisition. Click type, 1 MOA windage and elevation adjustments.

Simmons Scopes

AETEC RIFLESCOPES				
Magnification (x obj. dia.)	Field of View (ft., 100 yds)	Dia./Length (in.)	Weight (oz.)	MSRP
2.8-10 x 44 Gloss	43.5/11.5	na	13.8	$155.99
2.8-10 x 44 Matte	43.5/11.5	na	13.8	$179.99
2.8-10 x 44 Ill. Ret.	43.5/11.5	na	12.3	$199.99
4-14 x 44 SF Matte	29.3/8.2	na	15	$219.99
4-14 x 44 SF	Ill. Ret. 29.3/8.2	na	15.5	$219.99
BLAZER RIFLESCOPES				
Magnification (x obj. dia.)	Field of View (ft., 100 yds)	Dia./Length (in.)	Weight (oz.)	MSRP
3-9 x 32	31.4/10.5	na	9.6	$43.99
3-9 x 40	31.4/10.5	na	10.8	$48.99
3-9 x 50	31.4/10	na	13.2	$53.99
4 x 32	23.6	na	8.8	$58.99
PRO-DIAMOND SHOTGUN SCOPES				
Magnification (x obj. dia.)	Field of View (ft., 100 yds)	Dia./Length (in.)	Weight (oz.)	MSRP
1.5-5 x 32 (Camo Pro Diamond)	67/20	na	9.3	$120
4X32	17	1/8.5	9.1	$79.95
PROHUNTER HANDGUN SCOPES				
Magnification (x obj. dia.)	Field of View (ft., 100 yds)	Dia./Length (in.)	Weight (oz.)	MSRP
2-6 x 32	14/4.5	na	9.7	$127.95
4 x 32	15	9	8	$93.95

PROHUNTER RIFLESCOPES				
Magnification (x obj. dia.)	Field of View (ft., 100 yds)	Dia./Length (in.)	Weight (oz.)	MSRP
3 - 9 x 40	31.4	1/11	10.8	$82.99
PROSPORT SCOPES				
Magnification (x obj. dia.)	Field of View (ft., 100 yds)	Dia./Length (in.)	Weight (oz.)	MSRP
3-9 x 40	31.4/10.5	na	10.8	$68.99
3-9 x 50	31.4/10.5	na	13.2	$78.99
4-12 x 40 AO	24.8/8.1	na	13.8	$86.99
6-18 x 50 A/O	14.7/5.3	na	8.3	$114.99
22 MAG RIMFIRE SCOPES				
Magnification (x obj. dia.)	Field of View (ft., 100 yds)	Dia./Length (in.)	Weight (oz.)	MSRP
3 - 9 x 32	31.4/10.5	na	9.6	$47.99
3 - 9 x 32 A/O	31.4/10.5	na	10.8	$67.99
4 x 32	21	na	8.8	$41.99

RED DOT SCOPES					
Description	Field of View	Eye Relief	Weight (oz.)	Reticle	MSRP
30mm	Variable	Unlimited	6.5	4 MOA Dot	$47–115
30mm	Variable	Unlimited	5.6	Multi Reticle	$47–115
42mm	Variable	Unlimited	8.25	4 MOA Dot	$47–115

Swarovski Scopes

SWAROVSKI Z6 5-30X50

Features: 30mm tube, fully multi-coated lenses, ¼-minute clicks, six-times magnification, Ballistic Turret for long shooting, wide choice of reticles. Other magnification ranges available. Z6i, or illuminated-reticle versions, have new top-side controls, day/night modes, 64 brightness levels, automatic shut-off.
MSRP: $2532–3443

Z5 5-25X52

SWAROVSKI Z3

SWAROVSKI Z5 3.5-18X44, 5-25X52 P

Features: compact 1-inch tube with five-times power range, fully multi-coated optics, quick-focus eyepiece, available with long-range reticles, ballistic turret.
MSRP: $1532–1776

SWAROVSKI Z3 SCOPE LINE

Features: Low-profile 1-inch tube, available in 3-9x36, 3-10x42, and 4-12x50 with fully multi-coated optics, standard and long-range second-plane reticles, quick-focus eyepiece and Ballistic Turret.
MSRP: $1087–1410

Swarovski Scopes

Z6

Swarovski's Z6 scopes offer 50% more magnification, field of view, and eye relief.

Features: Swarovski lenses with Swarotop lens coating; waterproof and fog-proof; 6x zoom; low-design reticle illumination unit; High Grid technology eyepiece; watertight forged aluminum housing; microstructure grooves in tube to reduce reflection; 4-point coil sighting system; ergonomically designed operating elements; two separate memory locations for day and night settings; large choice of reticles

Z6 1-6x24: $1888
Z6 1-6x24 EE: $1888
Z6 1.7-10x42: $2032
Z6 2-12x50: $2187–2257
Z6i 1-6x24: $2443
Z6i 1-6x24EE: $2443
Z6i 1.7-10x42: $2732
Z6i 2-12x50: $2807

Z6

Z6 7-10x42

AV SERIES SCOPES

AV scopes are lightweight 1-in. scopes featuring constant-size reticles, lightweight alloy tubes and satin finish. Totally waterproof even with caps removed, these scopes have fully multi-coated lenses.

3-10x42 4A Reticle AV: $1099
3-10x42 PLEx Reticle AV: $1099
3-10x42 TDS Plex Reticle AV: . $1177
3-9x36 4A Reticle AV: $988
3-9x36 PLEx Reticle AV: $988
4-12x50 RAIL 4A Reticle AV: . . $1177
4-12x50 RAIL TDS Plex Reticle AV: $1288
4-12x50 TDS Plex Reticle AV: $1254
4-12x50 PLEx Reticle AV: $1177
6-18x50 TDS Plex Reticle AV: $1388
6-18x50 4A Reticle AV: $1288
6-18x50 PLEX Reticle AV: $1288

3-10x42

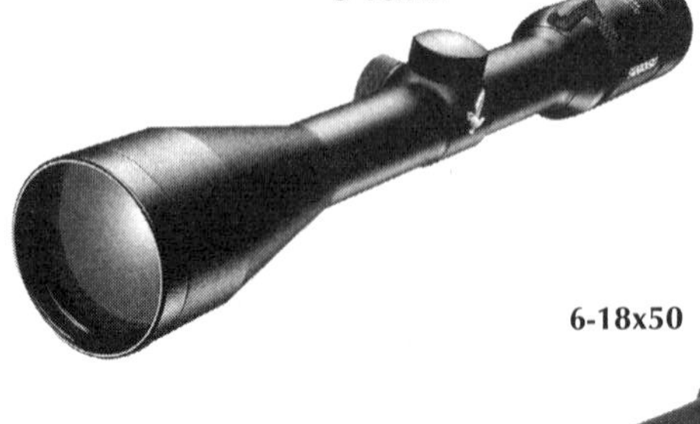

4-12x50

6-18x50

3-9x36

Swarovski Scopes

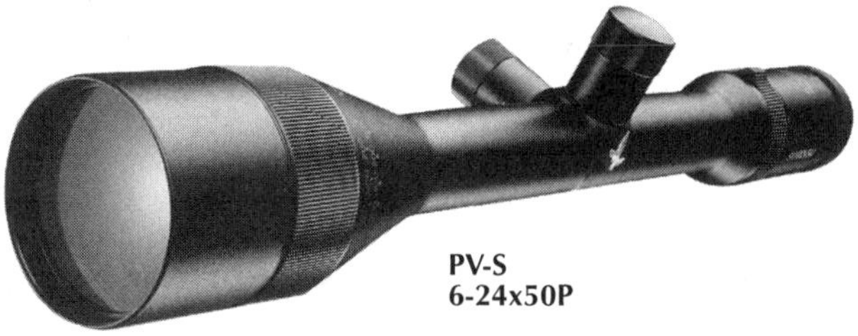

PV-S
6-24x50P

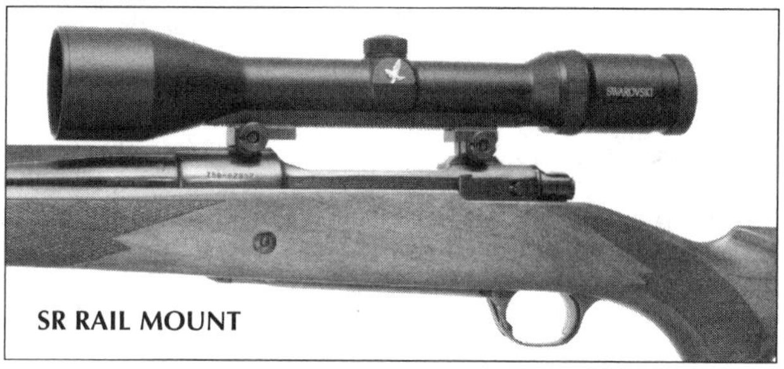

SR RAIL MOUNT

PF / PF-N SERIES

PF fixed magnification rifle scopes feature less weight, an extra wide field of view and a telescopic dampening system for the eyecup. They also feature a scratchproof surface. The Habicht PF-N versions come with an illuminated reticle.

PF 8x50 30mm w/4A Reticle:............................ $1100

SR RAIL PH SERIES

The Swarovski SR line uses an integral toothed rail on PH scopes that makes the tube stronger while eliminating the ring/tube juncture that can fail during heavy recoil.

1.5-6x42 RAIL Series #4A Reticle:............................ $1599

2.5-10x56 RAIL Series #4 Reticle PH:....................... $1966

3-12x50 RAIL Series TDS PLEx Reticle:............................ $1866

AV LIGHTWEIGHT	3-9x36	3-10x42	4-12x50	6-18x50
Magnification	3-9x	3.3-10x	4-12x	6-18x
Objective lens diameter (mm)	36	42	50	50
Objective lens diameter (in.)	1.42	1.55	1.97	1.97
Exit pupil, diameter (mm)	12-4	12.6-4.2	12.5-4.2	8.3-2.8
Eye relief (in.)	3.5	3.5	3.5	3.5
Field of view, real (m/100m)	13-4.5	11-3.9	9.7-3.3	17.4-6.5
Field of view, real (ft./100yds.)	39-13.5	33-11.7	29.1-9.9	17.4-6.5
Diopter compensation (dpt)	± 2.6	± 2.5	± 2.5	± 2.5
Transission (%)	94	94	94	92
Twilight factor (DIN 58388)	9-18	9-21	11-25	17-30
Impact Point correction per click (in./100yds.)	0.25	0.25	0.25	0.25
Max. elevation/windage adjustment range (ft./100yds.)	4.8	4.2	3.6	3.9
Length, approx (in.)	11.8	12.44	13.5	14.85
Weight, approx (oz.): L	11.6	12.7	13.9	20.3
LS	–	13.6	15.2	–
L=light alloy • LS=light alloy with rail				

PF & PV	PF 6x42	PF/PF-N 8X50	PF/PF-N 8X56	PV/PV-1 1.25-4X24	PV 1.5-6X42	PV/PV-N 2.5-10X42	PV/PV-N 2.5-10X56	PV/PV-N 3-1-1X50	PV 4-16X50P	PV 6-24X50P	PV-S 6-24X50P
Magnification	6x	8x	8x	1.25-4x	1.5-6x	2.5-10x	2.5-10x	3-12x	4-16x	6-24x	6-24x
Objective lens diameter (mm)	42	50	56	17-24	20-42	33-42	33-56	39-50	50	50	50
Objective lens diameter (in.)	1.65	1.97	2.20	0.67-0.94	0.79-1.65	1.3-1.65	1.3-2.20	1.54-1.97	1.97	1.97	1.97
Exit pupil, diameter (mm)	7	6.25	7	12.5-6	13.1-7	13.1-4.2	13.1-5.6	13.1-4.2	12.5-3.1	8.3-2.1	8.3-2.1
Eye relief (in.)	3.15	3.15	3.15	3.15	3.15	3.15	3.15	3.15	3.15	3.15	3.15
Field of view, real (m/100m)	7	5.2	5	32.8-10.4	21.8-7	13.2-4.2	13.2-4.1	11-3.5	9.1-2.6	6.2-1.8	6.2-1.8
Field of view, real (ft./100yds.)	21	15.6	15.6	98.4-31.2	65.4-21	39.6-12.6	39.6-12.3	33-10.5	27.3-7.8	18.6-5.4	18.6-5.4
Diopter compensation (dpt)	+2. -3	+2. -3	+2. -3	+2. -3	+2. -3	+2. -3	+2. -3	+2. -3	+2. -3	+2. -3	+2. -3
Transission (%)	94	94/92	93/91	93/91	93	94/92	93/91	94/92	90	90	90
Twilight factor (DIN 58388)	16	20	21	4-10	4-16	7-21	7-24	9-25	11-28	17-35	17-35
Impact Point correction per click (in./100yds.)	0.36	0.36	0.36	0.54	0.36	0.36	0.36	0.36	0.18	0.18	0.17
Max. elevation/windage adjustment range (ft./100yds.)	3.9	3.3	3.9	9.9	6.6	3.9	3.9	3.3	E:5.4/W:3	E:3.6/W:2.1	E:3.6/W:2.1
Length, approx (in.)	12.83	13.94	13.27	10.63	12.99	13.23	13.62	14.33	14.21	15.43	15.43
Weight, approx (oz.): L	12.0	14.8	15.9	12.7	16.2	15.2	18.0	16.9	22.2	23.6	24.5
LS	13.4	15.9	16.9	13.8	17.5	16.4	19.0	18.3	—	—	—
L=light alloy • LS=light alloy with rail											

SCOPES

Swift Scopes

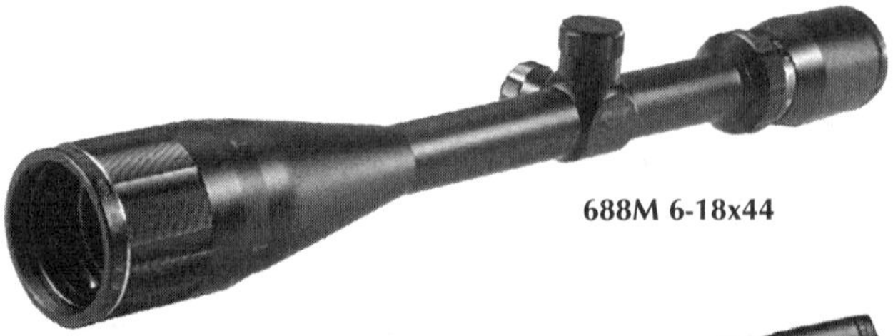

688M 6-18x44

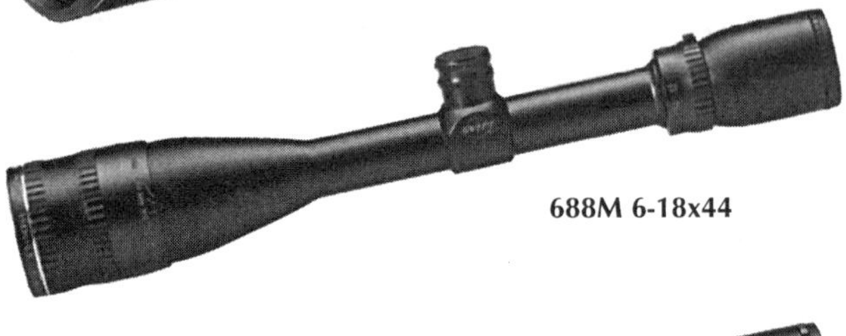

688M 6-18x44

685M 3-9x40

˚Swift Premier line features include full saddle construction; Speed Focus; fully multi-coated optics; clear dust caps; scopes are constructed to withstand the severe reverse recoil. Elevation and windage adjustments are mounted full saddle on hard anodized 1 in. tubes. Available in matte and silver finish.

PISTOL SCOPES				
Magnification (x obj. dia.)	Field of View (ft., 100 yds)	Dia./Length (in.)	Weight (oz.)	MSRP
2-6x32	14' @ 2x, 4.5' @ 6x	1/5.5	10.6	$219–300
4x32	6.6	1/9.4	9.9	$150–200
PREMIER RIFLESCOPES				
Magnification (x obj. dia.)	Field of View (ft., 100 yds)	Dia./Length (in.)	Weight (oz.)	MSRP
1.5-4.5x32	71 @ 1.5x, 25 @ 4.5x	1/10.41	12.7	$200–250
2-7x40	60 @ 2x, 17 @ 7x	1/12.2	14.8	$200–250
3-9x40	40 @ 3x, 14.2 @ 9x	1/12	13.1	$210–260
3.5-10x44	35 @ 3.5x, 11 @ 10x	1/12.6	15.2	$220–280
4-12x50	29.5' @ 4x, 9.5 @ 12x	1/13.8	15.8	$260–325
4-12x40	29.5' @ 4x, 11 @ 12x	1/12.4	15.4	$220–260
6-18x44	19.5' @ 6x, 7 @ 18x	1/15.4	22.6	$260–330
6-18x50	19' @ 6x, 6.7 @ 18x	1/15.8	20.9	$280–360
STANDARD RIFLESCOPES				
Magnification (x obj. dia.)	Field of View (ft., 100 yds)	Dia./Length (in.)	Weight (oz.)	MSRP
3-9x40	40 @ 3x,14 @ 9x	1/12.6	12.2	$170
4x32	25	1/10	8.9	$150
4x40	35	1/12.2	11.4	$140

Tasco Scopes

2.5-10x42 VARMINT

3-12X40 WORLD CLASS .22

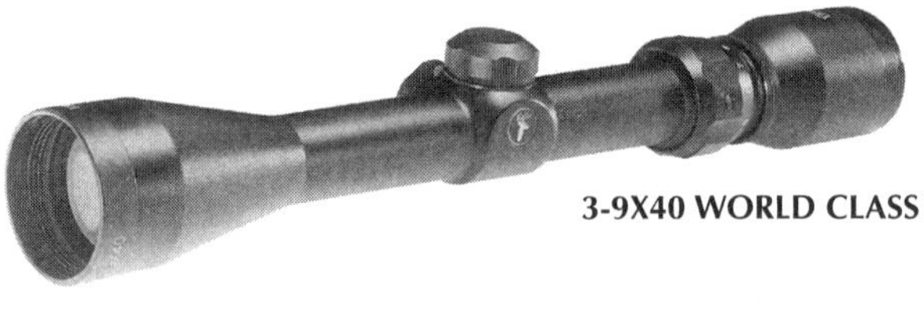

3-9X40 WORLD CLASS 40

GOLDEN ANTLER

Golden Antler riflescopes are engineered with 1 in. advanced construction for durability and feature HDC (High Definition Coating) on lens surfaces in addition to fully coated optics. Golden Antler scopes are waterproof/fogproof/shockproof. Backed by a Limited Lifetime Warranty.

PRONGHORN RIFLESCOPES

Wide view Pronghorn scopes feature magenta multi-coating on the objective and ocular lenses for increased light transmission and are waterproof, fogproof and shockproof.

RIMFIRE SCOPES

Tasco Rimfire scopes are designed for either .22 rifles or quality air guns, and feature lenses calibrated for short ranges and coated optics for a bright image. Rimfire scopes fit .22 and airgun receivers.

TARGET & VARMINT SCOPES

Tasco Target and Varmint riflescopes share high-quality, multi-coated optics and large objective lenses along with 1/4 or 1/8 min. click windage and elevation adjustments. Target and Varmint scopes are waterproof, fogproof and shockproof.

TITAN SERIES

Titan riflescopes are waterproof, fogproof and shockproof with premium, multi-coated, SuperCon optics and finger-adjustable windage and elevation controls.

WORLD CLASS RIFLESCOPES

World Class riflescopes feature Tasco

Tasco Scopes

SuperCon multi-layered coating on the objective and ocular lenses and fully coated optics. Models feature either ProShot, 30/30 or True MilDot reticles and are waterproof, fogproof and shockproof. The scopes are built with monotube construction and carry a Limited Lifetime Warranty.

22 RIFLESCOPES

Tailor-made for .22 rimfire rifles, featuring full-sized, 1 in. Advanced Monotube Construction; 50 yd. parallax setting and rings to fit standard .22 bases; magenta multi-layered lens coatings and fully coated optics; waterproof and fogproof construction.

GOLDEN ANTLER			
Magnification (x obj. dia.)	Field of View (ft., 100 yds)	Dia./Length (in.)	Weight (oz.)
4x32mm	32	1/12.75	11
3-9x32mm	39-13	1/13.25	12.2
2.5x32mm	43	1/11.4	10.1
3-9x40mm	41-15	1/12.75	13
TARGET & VARMINT SCOPES			
Magnification (x obj. dia.)	Field of View (ft., 100 yds)	Dia./Length (in.)	Weight (oz.)
2.5-10x42	35-9	1/14	19.1
6-24x40	17-4	1/16	19.1
6-24x42	13-3.7	1/16	19.6
10-40x50	11-2.5	1/15.5	25.5
TITAN SERIES			
Magnification (x obj. dia.)	Field of View (ft., 100 yds)	Dia./Length (in.)	Weight (oz.)
3.5-10x50	30-10.5	1/13	17.1
3-9x44	39-14	1/12.75	16.5
3-12x30	27-10	1/14	20.7
1.5-6x42	59 20	1/12	16.5
PROPOINT SIGHTS			
Magnification (x obj. dia.)	Field of View (ft., 100 yds)	Dia./Length (in.)	Weight (oz.)
1x25mm	40	1.18/5	5.5
1x30mm	68	1.18/4.75	5.4

WORLD CLASS RIFLESCOPES			
Magnification (x obj. dia.)	Field of View (ft., 100 yds)	Dia./Length (in.)	Weight (oz.)
3-9x40mm IR	34.50-10.50	1/12.50	16.26
1.5-4.5x32mm	77-23	1/11.25	12
2-8x32mm	50-17	1/10.5	12.5
3-9x40mm	41-15	1/12.75	13
PRONGHORN RIFLESCOPES			
Magnification (x obj. dia.)	Field of View (ft., 100 yds)	Dia./Length (in.)	Weight (oz.)
2.5x32	43	1/11.4	10.1
3-9x32	39-13	1/12	11
3-9x40	39-13	1/13	12.1
4x32	32	1/12	11
22 RIFLESCOPES			
Magnification (x obj. dia.)	Field of View (ft., 100 yds)	Dia./Length (in.)	Weight (oz.)
3-9x32	17.75-6	1/12.75	11.3
4x32	13.5	1/12.25	12.1
RIMFIRE SCOPES			
Magnification (x obj. dia.)	Field of View (ft., 100 yds)	Dia./Length (in.)	Weight (oz.)
4x20mm	23	¾/10.5	3.8
3-7x20mm	24-11	¾/11.5	5.7
4x15mm	20.5	¾/11	4

Trijicon Scopes

SCOPES

ACCUPOINT WITH CROSSHAIR RETICLE

Trijicon's AccuPoint riflescopes now come with a crosshair reticle. The AccuPoint with illuminated crosshair reticle does not require batteries for operation. Battery-free tritium technology provides amber illumination where the crosshairs intersect.

Features: Trijicon Manual Brightness Adjustment Override (allows the user to shade the tritium and fiber-optics during daylight to decrease the brightness of the illuminated reticle during increased light situations); aircraft quality, hard black matte finish anodized aluminum weather-resistant, nitrogen-filled scope body

MSRP: . . . . $815–$918

Trijicon Scopes

TRIJICON ACCUPOINT 5-20X50

Features: Trijicon's long-range scope for varmint hunters and tactical shooters has fully multi-coated optics, fiber-optic and tritium aiming point illumination, 30mm hard-anodized aluminum tube, choice of post, duplex or Mil Dot reticles, external turret controls and side parallax adjustment.

MSRP: $1224

TRIJICON RMR SIGHT

Features: Trijicon's new red-dot sight can be teamed up with the ACOG or AccuPoint for fast target acquisition or precise aim at long range. Available with adjustable LED insert or dual-illuminated, battery-free fiber optics.

LED: $663

Dual Illuminated: $556

ACCUPOINT 5-20X50

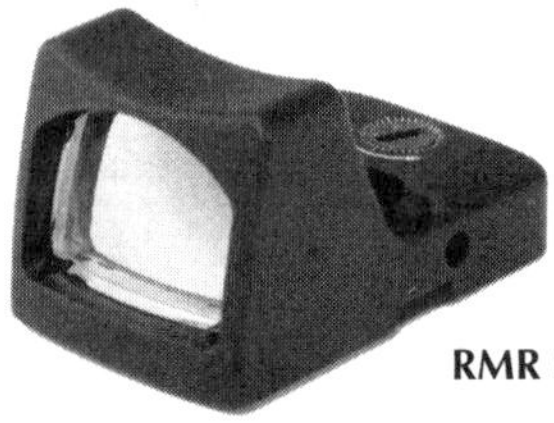

RMR SIGHT

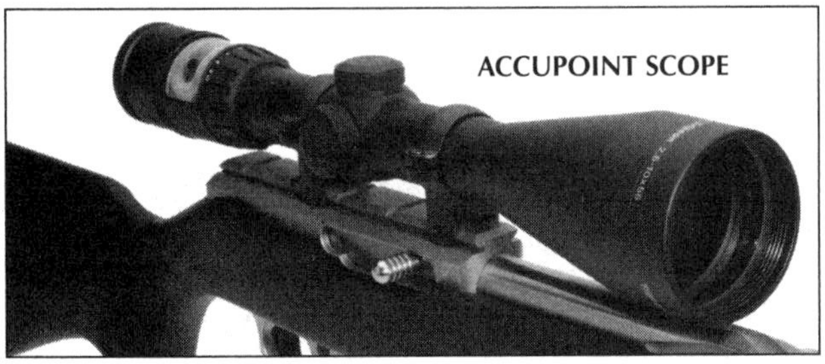

ACCUPOINT SCOPE

ACCUPOINT 3-9x40

ACCUPOINT SCOPES

AccuPoint's features a dual-illuminated aiming point—reticle illumination is supplied by advanced fiber optics or, in low-light conditions, by a self-contained tritium lamp. The AccuPoint scopes feature quick-focus eyepiece; water-resistant and nitrogen filled, multi-layer coated lenses; scope body crafted of hard anodized aluminum; manual brightness adjustment override; fiber-optic light collector. Choice of amber or red aiming point illuminated by a special tritium lamp.

ACCUPOINT 3–9X40 RIFLESCOPE

Utilizing Trijicon's exclusive battery-free, dual-illumination technology, and a fiber optic collector that automatically adjusts the brightness of the aiming point, the Trijicon AccuPoint 3–9x40 Riflescope has a super-precise, tritium-illuminated, amber-colored reticle to help ensure optimum clarity, regardless of the available light. This scope also features the revolutionary Bindon Aiming Concept, a both-eyes-open aiming method using telescopic magnification that allows a shooter to lock onto a moving target more quickly than with a traditional riflescope. Features include multi-layer coated lenses for excellent light transmission with no distortion; quick-focus eyepiece; long eye relief of 3.6 to 3.2 in.; manual brightness adjustment override; 1/4 MOA windage and elevation adjustments. The weather-resistant, nitrogen-filled scope body is crafted of aircraft-quality, hard anodized aluminum for maximum durability, and its black matte finish eliminates glare and helps to conceal the shooter's presence. Offered with either an amber or red reticle.

ACCUPOINT SCOPES				
Magnification (x obj. dia.)	Field of View (ft., 100 yds)	Dia./Length (in.)	Weight (oz.)	MSRP
3-9x40	33.8-11.3	1.18/12.2	13.4	$799
1.25-4x24	61.6-20.5	1.18/10.2	11.4	$799
2.5-10x56	37.6-10.1	1.18/13.8	22.1	$950

Vortex Scopes

VORTEX VIPER RIFLE-SCOPE

Features: Fully multi-coated optics with XR anti-reflective coating on XD premium glass, waterproof/fogproof with argon gas, one-piece 1-inch alloy tube. Fast-focus eyepiece and resettable ¼-minute adjustment dials. Magnification ranges from 2-7x32 to 6.5-20x50.

MSRP: . . . . starting at $359

VORTEX VIPER RIFLE-SCOPE

CROSSFIRE 4-12x40

STRIKEFIRE

CROSSFIRE SERIES

Reticle styles include V-Plex (on most models), V-Brite (on select models), Fine Crosshair (on target model) and Mil Dot (on long-range target & varmint model). ***Features:*** fully multi-coated optics; solid, one-piece turned aircraft-grade aluminum alloy tube; waterproof/fogproof construction; dry nitrogen purging to prevent internal fogging and corrosion; variable-zoom

1.5-4x32: $129
2-7x32: $139
2.5-10x50: $189
3-9x40: $139
3.5-10x44: $160
4-12x40: $159
6-24x50 AO: $249

STRIKEFIRE RED DOT

Vortex's StrikeFire red dot scopes are compact, waterproof and shockproof. Battery life ranges from 2,000 hours (83 days) to 3,000 hours (125 days), depending on power setting. ***Features:*** nitrogen-purged non-glare, black matte 30mm aluminum alloy tube; easily switches between intensity adjustable red and green dots; parallax free past 50 yards; unlimited eye relief; fully multi-coated lenses; flip-up lens caps; choice of rings for shotgun or AR mount

MSRP: . . . . starting at $179

DIAMONDBACK SCOPES

DIAMONDBACK SCOPES

Every glass surface of the Diamondback is fully multi-coated. By transmitting 91 percent of the light, you'll see the brightly detailed views you need when taking aim. Fast focus eyepiece is quick and easy to use. Pop-up dials let you easily set elevation and windage back to zero. Audible clicks are easily counted for fast, precise adjustment of elevation and windage. Zero reset accuracy. Machined for durability. Rugged one-piece tube, constructed of 6061 T6 aircraft-grade aluminum. Argon gas eliminates internal fogging.

Model	Field of view (ft/100yds)	Eye relief (in)	Click value (in@100yd)	Length (in)	Weight (oz.)	MSRP
2-7x35	64.3-19.3	3.5-3.1	1/4 MOA	11.6	14.2	$249
3.5-10x50	35.8-13.5	3.6-3.3	1/4 MOA	12.6	16.6	$299
1.75-5x32	68.3-23.1	3.7-3.5	1/4 MOA	10.3	12.8	$239
3-9x40	44.6-14.8	3.5-3.3	1/4 MOA	11.8	14.8	$259
4-12x40	32.4-11.3	3.4-3.1	1/4 MOA	12.1	14.8	$269

Weaver Scopes

TACTICAL 4-20X50

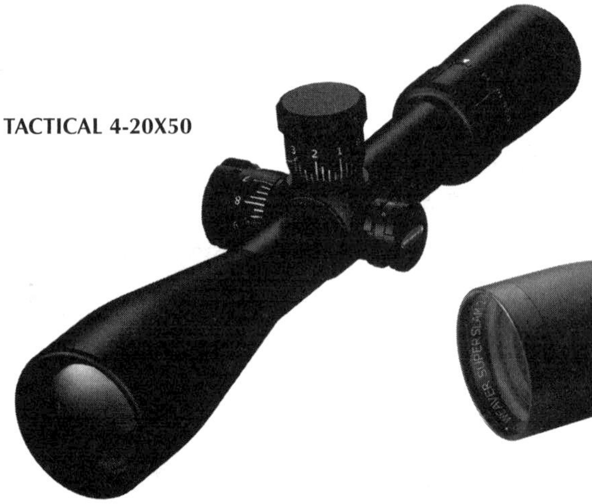

SUPER SLAM
2-10X42

WEAVER TACTICAL 3-15X50, 4-20X50

Features: five-times magnification, first-plane reticle, 30mm tube, turret parallax adjustment, Mil Dot reticle. Available in 4-20x50 or 3-15x50 in matte finish.
MSRP: $631

WEAVER SUPER SLAM 2-10X42

Features: One-piece 1-inch tubes, five times power range, SHR fully multi-coated lenses, EBX ballistic reticle, ¼-minute adjustments, 3-position, pull-up turrets (no caps), Argon-purged tubes, 3-point erector assembly, waterproof/fogproof/shockproof, in 2-10x42 to 4-20x50 power ranges in matte or silver.
MSRP: $555–869

K-6

CLASSIC
HANDGUN
1.5-4X20

RIMFIRE RV-7

CLASSIC HANDGUN & SHOTGUN SCOPES

Fixed-power scopes include 2x28 and 4x28 scopes in gloss black or silver. Variables in 1.5-4x20 and 2.5-8x28 come with a gloss black finish. Features: one-piece tubes, multi-coated lenses and generous eye relief.
2x28 Gloss Black or Silver: . . $249.99
4x28 Gloss Black or Silver: . . $249.99
1.5-4x20 Gloss Black: $307.49
2.5-8x28 Gloss
Black or Silver: $325.95
2.5-8x28 Matte: $325.95

CLASSIC K SERIES

Classic American scopes, the K2.5, K4 and K6 now have a sleeker look, weigh less but deliver brighter images. K scopes–including the target model, KT-15–have one-piece tubes.
K-4 (Matte): $202.49
K-6 (Gloss): $215.95
K-6 (Matte): $215.95

CLASSIC RIMFIRE RV4, RV-7 AND RV-9

Rimfire scopes are well suited .22s and airguns. They are designed with a sturdy one-piece aluminum housing and are waterproof and fogproof with fully multi-coated, nonglare lenses and 28mm objective lenses. Available in fixed or variable power.
4x28 Rimfire Matte Black: $181.49
2.5-7x28 Rimfire Matte
Black or Silver: $211.95
3-9x32 AO Matte:...............$344.49

GRAND SLAM SCOPES

The Grand Slam series features an advanced one-piece tube design with a "sure-grip" power ring and AO adjustment. An offset parallax indicator lets you remain in shooting position while adjusting the scope. The eyepiece has a fast-focus adjustment ring. Grand Slam configurations include: 4.75x40mm, a fixed-power scope; 1.5-5x32mm, the ideal scope for short-range rifles; 3.5-10x40mm, the traditional choice of big-game hunters; 3.5-10x50mm, which provides the brightest view in low-light situations; 4.5-14x40mm AO, possibly the most versatile Grand Slam; and 6-20x40mm AO, target/varminter model. Windage and elevation knobs have target-type finger adjustments. Grand Slam scopes are also equipped with

Weaver Scopes

GRAND SLAM
6-20X40

GRAND SLAM
3.5-10X50

T-10

T-SERIES MODEL T-6
RIFLESCOPE

T-SERIES TARGET/
VARMINT T-36

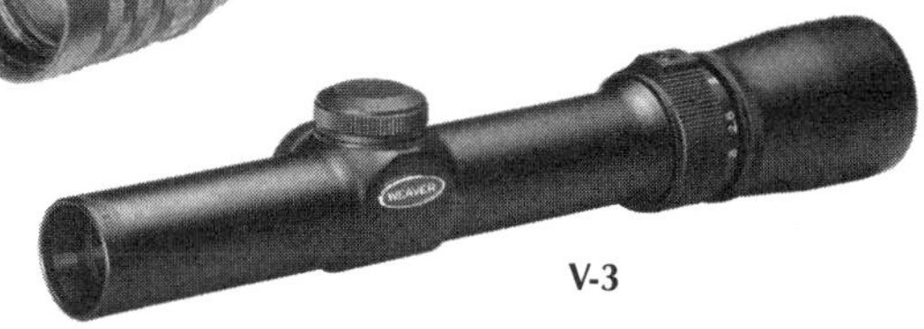

V-3

Micro-Trac, Weaver's four-point adjustment system. All Grand Slam scopes are offered with a plex reticle. The scopes have a non-glare black matte or silver and black finish.

6-20x40 AO Black or Silver: . $587.95
4.5-14x40 AO Black or Silver: $574.49
3.5-10x50 Black or Silver: . . . $530.49
3-10x40 Black or Silver: $437.95
1.5-5x32 Black: $481.95

T-24 TARGET

The T-10 target model (no AO) has 1/4-min. click adjustments and a 1/8 min. dot reticle. It weighs just 1 lb., has a 40mm objective lens and comes in black satin finish. The T-24 also has a 40mm front end. The parallax (AO) adjustment is the traditional forward ring. Weight 17 oz. Choose a 1/8 min. dot or a 1/2 min. dot.

T-24: $619.49

V-16 AND V-24

The V16 is popular for a variety of shooting applications, from close shots that require a wide field of view to long-range varmint or benchrest shooting. Adjustable objective allows a parallax-free view from 30 ft. to infinity. Features one-piece tube for strength and moisture resistance and multi-coated lenses for clear, crisp images. Two finishes and three reticle options.

Magnification/Objective: 4-16x42mm
Field of View: 26.8-6.8
Eye Relief: 3.1 in.
Length: 13.9 in.
Weight: 16.5 oz.
Reticle: Choice of Dual-X, 1/4 MOA Dot, or Fine Crosshair
Finish: Matte black
V-16 4-16x42: $481.95

V16

V-24 6-24x42 Black Matte: $578.95
V-24 6-24x42 With Mil Dot: . . . $558.95

V-3

Magnification/Objective: 1-3x20
Field of View: 100x34
Eye Relief: 3.5 in.
Length: 9 in.
Weight: 9.0 oz.
Finish: Matte black
Matte Black: $240.49

V-9

Magnification/Objective: 3-9x38
Field of View: 34-11 ft.
Eye Relief: 3.5 in.
Length: 12 in.
Weight: 11.0 oz.
Finish: Matte black, gloss
Matte Black or Gloss: $258.49

V-10

Magnification/Objective: 2-10x38mm
Field of View: 38.5-9.5
Eye Relief: 3.5 in.
Length: 12.2 in.
Weight: 11.2 oz.
Reticle: Dual-X
Finish: Matte black, silver
Matte Black, Silver or Gloss Black: $296.49

QUAD LOCK RINGS

All Quad-Lock rings utilize four straps per set for added gripping strength. These rings mount to all Weaver Top Mount Bases and their all-aluminum construction offers hunters a lightweight, sturdy option. The silver or matte Tip-Off Quad Lock rings fit a 3/8 in. dovetail receiver and three Quad Locks sets are available in silver (medium, high and high extension).

SURE GRIP
WINDAGE
ADJUSTABLE
RINGS

SURE GRIP WINDAGE ADJUSTABLE RINGS

With the Sure Grip Windage Adjustable Rings, hunters and shooters can rest assured that these rings will handle any recoil thrown at them. The four-screw system and steel cap offer shot-of-a-lifetime dependability. The windage adjustable models ensure zeroing in your scope to the critical optical clarity zone is certain.

Weaver Scopes

CLASSIC HANDGUN SCOPES (VARIABLE)								
Model	Magnification Power, Objective	Finish	Exit Pupil (mm)	Field of View (ft. @ 1000 yds.)	Eye Relief (in.)	Overall Length (in.)	Weight (oz.)	Reticle
849427	1.5-4x20mm	Gloss Black	13.33-5.5	15.5-6.5	4	9	8.2	Duplex
849428	2.5-8x28mm	Gloss Black	11.2-3.5	12.22-3.93	4	9.375	9.1	Duplex
849429	2.5-8x28mm	Matte Black	11.2-3.5	12.22-3.93	4	9.375	9.1	Duplex

CLASSIC HANDGUN SCOPES (FIXED)								
Model	Magnification Power, Objective	Finish	Exit Pupil (mm)	Field of View (ft. @ 1000 yds.)	Eye Relief (in.)	Overall Length (in.)	Weight (oz.)	Reticle
849423	2x28mm	Gloss Black	16	21	4.29	8.375	6.7	Duplex
849424	2x28mm	Silver	16	21	4.29	8.375	6.7	Duplex
849425	4x28mm	Matte Black	7	8.29	12-8	8.5	6.4	Duplex
849426	4x28mm	Silver	7	8.29	12-8	8.5	6.4	Duplex

CLASSIC SHOTGUN SCOPES								
Model	Magnification Power, Objective	Finish	Exit Pupil (mm)	Field of View (ft. @ 1000 yds.)	Eye Relief (in.)	Overall Length (in.)	Weight (oz.)	Reticle
849421	4x32mm	Matte Black	8	22.25	3.5	9.5	8.7	Duplex
849422	1.5-5x32	Matte Black	16-6.4	62-18.5	4.25-3.375	10.375	10	Diamond

CLASSIC K SERIES								
Model	Magnification Power, Objective	Finish	Exit Pupil (mm)	Field of View (ft. @ 1000 yds.)	Eye Relief (in.)	Overall Length (in.)	Weight (oz.)	Reticle
849417	15x40mm AO	Gloss Black	2.8	7.4	3	13.25	14.8	Duplex
849416	6x38mm	Gloss Black	6.3	18.4	3.25	11.625	9.8	Duplex
849418	6x38mm	Matte Black	6.3	18.4	3.25	11.625	9.8	Duplex
849414	4x38mm	Gloss Black	9.5	23.1	3.3	11.5	9.9	Duplex
849415	4x38mm	Matte Black	9.5	23.1	3.3	11.5	9.9	Duplex
849413	2.5x20mm	Gloss Black	8	36.8	4	9.625	7.1	Duplex

CLASSIC RIMFIRE								
Model	Magnification Power, Objective	Finish	Exit Pupil (mm)	Field of View (ft. @ 1000 yds.)	Eye Relief (in.)	Overall Length (in.)	Weight (oz.)	Reticle
849431	2.5-7x28mm	Matte Black	11.2-4	41.25-15.7	3.5	11.5	9.75	Duplex
849432	2.5-7x28mm	Silver	11.2-4	41.25-15.7	3.7-3.3	11.5	9.75	Duplex
849430	4x28mm	Matte Black	7	21.8	3.25	10.25	8.5	Duplex

GRAND SLAM								
Model	Magnification Power, Objective	Finish	Exit Pupil (mm)	Field of View (ft. @ 1000 yds.)	Eye Relief (in.)	Overall Length (in.)	Weight (oz.)	Reticle
800469	6-20x40	Matte Black	6.6-2	16.5-5.25	3-2.75	14.25	1lb 1.75oz	Duplex Dot
800471	1.5-5x32	Matte Black	17.4-6.2	71-21	3.25-3.25	10.25	11.5	Duplex
800472	4.75x40	Matte Black	7.7	20	3.25	11	10.75	Duplex
800473	3-10x40	Matte Black	12.6-4	35-11.3	3.5-3	11.875	13	Duplex
800474	3.5-10x50	Matte Black	11.5-4.5	23.6-10.91	3.12-3	12.75	1lb 0.3oz	Duplex
800475	4.5-14x40	Matte Black	8.8-2.6	22.5-10.5	3.5-3	14.25	1lb 1.5oz	Duplex
800476	6-20x40	Matte Black	6.6-2	16.5-5.25	3-2.75	14.25	1lb 1.75oz	Fine Crosshair Dot
800588	3-10x40	Matte Black	2.6-4	35-11.3	3.5-3	11.875	13	Duplex
800589	3.5-10x50	Silver Matte	11.5-4.5	23.6-10.91	3.12-3	12.75	1lb 0.3oz	Duplex
800590	4.5-14x40 AO	Silver Matte	8.8-2.6	22.5-10.5	3.5-3	14.25	1lb 1.5oz	Duplex
800591	6-20x40 AO	Silver Matte	6.6-2	16.5-5.25	3-2.75	14.25	1lb 1.75oz	Duplex Dot
800592	6-20x40 AO	Silver Matte	6.6-2	16.5-5.25	3-2.75	14.25	1lb 1.75oz	Fine Crosshair Dot

Weaver Scopes

T SERIES								
Model	Magnification Power, Objective	Finish	Exit Pupil (mm)	Field of View (ft. @ 1000 yds.)	Eye Relief (in.)	Overall Length (in.)	Weight (oz.)	Reticle
849970	36x40 AO	Matte Black	1.16	3	3	15.125	17	Fine Crosshair Dot
849981	36x40 AO	Silver	1.16	3	3	15.125	17	Fine Crosshair Dot
849974	36x40 AO	Matte Black	1.16	3	3	15.125	17	1/8 MOA Dot
849969	36x40 AO	Silver	1.16	3	3	15.125	17	1/8 MOA Dot
849976	24x40mm	Black Satin	1.6	4.4	3	15.1	16.7	Fine Crosshair Dot
849811	10x40mm	Black Satin	4	9.3	3	15.1	16.7	Fine Crosshair Dot
849995	6x40mm	Black Satin	6	17	3	12.75	15	Fine Crosshair Dot

V SERIES								
Model	Magnification Power, Objective	Finish	Exit Pupil (mm)	Field of View (ft. @ 1000 yds.)	Eye Relief (in.)	Overall Length (in.)	Weight (oz.)	Reticle
V24 (849411)	6-24x42mm AO	Matte Black	7-1.175	15.7-4.36	3.25-3	14.125	1lb .75oz	Duplex Dot
V24 (849402)	3-9x38mm	Matte Black	12.67-4.2	34-11.35	3.25-3	12.25	11.25	Mil-Dot
V16 (849408)	4-16x42mm AO	Matte Black	10.5-2.63	24.4-6.98	3.13-3	14	1lb .75oz	Duplex
V16 (849409)	4-16x42mm AO	Matte Black	10.5-2.63	24.4-6.98	3.13-3	14	1lb .75oz	FC
V16 (849410)	4-16x42mm AO	Matte Black	10.5-2.63	24.4-6.98	3.13-3	14	1lb .75oz	FCD
V10 (849404)	2-10x38mm	Gloss Black	19-3.8	38-9.6	3.25-3	12.5	11	Duplex
V10 (849405)	2-10x38mm	Matte Black	19-3.8	38-9.6	3.25-3	12.5	11	Duplex
V10 (849406)	2-10x38mm	Silver	19-3.8	38-9.6	3.25-3	12.5	11	Duplex
V10 (849407)	2-10x50mm	Matte Black	12-5.0	37.4-9.1	3.25-3	13.75	15.5	Duplex
V9 (849401)	3-9x38mm	Gloss Black	12.67-4.2	34-11.35	3.25-3	12.25	11.25	Duplex
V9 (849402)	3-9x38mm	Matte Black	12.67-4.2	34-11.35	3.25-3	12.25	11.25	Duplex
V9 (849403)	3-9x50mm	Matte Black	10.5-5	28.5-9.75	3.25-3	132.5	15.5	Duplex
V3 (849400)	1-3x20mm	Matte Black	15-6.6	87-30.75	3.12-3.12	9.125	8.5	Duplex

Yukon Scopes

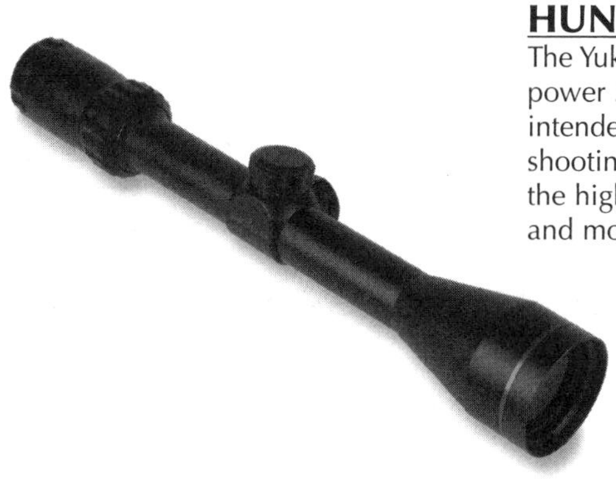

HUNTER 3-9x40

The Yukon Hunter's variable lower power 3-9x magnification range is intended for shorter distance, rapid fire shooting in light to dense cover and the higher power for longer distances and more open terrain.

Features: multicoated optics; long eye relief; oversized windage and elevation knobs; ¼-inch MOA; front diopter adjustment; nitrogen filled tube; waterproof and fog-proof; comes with two 30mm mounting rings

MSRP: $80–100

SCOPES

Zeiss Scopes

ENHANCED VICTORY DIAVARI 6-24x72 T* FL

Features: Zeiss FL (fluoride-ion) glass; Rapid-Z Ballistic Reticle systems; 90 mm eye relief; parallax free adjustable from 55 yds to infinite; choice of illuminated reticles 34 mm centre tube (objective tube: 80 mm; eyepiece tube: 45 mm); length 14.9 inches; weight without rail 37.4 oz

MSRP: $3400–3500

Zeiss Scopes

CONQUEST 3-9X50

CONQUEST 3.5-10x44
STAINLESS STEEL FINISH

CONQUEST 3-9x40

DIAVARI VM/V 3-9x42T

DIAVARI 1.1-4x24 T

DIAVARI 1.5-6x42 T

DIAVARI 2.5-10x50 T

DIAVARI VM/V 5-15x42T

VICTORY DIARANGE
3 - 12x56 T WITH LASER
RANGEFINDER

CONQUEST RIFLESCOPES

The Conquest series features MC anti-reflective coating, excellent low-light performance; arsenic/lead-free glass technology; Zeiss MC multicoating; Lifetime Transferable Warranty. Conquest scopes are waterproof and fogproof.

DIAVARI RIFLESCOPES

Light, compact riflescope available with illuminated vari-point reticle and wide field of view. The Diviari features easy-grip adjustment knobs and is available with bullet drop compensator.

VARIPOINT RIFLESCOPES

Compact scopes with the widest field-of-view offered by Zeiss (108 ft. at 100 yds.). The dot reticle is in the second image plane, so it's large and visible at low powers, small but distinct at high powers. The unilluminated reticle is highly visible.

VICTORY DIARANGE 3 - 12 X 56 T WITH LASER RANGEFINDER

The Victory Diarange 3-12x56 T with integrated laser range-finder is a new riflescope that delivers excellent optical performance and mechanical sturdiness, and the precise range to the target at the push of a button. Measures range up to 999 yds. High mechanical sturdiness as well as recoil proof, waterproof, nitrogen filled. Four different illuminated reticles for use in low-light conditions. Fast and comfortable mounting with Zeiss rail.

CONQUEST				
Magnification (x obj. dia.)	Field of View (ft., 100 yds)	Dia./Length (in.)	Weight (oz.)	MSRP
3-9x40 MC black	33.90-11.01	1/12.99	15.17	$399.99–574.99
3-9x40 MC stainless	33.90-11.01	1/12.99	15.17	$549.99
3-9x50 MC	37.5-12.9	1/12.36	16.58	$599.99–699.95
3-9x50 MC ss	37.5-12.9	1/12.36	16.58	$674.99
3.5-10x44 MC black	35.1-11.70	1/12.68	15.87	$699.99–774.99
3.5-10x44 MC silver	35.1-11.70	1/12.68	15.87	$749.99
3.5-10x50 MC	35.1-11.7	1/13.15	17.11	$749.99–824.99
3-12x56 MC black	27.6-9.9	1/15.3	25.8	$999.99
4.5-14x50 MC	25.5-8.84	1/14.02	19.75	$849.99–949.99
4.5-14x44 AO MC black	24.9-8.4	1/13.86	17.11	$799.99–949.99
4.5-14x44 AO MC silver	24.9-8.4	1/13.86	17.11	$849.99–924.99
6.5-20x50 AO MC black	17.7-5.7	1/15.59	21.83	$999.99–1024.99
6.5-20x50 AO MC silver	17.7-5.7	1/15.59	21.83	$1049.99–1124.99

DIAVARI				
Magnification (x obj. dia.)	Field of View (ft., 100 yds)	Dia./Length (in.)	Weight (oz.)	MSRP
V 6-24x56T	18.6-5.10	1.18/14.84	28.40	$2444–2667
VM/V 1.5-6x42 T	72-20.7	1.18/12.3	15	$1649.99
VM/V 2.5-10x50 T	43.5-12	1.18/12.5	15.9	$1799.99
VM/V 2.5-10x50 T w/ Illum Reticle	43.5-12	1.18/12.5	15.9	$2299.99
VM/V 3-12x56 T	37.5-10.5	1.18/13.54	18.38	$1899.99

VARIPOINT				
Magnification (x obj. dia.)	Field of View (ft., 100 yds)	Dia./Length (in.)	Weight (oz.)	MSRP
1.1-4x24 T VM/V	108-30.75	1.18/11.8	15.3	$2199.99
1.5-6x42 T VM/V	72-20.7	1.18/12.80	15	$2199.99
2.5-10x50 T VM/V w/ Illum	43.5-12	1.18/12.80	20.4	$2249.99

VICTORY DIARANGE WITH LASER RANGERFINDER				
Magnification (x obj. dia.)	Field of View (ft., 100 yds)	Dia./Length (in.)	Weight (oz.)	MSRP
3-12X56	7.5-10.5	-/14.2	32	$3999.99

SIGHTS

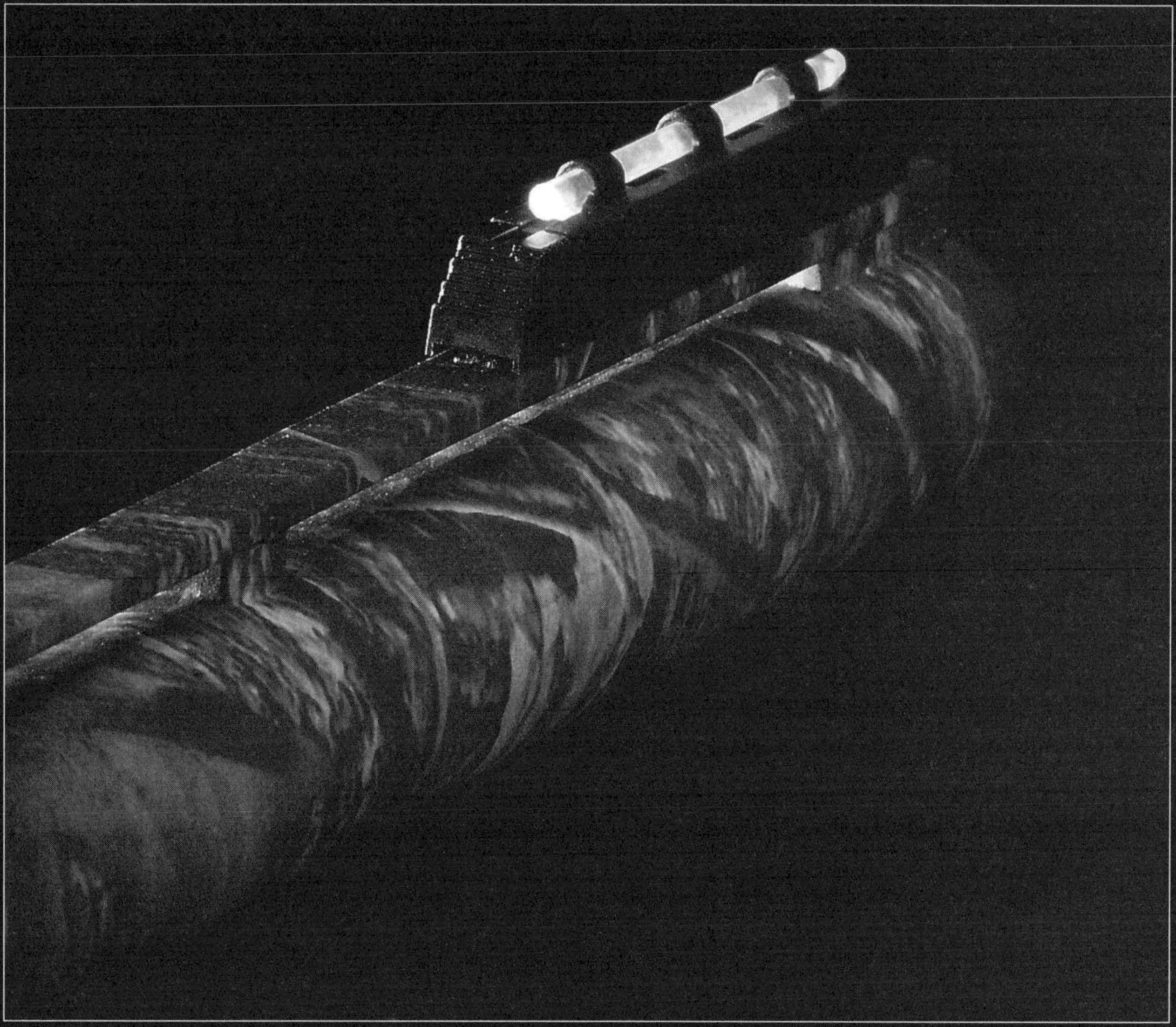

Aimpoint Sights

9000

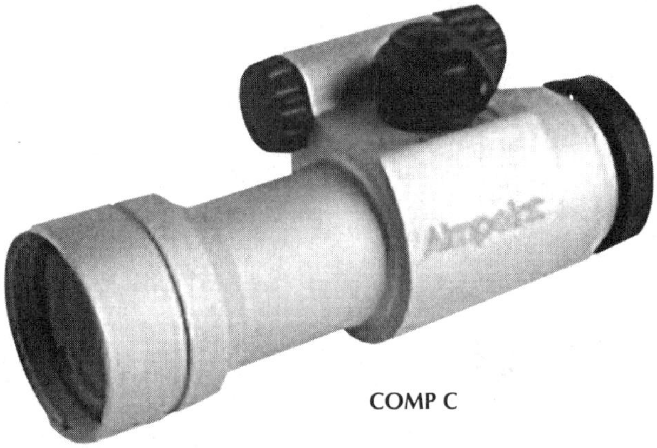

COMP C

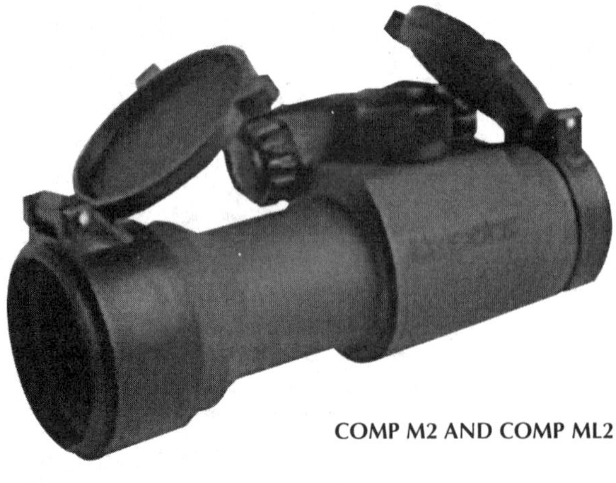

COMP M2 AND COMP ML2

9000

System: Passive Red Dot Collimator Reflex Sight
Optical: anti-reflex coated lens
Adjustment: 1 click = 10mm at 80 meters = 13mm at 100 meters = ½ in. at 100 yds
Length: 7.9 inches
Weight: 8.1 oz.
Objective diameter: 36mm
Diameter of dot: 2 MOA
Mounting system: 30mm ring
Magnification: 1X
Material: extruded aluminum; black finish
9000L: $433
9000SC: $433

COMP C3

System: 100% Parallax free
Optics: anti-reflex coated lenses
Eye relief: Unlimited
Batteries: 3V Lithium
Adjustment: 1 click = ½ in. at 100 yards
Length: 4¾ in.
Weight: 6.5 oz.
Objective diameter: 36mm
Dot diameter: 4 MOA
Mounting system: 30mm ring
Magnification: 1X
Material: Black or stainless finish
MSRP: $467

COMP ML2

System: Parallax free
Optical: Anti-reflex coated lens
Adjustment: 1 click = ½ in. at 100 yards
Length: 4.7 in.
Weight: 6.5 oz.
Objective diameter: 36mm
Diameter of dot: 4 MOA
Mounting system: 30mm ring
Magnification: 2X fixed
Material: anodized aluminum; black finish
Comp ML2: $495
Comp M2: $552

SIGHTS

Browning Sport Optics Sights

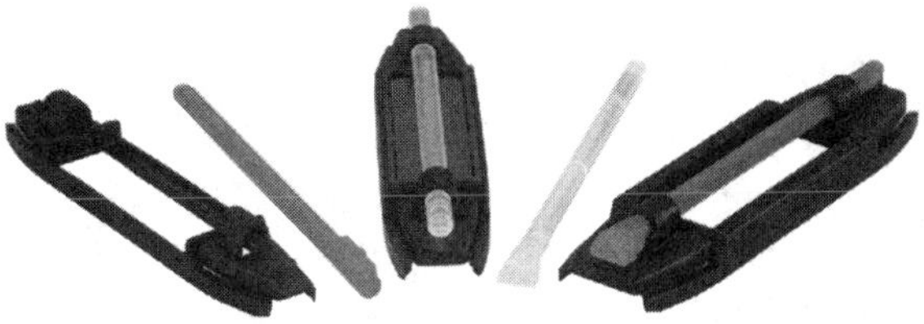

HIVIZ BIRD BUSTER MAGNETIC SHOTGUN SIGHT

HIVIZ BUCK MARK PISTOL SIGHT

HIVIZ COMP SIGHT

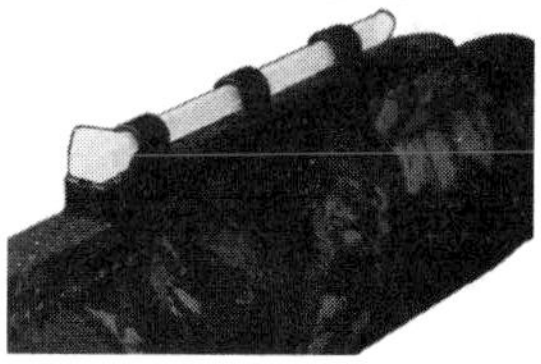

HIVIZ FLASH POINT SIGHT

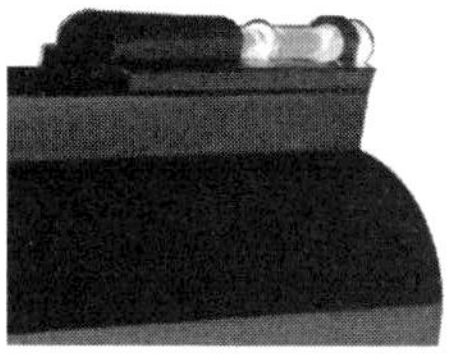

HIVIZ MAGNI-OPTIC SIGHT

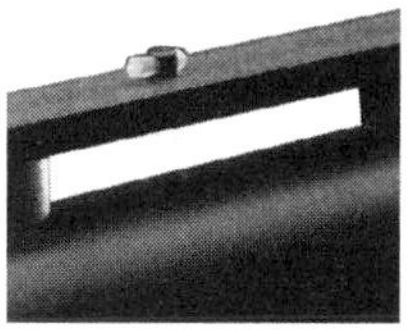

HIVIZ MID BRIGHT SIGHT

HIVIZ SPARK SIGHT

HIVIZ TRI-COMP SIGHT

HIVIZ TRIVIZ TURKEY SIGHT

HIVIZ BIRD BUSTER MAGNETIC SHOTGUN SIGHTS

Available with four interchangeable LitePipes. Fits all Browning shotguns and includes three sizes of magnetic bases. Comes in red, green or yellow.

MSRP: $19.99

HIVIZ BUCK MARK PISTOL SIGHT

Includes six LitePipes. Easy to install, replaces factory sight with single screw. Fits Browning Buck Mark Plus, Camper, Standard and Micro models.

MSRP: $39.99

HIVIZ COMP SIGHT

Interchangeable LitePipes—includes eight LitePipes of different diameters and colors. Base threads directly into shotgun bead.

MSRP: $39.99

HIVIZ MAGNI-OPTIC SIGHT

Enables any shotgunner to shoot with both eyes open for improved target acquisition and better hand/eye coordination.

MSRP: $39.99

HIVIZ MID BRIGHT SIGHT

Replaces the mid bead on many shotguns. Works well with Comp Sight, TriComp or Magnetic HiViz sights. Ensures proper barrel alignment and sight picture. Available in green or red.

MSRP: $8.95–12.45

HIVIZ SPARK SIGHT

Bright green fiber optic. Replaces factory bead. Thread sizes for most major shotguns.

MSRP: $6.95

HIVIZ TRI-COMP SIGHT

Solid steel construction with interchangeable triangular and round LitePipes.

MSRP: $34.99–39.95

HIVIZ TRIVIZ TURKEY SIGHT

Injection-molded optical-grade resin rear sight—fully adjustable for windage. Includes four green front sight LitePipes in different heights. Mounts on all common vent rib sizes.

MSRP: $33.50–36

MAGNETIC SHOTGUN SIGHTS

Available with four interchangeable LitePipes of different diameters for different light conditions. HiViz sights fit all Browning shotguns.

M2000

Beretta S686 Silver Essential, S686 Ultralight, S686 Silver Pigeon Field, S687 Silver Pigeon, S687 Gold Pigeon, AL-390 series, A304 series. Sig Arms SA-S Upland Hunter.

M3000

All Benelli shotgun models, Beretta S682 Gold Skeet and Gold Trap, Silver Pigeon Skeet, ASE models, Pintail, A303 Youth, SOS Sporting. Ithaca Model 37, Model 51. Krieghoff K-80. All Remington shotguns except 396 Sporting and 296 Skeet. Ruger Red Label. Weatherby Athena, Orion. Winchester Model 12 and Model 101. Perazzi all game models.

M4000

Fits Beretta S682 Gold Competition and Trap, ASE Gold Trap. Marocchi Conquista. All Mossberg shotgun models. Remington 396 Sporting and Skeet. SKB 505 and 585 Field. Winchester M 1300, M 1400 and Super X2.

MSRP: $22.00–27.95

Browning Sport Optics Sights

HIVIZ 4-IN-1 GAME SIGHT

Includes both front and rear sights, making the 4-in-1 perfect for deer, turkey, waterfowl and upland hunting. ***Features:*** injection-molded optical-grade resin sight construction; rear sight fully adjustable for windage and elevation; light-gathering LitePipes for low-light shooting; easily mounted
MSRP: $40

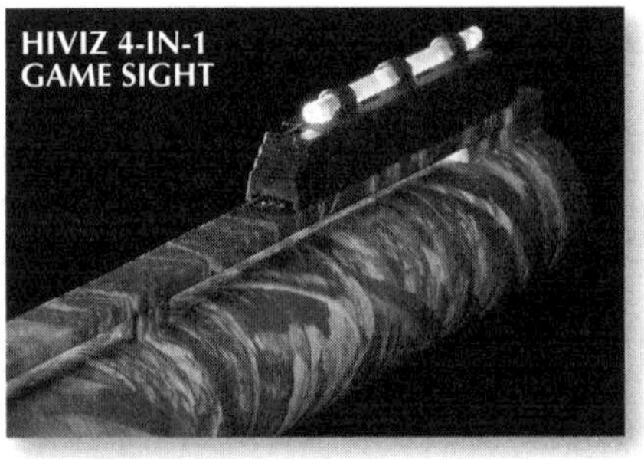

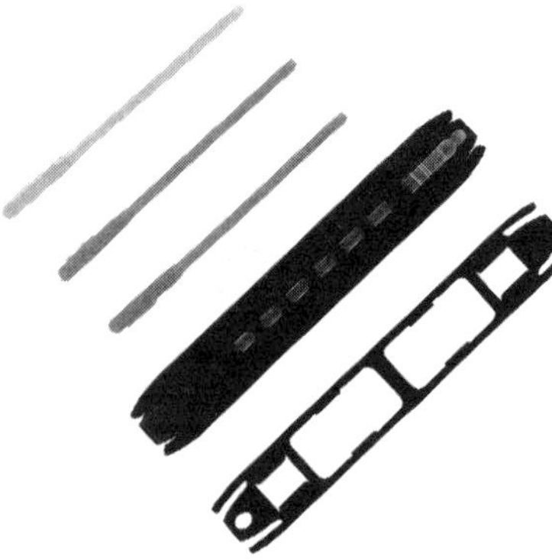

MAGNI-SPORT MAGNETIC SIGHT

Patent pending technology enables any shotgunner to shoot with both eyes open for improved target acquisition and better hand/eye coordination, refines shooting form, head-to-rib alignment and correct head position on the stock.
Features: one green and one red LitePipe; two sizes of magnetic base
MSRP: $25

BSA Sights

RED DOT SIGHTS

Perfect sight for pistols and shotguns; a small bright red dot appears in the center; available in BSA's Shadow Black rubber; choose either a push-button control, or 11-position click rheostat
PD30BK—30mm with rings: . . $41.95
PD30SIL—30mm with rings, Silver: $39.95
RD30—30mm Red Dot Sight: . $41.95
RD42CP—RD Red Dot Series: . . $50

Burris Sights

FASTFIRE RED DOT REFLEX SIGHT

Originally developed for semi-automatic handguns as a sight that could withstand the abuse of slide mounting, this tiny but tough, non-magnifying, reflex type red dot sight has proven to be a terrific fast target acquisition sight for turkey shotguns, deer slug guns, tactical and close range hunting carbines, muzzleloaders, paintball guns, home defense shotguns and even upland and waterfowl shotguns.

FastFire weighs just 2 ounces, and shrugs off recoil forces up to 1000 Gs. A target-directed light sensor automatically adjusts and controls the brightness of the 4MOA red dot for maximum visibility based on the ambient light conditions. Multicoating is sandwiched between two highly polished, optical quality glass lenses for protection from scratches and abrasion. Power is provided by a supplied standard lithium Type CR 2032 3-volt battery, and each FastFire sight is supplied with a mount for attachment to any Weaver-style or Picatinny-style base. In addition, 10 affordable handgun mounts are available.
MSRP: $313

Bushnell Sights

CAMO HOLOSIGHT

New model available in RealTree AP camo or matte black. Reticles available — standard, 65 MOA ring and 1 MOA dot.
Features: illuminated crosshairs; dedicated on/off button; reticle intensity memory; low-battery warning and auto shut-off; unlimited (½-in. to 10 feet) eye relief; waterproof, fog-proof, shockproof; standard AAA battery operation; XLP model with Rainguard lens coating; fits on handguns, shotguns and rifles with a Weaver-style mount
MSRP: $263

CenterPoint Precision Optics Sights

1X34MM
COMPACT RED DOT

1X25MM
COMPACT RED DOT

1X34MM, 1X25MM COMPACT RED DOT SIGHTS

CenterPoint's Red Dot sights offer a versatile dot sight for a wide range of pistols, shotguns and rifles. They are precision machined to exact tolerances from aircraft-grade aluminum alloy and feature all-weather, angled objectives for built-in rain protection and sunshield. Their 30mm tubes provide maximum light transmission, as well as wider windage and elevation adjustment. These sights also offer a Red/Green Dot with various brightness settings to account for changing light conditions and backgrounds, and feature finger adjustable windage and elevation dials. They come standard with lens covers and a Weaver/ Picatinny low profile mount.

List Prices
1x25mm Compact: $60.59
1x34mm: $60.59

Docter Sports Optics Sights

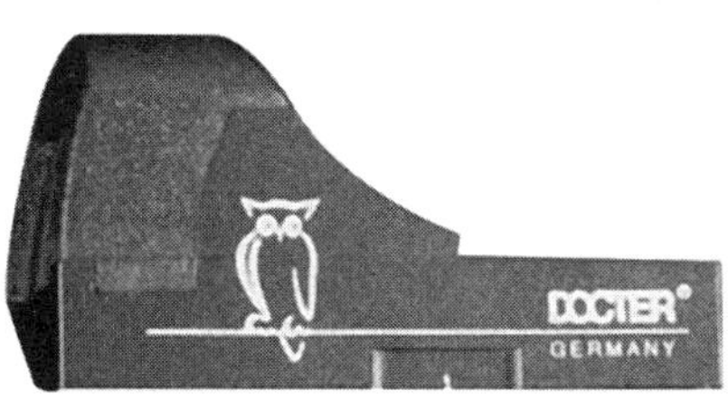

RED DOT SIGHT

Weighing just one ounce, it is not much bulkier than a standard rear aperture. There is no battery switch; batteries last up to five years without rest. Available in 3.5 or 7 M.D.A.
MSRP: $531.79

LaserLyte Sights

SUBCOMPACT LASER
ON SW HANDGUN

SUB-COMPACT LASER SIGHT

LaserLyte's FSL-0650-140, Sub-Compact Laser Sight is for owners of virtually all pistols and long guns with Picatinny, Weaver and Tactical rails. This ultra low-profile laser sight utilizes digital circuitry with a 650nm Hi-Definition laser module, wireless compression switch and adjustments for windage and elevation. With a range of up to 500 yds. at night, the Sub-Compact Laser Sight is set to become the standard. Miniature in size and weighing less than 1 ounce with batteries, the sight won't affect the firearm's ergonomics and adapts to many standard holsters. The sight incorporates a visible low battery indicator. When batteries are low the laser dot pulses, allowing the operator to use the laser for target acquisition. This extends the battery life by approximately 2.5 hours. The FSL sight offers 4 hours total run time with average use and 1.5 hours with continuous use before the low battery indicator alerts the user. The claw-type mounting system securely attaches the laser to the pistol's rails or onto LaserLyte's Rail Adapters for S&W Sigma VE, HK USP and USP Compact, Bersa and Hi-Point series. The Sub-Compact Laser Sight is precision CNC-machined from aerospace-grade aluminum.

MSRP: $99.95

Lyman Sights

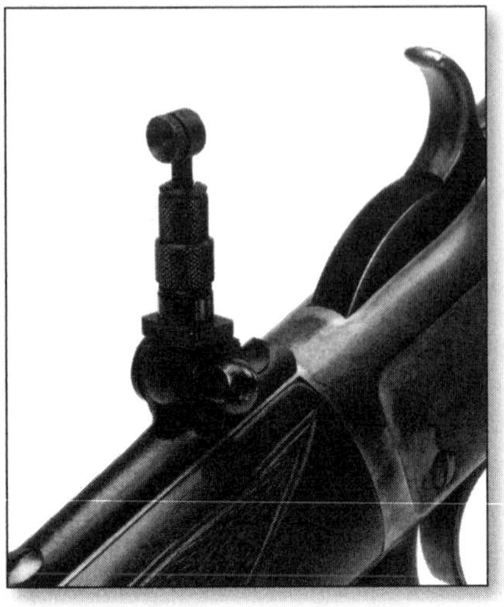

NO. 2 TANG SIGHT FOR UBERTI '66 & '73

Number 2 Tang Sights now includes two of the most popular lever-action rifles, Uberti Winchester Models '66 and '73. Sights are designed to fold down to allow use of the rifle's mid-sight for close work and then be flipped up for the long range rifle events or hunting.

Features: all steel construction, faithful to the original design; height index marks on the elevation post; two aperture sighting discs — .040 Target aperture and .093 diameter hunting aperture

MSRP: $87.50

SIGHTS

Lyman Sights

20 MJT-20 LJT GLOBE

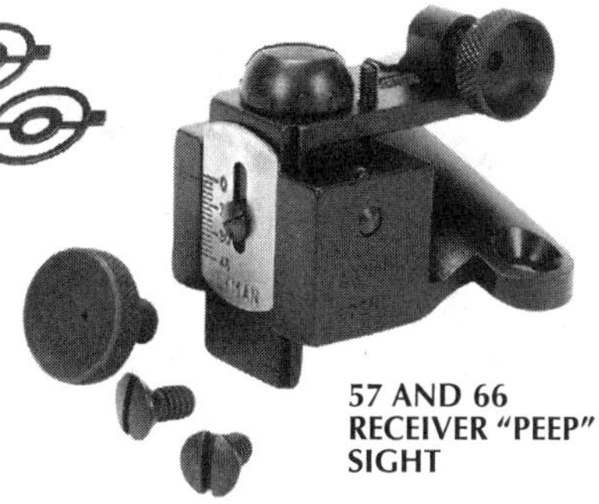

57 AND 66 RECEIVER "PEEP" SIGHT

66 WB RECEIVER SIGHT FOR 1886

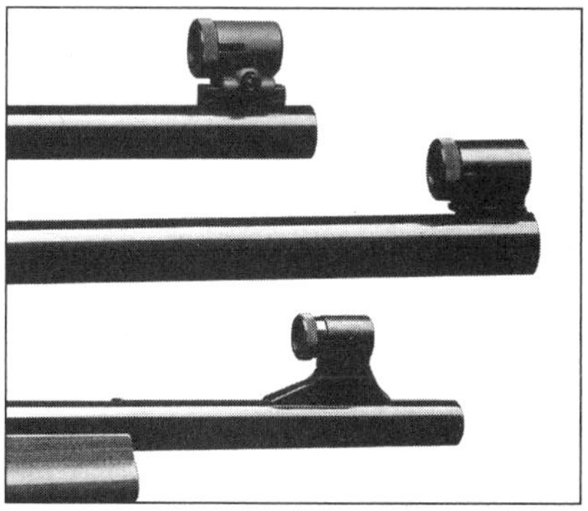

93 MATCH GLOBE FRONT SIGHT

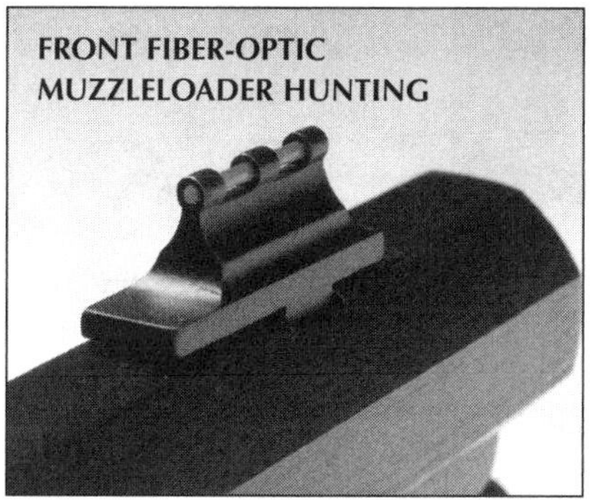

FRONT FIBER-OPTIC MUZZLELOADER HUNTING

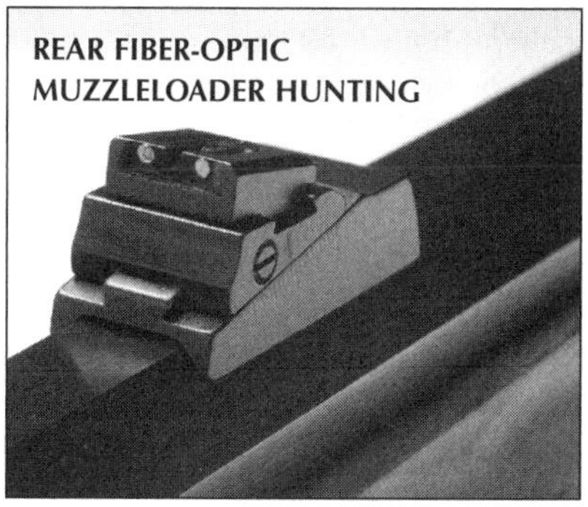

REAR FIBER-OPTIC MUZZLELOADER HUNTING

20 MJT-20 LJT GLOBE FRONT SIGHTS

The 20 MJT-20 LJT – 7/8 in. diameter Globe Front Sights are machined from one solid piece of steel designed to be mounted in a 3/8 in. barrel dovetail or dovetail base. 20 MJT height .700 in., 20 LJT height 7/8 in. from the bottom of dovetail to the aperture center supplied with seven Anschutz size steel apertures.
MSRP: $44.95

57 AND 66 RECEIVER "PEEP" SIGHTS

For flat receivers, such as lever action rifles or modern shotguns. Features include 1/4 minute audible click micrometer adjustments for elevation and windage, quick-release slide, coin-slotted "stayset" knobs and two interchangeable aperture discs (large hunting aperture and small target aperture). Weight: 4 oz.
MSRP: $93.25

66 WB RECEIVER SIGHT FOR 1886

Features semi-target knobs and 1/4 minute audible clicks for windage and elevation. Supplied with hunting and target aperture disks and quick release slide.
MSRP: $93.25

90 MJT TARGET RECEIVER SIGHT

Designed to mount on Lyman and other mounting bases. Adjustable zero scales and elevation stop screw permit instantaneous return to zero. Quick release slide with release button. Large 7/8 in. non glare .040 aperture. Elevation adjustable from 1.060 to 1.560 above bore centerline.
MSRP: $93.25

93 MATCH GLOBE FRONT SIGHT

Designed to fit any rifle, the 93 match sight (7/8 in. diameter) mounts on a standard dovetail base. Supplied with seven Anschutz size inserts. The sight height is .550 from the top of the dovetail to the center of the aperture.
MSRP: $57.95

FIBER-OPTIC MUZZLELOADER HUNTING SIGHTS

Lyman Products offers a new set of fiber-optic hunting sights for Lyman and many other muzzleloading rifles. Black-powder hunters can update their rifles with state-of-the-art fiber-optic technology. These bright, light-gathering sights let hunters take advantage of every minute in the field. They are especially helpful during the very productive dawn and dusk periods when game is most active. Designed to fit the Lyman Great Plains, Trade and Deerstalker Rifles, these state-of-the-art sights will also fit most other European-made black powder rifles, including Cabela's Hawken.
MSRP: $36

#37 HUNTING FRONT SIGHT

HUNTING FRONT SIGHTS

The #3 and #28 are designed to be mounted into the barrel dovetail. The #31 and #37 are designed to mount on ramps. #3 and #31 have 1/16 in. bead. #28 and #37 have 3/32 in. bead availability in ivory or gold.
MSRP: $11.25

Lyman Sights

NO. 2 TANG SIGHT

The No. 2 Tang will fit most new and old 94 models plus Winchester Models 1885, 1887, 1890 and 1894. (The No. 2 will also fit other models when adjusted to full height). A version is available for Marlin Models 336, 1894, 1895 and 30 series lever action-rifles. Marlin version includes adapter base. The No. 2 is all steel construction and features height index marks on the aperture post, with a maximum elevation of .800. It includes both a .093 quick sighting hunting aperture and a .040 Large Disk Target Aperture.

MSRP: $87.50

NO. 2 TANG SIGHT 1886

The Lyman No. 2 Tang Sight is now available for the Winchester 1886 lever action rifle. It fits the original Winchester Model 1886 and Browning replicas. Features include height index marks on the aperture post and an .800 maximum elevation adjustment. Also included is a .093 x ½ in. quick-sighting aperture and .040 x 5/8 in. target disk. Note: does not fit new rifles with Tang safety.

MSRP: $87.50

NO. 16 FOLDING LEAF SIGHT

This open rear sight with adjustable elevation blade is the perfect auxiliary sight for scope-mounted rifles. Folds close to the barrel when not in use. Designed to fit 3/8 in. dovetail slots.

MSRP: $15.95

NO. 2 TANG SIGHT

NO. 2 TANG SIGHT 1886

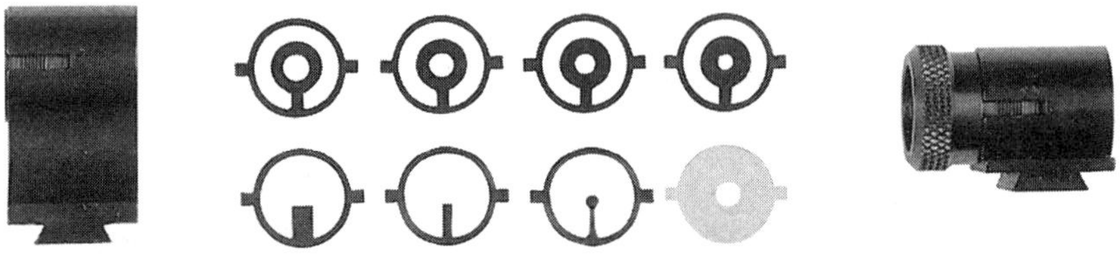

17 A TARGET FRONT SIGHT

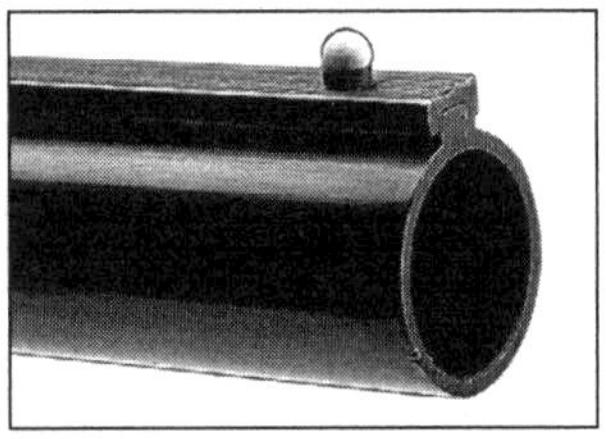

SHOTGUN SIGHT

SERIES 17A TARGET FRONT SIGHTS

Machined from solid steel and designed to be mounted in 3/8 in. dovetail slots. Supplied with eight interchangeable inserts. Sight Heights (bottom of dovetail to center of aperture): 17 AHB .404; 17AMI .494; 17AUG .584

MSRP: $34.95

SHOTGUN SIGHTS

Oversized ivory-like beads—easy to see under any light conditions. No. 10 Front Sights (press fit) for use on double barrel, or ribbed single barrel guns. No. 10D Front Sights (screw fit) for use on non-ribbed single barrel guns. No. 11 Middle Sight (press fit) small middle sight for use on double and ribbed single barrel guns.

MSRP: $6.75

Marble Arms Sights

CONTOUR FRONT SIGHTS

Marble's Contour Front Sights are strong, stable and give your rifle a true traditional look. Available in various widths and heights from .260 inches to .570 in. Choose a gold, ivory or fiber optic bead.

MSRP: $13–16

PEEP TANG SIGHTS

The Marble's Peep Tang Sight is adjustable for windage and elevation. The adjustments are micrometer precise. Each firm detent click equals four-tenths of an inch movement at 100 yards. Each sight includes three apertures and mounting screws.

MSRP: $119.95–125

UNIVERSAL REAR SIGHTS

The #20 Universal Rear Sight system combines a strong uni-base with both peep and U-shaped semi-buckhorn uprights. All components are machined from solid steel. Marble's barrel-mounted fiber optic rear sights can be used on modern rifles, slug shotguns and muzzleloaders. Available in all standard barrel contours and a variety of heights.

MSRP: $26.95

Nikon Sights

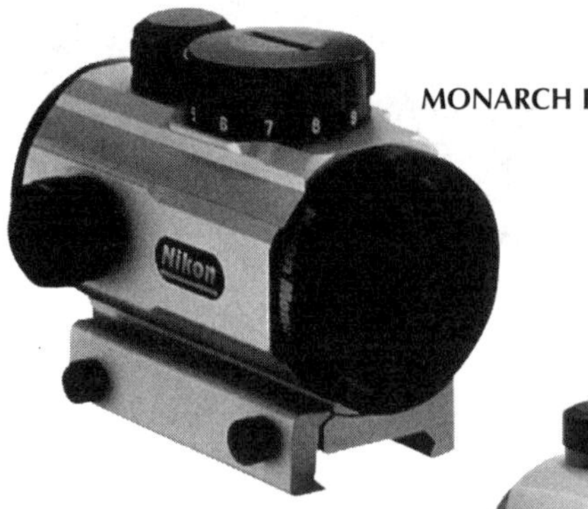

MONARCH DOT

MONARCH VSD BLACK

MONARCH VSD SILVER

MONARCH
VSD REALTREE

MONARCH DOT SIGHT

The Monarch Dot is waterproof, fogproof and shockproof. Objective and ocular lenses are 30mm diameter and fully multi-coated. Nikon Dot sights have zero magnification, providing unlimited eye relief and a 47.2′ field of view at 100 yds. Brightness is controlled by a lithium battery. The standard Monarch Dot Sight has a 6 MOA dot and is available in silver, black and Realtree camouflage.

VSD: $249.95
VSD in Camo: $279.95

MONARCH VARIABLE SIZE DOT SIGHT (VSD)

Waterproof, fogproof and shockproof construction of the Monarch 1x30mm VSD helps it handle the abuse of a magnum-shooting turkey gun or large caliber handgun. Select any of the five dot sizes—1, 4, 6, 8 or 10 MOA—with the simple twist of a knob. An 11-position rheostat allows almost limitless reticle brightness adjustment and guarantees performance in weak dawn light or bright mid-day sun. A large field-of-view—47½ ft. at 100 yds.—and fully multi-coated lenses work together to provide sharp, crystal clear images. The unlimited eye relief means that even the sneaky tom trying to slip in from behind is in serious trouble. A mounting system is included that works with any Weaver-style mount base. Adjustments are ½ MOA per click and the parallax is set at 50 yds. Available in Matte, Silver and Realtree APG HD. The Dot Sight measures 3.76 in. in length and runs on a single lithium battery that is included.

Matte and Silver: $250
Realtree APG: $280

Pachmayr Sights

ACCU-SET PISTOL SIGHTS

Low-profile, adjustable sights function properly with factory front sights. Constructed of carbon steel and available in blued finish. Available in plain black, white outline, or 3-dot. Micro-adjustable windage and elevation click screw for precise adjustments. Dovetail design slips easily into the factory dovetail groove and is held in place by a locking Allen screw.

MSRP: $45

Pentax Sights

GAMESEEKER DOT SIGHTS

Each of Pentax's Gameseeker Dot Sights features a 4 MOA dot, an ideal size for most shooters, as well as 11 brightness settings for various shooting conditions and a battery that provides 72 hours of continuous use. Also featuring PentaBright Technology, each Gameseeker dot sight offers a sharp, clear image that is parallax free for accurate target acquisition.

MSRP: $67–80

Phoenix Precision Sights

PREMIUM TARGET SIGHTS

CNC machined aircraft aluminum; Zero-able, ¼ min click numbered knobs; 70 min elevation adjustment; 60 min windage adjustment; adjustable scales engraved in 3 min increments; oil impregnated bronze guide and thread bushings.

AR-15 Flat Top 1-Piece Mount Rear Sight: $380

Standard Right Hand Rear Sight: $355

AR-15 FLAT TOP REAR SIGHT

STANDARD RIGHT HAND REAR SIGHT

Sightmark Sights

LASER DUAL SHOT

The Sightmark Dual Shot incorporates a laser that is in perfect parallel precision for shooting at fast moving targets.

Features: 0 to infinity usage capabilities; removable for separate use; parallax corrected with adjustable reticle brightness control; low power consumption; built-in Weaver mount; wide field of view

MSRP: $100

SIGHTS

Tasco Sights

PROPOINT SIGHT

SOLAR POWERED RED DOT SCOPE

TS RED DOT SCOPE

PROPOINT SIGHTS

ProPoint Sights are designed for competitive pistol and revolver shooters, turkey hunters and slug gun hunters. ProPoints deliver pinpoint accuracy with a rheostat-controlled illuminated red dot, unlimited eye relief and a clear field-of-view. ProPoints are powered by lithium batteries.

MSRP: $117.95–122.95

SOLAR POWERED RED DOT SCOPE

The Solar Cell Red Dot scope solar cell technology is available in a 1x30mm. For use during low light early morning or late afternoon hours, it can be switched from solar power to a back up battery. Standard features include fully coated lenses; an illuminated 5 MOA red dot reticle; Tasco Rubicon lens coating and unlimited eye relief. A rheostat lets the user dial in the brightness of the red dot to match hunting or shooting conditions.

MSRP: $97

TS RED DOT SCOPE

The TS Red Dot 1x32mm scope will function as well on the range as it will in the field. With a new single mounting ring design it mounts easily on rifles, shotguns or pistols. It is also the ideal scope for use on tactical firearms. Other key features include fully coated lenses; flip-up caps on the objective and ocular lenses; an illuminated 5 MOA red dot reticle and unlimited eye relief. The intensity of the red dot can be adjusted with an 11 position rheostat. It is covered by a lifetime limited warranty.

MSRP: $135–181

Trijicon Sights

4 x 32 ACOG

ACOG 6 x 48

R x 30 REFLEX

4x32 ACOG

Trijicon introduces the 4x32 ACOG to the consumer market for varmint or big game hunting.

Weight: 16.2 ounces

Size: 7.3″ L x 2.1″ W x 2.5″ H

Features: Bindon Aiming Concept (BAC); reticle with red chevron aiming point and incorporated bullet drop compensator (additional aiming points out to 800 meters); mounts to any MIL-STD-1913 rail with supplied mount; spacer system allows sight to be configured properly for varying weapon systems

MSRP: $1326

ACOG 6x48

The ACOG 6x48 was designed and developed specifically for hunters.

Weight: 32.5 ounces

Size: 9″ L x 2.9″ W x 3″ H; mounts to any MIL-STD-1913 rail with supplied mount

Features: battery free, powered by Trijicon's fiber optics and tritium-based technology; reticle with either a red or amber chevron aiming point; incorporated bullet drop compensator (additional aiming points estimated for trajectory of the 5.56mm M855 out to 800 meters or the 7.62mm M80 round out to 1200 meters); manual brightness adjustment override; Bindon Aiming Concept; spacer system allows sight to be configured properly for varying weapon systems

MSRP: $2500–2600

Rx30 REFLEX SIGHT

The RX30 is a non-magnified, self-luminous sight providing increased field-of-view capabilities for fast target acquisition for the military, law enforcement and hunters.

Weight: 12.5 ounces

Size: 4.87″ L x 2.07″ W x 2.22″ H

Features: large objective and field of view; 42mm clear aperture lens; no batteries required; dual-illuminated sight with both fluorescent fiber optics and a tritium lamp; +/- 30 MOA (one click per inch at 100 yards)

MSRP: $561

Trijicon Sights

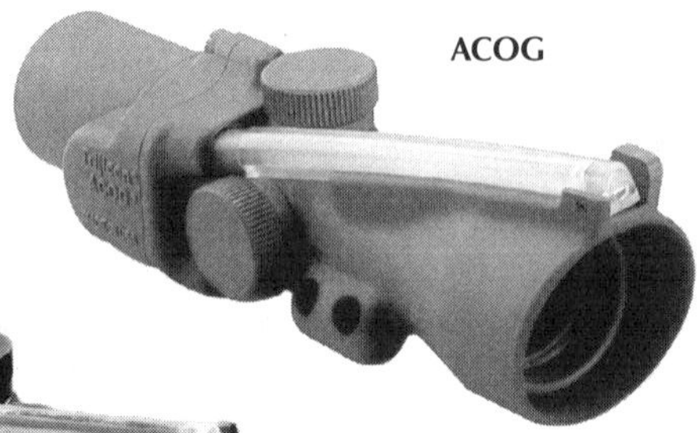
ACOG

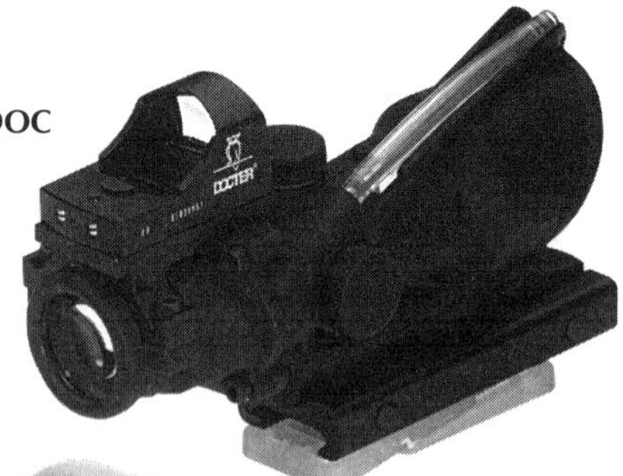
ACOG TA31DOC

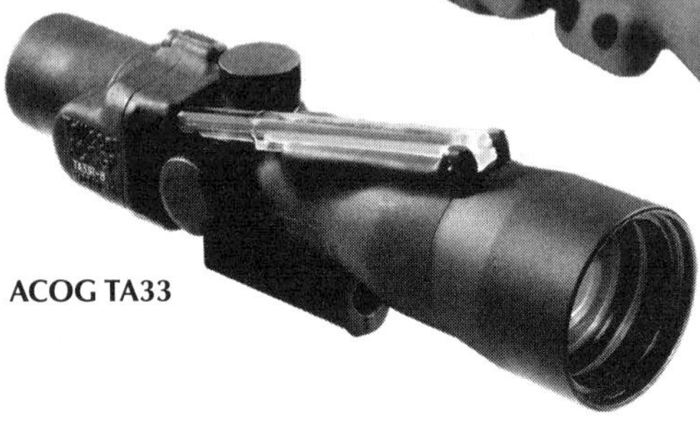
ACOG TA33

REDDOT

ACOG

The ACOGs are internally-adjustable, compact telescopic sights with tritium illuminated reticle patterns for use in low light or at night. Many models are dual-illuminated, featuring fiber optics which collect ambient light for maximum brightness in day-time shooting. The ACOGs combine traditional, precise distance marksmanship with close-in aiming speed.

MSRP: $1010–3163

ACOG TA31DOC

The TA31DOC combines the technology of the battle-tested Trijicon ACOG (4x32) gun sight with the Docter Optic Red Dot sight. The Trijicon ACOG model TA31DOC is an internally adjustable telescopic sight powered by Trijicon fiber optics and tritium-based technology. It's dual-illuminated reticle is designed to hold zero under the most extreme conditions and present a bright aiming point in all lighting conditions—providing excellent long-range precision targeting or even faster short range target selection using the Bindon Aiming Concept (BAC). With the field-proven Docter Optic 1x red dot sight mounted on top of the Trijicon ACOG TA31DOC, this innovative sighting system provides the user with lightening fast target acquisition in CQB situations while allowing for excellent situational awareness.

MSRP: $1850

ACOG TA33

The new Trijicon ACOG TA33 is a 3x30mm model designed for law enforcement and military applications where the combination of ample magnification, low light capability and long eye relief are needed. This aiming system is available with Bullet Drop Compensated reticles calibrated to the trajectory of the .223 and .308 cartridges and provides precision aiming for targets out to 600 meters. The extended eye relief allows the TA33 to be mounted on larger caliber weapons, giving the marksman ample eye relief for all shooting positions. The TA33 uses Trijicon's patented fiber optics and tritium-based technology, providing a dual illuminated reticle. It's totally battery-free, featuring a red or amber chevron aiming point. The TA33 also takes advantage of the innovative Bindon Aiming Concept. In tandem with scope magnification, this revolutionary both-eyes-open aiming method provides the shooter with "instinctive" target acquisition and increased hit potential. A forged, 7075-T6 aluminum alloy housing gives it durability, and multi-coated lenses provide maximum optical performance in any light. The unit is waterproof to 328 ft. and nitrogen-filled to eliminate fogging.

MSRP: $1010

NIGHT SIGHTS

Trijicon's self-luminous iron sights give shooters five times greater night fire accuracy. The light is provided by glowing tritium gas-filled lamps which are fully warranted up to twelve years for the green or yellow rear dots and up to five years for the orange dots. Trijicon night sights also feature a white outline around the glowing dots for the highest possible daylight visibility. The tritium lamps are protected by aluminum sleeves and polished synthetic sapphire windows. In addition a silicone rubber cushion helps protect the glass lamp within the aluminum sleeve. The metal body is manufactured for specific handgun makes and models. Night Sights are available for the following pistols, revolvers and rifles: Beretta, Browning, Colt, CZ, Desert Eagle, Firestar, Glock, H&K, Kimber, Remington, Ruger, SIG, Smith & Wesson, Walther, Taurus.

MSRP: $50–155

REDDOT SIGHT

Developed for quick target acquisition, the Trijicon RedDot Sight is designed for mounting atop the Trijicon ACOG (Advanced Combat Optical Gunsight). The sight features an innovative LED (light emitting diode) insert to sense the target's light level and control the light output of the LED. This technology ensures optimum visibility of the red dot against the target. Power is provided by a long-life lithium battery. Accuracy is enhanced with adjustments for windage and elevation. And, performance is assured with a stronger-than-aluminum, polymer alloy body. Tough, yet smaller and lighter than any alternative, the Trijicon RedDot Sight is suitable for all military and law enforcement applications.

MSRP: $425

Trijicon Sights

REFLEX

TRIPOWER

REFLEX SIGHTS

The dual-illuminated, Trijicon Reflex sight gives shooters next-generation technology for super-fast, any-light aiming without batteries. The Reflex sight features an amber aiming dot or triangle that is illuminated both by light from the target area and from a tritium lamp. Bright aiming point in low light, no light or bright light; quick target acquisition; big sight picture and realistic color.

MSRP: $434–638

TRIPOWER

The TriPower features a durable body forged in hard-anodized aircraft aluminum alloy, a sleek scope design and upgraded lens coatings. The Trijicon TriPower provides a quick and bright hunting optic. In tactical users, it provides clearly visible aiming point for the varied lighting conditions experienced in CQB (close-quarter battle).

MSRP: $765

Uberti Sights

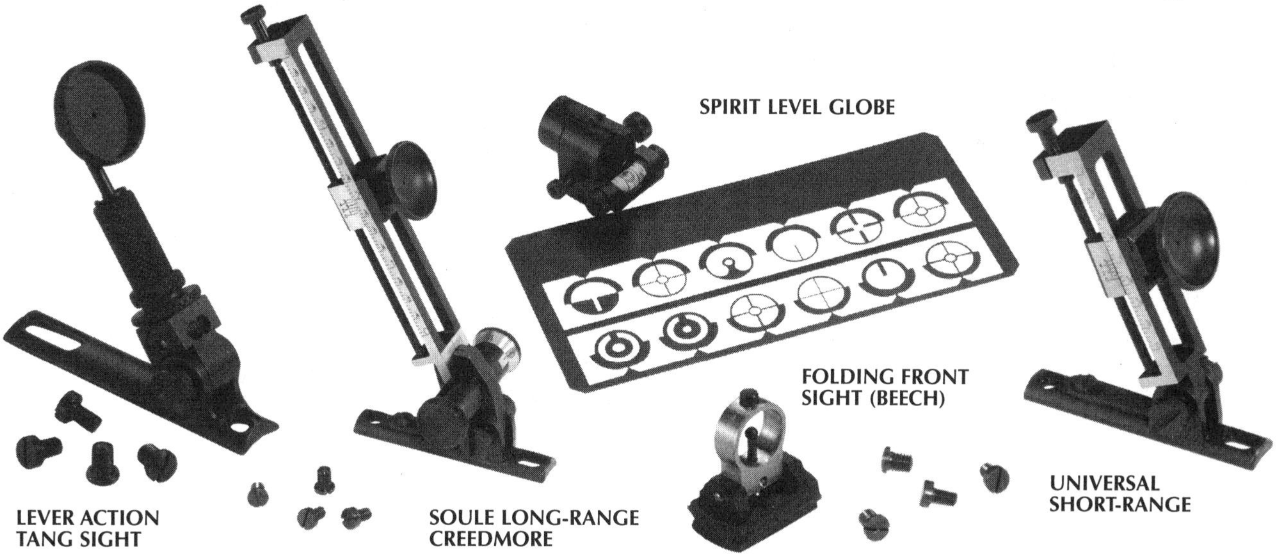

CREEDMORE TANG SIGHTS

For Sharps rifles in three heights—short-range sight good to 300 yards, mid-range to about 600 yards and long-range, about 1,200 yards. Front globe sight fitted with spirit level to level the rifle.

Soule Type Long-Range Creedmore: $299
Soule Type Mid-Range Creedmore: $289
Universal Long-Range Creedmore: $189
Universal Short-Range Creedmore: $169
Lever Action Tang Sight: $119
Spirit Level Globe Sight with 12 Inserts: $169
Globe Front Sight with 12 Inserts: $49–59
Folding Front Sight (Beech): . . . $79
Hadley Style Eyepiece: $99
Spirit Level Insert: $35
Glass Bubble Inserts (6): $35

Williams Sights

5D SERIES

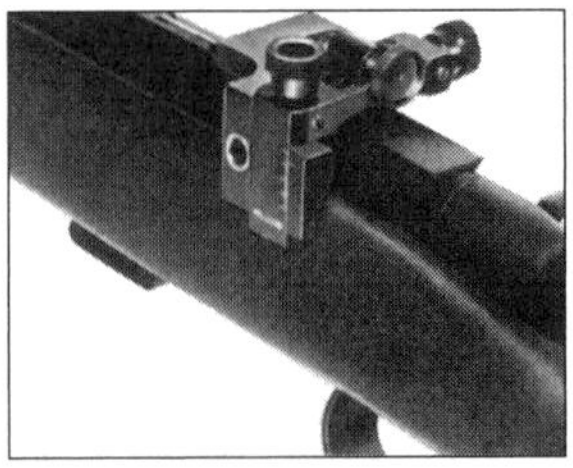

FP-GR-TK
ON REMINGTON 581

FP-94 SE ON WINCHESTER
94 SIDE EJECT

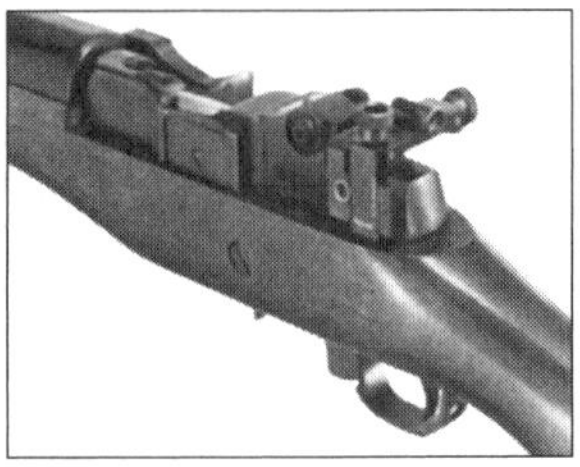

FP MINI-14-TK
WITH SUB-BASE

FP-KNIGHT-TK
SILVER ON MK-85

FP-AG-TK
ON BEEMAN
AIR RIFLE

FP RECEIVER SIGHT OPTIONS

STANDARD

TARGET KNOBS (TK)

SHOTGUN/BIG
GAME APERTURE

BLADE

TARGET - FP
(HIGH)

TARGET - FP
(LOW)

5D SERIES

5D models are available for most popular rifles and shotguns. These sights have the strength, light weight, and neat appearance of the FP, without the micrometer adjustments. 5D sights offer unobstructed vision with no knobs or side plates to blot out shooter's field of vision. Wherever possible, the manufacturers' mounting screw holes in the receivers of the guns have been utilized for easy installation. The upper staff of the Williams 5D sight is readily detachable. A set screw is provided as a stop screw so that the sight will return to absolute zero after reattaching. The Williams 5D sight is made of high grade alloy.

Most 5D models: $39.95

Target—FP (high)

Adjustable From 1.250 in. to 1.750 in. above centerline of bore.

MSRP: $79.95

FP SERIES

The "Foolproof" series of aperture sights have internal micrometer adjustments with positive internal locks. The alloy used to manufacture this sight has a tensile strength of 85,000 pounds. Yet, the FP is light and compact, weighing only 1½ oz. Target knobs are available on all models.

For most models: $72.95

With target knobs: $84.50

TARGET FP-ANSCHUTZ

Designed to fit many of the Anschutz Lightweight .22 Cal. Target and Sporter Models. No drilling and tapping required.

MSRP: $83.95

TARGET—FP (LOW)

Adjustable from ¾-1¼ in. above centerline of bore.

MSRP: $79.95

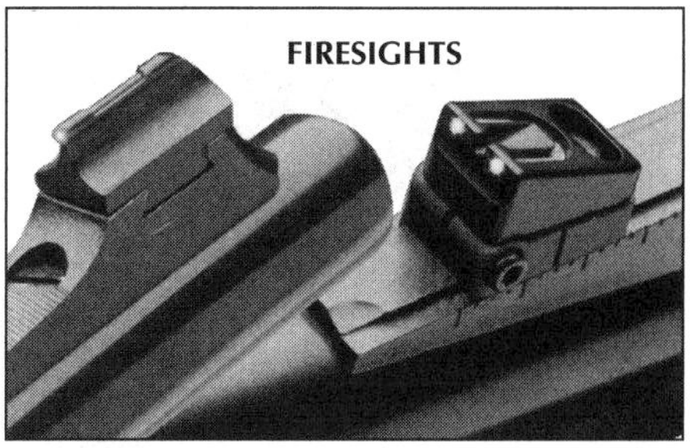
FIRESIGHTS

WGOS

WGRS-CVA ON CVA APOLLLO

.22 OR MUZZLELOADER FRONT FIRESIGHT BEAD

Wide steel front bead machined to accept a FireSights fiberoptic light gathering rod. Fits all standard 3/8 in. dovetails in a variety of heights.

MSRP: $18.95

AR-15 STYLE FIRESIGHT

Front metallic sight that is fully adjustable for elevation. No gunsmithing required.

MSRP: $45.95

BROWNING BLR FIRESIGHT SET

Replaces rear sight and front sight bead. Fully adjustable metallic sights. No gunsmithing required.

MSRP: $38

DOVETAIL FIRESIGHT SET

Light gathering fiber optics for most lever-action rifles with ramped front sights. Fully adjustable rear metallic FireSight fits all standard 3/8 in. dovetails on most Marlin and Winchester models. Front FireSight steel bead replaces existing factory bead.

Marlin 25N & 25MN: $30
Dovetail Fire Sight Set: $36.95

FIRESIGHTS

Steel front dovetail sight beads machined to accept FireSight light gathering rod. A must for all shooters in low-light situations. Comes in a variety of heights. CNC machined steel beads (not plastic).

MSRP: $18.95

LEVER ACTION FIRESIGHT PEEP SET

FireSight Steel bead and Williams FP94/36 micro adjustable peep sight for Winchester or Marlin centerfire lever action rifles. (Fits: Win94 top eject, 55, 63, 64, 65, 94-22; Marlin 36, 336, 1894, 1895SS, 1895G, 444SS, 444P)

MSRP: $82.95

MILITARY SIGHTS

Open and aperture for: SKS (no drilling required); AK47 (no drilling required)

MSRP: $20–26

RIFLE FIRESIGHT PEEP SETS

FireSight steel front bead and Williams WGRS rifle peep sight. Fully adjustable—no drilling and tapping required. Available for Ruger .22, Ruger 99/44, Marlin .336 and Ruger 96/22 and 96/22 Mag.

MSRP: $49.95

RUGER 10/22 FIRESIGHT SET

Customize your 10/22 with front and rear fiber optic FireSights. The front steel sight and the fully adjustable metallic rear sight are CNC machined for a perfect fit.

MSRP: $25.95

SKS RIFLE FIRESIGHT BEAD

Fiber optic, light gathering metallic front SKS sight. No gunsmithing required.

MSRP: $20.95

SKS RIFLE FIRESIGHT SET

Combines the FireSight Front bead with Williams fully adjustable metallic rear sight for an incredible sight picture. No gunsmithing required.

FireSight Set: $40
Front sight: $20.95

WGOS SERIES

Made from high tensile strength aluminum. Will not rust. All parts milled—no stampings. Streamlined and lightweight with tough anodized finish. Dovetailed windage and elevation. Easy to adjust, positive locks. Interchangeable blades available in four heights and four styles.

MSRP: $24.95

WGRS SERIES

Compact low profile; lightweight, strong, rustproof; positive windage and elevation locks in most cases these sights utilize dovetail or existing screws on top of the receiver for installation. They are made from an aluminum alloy that is stronger than many steels. Williams quality throughout.

Most models: $37.95

XS Sight Systems

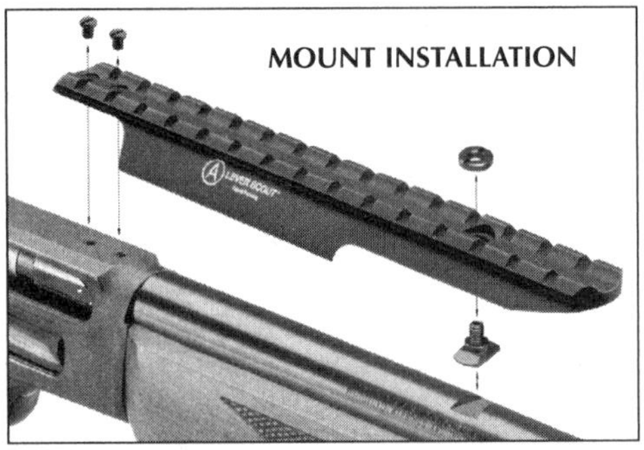

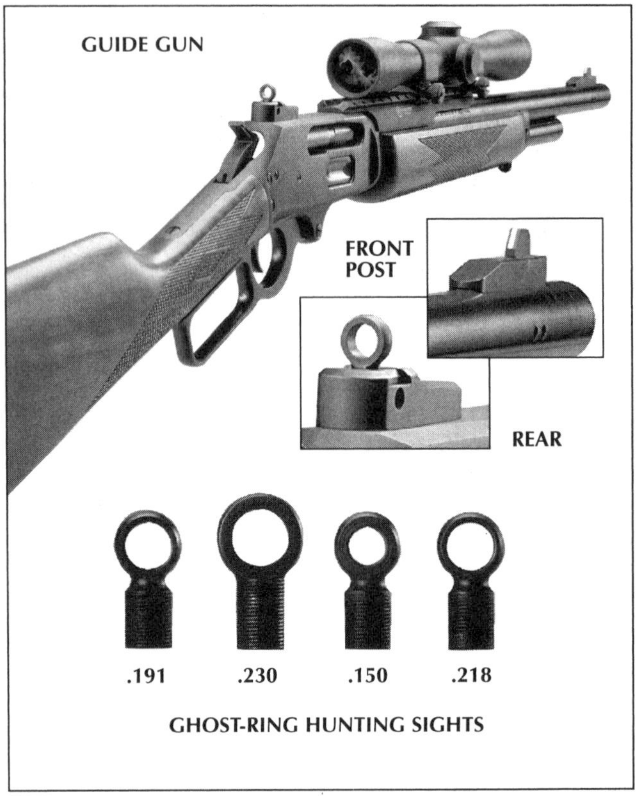

GHOST-RING SIGHTS & LEVER SCOUT MOUNTS

Scout Scope Mount with 8 in. long Weaver-style rail and cross slots on 1/2 in. centers. Scope mounts 1/8 in. lower than previously possible on Marlin Lever Guns. Drop-in installation, no gunsmithing required. Installs using existing rear dovetail & front two screw holes on receiver. Allows fast target acquisition with both eyes open—better peripheral vision. Affords use of Ghost-Ring Sights with scope dismounted. Recoil tested for even the stout .45/70 and .450 Loads. Available for Marlin Lever Models: 1895 Guide Series, new .450, .444P, the .336 and 1894.

MSRP: $65

XS Lever Scout Mount for Win 94: $70

GHOST-RING HUNTING SIGHTS

Fully adjustable for windage & elevation. Available for most rifles, including blackpowder. Minimum gunsmithing for most installations; matches most existing mounting holes. Compact design, CNC machined from steel and heat treated. Perfect for low light hunting conditions and brush/timer hunting, offers minimal target obstruction.

MSRP: . . . . $90 for most

SMLE SCOUT SCOPE MOUNTS

Offers Scout Scope Mount with 7 in. long Weaver style rail. Requires no machining of barrel to fit—no drilling or tapping. Tapered counter bore for snug fit of SMLE Barrels. Circular Mount is final filled with Brownells Acraglass.

MSRP: $60

XS 24/7 TRITIUM EXPRESS SIGHTS

The original fast acquisition sight. Now enhanced with new 24/7 tritium sight. These sights are the finest sights made for fast sight acquisition under any light conditions. Light or dark, just "dot the i" and put the dot on the target. Enhances low-light sight acquisition; Improves low-light accuracy; low profile, snag free design. Available for most pistols.

MSRP: $90–120

XS ADJUSTABLE EXPRESS SIGHT SETS

Incorporates Adjustable Rear Express Sight with a white stripe rear, or Pro Express Rear with a Vertical Tritium Bar; fits Bomar style cut, LPA style cut, or a Kimber Target cut rear sight. Affords same Express Sight principles as fixed sight models.

Adjustable Express w/White Stripe Rear and Big Dot Front or Standard Dot Front: $60

Adjustable Express w/White Stripe Rear and Big Dot Tritium or Standard Dot Tritium Front: $90

Adjustable Pro Express w/Tritium Rear and Big Dot Tritium or Standard Dot Tritium Front: $90

SIGHTS

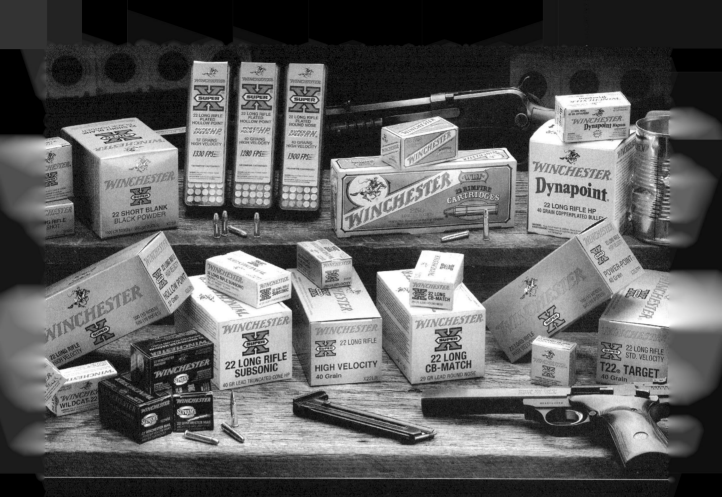

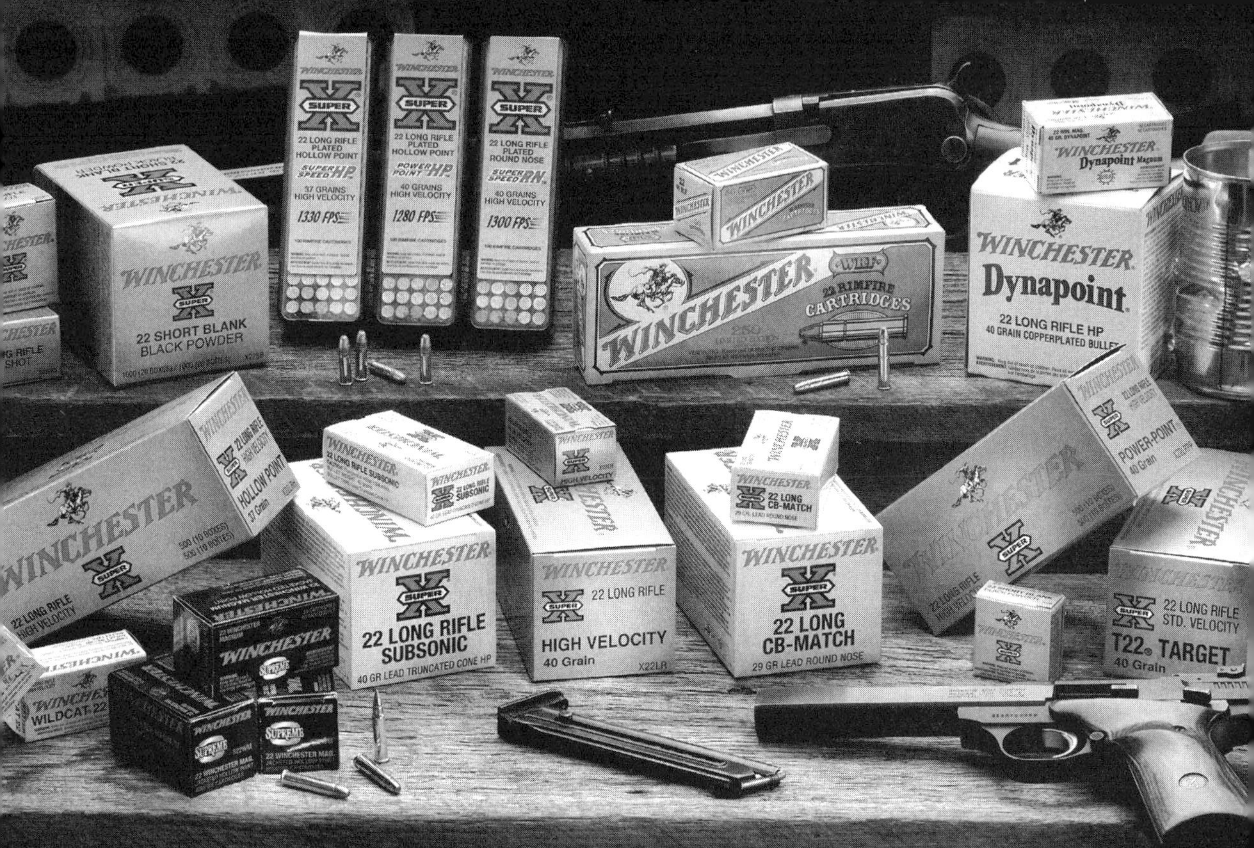

MUZZLELOADING AMMUNITION

Barnes Ammunition

BARNES BUSTER BULLETS

Features: full-jacketed lead-core handgun bullets for use on thick-skinned game – 300-gr. .429 (.44 Magnum), 325-gr. .451 (.454 Casull), 400-gr. .458 (.45-70 rifle), 400-gr. .500 (.500 S&W)

MSRP: $48–59

BARNES M/LE TAC-X

Features: All copper rifle bullets in .223, 6.8mm, .308, .50 BMG. Straight tracking through barriers and better weight retention than lead-core bullets.

MSRP: $39

BARNES SPIT-FIRE T-EZ MUZZLELOADER BULLETS

Features: poly-tipped .451-diameter 250 or 290-grain all-copper for 50-caliber muzzle-loaders

MSRP: $19.50–28.50

BARNES BANDED SOLID BULLETS

Features: 400-grain .410 solids for .450/400 for heavy African game, in a line that includes 13 other bullets, from .375 to .600.

MSRP: $18.79–61.99

BARNES TRIPLE-SHOCK X BULLET

Features: new 80-grain .243, 80- and 100-grain .257, 120-grain 6.5mm bullets for centerfire rifles, sleek boat-tail bullets with three belt grooves, polymer tip

MSRP: $44.99

BARNES LOADED AMMO

Features: Barnes now markets ammo in boxes by Weatherby, Black Hills, DPX Corbon and other known firms that load Barnes bullets. Same ammo as from those sources, but now direct from Barnes.

MSRP: . . . . . . .available on request

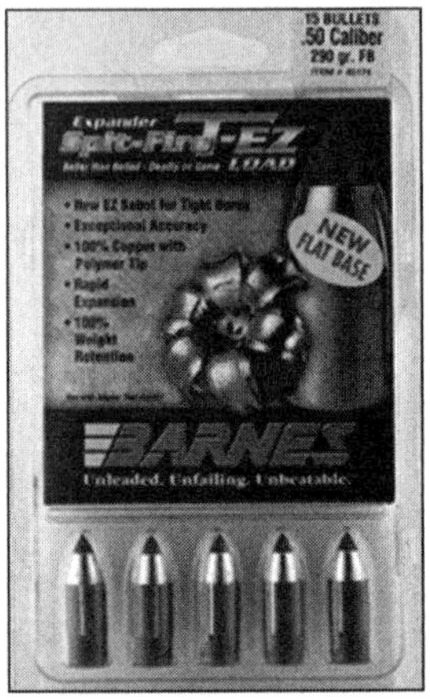

SPIT-FIRE T-EZ MUZZLELOADER BULLETS

Black Hills Ammunition

.22-250 AND .243 WIN. VARMINT GRENADE

The Black Hills Varmint Grenade projectile contains no lead but has a core composed of a compressed copper/tin mixture, which disintegrates upon striking the target. This load, designed for varmint shooters, is now available with a 36-grain bullet in the .22-250 cartridge (4250 fps), and 62-grain
bullet in .243 Winchester (3700 fps.).

MSRP: . . . $29.50 (per box of 20)

6.5-284 NORMA

Black Hills has reintroduced the 6.5-284 caliber in cooperation with Savage Arms, which is offering factory chambered rifles in this caliber. Features: 142-grain Sierra MatchKing bullet (2950 fps.).

MSRP: . . . .$56 (per box of 20)

BLACK HILLS TAC-XP PISTOL AMMO

Features: 9mm, .40 S&W and .45 ACP with Barnes Tac-XP copper HP bullets

MSRP: $53

BLACK HILLS TSX BULLETS AND MPG BULLETS IN RIFLE AMMO

Features: 55-grain Barnes TSX bullets in .223, 85-grain TSX in .243 cartridges Also: 55-grain Hornady FMJ bullets in new-manufacture .223, and Multi-Purpose-Green lead-free bullets in .223. MPGs are frangible in soft targets.

MSRP: $40–72

22-250 VARMINT GRENADE

243 WIN VARMINT GRENADE

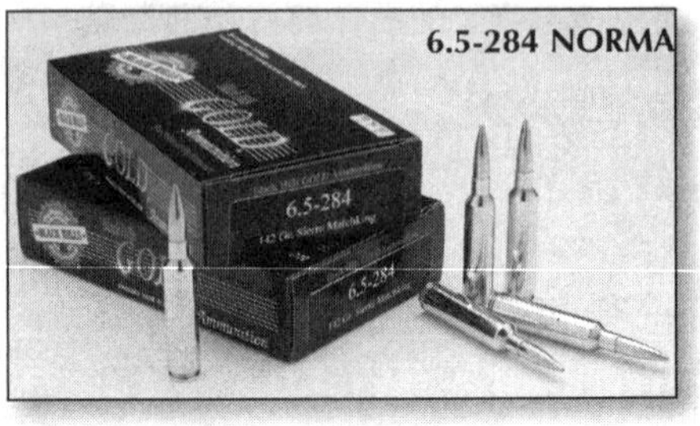
6.5-284 NORMA

Black Hills Ammunition

COWBOY ACTION HANDGUN AMMUNITION

Features: Carefully designed to meet the needs of cowboy-action shooters, this ammunition is made of new virgin brass and premium-quality hard-cast bullets. Velocities are moderate to provide low recoil and excellent accuracy.
Available in: .38-40, .44-40, .44 Russian, .44 Colt, .44 Special, .45 Schofield, .45 Colt, .45-70, .32 H&R, .32-20, .38 Long Colt, .38 Special, .38-55, .357 Mag.
MSRP: $274.50–369.50

FACTORY-NEW HANDGUN AMMUNITION

Features: Black Hills handgun ammunition combines the best of both worlds: quality and affordability. The choice of law-enforcement agencies due to its high level of consistency and dependability, and the affordable price accommodates the large volume of practice needed to achieve precision marksmanship.
Available in: .32 H&R Mag, .380 Auto, .45 ACP, 9mm Luger, .45 Auto Rim, .44 Mag, .40 S&W, .38 Special, .357 Mag
MSRP: $289.50–524.50

RIFLE AMMUNITION

FACTORY-NEW RIFLE AMMUNITION

Features: This high-performance ammunition is designed to deliver power and performance in several calibers.
Available in: .223 Rem, .308 Win Match, .300 Win Mag, .338 Lapua
MSRP: $289.50–1225.50

BLACK HILLS GOLD

Features: Coupling the finest components with bullets by manufacturers such as Hornady, Barnes and Nosler, these rounds set a high standard for high-performance hunting ammunition.
Available in: .22-250, .243 Win, .25-06 Rem, .270 Win, .270 Win Short Mag, .300 Win Short Mag, .308 Win, .30-06 Sprfd., .300 Win Mag, 7mm Rem Mag.
MSRP: $144.50–274.50

Brenneke USA Ammunition

610–776–0181

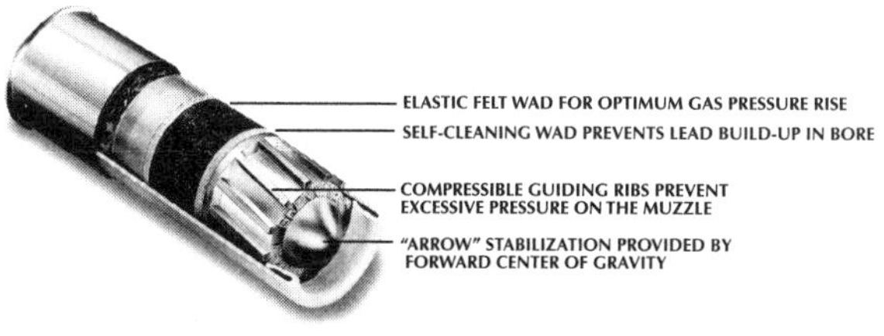
ELASTIC FELT WAD FOR OPTIMUM GAS PRESSURE RISE
SELF-CLEANING WAD PREVENTS LEAD BUILD-UP IN BORE
COMPRESSIBLE GUIDING RIBS PREVENT EXCESSIVE PRESSURE ON THE MUZZLE
"ARROW" STABILIZATION PROVIDED BY FORWARD CENTER OF GRAVITY

SHOTGUN AMMUNITION

BLACK MAGIC MAGNUM AND SHORT MAGNUM SLUGS

Features: 1 oz. (short mag) and 1 3/8 oz.; patented B.E.T. wad; CleanSpeed Coating reduces lead fouling inside the barrel; 3 inch is one of the heaviest slugs on the market ; for all barrel types; range 60 yds. (short mags) to 100 yds. (mag)
Available in: 12 ga., $2\frac{3}{4}$ and 3 in.
MSRP: $9.99–10.99

CLASSIC MAGNUM SLUGS

Features: 1 1/8 oz. original slug with felt wad, traditional since 1898; for all barrel types; range 70 yds.
Available in: 12 ga., $2\frac{3}{4}$ in.
MSRP: $10.99

GOLD MAGNUM SLUGS

Features: 1 3/8 oz.; original "Gold" slug with patented B.E.T. wad; special coating reduces lead fouling inside the barrel; for rifled barrels only; range 100+ yds.
Available in: 12 ga., 3 in.
MSRP: $11.99

HEAVY FIELD SHORT MAGNUM SLUGS

Features: 1 oz. (20 ga.) to 1 $\frac{1}{4}$ oz. (12 ga.) original "Emerald" slug with patented B.E.T. wad; for all barrel types; range 60 yds. (20 ga.) to 100 yds. (12 ga.)
Available in: 12 and 20 ga., $2\frac{3}{4}$ in.
MSRP: $9.99

K.O. SABOT

Features: 1 oz.; .63 diameter slug with red plastic wad; 58% more frontal area than standard .50 cal sabots; expansion up to .9 in.; for all barrel types; range 80 yds. ($2\frac{3}{4}$ in.) to 100 yds. (3 in.)
Available in: 12 ga., $2\frac{3}{4}$ and 3 in.
MSRP: $13.29–13.99

K.O. SLUG

Features: 1 oz. improved Foster type slug; for all barrel types; range up to 60 yds.
Available in: 12 ga., $2\frac{3}{4}$ in.
MSRP: $5.09–5.89

SUPERSABOT

Features: 1 1/8 oz, lead-free slug; expansion up to 1 in.; for rifled barrels only; range 80 yds. ($2\frac{3}{4}$ in.) to 100+ yds. (3 in.)
Available in: 12 ga., $2\frac{3}{4}$ and 3 in.
MSRP: $17.49–19.99

TACTICAL HOME DEFENSE

Features: 1 oz.; original "Bronze" slug with patented B.E.T. wad; for urban use; controlled penetration, low risk of dangerous exiting; for all barrel types; range CQB up to 35 yds.
Available in: 12 ga., $2\frac{3}{4}$ in.
MSRP: $6.30–7.50

CCI Ammunition

RIMFIRE AMMUNITION

GREEN TAG

Features: Our first and still most popular match rimfire product. Tight manufacturing and accuracy specs mean you get the consistency and accuracy that the unforgiving field of competition demands. And we load our rimfire match ammo to leave the muzzle subsonic. That means no buffeting in the transonic zone. Clean-burning propellants keep actions cleaner. Sure-fire CCI priming. Reusable plastic box with dispenser lid.
Available in: .22 LR 40 grain lead round nose
Box of 100: $15.29–20.99
Box of 500: $76.99–92.99

HMR TNT

Features: CCI extends the usefulness of the exciting 17 Hornady Magnum Rimfire by offering the first hollow point loading. A 17 grain Speer® TNT hollow point answers requests from varmint hunters and gives explosive performance over the 17's effective range. Clean-burning propellants keep actions cleaner. Sure-fire CCI priming. Reusable plastic box with dispenser lid.
Available in: 17 HMR 17 grain TNT hollow point
Box of 508: $15.99–18.99
Box of 500: $145.99

LONG HV AND SHORT HV

Features: Designed for rimfire guns that require .22 Long or .22 short ammunition. Clean-burning propellants keep actions cleaner. Sure-fire CCI priming. Reusable plastic box with dispenser lid.
Available in: .22 Short 29 gr solid lead bullet; .22 Short 27 gr hollow point bullet; .22 Long 29 gr solid lead bullet
Long Hv: $20.99
Short Hv: $11.99

MAXI-MAG

Features: CCI has built 22 Magnum RF ammo for over 30 years and is recognized as the technology leader in the specialized skills required to build the long RF Magnum case. MAXI-MAG offers a great power and range increase over the 22 Long Rifle and has become a favorite of varmint shooters everywhere.
Available in: .22 Mag RF
Box 50: $10.99–15.99

MINI-MAG HV

Features: CCI'S first rimfire product and still most popular. Mini-Mag and Mini-Mag hollow points are high-velocity products and offer excellent all-around performance for small game and varmints. Clean-burning propellants keep actions cleaner. Sure-fire CCI priming. Reusable plastic box with dispenser lid.
Available in: .22 LR—40 grain gilded lead round nose, 36 grain gilded lead hollow point
Box 100: $14.99

PISTOL MATCH

Features: Designed expressly for high-end semi-auto match pistols. Single-die tooling and great care in assembly lets you wring the last bit of accuracy from your precision pistol. Clean-burning propellants keep actions cleaner. Sure-fire CCI priming. Reusable plastic box with dispenser lid.
Available in: .22 LR 40 grain lead round nose
Box 50: $7.79–22.99

SELECT .22LR

Features: The 22 Long Rifle Select is built for semi-automatic competition. Reliable operation, accuracy and consistency make Select an ideal choice for competition shooters.
Available in: .22 LR
Box 100: $13.29–25.99

STANDARD VELOCITY

Features: Loaded to the same velocity as Green Tag and Pistol Match but priced less, this is the perfect practice load. Clean-burning propellants keep actions cleaner. Sure-fire CCI priming. Reusable plastic box with dispenser lid.
Available in: .22 LR 40 grain lead round nose
Box 100: $7.69–14.99

V-MAX 17 MACH 2

Features: The 17 Mach 2 is a 22 LR CCI Stinger case necked down to hold a 17 caliber bullet. CCI loads a super-accurate 17-grain polymer-tipped bullet, and drives it 60 percent faster than a 22 Long Rifle 40-grain hollow-point. The loaded cartridge is no longer than a 22 Long rifle, greatly expanding the gun actions that can accommodate 17 caliber rimfire cartridges. Reusable 50-count plastic box that protects and dispenses five cartridges at one time
Available in: 17 Mach 2 (V-Max also available in 17 HMR and 22 Mag RF)
Box 50: $7.99–11.99

HYDRA-SHOCK

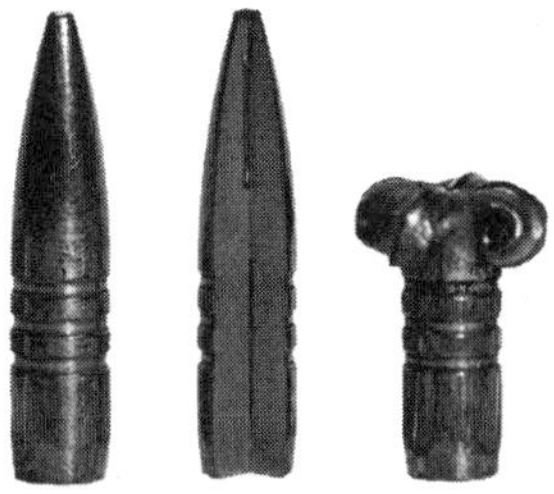

BARNES TRIPLE SHOCK X

ULTRA-SHOCK HEAVYWEIGHT

POWER-SHOK RIFLED SLUG

HANDGUN AMMUNITION

CASTCORE

Features: Heavyweight, flat-nosed, hard cast-lead bullet that smashes through bone.
Available in: 357 Mag, 41 Rem Mag, 44 Rem Mag (Premium Vital-Shok)
357: $24.99, 41: $35.99, 44: $35.99

EXPANDING FULL METAL JACKET

Features: Barrier-penetrating design combines a scored metal nose over an internal rubber tip that collapses on impact.
Available in: 40 S&W, 45 Auto, 9mm Luger (Premium Personal Defense)
40: $25.99, 9: $21.99, 40: $24.99

FULL METAL JACKET

Features: Good choice for range practice and reducing lead fouling in the barrel. Jacket extends from the nose to the base, preventing bullet expansion and barrel leading. Primarily as military ammunition and for recreational shooting.
Available in: 10mm Auto, 25 Auto, 32 Auto, 357 Sig, 38 Special, 38 Super +P, 380 Auto, 40 S&W, 45 Auto, 45 G.A.P., 9mm Luger, 9mm Makarov (American Eagle)
MSRP: $13.99–19.49

HYDRA-SHOK

Features: Unique center-post design delivers controlled expansion, and the notched jacket provides efficient energy transfer to penetrate barriers while retaining stopping power. Deep penetration satisfies even the FBI's stringent testing requirements.
Available in: 10mm Auto, 32 Auto, 357 Mag, 38 Special, 380 Auto, 40 S&W, 44 Rem Mag, 45 Auto, 45 G.A.P., 9mm Luger, 38 Special +P (Premium Personal Defense)
MSRP: $19.99–24.99

JACKETED HOLLOW POINT

Features: Ideal personal defense round in revolvers and semi-autos. Quick, positive expansion. Jacket ensures smooth feeding into autoloading firearms.
Available in: 357 Sig (Premium Personal Defense); 32 H&R Mag, 357 Mag, 40 S&W, 45 Auto, 9mm Luger (Personal Defense Handgun); 357 Mag, 41 Rem Mag, 44 Rem Mag (Power-Shok Handgun Hunting); 44 Rem Mag (American Eagle)
MSRP: $17.49–22.99

LEAD ROUND NOSE

Features: Great training round for practicing at the range. 100 lead with no jacket. Excellent accuracy and is very economical.
Available in: 32 S&W Long (Champion Handgun); 38 Special (American Eagle)
Box 500: $23.49–38.99

LEAD SEMI-WADCUTTER

Features: Most popular all-around choice for target and personal defense, a versatile design which cuts clean holes in targets and efficiently transfers energy.
Available in: 32 H&R Mag (Champion Handgun)
Box 20: $18.49

SEMI-WADCUTTER HOLLOW POINT

Features: For both small game and personal defense. Hollow point design promotes uniform expansion.
Available in: 44 Special, 45 Colt (Champion Handgun)
Box 20: $184922.49

RIFLE AMMUNITION

BARNES TRIPLE SHOCK X-BULLET (TSX)

Features: Superior expansion and deep penetration. The all-copper design provides high weight retention.
Available in: .243 Win., 25-06 Rem., *270 Win., 270 Win. Short Mag, 280 Rem, 300 H&H Mag, 300 Rem. Ultra Mag, 300 Weatherby Mag, 300 Win Mag, 300 Win Short Mag, 30-06 Spring., 308 Win, 338 Win Mag, 7mm Rem Mag, 7mm-08 Rem, 338 Fed (Premium Vital-Shok). 375 H&H Mag, 416 Rem Mag, 416 Rigby, 458 Win Mag (Premium Cape-Shok)*
Box 20: $44.99

FULL METAL JACKET BOAT-TAIL

Features: Accurate, non-expanding bullets. Flat shooting trajectory, leave a small exit hole in game, and put clean holes in paper. Smooth, reliable feeding into semi-automatics too.
Available in: 223 Rem (Power-Shok); 223 Rem, 30-06 Spring., 308 Win (American Eagle)
Box 20: $9.89

FUSION LITE

Features: Provides terminal energy with 50% less recoil. Jacket application process completely eliminates core-jacket separation and makes for high weight retention. Lower velocities. Slower speeds, holds nearly 100% of its weight.
Available in: .270 Win Mag 145-grain at 2200 fps; .30-06 Spring 170-grain at 2000 fps; .308 Win 170-grain at 2000 fps.
Box 20: $24.49–25.99

NOSLER ACCUBOND

Features: Combines the terminal performance of a bonded bullet with the accuracy and retained energy of a Ballistic Tip.
Available in: 25-06 Rem., 260 Rem, 270 Weatherby Mag, 270 Win, 270 Win. Short Mag, 280 Rem, 300 Win Mag, 300 Win Short Mag, 30-06

Federal Ammunition

Spring., 308 Win, 338 Rem, 338 Win Mag, 375 H&H Mag, 7mm Rem Mag, 7mm STW, 7mm Weatherby Mag, 7mm Win Short Mag, 7mm-08 Rem, 338 Fed (Premium Vital-Shok)
Box 20: $48.99–68.99

NOSLER BALLISTIC TIP

Features: Fast, flat-shooting wind-defying performance. Long-range shots at varmints, predators and small to medium game. Color-coded polycarbonate tip provides easy identification, prevents deformation in the magazine and drives back on impact for expansion.
Available in: .243 Win., 25-06 Rem., 260 Rem, 270 Win., 270 Win. Short Mag, 280 Rem, 300 Win Short Mag, 30-06 Spring., 308 Win, 7mm Rem Mag, 7mm Win Short Mag, 7mm-08 Rem (Premium Vital-Shok). 222 Rem., 22-250 Rem., 243 Win., 25-06 Rem., 204 Ruger (Premium V-Shok)
Box 20: $24.99–33.99

NOSLER PARTITION

Features: Proven choice for medium to large game animals. Partitioned copper jacket allows the front half of the bullet to mushroom, while the rear core remains intact, driving forward for deep penetration and stopping power.
Available in: 223 Rem., 243 Win., 25-06 Rem., 257 Roberts, 270 Win., 270 Win. Short Mag, 280 Rem., 300 H&H Mag, 300 Rem. Ultra Mag, 300 Weatherby Mag, 300 Win. Mag, 300 Win. Short Mag, 30-06 Spring., 30-30 Win., 308 Win., 338 Rem. Ultra Mag, 338 Win. Mag, 6mm Rem., 7mm Mauser, 7mm Rem. Mag, 7mm Win. Short Mag, 7mm-08 Rem., 338 Fed (Premium Vital-Shok). 375 H&H Mag (Premium Cape-Shok)
Box 20: $25.99–72.99

SIERRA GAMEKING BOAT-TAIL

Features: Long ranges are its specialty. Excellent choice for everything from varmints to big game animals. Tapered, boat-tail design provides extremely flat trajectories. Higher downrange velocity for more energy at the point of impact. Reduced wind drift.
Available in: 243 Win, 25-06 Rem, 260 Rem, 270 Win, 30-06 Spring., 308 Win, 7mm Rem. Mag (Premium Vital-Shok solid point); 243 Win (Premium Vital-Shok hollow point); 22-250 Rem, 223 Rem (Premium V-Shok)
Box 20: $28.49–39.99

SOFT POINT

Feature: Proven performer on small game and thin-skinned medium game. Aerodynamic tip for a flat trajectory. Exposed soft point expands rapidly for hard hits, even as velocity slows at longer ranges.
Available in: 222 Rem, 22-250 Rem, 223 Rem, 223 Rem, 243 Win, 270 Win, 270 Win Short Mag, 280 Rem, 300 Savage, 300 Win Short Mag, 30-06 Spring., 303 British, 308 Win, 375 H&H Mag, 6.5x55 Swedish, 6mm Rem, 7.62x39mm Soviet, 7mm Rem Mag, 7mm Win Short Mag, 8mm Mauser (Power-Shok)
Box 50: $25.49–27.99

SOFT POINT FLAT NOSE

Features: Great for thick cover, it expands reliably and penetrates deep on light to medium game. The flat nose prevents accidental discharge.
Available in: 30-30 Win, 32 Win Special (Power-Shok)
Box 20: $15.99

SOFT POINT ROUND NOSE

Features: The choice in heavy cover. Large exposed tip, good weight retention and specially tapered jacket provide controlled expansion.
Available in: 270 Win, 30 Carbine, 30-30 Win, 35 Rem, 7mm Mauser (Power-Shok)
Box 20: $15.49–26.99

TROPHY BONDED BEAR CLAW

Features: Ideal for medium to large dangerous game. The jacket and core are 100% fusion-bonded for reliable bullet expansion from 25 yards to extreme ranges. Bullet retains 95% of its weight for deep penetration. Hard solid copper base tapering to a soft, copper nose section for controlled expansion.
Available in: 270 Weatherby Mag, 270 Win, 270 Win Short Mag, 300 Rem Ultra Mag, 300 Weatherby Mag, 300 Win Mag, 300 Win. Short Mag, 30-06 Spring., 308 Win, 338 Win Mag, 35 Whelen, 375 H&H Mag, 7mm Rem Mag, 7mm Weatherby Mag (Premium Vital-Shok); 375 H&H Mag, 416 Rem Mag, 416 Rigby, 458 Win Mag, 470 Nitro Express, 458 Lott (Premium Cape-Shok)
Box 20: $39.99–340.99

TROPHY BONDED SLEDGEHAMMER

Features: Use it on the largest, most dangerous game in the world. Jack Carter design maximizes stopping power. Bonded bronze solid with a flat nose that minimizes deflection off bone and muscle for a deep, straight wound channel.
Available in: 375 H&H Mag, 416 Rem Mag, 416 Rigby, 458 Win Mag, 470 Nitro Express, 458 Lott (Premium Cape-Shok)
Box 20: $103.99–240.99

WOODLEIGH WELDCORE

Features: Respected by Safari hunters. Superb accuracy and excellent stopping power. Special heavy jacket provides 80-85% weight retention. Bullets are favored for large or dangerous game.
Available in: 470 Nitro Express (Premium Cape-Shok)
Box 5: $77.99

SHOTGUN AMMUNITION

GAME-SHOK GAME LOAD

Available in: 12, 16, 20 ga.; 2¾ in.; shot sizes 6, 7½, 8
Box 25: $8.69–10.39

GAME-SHOK HEAVY FIELD

Available in: 12, 20 ga.; 2¾ in.; shot sizes 4, 5, 6, 7½, 8
Box 25: $10.39–11.49

GAME-SHOK HI-BRASS

Available in: 12, 16, 20, 410 ga.; 2½, 2¾, 3 in.; shot sizes 4, 5, 6, 7½, 8
Box 25: $13.29–15.79

PREMIUM BLACK CLOUD STEEL

Available in: 12 ga.; 3, 3½ in.; shot sizes 2, BB, BBB
Box 25: $21.99

PREMIUM GOLD MEDAL TARGET—EXTRA-LITE PAPER (LR)
Available in: 12 ga.; 2¾ in.; shot sizes 7½, 8
Box 25: $38.99

PREMIUM GOLD MEDAL TARGET—EXTRA-LITE PLASTIC (LR)
Available in: 12 ga.; 2¾ in.; shot sizes 7½, 8
Box 25: $12.99

PREMIUM GOLD MEDAL TARGET—HANDICAP PAPER HV
Available in: 12 ga.; 2¾ in.; shot sizes 7½, 8
Box 25: $12.99

PREMIUM GOLD MEDAL TARGET—HANDICAP PLASTIC HV
Available in: 12 ga.; 2¾ in.; shot sizes 7½, 8
Box 25: $18.22

PREMIUM GOLD MEDAL TARGET—INTERNATIONAL PAPER
Available in: 12 ga.; 2¾ in.; shot sizes 7½
Box 25: $12.91

PREMIUM GOLD MEDAL TARGET—INTERNATIONAL PLASTIC
Available in: 12 ga.; 2¾ in.; shot sizes 7½, 8½
Box 25: $1599

PREMIUM GOLD MEDAL TARGET—PAPER
Available in: 12 ga.; 2¾ in.; shot sizes 7½, 8, 9
Box 25: $11.99–12.99

PREMIUM GOLD MEDAL TARGET—PLASTIC
Available in: 12, 20, 28, 410 ga.; 2½, 2¾ in.; shot sizes 7½, 8, 8½, 9
Box 25: $15.99

PREMIUM GOLD MEDAL TARGET—SPORTING CLAYS
Available in: 12 ga.; 2¾ in.; shot sizes 7½, 8, 8½
Box 25: $10.09–10.29

PREMIUM MAG-SHOK—HEAVYWEIGHT TURKEY
Available in: 12 ga.; 3, 3½ in.; shot sizes 5, 6, 7
Box 5: $20.99–31.99

PREMIUM MAG-SHOK HIGH VELOCITY LEAD
Available in: 10, 20 ga.; 3, 3½ in.; shot sizes 4, 5, 6
Box 10: $12.99–21.99

PREMIUM MAG-SHOK LEAD WITH FLITECONTROL
Available in: 12 ga.; 3, 3½ in.; shot sizes 4, 5, 6
Box 10: $17.99–21.99

PREMIUM MAG-SHOK LEAD WITH FLITECONTROL HIGH VELOCITY
Available in: 12 ga.; 2¾, 3, 3½ in.; shot sizes 4, 5, 6
Box 10: $12.99–21.99

PREMIUM ULTRA-SHOK HEAVY HIGH VELOCITY STEEL
Available in: 10, 12 ga.; 2¾, 3, 3½ in.; shot sizes 1, 2, 3, 4, BB, BBB, T
Box 25: $22.99–29.99

PREMIUM ULTRA-SHOK HEAVYWEIGHT
Available in: 12 ga.; 3, 3½ in.; shot sizes 2, 4, 6
Box 10: $48.99–54.99

PREMIUM ULTRA-SHOK HIGH DENSITY WATERFOWL
Available in: 10, 12, 20 ga.; 3, 3½ in.; shot sizes 2, 4, BB
Box 10: $26.99–41.99

PREMIUM ULTRA-SHOK HIGH VELOCITY STEEL
Available in: 12, 16, 20 ga.; 2¾, 3, 3½ in.; shot sizes 1, 2, 3, 4, 6, BB, BBB, T
Box 25: $21.99–25.99

PREMIUM ULTRA-SHOK SUBSONIC HIGH DENSITY
Available in: 12 ga.; 2¾ in.; shot sizes BB
Box 25: $19.18–21.06

PREMIUM WING-SHOK FLYER LOADS
Available in: 12 ga.; 2¾ in.; shot sizes 7½
Box 25: $22.99

PREMIUM WING-SHOK HIGH BRASS
Available in: 28 ga.; 2¾ in.; shot sizes 6, 7½, 8
Box 25: $25.99

PREMIUM WING-SHOK HIGH VELOCITY
Available in: 12 ga.; 2¾, 3 in.; shot sizes 4, 5, 6, 7½
Box 25: $18.99–21.99

PREMIUM WING-SHOK HIGH VELOCITY—PHEASANT
Available in: 12, 20 ga.; 2¾ in.; shot sizes 4, 5, 6, 7½
Box 25: $18.99–21.99

PREMIUM WING-SHOK HIGH VELOCITY—QUAIL FOREVER
Available in: 12, 20 ga.; 2¾ in.; shot sizes 7½, 8
Box 25: $18.99–19.99

PREMIUM WING-SHOK MAGNUM
Available in: 10, 12, 16, 20 ga.; 2¾, 3, 3½ in.; shot sizes 2, 4, 5, 6, BB
Box 25: $25.99–39.99

SPEED-SHOK STEEL
Available in: 12, 20 ga.; 2¾, 3, 3½ in.; shot sizes 2, 3, 4, 6, 7, BB
Box 25: $8.99–15.99

STRUT-SHOK
Available in: 12 ga.; 3, 3½ in.; shot sizes 2, 3, 4, 6, 7, BB
Box 10: $12.99–16.99

TOP GUN SUBSONIC TARGET
Available in: 12 ga.; 2¾ in.; shot sizes 7½
Box 25: $7.99

TOP GUN TARGET
Available in: 12, 20 ga.; 2¾ in.; shot sizes 7, 7½, 8, 9
Box 25: $7.89

Federal Ammunition

TOP GUN TARGET STEEL
Available in: 20 ga.; 2¾ in.; shot sizes 7
Box 25: $8.99

SHOTGUN AMMUNITION (SLUGS)

FUSION SABOT SLUGS
Features: Electro-chemical process applies a copper jacket to the lead core one molecule at a time. Yields a perfectly uniform jacket.
Available in: 20-gauge, 3 in., 5/8 oz. loads; 2¾ in., and 3 in., 12 ga. loads
Box 12: $12.79

POWER-SHOK RIFLED SLUG
Features: Hollow point slug type
Available in: 10, 12, 16, 20, 410 ga.; 2½, 2¾, 3, 3½ in.; ¼,¾, 7/8, 1, 1 ¼, 1¾ oz. slug wt.
Box 5: $5.79–7.09

POWER-SHOK SABOT SLUG
Features: Sabot hollow point slug type
Available in: 12 ga.; 2¾ in.; 1 oz. slug wt.
Box 5: $13.99–16.99

PREMIUM VITAL-SHOK BARNES EXPANDER
Features: Barnes Sabot slug type
Available in: 12, 20 ga.; 2¾, 3 in.; 5/8,¾, 1 oz. slug wt.
Box 5: $14.99–16.99

PREMIUM VITAL-SHOK TRUBALL RIFLED SLUG
Features: Truball rifled slug type
Available in: 12, 20 ga.; 2¾ in.;¾, 1 oz. slug wt.
Box 5: $5.79

Federal Fusion Ammunition

200-GRAIN .338 FEDERAL
Fusion has added a 200-grain, .338 Federal offering to its deer-focused rifle ammo lineup. This round (currently chambered by six major rifle manufacturers) will have a 200-grain (2660 fps.) load. The round is built on the.308 case and features a .338 diameter projectile.
MSRP: . . . . . $25–27 (per box of 20)

Federal Premium Ammunition

FEDERAL VITAL-SHOK TROPHY BONDED TIP
Features: Built on the Trophy Bonded Bear Claw platform to provide deep penetration and high weight retention. Sleek profile, with tapered heel and translucent polymer tip. Nickel-plated. Available as component and in Federal loaded ammunition.
Box of 20: $49.99–59.99

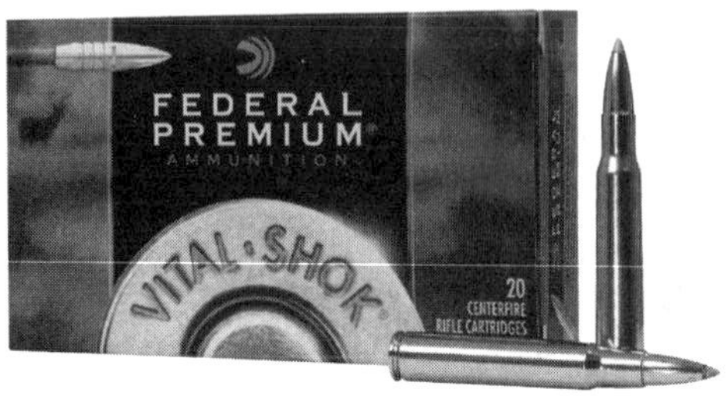

FEDERAL NYCLAD BULLETS
Features: in Federal Premium Personal Defense handgun ammunition, 125-grain .38 Special HP.
Box of 20: $19.99

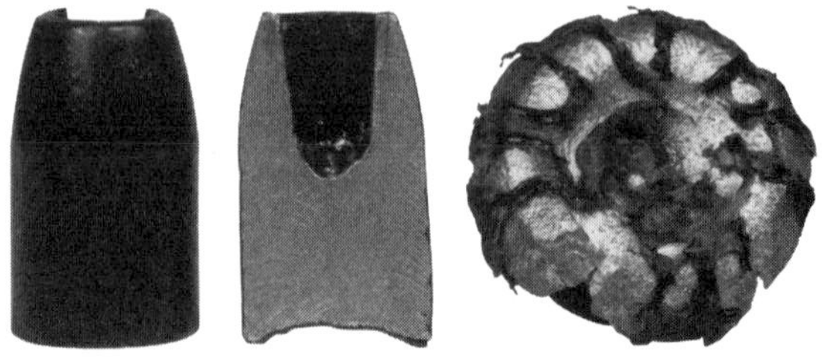

Federal Premium Ammunition

FEDERAL V-SHOK HEAVYWEIGHT COYOTE

Features: 12 gauge, BB shot, 1½ oz.
Box of 5: $22.99

FEDERAL BLACK CLOUD SS WATERFOWL

Features: FLIGHTCONTROL wad tightens patterns, FLIGHTSTOPPER steel shot pellets, 10, 20 and 12 gauge.
Box of 25: $19.99–28.99

FEDERAL ULTRAMATCH RIMFIRE TARGET

Features: 40-grain, 1080 fps match load for .22 rimfire competition.
Box of 50: $17.49

.327 FEDERAL MAGNUM

TNT GREEN

.327 FEDERAL MAGNUM

Federal Premium has partnered with Ruger to introduce a new personal defense revolver cartridge designed to deliver .357 Magnum ballistics from a .32-caliber diameter platform. The .327 Federal Magnum is designed for use in lightweight, small-frame revolvers like the Ruger SP101. The ammunition will be available in three loads: Federal Premium 85-gr Hydra-Shok JHP, American Eagle 100-gr SP and Speer 115-gr Gold Dot HP.
MSRP: . . . . $20 (per box of 20)

TNT GREEN

TNT Green brings non-tox technology to the Federal Premium V-Shok varmint hunting line. This is a totally lead-free bullet that couples explosive expansion with match-grade accuracy. Initial offerings will include .222, .22-250 and .223 options.
MSRP: . . . . $25 (per box of 20)

Federal Premium Ammunition

VITAL SHOK TROPHY BONDED TIP

VITAL-SHOK TROPHY BONDED TIP

The Vital-Shok Trophy Bonded Tip is built on the Trophy Bonded Bear Claw platform with numerous added features. A neon, translucent polymer tip and boat-tail design for flat trajectory and improved accuracy are combined with a solid copper shank to crush bone. Exterior skiving on the nickel-plated bullet provides optimum expansion at all ranges. The load also features a nickel plated case and bullet. Available in a full-line of offerings.
MSRP: . . . . . $50–56 (per box of 20)

Fiocchi Ammunition

SIZE #	9	8½	8	7½	6	5	4	3	2	1	BB	BBB	T	#4	00
DIA.IN.	.08	.085	.09	.095	.11	.12	.13	.14	.15	.16	.18	.19	.20	.24	.33
DIA.MM	2.03	2.16	2.29	2.41	2.79	3.05	3.30	3.56	3.81	4.06	4.57	4.83	5.08	6.10	8.38

HANDGUN AMMUNITION

7.63 MAUSER PISTOL CARTRIDGE

Features: The 7.63 Mauser cartridge was first introduced by the Waffenfabrik Mauser, Orbendorf, Germany in 1896 in the famous C-96 "Broomhandle" Mauser pistol. The C-96 was the first semi-automatic pistol to see wide spread military use in World War I, World War II, the Second Boer War, the Spanish Civil War and the Chinese Civil War. Such notables as Winston Churchill armed himself with the C-96 in 7.63 Mauser as his personal weapon in the Second Boer War. The unique shape of the C-96 pistol makes it one of the most recognizable pistols of our time; it's truly a classic pistol and cartridge combination. Fiocchi Ammunition USA now offers owners of these historic handguns new, high quality 7.63 Mauser ammunition.
Available in: 88-grain Full Metal Jacket (FMJ) with a muzzle velocity of 1425 feet per second (FPS) and 400 foot pounds of energy at the muzzle.
Box 50: $33.49

RIFLE AMMUNITION

EXTREMA 223 REM. HVA

Features: Fiocchi now offers the extremely popular 223 Remington cartridge loaded with super accurate and deadly Hornady V-Max 50-grain bullets in Fiocchi's Extrema rifle ammunition line. Extrema 223 Remington HVA has unmatched terminal ballistics that will make the cartridge a favorite of both the Western prairie dog and Eastern ground hog hunter.
Available in: 223 Rem, 50 grain
Box 50: $21.99

FIOCCHI CENTERFIRE RIFLE LINE

Features: new loads for .22 Hornet, .223, 6.5x55, .308, including lead-free designs.
MSRP: . . . . prices on request

FIOCCHI CENTERFIRE HANDGUN LINE

Features: new Expanding Mono-block bullet load in 9x19 pistol ammo. XTP loads in 9mm, .38 Special, .357 SIG, .44 Special (Cowboy Action), .44 Magnum and .45 ACP.
MSRP: . . . . prices on request

SHOTGUN AMMUNITION

PREMIUM NICKEL PLATED HUNTING LOADS

Features: Fiocchi offers the hunter a wide selection of hunting loads that incorporate nickel plated shot to help make hunting more successful. Nickel plated shot gives the hunter such benefits as denser, more consistent patterns with fewer stray pellets and increased range and penetration than non-plated shot.
Available in: 1¼ oz. Helice Loads (12 ga., 2¾ in., shot sizes 7, 7½, 8); 1½, 1¾ and 2 3/8 oz. Turkey Loads (12 ga., 2¾, 3 and 3½ in., shot sizes 4, 5, 6); ⅞ to 1¾ oz. Golden Pheasant Loads (12, 20, 16, 28 ga., 2¾ and 3 in., shot sizes 4, 5, 6, 7½, 8); and Buckshot Loads (12 ga., 2¾ in., shot sizes 00 Buck, 4 Buck)
Box 25: $9.34

PREMIUM TARGET LOADS

Features: Specifically for competitive shooters. Our Target Load Line is the offspring of a 50 year tradition of supporting the world of trap, skeet and now sporting clays, FITASC and Compaq.

Available in: 1 and 1⅛ oz. Paper Target Loads (12 ga., 2¾ in., shot sizes 7½, 8, 8½); ⅞ oz, 1⅛ oz. and 1 oz. Premium Target Loads (12, 20, 28, 410 ga., 2½ and 2¾ in., shot sizes 7½, 8, 8½, 9); 1 and 1⅛ oz. Multi-sport Loads (12 ga., 2¾ in., shot sizes 7½, 8, 9); 1 1/4 oz. Helice Loads (12 ga., 2¾ in., shot sizes 7, 7½, 8); 1⅛ oz. Power Spreaders (12 ga., 2¾ in., shot sizes 8, 8½); 1 oz. Interceptor Spreaders (12 ga., 2¾ in., shot sizes 8, 8½); ⅞ and 1 oz. Steel Target Loads (12, 20 ga., 2¾ in., shot sizes 7); and ¾ and ⅞ oz. Ultra Low Recoil Training Loads (12, 20 ga., 2¾ in., shot sizes 7½, 8)
MSRP: $9.59

STEEL HUNTING LOADS

Features: Fiocchi Steel shot hunting loads are manufactured with a combination of treated steel shot, protective wads and the appropriate powders to deliver a consistent dense pattern that is easy on your gun barrel but hard on your target.
Available in: 1⅛ to 1⅝ oz., 2¾ to 3½ in. 12 ga. loads in shot sizes 1, 2, 3, 4, BB, BBB, T; ⅞ oz., 3 in. 20 ga. loads in shot sizes 2, 3, 4
MSRP: $12.99

UPLAND GAME AND FIELD LOADS

Features: Fiocchi offers a full line of lead hunting loads from Dove Loads to powerful Hi Brass Loads.
Available in: ¾ to 1¾ oz. High Velocity Loads (12, 20, 16, 28, 410 ga., 2¾ and 3 in., shot sizes 4, 5, 6, 7½, 8, 9); 1 to 1¼ oz. Field Loads (12, 20, 16 ga., 2¾ in., shot sizes 4, 5, 6, 7½, 8, 9); ½ to 1⅛ oz. Dove Loads (12, 20, 16, 28, 410 ga., 2 to 3 ¼ in., shot sizes 6, 7½, 8, 9); and ¼ to 1 1/16 oz. Specialty Shotshell Loads (Flobert 9 Rimfire, 24, 32 ga., 1¾ and 2½ in., shot sizes 6, 7½, 8, 9)
MSRP: $9.89

WHITE RHINO SHOTSHELLS

Features: Fiocchi's White Rhino uses B&P (Baschieri & Pellagri) wads and 5-percent antimony lead shot. Its additional 50 feet per second velocity over standard trap loads make it a favorite for "handicap trap" and those long distance shots on the sporting clays course. The B&P shot cup, with its softer plastic and better sealing ability, means there's less gas escaping around the wad ensuring higher velocity.
Available in: 12 ga.
MSRP: $10.39

GOLDEN WATERFOWL

GOLDEN PHEASANT

GOLDEN PHEASANT SHOT SHELLS

Golden Pheasant shot shells utilize a special hard, nickel-plated lead shot, based on Fiocchi's strict ballistic tolerances that ensure proven shot consistency — resulting in deeper penetration, longer ranges and much tighter patterns. Available in 12, 16, 20 and 28 gauge.
MSRP: . . . . . $17–19 (per box of 25)

GOLDEN WATERFOWL SHOT SHELLS

The Fiocchi Golden Waterfowl shot shells are 3-inch, 12 gauge shells loaded with 1¼ ounces of steel shot in the hunter's choice of shot sizes BBB, BB, 1, 2, 3 or 4. Rated at 1,400 fps muzzle velocity.
MSRP: . . . . . $19–22 (per box of 25)

Harvester Muzzleloading Ammunition

SCORPION PT GOLD

Scorpion PT Gold Ballistic Tip Bullets are electroplated with copper plating that does not separate from lead core. The PT Gold offers greater accuracy at longer ranges than a hollow point. The 3% antimony makes the bullet harder than pure lead. Available in 50 caliber, 260- and 300-grain sizes.

MSRP: $11–22 (per box of 12 or 50)

Hornady Ammunition

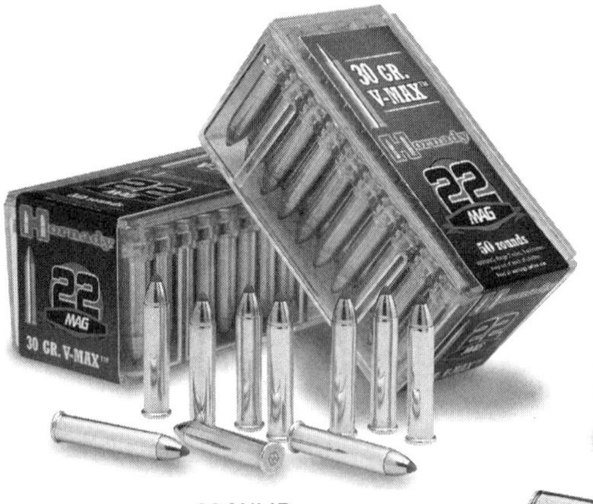

22 WMR

.300 RCM & .338 RCM

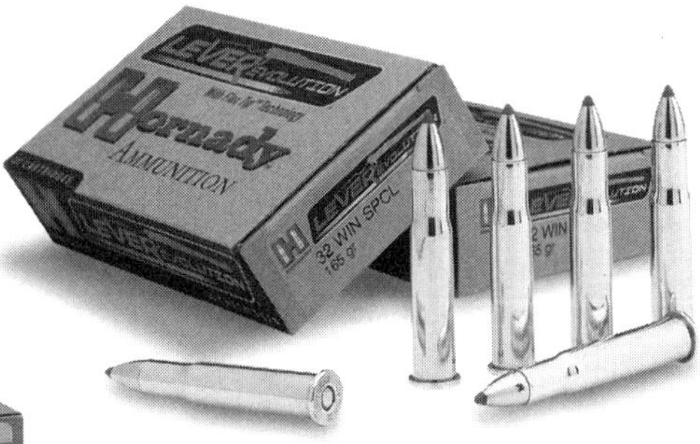

.32 WIN SPECIAL

.22 WMR

Hornady .22 WMR rimfire ammunition features a 30-grain V-MAX bullet that leaves the muzzle at 2,200 feet per second with excellent terminal performance out to 125 yards. Hornady's .22 WMR improves the accuracy of any .22 WMR rifle.

MSRP: . . . . . $15 (per dry box of 50)

.300 RCM AND .338 RCM

Most magnum cartridges require 24- to 26-inch-long barrels to achieve advertised performance. Hornady Ruger Compact Magnum cartridges achieve true magnum levels of velocity, accuracy and terminal performance in short action guns featuring a compact 20-inch barrel. Based on the beltless .375 Ruger case, the .300 and .338 RCMs feature cartridge geometry that provides for an extremely efficient cartridge case.

MSRP: . . . . . $40–50 (per box of 20)

.32 WIN SPECIAL

Hornady's .32 Winchester Special LEVERevolution cartridge features a 165-grain Flex Tip eXpanding (FTX) bullet that delivers a muzzle velocity of 2410 fps. This velocity combined with an impressive ballistic coefficient allows the .32 Winchester Special LEVERevolution to be effective out to 300 yards.

MSRP: . . . . $29 (per box of 20)

Hornady Ammunition

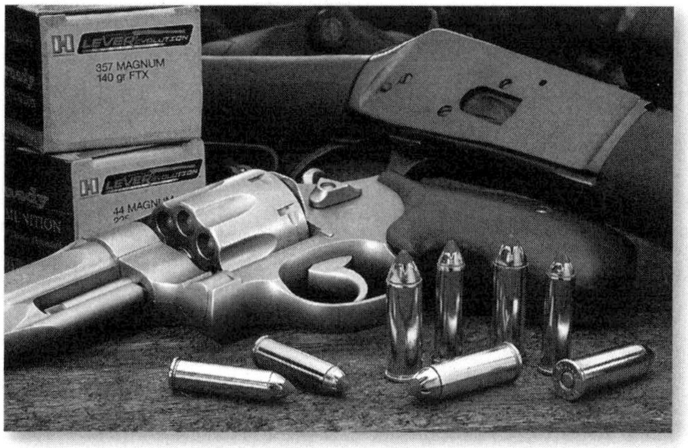

.357 MAG - 44 MAG

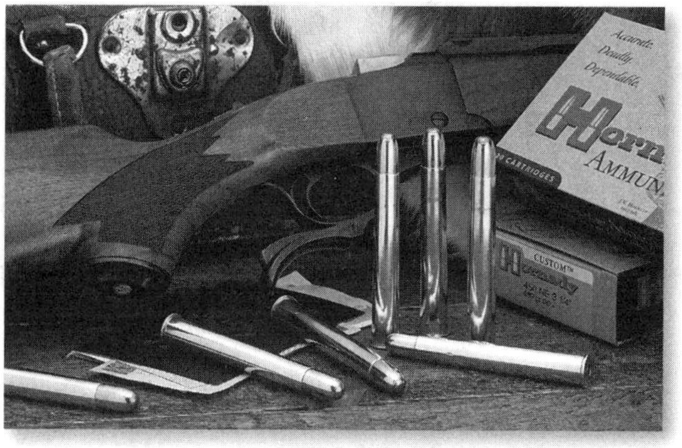

.450 NITRO EXPRESS

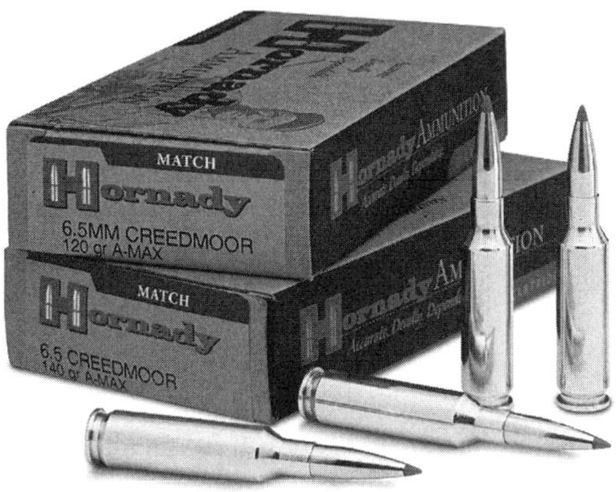

6.5 CREEDMOOR

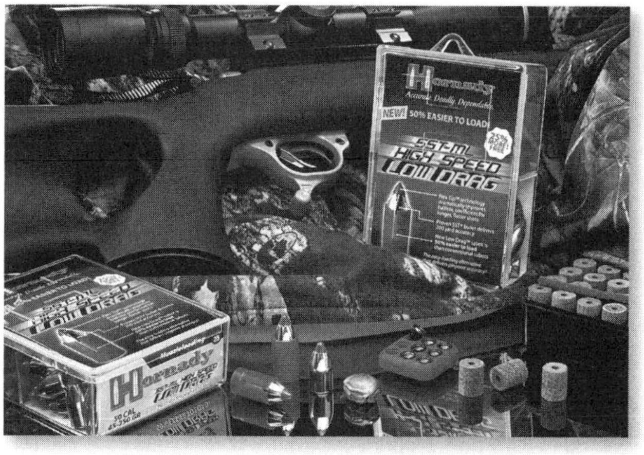

SST-ML HIGH SPEED LOW DRAG SABOT

.357 MAG / .44 MAG

The .357 and .44 Magnum LEVERevolution cartridges feature 140- and 225-grain FTX bullets, launching at 850 to 1,900 fps. respectively. Now hunters who use both handguns and lever guns no longer have to use two different cartridges to get results.

MSRP: . . . . . $24–26 (per box of 20)

.450 NITRO EXPRESS 3¼-INCH

Hornady's .450 Nitro Express 3¼-in. ammunition features a 480-grain bullet with a muzzle velocity of 2,150 fps. Hornady's .450 NE offers two bullet styles — the Dangerous Game Solid (DGS), a non-expanding solid for deep penetration and the 480-grain Dangerous Game eXpanding (DGX) that expands to allow more energy to be transferred upon impact.

MSRP: . . . . $120 (per box of 20)

6.5 CREEDMOOR

The 6.5 Creedmoor was built for match rifles, including the Tubb 2000 and DPMS LR Series, with a case slightly shorter than the .260 Remington, eliminating any "Cartridge Overall Length" issues when using .308 Winchester length magazines.

Sharper 30-degree shoulder and aggressive body taper allow the 6.5 Creedmoor to deliver higher velocities than other 6mm and 6.5mm cartridges, and yet it operates at standard .308 Winchester pressures, thus increasing barrel and case life.

MSRP: . . . . $33 (per box of 20)

SST-ML HIGH SPEED LOW DRAG SABOT

Hornady's Low Drag Sabot reduces loading effort while preserving terminal performance. The SST-ML High Speed Low Drag Sabot fully engages the rifling to deliver pinpoint accuracy at 200 yards and beyond.

MSRP: . . . . $16 (per box of 20)

Hornady Ammunition

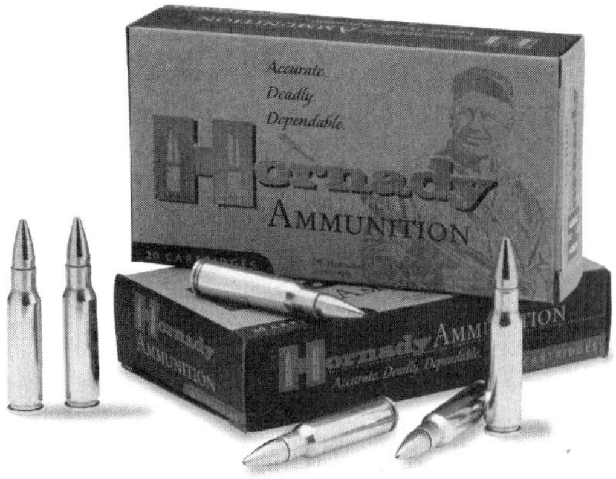

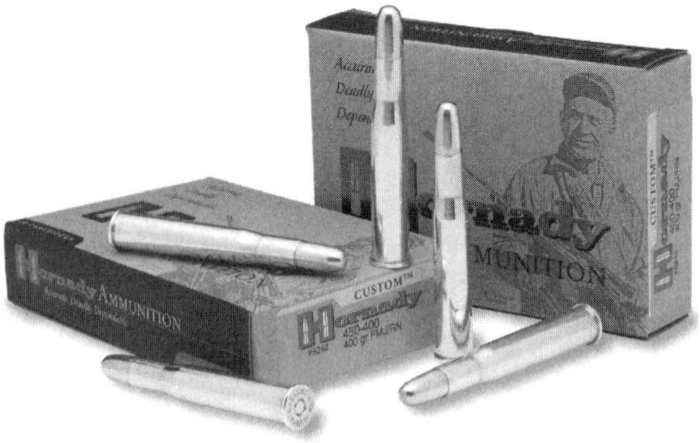

HANDGUN AMMUNITION

500 SMITH & WESSON

Features: Packs a 350 gr. Hornady XTP Mag bullet, one of the most accurate and deadly projectiles. The XTP Mag delivers dead-on, accuracy and reliable expansion for deep, terminal penetration at a wide range of velocities.
Box 20: $29.99–34.99

RIFLE AMMUNITION

6.8MM SPC

Features: Developed at the request of the U.S. Special Forces. Perfect sporting cartridge for game up to the size of whitetail and mule deer. Same power class as the .300 Savage, but delivers a flatter trajectory and less recoil. Features either a 110 gr. BTHP bullet, specifically designed for the cartridge, or a proven 110 gr. V-MAX bullet. 110 gr. BTHP delivers excellent expansion and maximum energy transfer at all velocities, while the 110 gr. VMAX has all the characteristics of our Varmint Express ammo—flat trajectories and rapid, violent expansion.
Box 20: $19.99

9.3 X 74R

Features: Originally designed in Germany during the early 1900s. Offers a 286-grain Spire Point Recoil-Proof bullet loaded to factory specifications and designed to deliver controlled expansion and devastating terminal performance on big game from a double rifle, while regulating. High-tech propellant. Provides maximum case fill for consistent ignition while providing temperature sensitivity in extreme climates.
Box 20: $25.99

17HMR XTP

Features: Delivers deeper penetration, less pelt damage and a quick kill. This new XTP bullet was purposed and designed as a hunting load. It's a great choice for small game and varmint hunting where salvaging the pelt is important. Has a 20-gr. XTP bullet.
Box 50: $12.99

17 HORNADY MACH 2

Features: Provides target-erasing accuracy and a frozen clothesline trajectory — nearly seven inches flatter at 150 yards than a standard High Velocity 22 Long Rifle cartridge. Delivers 2,100 fps, far outperforming a standard High Velocity 22 Long Rifle's 1,255 fps velocity at the muzzle.
Box 50: $7.49–7.99

.30 T/C

Features: Designed for Thompson Center's Icon bolt-action rifle. Hornady perfected the balance between case volume, bore volume and burn rates for both the 150- and 165-grain offerings. Slightly smaller in capacity than the 308 Winchester, but delivers ballistic performance exceeding the 30-06. With a muzzle velocity of 3000 fps, the 150-grain load outperforms the 308 Win by 180 fps and outperforms the 30-06 by nearly 100 fps. Provides a 15% reduction in perceived recoil, ultra-smooth feeding, full magazine capacity, a short bolt throw, longer barrel life and delivers full ballistic potential in a short action case. Packaged in boxes of 20.
Box 30: $13.99–16.99

204 RUGER, 45-GR. SP

Features: Designed to provide controlled expansion for deeper penetration on larger varmints. Built around Hornady's proven Spire Point design, the 204 45 gr SP cartridge provides flat trajectories, enhanced penetration and a new dimension to the 204 Ruger's personality.
Box 20: $18.49

.375 RUGER

Features: Delivers performance that exceeds the .375 H&H. Designed to provide greater knockdown power with a shorter cartridge from a standard action and a 20 in. barrel. Improves on the velocity of the .375 H&H by 150 fps. Three different loads, including a 270-grain Spire Point Recoil-Proof, 300-grain Round Nose and a 300-grain Solid. Spire Point Recoil-Proof bullet. Longer ogive and less exposed lead which helps protect the bullet from deformation under recoil in rifle magazines.
Box 100: $14.49–16.90

405 WINCHESTER 300-GR. SP

Features: When Theodore Roosevelt picked the 405 almost a century ago, he was looking for the perfect big game gun. The "modern" 405 delivers performance Roosevelt never even dreamed of. Two new No. 1H Tropical Single Shot Rifles chambered for this world-class big game load. The most powerful rimmed cartridge ever developed for the lever action rifle.
Box 50: $47.99

450 BUSHMASTER

Features: Fires Hornady's 0.452-in., 250 gr. SST with Flex Tip technology. Overall cartridge matches the 223 Remington at 2.250 inch. Flat trajectories and tremendous downrange ener-

gy. Soft polymer tipped SST bullet eliminates tip deformation and also initiates expansion over a wide range of impact velocities.
Box 50: $24.99

450/400 NITRO EXPRESS 3-IN.

Features: Comes loaded with either a 400-grain RN expanding bullet or FMJ-RN Solid. Regulate in double rifles. Ideal ammo for hunting hippo, buffalo and other thick-skinned game. Also features cutting-edge propellant technology ensuring consistent performance in all weather types.
Box 20: $32.49

LEVEREVOLUTION AMMUNITION

Features: Feature elastomer Flex Tip Technology that is safe in your tubular magazine. Flatter trajectories for fantastic downrange energy. Provides up to 250 feet-per-second faster muzzle velocity than conventional lever gun loads; exceptional accuracy and overwhelming downrange terminal performance; up to 40% more energy.
Available in: .30-30 Win., .308 Marlin Express, .35 Rem., .444 Marlin, .45-70 Gov't., .450 Marlin.
Box 100: $28.99

SHOTGUN AMMUNITION

SST SHOTGUN SLUG

Features: Delivers sub-2-in. groups at 100 yards. Flattest trajectory on the market. The polymer tip slices through the air, minimizing drop and wind drift. The tip initiates violent expansion, transferring its energy payload to the target. For use only in fully rifled barrels.
Available in: 12 and 20 ga.
Box 100: $26.99

Jarrett Rifles Ammunition

RIFLE AMMUNITION

Features: Jarrett's high-performance cartridges are in 10-round boxes. The cases are from Norma with Jarrett's headstamp.
Available in: 243 Win 85gr. Nosler Partition; 243 Win 85gr. Sierra HPBT; 270 Win 140gr. Nosler Accubond; 270 Win 150gr. Swift A Frame; 300 Jarrett 165gr. Nosler Ballistic Tip; 300 Jarrett 180gr. Nosler Accubond; 300 Jarrett 200gr. Nosler Partition; 300 WM 165gr. HPBT; 300 WM 180gr. Nosler Accubond; 300 WM 200gr. Nosler Partition; 30-06 Sprg. 165gr. Nosler Ballistic Tip; 30-06 Sprg. 180gr. Swift Scirocco; 375 H&H 300gr. Swift A Frame; 375 H&H 300gr. TCCI Solid; 416 Rem Mag 400gr. Swift A Frame; 416 Rem Mag 400gr. TCCI Solid; 7mm Rem Mag 140gr. Nosler Ballistic Tip; 7mm Rem Mag 160gr. Nosler Accubond; 7mm Rem Mag 175gr. Swift A Frame
From $26.68–76.05

Kynoch Ammunition

RIFLE AMMUNITION

Features: To reproduce the renowned quality of the nitro express cartridges, painstaking care has been taken to duplicate the original loads. Modern powder has been blended and tested with a wide range of boxer primers to obtain both the correct internal and external ballistics. This work has been meticulously conducted in conjunction with the Proof House, and all new Kynoch ammunition carries Birmingham Proof House CIP approval. This approval conforms to the specifications of the original loadings as proofed in Birmingham. Load development was conducted simultaneously with extensive testing at the firing range. The new Kynoch loads have been test fired in back to back comparison with the original IMI produced Kynoch ammunition of the 1960s. The choice of bullets for these loads has been the subject of extensive testing for both the external and terminal ballistic performance. Additional accommodations were made for dimensional variations from published nominal standards in the bore and rifling, which can frequently occur in older rifles. Kynoch ammunition is now standardized on Woodleigh Weldcore Softnose and Solid bullets. Woodleigh bullets are recognized worldwide as the most reliable big game bullets currently manufactured.
Available in: .700 Nitro Express, 1000 grains; .600 Nitro Express, 900 grains ; .577 Nitro Express, 750 grains; .500 Nitro Express, 570 grains; .500 Jeffery, 535 grains; .505 Gibbs, 525 grains; .476 Westley Richards, 520 grains; .475 No. 2 Jeffery, 500 grains; .475 No. 2 Eley, 480 grains; .500/.465 Nitro Express, 480 grains; .577/.450 Martini Henry, 480 grains; .450 Rigby, 480 grains; .450 No. 2 Nitro Express, 480 grains; .450 Nitro Express, 480 grains; .425 Westley Richards, 410 grains; .404 Jeffery, 400 grains; .416 Rigby, 410 grains; .450/.400 3 ¼ inch, 400 grains; .450/.400 3 inch, 400 grains; .405 Winchester, 300 grains; .400 Purdey, 230 grains; .375 Flanged, 235, 270, 300 grains; .375 Flanged 2½ inch, 270 grains; .400/.360 Westley Richards, 285 grains; .350 Rigby, 225 grains;9.5x57 Mannlicher (.375 rimless), 270 grains; .318 Westley Richards (Box of 10), 187, 250 grains; .303 British, 215 grains; .300 Flanged, 180, 220 grains
MSRP: $32.99–83.99

Lapua Ammunition

LAPUA NATURALIS AND MEGA BULLETS

Features: Polymer-tipped Naturalis bullets with solid-copper design are designed for near-100% weight retention. The bonded, lead-core Mega bullet is an option. Lapua offers two target bullets as well, and cases that include the .220 Russian, 6mm BR Norma, 6.5 Grendel and 6.5/284. Loaded cartridges range from the .22 Long Rifle Match to sniper loads for the .338 Lapua.

Naturalis: $81–119
Mega: $38–70

Magtech Ammunition

SOLID COPPER
HOLLOWPOINT

FIRST DEFENSE

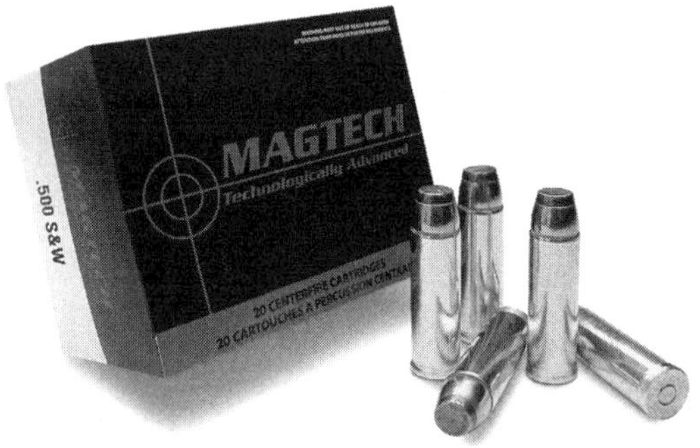

500 S&W

HANDGUN AMMUNITION

CLEANRANGE

Features: CleanRange loads are specially designed to eliminate airborne lead and the need for lead retrieval at indoor ranges. That means an overall cleaner shooting environment and lower maintenance costs for trap owners, as well as cleaner guns and brass casings for shooters. CleanRange ammunition was developed using a state-of-the-art combination of high-tech, lead-free primers and specially designed Fully Encapsulated Bullets. This unique mix of components eliminates lead and heavy metal exposure at the firing point. No more lead in the air.

Available in: .38 SPL, .380 Auto, 9mm Luger, .40 S&W, .45 Auto
Box 50: $20.49–30.99

COWBOY ACTION

Features: "Old West" Cowboy Action Loads were developed specifically for cowboy action shooting enthusiasts. These flat-nose bullets deliver reliable knockdown power that puts steel targets down on the first shot. Superior components and construction assure trouble-free performance in both single-action revolvers and lever-action rifles.

Available in: .38 SPL, .357 Mag, .44 SPL, .45 Colt, .44-40 Win
Box 50: $32.49

FIRST DEFENSE

Features: First Defense rounds are designed with a 100% solid copper bullet, unlike traditional hollow points that contain a lead core covered by a copper jacket. Copper jackets could tear away when fired, causing a loss of weight and a corresponding loss of power. However, Magtech First Defense solid copper bullets have no jacket to split or tear away, ensuring every round you fire meets its target with maximum impact and effectiveness.

Available in: 9mm Luger, .38 SPL+P, .380 Auto, .357 Mag, .40 S&W, .45 Auto+P
Box 20: $18.29–25.49

GUARDIAN GOLD

Features: Thanks to its tremendous stopping power, deep penetration, awesome expansion and dead-on accuracy, Guardian Gold is fast becoming a favorite among those seeking reliable, affordable personal protection. Simply put, Guardian Gold gives you the advantage against those who may seek to do harm to you or your family. Every round of Guardian Gold undergoes an extensive quality control process before it ever leaves the factory. After passing initial inspection, each case is primed with reliable ignition primers, loaded with the finest clean-burning propellants and assembled with the specified bullet. Only after passing each and every stage is the loaded round approved for final packaging.

Available in: 9mm Luger, 9mm Luger+P, 38 SPL+P, .380 Auto+P, .357 Mag, .40 S&W, .45 Auto+P
Box 20: $13.79–14.99

SPORT SHOOTING

Features: Magtech pistol and revolver ammunition is ideal for all of your recreational shooting needs. Each cartridge is assembled using only the highest quality components and rigorous quality control is exercised in every stage of the manufacturing process. Originally designed to be the ultimate high performance law enforcement and self-defense handgun bullet, the 100% solid copper hollow-point projectile also meets the critical requirement of stopping power for handgun hunting applications. The 100% solid copper bullet features a six-petal hollow-point specifically designed to deliver tight groups, superior expansion, and increased penetration over jacketed lead-core bullets. The one piece design of the solid copper bullet delivers virtually 100% weight retention, even through some of the toughest bone and tissue structure of your favorite thin skinned, big game animal.

Available in: .25 Auto FMJ, .32 Auto FMJ,.32 Auto JHP, .32 Auto LRN,.38 Super Auto+P FMJ,.380 Auto FMJ, .380 Auto JHP, .380 Auto LRN, 9mm Luger FMJ, 9mm Luger JHP, 9mm Luger JSP Flat, 9mm Luger LRN, 9mm Luger JSP Flat w/o grooves, 9mm Luger FMJ Flat Sub, 9mm Luger+P+ JHP, 9mm Luger JHP Sub, 9mm Luger JSP, 9x21mm FMJ, 9x21mm LRN, .40 S&W JHP,.40 S&W FMJ Flat, .40 S&W LSWC, .40 S&W JHP, .40 S&W FMJ Flat, .45 G.A.P. FMJ, .45 Auto FMJ, .45 Auto FMJ-SWC, .45 Auto LSWC (Pistol Cartridges); .32 S&W LRN, .32 S&W Long LRN, .32 S&W Long LWC, .32 S&W Long SJHP, .38 S&W LRN, .38 SPL LRN, .38 SPL LWC, .38 SPL SJSP Flat, .38 SPL+P SJSP Flat, .38 SPL SJHP, .38 SPL+P SJHP, .38 SPL-Short LRN, .38 SPL+P SJHP, .38 SPL LSWC, .38 SPL+P SJSP Flat, .38 SPL FMJ Flat, .38 SPL FMJ Flat, .38 SPL FMJ, .357 Mag SJSP Flat w/ nickel, .357 Mag SJHP, .357 Mag LSWC, .357 Mag FMJ Flat, .357 Mag SJSP Flat w/o nickel, .357 Mag FMJ Flat, .44 Rem Mag SJSP Flat, .44 Rem Mag FMJ Flat, .44 Rem Mag SCHP, .454 Casull SJSP Flat,.454 Casull FMJ Flat, .454 Casull SCHP, .454 Casull SJSP Flat, .500 S&W SJSP Flat, .500 S&W SCHP, .500 S&W FMJ Flat, .500 S&W SJSP-Flat Light (Revolver Cartridges)
Box 50: $14.29–20.99

MDM Muzzleloaders Ammunition

DYNO-CORE MAGNUM

DYNO-CORE PREMIUM

DYNO-CORE MAGNUM MUZZLELOADING BULLETS

The Dyno-Core Magnum uses a polymer tip and base that is surrounded by a grooved lead cylinder. Upon impact, the tip is driven back into the bullet causing tremendous expansion. This full-bore, conical bullet is pre-lubricated with Dyno-Kote, a dry lube finish with no greasy, wax-based lubricants, for easy loading and quick follow-up shots.
MSRP: $12.95

DYNO-CORE PREMIUM MUZZLELOADING BULLETS

The Dyno-Core Premium, a non-lead muzzleloading bullet that uses dual core tungsten technology to enhance performance. Terminal ballistics resemble those found in centerfire rifle bullets. This is a saboted non-lead bullet with a copper jacket, offered in an easy-to-load Tri-Petal sabot. Available in 50 caliber, 222 grains and 285 grains.
MSRP: $13

Nosler Ammunition

Features: For over 50 years, the professionals at Nosler have been making precision bullets for competition shooters, varmint hunters and big game hunters. Now they've taken Nosler premium hunting bullet technology and created a Custom line of premium Nosler ammunition. Available in over 120 loads, this Nosler ammunition is only sold direct from Nosler and MidwayUSA (www.midwayusa.com).
Available in: 6.5mm, 22 Hornet, 204, 221 Rem Fireball, 222 Rem, 220 Swift, 240 Weatherby Mag, 257 Roberts +P, 257 Weatherby Mag, 260 Rem, 6.5mm - 284 Norma, 264 Win Mag, 270, 270 Weatherby Mag, 280 Rem, 7mm Rem Mag, 7mm Rem Short Action Ultra Mag, 7mm Weatherby Mag, 7mm STW, 308 Win, 30-06 Spring., 300 Rem Short Action Ultra Mag, 300 H&H Mag, 300 Win Mag, 300 Weatherby Mag, 300 Rem Ultra Mag, 30-378 Weatherby Mag, 8x57mm Mauser (8mm Mauser), 8mm Rem Mag, 338-06 A-Square, 338 Win Mag, 338 Rem Ultra Mag, 338 Lapua Mag, 338-378 Weatherby Mag, 340 Weatherby Mag, 35 Whelen, 350 Rem Mag, 9.3mm, 9.3x62mm Mauser, 9.3x74mm Rimmed, 375 H&H Mag, 375 Weatherby Mag, 375 Rem Ultra Mag, 378 Weatherby Mag.
Box 20: $26–59

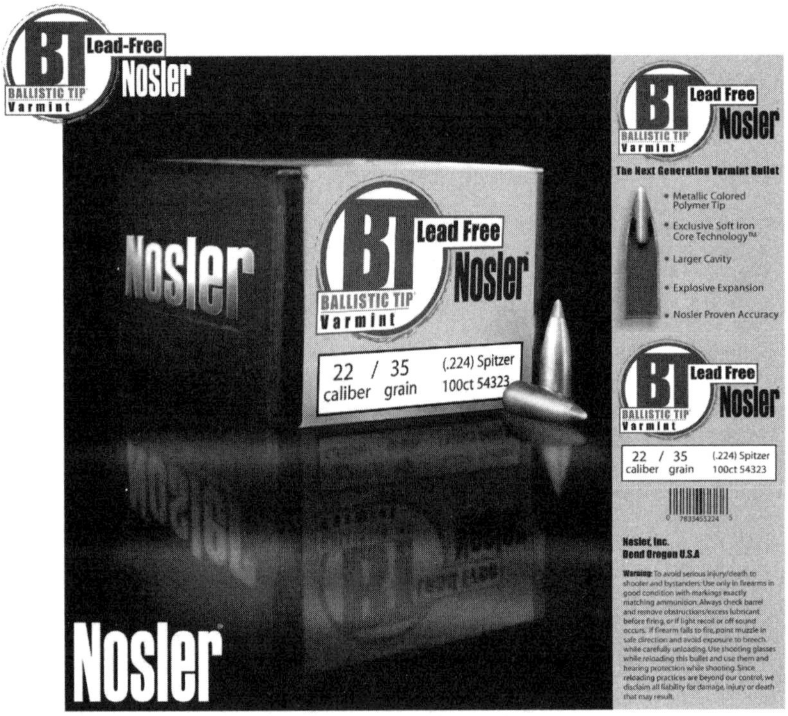

NOSLER BULLETS GROW HUNTING LINES

Features: 286-grain 9.3mm and 500-grain .470 solids for dangerous game, new .243, .270, 7mm and .338 lead-free E-Tips, 140-grain 7mm AccuBond, 150-grain .308 Ballistic Silvertip round-nose, 105-grain 6mm HPBT and 175-grain .308 HPBT match bullets. Also, .25-06 and 7mm-08 loads in the Nosler Custom ammunition line.
MSRP: $15.10–20.60

Norma Ammunition

NORMA AFRICAN PH AMMO

Features: loaded cartridges with Woodleigh softnose and solid bullets, in chamberings popular for dangerous game, including .375 H&H, .404 Jeffery, .416 Rem. Mag., .416 Rigby, .450 Rigby, .458 Lott, .470 NE, .500 NE, .505 Gibbs.
MSRP: $75–227

NORMA ORYX BULLETS IN SMALL-BORE LOADS, OTHER ADDITIONS

Features: Norma's 55-grain Oryx softnose is now available in Norma ammo -- .222, .223, .22-250, .220 Swift. Also, Norma now loads the 6XC with the 95-grain Nosler BST and 100-grain Oryx, the .270 and .270 WSM with 156-grain Vulcan bullets. The 8x68 gets a 200-grain Swift A-Frame.
MSRP: $42–72

GREEN PISTOL

GOLD HANDGUN

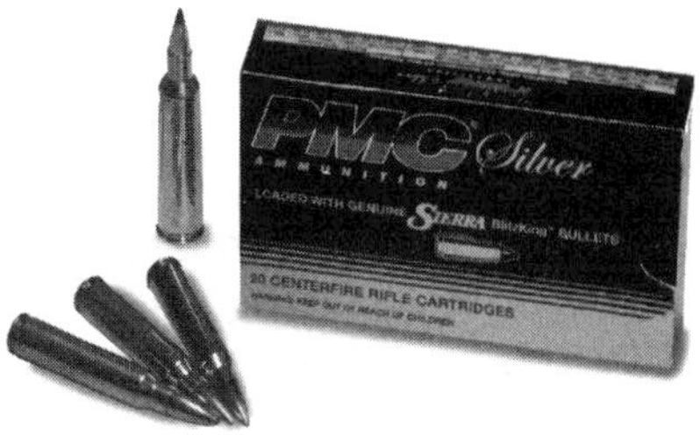

SILVER RIFLE

BRONZE LINE

Features: The same quality and dependability built into PMC's Starfire ammunition is incorporated throughout its extensive line of training ammunition and standard hollow point or soft point ammunition. All PMC cartridges pass through the rigorous inspection of the company's electronic powder check station. This station accurately measures the propellant charge in each round. If the propellant in any cartridge varies by a tiny amoun—just two tenths of one grain—the system stops and that cartridge is discarded. No other ammunition manufacturer can truthfully assure you greater uniformity and reliability.
Available in: Variety of bullet types in .25 Auto, .32 Auto, .380 Auto, .38 SPL, .38 Super+P, 9mm Luger, .357 Mag, 10mm Auto, .40 S&W, .44 S&W Special, .44 Rem Mag, .45 Auto.
MSRP: $307.99

GOLD LINE, STARFIRE

Features: The secret of Starfire's impressive performance lies in a unique, ity design that is like no other. Upon impact, the pre-notched jacket mouth begins to peel back, separating into five uniform copper petals and allowing expansion to begin. Pressure from incoming material creates lateral pressure on the ribs in the cavity wall, forcing them apart and allowing nearly instantaneous expansion of the lead core to the depth of the deep hollow point cavity. The sharp ribs are then exposed and form the leading edge of the expanded bullet, helping it cut its way through. The result is broad temporary and permanent wound cavities and impressive stopping power.
Available in: .380 Auto, .38 SPL+P, .38 SPL, .357 Mag, 9mm Luger, .40 S&W, .44 Rem Mag, .45 Auto.
Box 50: $15

SILVER LINE, ERANGE

Features: PMC's eRange environmentally friendly ammunition utilizes a reduced hazard primer that is the first of this type in the industry, an encapsulated metal jacket (EMJ) bullet that completely encloses the surface of the per alloy, and powder with clean burning characteristics and smooth fire for increased barrel life.
Available in: .380 Auto, .38 SPL+P, .357 Mag, 9mm Luger, .40 S&W, .44 Rem .45 Auto.
Box 50: $19.25

RIFLE AMMUNITION

BRONZE LINE

Features: For shooters and hunters who appreciate affordable quality ammunition, the PMC Bronze Line offers reliable performance for every shooting application, from target shooting to hunting. This long-popular ammunition line makes it possible for hunters and riflemen to enjoy high volume shooting without emptying their wallets.
Available in: Full Metal Jacket (FMJ) bullet types in .223 Rem, .30 Carbine, .308 Win and .50 cal. in commercial and military packaging.
Box 20: $6–31

Remington Ammunition

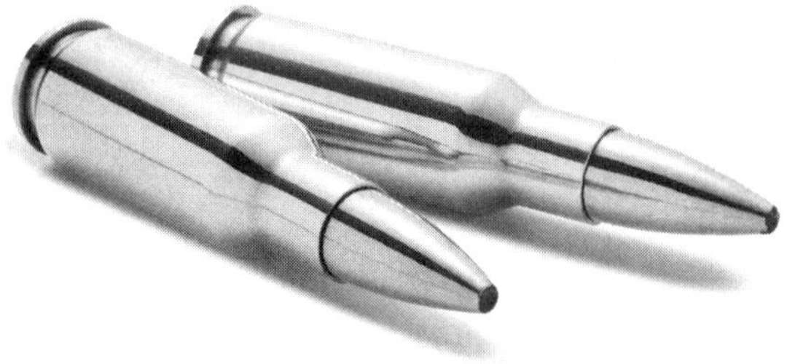

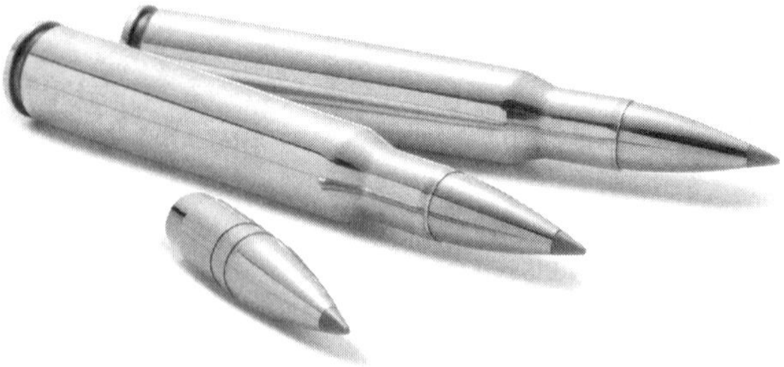

REMINGTON PREMIER .30 REM AR

Features: A short, 30-caliber round whose 125-grain bullets match the speed of .308 150s, for hunting deer-size game with the AR-15 modular repeating rifle. Ammo comes with Core-Lokt and AccuTip bullets (125 grains) and, in UMC loads, with full metal case (123 grains) bullets.
MSRP: $33–47

REMINGTON PREMIER COPPER SOLID

Features: This polymer-tipped copper bullet is of boat-tail design, and available in .243 Win (80 grains) to .300 Rem Ultra Mag (180 grains).
MSRP: $10.30–60

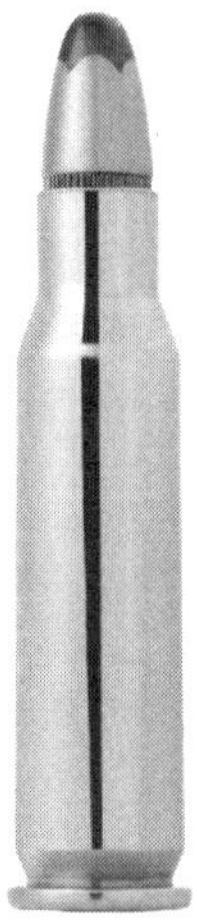

.308 MARLIN EXPRESS

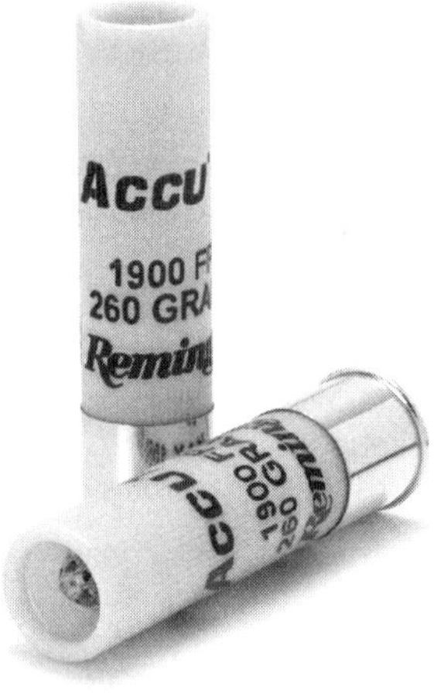

ACCUTIP 20 GA.

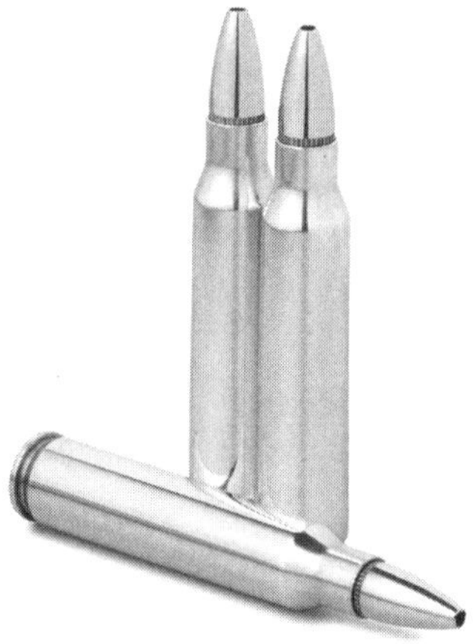

DISINTIGRATOR VARMINT AMMUNITION

REMINGTON .308 MARLIN EXPRESS

Features: 150-grain Core-Lokt soft-point bullet at 2725 fps.
MSRP: $22.49

REMINGTON ACCUTIP 20 GA.

Features: Bonded Sabot 260-grain slug now comes in 20 gauge, in 2 ¾- and 3-inch loads,(385 grains in 12 gauge, also in 2 ¾- and 3-inch).
MSRP: $14–29

REMINGTON DISINTEGRATOR VARMINT AMMUNITION

Features: Fragible bullet design with iron/tin bullet core (no lead), designed to disintegrate upon impact on varmints. These 45-grain JHP bullets are offered in .223 and .22-250.
MSRP: $24.49

7MM REM. ULTRA MAG POWER LEVEL AMMUNITION

The .300 Remington Ultra Mag Power Level ammunition introduced in 2007 is now available in 7mm Remington. Power Level III is the Full Power 7mm Remington Ultra Mag for big, tough game at extreme ranges. Power Level II is designed to take medium and large big game animals at extended ranges, offering reduced velocity, energy and recoil levels when the extreme performance of Power Level III ammunition is not required. Power Level I offers 270 Win./280 Rem. caliber performance for medium-sized big game animals at long range. It offers reduced velocity, energy and recoil levels when the magnum performance of Power Level III or Power Level II ammunition is not required.

MSRP: . . . . $28 (per box of 20)

6.8 MM SPC

RIMFIRE AMMUNITION

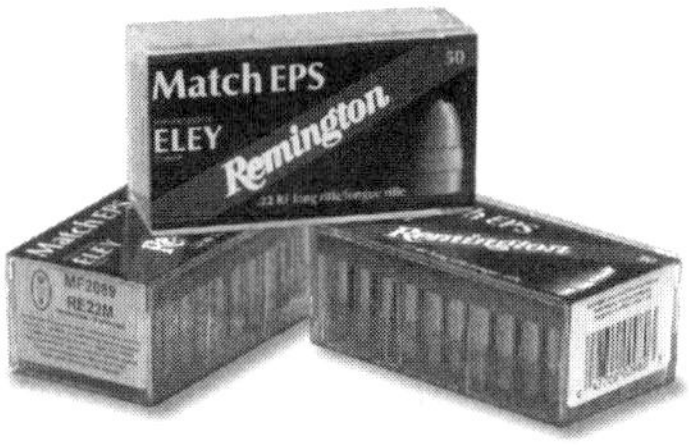

REMINGTON-ELEY COMPETITION

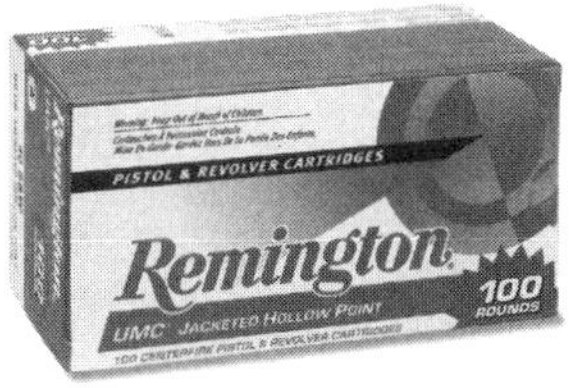

HANDGUN AMMUNITION

CENTERFIRE RIFLE AMMUNITION

.17 REMINGTON FIREBALL

Extremely well-balanced cartridge that provides flat trajectory, with match grade accuracy. When loaded with Remington's accurate 20-grain AccuTip-V bullet, the .17 Remington Fireball has a muzzle velocity of 4000 fps. The cartridge uses 50 percent less powder and generates 86 percent less recoil than the .22-250. The Remington .17 Fireball is well suited to short action firearms with 223 Remington bolt dimensions.

MSRP: $726.99

MANAGED-RECOIL

Features: Managed-Recoil ammunition delivers Remington field proven hunting performance out to 200 yards with half the recoil. Bullets provide 2x expansion with over 75% weight retention on shots inside 50 yards and out to 200 yards.

Available in: .270 Win., 7mm Remington Mag., .30-30 Win., .30-06 Springfield, .308 Win., .300 Win Mag.

Box 20: $16.99

PREMIER ACCUTIP

Features: Featuring precision-engineered polymer tip bullets designed for match-grade accuracy (sub minute-of-angle), Premier AccuTip offers an unprecedented combination of super-flat trajectory and deadly down-range performance.

Available in: .243 Win., .260 Remington, .270 Win., .280 Remington, 7mm-08 Remington, 7mm Remington Mag., .30-06, .300 Win Mag., .308 Win.

Box 50: $17.99

PREMIER A-FRAME

Features: Loaded with dual-core A-Frame bullets for reliable expansion at long-range decreased velocities, but without over-expansion at short-range high velocities.

Available in: .270 Win., 7mm Remington Mag., 7mm STW, 7mm Remington Ultra Mag., .30-06, .300 Win Mag., 8mm Remington Mag., .338 Win Mag., .338 Remington Ultra Mag., .375 H&H Mag., .375 Remington Ultra Mag., .416 Remington Mag.

Box 20: $71.99–80.99

PREMIER CORE-LOKT ULTRA BONDED

Features: The bonded bullet retains up to 95% of its original weight with maximum penetration and energy transfer. Featuring a progressively tapered jacket design, the Core-Lokt Ultra Bonded bullet initiates and controls expansion nearly 2x.

Available in: .243 Win., .25-06 Remington, .260 Remington, 6.8mm Remington SPC, .270 Win., 7mm Remington Mag., 7mm Rem SA Ultra

Remington Ammunition

Mag., 7mm Rem Ultra Mag., .30-06, .300 Win Mag., .308 Win., .300 Rem SA Ultra Mag., .300 Rem Ultra Mag., .338 Win Mag.
Box 20: $18.29–50.99

PREMIER MATCH

Features: Loaded with match-grade bullets, this ammunition employs special loading practices to ensure world-class performance and accuracy with every shot.
Available in: .223 Remington, 6.8mm Rem. SPC, .300 Rem. SA Ultra Mag., .300 Win Mag., .308 Win.

PREMIER SCIROCCO BONDED

Features: The Swift Scirocco Bonded bullet combines polymer tip ballistics with weight retention. The expansion-generating polymer tip and the boat tail base defy air resistance at the front end, and reduce drag at the back.
Available in: .243 Win., .270 Win., 7mm Remington Mag., .30-06, .300 Win Mag., .308 Win., .300 Rem Ultra Mag., .300 WSM
Box 20: $26.99–28.99

HANDGUN AMMUNITION

CORE-LOKT HIGH-PERFORMANCE

Features: The Core-Lokt Ultra bullet features bonded bullet construction, patented spiral nose cuts jacket taper and patented driving band that initiates precise bore alignment for match-grade accuracy.
Available in: .357 Mag, 165 gr.
MSRP: $23.49–377.9

EXPRESS HANDGUN AMMUNITION

Features: Remington's exceptionally broad line of handgun ammunition covers a comprehensive range of calibers, bullet weights and bullet styles. Available styles include: Full Metal Case, Lead Round Nose, Jacketed Hollow Point, Lead Hollow Point, Semi-Jacketed Hollow Point, Semi-Wadcutter Lead, Soft Point and Wadcutter Match.
Available in: .25 (6.35mm) Auto., .32 S&W, .32 S&W Long, .32 (7.65mm) Auto., .357 Mag, 9mm Luger, 9mm Luger (+P), 9mm Luger (Subsonic), .380 Auto, .38 S&W, .38 Special, .38 Short Colt, .357 Sig, .40 S&W, .44 Remington Magnum, .44 S&W Special, .45 Colt, .45 Automatic
Box 5: $4.49

GOLDEN SABER HPJ

Features: A unique "Driving Band" makes the difference on the Golden Saber HPJ. The bullet diameter directly ahead of the Driving Band is reduced from groove to bore diameter, so the bullet is precisely aligned before the driving band engages the rifling. The result: match-grade accuracy and reduced barrel friction that conserves velocity. In addition, the Driving Band locks the jacket and core together for maximum weight retention and core/jacket integrity.
Available in: .357 Mag., 9mm Luger, .380 Auto, .38 Special (+P), .40 S&W, .45 Auto., .45 Auto+P
MSRP: $17.79–225.99

RIMFIRE AMMUNITION

.22 RIMFIRE

Features: Whether it's getting young shooters started, practice plinking, small-game hunting or keeping match shooters scoring high, Remington's rimfire quality stands tall. As in their centerfire ammo, they put the maximum level of quality into their .22s so you can get the maximum performance out of them.
Available in: Subsonic (22 Subsonic Long Rifle Hollow Point); Standard Velocity/Target (22 Long Rifle Lead Round Nose); High Velocity Golden Bullet (22 Long Rifle Plated Lead Round Nose, 22 Long Rifle Plated Hollow Point, 22 Short Plated Lead Round Nose); Hyper Velocity (22 Yellow Jacket LR Truncated Cone Hollow Point, 22 Viper LR Truncated Cone Solid); Hi-Speed (22 Thunderbolt LR Lead Round Nose, 22 Cyclone LR Hollow Point, 22 Game Loads Hollow Point)
Box 50: $11.79

PREMIER GOLD BOX RIMFIRE

Features: This ammunition uses the AccuTip-V bullet with precision-engineered polymer tip for match-type accuracy, high on-game energy and rapid expansion.
Available in: .17 HMR, .17 Mach 2, .22 Win Mag.
Box 50: $17.99

MAGNUM RIMFIRE

Features: Premier Gold Box Rimfire ammunition features AccuTip-V bullets. Choice of Jacketed Hollow Point or Pointed Soft Point.
Available in: .17 HMR or .22 Win Mag.
Box 50: $11.79

REMINGTON-ELEY COMPETITION RIMFIRE

Features: Building on the rimfire expertise of Eley, Ltd., and its reputation among dedicated rimfire shooters as the world's most accurate and reliable ammunition, Remington and Eley offer three grades of their premier 22 Long Rifle ammunition: Target Rifle, Club Xtra and Match EPS.
Available in: .22 LR only
Box 1,000: $141.97

SHOTGUN AMMUNITION

EXPRESS EXTRA LONG RANGE UPLAND LOADS

Features: The hunter's choice for a wide variety of game-bird applications, available in an exceptionally broad selection of loadings, from 12-gauge to .410 bore, with shot size options ranging from BB's all the way down to 9s - suitable for everything from quail to farm predators.
Available in: 12, 16, 20, 28, .410 ga.; 2½, 2¾, 3 in.; shot sizes BB, 2, 4, 5, 6, 7½, 9
Box 5: $4.49

GUN CLUB TARGET LOADS

Features: Excellent choice for economical shooting. Loaded with Gun Club Grade Shot, Premier STS Primers, and Power Piston One-Piece Wads, these high-quality shells receive the same care in loading as top-of-the-line Premier STS and Nitro 27 shells. Many shooters are discovering that they can get acceptable reloading life while stretching their shooting dollar.
Available in: 12, 20 ga.; 2¾ in.; shot sizes 7½, 8, 9
Box 25: $6.19

LEAD GAME LOADS

Features: For a wide variety of field gaming, these budget-stretching loads include the same quality components as other Remington shotshells, and are available in four different gauges to match up with your favorite upland shotguns.
Available in: 12, 16, 20, .410 ga.; 2½, 2¾ in.; shot sizes 6, 7½, 8
MSRP: $20.99

MANAGED RECOIL STS TARGET LOADS

Features: Managed-Recoil STS target loads offer dramatically reduced recoil—40% less in the 12-ga. load—with target-grinding STS consistency and pattern density. Ideal for new shooters and high-volume practice.
Available in: 12, 20 ga.; 2¾ in.; shot sizes 8½
Box 25: $8.89

NITRO BUFFERED TURKEY LOADS

Features: Contain Nitro Mag extra-hard lead shot that is as hard and round as copper-plated shot. Nitro Turkey Magnums will pattern as well as other copper-plated, buffered loads without the higher cost. Utilizing a specially blended powder recipe and Remington's advanced Power Piston® one-piece wad, the loads delivers a full 1 7/8 oz. payload at 1210 fps while delivering 80% pattern densities with outstanding knockdown power.
Available in: 12 ga.; 3, 3½ in.; shot sizes 2, 4, 6
Box 10: $15.79

NITRO-MAG BUFFERED MAGNUM TURKEY LOADS

Features: The original buffered magnum shotshells from Remington. The shot charge is packed with a generous amount of shock-absorbing polymer buffering and surrounded by our patented Power Piston wad to protect the specially hardened shot all the way down the barrel for dense, even patterns and uniform shot strings.
Available in: 12, 20 ga.; 2¾, 3 in.; shot sizes 2, 4, 6
Box 25: $28.99–32.99

NITRO PHEASANT LOADS

Features: Uses Remington's own Copper-Lokt® copper-plated lead shot with high antimony content. Hard shot stays rounder for truer flight, tighter patterns, and greater penetration. Available in both high-velocity and magnum loadings.
Available in: 12, 20 ga.; 2¾, 3 in.; shot sizes 4, 5, 6
Box 25: $21.99

NITRO-STEEL HIGH VELOCITY MAGNUM WATERFOWL LOADS

Features: Greater hull capacity means heavier charges and larger pellets, which makes these loads ideal for large waterfowl. Nitro-Steel™ delivers denser patterns for greater lethality and is zinc-plated to prevent corrosion.
Available in: 10, 12, 16, 20 ga.; 2¾, 3, 3½ in.; shot sizes T, BBB, BB, 1, 2, 3, 4
Box 25: $26.99

PHEASANT LOADS

Features: For the broadest selection in game-specific upland lead shotshells, Remington Pheasant Loads are the perfect choice. Their high-velocity and long-range performance are just right for any pheasant hunting situation. Standard high-base payloads feature Power Piston® one-piece wads.
Available in: 12, 16, 20 ga.; 2¾ in.; shot sizes 4, 5, 6, 7½
Box 25: $18.99

PREMIER DUPLEX MAGNUM TURKEY LOADS

Features: Premier Duplex has No. 4 size shot carefully layered on top of No. 6 shot. When ranges vary, they combine retained energy and penetration from the larger pellets with pattern density from the smaller ones. Duplex patterns are extremely well balanced.
Available in: 12 ga.; 2¾, 3½ in.; shot sizes 4x6
Box 10: $17.99–20.99

PREMIER HIGH-VELOCITY MAGNUM TURKEY LOADS

Features: Utilizing a specially blended powder recipe, Remington's advanced Power Piston one piece wad and hardened copper plated shot, these new high velocity loads result in extremely dense patterns and outstanding knockdown power at effective ranges.
Available in: 12 ga.; 3, 3½ in.; shot sizes 4, 5, 6
Box 10: $18.99–22.99

PREMIER MAGNUM TURKEY LOADS

Features: Premier® Magnum Turkey Loads provide that extra edge to reach out with penetrating power and dense, concentrated patterns. Its magnum-grade, Copper-Lokt shot is protected by our Power Piston® wad and cushioned with special polymer buffering. Available with some of the heaviest payloads of 4s, 5s, and 6s on the market.
Available in: 10, 12, 20 ga.; 2¾, 3, 3½ in. ; shot sizes 4, 5, 6
Box 10: $14.99–22.99

PREMIER NITRO 27 HANDICAP TRAP LOADS

Features: Designed specifically for back-fence trap and long-range sporting clays. Delivers consistent handicap velocity and pattern uniformity. New, improved powder loading significantly reduces felt recoil while retaining high velocity - both factors allow avid trap shooters to stay fresh for the shootoff. They score just as high on fast-moving doves.
Available in: 12 ga.; 2¾ in.; shot sizes 7½, 8
MSRP: $35.99

PREMIER NITRO GOLD SPORTING CLAYS TARGET LOADS

Features: To meet the special demands of avid sporting clays shooters, we developed a new Premier Nitro Gold Sporting Clays target load. At 1300 fps, the extra velocity gives you an added advantage for those long crossers—making target leads closer to normal for ultimate target-crushing satisfaction. Also makes a great high-velocity dove load.
Available in: 12 ga.; 2¾ in.; shot sizes 7½, 8

PREMIER STS TARGET LOADS

Features: STS Target Loads have taken shot-to-shot consistency to a new performance level, setting the standard at all major skeet, trap, and sporting clays shoots across the country, while providing handloaders with unmatched reloading ease and hull longevity. Available in most gauges,

Remington Ammunition

WATERFOWL LOADS

UPLAND LOADS

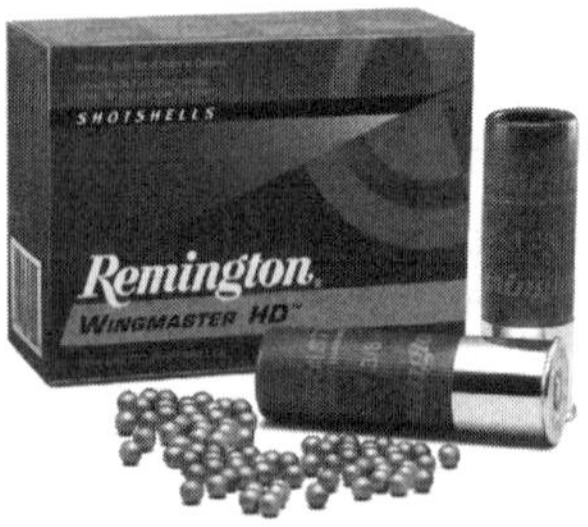

WINGMASTER HD SHOTSHELLS

SLUGS

our Premier STS shells are the most reliable, consistent and most reloadable shells you can shoot.
Available in: 12, 20, 28, .410 ga.; $2\frac{1}{2}$, $2\frac{3}{4}$, 3, $3\frac{1}{4}$ in.; shot sizes $7\frac{1}{2}$, 8, $8\frac{1}{2}$, 9
Box 25: $11.99–12.99

SHURSHOT HEAVY FIELD AND HEAVY DOVE LOADS

Features: A sure bet for all kinds of upland game, ShurShot loads have earned the reputation as one of the best-balanced, best-patterning upland field loads available. And for good reason. These shells combine an ideal balance of powder charge and shot payload to deliver effective velocities and near-perfect patterns with mild recoil for high-volume upland hunting situations.
Available in: 12, 20 ga.; $2\frac{3}{4}$ in.; shot sizes 6, $7\frac{1}{2}$, 8
MSRP: $12.99–16.99

SHURSHOT HIGH BASE PHEASANT LOADS

Features: The ShurShot High Base Pheasant loads deliver an ideal combination of velocity and payload. Loaded with our reliable Power Piston® Wad and hard lead shot.
Available in: 12 ga.; $2\frac{3}{4}$ in.; shot sizes 4, 5
MSRP: $15.99–16.99

SPORT LOADS

Features: Remington Sport Loads are an economical, multi-purpose utility load for a variety of shotgunning needs. Loaded with Power Piston wads, and plastic Unibody hulls, these shells perform effectively for skeet, trap and sporting clays, as well as quail, doves, and woodcock.
Available in: 12, 20 ga.; $2\frac{3}{4}$ in.; shot sizes 8

SPORTSMAN HI-SPEED STEEL WATERFOWL LOADS

Features: Sportsman Hi-Speed Steel's sealed primer, high quality steel shot, and consistent muzzle velocities combine to provide reliability in adverse weather, while delivering exceptional pattern density and retained energy. A high-speed steel load that is ideal for short-range high-volume shooting during early duck seasons, or over decoys.
Available in: 10, 12, 20 ga.; $2\frac{3}{4}$, 3, $3\frac{1}{2}$ in.; shot sizes BB, 1, 2, 3, 4, 6, 7
Box 10: $38.97

WINGMASTER HD TURKEY LOADS

Comprised of tungsten, bronze and iron, Wingmaster HD pellets are specifically engineered with a density of 12 grams/cc, 10 percent denser than lead. Wingmaster HD loads also feature a precise balance of payload and velocity that provide turkey hunters with a shotshell that generates nearly 200 ft.-lbs. more energy at 40 yds. than competitive tungsten based shot. This results in deeper penetrating pellets.
Available in: 12 ga. $3\frac{1}{2}$ in., $1\frac{7}{8}$ oz.; 12 ga. 3 in., $1\frac{5}{8}$ oz.; or 20 ga. 3 in., $1\frac{1}{4}$ oz. Size 4 or 6 shot.
Box 10: $14.99–22.60

WINGMASTER HD WATERFOWL LOADS

Features: Wingmaster HD nontoxic shot stretches the kill zone with an ultra-tuned combination of density, shape and energy. At 12.0 grams/cc, it's 10% denser than lead and the scientifically proven optimum density for pellet count and pattern density. Plus, its smooth, round shape delivers awesome aerodynamics and sustained payload energy. Wingmaster HD is also 16% softer than Premier Hevi-Shot, which makes it easier on your barrel. And it's more responsive to chokes, allowing you to open up the pattern for close-range hunting or stretch shotgun range to its farthest reaches. Also available in Turkey and Predator Loads.
Available in: 10, 12, 20 ga.; $2\frac{3}{4}$, 3, $3\frac{1}{2}$ in.; shot sizes BB, 2, 4, 6
Box 5: $13.00

SHOTGUN AMMUNITION (BUCKSHOT)

EXPRESS BUCKSHOT AND EXPRESS MAGNUM BUCKSHOT

Features: A combination of heavy cushioning behind the shot column and a granulated polymer buffering helps maintain pellet roundness for tight, even patterns. Packed in 5-round boxes.
Available in: 12, 20 ga.; $2\frac{3}{4}$, 3, $3\frac{1}{2}$ in.; shot sizes 0, 00, 000, 1, 3, 4
MSRP: $5.39–6.79

MANAGED-RECOIL EXPRESS BUCKSHOT

Features: With less felt recoil than full velocity loads, Express Managed-Recoil Buckshot is an ideal close-range performer. Less recoil means second shot recovery is quicker, allowing the user to get back on target more easily. These loads are buffered for dense patterns, allowing for highly effective performance at up to 40 yards.
Available in: 12 ga.; $2\frac{3}{4}$ in.; shot sizes 00
Box : $22.99

SHOTGUN AMMUNITION (SLUGS)

BUCKHAMMER LEAD SLUGS

Features: Specifically designed for rifled barrels and rifled choke tubes,

these high-performance slugs are capable of producing 3-inch or better groups at 100-yards with nearly 100% weight retention and controlled expansion to nearly one-inch in diameter. Unlike traditional sabot slugs, the BuckHammer's unique attached stabilizer allows for a full bore diameter lead slug that delivers devastating terminal performance with unsurpassed accuracy.
Available in: 12, 20 ga.; 2¾, 3 in.; 1, 1¼, 1⅜ oz.
Box 20: $7.79–8.79

MANAGED-RECOIL BUCKHAMMER LEAD SLUGS

Features: BuckHammer lead slugs generate 40% less felt-recoil without sacrificing its devastating on-game performance. Specially designed for fully rifled barrels and rifled choke tubes, these lower-recoil slugs still deliver the same outstanding accuracy as our standard BuckHammer loads with near 100% weight retention and controlled expansion to nearly 1-inch in diameter. For use at the range or in the field the Managed Recoil BuckHammer slug maintains an impressive 1032 ft-lbs of deer stopping energy at 100-yards.
Available in: 12, 20 ga.; 2¾.; ⅞, 1⅛ oz.
Box 20: $7.79

MANAGED-RECOIL COPPER SOLID SABOT SLUGS

Features: With 40% less recoil, these slugs are perfect for anyone who wants outstanding on-game results without the rearward punch. Or, use them to sight-in, then step up to full loads. There's no finer slug load for young or recoil-sensitive hunters.
Available in: 12 ga.; 2¾ in.; 1 oz.
Box 20: $20.99

PREMIER COPPER SOLID SABOT SLUGS

Features: Coupling the angled petal score design of the Copper Solid Muzzleloader bullet with the ballistic coefficient of a deep penetrating slug round, the 12 and 20-gauge Copper Solid Sabot Slugs deliver maximum performance: 100-percent weight retention, 2X controlled expansion and super accuracy.
Available in: 12, 20 ga.; 2¾, 3 in.; ⅝, 1 oz.
MSRP: $44.99–55.99

PREMIER CORE-LOKT ULTRA BONDED SABOT SLUGS

Features: Ultra-high velocities deliver devastating on-game performance and the tightest groups—1.8" —of any shotgun slug with ultra-flat trajectories. Remington® patented spiral nose cuts ensure consistent 2x expansion over a wide range of terminal velocities, while the sleek, ogive nose delivers high down-range energy retention. The 385-grain bonded bullet yields near 100% weight retention. Flattest shooting slug in existence—10% better than the nearest competition. Designed for use in fully rifled barrels only.
Available in: 12, 20 ga.; 2¾, 3 in.; 260, 385 gr..
MSRP: $65.99

SLUGGER HIGH VELOCITY SLUGS

Features: This is the first high-velocity Foster-style lead slug. This higher velocity slug exits the barrel at 1800 fps, 13% faster than standard 1 oz. slugs. The 7/8 oz. Slugger High Velocity delivers 200 ft-lbs more energy at 50 yards with flatter trajectory on deer than standard 1 oz. slugs. Designed for the avid deer hunter using smooth bore guns.
Available in: 12, 20 ga.; 2¾, 3 in.; ½, ⅞ oz.
Box 50: $5.29

SLUGGER MANAGED-RECOIL RIFLED SLUGS

Features: Slugger Managed-Recoil Rifled Slugs offer remarkably effective performance but with 45% less felt recoil than full velocity Sluggers. With effective energy out to 80 yards, these 1-ounce slugs easily handle the majority of shotgun deer hunting ranges.
Available in: 12 ga.; 2¾ in.; 1 oz.
MSRP: $14.99

SLUGGER RIFLED SLUGS

Features: Remington redesigned their 12-gauge Slugger Rifled Slug for a 25% improvement in accuracy. Also, at 1760 fps muzzle velocity, the 3 in. 12-ga. Magnum slugs shoot 25% flatter than regular 12-ga. slugs. Packed in convenient, easy-carrying 5-round boxes. Also available in a reduced recoil loading.
Available in: 12, 16, 20, .410 ga.; 2¾, 3 in.; ⅕, ⅘, ⅝, 1 oz.
Box 50: $5.29–6.39

RWS Ammunition

.375 H&H MAG. UNI

This cartridge is loaded with a 301-grain RWS UNI bullet. It leaves the muzzle at 2,590 fps and produces 4,468 ft./lbs. of muzzle energy. It has a softer lead tip core united to a harder and heavier tail core section. The harder rear core is blended to join with the softer front to retard its mushrooming ability and to increase its penetration force. Deep penetration, followed by delayed shock, is a very effective and reliable technique for taking large, dangerous game. The RWS UNI bullet contains a hard nickel-plated jacket with a deep groove cut into its mid-section to initiate the delayed fragmentation effect. The torpedo-shaped tail, with its large base area, improves the external-ballistic performance by giving the projectile precise flight stability. After deeply penetrating and fragmenting, the residual body of the projectile is designed to continue through the animal's body making a clean exit after transferring its high amount of energy.
MSRP: . . . . . $75–78 (per box of 20)

RWS Ammunition

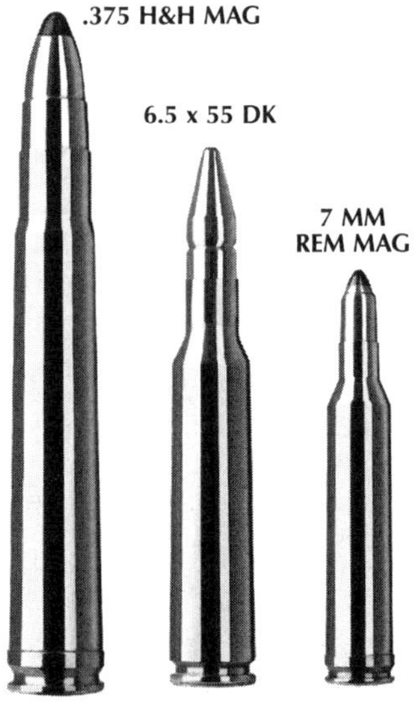

6.5x55 DK 140-GRAIN

The load is a twin-core projectile consisting of two lead cores of different hardness (a softer tip core backed by a harder tail core) surrounded by a jacket of tombac (an alloy of copper and zinc). For the separation from the softer tip core, the harder tail core is provided with an additional tough tombac jacket, and the weight ratio of the cores is 50:50 to ensure stability in flight. A groove in the rear section of the bullet bonds the tail core to the outer and inner jackets, and a groove in the front section (just above the inner jacket) serves as the breaking point for the front jacket. In use, the harder rear section of the bullet drives the softer front into the game animal, causing the front core to burst and deliver a high shock effect to the animal's nervous system while limiting fragmentation to the bullet's front section. The rear section travels through the animal and makes a clean exit, thereby increasing the knockdown power. The RWS 6.5x55 DK launches its 140-grain bullet at 2,855 fps and generates 2,534 ft./lbs. of energy from the muzzle. At 100 yards, it continues at a swift 2,557 fps with 2,032 ft./lbs. energy.
MSRP: . . . . $39 (per box of 20)

7MM REM. MAG. ID

Specifically developed using RWS' patented "Quick Knock Down" ID Classic bullet concept, the RWS 7mm Remington Magnum ID is engineered with a soft lead tip plug that quickly and more effectively mushrooms against a harder, heavier rear lead base on impact, swiftly expanding to transfer the bullet's more than 2000 foot-pounds of energy to the body of the animal. This two-lead core is "married" inside specially designed nickel-plated jacket. Engineered with a precision increase in thickness toward its tail, the bullet has a torpedo shaped tail to provide optimum ballistic characteristics and higher flight stability for the cartridge's 2920 foot per second muzzle velocity.
MSRP: . . . . $59 (per box of 20)

RIMFIRE AMMUNITION

RWS .22 L.R. HV HOLLOW POINT

Features: This higher velocity hollow point offers the shooter greater shocking power in game. Suitable for both small game and vermin.
Box 50: $8.49–11.49

RWS .22 L.R. RIFLE MATCH

Features: Perfect for the club level target competitor. Accurate and affordable.
Box 50: $10.29

RWS .22 L.R. SUBSONIC HOLLOW POINT

Features: Subsonic ammunition is a favorite ammunition of shooters whose shooting range is limited to where the noise of a conventional cartridge would be a problem.
Box 500: $77.99

RWS .22 L.R. TARGET RIFLE

Features: An ideal training and field cartridge, the .22 Long Rifle Target also excels in informal competitions. The target .22 provides the casual shooter with accuracy at an economical price.
Box 50: $8.49

RWS .22 MAGNUM FULL JACKET

Features: Outstanding penetration characteristics of this cartridge allow the shooter to easily tackle game where penetration is necessary.
Box 50: $30.77

RWS .22 MAGNUM HOLLOW POINT

Features: The soft point allows good expansion on impact, while preserving the penetration characteristics necessary for larger vermin and game.

RWS .22 R50

Features: For competitive shooters demanding the ultimate in precision. This cartridge has been used to establish several world records and is used by Olympic Gold Medalists.
Box 50: $20.99

RWS .22 SHORT R25

Features: Designed for world class Rapid Fire Pistol events, this cartridge provides the shooter with outstanding accuracy and minimal recoil. Manufactured to exacting standards, so the shooter can be assured of consistent performance.
Box 50: $6.96

Sierra Ammunition

SIERRA PALMA AND LONG-RANGE BULLETS

Features: A 155-grain Palma Match bullet joins Sierra's MatchKing series that dominates high-power competition. The long-range line now includes 77-, 80-, and 90-grain .224s, 210- and 240-grain .308s and 300-grain .338s.

MSRP: $31–143

Swift Ammunition

SWIFT SCIROCCO 100-GRAIN .257

Features: Newest of sleek, polymer-tipped bullets for long shooting at big game, the 100-grain .25 is one of 10 Sciroccos, .224 to .338.

MSRP: $50

Weatherby Ammunition

WEATHERBY AMMO FOR DEER HUNTERS

Features: Weatherby now offers Barnes Tipped TSX bullets in Norma-loaded ammo for the .257, .270, 7mm, .300 and .30-378 Weatherby rounds. These lead-free bullets range in weight from 80 to 130 grains.

MSRP: $39–169

Winchester Ammunition

WINCHESTER PDX1 PISTOL AMMO

Features: Bonded jacketed hollowpoint loads in .38 Special, 9mm, .40 S&W and .45 ACP upset to 1 ½ times diameter in six-petal mushroom. Available in nickel-plated Personal Protection Ammunition

MSRP: $13–14

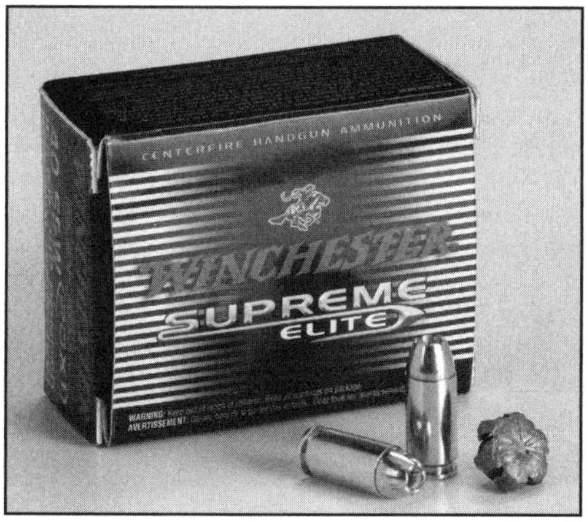

WINCHESTER POWERMAX BONDED

Features: Loads for the .270, .270 WSM, .30-30, .308, .30-06, .300 WSM and .300 Win. Mag. include PHP bullets with bonded lead core. Designed expressly for deer hunters.

MSRP: $18–33

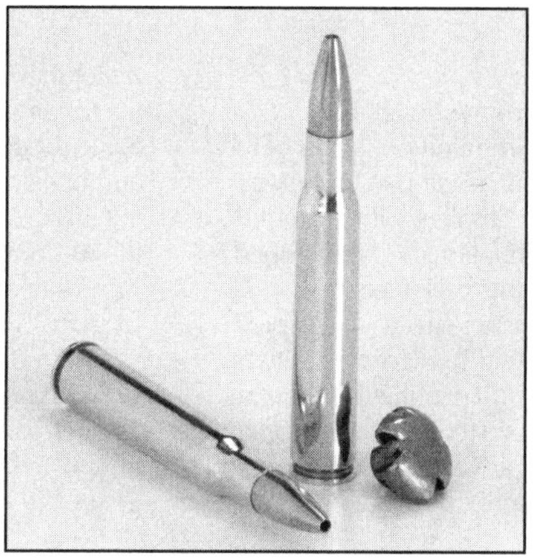

Winchester Ammunition

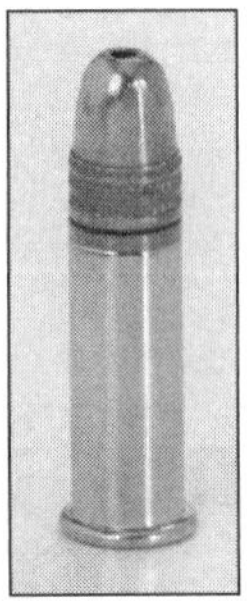

22 XPEDITER

WINCHESTER 22 XPEDITER

Features: 32-grain, plated hollowpoint bullets in nickel-plated cases distinguish this fastest of Winchester .22 Long Rifle rounds. Muzzle velocity: 1640 fps.
MSRP: . . . . price on request

WINCHESTER DUAL BOND HANDGUN AMMO

Features: Hunting ammunition for the .454 Casull, .460 S&W and .500 S&W includes this "bullet within a bullet" with inner and outer jackets, mechanically bonded. Hollowpoint design delivers 12-petal upset.
MSRP: $12.50–63

E-TIP

The E-Tip lead-free bullet from Winchester Ammunition is one of the latest products developed for big-game hunters and complies with current state non-toxic regulations. Co-developed with Nosler, this bullet features an E2 energy expansion cavity, which promotes consistent upset at a variety of impact ranges. The bullet is made of gilding metal instead of pure copper, which helps prevent barrel fouling and provides for a high performance sporting bullet that is lead-free. The polycarbonate tip prevents deformation in the magazine, boosts aerodynamic efficiency and initiates expansion. The E-Tip will initially be available in 180-grain bullets in .30-06 Springfield, .300 WSM, .300 Win-Mag and .308 Winchester.
MSRP: . . . . . $40–50 (per box of 20)

RACKMASTER SLUG, 3-IN.

The 1 1/8 oz., 3-in. Rackmaster 12-ga. Slug provides increased velocity and greater lethal range. With a velocity of 1,700 feet per second (fps), this high-accuracy shotgun slug features the innovative Winglide stabilizer, which was specifically engineered to improve in-bore alignment and enhance down-range accuracy. Can be used in smooth bore or fully-rifled slug barrels, or a rifled choke tube.
MSRP: . . . . $8.29 (per box of 5)

THEODORE ROOSEVELT COMMEMORATIVE AMMUNITION

Celebrating 150 years of Roosevelt's influence and achievement as arguably the greatest conservation hero North America has ever produced, the Theodore Roosevelt cartridges feature a nickel-plated shell casing bearing a special Roosevelt head-stamp in three popular calibers: .30-30 Win., .45 Colt and Roosevelt's favorite big bore lever-gun round, the .405 Winchester.The .30-30 Win. rounds are loaded with 150-grain Power-Point bullets and the .405 Winchester with 300-grain jacketed flat point bullets: both are boxed in 20-round packages. The .45 Colt is loaded with a 250-grain flat nose lead bullet and comes in a 50-count box. All Theodore Roosevelt cartridges are packaged in foil-embossed boxes.

MSRP: . . . .$42–$56

XP3 3-IN. SHOTGUN SLUG

The Supreme Elite XP3 3-inch Slug features a one-piece, 300-grain sabot designed to deliver high energy and deep penetration on big game. Winchester developed the accurate lead-free-alloy projectile to extend consistent, ethical and lethal big game hunting ranges beyond 175 yards in 12-gauge rifled barrel slug guns.

MSRP: . . . . . . $16–20 (per box of 5)

HANDGUN AMMUNITION

COWBOY LOADS LEAD

Features: Designed for cowboy action shooters who need high accuracy and consistent performance.
Available in: 38 SPL, 44-40 Win, 44 S&W SPL, 45 Colt
Box 50: $35.99–38.99

SUPER-CLEAN NT (TIN)

Features: Specially designed jacketed soft point tin core bullet shoots and performs like lead. Meets the totally non-toxic needs of indoor ranges.
Available in: 40 S&W, 9mm Luger
Box 50: $46.49

SUPER-X FULL METAL JACKET

Available in : 30 Luger
Box 5: $3.59–7.19

SUPER-X JHP

Available in: 357 Magnum, 38 Special +P, 454 Casull, 45 Winchester Magnum, 460 S&W Magnum

SUPER-X BLANK - BLACK POWDER

Available in: 32 S&W
Box 50: $32.99–35.99

SUPER-X BLANK - SMOKELESS

Available in: 38 Special
Box 50: $35.99

SUPER-X EXPANDING POINT

Available in: 25 Auto
Box 50: $40.99

SUPER-X HOLLOW SOFT POINT

Available in: 30 Carbine, 44 Rem-Mag
Box 50: $3.59–8.99

Winchester Ammunition

SUPER-X JACKETED SOFT POINT
Available in: 357 Mag
Box 50: $11.49

SUPER-X LEAD ROUND NOSE
Available in: 32 Short Colt, 32 S&W, 32 S&W Long, 38 Special, 38 S&W, 44 S&W Special, 45 Colt
Box 500: $30.99

SUPER-X LEAD SEMI-WAD CUTTER
Available in: 38 Special
Box 50: $32.99–34.99

SUPER-X LEAD SEMI-WAD CUTTER HP
Available in: 38 Special+P

SUPER-X MATCH
Available in: 38 Special Super Match
Box 50: $32.99

SUPER-SILVERTIP HOLLOW POINT
Available in: 10mm Auto, 32 Auto, 357 Mag, 380 Auto, 38 Super Auto +P, 38 Special +P, 38 Special, 40 S&W, 41 Rem Mag, 44 S&W Special , 45 Auto, 45 Colt, 45 G.A.P., 9x23 Winchester, 9mm Luger
Box 50: $31.99–43.99

SUPER-X JACKETED HOLLOW POINT
Available in: 500 S&W
Box 50: $11.49

SUPER-X LEAD FLATNOSE
Available in: 45 Colt
Box 50: $3.59–8.99

SUPREME PARTITION GOLD
Features: Proven partition technology, consistent, dramatic bullet expansion, deep penetration regardless of barrel length, maximum weight retention
Available in: 357 Mag, 44 Rem Mag, 454 Casull, 460 S&W Mag
Box 20: $28.99–36.99

SUPREME PLATINUM TIP HOLLOW POINT
Features: Patented notched reverse taper bullet jacket, plated heavy wall jacket and two-part hollow point cavity for uniform bullet expansion, massive energy depot
Available in: 41 Rem Mag, 44 Rem Mag, 454 Casull, 500 S&W
Box 20: $28.49

SUPREME T-SERIES
Features: Reverse Taper Jacket design; consistent, reliable bullet expansion through common barrier test events; excellent accuracy; positive functioning
Available in: 380 Auto, 38 Special +P, 38 Special, 40 S&W, 45 Auto, 9mm Luger
Box 20: $28.49

WINCLEAN
Features: The patented lead and heavy-metal free primers, Brass Enclosed Base bullets and clean-burning propellants not only eliminate airborne lead at the firing point, they also generate less barrel, action and shell case residue.
Available in: Brass Enclosed Base (357 Sig WinClean, 380 Auto, 40 S&W, 45 Auto, 45 GAP, 9mm Luger, 9mm Luger WinClean), Jacketed Soft Point (357 Mag, 38 Special)
Box 50: $17.49–22.49

RIFLE AMMUNITION

SUPER-X FLAT POINT
Available in: 405 Winchester
Box 50: $39.99

SUPER-X HOLLOW POINT
Available in: 204 Ruger, 218 Bee, 22 Hornet, 30-30 Win
Box 50: $31.99

SUPER-X HOLLOW SOFT POINT
Available in: 30 Carbine, 44 Rem Mag
Box 50: $45.49

SUPER-X JACKETED SOFT POINT
Available in: 357 Mag
Box 50: $47.49

SUPER-X JHP
Available in: 45-70 Gov't
Box 50: $3.59–8.99

SUPER-X LEAD
Available in: 32-20 Win
Box 20: $27.99–28.49

SUPER-X POSITIVE EXPANDING POINT
Available in: 25-06 Rem, 25 WSSM
Box 20: $27.99–28.49

SUPER-X POWER POINT
Available in: 22-250 Remington, 223 Remington, 223 WSSM, 243 Winchester, 243 WSSM, 257 Roberts + P, 264 Winchester Magnum, 270 Winchester, 270 Winchester, 270 WSM, 284 Winchester, 300 Savage, 30-06 Springfield, 30-06 Springfield, 300 WSM, 300 WSM Winchester Short Mag, 30-30 Winchester, 30-30 Winchester, 30-30 Win, 303 British, 30-40 Krag, 307 Winchester, 308 Winchester, 308 Winchester, 300 Winchester Magnum, 300 Winchester Magnum, 325 Winchester Short Magnum, 32 Winchester Special, 338 Winchester Magnum, 356 Winchester, 35 Remington, 375 Winchester, 6mm Remington, 7mm-08 Remington, 7mm Mauser (7 x 57), 7mm Remington Magnum, 7mm Remington Magnum, 7mm WSM, 8mm Mauser (8 x 57)
Box 500: $32.99

SUPER-X SILVERTIP
Available in: 250 Savage, 270 Winchester, 30-06 Springfield, 30-30 Winchester, 308 Winchester, 348 Winchester, 358 Winchester
Box 50: $31.99

SUPER-X SILVERTIP HOLLOW POINT
Available in: 44 Rem Mag
Box 50: $31.99

SUPER-X SOFT POINT
Available in: 22 Hornet, 25-20 Winchester, 25-35 Winchester, 38-40 Winchester, 38-55 Winchester, 44-40 Winchester, 458 Winchester, 6.5x55 Swedish, 7.62x39mm Russian

SUPER-X SUPER CLEAN NT TIN
Available in: 5.56mm
Box 50: $3.59–7.19

SUPREME ACCUBOND CT
Features: Fully bonded lead alloy core, high weight retention, pinpoint accuracy, boattail design, Lubalox coating/red polymer tip
Available in: 25-06 Remington, 25

WSSM, 270 Winchester, 270 WSM, 30-06 Springfield, 300 Winchester Magnum, 300 WSM, 325 Winchester Short Magnum, 338 Winchester Magnum, 7mm Remington Magnum, 7mm WSM
Box 50: $38.99–58.99

SUPREME BALLISTIC SILVERTIP

Features: Solid based boat tail design delivers excellent long range accuracy. In .22 calibers, the Ballistic plastic polycarbonate Silvertip bullet initiates rapid fragmentation. In medium to larger calibers special jacket contours extend range and reduce cross-wind drift. Harder lead core ensures proper bullet expansion.
Available in: 204 Ruger, 22-250 Remington, 223 Remington, 223 WSSM, 243 Winchester, 243 WSSM, 25-06 Remington, 25 WSSM, 270 Winchester, 270 WSM, 280 Remington, 300 Winchester Magnum, 30-06 Springfield, 300 WSM, 30-30 Winchester, 308 Winchester, 325 Winchester Short Magnum, 338 Winchester Magnum, 7mm Remington Magnum, 7mm-08 Remington, 7mm Remington Magnum, 7mm WSM

SUPREME E-TIP

Available in: 30-06 Springfield, 300 Winchester Magnum, 300 WSM, 308 Winchester
Box 20: $38.99–49.99

SUPREME NOSLER PARTITION AND NOSLER SOLID

Available in: 375 H&H, 416 Rigby, 416 Rem Mag, 458 Win Mag
Box 20: $59.99

SUPREME HOLLOWPOINT BOATTAIL MATCH

Available in: 300 Winchester Match
MSRP: $10.99–92.99

SUPREME PARTITION GOLD

Features: Proven partition technology, consistent, dramatic bullet expansion, deep penetration regardless of barrel length, maximum weight retention
Available in: 45-70 Government
Box 5: $16.99

SUPREME ELITE XP3

Features: The XP3 bullet starts with a 2-stage expansion design, then combines all the best-known bullet technology into one bullet. It delivers precision accuracy, awesome knockdown power, and deep penetration all in one package—and it's as effective on thin-skinned game, like deer and antelope, as it is on tough game, like elk, moose, bear, and African animals, at short and long ranges.
Available in: 243 Winchester, 243 WSSM, 270 WSM, 270 Winchester, 30-06 Springfield, 3000 WSM, 300 Winchester Magnum, 308 Winchester, 325 WSM, 7mm Rem Magnum, 7mm WSM Box 5: 15.99–19.99

RIMFIRE AMMUNITION

DYNAPOINT

Available in: 22 LR
Box 500: $26.99

SUPREME JHP AND SUPREME V-MAX

Available in: 17HMR, 22 Win Mag
Box 20: $16.29–22.99

SUPER-X #12 SHOT

Available in: 17HMR, 22 Short, 22 Long, 22 LR, 22 Win Mag
Box 50: $9.29

SUPER-X BLANK

Available in: 17HMR, 22 Short, 22 Long, 22 LR, 22 Win Mag
Box 50: $7.79

SUPER-X FULL METAL JACKET

Available in: 17HMR, 22 Short, 22 Long, 22 LR, 22 Win Mag
Box 50: $11.49

SUPER-X JHP

Available in: 17HMR, 22 Short, 22 Long, 22 LR, 22 Win Mag
Box 50: $16.49

SUPER-X LEAD HOLLOW POINT

Available in: 17HMR, 22 Short, 22 Long, 22 LR, 22 Win Mag
Box 50: $3.59–8.89

SUPER-X LEAD ROUND NOSE

Available in: 17HMR, 22 Short, 22 Long, 22 LR, 22 Win Mag
Box 500: $30.99

SUPER-X LEAD ROUND NOSE, STANDARD VELOCITY

Available in: 17HMR, 22 Short, 22 Long, 22 LR, 22 Win Mag
Box 20: $19.79

SUPER-X POWER-POINT

Available in: 17HMR, 22 Short, 22 Long, 22 LR, 22 Win Mag
Box 500: $32.99

SUPER-X POWER-POINT, LEAD HOLLOW POINT

Available in: 17HMR, 22 Short, 22 Long, 22 LR, 22 Win Mag
Box 100: $8.39

XPERT LEAD HOLLOW POINT

Available in: 22 LR
Box 500: $25.99

WILDCAT DYNAPOINT PLATED

Available in: 22 LR, 22 Win Mag, 22 WRF
Box 10: $9.25

WILDCAT LEAD FLAT NOSE

Available in: 22 LR, 22 Win Mag, 22 WRF
Box 50: $2.00

WILDCAT LEAD ROUND NOSE

Available in: 22 LR, 22 Win Mag, 22 WRF
Box 25: $26.49

SHOTGUN AMMUNITION

AA TARGET LOADS

Features: The hunter's choice for a wide variety of game-bird applications, available in an exceptionally broad selection of loadings, from 12-gauge to .410 bore, with shot size options ranging from BB's all the way down to 9s—suitable for everything from quail to farm predators.

Winchester Ammunition

Available in: 12, 20, 28, .410 ga.; 2½, 2¾; shot sizes 7½, 8, 8½, 9
Box 25: $8.49–10.99

SUPER-TARGET TARGET LOADS

Available in: 12, 20 ga.; 2¾ in.; shot sizes 7, 7½, 8
Box 500: $34.99

SUPER-X GAME AND FIELD LOADS

Available in: 12, 16, 20, 28, .410 ga.; 2½, 2¾, 3 in.; shot sizes 4, 5, 6, 7½, 8, 9
Box 25: $15.54

SUPER-X SUPER PHEASANT LOADS

Available in: 12, 20 ga.; 2¾, 3 in.; shot sizes 4, 5, 6
Box 25: $11.49

SUPER-X SUPER PHEASANT STEEL LOADS

Available in: 12 ga.; 3 in.; shot sizes 4
Box 25: $20.99

SUPER-X TRIALS AND BLANKS

Available in: 10, 12 ga.; 2¾, 2 7/8 in.; shot sizes (blank)
Box 25: $16.68

SUPER-X TURKEY LOADS

Available in: 12 ga.; 2¾, 3 in.; shot sizes 4, 5, 6
Box 10: $10.99

SUPER-X WATERFOWL LOADS

Available in: 10, 12, 20 ga.; 2¾, 3, 3 ½ in.; shot sizes T, BBB, BB, 1, 2, 3, 4
Box 25: $24.20

SUPREME GAME AND FIELD LOADS

Available in: 12, 20 ga.; 2¾, 3 in.; shot sizes 4, 5, 6
Box 25: $22–38

SUPREME TURKEY LOADS

Available in: 10, 12 20 ga.; 2¾, 3, 3 ½ in.; shot sizes 4, 5, 6
Box 10: $19.99

SUPREME ELITE XTENDED RANGE HD COYOTE

Available in: 12 ga.; 3 in.; shot sizes B
Box 5: $19.99

SUPREME ELITE XTENDED RANGE HD TURKEY

Available in: 12, 20 ga.; 2¾, 3, 3 ½ in.; shot sizes 4, 5, 6
Box 10: $19.99

SUPREME ELITE XTENDED RANGE HD WATERFOWL

Available in: 12, 20 ga.; 2¾, 3, 3 ½ in.; shot sizes B, 2, 4

WINLITE LOW RECOIL, LOW NOISE TARGET LOADS

Available in: 12, 20 ga.; 2¾ in.; shot sizes 8
Box 5: $4.99–5.19

XPERT HI-VELOCITY STEEL LOADS

Available in: 12, 16, 20, 28, .410 ga.; 2¾, 3, 3 ½ in.; shot sizes BB, 1, 2, 3, 4
Box 25: $812.29

XPERT STEEL LOADS

Available in: 12, 20 ga.; 2¾ in.; shot sizes 6, 7
Box 25: $7.69

SHOTGUN AMMUNITION (BUCKSHOT)

SUPER-X BUCKSHOT

Available in: 12, 16, 20, .410 ga.; 2½, 2¾, 3, 3 ½ in.; shot sizes 4, 3, 1, 00, 000
Box 5: $719

SUPREME BUCKSHOT

Available in: 12 ga.; 2¾, 3, 3 ½ in.; shot sizes 4, 00
Box 10: $13.79

WINLITE LOW RECOIL BUCKSHOT

Available in: 12 ga.; 2¾ in.
Box 5: $4.99

SHOTGUN AMMUNITION (SLUGS)

SUPER-X SLUGS

Available in: 12, 16, 20, .410 ga.; 2½, 2¾, 3 in.; 1/5, ¼, 5/8, ¾, 1 oz.
Box 5: $5.89

SUPREME ELITE XP3 SABOT SHOTGUN SLUGS

Available in: 12 ga.; 2¾, 3 in.; 300 gr.
Box 5: $15.99–19.99

SUPREME PLATINUM TIP HOLLOW POINT SLUGS

Available in: 12, 20, ga.; 2¾, 3 in.; 260 or 400 gr.
Box 20: $28.49

SUPREME RACKMASTER RIFLED SLUGS

Available in: 12 ga.; 2¾, 3 in.; 1 1/8 oz.
Box 5: $8.29–8.99

SUPREME WINCHESTER SLUGS

Available in: 12, 20, ga.; 2¾, 3 in.; 260 or 385 gr.
Box 10: $13.79

WINLITE LOW RECOIL SLUGS

Available in: 12 ga.; 2¾ in.; 1 oz. or 400 gr.
Box 5: $5.19

Barnes Bullets MUZZLELOADING AMMUNITION

EXPANDER MZ MUZZLELOADER BULLETS AND ALIGNERS

Features: Semi-spitzer ogive, boat-tail base. Six copper petals w/ double-diameter expansion. Full weight retention.
Available in: .50 Caliber (245, 285 gr.)
Box 24: $24.99

SPIT-FIRE MZ

Features: Semi-spitzer ogive, boattail base. Six copper petals with double-diameter expansion. Full weight retention.
Available in: .50 Caliber (245, 285 gr.)
Box 24: $28.99

SPIT-FIRE TMZ

Features: Boattail, All copper with polymer tip. Expands at 1050 fps.; remains intact at extreme velocities.
Available in: .50 Caliber (250, 290 gr.)
Box 24: $26.99

CVA

POWERBELT COPPER

Features: Thin copper plating reduces bore friction while allowing for optimal bullet expansion. Available in four tip designs: Hollow Point, AeroTip, Flat Point and Steel Tip.
Available in: .45 caliber (175,195, 195, 225, 225, 275, 275 gr.); 50 caliber (223, 245, 295, 348, 405 gr.); .54 caliber (295, 348, 405, 444 gr.)
MSRP: $16.99

POWERBELT PLATINUM AEROTIP

Features: Proprietary hard plating and aggressive bullet taper design for improved ballistic coefficient. A large size fluted gas check produces higher and more consistent pressures.
Available in: .45 caliber (223, 300 gr.); .50 caliber (270, 300, 338 gr.)
MSRP: $20.99–21.99

POWERBELT PURE LEAD

Pure lead, available in four different grain weights in Hollow Point and 444 in Flat Point.
Available in: .50 caliber (295, 348, 405 gr.); .54 caliber (295, 348 , 405 gr.)
MSRP: $13.19–15.99

Federal Ammunition

FUSION MUZZLELOADER SLUGS

Features: The Fusion bullet process now is available for hunters using .50-caliber muzzleloaders. A .45-caliber slug is offered in three grain weights paired with a .50-cal crush rib sabot. The Fusion bullet is deep penetrating, with high weight retention at 95 percent and high accuracy. In addition, the crush rib sabot reduces loading friction up to 50 percent.
Available in: .50 caliber in 240, 260 and 300 grain
Box 500: $32.99

Harvester

SABER TOOTH BELTED BULLETS

Features: Copper-Clad belted bullet in Harvester Crush Rib Sabot.
Available in: .50 cal. (250, 270, 300 gr.)
Box 15: $11.29–11.49

SCORPION

Features: Electroplated copper plating does not separate from lead core. Loaded in Harvester Crush Rib Sabots.
Available in: Funnel Point Mag. and Polymer Ballistic Tip—.50 caliber (240, 260, 300 gr.); .54 caliber (240, ***260, 300 gr.)***
Box 12: $7.39–9.99

SABOER TOOTH
BELTED BULLETS

SCORPION

Hornady Mfg. Co.

GREAT PLAINS MAXI HOLLOW BASE HOLLOW POINTS

Features: Pre-scored hollow points, a short ogive and three diameter bearing surface.
Available in: .45 caliber (285 gr.); .50 caliber (385, 410 gr.); .54 caliber (390, 425, 525 gr.)
Box 20: $10.49–11.79

HP/XTP BULLET/SABOT

Features: Hornady XTP bullet/sabot combination with controlled expansion XTP bullet.
Available in: .45 caliber (180 gr.); .50 caliber (180, 240, 300 gr.); ***.54 caliber (300 gr.)***
Box 20: $12.49–12.99

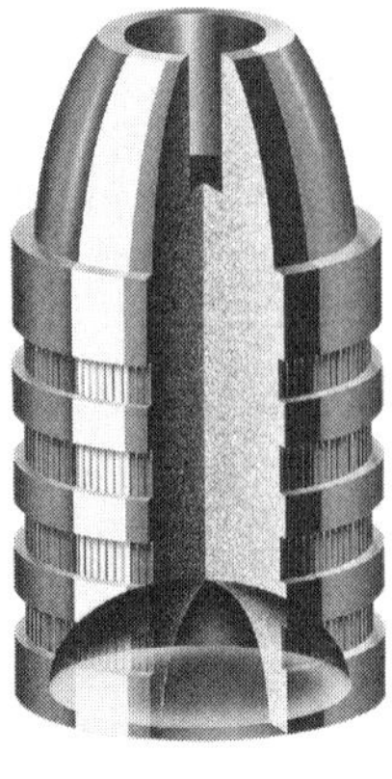

GREAT PLAINS MAXI HOLLOW BASE HOLLOW POINTS

HP/XTP BULLET/SABOT

Knight Rifles

JACKETED BULLETS WITH SABOTS

Features: Copper jacketed, hollow point bullet with sabot.
Available in: .50 cal. (240, 260, 300 gr.)
Box 20: $14.99

LEAD BULLETS WITH SABOTS

Features: Pure lead bullet with sabot.
Available in: .50 caliber (260, 310 gr.)
Box 20: $10.99

RED HOT BULLETS

Features: Saboted Barnes solid copper bullet with superior expansion.
Available in: .45 caliber (175, 195 gr.); .50 caliber (250, 300, 250, 250 gr.); .52 caliber (275 grain, 350, 375 gr.)
Box 18: $23.99

ULTIMATE SLAM HYDRA-CON

Features: Pure lead bullet.
Available in: .50 caliber (440 gr.); .52 caliber (530 gr.)
Box 12: $17.99

ULTIMATE SLAM PBT (POLYMER BOAT TAIL)

Features: Sabot with all copper polymer tip bullet; expands into six razor-sharp copper petals while retaining 100 percent of original weight.
Available in: .50 caliber (250, 250, 290 gr.)
Box 18: $23.99

ULTIMATE SLAM SPITZER BOAT TAIL

Features: Sabot loaded with Barnes Spitzer Boat tail bullet.
Available in: .50 caliber (245, 285 gr.)
Box 18: $19.99

Nosler

BLACK POWDER PARTITION-HG SABOT

Features: HG Sabot with Nosler Partition jacketed hollow point bullet.
Available in: .50 cal. (250, 260, 300 gr.)
$12.12

Remington

XBLS MUZZLELOADING SABOTS

Features: Remington Expander-LT bullets with sealed hydraulic chamber in the nose to ensure expansion.
Available in: .50 caliber (275, 300 gr.)
Box 15: $10.33

Thompson/Center Arms

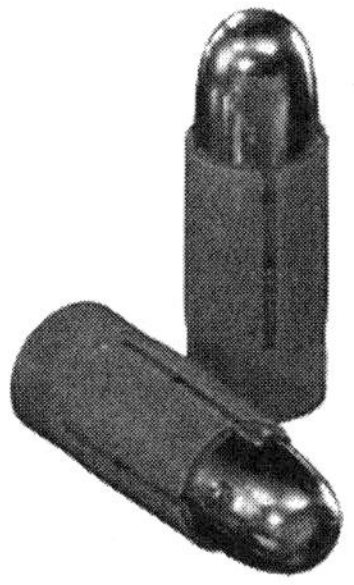

BONE CRUSHER SABOT

MAXIBALL

MAXI HUNTER

SHOCK WAVE

BONE CRUSHER SABOT

Features: .458 diameter solid projectile for 50 caliber muzzloaders
Available in: .50 caliber (400 gr.)
Box 15: $29.00

MAGNUM EXPRESS SABOTS

Features: Mag express sabots separate from the projectile quickly. Sabots are available preassembled with XTP bullets.
Available in: .50 caliber (300 gr.); .54 caliber (250 gr.)
Box 30: $14.07

MAXIBALL

Features: Features: Maximum expansion on deer sized game. Lubricating grooves (maxi wide grooves).
Available in: .45caliber (240 gr.); .50 caliber (320, 370 gr.); .54 (430 gr.); .58 caliber (555 gr.)
Box 20: $14.99

MAXI-HUNTER

Features: Maximum expansion on deer sized game. Lubricating grooves (maxi hunter multiple grooves).
Available in: .45 caliber (255 gr.); .50 caliber (275, 350 gr.); .54 caliber (435 gr.); .58 caliber (560 gr.)
Box 20: $14.99

SHOCK WAVE

Features: Polymer tip spire point bullet with sabot. Incorporates harder lead core with walls interlocked with the jacket for maximum weight retention and expansion. Available with spire point or bonded bullets
Available in: .45 caliber (200, 245 gr.); .50 caliber (200, 250, 250, 370, 300 gr.)
Box 15: $15.74

Winchester

BLACK POWDER PARTITION GOLD & SUPREME PLATINUM TIP

Features: Sabot loaded with Supreme Platinum Tip Hollow Point Bullets or Partition Gold bullet.
Available in: .50 caliber (260, 400 gr.)
Box 5: $11.00

HANDLOADING

Barnes Bullets

All Copper X-Bullets

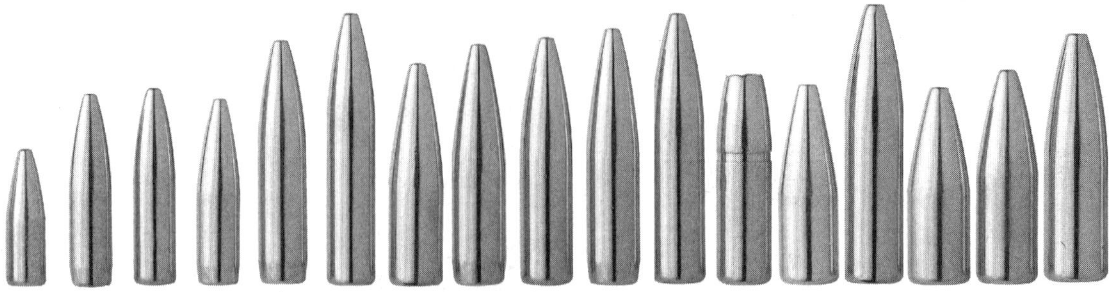

Caliber & Description	22 S	6mm BT	6mm S	25 BT	7mm BT	7mm S	30 S	30 BT	30 S	30 BT	30 S	30/30 FN	338 S	338 S	35 S	35 S	9.3mm S
Diameter, Inches	.224	.243	.243	.257	.284	.284	.308	.308	.308	.308	.308	.308	.338	.338	.358	.358	.366
Weight, Grains	50	85	90	90	150	175	150	165	180	180	200	150	160	250	180	200	250
Density	.142	.206	.218	.195	.266	.310	.226	.247	.271	.271	.301	.226	.200	.313	.201	.223	.267
Ballistic Coefficient	.220	.401	.382	.343	.529	.530	.386	.505	.511	.552	.550	.269	.337	.521	.298	.346	.428
Catalog Number	22450	24310	24315	25710	28428	28445	30815	30827	30835	30840	30845	30819	33878	33890	35810	35815	36605

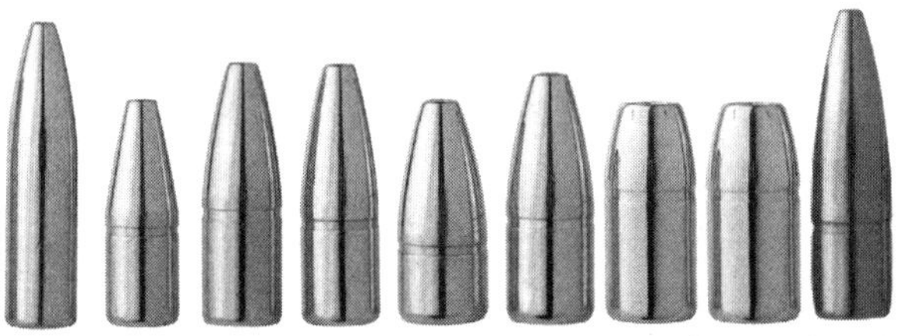

Caliber & Description	9.3mm S	375 S	405 Win S	416 S	458 S	458 Mag S	45/70 FN	45/70 FN	50 BT
Diameter, Inches	.366	.375	.411	.416	.284	.458	.458	.458	.510
Weight, Grains	286	210	300	300	300	350	250	300	647
Density	.305	.213	.254	.247	.204	.283	.170	.206	.355
Ballistic Coefficient	.468	.341	.313	.394	.340	.402	.172	.204	.592
Catalog Number	36615	37575	41178	41680	45802	45805	45831	45832	51064

LEGEND
- **BMG** – Browning Machinegun
- **BT** – Boattail
- **FB** – Flat Base
- **FMJ** – Full Metal Jacket
- **FN** – Flat Nose
- **RN** – Round Nose
- **S** – Spitzer
- **SP** – Soft Point

From: $29.11–41.59

Triple-Shock X-Bullet

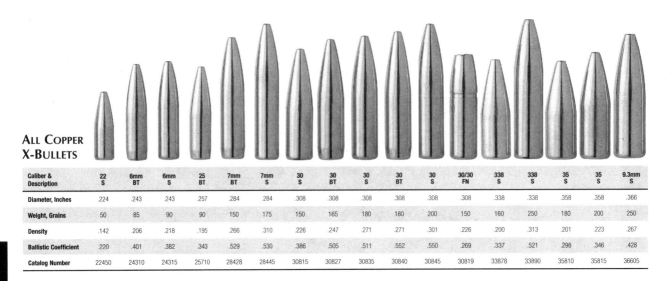

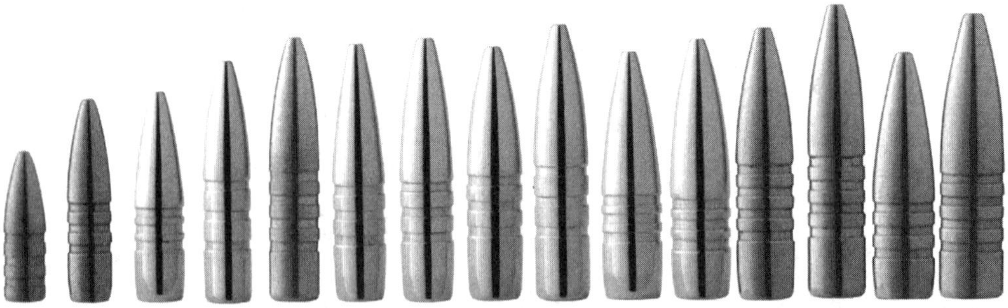

Caliber & Description	22 FB	6mm BT	25 BT	25 FB	6.5mm FB	270 BT	270 BT	7mm BT	7mm FB	30 BT	30 BT	30 BT	30 FB	338 BT	338 FB
Diameter, Inches	.224	.243	.257	.257	.264	.277	.277	.284	.308	.308	.308	.308	.308	.338	.338
Weight, Grains	53	85	100	115	130	130	140	140	160	180	168	180	200	185	225
Density	.151	.206	.216	.249	.266	.242	.261	.248	.283	.226	.253	.271	.301	.231	.281
Ballistic Coefficient	.231	.333	.420	.429	.479	.466	.497	.5477	.508	.428	.476	.552	.550	.437	.482
Catalog Number	22443	24341	25742	25743	26442	27742	27744	28444	28446	30841	30844	30846	30848	33843	33846

From: $25.13–35.66

Barnes Bullets

LEGEND

- **BMG** – Browning Machinegun
- **BT** – Boattail
- **FB** – Flat Base
- **FMJ** – Full Metal Jacket
- **FN** – Flat Nose
- **RN** – Round Nose
- **S** – Spitzer
- **SP** – Soft Point

XLC COATED XBULLETS

Caliber & Description	22 HORNET BT	22 S	6mm S	25 BT	6.5mm S	6.5mm S	270 BT	7mm BT	7mm S	30 BT
Diameter, Inches	.224	.224	.243	.257	.4264	.264	.277	.284	.284	.308
Weight, Grains	45	53	95	100	120	140	130	140	160	130
Density	.128	.151	.230	.216	.246	.287	.242	.248	.283	.196
Ballistic Coefficient	.203	.231	.398	.420	.441	.522	.466	.477	.508	.374
Catalog Number	22452	22455	24355	25754	26451	26453	27754	28455	28458	30851

From: $26–50

Rather than loading everything at home before going to the range, build a loading box for your scale, powder measure and an inexpensive press. Then take some sized and primed brass, powder and bullets to the range for initial load development. This way you can throw charges and seat bullets as needed. No more pulling bullets from loads that did not work or shooting up loads made at home just to get rid of them.

COPPER-JACKET/ LEAD CORE ORIGINAL

Caliber & Description	6mm RNSP	348 WIN FNSP	348 WIN FNSP	357 WIN FNSP	38/55 FNSP	38/55 FNSP	401 WIN RNSP	40/65 WIN FNSP	45/70 SSP	45/70 FNSP	45/70 SSP	45/70 FNSP	458 MAG RNSP	50/110 WIN FNSP	50/110 WIN FNSP
Diameter, Inches	.243	.348	.348	.375	.375	.377	.406	.406	.458	.458	.458	.458	.458	.510	.510
Jacket, Inches	.030	.032	.032	.032	.032	.032	.032	.032	.032	.032	.032	.032	.049	.032	.032
Weight, Grains	115	220	250	255	255	255	250	250	300	300	400	400	600	300	450
Density	.290	.260	.295	.259	.259	.256	.217	.217	.204	.204	.272	.272	.409	.165	.247
Ballistic Coefficient	.322	.301	.327	.290	.290	.290	.241	.231	.291	.227	.389	.302	.454	.183	.274
Catalog Number	24330	34805	34810	375W20	38/5510	38/5520	40610	40611	457010	457020	457030	457040	45860	5011010	5011020

From: $19.59–55.30

Barnes Bullets

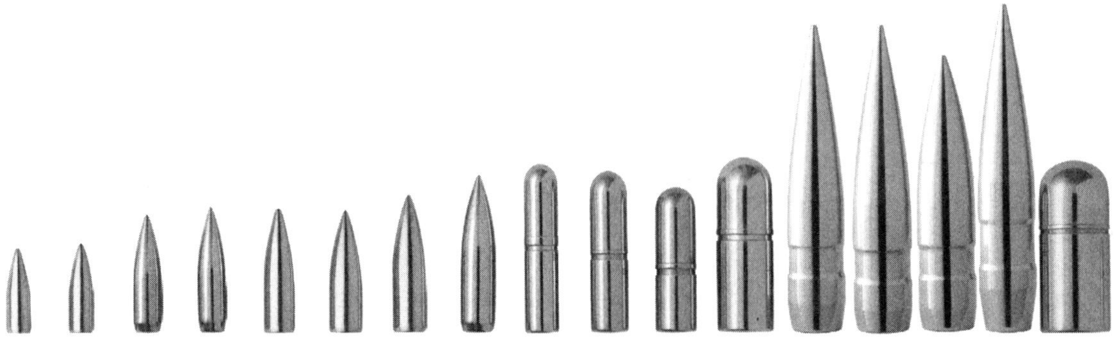

Solids

Caliber & Description	22 FB	22 FB	6mm BT	25 BT	7mm BT	7mm FB	30 FB	30 BT	30 FB	338 BT	9.3mm S	577 NITRO FN	50 BMG BT	50 BMG BT	50 BMG BT	50 BMG BT	600 NITRO FB
Diameter, Inches	.224	.224	.243	.257	.284	.284	.308	.308	.308	.338	.366	.585	.510	.510	.510	.510	.620
Weight, Grains	45	50	75	90	150	100	125	165	220	250	286	750	750	750	750	800	900
Density	.128	.142	.181	.195	.266	.177	.188	.248	.331	.313	.305	.313	.412	.412	.412	.439	.334
Ballistic Coefficient	.212	.235	.330	.324	.529	.343	.372	.481	.305	.326	.342	.351	1.070	—	—	1.095	.380
Catalog Number	22401	22402	24301	25720	28428	28401	30812	30822	30842	33825	36612	58520	510750A	510750	510750T	510800A	62020

From: $17.91–58.17

HANDGUN BULLETS

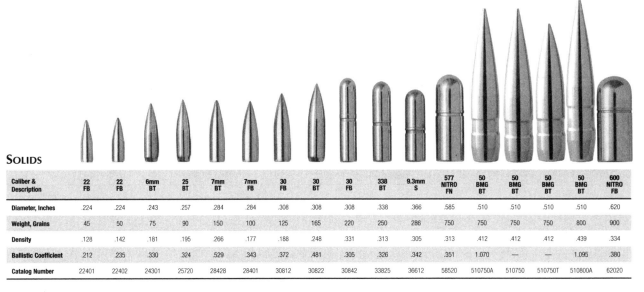

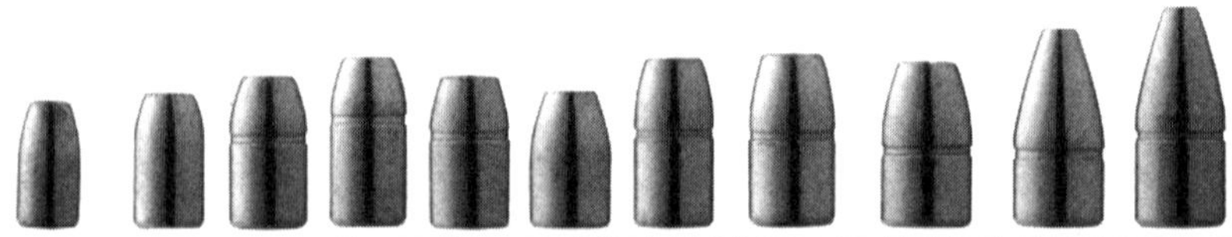

XPB Pistol Bullets

Caliber & Description	9mm XPB	40 S&W XPB	44 MAG XPB	44 MAG XPB	45 LONG COLT XPB	44 ACP XPB	454 CASULL XPB	480 RUGER 475 LINBAUGH XPB	50 XPB	50 XPB	50 XPB
Diameter, Inches	.355	.400	.429	.429	.451	.451	.451	.475	.500	.500	.500
Weight, Grains	115	155	200	225	225	185	250	275	275	325	375
Density	.130	.138	.155	.175	.158	.130	.176	.174	.157	.186	.214
Ballistic Coefficient	.167	.189	.172	.195	.146	.167	.141	.155	.141	.228	.261
Catalog Number	35515	40055	42920	42922	45120	45185	45123	48010	50025	50026	50028

LEGEND

- **BMG** – Browning Machinegun
- **BT** – Boattail
- **FB** – Flat Base
- **FMJ** – Full Metal Jacket
- **FN** – Flat Nose
- **RN** – Round Nose
- **S** – Spitzer
- **SP** – Soft Point

From: $14.61–23.02

Berger Bullets

Famous for their superior performance in benchrest matches, Berger bullets also include hunting designs. From .17 to .30, all Bergers feature 14 jackets with wall concentricity tolerance of .0003. Lead cores are 99.9% pure and swaged in dies to within .0001 of round. Berger's line includes several profiles: Low Drag, Very Low Drag, Length Tolerant and Maximum-Expansion, besides standard flat-base and standard boat-tail.

LEGEND
BT – Boattail
HBC – High Ballistic Coefficient
VLD – Very Low Drag

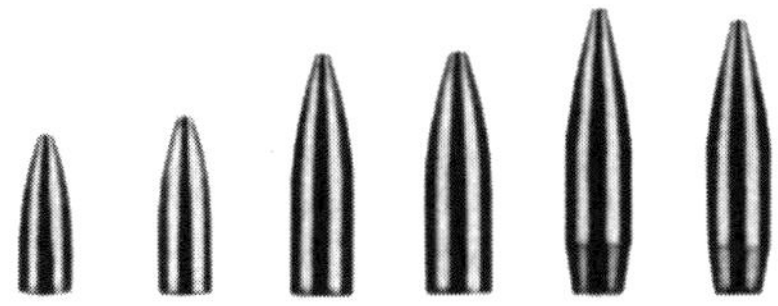

Caliber & Description	17	17	20	20	20 BT Varmint	20 BT Varmint
Weight, Grains	20	25	30	35	40	50

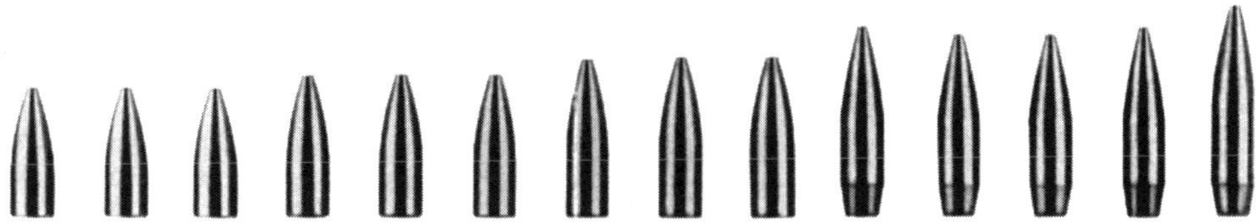

Caliber & Description	22 Varmint	22 Varmint	22 Varmint	22	22	22	22	22	22	22 VLD	22 BT	22 BT	22 VLD	22 VLD
Weight, Grains	30	35	40	50	52	55	60	62	64	70	70	73	75	80

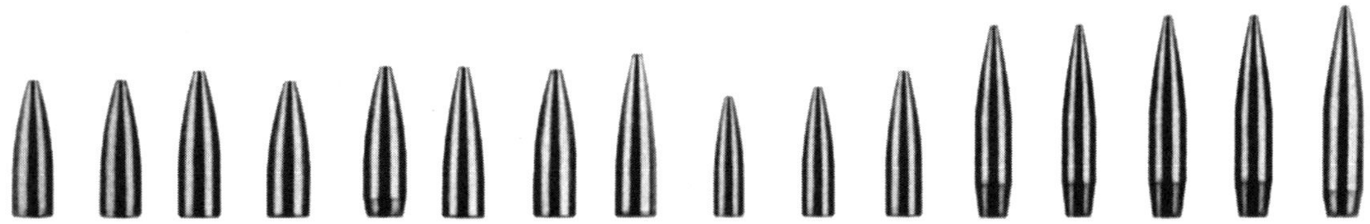

Caliber & Description	6mm	6mm	6mm	6mm Short	6mm BT	6mm HBCFB	6mm	6mm HBCFB	6mm	6mm	6mm HBCFB	6mm BT	6mm VLD	6mm LTB	6mm VLD	6mm VLD
Weight, Grains	60	62	65	65	65	65	68	69	70	80	88	90	95	105	105	115

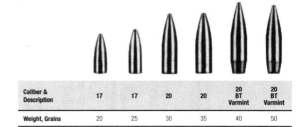

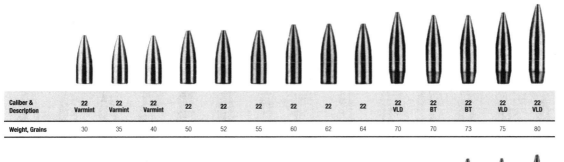

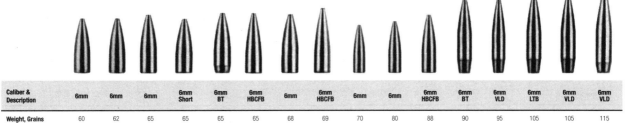

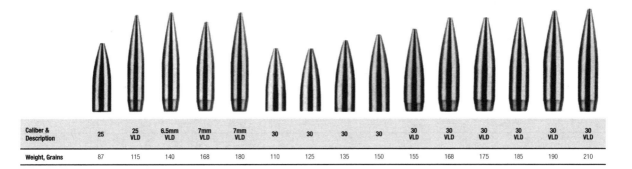

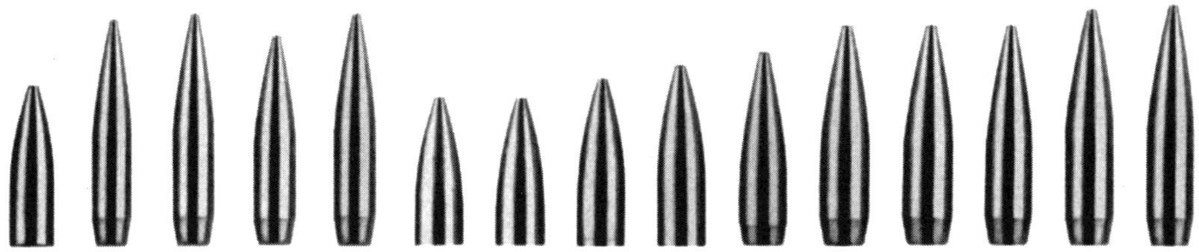

Caliber & Description	25	25 VLD	6.5mm VLD	7mm VLD	7mm VLD	30	30	30	30	30 VLD	30 VLD	30 VLD	30 VLD	30 VLD	30 VLD
Weight, Grains	87	115	140	168	180	110	125	135	150	155	168	175	185	190	210

From: $23.96–275.67

Empty glucose test-strip containers are great for storing and organizing handloading items. They have a handy flip lid, and they're just right for small parts. You can label with a Sharpie or print a laser label for each one so it doesn't smear.

Hornady Bullets

The 200-grain .40 and 250- and 300-grain .45 bullets are meant for use in sabot sleeves. They feature a jacketed lead core with the signature red polymer tip. The SST has led also to Hornady's newest big game bullet, the Interbond. Essentially, it's an SST with a thicker jacket that has an inner "expansion control ring" near the front of the shank. Jacket and core are also bonded to ensure deep penetration and high weight retention. Though it typically opens to double its initial diameter, the Interbond bullet can be expected to hold 90 percent of its weight in the animal.

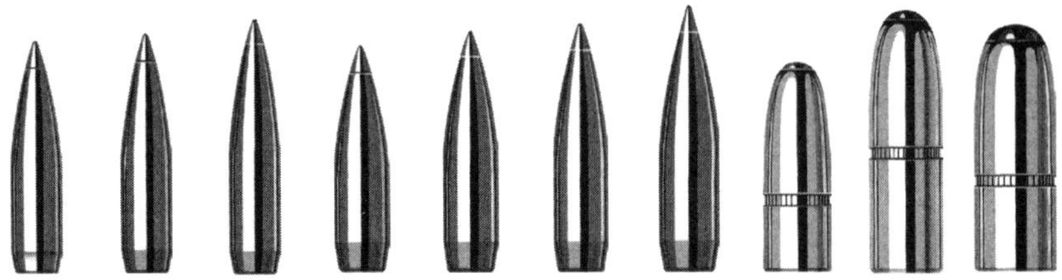

InterBond

Caliber & Description	270	7mm	7mm	30	3 0	30	338	375 RN	416 RN	45 RN
Diameter, Inches	.277	.284	.284	.308	.308	.308	.338	.375	.416	.458
Weight, Grains	130	139	154	150	165	180	225	300	400	500
Catalog Number	27309	28209	28309	30309	30459	30709	33209	37209	41659	45049

From: $56.08–76.52

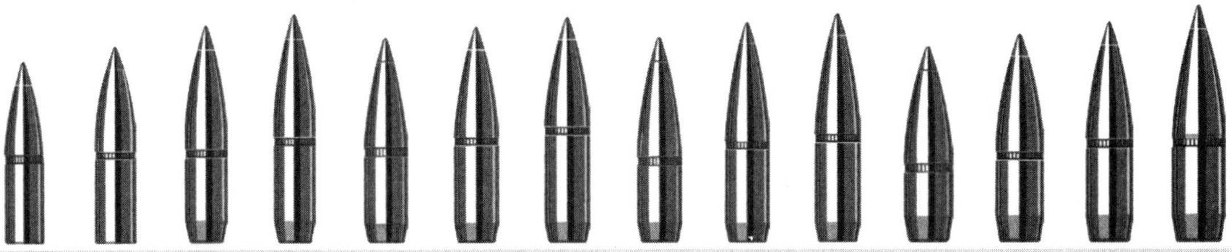

SST

Caliber & Description	6mm InterLock	25 InterLock	6.5mm InterLock	6.5mm InterLock	270 InterLock	270 InterLock	270 InterLock	7mm InterLock	7mm InterLock	7mm InterLock	30 InterLock	30 InterLock	30 InterLock	338 InterLock
Diameter, Inches	.243	.257	.264	.264	.277	.277	.277	.284	.284	.284	.308	.308	.308	.338
Weight, Grains	95	117	129	140	130	140	150	139	154	162	150	165	180	225
Catalog Number	24532	25522	26202	26302	27302	27352	27402	28202	28302	28452	30302	30452	30702	33202

From: $36.41–46.48

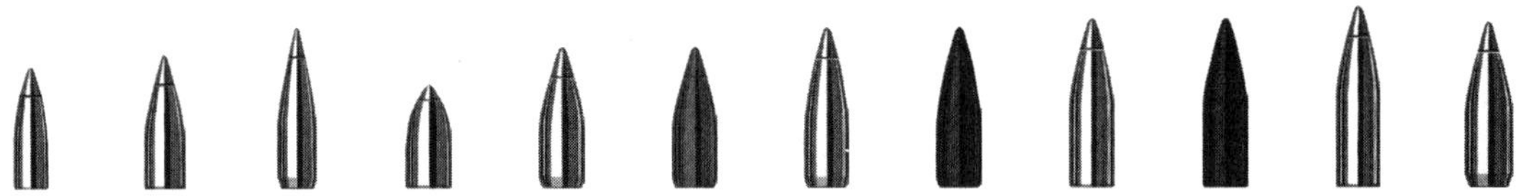

V-Max

Caliber & Description	17	20	20	22	22	22 w/Moly	22	22 w/Moly	22	22 w/Moly	22	6mm
Diameter, Inches	.172	.204	.204	.224	.224	.224	.224	.224	.224	.224	.224	.243
Weight, Grains	20	32	40	35	40	40	50	50	55	55	60	58
Catalog Number	21710	22004	22006	22252	22241	22413	22261	22613	22271	22713	22281	22411

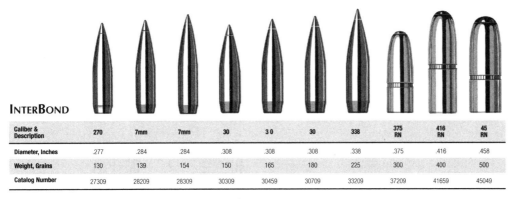

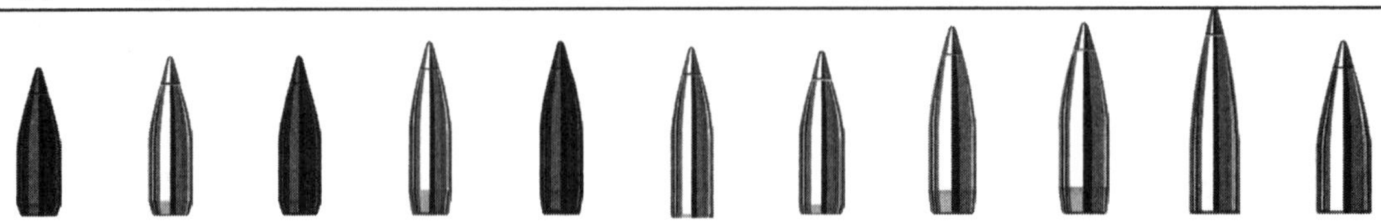

Caliber & Description	6mm w/Moly	6mm	6mm w/Moly	6mm w/Moly	6mm w/Moly	6mm	25	6.5mm	270	7mm	30
Diameter, Inches	.243	.243	.243	.243	.243	.243	.257	.264	.277	.284	.308
Weight, Grains	58	65	65	75	75	87	75	95	110	120	110
Catalog Number	24113	22415	24154	22420	24204	22440	22520	22601	22720	22810	23010

From: $21.75–55.68

Hornady Bullets

Traditional Varmint

Caliber & Description	17 HP	17 Moly	22 JET	22 HORNET	22 BEE	22 HORNET	22 SPSX	22 SP	22 SPSX	22 SP	22 SP w/c	22 SP	22 HP
Diameter, Inches	.172	.172	.222	.223	.224	.224	.224	.224	.224	.224	.224	.224	.224
Weight, Grains	25	25	40	45	45	45	50	50	55	55	55	60	60
Catalog Number	1710	17103	2210	2220	2229	2230	2240	2245	2260	2265	2266	2270	2275

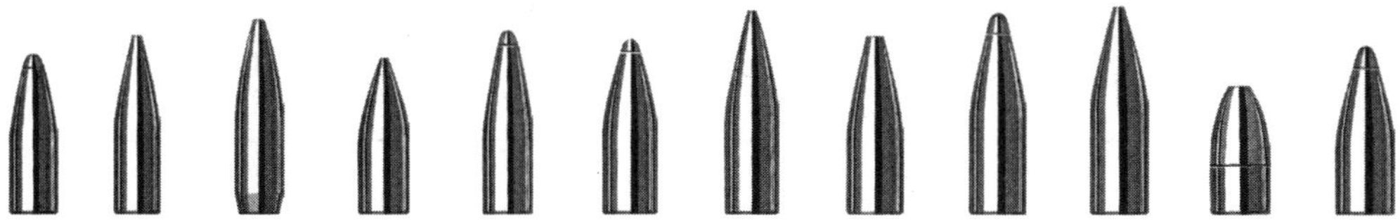

Caliber& Description	6mm SP	6mm HP	6mm BTHP	25 HP	25 SP	270 SP	270 HP	7mm HP	7mm SP	7mm HP	30 SJ	30 SP
Diameter, inches	.243	.243	.243	.257	.257	.277	.277	.284	.284	.284	.308	.308
Weight, Grains	70	75	87	75	87	100	110	100	120	120	100	110
Catalog Number	2410	2420	2442	2520	2530	2710	2720	2800	2810	2815	3005	3010

From: $17.53–55.68

Traditional Hunting

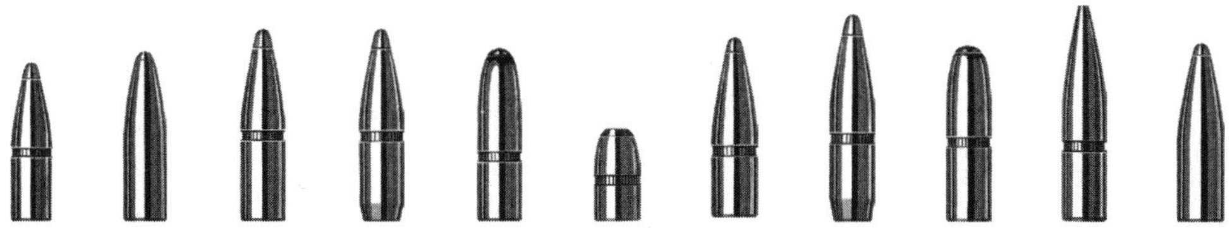

Caliber & Description	22 SP	6mm SP	6mm SP InterLock	6mm BTSP InterLock	6mm RN InterLoc	25 FP	25 SP InterLock	25 BTSP InterLock	25 RN InterLock	25 HP InterLock	6.5mm SP
Diameter, Inches	.227	.243	.243	.243	.243	.257	.257	.257	.257	.257	.264
Weight, Grains	70	87	100	100	100	60	100	117	117	120	100
Catalog Number	2280	2440	2450	2453`	2455	2510	2540	2552	2550	2560	2610

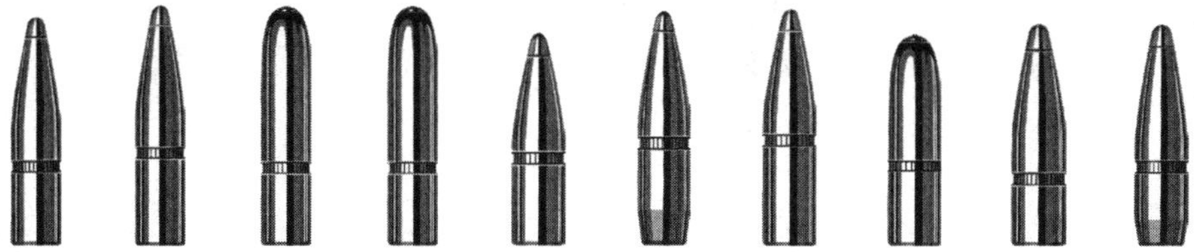

Caliber & Description	6.5mm SP InterLock	6.5mm SP InterLock	6.5mm RN InterLock	6.5mm RN Carcano	270 SP InterLock	270 BTSP InterLock	270 SP InterLock	270 RN InterLock	7mm SP InterLock	7mm BTSP InterLock
Diameter, Inches	.264	.264	.264	.267	.277	.277	.277	.277	.284	.284
Weight, Grains	129	140	160	160	130	140	150	150	139	139
Catalog Number	2620	2630	2640	2645	2730	2735	2740	2745	2820	2825

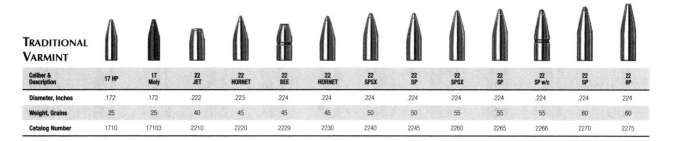

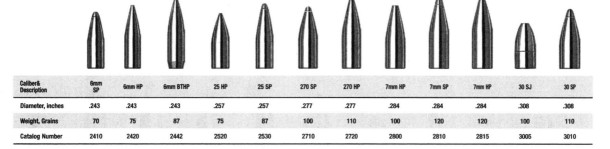

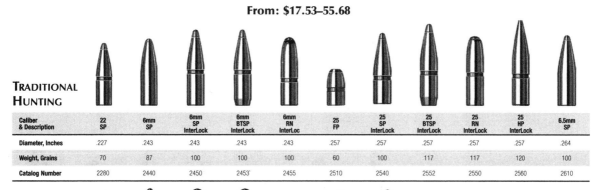

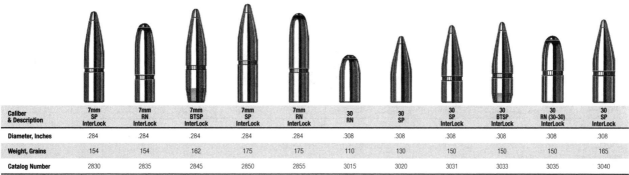

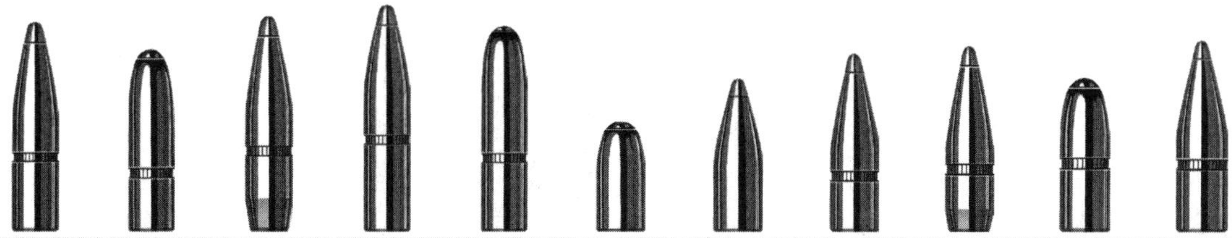

Caliber & Description	7mm SP InterLock	7mm RN InterLock	7mm BTSP InterLock	7mm SP InterLock	7mm RN InterLock	30 RN	30 SP	30 SP InterLock	30 BTSP InterLock	30 RN (30-30) InterLock	30 SP InterLock
Diameter, Inches	.284	.284	.284	.284	.284	.308	.308	.308	.308	.308	.308
Weight, Grains	154	154	162	175	175	110	130	150	150	150	165
Catalog Number	2830	2835	2845	2850	2855	3015	3020	3031	3033	3035	3040

Hornady Bullets

Traditional Hunting (cont.)

Caliber & Description	30 BTSP InterLock	30 FP (30-30) InterLock	30 SP InterLock	30 BTSP InterLock	30 RN InterLock	30 BTSP InterLock	30 RN InterLock	7.62 X 39mm SP	303 SP InterLock	303 RN InterLock
Diameter, Inches	.308	.308	.308	.308	.308	.308	.308	.310	.312	.312
Weight, Grains	165	170	180	180	180	190	220	123	150	174
Catalog Numbers	3045	3060	3070	3072	3075	3085	3090	3140	3120	3130

Caliber & Description	32 FP InterLock	8mm SP InterLock	8mm SP InterLock	8mm RN InterLock	8mm SP InterLock	338 SP InterLock	338 SP InterLock	338 SP InterLock	338RN InterLock	348 FP InterLock
Diameter, Inches	.321	.323	.323	.323	.323	.338	.338	.338	.338	.348
Weight, Grains	170	125	150	170	195	200	225	250	250	200
Catalog Number	3210	3230	3232	3235	3236	3310	3320	3335	3330	3410

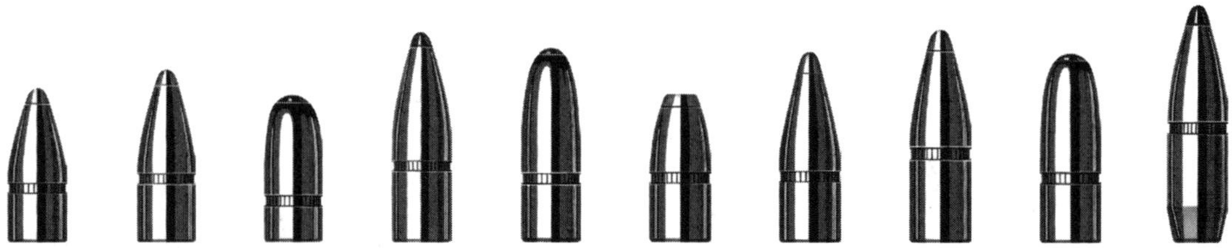

Caliber & Description	35. SP-SSP InterLock	35 SP InterLock	35 RN InterLock	35 SP InterLock	35 RN InterLock	375 FP (375 Win.)	375 SP InterLock	375 SP InterLock	375RN InterLock	375 BTSP InterLock
Diameter, Inches	.358	.358	.358	.358	.358	.375	.375	.375	.375	.375
Weight, Grains	180	200	200	250	250	220	225	270	270	300
Catalog Number	3505	3510	3515	3520	3525	3705	3706	3710	3715	3725

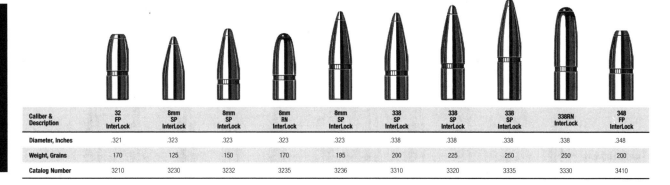

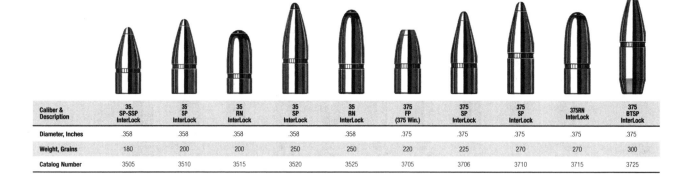

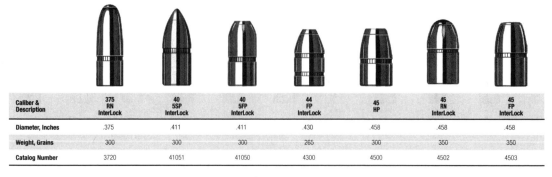

Caliber & Description	375 RN InterLock	40 5SP InterLock	40 5FP InterLock	44 FP InterLock	45 HP	45 RN InterLock	45 FP InterLock
Diameter, Inches	.375	.411	.411	.430	.458	.458	.458
Weight, Grains	300	300	300	265	300	350	350
Catalog Number	3720	41051	41050	4300	4500	4502	4503

From: $24.93–54.59

Hornady Bullets

Traditional Hunting FMJ Bullets

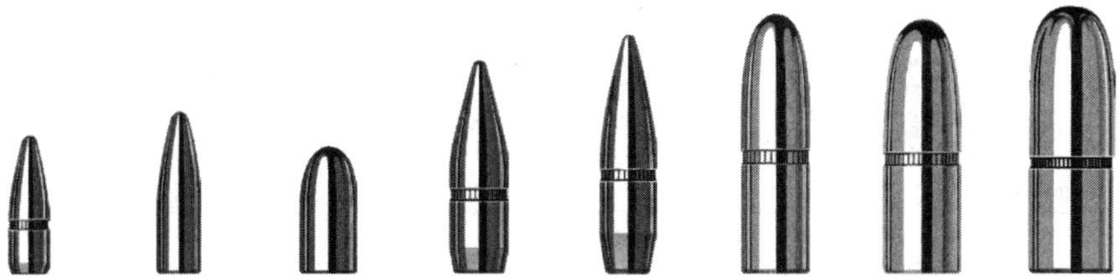

Caliber & Description	22 BT w/c	6MM	30	30 BT	303 BT	375 RN ENC	416 RN ENC	45 RN ENC
Diameter, Inches	.224	.243	.308	.308	.312	.375	.416	.458
Weight, Grains	55	80	110	150	174	300	400	500
Catalog Number	2267	2430	3017	3037	3131	37277	41677	45077

From: $17.77–34.55

BTHP Match

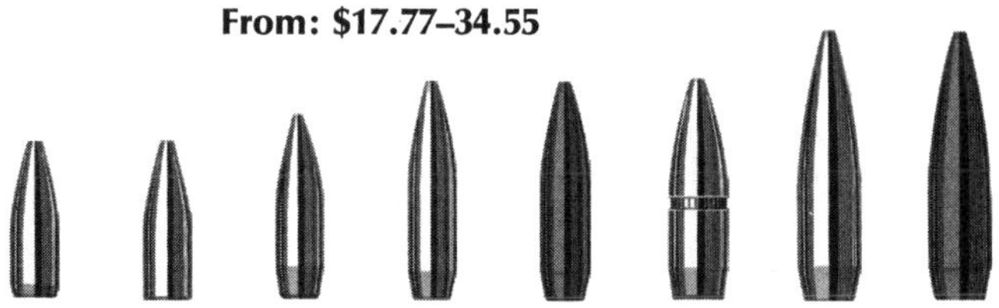

Caliber & Description	22	22	22	22	22 w/Moly	6.8mm w/c	30	30 w/Moly
Diameter, Inches	.224	.224	.224	.224	.224	.277	.308	.308
Weight, Grains	52	53	68	75	75	115	168	168
Catalog Number	2249	2250	2278	2279	22793	2715	30501	30503

From: $20.79–145.97

IA-Max Match

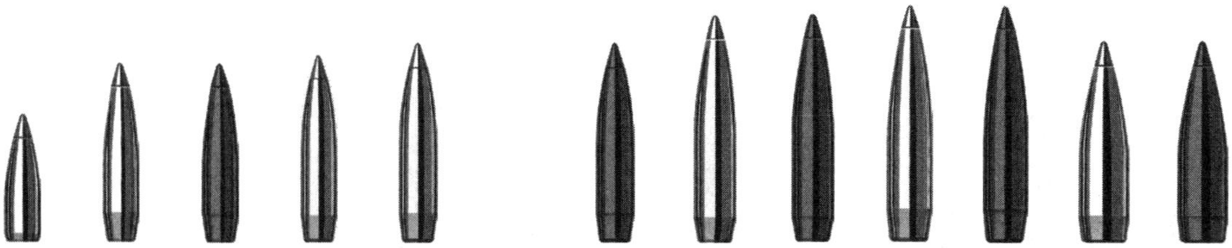

Caliber & Description	22	22	22 w/Moly	22	6mm	6mm w/Moly	6.5mm	6.5mm w/Moly	7mm	7mm w/Moly	30	30 w/Moly
Diameter, Inches	.224	.224	.224	.224	.243	.243	.264	.264	.284	.284	.308	.308
Weight, Grains	52	75	75	80	105	105	140	140	162	162	155	155
Catalog Number	22492	22792	22794	22832	24562	24564	26332	26334	28402	28404	30312	30314

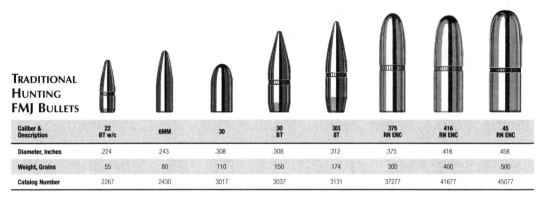

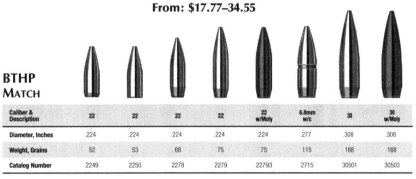

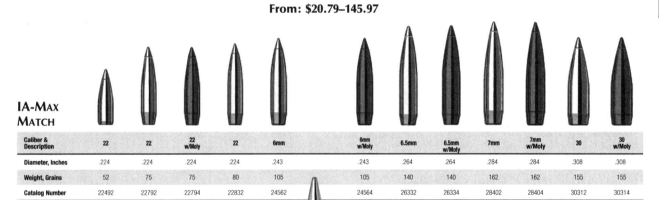

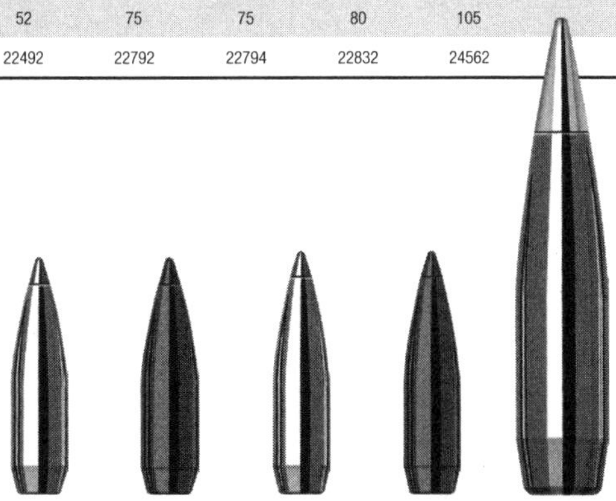

Caliber & Description	30	30 w/Moly	30	30 w/Moly	50
Diameter, Inches	.308	.308	.308	.308	.510
Weight, Grains	168	168	178	178	750
Catalog Number	30502	30504	30712	30714	5165

From: $24.84–45.97

LEGEND

B – Bulk
BT – Boattail
C/T – Combat Target
CL – Crimp Lock™
ENC – Encapsulated
FMJ – Full Metal Jacket
FP – Flat Point
HBWC – Hollow Base Wadcutter
HP – Hollow Point
HM – Heavy Magnum™
I – InterLock™ Bullet
IB – InterBond™ Bullet
JFP – Jacketed Flat Point
L – Swaged Lead Bullet
LM – Light Magnum™
LRN – Lead Round Nose
w/Moly – Moly-Coated
RN – Round Nose
SIL – Silhouette
SJ – Short Jacket
SP – Spire Point
SST – Super Shock Tipped™
SSP – Single Shot Pistol
SWC – Semi-Wadcutter
SX – Super Explosive
VX – Varmint Express™
XTP – Extreme Terminal Performance™
+P – Plus Pressure

Hornady Bullets

HANDLOADING

HANDGUN BULLETS

XTP Bullets

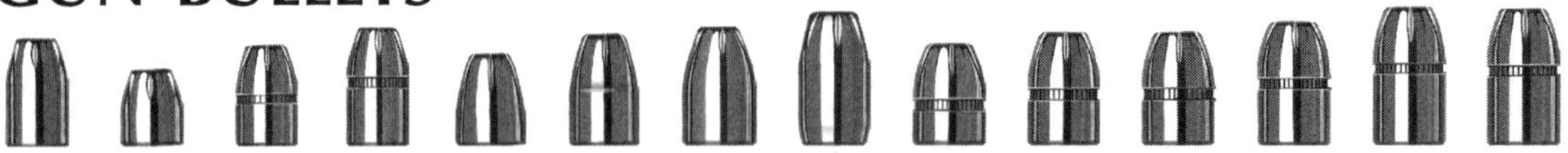

Caliber & Description	30 HP	32 HP	32 HP	32 HP	9mm HP	9mm HP	9mm HP	9mm BTHP	38 HP	38 HP	38 FP	38 HP	38 HP	38 FP
Diameter, Inches	.308	.312	.312	.312	.355	.355	.355	.355	.357	.357	.357	.357	.357	.357
Weight, Grains	90	60	85	100	90	115	124	147	110	125	125	140	158	158
Catalog Number	31000	32010	32050	32070	35500	35540	35571	35580	35700	35710	35730	35740	35750	35780

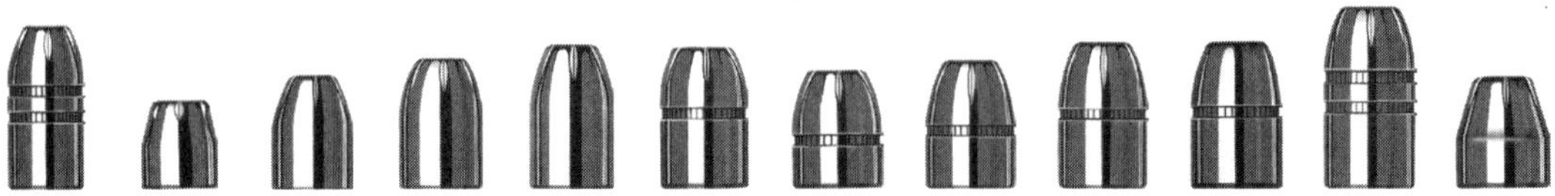

Caliber & Description	38 HP	9X18mm HP	10mm HP	10mm HP	10mm HP	41 HP	44 HP	44 HP	44 HP	44 CL-SIL	44 HP	45 HP
Diameter, Inches	.357	.365	.400	.400	.400	.410	.430	.430	.430	.430	.430	.451
Weight, Grains	180	95	155	180	200	210	180	200	240	240	300	185
Catalog Number	35771	36500	40000	40040	40060	41000	44050	44100	44200	4425	44280	45100

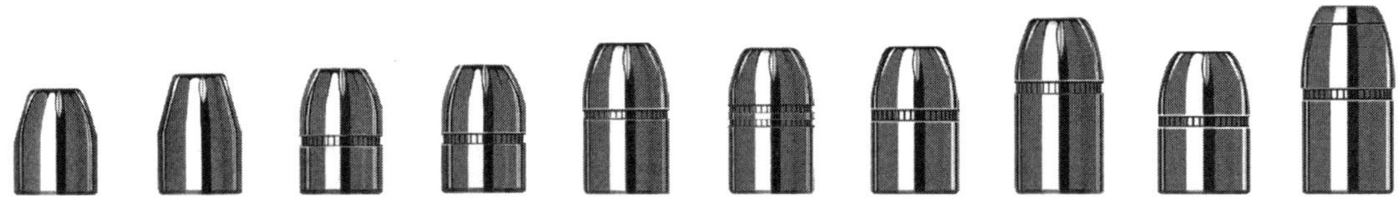

Caliber & Description	45 HP	45 HP	45 MAG	45 HP	45 MAG	45 HP	475 MAG	475 MAG	50 MAG	50 FP
Diameter, Inches	.451	.451	.452	.452	.452	.452	.475	.475	.500	.500
Weight, Grains	200	230	240	250	300	300	325	400	350	500
Catalog Number	45140	45160	45220	45200	45235	45230	47500	47550	50100	50105

From: $19.11–53.15

FMJ Bullets

Caliber & Description	9mm RN-ENC	9mm FP-ENC	9mm RN-ENC	45 SWC-ENC	45 CT-ENC	45 RN-ENC	45 FP-ENC
Diameter, Inches	.355	.355	.355	.451	.451	.451	.451
Weight, Grains	115	124	124	185	200	230	230
Catalog Number	35557	35567	35577	45137	45157	45177	45187

From: $20.65–29.37

HAP Bullets

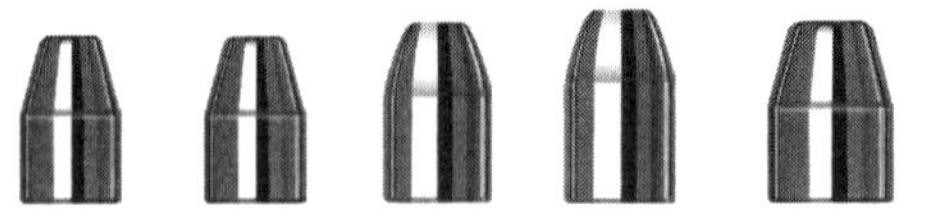

Caliber & Description	9mm	9mm	10mm	10mm	45
Diameter, Inches	.356	.356	.400	.400	.451
Weight, Grains	121	125	180	200	230
Catalog Number	35530B	35572B	40042B	40061B	45161B

From: $345–510

LEGEND

- **B** – Bulk
- **BT** – Boattail
- **C/T** – Combat Target
- **CL** – Crimp Lock™
- **ENC** – Encapsulated
- **FMJ** – Full Metal Jacket
- **FP** – Flat Point
- **HBWC** – Hollow Base Wadcutter
- **HP** – Hollow Point
- **HM** – Heavy Magnum™
- **I** – InterLock™ Bullet
- **IB** – InterBond™ Bullet
- **JFP** – Jacketed Flat Point
- **L** – Swaged Lead Bullet
- **LM** – Light Magnum™
- **LRN** – Lead Round Nose
- **w/Moly** – Moly-Coated
- **RN** – Round Nose
- **SIL** – Silhouette
- **SJ** – Short Jacket
- **SP** – Spire Point
- **SST** – Super Shock Tipped™
- **SSP** – Single Shot Pistol
- **SWC** – Semi-Wadcutter
- **SX** – Super Explosive
- **VX** – Varmint Express™
- **XTP** – Extreme Terminal Performance™
- **+P** – Plus Pressure

Frontier/ Lead Bullets

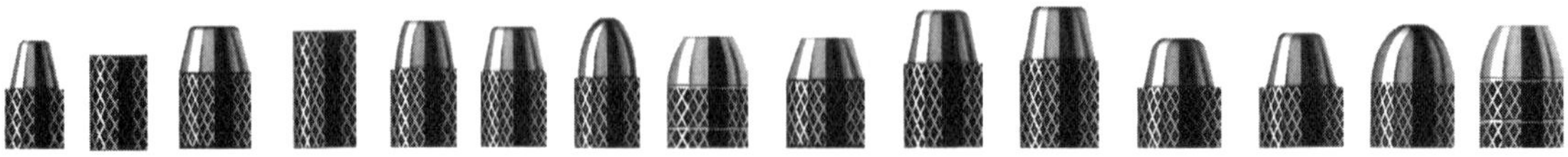

Caliber & Description	32 SWC	32 HBWC	38 FP Cowboy	38 HBWC	38 SWC	38 HP-SWC	38 LRN	44 FP Cowboy	44 FP Cowboy	44 SWC	44 HP-SWC	45 SWC	45 L-C/T	45 LRN	45 FP Cowboy
Diameter, Inches	.314	.314	.358	.358	.358	.358	.358	.427	.430	.430	.430	.452	.452	.452	.454
Weight, Grains	90	90	140	148	158	158	158	205	180	240	240	200	200	230	255
Catalog Number	10008	10028	10078	10208	10408	10428	10508	11208	11058	11108	11118	12108	12208	12308	12458

From: $29.73–47.01

Lapua Bullets

Lapua precision bullets are made from the best raw materials and meet the toughest precision specifications. Each bullet is subject to visual inspection and tested with advanced measurement devices.

D46
The D46 bullet is manufactured to the strictest tolerances for concentricity and uniformity of shape and weight.
From: $34.99–305.59

D166
The Lapua's unique D166 construction has remained the same since the late 1930s: superb accurate FMJBT bullet for 7.62x53R and 7.62x54R cartridges.
From: $44.00

FMJ SPITZER
The FMJ S is exceptionally accurate. Ten rounds (S374 in .308 Win) from 100 meters easily achieve groupings less than 30 mm.
From: $25.99–244.99

HOLLOW POINT
This HPCE bullet cuts a clean and easily distinguishable hole in your target. With ten rounds (G477 in .308 Win) fired at 100 meters, this bullet typically achieves groupings of under 25 mm— sometimes even less than 15 mm.
From: $25.59–220.59

LOCK BASE
The construction of the Lock Base bullet makes it possible to use maximum pressures and achieve higher velocities without damaging the base of the bullet. FMJBT configuration reduces drag and provides a flatter trajectory.
From: $34.59–301.59

MEGA
Mega is a soft-point bullet with a protective copper jacket with quadruple expansion on impact, which causes rapid energy transfer. Mega's lead alloy core achieves up to 97% weight retention.
From: $33.99–34.99

SCENAR
The Scenar hollow-point, boat-tail bullet provides low drag and a superb ballistic coefficient. These bullets deliver superb performance at long ranges and benchrest shooting. All Scenar bullets are also available in a coated Silver Jacket version.
From: $32.50–316.59

D46

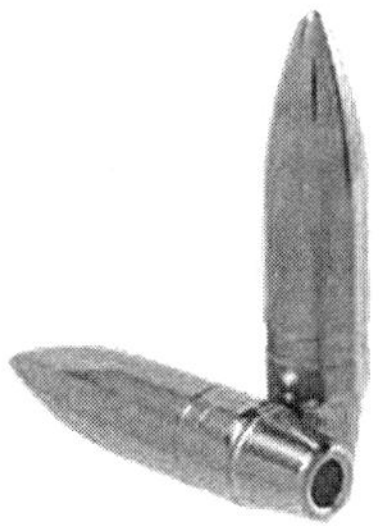
D166

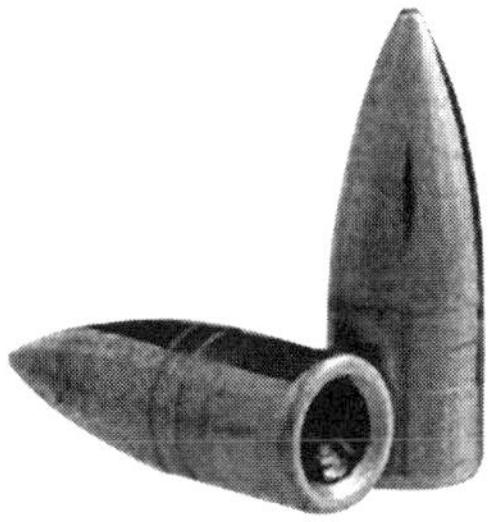
FMJ S

HOLLOW POINT

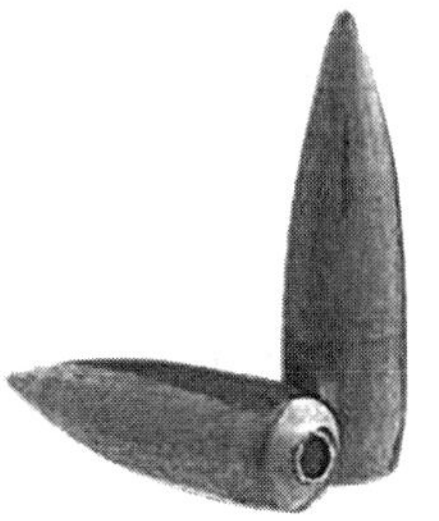
LOCK BASE

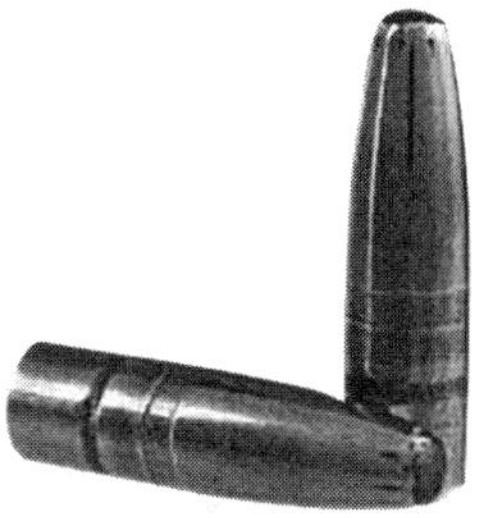
MEGA

SCENAR

Nosler Bullets

30-CALIBER, 168-GRAIN BALLISTIC TIP

Nosler has added a 30-caliber, 168-grain Ballistic Tip bullet to its lineup for deer and antelope hunters. The bullet's polycarbonate tip resists deformation in the magazine and initiates expansion upon impact. The fully tapered jacket and special lead alloy core allows controlled expansion and optimum weight retention at all practical velocity levels. A heavy jacket base acts as a platform for a large diameter mushroom. The Ballistic Tip is a ballistically engineered Solid Base boat tail configuration that combines with the streamlined polycarbonate tip for long-range performance in the popular .30 caliber hunting cartridge. Color-coded by caliber, the green polycarbonate tip is nestled in the jacket mouth and streamlined. The heavy jacketed base prevents bullet deformation during firing.

MSRP: . . . . $21 (per box of 50)

30 CAL BALLISTIC TIP

.458 PARTITION

Nosler now offers the largest Partition bullet to date. Designed for .458 Winchester Magnum and .460 Weatherby Magnum, the .458 Partition is ideal for dangerous game like Cape buffalo. It provides excellent accuracy, controlled expansion and weight retention. When the front lead is released it causes tissue damage by fragmentation, while the mushroomed bullet penetrates enough to exit the animal or stop under the skin on the off-side hide.

MSRP: . . . . $110 (per box of 25)

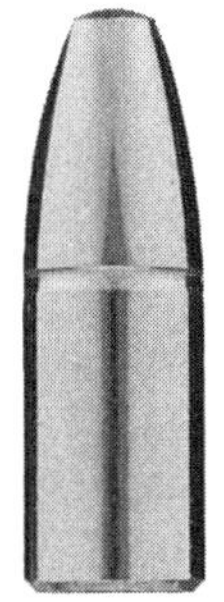

.458 PARTITION

E-TIP

The Nosler E-Tip is a lead-free bullet built on a highly concentric gilding metal frame. The polycarbonate tip prevents deformation in the magazine, boosts aerodynamic efficiency, and initiates expansion. Nosler's exclusive Energy Expansion Cavity allows for immediate and uniform expansion

yet retains 95%+ weight for improved penetration. E-Tip also features a precisely formed boat tail that serves to reduce drag and provides a more efficient flight profile for higher retained energy at long range. The E-Tip's alloy provides less fouling. Available in 30 cal. 180-grain and 150-grain.

MSRP: . . . . . $29–36 (per box of 50)

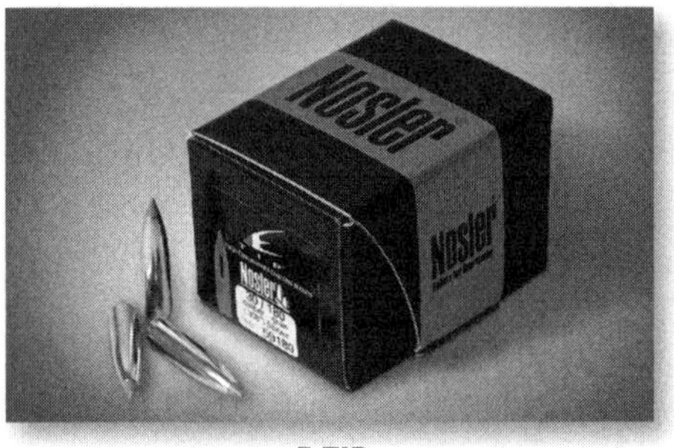

E-TIP

SOLIDS

Nosler Solid Bullets feature a unique design and homogenous lead-free alloy construction to provide an impressively straight wound channel. Engineered with multiple seating grooves, Solids provide optimal load versatility with minimal fouling. Nosler Solids are designed to match the ballistic performance of the Nosler Partition bullets in the same caliber and weight, resulting in near identical points of impact for both bullets at typical hunting ranges. For dangerous game, hunters can use a Partition load on the first shot, followed by Solids and have confidence in shot placement and bullet performance. Available in .375 cal. (260 and 300 gr.), .416 cal. (400 gr.) and .458 (500 gr.).

MSRP: . . . . . $60–76 (per box of 25)

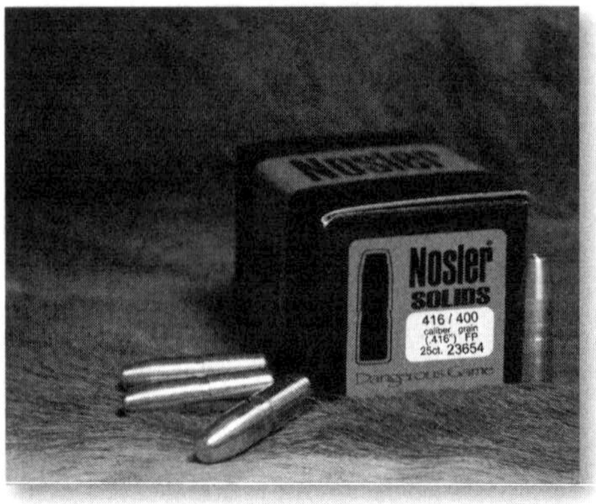

SOLIDS

Nosler Bullets

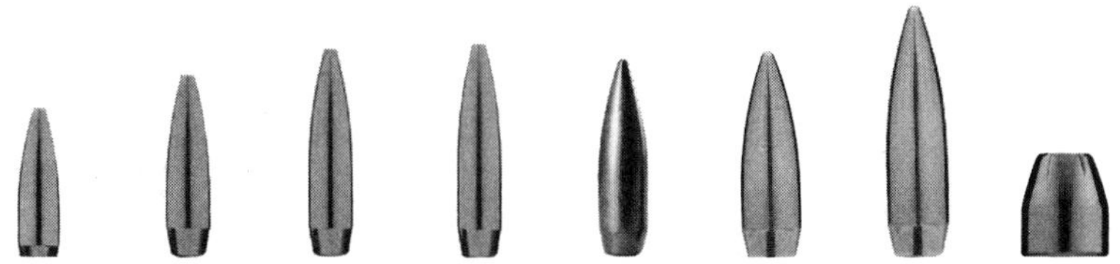

Custom Competition

Caliber & Description	22 HPBT	22 HPBT	22 HPBT	22 HPBT	6.5mm HPBT	30 HPBT	30 HPBT	45 JHP
Diameter, Inches	.220	.224	.224	.224	.264	.308	.308	.451
Weight, Grains	52	69	77	80	140	155	168	185
Density	.148	.196	.219	.228	.287	233	.253	.130
Ballistic Coefficient	.220	.305	.340	.415	.529	.450	.462	.142
Catalog Number	53294	17101 53065	22421 53064	25116 53080	26725	53155 53169	53164 53168	44847

From: $22.00–51.50

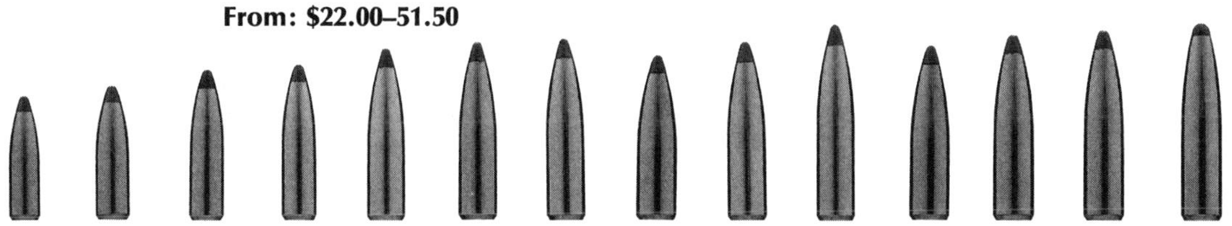

Partition

Caliber& Description	22 S	6mm S	6mm S	6mm S	25 S	25 S	25 S	6.5mm S	6.5mm S	6.5mm S	270 S	270 S	270 S	270 SS
Diameter, Inches	.220	.243	.243	.243	.257	.257	.257	.264	.264	.264	.277	.277	.277	.277
Weight, Grains	60	85	95	100	100	115	20	100	125	140	130	140	150	160
Density	.171	.206	.230	.242	.216	.249	.260	.205	.256	.287	.242	.261	.279	.298
Ballistic Coefficient	.228	.315	.365	.384	.377	.389	.391	.326	.449	.490	.416	.432	.465	.434
Catalog Number	16316	16314	16315	35642	16317	16318	35643	16319	16320	16321	16322	35200	16323	16324

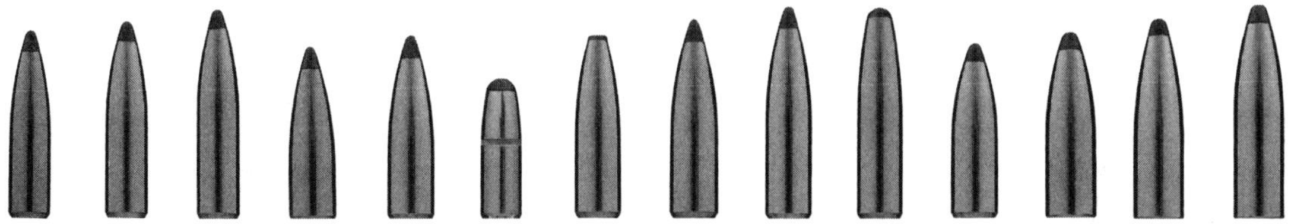

Caliber & Description	7mm S	7mm S	7mm S	30 S	30 S	30 RN	30 PP	30 S	30 S	30 SS	8mm S	338 S	338 S	338 S
Diameter, Inches	.284	.285	.284	.308	.308	.308	.308	.308	.308	.308	.323	.338	.338	.338
Weight, Grains	150	160	175	150	165	170	180	180	200	220	200	210	225	250
Density	.266	.283	.301	.226	.248	.256	.271	.271	.301	.331	.274	.263	.281	.313
Ballistic Coefficient	.456	.475	.519	.387	.410	.252	.361	.474	.481	.351	.350	.400	.454	.473
Catalog Number	16326	16327	35645	16329	16330	16333	25396	16331	35626	16332	35277	16337	16336	35644

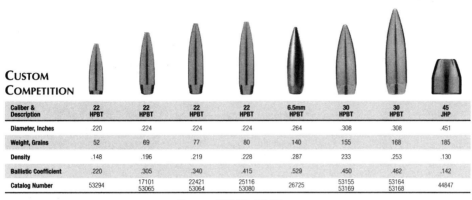

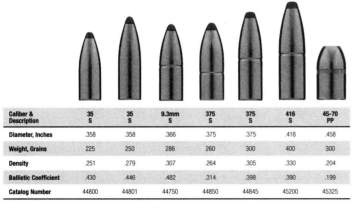

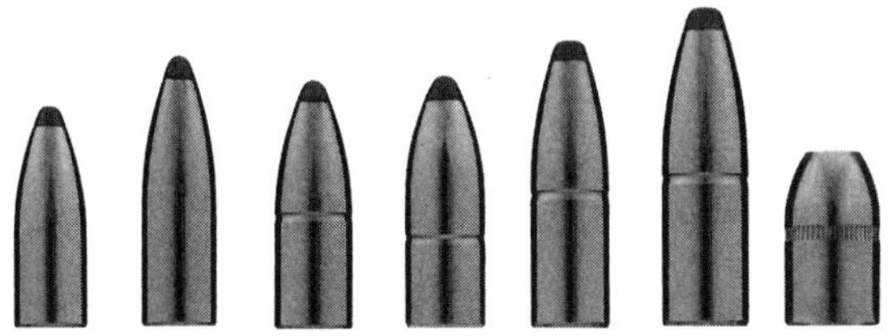

Caliber & Description	35 S	35 S	9.3mm S	375 S	375 S	416 S	45-70 PP
Diameter, Inches	.358	.358	.366	.375	.375	.416	.458
Weight, Grains	225	250	286	260	300	400	300
Density	.251	.279	.307	.264	.305	.330	.204
Ballistic Coefficient	.430	.446	.482	.314	.398	.390	.199
Catalog Number	44800	44801	44750	44850	44845	45200	45325

From: $23.40–80.60

LEGEND

Type of Bullet
- **BT** – Boat Tail
- **HP** – Hollow Point
- **J** – Jacketed
- **PP** – Protected Point
- **RN** – Round Nose
- **S** – Spitzer
- **SS** – Semi Spitzer
- **W** – Whelen

Type of Tip
- **PT** – Purple Tip
- **BT** – Blue Tip
- **BrT** – Brown Tip
- **BuT** – Buckskin Tip
- **GT** – Green Tip
- **GuT** – Gunmetal Tip
- **MT** – Maroon Tip
- **OT** – Olive Tip
- **RT** – Red Tip
- **SLT** – Soft Lead Tip
- **YT** – Yellow Tip

Nosler Bullets

Ballistic Tip Hunting

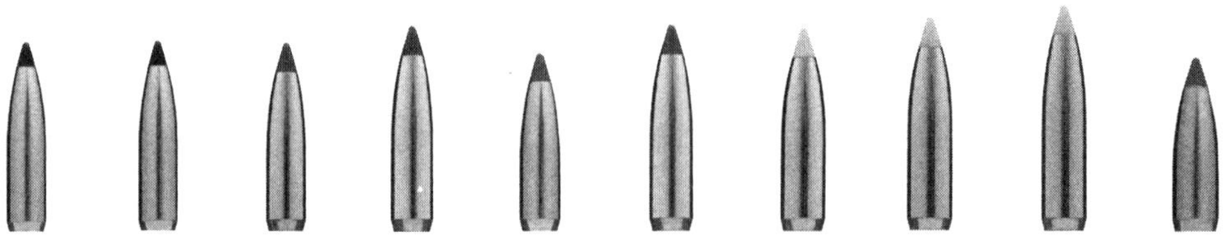

Caliber & Description	6mm SPT	6mm SPT	25 SBT	25 SBT	6.5mm SBrT	6.5mm SBrT	270 SYT	270 SYT	270 SYT	7mm SRT
Diameter, inches	.243	.243	.257	.257	.264	.264	.277	.277	.284	.284
Weight, Grains	90	95	100	115	100	120	130	140	150	120
Density	.218	.230	.216	.249	.205	.246	.242	.261	.279	.213
Ballistic Coefficient	.365	.379	.393	.453	.350	.458	.433	.456	.496	.417
Catalog Number	24090	24095	25100	25115	26100	26120	27130	27140	27150	28120

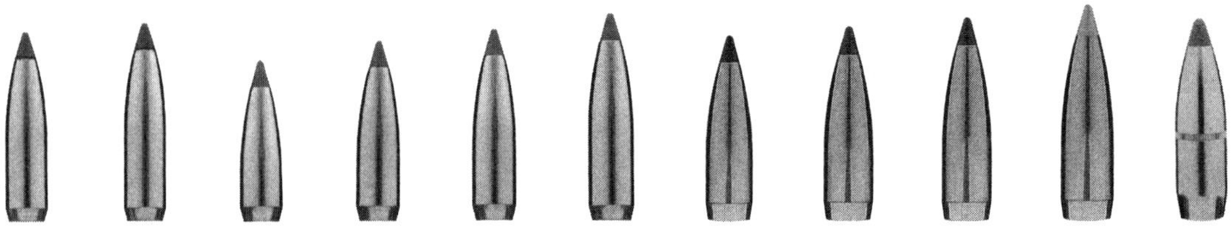

Caliber & Description	7mm SRT	7mm SRT	30 SRT	30 SRT	30 SRT	30 SRT	8mm SGuT	338 SMT	338 SMT	35 WBu	9.3mm SOT
Diameter, inches	.284	.284	.308	.308	.308	.308	.323	.338	.338	.358	.366
Weight, Grains	140	150	125	150	165	180	180	180	200	225	250
.248	.248	.266	.188	.226	.248	.271	.247	.225	.250	.251	.267
Ballistic Coefficient	.485	.493	.366	.435	.475	.507	.357	.372	.414	.421	.494
Catalog Number	28140	28150	30125	30150	30165	30180	32180	33180	33200	35225	36250

From: $15.10–20.50

Ballistic Tip Varmint

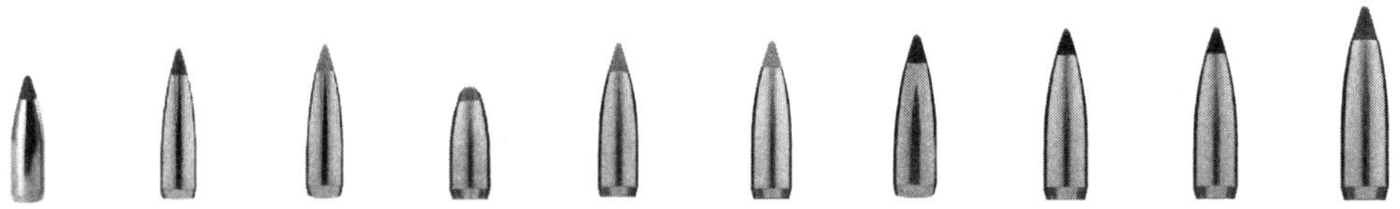

Caliber & Description	20 SRT	22 SOT	22 SOT	22 SOT	22 SOT	22 SOT	6mm SPT	6mm SPT	6mm SPT	25 SBT
Diameter, inches	.204	.224	.224	.227	.224	.224	.243	.243	.243	.257
Weight, Grains	32	40	40	45	50	55	55	70	80	85
Density	.110	.137	.114	.128	.142	.157	.133	.169	.194	.183
Ballistic Coefficient	.206	.239	.221	.144	.238	.267	.276	.310	.329	.329
Catalog Number	35216	52111	39510 39555	35487	39522 39557	39526 39560	24055 39565	39532 39570	24080	43004

From: $20.20–27.30

CT Ballistic Silvertip Hunting

Caliber & Description	6mm S	25 S	25 S	270 S	270 S	7mm S	7mm S	30 S	30 S	30 S	338 S
Diameter, inches	.243	.257	.257	.277	.277	.284	.284	.308	.308	.308	.338
Weight, Grains	95	85	115	130	150	140	150	150	168	180	200
Density	.230	.183	.249	.242	.279	.248	.266	.226	.253	.271	.250
Ballistic Coefficient	.379	.329	.453	.433	.496	.485	.493	.435	.490	.507	.414
Catalog Number	51040	51045	51050	51075	51100	51105	51110	51150	51160	51170	51200

From: $17.60–26.80

Nosler Bullets

HANDLOADING

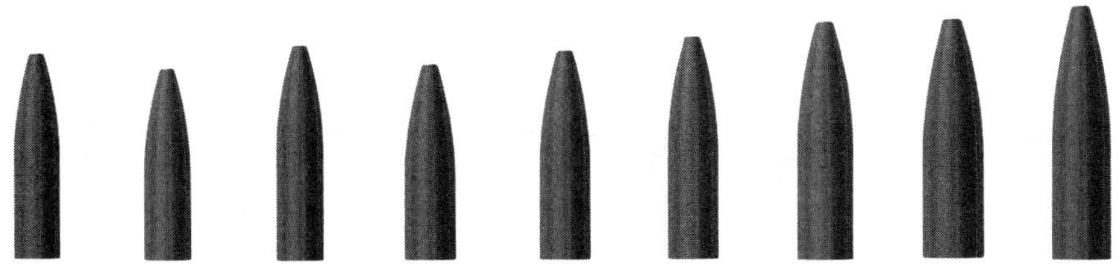

CT Fail Safe

Caliber & Description	270 SHP	7mm SHP	7mm SHP	30 SHP	30 SHP	30 SHP	338 SHP	375 SHP	375 SHP
Diameter, inches	.277	.284	.284	.308	.308	.308	.338	.375	.375
Weight, Grains	140	140	160	150	165	180	230	270	300
Density	.261	.248	.283	.266	.248	.271	.288	.274	.305
Ballistic Coefficient	.322	.323	.382	.310	.314	.391	.436	.393	.441
Catalog Number	53140	53150	53160	53170	53175	53180	53230	53350	53360

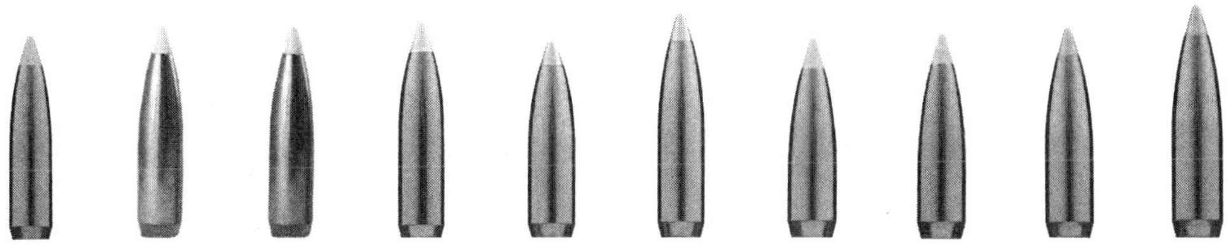

Accubond

Caliber & Description	25 SWT	6.5mm SWT	270 SWT	270 SWT	7mm SWT	7mm SWT	30 SWT	30 SWT	30 SWT	30 SWT
Diameter, inches	.257	.264	.277	.277	.284	.284	.308	.308	.308	.308
Weight, Grains	110	130	130	140	140	160	150	165	180	200
Density	.238	.266	.242	.261	.248	.283	.226	.248	.271	.301
Ballistic Coefficient	.418	.488	.435	.496	.485	.531	.435	.475	.507	.588
Catalog Number	53742	56902	54987	54765	59992	54932	56719	55602	54825	54618

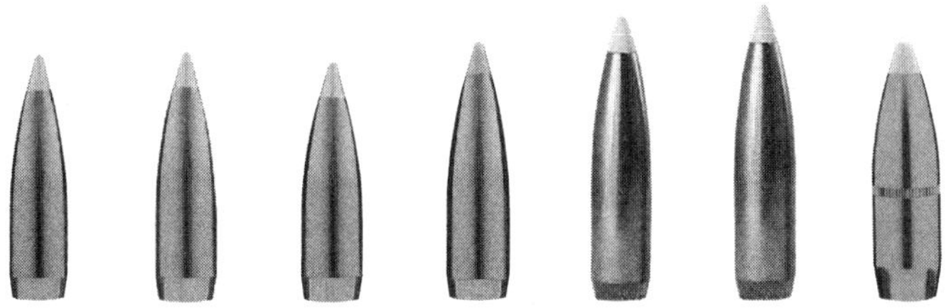

Caliber & Description	8mm SWT	338 SWT	338 SWT	338 SWT	35 SWT	9.3mm SWT	357 SWT
Diameter, inches	.323	.338	.338	.338	.358	.366	.375
Weight, Grains	200	180	200	225	225	250	260
Density	.274	.225	.250	.281	.251	.267	.264
Ballistic Coefficient	.379	.372	.414	.550	.423	.496	.473
Catalog Number	54374	57625	56382	54357	50712	59756	54413

From: $25.10–46.30

LEGEND

Type of Bullet
- **BT** – Boat Tail
- **HP** – Hollow Point
- **J** – Jacketed
- **PP** – Protected Point
- **RN** – Round Nose
- **S** – Spitzer
- **SS** – Semi Spitzer
- **W** – Whelen

Type of Tip
- **PT** – Purple Tip
- **BT** – Blue Tip
- **BrT** – Brown Tip
- **BuT** – Buckskin Tip
- **GT** – Green Tip
- **GuT** – Gunmetal Tip
- **MT** – Maroon Tip
- **OT** – Olive Tip
- **RT** – Red Tip
- **SLT** – Soft Lead Tip
- **YT** – Yellow Tip

Nosler Bullets

HANDGUN BULLETS

SPORTING HANDGUN

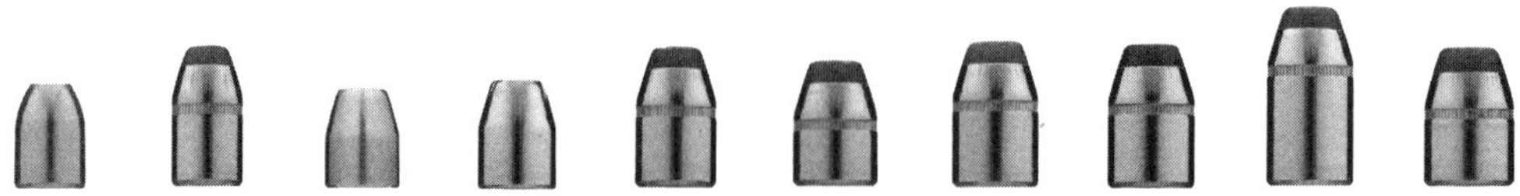

Caliber & Description	9mm JHP	38 JHP	10mm JHP	10mm JHP	41 JHP	44 JHP	44 JHP	44 JHP	44 JHP	44 Colt JHP
Diameter, Inches	.355	.357	.400	.400	.410	.429	.429	.429	.429	.451
Weight, Grains	115	158	135	150	210	200	240	240	300	250
Density	.130	.177	.121	.134	.178	.155	.186	.186	.233	.176
Ballistic Coefficient	.109	.182	.093	.106	.170	.151	.173	.177	.206	.177
Catalog Number	44848	44841	44852	44860	43012	44846	44842	44868	42069	43013

From: $40.30–49.40

Sierra Bullets

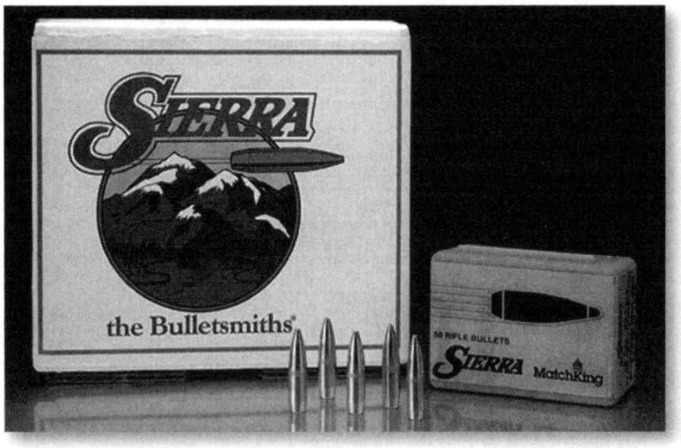

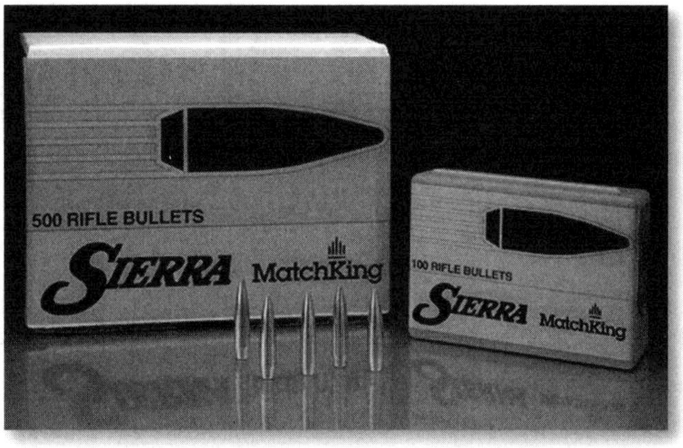

.22 CAL., 77 GR. HPBT MATCHKING CANNELURED

Sierra now offers its .22 caliber, 77 grain HPBT MatchKing in a cannelured version for the civilian market. Due to the fact that the 77-grain bullet is the heaviest magazine length tolerant .22 caliber bullet Sierra makes, it is a big favorite with the AR crowd. For years, many have requested a cannelured version for civilian use.

Cannelured: . . . $18 (per box of 50)
. . . . $137 (per box of 500)

6MM 95 GR. HPBT MATCHKING

Sierra's 6mm, 95 grain HPBT bullet was designed to fill the need for a lighter weight alternative to the Sierra 6mm 107 MatchKing. The bullet is built off the 6mm 107 HPBT MatchKing design with a long ogive, small meplat and improved boat tail to preserve downrange efficiency, enhance accuracy and reduce wind-drift. Sierra recommends a 9 in. twist rate or faster.

Matchking: . . . $30 (per box of 100)
. . . . $140–170 (per box of 500)

GAMEKING

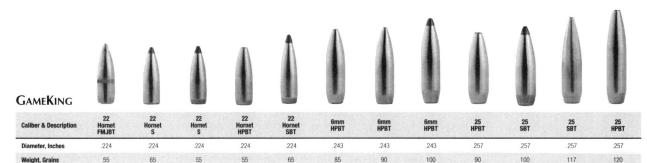

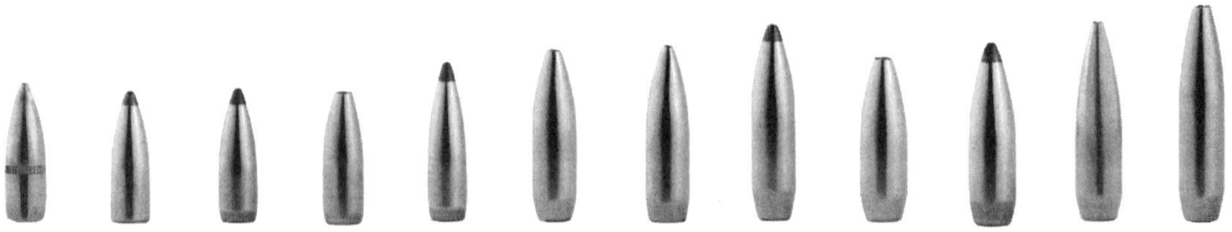

Caliber & Description	22 Hornet FMJBT	22 Hornet S	22 Hornet S	22 Hornet HPBT	22 Hornet SBT	6mm HPBT	6mm HPBT	6mm HPBT	25 HPBT	25 SBT	25 SBT	25 HPBT
Diameter, Inches	.224	.224	.224	.224	.224	.243	.243	.243	.257	.257	.257	.257
Weight, Grains	55	65	55	55	65	85	90	100	90	100	117	120
Catalog Number	1355	1395	1365	1390	1395	1530	1535	1560	1615	1625	1630	1650

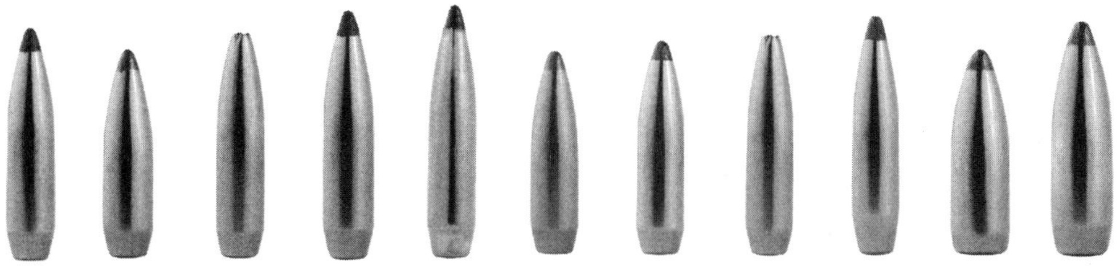

Caliber & Description	6.5mm SBT	270 SBT	270 SBT	270 SBT	270 SBT	7mm SBT	7mm SBT	7mm HPBT	7mm SBT	7mm SBT	7mm SBT
Diameter, Inches	.264	.270	.270	.270	.270	.284	.284	.284	.284	.284	.284
Weight, Grains	140	130	140	140	150	150	160	160	175	250	300
Catalog Number	1730	1820	1835	1845	1840	1913	1920	1925	1940	2950	3000

GameKing (cont.)

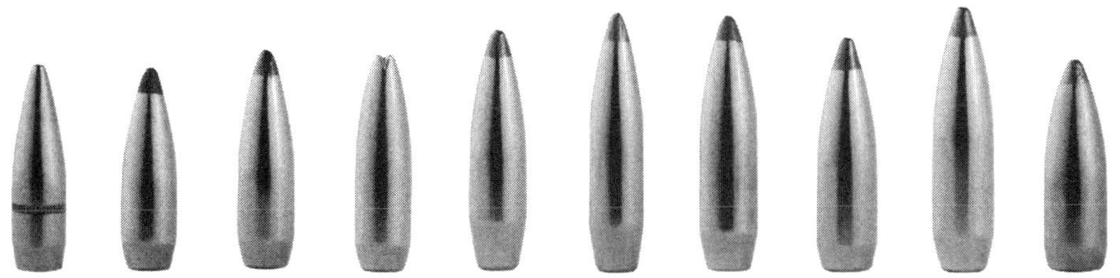

Caliber & Description	30 FMJBT	30 SBT	30 SBT	30 HPBT	30 SBT	30 SBT	8mm SBT	.338 SBT	.338 SBT	.35 SBT
Diameter, Inches	.308	.308	.308	.308	.308	.308	.323	.338	.338	.358
Weight, Grains	150	150	165	165	180	200	220	215	250	225
Catalog Number	2115	2125	2145	2140	2160	2165	2420	2610	2600	2850

From: $19.29–22.77

MatchKing

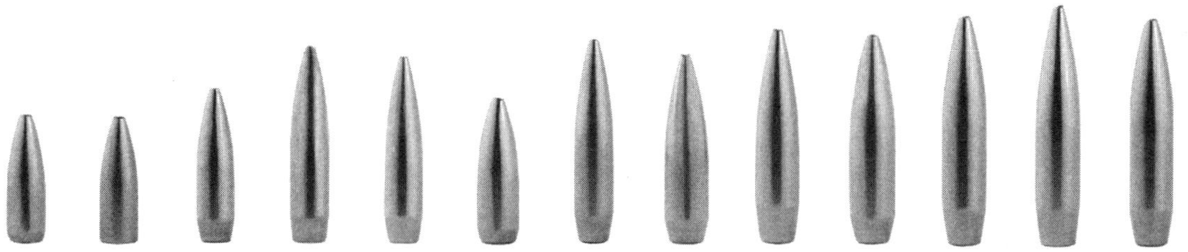

Caliber & Description	22 Hornet HPBT	22 Hornet HP	22 HPBT	22 LRHPBT	22 LRHPBT	6mm HPBT	6mm HPBT	25 HPBT	6.5mm HPBT	6.5mm HPBT	6.5mm HPBT	6.5mm HPBT	270 HPBT
Diameter, Inches	.224	.224	.224	.224	.224	.243	.243	.257	.264	.264	.264	.264	.277
Weight, Grains	52	53	69	77	80	70	107	100	107	120	140	142	135
Catalog Number	1410	53	1380	9377	9390	1570	1628	1715	1725	1740	1742	1833	

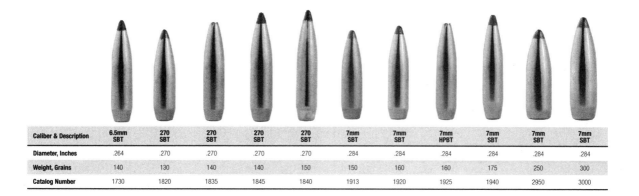

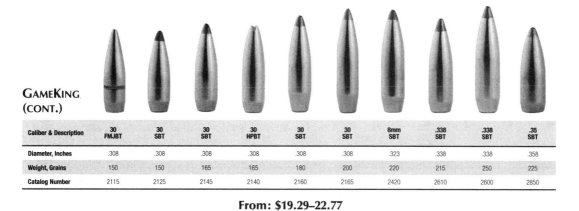

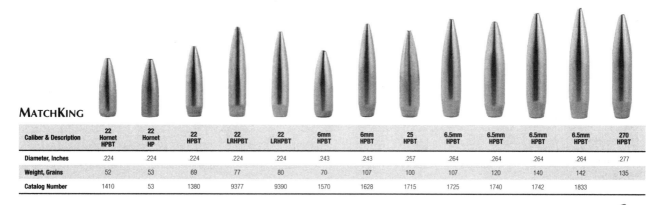

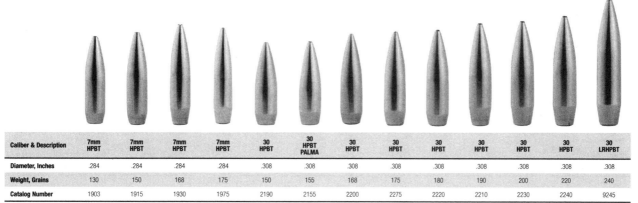

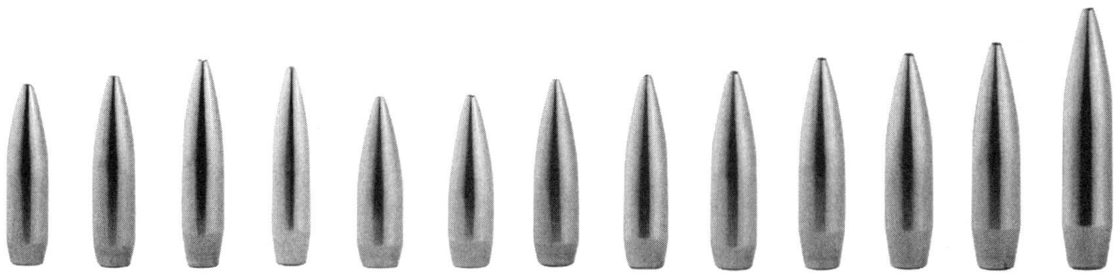

Caliber & Description	7mm HPBT	7mm HPBT	7mm HPBT	7mm HPBT	30 HPBT	30 HPBT PALMA	30 HPBT	30 HPBT	30 HPBT	30 HPBT	30 HPBT	30 HPBT	30 LRHPBT
Diameter, Inches	.284	.284	.284	.284	.308	.308	.308	.308	.308	.308	.308	.308	.308
Weight, Grains	130	150	168	175	150	155	168	175	180	190	200	220	240
Catalog Number	1903	1915	1930	1975	2190	2155	2200	2275	2220	2210	2230	2240	9245

Sierra Bullets

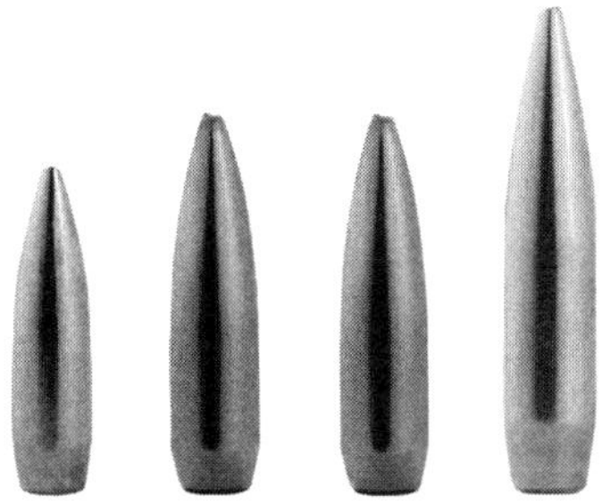

Caliber & Description	303 S	8mm HPBT	338 HBPT	338 LRHPBT
Diameter, Inches	.308	.308	.308	.308
Weight, Grains	174	200	200	300
Catalog Number	2315	2415	2145	9300

From: $21.03–37.09

LEGEND
BT – Boattail
FMJ – Full Metal Jacket
FN – Flat Nose
FPJ – Full Profile Jacket
HP – Hollow Point
JFP – Jacketed Flat Point
JHC – Jacketed Hollow Cavity
JHP – Jacketed Hollow Point
JSP – Jacketed Soft Point
RN – Round Nose
S – Spitzer
SMP – Semi-Pointed
SSP – Single Shot Pistol

HANDLOADING

Pro-Hunter

Caliber & Description	6mm S	25 S	25 S	6.5mm HP	270 S	270 S	7mm S	7mm S	7mm HPFN	30 (03-03) HPFN	30 (03-03) FNPJ	30 (03-03) FNPJ
Diameter, Inches	.243	.257	.257	.264	.277	.277	.284	.284	.284	.308	.308	.308
Weight, Grains	150	100	117	120	110	130	120	140	300	125	150	170
Catalog Number	1540	1620	1640	1720	1810	1830	1900	1910	8900	2020	2000	2010

Caliber & Description	30 RN	30 FMJ	30 S	30 S	30 RN	30 S	30 RN	30 RN
Diameter, Inches	.308	.308	.308	.308	.308	.308	.323	.338
Weight, Grains	110	110	125	150	150	180	180	220
Catalog Number	2100	2105	2120	2130	2135	2150	2170	2180

LEGEND
BT – Boattail
FMJ – Full Metal Jacket
FN – Flat Nose
FPJ – Full Profile Jacket
HP – Hollow Point
JFP – Jacketed Flat Point
JHC – Jacketed Hollow Cavity
JHP – Jacketed Hollow Point
JSP – Jacketed Soft Point
RN – Round Nose
S – Spitzer
SMP – Semi-Pointed
SSP – Single Shot Pistol

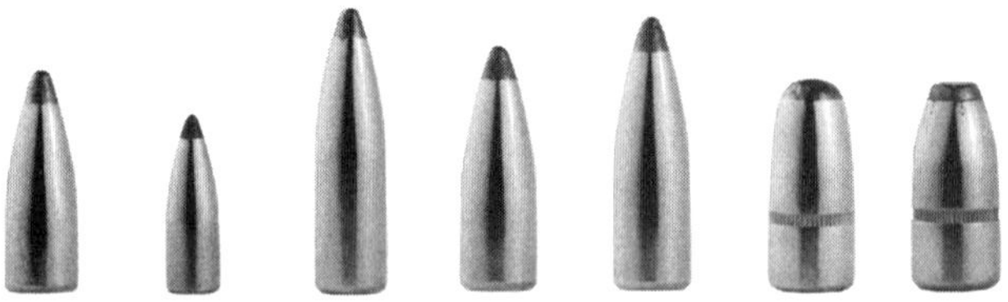

Caliber & Description	303 S	303 S	303 S	8mm S	8mm S	35 RN	375 FN
Diameter, Inches	.311	.311	.311	.323	.323	.358	.375
Weight, Grains	125	150	180	150	175	200	200
Catalog Number	2305	2300	2310	2400	2410	2800	2900

Varminter

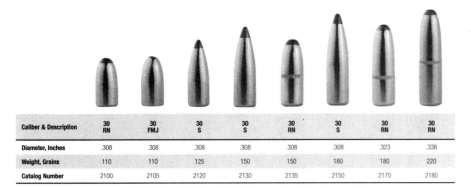

Caliber & Description	22 Hornet	22 Hornet	22 Hornet	22 Hornet
Diameter, Inches	.223	.223	.223	.223
Weight, Grains	40	45	40	45
Catalog Number	1100	1110	1200	1210

From: $24.53–33.38

HANDGUN BULLETS

Varminter (cont.)

Caliber & Description	22 Hornet HP	22 Hornet S	22 Hornet SMP	22 Hornet S	22 Hornet Blitz	22 Hornet SMP	22 Hornet HP	22 Hornet SMP	6mm HP	6mm HP	6mm Blitz	6mm S	.25 HP	.25 S	6.5mm HP	6.5mm HP	270 HP	7mm HP	30 HP
Diameter, Inches	.224	.224	.224	.224	.224	.224	.224	.224	.243	.243	.243	.257	.257	.264	.264	.264	.277	.284	.308
Weight, Grains	40	45	50	50	55	55	60	63	60	75	80	85	75	87	85	100	90	100	110
Catalog Number	1385	1310	1320	1330	1345	1350	1375	1370	1500	1510	1515	1520	1600	1610	1700	1710	1800	1895	2110

From: $17.52–26.54

Sports Master

Caliber & Description	30 RN	32 JHCPJ	9mm JHPPJ	9mm JHPPJ	9mm JHPPJ	38 Blitz JHCPJ	38 JSP	38 JHCPJ	38 JHCPJ	38 JSP	38 JHCPJ	38 JHCPJ
Diameter, Inches	.224	.224	.224	.224	.224	.243	.243	.257	.264	.264	.264	.264
Weight, Grains	52	53	69	77	80	70	107	100	107	120	140	142
Catalog Number	1410	53	1380	9377	9390	1570	1628	1715	1725	1740	1742	1833

Caliber & Description	10mm JHPPJ	10mm JHPPJ	10mm JHPPJ	10mm JHPPJ	41 JHCPC	41 JHCPC	44 JHCPJ	44 JHCPJ	44 JHCPJ	44 JSPPJ	45 JHPPJ	45 JHPPJ	45 JHCPJ	45 JSP	50 JHPPJ	50 JHPPJ
Diameter, Inches	.400	.400	.400	.400	.410	.410	.4295	.4295	.4295	.4295	.4515	.4515	.4515	.4515	.5000	.5000
Weight, Grains	135	150	165	180	170	210	180	210	240	300	185	230	240	300	350	400
Catalog Number	8425	8430	8445	8460	8500	8520	8600	8620	8610	8630	8800	8805	8820	8830	5350	5400

From: $20.29–34.65

BlitzKing

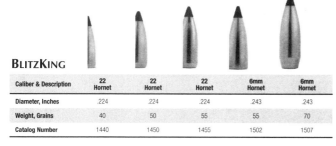

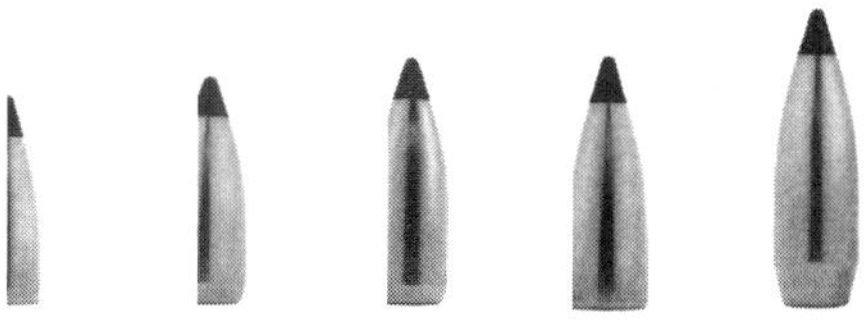

Caliber & Description	22 Hornet	22 Hornet	22 Hornet	6mm Hornet	6mm Hornet
Diameter, Inches	.224	.224	.224	.243	.243
Weight, Grains	40	50	55	55	70
Catalog Number	1440	1450	1455	1502	1507

From: $22.80–26.29

LEGEND
BT – Boattail
FMJ – Full Metal Jacket
FN – Flat Nose
FPJ – Full Profile Jacket
HP – Hollow Point
JFP – Jacketed Flat Point
JHC – Jacketed Hollow Cavity
JHP – Jacketed Hollow Point
JSP – Jacketed Soft Point
RN – Round Nose
S – Spitzer
SMP – Semi-Pointed
SSP – Single Shot Pistol

Speer Bullets

Boat Tail Bullets

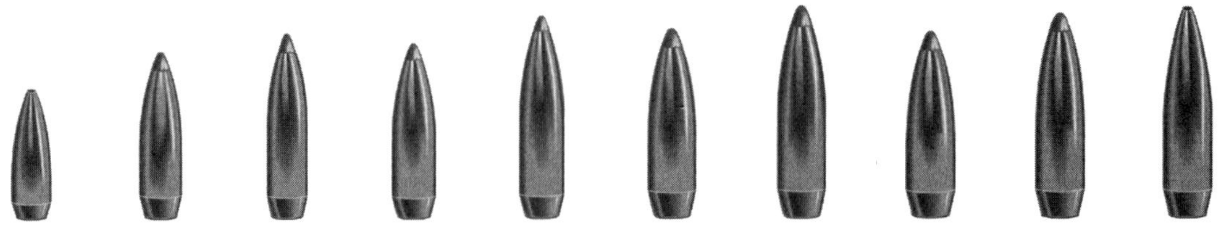

Caliber & Description	22 Match* HP	6mm SSP	6mm S SP	25 SHP	25 SSP	270 SSP	270 SSP	7mm SSP	7mm SSP	7mm Match* HP
Diameter, Inches	.224	.243	.243	.257	.257	.277	.277	.284	.284	.284
Weight, Grains	52	85	100	100	120	130	150	130	145	145
Ballistic Coefficient	.230	.380	.446	.393	.480	.412	.489	.424	.472	.468
Catalog Number	1036	1213	1220	1408	1410	1458	1604	1624	1628	1631

*Match bullets are not recommended for use on game animals.

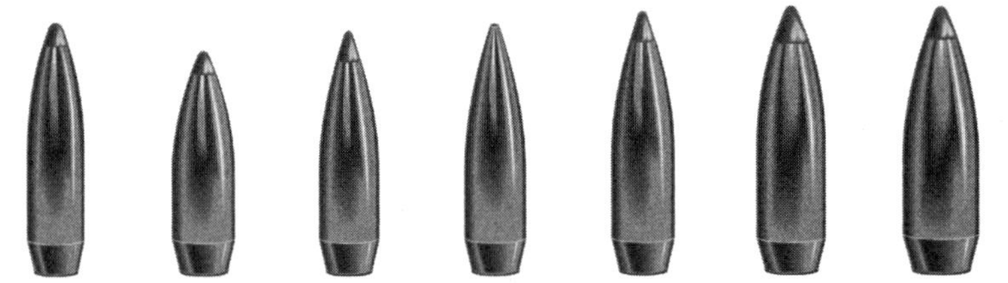

Caliber & Description	7mm SSP	30 SSP	30 SSP	30 Match* HP	30 SSP	338 SSP	375 SSP
Diameter, Inches	.284	.308	.308	.308	.308	.338	.375
Weight, Grains	160	150	165	168	180	225	270
Ballistic Coefficient	.519	.417	.520	.534	.545	.497	.478
Catalog Number	1634	2022	2034	2040	2052	2406	2472

*Match bullets are not recommended for use on game animals.

From: $18.99–31.99

Grand Slam

Caliber & Description	6mm SP	25 HCSP	6.5mm HCSP	270 HCSP	270 HCSP	7mm HCSP	7mm HCSP	7mm HCSP	30 HCSP	30 HCSP
Diameter, Inches	.243	.257	.264	.277	.277	.284	.284	.284	.308	.308
Weight, grains	100	120	140	130	150	145	160	175	150	165
BC	.327	.356	.385	.332	.378	.353	.389	.436	.295	.354
Part Number	1222	1415	1444	1465	1608	1632	1638	1643	2026	2038

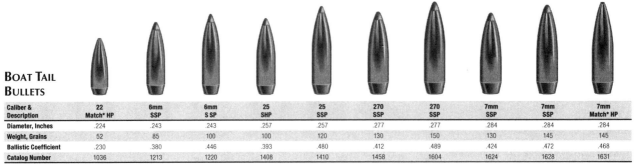

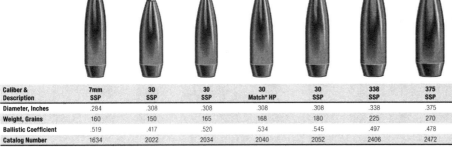

Caliber & Description	30 HCSP	30 HCSP	30 HCSP	30 HCSP	30 HCSP	30 HCSP
Diameter, Inches	.308	.308	.338	.338	.358	.375
Weight, grains	180	200	225	250	250	285
BC	.374	.453	.382	.436	.353	.354
Part Number	2063	2212	2407	2408	2455	2473

From: $23.99–53.99

Speer Bullets

Hot-Cor Bullets*

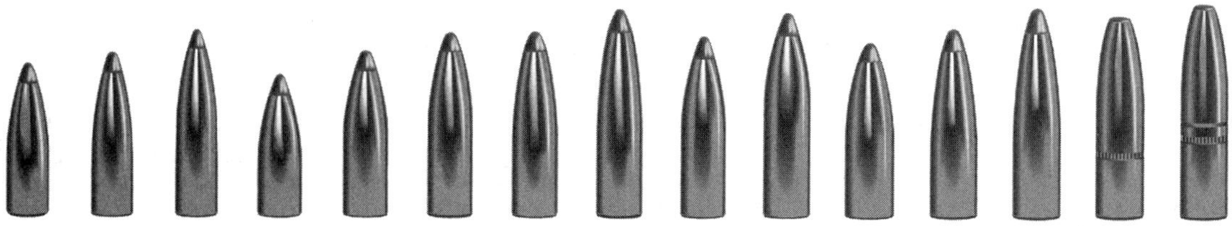

Caliber & Description	6mm SSP	6mm SSP	6mm SSP	25 SSP	25 SSP	25 SSP	6.5mm SSP	6.5mm SSP	270 SSP	270 SSP	7mm SSP	7mm SSP	7mm S SP	7mm Mag-Tip™ SP	7mm Mag-Tip™ SP
Diameter, Inches	.243	.243	.243	.257	.257	.257	.264	.264	.277	.277	.284	.284	.284	.284	.284
Weight, grains	80	90	105	87	100	120	120	140	130	150	130	145	160	160	175
BC	.325	.365	.424	.300	.334	.405	.392	.498	.383	.455	.368	.416	.504	.340	.382
Part Number	1211	1217	1229	1241	1405	1411	1435	1441	1459	1605	1623	1629	1635	1637	1641
Bullets/box	100	100	100	100	100	100	100	100	100	100	100	100	100	100	100
Bullet Construction	HC	HC	HC	HC	HC	HC	HC	HC	HC	HC	HC	HC	HC	HC	HC

** Not recommended for lever-action rifles.*

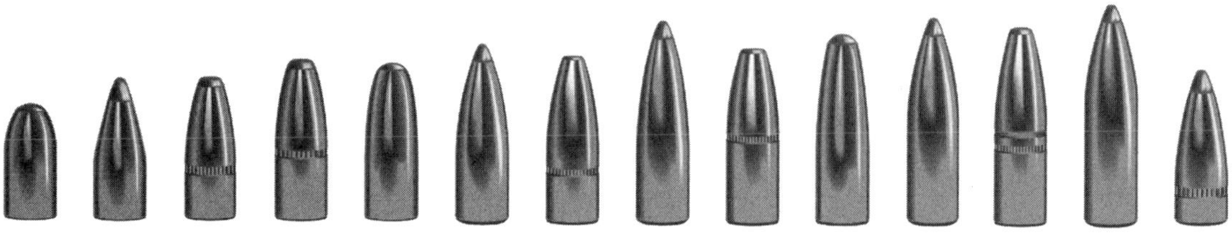

Caliber & Description	30 Carbine SP	30 Spire SP	30 FNSP	30 FNSP	30 RNSP	30 SSP	30 Mag-Tip™ SP	30 SSP	30 FNSP	30 RNSP	30 SSP	30 Mag-Tip™ SP	30 SSP	7.62x39 S SP
Diameter, Inches	.308	.308	.308	.308	.308	.308	.308	.308	.308	.308	.308	.308	.308	.310
Weight, Grains	110	110	130	150	150	150	150	165	170	180	180	180	200	123
Ballistic Coefficient	.136	.245	.213	.255	.235	.377	.278	.444	.298	.312	.441	.349	.478	.283
Catalog Number	1845	1855	2007	2011	2017	2023	2025	2035	2041	2047	2053	2059	2211	2213

** Not recommended for lever-action rifles.*

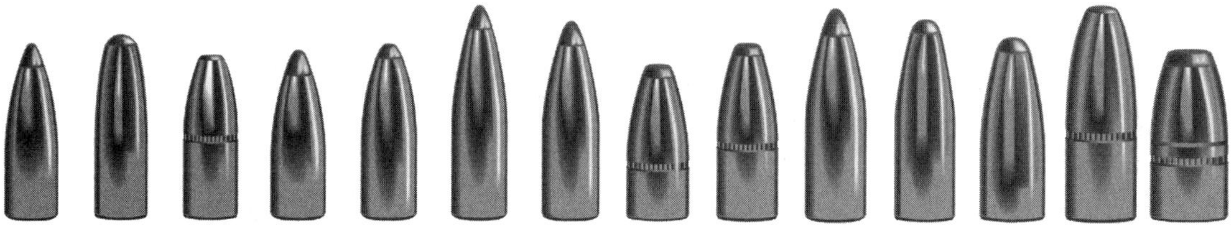

Caliber & Description	303 SSP	303 RNSP	32 Special FNSP	8mm SSP	8mm SSSP	8mm S SP	338 S SP	35 FNSP	35 FNSP	35 SSP	9.3mm SSSP	375 SSSP	416 Mag-Tip™ SP	45 FNSP
Diameter, Inches	.311	.311	.321	.323	.323	.323	.338	.358	.358	.358	.366	.375	.416	.458
Weight, Grains	150	180	170	150	170	200	200	180	220	250	270	235	350	350
Ballistic Coefficient	.351	.299	.236	.343	.311	.440	.426	.236	.296	.422	.361	.301	.332	.218
Catalog Number	2217	2223	2259	2277	2283	2285	2405	2435	2439	2453	2459	2471	2477	2478

From: $15.29–32.49

Jacketed Bullets

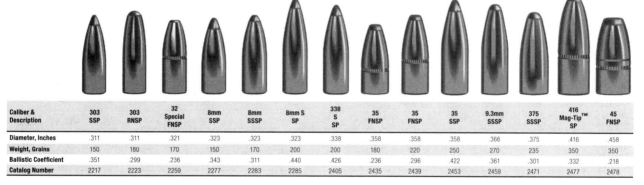

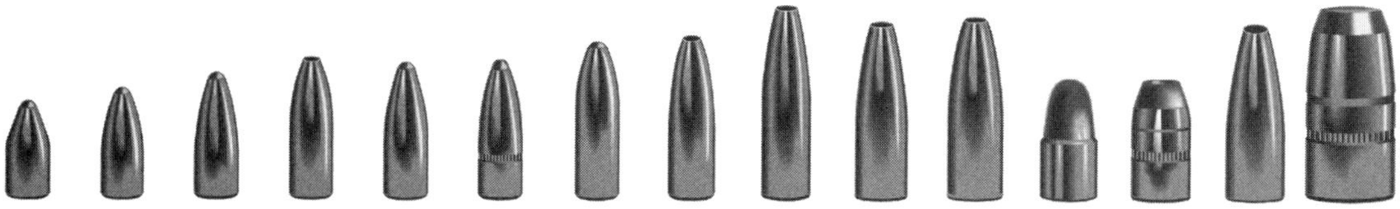

Caliber & Description	22 Spire SP	22 SSP	22 SSP	22 HP	22 SSP	22 SSP (cann)	22 SSSP	6mm HP	25 HP	270 HP	7mm HP	30 Plinker® SP	30 HP	30 HP	45 FNSP
Diameter, Inches	.224	.224	.224	.224	.224	.224	.224	.243	.257	.277	.284	.308	.308	.308	.458
Weight, Grains	40	45	50	52	55	55	70	75	100	100	115	100	110	130	400
Ballistic Coefficient	.144	.143	.207	.168	.212	.212	.219	.192	.263	.201	.250	.144	.128	.244	.259
Catalog Number	1017	1023	1029	1035	1047	1049	1053	1205	1407	1447	1617	1805	1835	2005	2479

From: $16.99–139.99

Speer Bullets

MHP Bullets

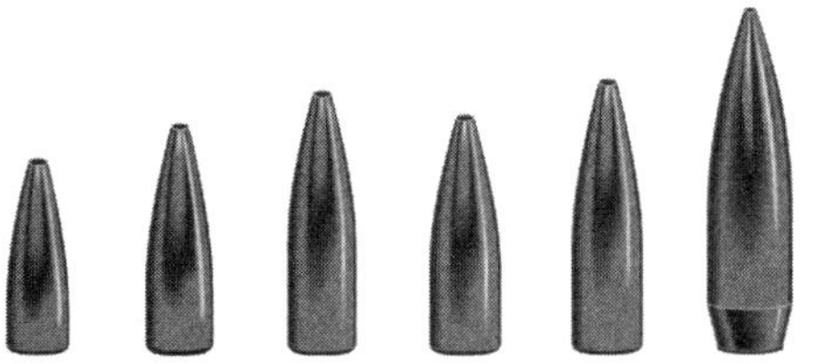

Caliber & Description	22 MH HP	6mm MHPHP	25 MHP HP	270 MHP HP	7mm MHPHP	30 MHP Match* BTHP
Diameter, Inches	.224	.243	.257	.277	.284	.308
Weight, grains	50	70	87	90	110	168
Ballistic Coefficient	.234	.296	.344	.310	.398	.541
Catalog Number	1031	1207	1247	1457	1615	2039

From: $18.99–31.49

TNT Bullets

Caliber & Description	22 Hornet TNT	22 TNT HP	22 TNT HP Hi-Vel.	6mm TNT HP	25 TNT HP	6.5mm TNT HP	270 TNT HP	7mm TNT HP	30 TNT HP
Diameter, Inches	.224	.224	.224	.243	.257	.264	.277	.284	.308
Weight, grains	33	50	55	70	87	90	90	110	125
Ballistic Coefficient	.080	.228	.233	.279	.337	.281	.303	.384	.341
Catalog Number	1014	1030	1032	1206	1246	1445	1446	1616	1986

From: $22.49–147.99

Special Purpose Bullets*

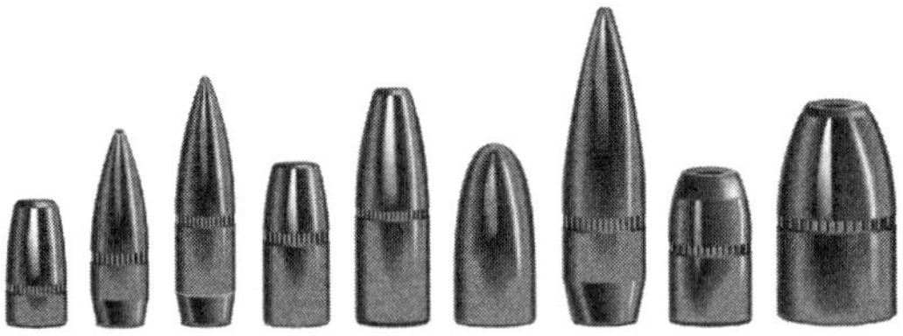

Caliber & Description	218 Bee FNSP	22 FMJ BT	22 FMJ BT	25-20 Win FNSP	7-30 Waters FNSP	30 Carbine TMJ	30 FMJ BT	32-20 Win FNHP	45 UCHP
Diameter, Inches	.224	.224	.224	.257	.284	.308	.308	.312	.458
Weight, grains	46	55	62	75	130	110	150	100	300
Ballistic Coefficient	.087	.269	.307	.135	.257	.179	.425	.167	.206
Catalog Number	1024	1044	1050	1237	1625	1846	2018	3981	2482

** Recommended for twist rates of 1 in 10" or faster.*

From: $16.98–28.89

Trophy Bonded Bear Claw

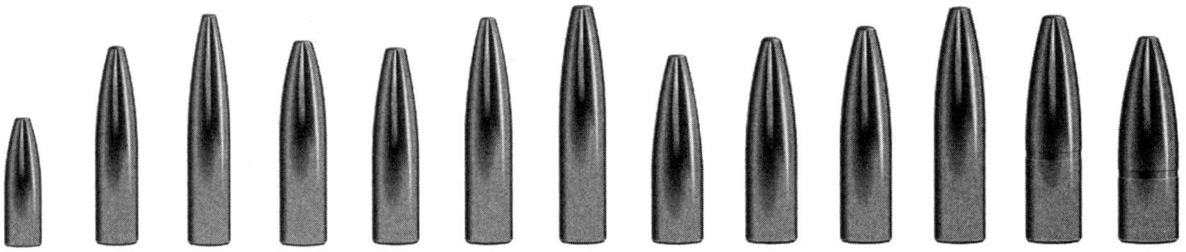

Caliber & Description	22	25	6.5mm	270	7mm	7mm	7mm	30	30	30	30	338	35 Whelen
Diameter, Inches	.224	.257	.264	.277	.284	.284	.284	.308	.308	.308	.308	.338	.358
Weight, Grains	55	115	140	140	140	160	175	150	165	180	200	225	225
Ballistic Coefficient	.201	.372	.405	.392	.360	.380	.400	.335	.342	.357	.392	.376	.350
Catalog Number	1725	1730	1735	1740	1745	1750	1755	1759	1760	1765	1770	1775	1777

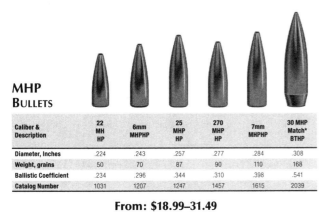

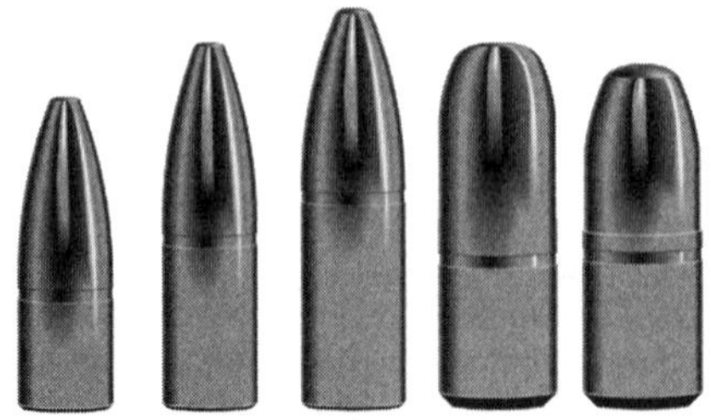

Caliber & Description	375 TBBC	375 TBBC	416 TBBC	458 TBBC	470 Nitro Express TBBC
Diameter, Inches	.375	.375	.416	.458	.474
Weight, Grains	250	300	400	500	500
Ballistic Coefficient	.286	.336	.374	.340	.330
Catalog Number	1778	1780	1785	1790	1795

From: $26.93–84.99

LEGEND

- **BT** — Boat Tail
- **FB** — Fusion Bonded
- **FMJ** — Full Metal Jacket
- **FN** — Flat Nose
- **GD** — Gold Dot®
- **HC** — Hot-Cor®
- **HP** — Hollow Point
- **L** — Lead
- **MHP™** — Molybdenum Disulfide Impregnated
- **S** — Spitzer
- **SS** — Semi-Spitzer
- **SB™** — For Short-Barrel Firearms
- **SP** — Soft Point
- **TMJ®** — Encased-Core Full Jacket
- **RN** — Round Nose
- **SWC** — Semi-Wadcutter
- **UC** — Uni-Cor®
- **WC** — Wadcutter

Speer Bullets

HANDGUN BULLETS

Gold Dot Bullets

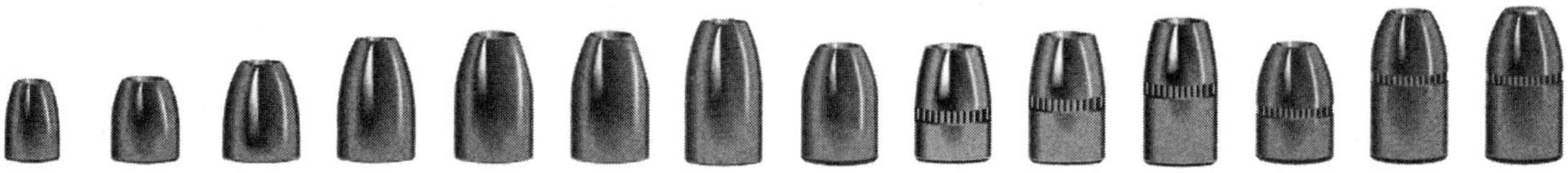

Caliber & Description	25 Auto HP	32 Auto HP	380 Auto HP	9mm Luger HP	9mm Luger HP	9mm Luger HPSB	9mm Luger HP	357 SIG/38 Super HP	38 Special HPSB	38 Spl 357 Mag HPSB	38 Spl 357 Mag HPSB	357 Mag HP	357 Mag HP	357 Mag SP
Diameter, Inches	.251	.312	.355	.355	.355	.355	.355	.355	.357	.357	.357	.357	.357	.357
Weight, Grains	35	60	90	115	124	124	147	125	110	135	147	125	158	170
Ballistic Coefficient	.091	.118	.101	.125	.134	—	.164	.141	.117	.141	.153	.140	.168	.185
Catalog Number	3985	3986	3992	3994	3998	4000	4002	4360	4009	4014	4016	4012	4215	4230

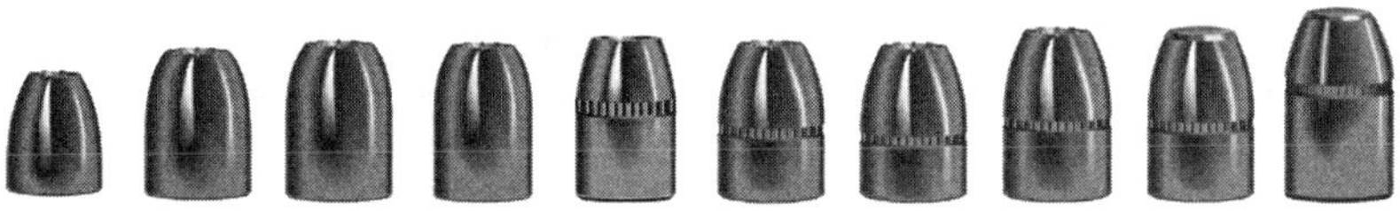

Caliber & Description	9x18mm Makarov HP	40/10mm HP	40/10mm HP	40/10mm HP	41 Mag HP	44 Special HP	44 Mag HP	44 Mag HP	44 Mag SP	44 Mag SP
Diameter, Inches	.364	.400	.400	.400	.410	.429	.429	.429	.429	.429
Weight, Grains	90	155	165	180	210	200	210	240	240	270
Ballistic Coefficient	.107	.123	.138	.143	.183	.145	.154	.175	.175	.193
Catalog Number	3999	4400	4397	4406	4430	4427	4428	4455	4456	4461

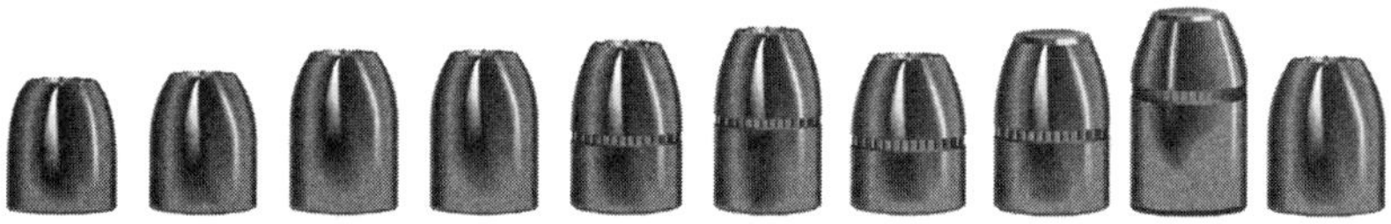

Caliber & Description	45 Auto Gold Dot HP	45 Auto Gold Dot HP	45 Auto Gold Dot HP	45 Auto Gold Dot HP SB	45 Colt Gold Dot HP	454 Casull Gold Dot HP	480 Ruger Gold Dot HP	480 Ruger Gold Dot SP	475 Linebaugh® Gold Dot SP†	50 Action Express Gold Dot HP
Diameter, Inches	.451	.451	.451	.451	.452	.452	.475	.475	.475	.500
Weight, Grains	185	200	230	230	250	300	275	325	400	300
Ballistic Coefficient	.109	.138	.143	—	.165	.233	.162	.191	.242	.155
Catalog Number	4470	4478	4483	—	4484	3974	3973	3978	3976	4493

†=475 Linebaugh is a registered trademark of Timothy B. Sundles

From: $15.29–27.99

Jacketed Bullets

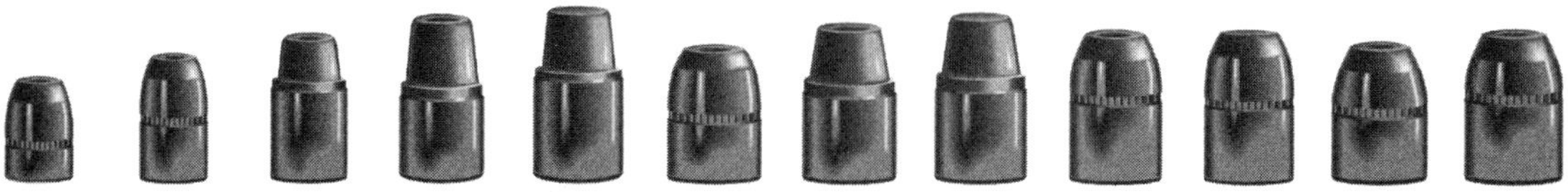

Caliber & Description	32 Revolver JHP	32 Revolver JHP	38 Spl 357 Magnum SWC-JHP	41 Magnum SWC-JHP	41 Magnum SWC-JSP	44 Magnum JHP	44 Magnum SWC-JHP	44 Magnum SWC-JSP	44 Magnum JHP	44 Magnum JSP	45 Colt JHP	45 Colt JHP
Diameter, Inches	.312	.312	.357	.410	.410	.429	.429	.429	.429	.429	.451	.451
Weight, grains	85	100	146	200	220	200	225	240	240	240	225	260
BC	.121	.167	.159	.113	.137	.122	.146	.157	.165	.164	.169	.183
Part Number	3987	3981	4205	4405	4417	4425	4435	4447	4453	4457	4479	4481
Bullets/box	100	100	100	100	100	100	100	100	100	100	100	100
Bullet Construction	C	C	C	C	C	C	C	C	C	C	C	C

From: $14.99–93.00

Speer Bullets

Uni-Cor Bullets

Caliber & Description	25 Auto TMJ	380 Auto TMJ	9mm Luger TMJ	9mm Luger UCSP	9mm Luger TMJ Match	9mm Luger TMJ	357 SIG 38 Super TMJ	38 Spl 357 Magnum UCHP	38 Spl 357 Magnum UCSP	38 Spl 357 Magnum UCHP	38 Spl 357 Magnum TMJ	38 Spl 357 Magnum UCHP	357 Magnum UCHP	357 Magnum UCSP	357 Magnum TMJ	357 Magnum Sil. Match TMJ	357 Magnum Sil. Match TMJ
Diameter, Inches	.251	.355	.355	.355	.355	.355	.355	.357	.357	.357	.357	.357	.357	.357	.357	.357	.357
Weight, grains	50	95	115	124	130	147	125	110	125	125	125	140	158	158	158	180	200
BC	.110	.131	.151	.115	.165	.188	.147	.113	.129	.129	.146	.145	.163	.164	.173	.230	.236
Part Number	3982	4001	3995	3997	4010	4006	4362	4007	4011	4013	4015	4203	4211	4217	4207	4229	4231
Bullets/box	100	100	100	100	100	100	100	100	100	100	100	100	100	100	100	100	100
Bullet Construction	UC	UC	UC	UC	UC	UC	UC	UC	UC	UC	UC	UC	UC	UC	UC	UC	UC

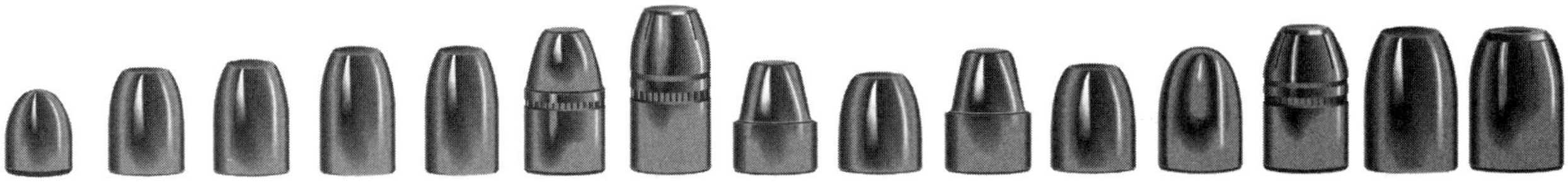

9x18 Makarov TMJ	40/10mm TMJ	40/10mm TMJ	40/10mm TMJ	40/10mm TMJ	44 Magnum Sil. Match TMJ	44 Magnum UCSP	45 Auto SWC Match TMJ	45 Auto FN TMJ	45 Auto SWC Match TMJ	45 Auto FN TMJ	45 Auto RN TMJ	45 Colt UCSP	50 Action Express FN TMJ	50 Action Express UCHP
.364	.400	.400	.400	.400	.429	.429	.451	.451	.451	.451	.451	.451	.500	.500
95	155	165	180	200	240	300	185	185	200	200	230	300	300	325
.127	.125	.135	.143	.168	.206	.213	.090	.094	.128	.102	.153	.199	.157	.169
4375	4399	4410	4402	4403	4459	4463	4473	4476	4475	4471	4480	4485	4490	4495
100	100	100	100	100	100	50	100	100	100	100	100	50	50	50
UC	UC	UC	UC	UC	UC	UC	UC	UC	UC	UC	UC	UC	UC	UC

From: $16.79–90.99

Lead Handgun Bullets

Caliber & Description	32 S&W HBWC	9mm Luger RN	38 Bevel-Base WC	38 Double-Ended WC	38 Hollow-Base WC	38 SWC	38 SWC HP	38 RN	44 SWC	45 Auto SWC	45 Auto RN	45 Colt SWC
Diameter, Inches	.314	.356	.358	.358	.358	.358	.358	.358	.430	.452	.452	.452
Weight, grains	98	125	148	148	148	158	158	158	240	200	230	250
Part No	–	4601	4605	–	4617	4623	4627	4647	4660	4677	4690	4683
Box Count	–	100	100	–	100	100	100	100	100	100	100	100
Bulk Part No.	4600	4602	4606	4611	4618	4624	4628	4648	4661	4678	4691	4684
Bulk Count	1000	500	500	500	500	500	500	500	500	500	500	500

From: $19.79–57.99

LEGEND

- **BT** —Boat Tail
- **FB** —Fusion Bonded
- **FMJ** —Full Metal Jacket
- **FN** —Flat Nose
- **GD** —Gold Dot®
- **HC** —Hot-Cor®
- **HP** —Hollow Point
- **L** —Lead
- **MHP™** —Molybdenum Disulfide Impregnated
- **S** —Spitzer
- **SS** —Semi-Spitzer
- **SB™** —For Short-Barrel Firearms
- **SP** —Soft Point
- **TMJ®** —Encased-Core Full Jacket
- **RN** —Round Nose
- **SWC** —Semi-Wadcutter
- **UC** —Uni-Cor®
- **WC** —Wadcutter

Swift Bullets

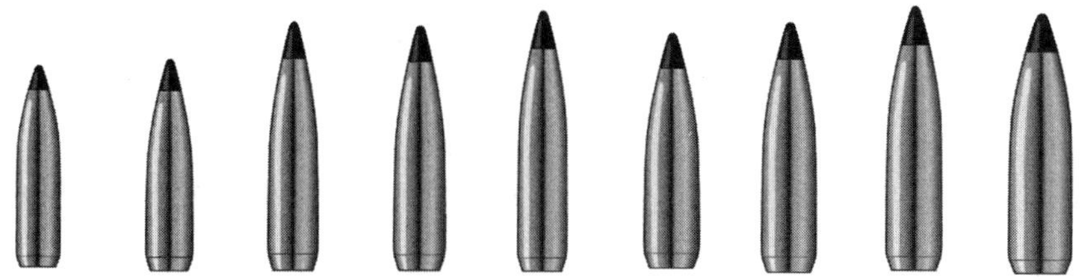

SCIROCCO

Caliber & Description	224 BTS	6mm BTS	6.5mm BTS	270 BTS	7mm BTS	30 BTS	30 BTS	30 BTS	338 BTS
Diameter, Inches	.224	.243	.264	.277	.284	.308	.308	.308	.357
Weight, Grains	75	90	130	130	150	150	165	180	210
Density	.214	.218	.265	.242	.266	.226	.248	.271	.263
Ballistic Coefficient	.419	.419	.571	.450	.515	.430	.470	.520	.507

From: $48.50–64.50

LEGEND
- **BT** – Boattail
- **FN** – Flat Nose
- **HP** – Hollow Point
- **RN** – Round Nose
- **S** – Spitzer
- **SS** – Semi-Spitzer

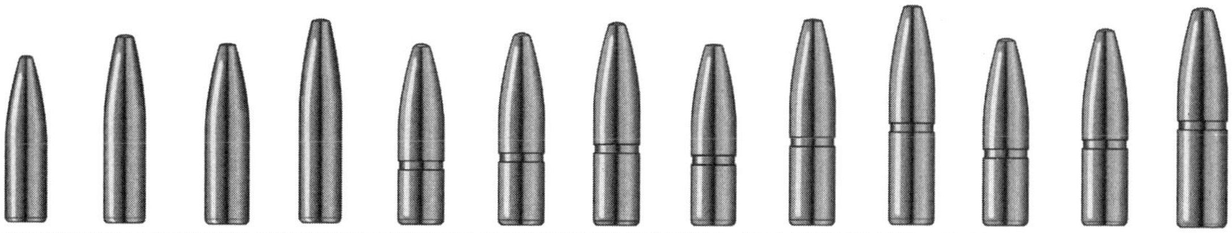

A-FRAME

Caliber & Description	25 SS	25 SS	6.5mm SS	6.5mm SS	270 SS	270 SS	270 SS	7mm SS	7mm SS	7mm SS	30 SS	30 SS	30 SS
Diameter, Inches	.257	.257	.264	.264	.277	.277	.277	.284	.284	.284	.308	.308	.308
Weight, Grains	100	120	120	140	130	140	150	140	160	175	165	180	200
Density	.216	.260	.246	.287	.242	.261	.279	.248	.283	.310	.248	.271	.301
Ballistic Coefficient	.318	.382	.344	.401	.323	.414	.444	.335	.450	.493	.367	.400	.444

THE SWIFT BULLET COMPANY

The Scirocco rifle bullet starts with a tough, pointed polymer tip that reduces air resistance, prevents tip deformation, and blends into the radius of its secant ogive nose section. A moderate 15-degree boat-tail base reduces drag and eases seating. The thick base prevents bullet deformation during launch. Scirocco's shape creates two other significant advantages. One is an extremely high ballistic coefficient. The other, derived from the secant ogive nose, is a comparatively long bearing surface for a sharply pointed bullet, a feature that improves rotational stability.

Inside, the Scirocco has a bonded-core construction with a pure lead core encased in a tapered, progressively thickening jacket of pure copper. Pure copper was selected because it is more malleable and less brittle than less expensive gilding metal. Both jacket and core are bonded by Swift's proprietary process so that the bullet expands without break-up as if the two parts were the same metal. In tests, the bullet mushroomed effectively at velocities as low as 1440 fps, yet stayed together at velocities in excess of 3,000 fps, with over 70 percent weight retention.

Swift A-Frame bullet, with its midsection wall of copper, is still earning praise for its deep-driving dependability in tough game. Less aerodynamic than the Scirocco, it produces a broad mushroom while carrying almost all its weight through muscle and bone. Available in a wide range of weights and diameters, it is also a bonded-core bullet.

.243 SCIROCCO, 90-GRAIN

Swift's 90-gr. Scirocco bullet makes 6mm or .243 diameter shooters more effective than ever with a bonded core and state-of-the-art shape that delivers buck-bagging energy clear to the county line. The computer-designed shape includes a boat tail base, long frontal profile and pointed tip that pierces the atmosphere at high velocity. Wind deflection is hardly a factor because the bullet gets downrange with a shorter flight time due to its high ballistic coefficient. The plastic tip drives in for expansion at just the right instant. A thick jacket and bonded core combine to assure 80%+ weight retention and game-taking penetration.

MSRP: . . . . $51 (per box of 100)

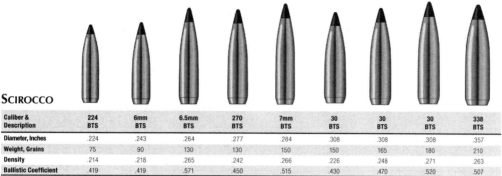

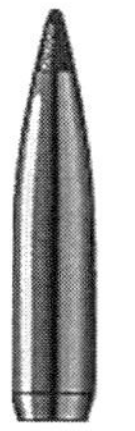

Swift Bullets

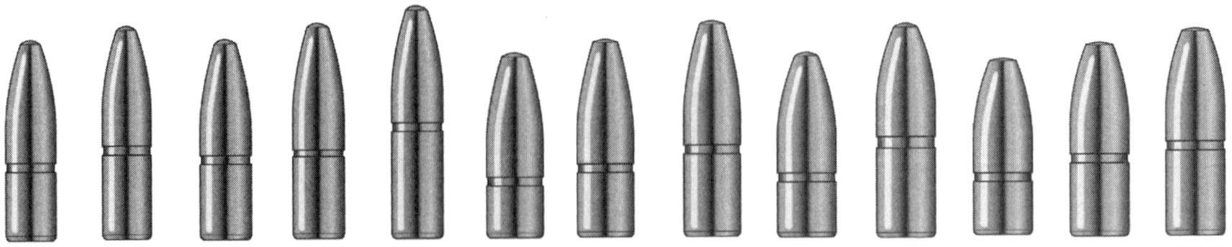

A-Frame (cont.)

Caliber & Description	8mm SS	8mm SS	338 SS	338 SS	338 SS	35 SS	35 SS	35 SS	9.3mm SS	9.3mm SS	375 SS	375 SS	375 SS
Diameter, Inches	.323	.323	.338	.338	.338	.358	.358	.358	.366	.366	.375	.375	.375
Weight, Grains	200	220	225	250	275	225	250	280	250	300	250	270	300
Density	.274	.301	.281	.313	.344	.251	.279	.312	.267	.320	.254	.274	.305
Ballistic Coefficient	.375	.393	.384	.427	.469	.312	.347	.388	.285	.342	.271	.349	.325

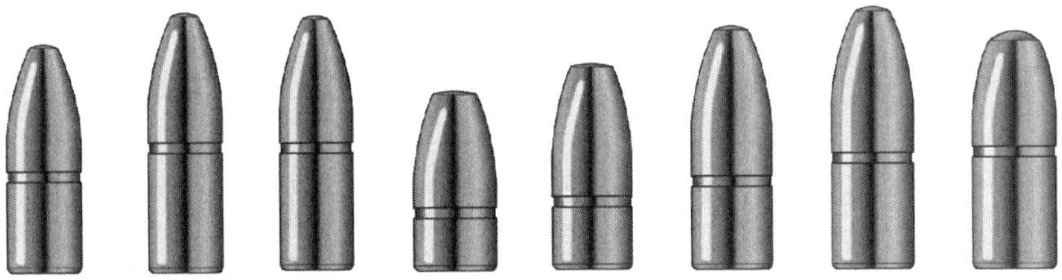

Caliber & Description	416 SS	416 SS	404 SS	458 FN	458 FN	458 SS	458 SS	470 AFRN
Diameter, Inches	.416	.416	.423	.458	.458	.458	.458	.475
Weight, Grains	350	400	400	350	400	450	500	500
Density	.289	.330	.319	.238	.72	.307	.341	.329
Ballistic Coefficient	.321	.367	.375	.170	.258	.325	.361	.364

From: $16.00–92.50

HANDGUN BULLETS

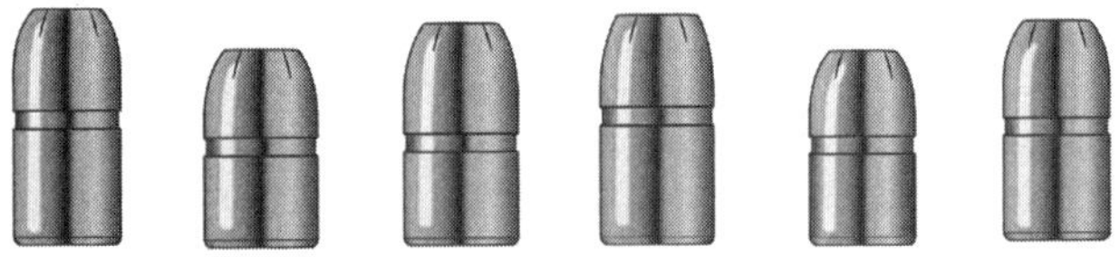

A-Frame

Caliber & Description	44 HP	444 HP	44 HP	45 HP	45 HP	45 HP
Diameter, Inches	.416	.416	.423	.458	.458	.458
Weight, Grains	350	400	400	350	400	450
Density	.289	.330	.319	.238	.72	.307
Ballistic Coefficient	.321	.367	.375	.170	.258	.325

$50.50

LEGEND
- **BT** – Boattail
- **FN** – Flat Nose
- **HP** – Hollow Point
- **RN** – Round Nose
- **S** – Spitzer
- **SS** – Semi-Spitzer

After charging cases with powder, it's a good idea to check all powder levels to be sure you have not double-charged a case or missed charging a case.

Woodleigh Premium Bullets

FULL METAL JACKET

Fashioned from gilding metal-clad steel 2mm thick, jackets on FMJ bullets are heavy at the nose for extra impact resistance. The jacket then tapers toward the base to assist rifling engraving. **From: $41.99–226.99**

WELDCORE SOFT NOSE

A product of Australia, Woodleigh Weldcore Soft Nose bullets are made from 90/100 gilding metal (90% copper; 10% zinc) 1.6 mm thick. Maximum retained weight is obtained by fusing the pure lead to the gilding metal jacket. **From: $74.99–219.99**

98% & 95%
RETAINED WEIGHT
300 WIN MAG 180GR PP

458 X 500GN SN
RECOVERED FROM BUFFALO

270 WIN 150GN PP
86% RETAINED WEIGHT

94% RETAINED WEIGHT
300 WIN MAG 180GR PP

500/465 RECOVERED
FROM BUFFALO

Caliber Diameter	Type	Weight Grain	SD	BC
700 Nitro	SN	1000	.292	.340
.700″	FMJ	1000	.292	.340
600 Nitro	SN	900	.334	.371
.620″	FMJ	900	.334	.334
577 Nitro	SN	750	.313	.346
.585″	FMJ	750	.313	.351
	SN	650	.271	.292
	FMJ	650	.271	.292
577 B.P. .585″	SN	650	.271	.320
500 Nitro	SN	570	.313	.474
.510″	FMJ	570	.313	.434
500 B.P. .510″	SN	440	.242	.336
500	PP	535	.304	.460
Jeffery	SN	535	.304	.460
.510″	FMJ	535	.304	.422
505	PP	600	.336	.450
Gibbs	SN	525	.294	.445
.505″	FMJ	525	.294	.408
	FMJ	600	.366	.450
475 No2	SN	500	.300	.420
Jeffery .488″	FMJ	500	.300	.416
475 No2	SN	480	.303	.400
.483″	FMJ	480	.303	.410
476 W.R.	SN	520	.328	.420
.476″	FMJ	520	.328	.455
475 Nitro	SN	480	.227	.307
.476″	FMJ	480	.227	.257
470 Nitro	SN	500	.318	.411
.474″	FMJ	500	.318	.410
465 Nitro	SN	480	.318	.410
.468″	FMJ	480	.318	.407
450 Nitro	SN	480	.327	.419
.458″	FMJ	480	.327	.410
458 Mag.	SN	500	.341	.430
.458″	SN	550	.375	.480
	FMJ	500	.341	.405
	FMJ	550	.375	.426
	PP	400	.272	.420
	RN	350	.238	.305
45/70 .458″	FN	405	.276	.250
11.3x62 Schuler .440″	SN	401	.296	.411
425 W.R.	SN	410	.310	.344
.435″	FMJ	410	.310	.336
404	SN	400	.319	.354
Jeffery	FMJ	400	.319	.358
.423″	SN	350	.279	.357
10.75x68mm	SN	347	.277	.355
.423″	FMJ	347	.277	.307
416	SN	410	.338	.375
Rigby	FMJ	410	.338	.341
.416″	PP	340	.281	.425
	SN	450	.372	.402
450/400	SN	400	.338	.384
Nitro .411″ or .408″	FMJ	400	.338	.433
.408	SN	400	.338	.384
.408	FMJ	400	.338	.433

Caliber Diameter	Type	Weight Grain	SD	BC
375 Mag.	PP	235	.239	.331
.375″	RN	270	.275	.305
	SP	270	.275	.380
	PP	270	.275	.352
	RN	300	.305	.340
	SP	300	.305	.425
	PP	300	.305	.420
	FMJ	300	.305	.307
	RN	350	.354	.354
	PP	350	.354	.440
	FMJ	350	.354	.372
405 Win., .411″	SN	300	.254	.194
9.3mm	SN	286	.305	.331
.366″	PP	286	.305	.381
	FMJ	286	.305	.324
	SN	250	.267	.296
360 No2	SN	320	.341	.378
.366″	FMJ	320	.341	.362
	PP	320	.343	.428
358 Cal	SN	225	.250	.277
.358″	FMJ	225	.250	.298
	SN	250	.285	.365
	SN	310	.346	.400
	FMJ	310	.346	.378
338 Mag	PP	225	.281	.425
.338″	SN	250	.313	.332
	PP	250	.313	.470
	FMJ	250	.313	.326
	SN	300	.375	.416
	FMJ	300	.375	.398
333	SN	250	.328	.400
Jeffery	SN	300	.386	.428
.333″	FMJ	300	.386	.419
318 W.R.	SN	250	.328	.420
.330″	FMJ	250	.328	.364
8mm	SN	196	.268	.370
.323″	SN	220	.302	.363
	SN	250	.343	.389
8X57	SN	200	.282	.370
303	SN	174	.257	.342
British .312	PP	215	.316	.359
308 Cal	FMJ	220	.331	.359
.308″	RN	220	.331	.367
	PP	180	.273	.376
	PP	165	.250	.320
	PP	150	.226	.301
Win Mag.	PP	180	.273	.435
	PP	200	.301	.450
275 H&H	PP	160	.275	.474
.287″	PP	175	.301	.518
7mm	PP	140	.247	.436
.284″	PP	160	.282	.486
	PP	175	.312	.530
270 Win	PP	130	.241	.409
.277″	PP	150	.278	.463

SP = Semi-point
PP = Protected Point
FN = Flat Nose
RN = Round Nose
FMJ = Full Metal Jacket
All PP, FN, RN, SP, SN bullets are Weldcore Softnose

MTM Case-Gard Handloading

MINI DIGITAL RELOADING SCALE

The pocket-sized DS-1200 scale features an extended, 3-minute auto shut-off; powder pan, custom designed to facilitate bullet, powder and arrow weighing; easy to read, backlit LCD display; plus\minus .1 grain accuracy; up to 1200 grain capacity; measures in grains, grams, carats and ounces; stainless steel sensory platform; high-impact, plastic sensory cover that doubles as large powder pan. Uses two standard AAA batteries. Calibration weight and detailed instructions included, along with a foam lined case for storage and travel.

FROM:. $37–42

Accurate Powder

Price		NG*	Avgerage Length/Thickness in./mm.	Avgerage Diameter inches	Avgerage Diameter millimeters	Bulk Density gram/cc	VMD cc/grain	Comparative Powders*** Ball	Comparative Powders*** Extruded
BALL PROPELLANTS - Handguns/Shotshell									
$15.99	No. 2 Imp.	14.0	—	0.018	0.457	0.650	0.100	WIN 231	
$17.99	No. 5	18.0	—	0.027	0.686	0.950	0.068	WIN 540	
$17.99	No. 7	12.0	—	0.012	0.305	0.985	0.066	WIN 630	
$17.99	No. 9	10.0	—	1.015	0.381	0.935	0.069	WIN 296	
$18.99	1680	10.0	—	0.014	0.356	0.950	0.068	WIN 680	
$18.99	Solo 4100	10.0	—	0.011	0.279	0.960	0.068	WIN 296	
BALL PROPELLANTS - Rifle									
$18.99	2230	10.0	—	0.022	0.559	0.980	0.066	BL C2, WIN 748	
$18.99	2460	10.0	—	0.022	0.559	0.990	0.065	BL C2, WIN 748	
$18.99	2520	10.0	—	0.022	0.559	0.970	0.067	—	
$18.99	2700	10.0	—	0.022	0.559	0.960	0.068	WIN 760	
$18.99	MAGPRO	9.0	—	0.030	0.762	0.970	0.067	—	
EXTRUDED PROPELLANTS - Shotshell/Handguns									
$14.99	Nirto 100	21.0	0.010/ 0.254	0.058	1.473	0.505	0.128	—	
$14.99	Solo 1000	—	0.010/ 0.254	0.052	1.321	0.510	0.127	—	
EXTRUDED PROPELLANTS - Rifle/handgun									
$22.99	5744	20.00	0.048/ 1.219	0.033	0.838	0.880	0.074	—	
EXTRUDED PROPELLANTS - Rifle									
$20.99	2015	—	0.039/ 0.991	0.031	0.787	0.880	0.074	—	
$20.99	2495	—	0.068/ 1.727	0.029	0.737	0.880	0.074	—	
$20.99	4064	—	0.050/ 1.270	0.035	0.889	0.890	0.072	—	
$20.99	4350	—	0.083/ 0.038	0.038	0.965	0.890	0.072	—	
$20.99	3100	—	0.083/ 0.038	0.038	0.965	0.920	0.070	—	

**NG-NItroglycerin ***For comparison only, not a loading recommendation*

Alliant Powder Handloading

20/28 SMOKELESS SHOTSHELL POWDER

20/28 is a powder designed to deliver competition-grade performance to 20 and 28 gauge clay target shooters. 20/28 has a density formulated for use in all modern reloading components. Available in 1-lb., 4-lb. and 8-lb. canisters.

MSRP:

(1 lb.) $18
(4 lbs.) $66
(8 lbs.) $123

Alliant Smokeless Powders

410

Cleanest .410 bore powder on the market.
1 lb: $16.99
4 lbs: $62.99
8 lbs: $117.99

2400

Legendary for its performance in .44 magnum and other magnum pistol loads. Originally developed for the .22 Hornet, it's also the shooter's choice for .410 bore. ***Available in 8 lb., 4 lb. and 1 lb. canisters.***
1 lb: $16.99
4 lbs: $62.99
8 lbs: $117.99

AMERICAN SELECT

This ultra-clean burning premium powder makes a versatile target load and superior 1 oz. load for improved clay target scores. Great for Cowboy Action handgun loading, too. ***Available in 8 lb., 4 lb. and 1 lb. canisters.***
1 lb: $16.29
4 lbs: $59.99
8 lbs: $908.99

BLUE DOT

The powder of choice for magnum lead shotshell loads. 10, 12, 16 and 20 ga. Consistent and accurate. Doubles as magnum handgun powder. ***Available in 5 lb. and 1 lb. canisters.***
1 lb: $16.79
5 lbs: $73.99

BULLSEYE

America's best known pistol powder. Unsurpassed for .45 ACP target loads. ***Available in 8 lb., 4 lb. and 1 lb. canisters.***
1 lb: $15.79
4 lbs: $57.99
8 lbs: $108.99

E^3

The first of a new generation of high performance powders.
1 lb: $17.79
4 lbs: $63.99
8 lbs: $118.99

GREEN DOT

It delivers precise burn rates for uniformly tight patterns, and you'll appreciate the lower felt recoil. Versatile for target and field. ***Available in 8 lb., 4 lb. and 1 lb. canisters.***
1 lb: $16.29
4 lbs: $59.99
8 lbs: $108.99

HERCO

Since 1920, a proven powder for heavy shotshell loads, including 10, 12, 16, 20 and 28 ga. target loads. The ultimate in 12 ga., 1¼ oz. upland game loads. ***Available in 8 lb., 4 lb. and 1 lb. canisters.***
1 lb: $16.29
4 lbs: $59.99
8 lbs: $108.99

POWER PISTOL

Designed for high performance in semiautomatic pistols (9mm, .40 S&W and .357 SIG). ***Available in 4 lb. and 1 lb. canisters.***
1 lb: $15.79
5 lbs: $57.99

Alliant Shotshell Powders

RED DOT

America's #1 choice for clay target loads, now 50% cleaner. Since 1932, more 100 straights than any other powder. ***Available in 8 lb., 4 lb. and 1 lb. canisters.***

1 lb: $16.29
4 lb: $59.99
8 lb: $108.99

RELODER 7

Designed for small-caliber varmint loads, it meters consistently and meets the needs of the most demanding bench rest shooter. Great in .45-70 and .450 Marlin. ***Available in 5 lb. and 1 lb. canisters.***

1 lb: $21.49
5 lb: $96.99

RELODER 10X

Best choice for light bullet applications in .222 Rem, .223 Rem, .22-250 Rem and key bench rest calibers. Also great in light bullet .308 Win. loads. ***Available in 5 lb. and 1 lb. canisters***

1 lb: $21.49
5 lb: $96.99

RELODER 15

An all-around medium speed rifle powder. It provides excellent .223 and .308 cal. performance. Selected as the powder for U.S. Military's M118 Special Ball Long Range Sniper Round. ***Available in 5 lb. and 1 lb. canisters.***

1 lb: $21.49
5 lb: $96.99

RELODER 19

Provides superb accuracy in most medium and heavy rifle loads and is the powder of choice for 30-06 and .338 calibers. ***Available in 5 lb. and 1 lb. canisters.***

1 lb: $21.49
5 lb: $96.99

RELODER 22

This top performing powder for big-game loads provides excellent metering and is the powder of choice for .270, 7mm magnum and .300 Win. magnum. ***Available in 5 lb. and 1 lb. canisters.***

1 lb: $21.49
5 lb: $96.99

RELODER 25

This powder for big-game hunting features improved slower burning and delivers the high-energy heavy magnum loads needed. ***Available in 5 lb. and 1 lb. canisters.***

1 lb: $21.49
5 lb: $96.99

STEEL

Designed for waterfowl shotshells. Gives steel shot high velocity within safe pressure limits for 10 and 12 ga. loads. ***Available in 4 lb. and 1 lb. canisters.***

1 lb: $17.29
4 lb: $61.99

UNIQUE

Shotgun/handgun powder for 12, 16, 20 and 28 ga. loads. Use with most hulls, primers and wads. ***Available in 8 lb., 4 lb. and 1 lb. canisters.***

1 lb: $16.29
4 lb: $59.99
8 lb: $108.99

When handloading, spilled powder should never be picked up with a vacuum cleaner. Use only a brush and pan and dispose of the powder in a safe manner.

Hodgdon Smokeless Powder

CLAYS
Tailored for use in 12 ga., 7/8 oz., 1 oz. and 1 1/8 oz. loads. Performs well in many handgun applications, including .38 Special, .40 S&W and 45 ACP. Perfect for 1 1/8 oz. and 1 oz. loads.
14oz.: $16.49 / 4 lb: $67.99
8 lb: $121.99

CLAYS, INTERNATIONAL
Ideal for 12 and 20 ga. autoloaders who want reduced recoil.
14oz.: $16.29 / 4 lb: $67.99
8 lb: $121.99

CLAYS, UNIVERSAL
Loads nearly all of the straight-wall pistol cartridges as well as 12 ga. 1 1/4 oz. thru 28 ga. 3/4 oz. target loads.
1 lb: $19.99 / 4 lb: $70.99 /
8 lb: $127.99

EXTREME BENCHMARK
A fine choice for small rifle cases like the .223 Rem and PPC competition rounds. Appropriate also for the 300-30 and 7x57.
1 lb: $22.99 / 8 lb: $152.99

EXTREME H50 BMG
Designed for the 50 Browning Machine Gun cartridge. Highly insensitive to extreme temperature changes.
1 lb: $22.49 / 8 lb: $152.99

EXTREME H322
This powder fills the gap between H4198 and BL-C9(2). Performs best in small to medium capacity cases.
1 lb: $22.49 / 8 lb: $152.99

EXTREME H1000 EXTRUDED POWDER
Fills the gap between H4831 and H870. Works especially well in overbore capacity cartridges (1,000-yard shooters take note).
1 lb: $22.99 / 8 lb: $152.99

EXTREME H4198
H4198 was developed especially for small and medium capacity cartridges.
1 lb: $22.49 / 8 lb: $151.99

EXTREME H4350
Gives superb accuracy at optimum velocity for many large capacity metallic rifle cartridges.
1 lb: $22.49 / 8 lb: $151.99

EXTREME H4831
Outstanding performance with medium and heavy bullets in the 6mm's, 25/06, 270 and Magnum calibers. Also available with shortened grains (H4831SC) for easy metering.
1 lb: $22.49 / 8 lb: $151.99

EXTREME H4895
4895 gives desirable performance in almost all cases from 222 Rem. to 458 Win. Reduced loads, to as low as 3/5 maximum, still give target accuracy.
1 lb: $22.49 / 8 lb: $151.99

EXTREME VARGET
Features small extruded grain powder for uniform metering, plus higher velocities/normal pressures in such calibers as .223, 22-250, 306, 30-06, 375 H&H.
1 lb: $22.49 / 8 lb: $152.99

H110
A spherical powder made especially for the 30 M1 carbine. H110 also does very well in 357, 44 spec., 44 Mag. or 410 ga. shotshell. Recommended for consistent ignition.
From: $20.49

HP38
A fast pistol powder for most pistol loading. Especially recommended for mid-range 38 specials.
1 lb: $17.779 / 8 lb: $121.99

HS-6 AND HS-7
HS-6 and HS-7 for Magnum field loads are unsurpassed. Deliver uniform charges and are dense to allow sufficient wad column for best patterns.
1 lb: $19.99 / 8 lb: $139.99

LONGSHOT
Spherical powder for heavy shotgun loads.
1 lb: $19.79 / 4 lb: $73.99
8 lb: $137.99

PYRODEX PELLETS
Both rifle and pistol pellets eliminate powder measures, speeds shooting for black powder enthusiasts.
From: $9.89–24.99

RETUMBO
Designed for such cartridges as the 300 Rem. Ultra Mag., 30-378 Weatherby, the 7mm STW and other cases with large capacities and small bores. Expect up to 40-100 feet per second more velocity than other magnum powders.
1 lb: $22.49 / 8 lb: $151.99

SPHERICAL BL-C2
Best performance is in the 222, .308 other cases smaller than 30/06.
1 lb: $20.99 / 8 lb: $142.99

SPHERICAL H335
Similar to BL-C(2), H335 is popular for its performance in medium capacity cases, especially in 222 and 308 Winchester.
1 lb: $20.49 / 8 lb: $140.99

SPHERICAL H380
Fills a gap between 4320 and 4350. It is excellent in 22/250, 220 Swift, the 6mm's, 257 and 30/06.
1 lb: $20.49 / 8 lb: $140.99

SPHERICAL H414
In many popular medium to medium-large calibers, pressure velocity relationship is better.
1 lb: $20.49 / 8 lb: $140.99

TITEGROUP
Excellent for most straight-walled pistol cartridges, incl. 38 Spec., 44 Spec., 45 ACP. Low charge weights, clean burning; position insensitive and flawless ignition.
1 lb: $16.79 / 4 lb: $61.99 /
8 lb: $115.99

TITEWAD
This 12 ga. flattened spherical shotgun powder is ideal for 7/8 oz., 1 oz. and 1 1/8 oz. loads, with minimum recoil and mild muzzle report. The fastest fuel in Hodgdon's line.
1 lb: $14.59 / 4 lb: $58.99 /
8 lb: $106.99

TRIPLE SEVEN
Hodgdon Powder Company offers its sulfur-free Triple Seven powder in 50-grain pellets. Formulated for use with 209 shotshell primers, Triple Seven leaves no rotten egg smell, and the residue is easy to clean from the bore with water only. The pellets are sized for 50-caliber muzzleloaders and can be used singly (for target shooting or small game) as well as two at a time.
From: $9.99–27.49

IMR Powders

RIFLE POWDERS

IMR 3031—A propellant with many uses, IMR 3031 is a favorite of 308 match shooters using 168 grain match bullets. It is equally effective in small-capacity varmint cartridges from .223 Remington to .22-250 Remington and a great .30-30 Winchester powder.
1 lb: $22.99 / 8 lb: $152.99

IMR 4198—This fast-burning rifle powder gives outstanding performance in cartridges like the .222 Remington, 221 Fireball, .45-70 and .450 Marlin.
1 lb: $22.99 / 8 lb: $152.99

IMR 4227—The choice for true magnum velocities and performance. In rifles, this powder delivers excellent velocity and accuracy in such cartridges as the .22 Hornet and .221 Fireball.
1 lb: $22.99 / 8 lb: $152.99

IMR 4320—Short granulation, easy metering and perfect for the .223 Remington, .22-250 Remington, .250 Savage and other medium burn rate cartridges. It has long been a top choice for the vintage .300 Savage cartridge.
1 lb: $22.99 / 8 lb: $152.99

IMR 4350—The number one choice for the new short magnums, both Remington and Winchester versions. For magnums with light to medium bullet weights, IMR 4350 is the best choice.
1 lb: $22.99 / 8 lb: $160.99

IMR 4895—Originally a military powder featured in the .30-06, IMR 4895 is extremely versatile. From .17 Remington to the .243 Winchester to the .375 H&H Magnum, accuracy and performance are excellent. In addition, it is a long-time favorite of match shooters.
1 lb: $22.99 / 8 lb: $152.99

IMR 7828—The big magnum powder. This slow burner gives real magnum performance to the large overbored magnums, such as the .300 Remington Ultra Mag, the .30-378 Weatherby Magnum and 7mm Remington Ultra Magnum.
1 lb: $22.99 / 8 lb: $152.99

HANDGUN & SHOTGUN POWDERS

"Hi Skor" 700-X—This extruded flake-type powder is ideally suited for shotshells in 12 and 16 ga. where clay target and light field loads are the norm. It doubles as an excellent pistol target powder for such cartridges as the .38 Special, .45 ACP and many more.
14oz.: $15.49 / 4 lb: $64.99
8 lb: $117.99

"Hi Skor" 800-X—This large-grained flake powder is at its best when used in heavy field loads from 10 ga. to 28 ga. In handgun cartridges, 800-X performs superbly in cartridges such as the 10mm Auto, .357 Magnum and . 44 Remington Magnum.
1 lb: $18.29 / 4 lb: $65.99 /
8 lb: $119.99

PB—Named for the porous base structure of its grains by which the burning rate is controlled, PB is an extremely clean-burning, single-base powder. It gives very low pressure in 12 and 20 ga. shotshell target loads and performs well in a wide variety of handgun loads.
14oz.: $20.99 / 4 lb: $84.99
8 lb: $161.99

SR 4756—This fine-grained, easy-metering propellant has long been a favorite of upland and waterfowl handloaders. SR4756 performs extremely well in the big handgun cartridges.
1 lb: $21.99 / 8 lb: $138.99

SR 4759—This bulky handgun powder works great in the magnums, but really shines as a reduced load propellant for rifle cartridges. Its large-grain size gives good loading density for reduced loads, enhancing velocity uniformity.
1 lb: $21.99 / 8 lb: $138.99

SR 7625—SR7625 covers the wide range of shotshells from 10 ga. to 28 ga. in both target and field loadings. This versatile powder is equally useful in a large array of handgun cartridges for target, self-defense and hunting loads.
1 lb: $23.99 / 8 lb: $163.99

Word Play: The word "bullet" is sometimes erroneously used to refer to the combination of bullet, case, gunpowder and primer more properly known as a "cartridge" or "round."

Ramshot Powders

Ramshot (Western Powders, Inc.) powders are all double-base propellants, meaning they contain nitrocellulose and nitroglycerine. While some spherical or ball powders are known for leaving plenty of residue in barrels, these fuels burn very clean. They meter easily, as do all ball powders. Plastic canisters are designed for spill-proof use and include basic loading data on the labels.

RAMSHOT BIG GAME is a versatile propellant for cartridges as diverse as the .30-06 and the .338 Winchester, and for light-bullet loads in small-bore magnums.
1 lb: $19.99 / 8 lb: $132.99

RAMSHOT COMPETITION is for the clay target shooter. A fast-burning powder comparable to 700-X or Red Dot, it performs well in a variety of 12 ga. target loads, offering low recoil, consistent pressures and clean combustion.
1 lb: $16.79 / 4 lb: $66.99 / 8 lb $115.99
RAMSHOT ENFORCER is a match for high-performance handgun hulls like the .40 Smith & Wesson. It is designed for full-power loading and high velocities. Ramshot X-Terminator, a fast-burning rifle powder, excels in small-caliber, medium-capacity cartridges. It has the versatility to serve in both target and high-performance varmint loads.
1 lb: $16.99 / 4 lb: $66.99 / 8 lb: $115.99

RAMSHOT MAGNUM is the slowest powder of the Western line, and does its best work in cartridges with lots of case volume and small to medium bullet diameter. It is the powder of choice in 7mm and .30 Magnums.
1 lb: $19.99 / 8 lb: $134.99

RAMSHOT SILHOUETTE is ideal for the 9mm handgun cartridge, from light to heavy loads. It also works well in the .40 Smith & Wesson and combat loads for the .45 Auto.
1 lb: $18.99 / 4 lb: $65.99

RAMSHOT TAC was formulated for tactical rifle cartridges, specifically the .223 and .308. It has produced exceptional accuracy with a variety of bullets and charge weights.
1 lb: $19.99 / 8 lb: $134.99

RAMSHOT TRUE BLUE was designed for small- to medium-size handgun cartridges. Similar to Winchester 231 and Hodgdon HP-38, it has enough bulk to nearly fill most cases, thereby better positioning the powder for ignition.
1 lb: $18.99 / 8 lb: $66.99

RAMSHOT X-TERMINATOR is a clean burning powder designed for the .222 Rem., 223 Rem. and .22 Benchrest calibers.
1 lb: $19.99 / 8 lb: $134.99

RAMSHOT ZIP, a fast-burning target powder for cartridges like the .38 Special and .45 ACP, gives competitors uniform velocities.
1 lb: $18.99 / 8 lb: $66.99

VihtaVuori Powders

N110—A very fast-burning propellant that can be used in applications that previously used Hercules 2400, Hodgdon H110 or Winchester 296. Typical applications include: .22 Hornet, .25-20 Winchester, .357 S&W Magnum, .357 Maximum, .44 Magnum and .45 Winchester Magnum.
1 lb: $32.65

N120—A limited application propellant. This speed develops higher pressure than N110 in order to optimize burning. Burning rate falls near the various 4227s. It works well with light bullets in .22 caliber cartridges.
1 lb: $32.65

N130—Burning rate is between IMR 4227 and the discontinued Winchester 680. This is the powder used in factory-loaded .22 and 6mm PPC.
1 lb: $32.65 / 2 lb: $58.76

N133—This powder's speed is very close to IMR 4198 in quickness. Thus, it is ideal for the .222 Remington, .223 Remington, .45-70 Government and other applications where a relatively fast-burning rifle propellant is needed.
1 lb: $32.65 / 8 lb: $209.92

N135—This is a moderate-burning propellant. It will fit applications similar to Hercules Reloader 12, IMR-4895 or IMR 4064. Applications range from the .17 Remington to the .458 Winchester.
1 lb: $32.45 / 2 lb: $64.00

N140—This powder can usually be used in place of Hercules Reloader 15, IMR 4320 and Hodgdon H380. Applications include: .222 Remington Magnum, .22-250 Remington (factory powder), .30-.30 Winchester, .308 Winchester, .30-06 Springfield, .375 H&H Magnum and so on.
1 lb: $32.65 / 8 lb: $209.92

N150—This is a moderately slow powder that can help refine rifle cartridge ballistics when N140 is too fast and N160 is too slow. Works well in many applications previously filled by 760, H414 and IMR 4350.
1 lb: $32.65 / 8 lb: $209.92

N160—A relatively slow powder ideally suited to many magnum and standard rounds requiring a slow propellant. It has characteristics that make it work well for applications previously using various 4350s, Hercules Reloader 19 and the various 4831s. For example, some ideal applications are: .243 Winchester, .25-06 Remington, .264 Winchester Magnum, .270 Winchester (factory load), 7mm Remington Magnum, .30-06 Springfield, .300 Winchester Magnum, .338 Winchester Magnum, .375 H&H Magnum, etc.
1 lb: $32.65 / 2 lb: $64.00 / 8 lb: $209.92

N165—A very slow-burning magnum propellant for use with heavy bullets. Applications begin with heavy bullets in the .30-06, and include the .338 Winchester Magnum.
1 lb: $32.65

N170—VihtaVuori's slowest speed propellant and the slowest canister reloading powder generally available from any manufacturer.
1 lb: $32.65

N500 Series
VihtaVuori calls powders that have nitroglycerol added (maximum 25%) producing the high energy NC-powders that form the N500 series. Geometrically the powders in the N500 series are equal to the N100 series. Although these powders have a higher energy content, they do not cause greater wear to the gun. This is because the surface of the powder has been treated with an agent designed to reduce barrel wear. N500 series powders work well at different temperatures.

N530—Burning rate close to N135. Especially for .223 Remington. Excellent also for .45-70 Government.
1 lb: $34.99 / 2 lb: $68.00

N540—Burning rate like N140. Especially for the .308 Winchester.
1 lb: $34.99 / 2 lb: $68.00

N550—Burning rate like N150. Especially for the .308 Winchester and .30-06 Springfield.
1 lb: $34.99

N560—Burning rate like N160. Especially for .270 Winchester and 6.5 x 55 Swedish Mauser.
1 lb: $34.99

HANDLOADING

Battenfeld Technologies

FRANKFORD ARSENAL MICRO RELOADING SCALE

The Micro Reloading Scale is the perfect accessory for reloaders who want a light, accurate, portable scale. The unit is suitable for use on the reloading bench, yet is at home on the shooting range or in the field. The Micro Reloading Scale weighs objects up to 750 grains. It is accurate within ± .1 grains. The digital scale can be set to read in grains, grams, ounces, ct, dwt or ozt. It comes with a protective sleeve and is small enough to fit in your shirt pocket. A calibration weight and batteries are also included.
MSRP: $40

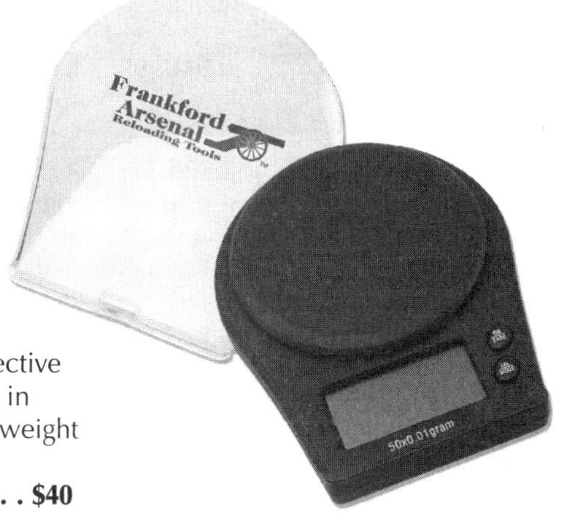

Dillon Precision Reloaders

MODEL RL550B

MODEL SL900

RL550B PROGRESSIVE LOADER

- Accommodates over 120 calibers
- Interchangeable toolhead assembly
- Auto/Powder priming systems
- Uses standard 7/8" x 14" dies
- Loading rate: 500-600 rounds per hour

MSRP: $419.95

SL900R

Based on Dillon's proven XL 650 O-frame design, the SL 900 progressive press features an automatic case insert system, an electric case collator, adjustable case-activated shot and powder bars. Should the operator forget to insert a wad during the reloading process, the SL 900 will not dispense shot into the powder-charged hull. Both powder and shot systems are based on Dillon's adjustable powder bar design, which is accurate to within a few tenths of a grain. Simply adjust the measures to dispense the exact charges required.

An interchangeable tool-head makes it quick and easy to change from one gauge to another using a collet-type sizing die that re-forms the base of the shotshell to factory specifications. The SL 900 also has an extra large, remote shot hopper that holds an entire 25-pound bag of shot, making it easy to fill with a funnel. The shot reservoir/dispenser helps ensure that a consistent volume of shot is delivered to each shell. The heat-treated steel crimp-die forms and folds the hull before the final taper crimp die radiuses and blends the end of the hull and locks the crimp into place.

MSRP: $829.95

Dillon Precision Reloaders

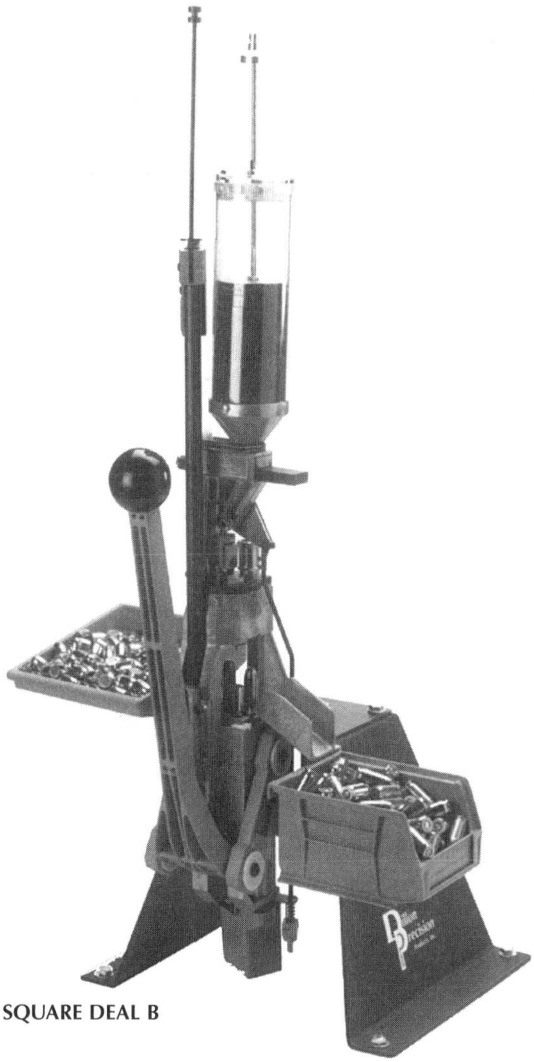

THE SQUARE DEAL B

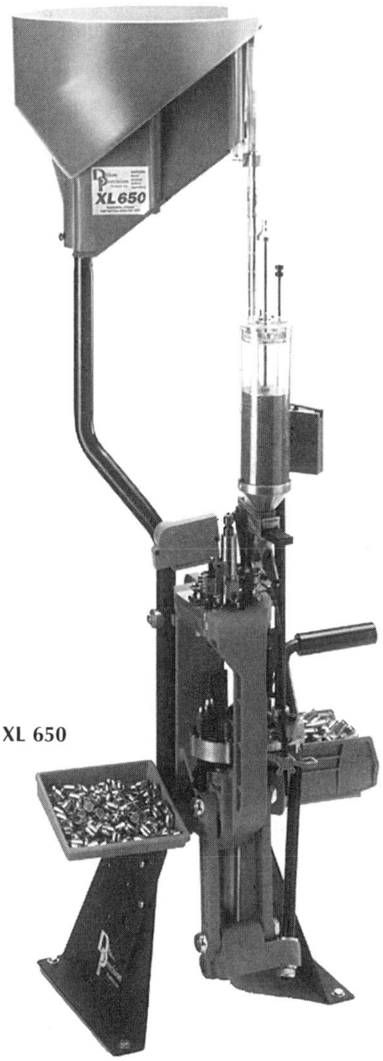

MODEL XL 650

THE SQUARE DEAL B

Designed to produce up to 400 or 500 handgun rounds per hour. The Square Deal B comes with a factory adjusted carbide die set. Square Deal B is available in all popular handgun calibers and you can change from one caliber to another in minutes with a Square Deal B caliber conversion kit. Features: Automatic indexing; auto powder/priming systems; available in 14 handgun calibers; loading dies standard.

MSRP: $365.95

MODEL XL 650

The XL 650 loads virtually every popular pistol and rifle cartridge utilizing standard dies. The optional powder charge check die on the third station sounds an alarm if the powder charge in a round is out of limits either high or low. An exclusive primer system uses a rotary indexing plate that positively controls each primer and keeps a steel shield between the primers and the operator. Features: Automatic indexing; five-station interchangeable tool-head; auto powder / priming systems; uses standard 7/8″ x 14″ dies rotary indexing plate for primers.

MSRP: $544.95

Forster Reloading

CO-AX LOADING PRESS B-3

CO-AX BENCH REST RIFLE DIES

HAND CASE TRIMMER

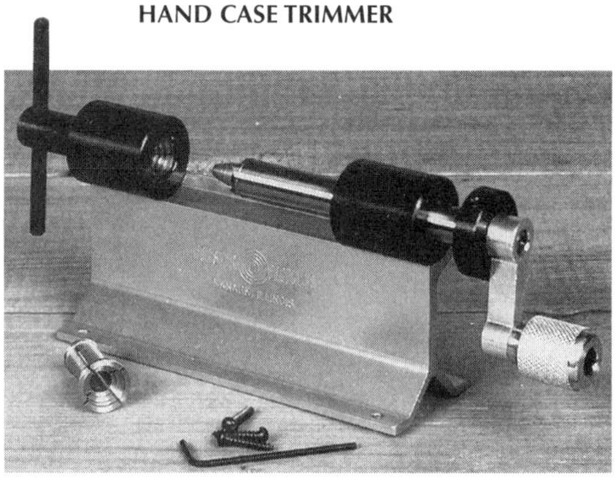

CO-AX CASE AND CARTRIDGE INSPECTOR

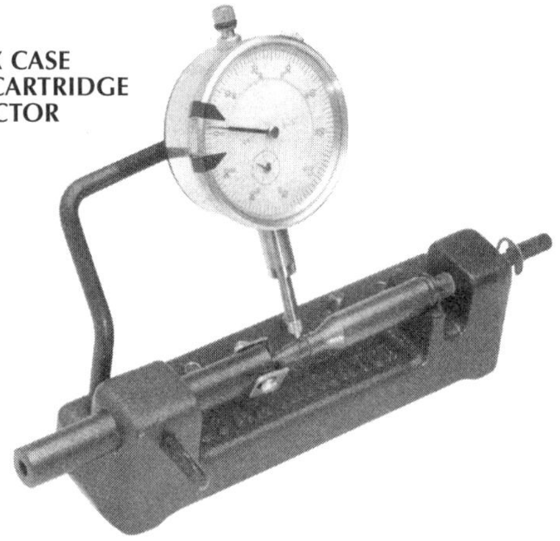

ULTRA BULLET SEATER DIE

CO-AX LOADING PRESS MODEL B-3

Designed to make reloading easier and more accurate, this press offers the following features: Snap-in and snap-out die change; positive spent primer catcher; automatic self-acting shell holder; floating guide rods; top priming device seats primers to factory specifications; uses any standard 7/8″ x 14″ dies.

MSRP: $396

CO-AX BENCH REST RIFLE DIES

Bench Rest Rifle Dies are glass-hard and polished mirror-smooth with special attention given to headspace, tapers and diameters. Sizing die has an elevated expander button to ensure better alignment of case and neck.

Bench Rest Die Set: $92
Bench Rest Seating Die: $56
Ultra Bench Rest Die Set: $129
Full Length Sizer: $44

ULTRA BULLET SEATER DIE

The micrometer-style Ultra Die is available in 61 calibers. Adjustment is identical to that of a precision micrometer—the head is graduated to .001″ increments with .025″ bullet movement per revolution. The cartridge case, bullet and seating stem are completely supported and perfectly aligned in a close-fitting chamber before and during the bullet seating operation.

MSRP: $92

.50 BMG TRIMMER

Handles more than 100 different big bore calibers–500 Nitro Express, 416 Rigby, 50 Sharps, 475 H&H, etc. Also available: .50 BMG Case Trimmer, designed specifically for reloading needs of .50 Cal. BMG shooters.

"Classic 50" Case Trimmer: . . . $112
.50 BMG Case Trimmer: $117

HAND CASE TRIMMER

Shell holder is a Brown & Sharpe-type collet. Case and cartridge conditioning accessories include inside neck reamer, outside neck turner, deburring tool, hollow pointer and primer pocket cleaners. The case trimmer trims all cases, ranging from .17 to .458 Winchester caliber.

MSRP: $79

CO-AX CASE AND CARTRIDGE INSPECTOR

Provides the ability to ensure uniformity by measuring three critical dimensions: neck wall thickness; case neck concentricity; bullet run-out. Measurements are in increments of one-thousandth of an inch. The Inspector checks both the bullet and case alignment in relation to the centerline (axis) of the entire cartridge or case.

MSRP: $107

BENCH REST
POWDER MEASURE

PRIMER POCKET
CLEANER

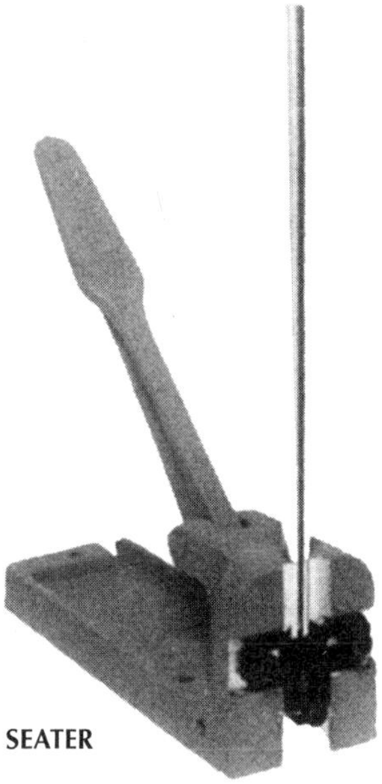

PRIMER SEATER

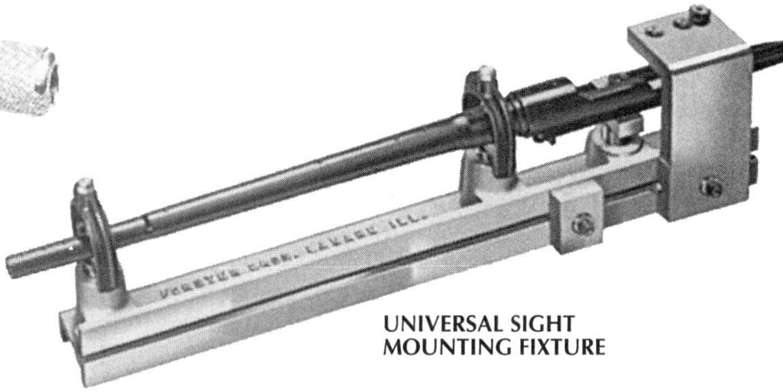

UNIVERSAL SIGHT
MOUNTING FIXTURE

BENCH REST POWDER MEASURE

When operated uniformly, this measure will throw uniform charges from 2½-grains Bullseye to 95-grains #4320. No extra drums are needed. Powder is metered from the charge arm, allowing a flow of powder without extremes in variation while minimizing powder shearing. Powder flows through its own built-in baffle, entering the charge arm uniformly.

MSRP: $144

PRIMER POCKET CLEANER

The Primer Pocket Cleaner helps ensure consistent ignition and reduce the incidence of misfires by removing powder and primer residue from the primer pockets of your cases. This tool is easy to use by holding the case mouth over the Primer Pocket Center with one hand while you quickly and easily clean the primer pockets by turning the Case Trimmer Handle.

MSRP: $9.40

PRIMER SEATER

Designed so that primers are seated co-axially (primer in line with primer pocket). Mechanical leverage allows primers to be seated fully without crushing. With the addition of one extra set of disc shell holders and one extra Primer Unit, all modern cases, rim or rimless, from .222 up to .458 Magnum, can be primed. Shell holders are easily adjusted to any case by rotating to contact rim or cannelure of the case.

MSRP: $94

UNIVERSAL SIGHT MOUNTING FIXTURE

The fixture handles any single-barrel gun—bolt-action, lever-action or pump-action—as long as the barrel can be laid into the "V" blocks of the fixture. Rifles with tube magazines are drilled in the same manner by removing the magazine tube. The fixture's main body is made of aluminum casting. The two "V" blocks are adjustable for height and are made of hardened steel ground accurately on the "V" as well as the shaft.

MSRP: $452

Hornady

MODEL 366

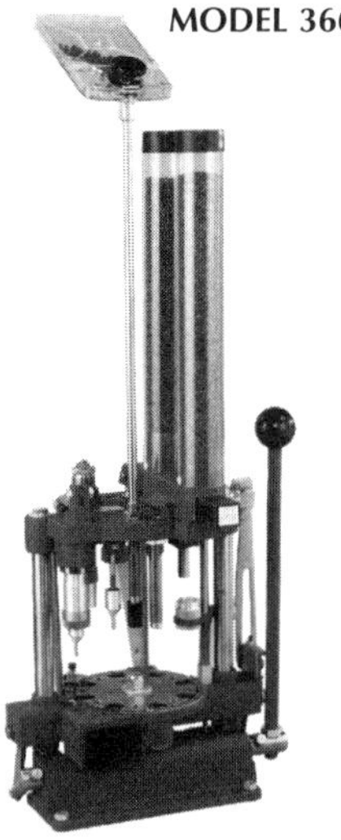

PROGRESSIVE PRESS

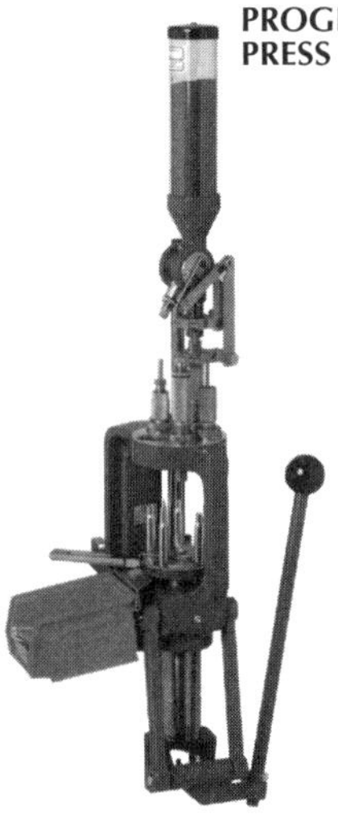

LOCK-N-LOAD CLASSIC PRESS

CUSTOM GRADE RELOADING DIES

MODEL 366 AUTO SHOTSHELL RELOADER

The 366 Auto features full-length resizing with each stroke, automatic primer feed, swing-out wad guide, three-state crimping featuring Taper-Loc for factory tapered crimp, automatic advance to the next station and automatic ejection. The turntable holds 8 shells for 8 operations with each stroke. Automatic charge bar loads shot and powder, dies and crimp starters for 6 point, 8 point and paper crimps.

12, 20, 28 ga.:. $670
.410:. $790

LOCK-N-LOAD AUTO PROGRESSIVE PRESS

The Lock-N-Load Automatic Progressive reloading press features the Lock-N-Load bushing system. Dies and powder measure are inserted into Lock-N-Load die bushings. The bushings remain with the die and powder measure and can be removed in seconds. Other features include: deluxe powder measure, automatic indexing, off-set handle, power-pac linkage, case ejector, five die bushings, shellplate, primer catcher, Positive Priming System, powder drop, Deluxe Powder Measure, automatic primer feed.

MSRP: $490

LOCK-N-LOAD CLASSIC PRESS

Lock-N-Load is available on Hornady's single stage and progressive reloader models. This bushing system locks the die into the press like a rifle bolt. Instead of threading dies in and out of the press, you simply lock and unlock them with a slight twist. Dies are held firmly in a die bushing that stays with the die and retains the die setting. Features: Easy-grip handle; O-style high-strength alloy frame; positive priming system.

MSRP: $145
Lock-N-Load Classic Press Kit: $383
Also Available:
Lock-N-Load 50 Cal. BMG Press: $329
Lock-N-Load 50 Cal. BMG Press Kit: $605

CUSTOM GRADE RELOADING DIES

An Elliptical Expander in Hornady dies minimizes friction and reduces case neck stretch. Other design features include a hardened steel decap pin and a bullet seater alignment sleeve. Dimension Reloading Dies include: collar and collar lock to center expander precisely; one-piece expander spindle with tapered bottom for easy cartridge insertion; wrench flats on die body; Sure-Loc lock rings and collar lock for easy tightening; and built-in crimper. The new Zip Spindle design features a series of light threads cut on the spindle and spindle collet. This design eliminates spindle slippage and takes the knucklebusting out of tightening the spindle lock while making spindle adjustments a snap.

Series I: $39
Series II Three-die Rifle Set: . . . $45
Series III: $45
Match Grade: $50

HANDHELD PRIMING TOOL

Hornady's handheld priming tool features a one-piece primer tray with an improved retaining system for the lid. It also sports integral molded bushings for ultra reliable function. The new primer tray also eliminates the need for separate bushings. The system comes with an additional tray designed for use with RCBS shell holders. The body has been modified for easier change-over, and the seater punch and spring are captured inside the body, allowing shell holders and primer trays to be changed without removing them.

MSRP: $45.48

UNIVERSAL SHELL HOLDERS

Shell Holders for the single stage press have been improved. The mouth of the shell holder has been widened with a radius to allow easier case insertion while maintaining maximum contact area once the case is in the shell holder. Made for use in any tool designed to use a shell holder.

MSRP: $8.17

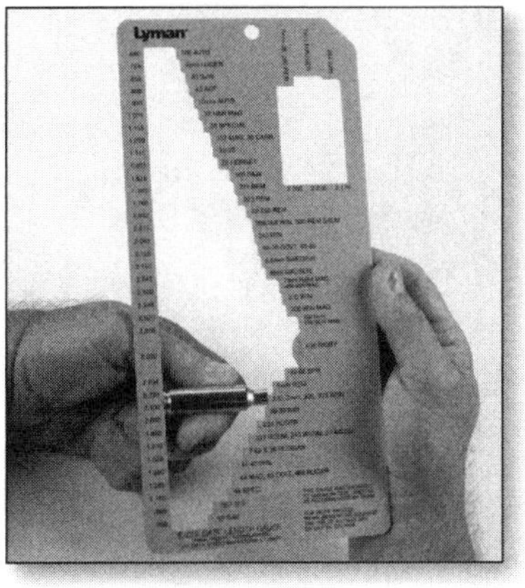

E-ZEE CASE GAUGE II

The E-Zee Case Gauge II measures over 70 popular American and metric rifle and pistol cases. New cartridges include the Winchester Short Magnums, the .204 Ruger and the .500 S&W. The simple slide-through design allows fast, easy and precise sorting of fired or resized cases based on SAAMI recommended maximum case length. Each E-Zee Case Gauge II is carefully crafted and CNC-finish machined. The gauge displays the maximum length dimension for each case in inches and has both inch and metric measuring scales.

E-ZEE Case Gauge II: $12–18

MODEL 1200 DPS II (DIGITAL POWDER SYSTEM)

The 1200 DPS dispenses powder quickly, with .1-grain precision. The 4500 Lube sizer, with a one-piece base casting and a built-in heating element (choose 110 or 220 volt). The long ball-knob handle offers the leverage for sizing and lubricating big bullets. It comes with a gas check seater.

1200 DPS:. $385–395
4500 Lube sizer: $195

CRUSHER II RELOADING PRESS

The only press for rifle or pistol cartridges that offers the advantage of powerful compound leverage combined with a true Magnum press opening. A unique handle design transfers power easily to the center of the ram. A $4\frac{1}{2}$ in. press opening accommodates even the largest cartridges.

MSRP: $162.50

CRUSHER II PRO KIT

Includes press, loading block, case lube kit, primer tray, Model 500 Pro scale, powder funnel and Lyman Reloading Handbook.

MSRP: $245

T-MAG II TURRET RELOADING PRESS

With the T-Mag II, up to six different reloading dies can be mounted on one turret—dies can be precisely mounted, locked in and ready to reload at all times. The T-Mag works with all $\frac{7}{8}$″ x 14″ dies. The T-Mag II turret with quick-disconnect release system is held in alignment by a $\frac{3}{4}$ in. steel stud. The T-Mag II features Lyman's Crusher II compound leverage system.

MSRP: $225
Extra Turret Head: $59.50

Also available:
Expert Kit: (T-MAG II Press, Universal Case Trimmer and pilot Multi-Pak, Model 500 powder scale and Model 50 powder measure, plus accessories. Available in calibers .30-06, .270 and .308

MSRP: $465

MODEL 1200 DPS II

CRUSHER II

T-MAG II PRESS W/ PRIMING ARM & CATCHER

Lyman Reloading Tools

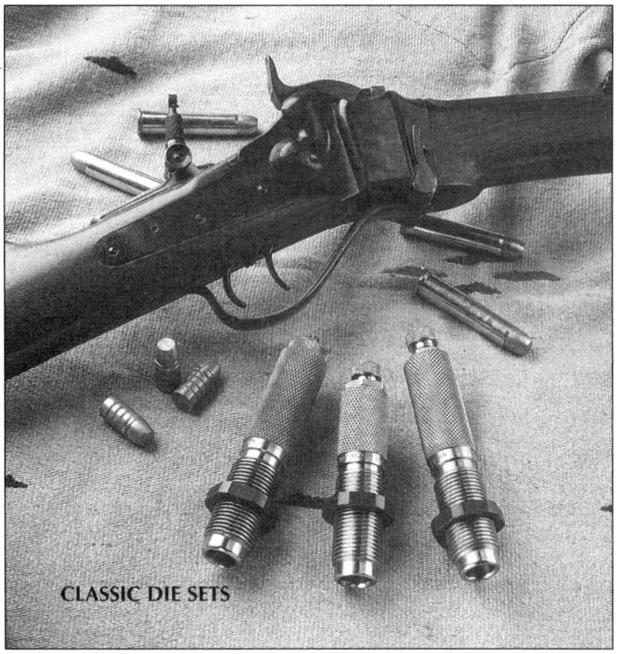
CLASSIC DIE SETS

DIE SET, 5.7X28MM

3-DIE CARBIDE PISTOL DIE SETS

Lyman originated the Tungsten Carbide (T-C) sizing die and the addition of extra seating screws for pistol die sets and the two step neck expanding die. Multi-Deluxe Die sets offer these features; a one-piece hardened steel decapping rod and extra seating screws for all popular bullet nose shapes; all-steel construction.

MSRP: $62.50

CLASSIC DIE SETS

Lyman Products offers new reloading dies sets for .40-60 Win, .45-65 Win and .45-75 Win cartridges. These cartridges have become popular with the introduction of the new '76 Winchester lever action reproductions. Most importantly, these new dies have been carefully engineered to modern standards to provide precise reloads with either black or smokeless powder.

MSRP: $62.50

DIE SET FOR 5.7X28MM FN PISTOL CARTRIDGE

Lyman has added a new die set for the 5.7x28mm FN pistol cartridge. Offered for those shooters who want to enjoy the economy and accuracy advantages of reloading this unique new pistol round, these new dies are precisely dimensioned to load ammo that will provide accurate and reliable function in autoloaders.

MSRP: $61.50

RIFLE DIE SETS

Lyman precision rifle dies feature fine adjustment threads on the bullet seating stem to allow for precision adjustments of bullet seating depth. Lyman dies fit all popular presses using industry standard 7/8″ x 14″ threads, including RCBS, Lee, Hornady, Dillon, Redding and others. Each sizing die for bottle-necked rifle cartridges is carefully vented. This vent hole is precisely placed to prevent air traps that can damage cartridge cases. Each sizing die is polished and heat-treated for toughness.

RIFLE 2-DIE SETS

Set consists of a full-length resizing die with de-capping stem and neck expanding button and a bullet-seating die for loading jacketed bullets in bottlenecked rifle cases. For those who load cast bullets, use a neck-expanding die, available separately.

MSRP: $40

RIFLE 3-DIE SETS

Straight wall rifle cases require these three die sets consisting of a full length resizing die with decapping stem, a two step neck expanding (M) die and a bullet seating die. These sets are ideal for loading cast bullets due to the inclusion of the neck-expanding die.

MSRP: $60
Classic Calibers: $61.50
Classic Neck Size Dies: $29

PREMIUM CARBIDE 4-DIE SETS FOR PISTOLS

Lyman 4-Die Sets feature a separate taper crimp die and powder charge/expanding die. The powder charge/expand die has a special hollow 2-step neck expanding plug which allows powder to flow through the die from a powder measure directly into the case. The powder charge/expanding die has a standard 7/8″ x 14″ thread and will accept Lyman's 55 Powder Measure, or most other powder measures.

MSRP: $76

Lyman Reloading Tools

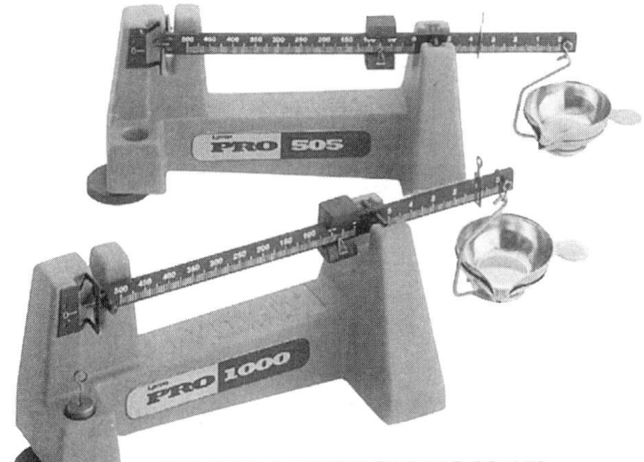

PRO 1000 & 505 RELOADING SCALES

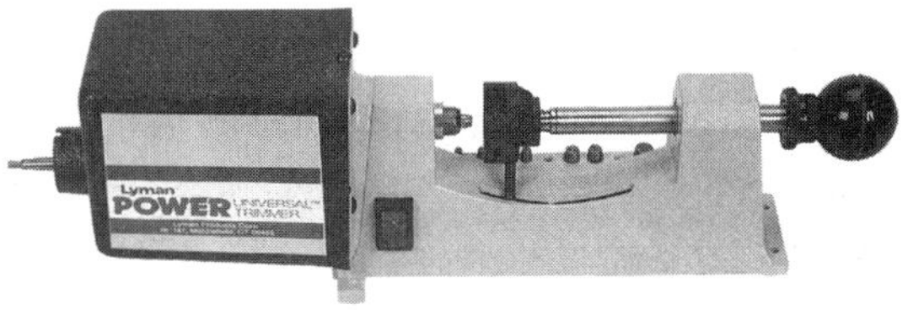

POWER CASE TRIMMER

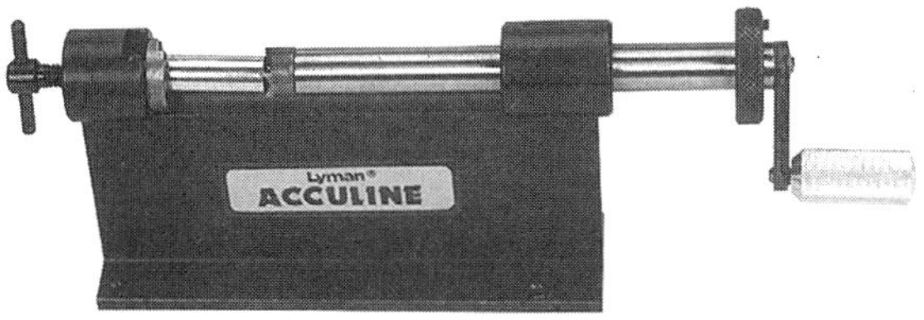

ACCU-TRIMMER

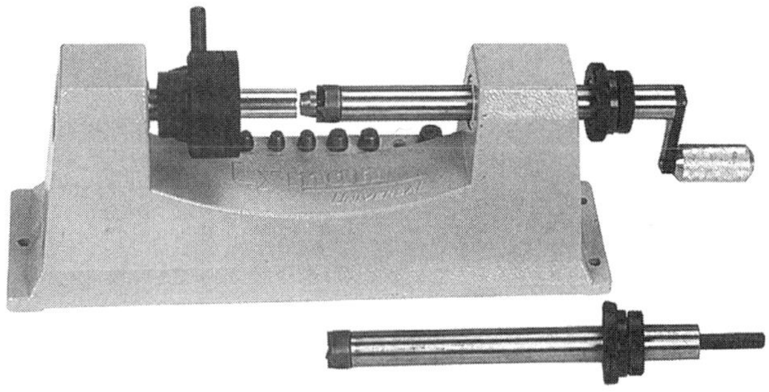

UNIVERSAL TRIMMER WITH NINE PILOT MULTI-PACK WITH POWER ADAPTER

PRO 1000 & 505 RELOADING SCALES

Features include improved platform system; hi-tech base design of high-impact styrene; extra-large, smooth leveling wheel; dual agate bearings; larger damper for fast zeroing; built-in counter weight compartment; easy-to-read beam.

Pro 1000 scale:............$79.95
Pro 500 scale:.............$64.95
Metric scale: $63

ACCU-TRIMMER

Lyman's Accu-Trimmer can be used for all rifle and pistol cases from .22 to .458 Winchester Magnum. Standard shellholders are used to position the case, and the trimmer incorporates standard Lyman cutter heads and pilots. Mounting options include bolting to a bench, C-clamp or vise.

Accu Trimmer w/ 9-pilot Multi-Pak: $55

POWER CASE TRIMMER

The Lyman Power Trimmer is powered by a fan-cooled electric motor designed to withstand the severe demands of case trimming. The unit, which features the Universal Chuckhead, allows cases to be positioned for trimming or easy removal. The Power Trimmer package includes Nine-Pilot Multi-Pack, two cutter heads and a pair of wire end brushes for cleaning primer pockets. Other features include safety guards, on-off rocker switch, heavy cast base with receptacles for nine pilots and bolt holes for mounting on a work bench. Power Trimmer is available for 110 or 220 volt systems.

110 V Model: $300
220 V Model: $310

UNIVERSAL TRIMMER

This trimmer with patented chuckhead accepts all metallic rifle or pistol cases, regardless of rim thickness. To change calibers, simply change the case head pilot. Other features include coarse and fine cutter adjustments, an oil-impregnated bronze bearing, and a rugged cast base to assure precision alignment. Optional carbide cutter available.

Trimmer Multi-Pack (9 pilots: 22, 24, 27, 28/7mm, 30, 9mm, 35, 44 and 4A):............... $94
Universal Trimmer Power Adapter: $24
Power Trimmer—115 V.:...... $286

Lyman Reloading Tools

TURBO TWIN TUMBLER

MODEL 2500
PRO MAGNUM TUMBLER

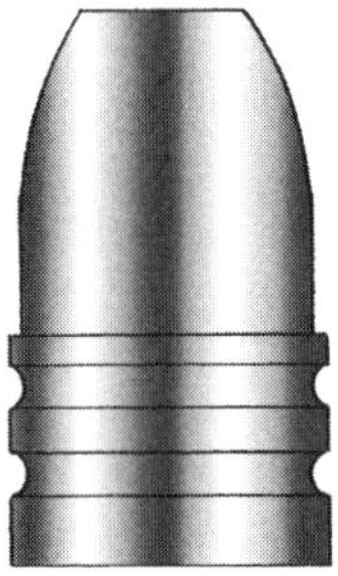

.40-60 WINCHESTER
BULLET MOLD

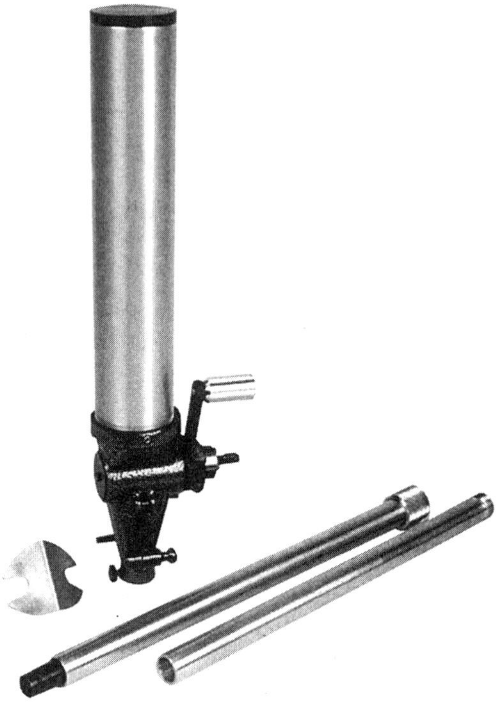

55 CLASSIC
BLACK POWDER MEASURE

MODEL 1200 CLASSIC TURBO TUMBLER

This case tumbler features an improved base and drive system, plus a stronger suspension system and built-in exciters for better tumbling action and faster cleaning.

Model 1200 Classic: $104–112
Model 1200 Auto-Flo: $108–117
Also available:
Model 600: $74
Model 2200 Auto-Flo: $154

MODEL 2500 PRO MAGNUM TUMBLER

The Lyman 2500 Pro Magnum tumbler handles up to 900 .38 Special cartridges at once.

2500 Pro Magnum Tumbler: $100–108
W/ Auto Flow feature: $137.50–140

TURBO TWIN TUMBLER

The Twin features Lyman 1200 Pro Tumbler with an extra 600 bowl system. Reloaders may use each bowl interchangeably for small or large capacity loads. 1200 Pro Bowl System has a built-in sifter lid for easy sifting of cases and media at the end of the polishing cycle. The Twin Tumbler features the Lyman Hi-Profile base design with built-in exciters and anti-rotation pads for faster, more consistent tumbling action.

MSRP: $88–92

.40-60 WINCHESTER BULLET MOLD

The .40-60 Winchester cartridge has become popular with the introduction of the '76 Winchester lever action reproductions. The mold is a proven ideal design that was popular back when these big-bore, lever-action rifles were originally introduced. It has been carefully updated and dimensioned to modern standards for precise reloads with either black or smokeless powder.

MSRP: $60

55 CLASSIC BLACK POWDER MEASURE

Lyman's 55 Classic Powder Measure is ideal for the Cowboy Action Competition or black powder cartridge shooters. The one-pound-capacity aluminum reservoir and brass powder meter eliminate static. The internal powder baffle assures highly accurate and consistent charges. The 24″ powder compacting drop tube allows the maximum charge in each cartridge. Drop tube works on calibers 38 through 50 and mounts easily to the bottom of the measure.

55 Classic Powder Measure (std model-no tubes): $140
55 Classic Powder Measure (with drop tubes): $158
Powder Drop Tubes only: . . . $33.25

Lyman Reloading Tools

POWER DEBURRING KIT

MASTER CASTING KIT

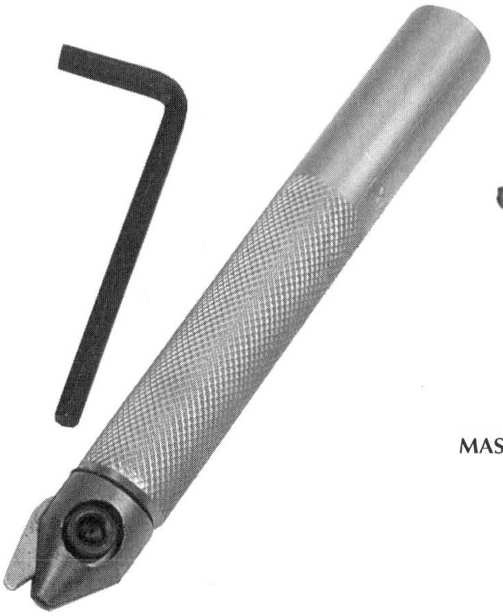

"INSIDE/OUTSIDE" DEBURRING TOOL

ACCULINE OUTSIDE NECK TURNER

To obtain perfectly concentric case necks, Lyman's Outside Neck Turner assures reloaders of uniform neck wall thickness and outside neck diameter. The unit fits Lyman's Universal Trimmer and AccuTrimmer. Rate of feed is adjustable and a mechanical stop controls length of cut. Mandrels are available for calibers from .17 to .375; cutter blade can be adjusted for any diameter from .195″ to .405.″

Outside Neck Turner w/extra blade, 6 mandrels: $37.50
Individual Mandrels: $5

"INSIDE/OUTSIDE" DEBURRING TOOL

This tool features an adjustable cutting blade that adapts easily to the mouth of any rifle or pistol case from .22 to .45 caliber with a simple hex wrench adjustment. Inside deburring is completed by a conical internal section with slotted cutting edges, thus providing uniform inside and outside deburring in one simple operation. The deburring tool is mounted on an anodized aluminum handle that is machine-knurled for a sure grip.

MSRP: $16.50

MASTER CASTING KIT

Designed especially to meet the needs of blackpowder shooters, this kit features Lyman's combination round ball and maxi ball mould blocks. It also contains a combination double cavity mould, mould handle, mini-mag furnace, lead dipper, bullet lube, a user's manual and a cast bullet guide. Kits are available in .45, .50 and .54 caliber.

MSRP: $235

POWER DEBURRING KIT

Features a high torque, rechargeable power driver plus a complete set of accessories, including inside and outside deburr tools, large and small reamers and cleaners and case neck brushes. No threading or chucking required. Set also includes battery recharger and standard flat and Phillips driver bits.

MSRP: $59.95

MEC Reloading

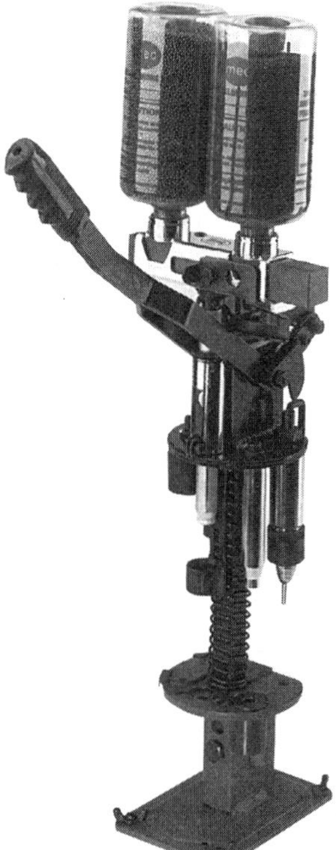

MODEL 600 JR. MARK V

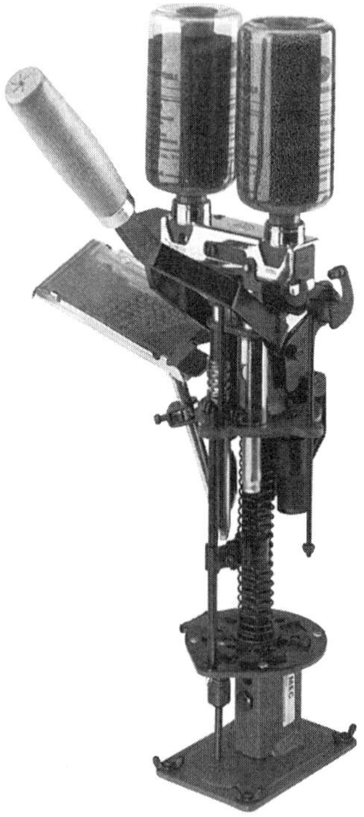

MODEL 650N

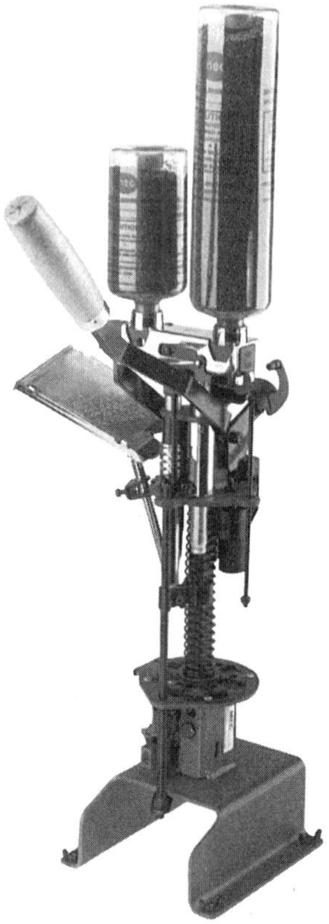

MODEL 8567N

MODEL 8120

MODEL 600 JR. MARK V

This single-stage reloader features a cam-action crimp die to ensure that each shell returns to its original condition. MEC's 600 Jr. Mark 5 can load 6 to 8 boxes per hour and can be updated with the 285 CA primer feed. Press is adjustable for 3 in. shells.

MSRP: $160.50–175.79

MODEL 650N

This reloader works on 6 shells at once. A reloaded shell is completed with every stroke. The MEC 650 does not resize except as a separate operation. Automatic primer feed is standard. Simply fill it with a full box of primers and it will do the rest. Reloader has 3 crimping stations: the first one starts the crimp, the second closes the crimp and the third places a taper on the shell. Available in 12, 16, 20 and 28 ga. and .410 bore. No die sets available.

MSRP: $305–334

MODEL 8567N GRABBER

This reloader features 12 different operations at all 6 stations, producing finished shells with each stroke of the handle. It includes a fully automatic primer feed and Auto-Cycle charging, plus MEC's exclusive 3-stage crimp. The "Power Ring" resizer ensures consistent, accurately sized shells without interrupting the reloading sequence. Simply put in the wads and shell casings, then remove the loaded shells with each pull of the handle. Optional kits to load 3 in. shells and steel shot make this reloader tops in its field. Resizes high and low base shells. Available in 12, 16, 20, 28 ga. and .410 bore.

MSRP: $429–470

MODEL 8120 SIZEMASTER

Sizemaster's "Power Ring" collet resizer returns each base to factory specifications. This resizing station handles brass or steel heads, both high and low base. An 8-fingered collet squeezes the base back to original dimensions, then opens up to release the shell easily. The E-Z Prime auto primer feed is standard equipment (not offered in .410 bore). Press is adjustable for 3 in. shells and is available in 10, 12, 16, 20, 28 ga. and .410 bore. Die sets are available at: $88.67 ($104.06 in 10 ga.).

MSRP: $231–253

MEC Reloading

STEELMASTER

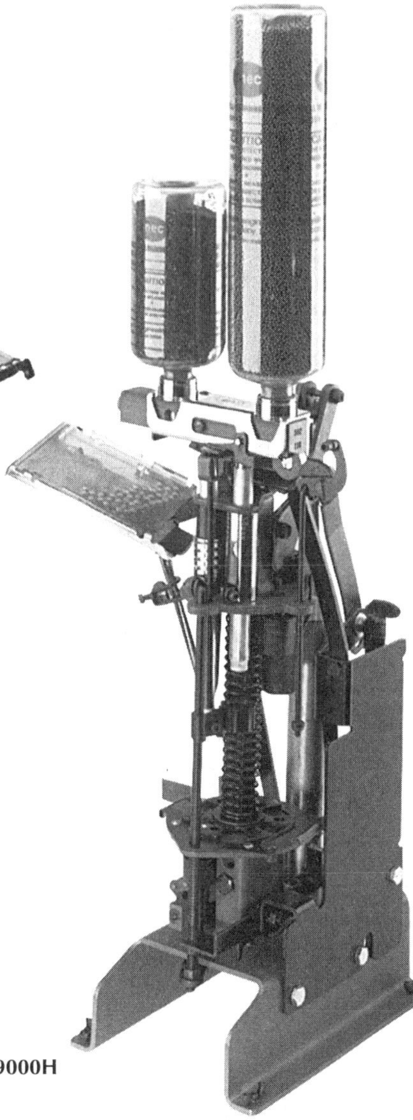

9000H

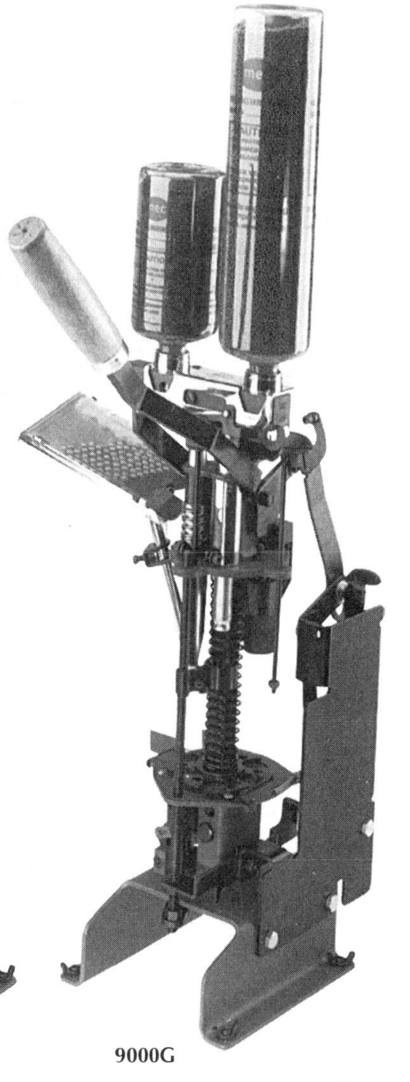

9000G

STEELMASTER SINGLE STATE

Equipped to load steel shotshells as well as lead ones. Every base is resized to factory specs by a precision "power ring" collet. Handles brass or steel heads in high or low base. The E-Z prime auto primer feed dispenses primers automatically and is standard equipment. Separate presses are available for 12 ga. 2¾", 3", 3½" and 10 ga.

8639 Steelmaster
10 & 12 ga.: $262–274
8755 Steelmaster
12 ga. 3½" only: $274

9000 SERIES SHOTSHELL RELOADER

MEC's 9000 Series features automatic indexing and finished shell ejection for quicker and easier reloading. The factory set speed provides uniform movement through every reloading stage. Dropping the primer into the reprime station no longer requires operator "feel." The reloader requires only a minimal adjustment from low to high brass domestic shells, any one of which can be removed for inspection from any station. Can be set up for automatic or manual indexing. Available in 12, 16, 20 and 28 ga. and .410 bore. No die sets are available.

MEC 9000HN: $1056–1650
MEC 9001HN without pump: $578–634
MEC 9000GN Series: $517–566
MEC Super Sizer: $87–95

Nosler Reloading

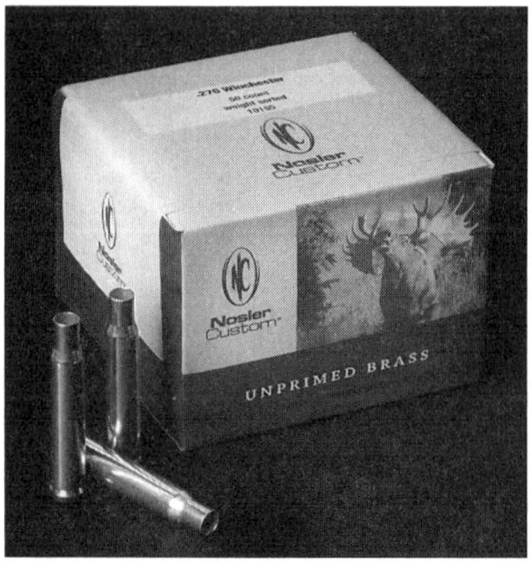

CUSTOM BRASS

Nosler offers cartridge brass in .260 Remington, .280 Ackley Improved, .300 H&H Magnum and .300 Short Action Ultra Mag. The cartridge brass is made to exact dimensional standards and tolerances for maximum accuracy/consistency and long case life. Flash holes are deburred, and necks are deburred and chamfered. Packaged in custom boxes of 50.

260 Rem: $50.95
.280 Ackley: $60.95
.300 H&H Mag:. $50.95
.300 Short Action: $58.95

RCBS Reloading Tools

ROCK CHUCKER SUPREME

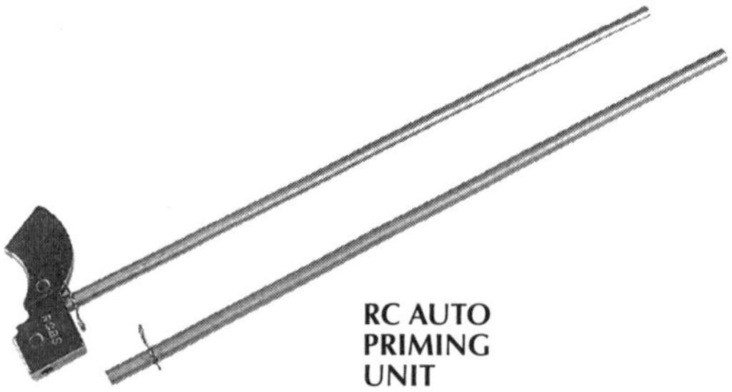

RC AUTO PRIMING UNIT

AMMOMASTER-2 SINGLE STAGE

PRESSES

ROCK CHUCKER SUPREME PRESS

With its easy operation, outstanding strength and versatility, a Rock Chucker Supreme press serves beginner and pro alike. It can also be upgraded to a progressive press with an optional Piggyback conversion unit.

- Heavy-duty cast iron for easy case-resizing
- Larger window opening to accommodate longer cartridges
- 1" ram held in place by 12½ sq. in. of rambearing surface
- Ambidextrous handle
- Compound leverage system
- 7/8" x 14" thread for all standard reloading dies and accessories

MSRP: $190.95

ROCK CHUCKER SUPREME AUTO PRIMING UNIT

RCBS's Rock Chucker Supreme Auto Priming Unit will allow the users of the current single stage model to advance to a tube-fed auto priming system. The new auto-priming option will expand the capabilities of one of the most popular reloading presses. It eliminates the need to handle primers and boasts a 100 primer capacity. The new feature is easy to install to existing presses, as the RC Supreme Auto Prime body attaches to the same place as the standard priming arm. The upgraded unit is operated with a push bar, and comes with a large and small primer pick up, feed tubes and primer seat plugs.

MSRP: $50

AMMOMASTER-2 RELOADING SYSTEM

The AmmoMaster offers handloaders the freedom to configure a press to particular needs and preferences. It covers the complete spectrum of reloading, from single stage through fully automatic progressive reloading, from .25 Auto to .50 caliber. The AmmoMaster Auto has all the features of a five-station press.

MSRP: $341.95

GRAND SHOTSHELL PRESS

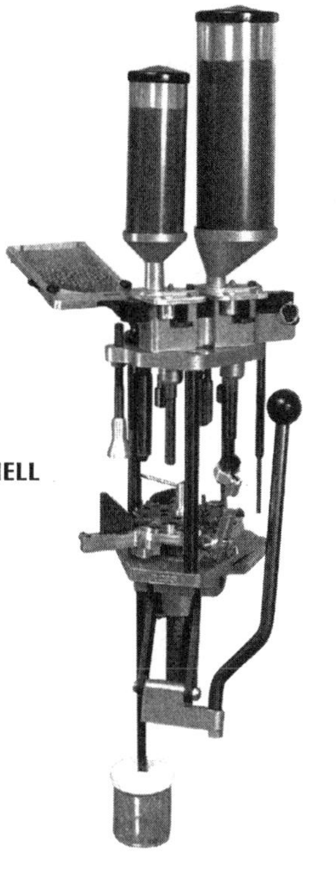

MINI-GRAND SHOTSHELL PRESS

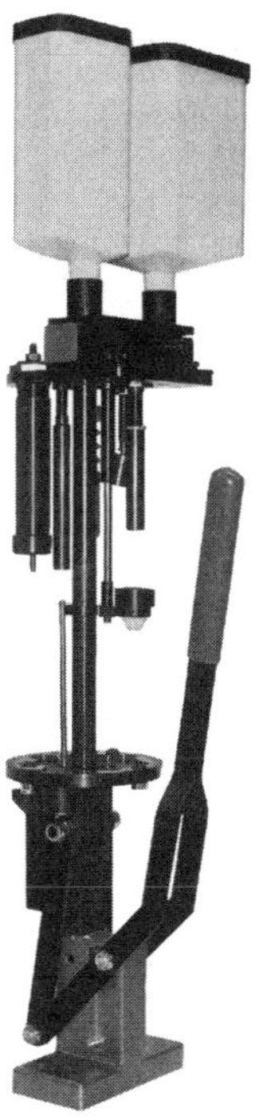

PRO-2000 PROGRESSIVE PRESS

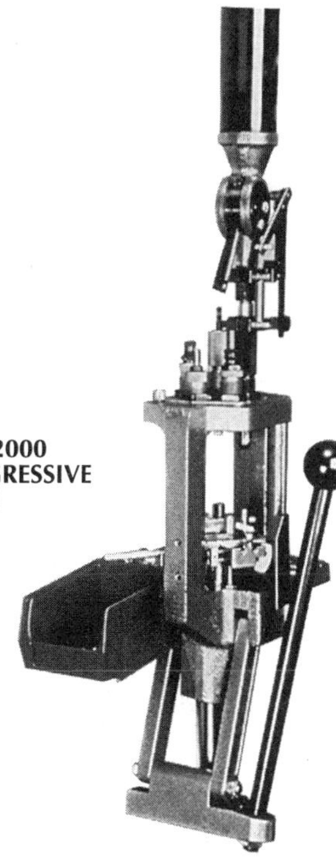

.50 BMG PACK

The Pack includes the press, dies and accessory items needed, all in one box. The press is the Ammo Master Single Stage rigged for 1½″ dies. It has a 1½″ solid steel ram and plenty of height for the big .50. The kit also has a set of RCBS .50 BMG, 1½″ reloading dies, including both full-length sizer and seater. Other items are a shell holder, ram priming unit and a trim die.

MSRP: $742.95

GRAND SHOTSHELL PRESS

Features: The combination of the Powder system and shot system and Case Holders allows the user to reload shells without fear of spillage. The powder system is case-actuated: no hull, no powder. Cases are easily removed with universal 12 and 20 ga. case holders allowing cases to be sized down to the rim. Priming system: Only one primer feeds at a time. Steel size ring: Provides complete resizing of high and low base hulls. Holds 25 lbs. of shot and 1½ lbs. of powder. Lifetime warranty.

MSRP: $878.36
Grand Conversion kit: $400.36

MINI-GRAND SHOTSHELL PRESS

The Mini-Grand shotgun press, a seven-station single-stage press, loads 12 and 20 ga. hulls, from 2¾ to 3½ in. in length. It utilizes RCBS, Hornady and Ponsness Warren powder and shot bushings, with a half-pound capacity powder hopper and 12½ lb. capacity shot hopper. The machine will load both lead and steel shot.

MSRP: $160.95

ROCK CHUCKER SUPREME MASTER RELOADING KIT

The Rock Chucker Master Reloading Kit includes all the tools and accessories needed to start handloading: Rock Chucker Press; RCBS 505 Reloading Scale; Speer Manual #13; Uniflow Powder Measure; deburring tool; case loading block; Primer Tray-2; Hand priming tool; powder funnel; case lube pad; case neck brushes; fold-up hex key set; Trim Pro Manual Case Trimmer Kit.

MSRP: $445.95

PARTNER PRESS

Easy-to-use, durable press in a compact package. Features compound linkage, durable steel links, priming arm. Reloads most standard calibers.

MSRP: $90.90
Partner Press Reloading Kit: $229.95

PRO-2000 PROGRESSIVE PRESS

Constructed of cast iron, the Pro-2000 features five reloading stations. The case-actuated powder measure assures repeatability of dispensing powder. A Micrometer Adjustment Screw allows precise return to previously recorded charges. All dies are standard 7/8″ x 14″, including the Expander Die. The press incorporates the APS Priming System. Allows full-length sizing in calibers from .32 Auto to.460 Weatherby Mag.

MSRP: $654.95
Deluxe Reloading Kit: $1177.95

RCBS Reloading Tools

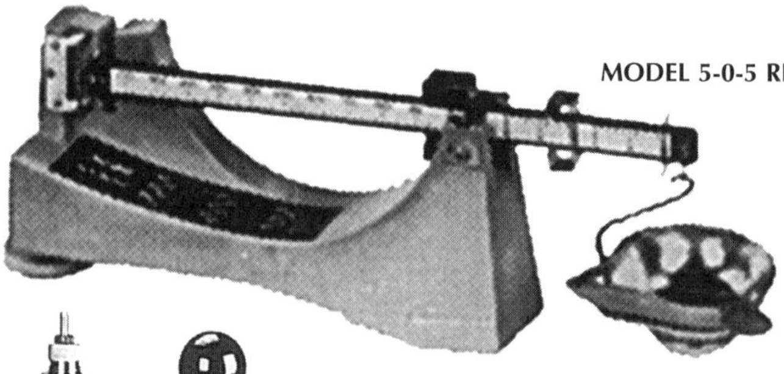

MODEL 5-0-5 RELOADING SCALE

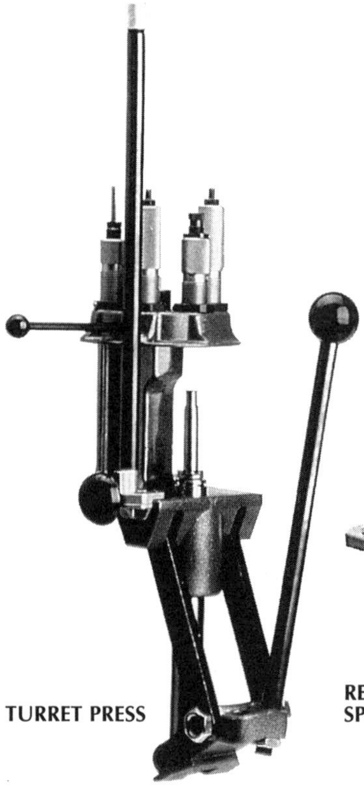

TURRET PRESS

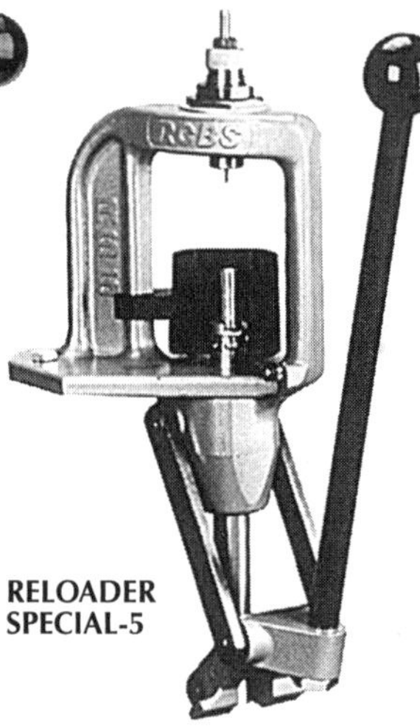

RELOADER SPECIAL-5

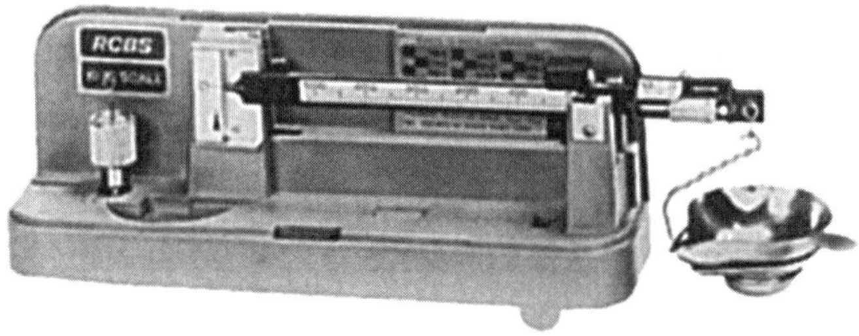

MODEL 1010 RELOADING SCALE

TURRET PRESS

With pre-set dies in the six-station turret head, the Turret Press can increase production from 50 to 200 rounds per hour. The frame, links, and toggle block are constructed of cast iron and the handle offers compound leverage for full-length sizing of any caliber from .25 ACP to .460 Weatherby Magnum. Six stations allow for custom set-up. The quick-change turret head makes caliber changes fast and easy. This press accepts all standard 7/8″ x 14″ dies and shell holders.

MSRP: $276.95
Turret Deluxe Reloading Kit: $543.95

RELOADER SPECIAL-5 PRESS

The Reloader Special press features a ball handle and primer arm so that cases can be primed and resized at the same time. Other features include a compound leverage system; solid aluminum "O" frame offset; corrosion-resistant baked-powder finish; 7/8″ x 14″ thread for all standard reloading dies and accessories; optional Piggyback II conversion unit.

MSRP: $155.95
Reloading Starter Kit: $353.95

PIGGYBACK III CONVERSION KIT

The Piggyback III conversion unit moves from single-stage reloading to 5-station, manual-indexing, progressive reloading in one step. The Piggyback III will work with the RCBS Rock Chucker, Reloader Special-3 and Reloader Special-5.

MSRP: $493.95

RELOADING SCALES

MODEL 5-0-5 RELOADING SCALE

This 511-grain capacity scale has a three-poise system with widely spaced, deep beam notches. Two smaller poises on right side adjust from 0.1 to 10 grains, larger one on left side adjusts in full 10-grain steps. The scale uses magnetic dampening to eliminate beam oscillation. The 5-0-5 also has a sturdy die-cast base with large leveling legs. Self-aligning agate bearings support the hardened steel beam pivots for a guaranteed sensitivity to 0.1 grains.

MSRP: $112.95

MODEL 1010 RELOADING SCALE

Normal capacity is 510 grains, which can be increased without loss of sensitivity by attaching the included extra weight up to 1010 grains. Features include micrometer poise for quick, precise weighing, special approach-to-weight indicator, easy-to-read graduation, magnetic dampener, agate bearings, anti-tip pan and a dustproof lid snaps on to cover scale for storage. Sensitivity is guaranteed to 0.1 grains.

MSRP: $189.95

RCBS Reloading Tools

CHARGEMASTER 1500

RANGEMASTER 750

APS PRIMER STRIP LOADER

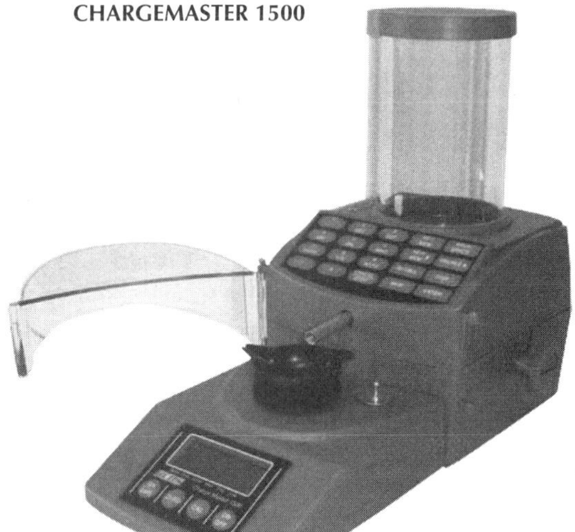

CHARGEMASTER COMBO

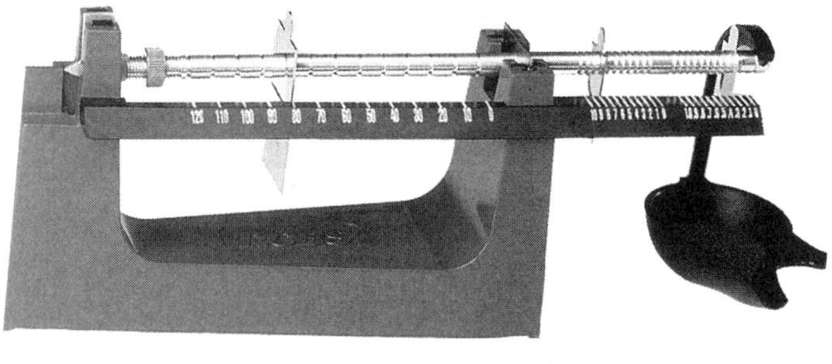

RC-130 MECHANICAL SCALE

CHARGEMASTER 1500 SCALE

High performance reloading scale with 1500-grain capacity. Scale reads in grains or grams; calibration weights included. Available in 110 or 220 volt—AC adaptor included. Can be upgraded to an automatic dispensing system with the RCBS ChargeMaster.

MSRP: $239.95

CHARGEMASTER COMBO

Performs as a scale or as a complete powder dispensing system. Scale can be removed and used separately. Dispenses from 2.0 to 300 grains. Reads and dispenses in grains or grams. Stores up to 30 charges in memory for quick recall of favorite loads. 110 volt or 220 volt adaptor included.

MSRP: $456.95

RANGEMASTER 750 SCALE

Compact, lightweight and portable with 750-grain capacity. Scale reads in grams or grains; calibration weights included. Accurate to ± 0.1 of a grain; fast calibration; Powered by AC or 9 volt battery—AC adaptor included. 110 or 220 volt model available.

MSRP: $152.95

RC-130 MECHANICAL SCALE

The RC130 features a 130-grain capacity and maintenance-free movement, plus a magnetic dampening system for fast readings. A 3-poise design incorporates easy adjustments with a beam that is graduated in increments of 10 grains and 1 grain. A micrometer poise measures in 0.1-grain increments with accuracy to ±0.1 grain.

MSRP: $56.95

HANDLOADING ACCESSORIES

APS PRIMER STRIP LOADER

For those who keep a supply of CCI primers in conventional packaging, the APS primer strip loader allows quick filling of empty strips. Each push of the handle seats 25 primers.

MSRP: $37.95

RCBS Reloading Tools

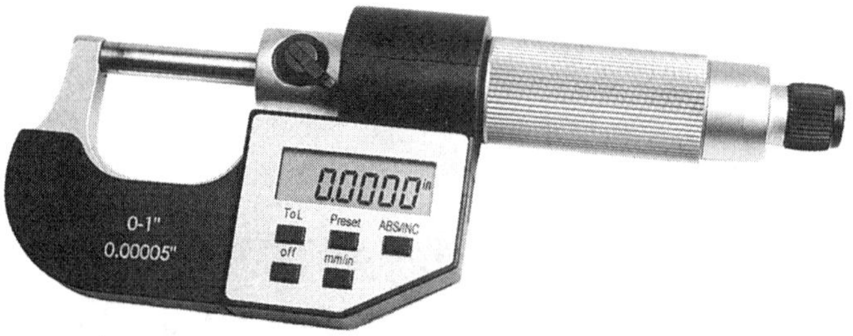

ELECTRONIC DIGITAL MICROMETER

SHELL HOLDER RACK

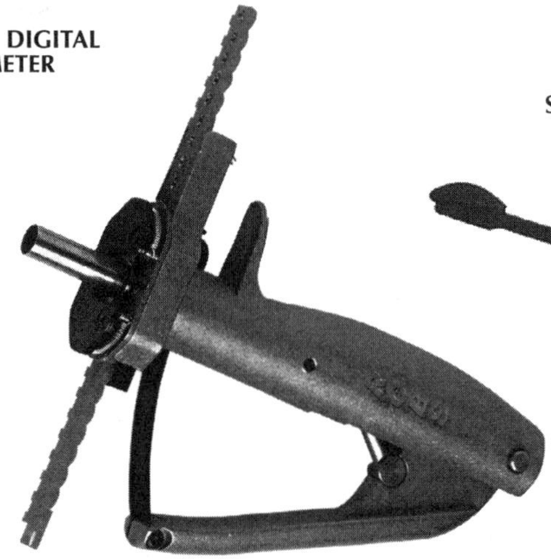

HAND PRIMING TOOL

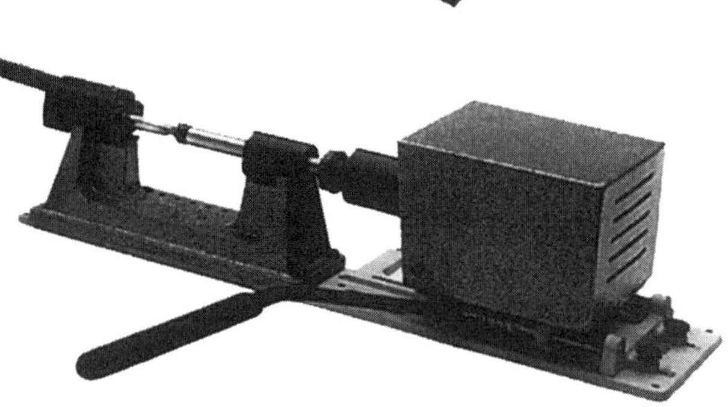

TRIM PRO CASE TRIMMER

ELECTRONIC DIGITAL MICROMETER

Instant reading; large, easy to read numbers for error reduction with instant inch/millimeter conversion; zero adjust at any position; thimble lock for measuring like objects; replaceable silver oxide cell—1.55 Volt; auto off after 5 minutes for longer battery life; adjustment wrench included; fitted wooden storage cases.

MSRP: $151.95

HAND PRIMING TOOL

A patented safety mechanism separates the seating operation from the primer supply, virtually eliminating the possibility of tray detonation. Fits in your hand for portable primer seating. Primer tray installation requires no contact with the primers. Uses the same RCBS shell holders as RCBS presses. Made of cast metal.

MSRP: $48.95

SHELL HOLDER RACK

RCBS has developed the Shell Holder Rack to give reloaders another unique way to stay organized. This item allows shooters quick and easy access to all shell holders, and eliminates digging through several loose holders to find the right one. The Shell Holder Rack has twelve positions that hold two shell holders on each post. There is also room to store six Trim Pro Shell Holders as well. Its clear cover keeps out the dust and dirt while allowing you to see what is stored in the rack. This rack can also be mounted on the wall or used on the bench. The wall mount spacing allows it to be hung off of standard 1-in. pegboard hooks as well. The support legs angle the bottom out for wall mounting or the top up for bench use. Several Shell Holder Racks can be snapped together if more shell holder storage is needed, and stickers are included to label shell holder posts.

MSRP: $14.95

POW'R PULL BULLET PULLER

The RCBS Pow'r Pull bullet puller features a three-jaw chuck that grips the case rim—just rap it on any solid surface like a hammer, and powder and bullet drop into the main chamber for re-use. A soft cushion protects bullets from damage. Works with most centerfire cartridges from .22 to .45 (not for use with rimfire cartridges).

MSRP: $19.95

TRIM PRO CASE TRIMMER

Cases are trimmed quickly and easily. The lever-type handle is more accurate to use than draw collet systems. A flat plate shell holder keeps cases locked in place and aligned. A micrometer fine adjustment bushing offers trimming accuracy to within .001 in. Made of die-cast metal with hardened cutting blades.

Power 120 Vac Kit: $347.95
Manual Kit: $125.95
Trim Pro Case Trimmer Stand: $25.95

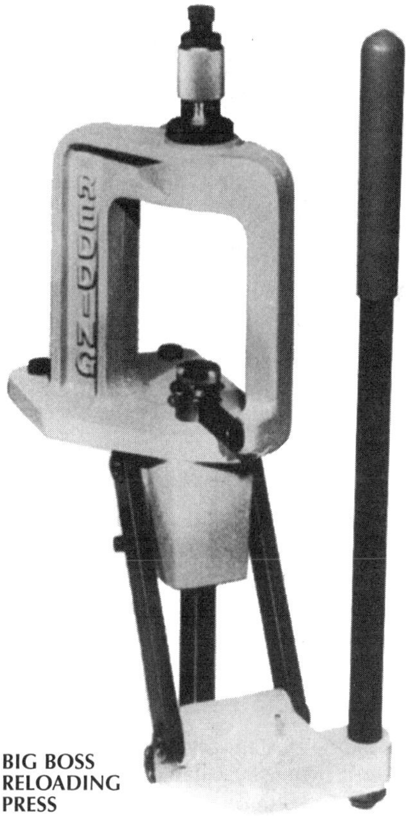

BIG BOSS RELOADING PRESS

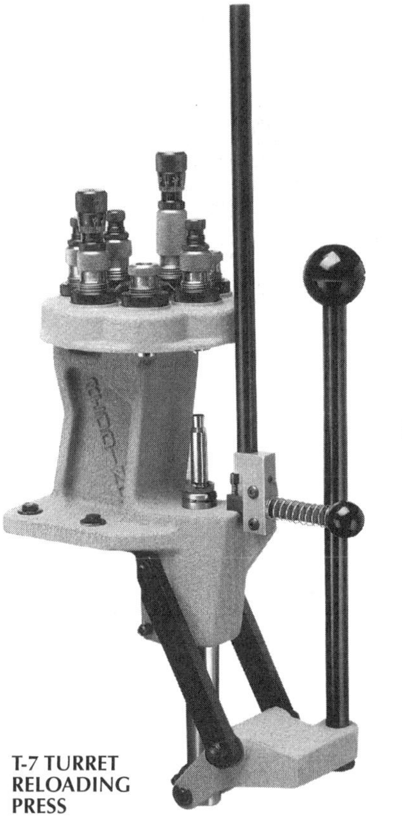

T-7 TURRET RELOADING PRESS

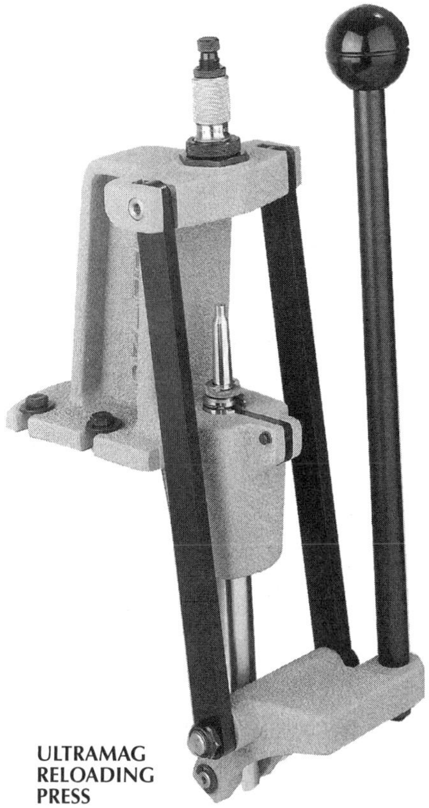

ULTRAMAG RELOADING PRESS

HANDLOADING PRESSES

BOSS RELOADING PRESS

This "O" type reloading press features a rigid cast iron frame whose 36 degree offset provides the best visibility and access of comparable presses. Its "Smart" primer arm moves in and out of position automatically with ram travel. The priming arm is positioned at the bottom of ram travel for lowest leverage and best feel. Model 721 accepts all standard 7/8″ x 14″ threaded dies and universal shell holders.

MSRP: $192
W/ Shellholder and 10A Dies: . $249
Boss Pro-Pak Reloading Kit: . . $477
W/o dies and shellholder: $429

BIG BOSS RELOADING PRESS

A larger version of the Boss reloading press built on a heavier frame with a longer ram stroke for reloading magnum cartridges. It features a 1 in. diameter ram with over 3.8 inches of stroke; Smart primer arm; offset ball handle; heavy duty cast iron frame; heavy duty compound linkage; steel adapter bushing accepts all standard 7/8″ x 14″ threaded dies.

MSRP: $262.50

T-7 TURRET RELOADING PRESS

Features 7 station turret head, heavy duty cast iron frame, 1 in. diameter ram, optional "Slide Bar Automatic Primer Feeder System." This feeder eliminates handling of primers during sizing and speeds up reloading operations.

T-7 Turret Press: $421.50
Kit (press, shellholder and 10A dies): $478.50
Slide Bar Automatic Primer Feeder System: $80

ULTRAMAG RELOADING PRESS

The Ultramag's compound leverage system is connected at the top of the press frame. This allows the reloader to develop tons of pressure without the usual concern of press frame deflection. Huge frame opening will handle 50 x 3¼-inch Sharps with ease.

MSRP: $439.50
Kit, includes shell holder and one set of 10A dies: . $496.50

DIES & BUSHINGS

BODY DIES

Designed to full-length resize the case body and bump the shoulder position for proper chambering without disturbing the case neck. They are intended for use only to resize cases that have become increasingly difficult to chamber after repeated firing and neck sizing. Small Base Body Dies are available in .223 Rem, 6mm P.P.C, 6mm B. R. Rem, 6mm/284 Win, .260 Rem, 6.5mm/284 Win, .284 Win, .308 Win, .30-06.

Category I: $340
Category II: $48.80
Category III: $60
Small Base Body Dies: $49.10

Redding Reloading Tools

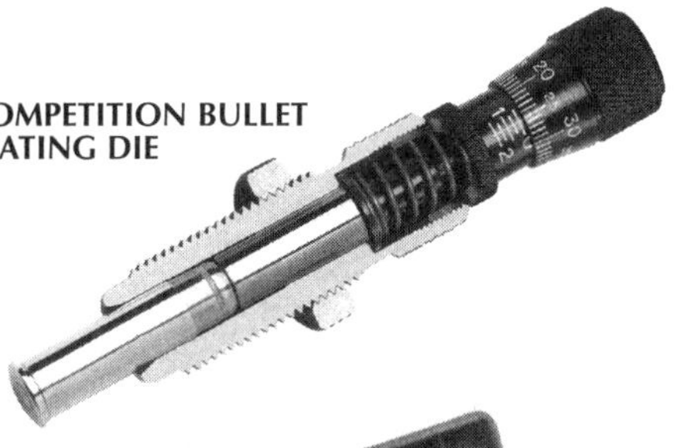

COMPETITION BULLET SEATING DIE

FORM & TRIM DIES

NECK SIZING DIES

NECK SIZING BUSHINGS

COMPETITION BUSHING STYLE - NECK SIZING DIE

PISTOL TRIM DIES

COMPETITION BULLET SEATING DIE FOR HANDGUN & STRAIGHT-WALL RIFLE CARTRIDGES

The precision seating stem moves well down into the die chamber to accomplish early bullet contact. The seating stem's spring loading provides positive alignment bias between the tapered nose and the bullet ogive. Thus spring loading and bullet alignment are maintained as the bullet and cartridge case move upward until the actual seating of the bullet begins. The Competition Bullet Seating Die features dial-in micrometer adjustment calibrated in .001-in. increments, is infinitely adjustable and has a "zero" set feature that allows setting desired load to zero. The die is compatible with all progressive reloading presses and has industry standard 7/8″ x 14″ threaded extended die bodies. An oversize bell-mouth chamfer with smooth radius has been added to the bottom of the die.

MSRP: $112.50

COMPETITION BUSHING-STYLE NECK SIZING DIE

This die allows you to fit the neck of your case perfectly in the chamber. As in the Competition Seating Die, the cartridge case is completely supported and aligned with the sizing bushing and remains supported in the sliding sleeve as it moves upward while the resizing bushing self-centers on the case neck. The micrometer adjustment of the bushing position delivers precise control to the desired neck length. All dies are supplied without bushings.

Category I:. $148.50
Category II: $177.00
Category III: $219.00

FORM & TRIM DIES

Redding trim dies file trim cases without unnecessary resizing because they are made to chamber dimensions. For case forming and necking brass down from another caliber, Redding trim dies can be the perfect intermediate step before full length resizing.

Series A: $39.30
Series B: $54.30
Series C: $66.60
Series D: $73.50

NECK SIZING BUSHINGS

Redding Neck Sizing Bushings are available in two styles. Both share the same external dimensions (1/2″ O.D. x 3/8″ long) and freely interchange in all Redding Bushing style Neck Sizing Dies. They are available in .001″ size increments throughout the range of .185″ thru .365″, covering all calibers from .17 to .338.

MSRP: $18.90
Heat treated steel bushings: .$33.60

NECK SIZING DIES

These dies size only the necks of bottleneck cases to prolong brass life and improve accuracy. These dies size only the neck and not the shoulder or body, fired cases should not be interchanged between rifles of the same caliber. Available individually or in Deluxe Die Sets.

Series A: $43.80
Series B: $59.40
Series C: $75.60
Series D: $85.20

PISTOL TRIM DIES

Redding trim dies for pistol calibers allow trimming cases without excessive resizing. Pistol trim dies require extended shellholders.

Series A: $39.30
Series B: $54.30
Series C: $66.60
Series D: $73.50

PROFILE CRIMP DIES

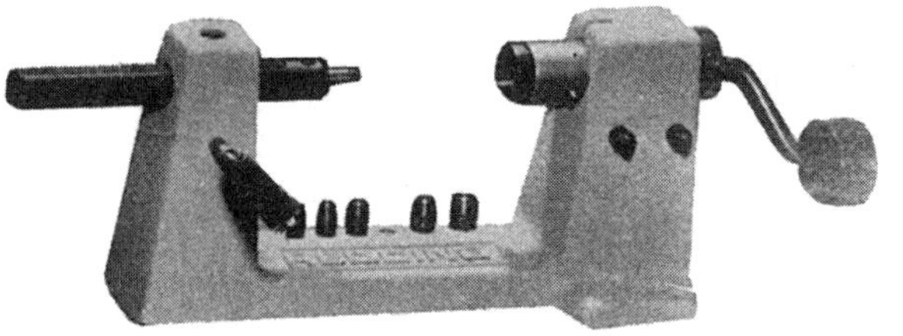

MODEL TR-1400 TRIMMER

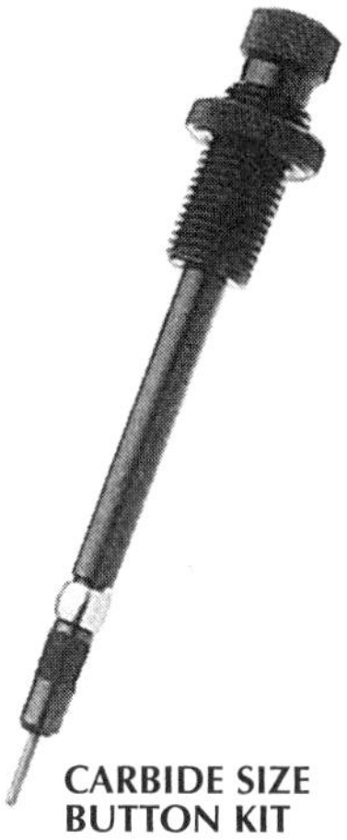

CARBIDE SIZE BUTTON KIT

TAPER & CRIMP DIES

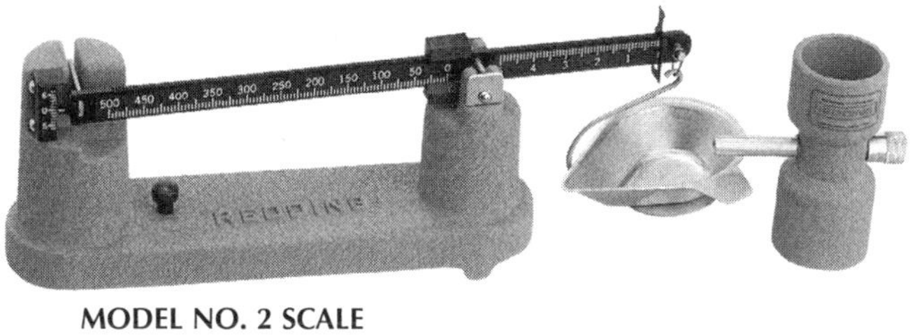

MODEL NO. 2 SCALE

PROFILE CRIMP DIES

For handgun cartridges which do not head-space on the case mouth. These dies were designed for those who want the best possible crimp. Profile crimp dies provide a tighter, more uniform roll type crimp, and require the bullet to be seated to the correct depth in a previous operation.

Series A: $33.90
Series B: $42
Series C: $51
Series D: $57.60

TAPER & CRIMP DIES

Designed for handgun cartridges which headspace on the case mouth where conventional roll crimping is undesirable. Also available for some revolver cartridges, for those who prefer the uniformity of a taper crimp. Available in the following rifle calibers: .223 Rem., 7.62MM x 39, .30-30, .308 Win, .30-06, .300, Win Mag.

Series A: $33.90
Series B: $42
Series C: $51
Series D: $57.60

TYPE S–BUSHING STYLE DIES

The new Type S - Bushing Style Neck Sizing Die provides reloaders with a simple means to precisely control case neck size and tension. The Type-S features: interchangeable sizing bushings available in .001 in. increments; adjustable decapping rod with standard size button; self-centering resizing bushing; decapping pin retainer. All dies are supplied without bushings.

Category I: $76.80
Category II: $94.20
Category III: $115.80

CASE TRIMMERS

MASTER CASE TRIMMER MODEL TR-1400

This unit features a universal collet that accepts all rifle and pistol cases. The frame is cast iron with storage holes in the base for extra pilots. Coarse and fine adjustments are provided for case length. The Master Case Trimmer also features: six pilots (.22, 6mm, .25, .270, 7mm and .30 cal.); universal collet; two neck cleaning brushes (.22 through .30 cal.); two primer pocket cleaners (large and small); tin coated replaceable cutter; accessory power screwdriver adaptor.

Master Case Trimmer: $136.50
Pilots: $6.00

POWDER SCALES

MODEL NO. 2 MASTER POWDER AND BULLET SCALE

Model No. 2 features 505-grain capacity and .1-grain accuracy, a dampened beam and hardened knife edges and milled stainless bearing seats for smooth, consistent operation and a high level of durability.

MSRP: $121.50

HANDLOADING ACCESSORIES

CARBIDE SIZE BUTTON KITS

Make inside neck sizing smoother and easier without lubrication. Now die sets can be upgraded with a carbide size button kit. Available for bottleneck cartridges .22 thru .338 cal. The carbide size button is free-floating on the decap rod, allowing it to self-center in the case neck. Kits contain: carbide size button, retainer and spare decapping pin. These kits also fit all Type-S dies.

MSRP: $37.50

MODEL 3 POWDER MEASURE

The Model 3 has a micrometer metering chamber in front for easy setting and reading. The frame is precision machined cast iron with hand honed fit between the frame and hard surfaced drum to easily cut and meter powders. The Model 3 features a large capacity clear powder reservoir; see-through drop tube; body w/ standard 7/8" x 14" thread to fit mounting bracket and optional bench stand; cast mounting bracket included.

Powder Measure 3 with universal metering chamber: $184.50
Powder Measure 3K, w/ two metering chambers: $218
Handgun Metering Chamber: $51.50

Redding Reloading Tools

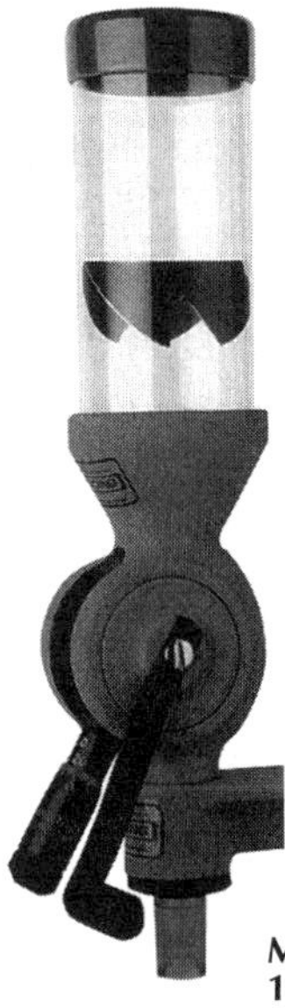

MODEL 10X-PISTOL AND SMALL RIFLE MEASURE

MODEL BR-30 MEASURE

EZ FEED SHELL HOLDERS

EXTENDED SHELL HOLDERS

HEADSPACE & BULLET COMPARATOR

COMPETITION MODEL 10X-PISTOL AND SMALL RIFLE POWDER MEASURE

Combines all of the features of Competition Model BR-30, with a drum and metering unit designed to provide uniform metering of small charge weights. To achieve the best metering possible at the targeted charge weight of approximately 10 grains, the diameter of the metering cavity is reduced and the metering plunger is given a hemispherical shape. Charge range: 1 to 25 grains. Drum assembly easily changed from right to left-handed operation.

MSRP: $276

COMPETITION MODEL BR-30 POWDER MEASURE

This powder measure features a drum and micrometer that limit the overall charging range from a low of 10 grains to a maximum of 50 grains. The diameter of Model 3BR's metering cavity has been reduced, and the metering plunger has a unique hemispherical shape, creating a powder cavity that resembles the bottom of a test tube. The result: irregular powder settling is alleviated and charge-to-charge uniformity is enhanced.

MSRP: $276

MATCH-GRADE POWDER MEASURE MODEL 3BR

Interchange Universal- or pistol-metering chambers. Measures charges up to 100 grains. Unit is fitted with lock ring for fast dump with large clear plastic reservoir. See-through drop tube accepts all calibers from .22 to .600. Precision-fitted rotating drum is critically honed to prevent powder escape. Knife-edged powder chamber shears coarse-grained powders with ease, ensuring accurate charges.

Match Grade 3BR measure: $232.50

3BR Kit, with both chambers: $288

Pistol Metering chamber (0-10 grains): $70.80

SHELLHOLDERS

EZ FEED SHELLHOLDERS

Redding shellholders are of a Universal "snap-in" design recommended for use with all Redding dies and presses, as well as all other popular brands. They are precision machined to very close tolerances and heat treated to fit cases and eliminate potential resizing problems. The outside knurling makes them easier to handle and change.

MSRP: $12

EXTENDED SHELL HOLDERS

Extended shellholders are required when trimming short cases under 1½ in. O.A.L. They are machined to the same tolerances as standard shellholders, except they're longer.

MSRP: $19.20

HANDLOADING TOOLS

INSTANT INDICATOR HEADSPACE & BULLET COMPARATOR

The Instant Indicator checks the headspace from the case shoulder to the base. Bullet seating depths can be compared and bullets can be sorted by checking the base of bullets to give dimension. Case length can be measured. Available for 33 cartridges from .222 Rem to .338 Win. Mag., including new WSSM cartridges.

W/ Dial Indicator: $168.30

W/o Dial Indicator: $130.20

CENTERFIRE RIFLE BALLISTICS

CENTERFIRE HANDGUN BALLISTICS

Centerfire Rifle Ballistics

Comprehensive Ballistics Tables for Currently Manufactured Sporting Rifle Cartridges

No more collecting catalogs and peering at microscopic print to find out what ammunition is offered for a cartridge, and how it performs relative to other factory loads! *Shooter's Bible* has assembled the data for you, in easy-to-read tables, by cartridge. Of course, this section will be updated every year to bring you the latest information.

Data is taken from manufacturers' charts; your chronograph readings may vary. Listings are current as of February the year *Shooter's Bible* appears (not the cover year). Listings are not intended as recommendations. For example, the data for the .44 Magnum at 400 yards shows its effective range is much shorter. The lack of data for a 285-grain .375 H&H bullet beyond 300 yards does not mean the bullet has no authority farther out. Besides ammunition, the rifle, sights, conditions and shooter ability all must be considered when contemplating a long shot. Accuracy and bullet energy both matter when big game is in the offing.

Barrel length affects velocity, and at various rates depending on the load. As a rule, figure 50 fps per inch of barrel, plus or minus, if your barrel is longer or shorter than 22 inches.

Bullets are given by make, weight (in grains) and type. Most type abbreviations are self-explanatory: BT=Boat-Tail, FMJ=Full Metal Jacket, HP=Hollow Point, SP=Soft Point—except in Hornady listings, where SP is the firm's Spire Point. TNT and TXP are trademarked designations of Speer and Norma. XLC identifies a coated Barnes X bullet. HE indicates a Federal High Energy load, similar to the Hornady LM (Light Magnum) and HM (Heavy Magnum) cartridges.

Arc (trajectory) is based on a zero range published by the manufacturer, from 100 to 300 yards. If a zero does not fall in a yardage column, it lies halfway between—at 150 yards, for example, if the bullet's strike is "+" at 100 yards and "-" at 200.

.17 REMINGTON TO .221 REMINGTON FIREBALL

CARTRIDGE BULLET	RANGE, YARDS:	0	100	200	300	400
.17 Remington						
Rem. 20 AccuTip BT	velocity, fps:	4250	3594	3028	2529	2081
	energy, ft-lb:	802	574	407	284	192
	arc, inches:		+1.3	+1.3	-2.5	-11.8
Rem. 20 Fireball	velocity, fps	4000	3380	2840	2360	1930
	energy, ft-lb	710	507	358	247	165
	arc, inches		+1.6	+1.5	-2.8	-13.5
Rem. 25 HP Power-Lokt	velocity, fps:	4040	3284	2644	2086	1606
	energy, ft-lb:	906	599	388	242	143
	arc, inches:		+1.8	0	-3.3	-16.6
.204 Ruger						
Federal 32 Nosler Ballistic Tip	velocity, fps	4030	3465	2968	2523	2119
	arc, inches		+0.7	0	-4.7	-14.9
Hornady 32 V-Max	velocity, fps:	4225	3632	3114	2652	2234
	energy, ft-lb:	1268	937	689	500	355
	arc, inches:		+0.6	0	-4.2	-13.4
Hornady 40 V-Max	velocity, fps:	3900	3451	3046	2677	2335
	energy, ft-lb:	1351	1058	824	636	485
	arc, inches:		+0.7	0	-4.5	-13.9
Rem. 32 AccuTip	velocity, fps:	4225	3632	3114	2652	2234
	Energy, ft-lb:	1268	937	689	500	355
	Arc, inches:		+0.6	0	-4.1	-13.1
Rem. 40 AccuTip	velocity, fps:	3900	3451	3046	2677	2336
	energy, ft-lb:	1351	1058	824	636	485
	arc, inches:		+0.7	0	-4.3	-13.2
Win. 32 Ballistic Silver Tip	velocity, fps	4050	3482	2984	2537	2132
	energy, ft-lb	1165	862	632	457	323
	arc, inches		+0.7	0	-4.6	-14.7
Win. 34 HP	velocity, fps:	4025	3339	2751	2232	1775
	energy, ft-lb:	1223	842	571	376	238
	arc, inches:		+0.8	0	-5.5	-18.1

CARTRIDGE BULLET	RANGE, YARDS:	0	100	200	300	400
.218 Bee						
Win. 46 Hollow Point	velocity, fps:	2760	2102	1550	1155	961
	energy, ft-lb:	778	451	245	136	94
	arc, inches:		0	-7.2	-29.4	
.22 Hornet						
Hornady 35 V-Max	velocity, fps:	3100	2278	1601	1135	929
	energy, ft-lb:	747	403	199	100	67
	arc, inches:		+2.8	0	-16.9	-60.4
Rem. 35 AccuTip	velocity, fps:	3100	2271	1591	1127	924
	energy, ft-lb:	747	401	197	99	66
	arc, inches:		+1.5	-3.5	-22.3	-68.4
Rem. 45 Pointed Soft Point	velocity, fps:	2690	2042	1502	1128	948
	energy, ft-lb:	723	417	225	127	90
	arc, inches:		0	-7.1	-30.0	
Rem. 45 Hollow Point	velocity, fps:	2690	2042	1502	1128	948
	energy, ft-lb:	723	417	225	127	90
	arc, inches:		0	-7.1	-30.0	
Win. 34 Jacketed HP	velocity, fps:	3050	2132	1415	1017	852
	energy, ft-lb:	700	343	151	78	55.
	arc, inches:		0	-6.6	-29.9	
Win. 45 Soft Point	velocity, fps:	2690	2042	1502	1128	948.
	energy, ft-lb:	723	417	225	127	90
	arc, inches:		0	-7.7	-31.3	
Win. 46 Hollow Point	velocity, fps:	2690	2042	1502	1128	948.
	energy, ft-lb:	739	426	230	130	92
	arc, inches:		0	-7.7	-31.3	
.221 Remington Fireball						
Rem. 50 AccuTip BT	velocity, fps:	2995	2605	2247	1918	1622
	energy, ft-lb:	996	753	560	408	292
	arc, inches:		+1.8	0	-8.8	-27.1

.222 Remington

CARTRIDGE BULLET	RANGE, YARDS:	0	100	200	300	400
Federal 50 Hi-Shok	velocity, fps:	3140	2600	2120	1700	1350
	energy, ft-lb:	1095	750	500	320	200
	arc, inches:		+1.9	0	-9.7	-31.6
Federal 55 FMJ boat-tail	velocity, fps:	3020	2740	2480	2230	1990
	energy, ft-lb:	1115	915	750	610	484.
	arc, inches:		+1.6	0	-7.3	-21.5
Hornady 40 V-Max	velocity, fps:	3600	3117	2673	2269	1911
	energy, ft-lb:	1151	863	634	457	324
	arc, inches:		+1.1	0	-6.1	-18.9
Hornady 50 V-Max	velocity, fps:	3140	2729	2352	2008	1710.
	energy, ft-lb:	1094	827	614	448	325
	arc, inches:		+1.7	0	-7.9	-24.4
Norma 50 Soft Point	velocity, fps:	3199	2667	2193	1771	
	energy, ft-lb:	1136	790	534	348	
	arc, inches:		+1.7	0	-9.1	
Norma 50 FMJ	velocity, fps:	2789	2326	1910	1547	
	energy, ft-lb:	864	601	405	266	
	arc, inches:		+2.5	0	-12.2	
Norma 62 Soft Point	velocity, fps:	2887	2457	2067	1716	
	energy, ft-lb:	1148	831	588	405	
	arc, inches:		+2.1	0	-10.4	
PMC 50 Pointed Soft Point	velocity, fps:	3044	2727	2354	2012	1651
	energy, ft-lb:	1131	908	677	494	333
	arc, inches:		+1.6	0	-7.9	-24.5
PMC 55 Pointed Soft Point	velocity, fps:	2950	2594	2266	1966	1693
	energy, ft-lb:	1063	822	627	472	350
	arc, inches:		+1.9	0	-8.7	-26.3
Rem. 50 Pointed Soft Point	velocity, fps:	3140	2602	2123	1700	1350.
	energy, ft-lb:	1094	752	500	321	202
	arc, inches:		+1.9	0	-9.7	-31.7
Rem. 50 HP Power-Lokt	velocity, fps:	3140	2635	2182	1777	1432.
	energy, ft-lb:	1094	771	529	351	228
	arc, inches:		+1.8	0	-9.2	-29.6
Rem. 50 AccuTip BT	velocity, fps:	3140	2744	2380	2045	1740
	energy, ft-lb:	1094	836	629	464	336.
	arc, inches:		+1.6	0	-7.8	-23.9
Win. 40 Ballistic Silvertip	velocity, fps:	3370	2915	2503	2127	1786
	energy, ft-lb:	1009	755	556	402	283
	arc, inches:		+1.3	0	-6.9	-21.5
Win. 50 Pointed Soft Point	velocity, fps:	3140	2602	2123	1700	1350
	energy, ft-lb:	1094	752	500	321	202
	arc, inches:		+2.2	0	-10.0	-32.3

.223 Remington

CARTRIDGE BULLET	RANGE, YARDS:	0	100	200	300	400
Black Hills 40 Nosler B. Tip	velocity, fps:	3600				
	energy, ft-lb:	1150				
	arc, inches:					
Black Hills 50 V-Max	velocity, fps:	3300				
	energy, ft-lb:	1209				
	arc, inches:					
Black Hills 52 Match HP	velocity, fps:	3300				
	energy, ft-lb:	1237				
	arc, inches:					
Black Hills 55 Softpoint	velocity, fps:	3250				
	energy, ft-lb:	1270				
	arc, inches:					
Black Hills 60 SP or V-Max	velocity, fps:	3150				
	energy, ft-lb:	1322				
	arc, inches:					
Black Hills 60 Partition	velocity, fps:	3150				
	energy, ft-lb:	1322				
	arc, inches:					
Black Hills 68 Heavy Match	velocity, fps:	2850				
	energy, ft-lb:	1227				
	arc, inches:					
Black Hills 69 Sierra MK	velocity, fps:	2850				
	energy, ft-lb:	1245				
	arc, inches:					
Black Hills 73 Berger BTHP	velocity, fps:	2750				
	energy, ft-lb:	1226				
	arc, inches:					
Black Hills 75 Heavy Match	velocity, fps:	2750				
	energy, ft-lb:	1259				
	arc, inches:					
Black Hills 77 Sierra MKing	velocity, fps:	2750				
	energy, ft-lb:	1293				
	arc, inches:					
Federal 50 Jacketed HP	velocity, fps:	3400	2910	2460	2060	1700
	energy, ft-lb:	1285	940	675	470	320
	arc, inches:		+1.3	0	-7.1	-22.7
Federal 50 Speer TNT HP	velocity, fps:	3300	2860	2450	2080	1750
	energy, ft-lb:	1210	905	670	480	340
	arc, inches:		+1.4	0	-7.3	-22.6
Federal 52 Sierra MatchKing BTHP	velocity, fps:	3300	2860	2460	2090	1760
	energy, ft-lb:	1255	945	700	505	360
	arc, inches:		+1.4	0	-7:2	-22.4
Federal 55 Hi-Shok	velocity, fps:	3240	2750	2300	1910	1550
	energy, ft-lb:	1280	920	650	445	295
	arc, inches:		+1.6	0	-8.2	-26.1
Federal 55 FMJ boat-tail	velocity, fps:	3240	2950	2670	2410	2170
	energy, ft-lb:	1280	1060	875	710	575
	arc, inches:		+1.3	0	-6.1	-18.3
Federal 55 Sierra GameKing BTHP	velocity, fps:	3240	2770	2340	1950	1610
	energy, ft-lb:	1280	935	670	465	315
	arc, inches:		+1.5	0	-8.0	-25.3
Federal 55 Trophy Bonded	velocity, fps:	3100	2630	2210	1830	1500.
	energy, ft-lb:	1175	845	595	410	275
	arc, inches:		+1.8	0	-8.9	-28.7
Federal 55 Nosler Bal. Tip	velocity, fps:	3240	2870	2530	2220	1920
	energy, ft-lb:	1280	1005	780	600	450
	arc, inches:		+1.4	0	-6.8	-20.8
Federal 55 Sierra BlitzKing	velocity, fps:	3240	2870	2520	2200	1910
	energy, ft-lb:	1280	1005	775	590	445
	arc, inches:		+-1.4	0	-6.9	-20.9
Federal 62 FMJ	velocity, fps:	3020	2650	2310	2000	1710
	energy, ft-lb:	1225	970	735	550	405
	arc, inches:		+1.7	0	-8.4	-25.5
Federal 64 Hi-Shok SP	velocity, fps:	3090	2690	2325	1990	1680
	energy, ft-lb:	1360	1030	770	560	400
	arc, inches:		+1.7	0	-8.2	-25.2
Federal 69 Sierra MatchKing BTHP	velocity, fps:	3000	2720	2460	2210	1980
	energy, ft-lb:	1380	1135	925	750	600
	arc, inches:		+1.6	0	-7.4	-21.9
Hornady 40 V-Max	velocity, fps:	3800	3305	2845	2424	2044
	energy, ft-lb:	1282	970	719	522	371
	arc, inches:		+0.8	0	-5.3	-16.6
Hornady 53 Hollow Point	velocity, fps:	3330	2882	2477	2106	1710
	energy, ft-lb:	1305	978	722	522	369
	arc, inches:		+1.7	0	-7.4	-22.7
Hornady 55 V-Max	velocity, fps:	3240	2859	2507	2181	1891.
	energy, ft-lb:	1282	998	767	581	437
	arc, inches:		+1.4	0	-7.1	-21.4
Hornady 55 TAP-FPD	velocity, fps:	3240	2854	2500	2172	1871
	energy, ft-lb:	1282	995	763	576	427

Centerfire Rifle Ballistics

.223 REMINGTON TO .22-250 REMINGTON

CARTRIDGE BULLET	RANGE, YARDS:	0	100	200	300	400
	arc, inches:		+1.4	0	-7.0	-21.4
Hornady 55 Urban Tactical	velocity, fps:	2970	2626	2307	2011	1739
	energy, ft-lb:	1077	842	650	494	369
	arc, inches:		+1.5	0	-8.1	-24.9
Hornady 60 Soft Point	velocity, fps:	3150	2782	2442	2127	1837.
	energy, ft-lb:	1322	1031	795	603	450
	arc, inches:		+1.6	0	-7.5	-22.5
Hornady 60 TAP-FPD	velocity, fps:	3115	2754	2420	2110	1824
	energy, ft-lb:	1293	1010	780	593	443
	arc, inches:		+1.6	0	-7.5	-22.9
Hornady 60 Urban Tactical	velocity, fps:	2950	2619	2312	2025	1762
	energy, ft-lb:	1160	914	712	546	413
	arc, inches:		+1.6	0	-8.1	-24.7
Hornady 75 BTHP Match	velocity, fps:	2790	2554	2330	2119	1926
	energy, ft-lb:	1296	1086	904	747	617
	arc, inches:		+2.4	0	-8.8	-25.1
Hornacy 75 TAP-FPD	velocity, fps:	2790	2582	2383	2193	2012
	energy, ft-lb:	1296	1110	946	801	674
	arc, inches:		+1.9	0	-8.0	-23.2
Hornady 75 BTHP Tactical	velocity, fps:	2630	2409	2199	2000	1814
	energy, ft-lb:	1152	966	805	666	548
	arc, inches:		+2.0	0	-9.2	-25.9
PMC 40 non-toxic	velocity, fps:	3500	2606	1871	1315	
	energy, ft-lb:	1088	603	311	154	
	arc, inches:		+2.6	0	-12.8	
PMC 50 Sierra BlitzKing	velocity, fps:	3300	2874	2484	2130	1809
	energy, ft-lb:	1209	917	685	504	363
	arc, inches:		+1.4	0	-7.1	-21.8
PMC 52 Sierra HPBT Match	velocity, fps:	3200	2808	2447	2117	1817
	energy, ft-lb:	1182	910	691	517	381
	arc, inches:		+1.5	0	-7.3	-22.5.
PMC 53 Barnes XLC	velocity, fps:	3200	2815	2461	2136	1840
	energy, ft-lb:	1205	933	713	537	398.
	arc, inches:		+1.5	0	-7.2	-22.2
PMC 55 HP boat-tail	velocity, fps:	3240	2717	2250	1832	1473
	energy, ft-lb:	1282	901	618	410	265
	arc, inches:		+1.6	0	-8.6	-27.7
PMC 55 FMJ boat-tail	velocity, fps:	3195	2882	2525	2169	1843
	energy, ft-lb:	1246	1014	779	574	415
	arc, inches:		+1.4	0	-6.8	-21.1
PMC 55 Pointed Soft Point	velocity, fps:	3112	2767	2421	2100	1806
	energy, ft-lb:	1182	935	715	539	398
	arc, inches:		+1.5	0	-7.5	-22.9
PMC 64 Pointed Soft Point	velocity, fps:	2775	2511	2261	2026	1806.
	energy, ft-lb:	1094	896	726	583	464
	arc, inches:		+2.0	0	-8.8	-26.1
PMC 69 Sierra BTHP Match	velocity, fps:	2900	2591	2304	2038	1791
	energy, ft-lb:	1288	1029	813	636	492
	arc, inches:		+1.9	0	-8.4	-25.3
Rem. 50 AccuTip BT	velocity, fps:	3300	2889	2514	2168	1851
	energy, ft-lb:	1209	927	701	522	380
	arc, inches:		+1.4	0	-6.9	-21.2
Rem. 55 Pointed Soft Point	velocity, fps:	3240	2747	2304	1905	1554
	energy, ft-lb:	1282	921	648	443	295
	arc, inches:		+1.6	0	-8.2	-26.2
Rem. 55 HP Power-Lokt	velocity, fps:	3240	2773	2352	1969	1627
	energy, ft-lb:	1282	939	675	473	323
	arc, inches:		+1.5	0	-7.9	-24.8
Rem. 55 AccuTip BT	velocity, fps:	3240	2854	2500	2172	1871
	energy, ft-lb:	1282	995	763	576	427
	arc, inches:		+1.5	0	-7.1	-21.7
Rem. 55 Metal Case	velocity, fps:	3240	2759	2326	1933	1587
	energy, ft-lb:	1282	929	660	456	307

CARTRIDGE BULLET	RANGE, YARDS:	0	100	200	300	400
	arc, inches:		+1.6	0	-8.1	-25.5
Rem. 62 HP Match	velocity, fps:	3025	2572	2162	1792	1471
	energy, ft-lb:	1260	911	643	442	298
	arc, inches:		+1.9	0	-9.4	-29.9
Rem. 69 BTHP Match	velocity, fps:	3000	2720	2457	2209	1975
	energy, ft-lb:	1379	1133	925	747	598
	arc, inches:		+1.6	0	-7.4	-21.9
Win. 40 Ballistic Silvertip	velocity, fps:	3700	3166	2693	2265	1879.
	energy, ft-lb:	1216	891	644	456	314
	arc, inches:		+1.0	0	-5.8	-18.4
Win. 45 JHP	velocity, fps:	3600				
	energy, ft-lb:	1295				
	arc, inches:					
Win. 50 Ballistic Silvertip	velocity, fps:	3410	2982	2593	2235	1907.
	energy, ft-lb:	1291	987	746	555	404
	arc, inches:		+1.2	0	-6.4	-19.8
Win. 53 Hollow Point	velocity, fps:	3330	2882	2477	2106	1770
	energy, ft-lb:	1305	978	722	522	369
	arc, inches:		+1.7	0	-7.4	-22.7
Win. 55 Pointed Soft Point	velocity, fps:	3240	2747	2304	1905	1554.
	energy, ft-lb:	1282	921	648	443	295
	arc, inches:		+1.9	0	-8.5	-26.7
Win. 55 Super Clean NT	velocity, fps:	3150	2520	1970	1505	1165
	energy, ft-lb:	1212	776	474	277	166
	arc, inches:		+2.8	0	-11.9	-38.9
Win. 55 FMJ	velocity, fps:	3240	2854			
	energy, ft-lb:	1282	995			
	arc, inches:					
Win. 55 Ballistic Silvertip	velocity, fps:	3240	2871	2531	2215	1923
	energy, ft-lb:	1282	1006	782	599	451
	arc, inches:		+1.4	0	-6.8	-20.8
Win. 64 Power-Point	velocity, fps:	3020	2656	2320	2009	1724
	energy, ft-lb:	1296	1003	765	574	423
	arc, inches:		+1.7	0	-8.2	-25.1
Win. 64 Power-Point Plus	velocity, fps:	3090	2684	2312	1971	1664
	energy, ft-lb:	1357	1024	760	552	393
	arc, inches:		+1.7	0	-8.2	-25.4

.5.6 x 52 R

Norma 71 Soft Point	velocity, fps:	2789	2446	2128	1835	
	energy, ft-lb:	1227	944	714	531	
	arc, inches:		+2.1	0	-9.9	

.22 PPC

A-Square 52 Berger	velocity, fps:	3300	2952	2629	2329	2049
	energy, ft-lb:	1257	1006	798	626	485
	arc, inches:		+1.3	0	-6.3	-19.1

.225 Winchester

Win. 55 Pointed Soft Point	velocity, fps:	3570	3066	2616	2208	1838.
	energy, ft-lb:	1556	1148	836	595	412
	arc, inches:		+2.4	+2.0	-3.5	-16.3

.224 Weatherby Magnum

Wby. 55 Pointed Expanding	velocity, fps:	3650	3192	2780	2403	2056
	energy, ft-lb:	1627	1244	944	705	516
	arc, inches:		+2.8	+3.7	0	-9.8

.22-250 Remington

Black Hills 50 Nos. Bal. Tip	velocity, fps:	3700				
	energy, ft-lb:	1520				
	arc, inches:					
Black Hills 60 Nos. Partition	velocity, fps:	3550				
	energy, ft-lb:	1679				
	arc, inches:					

CARTRIDGE BULLET	RANGE, YARDS:	0	100	200	300	400
Federal 40 Nos. Bal. Tip	velocity, fps:	4150	3610	3130	2700	2300
	energy, ft-lb:	1530	1155	870	645	470
	arc, inches:		+0.6	0	-4.2	-13.2
Federal 40 Sierra Varminter	velocity, fps:	4000	3320	2720	2200	1740
	energy, ft-lb:	1420	980	660	430	265
	arc, inches:		+0.8	0	-5.6	-18.4
Federal 55 Hi-Shok	velocity, fps:	3680	3140	2660	2220	1830
	energy, ft-lb:	1655	1200	860	605	410
	arc, inches:		+1.0	0	-6.0	-19.1
Federal 55 Sierra BlitzKing	velocity, fps:	3680	3270	2890	2540	2220
	energy, ft-lb:	1655	1300	1020	790	605
	arc, inches:		+0.9	0	-5.1	-15.6
Federal 55 Sierra GameKing BTHP	velocity, fps:	3680	3280	2920	2590	2280
	energy, ft-lb:	1655	1315	1040	815	630
	arc, inches:		+0.9	0	-5.0	-15.1
Federal 55 Trophy Bonded	velocity, fps:	3600	3080	2610	2190	1810.
	energy, ft-lb:	1585	1155	835	590	400.
	arc, inches:		+1.1	0	-6.2	-19.8
Hornady 40 V-Max	velocity, fps:	4150	3631	3147	2699	2293
	energy, ft-lb:	1529	1171	879	647	467
	arc, inches:		+0.5	0	-4.2	-13.3
Hornady 50 V-Max	velocity, fps:	3800	3349	2925	2535	2178
	energy, ft-lb:	1603	1245	950	713	527
	arc, inches:		+0.8	0	-5.0	-15.6
Hornady 53 Hollow Point	velocity, fps:	3680	3185	2743	2341	1974.
	energy, ft-lb:	1594	1194	886	645	459
	arc, inches:		+1.0	0	-5.7	-17.8
Hornady 55 V-Max	velocity, fps:	3680	3265	2876	2517	2183
	energy, ft-lb:	1654	1302	1010	772	582
	arc, inches:		+0.9	0	-5.3	-16.1
Hornady 60 Soft Point	velocity, fps:	3600	3195	2826	2485	2169
	energy, ft-lb:	1727	1360	1064	823	627
	arc, inches:		+1.0	0	-5.4	-16.3
Norma 53 Soft Point	velocity, fps:	3707	3234	2809	1716	
	energy, ft-lb:	1618	1231	928	690	
	arc, inches:		+0.9	0	-5.3	
PMC 50 Sierra BlitzKing	velocity, fps:	3725	3264	2641	2455	2103
	energy, ft-lb:	1540	1183	896	669	491
	arc, inches:		+0.9	0	-5.2	-16.2
PMC 50 Barnes XLC	velocity, fps:	3725	3280	2871	2495	2152
	energy, ft-lb:	1540	1195	915	691	514.
	arc, inches:		+0.9	0	-5.1	-15.9.
PMC 55 HP boat-tail	velocity, fps:	3680	3104	2596	2141	1737
	energy, ft-lb:	1654	1176	823	560	368
	arc, inches:		+1.1	0	-6.3	-20.2
PMC 55 Pointed Soft Point	velocity, fps:	3586	3203	2852	2505	2178
	energy, ft-lb:	1570	1253	993	766	579
	arc, inches:		+1.0	0	-5.2	-16.0
Rem. 50 AccuTip BT (also in EtronX)	velocity, fps:	3725	3272	2864	2491	2147
	energy, ft-lb:	1540	1188	910	689	512
	arc, inches:		+1.7	+1.6	-2.8	-12.8
Rem. 55 Pointed Soft Point	velocity, fps:	3680	3137	2656	2222	1832
	energy, ft-lb:	1654	1201	861	603	410
	arc, inches:		+1.9	+1.8	-3.3	-15.5
Rem. 55 HP Power-Lokt	velocity, fps:	3680	3209	2785	2400	2046.
	energy, ft-lb:	1654	1257	947	703	511
	arc, inches:		+1.8	+1.7	-3.0	-13.7
Rem. 60 Nosler Partition (also in EtronX)	velocity, fps:	3500	3045	2634	2258	1914
	energy, ft-lb:	1632	1235	924	679	488
	arc, inches:		+2.1	+1.9	-3.4	-15.5
Win. 40 Ballistic Silvertip	velocity, fps:	4150	3591	3099	2658	2257
	energy, ft-lb:	1530	1146	853	628	453
	arc, inches:		+0.6	0	-4.2	-13.4
Win. 50 Ballistic Silvertip	velocity, fps:	3810	3341	2919	2536	2182
	energy, ft-lb:	1611	1239	946	714	529.
	arc, inches:		+0.8	0	-4.9	-15.2
Win. 55 Pointed Soft Point	velocity, fps:	3680	3137	2656	2222	1832
	energy, ft-lb:	1654	1201	861	603	410
	arc, inches:		+2.3	+1.9	-3.4	-15.9
Win. 55 Ballistic Silvertip	velocity, fps:	3680	3272	2900	2558	2240
	energy, ft-lb:	1654	1307	1027	799	613
	arc, inches:		+0.9	0	-5.0	-15.4
Win. 64 Power-Point	velocity, fps:	3500	3086	2708	2360	2038
	energy, ft-lb:	1741	1353	1042	791	590
	arc, inches:		+1.1	0	-5.9	-18.0

.220 Swift

CARTRIDGE BULLET	RANGE, YARDS:	0	100	200	300	400
Federal 52 Sierra MatchKing BTHP	velocity, fps:	3830	3370	2960	2600	2230
	energy, ft-lb:	1690	1310	1010	770	575
	arc, inches:		+0.8	0	-4.8	-14.9
Federal 55 Sierra BlitzKing	velocity, fps:	3800	3370	2990	2630	2310.
	energy, ft-lb:	1765	1390	1090	850	650
	arc, inches:		+0.8	0	-4.7	-14.4
Federal 55 Trophy Bonded	velocity, fps:	3700	3170	2690	2270	1880
	energy, ft-lb:	1670	1225	885	625	430
	arc, inches:		+1.0	0	-5.8	-18.5
Hornady 40 V-Max	velocity, fps:	4200	3678	3190	2739	2329
	energy, ft-lb:	1566	1201	904	666	482
	arc, inches:		+0.5	0	-4.0	-12.9
Hornady 50 V-Max	velocity, fps:	3850	3396	2970	2576	2215.
	energy, ft-lb:	1645	1280	979	736	545
	arc, inches:		+0.7	0	-4.8	-15.1
Hornady 50 SP	velocity, fps:	3850	3327	2862	2442	2060.
	energy, ft-lb:	1645	1228	909	662	471
	arc, inches:		+0.8	0	-5.1	-16.1
Hornady 55 V-Max	velocity, fps:	3680	3265	2876	2517	2183
	energy, ft-lb:	1654	1302	1010	772	582
	arc, inches:		+0.9	0	-5.3	-16.1
Hornady 60 Hollow Point	velocity, fps:	3600	3199	2824	2475	2156
	energy, ft-lb:	1727	1364	1063	816	619
	arc, inches:		+1.0	0	-5.4	-16.3
Norma 50 Soft Point	velocity, fps:	4019	3380	2826	2335	
	energy, ft-lb:	1794	1268	887	605	
	arc, inches:		+0.7	0	-5.1	
Rem. 50 Pointed Soft Point	velocity, fps:	3780	3158	2617	2135	1710
	energy, ft-lb:	1586	1107	760	506	325
	arc, inches:		+0.3	-1.4	-8.2	
Rem. 50 V-Max boat-tail (also in EtronX)	velocity, fps:	3780	3321	2908	2532	2185
	energy, ft-lb:	1586	1224	939	711	530
	arc, inches:		+0.8	0	-5.0	-15.4
Win. 40 Ballistic Silvertip	velocity, fps:	4050	3518	3048	2624	2238.
	energy, ft-lb:	1457	1099	825	611	445
	arc, inches:		+0.7	0	-4.4	-13.9
Win. 50 Pointed Soft Point	velocity, fps:	3870	3310	2816	2373	1972
	energy, ft-lb:	1663	1226	881	625	432
	arc, inches:		+0.8	0	-5.2	-16.7

.223 WSSM

CARTRIDGE BULLET	RANGE, YARDS:	0	100	200	300	400
Win. 55 Ballistic Silvertip	velocity, fps:	3850	3438	3064	2721	2402
	energy, ft-lb:	1810	1444	1147	904	704
	arc, inches:		+0.7	0	-4.4	-13.6
Win. 55 Pointed Softpoint	velocity, fps:	3850	3367	2934	2541	2181
	energy, ft-lb:	1810	1384	1051	789	581
	arc, inches:		+0.8	0	-4.9	-15.1
Win. 64 Power-Point	velocity, fps:	3600	3144	2732	2356	2011
	energy, ft-lb:	1841	1404	1061	789	574
	arc, inches:		+1.0	0	-5.7	-17.7

Centerfire Rifle Ballistics

6MM PPC TO .243 WINCHESTER

6mm PPC

CARTRIDGE BULLET	RANGE, YARDS:	0	100	200	300	400
A-Square 68 Berger	velocity, fps:	3100	2751	2428	2128	1850
	energy, ft-lb:	1451	1143	890	684	516
	arc, inches:		+1.5	0	-7.5	-22.6

6x70 R

CARTRIDGE BULLET	RANGE, YARDS:	0	100	200	300	400
Norma 95 Nosler Bal. Tip	velocity, fps:	2461	2231	2013	1809	
	energy, ft-lb:	1211	995	810	654	
	arc, inches:		+2.7	0	-11.3	

6.8mm SPC

CARTRIDGE BULLET	RANGE, YARDS:	0	100	200	300	400
Hornady 110 V-Max	velocity, fps:	2550	2319	2100	1893	1700
	energy, ft-lb:	1588	1313	1077	875	706
	arc, inches:		+2.5	0	-10.4	-30.6

.243 Winchester

CARTRIDGE BULLET	RANGE, YARDS:	0	100	200	300	400
Black Hills 55 Nosler B. Tip	velocity, fps:	3800				
	energy, ft-lb:	1763				
	arc, inches:					
Black Hills 95 Nosler B. Tip	velocity, fps:	2950				
	energy, ft-lb:	1836				
	arc, inches:					
Federal 70 Nosler Bal. Tip	velocity, fps:	3400	3070	2760	2470	2200
	energy, ft-lb:	1795	1465	1185	950	755.
	arc, inches:		+1.1	0	-5.7	-17.1
Federal 70 Speer TNT HP	velocity, fps:	3400	3040	2700	2390	2100
	energy, ft-lb:	1795	1435	1135	890	685
	arc, inches:		+1.1	0	-5.9	-18.0
Federal 80 Sierra Pro-Hunter	velocity, fps:	3350	2960	2590	2260	1950
	energy, ft-lb:	1995	1550	1195	905	675
	arc, inches:		+1.3	0	-6.4	-19.7
Federal 85 Sierra GameKing	velocity, fps:	3320	3070	2830	2600	2380
BTHP	energy, ft-lb:	2080	1770	1510	1280	1070
	arc, inches:		+1.1	0	-5.5	-16.1
Federal 90 Trophy Bonded	velocity, fps:	3100	2850	2610	2380	2160.
	energy, ft-lb:	1920	1620	1360	1130	935
	arc, inches:		+1.4	0	-6.1	-19.2
Federal 100 Hi-Shok	velocity, fps:	2960	2700	2450	2220	1990
	energy, ft-lb:	1945	1615	1330	1090	880
	arc, inches:		+1.6	0	-7.5	-22.0
Federal 100 Sierra GameKing	velocity, fps:	2960	2760	2570	2380	2210
BTSP	energy, ft-lb:	1950	1690	1460	1260	1080
	arc, inches:		+1.5	0	-6.8	-19.8
Federal 100 Nosler Partition	velocity, fps:	2960	2730	2510	2300	2100
	energy, ft-lb:	1945	1650	1395	1170	975.
	arc, inches:		+1.6	0	-7.1	-20.9
Hornady 58 V-Max	velocity, fps:	3750	3319	2913	2539	2195
	energy, ft-lb:	1811	1418	1093	830	620
	arc, inches:		+1.2	0	-5.5	-16.4
Hornady 75 Hollow Point	velocity, fps:	3400	2970	2578	2219	1890
	energy, ft-lb:	1926	1469	1107	820	595
	arc, inches:		+1.2	0	-6.5	-20.3
Hornady 100 BTSP	velocity, fps:	2960	2728	2508	2299	2099
	energy, ft-lb:	1945	1653	1397	1174	979
	arc, inches:		+1.6	0	-7.2	-21.0
Hornady 100 BTSP LM	velocity, fps:	3100	2839	2592	2358	2138
	energy, ft-lb:	2133	1790	1491	1235	1014
	arc, inches:		+1.5	0	-6.8	-19.8
Norma 80 FMJ	velocity, fps:	3117	2750	2412	2098	
	energy, ft-lb:	1726	1344	1034	782	
	arc, inches:		+1.5	0	-7.5	
Norma 100 FMJ	velocity, fps:	3018	2747	2493	2252	
	energy, ft-lb:	2023	1677	1380	1126	
	arc, inches:		+1.5	0	-7.1	
Norma 100 Soft Point	velocity, fps:	3018	2748	2493	2252	
	energy, ft-lb:	2023	1677	1380	1126	
	arc, inches:		+1.5	0	-7.1	
Norma 100 Oryx	velocity, fps:	3018	2653	2316	2004	
	energy, ft-lb:	2023	1563	1191	892	
	arc, inches:		+1.7	0	-8.3	
PMC 80 Pointed Soft Point	velocity, fps:	2940	2684	2444	2215	1999
	energy, ft-lb:	1535	1280	1060	871	709
	arc, inches:		+1.7	0	-7.5	-22.1
PMC 85 Barnes XLC	velocity, fps:	3250	3022	2805	2598	2401
	energy, ft-lb:	1993	1724	1485	1274	1088
	arc, inches:		+1.6	0	-5.6	16.3
PMC 85 HP boat-tail	velocity, fps:	3275	2922	2596	2292	2009
	energy, ft-lb:	2024	1611	1272	991	761
	arc, inches:		+1.3	0	-6.5	-19.7
PMC 100 Pointed Soft Point	velocity, fps:	2743	2507	2283	2070	1869
	energy, ft-lb:	1670	1395	1157	951	776
	arc, inches:		+2.0	0	-8.7	-25.5
PMC 100 SP boat-tail	velocity, fps:	2960	2742	2534	2335	2144
	energy, ft-lb:	1945	1669	1425	1210	1021
	arc, inches:		+1.6	0	-7.0	-20.5
Rem. 75 AccuTip BT	velocity, fps:	3375	3065	2775	2504	2248
	energy, ft-lb:	1897	1564	1282	1044	842
	arc, inches:		+2.0	+1.8	-3.0	-13.3
Rem. 80 Pointed Soft Point	velocity, fps:	3350	2955	2593	2259	1951
	energy, ft-lb:	1993	1551	1194	906	676
	arc, inches:		+2.2	+2.0	-3.5	-15.8
Rem. 80 HP Power-Lokt	velocity, fps:	3350	2955	2593	2259	1951
	energy, ft-lb:	1993	1551	1194	906	676
	arc, inches:		+2.2	+2.0	-3.5	-15.8
Rem. 90 Nosler Bal. Tip	velocity, fps:	3120	2871	2635	2411	2199
(also in EtronX) or Scirocco	energy, ft-lb:	1946	1647	1388	1162	966
	arc, inches:		+1.4	0	-6.4	-18.8
Rem. 95 AccuTip	velocity, fps:	3120	2847	2590	2347	2118
	energy, ft-lb:	2053	1710	1415	1162	946
	arc, inches:		+1.5	0	-6.6	-19.5
Rem. 100 PSP Core-Lokt	velocity, fps:	2960	2697	2449	2215	1993
(also in EtronX)	energy, ft-lb:	1945	1615	1332	1089	882
	arc, inches:		+1.6	0	-7.5	-22.1
Rem. 100 PSP boat-tail	velocity, fps:	2960	2720	2492	2275	2069
	energy, ft-lb:	1945	1642	1378	1149	950
	arc, inches:		+2.8	+2.3	-3.8	-16.6
Speer 100 Grand Slam	velocity, fps:	2950	2684	2434	2197	
	energy, ft-lb:	1932	1600	1315	1072	
	arc, inches:		+1.7	0	-7.6	-22.4
Win. 55 Ballistic Silvertip	velocity, fps:	4025	3597	3209	2853	2525
	energy, ft-lb:	1978	1579	1257	994	779
	arc, inches:		+0.6	0	-4.0	-12.2
Win. 80 Pointed Soft Point	velocity, fps:	3350	2955	2593	2259	1951.
	energy, ft-lb:	1993	1551	1194	906	676
	arc, inches:		+2.6	+2.1	-3.6	-16.2
Win. 95 Ballistic Silvertip	velocity, fps:	3100	2854	2626	2410	2203
	energy, ft-lb:	2021	1719	1455	1225	1024
	arc, inches:		+1.4	0	-6.4	-18.9
Win. 95 Supreme Elite XP3	velocity, fps	3100	2864	2641	2428	2225
	energy, ft-lb	2027	1730	1471	1243	1044
	a rc, inches		+1.4	0	-6.4	-18.7
Win. 100 Power-Point	velocity, fps:	2960	2697	2449	2215	1993
	energy, ft-lb:	1945	1615	1332	1089	882
	arc, inches:		+1.9	0	-7.8	-22.6.
Win. 100 Power-Point Plus	velocity, fps:	3090	2818	2562	2321	2092
	energy, ft-lb:	2121	1764	1458	1196	972
	arc, inches:		+1.4	0	-6.7	-20.0

CARTRIDGE BULLET	RANGE, YARDS:	0	100	200	300	400
6MM REMINGTON						
Federal 80 Sierra Pro-Hunter	velocity, fps:	3470	3060	2690	2350	2040
	energy, ft-lb:	2140	1665	1290	980	735
	arc, inches:		+1.1	0	-5.9	-18.2
Federal 100 Hi-Shok	velocity, fps:	3100	2830	2570	2330	2100
	energy, ft-lb:	2135	1775	1470	1205	985
	arc, inches:		+1.4	0	-6.7	-19.8
Federal 100 Nos. Partition	velocity, fps:	3100	2860	2640	2420	2220
	energy, ft-lb:	2135	1820	1545	1300	1090
	arc, inches:		+1.4	0	-6.3	-18.7
Hornady 100 SP boat-tail	velocity, fps:	3100	2861	2634	2419	2231
	energy, ft-lb:	2134	1818	1541	1300	1088
	arc, inches:		+1.3	0	-6.5	-18.9
Hornady 100 SPBT LM	velocity, fps:	3250	2997	2756	2528	2311
	energy, ft-lb:	2345	1995	1687	1418	1186
	arc, inches:		+1.6	0	-6.3	-18.2
Rem. 75 V-Max boat-tail	velocity, fps:	3400	3088	2797	2524	2267
	energy, ft-lb:	1925	1587	1303	1061	856
	arc, inches:		+1.9	+1.7	-3.0	-13.1
Rem. 100 PSP Core-Lokt	velocity, fps:	3100	2829	2573	2332	2104.
	energy, ft-lb:	2133	1777	1470	1207	983
	arc, inches:		+1.4	0	-6.7	-19.8
Rem. 100 PSP boat-tail	velocity, fps:	3100	2852	2617	2394	2183.
	energy, ft-lb:	2134	1806	1521	1273	1058
	arc, inches:		+1.4	0	-6.5	-19.1
Win. 100 Power-Point	velocity, fps:	3100	2829	2573	2332	2104
	energy, ft-lb:	2133	1777	1470	1207	983
	arc, inches:		+1.7	0	-7.0	-20.4
.243 WSSM						
Win. 55 Ballistic Silvertip	velocity, fps:	4060	3628	3237	2880	2550
	energy, ft-lb:	2013	1607	1280	1013	794
	arc, inches:		+0.6	0	-3.9	-12.0
Win. 95 Ballistic Silvertip	velocity, fps:	3250	3000	2763	2538	2325
	energy, ft-lb:	2258	1898	1610	1359	1140
	arc, inches:		+1.2	0	5.7	16.9
Win. 95 Supreme Elite XP3	velocity, fps	3150	2912	2686	2471	2266
	energy, ft-lb	2093	1788	1521	1287	1083
	arc, inches		+1.3	0	-6.1	-18.0
Win. 100 Power Point	velocity, fps:	3110	2838	2583	2341	2112
	energy, ft-lb:	2147	1789	1481	1217	991
	arc, inches:		+1.4	0	-6.6	-19.7
.240 WEATHERBY MAGNUM						
Wby. 87 Pointed Expanding	velocity, fps:	3523	3199	2898	2617	2352
	energy, ft-lb:	2397	1977	1622	1323	1069
	arc, inches:		+2.7	+3.4	0	-8.4
Wby. 90 Barnes-X	velocity, fps:	3500	3222	2962	2717	2484
	energy, ft-lb:	2448	2075	1753	1475	1233
	arc, inches:		+2.6	+3.3	0	-8.0
Wby. 95 Nosler Bal. Tip	velocity, fps:	3420	3146	2888	2645	2414
	energy, ft-lb:	2467	2087	1759	1475	1229
	arc, inches:		+2.7	+3.5	0	-8.4
Wby. 100 Pointed Expanding	velocity, fps:	3406	3134	2878	2637	2408
	energy, ft-lb:	2576	2180	1839	1544	1287
	arc, inches:		+2.8	+3.5	0	-8.4
Wby. 100 Partition	velocity, fps:	3406	3136	2882	2642	2415
	energy, ft-lb:	2576	2183	1844	1550	1294
	arc, inches:		+2.8	+3.5	0	-8.4
.25-20 WINCHESTER						
Rem. 86 Soft Point	velocity, fps:	1460	1194	1030	931	858
	energy, ft-lb:	407	272	203	165	141
	arc, inches:		0	-22.9	-78.9	-173.0
Win. 86 Soft Point	velocity, fps:	1460	1194	1030	931	858.
	energy, ft-lb:	407	272	203	165	141
	arc, inches:		0	-23.5	-79.6	-175.9
.25-35 WINCHESTER						
Win. 117 Soft Point	velocity, fps:	2230	1866	1545	1282	1097
	energy, ft-lb:	1292	904	620	427	313
	arc, inches:		+2.1	-5.1	-27.0	-70.1
.250 SAVAGE						
Rem. 100 Pointed SP	velocity, fps:	2820	2504	2210	1936	1684.
	energy, ft-lb:	1765	1392	1084	832	630
	arc, inches:		+2.0	0	-9.2	-27.7
Win. 100 Silvertip	velocity, fps:	2820	2467	2140	1839	1569
	energy, ft-lb:	1765	1351	1017	751	547
	arc, inches:		+2.4	0	-10.1	-30.5
.257 ROBERTS						
Federal 120 Nosler Partition	velocity, fps:	2780	2560	2360	2160	1970
	energy, ft-lb:	2060	1750	1480	1240	1030
	arc, inches:		+1.9	0	-8.2	-24.0
Hornady 117 SP boat-tail	velocity, fps:	2780	2550	2331	2122	1925
	energy, ft-lb:	2007	1689	1411	1170	963
	arc, inches:		+1.9	0	-8.3	-24.4
Hornady 117 SP boat-tail LM	velocity, fps:	2940	2694	2460	2240	2031
	energy, ft-lb:	2245	1885	1572	1303	1071
	arc, inches:		+1.7	0	-7.6	-21.8
Rem. 117 SP Core-Lokt	velocity, fps:	2650	2291	1961	1663	1404
	energy, ft-lb:	1824	1363	999	718	512
	arc, inches:		+2.6	0	-11.7	-36.1
Win. 117 Power-Point	velocity, fps:	2780	2411	2071	1761	1488
	energy, ft-lb:	2009	1511	1115	806	576.
	arc, inches:		+2.6	0	-10.8	-33.0
.25-06 REMINGTON						
Black Hills 100 Nos. Bal. Tip	velocity, fps:	3200				
	energy, ft-lb:	2273				
	arc, inches:					
Black Hills 100 Barnes XLC	velocity, fps:	3200				
	energy, ft-lb:	2273				
	arc, inches:					
Black Hills 115 Barnes X	velocity, fps:	2975				
	energy, ft-lb:	2259				
	arc, inches:					
Federal 90 Sierra Varminter	velocity, fps:	3440	3040	2680	2340	2030
	energy, ft-lb:	2365	1850	1435	1100	825
	arc, inches:		+1.1	0	-6.0	-18.3
Federal 100 Barnes XLC	velocity, fps:	3210	2970	2750	2540	2330
	energy, ft-lb:	2290	1965	1680	1430	1205
	arc, inches:		+1.2	0	-5.8	-17.0
Federal 100 Nosler Bal. Tip	velocity, fps:	3210	2960	2720	2490	2280
	energy, ft-lb:	2290	1940	1640	1380	1150.
	arc, inches:		+1.2	0	-6.0	-17.5
Federal 115 Nosler Partition	velocity, fps:	2990	2750	2520	2300	2100
	energy, ft-lb:	2285	1930	1620	1350	1120
	arc, inches:		+1.6	0	-7.0	-20.8
Federal 115 Trophy Bonded	velocity, fps:	2990	2740	2500	2270	2050
	energy, ft-lb:	2285	1910	1590	1310	1075
	arc, inches:		+1.6	0	-7.2	-21.1
Federal 117 Sierra Pro Hunt.	velocity, fps:	2990	2730	2480	2250	2030
	energy, ft-lb:	2320	1985	1645	1350	1100
	arc, inches:		+1.6	0	-7.2	-21.4
Federal 117 Sierra GameKing BTSP	velocity, fps:	2990	2770	2570	2370	2190
	energy, ft-lb:	2320	2000	1715	1465	1240
	arc, inches:		+1.5	0	-6.8	-19.9

Centerfire Rifle Ballistics

.25-06 REMINGTON TO 6.5X55 SWEDISH

CARTRIDGE BULLET	RANGE, YARDS:	0	100	200	300	400
Hornady 117 SP boat-tail	velocity, fps:	2990	2749	2520	2302	2096
	energy, ft-lb:	2322	1962	1649	1377	1141
	arc, inches:		+1.6	0	-7.0	-20.7
Hornady 117 SP boat-tail LM	velocity, fps:	3110	2855	2613	2384	2168
	energy, ft-lb:	2512	2117	1774	1476	1220
	arc, inches:		+1.8	0	-7.1	-20.3
PMC 100 SPBT	velocity, fps:	3200	2925	2650	2395	2145
	energy, ft-lb:	2273	1895	1561	1268	1019
	arc, inches:		+1.3	0	-6.3	-18.6
PMC 117 PSP	velocity, fps:	2950	2706	2472	2253	2047
	energy, ft-lb:	2261	1900	1588	1319	1088
	arc, inches:		+1.6	0	-7.3	-21.5
Rem. 100 PSP Core-Lokt	velocity, fps:	3230	2893	2580	2287	2014
	energy, ft-lb:	2316	1858	1478	1161	901
	arc, inches:		+1.3	0	-6.6	-19.8
Rem. 115 Core-Lokt Ultra	velocity, fps:	3000	2751	2516	2293	2081
	energy, ft-lb:	2298	1933	1616	1342	1106
	arc, inches:		+1.6	0	-7.1	-20.7
Rem. 120 PSP Core-Lokt	velocity, fps:	2990	2730	2484	2252	2032
	energy, ft-lb:	2382	1985	1644	1351	1100
	arc, inches:		+1.6	0	-7.2	-21.4
Speer 120 Grand Slam	velocity, fps:	3130	2835	2558	2298	
	energy, ft-lb:	2610	2141	1743	1407	
	arc, inches:		+1.4	0	-6.8	-20.1
Win. 85 Ballistic Silvertip	velocity, fps	3470	3156	2863	2589	2331
	energy, ft-lb:	2273	1880	1548	1266	1026
	arc, inches:		+1.0	0	-5.2	-15.7
Win. 90 Pos. Exp. Point	velocity, fps:	3440	3043	2680	2344	2034
	energy, ft-lb:	2364	1850	1435	1098	827
	arc, inches:		+2.4	+2.0	-3.4	-15.0
Win. 110 AccuBond CT	velocity, fps:	3100	2870	2651	2442	2243
	energy, ft-lb:	2347	2011	1716	1456	1228
	arc, inches:		+1.4	0	-6.3	-18.5
Win. 115 Ballistic Silvertip	velocity, fps:	3060	2825	2603	2390	2188
	energy, ft-lb:	2391	2038	1729	1459	1223
	arc, inches:		+1.4	0	-6.6	-19.2
Win. 120 Pos. Pt. Exp.	velocity, fps:	2990	2717	2459	2216	1987
	energy, ft-lb:	2382	1967	1612	1309	1053
	arc, inches:		+1.6	0	-7.4	-21.8

.25 WINCHESTER SUPER SHORT MAGNUM

CARTRIDGE BULLET	RANGE, YARDS:	0	100	200	300	400
Win. 85 Ballistic Silvertip	velocity, fps:	3470	3156	2863	2589	2331
	energy, ft-lb:	2273	1880	1548	1266	1026
	arc, inches:		+1.0	0	-5.2	-15.7
Win. 110 AccuBond CT	velocity, fps:	3100	2870	2651	2442	2243.
	energy, ft-lb:	2347	2011	1716	1456	1228
	arc, inches:		+1.4	0	-6.3	-18.5
Win. 115 Ballistic Silvertip	velocity, fps:	3060	2844	2639	2442	2254
	energy, ft-lb:	2392	2066	1778	1523	1298
	arc, inches:		+1.4	0	-6.4	-18.6
Win. 120 Pos. Pt. Exp.	velocity, fps:	2990	2717	2459	2216	1987
	energy, ft-lb:	2383	1967	1612	1309	1053
	arc, inches:		+1.6	0	-7.4	-21.8

.257 WEATHERBY MAGNUM

CARTRIDGE BULLET	RANGE, YARDS:	0	100	200	300	400
Federal 115 Nosler Partition	velocity, fps:	3150	2900	2660	2440	2220.
	energy, ft-lb:	2535	2145	1810	1515	1260
	arc, inches:		+1.3	0	-6.2	-18.4
Federal 115 Trophy Bonded	velocity, fps:	3150	2890	2640	2400	2180
	energy, ft-lb:	2535	2125	1775	1470	1210
	arc, inches:		+1.4	0	-6.3	-18.8
Wby. 87 Pointed Expanding	velocity, fps:	3825	3472	3147	2845	2563
	energy, ft-lb:	2826	2328	1913	1563	1269
	arc, inches:		+2.1	+2.8	0	-7.1

CARTRIDGE BULLET	RANGE, YARDS:	0	100	200	300	400
Wby. 100 Pointed Expanding	velocity, fps:	3602	3298	3016	2750	2500
	energy, ft-lb:	2881	2416	2019	1680	1388
	arc, inches:		+2.4	+3.1	0	-7.7
Wby. 115 Nosler Bal. Tip	velocity, fps:	3400	3170	2952	2745	2547
	energy, ft-lb:	2952	2566	2226	1924	1656.
	arc, inches:		+3.0	+3.5	0	-7.9
Wby. 115 Barnes X	velocity, fps:	3400	3158	2929	2711	2504
	energy, ft-lb:	2952	2546	2190	1877	1601
	arc, inches:		+2.7	+3.4	0	-8.1
Wby. 117 RN Expanding	velocity, fps:	3402	2984	2595	2240	1921
	energy, ft-lb:	3007	2320	1742	1302	956
	arc, inches:		+3.4	+4.31	0	-11.1
Wby. 120 Nosler Partition	velocity, fps:	3305	3046	2801	2570	2350
	energy, ft-lb:	2910	2472	2091	1760	1471
	arc, inches:		+3.0	+3.7	0	-8.9

6.53 (.257) SCRAMJET

CARTRIDGE BULLET	RANGE, YARDS:	0	100	200	300	400
Lazzeroni 85 Nosler Bal. Tip	velocity, fps:	3960	3652	3365	3096	2844
	energy, ft-lb:	2961	2517	2137	1810	1526
	arc, inches:		+1.7	+2.4	0	-6.0
Lazzeroni 100 Nosler Part.	velocity, fps:	3740	3465	3208	2965	2735
	energy, ft-lb:	3106	2667	2285	1953	1661.
	arc, inches:		+2.1	+2.7	0	-6.7

6.5x50 JAPANESE

CARTRIDGE BULLET	RANGE, YARDS:	0	100	200	300	400
Norma 156 Alaska	velocity, fps:	2067	1832	1615	1423	
	energy, ft-lb:	1480	1162	904	701	
	arc, inches:		+4.4	0	-17.8	

6.5x52 CARCANO

CARTRIDGE BULLET	RANGE, YARDS:	0	100	200	300	400
Norma 156 Alaska	velocity, fps:	2428	2169	1926	1702	
	energy, ft-lb:	2043	1630	1286	1004	
	arc, inches:		+2.9	0	-12.3	

6.5x55 SWEDISH

CARTRIDGE BULLET	RANGE, YARDS:	0	100	200	300	400
Federal 140 Hi-Shok	velocity, fps:	2600	2400	2220	2040	1860
	energy, ft-lb:	2100	1795	1525	1285	1080
	arc, inches:		+2.3	0	-9.4	-27.2
Federal 140 Trophy Bonded	velocity, fps:	2550	2350	2160	1980	1810
	energy, ft-lb:	2020	1720	1450	1220	1015
	arc, inches:		+2.4	0	-9.8	-28.4
Federal 140 Sierra MatchKg. BTHP	velocity, fps:	2630	2460	2300	2140	2000
	energy, ft-lb:	2140	1880	1640	1430	1235
	arc, inches:		+16.4	+28.8	+33.9	+31.8
Hornady 129 SP LM	velocity, fps:	2770	2561	2361	2171	1994
	energy, ft-lb:	2197	1878	1597	1350	1138
	arc, inches:		+2.0	0	-8.2	-23.2
Hornady 140 SP Interlock	velocity, fps	2525	2341	2165	1996	1836
	energy, ft-lb:	1982	1704	1457	1239	1048
	arc, inches:		+2.4	0	-9.9	-28.5
Hornady140 SP LM	velocity, fps:	2740	2541	2351	2169	1999
	energy, ft-lb:	2333	2006	1717	1463	1242
	arc, inches:		+2.4	0	-8.7	-24.0
Norma 120 Nosler Bal. Tip	velocity, fps:	2822	2609	2407	2213	
	energy, ft-lb:	2123	1815	1544	1305	
	arc, inches:		+1.8	0	-7.8	
Norma 139 Vulkan	velocity, fps:	2854	2569	2302	2051	
	energy, ft-lb:	2515	2038	1636	1298	
	arc, inches:		+1.8	0	-8.4	
Norma 140 Nosler Partition	velocity, fps:	2789	2592	2403	2223	
	energy, ft-lb:	2419	2089	1796	1536	
	arc, inches:		+1.8	0	-7.8	
Norma 156 TXP Swift A-Fr.	velocity, fps:	2526	2276	2040	1818	
	energy, ft-lb:	2196	1782	1432	1138

CARTRIDGE BULLET	RANGE, YARDS:	0	100	200	300	400
	arc, inches:		+2.6	0	-10.9	
Norma 156 Alaska	velocity, fps:	2559	2245	1953	1687	
	energy, ft-lb:	2269	1746	1322	986	
	arc, inches:		+2.7	0	-11.9	
Norma 156 Vulkan	velocity, fps:	2644	2395	2159	1937	
	energy, ft-lb:	2422	1987	1616	1301	
	arc, inches:		+2.2	0	-9.7	
Norma 156 Oryx	velocity, fps:	2559	2308	2070	1848	
	energy, ft-lb:	2269	1845	1485	1183	
	arc, inches:		+2.5	0	-10.6	
PMC 139 Pointed Soft Point	velocity, fps:	2850	2560	2290	2030	1790
	energy, ft-lb:	2515	2025	1615	1270	985
	arc, inches:		+2.2	0	-8.9	-26.3
PMC 140 HP boat-tail	velocity, fps:	2560	2398	2243	2093	1949
	energy, ft-lb:	2037	1788	1563	1361	1181
	arc, inches:		+2.3	0	-9.2	-26.4
PMC 140 SP boat-tail	velocity, fps:	2560	2386	2218	2057	1903
	energy, ft-lb:	2037	1769	1529	1315	1126
	arc, inches:		+2.3	0	-9.4	-27.1
PMC 144 FMJ	velocity, fps:	2650	2370	2110	1870	1650
	energy, ft-lb:	2425	1950	1550	1215	945
	arc, inches:		+2.7	0	-10.5	-30.9
Rem. 140 PSP Core-Lokt	velocity, fps:	2550	2353	2164	1984	1814
	energy, ft-lb:	2021	1720	1456	1224	1023
	arc, inches:		+2.4	0	-9.8	-27.0
Speer 140 Grand Slam	velocity, fps:	2550	2318	2099	1892	
	energy, ft-lb:	2021	1670	1369	1112	
	arc, inches:		+2.5	0	-10.4	-30.6
Win. 140 Soft Point	velocity, fps:	2550	2359	2176	2002	1836
	energy, ft-lb:	2022	1731	1473	1246	1048.
	arc, inches:		+2.4	0	-9.7	-28.1

.260 Remington

CARTRIDGE BULLET	RANGE, YARDS:	0	100	200	300	400
Federal 140 Sierra GameKing BTSP	velocity, fps:	2750	2570	2390	2220	2060
	energy, ft-lb:	2350	2045	1775	1535	1315
	arc, inches:		+1.9	0	-8.0	-23.1
Federal 140 Trophy Bonded	velocity, fps:	2750	2540	2340	2150	1970
	energy, ft-lb:	2350	2010	1705	1440	1210
arc, inches:		+1.9	0	-8.4	-24.1	
Rem. 120 Nosler Bal. Tip	velocity, fps:	2890	2688	2494	2309	2131
	energy, ft-lb:	2226	1924	1657	1420	1210
	arc, inches:		+1.7	0	-7.3	-21.1
Rem. 120 AccuTip	velocity, fps:	2890	2697	2512	2334	2163
	energy, ft-lb:	2392	2083	1807	1560	1340
	arc, inches:		+1.6	0	-7.2	-20.7
Rem. 125 Nosler Partition	velocity, fps:	2875	2669	2473	2285	2105.
	energy, ft-lb:	2294	1977	1697	1449	1230
arc, inches:		+1.71	0	-7.4	-21.4	
Rem. 140 PSP Core-Lokt (and C-L Ultra)	velocity, fps:	2750	2544	2347	2158	1979
	energy, ft-lb:	2351	2011	1712	1448	1217
	arc, inches:		+1.9	0	-8.3	-24.0
Speer 140 Grand Slam	velocity, fps:	2750	2518	2297	2087	
	energy, ft-lb:	2351	1970	1640	1354	
	arc, inches:		+2.3	0	-8.9	-25.8

6.5/284

CARTRIDGE BULLET	RANGE, YARDS:	0	100	200	300	400
Norma 120 Nosler Bal. Tip	velocity, fps:	3117	2890	2674	2469	
	energy, ft-lb:	2589	2226	1906	1624	
	arc, inches:		+1.3	0	-6.2	
Norma 140 Nosler Part.	velocity, fps:	2953	2750	2557	2371	
	energy, ft-lb:	2712	2352	2032	1748	
	arc, inches:		+1.5	0	-6.8	

6.5 Remington Magnum

CARTRIDGE BULLET	RANGE, YARDS:	0	100	200	300	400
Rem. 120 Core-Lokt PSP	velocity, fps:	3210	2905	2621	2353	2102
	energy, ft-lb:	2745	2248	1830	1475	1177
	arc, inches:		+2.7	+2.1	-3.5	-15.5

.264 Winchester Magnum

CARTRIDGE BULLET	RANGE, YARDS:	0	100	200	300	400
Rem. 140 PSP Core-Lokt	velocity, fps:	3030	2782	2548	2326	2114
	energy, ft-lb:	2854	2406	2018	1682	1389
	arc, inches:		+1.5	0	-6.9	-20.2
Win. 140 Power-Point	velocity, fps:	3030	2782	2548	2326	2114.
	energy, ft-lb:	2854	2406	2018	1682	1389
	arc, inches:		+1.8	0	-7.2	-20.8

6.8mm Remington SPC

CARTRIDGE BULLET	RANGE, YARDS:	0	100	200	300	400
Rem. 115 Open Tip Match (and HPBT Match)	velocity, fps:	2800	2535	2285	2049	1828
	energy, ft-lb:	2002	1641	1333	1072	853
	arc, inches:		+2.0	0	-8.8	-26.2
Rem. 115 Metal Case	velocity, fps:	2800	2523	2262	2017	1789
	energy, ft-lb:	2002	1625	1307	1039	817
	arc, inches:		+2.0	0	-8.8	-26.2
Rem. 115 Sierra HPBT (2005; all vel. @ 2775)	velocity, fps:	2775	2511	2263	2028	1809
	energy, ft-lb:	1966	1610	1307	1050	835
	arc, inches:		+2.0	0	-8.8	-26.2.
Rem. 115 CL Ultra	velocity, fps:	2775	2472	2190	1926	1683
	energy, ft-lb:	1966	1561	1224	947	723
	arc, inches:		+2.1	0	-9.4	-28.2

.270 Winchester

CARTRIDGE BULLET	RANGE, YARDS:	0	100	200	300	400
Black Hills 130 Nos. Bal. T.	velocity, fps:	2950				
	energy, ft-lb:	2512				
	arc, inches:					
Black Hills 130 Barnes XLC	velocity, ft-lb:	2950				
	energy, ft-lb:	2512				
	arc, inches:					
Federal 130 Hi-Shok	velocity, fps:	3060	2800	2560	2330	2110
	energy, ft-lb:	2700	2265	1890	1565	1285
	arc, inches:		+1.5	0	-6.8	-20.0
Federal 130 Sierra Pro-Hunt.	velocity, fps:	3060	2830	2600	2390	2190
	energy, ft-lb:	2705	2305	1960	1655	1390
	arc, inches:		+1.4	0	-6.4	-19.0
Federal 130 Sierra GameKing	velocity, fps:	3060	2830	2620	2410	2220.
	energy, ft-lb:	2700	2320	1980	1680	1420
	arc, inches:		+1.4	0	-6.5	-19.0
Federal 130 Nosler Bal. Tip	velocity, fps:	3060	2840	2630	2430	2230
	energy, ft-lb:	2700	2325	1990	1700	1440
	arc, inches:		+1.4	0	-6.5	-18.8
Federal 130 Nos. Partition And Solid Base	velocity, fps:	3060	2830	2610	2400	2200
	energy, ft-lb:	2705	2310	1965	1665	1400
	arc, inches:		+1.4	0	-6.5	-19.1.
Federal 130 Barnes XLC And Triple Shock	velocity, fps:	3060	2840	2620	2420	2220
	energy, ft-lb:	2705	2320	1985	1690	1425
	arc, inches:		+1.4	0	-6.4	-18.9
Federal 130 Trophy Bonded	velocity, fps:	3060	2810	2570	2340	2130
	energy, ft-lb:	2705	2275	1905	1585	1310
	arc, inches:		+1.5	0	-6.7	-19.8
Federal 140 Trophy Bonded	velocity, fps:	2940	2700	2480	2260	2060
	energy, ft-lb:	2685	2270	1905	1590	1315
	arc, inches:		+1.6	0	-7.3	-21.5
Federal 140 Tr. Bonded HE	velocity, fps:	3100	2860	2620	2400	2200.
	energy, ft-lb:	2990	2535	2140	1795	1500

BALLISTICS

Centerfire Rifle Ballistics

.270 WINCHESTER TO .270 WINCHESTER

CARTRIDGE BULLET	RANGE, YARDS:	0	100	200	300	400
	arc, inches:		+1.4	0	-6.4	-18.9
Federal 140 Nos. AccuBond	velocity, fps:	2950	2760	2580	2400	2230
	energy, ft-lb:	2705	2365	2060	1790	1545
	arc, inches:		+1.5	0	-6.7	-19.6
Federal 150 Hi-Shok RN	velocity, fps:	2850	2500	2180	1890	1620
	energy, ft-lb:	2705	2085	1585	1185	870
	arc, inches:		+2.0	0	-9.4	-28.6
Federal 150 Sierra GameKing	velocity, fps:	2850	2660	2480	2300	2130
	energy, ft-lb:	2705	2355	2040	1760	1510
	arc, inches:		+1.7	0	-7.4	-21.4
Federal 150 Sierra GameKing	velocity, fps:	3000	2800	2620	2430	2260
HE	energy, ft-lb:	2995	2615	2275	1975	1700
	arc, inches:		+1.5	0	-6.5	-18.9
Federal 150 Nosler Partition	velocity, fps:	2850	2590	2340	2100	1880
	energy, ft-lb:	2705	2225	1815	1470	1175
	arc, inches:		+1.9	0	-8.3	-24.4
Hornady 130 SST	velocity, fps:	3060	2845	2639	2442	2254
(or Interbond)	energy, ft-lb:	2700	2335	2009	1721	1467
	arc, inches:		+1.4	0	-6.6	-19.1
Hornady 130 SST LM	velocity, fps:	3215	2998	2790	2590	2400
(or Interbond)	energy, ft-lb:	2983	2594	2246	1936	1662
	arc, inches:		+1.2	0	-5.8	-17.0
Hornady 140 SP boat-tail	velocity, fps:	2940	2747	2562	2385	2214
	energy, ft-lb:	2688	2346	2041	1769	1524
	arc, inches:		+1.6	0	-7.0	-20.2
Hornady 140 SP boat-tail LM	velocity, fps:	3100	2894	2697	2508	2327
	energy, ft-lb:	2987	2604	2261	1955	1684
	arc, inches:		+1.4	0	6.3	-18.3
Hornady 150 SP	velocity, fps:	2800	2684	2478	2284	2100
	energy, ft-lb:	2802	2400	2046	1737	1469
	arc, inches:		+1.7	0	-7.4	-21.6
Norma 130 SP	velocity, fps:	3140	2862	2601	2354	
	energy, ft-lb:	2847	2365	1953	1600	
	arc, inches:		+1.3	0	-6.5	
Norma 130 FMJ	velocity, fps:	2887	2634	2395	2169	
	energy, ft-lb:					
	arc, inches:		+1.8	0	-7.8	
Norma 150 SP	velocity, fps:	2799	2555	2323	2104	
	energy, ft-lb:	2610	2175	1798	1475	
	arc, inches:		+1.9	0	-8.3	
Norma 150 Oryx	velocity, fps:	2854	2608	2376	2155	
	energy, ft-lb:	2714	2267	1880	1547	
	arc, inches:		+1.8	0	-8.0	
PMC 130 Barnes X	velocity, fps:	2910	2717	2533	2356	2186
	energy, ft-lb:	2444	2131	1852	1602	1379
	arc, inches:		+1.6	0	-7.1	-20.4
PMC 130 SP boat-tail	velocity, fps:	3050	2830	2620	2421	2229
	energy, ft-lb:	2685	2312	1982	1691	1435
	arc, inches:		+1.5	0	-6.5	-19.0
PMC 130 Pointed Soft Point	velocity, fps:	2950	2691	2447	2217	2001
	energy, ft-lb:	2512	2090	1728	1419	1156
	arc, inches:		+1.6	0	-7.5	-22.1
PMC 150 Barnes X	velocity, fps:	2700	2541	2387	2238	2095
	energy, ft-lb:	2428	2150	1897	1668	1461
	arc, inches:		+2.0	0	-8.1	-23.1
PMC 150 SP boat-tail	velocity, fps:	2850	2660	2477	2302	2134
	energy, ft-lb:	2705	2355	2043	1765	1516
	arc, inches:		+1.7	0	-7.4	-21.4
PMC 150 Pointed Soft Point	velocity, fps:	2750	2530	2321	2123	1936
	energy, ft-lb:	2519	2131	1794	1501	1248
	arc, inches:		+2.0	0	-8.4	-24.6
Rem. 100 Pointed Soft Point	velocity, fps:	3320	2924	2561	2225	1916
	energy, ft-lb:	2448	1898	1456	1099	815
	arc, inches:		+2.3	+2.0	-3.6	-16.2
Rem. 115 PSP Core-Lokt mr	velocity, fps:	2710	2412	2133	1873	1636
	energy, ft-lb:	1875	1485	1161	896	683
	arc, inches:		+1.0	-2.7	-14.2	-35.6
Rem. 130 PSP Core-Lokt	velocity, fps:	3060	2776	2510	2259	2022
	energy, ft-lb:	2702	2225	1818	1472	1180
	arc, inches:		+1.5	0	-7.0	-20.9
Rem. 130 Bronze Point	velocity, fps:	3060	2802	2559	2329	2110
	energy, ft-lb:	2702	2267	1890	1565	1285
	arc, inches:		+1.5	0	-6.8	-20.0
Rem. 130 Swift Scirocco	velocity, fps:	3060	2838	2677	2425	2232
	energy, ft-lb:	2702	2325	1991	1697	1438
	arc, inches:		+1.4	0	-6.5	-18.8
Rem. 130 AccuTip BT	velocity, fps:	3060	2845	2639	2442	2254
	energy, ft-lb:	2702	2336	2009	1721	1467
	arc, inches:		+1.4	0	-6.4	-18.6
Rem. 140 Swift A-Frame	velocity, fps:	2925	2652	2394	2152	1923
	energy, ft-lb:	2659	2186	1782	1439	1150
	arc, inches:		+1.7	0	-7.8	-23.2
Rem. 140 PSP boat-tail	velocity, fps:	2960	2749	2548	2355	2171
	energy, ft-lb:	2723	2349	2018	1724	1465
	arc, inches:		+1.6	0	-6.9	-20.1
Rem. 140 Nosler Bal. Tip	velocity, fps:	2960	2754	2557	2366	2187
	energy, ft-lb:	2724	2358	2032	1743	1487
	arc, inches:		+1.6	0	-6.9	-20.0
Rem. 140 PSP C-L Ultra	velocity, fps:	2925	2667	2424	2193	1975
	energy, ft-lb:	2659	2211	1826	1495	1212
	arc, inches:		+1.7	0	-7.6	-22.5
Rem. 150 SP Core-Lokt	velocity, fps:	2850	2504	2183	1886	1618
	energy, ft-lb:	2705	2087	1587	1185	872
	arc, inches:		+2.0	0	-9.4	-28.6
Rem. 150 Nosler Partition	velocity, fps:	2850	2652	2463	2282	2108
	energy, ft-lb:	2705	2343	2021	1734	1480
	arc, inches:		+1.7	0	-7.5	-21.6
Speer 130 Grand Slam	velocity, fps:	3050	2774	2514	2269	
	energy, ft-lb:	2685	2221	1824	1485	
	arc, inches:		+1.5	0	-7.0	-20.9
Speer 150 Grand Slam	velocity, fps:	2830	2594	2369	2156	
	energy, ft-lb:	2667	2240	1869	1548	
	arc, inches:		+1.8	0	-8.1	-23.6
Win. 130 Power-Point	velocity, fps:	3060	2802	2559	2329	2110
	energy, ft-lb:	2702	2267	1890	1565	1285
	arc, inches:		+1.8	0	-7.1	-20.6
Win. 130 Power-Point Plus	velocity, fps:	3150	2881	2628	2388	2161
	energy, ft-lb:	2865	2396	1993	1646	1348
	arc, inches:		+1.3	0	-6.4	-18.9
Win. 130 Silvertip	velocity, fps:	3060	2776	2510	2259	2022
	energy, ft-lb:	2702	2225	1818	1472	1180
	arc, inches:		+1.8	0	-7.4	-21.6
Win. 130 Ballistic Silvertip	velocity, fps:	3050	2828	2618	2416	2224
	energy, ft-lb:	2685	2309	1978	1685	1428
	arc, inches:		+1.4	0	-6.5	-18.9
Win. 140 AccuBond	velocity, fps:	2950	2751	2560	2378	2203
	energy, ft-lb:	2705	2352	2038	1757	1508
	arc, inches:		+1.6	0	-6.9	-19.9
Win. 140 Fail Safe	velocity, fps:	2920	2671	2435	2211	1999
	energy, ft-lb:	2651	2218	1843	1519	1242
	arc, inches:		+1.7	0	-7.6	-22.3
Win. 150 Power-Point	velocity, fps:	2850	2585	2336	2100	1879
	energy, ft-lb:	2705	2226	1817	1468	1175
	arc, inches:		+2.2	0	-8.6	-25.0
Win. 150 Power-Point Plus	velocity, fps:	2950	2679	2425	2184	1957
	energy, ft-lb:	2900	2391	1959	1589	1276

CARTRIDGE BULLET	RANGE, YARDS:	0	100	200	300	400
	arc, inches:		+1.7	0	-7.6	-22.6
Win. 150 Partition Gold	velocity, fps:	2930	2693	2468	2254	2051
	energy, ft-lb:	2860	2416	2030	1693	1402
	arc, inches:		+1.7	0	-7.4	-21.6
Win. 150 Supreme Elite XP3	velocity, fps:	2950	2763	2583	2411	2245
	energy, ft-lb:	2898	2542	2223	1936	1679
	arc, inches:		+1.5	0	-6.9	-15.5

.270 Winchester Short Magnum

CARTRIDGE BULLET	RANGE, YARDS:	0	100	200	300	400
Black Hills 140 AccuBond	velocity, fps:	3100				
	energy, ft-lb:	2987				
	arc, inches:					
Federal 130 Nos. Bal. Tip	velocity, fps:	3300	3070	2840	2630	2430
	energy, ft-lb:	3145	2710	2335	2000	1705
	arc, inches:		+1.1	0	-5.4	-15.8
Federal 130 Nos. Partition	velocity, fps:	3280	3040	2810	2590	2380
And Nos. Solid Base	energy, ft-lb:	3105	2665	2275	1935	1635
And Barnes TS	arc, inches:		+1.1	0	-5.6	-16.3
Federal 140 Nos. AccuBond	velocity, fps	3200	3000	2810	2630	2450
	energy, ft-lb:	3185	2795	2455	2145	1865
	arc, inches:		+1.2	0	-5.6	-16.2
Federal 140 Trophy Bonded	velocity, fps:	3130	2870	2640	2410	2200
	energy, ft-lb:	3035	2570	2160	1810	1500
	arc, inches:		+1.4	0	-6.3	18.7
Federal 150 Nos. Partition	velocity, fps:	3160	2950	2750	2550	2370
	energy, ft-lb:	3325	2895	2515	2175	1870
	arc, inches:		+1.3	0	-5.9	-17.0
Norma 130 FMJ	velocity, fps:	3150	2882	2630	2391	
	energy, ft-lb:					
	arc, inches:		+1.5	0	-6.4	
Norma 130 Ballistic ST	velocity, fps:	3281	3047	2825	2614	
	energy, ft-lb:	3108	2681	2305	1973	
	arc, inches:		+1.1	0	-5.5	
Norma 140 Barnes X TS	velocity, fps:	3150	2952	2762	2580	
	energy, ft-lb:	3085	2709	2372	2070	
	arc, inches:		+1.3	0	-5.8	
Norma 150 Nosler Bal. Tip	velocity, fps:	3280	3046	2824	2613	
	energy, ft-lb:	3106	2679	2303	1972	
	arc, inches:		+1.1	0	-5.4	
Norma 150 Oryx	velocity, fps:	3117	2856	2611	2378	
	energy, ft-lb:	3237	2718	2271	1884	
	arc, inches:		+1.4	0	-6.5	
Win. 130 Bal. Silvertip	velocity, fps:	3275	3041	2820	2609	2408
	energy, ft-lb:	3096	2669	2295	1964	1673
	arc, inches:		+1.1	0	-5.5	-16.1
Win. 140 AccuBond	velocity, fps:	3200	2989	2789	2597	2413
	energy, ft-lb:	3184	2779	2418	2097	1810
	arc, inches:		+1.2	0	-5.7	-16.5
Win. 140 Fail Safe	velocity, fps:	3125	2865	2619	2386	2165
	energy, ft-lb:	3035	2550	2132	1769	1457
	arc, inches:		+1.4	0	-6.5	-19.0
Win. 150 Ballistic Silvertip	velocity, fps:	3120	2923	2734	2554	2380.
	energy, ft-lb:	3242	2845	2490	2172	1886.
	arc, inches:		+1.3	0	-5.9	-17.2
Win. 150 Power Point	velocity, fps:	3150	2867	2601	2350	2113
	energy, ft-lb:	3304	2737	2252	1839	1487
	arc, inches:		+1.4	0	-6.5	-19.4
Win. 150 Supreme Elite XP3	velocity, fps:	3120	2926	2740	2561	2389
	energy, ft-lb:	3242	2850	2499	2184	1901
	arc, inches:		+1.3	0	-5.9	-17.1

.270 Weatherby Magnum

CARTRIDGE BULLET	RANGE, YARDS:	0	100	200	300	400
Federal 130 Nosler Partition	velocity, fps:	3200	2960	2740	2520	2320
	energy, ft-lb:	2955	2530	2160	1835	1550
	arc, inches:		+1.2	0	-5.9	-17.3
Federal 130 Sierra GameKing	velocity, fps:	3200	2980	2780	2580	2400
BTSP	energy, ft-lb:	2955	2570	2230	1925	1655
	arc, inches:		+1.2	0	-5.7	-16.6
Federal 140 Trophy Bonded	velocity, fps:	3100	2840	2600	2370	2150.
	energy, ft-lb:	2990	2510	2100	1745	1440
	arc, inches:		+1.4	0	-6.6	-19.3
Wby. 100 Pointed Expanding	velocity, fps:	3760	3396	3061	2751	2462
	energy, ft-lb:	3139	2560	2081	1681	1346
	arc, inches:		+2.3	+3.0	0	-7.6
Wby. 130 Pointed Expanding	velocity, fps:	3375	3123	2885	2659	2444
	energy, ft-lb:	3288	2815	2402	2041	1724
	arc, inches:		+2.8	+3.5	0	-8.4
Wby. 130 Nosler Partition	velocity, fps:	3375	3127	2892	2670	2458.
	energy, ft-lb:	3288	2822	2415	2058	1744
	arc, inches:		+2.8	+3.5	0	-8.3
Wby. 140 Nosler Bal. Tip	velocity, fps:	3300	3077	2865	2663	2470.
	energy, ft-lb:	3385	2943	2551	2204	1896
	arc, inches:		+2.9	+3.6	0	-8.4
Wby. 140 Barnes X	velocity, fps:	3250	3032	2825	2628	2438
	energy, ft-lb:	3283	2858	2481	2146	1848
	arc, inches:		+3.0	+3.7	0	-8.7
Wby. 150 Pointed Expanding	velocity, fps:	3245	3028	2821	2623	2434
	energy, ft-lb:	3507	3053	2650	2292	1973
	arc, inches:		+3.0	+3.7	0	-8.7
Wby. 150 Nosler Partition	velocity, fps:	3245	3029	2823	2627	2439.
	energy, ft-lb:	3507	3055	2655	2298	1981
	arc, inches:		+3.0	+3.7	0	-8.

7-30 Waters

CARTRIDGE BULLET	RANGE, YARDS:	0	100	200	300	400
Federal 120 Sierra GameKing	velocity, fps:	2700	2300	1930	1600	1330.
BTSP	energy, ft-lb:	1940	1405	990	685	470
	arc, inches:		+2.6	0	-12.0	-37.6

7mm Mauser (7x57)

CARTRIDGE BULLET	RANGE, YARDS:	0	100	200	300	400
Federal 140 Sierra Pro-Hunt.	velocity, fps:	2660	2450	2260	2070	1890.
	energy, ft-lb:	2200	1865	1585	1330	1110
	arc, inches:		+2.1	0	-9.0	-26.1
Federal 140 Nosler Partition	velocity, fps:	2660	2450	2260	2070	1890.
	energy, ft-lb:	2200	1865	1585	1330	1110
	arc, inches:		+2.1	0	-9.0	-26.1
Federal 175 Hi-Shok RN	velocity, fps:	2440	2140	1860	1600	1380
	energy, ft-lb:	2315	1775	1340	1000	740
	arc, inches:		+3.1	0	-13.3	-40.1
Hornady 139 SP boat-tail	velocity, fps:	2700	2504	2316	2137	1965
	energy, ft-lb:	2251	1936	1656	1410	1192
	arc, inches:		+2.0	0	-8.5	-24.9
Hornady 139 SP Interlock	velocity, fps:	2680	2455	2241	2038	1846
	energy, ft-lb:	2216	1860	1550	1282	1052
	arc, inches:		+2.1	0	-9.1	-26.6
Hornady 139 SP boat-tail LM	velocity, fps:	2830	2620	2450	2250	2070
	energy, ft-lb:	2475	2135	1835	1565	1330
	arc, inches:		+1.8	0	-7.6	-22.1
Hornady 139 SP LM	velocity, fps:	2950	2736	2532	2337	2152.
	energy, ft-lb:	2686	2310	1978	1686	1429
	arc, inches:		+2.0	0	-7.6	-21.5
Norma 150 Soft Point	velocity, fps:	2690	2479	2278	2087	
	energy, ft-lb:	2411	2048	1729	1450	
	arc, inches:		+2.0	0	-8.8	
PMC 140 Pointed Soft Point	velocity, fps:	2660	2450	2260	2070	1890
	energy, ft-lb:	2200	1865	1585	1330	1110.
	arc, inches:		+2.4	0	-9.6	-27.3
PMC 175 Soft Point	velocity, fps:	2440	2140	1860	1600	1380
	energy, ft-lb:	2315	1775	1340	1000	740

Centerfire Rifle Ballistics

7MM MAUSER TO 7X65 R

CARTRIDGE BULLET	RANGE, YARDS:	0	100	200	300	400
	arc, inches:		+1.5	-3.6	-18.6	-46.8
Rem. 140 PSP Core-Lokt	velocity, fps:	2660	2435	2221	2018	1827
	energy, ft-lb:	2199	1843	1533	1266	1037
	arc, inches:		+2.2	0	-9.2	-27.4
Win. 145 Power-Point	velocity, fps:	2660	2413	2180	1959	1754
	energy, ft-lb:	2279	1875	1530	1236	990
	arc, inches:		+1.1	-2.8	-14.1	-34.4
7x57 R						
Norma 150 FMJ	velocity, fps:	2690	2489	2296	2112	
	energy, ft-lb:	2411	2063	1756	1486	
	arc, inches:		+2.0	0	-8.6	
Norma 154 Soft Point	velocity, fps:	2625	2417	2219	2030	
	energy, ft-lb:	2357	1999	1684	1410	
	arc, inches:		+2.2	0	-9.3	
Norma 156 Oryx	velocity, fps:	2608	2346	2099	1867	
	energy, ft-lb:	2357	1906	1526	1208	
	arc, inches:		+2.4	0	-10.3	
7mm-08 Remington						
Black Hills 140 AccuBond	velocity, fps:	2700				
	energy, ft-lb:					
	arc, inches:					
Federal 140 Nosler Partition	velocity, fps:	2800	2590	2390	2200	2020
	energy, ft-lb:	2435	2085	1775	1500	1265
	arc, inches:		+1.8	0	-8.0	-23.1
Federal 140 Nosler Bal. Tip	velocity, fps:	2800	2610	2430	2260	2100
And AccuBond	energy, ft-lb:	2440	2135	1840	1590	1360.
	arc, inches:		+1.8	0	-7.7	-22.3
Federal 140 Tr. Bonded HE	velocity, fps:	2950	2660	2390	2140	1900
	energy, ft-lb:	2705	2205	1780	1420	1120
	arc, inches:		+1.7	0	-7.9	-23.2
Federal 150 Sierra Pro-Hunt.	velocity, fps:	2650	2440	2230	2040	1860
	energy, ft-lb:	2340	1980	1660	1390	1150
	arc, inches:		+2.2	0	-9.2	-26.7
Hornady 139 SP boat-tail LM	velocity, fps:	3000	2790	2590	2399	2216
	energy, ft-lb:	2777	2403	2071	1776	1515
	arc, inches:		+1.5	0	-6.7	-19.4
Norma 140 Ballistic ST	velocity, fps:	2822	2633	2452	2278	
	energy, ft-lb:	2476	2156	1870	1614	
	arc, inches:		+1.8	0	-7.6	
PMC 139 PSP	velocity, fps:	2850	2610	2384	2170	1969
	energy, ft-lb:	2507	2103	1754	1454	1197
	arc, inches:		+1.8	0	-7.9	-23.3
Rem. 120 Hollow Point	velocity, fps:	3000	2725	2467	2223	1992
	energy, ft-lb:	2398	1979	1621	1316	1058
	arc, inches:		+1.6	0	-7.3	-21.7
Rem. 140 PSP Core-Lokt	velocity, fps:	2860	2625	2402	2189	1988
	energy, ft-lb:	2542	2142	1793	1490	1228
	arc, inches:		+1.8	0	-7.8	-22.9
Rem. 140 PSP boat-tail	velocity, fps:	2860	2656	2460	2273	2094
	energy, ft-lb:	2542	2192	1881	1606	1363
	arc, inches:		+1.7	0	-7.5	-21.7
Rem. 140 AccuTip BT	velocity, fps:	2860	2670	2488	2313	2145
	energy, ft-lb:	2543	2217	1925	1663	1431
	arc, inches:		+1.7	0	-7.3	-21.2
Rem. 140 Nosler Partition	velocity, fps:	2860	2648	2446	2253	2068
	energy, ft-lb:	2542	2180	1860	1577	1330
	arc, inches:		+1.7	0	-7.6	-22.0
Speer 145 Grand Slam	velocity, fps:	2845	2567	2305	2059	
	energy, ft-lb:	2606	2121	1711	1365	
	arc, inches:		+1.9	0	-8.4	-25.5
Win. 140 Power-Point	velocity, fps:	2800	2523	2268	2027	1802.
	energy, ft-lb:	2429	1980	1599	1277	1010
	arc, inches:		+2.0	0	-8.8	-26.0
Win. 140 Power-Point Plus	velocity, fps:	2875	2597	2336	2090	1859
	energy, ft-lb:	2570	1997	1697	1358	1075
	arc, inches:		+2.0	0	-8.8	26.0
Win. 140 Fail Safe	velocity, fps:	2760	2506	2271	2048	1839
	energy, ft-lb:	2360	1953	1603	1304	1051
	arc, inches:		+2.0	0	-8.8	-25.9
Win. 140 Ballistic Silvertip	velocity, fps:	2770	2572	2382	2200	2026
	energy, ft-lb:	2386	2056	1764	1504	1276
	arc, inches:		+1.9	0	-8.0	-23.8
7x64 Brenneke						
Federal 160 Nosler Partition	velocity, fps:	2650	2480	2310	2150	2000
	energy, ft-lb:	2495	2180	1895	1640	1415
	arc, inches:		+2.1	0	-8.7	-24.9
Norma 140 AccuBond	velocity, fps:	2953	2759	2572	2394	
	energy, ft-lb:	2712	2366	2058	1782	
	arc, inches:		+1.5	0	-6.8	
Norma 154 Soft Point	velocity, fps:	2821	2605	2399	2203	
	energy, ft-lb:	2722	2321	1969	1660	
	arc, inches:		+1.8	0	-7.8	
Norma 156 Oryx	velocity, fps:	2789	2516	2259	2017	
	energy, ft-lb:	2695	2193	1768	1410	
	arc, inches:		+2.0	0	-8.8	
Norma 170 Vulkan	velocity, fps:	2756	2501	2259	2031	
	energy, ft-lb:	2868	2361	1927	1558	
	arc, inches:		+2.0	0	-8.8	
Norma 170 Oryx	velocity, fps:	2756	2481	2222	1979	
	energy, ft-lb:	2868	2324	1864	1478	
	arc, inches:		+2.1	0	-9.2	
Norma 170 Plastic Point	velocity, fps:	2756	2519	2294	2081	
	energy, ft-lb:	2868	2396	1987	1635	
	arc, inches:		+2.0	0	-8.6	
PMC 170 Pointed Soft Point	velocity, fps:	2625	2401	2189	1989	1801
	energy, ft lb:	2601	2175	1808	1493	1224
	arc, inches:		+2.3	0	-9.6	-27.9
Rem. 175 PSP Core-Lokt	velocity, fps:	2650	2445	2248	2061	1883
	energy, ft-lb:	2728	2322	1964	1650	1378
	arc, inches:		+2.2	0	-9.1	-26.4
Speer 160 Grand Slam	velocity, fps:	2600	2376	2164	1962	
	energy, ft-lb:	2401	2006	1663	1368	
	arc, inches:		+2.3	0	-9.8	-28.6
Speer 175 Grand Slam	velocity, fps:	2650	2461	2280	2106	
	energy, ft-lb:	2728	2353	2019	1723	
	arc, inches:		+2.4	0	-9.2	-26.2
7x65 R						
Norma 150 FMJ	velocity, fps:	2756	2552	2357	2170	
	energy, ft-lb:	2530	2169	1850	1569	
	arc, inches:		+1.9	0	-8.2	
Norma 156 Oryx	velocity, fps:	2723	2454	2200	1962	
	energy, ft-lb:	2569	2086	1678	1334	
	arc, inches:		+2.1	0	-9.3	
Norma 170 Plastic Point	velocity, fps:	2625	2390	2167	1956	
	energy, ft-lb:	2602	2157	1773	1445	
	arc, inches:		+2.3	0	-9.7	
Norma 170 Vulkan	velocity, fps:	2657	2392	2143	1909	
	energy, ft-lb:	2666	2161	1734	1377	
	arc, inches:		+2.3	0	-9.9	
Norma 170 Oryx	velocity, fps:	2657	2378	2115	1871	
	energy, ft-lb:	2666	2135	1690	1321	
	arc, inches:		+2.3	0	-10.1	

.284 Winchester

CARTRIDGE BULLET	RANGE, YARDS:	0	100	200	300	400
Win. 150 Power-Point	velocity, fps:	2860	2595	2344	2108	1886
	energy, ft-lb:	2724	2243	1830	1480	1185
	arc, inches:		+2.1	0	-8.5	-24.8

.280 Remington

CARTRIDGE BULLET	RANGE, YARDS:	0	100	200	300	400
Federal 140 Sierra Pro-Hunt.	velocity, fps:	2990	2740	2500	2270	2060
	energy, ft-lb:	2770	2325	1940	1605	1320
	arc, inches:		+1.6	0	-7.0	-20.8
Federal 140 Trophy Bonded	velocity, fps:	2990	2630	2310	2040	1730
	energy, ft-lb:	2770	2155	1655	1250	925
	arc, inches:		+1.6	0	-8.4	-25.4
Federal 140 Tr. Bonded HE	velocity, fps:	3150	2850	2570	2300	2050
	energy, ft-lb:	3085	2520	2050	1650	1310
	arc, inches:		+1.4	0	-6.7	-20.0
Federal 140 Nos. AccuBond	velocity, fps:	3000	2800	2620	2440	2260
And Bal. Tip	energy, ft-lb:	2800	2445	2130	1845	1590
And Solid Base	arc, inches:		+1.5	0	-6.5	-18.9
Federal 150 Hi-Shok	velocity, fps:	2890	2670	2460	2260	2060
	energy, ft-lb:	2780	2370	2015	1695	1420
	arc, inches:		+1.7	0	-7.5	-21.8
Federal 150 Nosler Partition	velocity, fps:	2890	2690	2490	2310	2130
	energy, ft-lb:	2780	2405	2070	1770	1510.
	arc, inches:		+1.7	0	-7.2	-21.1
Federal 150 Nos. AccuBond	velocity, fps	2800	2630	2460	2300	2150
	energy, ft-lb:	2785	2455	2155	1885	1645
	arc, inches:		+1.8	0	-7.5	-21.5
Federal 160 Trophy Bonded	velocity, fps:	2800	2570	2350	2140	1940
	energy, ft-lb:	2785	2345	1960	1625	1340
	arc, inches:		+1.9	0	-8.3	-24.0
Hornady 139 SPBT LMmoly	velocity, fps:	3110	2888	2675	2473	2280.
	energy, ft-lb:	2985	2573	2209	1887	1604
	arc, inches:		+1.4	0	-6.5	-18.6
Norma 156 Oryx	velocity, fps:	2789	2516	2259	2017	
	energy, ft-lb:	2695	2193	1768	1410	
	arc, inches:		+2.0	0	-8.8	
Norma 170 Plastic Point	velocity, fps:	2707	2468	2241	2026	
	energy, ft-lb:	2767	2299	1896	1550	
	arc, inches:		+2.1	0	-9.1	
Norma 170 Vulkan	velocity, fps:	2592	2346	2113	1894	
	energy, ft-lb:	2537	2078	1686	1354	
	arc, inches:		+2.4	0	-10.2	
Norma 170 Oryx	velocity, fps:	2690	2416	2159	1918	
	energy, ft-lb:	2732	2204	1760	1389	
	arc, inches:		+2.2	0	-9.7	
Rem. 140 PSP Core-Lokt	velocity, fps:	3000	2758	2528	2309	2102
	energy, ft-lb:	2797	2363	1986	1657	1373
	arc, inches:		+1.5	0	-7.0	-20.5
Rem. 140 PSP boat-tail	velocity, fps:	2860	2656	2460	2273	2094
	energy, ft-lb:	2542	2192	1881	1606	1363
	arc, inches:		+1.7	0	-7.5	-21.7
Rem. 140 Nosler Bal. Tip	velocity, fps:	3000	2804	2616	2436	2263
	energy, ft-lb:	2799	2445	2128	1848	1593
	arc, inches:		+1.5	0	-6.8	-19.0
Rem. 140 AccuTip	velocity, fps:	3000	2804	2617	2437	2265
	energy, ft-lb:	2797	2444	2129	1846	1594
	arc, inches:		+1.5	0	-6.8	-19.0
Rem. 150 PSP Core-Lokt	velocity, fps:	2890	2624	2373	2135	1912
	energy, ft-lb:	2781	2293	1875	1518	1217
	arc, inches:		+1.8	0	-8.0	-23.6
Rem. 165 SP Core-Lokt	velocity, fps:	2820	2510	2220	1950	1701
	energy, ft-lb:	2913	2308	1805	1393	1060.
	arc, inches:		+2.0	0	-9.1	-27.4
Speer 145 Grand Slam	velocity, fps:	2900	2619	2354	2105	
	energy, ft-lb:	2707	2207	1784	1426	
	arc, inches:		+2.1	0	-8.4	-24.7
Speer 160 Grand Slam	velocity, fps:	2890	2652	2425	2210	
	energy, ft-lb:	2967	2497	2089	1735	
	arc, inches:		+1.7	0	-7.7	-22.4
Win. 140 Fail Safe	velocity, fps:	3050	2756	2480	2221	1977
	energy, ft-lb:	2893	2362	1913	1533	1216
	arc, inches:		+1.5	0	-7.2	-21.5
Win. 140 Ballistic Silvertip	velocity, fps:	3040	2842	2653	2471	2297
	energy, ft-lb:	2872	2511	2187	1898	1640
	arc, inches:		+1.4	0	-6.3	-18.4

7mm Remington Magnum

CARTRIDGE BULLET	RANGE, YARDS:	0	100	200	300	400
A-Square 175 Monolithic	velocity, fps:	2860	2557	2273	2008	1771
Solid	energy, ft-lb:	3178	2540	2008	1567	1219
	arc, inches:		+1.92	0	-8.7	-25.9
Black Hills 140 Nos. Bal. Tip	velocity, fps:	3150				
	energy, ft-lb:	3084				
	arc, inches:					
Black Hills 140 Barnes XLC	velocity, fps:	3150				
	energy, ft-lb:	3084				
	arc, inches:					
Black Hills 140 Nos. Partition	velocity, fps:	3150				
	energy, ft-lb:	3084				
	arc, inches:					
Federal 140 Nosler Bal. Tip	velocity, fps:	3110	2910	2720	2530	2360.
And AccuBond	energy, ft-lb:	3005	2630	2295	1995	1725
	arc, inches:		+1.3	0	-6.0	-17.4
Federal 140 Nosler Partition	velocity, fps:	3150	2930	2710	2510	2320
	energy, ft-lb:	3085	2660	2290	1960	1670
	arc, inches:		+1.3	0	-6.0	-17.5
Federal 140 Trophy Bonded	velocity, fps:	3150	2910	2680	2460	2250.
	energy, ft-lb:	3085	2630	2230	1880	1575
	arc, inches:		+1.3	0	-6.1	-18.1
Federal 150 Hi-Shok	velocity, fps:	3110	2830	2570	2320	2090
	energy, ft-lb:	3220	2670	2200	1790	1450
	arc, inches:		+1.4	0	-6.7	-19.9
Federal 150 Sierra GameKing	velocity, fps:	3110	2920	2750	2580	2410
BTSP	energy, ft-lb:	3220	2850	2510	2210	1930
	arc, inches:		+1.3	0	-5.9	-17.0
Federal 150 Nosler Bal. Tip	velocity, fps:	3110	2910	2720	2540	2370
	energy, ft-lb:	3220	2825	2470	2150	1865
	arc, inches:		+1.3	0	-6.0	-17.4
Federal 150 Nos. Solid Base	velocity, fps:	3100	2890	2690	2500	2310
	energy, ft-lb:	3200	2780	2405	2075	1775
	arc, inches:		+1.3	0	-6.2	-17.8
Federal 160 Barnes XLC	velocity, fps:	2940	2760	2580	2410	2240
	energy, ft-lb:	3070	2695	2360	2060	1785
	arc, inches:		+1.5	0	-6.8	-19.6
Federal 160 Sierra Pro-Hunt.	velocity, fps:	2940	2730	2520	2320	2140
	energy, ft-lb:	3070	2640	2260	1920	1620
	arc, inches:		+1.6	0	-7.1	-20.6
Federal 160 Nosler Partition	velocity, fps:	2950	2770	2590	2420	2250.
	energy, ft-lb:	3090	2715	2375	2075	1800
	arc, inches:		+1.5	0	-6.7	-19.4
Federal 160 Nos. AccuBond	velocity, fps:	2950	2770	2600	2440	2280.
	energy, ft-lb:	3090	2730	2405	2110	1845
	arc, inches:		+1.5	0	-6.6	-19.1
Federal 160 Trophy Bonded	velocity, fps:	2940	2660	2390	2140	1900
	energy, ft-lb:	3070	2505	2025	1620	1280.
	arc, inches:		+1.7	0	-7.9	-23.3

Centerfire Rifle Ballistics

7MM REMINGTON MAGNUM TO 7MM REMINGTON MAGNUM

CARTRIDGE BULLET	RANGE, YARDS:	0	100	200	300	400
Federal 165 Sierra GameKing	velocity, fps:	2950	2800	2650	2510	2370.
BTSP	energy, ft-lb:	3190	2865	2570	2300	2050
	arc, inches:		+1.5	0	-6.4	-18.4
Federal 175 Hi-Shok	velocity, fps:	2860	2650	2440	2240	2060
	energy, ft-lb:	3180	2720	2310	1960	1640
	arc, inches:		+1.7	0	-7.6	-22.1
Federal 175 Trophy Bonded	velocity, fps:	2860	2600	2350	2120	1900
	energy, ft-lb:	3180	2625	2150	1745	1400
	arc, inches:		+1.8	0	-8.2	-24.0
Hornady 139 SPBT	velocity, fps:	3150	2933	2727	2530	2341
	energy, ft-lb:	3063	2656	2296	1976	1692
	arc, inches:		+1.2	0	-6.1	-17.7
Hornady 139 SST	velocity, fps:	3150	2948	2754	2569	2391
(or Interbond)	energy, ft-lb:	3062	2681	2341	2037	1764
	arc, inches:		+1.1	0	-5.7	-16.7
Hornady 139 SST LM	velocity, fps:	3250	3044	2847	2657	2475
(or Interbond)	energy, ft-lb:	3259	2860	2501	2178	1890
	arc, inches:		+1.1	0	-5.5	-16.2
Hornady 139 SPBT HMmoly	velocity, fps:	3250	3041	2822	2613	2413
	energy, ft-lb:	3300	2854	2458	2106	1797.
	arc, inches:		+1.1	0	-5.7	-16.6
Hornady 154 Soft Point	velocity, fps:	3035	2814	2604	2404	2212
	energy, ft-lb:	3151	2708	2319	1977	1674
	arc, inches:		+1.3	0	-6.7	-19.3
Hornady 154 SST	velocity, fps:	3035	2850	2672	2501	2337
(or Interbond)	energy, ft-lb:	3149	2777	2441	2139	1867
	arc, inches:		+1.4	0	-6.5	-18.7
Hornady 162 SP boat-tail	velocity, fps:	2940	2757	2582	2413	2251
	energy, ft-lb:	3110	2735	2399	2095	1823
	arc, inches:		+1.6	0	-6.7	-19.7
Hornady 175 SP	velocity, fps:	2860	2650	2440	2240	2060.
	energy, ft-lb:	3180	2720	2310	1960	1640
	arc, inches:		+2.0	0	-7.9	-22.7
Norma 140 Nosler Bal. Tip	velocity, fps:	3150	2936	2732	2537	
	energy, ft-lb:	3085	2680	2320	2001	
	arc, inches:		+1.2	0	-5.9	
Norma 140 Barnes X TS	velocity, fps:	3117	2912	2716	2529	
	energy, ft-lb:	3021	2637	2294	1988	
	arch, inches:		+1.3	0	-6.0	
Norma 150 Scirocco	velocity, fps:	3117	2934	2758	2589	
	energy, ft-lb:	3237	2869	2535	2234	
	arc, inches:		+1.2	0	-5.8	
Norma 156 Oryx	velocity, fps:	2953	2670	2404	2153	
	energy, ft-lb:	3021	2470	2002	1607	
	arc, inches:		+1.7	0	-7.7	
Norma 170 Vulkan	velocity, fps:	3018	2747	2493	2252	
	energy, ft-lb:	3439	2850	2346	1914	
	arc, inches:		+1.5	0	-2.8	
Norma 170 Oryx	velocity, fps:	2887	2601	2333	2080	
	energy, ft-lb:	3147	2555	2055	1634	
	arc, inches:		+1.8	0	-8.2	
Norma 170 Plastic Point	velocity, fps:	3018	2762	2519	2290	
	energy, ft-lb:	3439	2880	2394	1980	
	arc, inches:		+1.5	0	-7.0	
PMC 140 Barnes X	velocity, fps:	3000	2808	2624	2448	2279
	energy, ft-lb:	2797	2451	2141	1863	1614
	arc, inches:		+1.5	0	-6.6	18.9
PMC 140 Pointed Soft Point	velocity, fps:	3099	2878	2668	2469	2279
	energy, ft-lb:	2984	2574	2212	1895	1614
	arc, inches:		+1.4	0	-6.2	-18.1
PMC 140 SP boat-tail	velocity, fps:	3125	2891	2669	2457	2255
	energy, ft-lb:	3035	2597	2213	1877	1580
	arc, inches:		+1.4	0	-6.3	-18.4

CARTRIDGE BULLET	RANGE, YARDS:	0	100	200	300	400
PMC 160 Barnes X	velocity, fps:	2800	2639	2484	2334	2189
	energy, ft-lb:	2785	2474	2192	1935	1703
	arc, inches:		+1.8	0	-7.4	-21.2
PMC 160 Pointed Soft Point	velocity, fps:	2914	2748	2586	2428	2276
	energy, ft-lb:	3016	2682	2375	2095	1840
	arc, inches:		+1.6	0	-6.7	-19.4
PMC 160 SP boat-tail	velocity, fps:	2900	2696	2501	2314	2135
	energy, ft-lb:	2987	2582	2222	1903	1620
	arc, inches:		+1.7	0	-7.2	-21.0
PMC 175 Pointed Soft Point	velocity, fps:	2860	2645	2442	2244	2957
	energy, ft-lb:	3178	2718	2313	1956	1644
	arc, inches:		+2.0	0	-7.9	-22.7
Rem. 140 PSP Core-Lokt mr	velocity, fps:	2710	2482	2265	2059	1865
	energy, ft-lb:	2283	1915	1595	1318	1081
	arc, inches:		+1.0	-2.5	-12.8	-31.3
Rem. 140 PSP Core-Lokt	velocity, fps:	3175	2923	2684	2458	2243
	energy, ft-lb:	3133	2655	2240	1878	1564
	arc, inches:		+2.2	+1.9	-3.2	-14.2
Rem. 140 PSP boat-tail	velocity, fps:	3175	2956	2747	2547	2356
	energy, ft-lb:	3133	2715	2345	2017	1726
	arc, inches:		+2.2	+1.6	-3.1	-13.4
Rem. 150 AccuTip	velocity, fps:	3110	2926	2749	2579	2415
	energy, ft-lb:	3221	2850	2516	2215	1943
	arc, inches:		+1.3	0	-5.9	-17.0
Rem. 150 PSP Core-Lokt	velocity, fps:	3110	2830	2568	2320	2085
	energy, ft-lb:	3221	2667	2196	1792	1448
	arc, inches:		+1.3	0	-6.6	-20.2
Rem. 150 Nosler Bal. Tip	velocity, fps:	3110	2912	2723	2542	2367
	energy, ft-lb:	3222	2825	2470	2152	1867
	arc, inches:		+1.2	0	-5.9	-17.3
Rem. 150 Swift Scirocco	velocity, fps:	3110	2927	2751	2582	2419
	energy, ft-lb:	3221	2852	2520	2220	1948
	arc, inches:		+1.3	0	-5.9	-17.0
Rem. 160 Swift A-Frame	velocity, fps:	2900	2659	2430	2212	2006
	energy, ft-lb:	2987	2511	2097	1739	1430
	arc, inches:		+1.7	0	-7.6	-22.4
Rem. 160 Nosler Partition	velocity, fps:	2950	2752	2563	2381	2207
	energy, ft-lb:	3091	2690	2333	2014	1730
	arc, inches:		+0.6	-1.9	-9.6	-23.6
Rem. 175 PSP Core-Lokt	velocity, fps:	2860	2645	2440	2244	2057
	energy, ft-lb:	3178	2718	2313	1956	1644
	arc, inches:		+1.7	0	-7.6	-22.1
Speer 145 Grand Slam	velocity, fps:	3140	2843	2565	2304	
	energy, ft-lb:	3174	2602	2118	1708	
	arc, inches:		+1.4	0	-6.7	
Speer 175 Grand Slam	velocity, fps:	2850	2653	2463	2282	
	energy, ft-lb:	3156	2734	2358	2023	
	arc, inches:		+1.7	0	-7.5	-21.7
Win. 140 Fail Safe	velocity, fps:	3150	2861	2589	2333	2092
	energy, ft-lb:	3085	2544	2085	1693	1361
	arc, inches:		+1.4	0	-6.6	-19.5
Win. 140 Ballistic Silvertip	velocity, fps:	3100	2889	2687	2494	2310
	energy, ft-lb:	2988	2595	2245	1934	1659.
	arc, inches:		+1.3	0	-6.2	-17.9
Win. 140 AccuBond CT	velocity, fps:	3180	2965	2760	2565	2377
	energy, ft-lb:	3143	2733	2368	2044	1756
	arc, inches:		+1.2	0	-5.8	-16.9
Win. 150 Power-Point	velocity, fps:	3090	2812	2551	2304	2071
	energy, ft-lb:	3181	2634	2167	1768	1429
	arc, inches:		+1.5	0	-6.8	-20.2
Win. 150 Power-Point Plus	velocity, fps:	3130	2849	2586	2337	2102
	energy, ft-lb:	3264	2705	2227	1819	1472
	arc, inches:		+1.4	0	-6.6	-19.6

CARTRIDGE BULLET	RANGE, YARDS:	0	100	200	300	400
Win. 150 Ballistic Silvertip	velocity, fps:	3100	2903	2714	2533	2359
	energy, ft-lb:	3200	2806	2453	2136	1853
	arc, inches:		+1.3	0	-6.0	-17.5
Win. 160 AccuBond	velocity, fps:	2950	2766	2590	2420	2257
	energy, ft-lb:	3091	2718	2382	2080	1809
	arc, inches:		+1.5	0	-6.7	-19.4
Win. 160 Partition Gold	velocity, fps:	2950	2743	2546	2357	2176
	energy, ft-lb:	3093	2674	2303	1974	1682
	arc, inches:		+1.6	0	-6.9	-20.1
Win. 160 Fail Safe	velocity, fps:	2920	2678	2449	2331	2025
	energy, ft-lb:	3030	2549	2131	1769	1457
	arc, inches:		+1.7	0	-7.5	-22.0
Win. 175 Power-Point	velocity, fps:	2860	2645	2440	2244	2057
	energy, ft-lb:	3178	2718	2313	1956	1644
	arc, inches:		+2.0	0	-7.9	-22.7

7MM REMINGTON SHORT ULTRA MAGNUM

CARTRIDGE BULLET	RANGE, YARDS:	0	100	200	300	400
Rem. 140 PSP C-L Ultra	velocity, fps:	3175	2934	2707	2490	2283
	energy, ft-lb:	3133	2676	2277	1927	1620
	arc, inches:		+1.3	0	-6.0	-17.7
Rem. 150 PSP Core-Lokt	velocity, fps:	3110	2828	2563	2313	2077
	energy, ft-lb:	3221	2663	2188	1782	1437
	arc, inches:		+2.5	+2.1	-3.6	-15.8
Rem. 160 Partition	velocity, fps:	2960	2762	2572	2390	2215
	energy, ft-lb:	3112	2709	2350	2029	1744
	arc, inches:		+2.6	+2.2	-3.6	-15.4
Rem. 160 PSP C-L Ultra	velocity, fps:	2960	2733	2518	2313	2117
	energy, ft-lb:	3112	2654	2252	1900	1592
	arc, inches:		+2.7	+2.2	-3.7	-16.2

7MM WINCHESTER SHORT MAGNUM

CARTRIDGE BULLET	RANGE, YARDS:	0	100	200	300	400
Federal 140 Nos. AccuBond	velocity, fps:	3250	3040	2840	2660	2470
	energy, ft-lb:	3285	2875	2515	2190	1900
	arc, inches:		+1.1	0	-5.5	-15.8
Federal 140 Nos. Bal. Tip	velocity, fps:	3310	3100	2900	2700	2520
	energy, ft-lb:	3405	2985	2610	2270	1975
	arc, inches:		+1.1	0	-5.2	15.2
Federal 150 Nos. Solid Base	velocity, fps:	3230	3010	2800	2600	2410
	energy, ft-lb:	3475	3015	2615	2255	1935
	arc, inches:		+1.3	0	-5.6	-16.3
Federal 160 Nos. AccuBond	velocity, fps:	3120	2940	2760	2590	2430
	energy, ft-lb:	3460	3065	2710	2390	2095
	arc, inches:		+1.3	0	-5.9	-16.8
Federal 160 Nos. Partition	velocity, fps:	3160	2950	2750	2560	2380
	energy, ft-lb:	3545	3095	2690	2335	2015
	arc, inches:		+1.2	0	-5.9	-16.9
Federal 160 Barnes TS	velocity, fps:	2990	2780	2590	2400	2220
	energy, ft-lb:	3175	2755	2380	2045	1750
	arc, inches:		+1.5	0	-6.6	-19.4
Federal 160 Trophy Bonded	velocity, fps:	3120	2880	2650	2440	2230
	energy, ft-lb:	3460	2945	2500	2105	1765
	arc, inches:		+1.4	0	-6.3	-18.5
Win. 140 Bal. Silvertip	velocity, fps:	3225	3008	2801	2603	2414
	energy, ft-lb:	3233	2812	2438	2106	1812
	arc, inches:		+1.2	0	-5.6	-16.4
Win. 140 AccuBond CT	velocity, fps:	3225	3008	2801	2604	2415
	energy, ft-lb:	3233	2812	2439	2107	1812
	arc, inches:		+1.2	0	-5.6	-16.4
Win. 150 Power Point	velocity, fps:	3200	2915	2648	2396	2157
	energy, ft-lb:	3410	2830	23351911		1550
	arc, inches:		+1.3	0	-6.3	-18.6
Win. 160 AccuBond	velocity, fps:	3050	2862	2682	2509	2342
	energy, ft-lb:	3306	2911	2556	2237	1950
	arc, inches:		1.4	0	-6.2	-17.9
Win. 160 Fail Safe	velocity, fps:	2990	2744	2512	2291	2081
	energy, ft-lb:	3176	2675	2241	1864	1538
	arc, inches:		+1.6	0	-7.1	-20.8

7MM WEATHERBY MAGNUM

CARTRIDGE BULLET	RANGE, YARDS:	0	100	200	300	400
Federal 160 Nosler Partition	velocity, fps:	3050	2850	2650	2470	2290
	energy, ft-lb:	3305	2880	2505	2165	1865
	arc, inches:		+1.4	0	-6.3	-18.4
Federal 160 Sierra GameKing BTSP	velocity, fps:	3050	2880	2710	2560	2400
	energy, ft-lb:	3305	2945	2615	2320	2050
	arc, inches:		+1.4	0	-6.1	-17.4
Federal 160 Trophy Bonded	velocity, fps:	3050	2730	2420	2140	1880
	energy, ft-lb:	3305	2640	2085	1630	1255
	arc, inches:		+1.6	0	-7.6	-22.7
Hornady 154 Soft Point	velocity, fps:	3200	2971	2753	2546	2348
	energy, ft-lb:	3501	3017	2592	2216	1885
	arc, inches:		+1.2	0	-5.8	-17.0
Hornady 154 SST (or Interbond)	velocity, fps:	3200	3009	2825	2648	2478
	energy, ft-lb:	3501	3096	2729	2398	2100
	arc, inches:		+1.2	0	-5.7	-16.5
Hornady 175 Soft Point	velocity, fps:	2910	2709	2516	2331	2154
	energy, ft-lb:	3290	2850	2459	2111	1803
	arc, inches:		+1.6	0	-7.1	-20.6
Wby. 139 Pointed Expanding	velocity, fps:	3340	3079	2834	2601	2380
	energy, ft-lb:	3443	2926	2478	2088	1748
	arc, inches:		+2.9	+3.6	0	-8.7
Wby. 140 Nosler Partition	velocity, fps:	3303	3069	2847	2636	2434
	energy, ft-lb:	3391	2927	2519	2159	1841
	arc, inches:		+2.9	+3.6	0	-8.5
Wby. 150 Nosler Bal. Tip	velocity, fps:	3300	3093	2896	2708	2527
	energy, ft-lb:	3627	3187	2793	2442	2127
	arc, inches:		+2.8	+3.5	0	-8.2
Wby. 150 Barnes X	veloctiy, fps:	3100	2901	2710	2527	2352
	energy, ft-lb:	3200	2802	2446	2127	1842
	arc, inches:		+3.3	+4.0	0	-9.4
Wby. 154 Pointed Expanding	velocity, fps:	3260	3028	2807	2597	2397
	energy, ft-lb:	3634	3134	2694	2307	1964
	arc, inches:		+3.0	+3.7	0	-8.8
Wby. 160 Nosler Partition	velocity, fps:	3200	2991	2791	2600	2417
	energy, ft-lb:	3638	3177	2767	2401	2075
	arc, inches:		+3.1	+3.8	0	-8.9
Wby. 175 Pointed Expanding	velocity, fps:	3070	2861	2662	2471	2288
	energy, ft-lb:	3662	3181	2753	2373	2034
	arc, inches:		+3.5	+4.2	0	-9.9

7MM DAKOTA

CARTRIDGE BULLET	RANGE, YARDS:	0	100	200	300	400
Dakota 140 Barnes X	velocity, fps:	3500	3253	3019	2798	2587
	energy, ft-lb:	3807	3288	2833	2433	2081
	arc, inches:		+2.0	+2.1	-1.5	-9.6
Dakota 160 Barnes X	velocity, fps:	3200	3001	2811	2630	2455
	energy, ft-lb:	3637	3200	2808	2456	2140
	arc, inches:		+2.1	+1.9	-2.8	-12.5

7MM STW

CARTRIDGE BULLET	RANGE, YARDS:	0	100	200	300	400
A-Square 140 Nos. Bal. Tip	velocity, fps:	3450	3254	3067	2888	2715
	energy, ft-lb:	3700	3291	2924	2592	2292
	arc, inches:		+2.2	+3.0	0	-7.3
A-Square 160 Nosler Part.	velocity, fps:	3250	3071	2900	2735	2576
	energy, ft-lb:	3752	3351	2987	2657	2357
	arc, inches:		+2.8	+3.5	0	-8.2
A-Square 160 SP boat-tail	velocity, fps:	3250	3087	2930	2778	2631
	energy, ft-lb:	3752	3385	3049	2741	2460
	arc, inches:		+2.8	+3.4	0	-8.0

Centerfire Rifle Ballistics

7MM STW TO .30-30 WINCHESTER

CARTRIDGE BULLET	RANGE, YARDS:	0	100	200	300	400
Federal 140 Trophy Bonded	velocity, fps:	3330	3080	2850	2630	2420
	energy, ft-lb:	3435	2950	2520	2145	1815
	arc, inches:		+1.1	0	-5.4	-15.8
Federal 150 Trophy Bonded	velocity, fps:	3250	3010	2770	2560	2350.
	energy, ft-lb:	3520	3010	2565	2175	1830
	arc, inches:		+1.2	0	-5.7	-16.7
Federal 160 Sierra GameKing	velocity, fps:	3200	3020	2850	2670	2530.
BTSP	energy, ft-lb:	3640	3245	2890	2570	2275
	arc, inches:		+1.1	0	-5.5	-15.7
Rem. 140 PSP Core-Lokt	velocity, fps:	3325	3064	2818	2585	2364
	energy, ft-lb:	3436	2918	2468	2077	1737
	arc, inches:		+2.0	+1.7	-2.9	-12.8
Rem. 140 Swift A-Frame	velocity, fps:	3325	3020	2735	2467	2215
	energy, ft-lb:	3436	2834	2324	1892	1525
	arc, inches:		+2.1	+1.8	-3.1	-13.8
Speer 145 Grand Slam	velocity, fps:	3300	2992	2075	2435	
	energy, ft-lb:	3506	2882	2355	1909	
	arc, inches:		+1.2	0	-6.0	-17.8
Win. 140 Ballistic Silvertip	velocity, fps:	3320	3100	2890	2690	2499
	energy, ft-lb:	3427	2982	2597	2250	1941
	arc, inches:		+1.1	0	-5.2	-15.2
Win. 150 Power-Point	velocity, fps:	3250	2957	2683	2424	2181
	energy, ft-lb:	3519	2913	2398	1958	1584
	arc, inches:		+1.2	0	-6.1	-18.1
Win. 160 Fail Safe	velocity, fps:	3150	2894	2652	2422	2204
	energy, ft-lb:	3526	2976	2499	2085	1727
	arc, inches:		+1.3	0	-6.3	-18.5

7MM REMINGTON ULTRA MAGNUM

CARTRIDGE BULLET	RANGE, YARDS:	0	100	200	300	400
Rem. 140 PSP Core-Lokt	velocity, fps:	3425	3158	2907	2669	2444
	energy, ft-lb:	3646	3099	2626	2214	1856
	arc, inches:		+1.8	+1.6	-2.7	-11.9
Rem. 140 Nosler Partition	velocity, fps:	3425	3184	2956	2740	2534
	energy, ft-lb:	3646	3151	2715	2333	1995
	arc, inches:		+1.7	+1.6	-2.6	-11.4
Rem. 160 Nosler Partition	velocity, fps:	3200	2991	2791	2600	2417
	energy, ft-lb:	3637	3177	2767	2401	2075
	arc, inches:		+2.1	+1.8	-3.0	-12.9

7.21 (.284) FIREHAWK

CARTRIDGE BULLET	RANGE, YARDS:	0	100	200	300	400
Lazzeroni 140 Nosler Part.	velocity, fps:	3580	3349	3130	2923	2724
	energy, ft-lb:	3985	3488	3048	2656	2308
	arc, inches:		+2.2	+2.9	0	-7.0
Lazzeroni 160 Swift A-Fr.	velocity, fps:	3385	3167	2961	2763	2574
	energy, ft-lb:	4072	3565	3115	2713	2354
	arc, inches:		+2.6	+3.3	0	-7.8

7.5X55 SWISS

CARTRIDGE BULLET	RANGE, YARDS:	0	100	200	300	400
Norma 180 Soft Point	velocity, fps:	2651	2432	2223	2025	
	energy, ft-lb:	2810	2364	1976	1639	
	arc, inches:		+2.2	0	-9.3	
Norma 180 Oryx	velocity, fps:	2493	2222	1968	1734	
	energy, ft-lb:	2485	1974	1549	1201	
	arc, inches:		+2.7	0	-11.8	

7.62X39 RUSSIAN

CARTRIDGE BULLET	RANGE, YARDS:	0	100	200	300	400
Federal 123 Hi-Shok	velocity, fps:	2300	2030	1780	1550	1350
	energy, ft-lb:	1445	1125	860	655	500.
	arc, inches:		0	-7.0	-25.1	
Federal 124 FMJ	velocity, fps:	2300	2030	1780	1560	1360
	energy, ft-lb:	1455	1135	875	670	510
	arc, inches:		+3.5	0	-14.6	-43.5
PMC 123 FMJ	velocity, fps:	2350	2072	1817	1583	1368
	energy, ft-lb:	1495	1162	894	678	507
	arc, inches:		0	-5.0	-26.4	-67.8

CARTRIDGE BULLET	RANGE, YARDS:	0	100	200	300	400
PMC 125 Pointed Soft Point	velocity, fps:	2320	2046	1794	1563	1350
	energy, ft-lb:	1493	1161	893	678	505.
	arc, inches:		0	-5.2	-27.5	-70.6
Rem. 125 Pointed Soft Point	velocity, fps:	2365	2062	1783	1533	1320
	energy, ft-lb:	1552	1180	882	652	483
	arc, inches:		0	-6.7	-24.5	
Win. 123 Soft Point	velocity, fps:	2365	2033	1731	1465	1248
	energy, ft-lb:	1527	1129	818	586	425
	arc, inches:		+3.8	0	-15.4	-46.3

.30 CARBINE

CARTRIDGE BULLET	RANGE, YARDS:	0	100	200	300	400
Federal 110 Hi-Shok RN	velocity, fps:	1990	1570	1240	1040	920
	energy, ft-lb:	965	600	375	260	210
	arc, inches:		0	-12.8	-46.9	
Federal 110 FMJ	velocity, fps:	1990	1570	1240	1040	920
	energy, ft-lb:	965	600	375	260	210
	arc, inches:		0	-12.8	-46.9	
Magtech 110 FMC	velocity, fps:	1990	1654			
	energy, ft-lb:	965	668			
	arc, inches:		0			
PMC 110 FMJ	(and RNSP)velocity, fps:	1927	1548	1248		
	energy, ft-lb:	906	585	380		
	arc, inches:		0	-14.2		
Rem. 110 Soft Point	velocity, fps:	1990	1567	1236	1035	923
	energy, ft-lb:	967	600	373	262	208
	arc, inches:		0	-12.9	-48.6	
Win. 110 Hollow Soft Point	velocity, fps:	1990	1567	1236	1035	923
	energy, ft-lb:	967	600	373	262	208
	arc, inches:		0	-13.5	-49.9	

.30 T/C HORNADAY

CARTRIDGE BULLET	RANGE, YARDS:	0	100	200	300	400
Hornady 150	velocity, fps	3000	2772	2555	2348	
	energy, ft-lb	2997	2558	2176	1836	
	arc, inches	-1.5	+1.5	0	-6.9	
Hornady 165	velocity, fps	2850	2644	2447	2258	
	energy, ft-lb	2975	2560	2193	1868	
	arc, inches	-1.5	+1.7	0	-7.6	

.30-30 WINCHESTER

CARTRIDGE BULLET	RANGE, YARDS:	0	100	200	300	400
Federal 125 Hi-Shok HP	velocity, fps:	2570	2090	1660	1320	1080
	energy, ft-lb:	1830	1210	770	480	320
	arc, inches:		+3.3	0	-16.0	-50.9
Federal 150 Hi-Shok FN	velocity, fps:	2390	2020	1680	1400	1180
	energy, ft-lb:	1900	1355	945	650	460
	arc, inches:		+3.6	0	-15.9	-49.1
Federal 170 Hi-Shok RN	velocity, fps:	2200	1900	1620	1380	1190
	energy, ft-lb:	1830	1355	990	720	535
	arc, inches:		+4.1	0	-17.4	-52.4
Federal 170 Sierra Pro-Hunt.	velocity, fps:	2200	1820	1500	1240	1060
	energy, ft-lb:	1830	1255	845	575	425
	arc, inches:		+4.5	0	-20.0	-63.5
Federal 170 Nosler Partition	velocity, fps:	2200	1900	1620	1380	1190
	energy, ft-lb:	1830	1355	990	720	535
	arc, inches:		+4.1	0	-17.4	-52.4
Hornady 150 Round Nose	velocity, fps:	2390	1973	1605	1303	1095
	energy, ft-lb:	1902	1296	858	565	399
	arc, inches:		0	-8.2	-30.0	
Hornady 160 Evolution	velocity, fps:	2400	2150	1916	1699	
	energy, ft-lb:	2046	1643	1304	1025	
	arc, inches:		+3.0	0.2	-12.1	
Hornady 170 Flat Point	velocity, fps:	2200	1895	1619	1381	1191
	energy, ft-lb:	1827	1355	989	720	535
	arc, inches:		0	-8.9	-31.1	

BALLISTICS

CARTRIDGE BULLET	RANGE, YARDS:	0	100	200	300	400
Norma 150 Soft Point	velocity, fps:	2329	2008	1716	1459	
	energy, ft-lb:	1807	1344	981	709	
	arc, inches:		+3.6	0	-15.5	
PMC 150 Starfire HP	velocity, fps:	2100	1769	1478		
	energy, ft-lb:	1469	1042	728		
	arc, inches:		0	-10.8		
PMC 150 Flat Nose	velocity, fps:	2300	1943	1627		
	energy, ft-lb:	1762	1257	881		
	arc, inches:		0	-7.8		
PMC 170 Flat Nose	velocity, fps:	2150	1840	1566		
	energy, ft-lb:	1745	1277	926		
	arc, inches:		0	-8.9		
Rem. 55 PSP (sabot) "Accelerator"	velocity, fps:	3400	2693	2085	1570	1187
	energy, ft-lb:	1412	886	521	301	172
	arc, inches:		+1.7	0	-9.9	-34.3
Rem. 150 SP Core-Lokt	velocity, fps:	2390	1973	1605	1303	1095
	energy, ft-lb:	1902	1296	858	565	399
	arc, inches:		0	-7.6	-28.8	
Rem. 170 SP Core-Lokt	velocity, fps:	2200	1895	1619	1381	1191
	energy, ft-lb:	1827	1355	989	720	535
	arc, inches:		0	-8.3	-29.9	
Rem. 170 HP Core-Lokt	velocity, fps:	2200	1895	1619	1381	1191.
	energy, ft-lb:	1827	1355	989	720	535
	arc, inches:		0	-8.3	-29.9	
Speer 150 Flat Nose	velocity, fps:	2370	2067	1788	1538	
	energy, ft-lb:	1870	1423	1065	788	
	arc, inches:		+3.3	0	-14.4	-43.7
Win. 150 Hollow Point	velocity, fps:	2390	2018	1684	1398	1177
	energy, ft-lb:	1902	1356	944	651	461
	arc, inches:		0	-7.7	-27.9	
Win. 150 Power-Point	velocity, fps:	2390	2018	1684	1398	1177
	energy, ft-lb:	1902	1356	944	651	461
	arc, inches:		0	-7.7	-27.9	
Win. 150 Silvertip	velocity,fps:	2390	2018	1684	1398	1177
	energy, ft-lb:	1902	1356	944	651	461
	arc, inches:		0	-7.7	-27.9	
Win. 150 Power-Point Plus	velocity, fps:	2480	2095	1747	1446	1209
	energy, ft-lb:	2049	1462	1017	697	487
	arc, inches:		0	-6.5	-24.5	
Win. 170 Power-Point	velocity, fps:	2200	1895	1619	1381	1191
	energy, ft-lb:	1827	1355	989	720	535.
	arc, inches:		0	-8.9	-31.1	
Win. 170 Silvertip	velocity, fps:	2200	1895	1619	1381	1191
	energy, ft-lb:	1827	1355	989	720	535
	arc, inches:		0	-8.9	-31.1	

.300 SAVAGE

CARTRIDGE BULLET	RANGE, YARDS:	0	100	200	300	400
Federal 150 Hi-Shok	velocity, fps:	2630	2350	2100	1850	1630
	energy, ft-lb:	2305	1845	1460	1145	885
	arc, inches:		+2.4	0	-10.4	-30.9
Federal 180 Hi-Shok	velocity, fps:	2350	2140	1940	1750	1570
	energy, ft-lb:	2205	1825	1495	1215	985
	arc, inches:		+3.1	0	-12.4	-36.1
Rem. 150 PSP Core-Lokt	velocity, fps:	2630	2354	2095	1853	1631
	energy, ft-lb:	2303	1845	1462	1143	806.
	arc, inches:		+2.4	0	-10.4	-30.9
Rem. 180 SP Core-Lokt	velocity, fps:	2350	2025	1728	1467	1252
	energy, ft-lb:	2207	1639	1193	860	626
	arc, inches:		0	-7.1	-25.9	
Win. 150 Power-Point	velocity, fps:	2630	2311	2015	1743	1500
	energy, ft-lb:	2303	1779	1352	1012	749
	arc, inches:		+2.8	0	-11.5	-34.4

.307 WINCHESTER

CARTRIDGE BULLET	RANGE, YARDS:	0	100	200	300	400
Win. 180 Power-Point	velocity, fps:	2510	2179	1874	1599	1362
	energy, ft-lb:	2519	1898	1404	1022	742
	arc, inches:		+1.5	-3.6	-18.6	-47.1

.30-40 KRAG

CARTRIDGE BULLET	RANGE, YARDS:	0	100	200	300	400
Rem. 180 PSP Core-Lokt	velocity, fps:	2430	2213	2007	1813	1632.
	energy, ft-lb:	2360	1957	1610	1314	1064
	arc, inches, s:		0	-5.6	-18.6	
Win. 180 Power-Point	velocity, fps:	2430	2099	1795	1525	1298
	energy, ft-lb:	2360	1761	1288	929	673
	arc, inches, s:		0	-7.1	-25.0	

7.62X54R RUSSIAN

CARTRIDGE BULLET	RANGE, YARDS:	0	100	200	300	400
Norma 150 Soft Point	velocity, fps:	2953	2622	2314	2028	
	energy, ft-lb:	2905	2291	1784	1370	
	arc, inches:		+1.8	0	-8.3	
Norma 180 Alaska	velocity, fps:	2575	2362	2159	1967	
	energy, ft-lb:	2651	2231	1864	1546	
	arc, inches:		+2.9	0	-12.9	

.308 MARLIN EXPRESS

CARTRIDGE BULLET	RANGE, YARDS:	0	100	200	300	400
Hornady 160	velocity, fps	2660	2438	2226	2026	1836
	energy, ft-lb	2513	2111	1761	1457	1197
	arc, inches	-1.5	+3.0	+1.7	-6.7	-23.5

.308 WINCHESTER

CARTRIDGE BULLET	RANGE, YARDS:	0	100	200	300	400
Black Hills 150 Nosler B. Tip	velocity, fps:	2800				
	energy, ft-lb:	2611				
	arc, inches:					
Black Hills 165 Nosler B. Tip (and SP)	velocity, fps:	2650				
	energy, ft-lb:	2573				
	arc, inches:					
Black Hills 168 Barnes X (and Match)	velocity, fps:	2650				
	energy, ft-lb:	2620				
	arc, inches:					
Black Hills 175 Match	velocity, fps:	2600				
	energy, ft-lb:	2657				
	arc, inches:					
Black Hills 180 AccuBond	velocity, fps:	2600				
	energy, ft-lb:	2701				
	arc, inches:					
Federal 150 Hi-Shok	velocity, fps:	2820	2530	2260	2010	1770
	energy, ft-lb:	2650	2140	1705	1345	1050
	arc, inches:		+2.0	0	-8.8	-26.3
Federal 150 Nosler Bal. Tip.	velocity, fps:	2820	2610	2410	2220	2040
	energy, ft-lb:	2650	2270	1935	1640	1380
	arc, inches:		+1.8	0	-7.8	-22.7
Federal 150 FMJ boat-tail	velocity, fps:	2820	2620	2430	2250	2070
	energy, ft-lb:	2650	2285	1965	1680	1430
	arc, inches:		+1.8	0	-7.7	-22.4
Federal 150 Barnes XLC	velocity, fps:	2820	2610	2400	2210	2030
	energy, ft-lb:	2650	2265	1925	1630	1370
	arc, inches:		+1.8	0	-7.8	-22.9
Federal 155 Sierra MatchKg. BTHP	velocity, fps:	2950	2740	2540	2350	2170
	energy, ft-lb:	2995	2585	2225	1905	1620
	arc, inches:		+1.9	0	-8.9	-22.6
Federal 165 Sierra GameKing BTSP	velocity, fps:	2700	2520	2330	2160	1990
	energy, ft-lb:	2670	2310	1990	1700	1450
	arc, inches:		+2.0	0	-8.4	-24.3
Federal 165 Trophy Bonded	velocity, fps:	2700	2440	2200	1970	1760
	energy, ft-lb:	2670	2185	1775	1425	1135
	arc, inches:		+2.2	0	-9.4	-27.7

Centerfire Rifle Ballistics

.308 WINCHESTER TO .308 WINCHESTER

CARTRIDGE BULLET	RANGE, YARDS:	0	100	200	300	400
Federal 165 Tr. Bonded HE	velocity, fps:	2870	2600	2350	2120	1890
	energy, ft-lb:	3020	2485	2030	1640	1310
	arc, inches:		+1.8	0	-8.2	-24.0
Federal 168 Sierra MatchKg. BTHP	velocity, fps:	2600	2410	2230	2060	1890
	energy, ft-lb:	2520	2170	1855	1580	1340
	arc, inches:		+2.1	0	+8.9	+25.9
Federal 180 Hi-Shok	velocity, fps:	2620	2390	2180	1970	1780
	energy, ft-lb:	2745	2290	1895	1555	1270
	arc, inches:		+2.3	0	-9.7	-28.3
Federal 180 Sierra Pro-Hunt.	velocity, fps:	2620	2410	2200	2010	1820
	energy, ft-lb:	2745	2315	1940	1610	1330
	arc, inches:		+2.3	0	-9.3	-27.1
Federal 180 Nosler Partition	velocity, fps:	2620	2430	2240	2060	1890
	energy, ft-lb:	2745	2355	2005	1700	1430
	arc, inches:		+2.2	0	-9.2	-26.5
Federal 180 Nosler Part. HE	velocity, fps:	2740	2550	2370	2200	2030
	energy, ft-lb:	3000	2600	2245	1925	1645
	arc, inches:		+1.9	0	-8.2	-23.5
Hornady 110 TAP-FPD	velocity, fps:	3165	2830	2519	2228	1957
	energy, ft-lb:	2446	1956	1649	1212	935
	arc, inches:		+1.4	0	-6.9	-20.9
Hornady 110 Urban Tactical	velocity, fps:	3170	2825	2504	2206	1937
	energy, ft-lb:	2454	1950	1532	1189	916
	arc, inches:		+1.5	0	-7.2	-21.2
Hornady 150 SP boat-tail	velocity, fps:	2820	2560	2315	2084	1866
	energy, ft-lb:	2648	2183	1785	1447	1160
	arc, inches:		+2.0	0	-8.5	-25.2
Hornady 150 SST (or Interbond)	velocity, fps:	2820	2593	2378	2174	1984
	energy, ft-lb:	2648	2240	1884	1574	1311
	arc, inches:		+1.9	0	-8.1	-22.9
Hornady 150 SST LM (or Interbond)	velocity, fps:	3000	2765	2541	2328	2127
	energy, ft-lb:	2997	2545	2150	1805	1506
	arc, inches:		+1.5	0	-7.1	-20.6
Hornady 150 SP LM	velocity, fps:	2980	2703	2442	2195	1964
	energy, ft-lb:	2959	2433	1986	1606	1285
	arc, inches:		+1.6	0	-7.5	-22.2
Hornady 155 A-Max	velocity, fps:	2815	2610	2415	2229	2051
	energy, ft-lb:	2727	2345	2007	1709	1448
	arc, inches:		+1.9	0	-7.9	-22.6
Hornady 155 TAP-FPD	velocity, fps:	2785	2577	2379	2189	2008
	energy, ft-lb:	2669	2285	1947	1649	1387
	arc, inches:		+1.9	0	-8.0	-23.3
Hornady 165 SP boat-tail	velocity, fps:	2700	2496	2301	2115	1937
	energy, ft-lb:	2670	2283	1940	1639	1375
	arc, inches:		+2.0	0	-8.7	-25.2
Hornady 165 SPBT LM	velocity, fps:	2870	2658	2456	2283	2078
	energy, ft-lb:	3019	2589	2211	1877	1583
	arc, inches:		+1.7	0	-7.5	-21.8
Hornady 165 SST LM (or Interbond)	velocity, fps:	2880	2672	2474	2284	2103
	energy, ft-lb:	3038	2616	2242	1911	1620
	arc, inches:		+1.6	0	-7.3	-21.2
Hornady 168 BTHP Match	velocity, fps:	2700	2524	2354	2191	2035
	energy, ft-lb:	2720	2377	2068	1791	1545
	arc, inches:		+2.0	0	-8.4	-23.9
Hornady 168 BTHP Match LM	velocity, fps:	2640	2630	2429	2238	2056
	energy, ft-lb:	3008	2579	2201	1868	1577
	arc, inches:		+1.8	0	-7.8	-22.4
Hornady 168 A-Max Match	velocity fps:	2620	2446	2280	2120	1972
	energy, ft-lb:	2560	2232	1939	1677	1450
	arc, inches:		+2.6	0	-9.2	-25.6
Hornady 168 A-Max	velocity, fps:	2700	2491	2292	2102	1921
	energy, ft-lb:	2719	2315	1959	1648	1377
	arc, inches:		+2.4	0	-9.0	-25.9
Hornady 168 TAP-FPD	velocity, fps:	2700	2513	2333	2161	1996
	energy, ft-lb:	2719	2355	2030	1742	1486
	arc, inches:		+2.0	0	-8.4	-24.3
Hornady 178 A-Max	velocity, fps:	2965	2778	2598	2425	2259
	energy, ft-lb:	3474	3049	2666	2323	2017
	arc, inches:		+1.6	0	-6.9	-19.8
Hornady 180 A-Max Match	velocity, fps:	2550	2397	2249	2106	1974
	energy, ft-lb:	2598	2295	2021	1773	1557
	arc, inches:		+2.7	0	-9.5	-26.2
Norma 150 Nosler Bal. Tip	velocity, fps:	2822	2588	2365	2154	
	energy, ft-lb:	2653	2231	1864	1545	
	arc, inches:		+1.6	0	-7.1	
Norma 150 Soft Point	velocity, fps:	2861	2537	2235	1954	
	energy, ft-lb:	2727	2144	1664	1272	
	arc, inches:		+2.0	0	-9.0	
Norma 165 TXP Swift A-Fr.	velocity, fps:	2700	2459	2231	2015	
	energy, ft-lb:	2672	2216	1824	1488	
	arc, inches:		+2.1	0	-9.1	
Norma 180 Plastic Point	velocity, fps:	2612	2365	2131	1911	
	energy, ft-lb:	2728	2235	1815	1460	
	arc, inches:		+2.4	0	-10.1	
Norma 180 Nosler Partition	velocity, fps:	2612	2414	2225	2044	
	energy, ft-lb:	2728	2330	1979	1670	
	arc, inches:		+2.2	0	-9.3	
Norma 180 Alaska	velocity, fps:	2612	2269	1953	1667	
	energy, ft-lb:	2728	2059	1526	1111	
	arc, inches:		+2.7	0	-11.9	
Norma 180 Vulkan	velocity, fps:	2612	2325	2056	1806	
	energy, ft-lb:	2728	2161	1690	1304	
	arc, inches:		+2.5	0	-10.8	
Norma 180 Oryx	velocity, fps:	2612	2305	2019	1755	
	energy, ft-lb:	2728	2124	1629	1232	
	arc, inches:		+2.5	0	-11.1	
Norma 200 Vulkan	velocity, fps:	2461	2215	1983	1767	
	energy, ft-lb:	2690	2179	1747	1387	
	arc, inches:		+2.8	0	-11.7	
PMC 147 FMJ boat-tail	velocity, fps:	2751	2473	2257	2052	1859
	energy, ft-lb:	2428	2037	1697	1403	1150
	arc, inches:		+2.3	0	-9.3	-27.3
PMC 150 Barnes X	velocity, fps:	2700	2504	2316	2135	1964
	energy, ft-lb:	2428	2087	1786	1518	1284
	arc, inches:		+2.0	0	-8.6	-24.7
PMC 150 Pointed Soft Point	velocity, fps:	2750	2478	2224	1987	1766
	energy, ft-lb:	2519	2045	1647	1315	1039
	arc, inches:		+2.1	0	-9.2	-27.1
PMC 150 SP boat-tail	velocity, fps:	2820	2581	2354	2139	1935
	energy, ft-lb:	2648	2218	1846	1523	1247
	arc, inches:		+1.9	0	-8.2	-24.0
PMC 168 Barnes X	velocity, fps:	2600	2425	2256	2095	1940
	energy, ft-lb:	2476	2154	1865	1608	1379
	arc, inches:		+2.2	0	-9.0	-26.0
PMC 168 HP boat-tail	velocity, fps:	2650	2460	2278	2103	1936
	energy, ft-lb:	2619	2257	1935	1649	1399
	arc, inches:		+2.1	0	-8.8	-25.6
PMC 168 Pointed Soft Point	velocity, fps:	2559	2354	2160	1976	1803
	energy, ft-lb:	2443	2067	1740	1457	1212
	arc, inches:		+2.4	0	-9.9	-28.7
PMC 168 Pointed Soft Point	velocity, fps:	2600	2404	2216	2037	1866
	energy, ft-lb:	2476	2064	1709	1403	1142
	arc, inches:		+2.3	0	-9.8	-28.7
PMC 180 Pointed Soft Point	velocity, fps:	2550	2335	2132	1940	1760
	energy, ft-lb:	2599	2179	1816	1504	1238
	arc, inches:		+2.5	0	-10.1	-29.5

CARTRIDGE BULLET	RANGE, YARDS:	0	100	200	300	400
PMC 180 SP boat-tail	velocity, fps:	2620	2446	2278	2117	1962
	energy, ft-lb:	2743	2391	2074	1790	1538
	arc, inches:		+2.2	0	-8.9	-25.4
Rem. 125 PSP C-L MR	velocity, fps:	2660	2348	2057	1788	1546
	energy, ft-lb:	1964	1529	1174	887	663
	arc, inches:		+1.1	-2.7	-14.3	-35.8
Rem. 150 PSP Core-Lokt	velocity, fps:	2820	2533	2263	2009	1774
	energy, ft-lb:	2648	2137	1705	1344	1048
	arc, inches:		+2.0	0	-8.8	-26.2
Rem. 150 PSP C-L Ultra	velocity, fps:	2620	2404	2198	2002	1818
	energy, ft-lb:	2743	2309	1930	1601	1320
	arc, inches:		+2.3	0	-9.5	-26.4
Rem. 150 Swift Scirocco	velocity, fps:	2820	2611	2410	2219	2037
	energy, ft-lb:	2648	2269	1935	1640	1381
	arc, inches:		+1.8	0	-7.8	-22.7
Rem. 165 AccuTip	velocity, fps:	2700	2501	2311	2129	1958.
	energy, ft-lb:	2670	2292	1957	1861	1401.
	arc, inches:		+2.0	0	-8.6	-24.8
Rem. 165 PSP boat-tail	velocity, fps:	2700	2497	2303	2117	1941.
	energy, ft-lb:	2670	2284	1942	1642	1379
	arc, inches:		+2.0	0	-8.6	-25.0
Rem. 165 Nosler Bal. Tip	velocity, fps:	2700	2613	2333	2161	1996
	energy, ft-lb:	2672	2314	1995	1711	1460
	arc, inches:		+2.0	0	-8.4	-24.3
Rem. 165 Swift Scirocco	velocity, fps:	2700	2513	2233	2161	1996
	energy, fps:	2670	2313	1994	1711	1459
	arc, inches:		+2.0	0	-8.4	-24.3
Rem. 168 HPBT Match	velocity, fps:	2680	2493	2314	2143	1979
	energy, ft-lb:	2678	2318	1998	1713	1460
	arc, inches:		+2.1	0	-8.6	-24.7
Rem. 180 SP Core-Lokt	velocity, fps:	2620	2274	1955	1666	1414
	energy, ft-lb:	2743	2066	1527	1109	799
	arc, inches:		+2.6	0	-11.8	-36.3
Rem. 180 PSP Core-Lokt	velocity, fps:	2620	2393	2178	1974	1782
	energy, ft-lb:	2743	2288	1896	1557	1269
	arc, inches:		+2.3	0	-9.7	-28.3
Rem. 180 Nosler Partition	velocity, fps:	2620	2436	2259	2089	1927.
	energy, ft-lb:	2743	2371	2039	1774	1485
	arc, inches:		+2.2	0	-9.0	-26.0
Speer 150 Grand Slam	velocity, fps:	2900	2599	2317	2053	
	energy, ft-lb:	2800	2249	1788	1404	
	arc, inches:		+2.1	0	-8.6	-24.8
Speer 165 Grand Slam	velocity, fps:	2700	2475	2261	2057	
	energy, ft-lb:	2670	2243	1872	1550	
	arc, inches:		+2.1	0	-8.9	-25.9
Speer 180 Grand Slam	velocity, fps:	2620	2420	2229	2046	
	energy, ft-lb:	2743	2340	1985	1674	
	arc, inches:		+2.2	0	-9.2	-26.6
Win. 150 Power-Point	velocity, fps:	2820	2488	2179	1893	1633
	energy, ft-lb:	2648	2061	1581	1193	888
	arc, inches:		+2.4	0	-9.8	-29.3
Win. 150 Power-Point Plus	velocity, fps:	2900	2558	2241	1946	1678
	energy, ft-lb:	2802	2180	1672	1262	938
	arc, inches:		+1.9	0	-8.9	-27.0
Win. 150 Partition Gold	velocity, fps:	2900	2645	2405	2177	1962
	energy, ft-lb:	2802	2332	1927	1579	1282.
	arc, inches:		+1.7	0	-7.8	-22.9
Win. 150 Ballistic Silvertip	velocity, fps:	2810	2601	2401	2211	2028
	energy, ft-lb:	2629	2253	1920	1627	1370.
	arc, inches:		+1.8	0	-7.8	-22.8
Win. 150 Fail Safe	velocity, fps:	2820	2533	2263	2010	1775
	energy, ft-lb:	2649	2137	1706	1346	1049
	arc, inches:		+2.0	0	-8.8	-26.2

CARTRIDGE BULLET	RANGE, YARDS:	0	100	200	300	400
Win. 150 Supreme Elite XP3	velocity, fps:	2825	2616	2417	2226	2044
	energy, ft-lb:	2658	2279	1945	1650	1392
	arc, inches:		+1.8	0	-7.8	-22.6
Win. 168 Ballistic Silvertip	velocity, fps:	2670	2484	2306	2134	1971
	energy, ft-lb:	2659	2301	1983	1699	1449
	arc, inches:		+2.1	0	-8.6	-24.8
Win. 168 HP boat-tail Match	velocity, fps:	2680	2485	2297	2118	1948
	energy, ft-lb:	2680	2303	1970	1674	1415
	arc, inches:		+2.1	0	-8.7	-25.1
Win. 180 Power-Point	velocity, fps:	2620	2274	1955	1666	1414
	energy, ft-lb:	2743	2066	1527	1109	799
	arc, inches:		+2.9	0	-12.1	-36.9
Win. 180 Silvertip	velocity, fps:	2620	2393	2178	1974	1782
	energy, ft-lb:	2743	2288	1896	1557	1269
	arc, inches:		+2.6	0	-9.9	-28.9

.30-06 SPRINGFIELD

CARTRIDGE BULLET	RANGE, YARDS:	0	100	200	300	400
A-Square 180 M & D-T	velocity, fps:	2700	2365	2054	1769	1524
	energy, ft-lb:	2913	2235	1687	1251	928
	arc, inches:		+2.4	0	-10.6	-32.4
A-Square 220 Monolythic Solid	velocity, fps:	2380	2108	1854	1623	1424
	energy, ft-lb:	2767	2171	1679	1287	990
	arc, inches:		+3.1	0	-13.6	-39.9
Black Hills 150 Nosler B. Tip	velocity, fps:	2900				
	energy, ft-lb:	2770				
	arc, inches:					
Black Hills 165 Nosler B. Tip	velocity, fps:	2750				
	energy, ft-lb:	2770				
	arc, inches:					
Black Hills 168 Hor. Match	velocity, fps:	2700				
	energy, ft-lb:	2718				
	arc, inches:					
Black Hills 180 Barnes X	velocity, fps:	2650				
	energy, ft-lb:	2806				
	arc, inches:					
Black Hills 180 AccuBond	velocity, ft-lb:	2700				
	energy, ft-lb:					
	arc, inches:					
Federal 125 Sierra Pro-Hunt.	velocity, fps:	3140	2780	2450	2140	1850
	energy, ft-lb:	2735	2145	1660	1270	955
	arc, inches:		+1.5	0	-7.3	-22.3
Federal 150 Hi-Shok	velocity, fps:	2910	2620	2340	2080	1840
	energy, ft-lb:	2820	2280	1825	1445	1130
	arc, inches:		+1.8	0	-8.2	-24.4
Federal 150 Sierra Pro-Hunt.	velocity, fps:	2910	2640	2380	2130	1900
	energy, ft-lb:	2820	2315	1880	1515	1205
	arc, inches:		+1.7	0	-7.9	-23.3
Federal 150 Sierra GameKing BTSP	velocity, fps:	2910	2690	2480	2270	2070
	energy, ft-lb:	2820	2420	2040	1710	1430
	arc, inches:		+1.7	0	-7.4	-21.5
Federal 150 Nosler Bal. Tip	velocity, fps:	2910	2700	2490	2300	2110
	energy, ft-lb:	2820	2420	2070	1760	1485
	arc, inches:		+1.6	0	-7.3	-21.1
Federal 150 FMJ boat-tail	velocity, fps:	2910	2710	2510	2320	2150
	energy, ft-lb:	2820	2440	2100	1800	1535
	arc, inches:		+1.6	0	-7.1	-20.8
Federal 165 Sierra Pro-Hunt.	velocity, fps:	2800	2560	2340	2130	1920
	energy, ft-lb:	2875	2410	2005	1655	1360
	arc, inches:		+1.9	0	-8.3	-24.3
Federal 165 Sierra GameKing BTSP	velocity, fps:	2800	2610	2420	2240	2070.
	energy, ft-lb:	2870	2490	2150	1840	1580
	arc, inches:		+1.8	0	-7.8	-22.4

Centerfire Rifle Ballistics

.30-06 SPRINGFIELD TO .30-06 SPRINGFIELD

CARTRIDGE BULLET	RANGE, YARDS:	0	100	200	300	400
Federal 165 Sierra GameKing HE	velocity, fps:	3140	2900	2670	2450	2240.
	energy, ft-lb:	3610	3075	2610	2200	1845
	arc, inches:		+1.5	0	-6.9	-20.4
Federal 165 Nosler Bal. Tip	velocity, fps:	2800	2610	2430	2250	2080
	energy, ft-lb:	2870	2495	2155	1855	1585
	arc, inches:		+1.8	0	-7.7	-22.3
Federal 165 Trophy Bonded	velocity, fps:	2800	2540	2290	2050	1830.
	energy, ft-lb:	2870	2360	1915	1545	1230
	arc, inches:		+2.0	0	-8.7	-25.4
Federal 165 Tr. Bonded HE	velocity, fps:	3140	2860	2590	2340	2100
	energy, ft-lb:	3610	2990	2460	2010	1625.
	arc, inches:		+1.6	0	-7.4	-21.9
Federal 168 Sierra MatchKg. BTHP	velocity, fps:	2700	2510	2320	2150	1980
	energy, ft-lb:	2720	2350	2010	1720	1460
	arc, inches:		+16.2	+28.4	+34.1	+32.3
Federal 180 Hi-Shok	velocity, fps:	2700	2470	2250	2040	1850
	energy, ft-lb:	2915	2435	2025	1665	1360
	arc, inches:		+2.1	0	-9.0	-26.4
Federal 180 Sierra Pro-Hunt. RN	velocity, fps:	2700	2350	2020	1730	1470
	energy, ft-lb:	2915	2200	1630	1190	860
	arc, inches:		+2.4	0	-11.0	-33.6
Federal 180 Nosler Partition	velocity, fps:	2700	2500	2320	2140	1970
	energy, ft-lb:	2915	2510	2150	1830	1550
	arc, inches:		+2.0	0	-8.6	-24.6
Federal 180 Nosler Part. HE	velocity, fps:	2880	2690	2500	2320	2150
	energy, ft-lb:	3315	2880	2495	2150	1845
	arc, inches:		+1.7	0	-7.2	-21.0
Federal 180 Sierra GameKing BTSP	velocity, fps:	2700	2540	2380	2220	2080
	energy, ft-lb:	2915	2570	2260	1975	1720
	arc, inches:		+1.9	0	-8.1	-23.1
Federal 180 Barnes XLC	velocity, fps:	2700	2530	2360	2200	2040.
	energy, ft-lb:	2915	2550	2220	1930	1670
	arc, inches:		+2.0	0	-8.3	-23.8
Federal 180 Trophy Bonded	velocity, fps:	2700	2460	2220	2000	1800
	energy, ft-lb:	2915	2410	1975	1605	1290
	arc, inches:		+2.2	0	-9.2	-27.0
Federal 180 Tr. Bonded HE	velocity, fps:	2880	2630	2380	2160	1940
	energy, ft-lb:	3315	2755	2270	1855	1505
	arc, inches:		+1.8	0	-8.0	-23.3
Federal 220 Sierra Pro-Hunt. RN	velocity, fps:	2410	2130	1870	1630	1420
	energy, ft-lb:	2835	2215	1705	1300	985
	arc, inches:		+3.1	0	-13.1	-39.3
Hornady 150 SP	velocity, fps:	2910	2617	2342	2083	1843
	energy, ft-lb:	2820	2281	1827	1445	1131
	arc, inches:		+2.1	0	-8.5	-25.0
Hornady 150 SP LM	velocity, fps:	3100	2815	2548	2295	2058
	energy, ft-lb:	3200	2639	2161	1755	1410
	arc, inches:		+1.4	0	-6.8	-20.3
Hornady 150 SP boat-tail	velocity, fps:	2910	2683	2467	2262	2066.
	energy, ft-lb:	2820	2397	2027	1706	1421
	arc, inches:		+2.0	0	-7.7	-22.2
Hornady 150 SST (or Interbond)	velocity, fps:	2910	2802	2599	2405	2219
	energy, ft-lb:	3330	2876	2474	2118	1803
	arc, inches:		+1.5	0	-6.6	-19.3
Hornady 150 SST LM	velocity, fps:	3100	2860	2631	2414	2208
	energy, ft-lb:	3200	2724	2306	1941	1624
	arc, inches:		+1.4	0	-6.6	-19.2
Hornady 165 SP boat-tail	velocity, fps:	2800	2591	2392	2202	2020
	energy, ft-lb:	2873	2460	2097	1777	1495
	arc, inches:		+1.8	0	-8.0	-23.3
Hornady 165 SPBT LM	velocity, fps:	3015	2790	2575	2370	2176
	energy, ft-lb:	3330	2850	2428	2058	1734
	arc, inches:		+1.6	0	-7.0	-20.1
Hornady 165 SST (or Interbond)	velocity, fps:	2800	2598	2405	2221	2046
	energy, ft-lb:	2872	2473	2119	1808	1534
	arc, inches:		+1.9	0	-8.0	-22.8
Hornady 165 SST LM	velocity, fps:	3015	2802	2599	2405	2219
	energy, ft-lb:	3330	2878	2474	2118	1803.
	arc, inches:		+1.5	0	-6.5	-19.3
Hornady 168 HPBT Match	velocity, fps:	2790	2620	2447	2280	2120.
	energy, ft-lb:	2925	2561	2234	1940	1677.
	arc, inches:		+1.7	0	-7.7	-22.2
Hornady 180 SP	velocity, fps:	2700	2469	2258	2042	1846
	energy, ft-lb:	2913	2436	2023	1666	1362
	arc, inches:		+2.4	0	-9.3	-27.0
Hornady 180 SPBT LM	velocity, fps:	2880	2676	2480	2293	2114
	energy, ft-lb:	3316	2862	2459	2102	1786
	arc, inches:		+1.7	0	-7.3	-21.3
Norma 150 Nosler Bal. Tip	velocity, fps:	2936	2713	2502	2300	
	energy, ft-lb:	2872	2453	2085	1762	
	arc, inches:		+1.6	0	-7.1	
Norma 150 Soft Point	velocity, fps:	2972	2640	2331	2043	
	energy, ft-lb:	2943	2321	1810	1390	
	arc, inches:		+1.8	0	-8.2	
Norma 180 Alaska	velocity, fps:	2700	2351	2028	1734	
	energy, ft-lb:	2914	2209	1645	1202	
	arc, inches:		+2.4	0	-11.0	
Norma 180 Nosler Partition	velocity, fps:	2700	2494	2297	2108	
	energy, ft-lb:	2914	2486	2108	1777	
	arc, inches:		+2.1	0	-8.7	
Norma 180 Plastic Point	velocity, fps:	2700	2455	2222	2003	
	energy, ft-lb:	2914	2409	1974	1603	
	arc, inches:		+2.1	0	-9.2	
Norma 180 Vulkan	velocity, fps:	2700	2416	2150	1901	
	energy, ft-lb:	2914	2334	1848	1445	
	arc, inches:		+2.2	0	-9.8	
Norma 180 Oryx	velocity, fps:	2700	2387	2095	1825	
	energy, ft-lb:	2914	2278	1755	1332	
	arc, inches:		+2.3	0	-10.2	
Norma 180 TXP Swift A-Fr.	velocity, fps:	2700	2479	2268	2067	
	energy, ft-lb:	2914	2456	2056	1708	
	arc, inches:		+2.0	0	-8.8	
Norma 180 AccuBond	velocity, fps:	2674	2499	2331	2169	
	energy, ft-lb:	2859	2497	2172	1881	
	arc, inches:		+2.0	0	-8.5	
Norma 200 Vulkan	velocity, fps:	2641	2385	2143	1916	
	energy, ft-lb:	3098	2527	2040	1631	
	arc, inches:		+2.3	0	-9.9	
Norma 200 Oryx	velocity, fps:	2625	2362	2115	1883	
	energy, ft-lb:	3061	2479	1987	1575	
	arc, inches:		+2.3	0	-10.1	
PMC 150 X-Bullet	velocity, fps:	2750	2552	2361	2179	2005
	energy, ft-lb:	2518	2168	1857	1582	1339
	arc, inches:		+2.0	0	-8.2	-23.7
PMC 150 Pointed Soft Point	velocity, fps:	2773	2542	2322	2113	1916
	energy, ft-lb:	2560	2152	1796	1487	1222.
	arc, inches:		+1.9	0	-8.4	-24.6
PMC 150 SP boat-tail	velocity, fps:	2900	2657	2427	2208	2000
	energy, ft-lb:	2801	2351	1961	1623	1332
	arc, inches:		+1.7	0	-7.7	-22.5
PMC 150 FMJ	velocity, fps:	2773	2542	2322	2113	1916
	energy, ft-lb:	2560	2152	1796	1487	1222
	arc, inches:		+1.9	0	-8.4	-24.6
PMC 168 Barnes X	velocity, fps:	2750	2569	2395	2228	2067
	energy, ft-lb:	2770	2418	2101	1818	1565
	arc, inches:		+1.9	0	-8.0	-23.0

BALLISTICS

CARTRIDGE BULLET	RANGE, YARDS:	0	100	200	300	400
PMC 180 Barnes X	velocity, fps:	2650	2487	2331	2179	2034
	energy, ft-lb:	2806	2472	2171	1898	1652
	arc, inches:		+2.1	0	-8.5	-24.3
PMC 180 Pointed Soft Point	velocity, fps:	2650	2430	2221	2024	1839
	energy, ft-lb:	2807	2359	1972	1638	1351
	arc, inches:		+2.2	0	-9.3	-27.0
PMC 180 SP boat-tail	velocity, fps:	2700	2523	2352	2188	2030
	energy, ft-lb:	2913	2543	2210	1913	1646
	arc, inches:		+2.0	0	-8.3	-23.9
PMC 180 HPBT Match	velocity, fps:	2800	2622	2456	2302	2158
	energy, ft-lb:	3133	2747	2411	2118	1861
	arc, inches:		+1.8	0	-7.6	-21.7
Rem. 55 PSP (sabot)	velocity, fps:	4080	3484	2964	2499	2080
"Accelerator"	energy, ft-lb:	2033	1482	1073	763	528.
	arc, inches:		+1.4	+1.4	-2.6	-12.2
Rem. 125 PSP C-L MR	velocity, fps:	2660	2335	2034	1757	1509
	energy, ft-lb:	1964	1513	1148	856	632
	arc, inches:		+1.1	-3.0	-15.5	-37.4
Rem. 125 Pointed Soft Point	velocity, fps:	3140	2780	2447	2138	1853
	energy, ft-lb:	2736	2145	1662	1269	953.
	arc, inches:		+1.5	0	-7.4	-22.4
Rem. 150 AccuTip	velocity, fps:	2910	2686	2473	2270	2077
	energy, ft-lb:	2820	2403	2037	1716	1436
	arc, inches:		+1.8	0	-7.4	-21.5
Rem. 150 PSP Core-Lokt	velocity, fps:	2910	2617	2342	2083	1843
	energy, ft-lb:	2820	2281	1827	1445	1131
	arc, inches:		+1.8	0	-8.2	-24.4
Rem. 150 Bronze Point	velocity, fps:	2910	2656	2416	2189	1974
	energy, ft-lb:	2820	2349	1944	1596	1298
	arc, inches:		+1.7	0	-7.7	-22.7
Rem. 150 Nosler Bal. Tip	velocity, fps:	2910	2696	2492	2298	2112.
	energy, ft-lb:	2821	2422	2070	1769	1485
	arc, inches:		+1.6	0	-7.3	-21.1
Rem. 150 Swift Scirocco	velocity, fps:	2910	2696	2492	2298	2111
	energy, ft-lb:	2820	2421	2069	1758	1485
	arc, inches:		+1.6	0	-7.3	-21.1
Rem. 165 AccuTip	velocity, fps:	2800	2597	2403	2217	2039
	energy, ft-lb:	2872	2470	2115	1800	1523
	arc, inches:		+1.8	0	-7.9	-22.8
Rem. 165 PSP Core-Lokt	velocity, fps:	2800	2534	2283	2047	1825.
	energy, ft-lb:	2872	2352	1909	1534	1220
	arc, inches:		+2.0	0	-8.7	-25.9
Rem. 165 PSP boat-tail	velocity, fps:	2800	2592	2394	2204	2023
	energy, ft-lb:	2872	2462	2100	1780	1500
	arc, inches:		+1.8	0	-7.9	-23.0
Rem. 165 Nosler Bal. Tip	velocity, fps:	2800	2609	2426	2249	2080.
	energy, ft-lb:	2873	2494	2155	1854	1588
	arc, inches:		+1.8	0	-7.7	-22.3
Rem. 168 PSP C-L Ultra	velocity, fps:	2800	2546	2306	2079	1866
	energy, ft-lb:	2924	2418	1984	1613	1299
	arc, inches:		+1.9	0	-8.5	-25.1
Rem. 180 SP Core-Lokt	velocity, fps:	2700	2348	2023	1727	1466
	energy, ft-lb:	2913	2203	1635	1192	859
	arc, inches:		+2.4	0	-11.0	-33.8
Rem. 180 PSP Core-Lokt	velocity, fps:	2700	2469	2250	2042	1846
	energy, ft-lb:	2913	2436	2023	1666	1362
	arc, inches:		+2.1	0	-9.0	-26.3
Rem. 180 PSP C-L Ultra	velocity, fps:	2700	2480	2270	2070	1882
	energy, ft-lb:	2913	2457	2059	1713	1415
	arc, inches:		+2.1	0	-8.9	-25.8
Rem. 180 Bronze Point	velocity, fps:	2700	2485	2280	2084	1899.
	energy, ft-lb:	2913	2468	2077	1736	1441
	arc, inches:		+2.1	0	-8.8	-25.5

CARTRIDGE BULLET	RANGE, YARDS:	0	100	200	300	400
Rem. 180 Swift A-Frame	velocity, fps:	2700	2465	2243	2032	1833
	energy, ft-lb:	2913	2429	2010	1650	1343
	arc, inches:		+2.1	0	-9.1	-26.6
Rem. 180 Nosler Partition	velocity, fps:	2700	2512	2332	2160	1995
	energy, ft-lb:	2913	2522	2174	1864	1590
	arc, inches:		+2.0	0	-8.4	-24.3
Rem. 220 SP Core-Lokt	velocity, fps:	2410	2130	1870	1632	1422
	energy, ft-lb:	2837	2216	1708	1301	988
	arc, inches, s:		0	-6.2	-22.4	
Speer 150 Grand Slam	velocity, fps:	2975	2669	2383	2114	
	energy, ft-lb:	2947	2372	1891	1489	
	arc, inches:		+2.0	0	-8.1	-24.1
Speer 165 Grand Slam	velocity, fps:	2790	2560	2342	2134	
	energy, ft-lb:	2851	2401	2009	1669	
	arc, inches:		+1.9	0	-8.3	-24.1
Speer 180 Grand Slam	velocity, fps:	2690	2487	2293	2108	
	energy, ft-lb:	2892	2472	2101	1775	
	arc, inches:		+2.1	0	-8.8	-25.1
Win. 125 Pointed Soft Point	velocity, fps:	3140	2780	2447	2138	1853
	energy, ft-lb:	2736	2145	1662	1269	953
	arc, inches:		+1.8	0	-7.7	-23.0
Win. 150 Power-Point	velocity, fps:	2920	2580	2265	1972	1704
	energy, ft-lb:	2839	2217	1708	1295	967
	arc, inches:		+2.2	0	-9.0	-27.0
Win. 150 Power-Point Plus	velocity, fps:	3050	2685	2352	2043	1760
	energy, ft-lb:	3089	2402	1843	1391	1032
	arc, inches:		+1.7	0	-8.0	-24.3
Win. 150 Silvertip	velocity, fps:	2910	2617	2342	2083	1843
	energy, ft-lb:	2820	2281	1827	1445	1131
	arc, inches:		+2.1	0	-8.5	-25.0
Win. 150 Partition Gold	velocity, fps:	2960	2705	2464	2235	2019
	energy, ft-lb:	2919	2437	2022	1664	1358.
	arc, inches:		+1.6	0	-7.4	-21.7
Win. 150 Ballistic Silvertip	velocity, fps:	2900	2687	2483	2289	2103
	energy, ft-lb:	2801	2404	2054	1745	1473
	arc, inches:		+1.7	0	-7.3	-21.2
Win. 150 Fail Safe	velocity, fps:	2920	2625	2349	2089	1848
	energy, ft-lb:	2841	2296	1838	1455	1137
	arc, inches:		+1.8	0	-8.1	-24.3
Win. 165 Pointed Soft Point	velocity, fps:	2800	2573	2357	2151	1956
	energy, ft-lb:	2873	2426	2036	1696	1402
	arc, inches:		+2.2	0	-8.4	-24.4
Win. 165 Fail Safe	velocity, fps:	2800	2540	2295	2063	1846
	energy, ft-lb:	2873	2365	1930	1560	1249
	arc, inches:		+2.0	0	-8.6	-25.3
Win. 168 Ballistic Silvertip	velocity, fps:	2790	2599	2416	2240	2072
	energy, ft-lb:	2903	2520	2177	1872	1601
	arc, inches:		+1.8	0	-7.8	-22.5
Win. 180 Ballistic Silvertip	velocity, fps:	2750	2572	2402	2237	2080
	energy, ft-lb:	3022	2644	2305	2001	1728
	arc, inches:		+1.9	0	-7.9	-22.8
Win. 180 Power-Point	velocity, fps:	2700	2348	2023	1727	1466
	energy, ft-lb:	2913	2203	1635	1192	859
	arc, inches:		+2.7	0	-11.3	-34.4
Win. 180 Power-Point Plus	velocity, fps:	2770	2563	2366	2177	1997
	energy, ft-lb:	3068	2627	2237	1894	1594
	arc, inches:		+1.9	0	-8.1	-23.6
Win. 180 Silvertip	velocity, fps:	2700	2469	2250	2042	1846
	energy, ft-lb:	2913	2436	2023	1666	1362
	arc, inches:		+2.4	0	-9.3	-27.0
Win. 180 AccuBond	velocity, fps:	2750	2573	2403	2239	2082
	energy, ft-lb:	3022	2646	2308	2004	1732
	arc, inches:		+1.9	0	-7.9	-22.8

Centerfire Rifle Ballistics

.30-06 SPRINGFIELD TO .300 WINCHESTER MAGNUM

CARTRIDGE BULLET	RANGE, YARDS:	0	100	200	300	400
Win. 180 Partition Gold	velocity, fps:	2790	2581	2382	2192	2010
	energy, ft-lb:	3112	2664	2269	1920	1615
	arc, inches:		+1.9	0	-8.0	-23.2
Win. 180 Fail Safe	velocity, fps:	2700	2486	2283	2089	1904
	energy, ft-lb:	2914	2472	2083	1744	1450
	arc, inches:		+2.1	0	-8.7	-25.5
Win. 150 Supreme Elite XP3	velocity, fps:	2925	2712	2508	2313	2127
	energy, ft-lb:	2849	2448	2095	1782	1507
	arc, inches:		+1.6	0	-7.2	-20.8
Win. 180 Supreme Elite XP3	velocity, fps:	2750	2579	2414	2256	2103
	energy, ft-lb:	3022	2658	2330	2034	1768
	arc, inches:		+1.9	0	-7.8	-22.5

.300 H&H MAGNUM

CARTRIDGE BULLET	RANGE, YARDS:	0	100	200	300	400
Federal 180 Nosler Partition	velocity, fps:	2880	2620	2380	2150	1930
	energy, ft-lb:	3315	2750	2260	1840	1480
	arc, inches:		+1.8	0	-8.0	-23.4
Win. 180 Fail Safe	velocity, fps:	2880	2628	2390	2165	1952
	energy, ft-lb:	3316	2762	2284	1873	1523
	arc, inches:		+1.8	0	-7.9	-23.2

.308 NORMA MAGNUM

CARTRIDGE BULLET	RANGE, YARDS:	0	100	200	300	400
Norma 180 TXP Swift A-Fr.	velocity, fps:	2953	2704	2469	2245	
	energy, ft-lb:	3486	2924	2437	2016	
	arc, inches:		+1.6	0	-7.3	
Norma 180 Oryx	velocity, fps:	2953	2630	2330	2049	
	energy, ft-lb:	3486	2766	2170	1679	
	arc, inches:		+1.8	0	-8.2	
Norma 200 Vulkan	velocity, fps:	2903	2624	2361	2114	
	energy, ft-lb:	3744	3058	2476	1985	
	arc, inches:	0	+1.8	0	-8.0	

.300 WINCHESTER MAGNUM

CARTRIDGE BULLET	RANGE, YARDS:	0	100	200	300	400
A-Square 180 Dead Tough	velocity, fps:	3120	2756	2420	2108	1820
	energy, ft-lb:	3890	3035	2340	1776	1324
	arc, inches:		+1.6	0	-7.6	-22.9
Black Hills 180 Nos. Bal. Tip	velocity, fps:	3100				
	energy, ft-lb:	3498				
	arc, inches:					
Black Hills 180 Barnes X	velocity, fps:	2950				
	energy, ft-lb:	3498				
	arc, inches:					
Black Hills 180 AccuBond	velocity, fps:	3000				
	energy, ft-lb:	3597				
	arc, inches:					
Black Hills 190 Match	velocity, fps:	2950				
	energy, ft-lb:	3672				
	arc, inches:					
Federal 150 Sierra Pro Hunt.	velocity, fps:	3280	3030	2800	2570	2360
	energy, ft-lb:	3570	3055	2600	2205	1860
	arc, inches:		+1.1	0	-5.6	-16.4
Federal 150 Trophy Bonded	velocity, fps:	3280	2980	2700	2430	2190
	energy, ft-lb:	3570	2450	2420	1970	1590
	arc, inches:		+1.2	0	-6.0	-17.9
Federal 180 Sierra Pro Hunt.	velocity, fps:	2960	2750	2540	2340	2160
	energy, ft-lb:	3500	3010	2580	2195	1860
	arc, inches:		+1.6	0	-7.0	-20.3
Federal 180 Barnes XLC	velocity, fps:	2960	2780	2600	2430	2260
	energy, ft-lb:	3500	3080	2700	2355	2050
	arc, inches:		+1.5	0	-6.6	-19.2
Federal 180 Trophy Bonded	velocity, fps:	2960	2700	2460	2220	2000
	energy, ft-lb:	3500	2915	2410	1975	1605
	arc, inches:		+1.6	0	-7.4	-21.9
Federal 180 Tr. Bonded HE	velocity, fps:	3100	2830	2580	2340	2110
	energy, ft-lb:	3840	3205	2660	2190	1790
	arc, inches:		+1.4	0	-6.6	-19.7
Federal 180 Nosler Partition	velocity, fps:	2960	2700	2450	2210	1990
	energy, ft-lb:	3500	2905	2395	1955	1585
	arc, inches:		+1.6	0	-7.5	-22.1
Federal 190 Sierra MatchKg. BTHP	velocity, fps:	2900	2730	2560	2400	2240
	energy, ft-lb:	3550	3135	2760	2420	2115
	arc, inches:		+12.9	+22.5	+26.9	+25.1
Federal 200 Sierra GameKing BTSP	velocity, fps:	2830	2680	2530	2380	2240
	energy, ft-lb:	3560	3180	2830	2520	2230
	arc, inches:		+1.7	0	-7.1	-20.4
Federal 200 Nosler Part. HE	velocity, fps:	2930	2740	2550	2370	2200
	energy, ft-lb:	3810	3325	2885	2495	2145
	arc, inches:		+1.6	0	-6.9	-20.1
Federal 200 Trophy Bonded	velocity, fps:	2800	2570	2350	2150	1950
	energy, ft-lb:	3480	2935	2460	2050	1690
	arc, inches:		+1.9	0	-8.2	-23.9
Hornady 150 SP boat-tail	velocity, fps:	3275	2988	2718	2464	2224
	energy, ft-lb:	3573	2974	2461	2023	1648
	arc, inches:		+1.2	0	-6.0	-17.8
Hornady 150 SST (and Interbond)	velocity, fps:	3275	3027	2791	2565	2352
	energy, ft-lb:	3572	3052	2593	2192	1842
	arc, inches:		+1.2	0	-5.8	-17.0
Hornady 165 SP boat-tail	velocity, fps:	3100	2877	2665	2462	2269
	energy, ft-lb:	3522	3033	2603	2221	1887
	arc, inches:		+1.3	0	-6.5	-18.5
Hornady 165 SST	velocity, fps:	3100	2885	2680	2483	2296
	energy, ft-lb:	3520	3049	2630	2259	1930
	arc, inches:		+1.4	0	-6.4	-18.6
Hornady 180 SP boat-tail	velocity, fps:	2960	2745	2540	2344	2157
	energy, ft-lb:	3501	3011	2578	2196	1859
	arc, inches:		+1.9	0	-7.3	-20.9
Hornady 180 SST	velocity, fps:	2960	2764	2575	2395	2222
	energy, ft-lb:	3501	3052	2650	2292	1974
	arc, inches:		+1.6	0	-7.0	-20.1
Hornady 180 SPBT HM	velocity, fps:	3100	2879	2668	2467	2275
	energy, ft-lb:	3840	3313	2845	2431	2068
	arc, inches:		+1.4	0	-6.4	-18.7
Hornady 190 SP boat-tail	velocity, fps:	2900	2711	2529	2355	2187
	energy, ft-lb:	3549	3101	2699	2340	2018
	arc, inches:		+1.6	0	-7.1	-20.4
Norma 150 Nosler Bal. Tip	velocity, fps:	3250	3014	2791	2578	
	energy, ft-lb:	3519	3027	2595	2215	
	arc, inches:		+1.1	0	-5.6	
Norma 150 Barnes TS	velocity, fps:	3215	2982	2761	2550	
	energy, ft-lb:	3444	2962	2539	2167	
	arc, inches:		+1.2	0	-5.8	
Norma 165 Scirocco	velocity, fps:	3117	2921	2734	2554	
	energy, ft-lb:	3561	3127	2738	2390	
	arc, inches:		+1.2	0	-5.9	
Norma 180 Soft Point	velocity, fps:	3018	2780	2555	2341	
	energy, ft-lb:	3641	3091	2610	2190	
	arc, inches:		+1.5	0	-7.0	
Norma 180 Plastic Point	velocity, fps:	3018	2755	2506	2271	
	energy, ft-lb:	3641	3034	2512	2062	
	arc, inches:		+1.6	0	-7.1	
Norma 180 TXP Swift A-Fr.	velocity, fps:	2920	2688	2467	2256	
	energy, ft-lb:	3409	2888	2432	2035	
	arc, inches:		+1.7	0	-7.4	
Norma 180 AccuBond	velocity, fps:	2953	2767	2588	2417	
	energy, ft-lb:	3486	3061	2678	2335	
	arc, inches:		+1.5	0	-6.7	

.300 WINCHESTER MAGNUM TO .300 WINCHESTER SHORT MAGNUM

CARTRIDGE BULLET	RANGE, YARDS:	0	100	200	300	400
Norma 180 Oryx	velocity, fps:	2920	2600	2301	2023	
	energy, ft-lb:	3409	2702	2117	1636	
	arc, inches:		+1.8	0	-8.4	
Norma 200 Vulkan	velocity, fps:	2887	2609	2347	2100	
	energy, ft-lb:	3702	3023	2447	1960	
	arc, inches:		+1.8	0	-8.2	
Norma 200 Oryx	velocity, fps:	2789	2510	2248	2002	
	energy, ft-lb:	3455	2799	2245	1780	
	arc, inches:		+2.0	0	-8.9	
PMC 150 Barnes X	velocity, fps:	3135	2918	2712	2515	2327
	energy, ft-lb:	3273	2836	2449	2107	1803
	arc, inches:		+1.3	0	-6.1	-17.7
PMC 150 Pointed Soft Point	velocity, fps:	3150	2902	2665	2438	2222
	energy, ft-lb:	3304	2804	2364	1979	1644
	arc, inches:		+1.3	0	-6.2	-18.3
PMC 150 SP boat-tail	velocity, fps:	3250	2987	2739	2504	2281
	energy, ft-lb:	3517	2970	2498	2088	1733
	arc, inches:		+1.2	0	-6.0	-17.4
PMC 180 Barnes X	velocity, fps:	2910	2738	2572	2412	2258
	energy, ft-lb:	3384	2995	2644	2325	2037
	arc, inches:		+1.6	0	-6.9	-19.8
PMC 180 Pointed Soft Point	velocity, fps:	2853	2643	2446	2258	2077
	energy, ft-lb:	3252	2792	2391	2037	1724
	arc, inches:		+1.7	0	-7.5	-21.9
PMC 180 SP boat-tail	velocity, fps:	2900	2714	2536	2365	2200
	energy, ft-lb:	3361	2944	2571	2235	1935
	arc, inches:		+1.6	0	-7.1	-20.3
PMC 180 HPBT Match	velocity, fps:	2950	2755	2568	2390	2219
	energy, ft-lb:	3478	3033	2636	2283	1968
	arc, inches:		+1.5	0	-6.8	-19.7
Rem. 150 PSP Core-Lokt	velocity, fps:	3290	2951	2636	2342	2068
	energy, ft-lb:	3605	2900	2314	1827	1859
	arc, inches:		+1.6	0	-7.0	-20.2
Rem. 150 PSP C-L MR	velocity, fps:	2650	2373	2113	1870	1646
	energy, ft-lb:	2339	1875	1486	1164	902
	arc, inches:		+1.0	-2.7	-14.3	-35.8
Rem. 150 PSP C-L Ultra	velocity, fps:	3290	2967	2666	2384	2120
	energy, ft-lb:	3065	2931	2366	1893	1496
	arc, inches:		+1.2	0	-6.1	-18.4
Rem. 180 AccuTip	velocity, fps:	2960	2764	2577	2397	2224
	energy, ft-lb:	3501	3053	2653	2295	1976
	arc, inches:		+1.5	0	-6.8	-19.6
Rem. 180 PSP Core-Lokt	velocity, fps:	2960	2745	2540	2344	2157
	energy, ft-lb:	3501	3011	2578	2196	1424
	arc, inches:		+2.2	+1.9	-3.4	-15.0
Rem. 180 PSP C-L Ultra	velocity, fps:	2960	2727	2505	2294	2093
	energy, ft-lb:	3501	2971	2508	2103	1751
	arc, inches:		+2.7	+2.2	-3.8	-16.4
Rem. 180 Nosler Partition	velocity, fps:	2960	2725	2503	2291	2089
	energy, ft-lb:	3501	2968	2503	2087	1744
	arc, inches:		+1.6	0	-7.2	-20.9
Rem. 180 Nosler Bal. Tip	velocity, fps:	2960	2774	2595	2424	2259
	energy, ft-lb:	3501	3075	2692	2348	2039
	arc, inches:		+1.5	0	-6.7	-19.3
Rem. 180 Swift Scirocco	velocity, fps:	2960	2774	2595	2424	2259
	energy, ft-lb:	3501	3075	2692	2348	2039
	arc, inches:		+1.5	0	-6.7	-19.3
Rem. 190 PSP boat-tail	velocity, fps:	2885	2691	2506	2327	2156
	energy, ft-lb:	3511	3055	2648	2285	1961
	arc, inches:		+1.6	0	-7.2	-20.8
Rem. 190 HPBT Match	velocity, fps:	2900	2725	2557	2395	2239
	energy, ft-lb:	3547	3133	2758	2420	2115
	arc, inches:		+1.6	0	-6.9	-19.9
Rem. 200 Swift A-Frame	velocity, fps:	2825	2595	2376	2167	1970
	energy, ft-lb:	3544	2989	2506	2086	1722
	arc, inches:		+1.8	0	-8.0	-23.5
Speer 180 Grand Slam	velocity, fps:	2950	2735	2530	2334	
	energy, ft-lb:	3478	2989	2558	2176	
	arc, inches:		+1.6	0	-7.0	-20.5
Speer 200 Grand Slam	velocity, fps:	2800	2597	2404	2218	
	energy, ft-lb:	3481	2996	2565	2185	
	arc, inches:		+1.8	0	-7.9	-22.9
Win. 150 Power-Point	velocity, fps:	3290	2951	2636	2342	2068
	energy, ft-lb:	3605	2900	2314	1827	1424
	arc, inches:		+2.6	+2.1	-3.5	-15.4
Win. 150 Fail Safe	velocity, fps:	3260	2943	2647	2370	2110
	energy, ft-lb:	3539	2884	2334	1871	1483
	arc, inches:		+1.3	0	-6.2	-18.7
Win. 165 Fail Safe	velocity, fps:	3120	2807	2515	2242	1985
	energy, ft-lb:	3567	2888	2319	1842	1445
	arc, inches:		+1.5	0	-7.0	-20.0
Win. 180 Power-Point	velocity, fps:	2960	2745	2540	2344	2157
	energy, ft-lb:	3501	3011	2578	2196	1859
	arc, inches:		+1.9	0	-7.3	-20.9
Win. 180 Power-Point Plus	velocity, fps:	3070	2846	2633	2430	2236
	energy, ft-lb:	3768	3239	2772	2361	1999
	arc, inches:		+1.4	0	-6.4	-18.7
Win. 180 Ballistic Silvertip	velocity, fps:	2950	2764	2586	2415	2250
	energy, ft-lb:	3478	3054	2673	2331	2023
	arc, inches:		+1.5	0	-6.7	-19.4
Win. 180 AccuBond	velocity, fps:	2950	2765	2588	2417	2253
	energy, ft-lb:	3478	3055	2676	2334	2028
	arc, inches:		+1.5	0	-6.7	-19.4
Win. 180 Fail Safe	velocity, fps:	2960	2732	2514	2307	2110
	energy, ft-lb:	3503	2983	2528	2129	1780
	arc, inches:		+1.6	0	-7.1	-20.7
Win. 180 Partition Gold	velocity, fps:	3070	2859	2657	2464	2280
	energy, ft-lb:	3768	3267	2823	2428	2078
	arc, inches:		+1.4	0	-6.3	-18.3
Win. 150 Supreme Elite XP3	velocity, fps:	3260	3030	2811	2603	2404
	energy, ft-lb:	3539	3057	2632	2256	1925
	arc, inches:		+1.1	0	-5.6	-16.2
Win. 180 Supreme Elite XP3	velocity, fps:	3000	2819	2646	2479	2318
	energy, ft-lb:	3597	3176	2797	2455	2147
	arc, inches:		+1.4	0	-6.4	-18.5

.300 Remington Short Ultra Magnum

CARTRIDGE BULLET	RANGE, YARDS:	0	100	200	300	400
Rem. 150 PSP C-L Ultra	velocity, fps:	3200	2901	2672	2359	2112
	energy, ft-lb:	3410	2803	2290	1854	1485
	arc, inches:		+1.3	0	-6.4	-19.1
Rem. 165 PSP Core-Lokt	velocity, fps:	3075	2792	2527	2276	2040
	energy, ft-lb:	3464	2856	2339	1828	1525
	arc, inches:		+1.5	0	-7.0	-20.7
Rem. 180 Partition	velocity, fps:	2960	2761	2571	2389	2214
	energy, ft-lb:	3501	3047	2642	2280	1959
	arc, inches:		+1.5	0	-6.8	-19.7
Rem. 180 PSP C-L Ultra	velocity, fps:	2960	2727	2506	2295	2094
	energy, ft-lb:	3501	2972	2509	2105	1753
	arc, inches:		+1.6	0	-7.1	-20.9
Rem. 190 HPBT Match	velocity, fps:	2900	2725	2557	2395	2239
	energy, ft-lb:	3547	3133	2758	2420	2115
	arc, inches:		+1.6	0	-6.9	-19.9

.300 Winchester Short Magnum

CARTRIDGE BULLET	RANGE, YARDS:	0	100	200	300	400
Black Hills 175 Sierra MKing	velocity, fps:	2950				
	energy, ft-lb:	3381				
	arc, inches:					

Centerfire Rifle Ballistics

.300 WINCHESTER SHORT MAGNUM TO .300 WEATHERBY MAGNUM

CARTRIDGE BULLET	RANGE, YARDS:	0	100	200	300	400
Black Hills 180 AccuBond	velocity, fps:	2950				
	energy, ft-lb:	3478				
	arc, inches:					
Federal 150 Nosler Bal. Tip	velocity, fps:	3200	2970	2755	2545	2345
	energy, ft-lb:	3410	2940	2520	2155	1830.
	arc, inches:		+1.2	0	-5.8	-17.0
Federal 165 Nos. Partition	velocity, fps:	3130	2890	2670	2450	2250
	energy, ft-lb:	3590	3065	2605	2205	1855.
	arc, inches:		+1.3	0	-6.2	-18.2
Federal 165 Nos. Solid Base	velocity, fps:	3130	2900	2690	2490	2290
	energy, ft-lb:	3590	3090	2650	2265	1920
	arc, inches:		+1.3	0	-6.1	-17.8
Federal 180 Barnes TS And Nos. Solid Base	velocity, fps:	2980	2780	2580	2400	2220
	energy, ft-lbs:	3550	3085	2670	2300	1970
	arc, inches:		+1.5	0	-6.7	-19.5
Federal 180 Grand Slam	velocity, fps:	2970	2740	2530	2320	2130
	energy, ft-lb:	3525	3010	2555	2155	1810
	arc, inches:		+1.5	0	-7.0	-20.5
Federal 180 Trophy Bonded	velocity, fps:	2970	2730	2500	2280	2080
	energy, ft-lb:	3525	2975	2500	2085	1725
	arc, inches:		+1.5	0	-7.2	-21.0
Federal 180 Nosler Partition	velocity, fps:	2975	2750	2535	2290	2126
	energy, ft-lb:	3540	3025	2570	2175	1825
	arc, inches:		+1.5	0	-7.0	-20.3
Federal 180 Nos. AccuBond	velocity, fps:	2960	2780	2610	2440	2280
	energy, ft-lb:	3500	3090	2715	2380	2075
	arc, inches:		+1.5	0	-6.6	-19.0
Federal 180 Hi-Shok SP	velocity, fps:	2970	2520	2115	1750	1430
	energy, ft-lb:	3525	2540	1785	1220	820
	arc, inches:		+2.2	0	-9.9	-31.4
Norma 150 FMJ	velocity, fps:	2953	2731	2519	2318	
	energy, ft-lb:					
	arc, inches:		+1.6	0	-7.1	
Norma 150 Barnes X TS	velocity, fps:	3215	2982	2761	2550	
	energy, ft-lb:	3444	2962	2539	2167	
	arc, inches:		+1.2	0	-5.7	
Norma 180 Nosler Bal. Tip	velocity, fps:	3215	2985	2767	2560	
	energy, ft-lb:	3437	2963	2547	2179	
	arc, inches:		+1.2	0	-5.7	
Norma 180 Oryx	velocity, fps:	2936	2542	2180	1849	
	energy, ft-lb:	3446	2583	1900	1368	
	arc, inches:		+1.9	0	-8.9	
Win. 150 Power-Point	velocity, fps:	3270	2903	2565	2250	1958
	energy, ft-lb:	3561	2807	2190	1686	1277
	arc, inches:		+1.3	0	-6.6	-20.2
Win. 150 Ballistic Silvertip	velocity, fps:	3300	3061	2834	2619	2414
	energy, ft-lb:	3628	3121	2676	2285	1941
	arc, inches:		+1.1	0	-5.4	-15.9
Win. 165 Fail Safe	velocity, fps:	3125	2846	2584	2336	2102
	energy, ft-lb:	3577	2967	2446	1999	1619
	arc, inches:		+1.4	0	-6.6	-19.6
Win. 180 Ballistic Silvertip	velocity, fps:	3010	2822	2641	2468	2301.
	energy, ft-lb:	3621	3182	2788	2434	2116
	arc, inches:		+1.4	0	-6.4	-18.6
Win. 180 AccuBond	velocity, fps:	3010	2822	2643	2470	2304
	energy, ft-lb:	3622	3185	2792	2439	2121
	arc, inches:		+1.4	0	-6.4	-18.5
Win. 180 Fail Safe	velocity, fps:	2970	2741	2524	2317	2120
	energy, ft-lb:	3526	3005	2547	2147	1797
	arc, inches:		+1.6	0	-7.0	-20.5
Win. 180 Power Point	velocity, fps:	2970	2755	2549	2353	2166
	energy, ft-lb:	3526	3034	2598	2214	1875
	arc, inches:		+1.5	0	-6.9	-20.1

CARTRIDGE BULLET	RANGE, YARDS:	0	100	200	300	400
Win. 150 Supreme Elite XP3	velocity, fps:	3300	3068	2847	2637	2437
	energy, ft-lb:	3626	3134	2699	2316	1978
	arc, inches:		+1.1	0	-5.4	-15.8
Win. 180 Supreme Elite XP3	velocity, fps:	3010	2829	2655	2488	2326
	energy, ft-lb:	3621	3198	2817	2473	2162
	arc, inches:		+1.4	0	-6.4	-18.3

.300 WEATHERBY MAGNUM

CARTRIDGE BULLET	RANGE, YARDS:	0	100	200	300	400
A-Square 180 Dead Tough	velocity, fps:	3180	2811	2471	2155	1863.
	energy, ft-lb:	4041	3158	2440	1856	1387
	arc, inches:		+1.5	0	-7.2	-21.8
A-Square 220 Monolythic Solid	velocity, fps:	2700	2407	2133	1877	1653
	energy, ft-lb:	3561	2830	2223	1721	1334
	arc, inches:		+2.3	0	-9.8	-29.7
Federal 180 Sierra GameKing BTSP	velocity, fps:	3190	3010	2830	2660	2490
	energy, ft-lb:	4065	3610	3195	2820	2480
	arc, inches:		+1.2	0	-5.6	-16.0
Federal 180 Trophy Bonded	velocity, fps:	3190	2950	2720	2500	2290
	energy, ft-lb:	4065	3475	2955	2500	2105
	arc, inches:		+1.3	0	-5.9	-17.5
Federal 180 Tr. Bonded HE	velocity, fps:	3330	3080	2850	2750	2410
	energy, ft-lb:	4430	3795	3235	2750	2320
	arc, inches:		+1.1	0	-5.4	-15.8
Federal 180 Nosler Partition	velocity, fps:	3190	2980	2780	2590	2400
	energy, ft-lb:	4055	3540	3080	2670	2305
	arc, inches:		+1.2	0	-5.7	-16.7
Federal 180 Nosler Part. HE	velocity, fps:	3330	3110	2810	2710	2520
	energy, ft-lb:	4430	3875	3375	2935	2540
	arc, inches:		+1.0	0	-5.2	-15.1
Federal 200 Trophy Bonded	velocity, fps:	2900	2670	2440	2230	2030
	energy, ft-lb:	3735	3150	2645	2200	1820
	arc, inches:		+1.7	0	-7.6	-22.2
Hornady 150 SST (or Interbond)	velocity, fps:	3375	3123	2882	2652	2434
	energy, ft-lb:	3793	3248	2766	2343	1973
	arc, inches:		+1.0	0	-5.4	-15.8
Hornady 180 SP	velocity, fps:	3120	2891	2673	2466	2268.
	energy, ft-lb:	3890	3340	2856	2430	2055
	arc, inches:		+1.3	0	-6.2	-18.1
Hornady 180 SST	velocity, fps:	3120	2911	2711	2519	2335
	energy, ft-lb:	3890	3386	2936	2535	2180
	arc, inches:		+1.3	0	-6.2	-18.1
Rem. 180 PSP Core-Lokt	velocity, fps:	3120	2866	2627	2400	2184
	energy, ft-lb:	3890	3284	2758	2301	1905
	arc, inches:		+2.4	+2.0	-3.4	-14.9
Rem. 190 PSP boat-tail	velocity, fps:	3030	2830	2638	2455	2279
	energy, ft-lb:	3873	3378	2936	2542	2190.
	arc, inches:		+1.4	0	-6.4	-18.6
Rem. 200 Swift A-Frame	velocity, fps:	2925	2690	2467	2254	2052
	energy, ft-lb:	3799	3213	2701	2256	1870
	arc, inches:		+2.8	+2.3	-3.9	-17.0
Speer 180 Grand Slam	velocity, fps:	3185	2948	2722	2508	
	energy, ft-lb:	4054	3472	2962	2514	
	arc, inches:		+1.3	0	-5.9	-17.4
Wby. 150 Pointed Expanding	velocity, fps:	3540	3225	2932	2657	2399
	energy, ft-lb:	4173	3462	2862	2351	1916
	arc, inches:		+2.6	+3.3	0	-8.2
Wby. 150 Nosler Partition	velocity, fps:	3540	3263	3004	2759	2528
	energy, ft-lb:	4173	3547	3005	2536	2128
	arc, inches:		+2.5	+3.2	0	-7.7
Wby. 165 Pointed Expanding	velocity, fps:	3390	3123	2872	2634	2409
	energy, ft-lb:	4210	3573	3021	2542	2126
	arc, inches:		+2.8	+3.5	0	-8.5

CARTRIDGE BULLET	RANGE, YARDS:	0	100	200	300	400
Wby. 165 Nosler Bal. Tip	velocity, fps:	3350	3133	2927	2730	2542
	energy, ft-lb:	4111	3596	3138	2730	2367
	arc, inches:		+2.7	+3.4	0	-8.1
Wby. 180 Pointed Expanding	velocity, fps:	3240	3004	2781	2569	2366
	energy, ft-lb:	4195	3607	3091	2637	2237
	arc, inches:		+3.1	+3.8	0	-9.0
Wby. 180 Barnes X	velocity, fps:	3190	2995	2809	2631	2459
	energy, ft-lb:	4067	3586	3154	2766	2417
	arc, inches:		+3.1	+3.8	0	-8.7
Wby. 180 Bal. Tip	velocity, fps:	3250	3051	2806	2676	2503
	energy, ft-lb:	4223	3721	3271	2867	2504
	arc, inches:		+2.8	+3.6	0	-8.4
Wby. 180 Nosler Partition	velocity, fps:	3240	3028	2826	2634	2449
	energy, ft-lb:	4195	3665	3193	2772	2396
	arc, inches:		+3.0	+3.7	0	-8.6
Wby. 200 Nosler Partition	velocity, fps:	3060	2860	2668	2485	2308
	energy, ft-lb:	4158	3631	3161	2741	2366
	arc, inches:		+3.5	+4.2	0	-9.8
Wby. 220 RN Expanding	velocity, fps:	2845	2543	2260	1996	1751
	energy, ft-lb:	3954	3158	2495	1946	1497
	arc, inches:		+4.9	+5.9	0	-14.6

.300 Dakota

CARTRIDGE BULLET	RANGE, YARDS:	0	100	200	300	400
Dakota 165 Barnes X	velocity, fps:	3200	2979	2769	2569	2377
	energy, ft-lb:	3751	3251	2809	2417	2070
	arc, inches:		+2.1	+1.8	-3.0	-13.2
Dakota 200 Barnes X	velocity, fps:	3000	2824	2656	2493	2336
	energy, ft-lb:	3996	3542	3131	2760	2423
	arc, inches:		+2.2	+1.5	-4.0	-15.2

.300 Pegasus

CARTRIDGE BULLET	RANGE, YARDS:	0	100	200	300	400
A-Square 180 SP boat-tail	velocity, fps:	3500	3319	3145	2978	2817
	energy, ft-lb:	4896	4401	3953	3544	3172
	arc, inches:		+2.3	+2.9	0	-6.8
A-Square 180 Nosler Part.	velocity, fps:	3500	3295	3100	2913	2734
	energy, ft-lb:	4896	4339	3840	3392	2988
	arc, inches:		+2.3	+3.0	0	-7.1
A-Square 180 Dead Tough	velocity, fps:	3500	3103	2740	2405	2095
	energy, ft-lb:	4896	3848	3001	2312	1753
	arc, inches:		+1.1	0	-5.7	-17.5

.300 Remington Ultra Magnum

CARTRIDGE BULLET	RANGE, YARDS:	0	100	200	300	400
Federal 180 Trophy Bonded	velocity, fps:	3250	3000	2770	2550	2340
	energy, ft-lb:	4220	3605	3065	2590	2180
	arc, inches:		+1.2	0	-5.7	-16.8
Rem. 150 Swift Scirocco	velocity, fps:	3450	3208	2980	2762	2556
	energy, ft-lb:	3964	3427	2956	2541	2175
	arc, inches:		+1.7	+1.5	-2.6	-11.2
Rem. 180 Nosler Partition	velocity, fps:	3250	3037	2834	2640	2454
	energy, ft-lb:	4221	3686	3201	2786	2407
	arc, inches:		+2.4	+1.8	-3.0	-12.7
Rem. 180 Swift Scirocco	velocity, fps:	3250	3048	2856	2672	2495
	energy, ft-lb:	4221	3714	3260	2853	2487
	arc, inches:		+2.0	+1.7	-2.8	-12.3
Rem. 180 PSP Core-Lokt	velocity, fps:	3250	2988	2742	2508	2287
	energy, ft-lb:	3517	2974	2503	2095	1741
	arc, inches:		+2.1	+1.8	-3.1	-13.6
Rem. 200 Nosler Partition	velocity, fps:	3025	2826	2636	2454	2279
	energy, ft-lb:	4063	3547	3086	2673	2308
	arc, inches:		+2.4	+2.0	-3.4	-14.6

.30-378 Weatherby Magnum

CARTRIDGE BULLET	RANGE, YARDS:	0	100	200	300	400
Wby. 165 Nosler Bal. Tip	velocity, fps:	3500	3275	3062	2859	2665
	energy, ft-lb:	4488	3930	3435	2995	2603
	arc, inches:		+2.4	+3.0	0	-7.4
Wby. 180 Nosler Bal. Tip	velocity, fps:	3420	3213	3015	2826	2645
	energy, ft-lb:	4676	4126	3634	3193	2797
	arc, inches:		+2.5	+3.1	0	-7.5
Wby. 180 Barnes X	velocity, fps:	3450	3243	3046	2858	2678
	energy, ft-lb:	4757	4204	3709	3264	2865
	arc, inches:		+2.4	+3.1	0	-7.4
Wby. 200 Nosler Partition	velocity, fps:	3160	2955	2759	2572	2392
	energy, ft-lb:	4434	3877	3381	2938	2541
	arc, inches:		+3.2	+3.9	0	-9.1

7.82 (.308) Warbird

CARTRIDGE BULLET	RANGE, YARDS:	0	100	200	300	400
Lazzeroni 150 Nosler Part.	velocity, fps:	3680	3432	3197	2975	2764
	energy, ft-lb:	4512	3923	3406	2949	2546
	arc, inches:		+2.1	+2.7	0	-6.6
Lazzeroni 180 Nosler Part.	velocity, fps:	3425	3220	3026	2839	2661
	energy, ft-lb:	4689	4147	3661	3224	2831
	arc, inches:		+2.5	+3.2	0	-7.5
Lazzeroni 200 Swift A-Fr.	velocity, fps:	3290	3105	2928	2758	2594
	energy, ft-lb:	4808	4283	3808	3378	2988
	arc, inches:		+2.7	+3.4	0	-7.9

7.65x53 Argentine

CARTRIDGE BULLET	RANGE, YARDS:	0	100	200	300	400
Norma 174 Soft Point	velocity, fps:	2493	2173	1878	1611	
	energy, ft-lb:	2402	1825	1363	1003	
	arc, inches:		+2.0	0	-9.5	
Norma 180 Soft Point	velocity, fps:	2592	2386	2189	2002	
	energy, ft-lb:	2686	2276	1916	1602	
	arc, inches:		+2.3	0	-9.6	

.303 British

CARTRIDGE BULLET	RANGE, YARDS:	0	100	200	300	400
Federal 150 Hi-Shok	velocity, fps:	2690	2440	2210	1980	1780
	energy, ft-lb:	2400	1980	1620	1310	1055
	arc, inches:		+2.2	0	-9.4	-27.6
Federal 180 Sierra Pro-Hunt.	velocity, fps:	2460	2230	2020	1820	1630
	energy, ft-lb:	2420	1995	1625	1315	1060
	arc, inches:		+2.8	0	-11.3	-33.2
Federal 180 Tr. Bonded HE	velocity, fps:	2590	2350	2120	1900	1700
	energy, ft-lb:	2680	2205	1795	1445	1160
	arc, inches:		+2.4	0	-10.0	-30.0
Hornady 150 Soft Point	velocity, fps:	2685	2441	2210	1992	1787
	energy, ft-lb:	2401	1984	1627	1321	1064
	arc, inches:		+2.2	0	-9.3	-27.4
Hornady 150 SP LM	velocity, fps:	2830	2570	2325	2094	1884
	energy, ft-lb:	2667	2199	1800	1461	1185
	arc, inches:		+2.0	0	-8.4	-24.6
Norma 150 Soft Point	velocity, fps:	2723	2438	2170	1920	
	energy, ft-lb:	2470	1980	1569	1228	
	arc, inches:		+2.2	0	-9.6	
PMC 174 FMJ (and HPBT)	velocity, fps:	2400	2216	2042	1876	1720
	energy, ft-lb:	2225	1898	1611	1360	1143
	arc, inches:		+2.8	0	-11.2	-32.2
PMC 180 SP boat-tail	velocity, fps:	2450	2276	2110	1951	1799
	energy, ft-lb:	2399	2071	1779	1521	1294
	arc, inches:		+2.6	0	-10.4	-30.1
Rem. 180 SP Core-Lokt	velocity, fps:	2460	2124	1817	1542	1311
	energy, ft-lb:	2418	1803	1319	950	687
	arc, inches, s:		0	-5.8	-23.3	
Win. 180 Power-Point	velocity, fps:	2460	2233	2018	1816	1629
	energy, ft-lb:	2418	1993	1627	1318	1060
	arc, inches, s:		0	-6.1	-20.8	

7.7x58 Japanese Arisaka

CARTRIDGE BULLET	RANGE, YARDS:	0	100	200	300	400
Norma 174 Soft Point	velocity, fps:	2493	2173	1878	1611	
	energy, ft-lb:	2402	1825	1363	1003	
	arc, inches:		+2.0	0	-9.5	

Centerfire Rifle Ballistics

7.7X58 JAPANESE ARISAKA TO .338 WINCHESTER MAGNUM

CARTRIDGE BULLET	RANGE, YARDS:	0	100	200	300	400
Norma 180 Soft Point	velocity, fps:	2493	2291	2099	1916	
	energy, ft-lb:	2485	2099	1761	1468	
	arc, inches:		+2.6	0	-10.5	

.32-20 Winchester

CARTRIDGE BULLET	RANGE, YARDS:	0	100	200	300	400
Rem. 100 Lead	velocity, fps:	1210	1021	913	834	769
	energy, ft-lb:	325	231	185	154	131
	arc, inches:		0	-31.6	-104.7	
Win. 100 Lead	velocity, fps:	1210	1021	913	834	769
	energy, ft-lb:	325	231	185	154	131
	arc, inches:		0	-32.3	-106.3	

.32 Winchester Special

CARTRIDGE BULLET	RANGE, YARDS:	0	100	200	300	400
Federal 170 Hi-Shok	velocity, fps:	2250	1920	1630	1370	1180
	energy, ft-lb:	1910	1395	1000	710	520
	arc, inches:		0	-8.0	-29.2	
Rem. 170 SP Core-Lokt	velocity, fps:	2250	1921	1626	1372	1175
	energy, ft-lb:	1911	1393	998	710	521
	arc, inches:		0	-8.0	-29.3	
Win. 170 Power-Point	velocity, fps:	2250	1870	1537	1267	1082
	energy, ft-lb:	1911	1320	892	606	442
	arc, inches:		0	-9.2	-33.2	

8mm Mauser (8x57)

CARTRIDGE BULLET	RANGE, YARDS:	0	100	200	300	400
Federal 170 Hi-Shok	velocity, fps:	2360	1970	1620	1330	1120
	energy, ft-lb:	2100	1465	995	670	475
	arc, inches:		0	-7.6	-28.5	
Hornady 195 SP	velocity, fps:	2550	2343	2146	1959	1782
	energy, ft-lb:	2815	2377	1994	1861	1375
	arc, inches:		+2.3	0	-9.9	-28.8.
Hornady 195 SP (2005)	velocity, fps:	2475	2269	2074	1888	1714
	energy, ft-lb:	2652	2230	1861	1543	1271
	arc, inches:		+2.6	0	-10.7	-31.3
Norma 123 FMJ	velocity, fps:	2559	2121	1729	1398	
	energy, ft-lb:	1789	1228	817	534	
	arc, inches:		+3.2	0	-15.0	
Norma 196 Oryx	velocity, fps:	2395	2146	1912	1695	
	energy, ft-lb:	2497	2004	1591	1251	
	arc, inches:		+3	0	-12.6	
Norma 196 Vulkan	velocity, fps:	2395	2156	1930	1720	
	energy, ft-lb:	2497	2023	1622	1289	
	arc, inches:		3.0	0	-12.3	
Norma 196 Alaska	velocity, fps:	2395	2112	1850	1611	
	energy, ft-lb:	2714	2190	1754	1399	
	arc, inches:		0	-6.3	-22.9	
Norma 196 Soft Point (JS)	velocity, fps:	2526	2244	1981	1737	
	energy, ft-lb:	2778	2192	1708	1314	
	arc, inches:		+2.7	0	-11.6	
Norma 196 Alaska (JS)	velocity, fps:	2526	2248	1988	1747	
	energy, ft-lb:	2778	2200	1720	1328	
	arc, inches:		+2.7	0	-11.5	
Norma 196 Vulkan (JS)	velocity, fps:	2526	2276	2041	1821	
	energy, ft-lb:	2778	2256	1813	1443	
	arc, inches:		+2.6	0	-11.0	
Norma 196 Oryx (JS)	velocity, fps:	2526	2269	2027	1802	
	energy, ft-lb:	2778	2241	1789	1413	
	arc, inches:		+2.6	0	-11.1	
PMC 170 Pointed Soft Point	velocity, fps:	2360	1969	1622	1333	1123
	energy, ft-lb:	2102	1463	993	671	476
	arc, inches:		+1.8	-4.5	-24.3	-63.8
Rem. 170 SP Core-Lokt	velocity, fps:	2360	1969	1622	1333	1123
	energy, ft-lb:	2102	1463	993	671	476
	arc, inches:		+1.8	-4.5	-24.3	-63.8.
Win. 170 Power-Point	velocity, fps:	2360	1969	1622	1333	1123
	energy, ft-lb:	2102	1463	993	671	476
	arc, inches:		+1.8	-4.5	-24.3	-63.8

.325 WSM

CARTRIDGE BULLET	RANGE, YARDS:	0	100	200	300	400
Win. 180 Ballistic ST	velocity, fps:	3060	2841	2632	2432	2242
	energy, ft-lb:	3743	3226	2769	2365	2009
	arc, inches:		+1.4	0	-6.4	-18.7
Win. 200 AccuBond CT	velocity, fps:	2950	2753	2565	2384	2210
	energy, ft-lb:	3866	3367	2922	2524	2170
	arc, inches:		+1.5	0	-6.8	-19.8
Win. 220 Power-Point	velocity, fps:	2840	2605	2382	2169	1968
	energy, ft-lb:	3941	3316	2772	2300	1893
	arc, inches:		+1.8	0	-8.0	-23.3

8mm Remington Magnum

CARTRIDGE BULLET	RANGE, YARDS:	0	100	200	300	400
A-Square 220 Monolythic Solid	velocity, fps:	2800	2501	2221	1959	1718
	energy, ft-lb:	3829	3055	2409	1875	1442
	arc, inches:		+2.1	0	-9.1	-27.6
Rem. 200 Swift A-Frame	velocity, fps:	2900	2623	2361	2115	1885
	energy, ft-lb:	3734	3054	2476	1987	1577
	arc, inches:		+1.8	0	-8.0	-23.9

.338-06

CARTRIDGE BULLET	RANGE, YARDS:	0	100	200	300	400
A-Square 200 Nos. Bal. Tip	velocity, fps:	2750	2553	2364	2184	2011
	energy, ft-lb:	3358	2894	2482	2118	1796
	arc, inches:		+1.9	0	-8.2	-23.6
A-Square 250 SP boat-tail	velocity, fps:	2500	2374	2252	2134	2019
	energy, ft-lb:	3496	3129	2816	2528	2263
	arc, inches:		+2.4	0	-9.3	-26.0
A-Square 250 Dead Tough	velocity, fps:	2500	2222	1963	1724	1507
	energy, ft-lb:	3496	2742	2139	1649	1261
	arc, inches:		+2.8	0	-11.9	-35.5
Wby. 210 Nosler Part.	velocity, fps:	2750	2526	2312	2109	1916
	energy, ft-lb:	3527	2975	2403	2074	1712
	arc, inches:		+4.8	+5.7	0	-13.5

.338 Winchester Magnum

CARTRIDGE BULLET	RANGE, YARDS:	0	100	200	300	400
A-Square 250 SP boat-tail	velocity, fps:	2700	2568	2439	2314	2193
	energy, ft-lb:	4046	3659	3302	2972	2669
	arc, inches:		+4.4	+5.2	0	-11.7
A-Square 250 Triad	velocity, fps:	2700	2407	2133	1877	1653
	energy, ft-lb:	4046	3216	2526	1956	1516
	arc, inches:		+2.3	0	-9.8	-29.8
Federal 210 Nosler Partition	velocity, fps:	2830	2600	2390	2180	1980
	energy, ft-lb:	3735	3160	2655	2215	1835
	arc, inches:		+1.8	0	-8.0	-23.3
Federal 225 Sierra Pro-Hunt.	velocity, fps:	2780	2570	2360	2170	1980
	energy, ft-lb:	3860	3290	2780	2340	1960
	arc, inches:		+1.9	0	-8.2	-23.7
Federal 225 Trophy Bonded	velocity, fps:	2800	2560	2330	2110	1900
	energy, ft-lb:	3915	3265	2700	2220	1800
	arc, inches:		+1.9	0	-8.4	-24.5
Federal 225 Tr. Bonded HE	velocity, fps:	2940	2690	2450	2230	2010
	energy, ft-lb:	4320	3610	3000	2475	2025
	arc, inches:		+1.7	0	-7.5	-22.0
Federal 225 Barnes XLC	velocity, fps:	2800	2610	2430	2260	2090
	energy, ft-lb:	3915	3405	2950	2545	2190
	arc, inches:		+1.8	0	-7.7	-22.2
Federal 250 Nosler Partition	velocity, fps:	2660	2470	2300	2120	1960
	energy, ft-lb:	3925	3395	2925	2505	2130.
	arc, inches:		+2.1	0	-8.8	-25.1

.338 WINCHESTER MAGNUM TO .338-378 WEATHERBY MAGNUM

CARTRIDGE BULLET	RANGE, YARDS:	0	100	200	300	400
Federal 250 Nosler Part HE	velocity, fps:	2800	2610	2420	2250	2080
	energy, ft-lb:	4350	3775	3260	2805	2395
	arc, inches:		+1.8	0	-7.8	-22.5
Hornady 225 Soft Point HM	velocity, fps:	2920	2678	2449	2232	2027
	energy, ft-lb:	4259	3583	2996	2489	2053
	arc, inches:		+1.8	0	-7.6	-22.0
Norma 225 TXP Swift A-Fr.	velocity, fps:	2740	2507	2286	2075	
	energy, ft-lb:	3752	3141	2611	2153	
	arc, inches:		+2.0	0	-8.7	
Norma 230 Oryx	velocity, fps:	2756	2514	2284	2066	
	energy, ft-lb:	3880	3228	2665	2181	
	arc, inches:		+2.0	0	-8.7	
Norma 250 Nosler Partition	velocity, fps:	2657	2470	2290	2118	
	energy, ft-lb:	3920	3387	2912	2490	
	arc, inches:		+2.1	0	-8.7	
PMC 225 Barnes X	velocity, fps:	2780	2619	2464	2313	2168
	energy, ft-lb:	3860	3426	3032	2673	2348.
	arc, inches:		+1.8	0	-7.6	-21.6
Rem. 200 Nosler Bal. Tip	velocity, fps:	2950	2724	2509	2303	2108
	energy, ft-lb:	3866	3295	2795	2357	1973
	arc, inches:		+1.6	0	-7.1	-20.8
Rem. 210 Nosler Partition	velocity, fps:	2830	2602	2385	2179	1983
	energy, ft-lb:	3734	3157	2653	2214	1834
	arc, inches:		+1.8	0	-7.9	-23.2
Rem. 225 PSP Core-Lokt	velocity, fps:	2780	2572	2374	2184	2003
	energy, ft-lb:	3860	3305	2815	2383	2004
	arc, inches:		+1.9	0	-8.1	-23.4
Rem. 225 PSP C-L Ultra	velocity, fps:	2780	2582	2392	2210	2036
	energy, ft-lb:	3860	3329	2858	2440	2071
	arc, inches:		+1.9	0	-7.9	-23.0
Rem. 225 Swift A-Frame	velocity, fps:	2785	2517	2266	2029	1808
	energy, ft-lb:	3871	3165	2565	2057	1633
	arc, inches:		+2.0	0	-8.8	-25.2
Rem. 250 PSP Core-Lokt	velocity, fps:	2660	2456	2261	2075	1898
	energy, ft-lb:	3927	3348	2837	2389	1999
	arc, inches:		+2.1	0	-8.9	-26.0
Speer 250 Grand Slam	velocity, fps:	2645	2442	2247	2062	
	energy, ft-lb:	3883	3309	2803	2360	
	arc, inches:		+2.2	0	-9.1	-26.2
Win. 200 Power-Point	velocity, fps:	2960	2658	2375	2110	1862
	energy, ft-lb:	3890	3137	2505	1977	1539
	arc, inches:		+2.0	0	-8.2	-24.3
Win. 200 Ballistic Silvertip	velocity, fps:	2950	2724	2509	2303	2108
	energy, ft-lb:	3864	3294	2794	2355	1972
	arc, inches:		+1.6	0	-7.1	-20.8
Win. 225 AccuBond	velocity, fps:	2800	2634	2474	2319	2170
	energy, ft-lb:	3918	3467	3058	2688	2353
	arc, inches:		+1.8	0	-7.4	-21.3
Win. 230 Fail Safe	velocity, fps:	2780	2573	2375	2186	2005
	energy, ft-lb:	3948	3382	2881	2441	2054
	arc, inches:		+1.9	0	-8.1	-23.4
Win. 250 Partition Gold	velocity, fps:	2650	2467	2291	2122	1960
	energy, ft-lb:	3899	3378	2914	2520	2134
	arc, inches:		+2.1	0	-8.7	-25.2

.340 WEATHERBY MAGNUM

CARTRIDGE BULLET	RANGE, YARDS:	0	100	200	300	400
A-Square 250 SP boat-tail	velocity, fps:	2820	2684	2552	2424	2299
	energy, ft-lb:	4414	3999	3615	3261	2935
	arc, inches:		+4.0	+4.6	0	-10.6
A-Square 250 Triad	velocity, fps:	2820	2520	2238	1976	1741
	energy, ft-lb:	4414	3524	2781	2166	1683
	arc, inches:		+2.0	0	-9.0	-26.8

CARTRIDGE BULLET	RANGE, YARDS:	0	100	200	300	400
Federal 225 Trophy Bonded	velocity, fps:	3100	2840	2600	2370	2150
	energy, ft-lb:	4800	4035	3375	2800	2310
	arc, inches:		+1.4	0	-6.5	-19.4
Wby. 200 Pointed Expanding	velocity, fps:	3221	2946	2688	2444	2213
	energy, ft-lb:	4607	3854	3208	2652	2174
	arc, inches:		+3.3	+4.0	0	-9.9
Wby. 200 Nosler Bal. Tip	velocity, fps:	3221	2980	2753	2536	2329
	energy, ft-lb:	4607	3944	3364	2856	2409
	arc, inches:		+3.1	+3.9	0	-9.2
Wby. 210 Nosler Partition	velocity, fps:	3211	2963	2728	2505	2293
	energy, ft-lb:	4807	4093	3470	2927	2452
	arc, inches:		+3.2	+3.9	0	-9.5
Wby. 225 Pointed Expanding	velocity, fps:	3066	2824	2595	2377	2170
	energy, ft-lb:	4696	3984	3364	2822	2352
	arc, inches:		+3.6	+4.4	0	-10.7
Wby. 225 Barnes X	velocity, fps:	3001	2804	2615	2434	2260
	energy, ft-lb:	4499	3927	3416	2959	2551
	arc, inches:		+3.6	+4.3	0	-10.3
Wby. 250 Pointed Expanding	velocity, fps:	2963	2745	2537	2338	2149
	energy, ft-lb:	4873	4182	3572	3035	2563
	arc, inches:		+3.9	+4.6	0	-11.1
Wby. 250 Nosler Partition	velocity, fps:	2941	2743	2553	2371	2197
	energy, ft-lb:	4801	4176	3618	3120	2678
	arc, inches:		+3.9	+4.6	0	-10.9

.330 DAKOTA

CARTRIDGE BULLET	RANGE, YARDS:	0	100	200	300	400
Dakota 200 Barnes X	velocity, fps:	3200	2971	2754	2548	2350
	energy, ft-lb:	4547	3920	3369	2882	2452
	arc, inches:		+2.1	+1.8	-3.1	-13.4
Dakota 250 Barnes X	velocity, fps:	2900	2719	2545	2378	2217
	energy, ft-lb:	4668	4103	3595	3138	2727
	arc, inches:		+2.3	+1.3	-5.0	-17.5

.338 REMINGTON ULTRA MAGNUM

CARTRIDGE BULLET	RANGE, YARDS:	0	100	200	300	400
Federal 210 Nosler Partition	velocity, fps:	3025	2800	2585	2385	2190
	energy, ft-lb:	4270	3655	3120	2645	2230
	arc, inches:		+1.5	0	-6.7	-19.5
Federal 250 Trophy Bonded	velocity, fps:	2860	2630	2420	2210	2020
	energy, ft-lb:	4540	3850	3245	2715	2260.
	arc, inches:		+0.8	0	-7.7	-22.6
Rem. 250 Swift A-Frame	velocity, fps:	2860	2645	2440	2244	2057
	energy, ft-lb:	4540	3882	3303	2794	2347
	arc, inches:		+1.7	0	-7.6	-22.1
Rem. 250 PSP Core-Lokt	velocity, fps:	2860	2647	2443	2249	2064
	energy, ft-lb:	4540	3888	3314	2807	2363
	arc, inches:		+1.7	0	-7.6	-22.0

.338 LAPUA

CARTRIDGE BULLET	RANGE, YARDS:	0	100	200	300	400
Black Hills 250 Sierra MKing	velocity, fps:	2950				
	energy, ft-lb:	4831				
	arc, inches:					
Black Hills 300 Sierra MKing	velocity, fps:	2800				
	energy, ft-lb:	5223				
	arc, inches:					

.338-378 WEATHERBY MAGNUM

CARTRIDGE BULLET	RANGE, YARDS:	0	100	200	300	400
Wby. 200 Nosler Bal. Tip	velocity, fps:	3350	3102	2868	2646	2434
	energy, ft-lb:	4983	4273	3652	3109	2631
	arc, inches:	0	+2.8	+3.5	0	-8.4
Wby. 225 Barnes X	velocity, fps:	3180	2974	2778	2591	2410.
	energy, ft-lb:	5052	4420	3856	3353	2902
	arc, inches:	0	+3.1	+3.8	0	-8.9

Centerfire Rifle Ballistics

.338-378 WEATHERBY MAGNUM TO 9.3X62

CARTRIDGE BULLET	RANGE, YARDS:	0	100	200	300	400
Wby. 250 Nosler Partition	velocity, fps:	3060	2856	2662	2475	2297
	energy, ft-lb:	5197	4528	3933	3401	2927
	arc, inches:	0	+3.5	+4.2	0	-9.8

8.59 (.338) TITAN

CARTRIDGE BULLET	RANGE, YARDS:	0	100	200	300	400
Lazzeroni 200 Nos. Bal. Tip	velocity, fps:	3430	3211	3002	2803	2613
	energy, ft-lb:	5226	4579	4004	3491	3033
	arc, inches:		+2.5	+3.2	0	-7.6
Lazzeroni 225 Nos. Partition	velocity, fps:	3235	3031	2836	2650	2471
	energy, ft-lb:	5229	4591	4021	3510	3052
	arc, inches:		+3.0	+3.6	0	-8.6
Lazzeroni 250 Swift A-Fr.	velocity, fps:	3100	2908	2725	2549	2379
	energy, ft-lb:	5336	4697	4123	3607	3143
	arc, inches:		+3.3	+4.0	0	-9.3

.338 A-SQUARE

CARTRIDGE BULLET	RANGE, YARDS:	0	100	200	300	400
A-Square 200 Nos. Bal. Tip	velocity, fps:	3500	3266	3045	2835	2634
	energy, ft-lb:	5440	4737	4117	3568	3081
	arc, inches:		+2.4	+3.1	0	-7.5
A-Square 250 SP boat-tail	velocity, fps:	3120	2974	2834	2697	2565.
	energy, ft-lb:	5403	4911	4457	4038	3652
	arc, inches:		+3.1	+3.7	0	-8.5
A-Square 250 Triad	velocity, fps:	3120	2799	2500	2220	1958
	energy, ft-lb:	5403	4348	3469	2736	2128
	arc, inches:		+1.5	0	-7.1	-20.4.

.338 EXCALIBER

CARTRIDGE BULLET	RANGE, YARDS:	0	100	200	300	400
A-Square 200 Nos. Bal. Tip	velocity, fps:	3600	3361	3134	2920	2715
	energy, ft-lb:	5755	5015	4363	3785	3274
	arc, inches:		+2.2	+2.9	0	-6.7
A-Square 250 SP boat-tail	velocity, fps:	3250	3101	2958	2684	2553
	energy, ft-lb:	5863	5339	4855	4410	3998
	arc, inches:		+2.7	+3.4	0	-7.8
A-Square 250 Triad	velocity, fps:	3250	2922	2618	2333	2066
	energy, ft-lb:	5863	4740	3804	3021	2370
	arc, inches:		+1.3	0	-6.4	-19.2

.348 WINCHESTER

CARTRIDGE BULLET	RANGE, YARDS:	0	100	200	300	400
Win. 200 Silvertip	velocity, fps:	2520	2215	1931	1672	1443.
	energy, ft-lb:	2820	2178	1656	1241	925
	arc, inches:		0	-6.2	-21.9	

.357 MAGNUM

CARTRIDGE BULLET	RANGE, YARDS:	0	100	200	300	400
Federal 180 Hi-Shok HP Hollow Point	velocity, fps:	1550	1160	980	860	770
	energy, ft-lb:	960	535	385	295	235
	arc, inches:		0	-22.8	-77.9	-173.8
Win. 158 Jacketed SP	velocity, fps:	1830	1427	1138	980	883
	energy, ft-lb:	1175	715	454	337	274
	arc, inches:		0	-16.2	-57.0	-128.3

.35 REMINGTON

CARTRIDGE BULLET	RANGE, YARDS:	0	100	200	300	400
Federal 200 Hi-Shok	velocity, fps:	2080	1700	1380	1140	1000
	energy, ft-lb:	1920	1280	840	575	445
	arc, inches:		0	-10.7	-39.3	
Hornady 200 Evolution	velocity, fps:	2225	1963	1721	1503	
	energy, ft-lb:	2198	1711	1315	1003	
	arc, inches:		+3.0	-1.3	-17.5	
Rem. 150 PSP Core-Lokt	velocity, fps:	2300	1874	1506	1218	1039
	energy, ft-lb:	1762	1169	755	494	359
	arc, inches:		0	-8.6	-32.6	
Rem. 200 SP Core-Lokt	velocity, fps:	2080	1698	1376	1140	1001
	energy, ft-lb:	1921	1280	841	577	445
	arc, inches:		0	-10.7	-40.1	
Win. 200 Power-Point	velocity, fps:	2020	1646	1335	1114	985
	energy, ft-lb:	1812	1203	791	551	431
	arc, inches:		0	-12.1	-43.9	

.356 WINCHESTER

CARTRIDGE BULLET	RANGE, YARDS:	0	100	200	300	400
Win. 200 Power-Point	velocity, fps:	2460	2114	1797	1517	1284
	energy, ft-lb:	2688	1985	1434	1022	732
	arc, inches:		+1.6	-3.8	-20.1	-51.2

.358 WINCHESTER

CARTRIDGE BULLET	RANGE, YARDS:	0	100	200	300	400
Win. 200 Silvertip	velocity, fps:	2490	2171	1876	1610	1379
	energy, ft-lb:	2753	2093	1563	1151	844
	arc, inches:		+1.5	-3.6	-18.6	-47.2

.35 WHELEN

CARTRIDGE BULLET	RANGE, YARDS:	0	100	200	300	400
Federal 225 Trophy Bonded	velocity, fps:	2600	2400	2200	2020	1840
	energy, ft-lb:	3375	2865	2520	2030	1690.
	arc, inches:		+2.3	0	-9.4	-27.3
Rem. 200 Pointed Soft Point	velocity, fps:	2675	2378	2100	1842	1606
	energy, ft-lb:	3177	2510	1958	1506	1145
	arc, inches:		+2.3	0	-10.3	-30.8
Rem. 250 Pointed Soft Point	velocity, fps:	2400	2197	2005	1823	1652
	energy, ft-lb:	3197	2680	2230	1844	1515
	arc, inches:		+1.3	-3.2	-16.6	-40.0

.358 NORMA MAGNUM

CARTRIDGE BULLET	RANGE, YARDS:	0	100	200	300	400
A-Square 275 Triad	velocity, fps:	2700	2394	2108	1842	1653
	energy, ft-lb:	4451	3498	2713	2072	1668
	arc, inches:		+2.3	0	-10.1	-29.8
Norma 250 TXP Swift A-Fr.	velocity, fps:	2723	2467	2225	1996	
	energy, ft-lb:	4117	3379	2748	2213	
	arc, inches:		+2.1	0	-9.1	
Norma 250 Woodleigh	velocity, fps:	2799	2442	2112	1810	
	energy, ft-lb:	4350	3312	2478	1819	
	arc, inches:		+2.2	0	-10.0	
Norma 250 Oryx	velocity, fps:	2756	2493	2245	2011	
	energy, ft-lb:	4217	3451	2798	2245	
	arc, inches:		+2.1	0	-9.0	

.358 STA

CARTRIDGE BULLET	RANGE, YARDS:	0	100	200	300	400
A-Square 275 Triad	velocity, fps:	2850	2562	2292	2039	1764
	energy, ft-lb:	4959	4009	3208	2539	1899.
	arc, inches:		+1.9	0	-8.6	-26.1

9.3x57

CARTRIDGE BULLET	RANGE, YARDS:	0	100	200	300	400
Norma 232 Vulkan	velocity, fps:	2329	2031	1757	1512	
	energy, ft-lb:	2795	2126	1591	1178	
	arc, inches:		+3.5	0	-14.9	
Norma 232 Oryx	velocity, fps:	2362	2058	1778	1528	
	energy, ft-lb:	2875	2182	1630	1203	
	arc, inches:		+3.4	0	-14.5	
Norma 285 Oryx	velocity, fps:	2067	1859	1666	1490	
	energy, ft-lb:	2704	2188	1756	1404	
	arc, inches:		+4.3	0	-16.8	
Norma 286 Alaska	velocity, fps:	2067	1857	1662	1484	
	energy, ft-lb:	2714	2190	1754	1399	
	arc, inches:		+4.3	0	-17.0	

9.3x62

CARTRIDGE BULLET	RANGE, YARDS:	0	100	200	300	400
A-Square 286 Triad	velocity, fps:	2360	2089	1844	1623	1369
	energy, ft-lb:	3538	2771	2157	1670	1189
	arc, inches:		+3.0	0	-13.1	-42.2
Norma 232 Vulkan	velocity, fps:	2625	2327	2049	1792	
	energy, ft-lb:	3551	2791	2164	1655	
	arc, inches:		+2.5	0	-10.8	

CARTRIDGE BULLET	RANGE, YARDS:	0	100	200	300	400
Norma 232 Oryx	velocity, fps:	2625	2294	1988	1708	
	energy, ft-lb:	3535	2700	2028	1497	
	arc, inches:		+2.5	0	-11.4	
Norma 250 A-Frame	velocity, fps:	2625	2322	2039	1778	
	energy, ft-lb:	3826	2993	2309	1755	
	arc, inches:		+2.5	0	-10.9	
Norma 286 Plastic Point	velocity, fps:	2362	2141	1931	1736	
	energy, ft-lb:	3544	2911	2370	1914	
	arc, inches:		+3.1	0	-12.4	
Norma 286 Alaska	velocity, fps:	2362	2135	1920	1720	
	energy, ft-lb:	3544	2894	2342	1879	
	arc, inches:		+3.1	0	-12.5	

9.3x64

CARTRIDGE BULLET	RANGE, YARDS:	0	100	200	300	400
A-Square 286 Triad	velocity, fps:	2700	2391	2103	1835	1602
	energy, ft-lb:	4629	3630	2808	2139	1631
	arc, inches:		+2.3	0	-10.1	-30.8

9.3x74 R

CARTRIDGE BULLET	RANGE, YARDS:	0	100	200	300	400
A-Square 286 Triad	velocity, fps:	2360	2089	1844	1623	
	energy, ft-lb:	3538	2771	2157	1670	
	arc, inches:		+3.6	0	-14.0	
Hornady 286	velocity, fps	2360	2136	1924	1727	1545
	energy, ft-lb	3536	2896	2351	1893	1516
	arc, inches	-1.5	0	-6.1	-21.7	-49.0
Norma 232 Vulkan	velocity, fps:	2625	2327	2049	1792	
	energy, ft-lb:	3551	2791	2164	1655	
	arc, inches:		+2.5	0	-10.8	
Norma 232 Oryx	velocity, fps:	2526	2191	1883	1605	
	energy, ft-lb:	3274	2463	1819	1322	
	arc, inches:		+2.9	0	-12.8	
Norma 285 Oryx	velocity, fps:	2362	2114	1881	1667	
	energy, ft-lb:	3532	2829	2241	1758	
	arc, inches:		+3.1	0	-13.0	
Norma 286 Alaska	velocity, fps:	2362	2135	1920	1720	
	energy, ft-lb:	3544	2894	2342	1879	
	arc, inches:		+3.1	0	-12.5	
Norma 286 Plastic Point	velocity, fps:	2362	2135	1920	1720	
	energy, ft-lb:	3544	2894	2342	1879	
	arc, inches:		+3.1	0	-12.5	

.375 Winchester

CARTRIDGE BULLET	RANGE, YARDS:	0	100	200	300	400
Win. 200 Power-Point	velocity, fps:	2200	1841	1526	1268	1089
	energy, ft-lb:	2150	1506	1034	714	
	arc, inches:		0	-9.5	-33.8	

.375 H&H Magnum

CARTRIDGE BULLET	RANGE, YARDS:	0	100	200	300	400
A-Square 300 SP boat-tail	velocity, fps:	2550	2415	2284	2157	2034
	energy, ft-lb:	4331	3884	3474	3098	2755
	arc, inches:		+5.2	+6.0	0	-13.3
A-Square 300 Triad	velocity, fps:	2550	2251	1973	1717	1496
	energy, ft-lb:	4331	3375	2592	1964	1491
	arc, inches:		+2.7	0	-11.7	-35.1
Federal 250 Trophy Bonded	velocity, fps:	2670	2360	2080	1820	1580
	energy, ft-lb:	3955	3100	2400	1830	1380
	arc, inches:		+2.4	0	-10.4	-31.7
Federal 270 Hi-Shok	velocity, fps:	2690	2420	2170	1920	1700
	energy, ft-lb:	4340	3510	2810	2220	1740
	arc, inches:		+2.4	0	-10.9	-33.3
Federal 300 Hi-Shok	velocity, fps:	2530	2270	2020	1790	1580
	energy, ft-lb:	4265	3425	2720	2135	1665
	arc, inches:		+2.6	0	-11.2	-33.3
Federal 300 Nosler Partition	velocity, fps:	2530	2320	2120	1930	1750
	energy, ft-lb:	4265	3585	2995	2475	2040
	arc, inches:		+2.5	0	-10.3	-29.9
Federal 300 Trophy Bonded	velocity, fps:	2530	2280	2040	1810	1610
	energy, ft-lb:	4265	3450	2765	2190	1725
	arc, inches:		+2.6	0	-10.9	-32.8
Federal 300 Tr. Bonded HE	velocity, fps:	2700	2440	2190	1960	1740
	energy, ft-lb:	4855	3960	3195	2550	2020
	arc, inches:		+2.2	0	-9.4	-28.0
Federal 300 Trophy Bonded Sledgehammer Solid	velocity, fps:	2530	2160	1820	1520	1280.
	energy, ft-lb:	4265	3105	2210	1550	1090
	arc, inches, s:		0	-6.0	-22.7	-54.6
Hornady 270 SP HM	velocity, fps:	2870	2620	2385	2162	1957
	energy, ft-lb:	4937	4116	3408	2802	2296
	arc, inches:		+2.2	0	-8.4	-23.9
Hornady 300 FMJ RN HM	velocity, fps:	2705	2376	2072	1804	1560
	energy, ft-lb:	4873	3760	2861	2167	1621
	arc, inches:		+2.7	0	-10.8	-32.1
Norma 300 Soft Point	velocity, fps:	2549	2211	1900	1619	
	energy, ft-lb:	4329	3258	2406	1747	
	arc, inches:		+2.8	0	-12.6	
Norma 300 TXP Swift A-Fr.	velocity, fps:	2559	2296	2049	1818	
	energy, ft-lb:	4363	3513	2798	2203	
	arc, inches:		+2.6	0	-10.9	
Norma 300 Oryx	velocity, fps:	2559	2292	2041	1807	
	energy, ft-lb:	4363	3500	2775	2176	
	arc, inches:		+2.6	0	-11.0	
Norma 300 Barnes Solid	velocity, fps:	2493	2061	1677	1356	
	energy, ft-lb:	4141	2829	1873	1234	
	arc, inches:		+3.4	0	-16.0	
PMC 270 PSP	velocity, fps:					
	energy, ft-lb:					
	arc, inches:					
PMC 270 Barnes X	velocity, fps:	2690	2528	2372	2221	2076
	energy, ft-lb:	4337	3831	3371	2957	2582
	arc, inches:		+2.0	0	-8.2	-23.4
PMC 300 Barnes X	velocity, fps:	2530	2389	2252	2120	1993
	energy, ft-lb:	4263	3801	3378	2994	2644
	arc, inches:		+2.3	0	-9.2	-26.1
Rem. 270 Soft Point	velocity, fps:	2690	2420	2166	1928	1707
	energy, ft-lb:	4337	3510	2812	2228	1747
	arc, inches:		+2.2	0	-9.7	-28.7
Rem. 300 Swift A-Frame	velocity, fps:	2530	2245	1979	1733	1512
	energy, ft-lb:	4262	3357	2608	2001	1523
	arc, inches:		+2.7	0	-11.7	-35.0
Speer 285 Grand Slam	velocity, fps:	2610	2365	2134	1916	
	energy, ft-lb:	4310	3540	2883	2323	
	arc, inches:		+2.4	0	-9.9	
Speer 300 African GS Tungsten Solid	velocity, fps:	2609	2277	1970	1690	
	energy, ft-lb:	4534	3453	2585	1903	
	arc, inches:		+2.6	0	-11.7	-35.6
Win. 270 Fail Safe	velocity, fps:	2670	2447	2234	2033	1842
	energy, ft-lb:	4275	3590	2994	2478	2035
	arc, inches:		+2.2	0	-9.1	-28.7
Win. 300 Fail Safe	velocity, fps:	2530	2336	2151	1974	1806
	energy, ft-lb:	4265	3636	3082	2596	2173
	arc, inches:		+2.4	0	-10.0	-26.9

.375 Dakota

CARTRIDGE BULLET	RANGE, YARDS:	0	100	200	300	400
Dakota 270 Barnes X	velocity, fps:	2800	2617	2441	2272	2109
	energy, ft-lb:	4699	4104	3571	3093	2666
	arc, inches:		+2.3	+1.0	-6.1	-19.9

Centerfire Rifle Ballistics

.375 DAKOTA TO .416 HOFFMAN

CARTRIDGE BULLET	RANGE, YARDS:	0	100	200	300	400
Dakota 300 Barnes X	velocity, fps:	2600	2316	2051	1804	1579
	energy, ft-lb:	4502	3573	2800	2167	1661
	arc, inches:		+2.4	-0.1	-11.0	-32.7

.375 Ruger

CARTRIDGE BULLET	RANGE, YARDS:	0	100	200	300	400
Hornady 300 Solid	velocity, fps	2660	2344	2050	1780	1536
	energy, ft-lb	4713	3660	2800	2110	1572
	arc, inches	-1.5	+2.4	0	-10.8	-32.6

.375 Weatherby Magnum

CARTRIDGE BULLET	RANGE, YARDS:	0	100	200	300	400
A-Square 300 SP boat-tail	velocity, fps:	2700	2560	2425	2293	2166
	energy, ft-lb:	4856	4366	3916	3503	3125
	arc, inches:		+4.5	+5.2	0	-11.9
A-Square 300 Triad	velocity, fps:	2700	2391	2103	1835	1602
	energy, ft-lb:	4856	3808	2946	2243	1710
	arc, inches:		+2.3	0	-10.1	-30.8
Wby. 300 Nosler Part.	velocity, fps:	2800	2572	2366	2140	1963
	energy, ft-lb:	5224	4408	3696	3076	2541
	arc, inches:		+1.9	0	-8.2	-23.9

.375 JRS

CARTRIDGE BULLET	RANGE, YARDS:	0	100	200	300	400
A-Square 300 SP boat-tail	velocity, fps:	2700	2560	2425	2293	2166.
	energy, ft-lb:	4856	4366	3916	3503	3125
	arc, inches:		+4.5	+5.2	0	-11.9
A-Square 300 Triad	velocity, fps:	2700	2391	2103	1835	1602
	energy, ft-lb:	4856	3808	2946	2243	1710
	arc, inches:		+2.3	0	-10.1	-30.8

.375 Remington Ultra Magnum

CARTRIDGE BULLET	RANGE, YARDS:	0	100	200	300	400
Rem. 270 Soft Point	velocity, fps:	2900	2558	2241	1947	1678
	energy, fps:	5041	3922	3010	2272	1689
	arc, inches:		+1.9	0	-9.2	-27.8
Rem. 300 Swift A-Frame	velocity, fps:	2760	2505	2263	2035	1822
	energy, fps:	5073	4178	3412	2759	2210
	arc, inches:		+2.0	0	-8.8	-26.1

.375 A-Square

CARTRIDGE BULLET	RANGE, YARDS:	0	100	200	300	400
A-Square 300 SP boat-tail	velocity, fps:	2920	2773	2631	2494	2360
	energy, ft-lb:	5679	5123	4611	4142	3710
	arc, inches:		+3.7	+4.4	0	-9.8
A-Square 300 Triad	velocity, fps:	2920	2596	2294	2012	1762
	energy, ft-lb:	5679	4488	3505	2698	2068
	arc, inches:		+1.8	0	-8.5	-25.5

.376 Steyr

CARTRIDGE BULLET	RANGE, YARDS:	0	100	200	300	400
Hornady 225 SP	velocity, fps:	2600	2331	2078	1842	1625
	energy, ft-lb:	3377	2714	2157	1694	1319
	arc, inches:		+2.5	0	-10.6	-31.4
Hornady 270 SP	velocity, fps:	2600	2372	2156	1951	1759
	energy, ft-lb:	4052	3373	2787	2283	1855
	arc, inches:		+2.3	0	-9.9	-28.9

.378 Weatherby Magnum

CARTRIDGE BULLET	RANGE, YARDS:	0	100	200	300	400
A-Square 300 SP boat-tail	velocity, fps:	2900	2754	2612	2475	2342
	energy, ft-lb:	5602	5051	4546	4081	3655
	arc, inches:		+3.8	+4.4	0	-10.0
A-Square 300 Triad	velocity, fps:	2900	2577	2276	1997	1747
	energy, ft-lb:	5602	4424	3452	2656	2034
	arc, inches:		+1.9	0	-8.7	-25.9
Wby. 270 Pointed Expanding	velocity, fps:	3180	2921	2677	2445	2225
	energy, ft-lb:	6062	5115	4295	3583	2968
	arc, inches:		+1.3	0	-6.1	-18.1
Wby. 270 Barnes X	velocity, fps:	3150	2954	2767	2587	2415
	energy, ft-lb:	5948	5232	4589	4013	3495
	arc, inches:		+1.2	0	-5.8	-16.7
Wby. 300 RN Expanding	velocity, fps:	2925	2558	2220	1908	1627.
	energy, ft-lb:	5699	4360	3283	2424	1764
	arc, inches:		+1.9	0	-9.0	-27.8
Wby. 300 FMJ	velocity, fps:	2925	2591	2280	1991	1725
	energy, ft-lb:	5699	4470	3461	2640	1983
	arc, inches:		+1.8	0	-8.6	-26.1

.38-40 Winchester

CARTRIDGE BULLET	RANGE, YARDS:	0	100	200	300	400
Win. 180 Soft Point	velocity, fps:	1160	999	901	827	
	energy, ft-lb:	538	399	324	273	
	arc, inches:		0	-23.4	-75.2	

.38-55 Winchester

CARTRIDGE BULLET	RANGE, YARDS:	0	100	200	300	400
Black Hills 255 FN Lead	velocity, fps:	1250				
	energy, ft-lb:	925				
	arc, inches:					
Win. 255 Soft Point	velocity, fps:	1320	1190	1091	1018	
	energy, ft-lb:	987	802	674	587	
	arc, inches:		0	-33.9	-110.6	

.41 Magnum

CARTRIDGE BULLET	RANGE, YARDS:	0	100	200	300	400
Win. 240 Platinum Tip	velocity, fps:	1830	1488	1220	1048	
	energy, ft-lb:	1784	1180	792	585	
	arc inches:		0	-15.0	-53.4	

.450/.400 (3")

CARTRIDGE BULLET	RANGE, YARDS:	0	100	200	300	400
A-Square 400 Triad	velocity, fps:	2150	1910	1690	1490	
	energy, ft-lb:	4105	3241	2537	1972	
	arc, inches:		+4.4	0	-16.5	

.450/.400 (3 1/4")

CARTRIDGE BULLET	RANGE, YARDS:	0	100	200	300	400
A-Square 400 Triad	velocity, fps:	2150	1910	1690	1490	
	energy, ft-lb:	4105	3241	2537	1972	
	arc, inches:		+4.4	0	-16.5	

.450/.400 Nitro Express

CARTRIDGE BULLET	RANGE, YARDS:	0	100	200	300	400
Hornady 400 RN	velocity, fps	2050	1815	1595	1402	
	energy, ft-lb	3732	2924	2259	1746	
	arc, inches	-1.5	0	-10.0	-33.4	

.404 Jeffery

CARTRIDGE BULLET	RANGE, YARDS:	0	100	200	300	400
A-Square 400 Triad	velocity, fps:	2150	1901	1674	1468	1299
	energy, ft-lb:	4105	3211	2489	1915	1499
	arc, inches:		+4.1	0	-16.4	-49.1

.405 Winchester

CARTRIDGE BULLET	RANGE, YARDS:	0	100	200	300	400
Hornady 300 Flatpoint	velocity, fps:	2200	1851	1545	1296	
	energy, ft-lb:	3224	2282	1589	1119	
	arc, inches:		0	-8.7	-31.9	
Hornady 300 SP Interlock	velocity, fps:	2200	1890	1610	1370	
	energy, ft-lb:	3224	2379	1727	1250	
	arc, inches:		0	-8.3	-30.2	

.416 Taylor

CARTRIDGE BULLET	RANGE, YARDS:	0	100	200	300	400
A-Square 400 Triad	velocity, fps:	2350	2093	1853	1634	1443
	energy, ft-lb:	4905	3892	3049	2371	1849
	arc, inches:		+3.2	0	-13.6	-39.8

.416 Hoffman

CARTRIDGE BULLET	RANGE, YARDS:	0	100	200	300	400
A-Square 400 Triad	velocity, fps:	2380	2122	1879	1658	1464
	energy, ft-lb:	5031	3998	3136	2440	1903
	arc, inches:		+3.1	0	-13.1	-38.7

BALLISTICS

CARTRIDGE BULLET	RANGE, YARDS:	0	100	200	300	400
.416 REMINGTON MAGNUM						
A-Square 400 Triad	velocity, fps:	2380	2122	1879	1658	1464
	energy, ft-lb:	5031	3998	3136	2440	1903
	arc, inches:		+3.1	0	-13.2	-38.7
Federal 400 Trophy Bonded Sledgehammer Solid	velocity, fps:	2400	2150	1920	1700	1500
	energy, ft-lb:	5115	4110	3260	2565	2005
	arc, inches:		0	-6.0	-21.6	-49.2
Federal 400 Trophy Bonded	velocity, fps:	2400	2180	1970	1770	1590
	energy, ft-lb:	5115	4215	3440	2785	2245
	arc, inches:		0	-5.8	-20.6	-46.9
Rem. 400 Swift A-Frame	velocity, fps:	2400	2175	1962	1763	1579
	energy, ft-lb:	5115	4201	3419	2760	2214
	arc, inches:		0	-5.9	-20.8	
.416 RIGBY						
A-Square 400 Triad	velocity, fps:	2400	2140	1897	1673	1478
	energy, ft-lb:	5115	4069	3194	2487	1940
	arc, inches:		+3.0	0	-12.9	-38.0
Federal 400 Trophy Bonded	velocity, fps:	2370	2150	1940	1750	1570
	energy, ft-lb:	4990	4110	3350	2715	2190
	arc, inches:		0	-6.0	-21.3	-48.1
Federal 400 Trophy Bonded Sledgehammer Solid	velocity, fps:	2370	2120	1890	1660	1460
	energy, ft-lb:	4990	3975	3130	2440	1895
	arc, inches:		0	-6.3	-22.5	-51.5
Federal 410 Woodleigh Weldcore	velocity, fps:	2370	2110	1870	1640	1440
	energy, ft-lb:	5115	4050	3165	2455	1895
	arc, inches:		0	-7.4	-24.8	-55.0
Federal 410 Solid	velocity, fps:	2370	2110	2870	1640	1440
	energy, ft-lb:	5115	4050	3165	2455	1895
	arc, inches:		0	-7.4	-24.8	-55.0
Norma 400 TXP Swift A-Fr.	velocity, fps:	2350	2127	1917	1721	
	energy, ft-lb:	4906	4021	3266	2632	
	arc, inches:		+3.1	0	-12.5	
Norma 400 Barnes Solid	velocity, fps:	2297	1930	1604	1330	
	energy, ft-lb:	4687	3310	2284	1571	
	arc, inches:		+3.9	0	-17.7	
.416 RIMMED						
A-Square 400 Triad	velocity, fps:	2400	2140	1897	1673	
	energy, ft-lb:	5115	4069	3194	2487	
	arc, inches:		+3.3	0	-13.2	
.416 DAKOTA						
Dakota 400 Barnes X	velocity, fps:	2450	2294	2143	1998	1859
	energy, ft-lb:	5330	4671	4077	3544	3068
	arc, inches:		+2.5	-0.2	-10.5	-29.4
.416 WEATHERBY						
A-Square 400 Triad	velocity, fps:	2600	2328	2073	1834	1624
	energy, ft-lb:	6004	4813	3816	2986	2343
	arc, inches:		+2.5	0	-10.5	-31.6
Wby. 350 Barnes X	velocity, fps:	2850	2673	2503	2340	2182
	energy, ft-lb:	6312	5553	4870	4253	3700
	arc, inches:		+1.7	0	-7.2	-20.9
Wby. 400 Swift A-Fr.	velocity, fps:	2650	2426	2213	2011	1820
	energy, ft-lb:	6237	5227	4350	3592	2941
	arc, inches:		+2.2	0	-9.3	-27.1
Wby. 400 RN Expanding	velocity, fps:	2700	2417	2152	1903	1676
	energy, ft-lb:	6474	5189	4113	3216	2493
	arc, inches:		+2.3	0	-9.7	-29.3
Wby. 400 Monolithic Solid	velocity, fps:	2700	2411	2140	1887	1656
	energy, ft-lb:	6474	5162	4068	3161	2435
	arc, inches:		+2.3	0	-9.8	-29.7
10.57 (.416) METEOR						
Lazzeroni 400 Swift A-Fr.	velocity, fps:	2730	2532	2342	2161	1987
	energy, ft-lb:	6621	5695	4874	4147	3508
	arc, inches:		+1.9	0	-8.3	-24.0
.425 EXPRESS						
A-Square 400 Triad	velocity, fps:	2400	2136	1888	1662	1465
	energy, ft-lb:	5115	4052	3167	2454	1906
	arc, inches:		+3.0	0	-13.1	-38.3
.44-40 WINCHESTER						
Rem. 200 Soft Point	velocity, fps:	1190	1006	900	822	756
	energy, ft-lb:	629	449	360	300	254
	arc, inches:		0	-33.1	-108.7	-235.2
Win. 200 Soft Point	velocity, fps:	1190	1006	900	822	756
	energy, ft-lb:	629	449	360	300	254
	arc, inches:		0	-33.3	-109.5	-237.4
.44 REMINGTON MAGNUM						
Federal 240 Hi-Shok HP	velocity, fps:	1760	1380	1090	950	860
	energy, ft-lb:	1650	1015	640	485	395
	arc, inches:		0	-17.4	-60.7	-136.0
Rem. 210 Semi-Jacketed HP	velocity, fps:	1920	1477	1155	982	880
	energy, ft-lb:	1719	1017	622	450	361
	arc, inches:		0	-14.7	-55.5	-131.3
Rem. 240 Soft Point	velocity, fps:	1760	1380	1114	970	878
	energy, ft-lb:	1650	1015	661	501	411
	arc, inches:		0	-17.0	-61.4	-143.0
Rem. 240 Semi-Jacketed Hollow Point	velocity, fps:	1760	1380	1114	970	878
	energy, ft-lb:	1650	1015	661	501	411
	arc, inches:		0	-17.0	-61.4	-143.0
Rem. 275 JHP Core-Lokt	velocity, fps:	1580	1293	1093	976	896
	energy, ft-lb:	1524	1020	730	582	490
	arc, inches:		0	-19.4	-67.5	-210.8
Win. 210 Silvertip HP	velocity, fps:	1580	1198	993	879	795
	energy, ft-lb:	1164	670	460	361	295
	arc, inches:		0	-22.4	-76.1	-168.0
Win. 240 Hollow Soft Point	velocity, fps:	1760	1362	1094	953	861
	energy, ft-lb:	1650	988	638	484	395
	arc, inches:		0	-18.1	-65.1	-150.3
Win. 250 Platinum Tip	velocity, fps:	1830	1475	1201	1032	931
	energy, ft-lb:	1859	1208	801	591	481
	arc, inches:		0	-15.3	-54.7	-126.6.
.444 MARLIN						
Rem. 240 Soft Point	velocity, fps:	2350	1815	1377	1087	941
	energy, ft-lb:	2942	1755	1010	630	472
	arc, inches:		+2.2	-5.4	-31.4	-86.7
Hornady 265 Evolution	velocity, fps:	2325	1971	1652	1380	
	energy, ft-lb:	3180	2285	1606	1120	
	arc, inches:		+3.0	-1.4	-18.6	
Hornady 265 FP LM	velocity, fps:	2335	1913	1551	1266	
	energy, ft-lb:	3208	2153	1415	943	
	arc, inches:		+ 2.0	-4.9	-26.5	
.45-70 GOVERNMENT						
Black Hills 405 FPL	velocity, fps:	1250				
	energy, ft-lb:					
	arc, inches:					
Federal 300 Sierra Pro-Hunt. HP FN	velocity, fps:	1880	1650	1430	1240	1110
	energy, ft-lb:	2355	1815	1355	1015	810
	arc, inches:		0	-11.5	-39.7	-89.1
PMC 350 FNSP	velocity, fps:					
	energy, ft-lb:					
	arc, inches:

Centerfire Rifle Ballistics

.45-70 GOVERNMENT TO .500/.465

CARTRIDGE BULLET	RANGE, YARDS:	0	100	200	300	400
Rem. 300 Jacketed HP	velocity, fps:	1810	1497	1244	1073	969
	energy, ft-lb:	2182	1492	1031	767	625
	arc, inches:		0	-13.8	-50.1	-115.7
Rem. 405 Soft Point	velocity, fps:	1330	1168	1055	977	918
	energy, ft-lb:	1590	1227	1001	858	758
	arc, inches:		0	-24.0	-78.6	-169.4
Win. 300 Jacketed HP	velocity, fps:	1880	1650	1425	1235	1105
	energy, ft-lb:	2355	1815	1355	1015	810
	arc, inches:		0	-12.8	-44.3	-95.5
Win. 300 Partition Gold	velocity, fps:	1880	1558	1292	1103	988
	energy, ft-lb:	2355	1616	1112	811	651
	arc, inches:		0	-12.9	-46.0	-104.9.

.450 BUSHMASTER

CARTRIDGE BULLET	RANGE, YARDS:	0	100	200	300	400
Hornady 250 SST-ML	velocity, fps	2200	1840	1524	1268	
	energy, ft-lb	2686	1879	1289	893	
	arc, inches	-2.0	+2.5	-3.5	-24.5	

.450 MARLIN

CARTRIDGE BULLET	RANGE, YARDS:	0	100	200	300	400
Hornady 350 FP	velocity, fps:	2100	1720	1397	1156	
	energy, ft-lb:	3427	2298	1516	1039	
	arc, inches:		0	-10.4	-38.9	

.450 NITRO EXPRESS (3¼")

CARTRIDGE BULLET	RANGE, YARDS:	0	100	200	300	400
A-Square 465 Triad	velocity, fps:	2190	1970	1765	1577	
	energy, ft-lb:	4952	4009	3216	2567	
	arc, inches:		+4.3	0	-15.4	

.450 #2

CARTRIDGE BULLET	RANGE, YARDS:	0	100	200	300	400
A-Square 465 Triad	velocity, fps:	2190	1970	1765	1577	
	energy, ft-lb:	4952	4009	3216	2567	
	arc, inches:		+4.3	0	-15.4	

.458 WINCHESTER MAGNUM

CARTRIDGE BULLET	RANGE, YARDS:	0	100	200	300	400
A-Square 465 Triad	velocity, fps:	2220	1999	1791	1601	1433
	energy, ft-lb:	5088	4127	3312	2646	2121
	arc, inches:		+3.6	0	-14.7	-42.5
Federal 350 Soft Point	velocity, fps:	2470	1990	1570	1250	1060
	energy, ft-lb:	4740	3065	1915	1205	870
	arc, inches:		0	-7.5	-29.1	-71.1
Federal 400 Trophy Bonded	velocity, fps:	2380	2170	1960	1770	1590
	energy, ft-lb:	5030	4165	3415	2785	2255
	arc, inches:		0	-5.9	-20.9	-47.1
Federal 500 Solid	velocity, fps:	2090	1870	1670	1480	1320
	energy, ft-lb:	4850	3880	3085	2440	1945
	arc, inches:		0	-8.5	-29.5	-66.2
Federal 500 Trophy Bonded	velocity, fps:	2090	1870	1660	1480	1310
	energy, ft-lb:	4850	3870	3065	2420	1915
	arc, inches:		0	-8.5	-29.7	-66.8
Federal 500 Trophy Bonded Sledgehammer Solid	velocity, fps:	2090	1860	1650	1460	1300
	energy, ft-lb:	4850	3845	3025	2365	1865
	arc, inches:		0	-8.6	-30.0	-67.8
Federal 510 Soft Point	velocity, fps:	2090	1820	1570	1360	1190
	energy, ft-lb:	4945	3730	2790	2080	1605
	arc, inches:		0	-9.1	-32.3	-73.9
Hornady 500 FMJ-RN HM	velocity, fps:	2260	1984	1735	1512	
	energy, ft-lb:	5670	4368	3341	2538	
	arc, inches:		0	-7.4	-26.4	
Norma 500 TXP Swift A-Fr.	velocity, fps:	2116	1903	1705	1524	
	energy, ft-lb:	4972	4023	3228	2578	
	arc, inches:		+4.1	0	-16.1	
Norma 500 Barnes Solid	velocity, fps:	2067	1750	1472	1245	
	energy, ft-lb:	4745	3401	2405	1721	
	arc, inches:		+4.9	0	-21.2	
Rem. 450 Swift A-Frame PSP	velocity, fps:	2150	1901	1671	1465	1289
	energy, ft-lb:	4618	3609	2789	2144	1659
	arc, inches:		0	-8.2	-28.9	
Speer 500 African GS Tungsten Solid	velocity, fps:	2120	1845	1596	1379	
	energy, ft-lb:	4989	3780	2828	2111	
	arc, inches:		0	-8.8	-31.3	
Speer African Grand Slam	velocity, fps:	2120	1853	1609	1396	
	energy, ft-lb:	4989	3810	2875	2163	
	arc, inches:		0	-8.7	-30.8	
Win. 510 Soft Point	velocity, fps:	2040	1770	1527	1319	1157
	energy, ft-lb:	4712	3547	2640	1970	1516
	arc, inches:		0	-10.3	-35.6	

.458 LOTT

CARTRIDGE BULLET	RANGE, YARDS:	0	100	200	300	400
A-Square 465 Triad	velocity, fps:	2380	2150	1932	1730	1551
	energy, ft-lb:	5848	4773	3855	3091	2485
	arc, inches:		+3.0	0	-12.5	-36.4
Hornady 500 RNSP or solid	velocity, fps:	2300	2022	1776	1551	
	energy, ft-lb:	5872	4537	3502	2671	
	arc, inches:		+3.4	0	-14.3	
Hornady 500 InterBond	velocity, fps:	2300	2028	1777	1549	
	energy, ft-lb:	5872	4535	3453	2604	
	arc, inches:		0	-7.0	-25.1	

.450 ACKLEY

CARTRIDGE BULLET	RANGE, YARDS:	0	100	200	300	400
A-Square 465 Triad	velocity, fps:	2400	2169	1950	1747	1567
	energy, ft-lb:	5947	4857	3927	3150	2534
	arc, inches:		+2.9	0	-12.2	-35.8

.460 SHORT A-SQUARE

CARTRIDGE BULLET	RANGE, YARDS:	0	100	200	300	400
A-Square 500 Triad	velocity, fps:	2420	2198	1987	1789	1613
	energy, ft-lb:	6501	5362	4385	3553	2890
	arc, inches:		+2.9	0	-11.6	-34.2

.450 DAKOTA

CARTRIDGE BULLET	RANGE, YARDS:	0	100	200	300	400
Dakota 500 Barnes Solid	velocity, fps:	2450	2235	2030	1838	1658
	energy, ft-lb:	6663	5544	4576	3748	3051
	arc, inches:		+2.5	-0.6	-12.0	-33.8

.460 WEATHERBY MAGNUM

CARTRIDGE BULLET	RANGE, YARDS:	0	100	200	300	400
A-Square 500 Triad	velocity, fps:	2580	2349	2131	1923	1737
	energy, ft-lb:	7389	6126	5040	4107	3351
	arc, inches:		+2.4	0	-10.0	-29.4
Wby. 450 Barnes X	velocity, fps:	2700	2518	2343	2175	2013
	energy, ft-lb:	7284	6333	5482	4725	4050
	arc, inches:		+2.0	0	-8.4	-24.1
Wby. 500 RN Expanding	velocity, fps:	2600	2301	2022	1764	1533.
	energy, ft-lb:	7504	5877	4539	3456	2608
	arc, inches:		+2.6	0	-11.1	-33.5
Wby. 500 FMJ	velocity, fps:	2600	2309	2037	1784	1557
	energy, ft-lb:	7504	5917	4605	3534	2690
	arc, inches:		+2.5	0	-10.9	-33.0

.500/.465

CARTRIDGE BULLET	RANGE, YARDS:	0	100	200	300	400
A-Square 480 Triad	velocity, fps:	2150	1928	1722	1533	
	energy, ft-lb:	4926	3960	3160	2505	
	arc, inches:		+4.3	0	-16.0	

CARTRIDGE BULLET	RANGE, YARDS:	0	100	200	300	400
.470 NITRO EXPRESS						
A-Square 500 Triad	velocity, fps:	2150	1912	1693	1494	
	energy, ft-lb:	5132	4058	3182	2478	
	arc, inches:		+4.4	0	-16.5	
Federal 500 Woodleigh Weldcore	velocity, fps:	2150	1890	1650	1440	1270
	energy, ft-lb:	5130	3965	3040	2310	1790
	arc, inches:		0	-9.3	-31.3	-69.7
Federal 500 Woodleigh Weldcore Solid	velocity, fps:	2150	1890	1650	1440	1270.
	energy, ft-lb:	5130	3965	3040	2310	1790
	arc, inches:		0	-9.3	-31.3	-69.7
Federal 500 Trophy Bonded	velocity, fps:	2150	1940	1740	1560	1400
	energy, ft-lb:	5130	4170	3360	2695	2160
	arc, inches:		0	-7.8	-27.1	-60.8
Federal 500 Trophy Bonded Sledgehammer Solid	velocity, fps:	2150	1940	1740	1560	1400
	energy, ft-lb:	5130	4170	3360	2695	2160
	arc, inches:		0	-7.8	-27.1	-60.8
Norma 500 Woodleigh SP	velocity, fps:	2165	1975	1795	1627	
	energy, ft-lb:	5205	4330	3577	2940	
	arc, inches:		0	-7.4	-25.7	
Norma 500 Woodleigh FJ	velocity, fps:	2165	1974	1794	1626	
	energy, ft-lb:	5205	4328	3574	2936	
	arc, inches:		0	-7.5	-25.7	
.470 CAPSTICK						
A-Square 500 Triad	velocity, fps:	2400	2172	1958	1761	1553
	energy, ft-lb:	6394	5236	4255	3445	2678
	arc, inches:		+2.9	0	-11.9	-36.1
.475 #2						
A-Square 480 Triad	velocity, fps:	2200	1964	1744	1544	
	energy, ft-lb:	5158	4109	3240	2539	
	arc, inches:		+4.1	0	-15.6	
.475 #2 JEFFERY						
A-Square 500 Triad	velocity, fps:	2200	1966	1748	1550	
	energy, ft-lb:	5373	4291	3392	2666	
	arc, inches:		+4.1	0	-15.6	

CARTRIDGE BULLET	RANGE, YARDS:	0	100	200	300	400
.495 A-SQUARE						
A-Square 570 Triad	velocity, fps:	2350	2117	1896	1693	1513
	energy, ft-lb:	6989	5671	4552	3629	2899
	arc, inches:		+3.1	0	-13.0	-37.8
.500 NITRO EXPRESS (3")						
A-Square 570 Triad	velocity, fps:	2150	1928	1722	1533	
	energy, ft-lb:	5850	4703	3752	2975	
	arc, inches:		+4.3	0	-16.1	
.500 A-SQUARE						
A-Square 600 Triad	velocity, fps:	2470	2235	2013	1804	1620
	energy, ft-lb:	8127	6654	5397	4336	3495
	arc, inches:		+2.7	0	-11.3	-33.5
.505 GIBBS						
A-Square 525 Triad	velocity, fps:	2300	2063	1840	1637	
	energy, ft-lb:	6166	4962	3948	3122	
	arc, inches:		+3.6	0	-14.2	
.577 NITRO EXPRESS						
A-Square 750 Triad	velocity, fps:	2050	1811	1595	1401	
	energy, ft-lb:	6998	5463	4234	3267	
	arc, inches:		+4.9	0	-18.5	
.577 TYRANNOSAUR						
A-Square 750 Triad	velocity, fps:	2460	2197	1950	1723	1516
	energy, ft-lb:	10077	8039	6335	4941	3825
	arc, inches:		+2.8	0	-12.1	-36.0
.600 NITRO EXPRESS						
A-Square 900 Triad	velocity, fps:	1950	1680	1452	1336	
	energy, ft-lb:	7596	5634	4212	3564	
	arc, inches:		+5.6	0	-20.7	
.700 NITRO EXPRESS						
A-Square 1000 Monolithic Solid	velocity, fps:	1900	1669	1461	1288	
	energy, ft-lb:	8015	6188	4740	3685	
	arc, inches:		+5.8	0	-22.2

Centerfire Handgun Ballistics

Data shown here is taken from manufacturers' charts; your chronograph readings may vary. Barrel lengths for pistol data vary, and depend in part on which pistols are typically chambered in a given cartridge. Velocity variations due to barrel length depend on the baseline bullet speed and the load. Velocity for the .30 Carbine, normally a rifle cartridge, was determined in a pistol barrel.

Listings are current as of February the year *Shooter's Bible* appears (not the cover year). Listings are not intended as recommendations. For example, the data for the .25 Auto gives velocity and energy readings to 100 yards. Few handgunners would call the little .25 a 100-yard cartridge.

Abbreviations: Bullets are designated by loading company, weight (in grains) and type, with these abbreviations for shape and construction: BJHP=brass-jacketed hollowpoint; FN=Flat Nose; FMC=Full Metal Case; FMJ=Full Metal Jacket; HP=Hollowpoint; L=Lead; LF=Lead-Free; +P=a more powerful load than traditionally manufactured for that round; RN=Round Nose; SFHP=Starfire (PMC) Hollowpoint; SP=Softpoint; SWC=Semi Wadcutter; TMJ=Total Metal Jacket; WC=Wadcutter; CEPP, SXT and XTP are trademarked designations of Lapua, Winchester and Hornady, respectively.

.25 AUTO TO .32 S&W LONG

CARTRIDGE BULLET	RANGE, YARDS:	0	25	50	75	100
.25 AUTO						
Federal 50 FMJ	velocity, fps:	760	750	730	720	700
	energy, ft-lb:	65	60	60	55	55
Hornady 35 JHP/XTP	velocity, fps:	900		813		742
	energy, ft-lb:	63		51		43
Magtech 50 FMC	velocity, fps:	760		707		659
	energy, ft-lb:	64		56		48
PMC 50 FMJ	velocity, fps:	754	730	707	685	663
	energy, ft-lb:	62				
Rem. 50 Metal Case	velocity, fps:	760		707		659
	energy, ft-lb:	64		56		48
Speer 35 Gold Dot	velocity, fps:	900		816		747
	energy, ft-lb:	63		52		43
Speer 50 TMJ (and Blazer)	velocity, fps:	760		717		677
	energy, ft-lb:	64		57		51
Win. 45 Expanding Point	velocity, fps:	815		729		655
	energy, ft-lb	66		53		42
Win. 50 FMJ	velocity, fps:	760		707		
	energy, ft-lb	64		56		
.30 LUGER						
Win. 93 FMJ	velocity, fps:	1220		1110		1040
	energy, ft-lb	305		255		225
7.62X25 TOKAREV						
PMC 93 FMJ	velocity and energy figures not available					
.30 CARBINE						
Win. 110 Hollow SP	velocity, fps:	1790		1601		1430
	energy, ft-lb	783		626		500
.32 AUTO						
Federal 65 Hydra-Shok JHP	velocity, fps:	950	920	890	860	830
	energy, ft-lb:	130	120	115	105	100
Federal 71 FMJ	velocity, fps:	910	880	860	830	810
	energy, ft-lb:	130	120	115	110	105
Hornady 60 JHP/XTP	velocity, fps:	1000		917		849
	energy, ft-lb:	133		112		96
Hornady 71 FMJ-RN	velocity, fps:	900		845		797
	energy, ft-lb:	128		112		100
Magtech 71 FMC	velocity, fps:	905		855		810
	energy, ft-lb:	129		115		103
Magtech 71 JHP	velocity, fps:	905		855		810
	energy, ft-lb:	129		115		103
PMC 60 JHP	velocity, fps:	980	849	820	791	763
	energy, ft-lb:	117				
PMC 70 SFHP	velocity, fps:	velocity and energy figures not available				
PMC 71 FMJ	velocity, fps:	870	841	814	791	763
	energy, ft-lb:	119				
Rem. 71 Metal Case	velocity, fps:	905		855		810
	energy, ft-lb:	129		115		97
Speer 60 Gold Dot	velocity, fps:	960		868		796
	energy, ft-lb:	123		100		84
Speer 71 TMJ (and Blazer)	velocity, fps:	900		855		810
	energy, ft-lb:	129		115		97
Win. 60 Silvertip HP	velocity, fps:	970		895		835
	energy, ft-lb	125		107		93
Win. 71 FMJ	velocity, fps:	905		855		
	energy, ft-lb	129		115		
.32 S&W						
Rem. 88 LRN	velocity, fps:	680		645		610
	energy, ft-lb:	90		81		73
Win. 85 LRN	velocity, fps:	680		645		610
	energy, ft-lb	90		81		73
.32 S&W LONG						
Federal 98 LWC	velocity, fps:	780	700	630	560	500
	energy, ft-lb:	130	105	85	70	55
Federal 98 LRN	velocity, fps:	710	690	670	650	640
	energy, ft-lb:	115	105	100	95	90
Lapua 83 LWC	velocity, fps:	240		189*		149*
	energy, ft-lb:	154		95*		59*
Lapua 98 LWC	velocity, fps:	240		202*		171*
	energy, ft-lb:	183		130*		93*
Magtech 98 LRN	velocity, fps:	705		670		635
	energy, ft-lb:	108		98		88
Magtech 98 LWC	velocity, fps:	682		579		491
	energy, ft-lb:	102		73		52
Norma 98 LWC	velocity, fps:	787	759	732		683
	energy, ft-lb:	136	126	118		102

BALLISTICS

Centerfire Handgun Ballistics

.32 S&W LONG TO 9MM LUGER

CARTRIDGE BULLET	RANGE, YARDS:	0	25	50	75	100
PMC 98 LRN	velocity, fps:	789	770	751	733	716
	energy, ft-lb:	135				
PMC 100 LWC	velocity, fps:	683	652	623	595	569
	energy, ft-lb:	102				
Rem. 98 LRN	velocity, fps:	705		670		635
	energy, ft-lb:	115		98		88
Win. 98 LRN	velocity, fps:	705		670		635
	energy, ft-lb:	115		98		88

.32 Short Colt

CARTRIDGE BULLET	RANGE, YARDS:	0	25	50	75	100
Win. 80 LRN	velocity, fps:	745		665		590
	energy, ft-lb	100		79		62

.32-20

CARTRIDGE BULLET	RANGE, YARDS:	0	25	50	75	100
Black Hills 115 FPL	velocity, fps:	800				
	energy, ft-lb:					

.32 H&R Mag

CARTRIDGE BULLET	RANGE, YARDS:	0	25	50	75	100
Black Hills 85 JHP	velocity, fps	1100				
	energy, ft-lb	228				
Black Hills 90 FPL	velocity, fps	750				
	energy, ft-lb					
Black Hills 115 FPL	velocity, fps	800				
	energy, ft-lb					
Federal 85 Hi-Shok JHP	velocity, fps:	1100	1050	1020	970	930
	energy, ft-lb:	230	210	195	175	165
Federal 95 LSWC	velocity, fps:	1030	1000	940	930	900
	energy, ft-lb:	225	210	195	185	170

9mm Makarov

CARTRIDGE BULLET	RANGE, YARDS:	0	25	50	75	100
Federal 90 Hi-Shok JHP	velocity, fps:	990	950	910	880	850
	energy, ft-lb:	195	180	165	155	145
Federal 90 FMJ	velocity, fps:	990	960	920	900	870
	energy, ft-lb:	205	190	180	170	160
Hornady 95 JHP/XTP	velocity, fps:	1000		930		874
	energy, ft-lb:	211		182		161
PMC 100 FMJ-TC	velocity, fps:	velocity and energy figures not available				
Speer 95 TMJ Blazer	velocity, fps:	1000		928		872
	energy, ft-lb:	211		182		161

9x21 IMI

CARTRIDGE BULLET	RANGE, YARDS:	0	25	50	75	100
PMC 123 FMJ	velocity, fps:	1150	1093	1046	1007	973
	energy, ft-lb:	364				

9mm Luger

CARTRIDGE BULLET	RANGE, YARDS:	0	25	50	75	100
Black Hills 115 JHP	velocity, fps:	1150				
	energy, ft-lb:	336				
Black Hills 115 FMJ	velocity, fps:	1150				
	energy, ft-lb:	336				
Black Hills 115 JHP +P	velocity, fps:	1300				
	energy, ft-lb:	431				
Black Hills 115 EXP JHP	velocity, fps:	1250				
	energy, ft-lb:	400				
Black Hills 124 JHP +P	velocity, fps:	1250				
	energy, ft-lb:	430				
Black Hills 124 JHP	velocity, fps:	1150				
	energy, ft-lb:	363				
Black Hills 124 FMJ	velocity, fps:	1150				
	energy, ft-lb:	363				
Black Hills 147 JHP subsonic	velocity, fps:	975				
	energy, ft-lb:	309				
Black Hills 147 FMJ subsonic	velocity, fps:	975				
	energy, ft-lb:	309				
Federal 105 EFMJ	velocity, fps:	1225	1160	1105	1060	1025
	energy, ft-lb:	350	315	285	265	245
Federal 115 Hi-Shok JHP	velocity, fps:	1160	1100	1060	1020	990
	energy, ft-lb:	345	310	285	270	250
Federal 115 FMJ	velocity, fps:	1160	1100	1060	1020	990
	energy, ft-lb:	345	310	285	270	250
Federal 124 FMJ	velocity, fps:	1120	1070	1030	990	960
	energy, ft-lb:	345	315	290	270	255
Federal 124 Hydra-Shok JHP	velocity, fps:	1120	1070	1030	990	960
	energy, ft-lb:	345	315	290	270	255
Federal 124 TMJ TMF Primer	velocity, fps:	1120	1070	1030	990	960
	energy, ft-lb:	345	315	290	270	255
Federal 124 Truncated FMJ Match	velocity, fps:	1120	1070	1030	990	960
	energy, ft-lb:	345	315	290	270	255
Federal 124 Nyclad HP	velocity, fps:	1120	1070	1030	990	960
	energy, ft-lb:	345	315	290	270	255
Federal 124 FMJ +P	velocity, fps:	1120	1070	1030	990	960
	energy, ft-lb:	345	315	290	270	255
Federal 135 Hydra-Shok JHP	velocity, fps:	1050	1030	1010	980	970
	energy, ft-lb:	330	315	300	290	280
Federal 147 Hydra-Shok JHP	velocity, fps:	1000	960	920	890	860
	energy, ft-lb:	325	300	275	260	240
Federal 147 Hi-Shok JHP	velocity, fps:	980	950	930	900	880
	energy, ft-lb:	310	295	285	265	255
Federal 147 FMJ FN	velocity, fps:	960	930	910	890	870
	energy, ft-lb:	295	280	270	260	250
Federal 147 TMJ TMF Primer	velocity, fps:	960	940	910	890	870
	energy, ft-lb:	300	285	270	260	245
Hornady 115 JHP/XTP	velocity, fps:	1155		1047		971
	energy, ft-lb:	341		280		241
Hornady 124 JHP/XTP	velocity, fps:	1110		1030		971
	energy, ft-lb:	339		292		259
Hornady 124 TAP-FPD	velocity, fps:	1100		1028		967
	energy, ft-lb:	339		291		257
Hornady 147 JHP/XTP	velocity, fps:	975		935		899
	energy, ft-lb:	310		285		264
Hornady 147 TAP-FPD	velocity, fps:	975		935		899
	energy, ft-lb:	310		285		264
Lapua 116 FMJ	velocity, fps:	365		319*		290*
	energy, ft-lb:	500		381*		315*
Lapua 120 FMJ CEPP Super	velocity, fps:	360		316*		288*
	energy, ft-lb:	505		390*		324*
Lapua 120 FMJ CEPP Extra	velocity, fps:	360		316*		288*
	energy, ft-lb:	505		390*		324*
Lapua 123 HP Megashock	velocity, fps:	355		311*		284*
	energy, ft-lb:	504		388*		322*
Lapua 123 FMJ	velocity, fps:	320		292*		272*
	energy, ft-lb:	410		342*		295*
Lapua 123 FMJ Combat	velocity, fps:	355		315*		289*
	energy, ft-lb:	504		397*		333*
Magtech 115 JHP +P	velocity, fps:	1246		1137		1056
	energy, ft-lb:	397		330		285
Magtech 115 FMC	velocity, fps:	1135		1027		961
	energy, ft-lb:	330		270		235
Magtech 115 JHP	velocity, fps:	1155		1047		971
	energy, ft-lb:	340		280		240
Magtech 124 FMC	velocity, fps:	1109		1030		971
	energy, ft-lb:	339		292		259
Norma 84 Lead Free Frangible (Geco brand)	velocity, fps:	1411				
	energy, ft-lb:	371				
Norma 124 FMJ (Geco brand)	velocity, fps:	1120				
	energy, fps:	341				
Norma 123 FMJ	velocity, fps:	1099	1032	980		899
	energy, ft-lb:	331	292	263		221

Centerfire Handgun Ballistics

9MM LUGER TO .380 AUTO

CARTRIDGE BULLET	RANGE, YARDS:	0	25	50	75	100
'Norma 123 FMJ	velocity, fps:	1280	1170	1086		972
	energy, ft-lb:	449	375	323		259
PMC 75 Non-Toxic Frangible	velocity, fps:	1350	1240	1154	1088	1035
	energy, ft-lb:	303				
PMC 95 SFHP	velocity, fps:	1250	1239	1228	1217	1207
	energy, ft-lb:	330				
PMC 115 FMJ	velocity, fps:	1157	1100	1053	1013	979
	energy, ft-lb:	344				
PMC 115 JHP	velocity, fps:	1167	1098	1044	999	961
	energy, ft-lb:	350				
PMC 124 SFHP	velocity, fps:	1090	1043	1003	969	939
	energy, ft-lb:	327				
PMC 124 FMJ	velocity, fps:	1110	1059	1017	980	949
	energy, ft-lb:	339				
PMC 124 LRN	velocity, fps:	1050	1006	969	937	908
	energy, ft-lb:	304				
PMC 147 FMJ	velocity, fps:	980	965	941	919	900
	enerby, ft-lb:	310				
PMC 147 SFHP	velocity, fps:	velocity and energy figures not available				
Rem. 101 Lead Free Frangible	velocity, fps:	1220		1092		1004
	energy, ft-lb:	334		267		226
Rem. 115 FN Enclosed Base	velocity, fps:	1135		1041		973
	energy, ft-lb:	329		277		242
Rem. 115 Metal Case	velocity, fps:	1135		1041		973
	energy, ft-lb:	329		277		242
Rem. 115 JHP	velocity, fps:	1155		1047		971
	energy, ft-lb:	341		280		241
Rem. 115 JHP +P	velocity, fps:	1250		1113		1019
	energy, ft-lb:	399		316		265
Rem. 124 JHP	velocity, fps:	1120		1028		960
	energy, ft-lb:	346		291		254
Rem. 124 FNEB	velocity, fps:	1100		1030		971
	energy, ft-lb:	339		292		252
Rem. 124 BJHP	velocity, fps:	1125		1031		963
	energy, ft-lb:	349		293		255
Rem. 124 BJHP +P	velocity, fps:	1180		1089		1021
	energy, ft-lb:	384		327		287
Rem. 124 Metal Case	velocity, fps:	1110		1030		971
	energy, ft-lb:	339		292		259
Rem. 147 JHP subsonic	velocity, fps:	990		941		900
	energy, ft-lb:	320		289		264
Rem. 147 BJHP	velocity, fps:	990		941		900
	energy, ft-lb:	320		289		264
Speer 90 Frangible	velocity, fps:	1350		1132		1001
	energy, ft-lb:	364		256		200
Speer 115 JHP Blazer	velocity, fps:	1145		1024		943
	energy, ft-lb:	335		268		227
Speer 115 FMJ Blazer	velocity, fps:	1145		1047		971
	energy, ft-lb:	341		280		241
Speer 115 FMJ	velocity, fps:	1200		1060		970
	energy, ft-lb:	368		287		240
Speer 115 Gold Dot HP	velocity, fps:	1200		1047		971
	energy, ft-lb:	341		280		241
Speer 124 FMJ Blazer	velocity, fps:	1090		989		917
	energy, ft-lb:	327		269		231
Speer 124 FMJ	velocity, fps:	1090		987		913
	energy, ft-lb:	327		268		230
Speer 124 TMJ-CF (and Blazer)	velocity, fps:	1090		989		917
	energy, ft-lb:	327		269		231
Speer 124 Gold Dot HP	velocity, fps:	1150		1030		948
	energy, ft-lb:	367		292		247
Speer 124 Gold Dot HP+P	velocity, ft-lb:	1220		1085		996
	energy, ft-lb:	410		324		273

CARTRIDGE BULLET	RANGE, YARDS:	0	25	50	75	100
Speer 147 TMJ Blazer	velocity, fps:	950		912		879
	energy, ft-lb:	295		272		252
Speer 147 TMJ	velocity, fps:	985		943		906
	energy, ft-lb:	317		290		268
Speer 147 TMJ-CF (and Blazer)	velocity, fps:	985		960		924
	energy, ft-lb:	326		300		279
Speer 147 Gold Dot	velocity, fps:	985		960		924
	energy, ft-lb:	326		300		279
Win. 105 Jacketed FP	velocity, fps:	1200		1074		989
	energy, ft-lb:	336		269		228
Win. 115 Silvertip HP	velocity, fps:	1225		1095		1007
	energy, ft-lb:	383		306		259
Win. 115 Jacketed HP	velocity, fps:	1225		1095		
	energy, ft-lb:	383		306		
Win. 115 FMJ	velocity, fps:	1190		1071		
	energy, ft-lb:	362		293		
Win. 115 EB WinClean	velocity, fps:	1190		1088		
	energy, ft-lb:	362		302		
Win. 124 FMJ	velocity, fps:	1140		1050		
	energy, ft-lb:	358		303		
Win. 124 EB WinClean	velocity, fps:	1130		1049		
	energy, ft-lb:	352		303		
Win. 147 FMJ FN	velocity, fps:	990		945		
	energy, ft-lb:	320		292		
Win. 147 SXT	velocity, fps:	990		947		909
	energy, ft-lb:	320		293		270
Win. 147 Silvertip HP	velocity, fps:	1010		962		921
	energy, ft-lb:	333		302		277
Win. 147 JHP	velocity, fps:	990		945		
	energy, ft-lb:	320		291		
Win. 147 EB WinClean	velocity, fps:	990		945		
	energy, ft-lb:	320		291		

9 x 23 Winchester

Win. 124 Jacketed FP	velocity, fps:	1460		1308		
	energy, ft-lb:	587		471		
Win. 125 Silvertip HP	velocity, fps:	1450		1249		1103
	energy, ft-lb:	583		433		338

.38 S&W

Rem. 146 LRN	velocity, fps:	685		650		620
	energy, ft-lb:	150		135		125
Win. 145 LRN	velocity, fps:	685		650		620
	energy, ft-lb:	150		135		125

.38 Short Colt

Rem. 125 LRN	velocity, fps:	730		685		645
	energy, ft-lb:	150		130		115

.38 Long Colt

Black Hills 158 RNL	velocity, fps:	650				
	energy, ft-lb:					

.380 Auto

Black Hills 90 JHP	velocity, fps:	1000				
	energy, ft-lb:	200				
Black Hills 95 FMJ	velocity, fps:	950				
	energy, ft-lb:	190				
Federal 90 Hi-Shok JHP	velocity, fps:	1000	940	890	840	800
	energy, ft-lb:	200	175	160	140	130
Federal 90 Hydra-Shok JHP	velocity, fps:	1000	940	890	840	800
	energy, ft-lb:	200	175	160	140	130
Federal 95 FMJ	velocity, fps:	960	910	870	830	790
	energy, ft-lb:	190	175	160	145	130

CARTRIDGE BULLET	RANGE, YARDS:	0	25	50	75	100
Hornady 90 JHP/XTP	velocity, fps:	1000		902		823
	energy, ft-lb:	200		163		135
Magtech 85 JHP + P	velocity, fps:	1082		999		936
	energy, ft-lb:	221		188		166
Magtech 95 FMC	velocity, fps:	951		861		781
	energy, ft-lb:	190		156		128
Magtech 95 JHP	velocity, fps:	951		861		781
	energy, ft-lb:	190		156		128
PMC 77 NT/FR	velocity, fps:	1200	1095	1012	932	874
	energy, ft-lb:	223				
PMC 90 FMJ	velocity, fps:	910	872	838	807	778
	energy, ft-lb:	165				
PMC 90 JHP	velocity, fps:	917	878	844	812	782
	energy, ft-lb:	168				
PMC 95 SFHP	velocity, fps:	925	884	847	813	783
	energy, ft-lb:	180				
Rem. 88 JHP	velocity, fps:	990		920		868
	energy, ft-lb:	191		165		146
Rem. 95 FNEB	velocity, fps:	955		865		785
	energy, ft-lb:	190		160		130
Rem. 95 Metal Case	velocity, fps:	955		865		785
	energy, ft-lb:	190		160		130
Rem. 102 BJHP	velocity, fps:	940		901		866
	energy, ft-lb:	200		184		170
Speer 88 JHP Blazer	velocity, fps:	950		920		870
	energy, ft-lb:	195		164		148
Speer 90 Gold Dot	velocity, fps:	990		907		842
	energy, ft-lb:	196		164		142
Speer 95 TMJ Blazer	velocity, fps:	945		865		785
	energy, ft-lb:	190		160		130
Speer 95 TMJ	velocity, fps:	950		877		817
	energy, ft-lb:	180		154		133
Win. 85 Silvertip HP	velocity, fps:	1000		921		860
	energy, ft-lb:	189		160		140
Win. 95 SXT	velocity, fps:	955		889		835
	energy, ft-lb:	192		167		147
Win. 95 FMJ	velocity, fps:	955		865		
	energy, ft-lb:	190		160		
Win. 95 EB WinClean	velocity, fps:	955		881		
	energy, ft-lb:	192		164		

.38 Special

CARTRIDGE BULLET	RANGE, YARDS:	0	25	50	75	100
Black Hills 125 JHP +P	velocity, fps:	1050				
	energy, ft-lb:	306				
Black Hills 148 HBWC	velocity, fps:	700				
	energy, ft-lb:					
Black Hills 158 SWC	velocity, fps:	850				
	energy, ft-lb:					
Black Hills 158 CNL	velocity, fps:	800				
	energy, ft-lb:					
Federal 110 Hydra-Shok JHP	velocity, fps:	1000	970	930	910	880
	energy, ft-lb:	245	225	215	200	190
Federal 110 Hi-Shok JHP +P	velocity, fps:	1000	960	930	900	870
	energy, ft-lb:	240	225	210	195	185
Federal 125 Nyclad HP	velocity, fps:	830	780	730	690	650
	energy, ft-lb:	190	170	150	130	115
Federal 125 Hi-Shok JSP +P	velocity, fps:	950	920	900	880	860
	energy, ft-lb:	250	235	225	215	205
Federal 125 Hi-Shok JHP +P	velocity, fps:	950	920	900	880	860
	energy, ft-lb:	250	235	225	215	205
Federal 125 Nyclad HP +P	velocity, fps:	950	920	900	880	860
	energy, ft-lb:	250	235	225	215	205
Federal 129 Hydra-Shok JHP+P	velocity, fps:	950	930	910	890	870
	energy, ft-lb:	255	245	235	225	215
Federal 130 FMJ	velocity, fps:	950	920	890	870	840
	energy, ft-lb:	260	245	230	215	205
Federal 148 LWC Match	velocity, fps:	710	670	630	600	560
	energy, ft-lb:	165	150	130	115	105
Federal 158 LRN	velocity, fps:	760	740	720	710	690
	energy, ft-lb:	200	190	185	175	170
Federal 158 LSWC	velocity, fps:	760	740	720	710	690
	energy, ft-lb:	200	190	185	175	170
Federal 158 Nyclad RN	velocity, fps:	760	740	720	710	690
	energy, ft-lb:	200	190	185	175	170
Federal 158 SWC HP +P	velocity, fps:	890	870	860	840	820
	energy, ft-lb:	280	265	260	245	235
Federal 158 LSWC +P	velocity, fps:	890	870	860	840	820
	energy, ft-lb:	270	265	260	245	235
Federal 158 Nyclad SWC-HP+P	velocity, fps:	890	870	860	840	820
	energy, ft-lb:	270	265	260	245	235
Hornady 125 JHP/XTP	velocity, fps:	900		856		817
	energy, ft-lb:	225		203		185
Hornady 140 JHP/XTP	velocity, fps:	825		790		757
	energy, ft-lb:	212		194		178
Hornady 140 Cowboy	velocity, fps:	800		767		735
	energy, ft-lb:	199		183		168
Hornady 148 HBWC	velocity, fps:	800		697		610
	energy, ft-lb:	210		160		122
Hornady 158 JHP/XPT	velocity, fps:	800		765		731
	energy, ft-lb:	225		205		188
Lapua 123 HP Megashock	velocity, fps:	355		311*		284*
	energy, ft-lb:	504		388*		322*
Lapua 148 LWC	velocity, fps:	230		203*		181*
	energy, ft-lb:	254		199*		157*
Lapua 150 SJFN	velocity, fps:	325		301*		283*
	energy, ft-lb:	512		439*		388*
Lapua 158 FMJLF	velocity, fps:	255		243*		232*
	energy, ft-lb:	332		301*		275*
Lapua 158 LRN	velocity, fps:	255		243*		232*
	energy, ft-lb:	332		301*		275*
Magtech 125 JHP +P	velocity, fps:	1017		971		931
	energy, ft-lb:	287		262		241
Magtech 148 LWC	velocity, fps:	710		634		566
	energy, ft-lb:	166		132		105
Magtech 158 LRN	velocity, fps:	755		728		693
	energy, ft-lb:	200		183		168
Magtech 158 LFN	velocity, fps:	800		776		753
	energy, ft-lb:	225		211		199
Magtech 158 SJHP	velocity, fps:	807		779		753
	energy, ft-lb:	230		213		199
Magtech 158 LSWC	velocity, fps:	755		721		689
	energy, ft-lb:	200		182		167
Magtech 158 FMC-Flat	velocity, fps:	807		779		753
	energy, ft-lb:	230		213		199
PMC 85 Non-Toxic Frangible	velocity, fps:	1275	1181	1109	1052	1006
	energy, ft-lb:	307				
PMC 110 SFHP +P	velocity, fps:	velocity and energy figures not available				
PMC 125 SFHP +P	velocity, fps:	950	918	889	863	838
	energy, ft-lb:	251				
PMC 125 JHP +P	velocity, fps:	974	938	906	878	851
	energy, ft-lb:	266				
PMC 132 FMJ	velocity, fps:	841	820	799	780	761
	energy, ft-lb:	206				
PMC 148 LWC	velocity, fps:	728	694	662	631	602
	energy, ft-lb:	175				
PMC 158 LRN	velocity, fps:	820	801	783	765	749
	energy, ft-lb:	235				

Centerfire Handgun Ballistics

.38 SPECIAL TO .357 MAGNUM

CARTRIDGE BULLET	RANGE, YARDS:	0	25	50	75	100
PMC 158 JSP	velocity, fps:	835	816	797	779	762
	energy, ft-lb:	245				
PMC 158 LFP	velocity, fps:	800		761		725
	energy, ft-lb:	225		203		185
Rem. 101 Lead Free Frangible	velocity, fps:	950		896		850
	energy, ft-lb:	202		180		162
Rem. 110 SJHP	velocity, fps:	950		890		840
	energy, ft-lb:	220		194		172
Rem. 110 SJHP +P	velocity, fps:	995		926		871
	energy, ft-lb:	242		210		185
Rem. 125 SJHP +P	velocity, ft-lb:	945		898		858
	energy, ft-lb:	248		224		204
Rem. 125 BJHP	velocity, fps:	975		929		885
	energy, ft-lb:	264		238		218
Rem. 125 FNEB	velocity, fps:	850		822		796
	energy, ft-lb:	201		188		176
Rem. 125 FNEB +P	velocity, fps:	975		935		899
	energy, ft-lb:	264		242		224
Rem. 130 Metal Case	velocity, fps:	950		913		879
	energy, ft-lb:	261		240		223
Rem. 148 LWC Match	velocity, fps:	710		634		566
	energy, ft-lb:	166		132		105
Rem. 158 LRN	velocity, fps:	755		723		692
	energy, ft-lb:	200		183		168
Rem. 158 SWC +P	velocity, fps:	890		855		823
	energy, ft-lb:	278		257		238
Rem. 158 SWC	velocity, fps:	755		723		692
	energy, ft-lb:	200		183		168
Rem. 158 LHP +P	velocity, fps:	890		855		823
	energy, ft-lb:	278		257		238
Speer 125 JHP +P Blazer	velocity, fps:	945		898		858
	energy, ft-lb:	248		224		204
Speer 125 Gold Dot +P	velocity, fps:	945		898		858
	energy, ft-lb:	248		224		204
Speer 158 TMJ +P (and Blazer)	velocity, fps:	900		852		818
	energy, ft-lb:	278		255		235
Speer 158 LRN Blazer	velocity, fps:	755		723		692
	energy, ft-lb:	200		183		168
Speer 158 Trail Blazer LFN	velocity, fps:	800		761		725
	energy, ft-lb:	225		203		184
Speer 158 TMJ-CF +P	velocity, fps:	900		852		818
(and Blazer)	energy, ft-lb:	278		255		235
Win. 110 Silvertip HP	velocity, fps:	945		894		850
	energy, ft-lb:	218		195		176
Win. 110 Jacketed FP	velocity, fps:	975		906		849
	energy, ft-lb:	232		201		176
Win. 125 Jacketed HP	velocity, fps:	945		898		
	energy, ft-lb:	248		224		
Win. 125 Jacketed HP +P	velocity, fps:	945		898		858
	energy, ft-lb:	248		224		204
Win. 125 Jacketed FP	velocity, fps:	850		804		
	energy, ft-lb:	201		179		
Win. 125 Silvertip HP + P	velocity, fps:	945		898		858
	energy, ft-lb:	248		224		204
Win. 125 JFP WinClean	velocity, fps:	775		742		
	energy, ft-lb:	167		153		
Win. 130 FMJ	velocity, fps:	800		765		
	energy, ft-lb:	185		169		
Win. 130 SXT +P	velocity, fps:	925		887		852
	energy, ft-lb:	247		227		210
Win. 148 LWC Super Match	velocity, fps:	710		634		566
	energy, ft-lb:	166		132		105
Win. 150 Lead	velocity, fps:	845		812		
	energy, ft-lb:	238		219		
Win. 158 Lead	velocity, fps:	800		761		725
	energy, ft-lb:	225		203		185
Win. 158 LRN	velocity, fps:	755		723		693
	energy, ft-lb:	200		183		168
Win. 158 LSWC	velocity, fps:	755		721		689
	energy, ft-lb:	200		182		167
Win. 158 LSWC HP +P	velocity, fps:	890		855		823
	energy, ft-lb:	278		257		238

.38-40

CARTRIDGE BULLET	RANGE, YARDS:	0	25	50	75	100
Black Hills 180 FPL	velocity, fps:	800				
	energy, ft-lb:					

.38 Super

CARTRIDGE BULLET	RANGE, YARDS:	0	25	50	75	100
Federal 130 FMJ +P	velocity, fps:	1200	1140	1100	1050	1020
	energy, ft-lb:	415	380	350	320	300
PMC 115 JHP	velocity, fps:	1116	1052	1001	959	923
	energy, ft-lb:	318				
PMC 130 FMJ	velocity, fps:	1092	1038	994	957	924
	energy, ft-lb:	348				
Rem. 130 Metal Case	velocity, fps:	1215		1099		1017
	energy, ft-lb:	426		348		298
Win. 125 Silvertip HP +P	velocity, fps:	1240		1130		1050
	energy, ft-lb:	427		354		306
Win. 130 FMJ +P	velocity, fps:	1215		1099		
	energy, ft-lb:	426		348		

.357 Sig

CARTRIDGE BULLET	RANGE, YARDS:	0	25	50	75	100
Federal 125 FMJ	velocity, fps:	1350	1270	1190	1130	1080
	energy, ft-lb:	510	445	395	355	325
Federal 125 JHP	velocity, fps:	1350	1270	1190	1130	1080
	energy, ft-lb:	510	445	395	355	325
Federal 150 JHP	velocity, fps:	1130	1080	1030	1000	970
	energy, ft-lb:	420	385	355	330	310
Hornady 124 JHP/XTP	velocity, fps:	1350		1208		1108
	energy, ft-lb:	502		405		338
Hornady 147 JHP/XTP	velocity, fps:	1225		1138		1072
	energy, ft-lb:	490		422		375
PMC 85 Non-Toxic Frangible	velocity, fps:	1480	1356	1245	1158	1092
	energy, ft-lb:	413				
PMC 124 SFHP	velocity, fps:	1350	1263	1190	1132	1083
	energy, ft-lb:	502				
PMC 124 FMJ/FP	velocity, fps:	1350	1242	1158	1093	1040
	energy, ft-lb:	512				
Rem. 104 Lead Free Frangible	velocity, fps:	1400		1223		1094
	energy, ft-lb:	453		345		276
Rem. 125 Metal Case	velocity, fps:	1350		1146		1018
	energy, ft-lb:	506		422		359
Rem. 125 JHP	velocity, fps:	1350		1157		1032
	energy, ft-lb:	506		372		296
Speer 125 TMJ (and Blazer)	velocity, fps:	1350		1177		1057
	energy, ft-lb:	502		381		307
Speer 125 TMJ-CF	velocity, fps:	1350		1177		1057
	energy, ft-lb:	502		381		307
Speer 125 Gold Dot	velocity, fps:	1375		1203		1079
	energy, ft-lb:	525		402		323
Win. 105 JFP	velocity, fps:	1370		1179		1050
	energy, ft-lb	438		324		257
Win. 125 FMJ FN	velocity, fps:	1350		1185		
	energy, ft-lb	506		390		

.357 Magnum

CARTRIDGE BULLET	RANGE, YARDS:	0	25	50	75	100
Black Hills 125 JHP	velocity, fps:	1500				
	energy, ft-lb:	625				
Black Hills 158 CNL	velocity, fps:	800				

BALLISTICS

Centerfire Handgun Ballistics

.357 MAGNUM TO .40 S&W

CARTRIDGE BULLET	RANGE, YARDS:	0	25	50	75	100
	energy, ft-lb:					
Black Hills 158 SWC	velocity, fps:	1050				
	energy, ft-lb:					
Black Hills 158 JHP	velocity, fps:	1250				
	energy, ft-lb:					
Federal 110 Hi-Shok JHP	velocity, fps:	1300	1180	1090	1040	990
	energy, ft-lb:	410	340	290	260	235
Federal 125 Hi-Shok JHP	velocity, fps:	1450	1350	1240	1160	1100
	energy, ft-lb:	580	495	430	370	335
Federal 130 Hydra-Shok JHP	velocity, fps:	1300	1210	1130	1070	1020
	energy, ft-lb:	490	420	370	330	300
Federal 158 Hi-Shok JSP	velocity, fps:	1240	1160	1100	1060	1020
	energy, ft-lb:	535	475	430	395	365
Federal 158 JSP	velocity, fps:	1240	1160	1100	1060	1020
	energy, ft-lb:	535	475	430	395	365
Federal 158 LSWC	velocity, fps:	1240	1160	1100	1060	1020
	energy, ft-lb:	535	475	430	395	365
Federal 158 Hi-Shok JHP	velocity, fps:	1240	1160	1100	1060	1020
	energy, ft-lb:	535	475	430	395	365
Federal 158 Hydra-Shok JHP	velocity, fps:	1240	1160	1100	1060	1020
	energy, ft-lb:	535	475	430	395	365
Federal 180 Hi-Shok JHP	velocity, fps:	1090	1030	980	930	890
	energy, ft-lb:	475	425	385	350	320
Federal 180 Castcore	velocity, fps:	1250	1200	1160	1120	1080
	energy, ft-lb:	625	575	535	495	465
Hornady 125 JHP/XTP	velocity, fps:	1500		1314		1166
	energy, ft-lb:	624		479		377
Hornady 125 JFP/XTP	velocity, fps:	1500		1311		1161
	energy, ft-lb:	624		477		374
Hornady 140 Cowboy	velocity, fps:	800		767		735
	energy, ft-lb:	199		183		168
Hornady 140 JHP/XTP	velocity, fps:	1400		1249		1130
	energy, ft-lb:	609		485		397
Hornady 158 JHP/XTP	velocity, fps:	1250		1150		1073
	energy, ft-lb:	548		464		404
Hornady 158 JFP/XTP	velocity, fps:	1250		1147		1068
	energy, ft-lb:	548		461		400
Lapua 150 FMJ CEPP Super	velocity, fps:	370		527*		303*
	energy, ft-lb:	664		527*		445*
Lapua 150 SJFN	velocity, fps:	385		342*		313*
	energy, ft-lb:	719		569*		476*
Lapua 158 SJHP	velocity, fps:	470		408*		359*
	energy, ft-lb:	1127		850*		657*
Magtech 158 SJSP	velocity, fps:	1235		1104		1015
	energy, ft-lb:	535		428		361
Magtech 158 SJHP	velocity, fps:	1235		1104		1015
	energy, ft-lb:	535		428		361
PMC 85 Non-Toxic Frangible	velocity, fps:	1325	1219	1139	1076	1025
	energy, ft-lb:	331				
PMC 125 JHP	velocity, fps:	1194	1117	1057	1008	967
	energy, ft-lb:	399				
PMC 150 JHP	velocity, fps:	1234	1156	1093	1042	1000
	energy, ft-lb:	512				
PMC 150 SFHP	velocity, fps:	1205	1129	1069	1020	980
	energy, ft-lb:	484				
PMC 158 JSP	velocity, fps:	1194	1122	1063	1016	977
	energy, ft-lb:	504				
PMC 158 LFP	velocity, fps:	800		761		725
	energy, ft-lb:	225		203		185
Rem. 110 SJHP	velocity, fps:	1295		1094		975
	energy, ft-lb:	410		292		232
Rem. 125 SJHP	velocity, fps:	1450		1240		1090
	energy, ft-lb:	583		427		330
Rem. 125 BJHP	velocity, fps:	1220		1095		1009
	energy, ft-lb:	413		333		283
Rem. 125 FNEB	velocity, fps:	1450		1240		1090
	energy, ft-lb:	583		427		330
Rem. 158 SJHP	velocity, fps:	1235		1104		1015
	energy, ft-lb:	535		428		361
Rem. 158 SP	velocity, fps:	1235		1104		1015
	energy, ft-lb:	535		428		361
Rem. 158 SWC	velocity, fps:	1235		1104		1015
	energy, ft-lb:	535		428		361
Rem. 165 JHP Core-Lokt	velocity, fps:	1290		1189		1108
	energy, ft-lb:	610		518		450
Rem. 180 SJHP	velocity, fps:	1145		1053		985
	energy, ft-lb:	542		443		388
Speer 125 Gold Dot	velocity, fps:	1450		1240		1090
	energy, ft-lb:	583		427		330
Speer 158 JHP Blazer	velocity, fps:	1150		1104		1015
	energy, ft-lb:	535		428		361
Speer 158 Gold Dot	velocity, fps:	1235		1104		1015
	energy, ft-lb:	535		428		361
Speer 170 Gold Dot SP	velocity, fps:	1180		1089		1019
	energy, ft-lb:	525		447		392
Win. 110 JFP	velocity, fps:	1275		1105		998
	energy, ft-lb:	397		298		243
Win. 110 JHP	velocity, fps:	1295		1095		
	energy, ft-lb:	410		292		
Win. 125 JFP WinClean	velocity, fps:	1370		1183		
	energy, ft-lb:	521		389		
Win. 145 Silvertip HP	velocity, fps:	1290		1155		1060
	energy, ft-lb:	535		428		361
Win. 158 JHP	velocity, fps:	1235		1104		1015
	energy, ft-lb:	535		428		361
Win. 158 JSP	velocity, fps:	1235		1104		1015
	energy, ft-lb:	535		428		361
Win. 180 Partition Gold	velocity, fps:	1180		1088		1020
	energy, ft-lb:	557		473		416

.40 S&W

CARTRIDGE BULLET	RANGE, YARDS:	0	25	50	75	100
Black Hills 155 JHP	velocity, fps:	1150				
	energy, ft-lb:	450				
Black Hills 165 EXP JHP	velocity, fps:	1150 (2005: 1100)				
	energy, ft-lb:	483				
Black Hills 180 JHP	velocity, fps:	1000				
	energy, ft-lb:	400				
Black Hills 180 JHP	velocity, fps:	1000				
	energy, ft-lb:	400				
Federal 135 Hydra-Shok JHP	velocity, fps:	1190	1050	970	900	850
	energy, ft-lb:	420	330	280	245	215
Federal 155 FMJ Ball	velocity, fps:	1140	1080	1030	990	960
	energy, ft-lb:	445	400	365	335	315
Federal 155 Hi-Shok JHP	velocity, fps:	1140	1080	1030	990	950
	energy, ft-lb:	445	400	365	335	315
Federal 155 Hydra-Shok JHP	velocity, fps:	1140	1080	1030	990	950
	energy, ft-lb:	445	400	365	335	315
Federal 165 EFMJ	velocity, fps:	1190	1060	970	905	850
	energy, ft-lb:	520	410	345	300	265
Federal 165 FMJ	velocity, fps:	1050	1020	990	960	935
	energy, ft-lb:	405	380	355	335	320
Federal 165 FMJ Ball	velocity, fps:	980	950	920	900	880
	energy, ft-lb:	350	330	310	295	280
Federal 165 Hydra-Shok JHP	velocity, fps:	980	950	930	910	890
	energy, ft-lb:	350	330	315	300	290
Federal 180 High Antim. Lead	velocity, fps:	990	960	930	910	890
	energy, ft-lb:	390	365	345	330	315

BALLISTICS

Centerfire Handgun Ballistics

.40 S&W TO .41 REMINGTON MAGNUM

CARTRIDGE BULLET	RANGE, YARDS:	0	25	50	75	100
Federal 180 TMJ TMF Primer	velocity, fps:	990	960	940	910	890
	energy, ft-lb:	390	370	350	330	315
Federal 180 FMJ Ball	velocity, fps:	990	960	940	910	890
	energy, ft-lb:	390	370	350	330	315
Federal 180 Hi-Shok JHP	velocity, fps:	990	960	930	910	890
	energy, ft-lb:	390	365	345	330	315
Federal 180 Hydra-Shok JHP	velocity, fps:	990	960	930	910	890
	energy, ft-lb:	390	365	345	330	315
Hornady 155 JHP/XTP	velocity, fps:	1180		1061		980
	energy, ft-lb:	479		387		331
Hornady 155 TAP-FPD	velocity, fps:	1180		1061		980
	energy, ft-lb:	470		387		331
Hornady 180 JHP/XTP	velocity, fps:	950		903		862
	energy, ft-lb:	361		326		297
Hornady 180 TAP-FPD	velocity, fps:	950		903		862
	energy, ft-lb:	361		326		297
Magtech 155 JHP	velocity, fps:	1025		1118		1052
	energy, ft-lb:	500		430		381
Magtech 180 JHP	velocity, fps:	990		933		886
	energy, ft-lb:	390		348		314
Magtech 180 FMC	velocity, fps:	990		933		886
	energy, ft-lb:	390		348		314
PMC 115 Non-Toxic Frangible	velocity, fps:	1350	1240	1154	1088	1035
	energy, ft-lb:	465				
PMC 155 SFHP	velocity, fps:	1160	1092	1039	994	957
	energy, ft-lb:	463				
PMC 165 JHP	velocity, fps:	1040	1002	970	941	915
	energy, ft-lb:	396				
PMC 165 FMJ	velocity, fps:	1010	977	948	922	899
	energy, ft-lb:	374				
PMC 180 FMJ/FP	velocity, fps:	985	957	931	908	885
	energy, ft-lb:	388				
PMC 180 SFHP	velocity, fps:	985	958	933	910	889
	energy, ft-lb:	388				
Rem. 141 Lead Free Frangible	velocity, fps:	1135		1056		996
	energy, ft-lb:	403		349		311
Rem. 155 JHP	velocity, fps:	1205		1095		1017
	energy, ft-lb:	499		413		356
Rem. 165 BJHP	velocity, fps:	1150		1040		964
	energy, ft-lb:	485		396		340
Rem. 180 JHP	velocity, fps:	1015		960		914
	energy, ft-lb:	412		368		334
Rem. 180 FN Enclosed Base	velocity, fps:	985		936		893
	energy, ft-lb:	388		350		319
Rem. 180 Metal Case	velocity, fps:	985		936		893
	energy, ft-lb:	388		350		319
Rem. 180 BJHP	velocity, fps:	1015		960		914
	energy, ft-lb:	412		368		334
Speer 105 Frangible	velocity, fps:	1380		1128		985
	energy, ft-lb:	444		297		226
Speer 155 TMJ Blazer	velocity, fps:	1175		1047		963
	energy, ft-lb:	475		377		319
Speer 155 TMJ	velocity, fps:	1200		1065		976
	energy, ft-lb:	496		390		328
Speer 155 Gold Dot	velocity, fps:	1200		1063		974
	energy, ft-lb:	496		389		326
Speer 165 TMJ Blazer	velocity, fps:	1100		1006		938
	energy, ft-lb:	443		371		321
Speer 165 TMJ	velocity, fps:	1150		1040		964
	energy, ft-lb:	484		396		340
Speer 165 Gold Dot	velocity, fps:	1150		1043		966
	energy, ft-lb:	485		399		342
Speer 180 HP Blazer	velocity, fps:	985		951		909
	energy, ft-lb:	400		361		330
Speer 180 FMJ Blazer	velocity, fps:	1000		937		886
	energy, ft-lb:	400		351		313
Speer 180 FMJ	velocity, fps:	1000		951		909
	energy, ft-lb:	400		361		330
Speer 180 TMJ-CF (and Blazer)	velocity, fps:	1000		951		909
	energy, ft-lb:	400		361		330
Speer 180 Gold Dot	velocity, fps:	1025		957		902
	energy, ft-lb:	420		366		325
Win. 140 JFP	velocity, fps:	1155		1039		960
	energy, ft-lb:	415		336		286
Win. 155 Silvertip HP	velocity, fps:	1205		1096		1018
	energy, ft-lb	500		414		357
Win. 165 SXT	velocity, fps:	1130		1041		977
	energy, ft-lb:	468		397		349
Win. 165 FMJ FN	velocity, fps:	1060		1001		
	energy, ft-lb:	412		367		
Win. 165 EB WinClean	velocity, fps:	1130		1054		
	energy, ft-lb:	468		407		
Win. 180 JHP	velocity, fps:	1010		954		
	energy, ft-lb:	408		364		
Win. 180 FMJ	velocity, fps:	990		936		
	energy, ft-lb:	390		350		
Win. 180 SXT	velocity, fps:	1010		954		909
	energy, ft-lb:	408		364		330
Win. 180 EB WinClean	velocity, fps:	990		943		
	energy, ft-lb:	392		356		

10 MM AUTO

CARTRIDGE BULLET	RANGE, YARDS:	0	25	50	75	100
Federal 155 Hi-Shok JHP	velocity, fps:	1330	1230	1140	1080	1030
	energy, ft-lb:	605	515	450	400	360
Federal 180 Hi-Shok JHP	velocity, fps:	1030	1000	970	950	920
	energy, ft-lb:	425	400	375	355	340
Federal 180 Hydra-Shok JHP	velocity, fps:	1030	1000	970	950	920
	energy, ft-lb:	425	400	375	355	340
Federal 180 High Antim. Lead	velocity, fps:	1030	1000	970	950	920
	energy, ft-lb:	425	400	375	355	340
Federal 180 FMJ	velocity, fps:	1060	1025	990	965	940
	energy, ft-lb:	400	370	350	330	310
Hornady 155 JHP/XTP	velocity, fps:	1265		1119		1020
	energy, ft-lb:	551		431		358
Hornady 180 JHP/XTP	velocity, fps:	1180		1077		1004
	energy, ft-lb:	556		464		403
Hornady 200 JHP/XTP	velocity, fps:	1050		994		948
	energy, ft-lb:	490		439		399
PMC 115 Non-Toxic Frangible	velocity, fps:	1350	1240	1154	1088	1035
	energy, ft-lb:	465				
PMC 170 JHP	velocity, fps:	1200	1117	1052	1000	958
	energy, ft-lb:	543				
PMC 180 SFHP	velocity, fps:	950	926	903	882	862
	energy, ft-lb:	361				
PMC 200 TC-FMJ	velocity, fps:	1050	1008	972	941	912
	energy, ft-lb:	490				
Rem. 180 Metal Case	velocity, fps:	1150		1063		998
	energy, ft-lb:	529		452		398
Speer 200 TMJ Blazer	velocity, fps:	1050		966		952
	energy, ft-lb:	490		440		402
Win. 175 Silvertip HP	velocity, fps:	1290		1141		1037
	energy, ft-lb:	649		506		418

.41 REMINGTON MAGNUM

CARTRIDGE BULLET	RANGE, YARDS:	0	25	50	75	100
Federal 210 Hi-Shok JHP	velocity, fps:	1300	1210	1130	1070	1030
	energy, ft-lb:	790	680	595	540	495
PMC 210 TCSP	velocity, fps:	1290	1201	1128	1069	1021
	energy, ft-lb:	774				

CARTRIDGE BULLET	RANGE, YARDS:	0	25	50	75	100
PMC 210 JHP	velocity, fps:	1289	1200	1127	1068	1020
	energy, ft-lb:	774				
Rem. 210 SP	velocity, fps:	1300		1162		1062
	energy, ft-lb:	788		630		526
Win. 175 Silvertip HP	velocity, fps:	1250		1120		1029
	energy, ft-lb:	607		488		412
Win. 240 Platinum Tip	velocity, ft-lb:	1250		1151		1075
	energy, ft-lb:	833		706		616

.44 Colt

CARTRIDGE BULLET	RANGE, YARDS:	0	25	50	75	100
Black Hills 230 FPL	velocity, fps:	730				
	energy, ft-lb:					

.44 Russian

CARTRIDGE BULLET	RANGE, YARDS:	0	25	50	75	100
Black Hills 210 FPL	velocity, fps:	650				
	energy, ft-lb:					

.44 Special

CARTRIDGE BULLET	RANGE, YARDS:	0	25	50	75	100
Black Hills 210 FPL	velocity, fps:	700				
	energy, ft-lb:					
Federal 200 SWC HP	velocity, fps:	900	860	830	800	770
	energy, ft-lb:	360	330	305	285	260
Federal 250 CastCore	velocity, fps:	1250	1200	1150	1110	1080
	energy, ft-lb:	865	795	735	685	645
Hornady 180 JHP/XTP	velocity, fps:	1000		935		882
	energy, ft-lb:	400		350		311
Magtech 240 LFN	velocity, fps:	750		722		696
	energy, ft-lb:	300		278		258
PMC 180 JHP	velocity, fps:	980	938	902	869	839
	energy, ft-lb:	383				
PMC 240 SWC-CP	velocity, fps:	764	744	724	706	687
	energy, ft-lb:	311				
PMC 240 LFP	velocity, fps:	750		719		690
	energy, ft-lb:	300		275		253
Rem. 246 LRN	velocity, fps:	755		725		695
	energy, ft-lb:	310		285		265
Speer 200 HP Blazer	velocity, fps:	875		825		780
	energy, ft-lb:	340		302		270
Speer 200 Trail Blazer LFN	velocity, fps:	750		714		680
	energy, ft-lb:	250		226		205
Speer 200 Gold Dot	velocity, fps:	875		825		780
	energy, ft-lb:	340		302		270
Win. 200 Silvertip HP	velocity, fps:	900		860		822
	energy, ft-lb:	360		328		300
Win. 240 Lead	velocity, fps:	750		719		690
	energy, ft-lb	300		275		253
Win. 246 LRN	velocity, fps:	755		725		695
	energy, ft-lb:	310		285		265

.44 Remington Magnum

CARTRIDGE BULLET	RANGE, YARDS:	0	25	50	75	100
Black Hills 240 JHP	velocity, fps:	1260				
	energy, ft-lb:	848				
Black Hills 300 JHP	velocity, fps:	1150				
	energy, ft-lb:	879				
Federal 180 Hi-Shok JHP	velocity, fps:	1610	1480	1370	1270	1180
	energy, ft-lb:	1035	875	750	640	555
Federal 240 Hi-Shok JHP	velocity, fps:	1180	1130	1080	1050	1010
	energy, ft-lb:	740	675	625	580	550
Federal 240 Hydra-Shok JHP	velocity, fps:	1180	1130	1080	1050	1010
	energy, ft-lb:	740	675	625	580	550
Federal 240 JHP	velocity, fps:	1180	1130	1080	1050	1010
	energy, ft-lb:	740	675	625	580	550
Federal 300 CastCore	velocity, fps:	1250	1200	1160	1120	1080
	energy, ft-lb:	1040	960	885	825	775
Hornady 180 JHP/XTP	velocity, fps:	1550		1340		1173
	energy, ft-lb:	960		717		550
Hornady 200 JHP/XTP	velocity, fps:	1500		1284		1128
	energy, ft-lb:	999		732		565
Hornady 240 JHP/XTP	velocity, fps:	1350		1188		1078
	energy, ft-lb:	971		753		619
Hornady 300 JHP/XTP	velocity, fps:	1150		1084		1031
	energy, ft-lb:	881		782		708
Magtech 240 SJSP	velocity, fps:	1180		1081		1010
	energy, ft-lb:	741		632		623
PMC 180 JHP	velocity, fps:	1392	1263	1157	1076	1015
	energy, ft-lb:	772				
PMC 240 JHP	velocity, fps:	1301	1218	1147	1088	1041
	energy, ft-lb:	900				
PMC 240 TC-SP	velocity, fps:	1300	1216	1144	1086	1038
	energy, ft-lb:	900				
PMC 240 SFHP	velocity, fps:	1300	1212	1138	1079	1030
	energy, ft-lb:	900				
PMC 240 LSWC-GCK	velocity, fps:	1225	1143	1077	1025	982
	energy, ft-lb:	806				
Rem. 180 JSP	velocity, fps:	1610		1365		1175
	energy, ft-lb:	1036		745		551
Rem. 210 Gold Dot HP	velocity, fps:	1450		1276		1140
	energy, ft-lb:	980		759		606
Rem. 240 SP	velocity, fps:	1180		1081		1010
	energy, ft-lb:	721		623		543
Rem. 240 SJHP	velocity, fps:	1180		1081		1010
	energy, ft-lb:	721		623		543
Rem. 275 JHP Core-Lokt	velocity, fps:	1235		1142		1070
	energy, ft-lb:	931		797		699
Speer 240 JHP Blazer	velocity, fps:	1200		1092		1015
	energy, ft-lb:	767		636		549
Speer 240 Gold Dot HP	velocity, fps:	1400		1255		1139
	energy, ft-lb:	1044		839		691
Speer 270 Gold Dot SP	velocity, fps:	1250		1142		1060
	energy, ft-lb:	937		781		674
Win. 210 Silvertip HP	velocity, fps:	1250		1106		1010
	energy, ft-lb:	729		570		475
Win. 240 Hollow SP	velocity, fps:	1180		1081		1010
	energy, ft-lb:	741		623		543
Win. 240 JSP	velocity, fps:	1180		1081		
	energy, ft-lb:	741		623		
Win. 250 Partition Gold	velocity, fps:	1230		1132		1057
	energy, ft-lb:	840		711		620
Win. 250 Platinum Tip	velocity, fps:	1250		1148		1070
	energy, ft-lb:	867		732		635

.44-40

CARTRIDGE BULLET	RANGE, YARDS:	0	25	50	75	100
Black Hills 200 RNFP	velocity, fps:	800				
	energy, ft-lb:					
Hornady 205 Cowboy	velocity, fps:	725		697		670
	energy, ft-lb:	239		221		204
Magtech 225 LFN	velocity, fps:	725		703		681
	energy, ft-lb:	281		247		232
PMC 225 LFP	velocity, fps:	725		723		695
	energy, ft-lb:	281		261		242
Win. 225 Lead	velocity, fps:	750		723		695
	energy, ft-lb:	281		261		242

.45 Automatic (ACP)

CARTRIDGE BULLET	RANGE, YARDS:	0	25	50	75	100
Black Hills 185 JHP	velocity, fps:	1000				
	energy, ft-lb:	411				

BALLISTICS

Centerfire Handgun Ballistics

.45 AUTOMATIC (ACP) TO .45 GAP

CARTRIDGE BULLET	RANGE, YARDS:	0	25	50	75	100
Black Hills 200 Match SWC	velocity, fps:	875				
	energy, ft-lb:	340				
Black Hills 230 FMJ	velocity, fps:	850				
	energy, ft-lb:	368				
Black Hills 230 JHP	velocity, fps:	850				
	energy, ft-lb:	368				
Black Hills 230 JHP +P	velocity, fps:	950				
	energy, ft-lb:	460				
Federal 165 Hydra-Shok JHP	velocity, fps:	1060	1020	980	950	920
	energy, ft-lb:	410	375	350	330	310
Federal 165 EFMJ	velocity, fps:	1090	1045	1005	975	942
	energy, ft-lb:	435	400	370	345	325
Federal 185 Hi-Shok JHP	velocity, fps:	950	920	900	880	860
	energy, ft-lb:	370	350	335	315	300
Federal 185 FMJ-SWC Match	velocity, fps:	780	730	700	660	620
	energy, ft-lb:	245	220	200	175	160
Federal 200 Exp. FMJ	velocity, fps:	1030	1000	970	940	920
	energy, ft-lb:	470	440	415	395	375
Federal 230 FMJ	velocity, fps:	850	830	810	790	770
	energy, ft-lb:	370	350	335	320	305
Federal 230 FMJ Match	velocity, fps:	855	835	815	795	775
	energy, ft-lb:	375	355	340	325	305
Federal 230 Hi-Shok JHP	velocity, fps:	850	830	810	790	770
	energy, ft-lb:	370	350	335	320	300
Federal 230 Hydra-Shok JHP	velocity, fps:	850	830	810	790	770
	energy, ft-lb:	370	350	335	320	305
Federal 230 FMJ	velocity, fps:	850	830	810	790	770
	energy, ft-lb:	370	350	335	320	305
Federal 230 TMJ TMF Primer	velocity, fps:	850	830	810	790	770
	energy, ft-lb:	370	350	335	315	305
Hornady 185 JHP/XTP	velocity, fps:	950		880		819
	energy, ft-lb:	371		318		276
Hornady 200 JHP/XTP	velocity, fps:	900		855		815
	energy, ft-lb:	358		325		295
Hornady 200 HP/XTP +P	velocity, fps:	1055		982		925
	energy, ft-lb:	494		428		380
Hornady 200 TAP-FPD	velocity, fps:	1055		982		926
	energy, ft-lbs:	494		428		380
Hornady 230 FMJ/RN	velocity, fps:	850		809		771
	energy, ft-lb:	369		334		304
Hornady 230 FMJ/FP	velocity, fps:	850		809		771
	energy, ft-lb:	369		334		304
Hornady 230 HP/XTP +P	velocity, fps:	950		904		865
	energy, ft-lb:	462		418		382
Hornady 230 TAP-FPD	velocity, fps:	950		908		872
	energy, ft-lb:	461		421		388
Magtech 185 JHP +P	velocity, fps:	1148		1066		1055
	energy, ft-lb:	540		467		415
Magtech 200 LSWC	velocity, fps:	950		910		874
	energy, ft-lb:	401		368		339
Magtech 230 FMC	velociy, fps:	837		800		767
	energy, ft-lb:	356		326		300
Magtech 230 FMC-SWC	velocity, fps:	780		720		660
	energy, ft-lb:	310		265		222
PMC 145 Non-Toxic Frangible	velocity, fps:	1100	1045	999	961	928
	energy, ft-lb:	390				
PMC 185 JHP	velocity, fps:	903	870	839	811	785
	energy, ft-lb:	339				
PMC 200 FMJ-SWC	velocity, fps:	850	818	788	761	734
	energy, ft-lb:	321				
PMC 230 SFHP	velocity, fps:	850	830	811	792	775
	energy, ft-lb:	369				

CARTRIDGE BULLET	RANGE, YARDS:	0	25	50	75	100
PMC 230 FMJ	velocity, fps:	830	809	789	769	749
	energy, ft-lb:	352				
Rem. 175 Lead Free Frangible	velocity, fps:	1020		923		851
	energy, ft-lb:	404		331		281
Rem. 185 JHP	velocity, fps:	1000		939		889
	energy, ft-lb:	411		362		324
Rem. 185 BJHP	velocity, fps:	1015		951		899
	energy, ft-lb:	423		372		332
Rem. 185 BJHP +P	velocity, fps:	1140		1042		971
	energy, ft-lb:	534		446		388
Rem. 185 MC	velocity, fps:	1015		955		907
	energy, ft-lb:	423		375		338
Rem. 230 FN Enclosed Base	velocity, fps:	835		800		767
	energy, ft-lb:	356		326		300
Rem. 230 Metal Case	velocity, fps:	835		800		767
	energy, ft-lb:	356		326		300
Rem. 230 JHP	velocity, fps:	835		800		767
	energy, ft-lb:	356		326		300
Rem. 230 BJHP	velocity, fps:	875		833		795
	energy, ft-lb:	391		355		323
Speer 140 Frangible	velocity, fps:	1200		1029		928
	energy, ft-lb:	448		329		268
Speer 185 Gold Dot	velocity, fps:	1050		956		886
	energy, ft-lb:	453		375		322
Speer 185 TMJ/FN	velocity, fps:	1000		909		839
	energy, ft-lb:	411		339		289
Speer 200 JHP Blazer	velocity, fps:	975		917		860
	energy, ft-lb:	421		372		328
Speer 200 Gold Dot +P	velocity, fps:	1080		994		930
	energy, ft-lb:	518		439		384
Speer 200 TMJ/FN	velocity, fps:	975		897		834
	energy, ft-lb:	422		357		309
Speer 230 FMJ (and Blazer)	velocity, fps:	845		804		775
	energy, ft-lb:	363		329		304
Speer 230 TMJ-CF (and Blazer)	velocity, fps:	845		804		775
	energy, ft-lb:	363		329		304
Speer 230 Gold Dot	velocity, fps:	890		845		805
	energy, ft-lb:	405		365		331
Win. 170 JFP	velocity, fps:	1050		982		928
	energy, ft-lb:	416		364		325
Win. 185 Silvertip HP	velocity, fps:	1000		938		888
	energy, ft-lb:	411		362		324
Win. 185 FMJ FN	velocity, fps:	910		861		
	energy, ft-lb:	340		304		
Win. 185 EB WinClean	velocity, fps:	910		835		
	energy, ft-lb:	340		286		
Win. 230 JHP	velocity, fps:	880		842		
	energy, ft-lb:	396		363		
Win. 230 FMJ	velocity, fps:	835		800		
	energy, ft-lb:	356		326		
Win. 230 SXT	velocity, fps:	880		846		816
	energy, ft-lb:	396		366		340
Win. 230 JHP subsonic	velocity, fps:	880		842		808
	energy, ft-lb:	396		363		334
Win. 230 EB WinClean	velocity, fps:	835		802		
	energy, ft-lb:	356		329		

.45 GAP

CARTRIDGE BULLET	RANGE, YARDS:	0	25	50	75	100
Federal 185 Hydra-Shok JHP	velocity, fps:	1090	1020	970	920	890
And Federal TMJ	energy, ft-lb:	490	430	385	350	320
Federal 230 Hydra-Shok	velocity, fps:	880	870	850	840	820
And Federal FMJ	energy, ft-lb:	395	380	3760	355	345

CARTRIDGE BULLET	RANGE, YARDS:	0	25	50	75	100
Win. 185 STHP	velocity, fps:	1000		938		887
	energy, ft-lb:	411		361		323
Win. 230 JHP	velocity, fps:	880		842		
	energy, ft-lb:	396		363		
Win. 230 EB WinClean	velocity, fps:	875		840		
	energy, ft-lb:	391		360		
Win. 230 FMJ	velocity, fps:	850		814		
	energy, ft-lb:	369		338		

.45 Winchester Magnum

CARTRIDGE BULLET	RANGE, YARDS:	0	25	50	75	100
Win. 260 Partition Gold	velocity, fps:	1200		1105		1033
	energy, ft-lb:	832		705		616
Win. 260 JHP	velocity, fps:	1200		1099		1026
	energy, ft-lb:	831		698		607

.45 Schofield

CARTRIDGE BULLET	RANGE, YARDS:	0	25	50	75	100
Black Hills 180 FNL	velocity, fps:	730				
	energy, ft-lb:					
Black Hills 230 RNFP	velocity, fps:	730				
	energy, ft-lb:					

.45 Colt

CARTRIDGE BULLET	RANGE, YARDS:	0	25	50	75	100
Black Hills 250 RNFP	velocity, fps:	725				
	energy, ft-lb:					
Federal 225 SWC HP	velocity, fps:	900	880	860	840	820
	energy, ft-lb:	405	385	370	355	340
Hornady 255 Cowboy	velocity, fps:	725		692		660
	energy, ft-lb:	298		271		247
Magtech 250 LFN	velocity, fps:	750		726		702
	energy, ft-lb:	312		293		274
PMC 250 LFP	velocity, fps:	800		767		736
	energy, ft-lb:	355		331		309
PMC 300 +P+	velocity, fps:	1250	1192	1144	1102	1066
	energy, ft-lb:	1041				
Rem. 225 SWC	velocity, fps:	960		890		832
	energy, ft-lb:	460		395		346
Rem. 250 RLN	velocity, fps:	860		820		780
	energy, ft-lb:	410		375		340
Speer 200 FMJ Blazer	velocity, fps:	1000		938		889
	energy, ft-lb:	444		391		351
Speer 230 Trail Blazer LFN	velocity, fps:	750		716		684
	energy, ft-lb:	287		262		239
Speer 250 Gold Dot	velocity, fps:	900		860		823
	energy, ft-lb:	450		410		376
Win. 225 Silvertip HP	velocity, fps:	920		877		839
	energy, ft-lb:	423		384		352
Win. 255 LRN	velocity, fps:	860		820		780
	energy, ft-lb:	420		380		345
Win. 250 Lead	velocity, fps:	750		720		692
	energy, ft-lb:	312		288		266

.454 Casull

CARTRIDGE BULLET	RANGE, YARDS:	0	25	50	75	100
Federal 300 Trophy Bonded	velocity, fps:	1630	1540	1450	1380	1300
	energy, ft-lb:	1760	1570	1405	1260	1130
Federal 360 CastCore	velocity, fps:	1500	1435	1370	1310	1255
	energy, ft-lb:	1800	1640	1500	1310	1260
Hornady 240 XTP-MAG	velocity, fps:	1900		1679		1483
	energy, ft-lb:	1923		1502		1172
Hornady 300 XTP-MAG	velocity, fps:	1650		1478		1328
	energy, ft-lb:	1813		1455		1175
Magtech 260 SJSP	velocity, fps:	1800		1577		1383
	energy, ft-lb:	1871		1437		1104
Rem. 300 Core-Lokt Ultra	velocity, fps:	1625		1472		1335
	energy, ft-lb:	1759		1442		1187
Speer 300 Gold Dot HP	velocity, fps:	1625		1477		1343
	energy, ft-lb:	1758		1452		1201
Win. 250 JHP	velocity, fps:	1300		1151		1047
	energy, ft-lb:	938		735		608
Win. 260 Partition Gold	velocity, fps:	1800		1605		1427
	energy, ft-lb:	1871		1485		1176
Win. 260 Platinum Tip	velocity, fps:	1800		1596		1414
	eneryg, ft-lb:	1870		1470		1154
Win. 300 JFP	velocity, fps:	1625		1451		1308
	energy, ft-lb:	1759		1413		1141

.460 Smith & Wesson

CARTRIDGE BULLET	RANGE, YARDS:	0	25	50	75	100
Hornady 200 SST	velocity, fps:	2250		2003		1772
	energy, ft-lb:	2248		1395		1081
Win. 260 Supreme Part. Gold	velocity, fps	2000		1788		1592
	energy, ft-lb	2309		1845		2012

.475 Linebaugh

CARTRIDGE BULLET	RANGE, YARDS:	0	25	50	75	100
Hornady 400 XTP-MAG	velocity, fps:	1300		1179		1093
	energy, ft-lb:	1501		1235		1060

.480 Ruger

CARTRIDGE BULLET	RANGE, YARDS:	0	25	50	75	100
Hornady 325 XTP-MAG	velocity, fps:	1350		1191		1076
	energy, ft-lb:	1315		1023		835
Hornady 400 XTP-MAG	velocity, fps:	1100		1027		971
	energy, ft-lb:	1075		937		838
Speer 275 Gold Dot HP	velocity, fps:	1450		1284		1152
	energy, ft-lb:	1284		1007		810
Speer 325 SP	velocity, fps:	1350		1224		1124
	energy, ft-lb:	1315		1082		912

.50 Action Express

CARTRIDGE BULLET	RANGE, YARDS:	0	25	50	75	100
Speer 300 Gold Dot HP	velocity, fps:	1550		1361		1207
	energy, ft-lb:	1600		1234		970
Speer 325 UCHP	velocity, fps:	1400		1232		1106
	energy, ft-lb:	1414		1095		883

.500 Smith & Wesson

CARTRIDGE BULLET	RANGE, YARDS:	0	25	50	75	100
Hornady 350 XTP Mag	velocity, fps:	1900		1656		1439
	energy, ft-lb:	2805		2131		1610
Hornady 500 FP-XTP	velocity, fps:	1425		1281		1164
	energy, ft-lb:	2254		1823		1505
Win. 350 Super-X	velocity, fps	1400		1231		1106
	energy, ft-lb	1523		1178		951
Win. 400 Platinum Tip	velocity, fps:	1800		1647		1505
	energy, ft-lb:	2877		2409		2012

Directory of Manufacturers & Suppliers

Accurate Arms Co., Inc.
c/o Western Powders, Inc.
P.O. Box 158
Miles City, MT 59301
Phone: 406-234-0422
http://www.accuratepowder.com

Accu-Tek Firearms
EXCEL INDUSTRIES, INC.
4510 Carter Court
Chino, CA 91710
Phone: 909-627-2404
http://www.accu-tekfirearms
.com

Aimpoint, Inc.
14103 Mariah Ct.
Chantilly, VA 20151
Phone: 703-263-9795
http://www.aimpoint.com

Alliant Powder
P.O. Box 6
Radford, VA 24143-0006
Phone: 800-276-9337
http://www.alliantpowder.com

Alpen Outdoors Corp.
10329 Dorset Street, Rancho
Cucamonga, CA 91730
Phone: 909-987-8370
http://www.alpenoutdoor.com

American Derringer Corp.
127 North Lacy Drive
Waco, TX 76715-4640
Phone: 254-799-9111
http://www.amderringer.com

J. G. Anschutz Co.
http://www.anschuetz-sport
.com
See Tristar Sporting Arms

Armalite, Inc.
P.O. Box 299
Geneseo, Il. 61254
Phone: 309-944-6939
Toll Free: 800-336-0184
http://www.armalite.com

ArmsCo
1247 Rand Rd
Des Plaines, IL 60016 US
Phone: 847-768-1000

Austin & Halleck
2150 South 950 East
Provo UT 84606
Phone: 877-543-3256
801-371-0412
http://www.topratedadventures.com

Barnes Bullets
P.O. Box 620
Mona, UT 84645
Phone: 800-574-9200
http://www.barnesbullets.com

Barrett Firearms Mfg.
P.O. Box 1077
Murfreesboro, TN 37133
Phone: 615-896-2938
http://www.barrettrifles.com

B. C. Outdoors
Eldorado Cartridge Corporation
P.O. Box 62173
Boulder City, NV 89006-2173
Phone: 702-293-6285
http://www.pmcammo.com

Berger Bullets, Inc.
4275 N. Palm St.
Fullerton, CA 92835
Phone: 714-447-5456
http://www.bergerbullets.com

Black Hills Ammunition
P.O. Box 3090
Rapid City, SD 57709-3090
Phone: 605-348-5150
http://www.black-hills.com

Bond Arms, Inc.
P.O. Box 1296
Granbury, TX 76048
Phone: 817-573-4445
http://www.bondarms.com

Brenneke of America Ltd.
P.O. Box 1481
Clinton, IA 52733-1481
Phone: 800-753-9733
http://www.brennekeusa.com

Ed. Brown Products, Inc.
P.O. Box 492,
Perry, MO 63462
Phone: 573-565-3261
http://www.edbrown.com

Browning
One Browning Place
Morgan, UT 84050
Phone: 800-333-3288
http://www.browning.com

Brown Precision, Inc.
P.O. Box 270 W.,
Los Molinos, CA 96055
Phone: 530-384-2506
http://www.brownprecision.com

Brunton
620 East Monroe Avenue
Riverton, WY 82501
Phone: 307-856-6559
http://www.brunton.com

BSA Optics, Inc.
3911 SW 47th Avenue, Suite
914
Fort Lauderdale, FL 33314
Phone: 954-581-2144
http://www.bsaoptics.com

Burris Company, Inc.
331 East 8th Street
P.O. Box 1747
Greeley, CO 80631
Phone: 970-356-1670
http://www.burrisoptics.com

Bushmaster Firearms International, LLC
P.O. Box 1479
Windham, ME 04062
Phone: 800-998-7928
http://www.bushmaster.com

Bushnell Outdoors Products
9200 Cody
Overland Park, KS 66214-1734
Phone: 800-423-3537
http://www.bushnell.com

Cabela's, Inc.
One Cabela Drive
Sidney, NE 69160
Phone: 800-331-3454
http://www.cabelas.com

Cci/Speer-Blount, Inc.
2299 Snake River Avenue
Lewiston, ID 83501
Phone: 800-627-3640
http://www.speer-bullets.com

CheyTac Associates Ltd.
363 Sunset Dr.
P.O. Box 822
Arco, ID 83213
Phone: 800-CHEYTAC (800-243-9822)
http://www.cheytac.com

Christensen Arms
192 E. 100 N
Fayettet, UT 84630
Phone: 888-517-8855
http://www.christensenarms.com

Cimarron Firearms Co., Inc.
105 Winding Oak Road
Fredericksburg, TX 78624
Phone: 830-997-9090
http://www.cimarron-firearms.com

Colt Blackpowder Arms Co.
110 8th St.
Brooklyn, NY 11215
Phone: 718-499-4678
http://www.gzanders.com

Colt's Manufacturing Company LLC
545 New Park Avenue
West Hartford, CT 06110 USA
Phone: 860-236-6311
http://www.coltsmfg.com

Cooper Arms, Inc.
P.O. Box 114
Stevensville, MT 59870
Phone: 406-777-0373
http://cooperfirearms.com

COR-BON/Glaser
P.O. Box 369
Sturgis, SD 57785
Phone: 800-626-7266
http://www.dakotaammo.net

Connecticut Valley Arms
5988 Peachtree Corners East
Norcross, GA 30071
Phone: 770-449-4687
http://www.cva.com

CZ-USA
P.O. Box 171073
Kansas City, KS 66117-0073
Phone: 800-955-4486
http://cz-usa.com

Dakota Arms
1310 Industry Road
Sturgis, SD 57785
Phone: 605-347-4686
http://www.dakotaarms.com

Dillon Precision Products, Inc.
8009 East Dillon's Way
Scottsdale, AZ 85260
Phone: 800-223-4570
http://www.dillonprecision.com

Dixie Gun Works
P.O. Box 130
Union City, TN 38281
Phone: 800-238-6785
http://www.dixiegunworks.com

Directory of Manufacturers & Suppliers

Downsizer Corporation
P.O. Box 710316
Santee, CA 92072-0316
Phone: 619-448-5510

Dynamit Nobel/RWS
81 Ruckman Road
Closter, NJ 07624
Phone: 201-767-1995
http://www.rwsairguns.com

Eagle Imports, Inc.
1750 Brielle Ave. Unit B-1
Wanamassa, NJ 07712
Phone: 732-493-0333
http://www.bersafirearmsusa.com

E.D.M. Arms
2410 West 350 North
Hurricane, UT 84737
Phone: 435-635-5233
http://www.edmarms.com

Entreprise Arms
5321 Irwindale Ave
Irwindale, CA 91706
Phone: 626-962-8712
http://www.entreprise.com

Euroarms of America, Inc.
P.O. BOX 3277
Winchester, VA 22601
Phone: 540-662-1863
http://www.euroarms.net

European American Armory Corp.
P.O. Box 560746
Rockledge, FL 32956-0746
Phone: 321-639-4842
http://www.eaacorp.com

Federal Cartridge Co.
900 Ehlen Dr
Anoka, MN 55303-1778
Phone: 763-421-7100
http://www.federalpremium.com

Skullman Enterprise AB
Flodman Guns
S - 647 95 Akers styckebruk
Jarsta, Sweden
Phone: +46-159-30861
http://www.flodman.com

Fiocchi of America
6930 N. Fremont Road
Ozark, MO 65721
Phone: 417-725-4118
http://www.fiocchiusa.com

FNH USA, Inc.
P.O. Box 697
McLean, VA 22101
Phone: 703-288-1292
http://www.fnhusa.com

Forster Products
310 East Lanark Avenue
Lanark, IL 61046
Phone: 815-493-6360
http://www.forsterproducts.com

Freedom Arms
314 Highway 239
P.O. Box 150
Freedom, WY 83120
Phone: 307-883-2468
http://www.freedomarms.com

Glock, Inc.
6000 Highlands Parkway
Smyrna, GA 30082
Phone: 770-432-1202
http://www.glock.com

Gonic Arms
134 Flagg Rd.
Gonic, NH 03839
Phone: 603-332-8456

Harrington & Richardson
H&R 1871, LLC
P.O. Box 1871
Madison, NC 27025
Phone: 866-776-9292
http://www.hr1871.com

H-S Precision
1301 Turbine Dr.,
Rapid City, SD 57703
Phone: 605-341-3006
http://www.hsprecision.com

Hammerli USA
Larry's Guns
56 West Gray Road
Gray, ME 04039
Phone: 207-657-4559
http://www.larrysguns.com

Heckler & Koch
7661 Commerce Ln.
Trussville, AL 35173
Phone: 706-568-1906
http://www.hk-usa.com

Henry Repeating Arms Co.
59 East 1st Street
Bayonne, NJ 07002
Phone: 201-858-4400
http://www.henryrepeating.com

Heritage Manufacturing
4600 NW 135th St.
Opa Locka, FL 33054
Phone: 305-685-5966
http://www.heritagemfg.com

High Standard Mfg. Co.
5200 Mitchelldale, Suite E-17
Houston, TX 77092
Phone: 800-272-7816
http://www.highstandard.com

Hodgdon Powder Co., Inc.
6231 Robinson
P.O. Box 2932
Shawnee Mission, KS 66202
Phone: 913-362-9455
http://www.hodgdon.com

Hornady Mfg. Co.
3625 Old Potash Hwy
P.O. Box 1848
Grand Island, NE 68802-1848
Phone: 800-338-3220
http://www.hornady.com

Ithaca Gun Co.
420 N. Warpole Street
Upper Sandusky, OH 43351
Phone: 877-6-ITHACA (877-648-4222)
http://www.ithacagun.com

Jarrett Rifles, Inc.
383 Brown Road
Jackson, SC 29831
Phone: 803-471-3616
http://www.jarrettrifles.com

Kahles
P.O. Box 21004
Cranston, RI 02920-1004
Phone: 866-606-8779
http://www.kahlesoptik.com

Kahr Arms
P.O. Box 220
Blauvelt, NY 10913
Phone: 845-652-8535
http://www.kahr.com

Kel-Tec Cnc
P.O. Box 236009
Cocoa, FL 32926
Phone: 321-631-0068
http://www.kel-tec-cnc.com

Kimber Manufacturing, Inc.
1 Lawton Street
Yonkers, NY 10705
Phone: 914-964-0771 Ext: 350
http://www.kimberamerica.com

Knight Rifles
21852 Hwy J46
Centerville, IA 52544
Phone: 641-856-2626
http://www.knightrifles.com

Krieghoff International, Inc.
P.O. Box 549
Ottsville, PA 18942
Phone: 610-847-5173
http://www.krieghoff.com

L.A.R. Manufacturing, Inc.
4133 West Farm Road
West Jordan, UT 84088-4997
Phone: 801-280-3505
http://www.largrizzly.com

Lazzeroni Arms Co.
P.O. Box 26696
Tucson, AZ 85726-6696
Phone: 888-492-7247
http://www.lazzeroni.com

Legacy Sports Intl.
4750 Longley Lane, Suite 208
Reno, NV 89502
Phone: 775-828-0555
http://www.legacysports.com

Lenartz Muzzleloading
8001 Whitneyville Rd SE
Alto, MI 49302
Phone: 616-891-0372
http://www.lenartztravel.com

Leupold & Stevens, Inc.
14400 NW Greenbrier Parkway
Beaverton, OR 97006-5790
Phone: 800-LEUP.O.LD (800-538-7653)
http://www.leupold.com

Lone Star Rifle Co., Inc.
11231 Rose Road
Conroe, Texas 77303
Phone: 936-228-2448
http://www.lonestarrifle.com

Lyman Products Corp.
475 Smith Street
Middletown, CT 06457
Phone: 800-225-9626
800-423-9704
860-632-2020
http://www.lymanproducts.com

Magnum Research, Inc.
7110 University Avenue N.E.
Minneapolis, MN 55432
Phone: 800-772-6168
http://www.magnumresearch.com

Magtech Ammunition Co., Inc
248 Apollo Drive, Suite 180
Lino Lakes, MN 55014
Phone: 800-466-7191
http://www.magtechammunition.com

Markesbery Muzzleloaders, Inc.
7065 Production Court
Florence, KY 41042
Phone: 859-534-5630
http://www.markesbery.com

Directory of Manufacturers & Suppliers

Marlin Firearms Co.
100 Kenna Drive
P.O. Box 248
North Haven, CT 06473-0905
Phone: 203-239-5621
800-544-8892
http://www.marlinfirearms.com

O.F. Mossberg & Sons, Inc.
7 Grasso Ave.
North Haven, CT 06473
Phone: 203-230-5300
http://www.mossberg.com

Navy Arms Company, Inc.
219 Lawn St
Martinsburg, WV 25405-5009
Phone: 304-262-1651
http://www.navyarms.com

New England Arms Corp.
P.O. Box 278
Kittery Point, ME 03905
Phone: 207-439-0593
http://www.newenglandarms.com

New England Firearms Co., Inc.
H&R 1871, LLC
P.O. Box 1871
Madison, NC 27025
Phone: 866-776-9292
http://www.hr1871.com

New Ultra Light Arms
P.O. Box 340
214 Price Street (Shipping)
Granville, WV 26534
Phone: 304-292-0600
http://www.newultralight.com

Nikon, Inc.
1300 Walt Whitman Rd.
Melville, NY 11747
Phone: 631-271-2145
http://www.nikon.com

North America Arms
2150 South 950 East
Provo, UT 84606
Phone: 800-821-5783
http://www.naaminis.com

Nosler, Inc.
P.O. Box 671
Bend, OR 97709
Phone: 800-285-3701
http://www.nosler.com

Olympic Arms, Inc.
624 Old Pacific Hwy. SE
Olympia, WA 98513
Phone: 800-228-3471
http://www.olyarms.com

Para-Ordnance Mfg, Inc.
980 Tapscott Road,
Toronto, ON M1X 1C3
Canada
Phone: 416-297-7855
http://www.paraord.com

Pentax Imaging Co.
600 12th St
Golden, CO 80401
Phone: 303-728-0230
http://www.pentaximaging.com

Perazzi USA
1010 W. Tenth St.
Azusa, Ca. 91702
Phone: 626-334-1234
http://www.perazzi.com

Pgw Defense Technologies
1-761 Marion St.
Winnipeg, Manitoba
Canada R2J0K6

RCBS
605 Oro Dam Blvd
Oroville, CA 95965
Phone: 800-533-5000
http://www.rcbs.com

Redding Reloading Equipment
1089 Starr Rd.
Cortland, NY 13045
Phone: 607-753-3331
http://www.redding-reloading
.com

Redfield USA
201 Plantation Oak Drive
Thomasville, GA 31792
Phone: 800-323-3191
http://www.redfieldoptics.co.uk

Remington Arms Company, Inc.
870 Remington Drive
P.O. Box 700
Madison, NC 27025-0700
Phone: 800-243-9700
http://www.remington.com

Rifles, Inc.
3580 Leal Road
Pleasanton, TX 78064
Phone: 830-569-2055
http://www.riflesinc.com

Rizzini
100 Burritt Street
New Britain, CT 06053
Phone: 860-225-6581
http://www.rizziniusa.com

Rogue Rifle Co.
1114 Birch Ave
Lewiston, ID 83501-5517
Phone: 208-746-5401

Rossi Firearms
BrazTech Intl.
16175 NW 49 Avenue
Miami, FL 33014
Phone: 305-474-0401
http://www.rossiusa.com

Sauer
SIG SAUER Inc.
Customer Service Dept.
18 Industrial Drive
Exeter, NH 03833-4557
Phone: 603-772-2302 (press #3 for Customer Service)
http://www.sigsauer.com

Savage Arms, Inc.
100 Springdale Road,
Westfield, MA 01085
Phone: 413-568-7001
http://www.savagearms.com

Shiloh Rifle Mfg.
P.O. Box 279
201 Centennial Drive
Big Timber, MT 59011
Phone: 406-932-4266
406-932-4454
http://www.shilohrifle.com

Sierra Bullets
1400 West Henry Street
Sedalia, MO 65301
Phone: 660-827-6300
http://www.sierrabullets.com

Sigarms, Inc.
SIG SAUER Inc.
Customer Service Dept.
18 Industrial Drive
Exeter, NH 03833-4557
Phone: 603-772-2302 (press #3 for Customer Service)
http://www.sigsauer.com

Sightron, Inc.
100 Jeffrey Way Suite A
Youngsville, NC 27596
Phone: 919-562-3000
http://www.sightron.com

Simmons Outdoor Corp.
9200 Cody
Overland Park, KS 66214-1734
Phone: 888-276-5945
http://www.simmonsoptics.com

SKB Shotguns
GU, Inc. / SKB Shotguns
4441 S 134th St
Omaha, NE 68137-1107
Phone: 800-752-2767
http://www.skbshotguns.com

Smith & Wesson
2100 Roosevelt Avenue
Springfield, MA 01104
Phone: 800-331-0852
http://smith-wesson.com

Springfield Armory
420 W. Main St.
Geneseo, IL 61254
Phone: 800-680-6866
http://www.springfield-armory.com

Sturm, Ruger & Company, Inc.
1 Lacey Pl
Southport, CT 06890-1207
Phone: 203-259-7843
http://www.ruger-firearms.com

Swarovski Optik, NA
2 Slater Rd
Cranston, RI 02920-4468
Phone: 401-734-1800
http://www.swarovskioptik.us

Swift Bullet Co.
One Thousand One Swift Avenue
P.O. Box 27
Quinter, KS 67752
Phone: 785-754-3959
http://www.swiftbullets.com

Swift Optics
2055 Gateway Pl
Suite 500
San Jose, CA 95110-1082
Phone: 408-293-2380

Szecsei & Fuchs
North American Office
450 Charles St.
Windsor, ON Canada
N8X 371
Phone: 519-966-1234
http://www.szecseidoublebol-trepeater.ca

Tactical Rifles – Dow Arms
38439 5th Ave #186
Zephyrhills, FL 33542-4328
Phone: 877-811-GUNS (877-811-4867)
http://www.tacticalrifles.net

Taurus Intl., Inc.
16175 NW 49 Avenue
Miami, FL 33014
Phone: 305-624-1115
http://www.taurususa.com

Directory of Manufacturers & Suppliers

Thompson/Center Arms
P.O. Box 5002
Rochester, NH 03866
Phone: 603-330-5659
http://www.tcarms.com

Traditions Firearms
1375 Boston Post Road
P.O. Box 776
Old Saybrook, CT 06475
Phone: 860-388-4656
http://www.traditionsfirearms.com

Trijicon
49385 Shafer Avenue
P.O. Box 930059
Wixom, MI 48393
Phone: 248-960-7700
http://www.trijicon.com

Tristar Sporting Arms, Ltd.
1816 Linn Street
North Kansas City, MO 64116
Phone: 816-421-1400
http://www.tristarsportingarms.com

U.S. Repeating Arms Co.
275 Winchester Ave.
Morgan, UT 84050
Phone: 800-333-3288
801.876.2711
http://www.winchesterguns.com

Vihtavuori/Lapua
1241 Ellis Street
Bensenville, IL 60106
Phone: 630-350-1116
http://www.vihtavuori-lapua.com

Walther
2100 Roosevelt Avenue
Springfield, MA 01104
Phone: 800-372-6454
http://www.waltheramerica.com

Weatherby, Inc.
1605 Commerce Way
Paso Robles, CA 93446
Phone: 805-227-2600
http://www.weatherby.com

Western Powders
P.O. Box 158
Miles City, MT 59301
Phone: 406-234-0422
http://www.accuratearms.com

White Rifles
P.O. Box 1044
Orem, UT 84059-1044
http://www.whiterifles.com

Wildey, Inc.
45 Angevine Rd
Warren, CT 06754
Phone: 860-355-9000
http://www.wildeyguns.com

Wild West Guns, Inc.
7100 Homer Drive
Anchorage, AK 99518
Phone: 800-992-4570
http://www.wildwestguns.com

Williams Gun Sight Co.
7389 Lapeer Rd.
Davison, MI 48423
Phone: 800-530-9028
http://www.williamsgunsight
.com

Winchester
427 N Shamrock St
East Alton, IL 62024-1174
Phone: 618-258-2000
http://www.winchester.com

XS Sight Systems
2401 Ludelle
Fort Worth, TX 76105
Phone: 888-744-4880
http://www.xssights.com

Zeiss Sports Optics
13005 North Kingston Avenue
Chester, VA 23836-8333
Phone: 800-441-3005
http://www.zeiss.com

Z-Hat Custom Dies
1991 Lilac St.
Casper, WY 82604
http://www.z-hat.com

Gun Finder Index

To help you find the model of your choice, the following index includes the firearms found in this edition of *Shooter's Bible*, listed by type of gun.

Gun Finder Index

Centerfire Single Shot

Rimfire Bolt Action and Single Shot

Rimfire Lever Action

Rimfire Semiautomatic and Slide Action

Double Rifles & Drillings

Competition Target Rifles

Rifle-Shotgun Combinations

SHOTGUNS

Autoloading

Gun Finder Index

Bolt & Lever Action

Over/Under

Side-by-Side

Single Barrel

Gun Finder Index

Gun Finder Index

Revolvers — Double Action

Revolvers — Single Action

Pistols—Single-Shot, Bolt-Action & Derringer

BLACKPOWDER/MUZLELOADER

In-Line Rifles

Gun Finder Index